W9-CKL-696

A WEALTH OF EXCLUSIVE VIDEOS!

Available to instructors upon adoption*

- Research in Action Videos, by Roger Klein
- ABC® Videos for Psychology
- Revealing Psychology™ Videos
- Psych in Film Videos
- Guest Lecture Series
- Lecture Starter Series

SEE INSIDE FOR DETAILS!

Timely and engaging video clips
ABC® News

Show students the relevance of psychology with these short, high-interest video segments. ABC videos are also available on our **ABC Social Psychology DVD**, along with other segments chosen to reflect the widest scope of social psychology topics.

A sampling of the segments included:

- Age Compression
- Artificial Eye
- Evaluating Patients with Brain Damage
- Gay Teens
- Mental Illness and Suicide
- Obedience to Authority
- Prescription Drug Abuse in Teenagers
- Ringtones and the Cochlea
- Rules of Attraction
- Sleepless in America

Exclusive ABC video clips:

- 20/20 clip, Life's Temptations (on self-control), featuring Roy Baumeister
- 20/20 clip, Soothing The Savage Beast (Is it better to hold in anger or vent it?), featuring Brad Bushman
- 20/20 clip, Feel Good About Failure? (surprising results from self-esteem research), featuring Roy Baumeister and Brad Bushman

Now playing—clips from the movies!
Psych in Film

The **Psych in Film DVD** for introductory psychology includes 35 clips with closed captioning. The **Social Psych in Film DVD** includes 25 clips. Both include clip overviews, discussion questions with suggested answers, and teaching tips.

A sampling of the clips included:

- Apollo Thirteen (Problem Solving)
- Bourne Identity (Amnesia)
- Dazed and Confused (Adolescent Behavior, Modeling)
- E.T. The Extraterrestrial (Developing Trust)
- Meet the Parents (Operant Conditioning)
- Mr. Baseball (Collectivist vs. Individualist Cultures)
- October Sky (Parenting Styles)
- Schindler's List (Learned Helplessness)
- Snow Falling on Cedars (Stereotyping, Prejudice)
- The Deer Hunter (Post-Traumatic Stress Disorder)
- The Lost Weekend (Substance Addiction)
- To Kill a Mockingbird (Crowd Behavior)

A sampling of Social Psych in Film segments:

- Babe—Pig in the City
- Bullies: Bullying and Aggression
- Faceism: Gender Stereotypes
- The Asch Conformity Study
- The "1984" Apple Computer Commercial: Use of Persuasion in TV Ads
- The Bobo Doll Study: Aggression and Modeling

Introduce your students to contemporary psychology researchers

Wadsworth Psychology Research in Action Videos
Volumes I and II

Roger D. Klein, author and producer

These videos provide undergraduate students with the opportunity to learn about cutting-edge research and meet the psychologists involved in this fascinating work. The videos offer an in-depth look at psychological laboratories and the applied work of both established and up-and-coming researchers. Award-winning author/producer Roger D. Klein, Ph.D., is an Associate Professor in the Educational Psychology Department at State University of New York, Buffalo. Dr. Klein specializes in media psychology and human learning.

A sampling of the clips available:

- **Internet Relationships**
  —Melanie Green, University of North Carolina, Chapel Hill
- **Reconstructive Memory**
  —Elizabeth Loftus, University of California, Irvine
- **Breast Cancer Groups**
  —Vicki Helgeson, Carnegie Mellon University
- **Socially Shared Cognition**
  —Richard Moreland, University of Pittsburgh
- **Visual-Spatial Processing**
  —Joan Stiles, University of California, San Diego
- **Culture and Emotion**
  —Jeanne Tsai, Stanford University
- **Effects of Drugs on Learning**
  —Daniel Cerutti, Duke University
- **Personality Traits**
  —Rodolfo Mendoza-Denton, University of California, Berkeley

- **Brain Organization, Structure, and Function**
  —Jon Kaas, Vanderbilt University

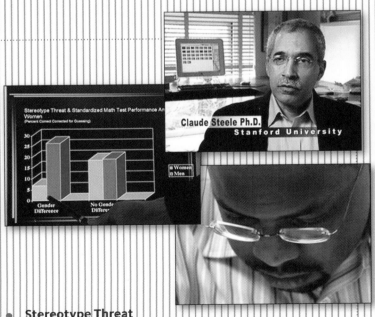

- **Implicit Association Test**
  —Mahzarin Banaji, Harvard University
- **Post-Traumatic Stress Disorder**
  —Elna Yadin, University of Pennsylvania
- **Sexual Prejudice**
  —Greg Herek, University of California, Davis
- **Health and Stress**
  —Sheldon Cohen, Carnegie Mellon University
- **Fear Conditioning**
  —Michael Fanselow, University of California, Los Angeles
- **Self-Control**
  —Roy Baumeister, Florida State University

- **Stereotype Threat**
  —Claude Steele, Stanford University

Use Video as a learning tool
Revealing Psychology™ Videos

These attention-grabbing, often humorous clips illustrate important concepts while simultaneously providing real-world examples of abstract psychological principles. The 13 clips range in length from 5 to 11 minutes. An instructor's guide with a video summary, points of emphasis, discussion questions, and suggested activities helps you use the clips to full advantage in your course.

Included clips:

- Body Image and Social Expectations
- Conformity
- Evolutionary Psychology and Social Communication
- Group Polarization

- Matching (Physical Attraction)
- Mating Strategies
- Personal Space
- Prisoner's Dilemma
- Risky Shift (Group Polarization)

- Who Lies More—Men or Women?
- Why Do Men and Women Lie?
- Why People Do Not Help
- Why People Help

Learn your colleagues' best teaching ideas
Guest Lecture Series: Volume I and II

Instructors from around the country offer their tried-and-true teaching suggestions on nearly 80 topics ranging from how to teach classical conditioning to the use of clickers in class.

A sampling of topics included:

- Making Pavlov Relevant
- Tricks for Teaching Research Methods
- F.I.B.E.R.: Teaching Critical Thinking
- Using PowerPoint® Effectively
- Blogging as an Effective Teaching Tool
- Inducing False Memories

- Role-Playing Techniques That Teach Psychology
- Helping Students to Develop Empathy
- Using Humor (Not Jokes)
- Demonstrating the Power of Obedience Within the Classroom
- "Door-in-The-Face" Technique
- Showing Students How to Think Like Scientists

More ways to spark student interest
Lecture Starter Series

Designed to stimulate discussion, these 34 clips feature footage from Films for the Humanities on such topics as research methods, the brain, displaying emotion, eating disorders, eyewitness memory, hearing, phobias, stress and disease, Tourette's syndrome, and many others.

Ordering Information
Contact your Cengage Learning representative with any questions and to ensure that you receive the appropriate videos to enhance your course.

Research in Action Videos
Volume I DVD: ISBN-10: 0-495-59520-9 | ISBN-13: 978-0-495-59520-5
Volume II DVD (Available in 2009)

ABC Videos: Introductory Psychology
Volume I DVD: ISBN-10: 0-495-50306-1 | ISBN-13: 978-0-495-50306-4
Volume II DVD: ISBN-10: 0-495-59637-X | ISBN-13: 978-0-495-59637-0
Volume III DVD (2009): ISBN-10: 0-495-60490-9 | ISBN-13: 978-0-495-60490-7

ABC Videos: Social Psychology
DVD: ISBN-10: 0-495-50301-0 | ISBN-13: 978-0-495-50301-9
VHS: ISBN-10: 0-495-03173-9 | ISBN-13: 978-0-495-03173-4

Revealing Psychology™
DVD: ISBN-10: 0-547-01453-1 | ISBN-13: 978-0-547-01453-1

Psych in Film, Version 2
DVD: ISBN-10: 0-618-27530-4 | ISBN-13: 978-0-618-27530-4
VHS: ISBN-10: 0-618-38115-5 | ISBN-13: 978-0-618-38115-9

Social Psych in Film
DVD: ISBN-10: 0-618-53995-6 | ISBN-13: 978-0-618-53995-6

Guest Lecture Series DVD
Volume I and II DVD: ISBN-10: 0-547-00401-X | ISBN-13: 978-0-547-00401-3

Lecture Starter CD-ROM
ISBN-10: 0-618-21998-6 | ISBN-13: 978-0-618-21998-8

Your students'

gateway to active learning

Streamlined, up-to-date, and more inviting than ever

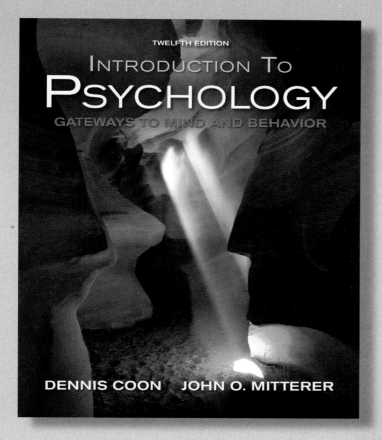

TWELFTH EDITION

INTRODUCTION TO

PSYCHOLOGY

GATEWAYS TO MIND AND BEHAVIOR

DENNIS COON   JOHN O. MITTERER

"This is an engaging text

that most students will find very accessible.

It has well-designed pedagogical features that

complement the accurate, up-to-date contents.

Concepts are well presented and easy to understand. . . . The

overall approach tends to draw in

the reader, making him/her feel part of the material."

Linda E. Flickinger, St. Clair County Community College

Written by Dennis Coon, a gifted psychology author whose animated style captivates readers, and coauthor John Mitterer, a distinguished teacher and researcher, this text attracts and holds the attention of even difficult-to-reach students. The Twelfth Edition consistently encourages students to engage in reflective cognitive processing through a heightened emphasis on critical thinking, the SQ4R learning system, and the relevance of psychology. This active learning approach—together with lively examples, coverage of the latest research findings, and media resources—opens the door to the study of psychology and helps to ensure that students find it to be fascinating, relevant, and accessible.

New Edition Highlights:

- Stronger emphasis on critical thinking—*See page P-2.*
- Integration of SQ4R's effective reflective processing step—*See page P-3.*
- Updated, streamlined content—*See page P-4.*
- Enhanced focus on psychology's everyday relevance—*See page P-5.*
- Excellent media resources, including videos, a lecture presentation tool, and an online teaching and learning system. *See the foldout insert at the front of this text and pages P-7 and P-8.*

SQ4R—proven to promote active learning and critical thinking

This book was the first college text to integrate the effective and nationally acclaimed SQ4R system. In this edition, students focus on each topic through an updated six-step process: Survey, Question, Read, Recite, Reflect, and Review. The result—success in the psychology course.

A *Gateway Theme* and *Gateway Questions* organize each chapter's topics and guide the discussion, helping students to read with purpose. A *Gateways to...* section at the end of the chapter lists key ideas that answer each question, reinforcing important take-home messages.

New! *Brainwaves* boxes promote critical thinking by encouraging reflection on brain mechanisms that underlie psychological phenomena. Topics include "Your Brain's 'Fat Point,'" "The Schizophrenic Brain," and "Tickling Your Own Fancy," which updates coverage of the self-stimulation phenomenon.

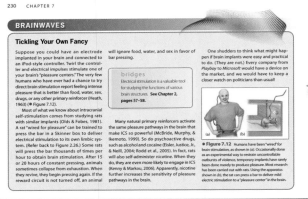

The active, questioning nature of the SQ4R method is in itself an inducement to think critically. In addition, features such as *Critical Thinking* boxes encourage deep thought, challenging students to question their commonsense beliefs and reflect on research findings that have relevance in their lives.

"This is a very good book that uses examples that undergraduate students can relate to. The science of learning is well implemented in this book."

Darlene Gould Colson, Norfolk State University

"Reflect"—tapping into the power of reflective processing

SQ4R's newest step, Reflect, is based on the insight from cognitive psychology that elaboration (reflective processing of new information) is one of the best ways to foster understanding and form lasting memories. Reflective thought is emphasized throughout the text.

Knowledge Builder exercises expand students' understanding of new ideas. They include *Reflect* questions that encourage students to associate new concepts with personal experience and prior knowledge. *Critical Thinking* questions promote a deeper form of reflection, while *Recite* sections enable students to review what they have learned.

Discovering Psychology boxes encourage self-discovery of concepts by asking students to try exercises for themselves and then reflect upon them. Topics include "Are You Color Blind?" "I'm Not Prejudiced, Right?" and "Behavioral Dieting," a new box that invites students to apply behavioral principles to control their own eating behavior.

Effects of Hypnosis

What can (and cannot) be achieved with hypnosis? Many abilities have been tested during hypnosis, leading to the following conclusions (Burgess & Kirsch, 1999; Chaves, 2000):

1. **Superhuman acts of strength.** Hypnosis has no more effect on physical strength than instructions that encourage a person to make his or her best effort.
2. **Memory.** There is some evidence that hypnosis can enhance memory (Wagstaff et al., 2004). However, it frequently increases the number of false memories as well. For this reason, many states now bar persons from testifying in court if they were hypnotized to improve their memory of a crime they witnessed.

> **bridges**
> Should the police use hypnosis to enhance the memories of witnesses? The evidence generally says no. **See Chapter 8, page 258.**

Bridges are brief cross-references that connect a topic mentioned in one chapter to further discussion in another chapter. This feature invites students to explore the interconnection of ideas that characterizes contemporary psychology.

The gateway to active learning

Current topics and research findings, framed with captivating writing

Students *like* to read this text. The authors use lively anecdotes and examples to convey new research findings, controversies, and psychology's key concepts and topics—and students eagerly turn the pages for more.

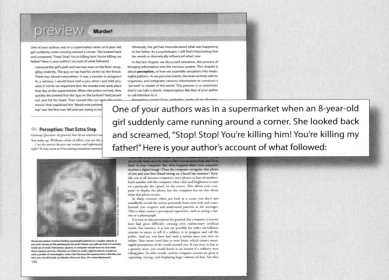

> One of your authors was in a supermarket when an 8-year-old girl suddenly came running around a corner. She looked back and screamed, "Stop! Stop! You're killing him! You're killing my father!" Here is your author's account of what followed:

New! Content and research updates

The Twelfth Edition is extensively updated, with two thirds of the references from 2000 or later. Highlights include:

- A reorganized section on **modern perspectives on behavior** to include three main perspectives: biological, behavioral, and sociocultural

- An expanded chapter on the brain and behavior, reflecting the **growing importance of neuroscience** in contemporary psychology

- Discussion of the **dual process hypothesis,** which assigns different functions to NREM and REM sleep

- Updated treatment of dreaming, including discussion of **Domhoff's neurocognitive theory** as well as **psychodynamic and activation-synthesis theories**

- Reorganized material on the neuroscience of memory; **flashbulb memories** now appear in a section on memory and emotion and are **linked to the role of the amygdala** in processing emotional memories

- Coverage of **mere presence,** including new glossary entries for social facilitation and social loafing. Invasions of personal space are now treated as a form of mere presence.

- Broader treatment of **prosocial behavior** to include affiliation, liking, loving, and the willingness to help strangers

- Coverage of **Robert Sternberg's triangular theory of love**

New! Streamlined chapters

- Chapter 3, "Human Development," combines and condenses material formerly presented in two separate chapters on child development and life-span development.

- Chapter 9, "Cognition, Language, Creativity and Intelligence" blends and streamlines the previous edition's chapters that covered these topics.

> *"Coon's and Mitterer's writing styles are appropriate for college undergraduates. (The book) is written in such a way that can be appealing regardless of any prior preparation. . . . It has sufficient application-type material to be interesting to students."*

Gloria Fisher, Mississippi College

Special focus on human diversity and the relevance of psychological research

Human Diversity boxes highlight similarities and differences in human expression, providing students with examples of how to be more reflective about human diversity. The book includes many topics and examples that encourage students to appreciate social, physical, and cultural differences—and to accept them as a natural part of being human.

The Clinical File boxes focus on therapies, disorders, mental health, and personal adjustment. For instance, "Coping with Chemo" discusses the application of classical conditioning to help patients cope with conditioned nausea from chemotherapy. "Telling Stories About Ourselves" discusses the narrative approach to personality, and "Sick of Being Sick" offers a fascinating look at Munchausen syndrome by proxy.

"I would describe this book to a colleague as multicultural and thorough .... The inclusion of different cultures in pictures, examples, and text was ingenious."

Kim Royster, Tidewater Community College

The gateway to active learning

Psychology in Action sections at the end of every chapter discuss ways that students can put their growing knowledge of psychology to work to improve their life experiences and their understanding of life issues. Topics include emotional intelligence, motivation, well-being, and effective parenting.

A comprehensive Chapter 18, "Applied Psychology," shows how psychological principles can be used to solve practical problems in such everyday settings as the workplace, the environment, school, and sports.

Discussions of topics associated with positive psychology—such as love, happiness, and self-confidence—are integrated throughout this text, showing students the many emotional and intellectual tools that psychology can offer them.

Time-saving resources for instructors

PowerLecture™: A 1-Stop Microsoft® PowerPoint® Tool

With ExamView® and JoinIn™ Student Response System
0-495-80676-5 • 978-0-495-80676-9
By Andrew Getzfeld,
New York University
This one-stop lecture and course preparation tool makes it easy for you to assemble, edit, and present custom lectures for your course, using Microsoft® PowerPoint®. The CD-ROM provides text-specific lecture outlines, art from the text, videos, animations, and copies of the **Instructor's Resource Manual** and **Test Bank** in Microsoft® Word format. Also included: **ExamView®**, which contains printed **Test Bank** questions in electronic format, making it easy to create customize tests; and **JoinIn™** content on slides, for use with your favorite student response system software and "clickers."

Instructor's Resource Manual
0-495-60314-7 • 978-0-495-60314-6
By Wanda McCarthy,
Clermont College, University of Cincinnati
This paperbound manual includes class activities, handouts, learning objectives, lecture enhancements, discussion topics, media suggestions, further reading suggestions, and Internet resources.

Test Bank
0-495-59916-6 • 978-0-495-59916-6
By Jeannette Murphey,
Meridian Community College
The **Test Bank** contains between 500 and 750 questions per chapter, including numerous multiple-choice, 30 true/false, 30 fill-in-the-blank, and 10 essay questions. The **Test Bank** is also included in electronic format on the **PowerLecture** CD-ROM.

CengageNOW™
for Introduction to Psychology, Twelfth Edition

CengageNOW™ is an online teaching and learning resource that gives you more control in less time and delivers better outcomes—NOW. **CengageNOW** offers you teaching and learning resources in one intuitive program organized around the essential activities you perform for class—lecturing, creating assignments, grading, quizzing, and tracking student progress and performance.

For students, **CengageNOW** *Personalized Study* is a diagnostic tool that utilizes text-specific assets to help students master the book's gateway concepts and prepare for exams. Students can use the program on their own, or you can assign it and track their progress in your online gradebook.

Also included with **CengageNOW**, the **Psychology Resource Center** features an array of teaching and learning resources. *See the inside front cover of this text for more details and information about packaging* **CengageNOW** *with each new text.*

WebTutor™ on WebCT® and Blackboard®
Printed Access WebCT: 0-495-80699-4 • 978-0-495-80699-8
Printed Access Blackboard: 0-495-80700-1 • 978-0-495-80700-1
Jump-start your course with customizable, text-specific content that can be easily loaded into your course management system. Contact your Cengage Learning representative for details and packaging information.

Psychology Videos
A diverse collection of classic and contemporary clips are available upon adoption, including *Research in Action Videos* and ABC® News segments. Please refer to the insert in the front of this text for details.

The gateway to active learning

Support for students outside class

Contact your Cengage Learning representative to package any of the resources described below with each new text, or use the order numbers provided.

Study Guide
ISBN-10: 0-495-80429-0
978-0-495-80429-1
Packaged with the text: 0-495-75843-4
978-0-495-75843-3
By Jori Reijonen
The **Study Guide** is structured around the text's SQ4R active learning system and offers many opportunities for practice, self-testing, and review, including fill-in-the-blank, matching, true/false, and mastery test questions.

Packaged with each new text!
Gateways to Psychology: Concept Maps and Concept Reviews
A handy reference to the gateway concepts presented in the text, this booklet presents the key transformative ideas that every student should know. The *Concept Maps* (by Christine M. Vanchella) help students see visually how ideas are interconnected. *Concept Reviews* for each chapter (by Shawn Talbot, Kellogg Community College) list main concepts, followed by 35 multiple-choice questions.

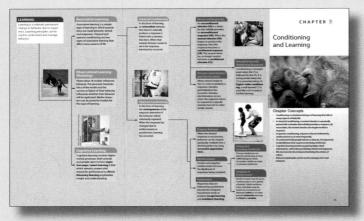

New! Audio Study Tools
Packaged with the text: 0-495-75844-2 • 978-0-495-75844-0
Cengage Learning **Audio Study Tools** give today's busy students a quick, convenient way to master key concepts and prepare for exams using their personal computer or MP3 player. In just ten minutes, students can review key terms and take audio practice quizzes. Access to **Audio Study Tools** can be packaged with the text, or purchased at **www.ichapters.com**.
CengageNOW™

Due to contractual reasons, certain ancillaries are available only in higher education or U.S. domestic markets. Minimum purchases may apply to receive the ancillaries at no charge. For more information, please contact your local Cengage Learning sales representative.

for Introduction to Psychology, Twelfth Edition
CENGAGENOW
See the inside front cover of this text for details.

Psychology Resource Center
Included with **CengageNOW**, the **Psychology Resource Center** features a full library of original and classic video clips plus interactive learning modules tied to the topics covered in an introductory psychology course. The **Psychology Resource Center** is easy to navigate; students simply browse by topic.

Book Companion Website
www.cengage.com/psychology/coon
When you adopt this text, you and your students can access an array of rich learning and test-prep online resources—including chapter-by-chapter tutorial quizzes, web links, and flash cards, and, for you, password-protected instructor resources.

Also Available

Writing Papers in Psychology, Eighth Edition
By Ralph L. Rosnow, Temple University, and Mimi Rosnow
ISBN-10: 0-495-50956-6 • ISBN-13: 978-0-495-50956-1

Writing With Style: APA Style Made Easy, Fourth Edition
By Lenore T. Szuchman
ISBN-10: 0-495-09972-4 • ISBN-13: 978-0-495-09972-7

Careers in Psychology: Opportunities in a Changing World, Third Edition
By Tara L. Kuther, Western Connecticut State University, and Robert D. Morgan, Texas Tech University
ISBN-10: 0-495-60074-1 • ISBN-13: 978-0-495-60074-9

Introduction to Positive Psychology
By William C. Compton, Middle Tennessee State University
ISBN-10: 0-534-64453-8 • ISBN-13: 978-0-534-64453-6

Challenging Your Preconceptions: Thinking Critically About Psychology, Second Edition
By Randolph A. Smith, Kennesaw State University
ISBN-10: 0-534-26739-4 • ISBN-13: 978-0-534-26739-1

Critical Thinking in Psychology: Separating Sense from Nonsense, Second Edition
By John Ruscio, Elizabethtown College
ISBN-10: 0-534-63459-1 • ISBN-13: 978-0-534-63459-9

Cross-Cultural Perspectives in Introductory Psychology, Fifth Edition
By William F. Price, North Country Community College, and Richley H. Crapo, Utah State University
ISBN-10: 0-534-54653-6 • ISBN-13: 978-0-534-54653-3

Introduction to Psychology

GATEWAYS TO MIND AND BEHAVIOR TWELFTH EDITION

Dennis Coon

John O. Mitterer

Brock University

WADSWORTH
CENGAGE Learning™

Australia • Brazil • Canada • Mexico • Singapore • Spain • United Kingdom • United States

Introduction to Psychology: Gateways to Mind and Behavior, **Twelfth Edition**
Dennis Coon / John O. Mitterer

Senior Publisher: Linda Schreiber

Senior Editors: Jane Potter, Jaime Perkins

Managing Development Editor: Jeremy Judson

Assistant Editors: Trina Tom, Ileana Shevlin

Editorial Assistant: Nicolas Albert

Associate Media Editor: Rachel Guzman

Executive Marketing Manager: Kim Russell

Marketing Manager: Tierra Morgan

Executive Marketing Communications Manager: Talia Wise

Sr. Content Project Manager, Editorial Production: Pat Waldo

Creative Director: Rob Hugel

Senior Art Director: Vernon Boes

Print Buyer: Karen Hunt

Permissions Acquisitions Manager, Images: Amanda Groszko

Permissions Acquisitions Manager, Text: Roberta Broyer

Production Service: Julie Ninnis, Graphic World Inc.

Text and Cover Designer: Liz Harasymczuk

Photo Researcher: Kathleen Olson

Copy Editor: Graphic World Inc.

Cover Image: Nick Wienholt

Compositor: Graphic World Inc.

© 2010, 2007 Wadsworth, Cengage Learning

For product information and technology assistance, contact us at **Cengage Learning Customer & Sales Support, 1-800-354-9706.**

For permission to use material from this text or product, submit all requests online at www.**cengage.com/permissions**. Further permissions questions can be e-mailed to **permissionrequest@cengage.com**.

Library of Congress Control Number: 2008938253

Student Edition:
ISBN-13: 978-0-495-59911-1
ISBN-10: 0-495-59911-5

Loose-leaf Edition:
ISBN-13: 978-0-495-59913-5
ISBN-10: 0-495-59913-1

Wadsworth
10 Davis Drive
Belmont, CA 94002-3098
USA

Cengage Learning is a leading provider of customized learning solutions with office locations around the globe, including Singapore, the United Kingdom, Australia, Mexico, Brazil, and Japan. Locate your local office at **international.cengage.com/region**.

Cengage Learning products are represented in Canada by Nelson Education, Ltd.

For your course and learning solutions, visit **www.cengage.com**.
Purchase any of our products at your local college store or at our preferred online store **www.ichapters.com**.

Printed in Canada
1 2 3 4 5 6 7 12 11 10 09

about the authors

After earning a doctorate in psychology from the University of Arizona, Dennis Coon taught for 22 years at Santa Barbara City College, California. Throughout his career, Dr. Coon has especially enjoyed the challenge of teaching introductory psychology. He and his wife, Sevren, have returned to Tucson, where he continues to teach, write, edit, and consult.

Dr. Coon is the author of *Introduction to Psychology* and *Psychology: A Journey,* as well as *Psychology: Modules for Active Learning.* Together, these texts have been used by more than 2 million students. Dr. Coon frequently serves as a reviewer and consultant to publishers, and he edited the best-selling trade book *Choices.* He also helped design modules for PsychNow!, Wadsworth's interactive CD-ROM.

In his leisure hours, Dr. Coon enjoys hiking, photography, painting, woodworking, and music. He also designs, builds, and plays classical and steel string acoustic guitars. He has published articles on guitar design and occasionally offers lectures on this topic, in addition to his more frequent presentations on psychology.

John O. Mitterer was awarded his Ph.D. in cognitive psychology from McMaster University. Currently, Dr. Mitterer teaches at Brock University, where he has taught more than 20,000 introductory psychology students. He is the recipient of the 2003 Brock University Distinguished Teaching Award, a 2003 Ontario Confederation of University Faculty Associations (OCUFA) Teaching Award, a 2004 National 3M Teaching Fellowship, and the 2005 Canadian Psychological Association Award for Distinguished Contributions to Education and Training in Psychology.

Dr. Mitterer's primary research focus is on basic cognitive processes in learning and teaching. He consulted for a variety of companies, such as Bell Northern Research, Unisys Corporation, IBM Canada, and computer-game developer Silicon Knights. His professional focus, however, is on applying cognitive principles to the improvement of undergraduate education. In support of his introductory psychology course, he has been involved in the production of textbooks and ancillary materials such as CD-ROMs and websites for both students and instructors. Dr. Mitterer has published and lectured on undergraduate instruction throughout Canada and the United States.

In his spare time, Dr. Mitterer strives to become a better golfer and to attain his life goal of seeing all the bird species in the world. To this end he recently traveled to Papua New Guinea, Brazil, Australia, and South Africa.

brief contents

contents

8 Memory 251

9 Cognition, Language, Creativity, and Intelligence 283

15 Therapies 495

preface to the twelfth edition

An Invitation to the Student

Greetings from your authors. We are delighted to be your guides as you explore the exciting field of psychology. We hope you will find that psychology is at once familiar, exotic, surprising, and challenging. What, really, could be more intriguing than our evolving understanding of human behavior?

Psychology is about each of us. It invites us to adopt a reflective attitude as we ask, "How can we step outside ourselves to look objectively at how we live, think, feel, and act?" Psychologists believe the answer is through intelligent thought, observation, and inquiry. As simple as that might seem, careful reflection takes practice to develop. It is the guiding light for all that follows.

Reading *Gateways to Mind and Behavior*

We trust you will find much that interests you in this book. To make your reading enjoyable, we tried to write as if we were talking with you. And to add to your interest, we will often invite you to relate psychology to your own experiences. But make no mistake, *Gateways to Mind and Behavior* is a sophisticated textbook that offers you an up-to-date introduction to psychology.

At the beginning of each chapter you will find a list of *Gateway Questions* to guide your reading. As you read a chapter, try to see if you can discover the answers to these questions. Then compare your answers with the ones listed in the chapter summary. The answers are what we think of as *Gateway concepts*. In other words, they open intellectual pathways and summarize psychology's "big ideas." Although you don't need to memorize the Gateway concepts, you can use them to review the most important points in each chapter. Ultimately, the Gateway concepts will provide a good summary of what you learned in this course. If you remember most of them 10 years after you finish reading this book, you will make us very happy, indeed.

Studying *Gateways to Mind and Behavior*

None of us likes to start a new adventure by reading a manual. We want to get right into a new computer game, step off the airplane and begin our vacation, or just start using our new camera or cell phone. You might be similarly tempted to just start reading this textbook.

Please be patient. Successfully learning psychology depends on how you study this book, as well as how you read it. *Gateways to Mind and Behavior* is your passport to an active adventure in learning, not just passive reading. To help you get off to a good start, we strongly encourage you to read our short Introduction, which precedes Chapter 1. The Introduction describes study skills, including the SQ4R method, that you can use to get the most out of this text and your psychology course. It also tells how you can

explore psychology through the Internet, electronic databases, and interactive CDs.

Each chapter of this book will take you into a different realm of psychology, such as personality, abnormal behavior, memory, consciousness, and human development. Each realm is complex and fascinating in its own right. *Gateways to Mind and Behavior* is your passport to an adventure in learning. In a very real sense, we wrote it about you, for you, and to you.

An Invitation to the Instructor

Thank you for choosing this book for your students and your course. Marcel Proust wrote, "The real voyage of discovery consists not in seeing new landscapes but in having new eyes." It is in this spirit that we encourage you to use this book's special features to help change the way your students see human behavior. Accordingly, we have written this book to promote an interest in human behavior, including an appreciation of the practical applications of psychology, the richness of human diversity, and the field of positive psychology. At the same time, we have structured this book to help students learn efficiently and apply critical-thinking skills. Without such skills, students cannot easily go, as Jerome Bruner put it, "beyond the information given" (Bruner, 1973).

To help students read more effectively, we open every chapter with a list of *Gateway Questions* that students can use as powerful advance organizers for digesting new information (e.g., Ausubel, 1978). These questions are addressed throughout the chapter and are explicitly answered in the chapter summaries. Featured in these summaries are psychology's *Gateway concepts*—the "take home" ideas every student should remember 10 years after reading this text. As a whole, they are capable of transforming the way students view human behavior.

Now widely emulated, earlier editions of *Gateways to Mind and Behavior* revolutionized textbooks by using psychology to help students learn more effectively. We continue that tradition of innovation in this edition. We have again updated our presentation of the SQ4R method to better promote active learning, long-term retention of ideas, and the reflective attitude that lies at the heart of critical thinking.

In the previous edition we replaced the "Relate" step of the SQ4R method with "Reflect," so that SQ4R now refers to Survey, Question, Read, Recite, Reflect, and Review. In every chapter, we have refined the Reflect step of the SQ4R method to strengthen connections among learning, elaborative processing, and critical thinking (Gadzella, 1995). For example, we have redesigned the chapter pedagogy to make it even clearer to students why it is valuable to engage in reflection while reading.

Readability and Narrative Emphasis

Selecting a textbook is half the battle in teaching a successful course. When a book overwhelms students or cools their interest, teaching and learning suffer. A good text does much of the work of imparting information to your students. This frees class time for your discussion, extra topics, or media presentations. It also leaves students asking for more.

Many introductory psychology students are reluctant readers. No matter how interesting a text may be, its value is lost if students fail to read it. That's why we've worked hard to make this a clear, readable, and engaging text. We want students to read this book with genuine interest and enthusiasm, not merely as an obligation.

To encourage students to read, we made a special effort to weave narrative threads through every chapter. Everyone loves a good story, and the story of psychology is among the most compelling to be told. Throughout *Gateways to Mind and Behavior,* we have used intriguing anecdotes and examples to propel reading and sustain interest. As students explore concepts, they are encouraged to think about ideas and relate them to current events and their own experiences.

Practical Applications

Gateways to Mind and Behavior is designed to give students a clear grasp of major concepts without burying them in details. At the same time, it offers a broad overview that reflects psychology's rich heritage of ideas. We think students will find this book informative and intellectually stimulating. Moreover, we have emphasized the many ways that psychology relates to practical problems in daily life.

A major feature of this book is the *Psychology in Action* section found at the end of each chapter. These high-interest discussions bridge the gap between theory and practical application. We believe it is fair for students to ask, "Does this mean anything to me? Can I use it? Why should I learn it if I can't?" The Psychology in Action features show students how to solve problems and manage their own behavior. This allows them to see the benefits of adopting new ideas, and it breathes life into psychology's concepts.

An Integrated Study Guide

The chapters of this text are divided into short segments by special sections called *Knowledge Builders.* These "mini study guides" challenge students to relate concepts to their own experiences, to quiz themselves, and to think critically about the principles they are learning. For this edition, we have reorganized the Knowledge Builders into *Recite* and *Reflect* sections, to better mirror the SQ4R method. Recite questions are somewhat easier than in-class test questions and are designed provide immediate feedback to students. Reflect questions come in two "flavors." *Critical Thinking* questions encourage critical reflection and come with answers. *Relate* questions are open-ended invitations to students to elaborate on just-read material by relating it to their personal experiences.

If students would like even more feedback and practice, *Chapter Quizzes* are available in a free booklet, *Gateways to Mind and Behavior: Concept Maps and Concept Reviews*; a traditional *Study Guide* is available; and students can use a web-based course-management tool called *WebTutor™* to take online quizzes or to practice with electronic flash cards. *Gateways to Mind and Behavior: Concept Maps and Concept Reviews* accompanies every new copy of the text and also includes Gateway concepts for every chapter, concept maps of key concepts, and concept reviews (consisting of a 30-item multiple-choice quiz for each chapter). This useful booklet is available to qualified adopters; please consult your local sales representative for details.

Electronic Resources

To encourage further exploration, students will find a section called *Web Resources* at the end of each chapter. The websites described there offer a wealth of information on topics related to psychology. All chapters include a list of relevant modules in *PsychNow! 2.0.* This excellent CD-ROM from Wadsworth provides students with a rich assortment of interactive learning experiences, animations, and simulations.

On the web, students can visit this text's *Book Companion Website,* where they will find quizzes, a final exam, chapter-by-chapter web links, flash cards, an audio glossary, and more (**www.cengage.com/psychology/coon**).

Students can also make use of *CengageNOW for Coon and Mitterer's Introduction to Psychology: Gateways to Mind and Behavior,* Twelfth Edition, a web-based, personalized study system that provides a pretest and a posttest for each chapter and separate chapter quizzes. *CengageNOW for Coon and Mitterer's Introduction to Psychology,* Twelfth Edition, can also create personalized study plans—which include rich media such as videos, animations, and learning modules—that point students to areas in the text that will help them master course content. An additional set of integrative questions helps students pull all the material together.

Human Diversity

Today's students reflect the multicultural, multifaceted nature of contemporary society. In *Gateways to Mind and Behavior,* students will find numerous discussions of human diversity, including differences in race, ethnicity, culture, gender, abilities, sexual orientation, and age. Too often, such differences needlessly divide people into opposing groups. Our aim throughout this text is to discourage stereotyping, prejudice, discrimination, and intolerance. We've tried to make this book gender neutral and sensitive to diversity issues. All pronouns and examples involving females and males are equally divided by gender. In artwork, photographs, and examples, we have tried to portray the rich diversity of humanity. In addition, a boxed feature, *Human Diversity,* appears throughout the book, providing students with examples of how to be more reflective about human diversity. In short, many topics and examples in this book encourage students to appreciate social, physical, and cultural differences and to accept them as a natural part of being human.

Positive Psychology

In January 2000, Martin Seligman and Mihaly Csikszentmihalyi co-edited a special issue of *American Psychologist* devoted to optimal functioning, happiness, and "positive psychology." Over the past 100 years, psychologists have paid ample attention to the negative side of human behavior. This is easy to understand because we urgently need to find remedies for human problems. However, Seligman and Csikszentmihalyi have urged us to also study positive psychology. What do we know, for instance, about love, happiness, creativity, well-being, self-confidence, and achievement? Throughout this book, we have attempted to answer such questions for students. Our hope is that students who read this book will gain an appreciation for the potential we all have for optimal functioning. Also, of course, we hope that they will leave introductory psychology with emotional and intellectual tools they can use to enhance their lives.

How Chapter Features Support the SQ4R Method

Introduction to Psychology was the first college text with an SQ4R, active-learning format. Through Dennis Coon's pioneering efforts, this book has made learning psychology a rewarding experience for more than 2 million students. With their feedback and generous help from many professors, we have continued to refine the unique features of *Gateways to Mind and Behavior.*

Notice how the steps of the SQ4R method—*survey, question, read, recite, reflect,* and *review*—are incorporated into the chapter design.

Survey Features at the beginning of each chapter help students build cognitive maps of upcoming topics, thus serving as advance organizers. Students begin with a chapter *Theme* and a list of Gateway Questions that identify the main points students should search for as they read. Next, a short *Preview* arouses interest, gives an overview of the chapter, and focuses attention on the task at hand. These chapter-opening features encourage students to read with a purpose and actively process information.

Question Throughout each chapter, frequent italicized *Guide Questions* also serve as advance organizers. That is, Guide Questions prompt students to look for important ideas as they read and thus promote active learning. They also establish a dialogue in which the questions and reactions of students are anticipated. This clarifies difficult points—in a lively give-and-take between questions and responses.

Read We've made every effort to make this a clear, readable text. To further aid comprehension, we've used a full array of traditional learning aids. These include boldface terms (with phonetic pronunciations), bullet summaries, a robust illustration program, summary tables, a name index, a subject index, and a detailed glossary. As an additional aid, figure and table references in the text are marked with small geometric shapes. These "placeholders" make it easier for students to return to reading after they have paused to view a table or figure.

An *Integrated Glossary* aids reading comprehension by providing precise definitions directly in context. When important terms first appear, they are immediately defined. In this way, students get clear definitions when and where they need them—in the general text itself. In addition, a parallel *Running Glossary* defines key terms in the margins of pages. The Running Glossary makes it easier for students to find, study, and review important terms.

Recite Every few pages, a Knowledge Builder gives students a chance to test their recall and understanding of preceding topics. As mentioned earlier, the Knowledge Builders are small, built-in study guides that include a Recite section (a short, noncomprehensive quiz), which helps students actively process information and assess their progress. Recite questions are not as difficult as in-class tests, and they are just a sample of what students could be asked about various topics. Students who miss any items are asked to backtrack and clarify their understanding before reading more. Completing Recite questions serves as a form of recitation to enhance learning.

Reflect Cognitive psychology tells us that elaboration, the reflective processing of new information, is one of the best ways to foster understanding and form lasting memories (Anderson, 2005; Gadzella, 1995; Goldstein, 2008). The more students elaborate ideas as they read and study, the richer their understanding will be and the better they will remember new concepts.

Self-reference, a particularly powerful form of elaboration, makes new information more meaningful by relating it to what is already known (Klein & Kihlstrom, 1986). *Discovering Psychology* boxes in this edition are "try-it" demonstrations that allow students to observe interesting facets of their own behavior or do self-assessment exercises. In this way, students can link new information to concrete experiences.

To help students further elaborate their new understanding, each Knowledge Builder includes a series of *Relate* questions that encourage students to associate new concepts with personal experiences and prior knowledge.

A course in psychology also naturally contributes to deeper forms of reflection, such as the development of critical-thinking abilities. As we described earlier, to further facilitate reflection, each Knowledge Builder also includes one or more *Critical Thinking Questions* to further facilitate reflection. These stimulating questions challenge students to think critically and analytically about psychology. Each is followed by a brief answer with which students can compare their own thoughts. Many of these answers are based on research and are informative in their own right.

In addition, several boxed highlights encourage other forms of reflective thought. The *Critical Thinking* boxes model a reflective approach to critical thinking in psychology. In addition, *Human Diversity* boxes encourage reflection on the variability of human experience, *The Clinical File* boxes help students think about clinical applications of psychology, and *Brainwaves* boxes, which are new to this edition, encourage reflection on brain mechanisms that underlie psychological phenomena.

Finally, *Bridges* appear throughout the text. Each Bridge links a topic under discussion to related information elsewhere in the book. This feature helps students reflect on the rich interconnection of ideas in contemporary psychology.

Review As noted previously, all important terms appear in a Running Glossary throughout the book, which aids review. As also noted, a Psychology in Action section shows students how psychological concepts relate to practical problems, including problems in their own lives. The information found in Psychology in Action helps reinforce learning by illustrating psychology's practicality.

Next, a point-by-point summary provides a concise synopsis of all major concepts. The *Chapter in Review* summary is organized around answers to the Gateway Questions found at the beginning of the chapter. This brings the SQ4R process full circle and provides closure with respect to the learning objectives of each chapter.

Critical Thinking

The active, questioning nature of the SQ4R method is, in itself, an inducement to think critically. Many of the Guide Questions that introduce topics in the text act as models of critical thinking. So do the Critical Thinking, Human Diversity, Discovering Psychology, The Clinical File, and Brainwaves boxes. Further, Chapter 1 contains a discussion of critical-thinking skills and a rational appraisal of pseudo-psychologies. In addition, the research methods portion of Chapter 1 is basically a short course on how to think clearly about behavior. It is augmented by tips about how to critically evaluate claims in the popular media. Chapter 9, which covers intelligence, cognition, language, and creativity, includes many topics related to critical thinking. Taken together, these features will help students gain thinking skills of lasting value.

Psychology: Gateways to Mind and Behavior — What's New?

Thanks to psychology's vitality, this text is improved in many ways. Most importantly, the book has been shortened to 18 chapters. Two developmental psychology chapters have been combined into one, as have two chapters on intelligence and cognition, language, and creativity. This major change is based on feedback suggesting that a 20-chapter book presents too much material to cover in most introductory courses.

This edition also features an updated SQ4R system, outlined elsewhere in this Preface. The refinements strengthen the link between remembering new information and thinking reflectively and critically about psychology.

Finally, the Twelfth Edition of *Introduction to Psychology: Gateways to Mind and Behavior* features some of the most recent and interesting information in psychology. Research references have been extensively updated, with fully two thirds of citations dated 2000 or newer. The following annotations highlight some of the new topics and features that appear in this edition.

Introduction: The Psychology of Studying

We have once again updated our SQ4R framework. The Knowledge Builders have been restructured so that students can more easily see how they relate to the SQ4R method. Specifically,

Learning Check questions are now *Recite* questions. A new section titled *Reflect* now includes *Relate* questions and *Critical Thinking* questions. This change is designed to make it clearer to students that relating new information to personal experiences and thinking critically about new ideas are both forms of reflective cognition. In addition, the Introduction shows students how to read effectively, study more efficiently, take good notes, prepare for tests, take tests, create study schedules, and avoid procrastination.

Chapter 1: Introduction to Psychology and Research Methods

- Chapter 1 has been extensively reorganized and updated and begins with a more engaging chapter-opening vignette.
- Critical thinking is now covered early in the chapter and is immediately followed by a discussion of the scientific method. This placement permits students to more tightly link critical thinking and scientific thought.
- The history of psychology is now presented after a discussion of critical thinking and the scientific method. This arrangement gives students a fuller context for understanding historical changes in psychology.
- Modern views on behavior have been reorganized into three major perspectives: biological, behavioral, and sociocultural.
- A new Critical Thinking highlight, "That's Interesting, but Is It Ethical?" provides increased coverage of research ethics in psychology.
- The material on placebo effects and the experimenter effect has been rewritten to include both research participant bias and experimenter bias. Placebo effects are treated as a form of research participant bias.
- The experimental method is now explored first, before other research methods. Nonexperimental methods (case studies, surveys, correlations, and natural observation) are then addressed as alternative research strategies.

Chapter 2: Brain and Behavior

- Chapter 2 has been enlarged to reflect the growing importance of neuroscience in contemporary psychology. Additional neuroscience content can also be found in subsequent chapters (most noticeably in the new Brainwaves boxes).
- The section on neural transmission now includes information about myelin and saltatory conduction.
- The explanation of neural networks has been expanded and includes a new explanatory figure.
- Artwork illustrating the structure of the nervous system has been unified for greater simplicity and clarity.
- Coverage of the spinal cord, which concludes with an appraisal of the possibility of spinal cord repair, is now followed by a Critical Thinking box, "Brain Repair."
- The discussion of neuroscience research methods has been rewritten to more clearly distinguish ablation from electrical stimulation.

- The lobes of the cerebral cortex are covered in a new order, and the entire topic has been revised, including an updated figure.
- A new Critical Thinking box, "Mirror, Mirror, in the Brain," discusses the discovery of mirror neurons and their possible significance.

Chapter 3: Human Development

- Chapter 3 combines major topics from Child Development (Chapter 3 of the previous edition) and Human Development (Chapter 4 of the previous edition). The resulting chapter moves from infancy through childhood to adulthood.
- Material on heredity and environmental influences has been reorganized and streamlined. Most notably, maturation is now treated in the heredity section, along with readiness.
- The section on the newborn has been reorganized for greater clarity.
- The discussion of Piaget's theory has also been reorganized. Transformations are now introduced in a subsection about the preoperational stage. Simple exercises have been added to make it easier for students to assimilate the concepts of internal representations and transformations.

Chapter 4: Sensation and Reality

- Chapter 4 begins with a new vignette about echolocation by bats that illustrates the limits of our senses.
- For greater clarity, the first section has been restructured to combine the previously separated topics of sensory limits and psychophysics.
- A more helpful metaphorical comparison is now drawn between the visual system and digital cameras.
- Material on blindsight is now presented in a Brainwaves box, "Blindsight: The 'What' and the 'Where' of Vision," which has been expanded to include a new figure illustrating the dorsal and ventral visual pathways.
- A new Discovering Psychology box titled "Going Biosonar" harks back to the chapter-opening vignette about bat echolocation by describing a blind human teenager who echolocates. Students are given instructions about how to navigate by echolocation.
- The discussion of hearing loss has been revised to follow current terminology (i.e., *sensorineural hearing loss* and *conductive hearing loss*).
- The material on gustation and olfaction has been rewritten. In particular, anosmia is now referred to as *dysosmia*.

Chapter 5: Perceiving the World

- Chapter 5 has been extensively reorganized to allow students to draw sharper distinctions between sensation and perception.
- The first section in the chapter explains in more detail why perception is a necessary extra step beyond sensation, and it includes a discussion of bottom-up and top-down processing.

- Because attention is an early stage of the perceptual process, we now discuss it earlier in the chapter.
- Student feedback suggests that it is easier to understand perceptual organization before tackling perceptual constancies. Accordingly, Gestalt principles are now covered before perceptual constancies are introduced.
- The section on depth perception has also been reorganized and streamlined. In particular, depth cues are now separated into binocular and monocular cues. Muscular depth cues have been omitted as a separate category because the heading mixed a binocular cue (convergence) with a monocular one (accommodation).

Chapter 6: States of Consciousness

- Chapter 6 features revised coverage of sleep and dreaming.
- The dual process hypothesis, which assigns different functions to NREM and REM sleep, is now discussed.
- The treatment of dreaming has been updated to include Domhoff's neurocognitive theory as a complement to psychodynamic and activation-synthesis theories.
- The section on hypnosis has also been rewritten for greater clarity.
- Meditation is now treated in a section along with REST (restricted environmental stimulation therapy), and both are related to the relaxation response.
- A new Brainwaves box, "How Drugs Affect the Brain," was fashioned from existing material and includes a new figure.
- Statistics have been updated throughout the chapter, such as those concerning rates of drug abuse and the percentage of accidents related to sleepiness.

Chapter 7: Conditioning and Learning

- Chapter 7 opens with an engaging new vignette about acquiring a phobia. This example better highlights differences between associative and cognitive learning, a distinction that is also more clearly reflected throughout the chapter.
- The section on classical conditioning has been streamlined for greater clarity.
- A new Brainwaves box, "Tickling Your Own Fancy," updates coverage of the self-stimulation phenomenon.
- Are animals aware of the past? A new Critical Thinking box, "Are Animals Stuck in Time?" explores this interesting question and also shows how operant conditioning can be used as a research technique.

Chapter 8: Memory

- The three-store memory model is now clearly labeled as the Atkinson-Schiffrin model.
- The term "dual memory" has been eliminated to avoid confusing students.
- The term "elaborative rehearsal" has been changed to "elaborative encoding" to better tie elaboration to encoding, one of the three fundamental memory processes.

- A new Critical Thinking box, "Do You Like Jam with Your Memory?" shows students how advertisers try to manipulate memory. It also serves as an interesting example of (re)constructive processing.
- Discussions of exceptional memory and strategies for improving memory have been extensively reorganized and rewritten.
- To help students remember why we forget, theories of forgetting are now organized into three categories: encoding failure, storage failure, and retrieval failure.
- Material on the neuroscience of memory has been reorganized. In particular, flashbulb memories are now included in a section on memory and emotion and linked to the role the amygdala plays in processing emotional memories.
- The section on improving memory has been reorganized into two subsections that tell students how they can improve encoding and retrieval.

Chapter 9: Intelligence, Cognition, Language, and Creativity

- This chapter is a condensation of Cognition, Language, and Creativity (Chapter 10 of the previous edition) and Intelligence (Chapter 11 of the previous edition).
- The chapter has also been streamlined for greater interest and readability.
- The distinction between multiple intelligences and intelligence as a *g*-factor is given more prominence.
- The coverage of artificial intelligence has been rewritten and is now included in the section on intelligence.

Chapter 10: Motivation and Emotion

- Chapter 10 opens with a new vignette featuring an interesting case study of alexithymia.
- The topic of hunger has been restructured into major sections that discuss internal and external factors affecting eating.
- A new Brainwaves box, "Your Brain's 'Fat Point,'" discusses setpoints and the role of leptin in hunger and feeding.
- The material on eating disorders has been reworked and now includes information about eating disorders in men.
- A new Discovering Psychology box, "Behavioral Dieting," more clearly invites students to apply behavioral principles to control their own eating behavior.
- To help students better organize their understanding, the Psychology in Action section on emotional intelligence has been reorganized around a revised definition of emotional intelligence.

Chapter 11: Gender and Sexuality

- The flow of topics in this chapter has been reorganized.
- Information about sexual development has been moved to the beginning of the chapter, which helps clarify the sequence of sexual development.
- Sexual orientation is discussed earlier in the chapter and is characterized as an intrinsic biological component of sexual development.

- Material on gender development is now presented in a single section of the chapter.
- A new Human Diversity box, "High Test," discusses how testosterone affects men.

Chapter 12: Personality

- Hereditary influences on personality have been moved forward into the first section of this chapter.
- A new The Clinical File box, "Telling Stories about Ourselves," explores narrative psychology and personality change.
- Information about when personality "hardens" has been rewritten.
- Direct and indirect aggression are clearly differentiated in the discussion of personality and gender.

Chapter 13: Health, Stress, and Coping

- A new table updates information about the top ten stressors.
- Material on the general adaptation syndrome and psychoneuroimmunology now appears at the beginning of this chapter.
- A new Discovering Psychology box, "Unhealthy Birds of a Feather," presents some new data on the social transmission of healthy and unhealthy behaviors.
- The Critical Thinking box, "It's All in Your Mind," has been rewritten.

Chapter 14: Psychological Disorders

- Chapter 14 has been reorganized for greater clarity. Specifically, the presentation of disorders has been rearranged. We now begin with psychotic disorders (to lead with a malady that is dramatic and highly interesting to students), and follow with mood disorders, anxiety disorders, and personality disorders. This ordering is easier for students to understand, and it matches the order of topics provided at the beginning of the chapter.
- A new Brainwaves box, "The Schizophrenic Brain," better highlights for students some differences between schizophrenic and normal brains.
- The Human Diversity box, "Running Amok with Cultural Maladies," has been updated.
- A new The Clinical File box, titled "Sick of Being Sick," introduces students to the fascinating topic of Munchausen syndrome by proxy.
- The discussion of insanity now occurs near the front of the chapter, where it makes better connections with related topics.
- The Critical Thinking box, "The Politics of Madness," has been repositioned to the end of the chapter.

Chapter 15: Therapies

- Chapter 15 has received a relatively light update.
- The section on cybertherapy has been rewritten and updated.
- A new description of interpersonal psychotherapy (IPT) has been added.
- The coverage of somatic therapies includes a discussion of electrical stimulation of the brain (other than ECT).

- A new The Clinical File box, "Overcoming the Gambler's Fallacy," introduces students to the problem of compulsive gambling and relates it to cognitive therapies.

Chapter 16: Social Thinking and Social Influence

- The two social psychology chapters (Chapters 16 and 17) have been extensively reorganized. Chapter titles have changed accordingly.
- Attribution (from the previous Chapter 16), attitudes, and attitude change (from the old Chapter 17) are discussed together, as forms of social thinking.
- The remaining topics from the former Chapter 16 now appear as an extended discussion of social influence, presented in order from mild to strong forms of influence.
- The effect of mere presence is now discussed, as are social facilitation and social loafing. Invasions of personal space are reinterpreted as a form of mere presence.
- The presentation of social influence then moves from conformity to compliance and obedience.
- Coercion, which is the final topic in this series, is composed mainly of material on brainwashing and cults from the old Chapter 17.

Chapter 17: Prosocial and Antisocial Behavior

- As the new chapter title implies, Chapter 17 now focuses on prosocial and antisocial behavior.
- The presentation of prosocial behavior has been broadened to include affiliation, liking, and loving, as well as a willingness to help strangers.
- An exploration of affiliation, liking, and loving now opens this chapter.
- Robert Sternberg's triangular theory of love is now included because it is highly interesting to students.
- A new Human Diversity box, "Purple America," invites students to think beyond stereotyping American citizens as either "red" or "blue" (Republican or Democrat).

Chapter 18: Applied Psychology

- The chapter-opening vignette now discusses how human factors have contributed to the iPod's success, a topic of great interest to students.
- The section on industrial/organizational psychology has been rewritten and restructured and now begins with the topic of leadership.
- A new Critical Thinking box, "From Glass Ceiling to Labyrinth," describes the challenges women face as business leaders.
- Material on flextime now includes a discussion of compressed workweeks and telecommuting.
- A new Discovering Psychology box, "Surviving Your Job Interview," offers concrete advice to students as they look for jobs.
- The discussion of environmental psychology has been revised and updated to include information about carbon footprints.

The Psychology in Action section has been rewritten to introduce students to human factors, with a focus on the study of human–computer interaction.

⬤⬤ A Complete Course—Teaching and Learning Supplements

A rich array of supplements accompanies *Introduction to Psychology: Gateways to Mind and Behavior,* including several that make use of the latest technologies. These supplements are designed to make teaching and learning more effective. Many are available free to professors or students. Others can be packaged with this text at a discount.

Student Support Materials

Introductory students must learn a multitude of abstract concepts, which can make a first course in psychology difficult. The materials listed here will greatly improve students' chances for success.

Gateways to Psychology: Concept Maps and Concept Reviews Concept Maps created by Christine M. Vanchella and quiz items updated by Shawn Talbot, Kellogg Community College. For each chapter of the text, this booklet includes the Gateway concepts, a concept map, and a 35-item multiple-choice practice exam (ISBN: 0-495-82929-3).

Study Guide The *Study Guide,* written by Thuy Karafa of Ferris State University and Dennis Coon, is an invaluable student resource. It contains a variety of study tools, including: Chapter Overviews, Recite and Review (fill-in-the-blank), Connections (matching), Check Your Memory (true/false), Final Survey and Review (fill-in-the-blank), and Mastery Test (ISBN: 0-495-80429-0).

Careers in Psychology: Opportunities in a Changing World, **Second Edition** This informative booklet, written by Tara L. Kuther, is a Wadsworth exclusive. The pamphlet describes the field of psychology, as well as how to prepare for a career in psychology. Career options and resources are also discussed. *Careers in Psychology* can be packaged with this text at no additional cost to students (ISBN: 0-495-09078-6).

Multimedia CD-ROMs

Interactive CD-ROMs make it possible for students to directly experience some of the phenomena they are studying. The following CDs from Wadsworth provide a wealth of engaging modules and exercises.

PsychNow!™ Interactive Experiences in Psychology 2.0 This exciting CD-ROM was created by Joel Morgovsky, Lonnie Yandell, Elizabeth Lynch, and project consultant Dennis Coon. At the end of each chapter of this text, students will find a list of *PsychNow!* modules they can access for additional, "hands-on" learning. *PsychNow!* provides stunning graphics and animations, interesting video clips, interactive exercises, and web links, bringing psychology to life. With *PsychNow!,* students can do more than just read about a topic—they can read, watch, listen, react, and reflect on the meaning of their own responses. *PsychNow!,* which is available for Macintosh and Windows, contains 39 fully interactive modules that will enhance their understanding, 8 "Interact Now" Collaborative Labs, and "Quiz Game Now" quizzes. Students can also conduct 15 different "Interactive Research Experiments" in areas such as neurocognition, perception, memory, concepts, and imagery. *PsychNow! 2.0* can be packaged with this text for a discount; contact your sales representative for details (ISBN: 0-534-59046-2).

Sniffy™ the Virtual Rat, Lite Version 2.0   There's no better way to master the basic principles of learning than working with a real laboratory rat. However, this is usually impractical in introductory psychology courses. *Sniffy the Virtual Rat* offers a fun, interactive alternative to working with lab animals. This innovative and entertaining software teaches students about operant and classical conditioning by allowing them to condition a virtual rat. Users begin by training Sniffy to press a bar to obtain food. Then they progress to studying the effects of reinforcement schedules and simple classical conditioning. In addition, special "Mind Windows" enable students to visualize how Sniffy's experiences in the Skinner Box produce learning. The Sniffy CD-ROM includes a Lab Manual that shows students how to set up various operant and classical conditioning experiments. *Sniffy™ the Virtual Rat, Lite Version 2.0* may be packaged with this text for a discount (ISBN: 0-534-63357-9).

Online Resources

The Internet is providing new ways to exchange information and enhance education. In psychology, Wadsworth is at the forefront in making use of this exciting technology.

Book Companion Website   As users of this text, you and your students will have access to the Book Companion Website for *Introduction to Psychology* at www.cengage.com/psychology/coon. Access is free and no pin is required. This outstanding site features chapter-by-chapter online tutorial quizzes, a final exam, chapter-by-chapter web links, flash cards, and more!

CENGAGENOW™   This web-based study aid, by Christopher B. Mayhorn, North Carolina State University, helps your students discover the areas of text where they need to focus their efforts through a series of diagnostic pretests and posttests, personalized study plans—which include rich media such as videos, animations, and learning modules—that parallel the modules in the book, eBook files, and other integrated media elements. New to this edition, students have access to the Psychology Resource Center included with CengageNow. The new Psychology Resource Center features powerful teaching and learning tools, bringing psychology to life with a full library of original and classic video clips plus interactive learning modules tied to all the topics covered in an introductory psychology course. Organized by topic, the Psychology Resource Center is easy to navigate by students to find learning resources, and instructors will also find it an amazing lecture resource to easily stream multimedia into their classrooms (ISBN: 0-495-80682-X).

WebTutor   This online supplement helps students succeed by taking them into an environment rich with study and mastery tools, communication aids, and additional course content. For students, *WebTutor* offers real-time access to a full array of study tools, including videos, animations, flash cards (with audio), practice quizzes and tests, online tutorials, exercises, asynchronous discussion, a whiteboard, and an integrated e-mail system. Students will also have integrated access to the *Newbury House Online Dictionary,* an interactive dictionary that gives users instant access to definitions (including audio pronunciations).

Professors can use *WebTutor* to offer virtual office hours, post syllabi, set up threaded discussions, track student progress on quizzes, and more. You can customize the content of *WebTutor* in any way you choose, including uploading images and other resources, adding web links, and creating course-specific practice materials (*WebTutor* on *WebCT,* ISBN: 0-495-80690-0; *WebTutor* on *Blackboard,* ISBN: 0-495-80691-9).

Essential Teaching Resources

As every professor knows, teaching an introductory psychology course is a tremendous amount of work. The supplements listed here should not only make life easier for you, they should also make it possible for you to concentrate on the more creative and rewarding facets of teaching.

Instructor's Resource Manual   The *Instructor's Resource Manual,* by Wanda McCarthy, Clermont College, University of Cincinnati, contains resources designed to streamline and maximize the effectiveness of your course preparation. In a three-ring binder format, this IRM is a treasure trove—from the introduction section, which includes a Resource Integration Guide, to a full array of chapter resources. Each chapter includes learning objectives, discussion questions, lecture enhancements, role-playing scenarios, "one-minute motivators," broadening-our-cultural-horizons exercises, journal questions, suggestions for further reading, media suggestions, and web links (ISBN: 0-495-60314-7).

Test Bank   The *Test Bank* was prepared by Jeannette Murphey of Meridian Community College. It includes over 4,500 multiple-choice questions organized by chapter and by learning objectives. All items, which are classified as factual, conceptual, or applied, include correct answers and page references from the text. All questions new to this edition are identified by an asterisk (ISBN: 0-495-59916-6).

PowerLecture with JoinIn and ExamView   This one-stop digital library and presentation tool includes preassembled Microsoft® PowerPoint® lecture slides by Andrew Getzfeld, New York University. In addition to a full *Instructor's Manual* and *Test Bank,* PowerLecture® also includes all videos from Wadsworth's Psychology Digital Video Library 3.0, which can be easily integrated into PowerPoint® for more interactive presentations. PowerLecture® brings together all your media resources in one place, including an image library with graphics from the book itself, video clips, and more. PowerLecture® also includes ExamView® testing software with all the test items from the printed Test Bank in electronic format, enabling you to create customized tests in print or online, as well as JoinIn™ Student Response System, offering instant assessment and better student results (ISBN: 0-495-80676-5).

Videotapes and Films

Wadsworth offers a variety of videotapes and films to enhance classroom presentations. Many video segments in the Wadsworth collection pertain directly to major topics in this text, making them excellent lecture supplements.

ABC Video for Introductory Psychology, Volume 1 and 2   Available to adopters, these ABC videos feature short, high-interest clips about current studies and research in psychology. These videos are perfect to start discussions or to enrich lectures. Topics include brain damage, measuring IQ, sleep patterns, obsessive-compulsive disorder, obedience to authority, rules of attraction and much more (Volume 1 ISBN: 0-495-50306-1; Volume 2 ISBN: 0-495-59637-X).

Wadsworth Film and Video Library for Introductory Psychology   Adopters can select from a variety of continually updated film and video options. The Wadsworth Film and Video Library includes selections from the *Discovering Psychology* series, the *Annenberg* series, and *Films for Humanities*. Contact your local sales representative or Wadsworth Marketing at 1-877-999-2350 for details.

Psychology Digital Video Library Version 3.0 CD-ROM   This CD-ROM contains a diverse selection of classic and contemporary clips, including "Little Albert," the "Action Potential of a Neuron," "Parts of the Brain," and many more! The digital library offers a convenient way to access an appropriate clip for every lecture. An accompanying *Digital Video Handbook* offers a detailed description, approximate running time, and references to related media clips. It also offers objective quizzing and critical-thinking questions for each clip, as well as instructions on how to embed clips into your PowerPoint presentations. Available exclusively to instructors who adopt Wadsworth psychology texts (ISBN: 0-495-09063-8).

Wadsworth Media Guide for Introductory Psychology   This essential instructor resource, edited by Russell J. Watson, contains hundreds of video and feature film recommendations for all major topics in introductory psychology (ISBN: 0-534-17585-6).

Supplementary Books

No text can cover all the topics that might be included in an introductory psychology course. If you would like to enrich your course, or make it more challenging, the Wadsworth titles listed here may be of interest.

Challenging Your Preconceptions: Thinking Critically about Psychology, Second Edition   This paperbound book (ISBN: 0-534-26739-4), written by Randolph Smith, helps students strengthen their critical-thinking skills. Psychological issues such as hypnosis and repressed memory, statistical seduction, the validity of pop psychology, and other topics are used to illustrate the principles of critical thinking.

Writing Papers in Psychology: A Student Guide   The Sixth Edition of *Writing Papers in Psychology* (ISBN: 0-534-52395-1), by Ralph L. Rosnow and Mimi Rosnow, is a valuable "how to" manual for writing term papers and research reports. This new edition has been updated to reflect the latest APA guidelines. The book covers each task with examples, hints, and two complete writing samples. Citation ethics, how to locate information, and new research technologies are also covered.

Cross-Cultural Perspectives in Psychology   How well do the concepts of psychology apply to various cultures? What can we learn about human behavior from cultures different from our own? These questions lie behind a collection of original articles written by William F. Price and Rich Crapo. The Fourth Edition of *Cross-Cultural Perspectives in Psychology* (ISBN: 0-534-54653-6) contains articles on North American ethnic groups as well as cultures from around the world.

Summary

We sincerely hope that both teachers and students will consider this book and its supporting materials a refreshing change from the ordinary. Creating them has been quite an adventure. In the pages that follow, we believe students will find an attractive blend of the theoretical and the practical, plus many of the most exciting ideas in psychology. Most of all, we hope that students using this book will discover that reading a college textbook can be entertaining and enjoyable.

◉ Acknowledgments

Psychology is a cooperative effort requiring the talents and energies of a large community of scholars, teachers, researchers, and students. Like most endeavors in psychology, this book reflects the efforts of many people. We deeply appreciate the contributions of the following professors who have, over the years, supported this text's evolution:

Faren R. Akins
University of Arizona

Avis Donna Alexander
John Tyler Community College

Clark E. Alexander
Arapahoe Community College

Tricia Alexander
Long Beach City College

Dennis Anderson
Butler Community College

Lynn Anderson
Wayne State University

Nancy L. Ashton
R. Stockton College of New Jersey

Scott A. Bailey
Texas Lutheran University

Frank Barbehenn
Bucks County Community College

Michael Bardo
University of Kentucky

Larry W. Barron
Grand Canyon University

Linda M. Bastone
Purchase College, SUNY

Brian R. Bate
Cuyahoga Community College

Hugh E. Bateman
Jones Junior College

Evelyn Blanch-Payne
Oakwood College

Cheryl Bluestone
Queensborough Community
College–CUNY

Galen V. Bodenhausen
Michigan State University

Aaron U. Bolin
Arkansas State University

Tom Bond
Thomas Nelson Community College

John Boswell
University of Missouri, St. Louis

Anne Bright
Jackson State Community College

Soheila T. Brouk
Gateway Technical College

Derek Cadman
El Camino Community College

James F. Calhoun
University of Georgia

Jane Marie Cirillo
Houston Community College-
Southeast

Dennis Cogan
Texas Tech University

Lorry Cology
Owens College

Darlene Colson
Norfolk State University

William N. Colson
Norfolk State College

Chris Cozby
California State University, Fullerton

Corinne Crandell
Broome County Community
College

Thomas L. Crandell
Broome County Community
College

Charles Croll
Broome Community College

Daniel B. Cruse
University of Miami

Betty J. Daughenbaugh
Wor-Wic Community College

Keith E. Davis
University of South Carolina–
Columbia

Diane DeArmond
University of Missouri, Kansas City

Patrick T. DeBoll
St. John's University

Dawn Delaney
University of Wisconsin–
Whitewater

Jack Demick
Suffolk University

Lorraine P. Dieudonne
Foothill College

H. Mitzi Doane
University of Minnesota–Duluth

Wendy Domjan
University of Texas at Austin

Roger A. Drake
Western State College of Colorado

John Dworetzky
Glendale Community College

Bill Dwyer
Memphis State University

Thomas Eckle
Modesto Community College

David Edwards
Iowa State University

Raymond Elish
Cuyahoga Community College

Diane Feibel
University of Cincinnati–Raymond
Walters College

Paul W. Fenton
University of Wisconsin, Stout

Dave Filak
Joliet Junior College

Gloria Fisher, Ph.D.
Mississippi College

Oney D. Fitzpatrick, Jr.
Lamar University

Linda E. Flickinger
Saint Clair County Community
College

William F. Ford
Bucks County Community College

Marie Fox
Metropolitan State College of
Denver

Chris Fraser
Gippsland Institute of Advanced
Education

Christopher Frost
Southwest Texas State University

Eugenio J. Galindro
El Paso Community College

Irby J. Gaudet
University of Southwestern
Louisiana

David Gersh
Houston Community College

David A. Gershaw
Arizona Western College

Andrew R. Getzfeld
New Jersey City University

Carolyn A. Gingrich
South Dakota State University

Perilou Goddard
Northern Kentucky University

Michael E. Gorman
Michigan Technological University

Peter Gram
Pensacola Junior College

David A. Gries
State University of New York,
Farmingdale

R.J. Grisham
Indian River Community College

John Grivas
Monash University

Anne Groves
Montgomery College

Michael B. Guyer
John Carroll University

Janice Hartgrove-Freile
North Harris College

Raquel Henry
Kingwood College

Callina Henson
Oakland Community College–
Auburn Hills

Anne Hester
Pennsylvania State University–
Hazleton Campus

Gregory P. Hickman
The Pennsylvania State University–
Fayette

Don Hockenbury
Tulsa Junior College

Sidney Hockman
Nassau Community College

Barbara Honhart
Lansing Community College

John C. Johanson
Winona State University

James A. Johnson
Sam Houston State University

Myles E. Johnson
Normandale Community College

Pat Jones
Brevard Community College

Richard Kandus
Menifee Valley Campus

Bruno M. Kappes
University of Alaska–Anchorage

Charles Karis
Northeastern University

John P. Keating
University of Washington

Patricia Kemerer
Ivy Tech Community College

Cindy Kennedy
Sinclair Community College

Shaila Khan
Tougaloo College

Richard R. Klene
University of Cincinnati

Ronald J. Kopcho
Mercer Community College

Mary Kulish
Thomas Nelson Community College

Billie Laney
Central Texas College

Phil Lau
DeAnza College

Robert Lawyer
Delgado Community College

Walter Leach
College of San Mateo

Christopher Legrow
Marshall University

Lindette I. Lent
Arizona Western College

Elizabeth Levin
Laurentian University

Julie Lewis
Georgian College

Elise B. Lindenmuth
York College of Pennsylvania

Linda Lockwood
Metropolitan State College of
Denver

Philip Lom
West Connecticut State University

Cheryl S. Lynch
University of Louisiana–Lafayette

Salvador Macias, III
University of South Carolina,
Sumter

Abe Marrero
Rogers State University

Al Mayer
Portland Community College

Michael Jason McCoy
Cape Fear Community College

Edward R. McCrary III
El Camino College

Yancy B. McDougal
University of South Carolina,
Spartanburg

Mark McGee
Texas A&M University

Angela McGlynn
Mercer County Community College

Mark McKinley
Lorain County Community College

Chelley Merrill
Tidewater Community College

Beth Moore
Madisonville Community College

Feleccia R. Moore-Davis
Houston Community College
System

Edward J. Morris
Owensboro Community College

Edward Mosley
Pasiac County Community College

James Murray
San Jacinto University

Gary Nallan
University of North Carolina–
Ashville

Andrew Neher
Cabrillo College

Don Nelson
Indiana State University

Steve Nida
Franklin University

Peggy Norwood
Tidewater Community College

James P. B. O'Brien
Tidewater Community College

Frances O'Keefe
Tidewater Community College

Steve G. Ornelas
Central Arizona College

Laura Overstreet
Tarrant County College

Darlene Pacheco
Moorpark College

Lisa K. Paler
College of New Rochelle

Debra Parish
Tomball College

Cora F. Patterson
University of Southwestern
Louisiana

Leon Peek
North Texas State University

John Pennachio
Adirondack Community College

Peter Phipps
Sullivan County Community
College

Steven J. Pollock
Moorpark College

Jack Powell
University of Hartford

Ravi Prasad
Texas Tech University

Derrick L. Proctor
Andrews University

Douglas Pruitt
West Kentucky Community College

Robin Raygor
Anoka-Ramsey Community College

Richard Rees
Glendale Community College

Paul A. Rhoads
Williams College

Harvey Richman
Columbus State University

Marcia Rossi
Tuskegee University

Kim Royster
Tidewater Community College

Jeffrey Rudski
Mulhenberg College

James J. Ryan
University of Wisconsin, La Crosse

John D. Sanders
Butler County Community College

Nancy Sauerman
Kirkwood Community College

Michael Schuller
Fresno City College

Pamela E. Scott-Johnson
Spelman College

Carol F. Shoptaugh
Southwest Missouri State University

Harold I. Siegel
Rutgers University

Richard Siegel
University of Massachusetts, Lowell

Nancy Simpson
Trident Technical College

Madhu Singh
Tougaloo College

Glenda Smith
North Harris Community College

Steven M. Smith
Texas A&M University

Francine Smolucha
Moraine Valley Community College

Michael C. Sosulski
College of DuPage

Lynn M. Sprott
Jefferson Community College

Donald M. Stanley
North Harris County College

Julie E. Stokes
California State University–
Fullerton

Catherine Grady Strathern
University of Cincinnati

Harvey Taub
Staten Island Community College

Christopher Taylor
University of Arizona

Carol Terry
University of Oklahoma

Laura Thompson
New Mexico State University

Richard Townsend
Miami-Dade Community College–
Kendall Campus

Bruce Trotter
Santa Barbara City College

Susan Troy
Northeast Iowa Community College

Pat Tuntland
Pima College

Paul E. Turner
David Lipscomb University

A.D. VanDeventer
Thomas Nelson Community College

Mark Vernoy
Palomar College

Charles Verschoor
Miami-Dade Community College–
Kendall Campus

Frank Vitro
Texas Women's University

John Vojtisek
Castleton State College

Paul J. Wellman
Texas A&M University

Carl D. Williams
University of Miami

Michael Zeller
Mankato State University

Francis Volking
Saint Leo University

Sharon Whelan
University of Kentucky

Don Windham
Roane State Community College

Margaret C. Zimmerman
Virginia Wesleyan College

Margaret L. Walker
Georgia State University

Robert Wiley
Montgomery College

Kaye D. Young
North Iowa Area Community
College

Otto Zinser
East Tennessee State College

David W. Ward
Arkansas Tech University

Thomas Wilke
University of Wisconsin, Parkside

Producing *Introduction to Psychology: Gateways to Mind and Behavior* and its supplements was a formidable task. We are especially indebted to each of the following individuals for supporting this book: At Cengage Learning, Susan Badger, Sean Wakely, Eve Howard, Vicki Knight, and Michele Sordi. We are also grateful to Jaime Perkins for his insight and support. Jaime has unmistakably contributed to this book. At home, Heather Mitterer, Kayleigh Hagerman, and Barbara Kushmier helped in oh so many ways.

We also wish to thank the individuals at Cengage Learning who have so generously shared their knowledge and talents over the past year. These are the people who made it happen: Jeremy Judson, Vernon Boes, Pat Waldo, Rachel Guzman, Ileana Shevlin, and Kim Russell.

It has been a pleasure to work with such a gifted group of professionals and many others at Cengage Learning. We especially want to thank Jeremy Judson. As our developmental editor, Jeremy has gracefully kept us on track and offered many deeply appreciated suggestions.

Dennis Coon
John O. Mitterer

The Psychology of Studying

Eric Audras/PhotoAlto/Jupiterimages

Well Hello There!

You're actually reading this! As your authors, we're impressed. Too often, students just jump in and read a textbook from the first assigned chapter to the last. That's a shame because a textbook needs to be studied, not just read. Think about it: How much do you typically remember after you've read straight through a whole textbook chapter? If the answer is "Nada," "Zilch," or simply "Not enough," it may be because reading a chapter is not really the same as studying it. Even if you're an excellent student, you may be able to improve your study skills. Students who get good grades tend to work smarter, not just longer or harder (Santrock & Halonen, 2007). To help you get a good start, let's look at several ways to improve studying.

"I'm too busy going to college to study."

⬤ The SQ4R Method— How to Tame a Textbook

What's the difference between reading a textbook and studying it? You have probably occasionally spent an evening just vegging out in front of a TV set. According to psychologist Donald Norman (1993), you were engaging in *experiential cognition.* This type of thinking occurs when you passively let an experience happen to you. There is nothing wrong with merely experiencing entertainment. But have you noticed that the next morning you often have trouble remembering what you watched the night before?

In contrast, suppose one of the programs was about, say, global warming, and it really got you thinking. You might have wondered how global warming will affect your own future plans. You might have questioned some of the program's more dire projections for the future. You might have thought back to another program on global warming and remembered some different perspectives. Now you are "going beyond the information given" (Bruner, 1973). For Norman (1993), this is *reflective cognition:* Rather than just experiencing something, you also actively think *about* what you experienced. The next morning, you may forget most of what you watched the night before, but the odds are you will remember the program on global warming. Thus, studying a textbook ideally involves not just experiencing it, but also actively reflecting on what you read.

One way to be more reflective while reading a textbook is to use the **SQ4R method.** SQ4R stands for *survey, question, read, recite, reflect,* and *review.* These six steps can help you learn as you read and reflect, remember more, and review effectively:

S = *Survey.* Skim through a chapter before you begin reading it. Start by looking at topic headings, figure captions, and summaries. Try to get an overall picture of what lies ahead. Because this book is organized into short sections, you can survey just one section at a time if you prefer.

Q = *Question.* As you read, turn each topic heading into one or more questions. For example, when you read the heading "Stages of Sleep" you might ask, "Is there more than one stage of sleep?" "What are the stages of sleep?" "How do they differ?" Asking questions helps you read with a purpose.

R1 = *Read.* The first R in SQ4R stands for read. As you read, look for answers to the questions you asked. Read in short "bites," from one topic heading to the next, then stop. For difficult material you may want to read only a paragraph or two at a time.

R2 = *Recite.* After reading a small amount, you should pause and recite or rehearse. Try to mentally answer your questions. Better yet, summarize what you just read in brief notes. Making notes will show you what you know and don't know, so you can fill gaps in your knowledge (Peverly et al., 2003).

If you can't summarize the main ideas, skim over each section again. Until you can remember what you just read, there's little point to reading more. After you've studied a short "bite" of text, turn the next topic heading into questions. Then read to the following heading. Remember to look for answers as you read and to recite or take notes before moving on. Ask yourself repeatedly, "What is the main idea here?"

Repeat the question–read–recite cycle until you've finished an entire chapter (or just from one Knowledge Builder to the next, if you want to read shorter units).

R3 = *Reflect.* As you read, try to reflect on what you are reading. One powerful way to do this is to relate new facts, terms, and concepts to information you already know well or to your own experiences. You've probably noticed that it is especially easy to remember ideas that are personally meaningful, so try to relate the ideas you encountered to your own life. This may be the most important step in the SQ4R method. The more genuine interest you can bring to your reading, the more you will learn (Hartlep & Forsyth, 2000).

R4 = *Review.* When you're done reading, skim back over a section or the entire chapter, or read your notes. Then check your memory by reciting and quizzing yourself again. Try to make frequent, active review a standard part of your study habits (⬤ Figure I.1).

| Survey | Question Read Recite Reflect | Question Read Recite Reflect | Question Read Recite Reflect | Question Read Recite Reflect | Review |

⬤ **Figure I.1** The SQ4R method promotes active learning and information processing. You should begin with a survey of the chapter or section, depending on how much you plan to read. Then you should proceed through cycles of questioning, reading, reciting, and reflecting, and conclude with a review of the section or the entire chapter.

Does this really work? Yes. Using a reflective reading strategy improves learning and course grades (Taraban, Rynearson, & Kerr, 2000). Simply reading straight through a chapter can give you "intellectual indigestion." That's why it's better to stop often to think, question, recite, reflect, review, and "digest" information as you read.

How to Use *Introduction to Psychology: Gateways to Mind and Behavior*

You can apply the SQ4R method to any text. However, we have specifically designed this textbook to help you actively learn psychology.

Survey

Each chapter opens with a chapter survey that includes a *Gateway Theme* and a list of *Gateway Questions* as well as a *Preview* of what will be covered. You can use these features to identify important ideas as you begin reading. The *Preview* should help you get interested in the topics you will be reading about. The *Gateway Theme* and *Gateway Questions* are a good guide to the kinds of information to look for as you read. In fact, answers to the *Gateway Questions* are a good summary of the core concepts in each chapter. If, years from now, you still remember those *Gateway* concepts, your authors will be very happy indeed. Anyway, after you've studied the *Gateway Questions*, take a few minutes to do your own survey of the chapter. You should notice that each major chapter heading is accompanied by one of the *Gateway Questions*. This will help you build a "mental map" of upcoming topics.

Question

How can I use the SQ4R method to make reading more interesting and effective? One of the key steps is to ask yourself a lot of questions while you read. *Dialogue Questions* like the one that began this paragraph will help you focus on seeking information as you read. These questions are very much like those running through the minds of students like you as they read this book. Try to anticipate these questions. Even better, be sure to ask your own questions. Try to actively interact with your textbooks as you read.

Read

As an aid to reading, important terms are printed in **boldface type** and defined where they first appear. (Some are followed by pronunciations—capital letters show which syllables are accented.) You'll also find a *running glossary* in the lower right-hand corner of pages you are reading, so you never have to guess about the meaning of technical terms. If you want to look up a term from a lecture or another chapter, check the main *Glossary*. This "mini-dictionary" is located near the end of the book. Perhaps you should take a moment to find it now. In addition, many figures and tables help you quickly grasp important concepts.

Recite and Reflect

To help you study in smaller "bites," this book is divided into short sections that end with *Knowledge Builders*, which make good stopping points. *Knowledge Builders* provide opportunities to check your memory for what you just read. They also invite you to think more deeply by presenting critical thinking questions and questions designed to help you relate material to your own life. (Don't forget to also take notes or recite and reflect on your own.)

This book also provides other opportunities for you to reflect more deeply about what you are reading. Each chapter ends with a *Psychology in Action* section. These discussions are filled with practical ideas you can relate to your own life. In many chapters, *Discovering Psychology* boxes also invite you to relate psychology to your own behavior. *Critical Thinking* boxes present intriguing questions you can use to sharpen your critical thinking skills. In addition, *Human Diversity* boxes encourage you to reflect on the rich variety of human experience; *Brainwaves* boxes show how the brain relates to psychology; and in *The Clinical File* boxes we will see how psychology can be applied to treat clinical problems.

Review

Each chapter concludes with a detailed review. There you will find a list of *Gateways* to psychology. These are summaries of psychology's "big ideas" and enduring principles. The first time you finish a chapter, don't feel obligated to memorize the *Gateways* concepts. However, be sure to take a moment to think about each statement. Ultimately, the *Gateways* will provide a good high-level summary of what you learned in this course. By making these ideas your own, you will gain something of lasting value: You will learn to see human behavior as psychologists do. Following each *Gateways* concept, you will find a more detailed, point-by-point summary of ideas presented in the chapter. These points will help you identify important ideas to remember.

For further review, you can use the running glossary in the margin, as well as boldface terms, figures, and tables. ● Table I.1 summarizes how this text helps you apply the SQ4R method. Even with all this help, there is still much more you can do on your own.

◖◗ Effective Note-Taking— Good Students, Take Note!

Reading strategies may be good for studying, but what about taking notes in class? Sometimes it's hard to know what's important. Just as studying a textbook is best done reflectively, so too is attending class (Norman, 1993). Like effective reading, good notes come from actively seeking information. People who are **active listeners** avoid distractions and skillfully gather ideas. Here's a listening/note-taking

SQ4R method An active study-reading technique based on these steps: survey, question, read, recite, reflect, and review.

Active listener A person who knows how to maintain attention, avoid distractions, and actively gather information from lectures.

Table I.1 ● Using the SQ4R Method

Survey
- Preview
- Gateway Theme
- Gateway Questions
- Chapter Preview
- Topic Headings
- Figure Captions

Question
- Topic Headings
- In-Text Dialogue Questions

Read
- Topic Headings
- Boldface Terms
- Running Glossary
- Figures and Tables

Recite
- Recite Questions (in Knowledge Builders)
- Practice Quizzes (online)
- Notes (make them while reading)

Reflect
- Critical Thinking Questions (in Knowledge Builders)
- Relate Questions (in Knowledge Builders)
- Psychology in Action Sections (throughout the text)
- Boxed Highlights (throughout the text)

Review
- Italicized Gateways Concepts
- Boldface Terms
- Running Glossary
- Figure and Tables
- Practice Quizzes (online)
- Study Guide

plan that works for many students. The letters LISAN, pronounced like the word *listen,* will help you remember the steps:

L = *Lead. Don't follow.* Read assigned materials before coming to class. Try to anticipate what your teacher will say by asking yourself questions. If your teacher provides course notes or PowerPoint overheads before lectures, review them before coming to class. Reflective questions can come from those materials or from study guides, reading assignments, or your own curiosity.

I = *Ideas.* Every lecture is based on a core of ideas. Usually, an idea is followed by examples or explanations. Ask yourself often, "What is the main idea now? What ideas support it?"

S = *Signal words.* Listen for words that tell you what direction the instructor is taking. For instance, here are some signal words:

There are three reasons why . . .	Here come ideas
Most important is . . .	Main idea
On the contrary . . .	Opposite idea
As an example . . .	Support for main idea
Therefore . . .	Conclusion

A = *Actively listen.* Sit where you can get involved and ask questions. Bring questions you want answered from the last lecture or from your text. Raise your hand at the beginning of class or approach your professor before the lecture. Do anything that helps you stay active, alert, and engaged.

N = *Note taking.* Students who take accurate lecture notes tend to do well on tests (Williams & Eggert, 2002). However, don't try to be a tape recorder. Listen to everything, but be selective and write down only key points. If you are too busy writing, you may not grasp what your professor is saying. When you're taking notes, it might help to think of yourself as a reporter who is trying to get a good story (Ryan, 2001).

Actually, most students take reasonably good notes—and then don't use them! Many students wait until just before exams to review. By then, their notes have lost much of their meaning. If you don't want your notes to seem like "chicken scratches," it pays to review them every day (Rowe, 2007).

Using and Reviewing Your Notes

When you review, you will learn more if you take the extra steps listed here (Knaus & Ellis, 2002; Rowe, 2007; Santrock & Halonen, 2007):

- As soon as you can, reflect on and improve your notes by filling in gaps, completing thoughts, and looking for connections among ideas.
- Remember to link new ideas to what you already know.
- Summarize your notes. Boil them down and *organize* them.
- After each class session, write down at least seven major ideas, definitions, or details that are likely to become test questions. Then make up questions from your notes and be sure you can answer them.

Summary

The letters LISAN are a guide to active listening, but listening and good note taking are not enough. You must also review, organize, reflect, extend, and think about new ideas. Use active listening to get involved in your classes and you will undoubtedly learn more (Rowe, 2007).

●● Study Strategies— Making a Habit of Success

Grades depend as much on effort as they do on "intelligence." However, don't forget that good students work more *efficiently,* not just harder. Many study practices are notoriously poor, such as recopying lecture notes, studying class notes but not the textbook (or the textbook but not class notes), outlining chapters, answering study questions with the book open, and "group study" (which often becomes a party). The best students emphasize *quality:* They study their books and notes in depth and attend classes regularly. It's a mistake to blame poor grades on events "beyond your control." Students who are motivated to succeed usually get better grades (Perry et al., 2001). Let's consider a few more things you can do to improve your study habits.

Study in a Specific Place

Ideally, you should study in a quiet, well-lit area free of distractions. If possible, you should also have at least one place where you *only study.* Do nothing else at that spot: Keep magazines, MP3 players, friends, cell phones, pets, posters, video games, puzzles, food, lovers, sports cars, elephants, pianos, televisions, YouTube, kazoos, and other distractions out of the area. In this way, the habit of studying will become strongly linked with one specific place. Then, rather than trying to force yourself to study, all you have to do is go to your study area. Once there, you'll find it is relatively easy to get started.

Use Spaced Study Sessions

It is reasonable to review intensely before an exam. However, you're taking a big risk if you are only "cramming" (learning new information at the last minute). Spaced practice is much more efficient (Anderson, 2005). **Spaced practice** consists of a large number of relatively short study sessions. Long, uninterrupted study sessions are called **massed practice.** (If you "massed up" your studying, you probably messed it up too.)

Cramming places a big burden on memory. Usually, you shouldn't try to learn anything new about a subject during the last day before a test. It is far better to learn small amounts every day and review frequently (Anderson, 2005).

Try Mnemonics

Learning has to start somewhere, and memorizing is often the first step. Many of the best ways to improve memory are covered in Chapter 8. Let's consider just one technique here.

A **mnemonic** (nee-MON-ik) is a memory aid. There are many ways to create mnemonics. Most mnemonics link new information to ideas or images that are easy to remember. For example, what if you want to remember that the Spanish word for duck is *pato* (pronounced POT-oh)? To use a mnemonic, you could picture a duck in a pot or a duck wearing a pot for a hat. Likewise, to remember that the cerebellum controls coordination, you might picture someone named "Sarah Bellum" who is very coordinated. For best results, make your mnemonic images exaggerated or bizarre, vivid, and interactive (Macklin & McDaniel, 2005).

Mnemonics make new information more familiar and memorable. Forming an image of a duck wearing a pot for a hat might help you remember that *pato* is the Spanish word for duck.

Test Yourself

A great way to improve grades is to take practice tests before the real one in class. In other words, studying should include **self-testing,** in which you pose questions to yourself. You can use flash cards, Learning Check questions, online quizzes, a study guide, or other means. As you study, ask many questions and be sure you can answer them. Studying without self-testing is like practicing for a basketball game without shooting any baskets.

For more convenient self-testing, your professor may make a *Study Guide* or a separate booklet of *Practice Quizzes* available. You can use either to review for tests. Practice quizzes are also available on the book companion website, as described later. However, don't use practice quizzes as a substitute for studying your textbook and lecture notes. Trying to learn from quizzes alone will probably *lower* your grades. It is best to use quizzes to find out what topics you need to study more (Brothen & Wambach, 2001).

Overlearn

Many students *underprepare* for exams, and most *overestimate* how well they will do. A solution to both problems is **overlearning,** in which you continue studying beyond your initial mastery of a topic. In other words, plan to do extra study and review *after* you think you are prepared for a test. One way to overlearn is approach all tests as if they will be essays. That way, you will learn more completely, so you really "know your stuff."

⬤⬤ Self-Regulated Learning— Academic All-Stars

Think of a topic you are highly interested in, such as music, sports, fashion, cars, cooking, politics, or movies. Whatever the topic, you have probably learned a lot about it—painlessly. How could you make your college work more like voluntary learning? An approach called self-regulated learning might be a good start. **Self-regulated learning** is deliberately reflective and active, self-guided study (Hofer & Yu, 2003). Here's how you can change passive studying into goal-oriented learning:

1. *Set specific, objective learning goals.* Try to begin each learning session with specific goals in mind. What knowledge or skills are you trying to master? What do you hope to accomplish (Knaus & Ellis, 2002)?

Spaced practice Practice spread over many relatively short study sessions.

Massed practice Practice done in a long, uninterrupted study session.

Mnemonic A memory aid or strategy.

Self-testing Evaluating learning by posing questions to yourself.

Overlearning Continuing to study and learn after you think you've mastered a topic.

Self-regulated learning Deliberately reflective and active, self-guided study.

2. *Plan a learning strategy.* How will you accomplish your goals? Make daily, weekly, and monthly plans for learning. Then put them into action.

3. *Be your own teacher.* Effective learners silently give themselves guidance and ask themselves questions. For example, as you are learning, you might ask yourself, "What are the important ideas here? What do I remember? What don't I understand? What do I need to review? What should I do next?"

4. *Monitor your progress.* Self-regulated learning depends on self-monitoring. Exceptional learners keep records of their progress toward learning goals (pages read, hours of studying, assignments completed, and so forth). They quiz themselves, use study guides, make sure they follow the SQ4R system, and find other ways to check their understanding while learning.

5. *Reward yourself.* When you meet your daily, weekly, or monthly goals, reward your efforts in some way, such as going to a movie or downloading some new music. Be aware that self-praise also rewards learning. Being able to say, "Hey, I did it!" or "Good work!" and knowing that you deserve it can be very rewarding. In the long run, success, self-improvement, and personal satisfaction are the real payoffs for learning.

6. *Evaluate your progress and goals.* It is a good idea to frequently evaluate your performance records and goals. Are there specific areas of your work that need improvement? If you are not making good progress toward long-range goals, do you need to revise your short-term targets?

7. *Take corrective action.* If you fall short of your goals you may need to adjust how you budget your time. You may also need to change your learning environment to deal with distractions such as watching TV, daydreaming, talking to friends, or testing the structural integrity of the walls with your stereo system.

If you discover that you lack necessary knowledge or skills, ask for help, take advantage of tutoring programs, or look for information beyond your courses and textbooks. Knowing how to regulate and control learning can be a key to lifelong enrichment and personal empowerment.

● Procrastination—Avoiding the Last-Minute Blues

All of these study techniques are fine. But what can I do about procrastination? A tendency to procrastinate is almost universal. (When campus workshops on procrastination are offered, many students never get around to signing up!) Even when procrastination doesn't lead to failure, it can cause much suffering. Procrastinators work only under pressure, skip classes, give false reasons for late work, and feel ashamed of their last-minute efforts. They also tend to feel frustrated, bored, and guilty more often (Blunt & Pychyl, 2005).

Why do so many students procrastinate? Many students equate grades with their *personal worth.* That is, they act as if grades tell whether they are good, smart people who will succeed in life. By procrastinating they can blame poor work on a late start, rather than a lack of ability (Beck, Koons, & Milgrim, 2000). After all, it wasn't their best effort, was it?

Perfectionism is a related problem. If you expect the impossible, it's hard to start an assignment. Students with high standards often end up with all-or-nothing work habits (Onwuegbuzie, 2000).

Time Management

Most procrastinators must eventually face the self-worth issue. Nevertheless, most can improve by learning study skills and better time management. We have already discussed general study skills, so let's consider time management in a little more detail.

A **weekly time schedule** is a written plan that allocates time for study, work, and leisure activities. To prepare your schedule, make a chart showing all the hours in each day of the week. Then fill in times that are already committed: sleep, meals, classes, work, team practices, lessons, appointments, and so forth. Next, fill in times when you will study for various classes. Finally, label the remaining hours as open or free times.

Each day, you can use your schedule as a checklist. That way you'll know at a glance which tasks are done and which still need attention (Knaus & Ellis, 2002).

You may also find it valuable to make a **term schedule** that lists the dates of all quizzes, tests, reports, papers, and other major assignments for each class.

The beauty of sticking to a schedule is that you know you are making an honest effort. It will also help you avoid feeling bored while you are working or guilty when you play.

Be sure to treat your study times as serious commitments, but respect your free times, too. And remember, students who study hard and practice time management *do* get better grades (Rau & Durand, 2000).

Goal Setting

As mentioned earlier, students who are active learners set **specific goals** for studying. Such goals should be clear-cut and measurable (Knaus & Ellis, 2002). If you find it hard to stay motivated, try setting goals for the semester, the week, the day, and even for single study sessions. Also, be aware that more effort early in a course can greatly reduce the "pain" and stress you will experience later. If your professors don't give frequent assignments, set your own day-by-day goals. That way, you can turn big assignments into a series of smaller tasks that you can actually complete (Ariely & Wertenbroch, 2002). An example would be reading, studying, and reviewing 8 pages a day to complete a 40-page chapter in 5 days. For this textbook, reading from one *Knowledge Builder* to the next each day might be a good pace. Remember, many small steps can add up to an impressive achievement.

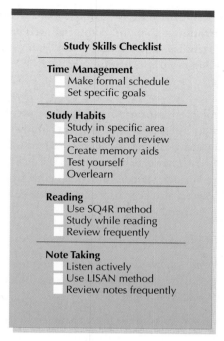

● **Figure I.2** Study skills checklist.

Make Learning an Adventure

A final point to remember is that you are most likely to procrastinate if you think a task will be unpleasant (Pychyl et al., 2000). Learning can be hard work. Nevertheless, many students find ways to make schoolwork interesting and enjoyable. Try to approach your schoolwork as if it were a game, a sport, an adventure, or simply a way to become a better person. The best educational experiences are challenging yet fun (Ferrari & Scher, 2000).

Virtually every topic is interesting to someone, somewhere. You may not be particularly interested in the sex life of South American tree frogs. However, a biologist might be fascinated. (Another tree frog might be, too.) If you wait for teachers to "make" their courses interesting, you are missing the point. Interest is a matter of *your attitude*. (See ● Figure I.2 for a summary of study skills.)

◉◉ Taking Tests—Are You "Test Wise"?

If I read and study effectively, is there anything else I can do to improve my grades? You must also be able to show what you know on tests. Here are some suggestions for improving your test-taking skills:

General Test-Taking Skills

You'll do better on all types of tests if you observe the following guidelines (Wood & Willoughby, 1995):

1. Read all directions and questions carefully. They may give you good advice or clues.
2. Quickly survey the test before you begin.
3. Answer easy questions before spending time on more difficult ones.
4. Be sure to answer all questions.
5. Use your time wisely.
6. Ask for clarification when necessary.

Objective Tests

Several additional strategies can help you do better on objective tests. Objective tests (multiple-choice and true–false items) require you to recognize a correct answer among wrong ones or a true statement versus a false one. Here are some strategies for taking objective tests:

1. First, relate the question to what you know about the topic. Then, read the alternatives. Does one match the answer you expected to find? If none match, reexamine the choices and look for a *partial* match.
2. Read *all* the choices for each question before you make a decision. Here's why: If you immediately think that *a* is correct and stop reading, you might miss seeing a better answer like "both *a* and *d*."
3. Read rapidly and skip items you are unsure about. You may find "free information" in later questions that will help you answer difficult items.
4. Eliminate certain alternatives. With a four-choice multiple-choice test, you have one chance in four of guessing right. If you can eliminate two alternatives, your guessing odds improve to 50-50.
5. Unless there is a penalty for guessing, be sure to answer any skipped items. Even if you are not sure of the answer, you may be right. If you leave a question blank, it is automatically wrong. When you are forced to guess, don't choose the longest answer or the letter you've used the least. Both strategies lower scores more than random guessing does.
6. There is a bit of folk wisdom that says "Don't change your answers on a multiple-choice test. Your first choice is usually right." This is *false*. If you change answers, you are more likely to gain points than to lose them. This is especially true if you are uncertain of your first choice or it was a hunch, and if your second choice is more reflective (Higham & Gerrard, 2005).
7. Remember, you are searching for the one *best* answer to each question. Some answers may be partly true, yet flawed in some way. If you are uncertain, try rating each multiple-choice alternative on a 1–10 scale. The answer with the highest rating is the one you are looking for.
8. Few circumstances are *always* or *never* present. Answers that include superlatives such as *most, least, best, worst, largest,* or *smallest* are often false.

Weekly time schedule A written plan that allocates time for study, work, and leisure activities during a 1-week period.

Term schedule A written plan that lists the dates of all major assignments for each of your classes for an entire semester or quarter.

Specific goal A goal with a clearly defined and measurable outcome.

Essay Tests

Essay questions are a weak spot for students who lack organization, don't support their ideas, or don't directly answer the question (Rowe, 2007). When you take an essay exam try the following:

1. Read the question carefully. Be sure to note key words, such as *compare, contrast, discuss, evaluate, analyze,* and *describe.* These words all demand a certain emphasis in your answer.

2. Answer the question. If the question asks for a definition and an example, make sure you provide both. Providing just a definition or just an example will get you half marks. Giving three examples instead of the one asked for will not earn you any extra marks.

3. Think about your answer for a few minutes and list the main points you want to make. Just write them as they come to mind. Then rearrange the ideas in a logical order and begin writing. Elaborate plans or outlines are not necessary.

4. Don't beat around the bush or pad your answer. Be direct. Make a point and support it. Get your list of ideas into words.

5. Look over your essay for errors in spelling and grammar. Save this for last. Your *ideas* are of first importance. You can work on spelling and grammar separately if they affect your grades.

Short-Answer Tests

Tests that ask you to fill in a blank, define a term, or list specific items can be difficult. Usually, the questions themselves contain little information. If you don't know the answer, you won't get much help from the questions.

The best way to prepare for short-answer tests is to overlearn the details of the course. As you study, pay special attention to lists of related terms.

Again, it is best to start with the questions you're sure you know. Follow that by completing items you think you probably know. Questions you have no idea about can be left blank.

Again, for your convenience, ● Figure I.2 provides a checklist summary of the main study skills we have covered.

⬤⬤ Using Digital Media— Netting New Knowledge

Google any psychological term ranging from *amnesia* to *zoophobia* and you will find a vast library of information, from serious websites, like that maintained by the American Psychological Association, to Wikipedia entries and personal blogs. Even if you don't own a computer, you can usually use one on campus to learn more about psychology. However, be aware that information on the Internet is not always accurate. It is wise to approach all websites with a healthy dose of skepticism.

Digital Gateways

The **Internet** is a network of interlinked computers. An important subpart of the Internet is the **World Wide Web (WWW)** or just plain "web," an interlinked system of information "sites" or "pages." If you know the URL (or "address") of a website, you can view the information it contains. Almost all web pages also have links to other websites. These **links** let you "jump" from one site to the next to find more information.

Google It

To find psychological information on the Internet, you'll need a computer and an Internet connection. If you don't own a computer, you can usually use one on campus. Various software browsers make it easier to navigate around the web. A **browser** allows you to see text, images, sounds, and video clips stored on other computers. Browsers also keep lists of your favorite URLs so that you can return to them.

The Book Companion Website

How would I find information about psychology on the Internet? Your first stop on the Internet should be the book companion website. Here's what you'll find there:

Online Quizzes. You can use these chapter-by-chapter multiple-choice and true–false quizzes to practice for tests and check your understanding.

Web Links. This area is a "launching pad" that will take you to other psychology-related sites on the Internet. If a site sounds interesting, a click of the mouse will take you to it.

Online Flash Cards. These online flash cards allow you to practice terms and concepts interactively.

Crossword Puzzles. Crosswords are a fun way to check your knowledge of key terms and their definitions.

The book companion website is located at www.cengage.com/psychology/coon. Be sure to visit this site for valuable information about how to improve your grades and enhance your appreciation of psychology.

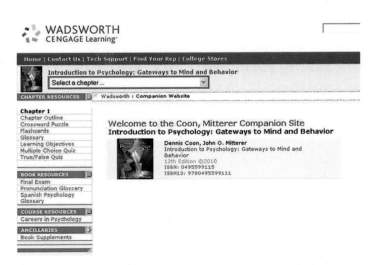

The book companion website gives you online access to a variety of valuable learning aids and interesting materials.

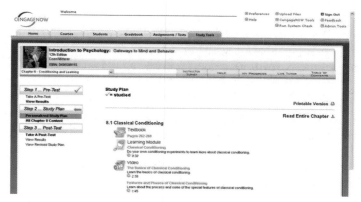

● **Figure I.3** A sample screen from *CengageNOW*.

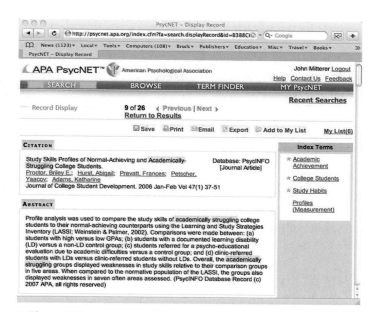

● **Figure I.4** This is a sample abstract from the PsycINFO database. If you search for the term *study skills*, you will find this article and many more in PsycINFO. (Reproduced with permission of the American Psychological Association, publisher of the PsycINFO database. PsycINFO Database Record © 2007 APA, all rights reserved. No further reproduction or distribution is permitted without written permission from the American Psychological Association.)

CengageNOW

Students can also make use of *CengageNOW for Coon/Mitterer's Psychology: Gateways to Mind and Behavior,* twelfth edition, a web-based, personalized study system that provides a pre-test and a post-test for each chapter. *CengageNOW,* located at academic .cengage.com/login, also creates personalized study plans—which include rich media such as videos, animations, and learning modules and links to the eBook that help you study the specific topics in the text where you need to study most (● Figure I.3).

Wadsworth's Psychology Resource Center

Do you like videos, simulations, and animations? Do you learn best when you get actively involved in psychology? The Wadsworth Psychology Resource Center brings psychology to life with a full library of original and classic video clips plus interactive learning modules tied to all of the topics covered in your introductory psychology course. Log in at www.cengage.com/login to visit the resource center.

Psychology Websites

You'll find the titles of interesting websites you may want to explore at the end of each chapter in this book, including this one. The best way to reach these sites is through the book companion website. We have not included website addresses in the book because they often change or may become inactive. At the website you'll find up-to-date links for websites listed in this book. The sites we've listed are generally of high quality. However, be aware that information on the Internet is not always accurate. It is wise to approach all websites with a healthy dose of skepticism.

PsycINFO

Psychological knowledge can also be found through specialized online databases. One of the best is PsycINFO, offered by the American Psychological Association. **PsycINFO** provides summaries of the scientific and scholarly literature in psychology. Each record in PsycINFO consists of an abstract (short summary), plus notes about the author, title, source, and other details (● Figure I.4). All entries are indexed using key terms. Thus, you can search for various top-

ics by entering words such as *drug abuse, postpartum depression,* or *creativity.*

You can gain access to PsycINFO in several ways. Almost every college and university subscribes to PsycINFO. If this is the case, you can usually search PsycINFO from a terminal in your college library or computer center for free. PsycINFO can also be directly accessed (for a fee) through the Internet via APA's PsycINFO Direct service. For more information on how to gain access to PsycINFO, check this website: **www.apa.org/psycinfo.**

The APA Website

The APA also maintains an online library of general interest articles on aging, anger, children and families, depression, divorce, emotional health, kids and the media, sexuality, stress, testing issues, women and men, and other topics. They are well worth consulting when you have questions about psychological issues. You'll find them at **www.apa.org.** For links to recent articles in newspapers and magazines, be sure to check the APA's PsycPORT page at **www.psycport.com.**

Internet An electronic network of interlinked computers.

World Wide Web (WWW) A system of information sites accessible through the Internet.

Links Connections built into websites that let you "jump" from one site to the next.

Browser Software that facilitates access to text, images, sounds, video, and other information stored in formats used on the Internet.

PsycINFO A searchable, online database that provides brief summaries of the scientific and scholarly literature in psychology.

Please do take some of the "digital gateways" described here. You might be surprised by the fascinating information that awaits you. Investigating psychology on your own is one of the best ways to enrich an already valuable course.

A Final Word

There is a distinction in Zen between "live words" and "dead words." Live words come from personal experience; dead words are "about" a subject. This book can only be a collection of dead words unless you accept the challenge of taking an intellectual step through this gateway to psychology. You will find many helpful, useful, and exciting ideas in the pages that follow. To make them yours, you must set out to *actively* learn as much as you can. The ideas presented here should get you off to a good start. Good luck!

For more information, consult any of the following books:

Hettich, P. I. (2005). *Connect college to career: Student guide to work and life transition*. Belmont, CA: Wadsworth.

Knaus, W. J., & Ellis, A. (2002). *The procrastination workbook: Your personalized program for breaking free from the patterns that hold you back*. Oakland, CA: New Harbinger Press.

Rosnow, R. L. (2006). *Writing papers in psychology: A student guide to research papers, essays, proposals, posters, and handouts* (7th ed.). Belmont, CA: Wadsworth.

Rowe, B. (2007). *College awareness guide: What students need to know to succeed in college*. Upper Saddle River, NJ: Prentice Hall.

Santrock, J. W., & Halonen, J. S. (2007). *Connections to college success*. Belmont, CA: Wadsworth.

KNOWLEDGE BUILDER
Study Skills

RECITE

1. The four Rs in SQ4R stand for "read, recite, reflect, and review." T or F?
2. When using the LISAN method, students try to write down as much of a lecture as possible so that their notes are complete. T or F?
3. Spaced study sessions are usually superior to massed practice. T or F?
4. According to research, you should almost always stick with your first answer on multiple-choice tests. T or F?
5. To use the technique known as overlearning, you should continue to study after you feel you have begun to master a topic. T or F?
6. Setting learning goals and monitoring your progress are important parts of _____ learning.
7. Procrastination is related to seeking perfection and equating self-worth with grades. T or F?

REFLECT

Critical Thinking

8. How are the SQ4R method and the LISAN method related?

Relate

Which study skills do you think would help you the most? Which techniques do you already use? Which do you think you should try? To what extent do you already engage in self-regulated learning? What additional steps could you take to become a more active, goal-oriented learner?

Answers: 1. T **2.** F **3.** T **4.** F **5.** T **6.** self-regulated **7.** T **8.** Both encourage people to actively seek information as a way of learning more effectively.

Web Resources

For an up-to-date list of direct links to interesting sites, including those listed here, visit the student companion site for this book at www.cengage.com/psychology/coon

How to Succeed as a Student Advice on how to be a college student. Topics from studying to housing to preparation for work are included.

Library Research in Psychology Hints on how to do library research in psychology.

Psychology Glossary You can use this glossary to get additional definitions for common psychological terms.

Study Skills More information on SQ4R, taking tests, note taking, and time management.

Interactive Learning

Introduction to Psychology: Gateways to Mind and Behavior **Book Companion Website**
www.cengage.com/psychology/coon

Visit your book companion website, where you will find flash cards, practice quizzes, web links, and more to help you study.

CENGAGENOW™ *Just what you need to know NOW!*

Spend time on what you need to master rather than on information you already have learned. Take a pre-test for this chapter, and CengageNOW will generate a personalized study plan based on your results. The study plan will identify the topics you need to review and direct you to online resources to help you master those topics. You can then take a post-test to help you determine the concepts you have mastered and what you will need to work on. Try it out! Go to www.cengage.com/login to sign in with an access code or to purchase access to this product.

CHAPTER 1

Introduction to Psychology and Research Methods

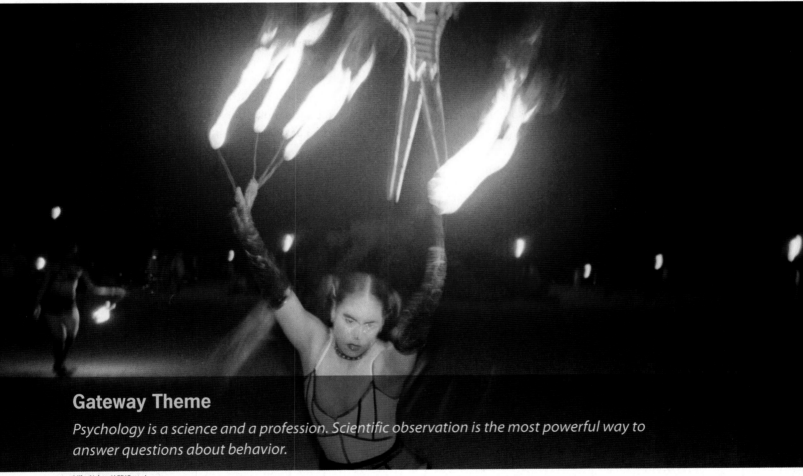

Gateway Theme

Psychology is a science and a profession. Scientific observation is the most powerful way to answer questions about behavior.

Mike Nelson/AFP/Getty Images

Gateway Questions

- *What is psychology, and what are its goals?*
- *What is critical thinking?*
- *How does psychology differ from false explanations of behavior?*
- *How is the scientific method applied in psychological research?*
- *How did the field of psychology emerge?*
- *What are the contemporary perspectives in psychology?*

- *What are the major specialties in psychology?*
- *How is an experiment performed?*
- *What is a double-blind experiment?*
- *What nonexperimental research methods do psychologists use?*
- *How good is the psychological information found in the popular media?*

Near the end of every summer, a remote stretch of Nevada desert hosts Burning Man, an eclectic weeklong festival attended by tens of thousands of, well, unusual folks. It's hard to explain just what this unique event is about except to say that attendees are encouraged to openly express themselves in any way they see fit. (Feel free to unleash your imagination on this one.) Revelers participate in a riotous cultural experience that climaxes with the burning of a giant wicker man. Old hippies mix with self-described rednecks, performance artists, musicians, sun worshippers, and individualists of every stripe.

Why, you might wonder, do people go to Burning Man, some of them year after year? But then again, you might equally wonder why people join the Army, or get married, or travel to different countries, or become suicide bombers, or live out their lives in monasteries, or go to school. You might even wonder, at least sometimes, why *you* do what you do. In other words, just like your authors, the odds are you are curious about human behavior. That may even be a part of the reason you are taking a course in psychology and reading this book.

Look around you: The Internet, television, newspapers, radio, and magazines are brimming with psychological topics. Psychology is an ever-changing panorama of people and ideas. You really can't call yourself educated without knowing something about it. And, although we might envy those who have walked on the moon or explored the ocean's depths, the ultimate frontier lies much closer to home. Psychology can help you better understand yourself and others. This book is a guided tour of human behavior. We hope you enjoy the adventure.

◐◑ Psychology—The ABCs of Behavior

Gateway Question: What is psychology, and what are its goals?

People have always been curious about human behavior. The word *psychology* itself is thousands of years old, coming from the ancient Greek roots *psyche,* which means "mind," and *logos,* meaning "knowledge or study." However, have you ever actually seen or touched a "mind"? Because the mind can't be studied directly, **psychology** is now defined as the scientific study of behavior and mental processes.

What does behavior *refer to in the definition of psychology?* Anything you do—eating, hanging out, sleeping, talking, or sneezing—is a behavior. So are studying, snowboarding, gambling, watching television, tying your shoelaces, wrapping presents, learning Spanish, and reading this book. Naturally, we are interested in *overt behaviors* (directly observable actions and responses). But psychologists also study *covert behaviors.* These are private, internal activities, such as thinking, dreaming, remembering, and other mental events (Jackson, 2008).

All in all, then, psychology studies behaviors from A to Z: aging, burnout, conformity, death, emotion, flexibility, groupthink, hypnosis, intelligence, joy, kinesthesis, love, memory, noise pollution, originality, personality, quantitative reasoning, repression, sexuality, therapy, unconscious, wisdom, vision, xenophobia, youth, zeitgeist, and much more.

Today, psychology is both a *science* and a *profession.* As scientists, some psychologists do research to discover new knowledge. Others are teachers who share their knowledge with students. Still others apply psychology to solve problems in mental health, education, business, sports, law, and medicine (Coolican et al., 2007). Later we will return to the profession of psychology. For now, let's focus on how knowledge is created. Whether they work in a class-

Psychologists are highly trained professionals. In addition to the psychological knowledge they possess, psychologists learn specialized skills in counseling and therapy, measurement and testing, research and experimentation, statistics, diagnosis, treatment, and many other areas.

room, a lab, or a clinic, all psychologists rely on critical thinking and information gained from scientific research.

Seeking Empirical Evidence

Many people regard themselves as expert "people watchers" and form their own "common-sense" theories of behavior. However, you may be surprised to learn how often self-appointed authorities and common-sense beliefs are wrong. Check your own expertise about human behavior by reading "Testing Common-Sense Beliefs."

Because of the limitations of common sense, psychologists have a special respect for **scientific observation,** which is based

CRITICAL THINKING

Testing Common-Sense Beliefs

It may appear that psychological research "discovers" what we already know from everyday experience. Why waste time and money confirming the obvious? Actually, common-sense beliefs are often wrong. See if you can tell which of the following common-sense beliefs are wrong (Landau & Bavaria, 2003):

- Babies love their mothers because mothers fulfill their babies' physiological need for food. True or False?
- Most humans use only 10 percent of their potential brainpower. True or False?
- Blind people have unusually sensitive organs of touch. True or False?

- The more motivated you are, the better you will do at solving a complex problem. True or False?
- The major cause of forgetting is that memory traces decay or fade as time passes. True or False?
- Psychotherapy has its greatest success in the treatment of psychotic patients who have lost touch with reality. True or False?
- Personality tests reveal your basic motives, including those you may not be aware of having. True or False?
- To change people's behavior toward members of ethnic minority groups, we must first change their attitudes. True or False?

Actually research has shown that *all* these beliefs are false. Yet in a survey, *all* the beliefs were accepted as common sense by many college students (Landau & Bavaria, 2003). How did you do?

We can all benefit from being more reflective as we evaluate our beliefs. It's valuable to think critically and ask whether a belief makes logical sense. Do any of the concepts in this book apply to the belief? Can you imagine how you could collect evidence that might get you closer to the truth? *Critical Thinking* boxes like this one will help you be more reflective as you think critically about human behavior.

on gathering *empirical evidence* (information gained from direct observation). Unlike personal observation, scientific observation is systematic and *intersubjective.* In other words, observations are planned and they can be confirmed by more than one observer. Basically, the empirical approach says, "Let's take a more objective look" (Stanovich, 2007). We study behavior directly and collect data (observed facts) so that we can draw valid conclusions. Would you say it's true, for instance, that "Absence makes the heart grow fonder"? Why argue about it? As psychologists, we would simply get some people who are separated ("absent hearts") and some who see each other every day ("present hearts") and find out who is fonder of their loved ones!

Here's an example of gathering empirical evidence: Have you ever wondered if people become more hostile when it's boiling hot outside? John Simister and Cary Cooper (2005) decided to find out. They obtained data on temperatures and criminal activity in

Los Angeles over a 4-year period. When they graphed air temperature and the frequency of aggravated assaults, a clear relationship emerged (● Figure 1.1). Assaults and temperatures rise and fall more or less in parallel (so there may be something to the phrase "hot under the collar").

Isn't the outcome of this study fairly predictable? Not if you started out believing otherwise. Sometimes the results of studies match our personal observations and common-sense beliefs and sometimes they come as a surprise. In this instance, you may have guessed the outcome. Your suspicions were confirmed by scientific observation. However, hostile actions that require more extreme physical exertion, such as fistfights, might become *less* likely at very high temperatures. Without systematically gathering data, we wouldn't know for sure if overheated Angelenos become more lethargic or more aggressive when it gets hot. Thus, the study tells us something interesting about frustration, discomfort, and aggression.

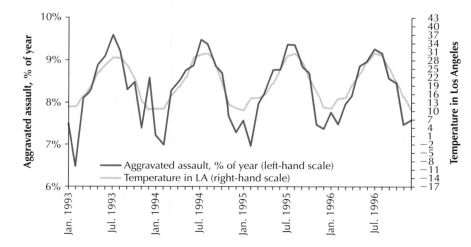

● **Figure 1.1** Results of an empirical study. The graph shows that aggravated assaults in Los Angeles become more likely as air temperature increases. This suggests that physical discomfort is associated with interpersonal hostility. (Data from Simister & Cooper, 2005.)

Psychology The scientific study of behavior and mental processes.

Scientific observation An empirical investigation structured to answers questions about the world in a systematic and intersubjective fashion (observations can be reliably confirmed by multiple observers).

The scientific study of dreaming was made possible by use of the EEG, a device that records the tiny electrical signals generated by the brain as a person sleeps. The EEG converts these electrical signals into a written record of brain activity. Certain shifts in brain activity, coupled with the presence of rapid eye movements, are strongly related to dreaming. (See Chapter 6, pages 186–188, for more information.)

Psychological Research

Many fields, such as history, law, art, and business, are also interested in human behavior. How is psychology different? Psychology's great strength is that it uses scientific observation to systematically answer questions about behavior (Stanovich, 2007). Of course, it may be impractical or unethical to study some topics. More often, questions go unanswered for lack of a suitable **research method** (a systematic process for answering scientific questions). In the past, for example, we had to take the word of people who say they never dream. Then the EEG (electroencephalograph, or brain-wave machine) was invented. Certain EEG patterns, and the presence of eye movements, can reveal that a person is dreaming. People who "never dream," it turns out, dream frequently. If they are awakened during a dream, they vividly remember it. Thus, the EEG helped make the study of dreaming more scientific.

Research Specialties

What kinds of topics do psychologists study? Here's a sample of what various psychologists might say about their work:

"I'm a *personality theorist*. I study personality traits, motivation, and individual differences. I am especially interested in the personality profiles of highly creative college students."

"In general, *developmental psychologists* study the course of human growth and development, from conception until death. I'm especially interested in the transition from the teenage years to early adulthood."

"Like other *learning theorists*, I study how and why learning occurs in humans and animals. Right now I'm investigating how patterns of punishment affect learning."

"As a *sensation and perception psychologist*, I investigate how we discern the world through our senses. I am using a perceptual theory to study how we are able to recognize faces in a crowd."

"*Comparative psychologists* study and compare the behavior of different species, especially animals. Personally, I'm fascinated by the communication abilities of porpoises."

"*Cognitive psychologists* are primarily interested in thinking. I want to know how reasoning, problem solving, memory, and other mental processes relate to computer game playing."

"*Biopsychologists* are interested in how behavior relates to biological processes, especially activities in the nervous system. I've been doing some exciting research on how the brain controls hunger."

"*Gender psychologists* study differences between females and males. I want to understand how gender differences are influenced by biology, child rearing, education, and stereotypes."

"*Social psychologists* explore human social behavior, such as attitudes, persuasion, riots, conformity, leadership, racism, and friendship. My own interest is interpersonal attraction. I place two strangers in a room and analyze how strongly they are attracted to each other."

"*Evolutionary psychologists* are interested in how our behavior is guided by patterns that evolved during the long history of humankind. I am studying some interesting trends in male and female mating choices."

"*Cultural psychologists* study the ways in which culture affects human behavior. The language you speak, the foods you eat, how your parents disciplined you, what laws you obey, who you regard as 'family,' whether you eat with a spoon or your fingers—these and countless other details of behavior are strongly influenced by culture."

"*Forensic psychologists* apply psychological principles to legal issues. I am interested in improving the reliability of eyewitness testimony during trials."

This small sample should give you an idea of the diversity of psychological research. It also hints at some of the information we will explore in this book.

Animals and Psychology

Research involving animals was mentioned in some of the preceding examples. Why is that? You may be surprised to learn that psychologists are interested in the behavior of *any* living creature—from flatworms to humans. Indeed, some comparative psychologists spend their entire careers studying rats, cats, dogs, parrots, or chimpanzees.

Although only a small percentage of psychological studies involve animals, they include many different types of research (Ord et al., 2005). Some psychologists use **animal models** to discover principles that apply to humans. For instance, animal studies have helped us understand stress, learning, obesity, aging, sleep, and many other topics. Psychology also benefits animals. For example, caring for domestic animals, as well as endangered species in zoos, relies on behavioral studies.

Some of the most interesting research with animals has focused on attempts to teach primates to communicate with sign language. Psychologist Penny Patterson has spent 35 years teaching Koko more than 1,000 signs. One of Koko's favorite signs ("stink") is shown here. (To learn more, visit www.koko.org.) Such research has helped illuminate the origins of human language and has even suggested better methods for teaching language to children with serious language impairment. (See Chapter 9, pages 291–292, for more information.)

Psychology's Goals

What do psychologists hope to achieve? Psychology's ultimate goal is to benefit humanity (O'Neill, 2005). Specifically, the goals of the science of psychology are to *describe, understand, predict,* and *control* behavior. What do psychology's goals mean in practice? Let's see.

Description

Answering psychological questions often begins with a careful description of behavior. **Description,** or naming and classifying, is typically based on making a detailed record of scientific observations.

But a description doesn't explain anything, does it? Right. Useful knowledge begins with accurate description, but descriptions fail to answer the important "why" questions. *Why* do more women attempt suicide, and *why* do more men complete it? *Why* are people more aggressive when they are uncomfortable? *Why* are bystanders often unwilling to help in an emergency?

Understanding

We have met psychology's second goal when we can explain an event. That is, **understanding** usually means we can state the causes of a behavior. For example, research on "bystander apathy" reveals that people often fail to help when *other* possible helpers are nearby. Why? Because a "diffusion of responsibility" occurs. Basically, no one feels personally obligated to pitch in. As a result, the more potential helpers there are, the less likely it is that anyone will help (Darley, 2000; Darley & Latané, 1968). Now we can explain a perplexing problem.

bridges
Bystander apathy and conditions that influence whether people will help in an emergency are of great interest to social psychologists. **See Chapter 17, pages 564–566 for details.**

Prediction

Psychology's third goal, **prediction,** is the ability to forecast behavior accurately. Notice that our explanation of bystander apathy makes a prediction about the chances of getting help. If you've ever been stranded on a busy freeway with car trouble, you'll recognize the accuracy of this prediction: Having many potential helpers nearby is no guarantee that anyone will stop to help.

Control

Description, explanation, and prediction seem reasonable, but is control a valid goal? "Control" may seem like a threat to personal freedom. However, to a psychologist, **control** simply refers to altering conditions that affect behavior. If a clinical psychologist helps a person overcome a terrible fear of spiders, control is involved. If

Some psychologists specialize in administering, scoring, and interpreting psychological tests, such as tests of intelligence, creativity, personality, or aptitude. This specialty, which is called psychometrics, is an example of using psychology to predict future behavior.

Research method A systematic approach to answering scientific questions.

Animal model In research, an animal whose behavior is used to derive principles that may apply to human behavior.

Description In scientific research, the process of naming and classifying.

Understanding In psychology, understanding is achieved when the causes of a behavior can be stated.

Prediction An ability to accurately forecast behavior.

Control Altering conditions that influence behavior.

you suggest changes in a classroom that help students learn better, you have exerted control. Control is also involved in designing automobiles to keep drivers from making fatal errors. Clearly, psychological control must be used wisely and humanely.

In summary, psychology's goals are a natural outgrowth of our desire to understand behavior. Basically, they boil down to asking the following questions:

- What is the nature of this behavior? (description)
- Why does it occur? (understanding and explanation)
- Can we forecast when it will occur? (prediction)
- What conditions affect it? (control)

KNOWLEDGE BUILDER
The Science of Psychology

RECITE

To check your memory, see if you can answer these questions. If you miss any, skim over the preceding material before continuing to make sure you understand what you just read.

1. Psychology is the _____ study of _____ and _____ processes.
2. The best psychological information is typically based on
   a. proven theories
   b. opinions of experts and authorities
   c. anthropomorphic measurements
   d. empirical evidence
3. In psychological research, animal _____ may be used to discover principles that apply to human behavior.
4. Which of the following questions relates most directly to the goal of *understanding* behavior?
   a. Do the scores of men and women differ on tests of thinking abilities?
   b. Why does a blow to the head cause memory loss?
   c. Will productivity in a business office increase if room temperature is raised or lowered?
   d. What percentage of college students suffer from test anxiety?

Match the following research areas with the topics they cover.

_____	5. Developmental psychology	A.	Attitudes, groups, leadership
_____	6. Learning	B.	Conditioning, memory
_____	7. Personality	C.	The psychology of law
_____	8. Sensation and perception	D.	Brain and nervous system
_____	9. Biopsychology	E.	Child psychology
_____	10. Social psychology	F.	Individual differences, motivation
_____	11. Comparative psychology	G.	Animal behavior
		H.	Processing sensory information

REFLECT

Critical Thinking

12. All sciences are interested in controlling the phenomena they study. T or F?

Relate

At first, many students think that psychology is primarily about abnormal behavior and psychotherapy. Did you? How would you describe the field now?

Answers: 1. scientific, behavior, mental 2. d 3. models 4. b 5. E 6. B 7. F 8. H 9. D 10. A 11. G 12. F Astronomy and archaeology are examples of sciences that do not share psychology's fourth goal.

Critical Thinking—Take It with a Grain of Salt

Gateway Question: What is critical thinking?

How does critical thinking play a role in psychology? Most of us would be skeptical when offered a "genuine" Rolex watch or expensive designer sunglasses for just a few dollars on eBay. Likewise, most of us easily accept our ignorance of subatomic physics. But because we deal with human behavior every day, we tend to think that we already know what is true in psychology. All too often, we are tempted to "buy" common-sense beliefs and even outrageous claims about psychics "channeling" dead people, the powers of "healing" crystals, "miraculous" herbal remedies, astrology, and so forth.

For these and many more reasons, learning to think critically is one of the lasting benefits of a college education. **Critical thinking** refers to an ability to reflect on, evaluate, compare, analyze, critique, and synthesize information. Critical thinkers are willing to challenge conventional wisdom by asking the hard questions. For example, everyone knows that women are more talkative than men, right? Critical thinkers might immediately ask: "How do we know that women talk more than men? Is there any empirical evidence that supports this 'wisdom'? (Be on the lookout later in this chapter for some evidence concerning this belief.) What could we do to find out for ourselves?

Thinking About Behavior

The heart of critical thinking is a willingness to actively *reflect* on ideas. Critical thinkers evaluate ideas by analyzing the evidence supporting their beliefs and probe for weaknesses in their reasoning. They question assumptions and look for alternate conclusions. True knowledge, they recognize, comes from constantly revising our understanding of the world. They are not afraid to admit they were wrong. As Susan Blackmore (2001) said when her studies caused her to abandon some long-held beliefs, "Admitting you are wrong is always hard—even though it's a skill that every psychologist has to learn."

Critical thinking relies on the following basic principles (Elder, 2006; Kida, 2006):

1. *Few "truths" transcend the need for empirical testing.* While religious beliefs and personal values may be held as matters of faith, without supporting evidence, most other ideas can be evaluated by applying the rules of logic, evidence, and the scientific method.
2. *Judging the quality of evidence is crucial.* Imagine that you are a juror in a courtroom, judging claims made by two battling lawyers. To decide correctly, you can't just weigh the amount of evidence. You must also critically evaluate the *quality* of the evidence. Then you can give greater weight to the most credible facts.
3. *Authority or claimed expertise does not automatically make an idea true.* Just because a teacher, guru, celebrity, or authority

is convinced or sincere doesn't mean you should automatically believe them. It is unscientific and self-demeaning to just take the word of an "expert" without asking, "What evidence convinced her or him? How good is it? Is there a better explanation?"

4. *Critical thinking requires an open mind.* Be prepared to consider daring departures and go wherever the evidence leads. However, don't become so "open-minded" that you are simply gullible. As astronomer Carl Sagan once noted, "It seems to me that what is called for is an exquisite balance between two conflicting needs: the most skeptical scrutiny of all hypotheses that are served up to us and at the same time a great openness to new ideas" (Kida, 2006, p. 51).

To put these principles into action, here are some questions to ask over and over again as you evaluate new information (Browne & Keeley, 2007; Elder, 2006):

1. What claims are being made? What are their implications?
2. What tests (if any) of these claims has been made? What was the nature and quality of the tests? Are they credible? Can they be repeated?
3. How good is the evidence? (In general, scientific observations provide the highest-quality evidence.)
4. Who did the tests? How reliable and trustworthy were the investigators? Do they have conflicts of interest? Do their findings appear to be objective? Has any other independent researcher duplicated the findings?
5. Finally, how much credibility can the claim be given? High, medium, low, provisional?

A course in psychology naturally enriches thinking skills. In this book, all upcoming chapters include Critical Thinking questions like the ones you have seen here. Take the time to tackle these questions. The effort will sharpen your thinking abilities and make learning more lively. For an immediate thinking challenge, let's take a critical look at several nonscientific systems that claim to explain behavior.

Pseudopsychologies—Palms, Planets, and Personality

Gateway Question: How does psychology differ from false explanations of behavior?

A **pseudopsychology** (SUE-doe-psychology) is any unfounded system that resembles psychology. Many pseudopsychologies give the appearance of science but are actually false. (*Pseudo* means "false.") Pseudopsychologies change little over time because followers seek evidence that appears to confirm their beliefs and avoid evidence that contradicts their beliefs. Scientists, in contrast, actively look for contradictions as a way to advance knowledge. They are skeptical critics of their own theories (Schick & Vaughn, 2004).

Can you give some examples of false psychologies? One early pseudopsychology, known as *phrenology,* was popularized in the nine-

Phrenology was an attempt to assess personality characteristics by examining various areas of the skull. Phrenologists used charts such as the one shown here as guides. Like other pseudopsychologists, phrenologists made no attempt to empirically verify their concepts.

teenth century by Franz Gall, a German anatomy teacher. Phrenology claimed that personality traits are revealed by the shape of the skull. Modern research has long since shown that bumps on the head have nothing to do with talents or abilities. In fact, the phrenologists were so far off that they listed the part of the brain that controls hearing as a center for "combativeness"! *Palmistry* is a similar false system that claims lines on the hand reveal personality traits and predict the future. Despite the overwhelming evidence against this, palmists can still be found separating the gullible from their money in many cities.

At first glance, a pseudopsychology called *graphology* might seem more reasonable. Some graphologists claim that personality traits are revealed by handwriting. Based on such claims, some companies use graphologists to select job candidates. This is troubling because graphologists score close to zero on tests of accuracy in rating personality (Furnham, Chamorro-Premuzic, & Callahan, 2003). In fact, graphologists do no better than untrained college students in rating personality and job performance (Neter & Ben-Shakhar, 1989). Even a graphological society recently concluded that handwriting analysis should not be used to select people for jobs (Simner & Goffin, 2003). (By the way, graphology's failure at revealing personality should be separated from its value for detecting forgeries.)

Graphology might seem harmless enough. However, imagine being denied a job because a graphologist didn't like your handwriting. This false system has been used to determine who is hired, given bank credit, or selected for juries. In these and similar situations, pseudopsychologies do, in fact, harm people.

Critical thinking An ability to reflect on, evaluate, compare, analyze, critique, and synthesize information.

Pseudopsychology Any false and unscientific system of beliefs and practices that is offered as an explanation of behavior.

Would you hire this man? Here's a sample of your author's handwriting. What do you think it reveals? Your interpretations are likely to be as accurate (or inaccurate) as those of a graphologist.

If pseudopsychologies have no scientific basis, how do they survive and why are they popular? There are several reasons, all of which can be illustrated by a critique of astrology.

Problems in the Stars

Astrology is arguably the most popular pseudopsychology. Astrology holds that the positions of the stars and planets at the time of one's birth determine personality traits and affect behavior. Like other pseudopsychologies, astrology has repeatedly been shown to have no scientific validity. The objections to astrology are numerous and devastating (Kelly, 1999):

1. A study of more than 3,000 predictions by famous astrologers found that only a small percentage were fulfilled. These "successful" predictions tended to be vague ("There will be a tragedy somewhere in the east in the spring") or easily guessed from current events (Culver & Ianna, 1988).

2. If astrologers are asked to match people with their horoscopes, they do no better than would be expected by chance. In one famous test, astrologers could not even use horoscopes to distinguish murderers from law-abiding people (Gauquelin, 1970).

3. There is no connection between people's astrological signs and their intelligence or personality traits (Hartmann, Reuter, & Nyborg, 2006). There is also no connection between the "compatibility" of couples' astrological signs and their marriage and divorce rates or between astrological signs and leadership, physical characteristics, or career choices (Martens & Trachet, 1998).

4. Astrologers have failed to explain why the moment of birth should be more important than, say, the moment of conception. (Perhaps it is because it is relatively easy to figure out the moment of birth and much trickier and touchy to determine the moment of conception.) Besides, the zodiac has shifted in the sky by one full constellation since astrology was first set up. (In other words, if astrology calls you a Scorpio you are really a Libra, and so forth.) However, most astrologers simply ignore this shift (Martens & Trachet, 1998).

In short, astrology doesn't work.

Then why does astrology often seem to work? The following discussion explains why.

Uncritical Acceptance

Even daily horoscopes printed in newspapers can seem uncannily accurate. However, such perceptions are typically based on **uncritical acceptance** (the tendency to believe positive or flattering descriptions of yourself). Horoscopes are generally made up of mostly flattering traits. Naturally, when your personality is described in *desirable* terms, it is hard to deny that the description has the "ring of truth." How much acceptance would astrology receive if a birth sign read like this:

> **Virgo:** You are the logical type and hate disorder. Your nitpicking is unbearable to your friends. You are cold, unemotional, and usually fall asleep while making love. Virgos make good doorstops.

Positive Instances

Even when an astrological description contains a mixture of good and bad traits it may seem accurate. To find out why, read the following personality description.

Your Personality Profile

You have a strong need for other people to like you and for them to admire you. You have a tendency to be critical of yourself. You have a great deal of unused energy which you have not turned to your advantage. While you have some personality weaknesses, you are generally able to compensate for them. Your sexual adjustment has presented some problems for you. Disciplined and controlled on the outside, you tend to be worrisome and insecure inside. At times you have serious doubts as to whether you have made the right decision or done the right thing. You prefer a certain amount of change and variety and become dissatisfied when hemmed in by restrictions and limitations. You pride yourself on being an independent thinker and do not accept other opinions without satisfactory proof. You have found it unwise to be too frank in revealing yourself to others. At times you are extroverted, affable, sociable, while at other times you are introverted, wary, and reserved. Some of your aspirations tend to be pretty unrealistic.*

Does this describe your personality? A psychologist read this summary individually to college students who had taken a personality test. Only 5 students out of 79 felt that the description was inaccurate. Another classic study found that people rated this "personality profile" as more accurate than their actual horoscopes (French et al., 1991).

Reread the description and you will see that it contains both sides of several personality dimensions ("At times you are extroverted . . . while at other times you are introverted"). Its apparent accuracy is an illusion based on the **fallacy of positive instances,** in which we remember or notice things that confirm our expectations and forget the rest. The pseudopsychologies thrive on this effect. For example, you can always find "Aquarius characteristics" in an Aquarius. If you looked, however, you could also find "Gemini characteristics," "Scorpio characteristics," or whatever. Perhaps this explains why, in an ironic twist, 94% of those sent the full 10-page horoscope of a famous mass murderer accepted it as their own (Gauquelin, 1970).

---

*Reprinted with permission of author and publisher from: R. E. Ulrich, T. J. Stachnik, and N. R. Stainton, "Student acceptance of generalized personality interpretations," *Psychological Reports,* 13, 1963, 831–834.

The fallacy of positive instances is also used by various "psychic mediums" who pretend to communicate with the deceased friends and relatives of audience members. An analysis shows that the number of "hits" (correct statements) made by these fakes tends to be very low. Nevertheless, many viewers are impressed because of the natural tendency to remember apparent hits and ignore misses. Of course, embarrassing misses are often edited out before the shows appear on television (Nickell, 2001).

Non Sequitur

YOU WILL BE TOLD WHAT YOU WANT TO HEAR. IT WILL BE SO GENERALIZED THAT IT COULD FIT ANYONE. YOU WILL PAY A RIDICULOUS AMOUNT OF MONEY FOR IT...

THE MOST ACCURATE FORTUNE EVER TOLD

Non Sequitur © 1993. Reprinted by permission of Universal Press Syndicate.

The Barnum Effect

Pseudopsychologies also take advantage of the **Barnum effect,** which is a tendency to consider personal descriptions accurate if they are stated in general terms (Kida, 2006). P. T. Barnum, the famed circus showman, had a formula for success: "Always have a little something for everybody." Like the all-purpose personality profile, palm readings, fortunes, horoscopes, and other products of pseudopsychology are stated in such general terms that they can hardly miss. There is always "a little something for everybody." To observe the Barnum effect, read *all 12* of the daily horoscopes found in newspapers for several days. You will find that predictions for other signs fit events as well as those for your own sign do. Try giving a friend the wrong horoscope sometime. Your friend may still be quite impressed with the "accuracy" of the horoscope.

Astrology's popularity shows that many people have difficulty separating valid psychology from systems that seem valid but are not. The goal of this discussion, then, has been to make you a more critical observer of human behavior and to clarify what is, and what is not, psychology. Here is what the "stars" say about your future:

> Emphasis now on education and personal improvement. A learning experience of lasting value awaits you. Take care of scholastic responsibilities before engaging in recreation. The word *psychology* figures prominently in your future.

Pseudopsychologies may seem like no more than a nuisance, but they can do harm. For instance, people seeking treatment for psychological disorders may become the victims of self-appointed "experts" who offer ineffective, pseudoscientific "therapies" (Kida, 2006; Lilienfeld et al., 2005). Valid psychological principles are based on scientific observation and evidence, not fads, opinions, or wishful thinking.

⬤⬤ Scientific Research—How to Think Like a Psychologist

Gateway Question: How is the scientific method applied in psychological research?

Suppose that your friend marries someone just like her. What do people say? "Ah . . . birds of a feather flock together." And what do they say if she gets divorced soon after? "Well, she should have known that opposites attract." Let's examine another *common-sense statement.* It is frequently said that "every cloud has

a silver lining." With this in mind, you use your lover's worrisome absences as a chance to spend more time with your family. You take comfort in this "silver lining" until a family member comments, "Where there's smoke, there's fire!" Much of what passes for common sense is equally vague and inconsistent. Notice also that most of these B.S. statements work best after the fact. (B.S., of course, stands for *Before Science.*)

Systematically recording facts and events is the heart of all sciences. To be *scientific,* our observations must be *systematic,* so that they reveal something about behavior (Stanovich, 2007). To use an earlier example, if you are interested in heat and aggression, you will learn little by driving around and making haphazard observations of aggressive behavior. To be of value, your observations must be planned and systematic.

The Scientific Method

The **scientific method** is a form of critical thinking based on careful collection of evidence, accurate description and measurement, precise definition, controlled observation, and repeatable results (Jackson, 2008). In its ideal form the scientific method has six elements:

1. Making observations
2. Defining a problem
3. Proposing a hypothesis
4. Gathering evidence/testing the hypothesis
5. Publishing results
6. Theory building

Let's take a closer look at some elements of the scientific method. All the basic elements of the scientific method are found in the example that follows.

Uncritical acceptance The tendency to believe generally positive or flattering descriptions of oneself.

Fallacy of positive instances The tendency to remember or notice information that fits one's expectations while forgetting discrepancies.

Barnum effect The tendency to consider a personal description accurate if it is stated in very general terms.

Scientific method A form of critical thinking based on careful measurement and controlled observation.

Applying the scientific method to the study of behavior requires careful observation. Here, a psychologist videotapes a session in which a child's thinking abilities are being tested.

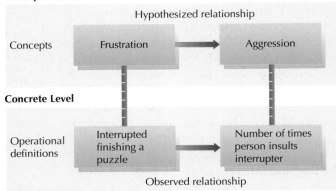

● **Figure 1.2** Operational definitions are used to link concepts with concrete observations. Do you think the examples given are reasonable operational definitions of frustration and aggression? Operational definitions vary in how well they represent concepts. For this reason, many different experiments may be necessary to draw clear conclusions about hypothesized relationships in psychology.

Observation

Many people believe that women are more chatty than men. Is there any truth to this belief? University of Arizona psychologist Mathias Mehl and his colleagues observed that the results of a few published reports do seem to support this stereotype.

Defining a Problem

However, the researchers noticed that none of the studies had actually recorded men's and women's normal conversations over long periods. Thus, they defined their problem as, "How can we record natural conversations without bothering people and perhaps biasing our observations?"

Proposing a Hypothesis

What exactly is a "hypothesis"? A **hypothesis** (hi-POTH-eh-sis) is a tentative statement about, or explanation of, an event or relationship. In common terms, a hypothesis is a *testable* hunch or educated guess about behavior. For example, you might hypothesize that "Frustration encourages aggression." How could you test this hypothesis? First you would have to decide how you are going to frustrate people. (This part might be fun.) Then you will need to find a way to measure whether or not they become more aggressive. (Not so much fun if you plan to be nearby.) Your observations would then provide evidence to confirm or disconfirm the hypothesis.

Because we cannot see or touch frustration, we must define it operationally. An **operational definition** states the exact procedures used to represent a concept. Operational definitions allow unobservable ideas, such as covert behaviors, to be tested in real-world terms (● Figure 1.2). For example, since you can't measure frustration directly, you might define frustration as "interrupting an adult before he or she can finish a puzzle and win an iPhone." And aggression might be defined as "the number of times a frus-

trated individual insults the person who prevented work on the puzzle." In other words, covert behaviors are operationally defined in terms of overt behavior so they can be observed and studied scientifically.

Gathering Evidence/Testing the Hypothesis

Now let's return to the question of whether women talk more than men do. To gather data, the researchers used an electronically activated recorder (EAR) to track people's conversations. This device recorded sounds for 30 seconds every 12.5 minutes. Participants could not tell when they were being recorded, so they acted and spoke normally. Researchers counted the number of words spoken when the recorder was on and used that to estimate the total number of words spoken each day. On average, women spoke 16,215 words a day, with men close behind at 15,699. This difference is too small to be meaningful, so we can conclude, as Mehl did, that there is no evidence that women talk more than men (Mehl et al., 2007).

Publishing Results

Scientific information must always be *publicly available.* That way, other researchers can read about the results and make their own observations if they doubt the study's findings. If others are able to *replicate* (repeat) the results of a study, those results become more credible.

The results of psychological studies are usually published in professional journals (● Table 1.1). That way, anyone willing to make appropriate observations can see whether or not a claim is true (Jackson, 2008). In a scholarly article, Mehl and his colleagues carefully describe the question they investigated, the methods they used, and the results of their study on male and female talkativeness. The article was published in the journal *Science* (Mehl et al., 2007).

Table 1.1 ● Outline of a Research Report

- **Abstract** Research reports begin with a very brief summary of the study and its findings. The abstract allows you to get an overview without reading the entire article.
- **Introduction** The introduction describes the question to be investigated. It also provides background information by reviewing prior studies on the same or related topics.
- **Method** This section tells how and why observations were made. It also describes the specific procedures used to gather data. That way, other researchers can repeat the study to see if they get the same results.
- **Results** The outcome of the investigation is presented. Data may be graphed, summarized in tables, or statistically analyzed.
- **Discussion** The results of the study are discussed in relation to the original question. Implications of the study are explored and further studies may be proposed.

Theory Building

What about theory building? In research, a **theory** acts as a map of knowledge. Good theories summarize observations, explain them, and guide further research (● Figure 1.3). Without theories of forgetting, personality, stress, mental illness, and the like, psychologists would drown in a sea of disconnected facts (Stanovich, 2007).

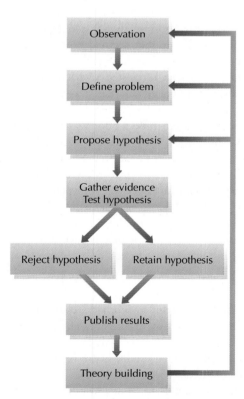

● **Figure 1.3** Psychologists use the logic of science to answer questions about behavior. Specific hypotheses can be tested in a variety of ways, including controlled experiments, naturalistic observation, correlational studies, clinical studies, and the survey method. Psychologists revise their theories to reflect the evidence they gather. New or revised theories then lead to new observations, problems, and hypotheses.

bridges

One of the major limitations of Freudian personality theory is that many of its concepts are not testable or falsifiable. **See Chapter 12, page 402.**

While Mehl and his colleagues did not present a theory of why humans talk more or less, they did discuss how their findings might affect such a theory. For instance, they pointed out that they only studied university students, and that older men and women might differ in how much they talk each day. Such findings invite others to study talkativeness in other age groups and to propose theories to explain any differences that might be observed.

KNOWLEDGE BUILDER
Critical Thinking and the Scientific Method in Psychology

RECITE

1. The fallacy of positive instances refers to graphology's accepted value for the detection of forgeries. T or F?
2. Personality descriptions provided by pseudopsychologies are stated in general terms, which provide "a little something for everybody." This fact is the basis of the
   a. palmist's fallacy
   b. uncritical acceptance pattern
   c. fallacy of positive instances
   d. Barnum effect
3. Most of psychology can rightfully be called common sense because psychologists prefer informal observation to systematic observation. T or F?
4. A psychologist does a study to see if exercising increases sense of well-being. In the study he will be testing an
   a. experimental hypothesis
   b. operational definition
   c. empirical definition
   d. anthropomorphic theory
5. _____ behaviors are operationally defined in terms of _____ behavior
   a. overt, covert
   b. observable, overt
   c. covert, overt
   d. covert, abstract

Continued

Hypothesis The predicted outcome of an experiment or an educated guess about the relationship between variables.

Operational definition Defining a scientific concept by stating the specific actions or procedures used to measure it. For example, "hunger" might be defined as "the number of hours of food deprivation."

Theory A system of ideas designed to interrelate concepts and facts in a way that summarizes existing data and predicts future observations.

A Brief History of Psychology— Psychology's Family Album

Gateway Question: How did the field of psychology emerge?

As we noted previously, people have been informally observing human behavior and philosophizing about it for thousands of years. In contrast, psychology's history as a science dates back only about 130 years to Leipzig, Germany. There, Wilhelm Wundt (VILL-helm Voont), the "father of psychology," set up a laboratory in 1879 to study conscious experience.

What happens, he wondered, when we experience sensations, images, and feelings? To find out, Wundt systematically observed and measured stimuli of various kinds (lights, sounds, weights). A **stimulus** is any physical energy that affects a person and evokes a response (stimulus: singular; stimuli [STIM-you-lie]: plural). Wundt then used **introspection,** or "looking inward," to probe his reactions to various stimuli. (Stop reading, close your eyes, carefully examine your thoughts, feelings, and sensations, and you will be introspecting.)

Wilhelm Wundt, 1832–1920. Wundt is credited with making psychology an independent science, separate from philosophy. Wundt's original training was in medicine, but he became deeply interested in psychology. In his laboratory, Wundt investigated how sensations, images, and feelings combine to make up personal experience.

Hulton Archive/Getty Images

Over the years, Wundt studied vision, hearing, taste, touch, memory, time perception, and many other topics. By insisting on systematic observation and measurement, he asked some interesting questions and got psychology off to a good start (Schultz & Schultz, 2008).

Structuralism

Wundt's ideas were carried to the United States by Edward Titchener (TICH-in-er). Titchener called Wundt's ideas **structuralism** and tried to analyze the structure of mental life into basic "elements" or "building blocks."

How could he do that? You can't analyze experience like a chemical compound, can you? Perhaps not, but the structuralists tried, mostly by using introspection. For instance, an observer might heft an apple and decide that she had experienced the elements "hue" (color), "roundness," and "weight." Another example of a question that might have interested a structuralist is, What basic tastes mix together to create complex flavors as different as broccoli, lime, bacon, and strawberry cheesecake?

Introspection proved to be a poor way to answer most questions (Benjafield, 2004). Why? Because no matter how systematic the observations, the structuralists frequently *disagreed.* And when they did, there was no way to settle differences. Think about it. If you and a friend both introspect on your perceptions of an apple and end up listing different basic elements, who would be right? Despite such limitations, "looking inward" is still used as one source of insight in studies of hypnosis, meditation, problem solving, moods, and many other topics.

Functionalism

American scholar William James broadened psychology to include animal behavior, religious experience, abnormal behavior, and other interesting topics. James's brilliant first book, *Principles of Psychology* (1890), helped establish the field as a separate discipline (Hergenhahn, 2005).

The term **functionalism** comes from James's interest in how the mind functions to help us adapt to the environment. James regarded consciousness as an ever-changing *stream* or *flow* of images and sensations—not a set of lifeless building blocks, as the structuralists claimed.

William James, 1842–1910. William James was the son of philosopher Henry James, Sr., and the brother of novelist Henry James. During his long academic career, James taught anatomy, physiology, psychology, and philosophy at Harvard University. James believed strongly that ideas should be judged in terms of their practical consequences for human conduct.

Archives of the History of American Psychology, University of Akron

John B. Watson, 1878–1958. Watson's intense interest in observable behavior began with his doctoral studies in biology and neurology. Watson became a psychology professor at Johns Hopkins University in 1908 and advanced his theory of behaviorism. He remained at Johns Hopkins until 1920 when he left for a career in the advertising industry!

Archives of the History of American Psychology, University of Akron

The functionalists admired Charles Darwin, who deduced that creatures evolve in ways that favor survival. According to Darwin's principle of **natural selection,** physical features that help animals adapt to their environments are retained in evolution. Similarly, the functionalists wanted to find out how the mind, perception, habits, and emotions help us adapt and survive.

What effect did functionalism have on modern psychology? Functionalism brought the study of animals into psychology. It also promoted educational psychology (the study of learning, teaching, classroom dynamics, and related topics). Learning makes us more adaptable, so the functionalists tried to find ways to improve education. For similar reasons, functionalism gave rise to industrial psychology, the study of people at work.

> **bridges**
> Today, educational psychology and industrial psychology remain two major applied specialties. **See Chapter 18 for more information about applied psychology.**

Behaviorism

Functionalism and structuralism were soon challenged by **behaviorism,** the study of observable behavior. Behaviorist John B. Watson objected strongly to the study of the "mind" or "conscious experience." He believed that introspection is unscientific because there is no way to settle disagreements between observers. Watson realized that he could study the behavior of animals even though he couldn't ask them questions or know what they were thinking (Watson, 1913/1994). He simply observed the relationship between *stimuli* (events in the environment) and an animal's **responses** (any muscular action, glandular activity, or other identifiable behavior). These observations were objective because they did not involve introspecting on subjective experience. Why not, he asked, apply the same objectivity to human behavior?

Watson soon adopted Russian physiologist Ivan Pavlov's (ee-VAHN PAV-lahv) concept of *conditioning* to explain most behavior. (A *conditioned response* is a learned reaction to a particular stimulus.) Watson claimed, "Give me a dozen healthy infants, well-formed, and my own special world to bring them up in and I'll

guarantee to take any one at random and train him to become any type of specialist I might select—doctor, lawyer, artist, merchant-chief, and yes, beggarman and thief" (Watson, 1913/1994).

Would most psychologists agree with Watson's claim? No, today it is regarded as an overstatement. Just the same, behaviorism helped make psychology a natural science, rather than a branch of philosophy (Benjafield, 2004).

Radical Behaviorism

The best-known behaviorist, B. F. Skinner (1904–1990), believed that our actions are controlled by rewards and punishments. To study learning, Skinner created his famous conditioning chamber, or "Skinner box." With it, he could present stimuli to animals and record their responses.

> **bridges**
> **See Chapter 7, pages 226–241, for more information about operant conditioning.**

Many of Skinner's ideas about learning grew out of work with rats and pigeons. Nevertheless, he believed that the same laws of behavior apply to humans. As a "radical behaviorist," Skinner also believed that mental events, such as thinking, are not needed to explain behavior (Schultz & Schultz, 2008).

Stimulus Any physical energy sensed by an organism.

Introspection To look within; to examine one's own thoughts, feelings, or sensations.

Structuralism The school of thought concerned with analyzing sensations and personal experience into basic elements.

Functionalism The school of psychology concerned with how behavior and mental abilities help people adapt to their environments.

Natural selection Darwin's theory that evolution favors those plants and animals best suited to their living conditions.

Behaviorism The school of psychology that emphasizes the study of overt, observable behavior.

Response Any muscular action, glandular activity, or other identifiable aspect of behavior.

B. F. Skinner, 1904–1990. Skinner studied simple behaviors under carefully controlled conditions. The "Skinner box" has been widely used to study learning in simplified animal experiments. In addition to advancing psychology, Skinner hoped that his radical brand of behaviorism would improve human life.

Yvonne Hemsey/Getty Images

Skinner was convinced that a "designed culture" based on positive reinforcement could encourage desirable behavior. (Skinner opposed the use of punishment because it doesn't teach correct responses.) Too often, he believed, misguided rewards lead to destructive actions that create problems such as overpopulation, pollution, and war.

Cognitive Behaviorism

Radical behaviorists have been criticized for ignoring the role that thinking plays in our lives. One critic even charged that Skinnerian psychology had "lost consciousness!" However, many criticisms have been answered by **cognitive behaviorism,** a view that combines cognition (thinking) and conditioning to explain behavior (Zentall, 2002). As an example, let's say you frequently visit a particular website because it offers free streaming videos. A behaviorist would say that you visit the site because you are rewarded by the pleasure of watching interesting videos each time you go there. A cognitive behaviorist would add that, in addition, you *expect* to find good videos at the site. This is the cognitive part of your behavior.

Behaviorists deserve credit for much of what we know about learning, conditioning, and the proper use of reward and punishment. Behaviorism is also the source of behavior therapy, which uses learning principles to change problem behaviors such as overeating, unrealistic fears, or temper tantrums. (See Chapter 15, pages 503–509, for more information.)

Gestalt Psychology

Imagine that you just played "Happy Birthday" on a low-pitched tuba. Next, you play it on a high-pitched flute. The flute duplicates none of the tuba's sounds. Yet we notice something interesting: The melody is still recognizable—as long as the *relationship* between notes remains the same.

Now, what would happen if you played the notes of "Happy Birthday" in the correct order, but at a rate of one per hour? What would we have? Nothing! The separate notes would no longer be a melody. Perceptually, the melody is somehow more than the individual notes that define it.

It was observations like these that launched the Gestalt school of thought. German psychologist Max Wertheimer (VERT-hi-mer) was the first to advance the Gestalt viewpoint. It is inaccurate, he said, to analyze psychological events into pieces, or "elements," as the structuralists did. Accordingly, **Gestalt psychologists** studied thinking, learning, and perception as whole units, not by analyz-

● **Figure 1.4** The design you see here is entirely made up of broken circles. However, as the Gestalt psychologists discovered, our perceptions have a powerful tendency to form meaningful patterns. Because of this tendency, you will probably see a triangle in this design, even though it is only an illusion. Your whole perceptual experience exceeds the sum of its parts.

Max Wertheimer, 1880–1941. Wertheimer first proposed the Gestalt viewpoint to help explain perceptual illusions. He later promoted Gestalt psychology as a way to understand not only perception, problem solving, thinking, and social behavior, but also art, logic, philosophy, and politics.

Archives of the History of American Psychology, University of Akron

ing experiences into parts. Their slogan was, "The whole is greater than the sum of its parts" (● Figure 1.4). In fact the German word *Gestalt* means "form, pattern, or whole."

Like a melody, many experiences cannot be broken into smaller units, as the Structuralists proposed. For this reason, studies of perception and personality have been especially influenced by the Gestalt viewpoint. Gestalt psychology also inspired a type of psychotherapy.

> **bridges**
> If you are curious about what Gestalt therapy is like, look ahead to Chapter 15, pages 501–502.

Psychoanalytic Psychology

As American psychology grew more scientific, an Austrian doctor named Sigmund Freud was developing radically different ideas which opened new horizons in art, literature, and history, as well as psychology (Jacobs, 2003). Freud believed that mental life is like an iceberg: Only a small part is exposed to view. He called the area of the mind that lies outside of personal awareness the **unconscious.** According to Freud, our behavior is deeply influenced by unconscious thoughts,

Sigmund Freud, 1856–1939. For more than 50 years, Freud probed the unconscious mind. In doing so, he altered modern views of human nature. His early experimentation with a "talking cure" for hysteria is regarded as the beginning of psychoanalysis. Through psychoanalysis, Freud added psychological treatment methods to psychiatry.

Hulton Archive/Getty Images

Abraham Maslow, 1908–1970. As a founder of humanistic psychology, Maslow was interested in studying people of exceptional mental health. Such self-actualized people, he believed, make full use of their talents and abilities. Maslow offered his positive view of human potential as an alternative to the schools of behaviorism and psychoanalysis.

Bettmann/Corbis

impulses, and desires—especially those concerning sex and aggression.

Freud theorized that many unconscious thoughts are **repressed** (held out of awareness) because they are threatening. But sometimes, he said, they are revealed by dreams, emotions, or slips of the tongue. ("Freudian slips" are often humorous, as when a student who is late for class says, "I'm sorry I couldn't get here any later.")

Freud believed that all thoughts, emotions, and actions are *determined*. In other words, nothing is an accident: If we probe deeply enough, we will find the causes of every thought or action. Freud was also among the first to appreciate that childhood affects adult personality ("The child is father to the man"). Most of all, perhaps, Freud is known for creating **psychoanalysis,** the first fully developed psychotherapy, or "talking cure." Freudian psychotherapy explores unconscious conflicts and emotional problems. (See Chapter 15, pages 498–499, for details.)

It wasn't very long before some of Freud's students began to promote their own theories. Several who modified Freud's ideas became known as neo-Freudians (*neo* means "new" or "recent"). **Neo-Freudians** accepted much of Freud's theory but revised parts of it. Many, for instance, placed less emphasis on sex and aggression and more on social motives and relationships. Some well-known neo-Freudians are Alfred Adler, Anna Freud (Freud's daughter), Karen Horney (HORN-eye), Carl Jung (yoong), Otto Rank (rahnk), and Erik Erikson. Today, Freud's ideas have been altered so much that few strictly psychoanalytic psychologists are left. However, his legacy is still evident in various **psychodynamic theories,** which continue to emphasize internal motives, conflicts, and unconscious forces (Gedo, 2002).

Humanistic Psychology

Humanism is a view that focuses on subjective human experience. Humanistic psychologists are interested in human potentials, ideals, and problems.

How is the humanistic approach different from others? Carl Rogers, Abraham Maslow, and other humanists rejected the Freudian idea that we are ruled by unconscious forces. They were also uncomfortable with the behaviorist emphasis on conditioning. Both views have a strong undercurrent of **determinism** (the idea that behavior is determined by forces beyond our control). In contrast, the humanists stress **free will,** our ability to make voluntary choices. Of course, past experiences do affect us. Nevertheless, humanists believe that people can freely *choose* to live more creative, meaningful, and satisfying lives.

Humanists are interested in psychological needs for love, self-esteem, belonging, self-expression, creativity, and spirituality. Such needs, they believe, are as important as our biological urges for food and water. For example, newborn infants deprived of human love may die just as surely as they would if deprived of food.

How scientific is the humanistic approach? Initially, humanists were less interested in treating psychology as a science. They stressed subjective factors, such as one's self-image, self-evaluation, and frame of reference. (*Self-image* is your perception of your own body, personality, and capabilities. *Self-evaluation* refers to appraising yourself as good or bad. A *frame of reference* is a mental perspective used to interpret events.) Today, humanists still seek to understand how we perceive ourselves and experience the world. However, most now do research to test their ideas, just as other psychologists do (Schneider, Bugental, & Pierson, 2001).

Maslow's concept of self-actualization is a key feature of humanism. **Self-actualization** refers to developing one's poten-

---

Cognitive behaviorism An approach that combines behavioral principles with cognition (perception, thinking, anticipation) to explain behavior.

Gestalt psychology A school of psychology emphasizing the study of thinking, learning, and perception in whole units, not by analysis into parts.

Unconscious Contents of the mind that are beyond awareness, especially impulses and desires not directly known to a person.

Repression The unconscious process by which memories, thoughts, or impulses are held out of awareness.

Psychoanalysis A Freudian approach to psychotherapy emphasizing the exploration of unconscious conflicts.

Neo-Freudian A psychologist who accepts the broad features of Freud's theory but has revised the theory to fit his or her own concepts.

Psychodynamic theory Any theory of behavior that emphasizes internal conflicts, motives, and unconscious forces.

Humanism An approach to psychology that focuses on human experience, problems, potentials, and ideals.

Determinism The idea that all behavior has prior causes that would completely explain one's choices and actions if all such causes were known.

Free will The idea that human beings are capable of freely making choices or decisions.

Self-actualization The ongoing process of fully developing one's personal potential.

Table 1.2 ● **The Early Development of Psychology**

Perspective	Date	Notable Events
Experimental psychology	1875	First psychology course offered by William James
	1878	First American Ph.D. in psychology awarded
	1879	Wilhelm Wundt opens first psychology laboratory in Germany
	1883	First American psychology lab founded at Johns Hopkins University
	1886	First American psychology textbook written by John Dewey
Structuralism	1898	Edward Titchener advances psychology based on introspection
Functionalism	1890	William James publishes *Principles of Psychology*
	1892	American Psychological Association founded
Psychodynamic psychology	1895	Sigmund Freud publishes first studies
	1900	Freud publishes *The Interpretation of Dreams*
Behaviorism	1906	Ivan Pavlov reports his research on conditioned reflexes
	1913	John Watson presents behavioristic view
Gestalt psychology	1912	Max Wertheimer and others advance Gestalt viewpoint
Humanistic psychology	1942	Carl Rogers publishes *Counseling and Psychotherapy*
	1943	Abraham Maslow publishes "A Theory of Human Motivation"

Mary Calkins, 1863–1930.

Christine Ladd-Franklin, 1847–1930.

tial fully and becoming the best person possible. According to humanists, everyone has this potential. Humanists seek ways to help it emerge. ● Table 1.2 presents a summary of psychology's early development.

bridges
Behaviorism, Gestalt psychology, psychoanalytic theory, and humanism have all given rise to various forms of psychotherapy. **See Chapter 15 for more information about how psychological disorders are treated.**

The Role of Women in Psychology's Early Days

Were all the early psychologists men? Even though most of the early psychologists were men, women have contributed to psychology from the beginning (Minton, 2000). By 1906, in the United States about 1 psychologist in 10 was a woman. Who were these "foremothers" of psychology? Three who became well known are Mary Calkins, Christine Ladd-Franklin, and Margaret Washburn.

Mary Calkins did valuable research on memory and was also the first woman president of the American Psychological Asso-

ciation, in 1905. Christine Ladd-Franklin studied color vision. In 1906 she was ranked among the 50 most important psychologists in America. In 1908 Margaret Washburn published an influential textbook on animal behavior, titled *The Animal Mind*.

Margaret Washburn, 1871–1939.

The first woman to be awarded a Ph.D. in psychology was Margaret Washburn, in 1894. Over the next 15 years many more women followed her pioneering lead. Today, more than half the members of the American Psychological Association are women, two out of three graduate students in psychology are women, and in recent years nearly 75 percent of all college graduates with a major in psychology have been women. Clearly, psychology has become fully open to both men and women (Hyde, 2004).

●● Psychology Today—Three Complementary Perspectives on Behavior

Gateway Question: What are the contemporary perspectives in psychology?

At one time, loyalty to each school of thought was fierce, and clashes were common. Now, some early systems, such as structuralism, have disappeared entirely while new ones have gained prominence. Also, viewpoints such as functionalism and Gestalt psychology have blended into newer, broader perspectives. Certainly, loyalties and specialties still exist. But today, many psychologists are *eclectic* (ek-LEK-tik), because they realize that a single perspective is unlikely to fully explain complex human behavior. As a result, psychologists commonly draw insight from a variety of perspectives, with insights from one often complementing insights from the other. The three broad views that shape modern psychology are the *biological, psychological,* and *sociocultural* perspectives (● Table 1.3).

Table 1.3 ● Contemporary Ways to Look at Behavior

Biological Perspective
Biopsychological View
Key Idea: *Human and animal behavior is the result of internal physical, chemical, and biological processes.*
Seeks to explain behavior through activity of the brain and nervous system, physiology, genetics, the endocrine system, and biochemistry; neutral, reductionistic, mechanistic view of human nature.

Evolutionary View
Key Idea: *Human and animal behavior is the result of the process of evolution.*
Seeks to explain behavior through evolutionary principles based on natural selection; neutral, reductionistic, mechanistic view of human nature.

Psychological Perspective
Behavioristic View
Key Idea: *Behavior is shaped and controlled by one's environment.*
Emphasizes the study of observable behavior and the effects of learning; stresses the influence of external rewards and punishments; neutral, scientific, somewhat mechanistic view of human nature.

Cognitive View
Key Idea: *Much human behavior can be understood in terms of the mental processing of information.*
Concerned with thinking, knowing, perception, understanding, memory, decision making, and judgment; explains behavior in terms of information processing; neutral, somewhat computer-like view of human nature.

Psychodynamic View
Key Idea: *Behavior is directed by forces within one's personality that are often hidden or unconscious.*
Emphasizes internal impulses, desires, and conflicts—especially those that are unconscious; views behavior as the result of clashing forces within personality; somewhat negative, pessimistic view of human nature.

Humanistic View
Key Idea: *Behavior is guided by one's self-image, by subjective perceptions of the world, and by needs for personal growth.*
Focuses on subjective, conscious experience, human problems, potentials, and ideals; emphasizes self-image and self-actualization to explain behavior; positive, philosophical view of human nature.

Sociocultural Perspective
Sociocultural View
Key Idea: *Behavior is influenced by one's social and cultural context.*
Emphasizes that behavior is related to the social and cultural environment within which a person is born, grows up, and lives from day to day; neutral, interactionist view of human nature.

The Biological Perspective

The **biological perspective** seeks to explain our behavior in terms of biological principles such as brain processes, evolution, and genetics. By using new techniques, *biopsychologists* are producing exciting insights about how the brain relates to thinking, feelings, perception, abnormal behavior, and other topics. Biopsychologists and others who study the brain and nervous system, such as biologists and biochemists, are part of the broader field of *neuroscience*. As mentioned earlier, *evolutionary psychologists* look at how human evolution and genetics might explain our current behavior.

The Psychological Perspective

The **psychological perspective** takes the view that behavior is shaped by psychological processes within each person. Although it continues to emphasize objective observation, just as the early behaviorists did, the psychological perspective now includes cognitive behaviorism and cognitive psychology. These perspectives

acknowledge that mental processes underlie much of our behavior. Cognitive psychology has gained greater prominence in recent years as researchers have devised ways to objectively study covert behaviors, such as thinking, memory, language, perception, problem solving, consciousness, and creativity. Cognitive psychologists and other researchers interested in cognition, such as computer scientists and linguists, form the broader field of *cognitive science*. With a renewed interest in thinking, it can be said that psychology has finally "regained consciousness" (Robins, Gosling, & Craik, 1998).

Biological perspective The attempt to explain behavior in terms of underlying biological principles.

Psychological perspective The traditional view that behavior is shaped by psychological processes occurring at the level of the individual.

Freudian psychoanalysis continues to evolve into the broader *psychodynamic view*. Although many of Freud's ideas have been challenged, psychodynamic psychologists continue to trace human behavior to unconscious processes. They also seek to develop therapies to help people lead happier, fuller lives. Humanistic psychologists do, too, although they stress subjective, conscious experience and the positive side of human nature, rather than unconscious processes.

Positive Psychology

Psychologists have always paid attention to the negative side of human behavior. This is easy to understand because of the pressing need to solve human problems. However, inspired by the humanists, more and more psychologists have recently begun to ask, What do we know about love, happiness, creativity, well-being, self-confidence, and achievement? Together, such topics make up **positive psychology,** the study of human strengths, virtues, and optimal behavior (Compton, 2005; Seligman & Csikszentmihalyi, 2000). Many topics from positive psychology can be found in this book. Ideally, they will help make your own life more positive and fulfilling (Simonton & Baumeister, 2005).

The Sociocultural Perspective

As you can see, it is helpful to view human behavior from more than one perspective. This is also true in another sense. The **sociocultural perspective** stresses the impact that social and cultural contexts have on our behavior. We are rapidly becoming a multicultural society, made up of people from many different nations. How has this affected psychology? Let us introduce you to Jerry, who is Japanese American and is married to an Irish-Catholic American. Here is what Jerry, his wife, and their children did one New Year's Day:

> We woke up in the morning and went to Mass at St. Brigid's, which has a black gospel choir. . . . Then we went to the Japanese-American Community Center for the Oshogatsu New Year's program and saw Buddhist archers shoot arrows to ward off evil spirits for the year. Next, we ate traditional rice cakes as part of the New Year's service and listened to a young Japanese-American storyteller. On the way home, we stopped in Chinatown and after that we ate Mexican food at a taco stand. (Njeri, 1991)

Jerry and his family reflect a new social reality: Cultural diversity is becoming the norm. More than 100 million Americans are now African American, Hispanic, Asian American, Native American, or Pacific Islander (United States Bureau of Census, 2007). In some large cities "minority" groups are already the majority.

In the past, psychology was based mostly on the cultures of North America and Europe. Now, we must ask, do the principles of Western psychology apply to people in all cultures? Are some psychological concepts invalid in other cultures? Are any universal? As psychologists have probed such questions, one thing has become clear: Most of what we think, feel, and do is influenced in one way or another by the social and cultural worlds in which we live (Lehman, Chiu, & Schaller, 2004).

Patrick Giardino/Corbis

To fully understand human behavior, personal differences based on age, race, culture, ethnicity, gender, and sexual orientation must be taken into account.

Cultural Relativity

Imagine that you are a psychologist. Your client, Linda, who is a Native American, tells you that spirits live in the trees near her home. Is Linda suffering from a delusion? Is she abnormal? Obviously, you will misjudge Linda's mental health if you fail to take her cultural beliefs into account. **Cultural relativity** (the idea that behavior must be judged relative to the values of the culture in which it occurs) can greatly affect the diagnosis and treatment of mental disorders (Draguns, Gielen, & Fish, 2004). Cases like Linda's teach us to be wary of using narrow standards when judging others or comparing groups.

---

bridges

Psychotherapy can be less effective if a therapist and client come from different cultures. **See Chapter 15, page 517, for a discussion of the impact of culture on therapy.**

A Broader View of Diversity

In addition to cultural differences, age, ethnicity, gender, religion, disability, and sexual orientation all affect the **social norms** that guide behavior. Social norms are rules that define acceptable and expected behavior for members of various groups. All too often, the unstated standard for judging what is "average," "normal," or "correct" has been the behavior of white, middle-class males (Reid, 2002). To fully understand human behavior, psychologists need to know how people differ, as well as the ways in which we are all alike. To be effective, psychologists must be sensitive to people who are ethnically and culturally different from themselves (APA, 2003). For the same reason, an appreciation of human diversity can enrich your life, as well as your understanding of psychology (Denmark, Rabinowitz, & Sechzer, 2005).

In a moment we will further explore what psychologists do. First, here are some questions to enhance your learning:

KNOWLEDGE BUILDER
History and Contemporary Perspectives

RECITE
Match:

_____ 1. Philosophy
_____ 2. Wundt
_____ 3. Structuralism
_____ 4. Functionalism
_____ 5. Behaviorism
_____ 6. Gestalt
_____ 7. Psychodynamic
_____ 8. Humanistic
_____ 9. Cognitive
_____ 10. Washburn
_____ 11. Biopsychology

A. Against analysis; studied whole experiences
B. "Mental chemistry" and introspection
C. Emphasizes self-actualization and personal growth
D. Interested in unconscious causes of behavior
E. Interested in how the mind aids survival
F. First woman Ph.D. in psychology
G. Studied stimuli and responses, conditioning
H. Part of psychology's "long past"
I. Concerned with thinking, language, problem solving
J. Used introspection and careful measurement
K. Relates behavior to the brain, physiology, and genetics
L. Also known as engineering psychology

12. Who among the following was not a historic woman psychologist?
   a. Calkins
   b. Ladd-Franklin
   c. Washburn
   d. Watson

13. A psychotherapist is working with a person from an ethnic group other than her own. She should be aware of how cultural relativity and _____ affect behavior.
   a. the anthropomorphic error
   b. operational definitions
   c. biased sampling
   d. social norms

REFLECT

Critical Thinking

14. Modern sciences such as psychology are built on observations that can be verified by two or more independent observers. Did structuralism meet this standard? Why or why not?

Relate

Which school of thought most closely matches your own view of behavior? Do you think any of the early schools offers a complete explanation of why we behave as we do? What about the three broad contemporary perspectives? Can you explain why so many psychologists are eclectic?

A group of psychologists were asked to answer this question: "Why did the chicken cross the road?" Their answers are listed next. Can you identify their theoretical orientations?

The chicken had been rewarded for crossing road in the past.

The chicken had an unconscious wish to become a pancake.

The chicken was trying to solve the problem of how to reach the other side of the road.

The chicken felt a need to explore new possibilities as a way to actualize its potentials.

The chicken's motor cortex was activated by messages from its hypothalamus.

no other person can observe.
examined the contents of his or her own mind, which is something that
14. *No, it did not. The downfall of structuralism was that each observer*
Answers: 1. H **2.** J **3.** B **4.** E **5.** G **6.** A **7.** D **8.** C **9.** I **10.** F **11.** K **12.** d **13.** d

⬤⬤ Psychologists—Guaranteed Not to Shrink

Gateway Question: What are the major specialties in psychology?

Psychologists are all shrinks, right? Nope. "Shrinks" (a slang term derived from "head shrinkers") are *psychiatrists,* a different type of mental health professional. A **psychologist** is highly trained in the methods, knowledge, and theories of psychology. Psychologists usually have a master's degree or a doctorate. These degrees typically require several years of postgraduate training.

Psychologists are often inaccurately portrayed in the media. Some films have featured psychologists who are more disturbed than their patients (such as Jack Nicholson's character in *Anger Management*) or psychologists who are bumbling buffoons (such as Billy Crystal's character in *Analyze This*). In the comedy *Prime*

© Mike Baldwin / Cornered

© Mike Baldwin/CartoonStock

"Thanks to you, Doc, I'm beginning to feel a lot more normal."

Positive psychology The study of human strengths, virtues, and effective functioning.

Sociocultural perspective The focus on the importance of social and cultural contexts in influencing the behavior of individuals.

Cultural relativity The idea that behavior must be judged relative to the values of the culture in which it occurs.

Social norms Rules that define acceptable and expected behavior for members of a group.

Psychologist A person highly trained in the methods, factual knowledge, and theories of psychology.

a therapist listens to a patient describe intimate details of her relationship with a man but fails to tell the patient that the man is her son. Such characters may be dramatic and entertaining, but they seriously distort public perceptions of responsible and hard-working psychologists (Schultz, 2004). Real psychologists follow an ethical code that stresses respect for people's privacy, dignity, confidentiality, and welfare (APA, 2002).

Even without media distortions, misconceptions about psychologists are common. For instance, most psychologists are not therapists in private practice. Instead, they are employed by schools, businesses, and social agencies. Likewise, only 16 percent work in clinics or hospitals. Contrary to common belief, clinical psychology is not the only specialty in the field. Only a little over half of all psychologists study mental disorders or do therapy. Others may teach, do research, give psychological tests, or serve as consultants to business, industry, government, or the military.

One perception of psychologists is accurate: Most do help people in one way or another. Psychologists interested in emotional problems specialize in clinical or counseling psychology (● Table 1.4). **Clinical psychologists** treat psychological problems or do research on therapies and mental disorders. In contrast, **counseling psychologists** tend to treat milder problems, such as troubles at work or school. However, such differences are fading, and many counseling psychologists now work full time as therapists.

To enter the profession of psychology, it is best to have a doctorate (Ph.D., Psy.D., or Ed.D.). Most clinical psychologists have a Ph.D. degree and follow a scientist-practitioner model. That is, they are trained to do either research or therapy. Many do both. Other clinicians earn the Psy.D. (Doctor of Psychology) degree, which emphasizes therapy skills rather than research (Peterson, 2001).

Have you ever wondered what it takes to become a psychologist? See "Is a Career in Psychology Right for You?"

Table 1.4 ● Kinds of Psychologists and What They Do

Specialty		Typical Activities
Biopsychology	B*	Does research on the brain, nervous system, and other physical origins of behavior
Clinical	A	Does psychotherapy; investigates clinical problems; develops methods of treatment
Cognitive	B	Studies human thinking and information processing abilities
Community	A	Promotes community-wide mental health through research, prevention, education, and consultation
Comparative	B	Studies and compares the behavior of different species, especially animals
Consumer	A	Researches packaging, advertising, marketing methods, and characteristics of consumers
Counseling	A	Does psychotherapy and personal counseling; researches emotional disturbances and counseling methods
Cultural	B	Studies the ways in which culture, subculture, and ethnic group membership affect behavior
Developmental	A, B	Conducts research on infant, child, adolescent, and adult development; does clinical work with disturbed children; acts as consultant to parents and schools
Educational	A	Investigates classroom dynamics, teaching styles, and learning; develops educational tests, evaluates educational programs
Engineering	A	Does applied research on the design of machinery, computers, airlines, automobiles, and so on, for business, industry, and the military
Environmental	A, B	Studies the effects of urban noise, crowding, attitudes toward the environment, and human use of space; acts as a consultant on environmental issues
Forensic	A	Studies problems of crime and crime prevention, rehabilitation programs, prisons, courtroom dynamics; selects candidates for police work
Gender	B	Does research on differences between males and females, the acquisition of gender identity, and the role of gender throughout life
Health	A, B	Studies the relationship between behavior and health; uses psychological principles to promote health and prevent illness
Industrial-organizational	A	Selects job applicants, does skills analysis, evaluates on-the-job training, improves work environments and human relations in organizations and work settings
Learning	B	Studies how and why learning occurs; develops theories of learning
Medical	A	Applies psychology to manage medical problems, such as the emotional impact of illness, self-screening for cancer, compliance in taking medicine
Personality	B	Studies personality traits and dynamics; develops theories of personality and tests for assessing personality traits
School	A	Does psychological testing, referrals, emotional and vocational counseling of students; detects and treats learning disabilities; improves classroom learning
Sensation and perception	B	Studies the sense organs and the process of perception; investigates the mechanisms of sensation and develops theories about how perception occurs
Social	B	Investigates human social behavior, including attitudes, conformity, persuasion, prejudice, friendship, aggression, helping, and so forth

*Research in this area is typically applied (A), basic (B), or both (A, B).

DISCOVERING PSYCHOLOGY

Is a Career in Psychology Right for You?

As you read this book we encourage you to frequently reflect on new ideas by relating them to your own life to better understand and remember them. Discovering Psychology boxes like this one are designed to help you be more reflective about how psychology relates to your own life. Answer the following questions to explore whether you would enjoy becoming a psychologist:

1. I have a strong interest in human behavior. True or False?

2. I am good at recognizing patterns, evaluating evidence, and drawing conclusions. True or False?
3. I am emotionally stable. True or False?
4. I have good communication skills. True or False?
5. I find theories and ideas challenging and stimulating. True or False?
6. My friends regard me as especially sensitive to the feelings of others. True or False?
7. I enjoy planning and carrying out complex projects and activities. True or False?

8. Programs and popular books about psychology interest me. True or False?
9. I enjoy working with other people. True or False?
10. Clear thinking, objectivity, and keen observation appeal to me. True or False?

If you answered "True" to most of these questions, a career in psychology might be a good choice. And remember that many psychology majors also succeed in occupations such as management, public affairs, social services, business, sales, and education.

Other Mental Health Professionals

Clinical psychologists are not the only people who work in the field of mental health. Often they coordinate their efforts with other specially trained professionals. What are the differences among psychologists, psychiatrists, psychoanalysts, counselors, and other mental health professionals? Certainly, they're not all "shrinks." Each has a specific blend of training and skills.

A **psychiatrist** is a medical doctor who treats mental disorders, usually by doing psychotherapy. Psychiatrists can also prescribe drugs, which is something psychologists usually cannot do. However, this is changing. Psychologists in New Mexico and Louisiana can now legally prescribe drugs. It will be interesting to see whether other states grant similar privileges (Munsey, 2006).

To be a psychoanalyst, you must have a moustache and goatee, spectacles, a German accent, and a well-padded couch—or so the media stereotype goes. Actually, to become a **psychoanalyst** you must have an M.D. or Ph.D. degree plus further training in Freudian psychoanalysis. In other words, either a physician or a psychologist may become an analyst by learning a specific type of psychotherapy.

In many states, counselors also do mental health work. A **counselor** is an adviser who helps solve problems with marriage, career, school, work, or the like. To be a licensed counselor (such as a marriage and family counselor, a child counselor, or a school counselor) typically requires a master's degree plus 1 or 2 years of full-time supervised counseling experience. Counselors learn practical helping skills and do not treat serious mental disorders.

Psychiatric social workers play an important role in many mental health programs, where they apply social science principles to help patients in clinics and hospitals. Most hold an M.S.W. (Master of Social Work) degree. Often, they assist psychologists and psychiatrists as part of a team. Their typical duties include evaluating patients and families; conducting group therapy; or visiting a patient's home, school, or job to alleviate problems.

The Profession of Psychology

Does a person have to have a license to practice psychology? At one time it was possible in many states for anyone to "hang out a shingle" as a "psychologist." Now psychologists must meet rigorous educational and legal requirements. To work as a clinical or counseling psychologist you must have a license issued by a state examining board. However, the law does not prevent you from calling yourself anything else you choose—therapist, rebirther, primal feeling facilitator, cosmic aura balancer, or Rolfer—or from selling your "services" to anyone willing to pay. Beware of people with self-proclaimed titles. Even if their intentions are honorable, they may have little training. A licensed psychologist who chooses to use a particular type of therapy is not the same as someone "trained" solely in that technique.

Ethics

Most psychologists take pride in following a professional code that stresses (1) high levels of competence, integrity, and responsibility; (2) respect for people's rights to privacy, dignity, confidentiality,

Clinical psychologist A psychologist who specializes in the treatment of psychological and behavioral disturbances or who does research on such disturbances.

Counseling psychologist A psychologist who specializes in the treatment of milder emotional and behavioral disturbances.

Psychiatrist A medical doctor with additional training in the diagnosis and treatment of mental and emotional disorders.

Psychoanalyst A mental health professional (usually a medical doctor) trained to practice psychoanalysis.

Counselor A mental health professional who specializes in helping people with problems not involving serious mental disorder; for example, marriage counselors, career counselors, or school counselors.

Psychiatric social worker A mental health professional trained to apply social science principles to help patients in clinics and hospitals.

and personal freedom; and, above all, (3) protection of the client's welfare. Psychologists are also expected to use their knowledge to contribute to society. Many do volunteer work in the communities in which they live (Barnett et al., 2007; APA, 2002).

Specialties in Psychology

Do all psychologists do therapy and treat abnormal behavior? No. About 58 percent are clinical and counseling psychologists. The rest are found in other specialties. At present, the American Psychological Association (APA) consists of more than 50 divisions, each reflecting special skills or areas of interest. Some of the major specialties are listed in ● Table 1.4. (Also see ● Figure 1.5.) Nearly 30 percent of all psychologists are employed full time at colleges

or universities, where they teach and do research, consulting, or therapy. Some do *basic research,* in which they seek knowledge for its own sake. For example, a psychologist might study memory simply to understand how it works. Others do *applied research* to solve immediate practical problems, such as finding ways to improve athletic performance. Some do both types of research.

In a moment we'll take a closer look at how research is done. Before that, here's a chance to do a little research on how much you've learned:

● **Figure 1.5** *(a)* Specialties in psychology (APA, 2005). Percentages are approximate. *(b)* Where psychologists work (APA, 2000). *(c)* This chart shows the main activities psychologists engage in at work (APA, 2000). Any particular psychologist might do several of these activities during a work week. As you can see, most psychologists specialize in applied areas and work in applied settings.

●● The Psychology Experiment—Where Cause Meets Effect

Gateway Question: How is an experiment performed?

To get beyond description and fully understand behavior, psychologists must to be able explain *why* we act the way we do. To discover the *causes* of behavior, we must usually conduct an **experiment.** An experiment is a formal trial undertaken to confirm or disconfirm a hypothesis about the causes of behavior (although causes are sometimes revealed by naturalistic observation or correlations). Experiments allow psychologists to carefully control conditions and bring cause-and-effect relationships into sharp focus. Hence, they are generally accepted as the most powerful scientific research tool. To perform an experiment you would do the following:

1. Directly vary a condition you think might affect behavior.
2. Create two or more groups of subjects. These groups should be alike in all ways *except* the condition you are varying.
3. Record whether varying the condition has any effect on behavior.

Suppose you want to find out if using cell phones while driving a car affects the likelihood of having an accident. First, you would form two groups. Then you could give the members of one group a test of driving ability while they are using a cell phone. The second group would take the same test without using a cell phone. By comparing average driving ability scores for the two groups, you could tell if cell phone use affects driving ability.

As you can see, the simplest psychological experiment is based on two groups of **experimental subjects** (animals or people whose behavior is investigated; human subjects are also called **participants**). One group is called the *experimental group;* the other becomes the *control group.* The control group and the experimental group are treated exactly alike except for the condition you intentionally vary. This condition is called the *independent variable.*

Variables and Groups

A **variable** is any condition that can change and that might affect the outcome of the experiment. Identifying causes and effects in an experiment involves three types of variables:

1. **Independent variables** are conditions altered or varied by the experimenter, who sets their size, amount, or value. Independent variables are suspected *causes* for differences in behavior.
2. **Dependent variables** measure the results of the experiment. That is, they reveal the *effects* that independent variables have on *behavior.* Such effects are often revealed by measures of performance, such as test scores.
3. **Extraneous variables** are conditions that a researcher wishes to prevent from affecting the outcome of the experiment.

We can apply these terms to our cell phone/driving experiment in this way: Cell phone use is the independent variable—we want to know if cell phone use affects driving ability. Driving ability (defined by scores achieved on a test of driving ability) is the dependent variable—we want to know if the ability to drive well depends on whether a person is using a cell phone. All other variables that could affect driving ability are extraneous. Examples of extraneous variables are the number of hours slept the night before the test, driving experience, or familiarity with the car used in the experiment. (You might be interested to know that people using cell phones drive no better than people who are legally drunk [Strayer, Drews, & Crouch, 2006].)

As you can see, an **experimental group** consists of participants exposed to the independent variable (cell phone use in the preced-

ing example). Members of the **control group** are exposed to all conditions except the independent variable.

Let's examine another simple experiment. Suppose you notice that you seem to study better while listening to your iPod. This suggests the hypothesis that music improves learning. We could test this idea by forming an experimental group that studies with music. A control group would study without music. Then we could compare their scores on a test.

Is a control group really needed? Can't people just study while listening to their iPods to see if they do better? Better than what? The control group provides a *point of reference* for comparison with the scores in the experimental group. Without a control group it would be impossible to tell if music had any effect on learning. If the average test score of the experimental group is higher than the average of the control group, we can conclude that music improves learning. If there is no difference, it's obvious that the independent variable had no effect on learning.

In this experiment, the amount learned (indicated by scores on the test) is the *dependent variable.* We are asking, Does the independent variable *affect* the dependent variable? (Does music affect or influence learning?)

Experimental Control

How do we know that the people in one group aren't more intelligent than those in the other group? It's true that personal differences might affect the experiment. However, they can be controlled by randomly assigning people to groups. **Random assignment** means that a participant has an equal chance of being in either the experimental group or the control group. Randomization evenly balances personal differences in the two groups. In our musical experiment, this could be done by simply flipping a coin for each participant: Heads, and the participant is in the experimental

---

Experiment A formal trial undertaken to confirm or disconfirm a hypothesis about cause and effect.

Experimental subjects Humans (also referred to as **participants**) or animals whose behavior is investigated in an experiment.

Variable Any condition that changes or can be made to change; a measure, event, or state that may vary.

Independent variable In an experiment, the condition being investigated as a possible cause of some change in behavior. The values that this variable takes are chosen by the experimenter.

Dependent variable In an experiment, the condition (usually a behavior) that is affected by the independent variable.

Extraneous variables Conditions or factors excluded from influencing the outcome of an experiment.

Experimental group In a controlled experiment, the group of subjects exposed to the independent variable or experimental condition.

Control group In a controlled experiment, the group of subjects exposed to all experimental conditions or variables *except* the independent variable.

Random assignment The use of chance (for example, flipping a coin) to assign subjects to experimental and control groups.

CRITICAL THINKING

That's Interesting, but Is It Ethical?

In one classic study, participants were ordered to give what they thought were painful electric shocks to another person (no shocks were actually given) (Milgram, 1963). Believing that they had hurt someone, many people left the experiment shaken and upset. A few suffered guilt and distress for some time afterward.

> **bridges**
>
> Stanley Milgram undertook his infamous studies to better understand just how willing people are to obey an authority. **See Chapter 16, pages 547–549.**

Such experiments raise serious ethical questions about behavioral research. Did the information gained justify the emotional costs? Was deception really necessary? As a reply to such questions, American Psychological Association guidelines state that "Psychologists must carry out investigations with respect for the people who participate and with concern for their dignity and welfare." Similar guidelines apply to animals, where investigators are expected to "ensure the welfare of animals and treat them humanely" (APA, 2002) (● Table 1.5).

To assure this, most university psychology departments have ethics committees that oversee research. Nevertheless, no easy answers exist for the ethical questions raised by psychology, and debate about specific experiments is likely to continue.

Table 1.5 ● Basic Ethical Guidelines for Psychological Researchers

Do no harm.
Accurately describe risks to potential participants.
Ensure that participation is voluntary.
Minimize any discomfort to participants.
Maintain confidentiality.
Do not unnecessarily invade privacy.
Use deception only when absolutely necessary.
Remove any misconceptions caused by deception (debrief).
Provide results and interpretations to participants.
Treat participants with dignity and respect.

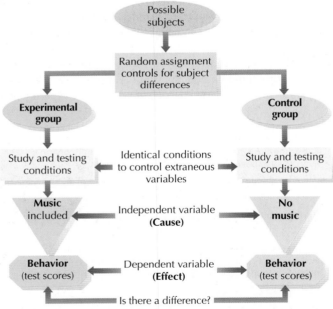

● **Figure 1.6** Elements of a simple psychological experiment to assess the effects on test scores of music during study.

group; tails, it's the control group. This would result in few average differences in the number of people in each group who are women or men, geniuses or dunces, hungry, hungover, tall, music lovers, or whatever.

Other *extraneous,* or outside, variables—such as the amount of study time, the temperature in the room, the time of day, the

amount of light, and so forth—must also be prevented from affecting the outcome of an experiment. But how? Usually this is done by making all conditions (except the independent variable) *exactly* alike for both groups. When all conditions are the same for both groups—*except* the presence or absence of music—then any difference in the amount learned *must* be caused by the music (● Figure 1.6). (Psychology experiments sometimes raise ethical questions. See "That's Interesting, but Is It Ethical" for more information.)

Cause and Effect

Now let's summarize. In an experiment, two or more groups of subjects are treated differently with respect to the independent variable. In all other ways they are treated the same. That is, extraneous variables are equated for all groups. The effect of the independent variable (or variables) on some behavior (the dependent variable) is then measured. In a carefully controlled experiment, the independent variable is the only possible *cause* for any *effect* noted in the dependent variable. This allows clear cause-and-effect connections to be identified (● Figure 1.7).

Evaluating Results

How can we tell if the independent variable really made a difference? This problem is handled statistically. Reports in psychology journals almost always include the statement, "Results were **statistically significant.**" What this means is that the obtained results would occur very rarely by chance alone. To be statistically significant, a difference must be large enough so that it would occur by

Dependent Variable

Experimental Group   Control Group

☐ Extraneous Variables
☐ Independent Variable

● **Figure 1.7** Experimental control is achieved by balancing extraneous variables for the experimental group and the control group. For example, the average age (A), education (B), and intelligence (C) of group members could be made the same for both groups. Then we could apply the independent variable to the experimental group. If their behavior (the dependent variable) changes (in comparison with the control group), the change must be caused by the independent variable.

chance in less than 5 experiments out of 100. (See the Statistics Appendix for more information.) Of course, findings also become more convincing when they can be *replicated* (repeated) by other researchers.

Meta-Analysis

As you might guess, numerous studies are done on important topics in psychology. Although each study adds to our understanding, the results of various studies don't always agree. Let's say we are interested in whether males or females tend to be greater risk takers. A computer search would reveal that more than 100 studies have investigated various types of risk-taking (for example, smoking, fast driving, or unprotected sex).

Is there a way to combine the results of the studies? Yes, a statistical technique called **meta-analysis** can be used to combine the results of many studies as if they were all part of one big study (Rosenthal & DiMatteo, 2001). In other words, a meta-analysis is a study of the results of other studies. In recent years, meta-analysis has been used to summarize and synthesize mountains of psychological research. This allows us to see the big picture and draw conclusions that might be missed in a single, small-scale study. Oh, and about that risk-taking question: A meta-analysis showed that males do tend to take more risks than females (Byrnes, Miller, & Schafer, 1999). (The most frequent last words uttered by deceased young males is rumored to be, "Hey, watch this!")

●● Double Blind—On Placebos and Self-Fulfilling Prophecies

Gateway Question: What is a double-blind experiment?

Suppose a researcher hypothesizes that the drug amphetamine (a stimulant) improves learning. She explains her hypothesis to her participants and gives experimental group participants an amphetamine pill before they begin studying. Control group members get

nothing. Later, she assesses how much each participant learned. Does this experiment seem valid? Actually, it is seriously flawed for several reasons.

Research Participant Bias

Why? The experimental group took the drug and the control group didn't. Differences in the amount they learned must have been caused by the drug, right? No, because the drug wasn't the only difference between the groups. For a start, because of what they were told, participants in the experimental group likely *expected* to learn more. Any observed differences between groups then may reflect differences in expectation, not the actual effect of the drug. In a well-designed experiment, you must be careful about what you tell participants. Small bits of information might create **research participant bias,** or changes in participants' behavior caused by the influence of their expectations.

Notice also that experimental group participants swallowed a pill, and control participants did not. This is another form of research participant bias. It could be that those who swallowed a pill unconsciously *expected* to do better. After all, pills are medicine, aren't they? This alone might have created a **placebo effect** (changes in behavior caused by belief that one has taken a drug). Suppose the researcher had not given the experimental group an amphetamine pill and instead had given them a **placebo** (plah-SEE-bo) or fake drug. Inactive substances such as sugar pills and saline (saltwater) injections are commonly used as placebos. If a placebo has any effect, it must be based on suggestion, rather than chemistry (Thompson, 2005).

Placebo effects can be quite powerful. For instance, a saline injection is 70 percent as effective as morphine in reducing pain. That's why doctors sometimes prescribe placebos—especially for complaints that seem to have no physical basis. Placebos have been shown to affect pain, anxiety, depression, alertness, tension, sexual arousal, cravings for alcohol, and many other processes (Wampold et al., 2005).

How could an inert substance have any effect? Placebos alter our expectations, both conscious and unconscious, about our own emotional and physical reactions. Because we associate taking medicine with feeling better, we expect placebos to make us feel better, too (Stewart-Williams, 2004). After a person takes a pla-

Statistical significance Experimental results that would rarely occur by chance alone.

Meta-analysis A statistical technique for combining the results of many studies on the same subject.

Research participant bias Changes in the behavior of research participants caused by the unintended influence of their own expectations.

Placebo effect Changes in behavior due to participant's expectations that a drug (or other treatment) will have some effect.

Placebo An inactive substance given in the place of a drug in psychological research or by physicians who wish to treat a complaint by suggestion.

Royalty-Free/Corbis

The placebo effect is a major factor in medical treatments. Would you also expect the placebo effect to occur in psychotherapy? (It does, which complicates studies on the effectiveness of new psychotherapies.)

cebo, there is a reduction in brain activity linked with pain, so the effect is not imaginary (Wager et al., 2004).

Controlling Research Participant Bias

How can you avoid research participant bias? To control for research participant bias, we could use a **single-blind experiment.** In this case, participants do not know if they are in the experimental or the control group or if they are receiving a real drug or a placebo. All participants are given the same instructions and everyone gets a pill or injection. People in the experimental group get a real drug, and those in the control group get a placebo. Because participants are *blind* as to the hypothesis under investigation and whether they received the drug, their expectations (conscious *and* unconscious) are the same. Any difference in their behavior must be caused by the drug. However, even this arrangement is not enough, because researchers themselves sometimes affect experiments by influencing participants. Let's see how this occurs.

Researcher Bias

How could a researcher influence subjects? As we saw earlier, when the experimenter explained her hypothesis to the participants, she likely biased the results of the study. But even if a researcher uses a single-blind procedure to avoid deliberately biasing participants, **researcher bias** (changes in behavior caused by the unintended influence of a researcher) remains a problem. In essence, experimenters run the risk of finding what they expect to find. This occurs because humans are very sensitive to hints about what is expected of them (Rosenthal, 1994).

Researcher bias even applies outside the laboratory. Psychologist Robert Rosenthal (1973) reports an example of how expectations influence people: At the U.S. Air Force Academy Preparatory School, 100 airmen were randomly assigned to five different math classes. Their teachers did not know about this random placement. Instead, each teacher was told that his or her students had unusually high or low ability. Students in the classes labeled "high ability" improved much more in math scores than those in "low-ability" classes. Yet initially all the classes had students of equal ability.

Although the teachers were not conscious of any bias, apparently they subtly communicated their expectations to students. Most likely, they did this through tone of voice, body language, and by giving encouragement or criticism. Their "hints," in turn, created a self-fulfilling prophecy that affected the students. A **self-fulfilling prophecy** is a prediction that prompts people to act in ways that make the prediction come true. For instance, many teachers underestimate the abilities of ethnic minority children, which hurts the students' chances for success (Weinstein, Gregory, & Strambler, 2004). In short, people sometimes become what we prophesy for them. It is wise to remember that others tend to live *up* or *down* to our expectations for them (Jussim & Harber, 2005).

The Double-Blind Experiment

Because of research participant bias and researcher bias, it is common to keep both participants and researchers "blind." In a **double-blind experiment** neither subjects nor researchers know who is in the experimental group or the control group, including who received a drug and who took a placebo. Typically, someone else conducts the experiment, including preparing the pills or injections so that actual researchers don't know until after testing who got what. This not only controls for research participant bias, it also keeps researchers from unconsciously influencing participants.

Double-blind testing has shown that about 50 percent of the effectiveness of antidepressant drugs, such as the "wonder drug" Prozac, is due to the placebo effect (Kirsch & Sapirstein, 1998). Much of the popularity of herbal health remedies is also based on the placebo effect (Seidman, 2001).

> ### bridges
>
> **For more information about how psychologists study placebos, see Chapter 13, page 449.**

KNOWLEDGE BUILDER
The Psychology Experiment

RECITE

1. To understand cause and effect, a simple psychological experiment is based on creating two groups: the _____ group and the _____ group.
2. There are three types of variables to consider in an experiment: _____ variables (which are manipulated by the experimenter), _____ variables (which measure the outcome of the experiment), and _____ variables (factors to be excluded in a particular experiment).
3. A researcher performs an experiment to learn if room temperature affects the amount of aggression displayed by college students under crowded conditions in a simulated prison environment. In this experiment, the independent variable is which of the following?
   a. room temperature
   b. the amount of aggression
   c. crowding
   d. the simulated prison environment

Continued

4. A procedure used to control both research participant bias and researcher bias in drug experiments is the
    a. correlation method
    b. extraneous prophecy
    c. double-blind technique
    d. random assignment of subjects

REFLECT

Critical Thinking

5. There is a loophole in the statement, "I've been taking vitamin C tablets, and I haven't had a cold all year. Vitamin C is great!" What is the loophole?
6. People who believe strongly in astrology have personality characteristics that actually match, to a degree, those predicted by their astrological signs. Can you explain why this occurs?

Relate

In a sense, we all conduct little experiments to detect cause-and-effect connections. If you are interested in cooking, for example, you might try adding a particular spice to a meal on one occasion but not another. The question then becomes, "Does the use of the spice (the independent variable) affect the appeal of the meal (the dependent variable)?" By comparing a spiced meal (the control group) with an unspiced meal (the experimental group) you could find out if that spice is worth using. Can you think of at least one informal experiment you've run in the last month? What were the variables? What was the outcome?

Answers: 1. experimental, control **2.** independent, dependent, extraneous **3.** *a* **4.** *c* **5.** The statement implies that vitamin C prevents colds. However, not getting a cold could just be a coincidence. A controlled experiment with a group given vitamin C and a control group not taking vitamin C would be needed to learn if vitamin C actually has any effect on susceptibility to colds. **6.** Belief in astrology can create a self-fulfilling prophecy in which people alter their behaviors and self-concepts to match their astrological signs (van Rooij, 1994).

● ● Nonexperimental Research Methods—Different Strokes

Gateway Question: What nonexperimental research methods do psychologists use?

Determining cause-and-effect relationships between variables lies at the heart of explaining not just *what* we do, but *why* we do it. For this reason, psychologists place a special emphasis on controlled experimentation (**experimental method**). However, because it is not always possible to conduct experiments, psychologists gather evidence and test hypotheses in many others ways (Jackson, 2008). They observe behavior as it unfolds in natural settings (**naturalistic observation**); they make measurements to discover relationships between events (**correlational method**); they study psychological problems and therapies in clinical settings (**clinical method**); and they use questionnaires to poll large groups of people (**survey method**). Let's see how each of these is used to advance psychological knowledge.

Naturalistic Observation

Psychologists sometimes actively observe behavior in a *natural setting* (the typical environment in which a person or animal lives). For example, in 1960 Jane Goodall observed a chimpanzee use a grass stem as a tool to remove termites from a termite mound (Van Lawick-Goodall, 1971). Notice that naturalistic observation only provides *descriptions* of behavior. In order to *explain* observations we may need information from other research methods. Just the same, Goodall's discovery showed that humans are not the only tool-making animals (Nakamichi, 2004).

Chimpanzees in zoos use objects as tools. Doesn't that demonstrate the same thing? Not necessarily. Naturalistic observation allows us to study behavior that hasn't been tampered with or altered by outside influences. Only by observing chimps in their natural environment can we tell if they use tools without human interference.

Limitations

Doesn't the presence of human observers affect the animals' behavior? Yes. The observer effect is a major problem. The **observer effect** refers to changes in a subject's behavior caused by an awareness of being observed. Naturalists must be very careful to keep their distance and avoid "making friends" with the animals they are watching. Likewise, if you are interested in why automobile drivers have traffic accidents, you can't simply get in people's cars and start taking notes. As a stranger, your presence would probably change the driver's behaviors. When possible, the observer effect can be minimized by concealing the observer.

Another solution is to use hidden recorders. One naturalistic study of traffic accidents was done with video cameras installed in

Single-blind experiment An arrangement in which participants remain unaware of whether they are in the experimental group or the control group.

Researcher bias Changes in subjects' behavior caused by the unintended influence of a researcher's actions.

Self-fulfilling prophecy A prediction that prompts people to act in ways that make the prediction come true.

Double-blind experiment An arrangement in which both participants and experimenters are unaware of whether participants are in the experimental group or the control group, including who might have been administered a drug or a placebo.

Experimental method Investigating causes of behavior through controlled experimentation.

Naturalistic observation Observing behavior as it unfolds in natural settings.

Correlational method Making measurements to discover relationships between events.

Clinical method Studying psychological problems and therapies in clinical settings.

Survey method Using questionnaires and surveys to poll large groups of people.

Observer effect Changes in a person's behavior brought about by an awareness of being observed.

100 cars (Dingus et al., 2006). It turns out that most accidents are caused by failing to look at the traffic in front of the car (eyes forward!). Hidden stationary video cameras have also provided valuable observations of many animal species. As recording devices have become miniaturized, it has even become possible to attach "critter cams" directly to many species, allowing observations to be in a wide range of natural environments (● Figure 1.8). For example, zoologist Christian Rutz and his colleagues outfitted shy New Caledonian crows with "crow cams" to better understand their use of tools to forage for food (Rutz et al., 2007). Apparently humans and other primates are not the only tool-using species.

Observer bias is a related problem in which observers see what they expect to see or record only selected details (Jackson, 2008). For instance, teachers in one classic study were told to watch normal elementary school children who had been labeled (for the study) as "learning disabled," "mentally retarded," "emotionally disturbed," or "normal." Sadly, teachers gave the children very different ratings, depending on the labels used (Foster & Ysseldyke, 1976). In some situations, observer bias can have serious consequences (Spano, 2005). For example, a police officer expecting criminal behavior might shoot a person who is reaching for his wallet because he appears to be reaching for a gun.

A special mistake to avoid while observing animals is the **anthropomorphic** (AN-thro-po-MORE-fik) **error.** This is the error of attributing human thoughts, feelings, or motives to animals—especially as a way of explaining their behavior (Wynne, 2004). The temptation to assume that an animal is "angry," "jealous," "bored,"

or "guilty" can be strong. If you have pets at home, you probably already know how difficult it is to avoid anthropomorphizing. But it can lead to false conclusions. For example, if your dog growls at your girlfriend every time she visits, you might assume the dog doesn't like her. But maybe she wears a perfume that irritates the dog's nose.

Psychologists doing naturalistic studies make a special effort to minimize bias by keeping an **observational record,** or detailed summary of data and observations. As suggested by the study of traffic accidents and the use of "critter cams," video recording often provides the most objective record of all. Despite its problems, naturalistic observation can supply a wealth of information and raise many interesting questions. In most scientific research it is an excellent starting point.

Correlational Studies

Let's say a psychologist notes an association between the IQs of parents and their children, or between beauty and social popularity, or between anxiety and test performance, or even between crime and the weather. In each case, two observations or events are **correlated** (linked together in an orderly way). The Los Angeles study of crime and temperature mentioned earlier in this chapter is an example of a **correlational study.** Such studies evaluate the degree of relationship, or correlation, between two existing traits, behaviors, or events. First, two factors are measured. Then a statistical technique is used to find their degree of correlation. For example, we could find the correlation between the number of hours spent practicing and sports performance during competitions. If the correlation is large, knowing how much a person practices would allow us to predict his or her success in competition. Likewise, success in competition could be used to predict the amount of practice.

Psychologists seek to identify relationships concerning memory, perception, stress, aging, therapy, and a host of similar topics. Much of this book is a summary of such relationships.

Correlation Coefficients

How is the degree of correlation expressed? The strength and direction of a relationship can be expressed as a **coefficient of correlation.** This can be calculated as a number falling somewhere between +1.00 and −1.00. Drawing graphs of relationships can also help clarify their nature (● Figure 1.9). If the number is zero or close to zero, the association between two measures is weak or nonexistent (● see Figure 1.9*c*). For example, the correlation between shoe size and intelligence is zero. (Sorry, size 12 readers.) If the correlation is +1.00, a perfect positive relationship exists (● see Figure 1.9*e*); if it is −1.00, a perfect negative relationship has been discovered (● see Figure 1.9*a*).

● **Figure 1.8** New Caledonian crows wearing tiny "crow cams" barely half the weight of a silver dollar have been recorded using twigs to forage for food (Rutz et al., 2007).

© Jolyon Troscianko 2006

bridges
For more details about calculating and graphing correlations, see the Statistics Appendix.

Correlations in psychology are rarely perfect. But the closer the coefficient is to $+1.00$ or -1.00, the stronger the relationship. For example, identical twins tend to have almost identical IQs. In contrast, the IQs of parents and their children are only generally similar. The correlation between the IQs of parents and children is .35; between identical twins it's .86.

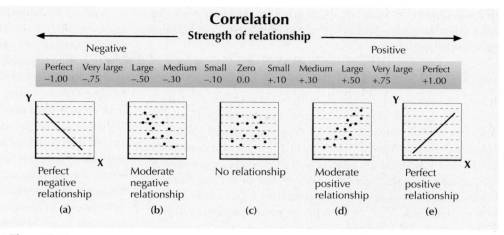

● **Figure 1.9** The correlation coefficient tells how strongly two measures are related. These graphs show a range of relationships between two measures, X and Y. If a correlation is negative, increases in one measure are associated with decreases in the other. (As Y gets larger, X gets smaller.) In a positive correlation, increases in one measure are associated with increases in the other. (As Y gets larger, X gets larger.) Graph *b* ("moderate negative relationship") might result from comparing grades in college (Y) with hours spent playing computer games (X): Higher anxiety is associated with lower scores. Graph *c* ("no relationship") would result from plotting a person's shoe size (Y) and his or her IQ (X). Graph *d* ("moderate positive relationship") could be a plot of grades in high school (Y) and grades in college (X) for a group of students: Higher grades in high school are associated with higher grades in college.

> **bridges**
> Correlations between the IQs of family members are used to estimate the degree to which intelligence is affected by heredity and environment. **See Chapter 9, pages 312–313.**

What do the terms "positive" and "negative" correlation mean? A **positive correlation** shows that higher scores in one measure are matched by higher scores in the other. For example, there is a moderate positive correlation between high school grades and college grades; students who do well in high school tend to do well in college (and the reverse) (see ● Figure 1.9*d*). In a **negative correlation,** higher scores in the first measure are associated with lower scores in the second. We might observe, for instance, a moderate negative correlation between the number of hours that students play computer games and grades. That is, more play is associated with lower grades. (This is the well-known computer-game-zombie effect; see ● Figure 1.9*b*).

Wouldn't that show that playing computer games too much causes lower grades? It might seem so, but as we saw previously, the best way to be confident that a cause-and-effect relationship exists is to perform a controlled experiment.

Correlation and Causation

Correlational studies help us discover relationships and make predictions. However, correlation *does not* demonstrate **causation** (a cause-effect relationship) (Elder, 2006). It could be, for instance, that students who aren't interested in their classes have more time for computer games. If so, then their lack of study and lower grades would *both* result from disinterest, not from excess game playing. Just because one thing *appears* to be related to another does not mean that a cause-and-effect connection exists.

Here is another example of mistaking correlation for causation: What if a psychologist discovers that the blood of patients with schizophrenia contains a certain chemical not found in the general population? Does this show that the chemical *causes* schizophrenia? It may seem so, but schizophrenia could cause the chemical to form. Or both schizophrenia and the chemical might be caused by some unknown third factor, such as the typical diet in mental hospitals (● Figure 1.10). To reiterate, just because one thing *appears*

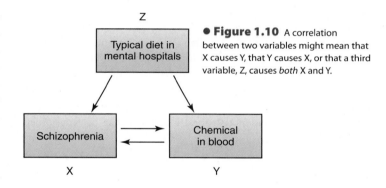

● **Figure 1.10** A correlation between two variables might mean that X causes Y, that Y causes X, or that a third variable, Z, causes *both* X and Y.

Observer bias The tendency of an observer to distort observations or perceptions to match his or her expectations.

Anthropomorphic error The error of attributing human thoughts, feelings, or motives to animals, especially as a way of explaining their behavior.

Observational record A detailed summary of observed events or a videotape of observed behavior.

Correlation The existence of a consistent, systematic relationship between two events, measures, or variables.

Correlational study A nonexperimental study designed to measure the degree of relationship (if any) between two or more events, measures, or variables.

Coefficient of correlation A statistical index ranging from -1.00 to $+1.00$ that indicates the direction and degree of correlation.

Positive correlation A statistical relationship in which increases in one measure are matched by increases in the other (or decreases correspond with decreases).

Negative correlation A statistical relationship in which increases in one measure are matched by decreases in the other.

Causation The act of causing some effect.

to cause another does not *confirm* that it does. The best way to be confident that a cause-and-effect relationship exists is to perform a controlled experiment.

The Clinical Method—One Case at a Time

It may be impractical, unethical, or impossible to use the experimental method to study rare events, such as unusual mental disorders, childhood "geniuses," or "rampage" school shootings (Harding, Fox, & Mehta, 2002). In such instances, a **case study** (an in-depth focus on a single subject) may be the best source of information. Clinical psychologists rely heavily on case studies, especially as a way to investigate mental disorders, such as depression or psychosis. Also, case studies of psychotherapy have provided many useful ideas about how to treat emotional problems (Wedding & Corsini, 2005).

Case studies may sometimes be thought of as *natural clinical tests* (accidents or other natural events that provide psychological data). Gunshot wounds, brain tumors, accidental poisonings, and similar disasters have provided much information about the human brain. One remarkable case from the history of psychology is reported by Dr. J. M. Harlow (1868). Phineas Gage, a young foreman on a work crew, had a 13-pound steel rod blown through the front of his brain by a dynamite explosion (● Figure 1.11). Amazingly, he survived the accident. Within 2 months Gage could walk, talk, and move normally, but the injury forever changed his personality. Instead of the honest and dependable worker he had been before, Gage became a surly, foul-mouthed liar. Dr. Harlow carefully recorded all details of what was perhaps the first in-depth case study of an accidental frontal lobotomy (the destruction of front brain matter).

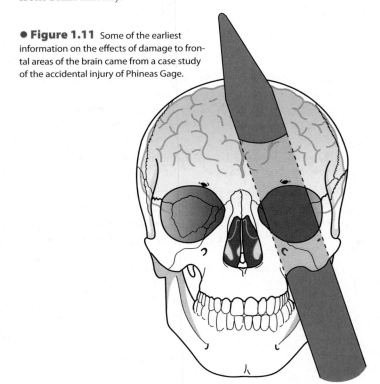

● **Figure 1.11** Some of the earliest information on the effects of damage to frontal areas of the brain came from a case study of the accidental injury of Phineas Gage.

When a Los Angeles carpenter named Michael Melnick suffered a similar injury, he recovered completely, with no lasting ill effects. Melnick's very different reaction to a similar injury shows why psychologists prefer controlled experiments and often use lab animals for studies of the brain. Case studies lack formal control groups. This, of course, limits the conclusions that can be drawn from clinical observations.

Nevertheless, case studies can provide special opportunities to answer interesting questions. For instance, a classic case study in psychology concerns identical quadruplets, known as the Genain sisters. In addition to having identical genes, all four women became schizophrenic before age 25 (Rosenthal & Quinn, 1977). The chances of identical quadruplets all becoming schizophrenic are about 1 in 1.5 billion.

The Genains, who have been studied for more than 40 years, were in and out of mental hospitals most of their lives. The fact that they share identical genes suggests that mental disorders are influenced by heredity. The fact that some of the sisters are more disturbed than others suggests that environmental conditions also affect mental illness. Indeed, Myra, the least ill of the four, was the only sister who was able to avoid her father, an alcoholic who terrorized, spied on, and sexually molested the girls. Thus, cases like theirs provide insights that can't be obtained by any other means (Mirsky et al., 2000).

> **bridges**
> See Chapter 14, pages 472–476, for more information about the causes of schizophrenia.

Survey Method—Here, Have a Sample

Sometimes psychologists would like to ask everyone in the world a few well-chosen questions: "Do you drink coffee? How often per week?" "What form of discipline did your parents use when you were a child?" "What is the most dishonest thing you've done?" Honest answers to such questions can reveal much about people's behavior. But, because it is impossible to question everyone, doing a survey is often more practical.

In the **survey method,** public polling techniques are used to answer psychological questions (Tourangeau, 2004). Typically, people in a representative sample are asked a series of carefully worded questions. A **representative sample** is a small group that accurately reflects a larger population. A good sample must include the same proportion of men, women, young, old, professionals, blue-collar workers, Republicans, Democrats, whites, African Americans, Native Americans, Latinos, Asians, and so on as found in the population as a whole.

A **population** is an entire group of animals or people belonging to a particular category (for example, all college students or all single women). Ultimately, we are interested in entire populations. But by selecting a smaller sample we can draw conclusions about the larger group without polling each and every person.

Representative samples are often obtained by *randomly* selecting who will be included (● Figure 1.12). (Notice that this is similar to randomly assigning participants to groups in an experiment.)

How accurate is the survey method? Modern surveys such as the Gallup and Harris polls are quite accurate. The Gallup poll has erred in its election predictions by only 1.5 percent since 1954. However, if a survey is based on a biased sample, it may paint a false picture. A **biased sample** does not accurately reflect the population from which it was drawn. Surveys done by magazines, websites, and online information services can be quite biased. Surveys on the use of guns done by *O: The Oprah Magazine* and *Guns and Ammo* magazine would probably produce very different results—neither of which would represent the general population. That's why psychologists using the survey method go to great lengths to ensure that their samples are representative. Fortunately, people can often be polled by telephone, which makes it easier to obtain large samples. Even if one person out of three refuses to answer survey questions, the results are still likely to be valid (Hutchinson, 2004).

In recent years, 93 percent of human subjects in psychology experiments have been recruited from introductory psychology courses (Sieber & Saks, 1989). The majority of these subjects have been white members of the middle class, and most of the researchers themselves have been white males (Guthrie, 2004). None of this automatically invalidates the results of psychology experiments. However, it may place some limitations on their meanings. (See "Is There a Gender Bias in Psychological Research?") The distinguished psychologist Edward Tolman once noted that much of psychology is based on two sets of subjects: rats and college sophomores. Tolman urged scientists to remember that rats are certainly not people and that college sophomores may not be!

Internet Surveys

Recently, psychologists have started doing surveys and experiments on the Internet. Web-based research can be a cost-effective way to reach very large groups of people. Internet studies have provided interesting information about topics such as anger, decision making, racial prejudice, what disgusts people, religion, sexual attitudes, and much more. Biased samples can limit web-based research (because it isn't easy to control who actually answers your online questionnaire), but psychologists are finding ways to gather valid information with it (Birnbaum, 2004; Whitaker, 2007).

Social Desirability

Even well-designed surveys may be limited by another problem. If a psychologist were to ask you detailed questions about your sexual history and current sexual behavior, how accurate would your replies be? Would you exaggerate? Would you be embar-

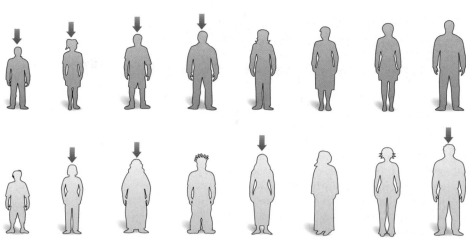

● **Figure 1.12** If you were conducting a survey in which a person's height might be an important variable, the upper, nonrandom sample would be very unrepresentative. The lower sample, selected using a table of random numbers, better represents the group as a whole.

rassed? Replies to survey questions are not always accurate or truthful. Many people show a distinct *courtesy bias* (a tendency to give "polite" or socially desirable answers). For example, answers to questions concerning sex, drinking or drug use, income, and church attendance tend to be less than truthful. Likewise, the week after an election, more people will say they voted than actually did (Hutchinson, 2004).

Summary

Despite their limitations, surveys frequently produce valuable information. For instance, the survey method has been used to find out about the attitudes of Muslims in the Middle East toward U.S. policies in the region and to clarify the debate about Islam and violence that has arisen since the terrorist attacks of 9/11 (Haddad, 2003). To sum up, the survey method can be a powerful research tool. Like other methods, it has limitations, but new techniques and strategies are providing valuable information about our behavior (Kahneman et al., 2004).

Is so much emphasis on science really necessary in psychology? In a word, yes. As we have seen, science is a powerful way of asking questions about the world and getting trustworthy answers. (● Table 1.6 summarizes many of the important ideas we have covered.)

Case study An in-depth focus on all aspects of a single person.

Survey method The use of public polling techniques to answer psychological questions.

Representative sample A small, randomly selected part of a larger population that accurately reflects characteristics of the whole population.

Population An entire group of animals or people belonging to a particular category (for example, all college students or all married women).

Biased sample A subpart of a larger population that does not accurately reflect characteristics of the whole population.

HUMAN DIVERSITY

Is There a Gender Bias in Psychological Research?

As you read through this book you may find yourself wondering whether or not a particular concept, theory, or research finding applies equally well to women and men, to members of various races or ethnic groups, or to people of different ages or sexual orientations. Human Diversity boxes like this one will help you be more reflective about our multicultural, multifaceted society. Here, let's begin with a basic question: Is there is a gender bias in the research process itself?

Many doctors continue to recommend that adults take an aspirin a day to help prevent a heart attack. Both men and women are given this advice. The problem? Not a single woman was included in the original sample on which the advice is based. Although females make up more than half the population, they continue to be neglected in psychological and medical research (Hyde, 2004).

This oversight is just one form of **gender bias in research.** This term refers to the tendency for females to be underrepresented as research subjects and female

topics to be ignored by many investigators. Consequently, the investigators assumed that conclusions based on men also apply to women. But without directly studying women it is impossible to know how often this assumption is wrong. A related problem occurs when researchers combine results from men and women. Doing so can hide important male–female differences. An additional problem is that unequal numbers of men and women may volunteer for some kinds of research. For example, in studies of sexuality, more male college students volunteer to participate than females (Wiederman, 1999). What a surprise!

Another form of gender bias in research occurs when women are underrepresented among the researchers themselves. In one example, Laurence Kohlberg (1969) proposed a theory about how we develop moral values. His studies suggested that women were morally "immature" because they were not as concerned with justice as men were. However, few women were involved in doing the studies and Kohlberg merely *assumed*

that theories based on men also apply to women. In response, Carol Gilligan (1982) provided evidence that women were more likely to make moral choices based on caring, rather than justice. From this point of view, it was men who were morally immature. Today, we recognize that both justice and caring perspectives may be essential to adult wisdom. (See Chapter 3, pages 104–106, for more details.)

Similar biases exist concerning the race, ethnicity, age, and sexual orientation of researchers and participants in psychological research (Denmark, Rabinowitz, & Sechzer, 2005; Guthrie, 2004). Far too many conclusions are created by and/or based on small groups of people who do not represent the rich tapestry of humanity. However, the solution to such problems is straightforward: We need to encourage a wider array of people to become researchers and, when possible, researchers need to include a wider array of people in their studies. In recognition of human diversity, many researchers are doing just that (Reid, 2002).

Table 1.6 ● Comparison of Psychological Research Methods

Method	Advantages	Disadvantages
Experimental Method	Clear cause-and-effect relationships can be identified; powerful controlled observations can be staged; no need to wait for natural event	May be somewhat artificial; some natural behavior not easily studied in laboratory (field experiments may avoid these objections)
Naturalistic Observation	Behavior is observed in a natural setting; much information is obtained, and hypotheses and questions for additional research are formed	Little or no control is possible; observed behavior may be altered by the presence of the observer; observations may be biased; causes cannot be conclusively identified
Correlational Method	Demonstrates the existence of relationships; allows prediction; can be used in lab, clinic, or natural setting	Little or no control is possible; relationships may be coincidental; cause-and-effect relationships cannot be confirmed
Clinical Method	Takes advantage of "natural clinical trials" and allows investigation of rare or unusual problems or events	Little or no control is possible; does not provide a control group for comparison; subjective interpretation is often necessary; a single case may be misleading or unrepresentative
Survey Method	Allows information about large numbers of people to be gathered; can address questions not answered by other approaches	Obtaining a representative sample is critical and can be difficult to do; answers may be inaccurate; people may not do what they say or say what they do

A Look Ahead

To help you get the most out of psychology, each chapter of this text includes a Psychology in Action section like the one that follows. There you will find ideas you can actually use, now or in the future. To complete the topics we have been discussing, let's take a critical look at information reported in the popular press. You should find this an interesting way to conclude our opening tour of psychology and its methods.

KNOWLEDGE BUILDER
Nonexperimental Research Methods

RECITE

1. Two major problems in naturalistic observation are the effects of the observer and observer bias. T or F?
2. The _____ fallacy involves attributing human feelings and motives to animals.
3. Correlation typically does not demonstrate causation. T or F?
4. Which correlation coefficient represents the strongest relationship?
   a. −0.86
   b. +0.66
   c. +0.10
   d. +0.09
5. Case studies can often be thought of as natural tests and are frequently used by clinical psychologists. T or F?
6. For the survey method to be valid, a representative sample of people must be polled. T or F?
7. A problem with the survey method is that answers to questions may not always be _____ or _____.

REFLECT

Critical Thinking

8. A psychologist conducting a survey at a shopping mall (The Gallery of Wretched Excess) flips a coin before stopping passersby. If the coin shows heads, he interviews the person; if it shows tails, he skips that person. Has the psychologist obtained a random sample?
9. Is attributing mischievous motives to a car that is not working properly a thinking error similar to anthropomorphizing?

Relate

Google "critter cam" and find one you can watch. What species are you watching? What behaviors might you observe and record?

See if you can identify at least one positive relationship and one negative relationship that involves human behavior.

Have you ever known someone who suffered a brain injury or disease? How did his or her behavior change? Was the change clear-cut enough to serve as a natural clinical test?

Have you ever been asked to complete a survey? Did you do it or did you refuse? If you refused, do you think your refusal influenced the final results of the survey? What would it say about accuracy if lots of people refused to complete the survey? If you completed the survey, were you honest about your answers? What would it say about accuracy if lots of people refused to answer accurately?

Answers: 1. T **2.** anthropomorphic **3.** T **4.** a **5.** T **6.** T **7.** accurate, truthful **8.** The psychologist's coin flips might produce a reasonably good sample of people *at the mall.* The real problem is that people who go to the mall may be mostly from one part of town, from upper income groups, or from some other nonrepresentative group. The psychologist's sample is likely to be seriously flawed. **9.** Yes. It appears to be difficult for humans to resist thinking of other species and even machines in human terms.

PSYCHOLOGY IN ACTION

Psychology in the Media—Separating Fact from Fiction

Gateway Question: How good is psychological information found in the popular media?

Psychology is a popular topic in contemporary media. Unfortunately, much of what you will encounter is based on entertainment value rather than critical thinking or science. Here are some suggestions for separating high-quality information from misleading fiction:

Suggestion 1: Be skeptical. Have you ever played the game called "telephone" or "pass it down"? You know, one person whispers a sentence to someone else who, in turn, whispers it on down the line. Usually, when the person at the end of the line repeats the message it has been humorously distorted. Similarly, modern media, and especially the Internet, function as a giant "echo chamber" awash with rumors, hoaxes, half-truths, and urban legends like the one about giant alligators living in New York sewers.

One of our all-time favorites was a story about the health department in Oregon seeking a Klingon interpreter for mental health patients who only speak in the fictional language used on the *Star Trek* TV series. This tale started when a newspaper reported that Klingon was on a list of languages that some psychiatric patients claimed they could speak. The article specifically noted that "in reality, no patient has yet tried to communicate in Klingon." Nevertheless, as the story echoed around the web, the idea that Oregon was looking for someone fluent in Klingon had become a "fact" (O'Neill, 2003).

Reports in the popular media tend to be made uncritically and with a definite bias toward reporting "astonishing" findings and telling interesting stories. Remember, saying "That's incredible" means "That's not believable"—which is often true.

Suggestion 2: Consider the source of information. It should come as no surprise that information used to sell a product often reflects a desire for profit rather than the objective truth. Here is a typical advertising claim: "Government tests prove that no sleep medicine is stronger or more effective than Coma." A statement like this usually means that there was *no difference* between Coma and the other products tested. No other sleep aid was stronger or more effective. But none was weaker either.

Keep the source in mind when reading the claims of makers of home biofeedback machines, sleep-learning devices, subliminal CDs, and the like. Remember that psychological services may be merchandised as well. Be wary of expensive courses that promise instant mental health and happiness, increased efficiency, memory, extrasensory perception (ESP) or psychic ability, control of the unconscious mind, an end to smoking, and so on. Usually they are promoted with a few testimonials and many unsupported claims (Lilienfeld, 2005).

Psychic claims should be viewed with special caution. Stage mentalists make a living by deceiving the public. Understandably, they are highly interested in promoting belief in their nonexistent powers. The same is true of the so-called psychic advisers promoted in TV commercials. These charlatans make use of the Barnum effect (the tendency to consider personal descriptions accurate if they are stated in general terms) to create an illusion

Gender bias (in research) A tendency for females and female issues to be underrepresented in research, psychological or otherwise.

that they know private information about the people who call them (Nickell, 2001).

Google magician James Randi's Million Dollar Challenge. Randi is offering $1,000,000 to anyone demonstrating such abilities under controlled conditions. Are you surprised to learn that no one has even passed the preliminary tests yet?

Suggestion 3: Beware of oversimplifications, especially those motivated by monetary gain.
Courses or programs that offer a "new personality in three sessions," "six steps to love and fulfillment in marriage," or some newly discovered "secret for unlocking the powers of the mind and the universe" should be immediately suspect.

An excellent example of oversimplification is provided by websites devoted to a video that promises to reveal "the secret to unlimited joy, health, money, relationships, love, youth: everything you have ever wanted." According to these sites, all you need to do is put your desires out to the universe and the universe must respond by granting your wishes. And all it will cost you is the price of the video. (It's no secret that the promoters are the real winners in this game.)

Suggestion 4: Remember, "for example" is no proof.
After reading this chapter you should be sensitive to the danger of selecting single examples. If you read, "Law student passes state bar exam using sleep-learning device," don't rush out to buy one. Systematic research showed long ago that these devices are of little or no value (Druckman & Bjork, 1994). A corollary to this suggestion is to ask if the reported observations are important or widely applicable.

Examples, anecdotes, single cases, and testimonials are all potentially deceptive. According to numerous testimonials, believers in the power of the "secret" described earlier have been showered with money, success, and happiness immediately after viewing the video. Unfortunately, such *individual cases* (or even several) tell nothing about what is true *in general* (Stanovich, 2007). How many people *didn't* win the lottery after buying the video? Similarly, studies of large groups of people show that smoking increases the likelihood of lung cancer. It doesn't matter if you know a lifelong heavy smoker who is 95 years old. The general finding is the one to remember.

Suggestion 5: Ask yourself if there was a control group.
The key importance of a control group in any experiment is frequently overlooked by the unsophisticated—an error to which you are no longer susceptible. The popular media are full of reports of "experiments" performed without control groups: "Talking to Plants Speeds Growth"; "Special Diet Controls Hyperactivity in Children"; "Graduates of Firewalking Seminar Risk Their Soles."

Consider the last example for a moment. Expensive commercial courses have long been promoted to teach people to walk barefoot on hot coals. (Why anyone would want to do this is itself an interesting question.) Firewalkers supposedly protect their feet with a technique called "neurolinguistic programming." Many people have paid good money to learn the technique, and most do manage a quick walk on the coals. But is the technique necessary? And is anything remarkable happening? We need a comparison group.

Fortunately, physicist Bernard Leikind has provided one. Leikind showed with volunteers that anyone (with reasonably callused feet) can walk over a bed of coals without being burned. The reason is that the coals, which are light, fluffy carbon, transmit little heat when touched. The principle involved is similar to briefly putting your hand in a hot oven. If you touch a pan, you will be burned because metal transfers heat efficiently. But if your hand stays in the heated air you'll be fine because air transmits little heat (Kida, 2006; Mitchell, 1987). Mystery solved.

Suggestion 6: Look for errors in distinguishing between correlation and causation.
As you now know, it is dangerous to presume that one

Firewalking is based on simple physics, not on any form of supernatural psychological control. The temperature of the coals may be as high as 1,200° F. However, coals are like the air in a hot oven: They are very inefficient at transferring heat during brief contact.

thing *caused* another just because they are correlated. In spite of this, you will see many claims based on questionable correlations. Here's an example of mistaking correlation for causation: Jeanne Dixon, a well-known astrologer, once answered a group of prominent scientists—who had declared that there is no scientific foundation for astrology—by saying, "They would do well to check the records at their local police stations, where they will learn that the rate of violent crime rises and falls with lunar cycles." Dixon, of course, believes that the moon affects human behavior.

If it is true that violent crime is more frequent at certain times of the month, doesn't that prove her point? Far from it. Increased crime could be due to darker nights, the fact that many people expect others to act crazier, or any number of similar factors. Besides, direct studies of the alleged "lunar effect" have shown that it doesn't occur (Dowling, 2005). Moonstruck criminals, influenced by "a bad moon rising," are a fiction (Iosif & Ballon, 2005).

Suggestion 7: Be sure to distinguish between observation and inference.
If you see a person *crying,* is it correct to assume that she or he is *sad?* Although it seems reasonable to make this assumption, it is actually quite risky. We can observe objectively that the person is crying, but to *infer* sadness may be in error. It could be that the individual has just peeled 5 pounds of onions. Or maybe he or she just won a million-dollar lottery or is trying contact lenses for the first time.

Psychologists, politicians, physicians, scientists, and other experts often go far beyond the available facts in their claims. This does not mean that their inferences, opinions, and interpretations have no value; the opinion of an expert on the causes of mental illness, criminal behavior, learning problems, or whatever can be revealing. But be careful to distinguish between fact and opinion.

Summary

We are all bombarded daily with such a mass of new information that it is difficult to absorb it. The available knowledge, even in a limited area like psychology, biology, medicine, or contemporary hip-hop music, is so vast that no single person can completely know and comprehend it. With this situation in mind, it becomes increasingly important that you become a critical, selective, and informed consumer of information.

KNOWLEDGE BUILDER
Psychology in the Media

RECITE

1. Popular media reports usually stress objective accuracy. T or F?
2. Stage mentalists and psychics often use deception in their "acts." T or F?
3. Blaming the lunar cycle for variations in the rate of violent crime is an example of mistaking correlation for causation. T or F?
4. If a psychology student uses a sleep-learning device to pass a mid-term exam, it proves that the device works. T or F?

REFLECT

Critical Thinking

5. Mystics have shown that fresh eggs can be balanced on their large ends during the vernal equinox when the sun is directly over the equator, day and night are equal in length, and the world is in perfect balance. What is wrong with their observation?

6. Many parents believe that children become "hyperactive" when they eat too much sugar, and some early studies seemed to confirm this connection. However, we now know that eating sugar rarely has any effect on children. Why do you think that sugar appears to cause hyperactivity?

Relate

Do you tend to assume that a statement must be true if it is in print, on television, or made by an authority? How actively do you evaluate and question claims found in the media? Could you be a more critical consumer of information? *Should* you be a more critical consumer of information?

Answers: 1. F **2.** T **3.** T **4.** F **5.** The mystics have neglected to ask if eggs can be balanced at other times. They can be balanced any time you like. The lack of a control group gives the illusion that something amazing is happening, but the equinox has nothing to do with egg balancing (Halpern, 2003). **6.** This is another case of mistaking correlation for causation. Children who are hyperactive may eat more sugar (and other foods) to fuel their frenetic activity levels.

chapter in review Gateways to Psychology

Psychology is the science of behavior and mental processes. Psychologists gather scientific data in order to describe, understand, predict, and control behavior.

- Psychologists are professionals who create and apply psychological knowledge. Psychologists engage in critical thinking as they systemically gather and analyze
- Psychology spans a wide variety of specialty areas of research.
- Some psychologists are directly interested in animal behavior. Others study animals as models of human behavior.
- As a science, psychology's goals are to describe, understand, predict, and control behavior.

Critical thinking is the ability to reflect on, evaluate, compare, analyze, critique, and synthesize information. Critical thinking is central to the scientific method, to psychology, and to effective behavior in general.

- To judge the validity of a claim, it is important to gather evidence for and against the claim and to evaluate the *quality* of the evidence.

Pseudopsychologies are unfounded systems that resemble psychology. Unlike psychology, pseudopsychologies change little over time because followers seek evidence that appears to confirm their beliefs and avoid evidence that contradicts their beliefs.

- Numerous pseudopsychologies are frequently confused with valid psychology. Belief in pseudopsychologies is based in part on uncritical acceptance, the fallacy of positive instances, and the Barnum effect.

Psychological research begins by defining problems and proposing hypotheses. Next, researchers gather evidence, test hypotheses, and

publish results. Scientific debate and theories suggest new hypotheses, which lead to further research.

- Because the scientific method is a powerful way to observe the natural world and draw valid conclusions, scientific research provides the highest quality information about behavior.
- In the scientific method, systematic observation is used to test hypotheses about behavior and mental events.
- Concepts must be defined operationally before they can be studied empirically.
- The results of scientific studies are made public so that others can evaluate them, learn from them, and use them to produce further knowledge.

The field of psychology emerged 130 years ago when researchers began to directly study and observe psychological events.

- The first psychological laboratory was established in Germany by Wilhelm Wundt, who studied conscious experience.
- The first school of thought in psychology was structuralism, a kind of "mental chemistry" based on introspection.
- Structuralism was followed by functionalism, behaviorism, and Gestalt psychology.
- Psychodynamic approaches, such as Freud's psychoanalytic theory, emphasize the unconscious origins of behavior.
- Humanistic psychology accentuates subjective experience, human potentials, and personal growth.
- Even though most of the early psychologists were men, women have contributed to psychology from the beginning.

Three complementary streams of thought in modern psychology are the biological perspective, including biopsychology and evolutionary psychology; the psychological perspective, including behaviorism, cognitive psychology, the psychodynamic approach, and humanism; and the sociocultural perspective.

- There is an eclectic blending of sviewpoints within psychology.
- Psychologists have recently begun to formally study positive aspects of human behavior, or positive psychology.
- Most of what we think, feel, and do is influenced by the social and cultural worlds in which we live.

There are dozens of specialties in psychology including clinical, counseling, industrial, educational, consumer, school, developmental, engineering, medical, environmental, forensic, community, psychometric, and experimental psychology.

- Although psychologists, psychiatrists, psychoanalysts, and counselors all work in the field of mental health, their training and methods differ considerably.
- Psychological research may be basic or applied.

Experiments involve two or more groups of subjects that differ only with regard to the independent variable. Effects on the dependent variable are then measured. All other conditions (extraneous variables) are held constant.

- Since the independent variable is the only difference between the experimental group and the control group, it is the only possible cause of a change in the dependent variable.
- The design of experiments allows cause-and-effect connections to be clearly identified.
- Psychological research must be done ethically, in order to protect the rights, dignity, and welfare of participants.
- To be taken seriously, the results of an experiment must be statistically significant (they would occur very rarely by chance alone).

In a double-blind experiment, neither the research participants nor the researchers collecting data know who was in the experimental group or the control group, allowing valid conclusions to be drawn.

- Research participant bias is a problem in some studies. The placebo effect is also a factor, especially in experiments involving drugs.
- A related problem is researcher bias. Researcher expectations can create a self-fulfilling prophecy, in which a participant changes in the direction of the expectation.

Psychologists also rely on naturalistic observation, the correlational method, case studies, and the survey method.

- Unlike controlled experiments, nonexperimental methods usually cannot demonstrate cause-and-effect relationships.
- Naturalistic observation is a starting place in many investigations.
- Two problems with naturalistic observation are the effects of the observer on the observed and observer bias.
- In the correlational method, relationships between two traits, responses, or events are measured and a correlation coefficient is computed to gauge the strength of the relationship.
- Correlations allow prediction but do not show cause and effect.
- Relationships in psychology may be positive or negative.
- Case studies provide insights into human behavior that can't be gained by other methods.
- In the survey method, people in a representative sample are asked a series of carefully worded questions.

- Obtaining a representative sample of people is crucial when the survey method is used to study large populations.

Information in the mass media varies greatly in quality and accuracy and should be approached with skepticism and caution.

- It is essential to critically evaluate information from popular sources (or from any source, for that matter) in order to separate facts from fallacies.
- Problems in media reports are often related to biased or unreliable sources of information, uncontrolled observation, misleading correlations, false inferences, oversimplification, use of single examples, and unrepeatable results.

Web Resources

For an up-to-date list of direct links to interesting sites, including those listed here, visit the student companion site for this book at www.cengage.com/psychology/coon

What Is Psychology? Discusses psychology as a science, with links to other articles about various branches of psychology.

Critical Thinking in Everyday Life: 9 Strategies Some useful critical thinking strategies, along with many other articles on aspects of critical thinking.

Today in the History of Psychology Events in the history of psychology by the date, including podcasts.

Careers in Psychology Marky Lloyd's Careers in Psychology Page.

The Experimental Method An introduction to experimental research methods.

Psychological Research on the Net Find and complete a survey study.

That's Infotainment! Article about sensationalism in the news media.

Interactive Learning

Introduction to Psychology: Gateways to Mind and Behavior Book Companion Website
www.cengage.com/psychology/coon

Visit your book companion website, where you will find flash cards, practice quizzes, web links, and more to help you study.

CENGAGENOW™ *Just what you need to know NOW!*

Spend time on what you need to master rather than on information you already have learned. Take a pre-test for this chapter, and CengageNOW will generate a personalized study plan based on your results. The study plan will identify the topics you need to review and direct you to online resources to help you master those topics. You can then take a post-test to help you determine the concepts you have mastered and what you will need to work on. Try it out! Go to www.cengage.com/login to sign in with an access code or to purchase access to this product.

CHAPTER 2

Brain and Behavior

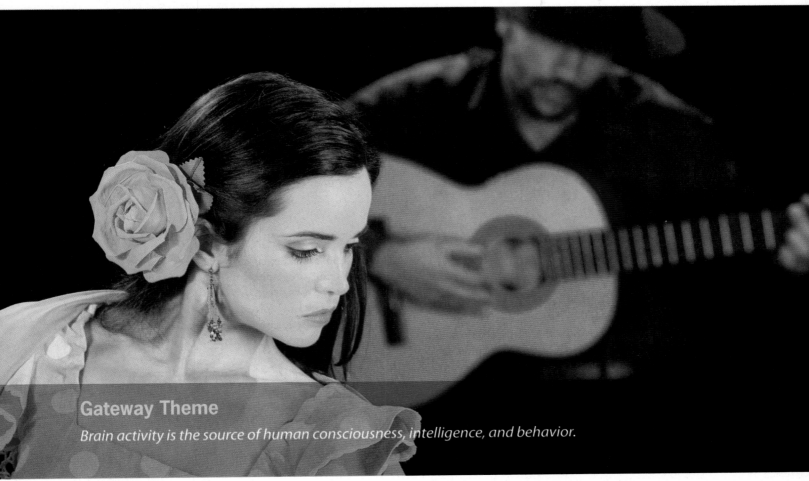

Gateway Theme

Brain activity is the source of human consciousness, intelligence, and behavior.

Hill Street Studios/Photolibrary

Gateway Questions

- *How do nerve cells operate and communicate?*
- *What are the major parts of the nervous system?*
- *How is the brain studied?*
- *Why is the human cerebral cortex so important, and what are its parts?*

- *What are the major parts of the subcortex?*
- *Does the glandular system affect behavior?*
- *In what ways do right- and left-handed individuals differ?*

47

Your authors recently shared an evening together in Tucson, Arizona, watching some fiery Spanish flamenco. We both had brains on our minds. (Really!) The guitarist and dancer were passionate and brilliant. If they had been athletes, you would say they were "in the zone." Of course, in everything from classical to jazz to hip-hop, musicians regularly make music that no machine could duplicate. A virtual Bruce Springsteen? A mechanical Beyoncé? We doubt it. That's why music is such a good example of the central role the brain plays in all that is human.

Your 3-pound brain is wrinkled like a walnut, the size of a grapefruit, and the texture of tofu. The next time you are in a market that sells beef brains, stop and have a look. What you will see is similar to your own brain, only smaller. How could such a squishy little blob of tissue allow us to make music of exquisite beauty? To seek a cure for cancer? To fall in love? Or to read a book like this one?

Each of the billions of nerve cells in your brain is linked to thousands of others. The resulting network allows you to process immense amounts of information. In fact, there may be more *possible* pathways between the neurons in your brain than there are stars in the visible universe! Undeniably, the human brain is the most amazing of all computers.

Scientists use the power of the brain to study the brain. Yet, even now we must wonder if the brain will ever completely understand itself. Nevertheless, answers to many age-old questions about the mind, consciousness, and knowledge lie buried within the brain. Let's visit this fascinating realm.

⬤⬤ Neurons—Building a "Biocomputer"

Gateway Question: How do nerve cells operate and communicate?

While they may seem far removed from your daily life, 100 billion tiny **neurons** (NOOR-ons: individual nerve cells) make up your brain. Neurons carry information from the senses to the brain, where they process it. They also activate muscles and glands. Yet, a single neuron is not very smart—it would take many just to make you blink. Millions of neurons must send messages at the same time to produce even the most fleeting thought. When a musician such as Eric Clapton plays a guitar riff, literally billions of neurons may be involved (Kalat, 2007).

Your brainpower arises because individual neurons link to one another in tight clumps and long "chains." Each neuron receives messages from many others and sends its own message on. Everything you think, feel, or do can be traced back to electrical impulses flashing through spidery networks of neurons. When neurons form vast networks, they produce intelligence and consciousness. Let's see how neurons operate and how the nervous system is "wired."

Parts of a Neuron

What does a neuron look like? What are its main parts? No two neurons are exactly alike, but most have four basic parts (● Figure 2.1). The **dendrites** (DEN-drytes), which look like tree roots, receive messages from other neurons. The **soma** (SOH-mah: cell body) does the same. In addition, the soma sends messages of its own (nerve impulses) down a thin fiber called the **axon** (AK-sahn).

Some axons are only .1 millimeter long. (That's about the width of a pencil line.) Others stretch up to a meter through the nervous system. (From the base of your spine to your big toe, for instance.)

Like miniature cables, axons carry messages through the brain and nervous system. Altogether, your brain contains about 3 million miles of axons (Rosenzweig, Breedlove, & Watson, 2004).

Axons "branch out" into smaller fibers ending in bulb-shaped **axon terminals.** By forming connections with the dendrites and somas of other neurons, axon terminals allow information to pass from neuron to neuron.

Now let's summarize with a metaphor. Imagine that you are standing in a long line of people who are holding hands. A person on the far right end of the line wants to silently send a message to the person on the left end. She does this by pressing the hand of the person to her left, who presses the hand of the person to his left, and so on. The message arrives at your right hand (your dendrites). You decide whether to pass it on. (You are the soma.) The message goes out through your left arm (the axon). With your left hand (the axon terminals), you squeeze the hand of the person to your left, and the message moves on.

The Nerve Impulse

Electrically charged molecules called *ions* (EYE-ons) are found inside each neuron (● Figure 2.2). Other ions lie outside the cell. Some ions have a positive electrical charge, and some are negative. When a neuron is inactive, more of these "plus" charges exist outside the neuron and more "minus" charges exist inside. As a result, the inside of each neuron in your brain has an electrical charge of about minus 70 millivolts. (A millivolt is one thousandth of a volt.) This charge allows each neuron in your brain to act like a tiny biological battery.

The electrical charge of an inactive neuron is called its **resting potential.** But neurons seldom get much rest: Messages arriving from other neurons raise and lower the resting potential. If the electrical charge rises to about minus 50 millivolts, the neuron

Synapse (see Figure 2.6 for an enlarged view)

Other neuron

Axon terminals

● Figure 2.1 A neuron, or nerve cell. In the right foreground you can see a nerve cell fiber in cross section. The upper left photo gives a more realistic picture of the shape of neurons. Nerve impulses usually travel from the dendrites and soma to the branching ends of the axon. The nerve cell shown here is a motor neuron. The axons of motor neurons stretch from the brain and spinal cord to muscles or glands of the body.

Myelin

Nerve impulse

Neurilemma

Nerve impulse

Soma (cell body)

Axon collateral (branch)

Axon

Myelin sheath

Nerve cell fiber {

Axon

Dendrites

will reach its **threshold,** or trigger point for firing. (See ● Figure 2.2.) It's as if the neuron says, "Ah ha! It's time to send a message to my neighbors." When a neuron reaches about −50 millivolts, an **action potential,** or nerve impulse, sweeps down the axon at up to 200 miles per hour (● Figure 2.3). That may seem fast, but it still takes at least a split second to react. That's one reason why hitting a 95-mile-per-hour major league fastball is so difficult.

What happens during an action potential? The axon membrane is pierced by tiny tunnels or "holes," called **ion channels.** Normally, these tiny openings are blocked by molecules that act like "gates" or "doors." During an action potential, the gates pop open. This allows sodium ions (Na^+) to rush into the axon (Carlson, 2007). The channels first open near the soma. Then gate after gate opens down the length of the axon as the action potential zips along (● Figure 2.4).

Each action potential is an *all-or-nothing event* (a nerve impulse occurs completely or not at all). You might find it helpful to picture the axon as a row of dominoes set on end. Tipping over the dominoes is an all-or-nothing act. Once the first domino drops, a wave of falling blocks will zip rapidly to the end of the line. Similarly, when a nerve impulse is triggered near the soma, a wave of activity (the action potential) travels down the length of the axon. This is what happens in long chains of neurons as a flamenco dancer's brain tells her feet what to do next, beat after beat.

After each nerve impulse, the cell briefly dips below its resting level and it becomes less willing to fire. This **negative after-potential** occurs because potassium ions (K^+) flow out of the neuron while the membrane gates are open. (See ● Figure 2.4.) After a nerve impulse, ions flow both into and out of the axon, recharging it for more action. In our model, it takes an instant for the row of dominoes to be set up again. Soon, however, the axon is ready for another wave of activity.

Neuron An individual nerve cell.

Dendrites Neuron fibers that receive incoming messages.

Soma The main body of a neuron or other cell.

Axon Fiber that carries information away from the cell body of a neuron.

Axon terminals Bulb-shaped structures at the ends of axons that form synapses with the dendrites and somas other neurons.

Resting potential The electrical charge of a neuron at rest.

Threshold The point at which a nerve impulse is triggered.

Action potential The nerve impulse.

Ion channels Tiny openings through the axon membrane.

Negative after-potential A drop in electrical charge below the resting potential.

● **Figure 2.2** Electrical probes placed inside and outside an axon measure its activity. (The scale is exaggerated here. Such measurements require ultra-small electrodes, as described in this chapter.) The inside of an axon at rest is about –60 to –70 millivolts, compared with the outside. Electrochemical changes in a neuron generate an action potential. When sodium ions (Na$^+$) that have a positive charge rush into the cell, its interior briefly becomes positive. This is the action potential. After the action potential, positive potassium ions (K$^+$) flow out of the axon and restore its negative charge. (See Figure 2.3 for further explanation.)

● **Figure 2.3** The inside of an axon normally has a negative electrical charge. The fluid surrounding an axon is normally positive. As an action potential passes along the axon, these charges reverse so that the interior of the axon briefly becomes positive. This process is described in more detail in Figure 2.4.

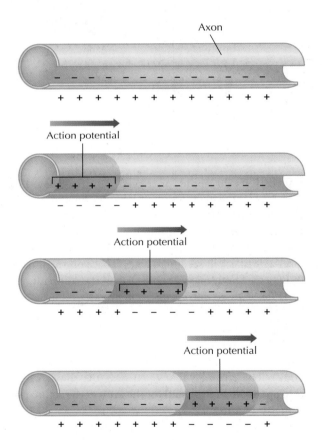

1. In its resting state, the axon has a negatively charged interior.

2. During an action potential, positively charged atoms (ions) rush into the axon. This briefly changes the electrical charge inside the axon from negative to positive. Simultaneously, the charge outside the axon becomes negative.

3. The action potential advances as positive and negative charges reverse in a moving zone of electrical activity that sweeps down the axon.

4. After an action potential passes, positive ions rapidly flow out of the axon to quickly restore its negative charge. An outward flow of additional positive ions returns the axon to its resting state.

Saltatory Conduction

The axons of some neurons (such as the one pictured in ● Figure 2.1) are coated with a fatty layer called **myelin** (MY-eh-lin). Small gaps in the myelin help nerve impulses move faster. Instead of passing down the entire length of the axon, the action potential leaps from gap to gap, a process called **saltatory conduction**. Without the added speed this allows, it would probably be impossible to brake in time to avoid many automobile accidents (or hit that major league fastball). When the myelin layer is damaged, a person may suffer from numbness, weakness, or paralysis. That, in fact, is what happens in multiple sclerosis, a disease that occurs when the immune system attacks and destroys the myelin in a person's body.

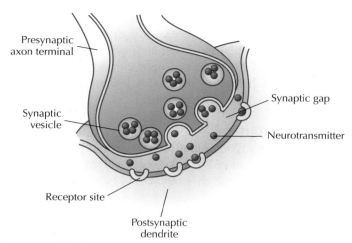

● **Figure 2.4** The interior of an axon. The right end of the top axon is at rest. Thus, it has a negative charge inside. An action potential begins when ion channels open and sodium ions (Na⁺) rush into the axon. In this drawing, the action potential would travel from left to right along the axon. In the lower axon, the action potential has moved to the right. After it passes, potassium ions (K⁺) flow out of the axon. This quickly renews the negative charge inside the axon so that it can fire again. Sodium ions that enter the axon during an action potential are pumped out more slowly. Removing them restores the original resting potential.

Synapses and Neurotransmitters

How does information move from one neuron to another? The nerve impulse is primarily electrical. That's why electrically stimulating the brain affects behavior. To prove the point, researcher José Delgado once entered a bullring with a cape and a radio transmitter. The bull charged. Delgado retreated. At the last instant the speeding bull stopped short. Why? Because Delgado had placed radio-activated electrodes (metal wires) deep within the bull's brain. These, in turn, stimulated "control centers" that brought the bull to a halt (Horgan, 2005).

In contrast to the nerve impulse, communication between neurons is chemical. The microscopic space between two neurons, over which messages pass, is called a **synapse** (SIN-aps) (● Figure 2.5). When an action potential reaches the tips of the axon terminals, **neurotransmitters** (NOOR-oh-TRANS-mit-ers) are released into the synaptic gap. Neurotransmitters are chemicals that alter activity in neurons.

Let's return to our metaphor of people standing in a line. To be more accurate, you and the others shouldn't be holding hands. Instead, each person should have a squirt gun in his or her left hand. To pass along a message, you would squirt the right hand of the person to your left. When that person notices this "message," he or she would squirt the right hand of the person to the left, and so on.

When chemical molecules cross over a synapse, they attach to special receiving areas on the next neuron. (See ● Figure 2.5.) These tiny **receptor sites** on the cell membrane are sensitive to neu-

● **Figure 2.5** A highly magnified view of a synapse. Neurotransmitters are stored in tiny sacs called synaptic vesicles (VES-ih-kels). When a nerve impulse reaches the end of an axon, the vesicles move to the surface and release neurotransmitters. These molecules cross the synaptic gap to affect the next neuron. The size of the gap is exaggerated here; it is actually only about one millionth of an inch. Some transmitter molecules excite the next neuron and some inhibit its activity.

rotransmitters. The sites are found in large numbers on nerve cell bodies and dendrites. Muscles and glands have receptor sites, too.

Do neurotransmitters always trigger an action potential in the next neuron? No, but they do change the likelihood of an action potential in the next neuron. Some transmitters *excite* the next neuron (move it closer to firing). Others *inhibit* it (make firing less likely).

More than 100 transmitter chemicals are found in the brain. Some examples are acetylcholine, epinephrine, norepinephrine, serotonin, dopamine, histamine, and various amino acids. Disturbances of any of these substances can have serious consequences. For example, too little dopamine can cause the shaking and muscle tremors of Parkinson's disease. Too much dopamine may cause the severe mental disorder known as schizophrenia (Di Forti, Lappin, & Murray, 2007).

Many drugs imitate, duplicate, or block neurotransmitters. For example, **acetylcholine** (ah-SEET-ul-KOH-leen) normally activates muscles. Without acetylcholine, our flamenco musicians couldn't even move, much less perform. That's exactly how the

Myelin A fatty layer coating some axons.

Saltatory conduction The process by which nerve impulses conducted down the axons of neurons coated with myelin jump from gap to gap in the myelin layer.

Synapse The microscopic space between two neurons, over which messages pass.

Neurotransmitter Any chemical released by a neuron that alters activity in other neurons.

Receptor sites Areas on the surface of neurons and other cells that are sensitive to neurotransmitters or hormones.

Acetylcholine The neurotransmitter released by neurons to activate muscles.

drug curare (cue-RAH-ree) causes paralysis. By attaching to receptor sites on muscles, curare competes with acetylcholine. This prevents acetylcholine from activating muscle cells. As a result, a person or animal given curare cannot move—a fact known to South American Indians of the Amazon River Basin, who use curare as an arrow poison for hunting.

Neural Regulators

More subtle brain activities are affected by chemicals called **neuropeptides** (NOOR-oh-PEP-tides). Neuropeptides do not carry messages directly. Instead, they *regulate* the activity of other neurons. By doing so, they affect memory, pain, emotion, pleasure, moods, hunger, sexual behavior, and other basic processes. For example, when you touch something hot, you jerk your hand away. The messages for this action are carried by neurotransmitters. At the same time, pain may cause the brain to release *enkephalins* (en-KEF-ah-lins). These opiate-like neural regulators relieve pain and stress. Related chemicals called *endorphins* (en-DORF-ins) are released by the pituitary gland. Together, these chemicals reduce the pain so that it is not too disabling (Drolet et al., 2001).

Such discoveries help explain the painkilling effect of placebos (fake pills or injections), which raise endorphin levels (Stewart-Williams, 2004). A release of endorphins also seems to underlie "runner's high," masochism, acupuncture, and the euphoria sometimes associated with childbirth, painful initiation rites, and even sport parachuting (Janssen & Arntz, 2001). In each case, pain and stress cause the release of endorphins. These in turn induce feelings of pleasure or euphoria similar to being "high" on morphine. People who say they are "addicted" to running may be closer to the truth than they realize.

> **bridges**
> **To learn more about how pain can sometimes produce feelings of relaxation or euphoria, see Chapter 4, pages 143–144.**

Ultimately, neural regulators may help explain depression, schizophrenia, drug addiction, and other puzzling topics. For example, women who suffer from severe premenstrual pain and distress have unusually low endorphin levels (Straneva et al., 2002).

Neural Networks

Let's put together what we now know about the nerve impulse and synaptic transmission to see how *neural networks* process information in our brains. ● Figure 2.6 shows a small part of a neural network. Five neurons synapse with a single neuron that, in turn, connects with three more neurons. At the point in time depicted in the diagram, the single neuron is receiving one stronger and two weaker excitatory messages (+) as well as two inhibitory ones (−). Does it fire an impulse? It depends: If enough "exciting" messages

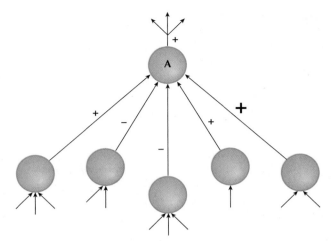

● **Figure 2.6** A small neural network. Neuron A receives inputs from two weaker and one stronger excitatory connections (+) and two inhibitory connections (−) and combines the inputs into a "decision" to launch an action potential, which may help trigger further synaptic transmissions in other neurons.

arrive close in time, the neuron will fire—but only if it doesn't get too many "inhibiting" messages that push it *away* from its trigger point. In this way, messages are *combined* before a neuron "decides" to fire its all-or-nothing action potential.

Let's try another metaphor. You are out shopping for new jeans with five friends. Three of them think you should buy the jeans (your best friend is especially positive) and two think you shouldn't. Because, on balance, their input is positive, you go ahead and buy the jeans. Maybe you even tell some other friends they should buy those jeans as well. Similarly, any single neuron in a neural network "listens" to the neurons that synapse with it and combines that input into an output. At any instant, a single neuron may weigh hundreds or thousands of inputs to produce an outgoing message. After the neuron recovers from the resulting action potential, it again combines the inputs, which may have changed in the meantime, into another output, and another, and another.

In this way, each neuron in your brain functions as a tiny computer. Compared with the average laptop computer, a neuron is terribly simple and slow. But multiply these events by 100 billion neurons and 100 trillion synapses, all operating at the same time, and you have an amazing computer—one that could easily fit inside a shoebox.

Neuroplasticity

The neural networks in your brain constantly change. The term **neuroplasticity** refers to the capacity of our brains to change in response to experience. New synapses may form between neurons or synaptic connections may grow stronger. (● Figure 2.6 shows one particularly strong synapse—the large +.) Other synaptic connections may weaken and might even die. Every new experience you have is reflected in changes in your brain. For example, rats raised in a complex environment have more synapses and longer dendrites in their brains than rats raised in a simpler environment (Kolb, Gibb, & Gorny, 2003). (See "You Can Change Your Mind, but Can You Change Your Brain?")

CRITICAL THINKING

You Can Change Your Mind, but Can You Change Your Brain?

You can always change your mind. But does that have anything to do with your brain? Philosophers have debated the relationship of the mind to the brain (and the rest of the body) for centuries. Biopsychologists argue that every mental event involves a brain event.

In one study, people suffering from spider phobias were treated with cognitive behavior therapy. (For more information, see Chapter 15, pages 505–507.)

After therapy, they could actually touch spiders (although they might not have been ready to appear on *Fear Factor*). Images of their brains revealed reduced activity in the brain areas involved in the phobia (Paquette et al., 2003). Not only did they change their minds about spiders, they literally changed their brains.

Another study focused on patients with language difficulties caused by damage to the left sides of their brains. To aid their recovery, the patients were given training in language comprehension. Not only did the training help improve their ability to understand language, but brain images revealed that the right sides of their brains had become more active to compensate for their left-brain damage (Musso et al., 1999). Again, a learning experience changed their brains.

Every time you learn something, you are reshaping your living brain. There is even a fancy phrase to describe what you are doing: *self-directed neuroplasticity*. Just think. As you study this psychology textbook you are changing your mind, and your brain, about psychology.

The Nervous System—Wired for Action

Gateway Question: What are the major parts of the nervous system?

Harry and Maya are playing catch with a football. This may look fairly simple. However, to merely toss the football or catch it, a huge amount of information must be sensed, interpreted, and directed to countless muscle fibers. As they play, Harry and Maya's neural circuits are ablaze with activity. Let's explore the "wiring diagram" that makes their game of catch possible.

As you can see in ● Figure 2.7, the **central nervous system (CNS)** consists of the brain and spinal cord. The brain carries out most of the "computing" in the nervous system. Harry must use his brain to anticipate when and where the football will arrive. Harry's brain communicates with the rest of his body through a large "cable" called the spinal cord. From there, messages flow through the **peripheral nervous system (PNS).** This intricate network of *nerves* carries information to and from the CNS.

Are nerves the same as neurons? No. Neurons are tiny cells. You would need a microscope to see one. **Nerves** are large bundles of neuron axons. You can easily see nerves without magnification.

Nerves in the peripheral nervous system can regrow if they are damaged. The axons of most neurons in nerves outside the brain and spinal cord are covered by a thin layer of cells called the **neurilemma** (NOOR-rih-LEM-ah). (Return to ● Figure 2.1.) The neurilemma forms a "tunnel" that damaged fibers can follow as they repair themselves. Because of this, patients can expect to regain some control over severed limbs once they have been reattached.

The Peripheral Nervous System

The peripheral system can be divided into two major parts (See ● Figure 2.7). The **somatic nervous system (SNS)** carries messages to and from the sense organs and skeletal muscles. In

(a)

(b)

● **Figure 2.7** Subparts of the nervous system. *(a)* Central nervous system. *(b)* Peripheral nervous system.

general, it controls voluntary behavior, such as when Maya tosses the football or Tiger Woods hits a golf ball. In contrast, the **autonomic nervous system (ANS)** serves the internal organs and glands. The word *autonomic* means "self-governing." Activities

Neuropeptides Brain chemicals that regulate the activity of neurons, such as enkephalins and endorphins.

Neuroplasticity The capacity of our brains to change in response to experience.

Central nervous system (CNS) The brain and spinal cord.

Peripheral nervous system (PNS) All parts of the nervous system outside the brain and spinal cord.

Nerve A bundle of neuron fibers.

Neurilemma A layer of cells that encases many axons.

Somatic nervous system (SNS) The system of nerves linking the spinal cord with the body and sense organs.

Autonomic nervous system (ANS) The system of nerves carrying information to and from the internal organs and glands.

governed by the autonomic nervous system are mostly "vegetative" or automatic, such as heart rate, digestion, and perspiration. Thus, messages carried by the somatic system can make your hand move, but they cannot cause your eyes to dilate. Likewise, messages carried by the ANS can stimulate digestion, but they cannot help you carry out a voluntary action, such as writing a letter. If Harry feels a flash of anger when he misses a catch, a brief burst of activity will spread through his autonomic system.

> ### bridges
> The ANS plays a central role in our emotional lives. In fact, without the ANS a person would feel little emotion. **See Chapter 10, pages 343–345 for more information about the ANS and emotion.**

The ANS and SNS work together to coordinate the body's internal reactions to events in the world outside. For example, if a snarling dog lunges at you, the somatic system will control your leg muscles so that you can run. At the same time, the autonomic system will raise your blood pressure, quicken your heart, and so forth. The ANS can be divided into the sympathetic and parasympathetic branches. Both are related to emotional responses, such as crying, sweating, heart rate, and other involuntary behavior (● Figure 2.8).

How do the branches of the autonomic system differ? The **sympathetic branch** is an "emergency" system. It prepares the body for "fight or flight" during times of danger or high emotion. In essence, it arouses the body for action.

The **parasympathetic branch** quiets the body and returns it to a lower level of arousal. It is most active soon after an emotional event. The parasympathetic branch also helps keep vital processes such as heart rate, breathing, and digestion at moderate levels.

Of course, both branches of the ANS are always active. At any given moment, their combined activity determines if your body is more or less relaxed or aroused.

The Spinal Cord

As mentioned earlier, the spinal cord connects the brain to other parts of the body. If you were to cut through this "cable," you would see columns of *white matter* (bundles of axons covered with myelin). This tissue is made up of axons that eventually leave the spinal cord to form the peripheral nervous system nerves. Thirty-one *spinal nerves* carry sensory and motor messages to and from the spinal cord. In addition, 12 pairs of *cranial nerves* leave the brain directly. Together, these nerves keep your entire body in communication with your brain.

Is the spinal cord's only function to connect the brain to the peripheral nervous system? Actually, the spinal cord can do some simple "computing" of its own. **Reflex arcs**, which occur when a stimulus provokes an automatic response, arise within the spinal cord, without any help from the brain (● Figure 2.9). Imagine that Maya steps on a thorn. (Yes, they're still playing catch.) Pain is detected in her foot by a **sensory neuron** (a nerve cell that carries messages from the senses toward the CNS). Instantly, the sensory neuron fires off a message to Maya's spinal cord.

● **Figure 2.8** Sympathetic and parasympathetic branches of the autonomic nervous system. Both branches control involuntary actions. The sympathetic system generally activates the body. The parasympathetic system generally quiets it. The sympathetic branch relays its messages through clusters of nerve cells outside the spinal cord.

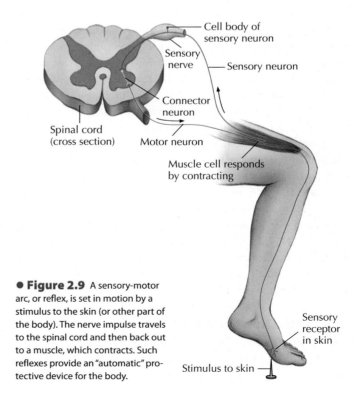

● **Figure 2.9** A sensory-motor arc, or reflex, is set in motion by a stimulus to the skin (or other part of the body). The nerve impulse travels to the spinal cord and then back out to a muscle, which contracts. Such reflexes provide an "automatic" protective device for the body.

Inside the spinal cord, the sensory neuron synapses with a *connector neuron* (a nerve cell that links two others). The connector neuron activates a *motor neuron* (a cell that carries commands from the CNS to muscles and glands). The muscle fibers are made up of *effector cells* (cells capable of producing a response). The muscle cells contract and cause Maya's foot to withdraw. Note that no brain activity is required for a reflex arc to occur. Maya's body will react automatically to protect itself.

In reality, even a simple reflex usually triggers more complex activity. For example, muscles of Maya's other leg must contract to support her as she shifts her weight. Even this can be done by the spinal cord, but it involves many more cells and several spinal nerves. Also, the spinal cord normally informs the brain of its actions. As her foot pulls away from the thorn, Maya will feel the pain and think, "Ouch, what was that?"

Perhaps you have realized how adaptive it is to have a spinal cord capable of responding on its own. Such automatic responses leave the brains of our football stars free to deal with more important information—such as the location of trees, lampposts, and attractive onlookers—as they take turns making grandstand catches.

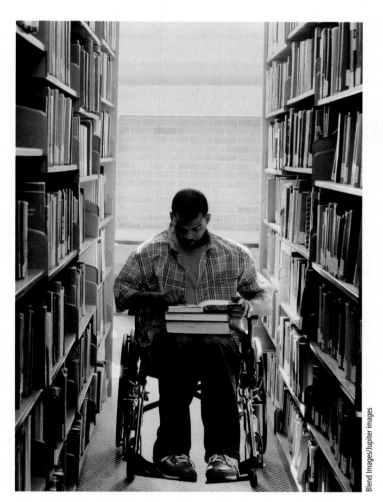

Blend Images/Jupiter images

Each year spinal cord injuries rob many thousands of people of the ability to move. Yet there is growing hope that nerve-grafting techniques may someday make it possible for some of these people to walk again.

While peripheral nerves can regrow, a serious injury to the brain or spinal cord is usually permanent. However, scientists are starting to make progress repairing damaged neurons in the CNS. For instance, they have partially repaired cut spinal cords in rats. First they close the gap with nerve fibers from outside the spinal cord. Then they biochemically coax the severed spinal nerve fibers to grow through the "tunnels" (neurilemma) provided by the implanted fibers. Within months, rats treated this way regain some use of their hind legs (Cheng, Cao, & Olson, 1996).

Similarly, medical researchers have already begun the first human trials in which nerve grafts will be used to repair damaged spinal cords (Féron et al., 2005). Imagine what that could mean to a person confined to a wheelchair. Although it is unwise to raise false hopes, solutions to such problems are beginning to emerge. Nevertheless, it is wise to take good care of your own CNS. That means using seat belts when you drive, wearing a helmet if you ride a motorcycle or bicycle, wearing protective gear for sports, and avoiding activities that pose a risk to your head or spinal cord.

Can brain damage also be repaired? While we will be exploring the brain itself in more detail later on in the chapter, we can, for now, answer with an optimistic but cautious *yes*. (See "Repairing Your Brain.")

Before we go on to explore some of the research tools biopsychologists use, take some time to check out how much you've learned.

KNOWLEDGE BUILDER
Neurons and the Nervous System
RECITE

1. The _____ and _____ are the receiving areas of a neuron where information from other neurons is accepted.
2. Nerve impulses are carried down the _____ to the _____ _____.
3. The _____ potential becomes a(n) _____ potential when a neuron passes the threshold for firing.
4. Neuropeptides are transmitter substances that help regulate the activity of neurons. T or F?
5. The somatic and autonomic systems are part of the _____ nervous system.
6. Sodium and potassium ions flow across the synapse to trigger a nerve impulse in the receiving neuron. T or F?
7. The simplest behavior sequence is a _____ _____.
8. The parasympathetic nervous system is most active during times of high emotion. T or F?

Continued

Sympathetic branch A branch of the ANS that arouses the body.

Parasympathetic branch A branch of the ANS that quiets the body.

Reflex arc The simplest behavior, in which a stimulus provokes an automatic response.

Sensory neuron A nerve cell that carries information from the senses toward the CNS.

Repairing Your Brain

Until only a few years ago, it was widely believed that we are born with all the brain cells we will ever have. This led to the depressing idea that we all slowly go downhill, as the brain loses thousands of neurons every day. It also led to limited options, such as nerve cell transplants, for the treatment of brain damage (Wong, Hodges, & Horsburgh, 2005). Imagine that Bobby M. suffered partial paralysis in his left arm due to a *stroke*. (A stroke occurs when an artery in the brain becomes blocked or bursts open. This interrupts blood flow and causes some brain tissue to die.) What could be done to help Bobby recover? One remedy involves injecting immature nerve cells into his damaged brain areas. This would allow the new cells to link up with existing neurons in order to repair Bobby's stroke damage (Borlongan, Sanberg, & Freeman, 1999; Zhang, Zhang, & Chopp, 2005).

Rather than facing a steady decline, we now know that a healthy 75-year-old brain has just as many neurons as it did when it was careening through life in the body of a 25-year-old. Although it is true that the brain loses cells daily, it simultaneously grows new neurons to replace them. This process is called **neurogenesis** (noor-oh-JEN-uh-sis; the production of new brain cells) (Kempermann, 2005). Each day, thousands of new cells originate deep within the brain, move to the surface, and link up with other neurons to become part of the brain's circuitry. This is stunning news to brain scientists, who must now figure out what the new cells do. Most likely they are involved in learning, memory, and our ability to adapt to changing circumstances (Gould & Gross, 2002).

The discovery of neurogenesis in adult brains has raised hope that new treatments can be found for some types of brain damage. For example, an approach called constraint-induced movement therapy could be used to speed Bobby M.'s recovery. In this case, Bobby's good right arm would be restrained, forcing his impaired left arm to be more active, which would increase neurogenesis in the damaged part of his brain (Taub, 2004). In another approach, drugs that speed up neurogenesis could be injected into the damaged area of Bobby's brain (Zhang, Zhang, & Chopp, 2005). Such techniques are beginning to offer new hope for people suffering from a variety of other disabilities, such as blindness and Parkinson's disease (Brinton & Wang, 2006; Burke et al., 2007).

But don't these treatments assume that Bobby's brain is still capable of neurogenesis? What if it isn't? Brilliant! Although a stroke most likely doesn't damage the brain's ability to repair itself, it is quite possible that other brain disorders do arise from impaired neurogenesis (Thompson et al., 2008). In fact, that is exactly the theory proposed by neuroscientists Carla Toro and Bill Deakin to explain the serious mental disorder schizophrenia (Toro & Deakin, 2007). The brains of schizophrenic persons are usually smaller than normal, indicating that they have fewer neurons. Toro and Deakin's idea is that the schizophrenic brain may be unable to continually create new neurons to replace old ones that have died. If they are right, new therapies to promote neurogenesis may hold the key to treating schizophrenia, one of the most devastating mental illnesses.

Critical Thinking

9. What effect would you expect a drug to have if it blocked passage of neurotransmitters across the synapse?

Relate

To cope with all the technical terms in this section, think of neurons as strange little creatures. How do they act? What excites them? How do they communicate? To remember the functions of major branches of the nervous system, think about what you *couldn't* do if each part were missing.

Answers: 1. dendrites, soma **2.** axon, axon terminals **3.** resting, action **4.** T **5.** T **6.** F **7.** reflex arc **8.** F **9.** Such a drug could have wide-ranging effects. If the drug blocked excitatory synapses, it would depress brain activity. If it blocked inhibitory messages, it would act as a powerful stimulant.

● Research Methods—Charting the Brain's Inner Realms

Gateway Question: How is the brain studied?

Biopsychology is the study of how biological processes, and especially those of the nervous system, relate to behavior. In their research, many biopsychologists try to relate specific parts of the brain to the control of particular cognitive or behavioral functions, such as being able to recognize faces or move your hands. That is, they try to learn where functions are localized (located) in the brain. Many techniques have been developed to help identify brain structures and the functions they control.

Mapping Brain Structure

Anatomists have learned much about brain structure by dissecting (cutting apart) autopsied human and animal brains and examining them under a microscope. Dissection reveals that the brain is made up of many anatomically distinct areas or "parts." Less intrusive newer methods, such as the CT scan and the MRI scan, can be used to map brain structures in living brains.

CT Scan

Computerized scanning equipment has revolutionized the study of brain structures and made it easier to identify brain diseases and injuries. At best, conventional X-rays produce only shadowy images of the brain. **Computed tomographic (CT) scanning** is a specialized type of X-ray that does a much better job of making the brain visible. In a CT scan, X-rays taken from a number of different angles are collected by a computer and formed into an image of the brain. A CT scan can reveal the location of strokes, injuries, tumors, and other brain disorders.

● **Figure 2.10** A colored MRI scan of the brain reveals many details. Can you identify any brain regions?

MRI Scan

Magnetic resonance imaging (MRI) uses a very strong magnetic field, rather than X-rays, to produce an image of the body's interior. During an MRI scan, the body is placed inside a magnetic field. Processing by a computer then creates a three-dimensional model of the brain or body. Any two-dimensional plane, or slice, of the body can be selected and displayed as an image on a computer screen. MRI scans produce more detailed images than are possible with CT scans, allowing us to peer into the living brain almost as if it were transparent (● Figure 2.10).

Exploring Brain Function

How does the brain allow us to think, feel, perceive, or act? To answer questions like these, we must **localize function** by linking these psychological or behavioral capacities with particular brain structures. In many instances, this has been done through **clinical case studies.** Such studies examine changes in personality, behavior, or sensory capacity caused by brain diseases or injuries. If damage to a particular part of the brain consistently leads to a particular loss of function, then we say the function is localized in that structure. Presumably, that part of the brain controls the same function in all of us.

Consider, for example, the story of Kate Adamson (Adamson, 2004). At the age of 33, she had a stroke that caused catastrophic damage to her brainstem. This event left her with *locked-in syndrome:* One moment she was fine, and the next she was totally paralyzed, trapped in her own body and barely able to breathe. As you can see, this clinical case suggests that our brainstems play a role in the control of vital life functions, such as movement and breathing.

But what happened to Kate? Oh, yes. Unable to move a muscle, but still fully awake and aware, Kate thought she was going to die. Her doctors, who thought she was *brain dead* (Laureys & Boly, 2007), did not administer painkillers as they inserted breathing and feeding tubes down her throat. However, in time Kate discovered that she could communicate by blinking her eyes. After a

recovery that has been miraculous by any measure, she even went on to appear before the U. S. Congress.

Instead of relying on clinical studies, researchers have learned much from **electrical stimulation of the brain (ESB)** (● Figure 2.11). For example, the surface of the brain can be "turned on" by stimulating it with a mild electrical current delivered through a thin insulated wire called an **electrode.** When this is done during brain surgery, the patient can describe what effect the stimulation had. (The brain has no pain receptors, so surgery can be done while a patient is awake. Only local painkillers are used for the scalp and skull.) (Any volunteers?) Even structures below the surface of the brain can be activated by lowering a stimulating electrode, insulated except at the tip, into a target area inside the brain. ESB can call forth behavior with astonishing power. Instantly, it can bring about aggression, alertness, escape, eating, drinking, sleeping, movement, euphoria, memories, speech, tears, and more.

Could ESB be used to control a person against his or her will? It might seem that ESB could be used to control a person like a robot. But the details of emotions and behaviors elicited by ESB are modified by personality and circumstances. Sci-fi movies to the contrary, it would be impossible for a ruthless dictator to enslave people by "radio controlling" their brains.

An alternate approach is **ablation** (ab-LAY-shun: surgical removal) of parts of the brain. (See ● Figure 2.11.) When ablation

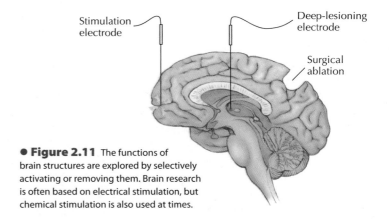

● **Figure 2.11** The functions of brain structures are explored by selectively activating or removing them. Brain research is often based on electrical stimulation, but chemical stimulation is also used at times.

Neurogenesis The production of new brain cells.

Computed tomographic (CT) scanning A computer-enhanced X-ray image of the brain or body.

Magnetic resonance imaging (MRI) A three-dimensional image of the brain or body, based on its response to a magnetic field.

Localization of function The research strategy of linking specific structures in the brain with specific psychological or behavioral functions.

Clinical case study A detailed investigation of a single person, especially one suffering from some injury or disease.

Electrical stimulation of the brain (ESB) Direct electrical stimulation and activation of brain tissue.

Electrode Any device (such as a wire, needle, or metal plate) used to electrically stimulate or destroy nerve tissue or to record its activity.

Ablation Surgical removal of tissue.

causes changes in behavior or sensory capacity, we also gain insight into the purpose of the missing "part." By using **deep lesioning** (LEE-zhun-ing), structures below the surface of the brain can also be removed. A strong electric current can be used to destroy a small amount of brain tissue when delivered via an electrode lowered into a target area inside the brain. (See ● Figure 2.11.) Again, changes in behavior give clues to the function of the affected area.

By using ESB, ablation, and deep lesioning, researchers are creating a three-dimensional brain map. This "atlas" shows the sensory, motor, and emotional responses that can be elicited from various parts of the brain. It promises to be a valuable guide for medical treatment, as well as for exploring the brain (Kalat, 2007; Yoshida, 1993).

To find out what individual neurons are doing, we need to do a microelectrode recording. A *microelectrode* is an extremely thin glass tube filled with a salty fluid. The tip of a microelectrode is small enough to detect the electrical activity of a *single* neuron. Watching the action potentials of just one neuron provides a fascinating glimpse into the true origins of behavior. (The action potential shown in ● Figure 2.2 was recorded with a microelectrode.)

Are any less invasive techniques available for studying brain function? Yes, several techniques allow us to observe the activity of parts of the brain without doing any damage at all. These include the EEG, PET scan, and fMRI. Such techniques allow biopsychologists to pinpoint areas in the brain responsible for thoughts, feelings, and actions.

EEG

Electroencephalography (ee-LEK-tro-in-SEF-ah-LOG-ruh-fee) measures the waves of electrical activity produced near the surface of the brain. Small disk-shaped metal plates are placed on a person's scalp. Electrical impulses from the brain are detected by these electrodes and sent to an **electroencephalograph (EEG)**. The EEG amplifies these very weak signals (brain waves) and records them on a moving sheet of paper or a computer screen (● Figure 2.12). Various brain-wave patterns can identify the presence of tumors, epilepsy, and other diseases. The EEG also reveals changes in brain activity during sleep, daydreaming, hypnosis, and other mental states. (For

example, Chapter 6, page 186, explains how changes in brain waves help define various stages of sleep.)

PET Scan

A newer technology, called positron emission tomography (PET), provides much more detailed images of activity both *near* the surface and *below* the surface of the brain. A **PET scan** detects positrons (subatomic particles) emitted by weakly radioactive glucose (sugar) as it is consumed by the brain. Because the brain runs on glucose, a PET scan shows which areas are using more energy. Higher energy use corresponds with higher activity. Thus, by placing positron detectors around the head and sending data to a computer, it is possible to create a moving, color picture of changes in brain activity. As you can see in ● Figure 2.13, PET scans reveal that very specific brain areas are active when you see, hear, speak, or think.

> ### bridges
> PET scans suggest that different patterns of brain activity accompany major psychological disorders, such as depression or schizophrenia. **See Chapter 14, pages 473–475.**

More active brains are good, right? Surprisingly, although we might assume that smart brains are hardworking brains, the reverse appears to be true. Using PET scans, psychologist Richard Haier and his colleagues found that the brains of people who perform well on a difficult reasoning test consume less energy than those of poor performers (Haier et al., 1988) (● Figure 2.14). Haier believes this shows that intelligence is related to brain efficiency: Less efficient brains work harder and still accomplish less (Haier, White, & Alkire, 2003). We've all had days like that!

Is it true that most people use only 10 percent of their brain capacity? This is one of the lasting myths about the brain. Brain scans show that all parts of the brain are active during waking hours. Obviously, some people make better use of their innate brainpower than others do. Nevertheless, there are no great hidden or untapped reserves of mental capacity in a normally functioning brain.

● **Figure 2.12** An EEG recording.

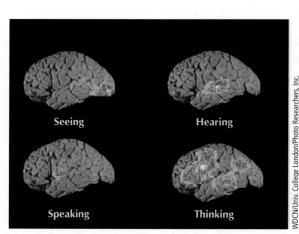

● **Figure 2.13** Colored PET scans reveal different patterns of brain activation when we engage in different tasks.

fMRI

A **functional MRI (fMRI)** uses MRI technology to make brain activity visible. Like PET scans, functional MRIs also provide images of activity throughout the brain. For example, if we scanned Carlos Santana while he played his guitar, areas of his brain that control his hands would be highlighted in an fMRI image.

Psychiatrist Daniel Langleben and his colleagues have even used fMRI images to tell if a person is lying (Langleben et al., 2005). As ● Figure 2.15 shows, the front of the brain is more active when a person is lying, rather than telling the truth. This may occur because it takes extra effort to lie and the resulting extra brain activity is detected with fMRI. Eventually, fMRI may help us distinguish between lies, false statements made with the intention to deceive, and *confabulations,* which are false claims made by persons who believe they are telling the truth (Hirstein, 2005; Langleben, Dattilio, & Gutheil, 2006). Clearly, it is just a matter of time until even brighter beacons are flashed into the shadowy inner world of thought.

● **Figure 2.14** In the images you see here, red, orange, and yellow indicate high consumption of glucose; green, blue, and pink show areas of low glucose use. The PET scan of the brain on the left shows that a man who solved 11 out of 36 reasoning problems burned more glucose than the man on the right, who solved 33.

● **Figure 2.15** Participants were asked to tell the truth or to lie while fMRI images of their brains were taken. When compared with telling the truth (shown in blue), areas toward the front of the brain were active during lying (shown in red). (Adapted from Langleben et al., 2005.)

KNOWLEDGE BUILDER
Brain Research

RECITE
1. Which of the following research techniques has the most in common with clinical studies of the effects of brain injuries?
   a. EEG recording
   b. deep lesioning
   c. microelectrode recording
   d. PET scan
2. CT scans cannot determine which part of your brain plays a role in speech because CT scans
   a. use X-rays
   b. reveal brain structure, not brain activity
   c. reveal brain activity, not brain structure
   d. use magnetic fields
3. _____ links brain structures to brain functions.
4. People only use 10 percent of their brain capacity. T or F?

REFLECT

Critical Thinking
5. Deep lesioning is used to ablate an area in the hypothalamus of a rat. After the operation, the rat seems to lose interest in food and eating. Why would it be a mistake to automatically conclude that the ablated area is a "hunger center"?

Relate
You suspect that a certain part of the brain is related to risk-taking. How could you use clinical studies, ablation, deep lesioning, and ESB to study the structure? You want to know which areas of the brain's surface are most active when a person sees a face. What methods will you use?

Answers: 1. b **2.** b **3.** Localization of function **4.** F **5.** Because other factors might explain the apparent loss of appetite. For example, the taste or smell of food might be affected, or the rat might simply have difficulty swallowing. It is also possible that hunger originates elsewhere in the brain and the ablated area merely relays messages that cause the rat to eat.

●● The Cerebral Cortex—My, What a Big Brain You Have!

Gateway Question: Why is the human cerebral cortex so important, and what are its parts?

In many ways we are pretty unimpressive creatures. Animals surpass humans in almost every category of strength, speed, and sensory sensitivity. However, we do excel in intelligence.

Deep lesioning Removal of tissue within the brain by use of an electrode.

Electroencephalograph (EEG) A device that detects, amplifies, and records electrical activity in the brain.

PET scan Positron emission tomography; a computer-generated image of brain activity based on glucose consumption in the brain.

Functional MRI (fMRI) Functional magnetic resonance imaging that records brain activity.

● **Figure 2.20** A circle is flashed to the left brain of a split-brain patient and he is asked what he saw. He easily replies, "A circle." He can also pick out the circle by merely touching shapes with his right hand, out of sight behind a screen. However, his left hand can't identify the circle. If a triangle is flashed to the patient's right brain, he can't say what he saw (speech is controlled by the left hemisphere). He also can't identify the triangle by touch with the right hand. Now, however, the left hand has no difficulty picking out the triangle. In other tests, the hemispheres reveal distinct skills, as listed above the drawing.

Left Hemisphere   **Right Hemisphere**

"Split Brains"

After the right and left brain are separated, each hemisphere will have its own separate perceptions, concepts, and impulses to act.

How does a split-brain person act after the operation? Having two "brains" in one body can create some interesting dilemmas. When one split-brain patient dressed himself, he sometimes pulled his pants up with one hand (*that* side of his brain wanted to get dressed . . .) and down with the other (. . . while *this* side didn't). Once, he grabbed his wife with his left hand and shook her violently. Gallantly, his right hand came to her aid and grabbed the aggressive left hand (Gazzaniga, 1970). However, such conflicts are actually rare. That's because both halves of the brain normally have about the same experience at the same time. Also, if a conflict arises, one hemisphere usually overrides the other.

Split-brain effects are easiest to see in specialized testing. For example, we could flash a dollar sign to the right brain and a question mark to the left brain of a patient named Tom. (● Figure 2.19 shows how this is possible.) Next, Tom is asked to draw what he saw, using his left hand, out of sight. Tom's left hand draws a dollar sign. If Tom is then asked to point with his right hand to a picture of what his hidden left hand drew, he will point to a question mark (Sperry, 1968). In short, for the split-brain person, one hemisphere may not know what is happening in the other. This has to be the ultimate case of the "right hand not knowing what the left hand is doing"! ● Figure 2.20 provides another example of split-brain testing.

Right Brain/Left Brain

Earlier it was stated that the hemispheres differ in abilities; in what ways are they different? The brain divides its work in interesting ways. Roughly 95 percent of us use our left brain for language (speaking, writing, and understanding). In addition, the left hemisphere is superior at math, judging time and rhythm, and coordinating the order of complex movements, such as those needed for speech.

In contrast, the right hemisphere can produce only the simplest language and numbers. Working with the right brain is like talking to a child who can say only a dozen words or so. To answer ques-

tions, the right hemisphere must use nonverbal responses, such as pointing at objects (● Figure 2.21).

Although it is poor at producing language, the right brain is especially good at perceptual skills, such as recognizing patterns, faces, and melodies; putting together a puzzle; or drawing a picture. It is also helps you express emotions and detect the emotions that other people are feeling (Borod et al., 2002; Stuss & Alexander, 2000).

Even though the right hemisphere is nearly "speechless," it is superior at some aspects of understanding language. If the right side of the brain is damaged, people lose their ability to understand jokes, irony, sarcasm, implications, and other nuances of language. Basically, the right hemisphere helps us see the overall context in which something is said (Beeman & Chiarello, 1998).

● **Figure 2.21** The left and right brain have different information processing styles. The right brain gets the big pattern; the left focuses on small details.

One Brain, Two Styles

In general, the left hemisphere is mainly involved with *analysis* (breaking information into parts). It also processes information *sequentially* (in order, one item after the next). The right hemisphere appears to process information *simultaneously* and *holistically* (all at once) (Springer & Deutsch, 1998).

To summarize further, you could say that the right hemisphere is better at assembling pieces of the world into a coherent picture; it sees overall patterns and general connections. The left brain focuses on small details. (See ● Figure 2.21.) The right brain sees the wide-angle view; the left zooms in on specifics. The focus of the left brain is local, the right is global (Hübner & Volberg, 2005).

Do people normally do puzzles or draw pictures with just the right hemisphere? Do they do other things with only the left? Numerous books have been written about how to use the right brain to manage, teach, draw, ride horses, learn, and even make love (Clark, Boutros, & Mendez, 2005). But such books drastically oversimplify right-brain and left-brain differences. People normally use both sides of the brain at all times. It's true that some tasks may make *more* use of one hemisphere or the other. But in most "real world" activities, the hemispheres share the work. Each does the parts it does best and shares information with the other side.

A smart brain is one that grasps both the details and the overall picture at the same time. For instance, during a concert a flamenco guitarist will use his left brain to judge time and rhythm and coordinate the order of his hand movements. At the same time, he will use his right brain to recognize and organize melodies.

Lobes of the Cerebral Cortex

Each of the two hemispheres of the cerebral cortex can be divided into several smaller *lobes*. Some of the **lobes of the cerebral cortex** are defined by larger fissures on the surface of the cortex. Others are regarded as separate areas because their functions are quite different (● Figure 2.22).

● **Figure 2.22**

The Frontal Lobes

The **frontal lobes** are associated with higher mental abilities and play a role in your sense of self. This area is also responsible for the control of movement. Specifically, an arch of tissue at the rear of the frontal lobes, called the **primary motor area** (or **primary motor cortex**), directs the body's muscles. If this area is stimulated with an electrical current, various parts of the body will twitch or move. The drawing wrapped around the motor cortex in ● Figure 2.23 is out of proportion because it reflects the *dexterity* of body areas, not their size. The hands, for example, get more area than the feet. (See ● Figure 2.23.) If you've ever wondered why your hands are more skilled or agile than your feet, it's partly because more motor cortex is devoted to the hands. Incidentally, due to neuroplasticity, learning and experience can alter these "motor maps." For instance, violin, viola, and cello players have larger "hand maps" in the cortex (Hashimoto et al., 2004).

Motor cortex is one brain area that contains **mirror neurons.** These are neurons that become active when we perform an action *and* when we merely observe someone else carrying out the same action. (For more information about mirror neurons, see "Mirror, Mirror in the Brain.")

The rest of the frontal lobes are often referred to as *frontal association areas*. Only a small portion of the cerebral cortex (the primary areas) directly controls the body or receives information from the senses. All the surrounding areas, which are called **association areas** (or **association cortex**), combine and process information. For example, if you see a rose, association areas will help you connect your primary sensory impressions with memories, so that you can recognize the rose and name it. Some association areas also contribute to higher mental abilities, such as language. For example, a person with damage to association areas in the left hemisphere may suffer **aphasia** (ah-FAZE-yah: an impaired ability to use language).

One type of aphasia is related to **Broca's** (BRO-cahs) **area,** a "speech center" that is part of the left frontal association area (for 5 percent of all people, the area is part of the right frontal association area). Damage to Broca's area causes *motor (or expressive)*

Lobes of the cerebral cortex Areas on the cortex bordered by major fissures or defined by their functions.

Frontal lobes A brain area associated with movement, the sense of self, and higher mental functions.

Primary motor area (primary motor cortex) A brain area associated with control of movement.

Mirror neuron A neuron that becomes active when a motor action is carried out *and* when another organism is observed carrying out the same action.

Association area (association cortex) All areas of the cerebral cortex that are not primarily sensory or motor in function.

Aphasia A speech disturbance resulting from brain damage.

Broca's area A language area related to grammar and pronunciation.

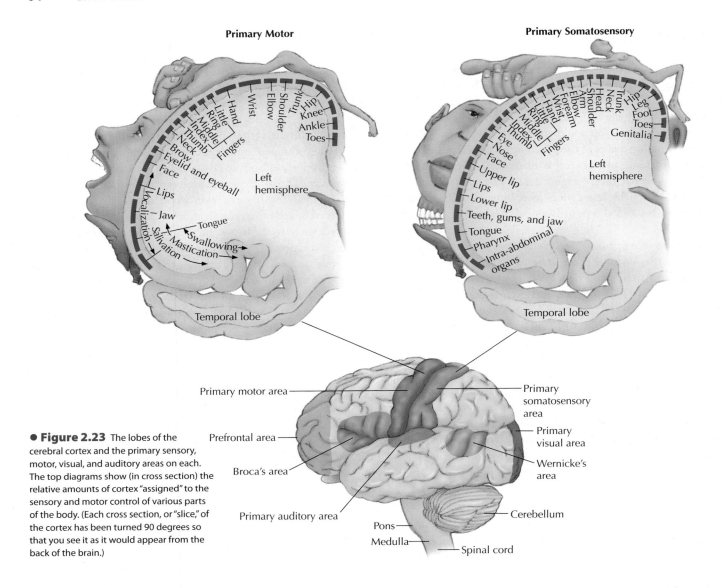

● **Figure 2.23** The lobes of the cerebral cortex and the primary sensory, motor, visual, and auditory areas on each. The top diagrams show (in cross section) the relative amounts of cortex "assigned" to the sensory and motor control of various parts of the body. (Each cross section, or "slice," of the cortex has been turned 90 degrees so that you see it as it would appear from the back of the brain.)

aphasia, a great difficulty in speaking or writing (Ward, 2006). Generally, the person knows what she or he wants to say but can't seem to fluently utter the words (Geschwind, 1979). Typically, a patient's grammar and pronunciation are poor and speech is slow and labored. For example, the person may say "bife" for bike, "seep" for sleep, or "zokaid" for zodiac.

The very front of the frontal association region is known as the **prefrontal area** (or **prefrontal cortex**). This part of the brain is related to more complex behaviors. If the frontal lobes are damaged, a patient's personality and emotional life may change dramatically. Remember Phineas Gage, the railroad foreman described in Chapter 1? It's likely that Gage's personality changed after he suffered brain damage because the prefrontal cortex generates our sense of self, including an awareness of our current emotional state (Moran et al., 2006; Kawasaki et al., 2005).

Reasoning or planning may also be affected (Goel & Dolan, 2004). Patients with damage to the frontal lobes often get "stuck" on mental tasks and repeat the same wrong answers over and over

(Stuss & Knight, 2002). PET scans suggest that much of what we call intelligence is related to increased activity in the frontal areas of the cortex (Duncan, 2005). Sadly, drug abuse can damage this important area of the brain (Liu et al., 1998).

The Parietal Lobes

Bodily sensations register in the **parietal** (puh-RYE-ih-tal) **lobes,** located just above the occipital lobes. Touch, temperature, pressure, and other somatic sensations flow into the **primary somatosensory** (SO-mat-oh-SEN-so-ree) **area** (or **primary somatosensory cortex**) of the parietal lobes. Again we find that the map of bodily sensations is distorted. In the case of somatosensory cortex, the drawing in ● Figure 2.23 reflects the *sensitivity* of body areas, not their size. For example, the lips are large in the drawing because of their great sensitivity, whereas the back and trunk, which are less sensitive, are much smaller. Notice that the hands are also large in the map of body sensitivity—which is obviously an aid to musicians, typists, watchmakers, massage therapists, lovers, and brain surgeons.

CRITICAL THINKING

Mirror, Mirror in the Brain

Italian researchers had just recorded an increase in the activity of a single neuron in the motor cortex of a monkey as it reached for food. A few seconds later, one of the researchers happened to reach for a snack of his own. The same neuron obligingly responded as if the monkey had reached for the food itself. Unexpectedly, a neuron involved in controlling a particular motor movement was also activated when the monkey merely observed that same motor movement in someone else. Just like that, the Italians discovered *mirror neurons* (Rizzolatti, Fogassi, & Gallese, 2006). Because they *mirror* actions performed by others, such neurons may explain how we can intuitively understand other people's behavior. They may also underlie our ability to learn new skills by imitation (Rizzolatti & Craighero, 2004).

The discovery of mirror neurons has triggered a flood of interest. Recently, researchers have confirmed that mirror neurons are found in various areas of the brain and appear to exist in the human brain as well (Bertenthal & Longo, 2007). In addition, neuroscientists speculate that newborn humans (and monkeys) are able to imitate others because networks of mirror neurons are activated when an infant watches someone perform an action. Then the same mirror network can be used to perform that action (Lepage & Théret, 2007). Similarly, human empathy (the ability to identify with another person's experiences and feelings) may arise from activation of mirror neurons (de C. Hamilton, 2008).

Mirror neurons may even partially explain *autism spectrum disorders*. In early childhood, children with autism begin to suffer from an impaired ability to interact and communicate with other people. Restricted and repetitive behavior such as head banging is also common. According to the "broken mirrors" hypothesis, autism may arise in infants whose mirror neuron system has been damaged by genetic defects or environmental risk factors (Ramachandran & Oberman, 2006). This explanation is attractive because autism's primary features of impaired communication and social interaction appear to be related to the role that mirror neurons play in reflecting the actions and words of others.

To date, these are just hypotheses that await empirical confirmation. More importantly, such possibilities have not yet led to any new therapies for autism. Nevertheless, the possibilities are exciting.

China Photos/Getty Images

The intense social isolation of autism spectrum disorder may arise because of damage to mirror neurons distributed throughout the brain.

The Temporal Lobes

The **temporal lobes** are located on each side of the brain. Auditory information projects directly to the **primary auditory area,** making it the main site where hearing first registers. If we did a PET scan of your brain while you listened to your favorite MP3, your primary auditory area would be the first to light up, followed by association areas in your temporal lobes. Likewise, if we could electrically stimulate the primary auditory area of your temporal lobe, you would "hear" a series of sound sensations.

An association area, called **Wernicke's** (VER-nick-ees) **area** (see ● Figure 2.23), lies on the left temporal lobe (again, for 5 percent of all people, the area is on the right temporal lobe). Wernicke's area also functions as a language site. If it is damaged, the result is a *receptive (or fluent) aphasia.* Although the person can hear speech, he or she has difficulty understanding the meaning of words. Thus, when shown a picture of a chair, someone with Broca's aphasia might say "tssair." In contrast, a Wernicke's patient might *fluently,* but incorrectly, identify the photo as "truck" (Ward, 2006).

The Occipital Lobes

At the back of the brain, we find the **occipital** (awk-SIP-ih-tal) **lobes,** the area of the cortex concerned with vision. Patients with tumors (cell growths that interfere with brain activity) in the

Prefrontal area (prefrontal cortex) The very front of the frontal lobes; involved in sense of self, reasoning, and planning.

Parietal lobes Area of the brain where body sensations register.

Primary somatosensory area (primary somatosensory cortex) A receiving area for body sensations.

Temporal lobes Areas on each side of the brain where hearing registers in the brain.

Primary auditory area Part of the temporal lobe where auditory information is first registered.

Wernicke's area A temporal lobe brain area related to language comprehension.

Occipital lobes Portion of the cerebral cortex where vision registers in the brain.

HUMAN DIVERSITY

His and Hers Brains?

Are men's and women's brains specialized in different ways? Yes, to some extent. Many physical differences between male and female brains have been found, although their significance remains debatable. In one series of studies, researchers observed brain activity while people did language tasks. Both men and women showed increased activity in Broca's area, on the left side of the brain, exactly as expected. Surprisingly, however, the left *and* the right brain were activated in more than half the women tested (Shaywitz & Gore, 1995) (● Figure 2.24).

Using both sides of the brain for language may be a big advantage. When Broca's area is damaged, some women can use the right side of their brains to compensate for the loss (Hochstenbach et al., 1998). Thus, when a man says, "I have half a mind to tell you what I think," he may be stating a curious truth. Despite this difference, the two sexes performed equally well on a task that involved sounding out words (Shaywitz et al., 1995). The researchers concluded that nature has given the brain different routes to the same ability.

In a study of men and women with similar IQ scores, brain images revealed major differences in brain areas involved in intelligence (Haier et al., 2004). In general, the men had more gray matter (neuron cell bodies), while the women had more white matter (axons coated in myelin). Further, the women had more gray and white matter concentrated in their frontal lobes than the men did. The men's gray matter was split between their frontal and parietal lobes, while their white matter was mostly in the temporal lobes. Whatever else these differences mean, they show that the human brain can be specialized in different ways to arrive at the same capabilities.

Shaywitz et al., 1995 NMR Research/Yale Medical School

● **Figure 2.24** Language tasks activate both sides of the brain in many women but only the left side in men.

---

primary visual area, the part of cortex to first receive input from the eyes, experience blind spots in their vision.

Do the primary visual areas of the cortex correspond directly to what is seen? Images are mapped onto the cortex, but the map is greatly stretched and distorted (Carlson, 2007). That's why it's important to avoid thinking of the visual area as being like a little TV screen in the brain. Visual information creates complex patterns of activity in nerve cells; it does *not* make a TV-like image.

One of the most fascinating results of brain injury is **visual agnosia** (ag-KNOW-zyah), an inability to identify seen objects. Visual agnosia is often caused by damage to the association areas on the occipital lobes (Farah, 2004). This condition is sometimes referred to as "mindblindness." For example, if we show Alice, an agnosia patient, a candle, she can see it and can describe it as "a long narrow object that tapers at the top." Alice can even draw the candle accurately, but she cannot name it. However, if she is allowed to feel the candle, she will name it immediately. In short, Alice can still see color, size, and shape. She just can't form the associations necessary to perceive the meanings of objects.

Are agnosias limited to objects? No. A fascinating form of "mindblindness" is **facial agnosia,** an inability to perceive familiar faces (Farah, 2006). One patient with facial agnosia couldn't recognize her husband or mother when they visited her in the hospital, and she was unable to identify pictures of her children. However, as soon as a visitor spoke she knew them immediately by their voices.

Areas devoted to recognizing faces lie in association areas on the underside of the occipital lobes. These areas appear to have no other function. Why would part of the brain be set aside solely for identifying faces? From an evolutionary standpoint it is not really so surprising. After all, we are social animals, for whom facial recognition is very important. This specialization is just one example of what a marvelous organ of consciousness we possess.

How much do individual brains differ? Could we find different specializations from brain to brain? Perhaps. "His and Hers Brains?" explains why.

In summary, the bulk of our daily experience and all of our understanding of the world can be traced to the different areas of the cortex. The human brain is among the most advanced and sophisticated of the brain-bearing species on earth. This, of course, is no guarantee that this marvelous "biocomputer" will be put to full use. Still, we must stand in awe of the potential it represents.

The Subcortex—At the Core of the (Brain) Matter

Gateway Question: What are the major parts of the subcortex?

You could lose large portions of your cerebral cortex and still survive. Not so with the **subcortex,** the brain structures immediately below the cerebral cortex. Serious damage to the subcortex (lower

brain) can be fatal. Hunger, thirst, sleep, attention, sex, breathing, and many other vital functions are controlled by parts of the subcortex. Let's take a quick tour of these brain areas, which can be divided into the brainstem (or hindbrain), the midbrain, and the forebrain. (The forebrain also includes the cerebral cortex, which we have already discussed because of its size and importance.) For our purposes the midbrain can be viewed as a link between the forebrain and the brainstem. Therefore, let us focus on the rest of the subcortex (● Figure 2.25).

The Hindbrain

Why are the lower brain areas so important? As the spinal cord joins the brain, it widens into the brainstem. The **brainstem** consists mainly of the medulla (meh-DUL-ah) and the cerebellum (ser-ah-BEL-uhm). The **medulla** contains centers important for the reflex control of vital life functions, including heart rate, breathing, swallowing, and the like. Various drugs, diseases, and injuries can disrupt the medulla and end or endanger life. That's why a karate chop to the back of the neck can be extremely dangerous.

The **pons,** which looks like a small bump on the brainstem, acts as a bridge between the medulla and other brain areas. In addition to connecting with many other locations, including the cerebellum, the pons influences sleep and arousal.

The cerebellum, which looks like a miniature cerebral cortex, lies at the base of the brain. The **cerebellum** primarily regulates posture, muscle tone, and muscular coordination. The cerebellum also stores memories related to skills and habits (Christian & Thompson, 2005). Again we see that experience shapes the brain: Musicians, who practice special motor skills throughout their lives, have larger than average cerebellums (Hutchinson et al., 2003).

> **bridges**
> In general, the cerebellum stores "know how" or "skill" memories. "Know what" memories, such as remembering a person's name or knowing what the cerebellum does, are stored elsewhere in the brain. **See Chapter 8, page 260.**

Primary visual area The part of occipital lobe that first receives input from the eyes.

Visual agnosia Inability to identify seen objects.

Facial agnosia Inability to perceive familiar faces.

Subcortex All brain structures below the cerebral cortex.

Brainstem The lowest portions of the brain, including the cerebellum, medulla, pons, and reticular formation.

Medulla The structure that connects the brain with the spinal cord and controls vital life functions.

Pons An area on the brainstem that acts as a bridge between the medulla and other structures.

Cerebellum A brain structure that controls posture and coordination.

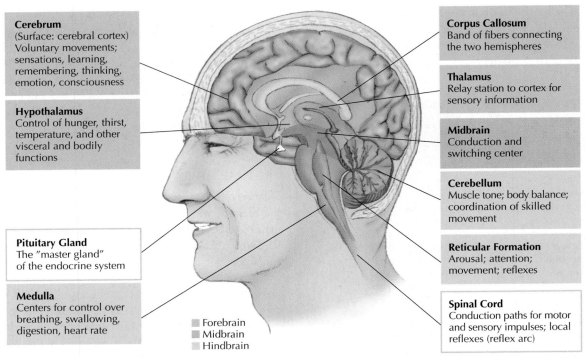

Cerebrum
(Surface: cerebral cortex)
Voluntary movements; sensations, learning, remembering, thinking, emotion, consciousness

Hypothalamus
Control of hunger, thirst, temperature, and other visceral and bodily functions

Pituitary Gland
The "master gland" of the endocrine system

Medulla
Centers for control over breathing, swallowing, digestion, heart rate

Corpus Callosum
Band of fibers connecting the two hemispheres

Thalamus
Relay station to cortex for sensory information

Midbrain
Conduction and switching center

Cerebellum
Muscle tone; body balance; coordination of skilled movement

Reticular Formation
Arousal; attention; movement; reflexes

Spinal Cord
Conduction paths for motor and sensory impulses; local reflexes (reflex arc)

Forebrain
Midbrain
Hindbrain

● **Figure 2.25** This simplified drawing shows the main structures of the human brain and describes some of their most important features. (You can use the color code in the foreground to identify which areas are part of the forebrain, midbrain, and hindbrain.)

What happens if the cerebellum is injured? Without the cerebellum, tasks like walking, running, or playing catch become impossible. The first symptoms of a crippling disease called *spinocerebellar degeneration* are tremor, dizziness, and muscular weakness. Eventually, victims have difficulty merely standing, walking, or feeding themselves.

Reticular Formation

A network of fibers and cell bodies called the **reticular** (reh-TICK-you-ler) **formation (RF)** lies inside the medulla and brainstem. As messages flow into the brain, the RF gives priority to some while turning others aside (Kalat, 2007). By doing so, the RF influences *attention*. The RF doesn't fully mature until adolescence, which may be why children have such short attention spans. The RF also modifies outgoing commands to the body. In this way the RF affects muscle tone, posture, and movements of the eyes, face, head, body, and limbs. At the same time, the RF controls reflexes involved in breathing, sneezing, coughing, and vomiting.

The RF also keeps us vigilant, alert, and awake. Incoming messages from the sense organs branch into a part of the RF called the **reticular activating system (RAS)**. The RAS bombards the cortex with stimulation, keeping it active and alert. For instance, let's say a sleepy driver rounds a bend and sees a deer standing in the road. The driver snaps to attention and applies the brakes. She can thank her RAS for arousing the rest of her brain and averting an accident. If you're getting sleepy while reading this chapter, try

pinching your ear—a little pain will cause the RAS to momentarily arouse your cortex.

The Forebrain

Like buried treasure, two of the most important parts of your body lie deep within your brain. The thalamus (THAL-uh-mus) and an area just below it called the hypothalamus (HI-po-THAL-uh-mus) are key parts of the forebrain. (See ● Figure 2.25.)

How could these be any more important than other areas already described? The **thalamus** acts as a final "switching station" for sensory messages on their way to the cortex. Vision, hearing, taste, and touch all pass through this small, football-shaped structure. Thus, injury to even small areas of the thalamus can cause deafness, blindness, or loss of any other sense, except smell.

The human hypothalamus is about the size of a small grape. Small as it may be, the **hypothalamus** is a kind of master control center for emotion and many basic motives (Carlson, 2007). The hypothalamus affects behaviors as diverse as sex, rage, body temperature, hormone release, eating and drinking, sleep, waking, and emotion. (See Chapter 10, pages 324–325.)

The hypothalamus is basically a "crossroads" that connects many areas of the brain. It is also the final pathway for many kinds of behavior. That is, the hypothalamus is the last place where many behaviors are organized or "decided on" before messages leave the brain, causing the body to react.

The Limbic System

As a group, the hypothalamus, parts of the thalamus, the amygdala, the hippocampus, and other structures make up the limbic system (● Figure 2.26). The **limbic system** has a major role in producing emotion and motivated behavior. Rage, fear, sexual response, and intense arousal can be localized to various points in the limbic system. Laughter, a delightful part of human social life, also has its origins in the limbic system (Cardoso, 2000).

During evolution, the limbic system was the earliest layer of the forebrain to develop. In lower animals, the limbic system helps organize basic survival responses: feeding, fleeing, fighting, or reproduction. In humans, a clear link to emotion remains. The **amygdala** (ah-MIG-dah-luh), in particular, is strongly related to fear. For example, during medical testing one woman reacted with a sudden outburst of fear and anger when the amygdala was stimulated, saying, "I feel like I want to get up from this chair! Please don't let me do it! I don't want to be mean! I want to get something and just tear it up!" (King, 1961).

The amygdala provides a primitive, "quick pathway" to the cortex. Like lower animals, we can be startled and, as such, are able to react to dangerous stimuli before we fully know what is going on. In situations where true danger exists, such as in military combat, the amygdala's rapid response may aid survival. However, disorders of the brain's fear system can be very disruptive. An example is the war veteran who involuntarily dives into the bushes when he hears a car backfire (Fellous & LeDoux, 2005; LaBar & LeDoux, 2002). The role of the amygdala in emotion may also explain why people who suffer from phobias and disabling anxiety often feel afraid without knowing why (LeDoux, 1999).

bridges

Unconscious fear produced by the amygdala seems to explain why people who survive horrible experiences, such as a plane crash, can have debilitating fears years later. **See the discussion of stress disorders in Chapter 14, page 483.**

Some parts of the limbic system have taken on additional, higher-level functions. A part called the **hippocampus** (HIP-oh-CAMP-us) is important for forming lasting memories (Kumaran & Maguire, 2005). The hippocampus lies inside the temporal lobes, which is why stimulating the temporal lobes can produce memory-like or dream-like experiences. The hippocampus also helps us navigate through space. The right side of your hippocampus will become more active, for instance, if you mentally plan a drive across town (Maguire, Frackowiak, & Frith, 1997).

Psychologists have discovered that animals will learn to press a lever to deliver a dose of electrical stimulation to the limbic system. The animals act like the stimulation is satisfying or pleasurable. Indeed, several areas of the limbic system act as reward, or "pleasure," pathways. Many are found in the hypothalamus, where they overlap with areas that control thirst, sex, and hunger. Commonly abused drugs, such as cocaine, amphetamine, heroin, nicotine, marijuana, and alcohol, activate many of the same pleasure pathways. This appears to be part of the reason why these drugs are so powerfully rewarding (Kandel, Schwartz, & Jessell, 2003). You might also be interested to know that music you would describe as "thrilling" activates pleasure systems in your brain. This may explain some of the appeal of music that can send shivers down your spine (Blood & Zatorre, 2001). (It may also explain why people will pay so much for concert tickets!)

Punishment, or "aversive," areas have also been found in the limbic system. When these locations are activated, animals show discomfort and will work hard to turn off the stimulation. Because much of our behavior is based on seeking pleasure and avoiding pain, these discoveries continue to fascinate psychologists.

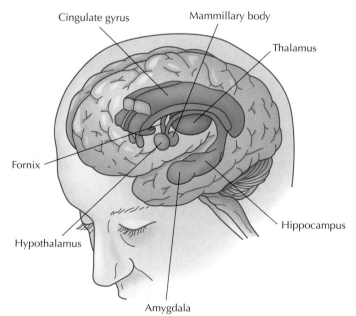

● **Figure 2.26** Parts of the limbic system. Although only one side is shown here, the hippocampus and the amygdala extend out into the temporal lobes at each side of the brain. The limbic system is a sort of "primitive core" of the brain strongly associated with emotion.

Labels: Cingulate gyrus, Mammillary body, Thalamus, Hippocampus, Amygdala, Hypothalamus, Fornix

Reticular formation (RF) A network within the medulla and brainstem; associated with attention, alertness, and some reflexes.

Reticular activating system (RAS) A part of the reticular formation that activates the cerebral cortex.

Thalamus A brain structure that relays sensory information to the cerebral cortex.

Hypothalamus A small area of the brain that regulates emotional behaviors and motives.

Limbic system A system in the forebrain that is closely linked with emotional response.

Amygdala A part of the limbic system associated with fear responses.

Hippocampus A part of the limbic system associated with storing memories.

The Magnificent Brain

Given the amount of information covered in our journey through the brain, a short review is in order. We have seen that the human brain is an impressive assembly of billions of sensitive cells and nerve fibers. The brain controls vital bodily functions, keeps track of the external world, issues commands to the muscles and glands, responds to current needs, regulates its own behavior, and even creates the "mind" and the magic of consciousness—*all* at the same time.

A final note of caution is now in order. For the sake of simplicity we have assigned functions to each "part" of the brain as if it were a computer. This is only a half-truth. In reality, the brain is a vast information-processing system. Incoming information scatters all over the brain and converges again as it goes out through the spinal cord, to muscles and glands. The overall system is much, much more complicated than our discussion of separate "parts" implies. In addition, the brain constantly revises its circuits in response to changing life experiences (Kolb & Whishaw, 2006).

We began our exploration of the brain with a virtuoso performance. Imagine the other extreme of being completely unable to move or speak. Even though you would remain alert and intelligent, you would be unable to communicate your simplest thoughts and feelings to others. Each year, this is the fate of thousands of people, like Kate Adamson, who are paralyzed by stroke, disease, or injury. In a very real sense, these people are *locked in,* prisoners in their own bodies (Smith & Delargy, 2005).

What if they could "will" a computer to speak for them? Right on! Researchers have developed brain–computer interfaces that translate a patient's EEG recordings into commands that can be used to control a computer (Hinterberger et al., 2003) and even access the Internet (Karim et al., 2006).

⬤⬤ The Endocrine System— My Hormones Made Me Do It

Gateway Question: Does the glandular system affect behavior?

Our behavior is not solely a product of the nervous system. The endocrine (EN-duh-krin) glands form an equally important parallel communication system in the body. The **endocrine system** is made up of glands that secrete chemicals directly into the bloodstream or lymph system (⬤ Figure 2.27). These chemicals, called **hormones,** are carried throughout the body, where they affect both internal activities and visible behavior. Hormones are related to neurotransmitters. Like other transmitter chemicals, hormones activate cells in the body. To respond, the cells must have receptor sites for the hormone. Hormones affect puberty, personality, dwarfism, jet lag, and much more.

How do hormones affect behavior? Although we are seldom directly aware of them, hormones affect us in many ways (Carlson, 2007). Here is a brief sample: Pregnancy and motherhood cause the release of hormones that lead to the dramatic changes involved in maternal behavior (Kingsley & Lambert, 2006). Hormone output from the adrenal glands rises during stressful situations; androgens ("male" hormones) are related to the sex drive in both males and females; hormones secreted during times of high emotion intensify memory formation; at least some of the emotional turmoil of adolescence is due to elevated hormone levels; different hormones prevail when you are angry, rather than fearful. Even disturbing personality patterns may be linked to hormonal irregularities (Evardone, Alexander, & Morey, 2007).

In fact, something as routine as watching a movie can alter hormone levels. After watching violent scenes from *The Godfather,* men had higher levels of the male hormone testosterone. For both men and women, watching a romantic film boosted a hormone that's linked to relaxation and reproduction (Schultheiss, Wirth, & Stanton, 2004). Because these are just samples, let's consider some additional effects hormones have on the body and behavior.

The pituitary is a pea-sized globe hanging from the base of the brain. (Return to ⬤ Figure 2.27.) One of the pituitary's more important roles is to regulate growth. During childhood, the pituitary secretes a hormone that speeds body development. If too little **growth hormone** is released, a person may remain far smaller than average. If this condition is not treated, a child may be 6 to 12 inches shorter than age-mates. As adults, some will have *hypo-*

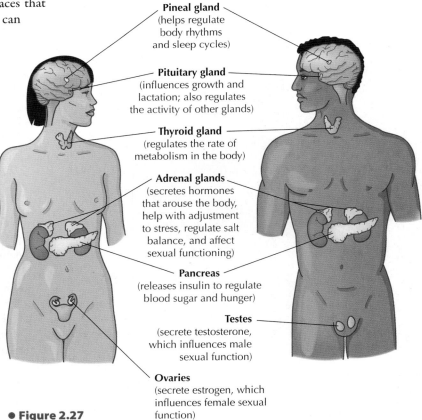

Pineal gland
(helps regulate body rhythms and sleep cycles)

Pituitary gland
(influences growth and lactation; also regulates the activity of other glands)

Thyroid gland
(regulates the rate of metabolism in the body)

Adrenal glands
(secretes hormones that arouse the body, help with adjustment to stress, regulate salt balance, and affect sexual functioning)

Pancreas
(releases insulin to regulate blood sugar and hunger)

Testes
(secrete testosterone, which influences male sexual function)

Ovaries
(secrete estrogen, which influences female sexual function)

● **Figure 2.27**

pituitary (HI-po-pih-TU-ih-ter-ee) *dwarfism*. Such individuals are perfectly proportioned, but tiny. Regular injections of growth hormone can raise a hypopituitary child's height by several inches, usually to the short side of average.

Too much growth hormone produces *gigantism* (excessive bodily growth). Secretion of too much growth hormone late in the growth period causes *acromegaly* (AK-row-MEG-uh-lee), a condition in which the arms, hands, feet, and facial bones become enlarged. Acromegaly produces prominent facial features, which some people have used as a basis for careers as character actors, wrestlers, and the like.

The pituitary also governs the functioning of other glands (especially the thyroid, adrenal glands, and ovaries or testes). These glands in turn regulate such bodily processes as metabolism, responses to stress, and reproduction. In women, the pituitary controls milk output during breast-feeding.

The **pituitary** is often called the "master gland" because it influences other endocrine glands. But the master has a master: The pituitary is directed by the hypothalamus, which lies directly above it. In this way, the hypothalamus can affect glands throughout the body. This, then, is the major link between the brain and hormones (Carlson, 2007).

The pineal (pin-EE-ul) gland was once considered a useless remnant of evolution. In certain fishes, frogs, and lizards, the gland is associated with a well-developed light-sensitive organ, or so-called third eye. In humans, the function of the **pineal gland** is just now coming to light (so to speak). The pineal gland releases a hormone called **melatonin** (mel-ah-TONE-in) in response to daily variations in light. Melatonin levels in the bloodstream rise at dusk and peak around midnight and fall again as morning approaches. As far as the brain is concerned, it's bedtime when melatonin levels rise (Kennaway & Wright, 2002).

bridges

Melatonin can be used to reset the body's "clock" and minimize jet lag for long-distance pilots, aircrews, and travelers. **See Chapter 10, pages 322–323.**

The **thyroid gland,** located in the neck, regulates metabolism. As you may remember from a biology course, metabolism is the rate at which energy is produced and expended in the body. By altering metabolism, the thyroid can have a sizable effect on personality. A person suffering from *hyperthyroidism* (an overactive thyroid) tends to be thin, tense, excitable, and nervous. An underactive thyroid (*hypothyroidism*) in an adult can cause inactivity, sleepiness, slowness, obesity, and depression (Joffe, 2006). In infancy, hypothyroidism limits development of the nervous system, leading to severe mental retardation. (See Chapter 9, pages 309–310.)

When you are frightened or angry, some important reactions prepare your body for action: Your heart rate and blood pressure rise, stored sugar is released into the bloodstream for quick energy, your muscles tense and receive more blood, and your blood is prepared to clot more quickly in case of injury. As we

Underactivity of the pituitary gland may produce a dwarf. Verne Troyer, best known for playing Mini-Me in the *Austin Powers* movies, has enjoyed an impressive career as an actor. Overactivity of the pituitary gland may produce a giant. Until his premature death in 2005, actor Matthew McGrory was best known for his role of Karl the Giant in the 2003 movie *Big Fish*.

Endocrine system Glands whose secretions pass directly into the bloodstream or lymph system.

Hormone A glandular secretion that affects bodily functions or behavior.

Growth hormone A hormone, secreted by the pituitary gland, that promotes body growth.

Pituitary gland The "master gland" whose hormones influence other endocrine glands.

Pineal gland Gland in the brain that helps regulate body rhythms and sleep cycles.

Melatonin Hormone released by the pineal gland in response to daily cycles of light and dark.

Thyroid gland Endocrine gland that helps regulate the rate of metabolism.

discussed earlier, these changes are controlled by the autonomic nervous system. Specifically, the sympathetic branch of the ANS causes the hormones *epinephrine* (ep-eh-NEF-rin) and *norepinephrine* to be released by the adrenal glands. (Epinephrine is also known as adrenaline, which may be more familiar to you.) **Epinephrine,** which is associated with fear, tends to arouse the body. **Norepinephrine** also tends to arouse the body, but it is linked with anger.

The **adrenal glands** are located just under the back of the rib cage, atop the kidneys. The *adrenal medulla,* or inner core of the adrenal glands, is the source of epinephrine and norepinephrine. The *adrenal cortex,* or outer "bark" of the adrenal glands, produces a set of hormones called corticoids (KOR-tih-coids). One of their jobs is to regulate salt balance in the body. A deficiency of certain corticoids can evoke a powerful craving for the taste of salt in humans. The corticoids also help the body adjust to stress, and they are a secondary source of sex hormones.

An oversecretion of the adrenal sex hormones can cause *virilism* (exaggerated male characteristics). For instance, a woman may grow a beard or a man's voice may become so low it is difficult to understand. Oversecretion early in life can cause *premature puberty* (full sexual development during childhood). One of the most remarkable cases on record is that of a 5-year-old Peruvian girl who gave birth to a son (Strange, 1965).

While we are on the topic of sex hormones, there is a related issue worth mentioning. One of the principal androgens, or "male" hormones, is testosterone, which is supplied in small amounts by the adrenal glands. (The testes are the main source of testosterone in males.) Perhaps you have heard about the use of anabolic steroids by athletes who want to "bulk up" or promote muscle growth. Most of these drugs are synthetic versions of testosterone.

Although there is some disagreement about whether steroids actually improve athletic performance, it is widely accepted that they may cause serious side effects. Problems include voice deepening or baldness in women and shrinkage of the testicles, sexual impotence, or breast enlargement in men (Millman & Ross, 2003). Dangerous increases in hostility and aggression ("roid rage") have also been linked with steroid use (Hartgens & Kuipers, 2004). Also common when steroids are used by younger adolescents are an increased risk of heart attack and stroke, liver damage, or stunted growth. Understandably, almost all major sports organizations ban the use of anabolic steroids.

In this brief discussion of the endocrine system we have considered only a few of the more important glands. Nevertheless, this should give you an appreciation of how completely behavior and personality are tied to the ebb and flow of hormones in the body.

A Look Ahead

In the upcoming "Psychology in Action" section, we will return to the brain to see how hand preference relates to brain organization. You'll also find out if being right- or left-handed affects your chances of living to a ripe old age.

Subcortex and Endocrine System

RECITE

1. Three major divisions of the brain are the brainstem or _____, the _____, and the _____.
2. Reflex centers for heartbeat and respiration are found in the
   a. cerebellum
   b. thalamus
   c. medulla
   d. RF
3. A portion of the reticular formation, known as the RAS, serves as an _____ system in the brain.
   a. activating
   b. adrenal
   c. adjustment
   d. aversive
4. The _____ is a final relay, or "switching station," for sensory information on its way to the cortex.
5. "Reward" and "punishment" areas are found throughout the _____ system, which is also related to emotion.
6. Undersecretion from the thyroid can cause both
   a. dwarfism
   b. gigantism
   c. obesity
   d. mental retardation
7. The body's ability to resist stress is related to the action of the adrenal _____.

REFLECT

Critical Thinking

8. Subcortical structures in humans are quite similar to corresponding lower brain areas in animals. Why would knowing this allow you to predict, in general terms, what functions are controlled by the subcortex?
9. Where in all the brain's "hardware" do you think the mind is found? What is the relationship between mind and brain?

Relate

If Mr. Medulla met Ms. Cerebellum at a party, what would they say their roles are in the brain? Would a marching band in a "reticular formation" look like a network? Would it get your attention? If you were standing in the final path for behavior leaving the brain, would you be in the thalamus? Or in the hy-*path*-alamus (please forgive the misspelling)? When you are emotional, do you wave your limbs around (and does your limbic system become more active)?

Name as many of the endocrine glands as you can. Which did you leave out? Can you summarize the functions of each of the glands?

Answers: 1. hindbrain, midbrain, forebrain **2.** c **3.** a **4.** thalamus **5.** limbic **6.** c, d (in infancy) **7.** cortex **8.** Because the subcortex must be related to basic functions common to all higher animals: motives, emotions, sleep, attention, and vegetative functions, such as heartbeat, breathing, and temperature regulation. The subcortex also routes and processes incoming information from the senses and outgoing commands to the muscles. **9.** This question, known as the mind–body problem, has challenged thinkers for centuries. One recent view is that mental states are "emergent properties" of brain activity. That is, brain activity forms complex patterns that are, in a sense, more than the sum of their parts. Or, to use a rough analogy, if the brain were a musical instrument, then mental life would be like music played on that instrument.

PSYCHOLOGY IN ACTION

Handedness—Are You Dexterous or Sinister?

Gateway Question: In what ways do right- and left-handed individuals differ?

Around the world, left-handedness has been frowned upon. "Lefties" have often been characterized as clumsy, awkward, unlucky, or insincere. The Latin word for left is actually *sinister!* In contrast, right-handedness is the paragon of virtue. The Latin word for right is *dexter,* and "righties" are more likely to be referred to as dexterous, coordinated, skillful, and just. But is there any basis in fact for these attitudes?

What causes **handedness** (a preference for the right or left hand)? Why are there more right-handed than left-handed people? How do left-handed and right-handed people differ? Does being left-handed create any problems—or benefits? The answers to these questions lead us back to the brain, where handedness begins. Let's see what research has revealed about handedness, the brain, and you.

Assessing Handedness

Write your name on a sheet of paper, first using your right hand and then your left. You were probably much more comfortable writing with your dominant hand. This is interesting because there's no real difference in the strength or dexterity of the hands themselves. The agility of your dominant hand is an outward expression of superior motor control on one side of the brain. If you are right-handed, there is literally more area on the left side of your brain devoted to controlling your right hand. If you are left-handed, the reverse applies.

The preceding exercise implies that you are either entirely right- or left-handed. But handedness is a matter of degree. To better assess your handedness, complete a few questions adapted from the Waterloo Handedness Questionnaire (Brown et al., 2006) by checking an answer for each question. The more "Rights" you check, the more right-handed you are.

Are You Right- or Left-Handed?

1. Which hand would you use to spin a top?
    ____Right   ____Left   ____Either

2. With which hand would you hold a paintbrush to paint a wall?
    ____Right   ____Left   ____Either

3. Which hand would you use to pick up a book?
    ____Right   ____Left   ____Either

4. With which hand would you use a spoon to eat soup?
    ____Right   ____Left   ____Either

5. Which hand would you use to flip pancakes?
    ____Right   ____Left   ____Either

6. Which hand would you use to pick up a piece of paper?
    ____Right   ____Left   ____Either

7. Which hand would you use to draw a picture?
    ____Right   ____Left   ____Either

8. Which hand would you use to insert and turn a key in a lock?
    ____Right   ____Left   ____Either

9. Which hand would you use to insert a plug into an electrical outlet?
    ____Right   ____Left   ____Either

10. Which hand would you use to throw a ball?
    ____Right   ____Left   ____Either

About 90 percent of all humans are right-handed; 10 percent are left-handed. Most people (about 75 percent) are strongly right- or left-handed. The rest show some inconsistency in hand preference. Which were you?

Is there such a thing as being left-footed? Excellent question. Do you have "two left feet"? **Sidedness** is often measured by assessing hand, foot, eye, *and* ear preference (Greenwood et al., 2006). We also generally prefer breathing through one nostril over the other and even have a preference for which direction we lean our head when kissing (Barrett, Greenwood, & McCullagh, 2006). (Do you kiss "right"?) Nevertheless, handedness remains the single most important behavioral indicator of sidedness.

If a person is strongly left-handed, does that mean the right hemisphere is dominant? Not necessarily. It's true that the right hemisphere controls the left hand, but a left-handed person's language-producing, **dominant hemisphere** may be on the opposite side of the brain.

Brain Dominance

About 97 percent of right-handers process speech in the left hemisphere and are left-brain dominant (● Figure 2.28). A good 68 percent of left-handers produce speech from the left hemisphere, just as right-handed people do. About 19 percent of all lefties and 3 percent of righties use their right brain for language. Some left-handers (approximately 12 percent) use both sides of the brain for language processing. All told, 94 percent of the population uses the left brain for language (Coren, 1992).

Is there any way for a person to tell which of his or her hemispheres is dominant? One classic clue is the way you write. Right-handed individuals who write with a straight hand, and lefties who write with a hooked hand, are usually left-brain dominant for language. Left-handed people who write with their hand below the line, and righties who use a hooked position, are usually right-brain dominant (Levy & Reid, 1976). Another hint is provided by hand gestures. If you gesture mostly with your right hand as you talk, you probably process language in your left hemisphere. Gesturing with your left hand is associated with right-brain language processing (Hellige, 1993).

Epinephrine An adrenal hormone that tends to arouse the body; epinephrine is associated with fear. (Also known as adrenaline.)

Norepinephrine An adrenal hormone that tends to arouse the body; norepinephrine is associated with anger. (Also known as noradrenaline.)

Adrenal glands Endocrine glands that arouse the body, regulate salt balance, adjust the body to stress, and affect sexual functioning.

Handedness A preference for the right or left hand in most activities.

Sidedness A combination of preference for hand, foot, eye, and ear.

Dominant hemisphere A term usually applied to the side of a person's brain that produces language.

● **Figure 2.28** Language is controlled by the left side of the brain in the majority of right- and left-handers.

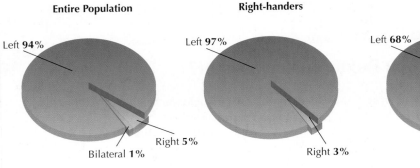

Entire Population

Left **94%**

Right **5%**

Bilateral **1%**

Right-handers

Left **97%**

Right **3%**

Left-handers

Left **68%**

Right **19%**

Bilateral **12%**

Are your friends right-brained or left-brained (● Figure 2.29)? Before you leap to any conclusions, be aware that writing position and gestures are not foolproof. The only sure way to check brain dominance is to do medical tests that involve assessing one cerebral hemisphere at a time (Kirveskari, Salmelin, & Hari, 2006).

Causes of Handedness

Is handedness inherited from parents? Yes, at least partly. Clear hand preferences are apparent even before birth, as can be seen in a fetal ultrasound image (● Figure 2.30). According to British psychologist Peter Hepper, prenatal handedness preferences persist for at least 10 years after birth (Hepper, McCartney, & Shannon, 1998; Hepper, Wells, & Lynch, 2005). This suggests that handedness cannot be dictated. Parents should never try to force a left-handed child to use the right hand. To do so may create speech or reading problems.

Studies of twins show that hand preferences are not directly inherited like eye color or skin color (Ooki, 2005; Reiss et al., 1999). Yet, two left-handed parents are more likely to have a left-handed child than two right-handed parents are (McKeever, 2000). The best evidence to date shows that handedness is influenced by a single gene on the X (female) chromosome (Jones & Martin, 2001).

On the other hand, environmental factors such as learning, birth traumas, and social pressure to use the right hand can also affect which hand you end up favoring (Bailey & McKeever, 2004; McKeever et al., 2000). In the past, many left-handed children were forced to use their right hand for writing, eating, and other skills. This is especially true in collectivist cultures like India and Japan, where left-handedness is viewed as especially negative. Not surprisingly, the proportion of left-handers in these societies is only about half that found in individualist cultures such as the United States and Canada (Ida & Mandal, 2003).

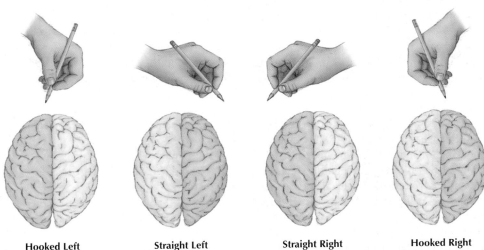

Hooked Left   Straight Left   Straight Right   Hooked Right

● **Figure 2.29** Research suggests that the hand position used in writing may indicate which brain hemisphere is used for language. (Redrawn from an illustration by M. E. Challinor.)

Advantage Right

Are there any drawbacks to being left-handed? A small minority of lefties owe their hand preference to birth traumas (such as prematurity, low birth weight, and breech birth). These individuals have higher rates of allergies, learning disorders, and other problems (Betancur et al., 1990). Similarly, people with inconsistent handedness (as opposed to consistent left-handers) may be at risk for more immune-related diseases (Bryden, Bruyn, & Fletcher, 2005).

Is it true that right-handed people live longer than left-handed people? It is true that there is a shortage of very old lefties. One possible explanation lies in the widespread finding that left-handers are more accident-prone (Dutta & Mandal, 2005). However, the supposed clumsiness of lefties may well be a result of living in

● **Figure 2.30** In this ultrasound image, a 4-month-old fetus sucks her right thumb. A study by psychologist Peter Hepper suggests that she will continue to prefer her right hand after she is born and that she will be right-handed as an adult.

a right-handed world. One study showed that left-handed locomotive engineers have higher accident rates and suggested that the cause was due to the design of locomotive controls (Bhushan & Khan, 2006). If it can be gripped, turned, or pulled, it's probably designed for the right hand. Even toilet handles are on the right side. On the other hand, the shortage of very old lefties may just reflect the fact that, in the past, more left-handed children were forced to become right-handed. That makes it look like many lefties don't survive to old age. In reality, they do, but many of them are masquerading as righties (Martin & Freitas, 2002)!

Advantage Left

Actually, there are some clear advantages to being left-handed. Throughout history a notable number of artists have been lefties, from Leonardo da Vinci and Michelangelo to Pablo Picasso and M. C. Escher. Conceivably, because the right hemisphere is superior at imagery and visual abilities, there is some advantage to using the left hand for drawing or painting (Springer & Deutsch, 1998). At the least, lefties are definitely better at visualizing three-dimensional objects. This may be why there are more left-handed architects, artists, and chess players than would be expected (Coren, 1992).

Similarly, being right-handed does not guarantee sports superiority, as you can see in ● Table 2.1.

By the way, chalk up a few more for the left-handers, who have also done well in handball (Dane & Erzurumluoglu, 2003) and professional tennis (Holtzen, 2000).

Lateralization refers to specialization in the abilities of the brain hemispheres. One striking feature of lefties is that they are gen-

Table 2.1 ● **Sports and Handedness**

Sport	Handedness Advantage
Baseball	No overall left or right advantage
Boxing	Left
Fencing	Left
Basketball	Mixed and ambidextrous
Ice hockey	Mixed and ambidextrous
Field hockey	Mixed and ambidextrous
Tennis	Strong left or strong right
Squash	Strong left or strong right
Badminton	Strong left or strong right

Adapted from Coren, 1992.

Left-handers have an advantage in sports such as fencing and boxing. Most likely, their movements are less familiar to opponents, who usually face right-handers (Coren, 1992).

erally less lateralized than the right-handed. In fact, even the physical size and shape of their cerebral hemispheres are more alike. If you are a lefty, you can take pride in the fact that your brain is less lopsided than most! In general, left-handers are more symmetrical on almost everything, including eye dominance, fingerprints—even foot size (Polemikos & Papaeliou, 2000).

In some situations, less lateralization may be a real advantage. For instance, individuals who are moderately left-handed or ambidextrous seem to have better than average pitch memory, which is a basic musical skill. Correspondingly, more musicians are ambidextrous than would normally be expected (Springer & Deutsch, 1998).

Math abilities may also benefit from fuller use of the right hemisphere. Students who are extremely gifted in math are much more likely to be left-handed or ambidextrous (Benbow, 1986). Even where ordinary arithmetic skills are concerned, lefties seem to excel (Annett, 2002; Annett & Manning, 1990).

The clearest advantage of being left-handed shows up when there is a brain injury. Because of their milder lateralization, left-handed individuals typically experience less language loss after damage to either brain hemisphere, and they recover more easily (Geschwind, 1979). Maybe having "two left feet" isn't so bad after all.

Lateralization Differences between the two sides of the body, especially differences in the abilities of the brain hemispheres.

CHAPTER 3

Human Development

Gateway Theme

The principles of development help us better understand not only children, but our own behavior as well.

Paul Kuroda/Superstock

Gateway Questions

- *How do heredity and environment affect development?*
- *What can newborn babies do?*
- *Of what significance is a child's emotional bond with adults?*
- *How important are parenting styles?*
- *How do children acquire language?*
- *How do children learn to think?*
- *Why is the transition from adolescence to adulthood especially challenging?*

- *How do we develop morals and values?*
- *What are the typical tasks and dilemmas through the life span?*
- *What is involved in well-being during later adulthood?*
- *How do people typically react to death?*
- *How do effective parents discipline and communicate with their children?*

With those words, Olivia catches her first glimpse of Samantha, her tiny newborn baby. Frankly, at the moment Samantha looks something like a prune, with pudgy arms, stubby legs, and lots of wrinkles. Yet she looks so perfect—at least in her parents' eyes. As Olivia and her husband Tom look at Samantha they wonder, "How will her life unfold? What kind of a person will she be?" "Will Samantha be a happy teenager?" "Will she marry, become a mother, find an interesting career?" Tom and Olivia can only hope that by the time Samantha is 83, she will have lived a full and satisfying life.

What if we could skip ahead through Samantha's life and observe her at various ages? What could we learn? Seeing the world through her eyes would be fascinating and instructive. For example, a child's viewpoint can make us more aware of things we take for granted. Younger children, in particular, are very literal in their use of language. When Samantha was 3, she thought her bath was too hot and said to Tom, "Make it warmer, daddy." At first, Tom was confused. The bath was already fairly hot. But then he realized that what she really meant was, "Bring the water closer to the temperature we call *warm*." It makes perfect sense if you look at it that way.

Research done by developmental psychologists tells a fascinating story about human growth and development. Let's let Olivia, Tom, and Samantha represent parents and children everywhere, as we see what psychology can tell us about the challenges of growing up, maturing, aging, and facing death. Tracing Samantha's development might even help you answer two very important questions: How did I become the person I am today? and Who will I become tomorrow?

Nature and Nurture— It Takes Two to Tango

Gateway Question: How do heredity and environment affect development?

When we think of development we naturally think of children "growing up" into adults. But even as adults we never really stop changing. **Developmental psychology,** the study of progressive changes in behavior and abilities, involves every stage of life from conception to death (or "the womb to the tomb"). Heredity and environment also affect us throughout life. Some events, such as when Samantha achieves sexual maturity, are mostly governed by heredity. Others, such as when Samantha learns to swim, read, or drive a car, are primarily a matter of environment.

But which is more important, heredity or environment? Actually, neither. Biopsychologist Donald Hebb once offered a useful analogy: To define the area of a rectangle, what is more important, height or width? Of course, both dimensions are absolutely essential. If either is reduced to zero, there is no rectangle. Similarly, if Samantha grows up to become a prominent civil rights lawyer, her success will be due to both heredity and environment.

While heredity gives each of us a variety of potentials and limitations, these are, in turn, affected by environmental influences, such as learning, nutrition, disease, and culture. Ultimately, the person you are today reflects a continuous *interaction*, or interplay, between the forces of nature and nurture (Kalat, 2007). Let's look in more detail at this dance.

Heredity

Heredity ("nature") refers to the genetic transmission of physical and psychological characteristics from parents to their children. An incredible number of personal features are set at conception, when a sperm and an ovum (egg) unite.

Identical twins. Twins who share identical genes (identical twins) demonstrate the powerful influence of heredity. Even when they are reared apart, identical twins are strikingly alike in motor skills, physical development, and appearance. At the same time, twins are less alike as adults than they were as children, which shows environmental influences are at work (Larsson, Larsson, & Lichtenstein, 2004).

Myrleen Ferguson Cate/PhotoEdit

How does heredity operate? The nucleus of every human cell contains **DNA, deoxyribonucleic acid** (dee-OX-see-RYE-bo-new-KLEE-ik). DNA is a long, ladder-like chain of pairs of chemical molecules (● Figure 3.1). The order of these molecules, or organic bases, acts as a code for genetic information. The DNA in

Developmental psychology The study of progressive changes in behavior and abilities from conception to death.

Heredity ("nature") The transmission of physical and psychological characteristics from parents to offspring through genes.

DNA Deoxyribonucleic acid, a molecular structure that contains coded genetic information.

● **Figure 3.1** *(Top left)* Linked molecules (organic bases) make up the "rungs" on DNA's twisted "molecular ladder." The order of these molecules serves as a code for genetic information. The code provides a genetic blueprint that is unique for each individual (except identical twins). The drawing shows only a small section of a DNA strand. An entire strand of DNA is composed of billions of smaller molecules. *(Bottom left)* The nucleus of each cell in the body contains chromosomes made up of tightly wound coils of DNA. (Don't be misled by the drawing: Chromosomes are microscopic, and the chemical molecules that make up DNA are even smaller.)

each cell contains a record of all the instructions needed to make a human—with room left over to spare. In 2003, a major scientific milestone was reached when the Human Genome Project completed sequencing all 3 billion chemical base pairs in human DNA (U.S. Department of Energy Office of Science, 2005).

Human DNA is organized into 46 **chromosomes.** (The word *chromosome* means "colored body.") These thread-like structures hold the coded instructions of heredity (● Figure 3.2). A notable exception is sperm cells and ova, which contain only 23 chromosomes. Thus, Samantha received 23 chromosomes from Olivia and 23 from Tom. This is her genetic heritage.

Genes are small areas of DNA that affect a particular process or personal characteristic. Sometimes, a single gene is responsible for an inherited feature, such as Samantha's eye color. Genes may be dominant or recessive. When a gene is **dominant,** the feature it controls will appear every time the gene is present. When a gene is **recessive,** it must be paired with a second recessive gene before its effect will be expressed. For example, if Samantha got a blue-eye gene from Tom and a brown-eye gene from Olivia, Samantha will be brown-eyed, because brown-eye genes are dominant.

If brown-eye genes are dominant, why do two brown-eyed parents sometimes have a blue-eyed child? If one or both parents have two brown-eye genes, the couple's children can only be brown-eyed. But what if each parent has one brown-eye gene and one blue-eye gene? In that case, both parents would have brown eyes. Yet there

is 1 chance in 4 that their children will get two blue-eye genes and have blue eyes (● Figure 3.3).

In actuality, few of our characteristics are controlled by single genes. Instead, most are **polygenic** (pol-ih-JEN-ik), or controlled by many genes working in combination. Through the expression of genes, heredity determines eye color, skin color, and susceptibility to some diseases. Also, genes can switch on (or off) at certain ages or developmental stages. In this way, heredity continues to exert a powerful influence throughout **maturation,** the physical growth and development of the body, brain, and nervous system. As the *human growth sequence* unfolds, genetic instructions influence body size and shape, height, intelligence, athletic potential, personality traits, sexual orientation, and a host of other details (Cummings, 2006) (● Table 3.1).

● **Figure 3.2** This image, made with a scanning electron microscope, shows several pairs of human chromosomes. (Colors are artificial.)

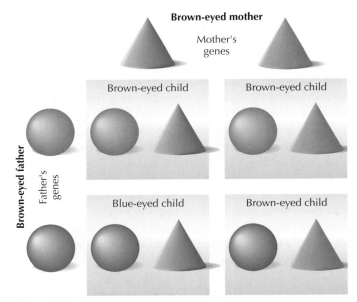

● **Figure 3.3** Gene patterns for children of brown-eyed parents, where each parent has one brown-eye gene and one blue-eye gene. Because the brown-eye gene is dominant, 1 child in 4 will be blue-eyed. Thus, there is a significant chance that two brown-eyed parents will have a blue-eyed child.

Table 3.1 ● Human Growth Sequence

Period	Duration	Descriptive Name
Prenatal period Germinal period Embryonic period Fetal period	From conception to birth First 2 weeks after conception 2–8 weeks after conception From 8 weeks after conception to birth	Zygote Embryo Fetus Neonate
Neonatal period **Infancy**	From birth to a few weeks after birth From a few weeks after birth until child is walking securely; some children walk securely at less than a year, while others may not be able to until age 17–18 months	Infant
Early childhood	From about 15–18 months until about 2–2½ years From age 2–3 to about age 6	Toddler Preschool child
Middle childhood	From about age 6 to age 12	School-age child
Pubescence **Puberty** **Adolescence**	Period of about 2 years before puberty Point of development at which biological changes of pubescence reach a climax marked by sexual maturity From the beginning of pubescence until full social maturity is reached (difficult to fix duration of this period)	Adolescent
Adulthood Young adulthood (19–25) Adulthood (26–40) Maturity (41 plus)	From adolescence to death; sometimes subdivided into other periods as shown at left	Adult
Senescence	No defined limit that would apply to all people; extremely variable; characterized by marked physiological and psychological deterioration	Adult (senile), "old age"

*Note: There is no exact beginning or ending point for various growth periods. The ages are approximate, and each period may be thought of as blending into the next.

Table courtesy of Tom Bond.

Readiness

At what ages will Samantha be ready to feed herself, to walk alone, or to say goodbye to diapers? Such milestones tend to be governed by a child's **readiness** for rapid learning. That is, minimum levels of maturation must occur before some skills can be learned. Parents are asking for failure when they try to force a child to learn skills too early (Schum et al., 2002). It is impossible, for instance, to teach children to walk or use a toilet before they have matured enough to control their bodies.

Consider the eager parents who toilet trained an 18-month-old child in 10 trying weeks of false alarms and "accidents." If they had waited until the child was 24 months old, they might have succeeded in just 3 weeks. Parents may control when toilet training starts, but maturation tends to dictate when it will be completed (Schum et al., 2002). The average age for *completed* toilet training is about 3 years (girls a little earlier, boys a little later) (Schum et al., 2001). So why fight nature? (The wet look is in.)

Environment

Our environment also exerts a profound influence on our development. **Environment ("nurture")** refers to the sum of all external conditions that affect a person. For example, the brain of a newborn baby has fewer *dendrites* (nerve cell branches) and *synapses* (connections between nerve cells) than an adult brain (● Figure 3.4). However, the newborn brain is highly *plastic* (capable of being altered by experience). During the first 3 years of life, millions of new connections form in the brain every day. At the same time, unused connections disappear. As a result, early learning environments literally shape the developing brain, through "blooming and pruning" of synapses (Nelson, 1999).

Although human culture is accelerating the rate at which human DNA is evolving, modern humans are still genetically quite similar to cave dwellers who lived 30,000 years ago (Hawks et al., 2007). Nevertheless, a bright baby born today could learn to become almost anything—a ballet dancer, an engineer, a gangsta rapper, or a biochemist who likes to paint in watercolors. But an

Chromosomes Thread-like "colored bodies" in the nucleus of each cell that are made up of DNA.

Genes Specific areas on a strand of DNA that carry hereditary information.

Dominant gene A gene whose influence will be expressed each time the gene is present.

Recessive gene A gene whose influence will be expressed only when it is paired with a second recessive gene.

Polygenic characteristics Personal traits or physical properties that are influenced by many genes working in combination.

Maturation The physical growth and development of the body and nervous system.

Readiness A condition that exists when maturation has advanced enough to allow the rapid acquisition of a particular skill.

Environment ("nurture") The sum of all external conditions affecting development, including especially the effects of learning.

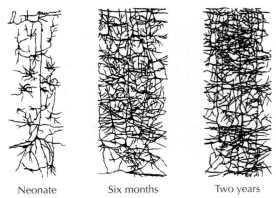

Neonate   Six months   Two years

● **Figure 3.4** A rapid increase in brain synapses continues until about age 4. At that point, children actually have more brain synapses than adults do. Then, after age 10, the number slowly declines, reaching adult levels at about age 16. (Reprinted by permission of the publisher from *The Postnatal Development of the Human Cerebral Cortex, Vols. I–III* by Jesse LeRoy Conel, Cambridge, MA: Harvard University Press, Copyright © 1939, 1975 by the President and Fellows of Harvard College.)

Upper Paleolithic baby could have only become a hunter or food gatherer.

Prenatal Influences

Environmental factors actually start influencing development before birth. Although the *intrauterine* environment (interior of the womb) is highly protected, environmental conditions can nevertheless affect the developing child. For example, when Olivia was pregnant, Samantha's fetal heart rate and movements increased when loud sounds or vibrations penetrated the womb (Kisilevsky et al., 2004).

If Olivia's health or nutrition had been poor, or if she had German measles, syphilis, or HIV; or used drugs; or was exposed to X-rays or radiation, Samantha's growth sequence might have been harmed. In such cases babies can suffer from **congenital problems,** or "birth defects." These environmental problems affect the

developing fetus and become apparent at birth. In contrast, **genetic disorders** are inherited from parents. Examples are sickle-cell anemia, hemophilia, cystic fibrosis, muscular dystrophy, albinism, and some types of mental retardation.

How is it possible for the embryo or the fetus to be harmed? No direct intermixing of blood takes place between a mother and her unborn child. Yet some substances—especially drugs—do reach the fetus. Anything capable of directly causing birth defects is called a **teratogen** (teh-RAT-uh-jen). Sometimes women are exposed to powerful teratogens, such as radiation, lead, pesticides, or polychlorinated biphenyls (PCBs), without knowing it. But pregnant women do have direct control over many teratogens. For example, a woman who takes cocaine runs a serious risk of injuring her fetus (Schuetze & Eiden, 2006). In short, when a pregnant woman takes drugs, her unborn child does too.

Unfortunately, in the United States this is one of the greatest risk factors facing unborn children (Coles & Black, 2006). If a mother is addicted to morphine, heroin, or methadone, her baby may be born with an addiction. Repeated heavy drinking during pregnancy causes *fetal alcohol syndrome (FAS).* Affected infants have low birth weight, a small head, bodily defects, and facial malformations. Many also suffer from emotional, behavioral, and mental handicaps (Golden, 2005).

Tobacco is also harmful. Smoking during pregnancy greatly reduces oxygen to the fetus. Heavy smokers risk miscarrying or having premature, underweight babies who are more likely to die soon after birth. Children of smoking mothers score lower on tests of language and mental ability (Huijbregts et al., 2006). In other words, an unborn child's future can go "up in smoke." That goes for marijuana as well (Viveros et al., 2005).

Some of the typical features of children suffering from fetal alcohol syndrome (FAS) include a small nonsymmetrical head, a short nose, a flattened area between the eyes, oddly shaped eyes, and a thin upper lip. Many of these features become less noticeable by adolescence. However, mental retardation and other problems commonly follow the FAS child into adulthood. The child shown here represents a moderate example of FAS.

Petit Format/Photo Researchers, Inc.

Because of the rapid growth of basic structures, the developing fetus is sensitive to a variety of diseases, drugs, and sources of radiation. This is especially true during the first trimester (3 months) of gestation (pregnancy).

Sensitive Periods

Early experiences can have particularly lasting effects. For example, children who are abused may suffer lifelong emotional problems (Goodwin, Fergusson, & Horwood, 2005). At the same time, extra care can sometimes reverse the effects of a poor start in life (Bornstein & Tamis-LeMonda, 2001). In short, environmental forces guide human development, for better or worse, throughout life.

Why do some experiences have more lasting effects than others? Part of the answer lies in **sensitive periods.** These are times when children are more susceptible to particular types of environmental influences. Events that occur during a sensitive period can permanently alter the course of development (Bruer, 2001). For example, forming a loving bond with a caregiver early in life seems to be crucial for optimal development. Likewise, babies who don't hear normal speech during their first year may have impaired language abilities (Thompson & Nelson, 2001).

Deprivation and Enrichment

Some environments can be described as *enriched* or *deprived.* **Deprivation** refers to a lack of normal nutrition, stimulation, comfort, or love. **Enrichment** exists when an environment is deliberately made more stimulating, loving, and so forth.

What happens when children suffer severe deprivation? Tragically, a few mistreated children have spent their first years in closets, attics, and other restricted environments. When first discovered, these children are usually mute, retarded, and emotionally damaged (Wilson, 2003). Fortunately, such extreme deprivation is unusual. Nevertheless, milder perceptual, intellectual, or emotional deprivation occurs in many families, especially those that must cope with poverty. Poverty can effect the development of children in at least two ways (Sobolewski & Amato, 2005). First, poor parents may not be able to give their children needed resources such as nutritious meals, health care, or learning materials (Bradley & Corwyn, 2002). As a result, impoverished children tend to be sick more often, their cognitive development lags, and they do poorly at school. Second, the stresses of poverty can also be hard on parents, leading to marriage problems, less positive parenting, and poorer parent-child relationships. The resulting emotional turmoil can damage a child's socioemotional development. In the extreme, it may increase the risk of mental illness and delinquent behavior (Bradley & Corwyn, 2002).

> ### bridges
> Adults experience a number of disruptive effects when they are deprived of perceptual stimulation. **See Chapter 6, page 198, for details.**

Adults who grew up in poverty often remain trapped in a vicious cycle of continued poverty. Because one in seven American families fall below the poverty line, this grim reality plays itself out in millions of American homes every day (Sobolewski & Amato, 2005).

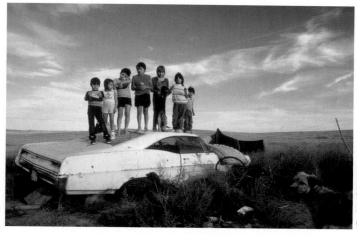

Allen Russell/Photolibrary

Children who grow up in poverty run a high risk of experiencing many forms of deprivation. There is evidence that lasting damage to social, emotional, and cognitive development occurs when children must cope with severe early deprivation.

Can an improved environment enhance development? To answer this question, psychologists have created *enriched environments* that are especially novel, complex, and stimulating. Enriched environments may be the "soil" from which brighter children grow. To illustrate, let's consider the effects of raising rats in a sort of "rat wonderland." The walls of their cages were decorated with colorful patterns, and each cage was filled with platforms, ladders, and cubbyholes. As adults, these rats were superior at learning mazes. In addition, they had larger, heavier brains, with a thicker cortex (Benloucif, Bennett, & Rosenzweig, 1995). Of course, it's a long leap from rats to people, but an actual increase in brain size is impressive. If extra stimulation can enhance the "intelligence" of a lowly rat, it's likely that human infants also benefit from enrichment. Many studies have shown that enriched environments improve abilities or enhance development. It would be wise for Tom and Olivia to make a point of nourishing Samantha's mind, as well as her body (Beeber et al., 2007).

What can parents do to enrich a child's environment? They can encourage exploration and stimulating play by paying attention to what holds the baby's interest. It is better to "child-proof" a house

Congenital problems Problems or defects that originate during prenatal development in the womb.

Genetic disorders Problems caused by defects in the genes or by inherited characteristics.

Teratogen Radiation, a drug, or other substance capable of altering fetal development in nonheritable ways that cause birth defects.

Sensitive period During development, a period of increased sensitivity to environmental influences. Also, a time during which certain events must take place for normal development to occur.

Deprivation In development, the loss or withholding of normal stimulation, nutrition, comfort, love, and so forth; a condition of lacking.

Enrichment In development, deliberately making an environment more stimulating, nutritional, comforting, loving, and so forth.

than to strictly limit what a child can touch. There is also value in actively enriching sensory experiences. Infants are not vegetables. Babies should be surrounded by colors, music, people, and things to see, taste, smell, and touch. It makes perfect sense to take them outside, to hang mobiles over their cribs, to place mirrors nearby, to play music for them, or to rearrange their rooms now and then. Children progress most rapidly when they have responsive parents and stimulating play materials at home (Beeber et al., 2007). In light of this, it is wise to view all of childhood as a *relatively sensitive period* (Nelson, 1999).

Reaction Range

One way to visualize the interplay of heredity and environment is through the concept of **reaction range,** the limits that one's environment places on the effects of heredity (● Figure 3.5). Let's suppose that Samantha was born with genes for a normal level of musical ability. If Samantha grows up in a musically deprived environment, she might well end up with lower than average adult musical ability. If Olivia and Tom provide her with an enriched environment, she will probably have normal, or even above normal, musical ability. While Samantha might not be genetically capable of becoming a child prodigy, the environment her parents provide for her will also determine her developmental path.

Reciprocal Influences

Nurture often affects the expression of hereditary tendencies through ongoing reciprocal influences. A good example of such influences is the fact that growing infants influence their parents' behavior at the same time they are changed by it.

Newborn babies differ noticeably in **temperament.** This is the inherited, physical core of personality. It includes sensitivity, irritability, distractibility, and typical mood (Kagan, 2004). About 40 percent of all newborns are *easy children* who are relaxed and agreeable. Ten percent are *difficult children* who are moody, intense, and easily angered. *Slow-to-warm-up children* (about 15 percent) are restrained, unexpressive, or shy. The remaining children do not fit neatly into a single category (Chess & Thomas, 1986).

Because of differences in temperament, some babies are more likely than others to smile, cry, vocalize, reach out, or pay attention. As a result, babies rapidly become active participants in their own development. For example, Samantha is an easy baby who smiles frequently and is easily fed. This encourages Olivia to touch, feed, and sing to Samantha. Olivia's affection rewards Samantha, causing her to smile more. Soon, a dynamic relationship blossoms between mother and child. Similarly, good parenting can reciprocally influence a very shy child who, in turn, becomes progressively less shy.

The reverse also occurs: Difficult children make parents unhappy and elicit more negative parenting (Parke, 2004). Alternately, negative parenting can turn a moderately shy child into a very shy one. This suggests that inherited temperaments are dynamically modified by learning (Kagan, 2005).

A person's **developmental level** is his or her current state of physical, emotional, and intellectual development. To summarize, three factors combine to determine your developmental level at any stage of life. These are *heredity, environment,* and your *own behavior,* each tightly interwoven with the others.

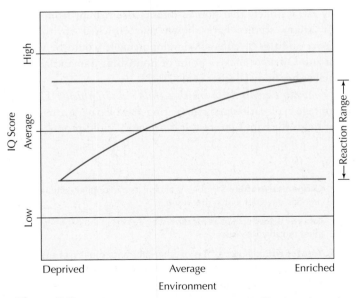

● **Figure 3.5** The effect of heredity on the development of human traits, such as intelligence, can often be influenced by environmental circumstances. A child with average genes for intelligence growing up in an average environment might have an average IQ score as an adult. However, growing up in a deprived environment might result in a somewhat lower IQ score and growing up in an enriched environment might result in a somewhat higher IQ score. In this way, the environment sets a range within which our hereditary potential is actually expressed. This range is called the *reaction range.*

KNOWLEDGE BUILDER
The Interplay of Heredity and Environment

RECITE

1. Areas of the DNA molecule called genes are made up of dominant and recessive chromosomes. T or F?
2. Most inherited characteristics can be described as polygenic. T or F?
3. If one parent has a one dominant brown-eye gene and one recessive blue-eye gene and the other parent has two dominant brown-eye genes, what is the chance that their child will have blue eyes?
   a. 25 percent
   b. 50 percent
   c. 0 percent
   d. 75 percent
4. The orderly sequence observed in the unfolding of many basic responses can be attributed to _____.
5. "Slow-to-warm-up" children can be described as restrained, unexpressive, or shy. T or F?
6. A _____ _____ is a time of increased sensitivity to environmental influences.
7. As a child develops there is a continuous _____ between the forces of heredity and environment.

REFLECT

Critical Thinking

8. Environmental influences can interact with hereditary programming in an exceedingly direct way. Can you guess what it is? *Continued*

The Newborn—More Than Meets the Eye

Gateway Question: What can newborn babies do?

At birth the human *neonate* (NEE-oh-NATE: newborn infant) will die if not cared for by adults. Newborn babies cannot lift their heads, turn over, or feed themselves. Does this mean they are inert and unfeeling? Definitely not! Contrary to common belief, newborn babies are not oblivious to their surroundings. Infants have mental capacities that continue to surprise researchers and delight parents. The emergence of many of these capacities, as well as a baby's physical abilities, is closely related to maturation of the brain, nervous system, and body. Likewise, a baby's early emotional life unfolds on a timetable that is largely controlled by maturation.

Neonates like Samantha can see, hear, smell, taste, and respond to pain and touch. Although their senses are less acute, babies are very responsive. Samantha will follow a moving object with her eyes and will turn in the direction of sounds.

Samantha also has a number of adaptive infant reflexes (Siegler, DeLoache, & Eisenberg, 2006). To elicit the *grasping reflex,* press an object in the neonate's palm and she will grasp it with surprising strength. Many infants, in fact, can hang from a raised bar, like little trapeze artists. The grasping reflex aids survival by helping infants

Newborn babies display a special interest in the human face. A preference for seeing their mother's face develops rapidly and encourages social interactions between mother and baby.

avoid falling. You can observe the *rooting reflex* (reflexive head turning and nursing) by touching Samantha's cheek. Immediately, she will turn toward your finger, as if searching for something.

How is such turning adaptive? The rooting reflex helps infants find a bottle or a breast. Then, when a nipple touches the infant's mouth, the *sucking reflex* (rhythmic nursing) helps her obtain needed food. Like other reflexes, this is a genetically programmed action. At the same time, food rewards nursing. Because of this, babies quickly learn to nurse more actively. Again, we see how the interplay of nature and nurture alters a baby's behavior.

The *Moro reflex* is also interesting. If Samantha's position is changed abruptly or if she is startled by a loud noise, she will make a hugging motion. This reaction has been compared to the movements baby monkeys use to cling to their mothers. (We leave it to the reader's imagination to decide if there is any connection.)

Perceptual and Cognitive Development

Thirty years ago, many people thought of newborn babies as mere bundles of reflexes, like the ones just described. But infants are capable of much more. For example, psychologist Andrew Meltzoff has found that babies are born mimics (Meltzoff, 2005). ● Figure 3.6 shows Meltzoff as he sticks out his tongue, opens his mouth, and purses his lips at a 20-day-old girl. Will she imitate him? Videotapes of babies confirm that they imitate adult facial gestures. As early as 9 months of age, infants can imitate actions a day after seeing them (Heimann & Meltzoff, 1996). Such mimicry obviously aids rapid learning in infancy.

How intelligent are neonates? Babies are smarter than many people think. From the earliest days of life, babies are learning how the world works. They immediately begin to look, touch, taste, and otherwise explore their surroundings. From an evolutionary perspective, a baby's mind is designed to soak up information, which it does at an amazing pace (Meltzoff & Prinz, 2002).

In the first months of life, babies are increasingly able to think, to learn from what they see, to make predictions, and to search for explanations. For example, Jerome Bruner (1983) observed that 3- to 8-week-old babies seem to understand that a person's voice and body should be connected. If a baby hears his mother's voice coming from where she is standing, the baby will remain calm. If her voice comes from a loudspeaker several feet away, the baby will become agitated and begin to cry.

Another look into the private world of infants can be drawn from testing their vision. However, such testing is a challenge because infants cannot talk. Robert Fantz invented a device called a *looking chamber* to find out what infants can see and what holds their attention (● Figure 3.7a). Imagine that Samantha is placed

Reaction range The limits environment places on the effects of heredity.

Temperament The physical core of personality, including emotional and perceptual sensitivity, energy levels, typical mood, and so forth.

Developmental level An individual's current state of physical, emotional, and intellectual development.

● **Figure 3.6** Infant imitation. In the top row of photos, Andrew Meltzoff makes facial gestures at an infant. The bottom row records the infant's responses. Videotapes of Meltzoff and of tested infants helped ensure objectivity.

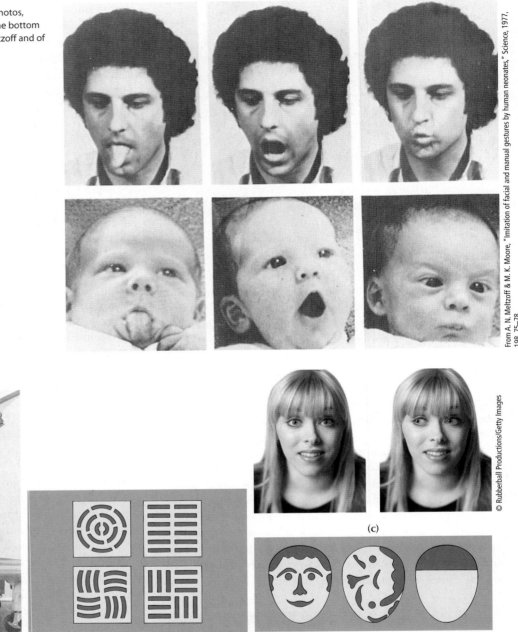

From A. N. Meltzoff & M. K. Moore, "Imitation of facial and manual gestures by human neonates," Science, 1977, 198, 75–78.

© Rubberball Productions/Getty Images

(a) (b) (c) (d)

● **Figure 3.7** (a) Eye movements and fixation points of infants are observed in Fantz's "looking chamber." (b) Thirteen-week-old infants prefer concentric and curved patterns like those on the left to nonconcentric and straight-line patterns like those on the right. (c) When they are just days old, infants pay more attention to the faces of people who are gazing directly at them. (d) Infants look at normal faces longer than at scrambled faces and at both faces longer than designs, like the one on the right. (Photo a courtesy of David Linton. Drawing from "The Origin of Form Perception" by Robert L. Fantz, Copyright © 1961 by Scientific American, Inc. All rights reserved.)

on her back inside the chamber, facing a lighted area above. Next, two objects are placed in the chamber. By observing the movements of Samantha's eyes and the images they reflect, we can tell what she is looking at. Such tests show that adult vision is about 30 times sharper, but babies can see large patterns, shapes, and edges.

Fantz found that 3-day-old babies prefer complex patterns, such as checkerboards and bull's-eyes, to simpler colored rectangles. Other researchers have learned that infants are excited by circles, curves, and bright lights (● Figure 3.7b) (Brown, 1990). Immediately after birth, Samantha will be aware of changes in the position

of objects (Slater et al., 1991). When she is 6 months old, she will be able to recognize categories of objects that differ in shape or color. By 9 months of age she will be able to tell the difference between dogs and birds or other groups of animals (Mandler & McDonough, 1998). By 1 year of age, she will see as well as her parents (Sigelman & Rider, 2006). So, there really is a person inside that little body!

Neonates can most clearly see objects about a foot away from them. It is as if they are best prepared to see the people who love and care for them (Gopnik, Meltzoff, & Kuhl, 2000). Perhaps that's why babies have a special fascination with human faces. Just

1. Fetal posture
(newborn)

2. Holds chin up
(1 month)

3. Holds chest up
(2 months)

4. Sits when supported
(4 months)

5. Sits alone
(7 months)

6. Stands holding furniture
(9 months)

7. Crawls
(10 months)

8. Walks if led
(11 months)

9. Stands alone
(11 months)

10. Walks alone
(12 months)

● **Figure 3.8** Motor development. Most infants follow an orderly pattern of motor development. Although the order in which children progress is similar, there are large individual differences in the ages at which each ability appears. The ages listed are averages for American children. It is not unusual for many of the skills to appear 1 or 2 months earlier than average or several months later (Harris & Liebert, 1991). Parents should not be alarmed if a child's behavior differs some from the average.

hours after they are born, babies begin to prefer seeing their mother's face, rather than a stranger's (Walton, Bower, & Bower, 1992). When babies are only 2 to 5 days old, they will pay more attention to a person who is gazing directly at them, rather than one who is looking away (Farroni et al., 2004) (● Figure 3.7*c*).

In a looking chamber, most infants will spend more time looking at a human face pattern than a scrambled face or a colored oval (● Figure 3.7*d*). When real human faces are used, infants prefer familiar faces to unfamiliar faces. However, this reverses at about age 2. At that time, unusual objects begin to interest the child. For instance, in a classic study Jerome Kagan (1971) showed face masks to 2-year-olds. Kagan found that the toddlers were fascinated by a face with eyes on the chin and a nose in the middle of the forehead. He believes the babies' interest came from a need to understand why the scrambled face differed from what they had come to expect. Such behavior is further evidence that babies actively try to make sense of their surroundings (Gopnik, Meltzoff, & Kuhl, 2000).

Motor Development

As we noted previously, the emergence of many basic abilities is closely tied to *maturation*, which will be evident, for example, as Samantha learns motor skills, such as crawling and walking. Of course, the *rate* of maturation varies from child to child. Nevertheless, the *order* of maturation is almost universal. For instance, Samantha will be able to sit without support from Tom before she has matured enough to crawl. Indeed, infants around the world typically sit before they crawl, crawl before they stand, and stand before they walk (● Figure 3.8).

What about my weird cousin Emo who never crawled? Like cousin Emo, a few children substitute rolling, creeping, or shuffling for

crawling. A very few move directly from sitting to standing and walking. Even so, their motor development is orderly. In general, muscular control spreads in a pattern that is *cephalocaudal* (SEF-eh-lo-KOD-ul: from head to toe) and *proximodistal* (PROK-seh-moe-DIS-tul: from the center of the body to the extremities). Even if cousin Emo flunked Elementary Crawling, his motor development followed the standard top-down, center-outward pattern (Piek, 2006).

Although maturation has a big impact, motor skills don't simply "emerge." Samantha must learn to control her actions. When babies are beginning to crawl or walk, they actively try new movements and select those that work. Samantha's first efforts may be flawed—a wobbly crawl or some shaky first steps. However, with practice, babies "tune" their movements to be smoother and more effective. Such learning is evident from the very first months of life (Piek, 2006; Thelen, 2000; ● Figure 3.9).

Emotional Development

Early emotional development also follows a pattern closely tied to maturation (Panksepp & Pasqualini, 2005). Even the basic emotions of *anger, fear,* and *joy*—which appear to be unlearned—take time to develop. General *excitement* is the only emotion newborn infants clearly express. However, as Tom and Olivia can tell you, a baby's emotional life blossoms rapidly. One researcher (Bridges, 1932) observed that all the basic human emotions appear before age 2. Bridges found that emotions appear in a consistent order and that the first basic split is between pleasant and unpleasant emotions (● Figure 3.10).

Experts do not yet agree on how quickly emotions unfold (Oster, 2005). For example, psychologist Carroll Izard thinks that infants can express several basic emotions as early as 10 weeks of

• **Figure 3.9** Psychologist Carolyn Rovee-Collier has shown that babies as young as 3 months old can learn to control their movements. In her experiments, babies lie on their backs under a colorful crib mobile. A ribbon is tied around the baby's ankle and connected to the mobile. Whenever babies spontaneously kick their legs, the mobile jiggles and rattles. Within a few minutes, infants learn to kick faster. Their reward for kicking is a chance to see the mobile move (Hayne & Rovee-Collier, 1995).

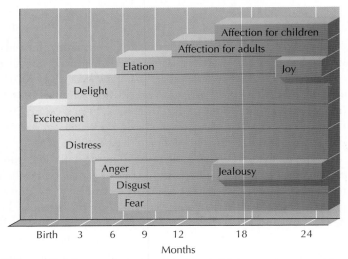

• **Figure 3.10** The traditional view of infancy holds that emotions are rapidly differentiated from an initial capacity for excitement. (After K. M. B. Bridges, 1932. Reprinted by permission of the Society for Research in Child Development, Inc.)

• **Figure 3.11** Infants display many of the same emotional expressions as adults do. Carroll Izard believes such expressions show that distinct emotions appear within the first months of life. Other theorists argue that specific emotions come into focus more gradually, as an infant's nervous system matures. Either way, parents can expect to see a full range of basic emotions by the end of a baby's first year.

age. When Izard looks carefully at the faces of babies, he sees abundant signs of emotion (• Figure 3.11). The most common infant expression, he found, is not excitement, but *interest*—followed by *joy, anger,* and *sadness* (Izard et al., 1995).

If Izard is right, then emotions are "hardwired" by heredity and related to evolution. Perhaps that's why smiling is one of a baby's most common reactions. Smiling probably helps babies survive by inviting parents to care for them (Izard et al., 1995).

At first, a baby's smiling is haphazard. By the age of 8 to 12 months, however, infants smile more frequently when another person is nearby (Jones & Hong, 2001). This **social smile** is especially rewarding to parents. Infants can even use their social smile to communicate inter-

est in an object, like the time Samantha smiled when her mother held up her favorite teddy bear (Venezia et al., 2004). On the other hand, when new parents see and hear a crying baby, they feel annoyed, irritated, disturbed, or unhappy. Babies the world over, it seems, rapidly become capable of letting others know what they like and dislike. (Prove this to yourself sometime by driving a baby buggy.)

With dazzling speed, human infants are transformed from helpless babies to independent persons. By her third year, Samantha will have a unique personality and she will be able to stand, walk, talk, and explore. At no other time after birth does development proceed more rapidly. During the same period, Samantha's relationships with other people will expand as well. Before we explore that topic, here's a chance to review what you've learned.

KNOWLEDGE BUILDER
The Neonate and Early Maturation
RECITE
1. If an infant is startled, he or she will make movements similar to an embrace. This is known as the
   a. grasping reflex
   b. rooting reflex
   c. Moro reflex
   d. adaptive reflex
2. During infancy, a capacity for imitating others first becomes evident at about 9 months of age. T or F?

Continued

3. After age 2, infants tested in a looking chamber show a marked preference for familiar faces and simpler designs. T or F?

4. General excitement or interest is the clearest emotional response present in newborn infants, but meaningful expressions of delight and distress appear soon after. T or F?

5. Neonates display a social smile as early as 10 days after birth. T or F?

REFLECT

Critical Thinking

6. If you were going to test newborn infants to see if they prefer their own mother's face to that of a stranger, what precautions would you take?

Relate

What infant reflexes have you observed? Can you give an example of how heredity and environment interact during motor development?

To know what a baby is feeling would it be more helpful to be able to detect delight and distress (Bridges) or joy, anger, and sadness (Izard)?

Answers: 1. c 2. F 3. F 4. T 5. F 6. In one study of the preferences of newborns, the hair color and complexion of strangers was matched to that of the mothers. Also, only the mother's or stranger's face was visible during testing. And finally, a scent was used to mask olfactory (smell) cues so that an infant's preference could not be based on the mother's familiar odor (Bushnell, Sai, & Mullin, 1989).

●● Social Development— Baby, I'm Stuck on You

Gateway Question: Of what significance is a child's emotional bond with adults?

Infants begin to develop self-awareness and to become aware of others at about the same time they first form an emotional bond with an adult. Each of these developments is an important step toward entering the social world. Parents are the most important influences in early social development. Later, playing with other children begins to extend a child's social life beyond the family.

Like all humans, babies are social creatures. Their early **social development** lays a foundation for relationships with parents, siblings, friends, and relatives. A first basic step into the social world

Ursula Markus/Photo Researchers, Inc.

A sense of self, or self-awareness, develops at about age 18 months. Before children develop self-awareness, they do not recognize their own image in a mirror. Typically, they think they are looking at another child. Some children hug the child in the mirror or go behind it looking for the child they see there (Lewis, 1995).

involves becoming aware of oneself as a person. When you look in a mirror, you recognize the image staring back as your own—except, perhaps, early on Monday mornings. Like many such events, initial self-awareness depends on maturation of the nervous system. In a typical test of self-recognition, infants are shown images of themselves on a TV. Most infants have to be 18 months old before they recognize themselves (Nielsen & Dissanayake, 2004).

Attachment

The real core of social development is found in the **emotional attachment,** or close emotional bond, that babies form with their primary caregivers. To investigate mother–infant relationships, Harry Harlow separated baby rhesus monkeys from their mothers at birth. The real mothers were replaced with **surrogate** (substitute) **mothers.** Some were made of cold, unyielding wire. Others were covered with soft terry cloth (● Figure 3.12).

When the infants were given a choice between the two mothers, they spent most of their time clinging to the cuddly terry-cloth mother. This was true even when the wire mother held a bottle, making her the source of food. The "love" and attachment displayed toward the cloth replicas was identical to that shown toward natural mothers. For example, when frightened by rubber snakes, wind-up toys, and other "fear stimuli," the infant monkeys ran to their cloth mothers and clung to them for security. These classic studies suggest that attachment begins with **contact comfort,** the pleasant, reassuring feeling infants get from touching something soft and warm, especially their mother.

● **Figure 3.12** An infant monkey clings to a cloth-covered surrogate mother. Baby monkeys become attached to the cloth "contact-comfort" mother but not to a similar wire mother. This is true even when the wire mother provides food. Contact comfort may also underlie the tendency of children to become attached to inanimate objects, such as blankets or stuffed toys. However, a study of 2- to 3-year-old blanket-attached children found that they were no more insecure than others (Passum, 1987). (So maybe Linus is okay after all.)

Harry Harlow, U. of WI Primate Laboratory

Social smile Smiling elicited by social stimuli, such as seeing a parent's face.

Social development The development of self-awareness, attachment to parents or caregivers, and relationships with other children and adults.

Emotional attachment An especially close emotional bond that infants form with their parents, caregivers, or others.

Surrogate mothers A substitute mother (often an inanimate dummy in animal research).

Contact comfort A pleasant and reassuring feeling human and animal infants get from touching or clinging to something soft and warm, usually their mother.

Most parents are familiar with the storm of crying that sometimes occurs when babies are left alone at bedtime. Bedtime distress can be a mild form of separation anxiety. As many parents know, it is often eased by the presence of "security objects," such as a stuffed animal or favorite blanket (Donate-Bartfield & Passman, 2004).

Michael Newman/PhotoEdit

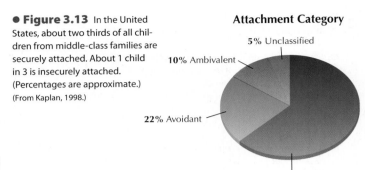

● **Figure 3.13** In the United States, about two thirds of all children from middle-class families are securely attached. About 1 child in 3 is insecurely attached. (Percentages are approximate.) (From Kaplan, 1998.)

Attachment Category

5% Unclassified
10% Ambivalent
22% Avoidant
63% Secure

There is a sensitive period (roughly the first year of life) during which attachment must occur for optimal development. Mothers usually begin to feel attached to their baby before birth. For their part, as babies mature, they become more and more capable of bonding with their mothers. For the first few months, babies respond more or less equally to everyone. By 2 or 3 months, most babies prefer their mothers to strangers. By around 7 months, babies generally become truly attached to their mothers, crawling after her if they can. Shortly thereafter they also begin to form attachments to other people as well, such as father, grandparents, or siblings (Sigelman & Rider, 2006). Returning to Samantha's story, we find that attachment keeps her close to Olivia, who provides safety, stimulation, and a secure "home base" from which Samantha can go exploring.

A direct sign that an emotional bond has formed appears around 8 to 12 months of age. At that time Samantha will display **separation anxiety** (crying and signs of fear) when she is left alone or with a stranger. Mild separation anxiety is normal. When it is more intense, it may reveal a problem. At some point in their lives, about 1 in 20 children suffer from *separation anxiety disorder* (Dick-Niederhauser & Silverman, 2006). These children are miserable when they are separated from their parents, whom they cling to or constantly follow. Some fear that they will get lost and never see their parents again. Many refuse to go to school, which can be a serious handicap. Children tend to grow out of the disorder (Kearney et al., 2003), but if separation anxiety is intense or lasts for more than a month, parents should seek professional help for their child (Masi, Mucci, & Millepiedi, 2001).

Attachment Quality

According to psychologist Mary Ainsworth (1913–1999), the quality of attachment is revealed by how babies act when their mothers return after a brief separation. Infants who are **securely attached** have a stable and positive emotional bond. They are upset by the mother's absence and seek to be near her when she returns. **Insecure-avoidant** infants have an anxious emotional bond. They tend to turn away from the mother when she returns. **Insecure-ambivalent** attachment is also an anxious emotional bond. In this case, babies have mixed feelings: They both seek to be near the returning mother and angrily resist contact with her (● Figure 3.13).

Attachment can have lasting effects. Infants who are securely attached at the age of 1 year show more resiliency, curiosity, problem-solving ability, and social skill in preschool (Collins & Gunnar, 1990). In contrast, attachment failures can be quite damaging. Consider, for example, the plight of children raised in severely overcrowded Romanian orphanages (Wilson, 2003). These children got almost no attention from adults for the first year or two of their lives. Some have now been adopted by American and Canadian families, but many are poorly attached to their new parents. Some, for instance, will wander off with strangers; they are anxious and remote, and they don't like to be touched or make eye contact with others (O'Conner et al., 2003). In short, for some children, a lack of affectionate care early in life leaves a lasting emotional impact well into adulthood. (See "What's Your Attachment Style?")

Promoting Secure Attachment

The key to secure attachment is a mother who is accepting and sensitive to her baby's signals and rhythms. Poor attachment occurs when a mother's actions are inappropriate, inadequate, intrusive, overstimulating, or rejecting. An example is the mother who tries to play with a drowsy infant or who ignores a baby who is looking at her and vocalizing. The link between sensitive caregiving and secure attachment appears to apply to all cultures (Posada et al., 2002).

What about attachment to fathers? Fathers of securely attached infants tend to be outgoing, agreeable, and happy in their marriage. In general, a warm family atmosphere—one that includes sensitive mothering *and* fathering—produces secure children (Belsky, 1996; Gomez & McLaren, 2007).

Day Care

Does commercial day care interfere with the quality of attachment? It depends on the quality of day care. Overall, *high-quality* day care does not adversely affect attachment to parents (National Institute of Child Health and Human Development, 1999). In fact, high-quality day care can actually improve children's social and mental skills (Mercer, 2006). Children in high-quality day care tend to have better relationships with their mothers and fewer behavior problems. They also have better cognitive skills and language abilities (Burchinal et al., 2000; Vandell, 2004).

However, all the positive effects just noted are *reversed* for low-quality day care. Low-quality day care *is* risky and it *may* weaken

DISCOVERING PSYCHOLOGY

What's Your Attachment Style?

Do our first attachments continue to affect us as adults? Some psychologists believe they do, by influencing how we relate to friends and lovers (Bridges, 2003; Sroufe et al., 2005). Read the following statements and see which best describes your adult relationships.

SECURE ATTACHMENT STYLE

In general, I think most other people are well intentioned and trustworthy.

I find it relatively easy to get close to others.

I am comfortable relying on others and having others depend on me.

I don't worry much about being abandoned by others.

I am comfortable when other people want to get close to me emotionally.

AVOIDANT ATTACHMENT STYLE

I tend to pull back when things don't go well in a relationship.

I am somewhat skeptical about the idea of true love.

I have difficulty trusting my partner in a romantic relationship.

Other people tend to be too eager to seek commitment from me.

I get a little nervous if anyone gets too close emotionally.

AMBIVALENT ATTACHMENT STYLE

I have often felt misunderstood and unappreciated in my romantic relationships.

My friends and lovers have been somewhat unreliable.

I love my romantic partner but I worry that she or he doesn't really love me.

I would like to be closer to my romantic partner, but I'm not sure I trust her or him.

Do any of the preceding statements sound familiar? If so, they may describe your adult attachment style. Most adults have a secure attachment style that is marked by caring, supportiveness, and understanding. However, it's not unusual to have an avoidant attachment style that reflects a tendency to resist intimacy and commitment to others (Collins et al., 2002). An ambivalent attachment style is marked by mixed feelings about love and friendship (Tidwell, Reis, & Shaver, 1996). Do you see any similarities between your present relationships and your attachment experiences as a child?

---

attachment. Poor-quality day care can even create behavior problems that didn't exist beforehand (Pierrehumbert et al., 2002). Parents are wise to carefully evaluate and monitor the quality of day care their children receive.

What should parents look for when they evaluate the quality of child care? Parents seeking quality should insist on *at least* the following: a small number of children per caregiver; small overall group size (12 to 15); trained caregivers; minimal staff turnover; and stable, consistent care (Howes, 1997). (Also, avoid any child-care center with the words *zoo, menagerie,* or *stockade* in its name.)

Attachment and Affectional Needs

A baby's **affectional needs** (needs for love and affection) are every bit as important as more obvious needs for food, water, and physical care. All things considered, creating a bond of trust and affection between the infant and at least one other person is a key event during the first year of life. Parents are sometimes afraid of "spoiling" babies with too much attention, but for the first year or two this is nearly impossible. In fact, a later capacity to experience warm and loving relationships may depend on it.

●● Parental Influences— Life with Mom and Dad

Gateway Question: How important are parenting styles?

From the first few years of life, when caregivers are the center of a child's world, through to adulthood, the style and quality of mothering and fathering are very important.

Parenting Styles

Psychologist Diana Baumrind (1991, 2005) has studied the effects of three major **parental styles,** which are identifiable patterns of parental caretaking and interaction with children. See if you recognize the styles she describes.

Authoritarian parents enforce rigid rules and demand strict obedience to authority. Typically they view children as having few rights but adult-like responsibilities. The child is expected to stay out of trouble and to accept, without question, what parents regard as right or wrong. ("Do it because I say so.") The children of authoritarian parents are usually obedient and self-controlled. But they also tend to be emotionally stiff, withdrawn, apprehensive, and lacking in curiosity.

Separation anxiety Distress displayed by infants when they are separated from their parents or principal caregivers.

Secure attachment A stable and positive emotional bond.

Insecure-avoidant attachment An anxious emotional bond marked by a tendency to avoid reunion with a parent or caregiver.

Insecure-ambivalent attachment An anxious emotional bond marked by both a desire to be with a parent or caregiver and some resistance to being reunited.

Affectional needs Emotional needs for love and affection.

Parental styles Identifiable patterns of parental caretaking and interaction with children.

Authoritarian parents Parents who enforce rigid rules and demand strict obedience to authority.

Overly permissive parents give little guidance, allow too much freedom, or don't hold children accountable for their actions. Typically, the child has rights similar to an adult's but few responsibilities. Rules are not enforced, and the child usually gets his or her way. ("Do whatever you want.") Permissive parents tend to produce dependent, immature children who misbehave frequently. Such children are aimless and likely to "run amok."

Baumrind describes **authoritative parents** as those who supply firm and consistent guidance, combined with love and affection. Such parents balance their own rights with those of their children. They control their children's behavior in a caring, responsive, non-authoritarian way. ("Do it for this reason.") Effective parents are firm and consistent, not harsh or rigid. In general, they encourage the child to act responsibly, to think, and to make good decisions. This style produces children who are *resilient* (good at bouncing back after bad experiences) and develop the strengths they need to thrive even in difficult circumstances (Kim-Cohen et al., 2004; Masten, 2001). The children of authoritative parents are competent, self-controlled, independent, assertive, and inquiring. They know how to manage their emotions and use positive coping skills (Eisenberg et al., 2003; Lynch et al., 2004). To read more about effective parenting, see this chapter's Psychology in Action section.

Maternal and Paternal Influences

Don't mothers and fathers parent differently? Yes. Although **maternal influences** (all the effects a mother has on her child) generally have a greater impact, fathers do make a unique contribution to parenting (Santrock, 2007). Although fathers are spending more time with their children, mothers still do most of the nurturing and caretaking, especially of young children (Craig, 2006).

Studies of **paternal influences** (the sum of all effects a father has on his child) reveal that fathers are more likely to play with their children and tell them stories. In contrast, mothers are typically responsible for the physical and emotional care of their children (● Figure 3.14).

It might seem that the father's role as a playmate makes him less important. Not so. Samantha's playtime with Tom is actually very valuable. From birth onward, fathers pay more visual attention to children than mothers do. Fathers are much more tactile (lifting, tickling, and handling the baby), more physically arousing (engaging in rough-and-tumble play), and more likely to engage in unusual play (imitating the baby, for example) (Crawley & Sherrod, 1984; Paquette et al., 2003). In comparison, mothers speak to infants more, play more conventional games (such as peekaboo), and, as noted, spend much more time in caregiving. Young children who spend a lot of time playing with their fathers tend to be more competent in many ways (Tamis-LeMonda et al., 2004).

Overall, fathers can be as affectionate, sensitive, and responsive as mothers are. Nevertheless, infants and children tend to get very different views of males and females. Females, who offer comfort, nurturance, and verbal stimulation, tend to be close at hand. Males come and go, and when they are present, action, exploration, and risk-taking prevail. It's no wonder, then, that the parental styles of mothers and fathers have a major impact on children's gender role development (Lindsay, Mize, & Pettit, 1997; Videon, 2005).

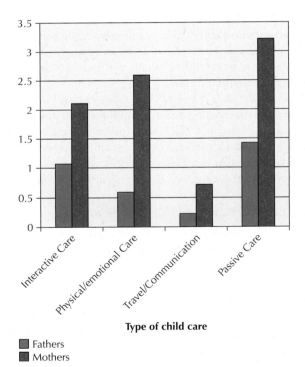

Type of child care

■ Fathers
■ Mothers

● **Figure 3.14** Mother-child and father-child interactions. This graph shows what occurred on routine days in a sample of more than 1,400 Australian homes. Mothers spend about twice as long each day on child care, compared with fathers. Further, mothers spend more time on physical and emotional care (such as feeding, bathing, soothing) than on interactive care (such as playing, reading, activities); fathers show the reverse pattern. Finally, mothers spend more time on travel (for instance, driving children to sports or music lessons), communication (such as talking to teachers about their children), and passive care (supervising children while they play). (Adapted from Craig, 2006.)

Fathering typically makes a contribution to early development that differs in emphasis from mothering.

Ethnic Differences: Four Flavors of Parenting

Do ethnic differences in parenting affect children in distinctive ways? Diana Baumrind's work provides a good overall summary of the effects of parenting. However, her conclusions are probably most valid for families whose roots lie in Europe. Child rearing in other ethnic groups often reflects different customs and beliefs. Cultural differences are especially apparent with respect to the meaning attached to a child's behavior. Is a particular behavior "good" or "bad"? Should it be encouraged or discouraged? The answer will depend greatly on parents' cultural values (Leyendecker et al., 2005).

Making generalizations about groups of people is always risky. Nevertheless, some typical differences in child-rearing patterns have been observed in North American ethnic communities (Kaplan, 1998; Parke, 2004).

African-American Families

Traditional African-American values emphasize loyalty and interdependence among family members, security, developing a positive identity, and not giving up in the face of adversity. African-American parents typically stress obedience and respect for elders (Dixon, Graber, & Brooks-Gunn, 2008). Child discipline tends to be fairly strict (Parke, 2004), but many African-American parents see this as a necessity, especially if they live in urban areas where safety is a concern. Self-reliance, resourcefulness, and an ability to take care of oneself in difficult situations are also qualities that African-American parents seek to promote in their children.

Hispanic Families

Like African-American parents, Hispanic parents tend to have relatively strict standards of discipline (Dixon, Graber, & Brooks-Gunn, 2008). They also place a high value on family values, family pride, and loyalty. Hispanic families are typically affectionate and indulgent toward younger children. However, as children grow older, they are expected to learn social skills and to be calm, obedient, courteous, and respectful. In fact, such social skills may be valued more than cognitive skills (Delgado & Ford, 1998). In addition, Hispanic parents tend to stress cooperation more than competition. Such values can put Hispanic children at a disadvantage in highly competitive, European-American culture.

Asian-American Families

Asian cultures tend to be group oriented, and they emphasize interdependence among individuals. In contrast, Western cultures value individual effort and independence. This difference is often reflected in Asian-American child-rearing practices (Chao & Tseng, 2002). Asian-American children are taught that their behavior can bring either pride or shame to the family. Therefore, they are obliged to set aside their own desires when the greater good of the family is at stake (Parke, 2004). Parents tend to act as teachers who encourage hard work, moral behavior, and achievement. For the first few years, parenting is lenient and permissive. However, after about age 5, Asian-American parents begin to expect respect, obedience, self-control, and self-discipline from their children.

Arab-American Families

In Middle Eastern cultures, children are expected to be polite, obedient, disciplined, and conforming. Punishment generally consists of spankings, teasing, or shaming in front of others. Arab-American fathers tend to be strong authority figures who demand obedience so that the family will not be shamed by a child's bad behavior. Success, generosity, and hospitality are highly valued in Arab-American culture. The pursuit of family honor encourages hard work, thrift, conservatism, and educational achievement. The welfare of the family is emphasized over individual identity. Thus, Arab-American children are raised to respect their parents, members of their extended family, and other adults as well (Erickson & Al-Timimi, 2001; Medhus, 2001).

Steven J. Gold

In other ethnic communities, norms for effective parenting often differ in subtle ways from parenting styles in Euro-American culture.

Overly permissive parents Parents who give little guidance, allow too much freedom, or do not require the child to take responsibility.

Authoritative parents Parents who supply firm and consistent guidance combined with love and affection.

Maternal influences The aggregate of all psychological effects mothers have on their children.

Paternal influences The aggregate of all psychological effects fathers have on their children.

Implications

Child rearing is done in a remarkable variety of ways around the world. In fact, many of the things we do in North America, such as forcing young children to sleep alone, would be considered odd or wrong in other cultures. In the final analysis, parenting can only be judged if we know what culture or ethnic community a child is being prepared to enter (Leyendecker et al., 2005).

KNOWLEDGE BUILDER
Social Development in Childhood

RECITE

1. Clear signs of self-awareness or self-recognition are evident in most infants by the time they reach 8 months of age. T or F?
2. The development of separation anxiety in an infant corresponds to the formation of an attachment to parents. T or F?
3. High-quality day care can actually improve children's social and mental skills. T or F?
4. Fathers are more likely to act as playmates for their children, rather than caregivers. T or F?
5. According to Diana Baumrind's research, effective parents are authoritarian in their approach to their children's behavior. T or F?
6. Asian-American parents tend to be more individually oriented than parents whose ethnic roots are European. T or F?

REFLECT

Critical Thinking

7. Can you think of another way to tell if infants have self-awareness?
8. Can emotional bonding begin before birth?

Relate

Do you think that your experiences as a child, such as your early attachment pattern, really affect your life as an adult? Can you think of any examples from your own life?

Do you know any parents who have young children and who are authoritarian, permissive, or authoritative? What are their children like?

Do you think parenting depends on ethnicity? If so, why? If not, why not?

emotionally attached to the unborn child (Santrock, 2007).
doctor's office or see an ultrasound image of the fetus begin to become of her. Likewise, prospective parents who hear a fetal heartbeat at the fetal movements, she becomes aware that a baby is coming to life inside **8.** It certainly can for parents. When a pregnant woman begins to feel ability that a child will do so jumps dramatically during the second year. showing recognition of the mirror image as his or her own? The prob- in front of a mirror. The question is, Will the child touch the red spot, secretly rub a spot of rouge on an infant's nose. The child is then placed **Answers: 1.** F **2.** T **3.** T **4.** T **5.** F **6.** F **7.** Another successful method is to

---

Language Development— Fast-Talking Babies

Gateway Question: How do children acquire language?

There's something almost miraculous about a baby's first words. As infants, how did we manage to leap into the world of language? Even a quick survey like this one reveals that both maturation (nature) and social development (nurture) provide a foundation for language learning. Let's begin with a quick survey of language development.

Language development is closely tied to maturation (Carroll, 2008; Gleason, 2005). As every parent knows, babies can cry from birth on. By 1 month of age they use crying to gain attention. Typically, parents can tell if an infant is hungry, angry, or in pain from the tone of the crying (Kaplan, 1998). Around 6 to 8 weeks of age, babies begin *cooing* (the repetition of vowel sounds such as "oo" and "ah").

By 7 months of age, Samantha's nervous system will mature enough to allow her to grasp objects, smile, laugh, sit up, and *babble*. In the babbling stage, the consonants *b, d, m,* and *g* are combined with the vowel sounds to produce meaningless language sounds: *dadadadada* or *bababa*. At first, babbling is the same around the world. But soon, the language spoken by parents begins to have an influence. That is, Japanese babies start to babble in a way that sounds like Japanese, Mexican babies babble in Spanish-like sounds, and so forth (Gopnik, Meltzoff, & Kuhl, 2000; Kuhl, 2004).

At about 1 year of age, children respond to real words such as *no* or *hi*. Soon afterward, the first connection between words and objects forms, and children may address their parents as "Mama" or "Dada." By age 18 months to 2 years, Samantha's vocabulary may include a hundred words or more. At first there is a *single-word stage,* during which children use one word at a time, such as "go," "juice," or "up." Soon after, words are arranged in simple two-word sentences called *telegraphic speech:* "Want-Teddy," "Mama-gone."

Language and the Terrible Twos

At about the same time that children begin to put two or three words together they become much more independent. Two-year-olds understand some of the commands parents make, but they are not always willing to carry them out. A child like Samantha may assert her independence by saying "No drink," "Me do it," "My cup, my cup," and the like. It can be worse, of course. A 2-year-old may look at you intently, make eye contact, listen as you shout "No, no," and still pour her juice on the cat.

During their second year, children become increasingly capable of mischief and temper tantrums. Thus, calling this time "the terrible twos" is not entirely inappropriate. One-year-olds can do plenty of things parents don't want them to do. However, it's usually 2-year-olds who do things *because* you don't want them to (Gopnik, Meltzoff, & Kuhl, 2000). Perhaps parents can take some comfort in knowing that a stubborn, negative 2-year-old is simply becoming more independent. When Samantha is 2, Olivia and Tom would be wise to remember that "this, too, shall pass."

After age 2, the child's comprehension and use of words takes a dramatic leap forward. From this point on, vocabulary and language skills grow at a phenomenal rate (Fernald, Perfors, & Marchman, 2006). By first grade, Samantha will be able to understand around 8,000 words and use about 4,000. She will have truly entered the world of language.

| 85 | 50 | 20 |
| Medium high positive | Neutral attention | Avert |

● **Figure 3.15** Infant engagement scale. These samples from a 90-point scale show various levels of infant engagement, or attention. Babies participate in prelanguage "conversations" with parents by giving and withholding attention and by smiling, gazing, or vocalizing. (From Beebe et al., 1982.)

The Roots of Language

What accounts for this explosion of language development? Linguist Noam Chomsky (1975, 1986) has long claimed that humans have a **biological predisposition** or hereditary readiness to develop language. According to Chomsky, language patterns are inborn, much like a child's ability to coordinate walking. If such inborn language recognition does exist, it may explain why children around the world use a limited number of patterns in their first sentences. Typical patterns include (Mussen et al., 1979):

Identification:	"See kitty."
Nonexistence:	"Allgone milk."
Possession:	"My doll."
Agent-Action:	"Mama give."
Negation:	"Not ball."
Question:	"Where doggie?"

Does Chomsky's theory explain why language develops so rapidly? It is certainly part of the story. But many psychologists feel that Chomsky underestimates the importance of learning (Tomasello, 2003) and the social contexts that shape language development (Hoff, 2006). *Psycholinguists* (specialists in the psychology of language) have shown that imitation of adults and rewards for correctly using words (as when a child asks for a cookie) are an important part of language learning. Also, babies actively participate in language learning by asking questions, such as "What dis?" (Domingo & Goldstein-Alpern, 1999).

When a child makes a language error, parents typically repeat the child's sentence with needed corrections (Bohannon & Stanowicz, 1988; Hoff, 2006) or ask a clarifying question to draw the child's attention to the error (Saxton, Houston-Price, & Dawson, 2005). More important is the fact that parents and children begin

to communicate long before the child can speak. A readiness to interact *socially* with parents may be as important as innate language recognition. The next section explains why.

Early Communication

How do parents communicate with infants before they can talk? Parents go to a great deal of trouble to get babies to smile and vocalize (● Figure 3.15). In doing so, they quickly learn to change their actions to keep the infant's attention, arousal, and activity at optimal levels. A familiar example is the "I'm-Going-to-Get-You Game." In it, the adult says, "I'm gonna getcha . . . . I'm gonna getcha . . . . I'm gonna getcha . . . . Gotcha!" Through such games, adults and babies come to share similar rhythms and expectations (Carroll, 2008). Soon a system of shared **signals** is created, including touching, vocalizing, gazing, and smiling. These help lay a foundation for later language use (Tamis-LeMonda, Bornstein, & Baumwell, 2001). Specifically, signals establish a pattern of "conversational" *turn-taking* (alternate sending and receiving of messages).

Olivia	*Samantha*
	(smiles)
"Oh what a nice little smile!"	
"Yes, isn't that nice?"	
"There."	
"There's a nice little smile."	(burps)
"Well, pardon you!"	
"Yes, that's better, isn't it?"	
"Yes."	(vocalizes)
"Yes."	(smiles)
"What's so funny?"	

Biological predisposition The presumed hereditary readiness of humans to learn certain skills, such as how to use language, or a readiness to behave in particular ways.

Signal In early language development, any behavior, such as touching, vocalizing, gazing, or smiling, that allows nonverbal interaction and turn-taking between parent and child.

From the outside, such exchanges may look meaningless. In reality, they represent real communication. Samantha's vocalizations and attention provide a way of interacting emotionally with Olivia and Tom. Infants as young as 4 months engage in vocal turn-taking with adults (Jaffe et al., 2001). The more children interact with parents, the faster they learn to talk and the faster they learn thinking abilities (Dickinson & Tabors, 2001; Hoff & Tian, 2005). One study found that 6-week-old babies gaze at an adult's face in rhythm with the adult's speech (Crown et al., 2002). Unmistakably, social relationships contribute to early language learning (Hoff, 2006).

Parentese

When they talk to infants, parents use an exaggerated pattern of speaking called **motherese** or **parentese.** Typically, they raise their tone of voice; use short, simple sentences; repeat themselves more; and use frequent gestures (Gogate, Bahrick, & Watson, 2000). They also slow their rate of speaking and use exaggerated voice inflections: "Did Samantha eat it A-L-L UP?"

What is the purpose of such changes? Parents are apparently trying to help their children learn language (Soderstrom, 2007). When a baby is still babbling, parents tend to use long, adult-style sentences. But as soon as the baby says its first word they switch to parentese. By the time babies are 4 months old they prefer parentese over normal speech (Cooper et al., 1997).

In addition to being simpler, parentese has a distinct "musical" quality (Trainor & Desjardins, 2002). No matter what language mothers speak, the melodies, pauses, and inflections they use to comfort, praise, or give warning are universal. Psychologist Anne

As with motherese, parents use a distinctive style when singing to an infant. Even people who speak another language can tell if a tape-recorded song was sung to an infant or an adult. Likewise, lullabies remain recognizable when electronic filtering removes words (Trehub et al., 1993a, 1993b).

Fernald has found that mothers of all nations talk to their babies with similar changes in pitch. For instance, we praise babies with a rising, then falling pitch ("BRA-vo!" "GOOD girl!"). Warnings are delivered in a short, sharp rhythm ("Nein! Nein!" "Basta! Basta!" "Not! Dude!"). To give comfort, parents use low, smooth, drawn-out tones ("Oooh poor baaa-by," "Oooh pobrecito"). A high-pitched, rising melody is used to call attention to objects ("See the pretty BIRDIE?") (Fernald, 1989).

Parentese helps parents get babies' attention, communicate with them, and teach them language (Thiessen, Hill, & Saffran, 2005). Later, as a child's speaking improves, parents tend to adjust their speech to the child's language ability. Especially from 18 months to 4 years of age, parents seek to clarify what a child says and prompt the child to say more.

In summary, some elements of language are innate. Nevertheless, our inherited tendency to learn language does not determine if we will speak English or Vietnamese, Spanish or Russian. Environmental forces also influence whether a person develops simple or sophisticated language skills. The first 7 years of life are a sensitive period in language learning (Eliot, 1999). Clearly, a full flowering of speech requires careful cultivation.

KNOWLEDGE BUILDER
Language Development in Childhood

RECITE

1. The development of speech and language usually occurs in which order?
   a. crying, cooing, babbling, telegraphic speech
   b. cooing, crying, babbling, telegraphic speech
   c. babbling, crying, cooing, telegraphic speech
   d. crying, babbling, cooing, identification
2. Simple two-word sentences are characteristic of _____ _____ speech.
3. Noam _____ has advanced the idea that language acquisition is built on innate patterns.
4. Prelanguage turn-taking and social interactions would be of special interest to a psycholinguist. T or F?
5. The style of speaking known as _____ is higher in pitch and has a musical quality.

REFLECT

Critical Thinking

6. The children of professional parents hear more words per hour than the children of welfare parents, and they also tend to score higher on tests of mental abilities. How else could their higher scores be explained?

Relate

In order, see if you can name and imitate the language abilities you had as you progressed from birth to age 2 years. Now see if you can label and imitate some basic elements of parentese.

In your own words, state at least one argument for and against Chomsky's view of language acquisition.

You are going to spend a day with a person who speaks a different language than you do. Do you think you would be able to communicate with the other person? How does this relate to language acquisition?

Answers: 1. a **2.** telegraphic **3.** Chomsky **4.** T **5.** Parentese or motherese **6.** Children in professional homes receive many educational benefits that are less common in welfare homes. Yet, even when such differences are taken into account, brighter children tend to come from richer language environments (Hart & Risley, 1999).

Cognitive Development— Think Like a Child

Gateway Question: How do children learn to think?

Now that we have Samantha talking, let's move on to a broader view of intellectual development. Jean Piaget (Jahn pea-ah-ZHAY) provided some of the first great insights into how children develop thinking abilities when he proposed that children's cognitive skills progress through a series of maturational stages. Also, many psychologists have become interested in how children learn the intellectual skills valued by their culture. Typically, children do this with guidance from skilled "tutors" (parents and others).

How different is a child's understanding of the world from that of an adult? According to the Swiss psychologist and philosopher Jean Piaget (1951, 1952), their thinking is, generally speaking, less abstract. They tend to base their understanding on particular examples and objects they can see or touch. Also, children use fewer generalizations, categories, and principles.

Piaget's Theory of Cognitive Development

Jean Piaget believed that all children mature through a series of distinct stages in intellectual development. Many of his ideas came from observing his own children as they solved various thought problems. (It is tempting to imagine that Piaget's illustrious career was launched one day when his wife said to him, "Watch the children for a while, will you, Jean?")

Mental Processes

Piaget was convinced that intellect grows through processes he called assimilation and accommodation. **Assimilation** refers to using existing mental patterns in new situations. Let's say that Benjamin pounds on blocks with his favorite toy, a plastic hammer. For his birthday Benjamin gets an oversized toy wrench. If he uses the wrench for pounding, it has been assimilated to an existing knowledge structure.

In **accommodation,** existing ideas are modified to fit new requirements. For instance, a younger child might think that a dime is worth less than a (larger) nickel. However, as children begin to spend money, they must alter their ideas about what "more" and "less" mean. Thus, new situations are assimilated to existing ideas, and new ideas are created to accommodate new experiences.

Piaget's ideas have deeply affected our view of children (Feldman, 2004). The following is a brief summary of what he found.

The Sensorimotor Stage (0–2 Years)

Look up from this book until your attention is attracted to something else in the room. Now close your

Jean Piaget—philosopher, psychologist, and keen observer of children.

Farrell Grehan/Corbis

eyes. Is it still there? How do you know? As an adult, you can keep an image of the object in your "mind's eye." According to Piaget, newborn babies cannot create *internal representations* such as mental images. As a result, they lack **object permanence,** an understanding that objects continue to exist when they are out of sight.

bridges

Concepts and language are other types of internal representation. **See Chapter 9, page 284, for more information.**

For this reason, in the first 2 years of life, Samantha's intellectual development will be largely nonintellectual and nonverbal. She will be mainly concerned with learning to coordinate information from her senses with her motor movements. But sometime during their first year, babies begin to actively pursue disappearing objects. By age 2, they can anticipate the movement of an object behind a screen. For example, when watching an electric train, Samantha will look ahead to the end of a tunnel, rather than staring at the spot where the train disappeared.

In general, developments in this stage indicate that the child's conceptions are becoming more *stable*. Objects cease to appear and disappear magically, and a more orderly and predictable world replaces the confusing and disconnected sensations of infancy.

The Preoperational Stage (2–7 Years)

Close your eyes again. Imagine the room you sleep in. What would it look like if you were perched on the ceiling? You have now mentally *transformed* your image of the room. According to Piaget, even though preoperational children can form mental images or ideas, they cannot easily **transform** those images or ideas in their minds.

Motherese (or parentese) A pattern of speech used when talking to infants, marked by a higher-pitched voice; short, simple sentences; repetition, slower speech; and exaggerated voice inflections.

Assimilation In Piaget's theory, the application of existing mental patterns to new situations (that is, the new situation is assimilated to existing mental schemes).

Accommodation In Piaget's theory, the modification of existing mental patterns to fit new demands (that is, mental schemes are changed to accommodate new information or experiences).

Sensorimotor stage Stage of intellectual development during which sensory input and motor responses become coordinated.

Object permanence Concept, gained in infancy, that objects continue to exist even when they are hidden from view.

Preoperational stage Period of intellectual development during which children begin to use language and think symbolically, yet remain intuitive and egocentric in their thought.

Transformation The ability to mentally change the shape or form of a mental image or idea.

Before the age of 6 or 7, children begin to think *symbolically* and use language. But the child's thinking is still very concrete and **intuitive** (it makes little use of reasoning and logic). (Do you remember thinking as a child that the sun and the moon followed you when you took a walk?).

Let's visit Samantha at age 5: If you show her a short, wide glass full of milk and a taller, narrow glass (also full), she will most likely tell you that the taller glass contains more milk (even if it doesn't). Samantha will tell you this even if she watches you pour milk from the short glass into an empty, tall glass. Older children can easily mentally *reverse* the pouring of the milk to see that the shape of container is irrelevant to the volume of milk it contains. But Samantha is preoperational; she cannot engage in the mental operation of transforming the tall glass of milk back into a short, wide glass. Thus, she is not bothered by the fact that the milk appears to be transformed from a smaller to a larger amount. Instead, she responds only to the fact that *taller* seems to mean *more* (● Figure 3.16).

After about age 7, children are no longer fooled by this situation. Perhaps that's why 7 has been called the "age of reason." From age 7 on, we see a definite trend toward more logical, adult-like thought (Flavell, 1992).

During the preoperational stage, the child is also quite **egocentric** (unable to take the viewpoint of other people). The child's ego seems to stand at the center of his or her world. To illustrate, show Samantha a two-sided mirror. Then hold it between you and her, so she can see herself in it. If you ask her what she thinks *you* can see, she imagines that you see *her* face reflected in the mirror, instead of your own. She cannot mentally transform the view she sees into the view you must be seeing.

Crossing a busy street can be dangerous for the preoperational child. Because their thinking is still egocentric, younger children cannot understand why the driver of a car can't see them if they can see the car. Children under the age of 7 also cannot consistently judge speeds and distances of oncoming cars. Adults can easily overestimate the "street smarts" of younger children. It is advisable to teach children to cross with a light, in crosswalks, or with assistance.

Such egocentrism explains why children can seem exasperatingly selfish or uncooperative at times. If Benjamin blocks your view by standing in front of the TV, he assumes that you can see it if he can. If you ask him to move so you can see better, he may move so that he can see better! Benjamin is not being selfish in the ordinary sense. He just doesn't realize that your view differs from his.

In addition, the child's use of language is not as sophisticated as it might seem. Children have a tendency to confuse words with the objects they represent. If Benjamin calls a toy block a "car" and you use it to make a "house," he may be upset. To children, the name of an object is as much a part of the object as its size, shape, and color. This seems to underlie a preoccupation with name-calling. To the preoperational child, insulting words may really hurt. Samantha was once angered by her older brother. Searching for a way to retaliate against her larger and stronger foe, she settled on, "You panty-girdle!" It was the worst thing she could think of saying.

The Concrete Operational Stage (7–11 Years)

The hallmark of this stage is the ability to carry out mental operations such as *reversing* thoughts. A 4-year-old boy in the preoperational stage might have a conversation like this (showing what happens when a child's thinking *lacks* reversibility):

> *"Do you have a brother?"*
> *"Yes."*
> *"What's his name?"*
> *"Sam."*
> *"Does Sam have a brother?"*
> *"No."*

Reversibility of thought allows children in the concrete operational stage to recognize that if $4 \times 2 = 8$, then 2×4 does, too. Younger children must memorize each relationship separately.

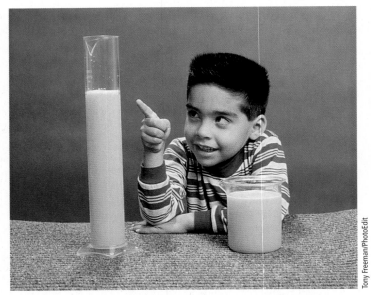

● **Figure 3.16** Children under age 7 intuitively assume that a volume of liquid increases when it is poured from a short, wide container into a taller, thinner one. This boy thinks the tall container holds more than the short one. Actually each holds the same amount of liquid. Children make such judgments based on the height of the liquid, not its volume.

Thus, a preoperational child may know that $4 \times 9 = 36$, without being able to tell you what 9×4 equals.

The development of mental operations allows mastery of **conservation** (the concept that mass, weight, and volume remain unchanged when the shape of objects changes). Children have learned conservation when they understand that rolling a ball of clay into a "snake" does not increase the amount of clay. Likewise, pouring liquid from a tall, narrow glass into a shallow dish does not reduce the amount of liquid. In each case the volume remains the same despite changes in shape or appearance. The original amount is *conserved*. (See ● Figure 3.16.)

During the concrete operational stage, children begin to use concepts of time, space, and number. The child can think logically about very concrete objects or situations, categories, and principles. Such abilities help explain why children stop believing in Santa Claus when they reach this stage. Because they can conserve volume, they realize that Santa's sack couldn't possibly hold enough toys for millions of girls and boys.

The Formal Operations Stage (11 Years and Up)

After about the age of 11, children begin to break away from concrete objects and specific examples. Thinking is based more on abstract principles, such as "democracy," "honor," or "correlation." Children who reach this stage can think about their own thoughts, and they become less egocentric. Older children and young adolescents also gradually become able to consider hypothetical possibilities (suppositions, guesses, or projections). For example, if you ask a younger child, "What do you think would happen if it suddenly became possible for people to fly?" the child might respond, "People can't fly." Older children are better able to consider such possibilities.

Full adult intellectual ability is attained during the stage of formal operations. Older adolescents are capable of inductive and deductive reasoning, and they can comprehend math, physics, philosophy, psychology, and other abstract systems. They can learn to test hypotheses in a scientific manner. Of course, not everyone reaches this level of thinking. Also, many adults can think formally about some topics, but their thinking becomes concrete when the topic is unfamiliar. This implies that formal thinking may be more a result of culture and learning than maturation. In any case, after late adolescence, improvements in intellect are based on gaining specific knowledge, experience, and wisdom, rather than on any leaps in basic thinking capacity.

How can parents apply Piaget's ideas? Piaget's theory suggests that the ideal way to guide intellectual development is to provide experiences that are only slightly novel, unusual, or challenging. Remember, a child's intellect develops mainly through accommodation. It is usually best to follow a *one-step-ahead strategy,* in which your teaching efforts are aimed just beyond a child's current level of comprehension (Brainerd, 2003).

Parents should avoid *forced teaching,* or "hothousing," which is like trying to force plants to bloom prematurely. Forcing children to learn reading, math, gymnastics, swimming, or music at an accelerated pace can bore or oppress them. True intellectual enrichment respects the child's interests. It does not make the child feel pressured to perform (Alvino et al., 1996).

For your convenience, ● Table 3.2 briefly summarizes each Piagetian stage. To help you remember Piaget's theory, the table describes what would happen at each stage if we played a game of Monopoly with the child. You'll also find brief suggestions about how to relate to children in each stage.

Piaget Today

Piaget's theory is a valuable "road map" for understanding how children think. However, many psychologists are convinced that Piaget gave too little credit to the effects of the learning environment. For example, children who grow up in villages where pottery is made can correctly answer questions about the conservation of clay at an earlier age than Piaget would have predicted.

According to learning theorists, children continuously gain specific knowledge; they do not undergo stage-like leaps in general mental ability (Siegler, 2004). On the other hand, the growth in

"Young man, go to your room and stay there until your cerebral cortex matures."

Intuitive thought Thinking that makes little or no use of reasoning and logic.

Egocentric thought Thought that is self-centered and fails to consider the viewpoints of others.

Concrete operational stage Period of intellectual development during which children become able to use the concepts of time, space, volume, and number, but in ways that remain simplified and concrete, rather than abstract.

Conservation In Piaget's theory, mastery of the concept that the weight, mass, and volume of matter remains unchanged (is conserved) even when the shape or appearance of objects changes.

Formal operations stage Period of intellectual development characterized by thinking that includes abstract, theoretical, and hypothetical ideas.

Table 3.2 ● **Piaget—A Guide for Parents**

Piaget	Monopoly Game	Guidelines for Parents
Sensorimotor Stage (0–2 Years) The stage during which sensory input and motor responses become coordinated.	The child puts houses, hotels, and dice in her mouth and plays with "Chance" cards.	Active play with a child is most effective at this stage. Encourage explorations in touching, smelling, and manipulating objects. Peekaboo is a good way to establish the permanence of objects.
Preoperational Stage (2–7 Years) The period of cognitive development when children begin to use language and think symbolically, yet remain intuitive and egocentric.	The child plays Monopoly, but makes up her own rules and cannot understand instructions.	Specific examples and touching or seeing things continues to be more useful than verbal explanations. Learning the concept of conservation may be aided by demonstrations with liquids, beads, clay, and other substances.
Concrete Operational Stage (7–11 Years) The period of cognitive development during which children begin to use concepts of time, space, volume, and number, but in ways that remain simplified and concrete.	The child understands basic instructions and will play by the rules but is not capable of hypothetical transactions dealing with mortgages, loans, and special pacts with other players.	Children are beginning to use generalizations, but they still require specific examples to grasp many ideas. Expect a degree of inconsistency in the child's ability to apply concepts of time, space, quantity, and volume to new situations.
Formal Operations Stage (11 Years and Up) The period of intellectual development marked by a capacity for abstract, theoretical, and hypothetical thinking.	The child no longer plays the game mechanically; complex and hypothetical transactions unique to each game are now possible.	It is now more effective to explain things verbally or symbolically and to help children master general rules and principles. Encourage the child to create hypotheses and to imagine how things could be.

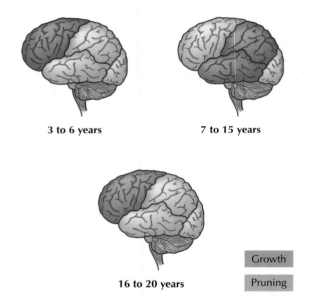

3 to 6 years   7 to 15 years

16 to 20 years

Growth

Pruning

● **Figure 3.17** Between the ages of 3 and 6 a tremendous wave of growth occurs in connections among neurons in the frontal areas of the brain. This corresponds to the time when children make rapid progress in their ability to think symbolically. Between ages 7 and 15, peak synaptic growth shifts to the temporal and parietal lobes. During this period children become increasingly adept at using language, a specialty of the temporal lobes. In the late teens, the brain actively destroys unneeded connections, especially in the frontal lobes. This pruning of synapses sharpens the brain's capacity for abstract thinking (Restak, 2001).

connections between brain cells occurs in waves that parallel some of Piaget's stages (● Figure 3.17). Thus, the truth may lie somewhere between Piaget's stage theory and modern learning theory.

On a broad scale, many of Piaget's *observations* have held up well. However, his *explanations* of childhood thinking abilities continue to be debated (Feldman, 2004). Where early infancy is concerned, even Piaget's observations may need updating. It looks like Piaget greatly underestimated the mental abilities of infants.

Infant Cognition

What evidence is there that Piaget underestimated infant abilities? Piaget believed that infants under the age of 1 year cannot think (use internal representations). Babies, he said, can have no memory of people and objects that are out of sight. Yet, we now know that infants begin forming representations of the world very early in life. For example, babies as young as 3 months of age appear to know that objects are solid and do not disappear when out of view (Baillargeon, 2004).

Why did Piaget fail to detect the thinking skills of infants? Most likely, he mistook babies' limited *physical* skills for *mental* incompetence. Piaget's tests required babies to search for objects or reach out and touch them. Newer, more sensitive methods are uncovering abilities Piaget missed. One such method takes advantage of the fact that babies, like adults, act surprised when they see something "impossible" or unexpected occur. To use this effect, psychologist Renee Baillargeon (1991, 2004) puts on little "magic shows" for infants. In her "theater," babies watch as possible and impossible events occur with toys or other objects. Some 3-month-old infants act surprised and gaze longer at impossible events. An example is seeing two solid objects appear to pass through each other. By the time they are 8 months old, babies can remember where objects are (or should be) for at least 1 minute (● Figure 3.18).

Piaget believed that abilities like those described in ● Figure 3.18 emerge only after a long period of sensorimotor development. How-

● **Figure 3.18** The panels on the left show a possible event, in which an infant watches as a toy is placed behind the right of two screens. After a delay of 70 seconds, the toy is brought into view from behind the right screen. In the two panels on the right, an impossible event occurs. The toy is placed behind the left screen and retrieved from behind the right. (A duplicate toy was hidden there before testing.) Eight-month-old infants react with surprise when they see the impossible event staged for them. Their reaction implies that they remember where the toy was hidden. Infants appear to have a capacity for memory and thinking that greatly exceeds what Piaget claimed is possible during the sensorimotor period. (Adapted from Baillargeon et al., 1989.)

ever, it's clear that babies quickly acquire the capacity to form concepts about the world (Eimas, Quinn, & Cowan, 1994). It looks as if further study is likely to refine and amend the ideas that grew from Piaget's fateful decision to "watch the children for a while."

Another criticism of Piaget is that he underestimated the impact of culture on mental development. The next section tells how Samantha will master the intellectual tools valued by her culture.

Vygotsky's Sociocultural Theory

While Piaget stressed the role of maturation in cognitive development, Russian scholar Lev Vygotsky (1896–1934) focused on the impact of sociocultural factors. Vygotsky's key insight is that children's thinking develops through dialogues with more capable persons (Vygotsky, 1962, 1978).

How does that relate to intellectual growth? So far, no one has ever published *A Child's Guide to Life on Earth*. Instead, children must learn about life from various "tutors," such as parents, teachers, and older siblings. Even if *A Child's Guide to Life on Earth* did exist, we would need a separate version for every culture. It is not enough for children to learn how to think. They must also learn specific intellectual skills valued by their culture.

Like Piaget, Vygotsky believed that children actively seek to discover new principles. However, Vygotsky emphasized that many of a child's most important "discoveries" are guided by skillful tutors. Psychologist David Shaffer (2002) offers the following example:

Annie, a 4-year-old, has just received her first jigsaw puzzle as a birthday present. She attempts to work the puzzle but gets nowhere until her father comes along, sits down beside her, and gives her some tips. He suggests that it would be a good idea to put together the corners first, points to the pink area at the edge of one corner piece and says, "Let's look for another pink piece." When Annie seems frustrated, he places two inter-

locking pieces near each other so that she will notice them, and when Annie succeeds, he offers words of encouragement. As Annie gradually gets the hang of it, he steps back and lets her work more and more independently. (p. 260)

Interactions like this are most helpful when they take place within a child's **zone of proximal development.**

What did Vygotsky mean by that? The word *proximal* means close or nearby. Vygotsky realized that, at any given time, some tasks are just beyond a child's reach. The child is close to having the mental skills needed to do the task, but it is a little too complex to be mastered alone. However, children working within this zone can make rapid progress if they receive sensitive guidance from a skilled partner (LeBlanc & Bearison, 2004). (Notice that this is similar to the one-step-ahead strategy described earlier.)

Vygotsky also emphasized a process he called **scaffolding.** A scaffold is a framework or temporary support. Vygotsky believed that adults help children learn how to think by "scaffolding," or supporting, their attempts to solve problems or discover principles (Daniels, 2005). To be most effective, scaffolding must be responsive to a child's needs. For example, as Annie's father helped her with the puzzle, he tailored his hints and guidance to match her evolving abilities. The two of them worked together, step by step, so that Annie could better understand how to assemble a puzzle. In a sense, Annie's father set up a series of temporary bridges that helped her move into new mental territory. As predicted by Vygotsky's theory, the reading skills of 8- to 10-year-old children

Zone of proximal development Refers to the range of tasks a child cannot yet master alone, but that she or he can accomplish with the guidance of a more capable partner.

Scaffolding The process of adjusting instruction so that it is responsive to a beginner's behavior and supports the beginner's efforts to understand a problem or gain a mental skill.

are closely related to the amount of verbal scaffolding their mothers provided at ages 3 and 4 (Dieterich et al., 2006).

During their collaborations with others, children learn important cultural beliefs and values. For example, imagine that a boy wants to know how many baseball cards he has. His mother helps him stack and count the cards, moving each card to a new stack as they count it. She then shows him how to write the number on a slip of paper so he can remember it. This teaches the child not only about counting, but also that writing is valued in our culture. In other parts of the world, a child learning to count might be shown how to make notches on a stick or tie knots in a cord.

Implications

Vygotsky saw that grown-ups play a crucial role in what children know. As they try to decipher the world, children rely on adults to help them understand how things work. Vygotsky further noticed that adults unconsciously adjust their behavior to give children the information they need to solve problems that interest the child. In this way, children use adults to learn about their culture and society (Gopnik, Meltzoff, & Kuhl, 2000; LeBlanc & Bearison, 2004).

KNOWLEDGE BUILDER
Cognitive Development in Childhood

RECITE
Match each item with one of the following stages.

A. Sensorimotor B. Preoperational C. Concrete operational D. Formal operations

1. _____ egocentric thought
2. _____ abstract or hypothetical
3. _____ purposeful movement
4. _____ intuitive thought
5. _____ conservation
6. _____ reversibility thought
7. _____ object permanence
8. _____ nonverbal development

9. *Assimilation* refers to applying existing thought patterns or knowledge to new situations. T or F?
10. Newer methods for testing infant thinking abilities frequently make note of whether an infant is _____ by seemingly _____ events.
11. Vygotsky called the process of providing a temporary framework of supports for learning new mental abilities _____ _____.

REFLECT

Critical Thinking
12. Using Piaget's theory as a guide, at what age would you expect a child to recognize that a Styrofoam cup has weight?

Relate
You are going to make cookies with children of various ages. See if you can name each of Piaget's stages and give an example of what a child in that stage might be expected to do.

You have been asked to help a child learn to use a pocket calculator to do simple addition. How would you go about identifying the child's zone of proximal development for this task? How would you scaffold the child's learning?

Answers: 1. B 2. D 3. A 4. B 5. C 6. C 7. A 8. A 9. T 10. surprised, impossible 11. scaffolding 12. Seventy-five percent of 4- to 6-year-olds say that a Styrofoam cup has no weight after lifting it! Most children judge weight intuitively (by the way an object feels) until they begin to move into the concrete operational stage (Smith, Carey, & Wiser, 1985).

⬤⬤ Adolescence and Young Adulthood— The Best of Times, the Worst of Times

Gateway Question: Why is the transition from adolescence to adulthood especially challenging?

Adolescence and young adulthood is a time of change, youthful exploration, and exuberance. It can also be a time of worry and problems, especially in today's world. It might even be fair to describe this period as "the best of times, the worst of times." During adolescence, a person's identity and moral values come into sharper focus even as the transition to adulthood is occurring at ever-later ages.

Adolescence is the culturally defined period between childhood and adulthood. Socially, the adolescent is no longer a child, yet not quite an adult. Almost all cultures recognize this transitional status. However, the length of adolescence varies greatly from culture to culture. For example, most 14-year-old girls in North America live at home and go to school. In contrast, many 14-year-old females in rural villages of many poorer countries are married and have children. In our culture, 14-year-olds are adolescents. In others, they may be adults.

Is marriage the primary criterion for adult status in North America? No, it's not even one of the top three criteria. Today, the most widely accepted standards are (1) taking responsibility for oneself, (2) making independent decisions, and (3) becoming financially independent. In practice, this typically means breaking away from parents by taking a job and setting up a separate residence (Arnett, 2001).

Puberty

Many people confuse adolescence with puberty. However, puberty is a *biological* event, not a social status. During **puberty,** hormonal changes promote rapid physical growth and sexual maturity. Biologically, most people reach reproductive maturity in the early teens. Social and intellectual maturity, however, may lie years ahead. Young adolescents often make decisions that affect their entire lives, even though they are immature mentally and socially. The tragically high rates of teenage pregnancy and drug abuse are prime examples. Despite such risks, most people do manage to weather adolescence without developing any serious psychological problems (Steinberg, 2001).

How much difference does the timing of puberty make? For boys, maturing early is generally beneficial. Typically, it enhances their self-image and gives them an advantage socially and athletically. Early-maturing boys tend to be more relaxed, dominant, self-assured, and popular. However, early puberty does carry some risks because early-maturing boys are also more likely to get into trouble with drugs, alcohol, and antisocial behavior (Steinberg, 2001).

For girls, the advantages of early maturation are less clear-cut. In elementary school, fast-maturing girls are *less* popular and have poorer self-images, perhaps because they are larger and heavier than their classmates (Deardorff et al., 2007). By junior high, how-

HUMAN DIVERSITY

Ethnic Diversity and Identity

Ethnic heritage can have a powerful influence on personal identity (Weisskirch, 2005). For adolescents of ethnic descent, the question is often not just "Who am I?" Rather, it is "Who am I at home? Who am I at school? Who am I with friends from my neighborhood?"

As ethnic minorities in America continue to grow in status and prominence, adolescents are less and less likely to feel rejected or excluded because of their ethnic heritage as they try to find their place in society. This is fortunate since ethnic adolescents have often faced degrading stereotypes concern-

ing their intelligence, sexuality, social status, manners, and so forth. The result can be lowered self-esteem and confusion about roles, values, and personal identity (de las Fuentes & Vasquez, 1999). At the same time, the increasingly multicultural nature of contemporary American society raises new questions for adolescents about what it means to be American (Schwartz, 2008).

In forming an identity, adolescents of ethnic descent face the question of how they should think of themselves. Is Lori an American or a Chinese American or both?

Is Jaime a Latino, a Chicano, or a Mexican American? The answer typically depends on how strongly adolescents identify with their family and ethnic community. Teens who take pride in their ethnic heritage have higher self-esteem, a better self-image, and a stronger sense of personal identity (Roberts et al., 1999; Tse, 1999). They are also less likely to engage in drug use (Marsiglia et al., 2004) or violent behavior (French, Kim, & Pillado, 2006).

Group pride, positive models, and a more tolerant society could do much to keep a broad range of options open to *all* adolescents.

---

ever, early development includes sexual features. This leads to a more positive body image, *greater* peer prestige, and adult approval (Brooks-Gunn & Warren, 1988). Early-maturing girls tend to date sooner and are more independent and more active in school. However, like their male counterparts, they are also more often in trouble at school and more likely to engage in early sex (Flannery et al., 1993).

As you can see, there are costs and benefits associated with early puberty. One added cost of early maturation is that it may force premature identity formation. When Samantha is a teenager and she begins to look like an adult, she may be treated like an adult.

Ideally, this change can encourage greater maturity and independence. However, if the search for identity ends too soon, it may leave Samantha with a distorted, poorly formed sense of self (● Figure 3.19).

The Search for Identity

Identity formation is a key task of adolescence (Schwartz, 2008). Of course, problems of identity occur at other times too. But in a very real sense, puberty signals that it's time to begin forming a new, more mature self-image (Douvan, 1997). Many problems stem from unclear standards about the role adolescents should play within society. Are they adults or children? Should they be autonomous or dependent? Should they work or play? Such ambiguities make it difficult for young people to form clear images of themselves and of how they should act (Alsaker, 1995).

Answering the question "Who am I?" is also spurred by cognitive development. After adolescents have attained the stage of formal operations, they are better able to ask questions about their place in the world and about morals, values, politics, and social relationships. Then too, being able to think about hypothetical possibilities allows the adolescent to contemplate the future and ask more realistically, "Who will I be?" (Côté, 2006b). (See "Ethnic Diversity and Identity.")

● **Figure 3.19** Dramatic differences in physical size and maturity are found in adolescents of the same age. The girls pictured are all 13, the boys 16. Maturation that occurs earlier or later than average can affect the "search for identity." (Reprinted with permission of Nelson Prentiss.)

Adolescence The culturally defined period between childhood and adulthood.

Puberty The biologically defined period during which a person matures sexually and becomes capable of reproduction.

CRITICAL THINKING

The Twixters

As you read this text, we encourage you to reflect on new ideas and concepts by thinking critically about them. Consider, for example, the term *adulthood*. Is becoming an adult strictly a biological event? Meet 22-year-old Kirsten:

"When our mothers were our age, they were engaged. . . . They at least had some idea what they were going to do with their lives. . . . I, on the other hand, will have a dual degree in majors that are ambiguous at best and impractical at worst (English and political science), no ring on my finger and no idea who I am, much less what I want to do. . . . I realize that having nothing ahead to count on means I now have

to count on myself; that having no direction means forging one of my own." (Page, 1999).

Kirsten is a "twixter": twentysomething, still living at home, not yet married, with no children, and no settled career. In England, twixters are called "kippers" (Kids In Parents' Pockets Eroding Retirement Savings). In Australia they are "boomerang kids" (they always come back home). And in Germany they are "Nesthocker" (nest squatters). Are twixters adolescents who are taking longer to find their identity? Or are they young adults avoiding their need to enter the adult world? Are they self-indulgent individuals trapped in a "maturity gap" (Galambos, Barker, & Tilton-Weaver, 2003)? Or are they part of a new

social status that could be called "emerging adulthood" (Arnett & Tanner, 2006)?

According to psychologist Jeffrey Arnett, emerging adulthood is increasingly common in affluent Westernized cultures that allow young people to take longer to settle into their adult roles (Arnett, 2000, 2004). However, in less affluent countries, as in poorer parts of America, most adolescents continue to "become adults" at much younger ages (Arnett & Galambos, 2003). Thus, words like *adolescent* or *adulthood* cannot be defined solely in terms of physical maturation. Sociocultural factors also play a role in defining when we stop being children or become adults (Arnett, 2004).

© Zits Partnership. Reprinted with special permission of King Features Syndicate.

The Transition to Adulthood

Today the challenge of identity formation is further complicated by the fact that more and more young people are deferring young adulthood, preferring to prolong identity explorations into their 20s before they commit to long-term choices in love and work (Arnett, 2000, 2004; Arnett & Tanner, 2006). According to sociologist James Côté, Western industrialized societies, like the United States and Canada, are becoming increasingly tolerant of this period of extended adolescence (Côté, 2006a). (See "The Twixters.")

Samantha may live with Olivia and Tom until her mid-20s, delaying her transition to adulthood. Alternately, she may make the transition to young adulthood during the traditional 18-to-21 period. Regardless, she will eventually face the primary adult issues of marriage, children, and career. How she manages, especially in her core relationships, will determine whether she feels a sense of intimacy or feels isolated from others.

In many ways adolescence and young adulthood are more emotionally turbulent than midlife or old age. One important aspect of the emotional turbulence of adolescence and young adulthood is the struggle with right and wrong—in other words, the need to develop moral values.

⬤ Moral Development—
Growing a Conscience

Gateway Question: How do we develop morals and values?

A person with a terminal illness is in great pain. She is pleading for death. Should extraordinary medical efforts be made to keep her alive? A friend of yours desperately needs to pass a test and asks you to help him cheat. Will you do it? These are *moral* questions, or questions of conscience.

Moral development starts in childhood and continues into adulthood (Turiel, 2006). Through this process, we acquire values, beliefs, and thinking patterns that guide responsible behavior. Moral values are especially likely to come into sharper focus during adolescence and the transition to adulthood, as capacities for self-control and abstract thinking increase (Hart & Carlo, 2005). Let's take a brief look at this interesting aspect of personal development.

Levels of Moral Development

How are moral values acquired? In an influential account, psychologist Lawrence Kohlberg (1981) held that we learn moral values through thinking and reasoning. To study moral development, Kohlberg posed dilemmas to children of different ages. The following is one of the moral dilemmas he used (Kohlberg, 1969, adapted).

> A woman was near death from cancer, and there was only one drug that might save her. It was discovered by a druggist who was charging 10 times what it cost to make the drug. The sick woman's husband could only pay $1,000, but the druggist wanted $2,000. He asked the druggist to sell it cheaper or to let him pay later. The druggist said no. So the husband became desperate and broke into the store to steal the drug for his wife. Should he have done that? Was it wrong or right? Why?

Each child was asked what action the husband should take. Kohlberg classified the reasons given for each choice and identified three levels of moral development. Each is based not so much on the choices made, but on the reasoning used to arrive at a choice.

At the lowest, **preconventional level,** moral thinking is guided by the consequences of actions (punishment, reward, or an exchange of favors). For example, a person at this level might reason that "The man shouldn't steal the drug because he could get caught and sent to jail" (avoiding punishment) or "It won't do him any good to steal the drug because his wife will probably die before he gets out of jail" (self-interest).

At the second, or **conventional level,** reasoning is based on a desire to please others or to follow accepted authority, rules, and values. For example, a person at this intermediate level might say "He shouldn't steal the drug because others will think he is a thief. His wife would not want to be saved by thievery" (avoiding disapproval) or "Although his wife needs the drug, he should not break the law to get it. Everyone has to obey the law. His wife's condition does not justify stealing" (traditional morality of authority).

At the highest, or **postconventional level,** moral behavior is directed by self-chosen ethical principles that tend to be general, comprehensive, or universal. People at this level place high value on justice, dignity, and equality. For example, a highly principled person might say "He should steal the drug and then inform the authorities that he has done so. He will have to face a penalty, but he will have saved a human life" (self-chosen ethical principles).

Does everyone eventually reach the highest level? People advance at different rates, and many fail to reach the postconventional level of moral reasoning. In fact, many do not even reach the conventional level. For instance, one English survey revealed that 11 percent of men and 3 percent of women would commit murder for $1 million if they could be sure of getting away with the crime ("They'd kill," 1991).

The preconventional level is most characteristic of young children and delinquents (Forney, Forney, & Crutsinger, 2005). Conventional, group-oriented morals are typical of older children and most adults. Kohlberg estimated that only about 20 percent of the adult population achieves postconventional morality, representing self-direction and higher principles. (It would appear that few of these people enter politics!)

Developing a "moral compass" is an important part of growing up. Many of the choices we make every day involve fundamental questions of right and wrong. Being able to think clearly about such questions is essential to becoming a responsible adult.

Justice or Caring?

Carol Gilligan (1982) pointed out that Kohlberg's system is concerned mainly with *justice.* Based on studies of women who faced real-life dilemmas, Gilligan argued that there is also an ethic of *caring* about others. As one illustration, Gilligan presented the following story to 11- to 15-year-old American children.

The Porcupine and the Moles
Seeking refuge from the cold, a porcupine asked to share a cave for the winter with a family of moles. The moles agreed. But because the cave was small, they soon found they were being scratched each time the porcupine moved about. Finally, they asked the porcupine to leave. But the porcupine refused, saying, "If you moles are not satisfied, I suggest that you leave."

Boys who read this story tended to opt for justice in resolving the dilemma: "It's the moles' house. It's a deal. The porcupine leaves." In contrast, girls tended to look for solutions that would keep all parties happy and comfortable, such as "Cover the porcupine with a blanket."

Gilligan's point is that male psychologists have, for the most part, defined moral maturity in terms of justice and autonomy. From this perspective, a woman's concern with relationships can look like a weakness rather than a strength. (A woman who is concerned about what pleases or helps others would be placed at the conventional level in Kohlberg's system.) But Gilligan believes that caring is also a major element of moral development, and she

---

Moral development The development of values, beliefs, and thinking abilities that act as a guide regarding what is acceptable behavior.

Preconventional moral reasoning Moral thinking based on the consequences of one's choices or actions (punishment, reward, or an exchange of favors).

Conventional moral reasoning Moral thinking based on a desire to please others or to follow accepted rules and values.

Postconventional moral reasoning Moral thinking based on carefully examined and self-chosen moral principles.

suggests that males may lag in achieving it (Botes, 2000; Gilligan & Attanucci, 1988).

Does the evidence support Gilligan's position? Several studies have found little or no difference in men's and women's overall moral reasoning abilities (Glover, 2001; Wilson, 1995). Indeed, both men and women may use caring *and* justice to make moral decisions. The moral yardstick they use appears to depend on the situation they face (Wark & Krebs, 1996). Just the same, Gilligan deserves credit for identifying a second major way in which moral choices are made. It can be argued that our best moral choices combine justice and caring, reason and emotion—which may be what we mean by wisdom (Pasupathi & Staudinger, 2001).

KNOWLEDGE BUILDER
Adolescence, Young Adulthood, and Moral Development

RECITE

1. In North America the primary criterion for the transition from adolescence to adulthood is marriage. T or F?
2. Identify formation is spurred by _____ and _____.
3. According to Jeffrey Arnett, the trend in affluent Westernized cultures toward allowing young people to take longer to settle into their adult roles is best referred to as
   a. emerging adulthood
   b. hurried childhood
   c. a maturity gap
   d. extended adolescence
4. According to Kohlberg, the conventional level of moral development is marked by a reliance on outside authority. T or F?
5. Self-interest and avoiding punishment are elements of postconventional morality. T or F?
6. About 80 percent of all adults function at the postconventional level of moral reasoning. T or F?
7. Gilligan regards gaining a sense of justice as the principal basis of moral development. T or F?

REFLECT

Critical Thinking

8. Are labels like "adolescent" or "young adult" reflective of heredity or environment?

Relate

To what extent does the concept of identity formation apply to your own experience during adolescence?

Do you know any twixters? (Are you one?) Do you think twixters are adolescents taking longer to find their identity or young adults avoiding their need to establish themselves in the world of adults?

At what stage of moral development do you think most terrorists function?

Answers: 1. F **2.** puberty, cognitive development **3.** a **4.** T **5.** F **6.** F **7.** F **8.** Environment, rather than heredity, is the better answer. Even better, the meanings of terms like "adolescence" or "adult" vary considerably from culture to culture, indicating that it is really a matter of definition (Côté, 2006a).

🔵 The Story of a Lifetime— Rocky Road or Garden Path?

Gateway Question: What are the typical tasks and dilemmas through the life span?

Erik Erikson's psychosocial theory provides a good overview of the major psychological conflicts that occur during a "typical" life. In later adulthood we all face many additional challenges, including physical aging. Regardless, it is possible to age successfully. We also must face our own mortality and inevitable death.

Every life is marked by a number of developmental milestones. These are notable events, markers, or turning points in personal development. Some examples include graduating from school, voting for the first time, getting married, watching a child leave home (or move back!), the death of a parent, becoming a grandparent, retirement, and one's own death. Thus far, we have traced Samantha's progress through childhood, adolescence, and young adulthood. What challenges lie ahead for her?

Erikson's Psychosocial Theory

Perhaps the best way to get a preview of Samantha's life is to consider some of the major psychological challenges she is likely to encounter. Broad similarities can be found in the life stages of infancy, childhood, adolescence, young adulthood, middle adulthood, and old age. Each stage confronts a person with new **developmental tasks** that must be mastered for optimal development. Examples are learning to read in childhood, adjusting to sexual maturity in adolescence, and establishing a vocation as an adult.

In an influential book titled *Childhood and Society* (1963), personality theorist Erik Erikson (1903–1994) suggests that we face a specific *psychosocial dilemma,* or "crisis," at each stage of life. A **psychosocial dilemma** is a conflict between personal impulses and the social world. Resolving each dilemma creates a new balance between a person and society. A string of "successes" produces healthy development and a satisfying life. Unfavorable outcomes throw us off balance, making it harder to deal with later crises. Life becomes a "rocky road," and personal growth is stunted. ● Table 3.3 lists Erikson's dilemmas.

Table 3.3 ● Erikson's Psychosocial Dilemmas

Age	Characteristic Dilemma
Birth to 1 year	Trust versus mistrust
1 to 3 years	Autonomy versus shame and doubt
3 to 5 years	Initiative versus guilt
6 to 12 years	Industry versus inferiority
Adolescence	Identity versus role confusion
Young adulthood	Intimacy versus isolation
Middle adulthood	Generativity versus stagnation
Late adulthood	Integrity versus despair

Personality theorist Erik Erikson (1903–1994) is best known for his life-stage theory of human development.

What are the major developmental tasks and life crises? A brief description of each psychosocial dilemma follows.

Stage One, First Year of Life: Trust versus Mistrust

During the first year of life, children are completely dependent on others. Erikson believes that a basic attitude of trust or mistrust is formed at this time. **Trust** is established when babies are given warmth, touching, love, and physical care. **Mistrust** is caused by inadequate or unpredictable care and by parents who are cold, indifferent, or rejecting. Basic mistrust may later cause insecurity, suspiciousness, or an inability to relate to others. Notice that trust comes from the same conditions that help babies become securely attached to their parents.

Stage Two, 1–3 Years: Autonomy versus Shame and Doubt

In stage two, children express their growing self-control by climbing, touching, exploring, and trying to do things for themselves. Tom and Olivia fostered Samantha's sense of **autonomy** by encouraging her to try new skills. However, her first efforts were sometimes crude, involving spilling, falling, wetting, and other "accidents." If Tom and Olivia had ridiculed or overprotected Samantha, they might have caused her to feel **shameful** about her actions and **doubt** her abilities.

Stage Three, 3–5 Years: Initiative versus Guilt

In stage three, children move beyond simple self-control and begin to take initiative. Through play, children learn to make plans and carry out tasks. Parents reinforce **initiative** by giving children free-

dom to play, ask questions, use imagination, and choose activities. Feelings of **guilt** about initiating activities are formed if parents criticize severely, prevent play, or discourage a child's questions.

Stage Four, 6–12 Years: Industry versus Inferiority

Many events of middle childhood are symbolized by that fateful day when you first entered school. With dizzying speed your world expanded beyond your family, and you faced a whole series of new challenges.

The elementary school years are a child's "entrance into life." In school, children begin to learn skills valued by society, and success or failure can affect a child's feelings of adequacy. Children learn a sense of **industry** if they win praise for productive activities, such as building, painting, cooking, reading, and studying. If a child's efforts are regarded as messy, childish, or inadequate, feelings of **inferiority** result. For the first time, teachers, classmates, and adults outside the home become as important as parents in shaping attitudes toward oneself.

Stage Five, Adolescence: Identity versus Role Confusion

As we have noted, adolescence is often a turbulent time. Erikson considers a need to answer the question "Who am I?" the primary task during this stage of life. As Samantha matures mentally and physically, she will have new feelings, a new body, and new attitudes. Like other adolescents, she will need to build a consistent **identity** out of her talents, values, life history, relationships, and the demands of her culture (Côté & Levine, 2002). Her conflicting experiences as a student, friend, athlete, worker, daughter, lover, and so forth must be integrated into a unified sense of self. Persons who fail to develop a sense of identity suffer from **role confusion,** an uncertainty about who they are and where they are going.

Stage Six, Young Adulthood: Intimacy versus Isolation

What does Erikson believe is the major conflict in early adulthood? In stage six, the individual feels a need for *intimacy* in his or her life. After establishing a stable identity, a person is prepared to

Developmental task Any skill that must be mastered, or personal change that must take place, for optimal development.

Psychosocial dilemma A conflict between personal impulses and the social world.

Trust versus mistrust A conflict early in life about learning to trust others and the world.

Autonomy versus shame and doubt A conflict created when growing self-control (autonomy) is pitted against feelings of shame and doubt.

Initiative versus guilt A conflict between learning to take initiative and overcoming feelings of guilt about doing so.

Industry versus inferiority A conflict in middle childhood centered around lack of support for industrious behavior, which can result in feelings of inferiority.

Identity versus role confusion A conflict of adolescence, involving the need to establish a personal identity.

share meaningful love or deep friendship with others. By **intimacy,** Erikson means an ability to care about others and to share experiences with them. In line with Erikson's view, 75 percent of college-age men and women rank a good marriage and family life as important adult goals (Bachman & Johnson, 1979). And yet, marriage or sexual involvement is no guarantee of intimacy: Many adult relationships remain shallow and unfulfilling. Failure to establish intimacy with others leads to a deep sense of **isolation** (feeling alone and uncared for in life). This often sets the stage for later difficulties.

Stage Seven, Middle Adulthood: Generativity versus Stagnation

According to Erikson, an interest in guiding the next generation provides emotional balance in mature adulthood. Erikson called this quality **generativity.** It is expressed by caring about oneself, one's children, and future generations. Generativity may be achieved by guiding one's own children or by helping other children (as a teacher or coach, for example). Productive or creative work can also express generativity. In any case, a person's concerns and energies must broaden to include the welfare of others and society as a whole. Failure to do this is marked by a **stagnant** concern with one's own needs and comforts. Life loses meaning, and the person feels bitter, dreary, and trapped (Friedman, 2004).

Stage Eight, Late Adulthood: Integrity versus Despair

What does Erikson see as the conflicts of old age? Old age is a time of reflection. According to Erikson, when Samantha grows old she must be able to look back over her life with acceptance and satisfaction. People who have lived richly and responsibly develop

According to Erikson, an interest in future generations characterizes optimal adult development.

a sense of **integrity** (self-respect). This allows them to face aging and death with dignity. If previous life events are viewed with regret, the elderly person experiences **despair** (heartache and remorse). In this case, life seems like a series of missed opportunities. The person feels like a failure and knows it's too late to reverse what has been done. Aging and the threat of death then become sources of fear and depression.

The Life Span in Perspective

To squeeze a lifetime into a few pages, we had to ignore countless details. Although much is lost, the result is a clearer picture of an entire life cycle. Is Erikson's description, then, an exact map of Samantha's past and her future—or your own? Probably not. Still, psychosocial dilemmas are major events in many lives. Knowing about them may allow you to anticipate typical trouble spots in your own life. You may also be better prepared to understand the problems and feelings of friends and relatives at various points in the life cycle.

⬤⬤ Later Adulthood: Will You Still Need Me When I'm 64?

Gateway Question: What is involved in well-being during later adulthood?

Although Erikson's dilemmas extend into adulthood, they are not the only challenges adults face. Others are all too familiar: marital strife, divorce, career difficulties, unemployment, health problems, financial pressures, legal conflicts, and personal tragedies—to name but a few. How do people maintain a state of well-being as they run the gauntlet of modern life? Psychologist Carol Ryff (1995; Ryff, Singer, & Palmersheim, 2004) believes that well-being during adulthood has six elements:

1. Self-acceptance
2. Positive relations with others
3. Autonomy (personal freedom)
4. Environmental mastery
5. A purpose in life
6. Continued personal growth

Ryff found that for many older adults, age-related declines are offset by positive relationships and greater mastery of life's demands (Ryff & Keyes, 1995). Thus, sharing life's joys and sorrows with others, coupled with a better understanding of how the world works, can help carry people through midlife and into their later years (Ryff & Singer, 2000; Ryff, Singer, & Palmersheim, 2004). Despite the emphasis on youth in our culture, middle age and beyond can be a rich period of life in which people feel secure, happy, and self-confident (Rubenstein, 2002).

A Midlife Crisis?

But don't people face a "midlife crisis" at this point in their lives? Yes and no. Serious difficulties at the midpoint of life are certainly not universal. Most people thrive during middle adulthood and have no special problems. Only about a quarter of men and women believe they have experienced a midlife crisis (Wethington, Kessler, & Pixley, 2004).

Nevertheless, midlife does pose special challenges. According to Roger Gould (1975), a psychiatrist interested in adult personality, North American adults actually experience two "crisis" points in their development.

Crisis of Questions

According to Gould, around the age of 30 many people experience a minor life crisis. The heart of this crisis is a serious questioning of what life is all about. People tend to ask themselves, "Is this it?" and confidence in previous choices and values can waver. Unsettled by these developments, the person actively searches for a style of living that will bring more meaning to life. Marriages are particularly vulnerable during this time of dissatisfaction. Extramarital affairs and divorces are common symptoms of the "crisis of questions."

Crisis of Urgency

People in their late 30s and 40s are typically beginning to become more aware of the reality of death. Having a limited number of years to live begins to exert pressure on the individual. Intensified attempts are made to succeed at a career or to achieve one's life goals. Generativity, in the form of nurturing, teaching, or serving others, helps alleviate many of the anxieties of this stage.

If a midlife crisis does occur, what does it look like? Psychologist Daniel Levinson carried out a classic in-depth study of adulthood and identified several periods when people typically make major transitions. A **transition period** ends one life pattern and opens the door to new possibilities (Levinson, 1986). At such times, people address concerns about their identity, their work, and relationships to others.

Levinson's first study focused on men. As they approached the midlife transition (between the ages of 37 and 41), most men went through a period of instability, anxiety, and change. (Notice that this corresponds closely to Gould's crisis-of-urgency period.) In a later study, Levinson found that most of what he learned about men also applies to women (Levinson & Levinson, 1996).

Of the men Levinson studied, roughly half defined the midlife period as a "last chance" to achieve their goals. Such goals were often stated as a key event, such as reaching a certain income or becoming a supervisor, a full professor, a shop steward, and so forth. For these men the midlife period was stressful but manageable.

A smaller percentage of men experienced a serious midlife decline. Many of these men had to face the fact that they had chosen a dead-end job or lifestyle. Others had achieved financial success but felt that what they were doing was pointless.

In a third pattern, a few hardy individuals appeared to "break out" of a seriously flawed life structure. For them, a decision to "start over" was typically followed by 8 to 10 years of rebuilding.

In what ways does the midlife transition differ for women? Compared with men, women were less likely to enter adulthood with specific "goals." As a result, they were less likely to define "success"

in terms of some key event. Rather than focusing on external goals, women tended to seek changes in personal identity at midlife. For example, a woman might become more self-reliant and independent—qualities she might have regarded as "masculine" earlier in life (Levinson & Levinson, 1996). But make no mistake, midlife can be challenging for women, too (Wethington, 2000). In another survey of middle-aged women, two thirds said they made major changes in their lives between ages 37 and 43 (Stewart & Vandewater, 1999).

Midcourse Corrections

In summary, people tend to move through cycles of stability and transition in their adult lives (Ornstein & Isabella, 1990). However, it is more common to make a "midcourse correction," at midlife than it is to survive a "crisis" (Lachman, 2004). Ideally, the midlife transition involves reworking old identities, achieving valued goals, finding one's own truths, and preparing for old age. Taking stock may be especially valuable at midlife, but reviewing past choices to prepare for the future is helpful at any age (Lewchanin & Zubrod, 2001). For some people, difficult turning points in life can serve as "wake-up calls" that create opportunities for personal growth (Wethington, 2003).

Old Age

After the late 50s, personal development is complicated by physical aging. However, it is wrong to believe that most elderly people are sickly, infirm, or senile. (Nowadays, 60 is the new 40, an idea both of your authors whole-heartedly agree with!) Only about 5 percent of those older than 65 are in nursing homes. Mentally, many elderly persons are at least as capable as the average young adult. On intellectual tests, top scorers over the age of 65 match the average for men younger than 35. What sets these silver-haired stars apart? Typically they are people who have continued to work and remain intellectually active (Salthouse, 2004). Gerontologist Warner Schaie (1994, 2005) found that you are most likely to stay mentally sharp in old age if:

1. You remain healthy.
2. You live in a favorable environment. (You are educated and have a stimulating occupation, an above-average income, and an intact family.)
3. You are involved in intellectually stimulating activities (reading, travel, cultural events, continuing education, clubs, professional associations).

Intimacy versus isolation The challenge of overcoming a sense of isolation by establishing intimacy with others.

Generativity versus stagnation A conflict of middle adulthood in which self-interest is countered by an interest in guiding the next generation.

Integrity versus despair A conflict in old age between feelings of integrity and the despair of viewing previous life events with regret.

Transition period Time span during which a person leaves an existing life pattern behind and moves into a new pattern.

At age 77, John Glenn became the oldest person to fly into space, in October 1998. Glenn was also the first American astronaut to orbit Earth, in 1962. As Glenn's space adventure shows, aging does not inevitably bring an end to engaging in challenging activities.

4. You have a flexible personality.
5. You are married to a smart spouse.
6. You maintain your perceptual processing speed.
7. You were satisfied with your accomplishments in midlife.

A shorter summary of this list is "Those who live by their wit die with their wits."

Successful Aging

What are the keys to successful aging? They are not unlike the elements of well-being at midlife. Four psychological characteristics shared by the healthiest, happiest older people are (de Leon, 2005; Vaillant, 2002):

> Optimism, hope, and an interest in the future
> Gratitude and forgiveness; an ability to focus on what is good in life
> Empathy; an ability to share the feelings of others and see the world through their eyes
> Connection with others; an ability to reach out, to give and receive social support

Actually, these are excellent guidelines for well-being at any stage of adulthood.

In summary, enlightened views of aging call for an end to the forced obsolescence of the elderly. As a group, older people represent a valuable source of skill, knowledge, and energy that we can't afford to cast aside. As we face the challenges of this planet's uncertain future, we need all the help we can get!

Aging and Ageism

You have almost certainly encountered ageism in one way or another. **Ageism,** which refers to discrimination or prejudice based on age, can oppress the young as well as the old. For instance, a person applying for a job may just as well be told "You're too young" as "You're too old." In some societies ageism is expressed as respect for the elderly. In Japan, for instance, aging is seen as positive, and greater age brings more status and respect. In most Western nations, however, ageism tends to have a negative impact on older individuals (Ng, 2002).

Ageism is often expressed through patronizing language. Older people are frequently spoken to in an overly polite, slow, loud, and simple way implying that they are infirm, even when they are not (Nelson, 2005). Popular stereotypes of the "dirty old man," "meddling old woman," "senile old fool," and the like also help perpetuate myths about aging. But such stereotypes are clearly wrong: A tremendous diversity exists among the elderly—ranging from the infirm to aerobic-dancing grandmothers.

In many occupations, older workers perform well in jobs that require *both* speed and skill. Of course, people do experience a gradual loss of *fluid abilities* (those requiring speed or rapid learning) as they age but often this can be offset by many *crystallized abilities* (learned knowledge and skills), such as vocabulary and stored-up facts, which may actually improve—at least into the 60s (Schaie, 2005). Overall, very little loss of job performance occurs as workers grow older. In the professions, wisdom and expertise can usually more than compensate for any loss of mental quickness (Ericsson, 2000). Basing retirement solely on a person's age makes little sense.

●● Death and Dying—The Final Challenge

Gateway Question: How do people typically react to death?

DEAR ABBY: Do you think about dying much? *(signed)* CURIOUS
DEAR CURIOUS: No, it's the last thing I want to do.
"I'm not afraid of dying. I just don't want to be there when it happens."
   Woody Allen
"Why not? Why not?" LSD guru Timothy Leary (his last words before dying)

The statistics on death are very convincing: Everyone dies. In spite of this, most of us are poorly informed about a process that is as basic as birth. We have seen throughout this chapter that it is valuable to understand major trends in the course of development. With this in mind, let us now explore emotional responses to death, the inevitable conclusion of every life.

Death may be inevitable, but it can be faced with dignity and sometimes even humor. Mel Blanc's famous sign-off, "That's all folks," is engraved on a marble headstone over his grave. Blanc was the voice of Bugs Bunny, Porky Pig, and many other cartoon characters.

It might seem that as people grow older they would fear death more. However, older persons actually have fewer death fears than younger people. Older people more often fear the *circumstances* of dying, such as pain or helplessness, rather than death itself (Thorson & Powell, 1990). These findings seem to show a general lack of death fears, but they may actually reflect a widespread denial of death. Notice how denial is apparent in the language used to talk about death: Often we speak of a dead person as having "passed away," "expired," "gone to God," or "breathed one's last."

Many people have little direct experience with death until they, themselves, are fairly old. The average person's exposure to death consists of the artificial and unrealistic portrayals of death on TV. By the time the average person is 17 years old, she or he will have witnessed thousands of TV deaths. With few exceptions these are *homicides,* not deaths due to illness or aging.

Reactions to Impending Death

A direct and highly influential account of emotional responses to death comes from the work of Elisabeth Kübler-Ross (1926–2004). Kübler-Ross was a **thanatologist** (THAN-ah-TOL-oh-jist: one who studies death). Over the years she spent hundreds of hours at the bedsides of the terminally ill, where she observed five basic emotional reactions to impending death (Kübler-Ross, 1975).

1. **Denial and isolation.** A typical first reaction is to deny death's reality and isolate oneself from information confirming that death is really going to occur. Initially the person may be sure that "It's all a mistake." "Surely," she or he thinks, "the lab reports have been mixed up or the doctor made an error." This sort of denial may proceed to attempts to avoid any reminder of the situation.
2. **Anger.** Many dying individuals feel anger and ask, "Why me?" As they face the ultimate threat of having life torn away, their anger may spill over into rage toward the living. Even good friends may temporarily evoke anger because their health is envied.
3. **Bargaining.** In another common reaction, the terminally ill bargain with themselves or with God. The dying person thinks, "Just let me live a little longer and I'll do anything to earn it." Individuals may bargain for time by trying to be "good" ("I'll never smoke again"), by righting past wrongs, or by praying that if they are granted more time they will dedicate themselves to their religion.
4. **Depression.** As death draws near and the person begins to recognize that it cannot be prevented, feelings of futility, exhaustion, and deep depression may set in. The person realizes she or he will be separated from friends, loved ones, and the familiar routines of life, and this causes a profound sadness.
5. **Acceptance.** If death is not sudden, many people manage to come to terms with dying and accept it calmly. The person who accepts death is neither happy nor sad, but at peace with the inevitable. Acceptance usually signals that the struggle with death has been resolved. The need to talk about death ends, and silent companionship from others is frequently all the person desires.

Not all terminally ill persons display all these reactions, nor do they always occur in this order. Individual styles of dying vary greatly. Generally, there does tend to be a movement from initial shock, denial, and anger toward eventual acceptance. However, some people who seem to have accepted death may die angry and raging against the inevitable. Conversely, the angry fighter may let go of the struggle and die peacefully. In general, one's approach to dying will mirror his or her style of living (Yedidia & MacGregor, 2001).

It is a mistake, then, to think that Kübler-Ross's list is a series of stages to go through in order or that there is something wrong if a person does not show all these emotions. Rather, the list describes typical reactions to impending death. Note, as well, that many of the same reactions accompany any major loss, be it divorce, loss of a home due to fire, death of a pet, or loss of a job.

Implications

How can I make use of this information? First, it can help both the dying and survivors to recognize and cope with periods of depression, anger, denial, and bargaining. Second, it helps to realize that close friends or relatives may feel many of the same emotions before or after a person's death because they, too, are facing a loss.

Perhaps the most important thing to recognize is that the dying person needs to share feelings with others and to discuss death openly. Too often, dying persons feel isolated and separated from others. Adults tend to "freeze up" with someone who is dying. For such people, thanatologist Kirsti Dyer (2001) has this advice:

- Be yourself and relate person to person.
- Be ready to listen again and again.
- Be respectful.
- Be aware of feelings and nonverbal cues.
- Be comfortable with silence.
- Be genuine.
- Most of all, be there.

Understanding what the dying person is going through may make it easier for you to offer support at this important time. A simple willingness to be with the person and to honestly share his or her feelings can help bring dignity, acceptance, and meaning to death (Holstein, 1997). Today, many terminally ill individuals also benefit from *hospice* care, which can improve the quality of life in a person's final days. Hospices typically offer support, guidance, pain relief, and companionship. In short, the dying person is made comfortable and feels loved and respected (Lynn, 2001). As each of us faces the end of life, to die well may be no less an accomplishment than to live well.

Ageism Discrimination or prejudice based on a person's age.

Thanatologist A specialist who studies emotional and behavioral reactions to death and dying.

KNOWLEDGE BUILDER
Challenges Across the Lifespan

RECITE

As a way to improve your memory, you might find it helpful to summarize Erikson's eight life stages. Complete this do-it-yourself summary and compare your answers to those given below.

Stage	Crisis	Favorable Outcome
First year of life	1. _____ vs. 2. _____	Faith in the environ-ment and in others
Ages 1–3	Autonomy vs. 3. _____	Feelings of self-control and adequacy
Ages 3–5	4. _____ vs. guilt	Ability to begin one's own activities
Ages 6–12	Industry vs. 5. _____	Confidence in productive skills, learning how to work
Adolescence	6. _____ vs. role confusion	An integrated image of oneself as a unique person
Young adulthood	Intimacy vs. 7. _____	Ability to form bonds of love and friendship with others

Middle adulthood	Generativity vs. 8. _____	Concern for family, society, and future generations
Late adulthood	9. _____ vs. 10. _____	Sense of dignity and fulfillment, willing-ness to face death

11. Nearly everyone experiences a midlife crisis sometime around age 40. T or F?
12. After age 65, a large proportion of older people show significant signs of mental disability and most require special care. T or F?
13. Job performance tends to decline rapidly in older workers. T or F?
14. In the reaction that Kübler-Ross describes as bargaining, the dying individual asks, "Why me?" T or F?

REFLECT

Critical Thinking

15. Trying to make generalizations about development throughout life is complicated by at least one major factor. What do you think it is?

Relate

See if you can think of a person you know who is facing one of Erikson's psychosocial dilemmas. Now see if you can think of specific people who seem to be coping with each of the other dilemmas.

See if you can describe three instances of ageism you have witnessed.

Answers: 1. Trust **2.** mistrust **3.** shame or doubt **4.** Initiative **5.** Inferiority **6.** Identity **7.** isolation **8.** stagnation **9.** Integrity **10.** despair **11.** F **12.** F **13.** F **14.** F **15.** Different *cohorts* (groups of people born in the same year) live in different historical times. People born in various decades may have very different life experiences. This makes it difficult to identify universal patterns (Stewart & Ostrove, 1998).

PSYCHOLOGY IN ACTION

Effective Parenting—Raising Healthy Children

Gateway Question: How do effective parents discipline and communicate with their children?

Authoritative parents help their children grow up with a capacity for love, joy, fulfillment, responsibility, and self-control through *positive parent-child interactions*. Positive interactions occur when parents spend enjoyable time encouraging their children in a loving and mutually respectful fashion (Dinkmeyer, McKay, & Dinkmeyer, 1997).

As any parent can tell you, it is all well and good to talk about positive interactions until little Johnny misbehaves (and he will, count on it!). As children mature and become more independent, parents must find ways to control their children's behavior. ("No, you may not smear banana pudding on daddy's face.") When parents fail to provide *discipline* (guidance regarding acceptable behavior), children become antisocial, aggressive, and insecure.

And yet, it is not easy to have a positive interaction while disciplining your child. This is one reason why overly permissive parents avoid disciplining their children.

Effective discipline is created through communication that is fair but loving, authoritative yet sensitive. It socializes a child without destroying the bond of love and trust between parent and child. Children should feel free to express their deepest feelings. However, this

Image 100/SuperStock

does not mean they can do whatever they please. Rather, the child is allowed to move freely within consistent, well-defined boundaries for acceptable behavior.

Effective Discipline

Parents typically discipline children in one of three ways. **Power assertion** refers to physical punishment or a show of force, such as taking away toys or privileges. As an alternative, some parents use **withdrawal of love** (withholding affection) by refusing to speak to a child, threatening to leave, rejecting the child, or otherwise acting as if the child is temporarily unlovable. **Management techniques** combine praise, recognition, approval, rules, reasoning, and the like to encourage desirable behavior. Each of these approaches can control a child's behavior, but their side effects differ considerably.

What are the side effects? Power-oriented techniques—particularly harsh or severe

Calvin
and
Hobbes

physical punishment—are associated with fear, hatred of parents, and a lack of spontaneity and warmth. Most children show no signs of long-term damage from spanking—*if* spanking is backed up by supportive parenting (Baumrind, Larzelere, & Cowan, 2002). However, emotional damage does occur if spankings are severe, frequent, or coupled with harsh parenting. In addition, frequent spanking tends to increase aggression, and it leads to *more* problem behaviors, not fewer (McLoyd & Smith, 2002). After reviewing many studies, psychologist Elizabeth Gershoff concludes that parents should minimize spanking or avoid it entirely (Gershoff, 2002).

> ### bridges
> Punishment also has important effects on learning. **For more tips on how to use punishment wisely, see Chapter 7, pages 240–241.**

Withdrawal of love produces children who tend to be self-disciplined. You could say that such children have developed a good conscience. Often, they are described as "model" children or as unusually "good." But as a side effect, they are also frequently anxious, insecure, and dependent on adults for approval.

Management techniques also have limitations. Most important is the need to carefully adjust to a child's level of understanding. Younger children don't always see the connection between rules, explanations, and their own behavior. Nevertheless, management techniques receive a big plus in another area: There is a direct connection between discipline and a child's self-esteem.

How does discipline affect self-esteem? If you regard yourself as a worthwhile person, you have **self-esteem.** High self-esteem is essential for good emotional health. In elementary school, children with high self-esteem tend to be more popular, cooperative, and successful in class. Children with low self-esteem are more withdrawn and tend to perform below average (Amato & Fowler, 2002).

Low self-esteem is related to physical punishment and the withholding of love. And why not? What message do children receive if a parent beats them or tells them they are not worthy of love? Thus, it is best to minimize physical punishment and avoid withdrawal of love. In contrast, high self-esteem is promoted by management techniques. Children who feel that their parents support them emotionally tend to have high self-esteem (Amato & Fowler, 2002; Nielsen & Metha, 1994).

Can self-esteem ever get too high? Yes it can. According to clinical psychologist Maggie Mamen, many modern parents try to "empower" their children by imposing few limits on behavior, making them feel special, and giving them everything they want (Mamen, 2004). But such good intentions can backfire, leaving parents with children who have developed an artificially high level of self-esteem and a sense of entitlement. That is, overly permissive parenting produces spoiled, self-indulgent children who have little self-control (Baumrind, 1991). Their sense of entitlement can lead them to bully other children to get their way or even to engage in criminal activity. As adults, such children may become addicted to seeking ways to enhance their self-esteem. For example, they may place excessive importance on being physically attractive, leading to stress, drug and alcohol use, and eating disorders (Crocker & Park, 2004).

Consistent Discipline. Individual parents choose limits on behavior that are more "strict" or less "strict." But this choice is less important than **consistency** (maintaining stable rules of conduct). Consistent discipline gives a child a sense of security and stability. Inconsistency makes the child's world seem insecure and unpredictable.

What does consistent discipline mean in practice? To illustrate the errors parents often make, let's consider a few examples of inconsistency (Fontenelle, 1989). The following are mistakes to avoid:

> Saying one thing and doing something else. You tell the child, "Bart, if you don't eat your brussels sprouts you can't have any dessert." Then you feel guilty and offer him some dessert.
>
> Making statements you don't mean. "If you don't quiet down, I'm going to stop the car and make you walk home."
>
> Changing *no* to *yes,* especially to quiet a nagging child. A good example is the parent who first refuses to buy the child a toy and later gives in and buys it.
>
> Responding differently to the same misbehavior. One day a child is sent to his room for fighting with his sister. The next day the fighting is overlooked.

Inconsistency makes children feel angry and confused because they cannot control the consequences of their own behavior. Inconsistency also gives children the message: "Don't believe what I say because I usually don't mean it."

Power assertion The use of physical punishment or coercion to enforce child discipline.

Withdrawal of love Withholding affection to enforce child discipline.

Management techniques Combining praise, recognition, approval, rules, and reasoning to enforce child discipline.

Self-esteem Regarding oneself as a worthwhile person; a positive evaluation of oneself.

Consistency With respect to child discipline, the maintenance of stable rules of conduct.

Using Discipline Constructively. At one time or another, most parents use power assertion, withdrawal of love, or management techniques to control their children. Each mode of discipline has its place. However, physical punishment and withdrawal of love should always be used with caution. Here are some guidelines:

1. Parents should separate disapproval of the act from disapproval of the child. Instead of saying, "I'm going to punish you because *you are bad,*" say, "I'm upset about *what you did.*"
2. State specifically what misbehavior you are punishing. Explain why you have set limits on this kind of conduct.
3. Punishment should never be harsh or injurious. Don't physically punish a child while you are angry. Also remember that the message "I don't love you right now" can be more painful and damaging than any spanking.
4. Punishment, such as a scolding or taking away privileges, is most effective when done immediately. This statement is especially true for younger children.
5. Spanking and other forms of physical punishment are not particularly effective for children younger than age 2. The child will only be confused and frightened. Spankings also become less effective after age 5 because they tend to humiliate the child and breed resentment.
6. As discussed earlier, many psychologists believe that children should never be spanked. If you do use physical punishment, reserve it for situations that pose an immediate danger to younger children; for example, when a child runs into the street.
7. Remember, too, that it is usually more effective to reward children when they are being good than it is to punish them for misbehavior.

After age 5, management techniques are the most effective form of discipline, especially techniques that emphasize communication and the relationship between parent and child.

Communicating Effectively with Children

Creative communication is another important ingredient of successful child management (Bath, 1996). Child expert Haim Ginott (1965) believed that making a distinction between feelings and behavior is the key to clear communication. Because children (and parents, too) do not choose how they feel, it is important to allow free expression of feelings.

Accepting Feelings. The child who learns to regard some feelings as "bad," or unacceptable, is being asked to deny a very real part of his or her experience. Ginott encouraged parents to teach their children that all feelings are appropriate; it is only actions that are subject to disapproval. Consider this typical conversation excerpted from Ginott's classic book (1965):

> Son: I am stupid, and I know it. Look at my grades in school.
>
> Father: You just have to work harder.
>
> Son: I already work harder and it doesn't help. I have no brains.
>
> Father: You are smart, I know.
>
> Son: I am stupid, I know.
>
> Father: (loudly) You are not stupid!
>
> Son: Yes, I am!
>
> Father: You are not stupid. Stupid!

By debating with the child, the father misses the point that his son *feels* stupid. It would be far more helpful for the father to encourage the boy to talk about his feelings. For instance, he might say, "You really feel that you are not as smart as others, don't you? Do you feel this way often?" In this way, the child is given a chance to express his emotions and to feel understood. The father might conclude by saying, "Look, son, in my eyes you are a fine person. But I understand how you feel. Everyone feels stupid at times." He might also offer some encouragement: "You're improving. Look at the progress you've made."

I-Messages. Child psychologist Thomas Gordon (2000) believes that parents should send *I-messages* to their children, rather than *you-messages*.

What's the difference? **You-messages** take the form of threats, name-calling, accusing, bossing, lecturing, or criticizing. Generally, you-messages tell children what's "wrong" with them. An **I-message** tells children what effect their behavior had on you. For example, after a hard day's work, Maria wants to sit down and rest awhile. She begins to relax with a newspaper when her 5-year-old daughter starts banging loudly on a toy drum. Many parents would respond with a you-message such as "You go play outside this instant." (bossing) or "Don't you ever make such a racket when someone is reading." (lecturing).

Gordon suggests sending an I-message such as, "I am very tired, and I would like to read. I feel upset and can't read with so much noise." This forces the child to accept responsibility for the effects of her actions (Dinkmeyer, McKay, & Dinkmeyer, 1997).

Using Natural and Logical Consequences. Sometimes events automatically discourage misbehavior. For example, a child who refuses to eat dinner will get uncomfortably hungry. A child who throws a temper tantrum may gain nothing but a sore throat and a headache if the tantrum is ignored (Fontenelle, 1989). In such instances, a child's actions have **natural consequences** (intrinsic effects). In situations that don't produce natural consequences, parents can set up **logical consequences** (rational and reasonable effects). For example, a parent might say, "We'll go to the zoo when you've picked up all those toys," or "You can play with your dolls as soon as you've taken your bath," or "You two can stop arguing or leave the table until you're ready to join us."

The concept of logical, parent-defined consequences can be combined with I-messages to handle many day-to-day instances of misbehavior. The key idea is to use an I-message to set up consequences and then give the child a choice to make: "Michelle, we're trying to watch TV. You can settle down and watch with us or go play elsewhere. You decide which you'd rather do" (Dinkmeyer, McKay, & Dinkmeyer, 1997).

How could Maria have dealt with her 5-year-old—the one who was banging on a drum? A response that combines an I-message with logical consequences would be, "I would like for you to stop banging on that drum; otherwise, please take it outside." If the child continues to bang on the drum inside the house, then she has caused the toy to be put away. If she takes it outside, she has made a decision to play with the drum in a way that respects her mother's wishes. In this way, both parent and child have been allowed to maintain a sense of self-respect and a needless clash has been averted.

After you have stated consequences and let the child decide, be sure to respect the child's choice. If the child repeats the misbehavior, you can let the consequences remain in effect longer. But later, give the child another chance to cooperate.

With all child management techniques, remember to be firm, kind, consistent, respectful, and encouraging. And most of all, try every day to live the message you wish to communicate.

Effective Parenting

RECITE

1. Effective discipline gives children freedom within a structure of consistent and well-defined limits. T or F?
2. One good way to maintain consistency in child management is to overstate the consequences for misbehavior. T or F?
3. Spankings and other physical punishments are most effective for children under the age of 2. T or F?
4. Giving recognition for progress and attempts to improve is an example of parental _____.
5. I-messages are a gentle way of accusing a child of misbehavior. T or F?
6. In situations where natural consequences are unavailable or do not discourage misbehavior, parents should define logical consequences for a child. T or F?

REFLECT

Critical Thinking

7. Several Scandinavian countries have made it illegal for parents to spank their own children. Does this infringe on the rights of parents?

8. If power assertion is a poor way to discipline children, why do so many parents use it?

Relate

What do you think are the best ways to discipline children? How would your approach be classified? What are its advantages and disadvantages?

Parents can probably never be completely consistent. Think of a time when your parents were inconsistent in disciplining you. How did it affect you?

Think of a you-message you have recently given a child, family member, roommate, or spouse. Can you change it into an I-message?

Answers: 1. T **2.** F **3.** F **4.** encouragement **5.** F **6.** T **7.** Such laws are based on the view that it should be illegal to physically assault any person, regardless of their age. Although parents may believe they have a "right" to spank their children, it can be argued that children need special protection because they are small, powerless, and dependent (Durrant & Janson, 2005). **8.** Most parents discipline their children in the same ways that they themselves were disciplined. Parenting is a responsibility of tremendous importance, for which most people receive almost no training.

chapter in review   Gateways to Human Development

Heredity (nature) and environment (nurture) are interacting forces that are both necessary for human development. However, caregivers can only influence environment.

- The chromosomes and genes in each cell of the body carry hereditary instructions. Most characteristics are polygenic and reflect the combined effects of dominant and recessive genes.
- Maturation of the body and nervous system underlies the orderly development of motor skills, cognitive abilities, emotions, and language.
- Many early skills are subject to the principle of readiness.
- Prenatal development is influenced by environmental factors, such as various teratogens, including diseases, drugs, and radiation, as well as the mother's diet, health, and emotions.
- During sensitive periods in development, infants are more sensitive to specific environmental influences.
- Early perceptual, intellectual, or emotional deprivation seriously retards development, whereas deliberate enrichment of the environment has a beneficial effect on infants.
- In general, environment sets a reaction range within which maturation unfolds.
- Temperament is hereditary. Most infants fall into one of three temperament categories: easy children, difficult children, and slow-to-warm-up children.
- A child's developmental level reflects heredity, environment, and the effects of the child's own behavior.

Although neonates will die if not cared for at birth they are far from helpless. They possess adaptive reflexes, are responsive to their senses, begin to learn immediately, and are aware of their actions.

- Infant development is strongly influenced by heredity. However, environmental factors such as nutrition, parenting, and learning are also important.
- The human neonate has a number of adaptive reflexes, including the grasping, rooting, sucking, and Moro reflexes.
- Tests in a looking chamber reveal a number of visual preferences in the newborn. The neonate is drawn to bright lights and circular or curved designs.
- Infants prefer human face patterns, especially familiar faces. In later infancy, interest in the unfamiliar emerges.
- The rate of maturation varies from person to person. Also, learning contributes greatly to the development of basic motor skills.

You-message Threatening, accusing, bossing, lecturing, or criticizing another person.

I-message A message that states the effect someone else's behavior has on you.

Natural consequences The effects that naturally tend to follow a particular behavior.

Logical consequences Reasonable consequences that are defined by parents.

- Emotions develop in a consistent order, starting with generalized excitement in newborn babies. Three of the basic emotions—fear, anger, and joy—may be unlearned.

Early social development lays a foundation for relationships with parents, siblings, friends, and relatives and the emotional attachment of human infants is a critical early event.

- Opportunities for social interaction increase as infants develop self-awareness and they begin to actively seek guidance from adults.
- Infant attachment is reflected by separation anxiety. The quality of attachment can be classified as secure, insecure-avoidant, or insecure-ambivalent.
- Secure attachment is fostered by consistent care from parents who are sensitive to a baby's signals and rhythms.
- High-quality day care is not harmful and can even be helpful to preschool children. Low-quality care can be risky.
- Meeting a baby's affectional needs is as important as meeting needs for physical care.

Studies suggest that parental styles have a substantial impact on emotional and intellectual development.

- Three major parental styles are authoritarian, permissive, and authoritative (effective). Authoritative parenting appears to benefit children the most.
- Whereas mothers typically emphasize caregiving, fathers tend to function as playmates for infants. Both caregiving styles contribute to the competence of young children.
- The ultimate success of various parenting styles depends on what culture or ethnic community a child will enter.
- Parenting styles vary across cultures.

Language development proceeds from crying to cooing, then babbling, the use of single words, and then to telegraphic speech.

- Learning to use language is a cornerstone of early intellectual development.
- The underlying patterns of telegraphic speech suggest a biological predisposition to acquire language. This innate tendency is augmented by learning.
- Prelanguage communication between parent and child involves shared rhythms, nonverbal signals, and turn-taking.
- Motherese or parentese is a simplified, musical style of speaking that parents use to help their children learn language.

The intellect of a child is less abstract than that of an adult. Jean Piaget theorized that children mature through a fixed series of cognitive stages by applying a combination of assimilation and accommodation. Lev Vygotsky emphasized the role of interactions with more competent partners.

- Piaget held that children mature through a fixed series of cognitive stages. The stages and their approximate age ranges are sensorimotor (0–2), preoperational (2–7), concrete operational (7–11), and formal operations (11–adult).

- Caregivers should offer learning opportunities that are appropriate for a child's level of cognitive development.
- Learning principles provide an alternate explanation that assumes cognitive development is continuous; it does not occur in stages.
- Recent studies of infants under the age of 1 year suggest that they are capable of thought well beyond that observed by Piaget.
- Lev Vygotsky's sociocultural theory emphasizes that a child's mental growth takes place in a child's zone of proximal development, where a more skillful person may scaffold the child's progress. As children rely on adults to help them discover new skills and principles they learn cultural beliefs and values.

Adolescents must form their identity and values at a time when they are also dealing with puberty and transition to adulthood is occurring at ever-later ages.

- The timing of puberty can complicate the task of identity formation, a major task of adolescence.
- Transitioning from childhood to adulthood requires the formation of a personal identity, the major life task of adolescence.
- Identity formation is even more challenging for adolescents of ethnic descent.
- In Western industrialized societies the transition into adulthood is further complicated as it is increasingly delayed well into the 20s.

As in other types of development, we develop morals and values as we grow through several levels.

- Lawrence Kohlberg identified preconventional, conventional, and postconventional levels of moral reasoning.
- Developing mature moral standards is also an important task of adolescence.
- Most people function at the conventional level of morality, but some never get beyond the selfish, preconventional level. Only a minority of people attain the highest, or postconventional level, of moral reasoning.
- Carol Gilligan distinguished between Kohlberg's justice perspective and a caring perspective. Mature adult morality likely involves both.

Erik Erikson identified a series of challenges that occur across the lifespan. These range from a need to gain trust in infancy to the need to live with integrity in old age.

- Personal development does not end after adolescence. Periods of stability and transition occur throughout adulthood.
- We face a specific "crisis," or psychosocial dilemma, at each life stage.
- Successful resolution of the dilemmas produces healthy development, whereas unsuccessful outcomes make it harder to deal with later crises.

Well-being during adulthood consists of six elements: self-acceptance, positive relations with others, autonomy, environmental mastery, having a purpose in life, and continued personal growth.

- Physical aging starts early in adulthood. Every adult must find ways to successfully cope with aging.
- Only a minority of people have a midlife crisis, but midlife course corrections are more common.
- Even if no crisis occurs, people tend to move through repeated cycles of stability and transition throughout adulthood.
- Intellectual declines associated with aging are limited, at least through one's 70s. This is especially true of individuals who remain mentally active.
- Successful lives are based on happiness, purpose, meaning, and integrity.
- Ageism refers to prejudice, discrimination, and stereotyping on the basis of age. It affects people of all ages but is especially damaging to older people. Most ageism is based on stereotypes, myths, and misinformation.

Typical emotional reactions to impending death include denial, anger, bargaining, depression, and acceptance, but not necessarily in that order or in every case.

- Death is a natural part of life. There is value in understanding it and accepting it.

Positive parent-child interactions occur when parents spend enjoyable time encouraging their children in a loving and mutually respectful fashion.

- Effective parental discipline tends to emphasize child management techniques (especially communication), rather than power assertion or withdrawal of love.
- Consistency is also an important aspect of effective parenting.
- Effective parents allow their children to express their feelings but place limits on their behavior.
- Much misbehavior can be managed by use of I-messages and the application of natural and logical consequences.

Web Resources

For an up-to-date list of direct links to interesting sites, including those listed here, visit the student companion site for this book at www.cengage.com/psychology/coon

Human Genome Project Learn more about your human genetic heritage.

Crack Babies A photostory by Ken Kobre.

Scaffolding as a Teaching Strategy Download a paper on the application of Vygotsky's idea of scaffolding to teaching.

A Positive Approach to Identity Formation of Biracial Children Join the debate about multiethnicity and identity formation.

Delayed Adulthood Read two articles about delayed adulthood.

Kohlberg Dilemmas Try your hand at answering several moral dilemmas.

Hospice A website of information about death, bereavement, and hospices.

Discipline: Logical & Natural Consequences Read about ways to effectively structure discipline.

Interactive Learning

Introduction to Psychology: Gateways to Mind and Behavior **Book Companion Website**
www.cengage.com/psyc hology/coon

Visit your book companion website, where you will find flash cards, practice quizzes, web links, and more to help you study.

CENGAGENOW™ *Just what you need to know NOW!*

Spend time on what you need to master rather than on information you already have learned. Take a pre-test for this chapter, and CengageNOW will generate a personalized study plan based on your results. The study plan will identify the topics you need to review and direct you to online resources to help you master those topics. You can then take a post-test to help you determine the concepts you have mastered and what you will need to work on. Try it out! Go to www.cengage.com.com/login to sign in with an access code or to purchase access to this product.

CHAPTER 4

Sensation and Reality

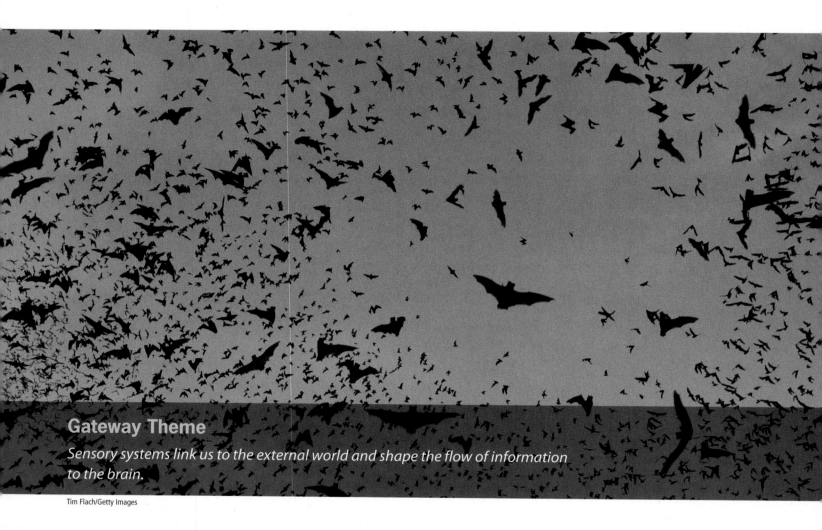

Gateway Theme

Sensory systems link us to the external world and shape the flow of information to the brain.

Tim Flach/Getty Images

Gateway Questions

- *In what ways are our senses limited?*
- *How does the visual system function?*
- *How do we perceive colors?*
- *How do we adjust to the dark?*
- *What are the mechanisms of hearing?*

- *How do the chemical senses operate?*
- *What are the somesthetic senses?*
- *Why are we more aware of some sensations than others?*
- *How can pain be reduced in everyday situations?*

One of your authors once stood at dusk at the mouth of a huge limestone cave on the island of Borneo. For some 20 minutes, fruit bats streamed out of the cave until a dense cloud of half a million bats swirled overhead in the gathering darkness. Besides the sheer spectacle, what most struck him was the silence. Aside from the occasional whisper of bat wings swishing by his ear, he heard nothing. And yet every single bat was shouting—at a pitch so high a human being couldn't hear it. Echoes from those shouts allowed the bats to avoid colliding with each other. At that moment, he was keenly aware of the limitations of his senses.

Do you imagine that the ear is like a digital recorder or the eye is like a camera, giving us a completely accurate "picture" of reality? Perhaps you already understand that this view greatly oversimplifies how we sense and perceive the world. Certainly, as our bat story shows, the senses do not capture complete information about the environment. While this may seem to be some sort of evolutionary oversight, just the opposite is the case. We collect enough sensory information to survive while reducing the amount of sensory information bombarding the brain. This selectivity helps prevent the brain from overloading.

Regardless, at this very moment you are bathed in a swirling kaleidoscope of electromagnetic radiation, heat, pressure, vibrations, molecules, and mechanical forces. Without the senses, all of this would seem like nothing more than a void of silence and darkness. The next time you drink in the beauty of a sunset, a flower, or a friend, remember this: Sensation makes it all possible.

◖◗ Psychophysics—The Limits of Sensibility

Gateway Question: In what ways are our senses limited?

Physical energy, in the form of light waves or heat or sound waves, stimulates your senses. An instant later you see a snowball whiz past your nose or feel the warmth of the sun on your face or hear a catchy tune on the radio. In that instant, a remarkable series of events will have transpired as you detect, analyze, and interpret sensory information.

In an approach called **psychophysics,** physical energy (such as sound waves or electromagnetic radiation) is measured and related to dimensions of the resulting sensations we experience (such as loudness or brightness). Psychophysical investigations have revealed much about our sensory capacities and their limits.

Our eyes, for example, provide us with stunningly wide access to the world. In one instant you can view a star light-years away, and in the next, you can peer into the microscopic universe of a dewdrop. Yet, vision also dramatically narrows what we can observe. Like the other senses, vision acts as a *data reduction system.* Your senses send only the most important data to your brain (Sekuler & Blake, 2006). Before we examine specific senses in more detail, let's explore how the senses reduce the amount of information the brain must process.

Transduction

How does data reduction take place? To begin, our senses limit what we can experience because they do not *transduce* all the physical energies surrounding us. Sensory receptors, such as the eyes and ears, are biological **transducers,** devices that convert one kind of energy into another (Fain, 2003). For example, a guitar transduces string vibrations into sound waves. Pluck a string and the guitar will produce a sound. However, stimuli that don't cause the string to move will have no effect. For instance, if you shine a light on the string, or pour cold water on it, the guitar will remain silent. (The owner of the guitar, however, might get quite loud at this point!) Thus, the eye transduces electromagnetic radiation, the ear transduces sound waves, and so on. Many other types of stimuli cannot be sensed directly because we have no sense receptors to transduce their energy.

For example, humans cannot sense the bioelectric fields of other living beings, but sharks have special organs that can (Fields, 2007). (Do they *hear* the fields or *feel* them or what?) Similarly, humans can transduce only *visible light,* which is a tiny slice of the *electromagnetic spectrum* (entire spread of electromagnetic wavelengths). The spectrum also includes infrared and ultraviolet light, radio waves, television broadcasts, gamma rays, and other energies (look ahead at ● Figure 4.3). In contrast, the eyes of honeybees transduce parts of the electromagnetic spectrum invisible to humans. As you can see, our rich sensory experience is only a small part of what *could* be sensed and what some animals *can* sense.

Absolute Thresholds

Before you can experience a sensation, a stimulus (physical energy) must be above a certain minimum intensity. The necessary minimum defines the **absolute threshold** for a sensory system. For

---

Psychophysics Study of the relationship between physical stimuli and the sensations they evoke in a human observer.

Transducers Devices that convert one kind of energy into another.

Absolute threshold The minimum amount of physical energy necessary to produce a sensation.

Table 4.1 ● Absolute Thresholds

Sensory Modality	Absolute Threshold
Vision	Candle flame seen at 30 miles on a clear dark night
Hearing	Tick of a watch under quiet conditions at 20 feet
Taste	1 teaspoon of sugar in 2 gallons of water
Smell	1 drop of perfume diffused into a three-room apartment
Touch	A bee's wing falling on your cheek from 1 centimeter above

From Galanter, 1962.

© Robert Rattner

Absolute thresholds define the sensory worlds of humans and animals, sometimes with serious consequences. The endangered Florida manatee ("sea cow") is a peaceful, plant-eating creature that can live for more than 60 years. For the last decade, the number of manatees killed by boats has climbed alarmingly. The problem? Manatees have poor sensitivity to the low-frequency sounds made by slow-moving boats. Current laws require boats to slow down in manatee habitats, which may actually increase the risk to these gentle giants (Gerstein, 2002).

example, very soft sounds (which could be heard if they were just a little louder) fall below the absolute threshold for human hearing. Of course, owls have much lower absolute thresholds for hearing, which allows them to hunt at night.

What is the quietest sound that humans can hear? The weakest light that we can see? The lightest touch that we can feel? Testing for absolute thresholds shows just how sensitive we are. For example, it only takes three photons of light striking visual receptors at the back of the eye to produce a sensation. A photon (FOE-tahn: one quantum of energy) is the smallest possible "package" of light. Responding to three photons is like seeing a candle flame 30 miles away! ● Table 4.1 gives approximate absolute thresholds for the five major senses.

Some sensory systems have upper limits as well as lower ones. For example, if we test for pitch sensitivity (higher and lower tones), we find that humans can hear sounds down to 20 hertz (vibrations per second) and up to about 20,000 hertz. This is an impressive range—from the lowest rumble of a pipe organ to the highest squeak of a stereo "tweeter." On the lower end, the threshold is as low as practical. If your ears could sense tones below 20 hertz, you would hear the movements of your own muscles. Imagine how disturbing it would be to hear your body creak and groan like an old ship as you move.

The 20,000 hertz upper threshold for human hearing, on the other hand, could easily be higher. Bats, dogs, cats, and other animals can hear sounds well above this limit. That's why a "silent" dog whistle (which may make sounds as high as 40,000 to 50,000 hertz) can be heard by dogs but not by humans. For dogs the sound exists. For humans it is beyond awareness. It's easy to see how thresholds define the limits of the sensory world in which we live. (If you want to buy a stereo system for your dog, you will have a hard time finding one that reproduces sounds above 20,000 hertz!)

Wouldn't the absolute threshold be different for different people? Not only do absolute thresholds vary for different people, they also change from time to time for a single person. The type of stimulus, the state of your nervous system, and the costs of false "detections" all make a difference (Goldstein, 2007). Emotional factors are also important. Unpleasant stimuli, for example, may *raise* the threshold for recognition.

Is "subliminal" perception possible? Yes, under limited circumstances. Anytime information is processed below the normal *limen* (LIE-men: threshold or limit) for awareness, it is *subliminal*. **Subliminal perception** was demonstrated by a study in which college

students saw photos of a person flashed on a screen. Each time before the face appeared, it was preceded by a subliminal image that was shown for just a fraction of a second. Some were images that made viewers feel good (such as cute kittens). Others made them feel bad (for example, a face on fire). All the emotional images were flashed too briefly to be recognized. Nevertheless, they altered the impressions students formed of the target person (Krosnick et al., 1992). Apparently, some emotional impact gets through, even when a stimulus is below the level of conscious awareness (Arndt, Allen, & Greenberg, 2001). To find out if such effects could be applied to advertising, read "Subliminal Seduction or Subliminal Myths?"

Difference Thresholds

Psychophysics also involves the study of **difference thresholds.** Here we are asking, "How much must a stimulus change (increase or decrease) before it becomes just noticeably different?" The study of **just noticeable differences** (**JNDs**) led to one of psychology's first natural "laws." **Weber's** (VAY-bears) **law** can be roughly stated as follows: The amount of change needed to produce a JND is a constant proportion of the original stimulus intensity. Here are some Weber's proportions for common judgments:

Pitch	1/333 (1/3 of 1 percent)
Weight	1/50 (2 percent)
Loudness	1/10 (10 percent)
Taste	1/5 (20 percent)

Notice how much more sensitive hearing is than taste. Very small changes in pitch and loudness are easy to detect. If a voice or a musical instrument is off pitch by 1/3 of 1 percent, you'll probably notice it. For taste, we find that a 20-percent change is necessary to produce a JND. If a cup of coffee has 5 teaspoons of sugar in it, you will have to add 1 more (1/5 of 5) before it will be noticeably sweeter. If you're salting soup, it takes a lot of cooks to spoil the broth!

CRITICAL THINKING

Subliminal Seduction or Subliminal Myth?

Could subliminal perception ever be used against us? The sensationalistic book *Subliminal Seduction* (Key, 1973) voiced popular fears of attempts to influence us through subliminal messages embedded in advertising. But could it work?

In a famous early attempt, a New Jersey theater flashed the words *Eat popcorn* and *Drink Coca-Cola* on the screen for 1/3,000 second every 5 seconds during movies. Dramatic claims that popcorn and Coke sales increased as a result later turned out to be falsehoods. The advertising "expert" responsible admitted he faked the whole thing. By lying about his ability to control audiences, he had hoped to gain customers for his marketing business (Pratkanis, 1992; Shrum, 2004). Regardless, the possibility of subliminal seduction was so horrifying that such advertising was banned in the United States, Britain, and Australia (Karremans, Stroebe, & Claus, 2006).

Despite these fears, some businesses actually sell subliminal messages to people who want them to work. Each year, consumers spend many millions of dollars on so-called subliminal self-help tapes and CDs (Pratkanis & Aronson, 2001). "Subliminal messages" embedded in relaxing music or the soothing sounds of ocean waves purportedly influence "subconscious motivation" to help listeners lose weight, relieve pain, find romance, succeed financially, improve grades, and so forth.

In one study, students who listened to subliminal messages meant to improve their study habits, and, hence, their grades,

performed no better than students who just listened to relaxing ocean sounds without subliminal messages and students who listened to nothing at all (Russell, Rowe, & Smouse, 1991). In this instance, subliminal messages had no effect, even when people wanted to be influenced. In most cases, people who think they have been helped by subliminal messages have likely experienced nothing more than a placebo effect (Froufe & Schwartz, 2001).

However, before writing off subliminal advertising altogether, let's consider the work of psychologist Johan Karremans and his colleagues (Karremans, Stroebe, & Claus, 2006).

They suggest that only simple messages, such as single words, can be processed subliminally, which is why subliminal self-help materials are usually ineffective. They also provide evidence that subliminally flashing the brand name of a drink can increase the likelihood that people will buy it, but only if they are already thirsty. Perhaps subliminal advertising can work under limited circumstances. Nevertheless, advertisers are still better off using the loudest, clearest, most attention-demanding stimuli available—as most do (Smith & Rogers, 1994).

"I'll be right back after these subliminal messages."

Sensory Analysis and Coding

What we experience is greatly influenced by **sensory analysis.** As they process information, the senses divide the world into important **perceptual features** (basic stimulus patterns). For vision, such features include lines, shapes, edges, spots, colors, and other patterns (Hubel & Wiesel, 2005). Look at ● Figure 4.1 and notice how eye-catching the single vertical line is among a group of slanted lines. This effect, which is called *pop-out,* occurs because your visual system is highly sensitive to perceptual features such as line orientation (Adler & Orprecio, 2006).

In some instances, the senses act as *feature detectors* because they are attuned to very specific stimuli. Frog eyes, for example, are highly sensitive to small, dark, moving spots. In other words,

Subliminal perception Perception of a stimulus below the threshold for conscious recognition.

Difference threshold A change in stimulus intensity that is detectable to an observer.

Just noticeable difference (JND) Any noticeable difference in a stimulus.

Weber's law The just noticeable difference is a constant proportion of the original stimulus intensity.

Sensory analysis Separation of sensory information into important elements.

Perceptual features Basic elements of a stimulus, such as lines, shapes, edges, or colors.

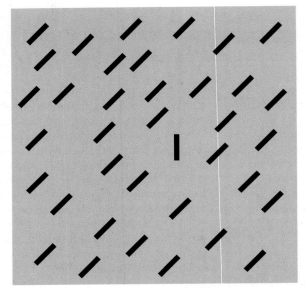

● **Figure 4.1** Visual pop-out. Pop-out is so basic that babies as young as 3 months respond to it. (Adapted from Adler & Orprecio, 2006.)

they are basically "tuned" to detect bugs flying nearby (Lettvin, 1961). But the insect (spot) must be moving, or the frog's "bug detectors" won't work. A frog could starve to death surrounded by dead flies.

After they have selected and analyzed information, sensory systems must *code* it. **Sensory coding** refers to changing important features of the world into messages understood by the brain (Hubel & Wiesel, 2005). To see coding at work, try closing your eyes for a moment. Then take your fingertips and press firmly on your eyelids. Apply enough pressure to "squash" your eyes slightly. Do this for about 30 seconds and observe what happens. (Readers with eye problems or contact lenses should not try this.)

Did you "see" stars, checkerboards, and flashes of color? These are called *phosphenes* (FOSS-feens: visual sensations caused by mechanical excitation of the retina). They occur because the eye's receptor cells, which normally respond to light, are also somewhat sensitive to pressure. Notice though, that the eye is only prepared to code stimulation—

including pressure—into visual features. As a result, you experience light sensations, not pressure. Also important in producing this effect is *sensory localization* in the brain.

Sensory localization means that the type of sensation you experience depends on which brain area is activated. Some brain areas receive visual information, others receive auditory information, and still others receive taste or touch. (See Chapter 2, pages 63–67.) Knowing which brain areas are active tells us, in general, what kinds of sensations you are feeling.

Sensory localization makes it possible to artificially restore sight, hearing, or other senses. For example, in July 2006, a woman named Cheri Robinson became the sixteenth person in the world with an implant that allows a miniature television camera to send electrical signals to her brain's visual cortex (● Figure 4.2). She can now "see" 100 dots of light. Like a sports scoreboard, these lights can be used to form crude letters (Warren & Normann, 2005). Eventually, increasing the number of dots could make reading and "seeing" large objects, such as furniture and doorways, possible.

It is fascinating to realize that "seeing" and "hearing" take place in the brain, not in the eye or ear. Information arriving from the sense organs creates **sensations.** When the brain organizes sensations into meaningful patterns, we speak of **perception,** which will be covered in Chapter 5. It's now time to examine each of the senses in more detail. In the next section, we will begin with vision, which is perhaps the most magnificent sensory system of all. Before you read more, it might be a good idea to stop and review some of the ideas we have covered.

KNOWLEDGE BUILDER
Sensation and Psychophysics

RECITE
1. Sensory receptors are biological _____, or devices for converting one type of energy to another.
2. The minimum amount of stimulation necessary for a sensation to occur defines the _____ _____.

Continued

Actual image

Cameras

Visual cortex

Electrodes

Perceived image

● **Figure 4.2** An artificial visual system.

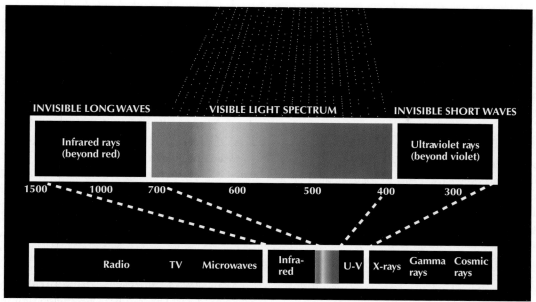

● **Figure 4.3** The visible spectrum.

3. Subliminal stimuli have been shown to have an effect on the behavior of viewers. T or F?
4. Lettvin found that a frog's eyes are especially sensitive to phosphenes. T or F?
5. Important features of the environment are transmitted to the brain through a process known as
   a. phosphenation
   b. coding
   c. detection
   d. programming

REFLECT

Critical Thinking

6. Is a doorbell a transducer?
7. If the human ear were more sensitive than it is now, our hearing would be impaired. How could this be true?
8. When promoters of self-help "subliminal tapes" are challenged to provide evidence that their products work, what study do you think they most often cite?

Relate

How does sensation affect what you are experiencing right now? What if data reduction didn't occur? What if you could transduce other energies? What if your senses were tuned to detect different perceptual features? What if your absolute thresholds were higher or lower for each sense? How would the sensory world you live in change?

faked "Eat popcorn/drink Coca-Cola" study (Pratkanis, 1992).

constant roaring or hissing noise. **8.** Good guess! That's right, it's still the hydrogen atom) can be heard. Therefore, if your ears were more sensitive, they would convert the random movement of air molecules into a person in the house. **7.** Under ideal conditions, vibrations of the eardrum as small as one billionth of a centimeter (one tenth the diameter of a sound waves that are transduced into nerve impulses by the ears of the in order to strike a bell; the physical vibrations of the bell then produce into an electrical signal that is converted again into mechanical energy sense, it is. The button converts mechanical energy from your finger **Answers: 1.** transducers **2.** absolute threshold **3.** T **4.** F **5.** b **6.** In a broad

●● Vision—Catching Some Rays

Gateway Question: How does the visual system function?

In the morning when you awaken and open your eyes you effortlessly become aware of the visual richness of the world around you. But the ease with which normally sighted people can *see* conceals incredible complexity. Vision is an impressive sensory system, worthy of a detailed discussion.

What are the basic dimensions of light and vision? As we have noted, various wavelengths of light make up the **visible spectrum** (the narrow spread of electromagnetic energies to which the eyes respond). Visible light starts at "short" wavelengths of 400 *nanometers* (nan-OM-et-er: one billionth of a meter), which we sense as purple or violet. Longer light waves produce blue, green, yellow, orange, and red, which has a wavelength of 700 nanometers (● Figure 4.3).

The term *hue* refers to the basic color categories of red, orange, yellow, green, blue, indigo, and violet. As just noted, various hues (or color sensations) correspond to the wavelength of the light that reaches our eyes (Sekuler & Blake, 2006). White light, in contrast, is a mixture of many wavelengths. Hues (colors) from a narrow band of wavelengths are very *saturated*, or "pure." (An

Sensory coding Codes used by the sense organs to transmit information to the brain.

Sensation A sensory impression; also, the process of detecting physical energies with the sensory organs.

Perception The mental process of organizing sensations into meaningful patterns.

Visible spectrum The narrow spread of the electromagnetic spectrum to which the eyes are sensitive.

intense "fire-engine" red is more saturated than a muddy "brick" red.) A third dimension of vision, *brightness,* corresponds roughly to the amplitude, or height of light waves. Waves of greater amplitude are "taller," carry more energy, and cause the colors we see to appear brighter or more intense. For example, the same "brick" red would look bright under intense, high-energy illumination and drab under dim light.

Structure of the Eye

Although the visual system is much more complex than any digital camera, both cameras and eyes have a *lens* to focus images on a light-sensitive layer at the back of a closed space. In a camera, this layer is the digital image sensor. In the eye, it is a layer of *photoreceptors* (light-sensitive cells) in the **retina,** an area about the size and thickness of a postage stamp (● Figure 4.4).

How does the eye focus? Most focusing is done at the front of the eye by the *cornea,* a clear membrane that bends light inward. The lens makes additional, smaller adjustments. Your eye's focal point changes when muscles attached to the lens alter its shape. This

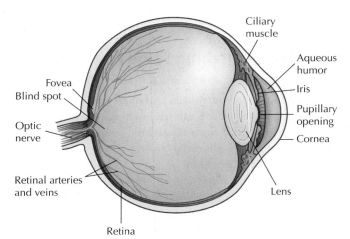

● **Figure 4.4** The human eye, a simplified view.

process is called **accommodation.** In cameras, focusing is done more simply—by changing the distance between the lens and the image sensor.

Visual Problems

Focusing is also affected by the shape of the eye. If your eye is too short, nearby objects will be blurred, but distant objects will be sharp. This is called **hyperopia** (HI-per-OPE-ee-ah: farsightedness). If your eyeball is too long, images fall short of the retina and you won't be able to focus distant objects. This results in **myopia** (my-OPE-ee-ah: nearsightedness). When the cornea or the lens is misshapen, part of vision will be focused and part will be fuzzy. In this case, the eye has more than one focal point, a problem called **astigmatism** (ah-STIG-mah-tiz-em). All three visual defects can be corrected by reshaping the cornea through laser eye surgery or by placing glasses (or contact lenses) in front of the eye to change the path of light (● Figure 4.5).

As people age, the lens becomes less flexible and less able to accommodate. The result is **presbyopia** (prez-bee-OPE-ee-ah: old vision, or farsightedness due to aging). Perhaps you have seen a grandparent or older friend reading a newspaper at arm's length because of presbyopia. If you now wear glasses for nearsightedness, you may need bifocals as you age. (Just like your authors. Sigh.) Bifocal lenses correct near vision *and* distance vision.

Light Control

There is one more major similarity between the eye and a camera. In front of the lens in both is a mechanism that controls the amount of light entering. In the eye, this mechanism is the *iris*; in a camera, it is the diaphragm (● Figure 4.6). The **iris** is a colored circular muscle that gives your eyes their blue or brown or green color. By expanding and contracting, the iris changes the size of the **pupil** (the opening at the center of the eye).

With some cameras, you can adjust the sensitivity of the digital image sensor. The sensitivity of the retina also changes in brighter

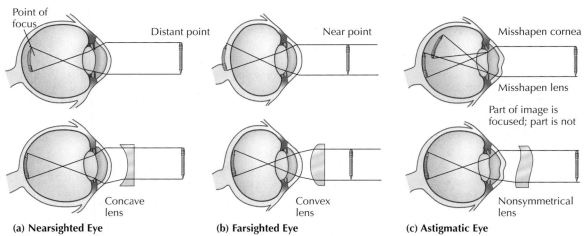

(a) **Nearsighted Eye**   (b) **Farsighted Eye**   (c) **Astigmatic Eye**

● **Figure 4.5** Visual defects and corrective lenses: *(a)* A myopic (longer than usual) eye. The concave lens spreads light rays just enough to increase the eye's focal length. *(b)* A hyperopic (shorter than usual) eye. The convex lens increases refraction (bending), returning the point of focus to the retina. *(c)* An astigmatic (lens or cornea not symmetrical) eye. In astigmatism, parts of vision are sharp and parts are unfocused. Lenses to correct astigmatism are unsymmetrical.

● **Figure 4.6** The iris and diaphragm.

Fibers of the optic nerve

Ganglion cell

Amacrine cell

Retina

Bipolar neuron

Horizontal cell

Photoreceptor cells:
Cone
Rod

Pigment layer of retina

Choroid layer

Sclera

Direction of light

Direction of nerve impulses

Retina

Optic nerve

Omikron/Photo Researchers, Inc.

● **Figure 4.7** Anatomy of the retina. The retina lies behind the vitreous humor, which is the jelly-like substance that fills the eyeball. The rods and cones are much smaller than implied here. The smallest are 1 micron (one millionth of a meter) wide. The lower-left photograph shows rods and cones as seen through an electron microscope. In the photograph the cones are colored green and the rods blue.

120 million, can't detect colors (● Figure 4.7). Pure rod vision is black and white. However, the rods are much more sensitive to light than the cones are. The rods therefore allow us to see in very dim light.

Notice in ● Figure 4.7 that light does not fall directly on the rods and cones. It must pass through the outer layers of the retina. Note, too, that the rods and cones face the *back* of the eye! Only about one half of the light falling on the front of the eye ever reaches the rods and cones—testimony to the eye's amazing light sensitivity.

Surprisingly, the retina has a "hole" in it: Each eye has a **blind spot** because there are no receptors where the optic nerve passes out of the eye and blood vessels enter (● Figure 4.7). The blind spot shows that vision depends greatly on the brain. If you close one eye, part of what you see will fall on the blind spot of your open eye (● Figure 4.8*a*). Why isn't there a gap in your vision? The answer is that the visual cortex of the brain actively fills in the gap with patterns from surrounding areas (● Figure 4.8*b*). By closing one eye, you can visually "behead" other people by placing their images on your blind spot. (Just a hint for some classroom fun.) The brain can also "erase" distracting information. Roll your eyes all the way to the right and then close your right eye. You should clearly see your nose in your left eye's field of vision. Now, open your right eye again and your nose will nearly disappear as your brain disregards its presence.

It's tempting to think of vision as a movie-like projection of "pictures" to the brain. However, this mistaken notion immediately raises the question, "Who's watching the movie?" From the retina on, vision becomes quite unlike a digital camera, which merely records and displays the digital images it has captured. Instead, vision is a complex system

or dimmer light, but the retina can only adapt slowly. By making rapid adjustments, the iris allows us to move quickly from darkness to bright sunlight, or the reverse. In dim light the pupils dilate (enlarge), and in bright light they constrict (narrow). When the iris is wide open, the pupil is 17 times larger than at its smallest. Were it not for this, you would be blinded for some time after walking into a darkened room.

Rods and Cones

The eye has two types of "image sensors," consisting of receptor cells called *rods* and *cones* (Goldstein, 2007). The 5 million **cones** in each eye work best in bright light. They also produce color sensations and fine details. In contrast, the **rods,** numbering about

Retina The light-sensitive layer of cells at the back of the eye.

Accommodation Changes in the shape of the lens of the eye.

Hyperopia Difficulty focusing nearby objects (farsightedness).

Myopia Difficulty focusing distant objects (nearsightedness).

Astigmatism Defects in the cornea, lens, or eye that cause some areas of vision to be out of focus.

Presbyopia Farsightedness caused by aging.

Iris Circular muscle that controls the amount of light entering the eye.

Pupil The opening at the front of the eye through which light passes.

Cones Visual receptors for colors and daylight visual acuity.

Rods Visual receptors for dim light that produce only black and white sensations.

Blind spot An area of the retina lacking visual receptors.

● **Figure 4.8** Experiencing the blind spot. *(a)* With your right eye closed, stare at the upper-right cross. Hold the book about 1 foot from your eye and slowly move it back and forth. You should be able to locate a position that causes the black spot to disappear. When it does, it has fallen on the blind spot. With a little practice you can learn to make people or objects you dislike disappear too! *(b)* Repeat the procedure described, but stare at the lower cross. When the white space falls on the blind spot, the black lines will appear to be continuous. This may help you understand why you do not usually experience a blind spot in your visual field.

for analyzing patterns of light. Thanks to the Nobel Prize–winning work of biopsychologists David Hubel and Torsten Wiesel, we now know that vision acts more like an incredibly advanced computer than a television or movie camera.

Hubel and Wiesel directly recorded the activities of single cells in the brain's visual cortex in cats and monkeys. As they did, they noted the area of the retina to which each cell responded. Then they aimed lights of various sizes and shapes at the retina and recorded how often the corresponding brain cell fired nerve impulses (● Figure 4.9*a*).

The results were fascinating. Many brain cells responded only to lines of a certain width or orientation. These same cells didn't get the least bit "excited" over a dot of light or overall illumination (● Figure 4.9*b*). Other cells responded only to lines at certain angles, or lines of certain lengths, or lines moving in a particular direction (Hubel & Wiesel, 1979).

The upshot of such findings is that cells in the brain, like the frog's retina described earlier, act as feature detectors. The brain seems to first analyze information into lines, angles, shading, movement, and other basic features. Then, other brain areas combine these features into meaningful visual experiences. (This concept is discussed further in Chapter 5.) Reading this page is a direct result of such feature analysis. Given the size of the task, it's little wonder that as much as 30 percent of the human brain may be involved in vision. (To further follow the pathways visual infor-

mation takes through the brain, see "Blindsight: The 'What' and the 'Where' of Vision.")

Visual Acuity

The rods and cones also affect **visual acuity,** or sharpness. The cones lie mainly at the center of the eye. In fact, the **fovea** (FOE-vee-ah: a small cup-shaped area in the middle of the retina) contains only cones—about 50,000 of them. Like a newspaper photograph made of many small dots, the tightly packed cones in the fovea produce the sharpest images. Normal acuity is designated as 20/20 vision: At 20 feet in distance, you can distinguish what the average person can see at 20 feet (● Figure 4.11). If your vision is 20/40, you can only see at 20 feet what the average person can see at 40 feet. If your vision is 20/200, everything is a blur and you need glasses! Vision that is 20/12 would mean that you can see at 20 feet what the average person must be 8 feet nearer to see, indicating better than average acuity. American astronaut Gordon Cooper, who claimed to see railroad lines in northern India from 100 miles above, had 20/12 vision.

Peripheral Vision

What is the purpose of the rest of the retina? Areas outside the fovea also get light, creating a large region of **peripheral** (side) **vision.** The rods are most numerous about 20 degrees from the center of the retina, so much of our peripheral vision is rod vision. Although

● **Figure 4.9** *(a)* A "typical" brain cell responds to only a small area of the total field of vision. In this example, the cell responds to stimuli that fall above and left of the center of vision. The bar graph *(b)* illustrates how a brain cell may act as a feature detector. Notice how the cell primarily responds to just one type of stimulus. (Adapted from Hubel, 1979.)

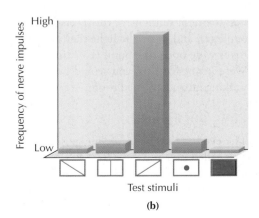

BRAINWAVES

Blindsight: The "What" and the "Where" of Vision

As you read this book, you may find yourself wondering why psychologists are so interested in the brain. Brainwaves boxes like this one are designed to help you think about how the biopsychological perspective contributes to a better understanding of human behavior.

Meet a woman we will call D. F., who suffered brain damage that caused severe *visual agnosia* (Goodale et al., 1991). If D. F. was shown an object, she could not recognize it. Remarkably, even though she couldn't recognize objects, D. F. could successfully manipulate them. For example, in one test she was given a card and asked to insert it into a slot at a certain angle. Although she could not describe the slot's orientation, she had no difficulty inserting the card into it. You could say that D. F. displayed *blindsight:* When shown an object, she was *blind* to *what* the object

was, but she had enough *sight* to know *where* it was in her visual field (James et al., 2003).

What patients like D. F. teach us is that the brain has assigned the job of seeing to different brain regions (Deco, Rolls, & Horowitz, 2004). One series of regions, the *ventral pathway*, is responsible for the "what" of vision, whereas another series of regions, the *dorsal pathway*, is responsible for the "where" of vision (● Figure 4.10). D. F. suffered damage in her ventral pathway so she could not process the "what" of vision, but her intact dorsal pathway could still process the "where" of vision.

What happens if someone suffers brain damage to the dorsal pathway? In a rare case, a woman with just such damage had great difficulty crossing the street. Although she had no trouble recognizing cars (the what), she could not tell *where* they were. She could not even distinguish approaching cars from parked cars (Zeki, 1991).

● **Figure 4.10** The ventral and dorsal visual pathways.

● **Figure 4.11** Tests of visual acuity. Here are some common tests of visual acuity. In *(a)* sharpness is indicated by the smallest grating still seen as individual lines. The Snellen chart *(b)* requires that you read rows of letters of diminishing size until you can no longer distinguish them. The Landolt rings *(c)* require no familiarity with letters. All that is required is a report of which side has a break in it.

rod vision is not very sharp, the rods are quite sensitive to *movement* in peripheral vision. To experience this characteristic of the rods, look straight ahead and hold your hand beside your head, at about 90 degrees. Wiggle your finger and slowly move your hand forward until you can detect motion. You will become aware of the movement before you can actually "see" your finger.

Seeing "out of the corner of the eye" is important for sports, driving, and walking down dark alleys. People who suffer from *tunnel vision* (a loss of peripheral vision) feel as if they are wearing blinders (Godnig, 2003). Tunnel vision can also occur temporarily when we are overloaded by a task. For example, if you were playing a demanding video game you might be excused for not noticing that a friend had walked up beside you.

The rods are also highly responsive to dim light. Because most rods are 20 degrees to each side of the fovea, the best night vision comes from looking *next to* an object you wish to see. Test this yourself some night by looking at, and next to, a very dim star.

⬤⬤ Color Vision—There's More to It Than Meets the Eye

Gateway Question: How do we perceive colors?

What would you say is the brightest color? Red? Yellow? Blue? Actually, there are two answers to this question, one for the rods and one for the cones. The cones are most sensitive to the *yellowish green* part of the spectrum. In other words, if all colors are tested in daylight (with each reflecting the same amount of light), then yellowish green appears *brightest*. Yellow-green fire trucks and the bright yellow vests worn by roadside work crews are a reflection of this fact.

To what color are the rods most sensitive? Remember that the rods do not produce color sensations. If you were looking at a very dim colored light, you wouldn't see any color. Even so, one light would appear brighter than the others. When tested this way, the rods are most sensitive to *blue-green* lights. Thus, at night or in dim light, when rod vision prevails, the brightest-colored light will be one that

---

Visual acuity The sharpness of visual perception.

Fovea An area at the center of the retina containing only cones.

Peripheral vision Vision at the edges of the visual field.

is blue or blue-green. For this reason, police and highway patrol cars in many states now have blue emergency lights for night work. Also, you may have wondered why the taxiway lights at airports are blue. It seems like a poor choice, but blue is actually highly visible to pilots.

Color Theories

How do the cones produce color sensations? The **trichromatic** (TRY-kro-MAT-ik) **theory** of color vision holds that there are three types of cones, each most sensitive to either red, green, or blue. Other colors result from combinations of these three.

A basic problem with the trichromatic theory is that four colors of light—red, green, blue, and yellow—seem to be primary (you can't get them by mixing other colors). Also, why is it impossible to have a reddish green or a yellowish blue? These problems led to the development of a second view, known as the **opponent-process theory,** which states that vision analyzes colors into "either-or" messages (Goldstein, 2007). That is, the visual system can produce messages for either red or green, yellow or blue, black or white. Coding one color in a pair (red, for instance) seems to block the opposite message (green) from coming through. As a result, a reddish green is impossible, but a yellowish red (orange) can occur.

According to opponent-process theory, fatigue caused by making one response produces an afterimage of the opposite color as the system recovers. *Afterimages* are visual sensations that persist after a stimulus is removed—like seeing a spot after a flashbulb goes off. To see an afterimage of the type predicted by opponent-process theory, look at ● Figure 4.12 and follow the instructions there.

Which color theory is correct? Both! The three-color theory applies to the retina, where three different types of cone have been found. Each contains a different type of *iodopsin* (i-oh-DOP-sin), a light-sensitive pigment that breaks down when struck by light. This triggers action potentials and sends neural messages to the brain. The three types of cones are most sensitive to red, green, or blue. Other colors result from combinations of these three. (Black and white sensations are produced by the rods, which contain a

chemical called *rhodopsin* (row-DOP-sin), another light-sensitive visual pigment.) As predicted, each form of iodopsin is most sensitive to light in roughly the red, green, or blue region. The three types of cones fire nerve impulses at different rates to produce various color sensations (● Figure 4.13).

In contrast, the opponent-process theory better explains what happens in optic pathways and the brain *after* information leaves the eye. For example, some nerve cells in the brain are excited by the color red and inhibited by the color green. So both theories are "correct." One explains what happens in the eye itself. The other explains how colors are analyzed after messages leave the eye (Gegenfurtner & Kiper, 2003).

Constructing Colors

The preceding explanations present a fairly mechanical view of how colors are sensed. In reality, color experiences are more complex. For example, the apparent color of an object is influenced by the colors of other nearby objects. This effect is called **simultaneous color contrast.** It occurs because brain cell activity in one area of the cerebral cortex can be altered by activity in nearby areas. Simultaneous contrast can make it difficult to paint a picture or decorate a room. If you add a new color to a canvas or a room, all the existing colors will suddenly look different. Typically, each time a new color is added, all the other colors must be adjusted (● Figure 4.14).

More striking than simultaneous contrast is the fact that color experiences are *actively constructed* in the brain. The brain does not simply receive prepackaged color messages. It must generate color from the data it receives. As a result, it is possible to experience color where none exists. (See ● Figure 4.15 for an example.) Indeed, all our experiences are at least partially constructed from the information surrounding us. (We'll explore this idea further later in this chapter.)

● **Figure 4.12** Negative afterimages. Stare at the dot near the middle of the flag for at least 30 seconds. Then look immediately at a plain sheet of white paper or a white wall. You will see the American flag in its normal colors. Reduced sensitivity to yellow, green, and black in the visual system, caused by prolonged staring, results in the appearance of complementary colors. Project the afterimage of the flag on other colored surfaces to get additional effects.

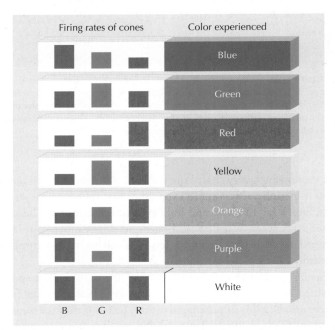

● **Figure 4.13** Firing rates of blue, green, and red cones in response to different colors. The taller the colored bar, the higher the firing rates for that type of cone. As you can see, colors are coded by differences in the activity of all three types of cones in the normal eye. (Adapted from Goldstein, 2007.)

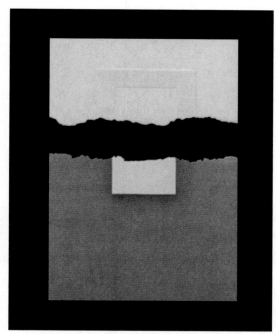

● **Figure 4.14** Notice how different the gray-blue color looks when it is placed on different backgrounds. Unless you are looking at a large, solid block of color, simultaneous contrast is constantly affecting your color experiences.

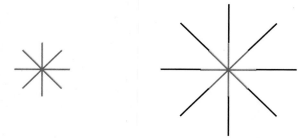

● **Figure 4.15** On the left is a "star" made of red lines. On the right, the red lines are placed on top of longer black lines. Now, in addition to the red lines, you will see a glowing red disk, with a clear border. Of course, no red disk is printed on this page. No ink can be found between the red lines. The glowing red disk exists only in your mind. (After Hoffman, 1999, p. 111.)

Color Blindness and Color Weakness

Do you know anyone who regularly draws hoots of laughter by wearing clothes of wildly clashing colors? Or someone who sheepishly tries to avoid saying what color an object is? If so, you probably know someone who is color blind.

What is it like to be color blind? What causes color blindness? A person who is **color blind** cannot perceive colors. It is as if the world is a black-and-white movie. The color-blind person either lacks cones or has cones that do not function normally (Deeb, 2004). Such total color blindness is rare. In **color weakness,** or partial color blindness, a person can't see certain colors. Approximately 8 percent of Caucasian males are red-green color blind (but fewer Asian American, African American, and Native American males, and less than 1 percent of women, are) (Delpero et al., 2005). These people see both reds and greens as the same color, usually a yellowish brown (● Figure 4.16). Another type of color

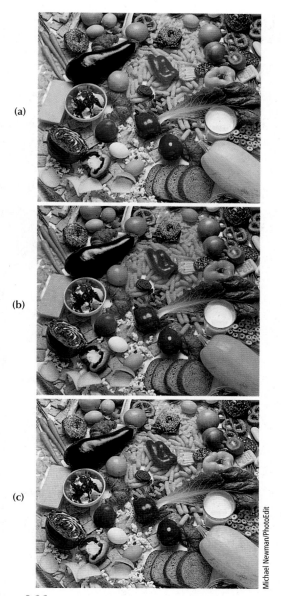

● **Figure 4.16** Color blindness and color weakness. *(a)* Photograph illustrates normal color vision. *(b)* Photograph is printed in blue and yellow and gives an impression of what a red-green color-blind person sees. *(c)* Photograph simulates total color blindness. If you are totally color blind, all three photos will look nearly identical.

Michael Newman/PhotoEdit

weakness, involving yellow and blue, is extremely rare (Hsia & Graham, 1997). (See "Are You Color Blind?")

Color blindness is caused by changes in the genes that control red, green, and blue pigments in the cones. Red-green color weak-

Trichromatic theory Theory of color vision based on three cone types: red, green, and blue.

Opponent-process theory Theory of color vision based on three coding systems (red or green, yellow or blue, black or white).

Simultaneous color contrast Changes in perceived hue that occur when a colored stimulus is displayed on backgrounds of various colors.

Color blindness A total inability to perceive colors.

Color weakness An inability to distinguish some colors.

DISCOVERING PSYCHOLOGY

Are You Color Blind?

How can I tell if I am color blind? Surprisingly, it is not as obvious as you might think; some of us reach adulthood without knowing. The *Ishihara test* is commonly used to measure color blindness and weakness. In the test, numbers and other designs made of dots are placed on a background also made of dots (● Figure 4.17). The background and the numbers are of different colors (red and green, for example). A person who is color blind sees only a jumble of dots. If you have normal color vision you can detect the numbers or designs (Birch & McKeever, 1993; Coren, Ward, & Enns, 2004). The chart below ● Figure 4.17 lists what people with normal color vision and color blindness see. Because this chart is just a replica, it is not a definitive test of color blindness. Nevertheless, if you can't see all the embedded designs, you may be color blind or color weak.

● **Figure 4.17** A replica of the Ishihara test for color blindness.

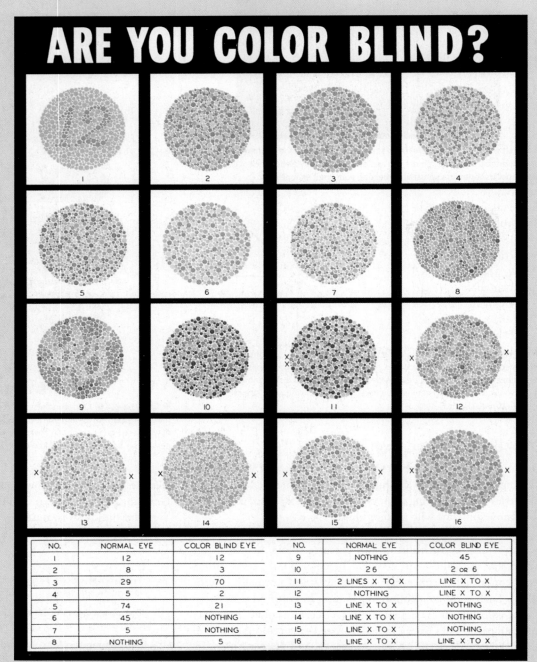

NO.	NORMAL EYE	COLOR BLIND EYE	NO.	NORMAL EYE	COLOR BLIND EYE
1	12	12	9	NOTHING	45
2	8	3	10	26	2 OR 6
3	29	70	11	2 LINES X TO X	LINE X TO X
4	5	2	12	NOTHING	LINE X TO X
5	74	21	13	LINE X TO X	NOTHING
6	45	NOTHING	14	LINE X TO X	NOTHING
7	5	NOTHING	15	LINE X TO X	NOTHING
8	NOTHING	5	16	LINE X TO X	LINE X TO X

ness is a recessive, sex-linked trait. That means it is carried on the *X*, or female, chromosome. Women have two *X* chromosomes, so if they receive only one defective color gene, they still have normal vision. Color-weak men, however, have only one *X* chromosome, so they can inherit the defect from their mothers (who usually don't display any color weakness).

How can color-blind individuals drive? Don't they have trouble with traffic lights? Red-green color-blind individuals have normal vision for yellow and blue, so the main problem is telling red lights from green. In practice, that's not difficult. The red light is always on top, and the green light is brighter than the red. Also, "red" traffic signals have yellow light mixed in with the red and a "green" light that is really blue-green.

⬤⬤ Dark Adaptation—Let There Be Light!

Gateway Question: How do we adjust to the dark?

What happens when the eyes adjust to a dark room? **Dark adaptation** is the dramatic increase in retinal sensitivity to light that occurs after a person enters the dark (Goldstein, 2007). Consider walking into a theater. If you enter from a brightly lighted lobby, you practically need to be led to your seat. After a short time, however, you can see the entire room in detail (including the couple kissing over in the corner). It takes about 30 to 35 minutes of complete darkness to reach maximum visual sensitivity (⬤ Figure 4.18). At that point, your eye will be 100,000 times more sensitive to light.

What causes dark adaptation? Remember that both rods and cones contain light-sensitive visual pigments. When struck by light, visual pigments *bleach,* or break down chemically. The afterimages you have seen after looking at a flashbulb are a result of this bleaching. To restore light sensitivity, the visual pigments must recombine, which takes time. Night vision is due mainly to an increase in rhodopsin, the rod pigment. When completely dark adapted, the human eye is almost as sensitive to light as the eye of an owl.

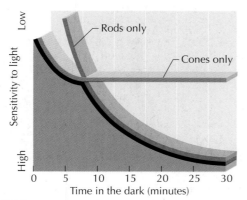

⬤ **Figure 4.18** Typical course of dark adaptation. The black line shows how the threshold for vision lowers as a person spends time in the dark. (A lower threshold means that less light is needed for vision.) The green line shows that the cones adapt first, but they soon cease adding to light sensitivity. Rods, shown by the red line, adapt more slowly. However, they continue to add to improved night vision long after the cones are fully adapted.

As you might have noticed, a few seconds of exposure to bright white light can completely wipe out dark adaptation. That's why you should be sure to avoid looking at oncoming headlights when you are driving at night—especially the new bluish-white xenon lights.

Under normal conditions, glare recovery takes about 20 seconds, plenty of time for an accident. After a few drinks, it may take 30 to 50 percent longer because alcohol dilates the pupils, allowing more light to enter. Note, too, that dark adaptation occurs more slowly as we grow older. This is one reason why injuries caused by falling in the dark become more common among the elderly (Jackson, Owsley, & McGwin, 1999).

Is there any way to speed up dark adaptation? The rods are *insensitive* to extremely red light. That's why submarines, airplane cockpits, and ready rooms for fighter pilots are illuminated with red light. In each case, people can move quickly into the dark without having to adapt. Because the red light doesn't stimulate the rods, it is as if they had already spent time in the dark.

Can eating carrots really improve vision? One chemical "ingredient" of rhodopsin is *retinal,* which the body makes from vitamin A. (Retinal is also called *retinene.*) When too little vitamin A is available, less rhodopsin is produced. Thus, a person lacking vitamin A may develop night blindness. In **night blindness,** the person can see normally in bright light while using the cones, but becomes blind at night when the rods must function. Carrots are an excellent source of vitamin A, so they could improve night vision for someone suffering a deficiency, but not the vision of anyone with an adequate diet (Carlson, 2005).

KNOWLEDGE BUILDER
Vision
RECITE
1. The _____ _____ is made up of electromagnetic radiation with wavelengths between 400 and 700 nanometers.
2. Hyperopia is related to
   a. farsightedness
   b. having an elongated eye
   c. corneal astigmatism
   d. lack of cones in the fovea
3. Hubel and Wiesel found that cells in the visual cortex of the brain function as _____ _____.
4. In dim light, vision depends mainly on the _____. In brighter light, color and fine detail are produced by the _____.
5. The fovea has the greatest visual acuity due to the large concentration of rods found there. T or F?
6. The term "20/20 vision" means that a person can see at 20 feet what can normally be seen from 20 feet. T or F?

Continued

Dark adaptation Increased retinal sensitivity to light.

Night blindness Blindness under conditions of low illumination.

DISCOVERING PSYCHOLOGY

Going Biosonar

Although Ben Underwood has been blind since the age of 3, he has learned to use echolocation to do many things that normally sighted children take for granted.

This chapter opened with a story about *echolocation* (also known as *biosonar*), the remarkable ability of bats to use the echoes of their own voices to judge distance. Not human at all, right? Don't tell that to teenager Ben Underwood, who has been sightless since the age of 3, when retinal cancer claimed his eyes (Engber, 2006). In 2006, Ben proudly proclaimed during a television interview, "I'm not blind, I just can't see." Sure enough, Ben can ride a bike, climb trees, skate, and even play video games. He does it by using echolocation.

It turns out that bat echolocation is especially powerful because bats use very high-pitched sounds. But any sounds will do, and Ben makes clicking sounds with his tongue. With practice he has learned to use his own echoes to navigate through the world. Although Ben discovered echolocation all by himself (!), it turns out that researchers have known about human echolocation for 50 years and have even proposed training blind people to echolocate (Kellogg, 1962).

Although blind people may be better at echolocating, there is no reason why the rest of us can't do it as well (Rosenblum, Gordon, & Jarquin, 2000). Try this: Blindfold yourself and have a friend move a large plate or pan closer or farther away from you. All the while, make some noise. Click like Ben does or sing a song or whistle. Don't expect to hear your own echo as a separate sound. Noticeable echoes only occur when sounds bounce off objects far away. Instead, expect to hear slight differences when an object is moved. With some practice, you can tell when the plate or pan is closer and when it is farther away. Congratulations, you've gone biosonar.

---

7. For the cones, the most visible color is
   a. reddish orange
   b. blue-green
   c. yellow-orange
   d. yellowish green
8. The eyes become more sensitive to light at night because of a process known as _____
   _____.

REFLECT

Critical Thinking

9. William James once said, "If a master surgeon were to cross the auditory and optic nerves, we would hear lightning and see thunder." Can you explain what James meant?
10. Sensory transduction in the eye takes place first in the cornea, then in the lens, then in the retina. T or F?

Relate

Pretend you are a beam of light. What will happen to you at each step as you pass into the eye and land on the retina? What will happen if the eye is not perfectly shaped? How will the retina know you've arrived? How will it tell what color of light you are? What will it tell the brain about you?

Answers: 1. visible spectrum 2. a 3. feature detectors 4. rods, cones 5. F 6. T 7. d 8. dark adaptation 9. The explanation is based on localization of function: if a lightning flash caused rerouted messages from the eyes to activate auditory areas of the brain, we would experience a sound sensation. Likewise, if the ears transduced a thunderclap and sent impulses to the visual area, a sensation of light would occur. 10. False. The cornea and lens bend and focus light rays, but they do not change light to another form of energy. No change in the *type* of energy takes place until the retina converts light to nerve impulses.

⬤⬤ Hearing—Good Vibrations

Gateway Question: What are the mechanisms of hearing?

Rock, classical, jazz, rap, country, electronic, hip-hop—whatever your musical taste, you have probably been moved by the riches of sound. Hearing also collects information from all around the body, such as detecting the approach of an unseen car (Yost, 2007). Vision, in all its glory, is limited to stimuli in front of the eyes (unless, of course, your "shades" have rearview mirrors attached).

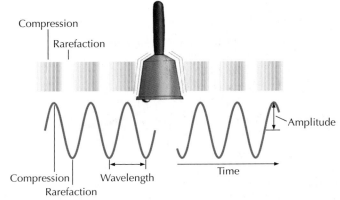

● **Figure 4.19** Waves of compression in the air, or vibrations, are the stimulus for hearing. The frequency of sound waves determines their pitch. The amplitude determines loudness.

External Ear (air conduction) — **Inner Ear** (fluid conduction)

(bone conduction by ossicles)

Auditory canal · Incus · Malleus · Stapes · Vestibular apparatus · Auditory nerve · Pinna · Cochlea · Tympanic membrane (eardrum) · Round window · Oval window

Scala vestibuli (with perilymph) · Cochlear canal (with endolymph) · Scala tympani (with perilymph)

Cochlea in Cross Section

Stapes · Oval window · Round window · Cochlear canal · **Cochlea "Unrolled"** · Perilymph (fluid inside cochlea)

Auditory nerve fibers · Basilar membrane · Hair cells · **Organ of Corti**

● **Figure 4.20** Anatomy of the ear. The entire ear is a mechanism for changing waves of air pressure into nerve impulses. The inset in the foreground (Cochlea "Unrolled") shows that as the stapes moves the oval window, the round window bulges outward, allowing waves to ripple through fluid in the cochlea. The waves move membranes near the hair cells, causing cilia or "bristles" on the tips of the cells to bend. The hair cells then generate nerve impulses carried to the brain. (See an enlarged cross section of cochlea in ● Figure 4.21.)

waves collide with the *tympanic membrane* (eardrum), setting it in motion. This, in turn, causes three small bones (the *auditory ossicles*) (OSS-ih-kuls) to vibrate (● Figure 4.20). The ossicles are the malleus (MAL-ee-us), incus, and stapes (STAY-peas). Their common names are the hammer, anvil, and stirrup. The ossicles link the eardrum with the *cochlea* (KOCK-lee-ah: a snail-shaped organ that makes up the inner ear). The stapes is attached to a membrane on the cochlea called the *oval window*. As the oval window moves back and forth, it makes waves in a fluid inside the cochlea.

Inside the cochlea tiny **hair cells** detect waves in the fluid. The hair cells are part of the **organ of Corti** (KOR-tee), which makes up the center part of the cochlea (● Figure 4.21). A set of *stereocilia* (STER-ee-oh-SIL-ih-ah), or "bristles," atop each hair cell brush against the tectorial membrane when waves ripple through fluid surrounding the organ of Corti. As the stereocilia are bent, transduction takes place and nerve impulses are triggered, which then flow to the brain. (Are your ears "bristling" with sound?)

How are higher and lower sounds detected? The **frequency theory** of hearing states that as pitch rises, nerve impulses of a corresponding frequency are fed into the auditory nerve. That is, an 800-hertz tone produces 800 nerve impulses per second. (*Hertz*

What is the stimulus for hearing? If you throw a stone into a quiet pond, a circle of waves will spread in all directions. In much the same way, sound travels as a series of invisible waves of *compression* (peaks) and *rarefaction* (RARE-eh-fak-shun: valleys) in the air. Any vibrating object—a tuning fork, the string of a musical instrument, or the vocal cords—will produce sound waves (rhythmic movement of air molecules). (To learn how to use sound waves to act like a bat, read "Going Biosonar.") Other materials, such as fluids or solids, can also carry sound. But sound does not travel in a vacuum or the airless realm of outer space. Movies that show characters reacting to the "roar" of alien starships or titanic battles in deep space are in error.

The *frequency* of sound waves (the number of waves per second) corresponds to the perceived *pitch* (higher or lower tone) of a sound. The *amplitude,* or physical "height," of a sound wave tells how much energy it contains. Psychologically, amplitude corresponds to sensed *loudness* (sound intensity) (● Figure 4.19).

How We Hear Sounds

How are sounds converted to nerve impulses? Hearing involves an elaborate chain of events that begins with the *pinna* (PIN-ah: the visible, external part of the ear). In addition to being a good place to hang earrings or balance pencils, the pinna acts like a funnel to concentrate sounds. After they are guided into the ear canal, sound

Hair cells Receptor cells within the cochlea that transduce vibrations into nerve impulses.

Organ of Corti Center part of the cochlea, containing hair cells, canals, and membranes.

Frequency theory Holds that tones up to 4,000 hertz are converted to nerve impulses that match the frequency of each tone.

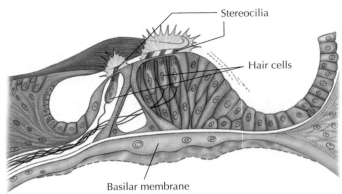

● **Figure 4.21** A closer view of the hair cells shows how movement of fluid in the cochlea causes the bristling "hairs" or cilia to bend, generating a nerve impulse.

● **Figure 4.22** Here we see a simplified side view of the cochlea "unrolled." Remember that the basilar membrane is the elastic "roof" of the lower chamber of the cochlea. The organ of Corti, with its sensitive hair cells, rests atop the basilar membrane. The colored line shows where waves in the cochlear fluid cause the greatest deflection of the basilar membrane. (The amount of movement is exaggerated in the drawing.) Hair cells respond most in the area of greatest movement, which helps identify sound frequency.

refers to the number of vibrations per second.) This explains how sounds up to about 4,000 hertz reach the brain. But what about higher tones? **Place theory** states that higher and lower tones excite specific areas of the cochlea. High tones register most strongly at the base of the cochlea (near the oval window). Lower tones, on the other hand, mostly move hair cells near the narrow outer tip of the cochlea (● Figure 4.22). Pitch is signaled by the area of the cochlea most strongly activated. Place theory also explains why hunters sometimes lose hearing in a narrow pitch range. "Hunter's notch," as it is called, occurs when hair cells are damaged in the area affected by the pitch of gunfire.

Hearing Loss

What causes other types of hearing loss? The two most common types of hearing loss afflict some 278 million people worldwide (Tennesen, 2007). **Conductive hearing loss** occurs when the transfer of vibrations from the outer ear to the inner ear is weak.

● **Figure 4.23** A highly magnified electron microscope photo of the cilia (orange bristles) on the top of human hair cells. (Colors are artificial.)

For example, the eardrums or ossicles may be damaged or immobilized by disease or injury. In many cases, conductive hearing loss can be overcome with a hearing aid, which makes sounds louder and clearer.

Sensorineural hearing loss results from damage to the inner ear hair cells or auditory nerve. The hair cells, which are about as thin as a cobweb, are very fragile (● Figure 4.23). By the time you are 65, more than 40 percent of them will be gone, mainly those that transduce high pitches (Chisolm, Willott, & Lister, 2003). This explains why younger students are beginning to download very high-pitched ring tones for their cell phones: If their teacher has aging ears, the students can hear the ring tone while their teacher cannot. (Your authors may have experienced this effect without knowing it!)

Many jobs, hobbies, and pastimes can cause **noise-induced hearing loss,** a common form of sensorineural hearing impairment that occurs when very loud sounds damage hair cells (as in hunter's notch). If you work in a noisy environment or enjoy loud music, motorcycling, snowmobiling, hunting, or similar pursuits, you are risking noise-induced hearing loss. Consider taking precautions because dead hair cells are never replaced: When you abuse them, you lose them.

So sensorineural hearing loss cannot be treated? Not easily, because hearing aids are of little or no help. However, in many cases of sensorineural hearing loss, the auditory nerve is actually intact. This finding has spurred the development of cochlear implants that bypass hair cells and stimulate the auditory nerves directly.

As you can see in ● Figure 4.24, wires from a microphone carry electrical signals to an external coil. A matching coil under the skin picks up the signals and carries them to one or more areas of the cochlea. The latest implants make use of place theory to separate higher and lower tones. This has allowed some formerly deaf persons to hear human voices, music, and other higher-frequency sounds. About 60 percent of all multichannel implant patients can understand some spoken words and appreciate music (Leal et al., 2003; Tye-Murray, Spencer, & Woodworth, 1995). Some deaf

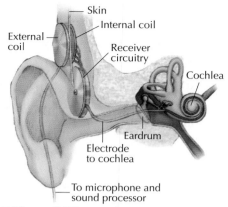

● **Figure 4.24** A cochlear implant, or "artificial ear."

● **Figure 4.25** Loudness ratings and potential hearing damage.

children learn to speak. Those who receive a cochlear implant before age 2 learn spoken language at a near normal rate (Dorman & Wilson, 2004).

At present, artificial hearing remains crude. All but the most successful cochlear implant patients describe the sound as "like a radio that isn't quite tuned in." In fact, 30 percent of all adults who have tried implants have given up on them. But cochlear implants are improving. And even now it is hard to argue with enthusiasts like Kristen Cloud. Shortly after Kristen received an implant, she was able to hear a siren and avoid being struck by a speeding car. She says simply, "The implant saved my life."

How loud must a sound be to be hazardous? The danger of hearing loss depends on both the loudness of sound and how long you are exposed to it. Daily exposure to 85 decibels or more may cause permanent hearing loss (Sekuler & Blake, 2006). Even short periods at 120 decibels (a rock concert) may cause a *temporary threshold shift* (a partial, transitory loss of hearing). Brief exposure to 150 decibels (a jet airplane nearby) can cause permanent hearing loss.

You might find it interesting to check the decibel ratings of some of your activities in ● Figure 4.25. Don't be fooled by the numbers, though. Decibels are plotted on a logarithmic scale (like earthquake intensity!). Every 20 decibels increases the sound pressure by a factor of 10. In other words, a rock concert at 120 decibels is not just twice as powerful as a normal voice at 60 decibels. It is actually 1,000 times stronger. Be aware that amplified musical concerts, iPod-style headphones, and "boom-box" car stereos can also damage your hearing.

If *tinnitus* (tin-NYE-tus: a ringing or buzzing sensation) follows exposure to loud sounds, chances are that hair cells have been damaged. Almost everyone has tinnitus at times, especially with increasing age. But after repeated sounds that produce this warning, you can expect to become permanently hard-of-hearing. A study of people who regularly go to amplified concerts found that 44 percent had tinnitus and most had some hearing loss (Meyer-Bisch, 1996).

The next time you are exposed to a very loud sound, remember ● Figure 4.24 and take precautions against damage. (Remember, too, that for temporary ear protection, fingers are always handy.)

Smell and Taste—The Nose Knows When the Tongue Can't Tell

Gateway Question: How do the chemical senses operate?

Unless you are a wine taster, a perfume blender, a chef, or a gourmet, you may think of **olfaction** (smell) and **gustation** (taste) as minor senses. Certainly you could survive without these two *chemical senses* (receptors that respond to chemical molecules). But don't be deceived. Life without these senses can be difficult (Drummond, Douglas, & Olver, 2007). One person, for instance, almost died because he couldn't smell the smoke when his apartment building caught fire. Without the chemical senses, people may be unable to cook, may have difficulty maintaining a healthy body weight due to diminished appetites, and may even be poi-

Place theory Theory that higher and lower tones excite specific areas of the cochlea.

Conductive hearing loss Poor transfer of sounds from the eardrum to the inner ear.

Sensorineural hearing loss Loss of hearing caused by damage to the inner ear hair cells or auditory nerve.

Noise-induced hearing loss Damage caused by exposing the hair cells to excessively loud sounds.

Olfaction The sense of smell.

Gustation The sense of taste.

soned by spoiled food (Brisbois et al., 2006; Gilbert & Wysocki, 1987). Besides, olfaction and gustation add pleasure to our lives. Skilled novelists always include descriptions of odors and tastes in their writings because they are among the most memorable sensations. Perhaps authors intuitively realize that a scene is incomplete without smells and tastes. Likewise, this chapter would be incomplete without a description of the chemical senses.

The Sense of Smell

Smell receptors respond to airborne molecules. As air enters the nose, it flows over roughly 5 million nerve fibers embedded in the lining of the upper nasal passages. Molecules passing over the fibers trigger nerve signals that are sent to the brain. The extreme close-up of an olfactory receptor cell in ● Figure 4.26c shows the thread-like fibers that project into the air flow inside the nose. Receptor proteins on the surface of the fibers are sensitive to various airborne molecules. When a fiber is stimulated, it sends signals to the brain.

How are different odors produced? This is still an unfolding mystery. One hint comes from a type of **dysosmia** (dis-OZE-me-ah: defective smell), a sort of "smell blindness" for a single odor. Loss of sensitivity to specific types of odors suggests there are receptors for specific odors. Indeed, the molecules that produce a particular odor are quite similar in shape. Specific shapes produce the following types of odors: floral (flower-like), camphoric (camphor-like), musky (have you ever smelled a sweaty musk ox?), minty (mint-like), and etherish (like ether or cleaning fluid).

Does this mean that there are five different types of olfactory receptors? Actually, in humans, about 1,000 types of smell receptors are believed to exist (Bensafi et al., 2004). It appears that different-

shaped "holes," or "pockets," exist on the surface of olfactory receptors. Like a piece fits in a puzzle, chemicals produce odors when part of a molecule matches a hole of the same shape. This is the **lock and key theory of olfaction.**

Further, molecules trigger activity in different *combinations* of odor receptors. Thus, humans can detect at least 10,000 different odors. Just as you can make many thousands of words from the 26 letters of the alphabet, many combinations of receptors are possible, resulting in many different odors. Scents are also identified, in part, by the *location* of the receptors in the nose that are activated by a particular odor. And finally, the *number of activated receptors* tells the brain how strong an odor is (Bensafi et al., 2004). The brain uses these distinctive patterns of messages it gets from the olfactory receptors to recognize particular scents (Laurent et al., 2001).

What causes dysosmia? Five people out of 100 experience some degree of dysosmia (Bramerson et al., 2004). Risks include infections, allergies, and blows to the head (which may tear the olfactory nerves). Exposure to chemicals such as ammonia, photo-developing solutions, and hairdressing potions can also cause dysosmia. If you value your sense of smell, be careful what you breathe (Drummond, Douglas, & Olver, 2007; Herz, 2001).

It might seem that various odors are inherently good or bad smelling. But newborn infants show no signs to reacting more strongly to "good" versus "bad" odors. The U.S. military once tried to create a stink bomb that could be used for clearing people out of an area. No matter how foul the smell, nothing could be found that was universally repelling. It appears that likes and dislikes for various scents are learned (Herz, 2001). For example, a person who smelled roses for the first time at her mother's funeral might dislike the scent of roses. Or one who smelled a skunk for the first time during a backyard birthday party might like the scent of

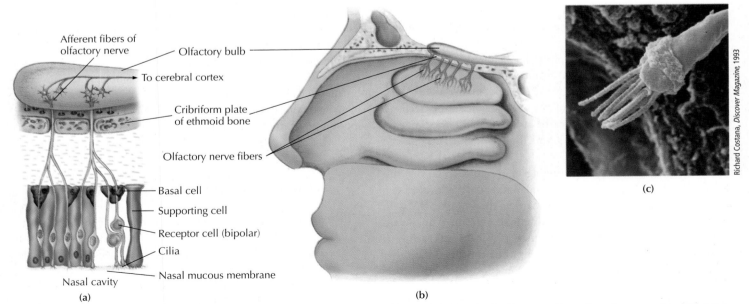

● **Figure 4.26** Receptors for the sense of smell (olfaction). *(a)* Olfactory nerve fibers respond to gaseous molecules. Receptor cells are shown in cross section to the left. *(b)* Olfactory receptors are located in the upper nasal cavity. *(c)* On the right, an extreme close-up of an olfactory receptor shows fibers that sense gaseous molecules of various shapes.

skunk. If you don't like the fetid, rotten odor of "ripe" cheeses, you just grew up in the wrong culture!

Pheromones: A Special Scent?

Among mammals, **pheromones** (FAIR-oh-moans: airborne chemical signals) greatly affect mating, sexual behavior, recognizing family members, and territorial marking (Kalat, 2007). For example, when a female pig is exposed to the pheromones in a male pig's breath, she immediately becomes sexually receptive.

The *vomeronasal* (voh-MARE-oh-NAZE-ul) *organ* (VNO) is the sense organ for pheromones. Until recently, humans were assumed to have only a vestigial VNO or none at all. Now, however, scientists believe they have located the VNO in humans (Hays, 2003). The suspected human vomeronasal organ looks like a small pit inside the nose (one on each side of the septum). These pits are lined with nerve cells and respond to chemicals that are suspected pheromones (Benson, 2002).

Does this mean that someone could use pheromones to "turn on" their girlfriend or boyfriend? It is doubtful that human pheromones directly release sexual behavior. At best the effect would be indirect because pheromones are not smelled, felt, seen, tasted, or heard. In humans, they appear to unconsciously produce general moods, such as well-being, attraction, unease, or anxiety (Olsson et al., 2006). When people say that their relationships are influenced by good or bad "chemistry," there may be some truth to it. Pheromones could add to the intoxicating feelings of romantic attraction or the sourness of instant dislike.

In fact, one group of researchers believe that adding a pheromone to aftershave lotion can make men more sexually attractive (McCoy & Pitino, 2002). (However, the most likely human pheromones are found in underarm sweat, which is not exactly an enticing thought.) Even then, social context appears to influence the effect. For instance, the ability of pheromones to induce a positive mood depends on whether a person of the opposite sex is nearby (Jacob, Hayreh, & McClintock, 2001).

Evidence for the existence of human pheromones remains preliminary and controversial. (Men shouldn't expect "Boar's Breath" cologne to be offered anytime soon!) Nevertheless, the possibilities are intriguing (Ebster & Kirk-Smith, 2005). For instance, human pheromones appear to explain why the menstrual cycles of women who live together tend to become synchronized. It's also possible that pheromones may one day be used to decrease anxiety, curb hunger, relieve premenstrual discomforts, or aid sex therapy. Only further study will tell whether searching for these special scents makes sense.

Taste and Flavors

There are at least four basic taste sensations: *sweet, salt, sour,* and *bitter.* We are most sensitive to bitter, less sensitive to sour, even less sensitive to salt, and least sensitive to sweet. This order may have helped prevent poisonings when most humans foraged for food, because bitter and sour foods are more likely to be inedible.

Most experts now believe that a fifth taste quality exists (Chandrashekar et al., 2006). The Japanese word *umami* (oo-MAH-me)

describes a pleasant savory or "brothy" taste associated with certain amino acids in chicken soup, some meat extracts, kelp, tuna, human milk, cheese, and soybeans. The receptors for *umami* are sensitive to glutamate, a substance found in monosodium glutamate (MSG) (Sugimoto & Ninomiya, 2005). Perhaps MSG's reputation as a "flavor enhancer" is based on the pleasant *umami* taste (McCabe & Rolls, 2007). At the very least, we may finally know why chicken soup is such a "comfort food."

If there are only four or five tastes, how can there be so many different flavors? Flavors seem more varied because we tend to include sensations of texture, temperature, smell, and even pain ("hot" chili peppers) along with taste. Smell is particularly important in determining flavor (Shepherd, 2006). If you plug your nose and eat small bits of apple, potato, and onion, they will "taste" almost exactly alike. So do gourmet jelly beans! It is probably fair to say that subjective flavor is half smell. That's why food loses its "taste" when you have a cold.

Taste buds (taste-receptor cells) are mainly located on the top side of the tongue, especially around the edges. However, a few are found elsewhere inside the mouth (● Figure 4.27). As food is chewed, it dissolves and enters the taste buds, where it sets off nerve impulses to the brain (Northcutt, 2004). Much like smell, sweet and bitter tastes appear to be based on a lock-and-key match between molecules and intricately shaped receptors. Saltiness and sourness, however, are triggered by a direct flow of charged atoms into the tips of taste cells (Lindemann, 2001).

People seem to have very different tastes. Why is that? Some differences are genetic. The chemical phenylthiocarbamine (FEEN-il-thigh-oh-CAR-bah-meen), or PTC, tastes bitter to about 70 percent of those tested and has no taste for the other 30 percent. Sensitivity to tastes has a genetic basis (Bartoshuk, 2000). In general, taste sensitivity is related to how many taste buds you have on your tongue. Some people have as few as 500 taste buds, whereas others have as many as 10,000. Those with many taste buds are "supertasters" who need only half as much sugar in their coffee to make it sweet (Bartoshuk et al., 2004).

Supertasters tend to have stronger tastes for sweet, bitter, and irritants such as alcohol and capsaicin (the chemical that makes chilies hot). Women are more often supertasters. Nontasters tend to prefer sweets and fatty foods, which may be why supertasters tend to be slimmer than nontasters.

The sense of taste also varies with age. Taste cells only live for several days. With aging, cell replacement slows, so the sense of taste diminishes. That's why many foods you disliked in childhood may seem appetizing now. Children who will not eat broccoli,

Dysosmia Loss or impairment of the sense of smell.

Lock and key theory of olfaction Holds that odors are related to the shapes of chemical molecules.

Pheromone An airborne chemical signal.

Taste bud The receptor organ for taste.

Circular papilla   Filamentous papilla

Omikron/Photo Researchers, Inc.

(a)

Taste bud

Hairlike ending of taste receptor

Sensory nerve

(b)   (c)   (d)

● **Figure 4.27** Receptors for taste: *(a)* The tongue is covered with small protrusions called *papillae. (b)* Most taste buds are found around the top edges of the tongue (shaded area). However, some are located elsewhere, including under the tongue. Stimulation of the central part of the tongue causes no taste sensations. All four primary taste sensations occur anywhere that taste buds exist. *(c)* An enlarged drawing shows that taste buds are located near the base of papillae. *(d)* Detail of a taste bud. These receptors also occur in other parts of the digestive system, such as the lining of the mouth.

spinach, liver, and so on may be having a very different taste experience than an adult. Aside from this fact, however, most taste preferences are acquired. Would you eat the coagulated secretion of the modified skin glands of a cow after it had undergone bacterial decomposition? If you would, you are a *cheese* fancier!

KNOWLEDGE BUILDER
Hearing, Smell, and Taste

RECITE

1. The frequency of a sound wave corresponds to how loud it is. T or F?
2. Which of the following is not a part of the cochlea?
   a. ossicles
   b. pinna
   c. tympanic membrane
   d. all of the above
3. Which of the following is *not* important for the transduction of sound?
   a. pinna
   b. ossicles
   c. phosphenes
   d. oval window
   e. hair cells
4. According to the place theory of hearing, higher tones register most strongly near the base of the cochlea. T or F?
5. Sensorineural hearing loss occurs when the auditory ossicles are damaged. T or F?
6. Daily exposure to sounds with a loudness of _____ decibels may cause permanent hearing loss.
7. Cochlear implants have been used primarily to overcome
   a. conductive hearing loss
   b. hunter's notch
   c. sensorineural hearing loss
   d. tinnitus
8. Olfaction appears to be at least partially explained by the _____ _____ _____ theory of molecule shapes and receptor sites.
9. From the standpoint of survival, we are fortunate that we are least sensitive to bitter tastes. T or F?

REFLECT

Critical Thinking

10. Why do you think your voice sounds so different when you hear a tape recording of your speech?
11. Smell and hearing differ from vision in a way that may aid survival. What is it?

Relate

Close your eyes and listen to the sounds around you. As you do, try to mentally trace the events necessary to convert vibrations in the air into the sounds you are hearing. Review the discussion of hearing if you leave out any steps.

What is your favorite food odor? What is your favorite taste? Can you explain how you are able to sense the aroma and taste of foods?

Answers: 1. F **2.** d **3.** c **4.** T **5.** F **6.** 85 **7.** c **8.** lock and key **9.** F **10.** The answer lies in another question: How else might vibrations from the voice reach the cochlea? Other people hear your voice only as it is carried through the air. You hear not only that sound, but also vibrations conducted by the bones of your skull. **11.** Both smell and hearing can detect stimuli (including signals of approaching danger) around corners, behind objects, and behind the head.

The Somesthetic Senses—Flying by the Seat of Your Pants

Gateway Question: What are the somesthetic senses?

A gymnast "flying" through a routine on the uneven bars may rely as much on the **somesthetic senses** as on vision (*soma* means "body"; *esthetic* means "feel"). Even the most routine activities, such as walking, running, or passing a sobriety test, would be impossible without somesthetic information from the body. You would find it very difficult to move, stay upright, or even stay alive without touch, pain, balance, and other bodily senses. They are an essential part of our sensory world.

What are the somesthetic senses? Somesthetic sensitivity includes the **skin senses** (touch), the **kinesthetic senses** (receptors in muscles and joints that detect body position and movement), and the **vestibular senses** (receptors in the inner ear for balance, gravity, and acceleration). Let's begin with the skin senses.

The Skin Senses

It's difficult to imagine what life would be like without the sense of touch, but the plight of Ian Waterman gives a hint. After an illness, Waterman permanently lost all feeling below his neck. Now, in order to know what position his body is in he has to be able to see it. If he moves with his eyes closed, he has no idea where he is moving. If the lights go out in a room, he's in big trouble (Cole, 1995).

Skin receptors produce at least five different sensations: *light touch, pressure, pain, cold,* and *warmth*. Receptors with particular shapes appear to specialize somewhat in various sensations (● Figure 4.28). However, free nerve endings alone can produce all five sensations (Carlson, 2005). Altogether, the skin has about 200,000 nerve endings for temperature, 500,000 for touch and pressure, and 3 million for pain.

Does the number of receptors in an area of skin relate to its sensitivity? Yes. Your skin could be "mapped" by applying heat, cold, touch, pressure, or pain to points all over your body. Such testing would show that the number of skin receptors varies and that sensitivity generally matches the number of receptors in a given area. As a rough-and-ready illustration, try this two-point touch test:

> The density of touch receptors on various body areas can be checked by having a friend apply two pencil points to the skin with varying distances between them. Without looking, you should respond "one" or "two" each time. Record the distance between the pencils each time you feel two points.

You should find that two points are recognizable when they are 1/10 inch apart on the fingertips, 1/4 inch on the nose, and 3 inches at the middle of the back. Generally speaking, important areas such as the lips, tongue, face, hands, and genitals have a higher density of receptors. Of course, the sensation you ultimately feel will depend on brain activity.

Pain

The number of pain receptors also varies, right? Yes, like the other skin senses, pain receptors vary in their distribution. About 230 pain points per square centimeter (about a half inch) are found behind the knee, 180 per centimeter on the buttocks, 60 on the pad of the thumb, and 40 on the tip of the nose. (Is it better, then, to be pinched on the nose or behind the knee? It depends on what you like!)

Pain fibers are also found in the internal organs. Stimulation of these fibers causes **visceral pain.** Curiously, visceral pain is often felt on the surface of the body, at a site some distance from the point of origin. Experiences of this type are called **referred pain** (● Figure 4.29). For example, a person having a heart attack may feel pain in the left shoulder, arm, or even the little finger.

Pain from the skin, muscles, joints, and tendons is known as **somatic** (bodily) **pain.** Somatic pain carried by *large nerve fibers* is sharp, bright, fast, and seems to come from specific body areas (McMahon & Koltzenburg, 2005). This is the body's **warning system.** Give yourself a small jab with a pin and you will feel this type of pain. As you do this, notice that warning pain quickly disappears. Much as we may dislike warning pain, it is usually a signal that the body has been, or is about to be, damaged. Without warning pain, we would be unable to detect or prevent injury. Children who are born with a rare inherited insensitivity to pain repeatedly burn themselves, break bones, bite off parts of their tongues, and become ill without knowing it (Cox et al., 2006). As you might imagine, it's also hard for people with *congenital pain insensitivity* to have empathy for the pain of others (Danziger, Prkachin, & Willer, 2006).

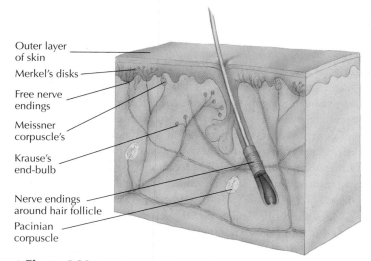

Outer layer of skin
Merkel's disks
Free nerve endings
Meissner corpuscle's
Krause's end-bulb
Nerve endings around hair follicle
Pacinian corpuscle

● **Figure 4.28** The skin senses include touch, pressure, pain, cold, and warmth. This drawing shows different forms the skin receptors can take. The only clearly specialized receptor is the Pacinian corpuscle, which is highly sensitive to pressure. Free nerve endings are receptors for pain and any of the other sensations. For reasons that are not clear, cold is sensed near the surface of the skin and warmth is sensed deeper (Carlson, 2005).

Somesthetic sense Sensations produced by the skin, muscles, joints, viscera, and organs of balance.

Skin senses The senses of touch, pressure, pain, heat, and cold.

Kinesthetic senses The senses of body movement and positioning.

Vestibular senses The senses of balance, position in space, and acceleration.

Skin receptors Sensory organs for touch, pressure, pain, cold, and warmth.

Visceral pain Pain originating in the internal organs.

Referred pain Pain that is felt in one part of the body but comes from another.

Somatic pain Pain from the skin, muscles, joints, and tendons.

Warning system Pain based on large nerve fibers; warns that bodily damage may be occurring.

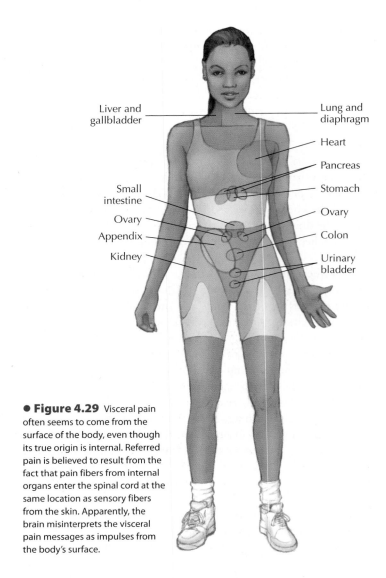

Liver and
gallbladder

Lung and
diaphragm

Heart

Pancreas

Small
intestine

Stomach

Ovary

Ovary

Appendix

Colon

Kidney

Urinary
bladder

● **Figure 4.29** Visceral pain often seems to come from the surface of the body, even though its true origin is internal. Referred pain is believed to result from the fact that pain fibers from internal organs enter the spinal cord at the same location as sensory fibers from the skin. Apparently, the brain misinterprets the visceral pain messages as impulses from the body's surface.

A second type of somatic pain is carried by *small nerve fibers.* This type is slower, nagging, aching, widespread, and very unpleasant (McMahon & Koltzenburg, 2005). It gets worse if the pain stimulus is repeated. This is the body's **reminding system.** It reminds the brain that the body has been injured. For instance, lower back pain often has this quality. Sadly, the reminding system can cause agony long after an injury has healed, or in terminal illnesses, when the reminder is useless. This chapter's Psychology in Action section describes some ways to control pain. If you got carried away with the earlier pin demonstration, maybe you should read ahead now!

Dynamic Touch

A carpenter swings a hammer with practiced precision. A juggler fluidly tosses and catches five balls. An ice hockey player embeds his stick in an opposing player's helmet. In sports and everyday life, touch is rarely static. Most skilled performances rely on **dynamic touch,** which combines sensations from skin receptors with kinesthetic information from the muscles and tendons.

● **Figure 4.30** Hold a variety of elongated objects upright between your fingertips. Close your eyes and move each object about. Your ability to estimate the size, length, shape, and orientation of each object will be quite accurate. (After Turvey, 1996.)

Studies have shown that dynamic touch provides surprisingly detailed information about objects, such as their size and shape (● Figure 4.30). How are we able to make such judgments? Psychologist M. T. Turvey has found that most bodily motions form an arc or a combination of arcs (Turvey, 1996). Dynamic touch is largely a matter of sensing the *inertia* of objects as they move through these arcs. The fact that dynamic touch is a reliable source of information is what makes it possible for us to use a wide range of tools, utensils, and objects as if they were extensions of our bodies (Hove, Riley, & Shockley, 2006).

The Vestibular System

Space flight might look like fun. But if you ever get a ride into space, it is about 70 percent likely that your first experience in orbit will be throwing up. Weightlessness and space flight affect the vestibular system, often causing severe motion sickness (● Figure 4.31). Within the vestibular system, fluid-filled sacs called *otolith* (OH-toe-lith) *organs* are sensitive to movement, acceleration, and gravity. The otolith organs contain tiny crystals in a soft, gelatin-like mass. The tug of gravity or rapid head movements can cause the mass to shift. This, in turn, stimulates hair-like receptor cells, allowing us to sense gravity, acceleration, and movement through space (Lackner & DiZio, 2005).

Three fluid-filled tubes called the *semicircular canals* are the sensory organs for balance. If you could climb inside these tubes, you would find that head movements cause the fluid to swirl about. As the fluid moves, it bends a small "flap," or "float," called the *crista,* that detects movement in the semicircular canals. A crista can be found within each *ampulla* (am-PULL-ah), a wider part of the canal. The bending of each crista again stimulates hair cells and signals head rotation.

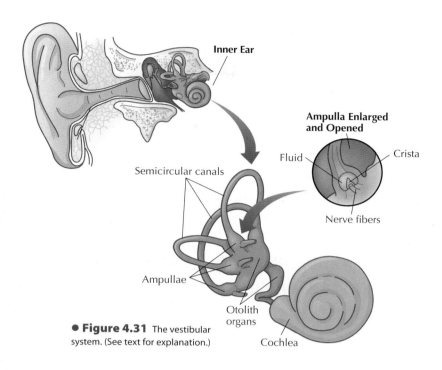

● **Figure 4.31** The vestibular system. (See text for explanation.)

Weightlessness presents astronauts with a real challenge in sensory adaptation.

What causes motion sickness? According to **sensory conflict theory,** dizziness and nausea occur when sensations from the vestibular system don't match sensations from the eyes and body (Flanagan, May, & Dobie, 2004). On solid ground, information from the vestibular system, vision, and kinesthesis usually matches. However, in a heaving, pitching boat, car, or airplane, a serious mismatch can occur—causing disorientation and heaving of another kind.

Many people become nauseated the first time they experience virtual reality. Why? Because virtual reality also creates a sensory conflict: Computer-generated visual images change as if the viewer's body is in motion, but the vestibular system tells viewers that they are standing still (Merhi et al., 2007). The result? The scenery may not be real but the nausea is.

Why would sensory conflict cause nausea? You can probably blame (or thank) evolution. Many poisons disturb the vestibular system, vision, and the body. Therefore, we may have evolved so that we react to sensory conflict by vomiting to expel poison. The value of this reaction, however, may be of little comfort to anyone who has ever been "green" and miserable with motion sickness.

In space, sensory conflict can be especially intense. During weightlessness, merely pulling on one's shoes can result in a backward somersault. Under such conditions, the otolith organs send unexpected signals to the brain, and head movements are no longer confirmed by the semicircular canals. Few of the messages the brain receives from the vestibular system and kinesthetic receptors agree with a lifetime of past experience.

What can be done to minimize motion sickness? Whether you are in outer space, playing a particularly intense video game, or just sitting in the backseat of a moving car, motion sickness is a very unpleasant experience. If you face motion sickness, there are a few things you can try that should help (Harm, 2002). If you know beforehand that you might be at risk, consider taking nonprescription motion sickness pills. If you are trapped in the moment, try

Reminding system Pain based on small nerve fibers; reminds the brain that the body has been injured.

Dynamic touch Touch experienced when the body is in motion; a combination of sensations from skin receptors, muscles, and joints.

Sensory conflict theory Explains motion sickness as the result of a mismatch between information from vision, the vestibular system, and kinesthesis.

minimizing sensory conflict by moving your head as little as possible. Either close your eyes, fixate on an unmoving point (such as the horizon), or look above the horizon at the unmoving sky. Also, lie down if you can. The otoliths are less sensitive to vertical movements when you are horizontal, and your head will move less. Finally, anxiety intensifies motion sickness. Try slow, deep breathing and other relaxation techniques that you can use when needed.

> **bridges**
> Relaxation methods are described in Chapter 15 of this book.

⬤⬤ Adaptation, Attention, and Gating—Tuning In and Tuning Out

Gateway Question: Why are we more aware of some sensations than others?

You are surrounded by sights, sounds, odors, tastes, and touch sensations. Which are you aware of? Each of the senses we have described is continuously active. Even so, many sensory events never reach awareness because of *sensory adaptation, selective attention,* and *sensory gating.* Let's see how information is filtered by these processes.

Sensory Adaptation

Think about walking into a house where fried fish, sauerkraut, and head cheese were prepared for dinner. (Some dinner!) You would probably pass out at the door, yet people who had been in the house for some time wouldn't be aware of the food odors. Similarly, smokers often don't get how much nonsmokers are bothered by the smell of tobacco smoke. Why? Because sensory receptors respond less to unchanging stimuli, a process called **sensory adaptation.**

Fortunately, the olfactory (smell) receptors adapt quickly. When exposed to a constant odor, they send fewer and fewer nerve impulses to the brain until the odor is no longer noticed. Adaptation to pressure from a wristwatch, waistband, ring, or glasses is based on the same principle. Sensory receptors generally respond best to *changes* in stimulation. No one wants or needs to be reminded 16 hours a day that his shoes are on.

If change is necessary to prevent sensory adaptation, why doesn't vision undergo adaptation like the sense of smell does? If you stare at something, it certainly doesn't go away. The rods and cones, like other receptor cells, would respond less to a constant stimulus. However, the eye normally makes thousands of tiny movements every minute. These movements are caused by *physiological nystagmus* (nis-TAG-mus: involuntary tremors of the eye muscles). Although they are too small to be seen, the movements shift visual images from one receptor cell to another.

Constant eye movement ensures that images always fall on fresh, unfatigued rods and cones. Evidence for this comes from

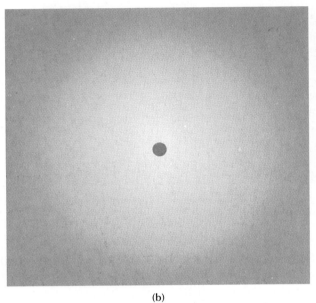

● **Figure 4.32** Stabilized images. *(a)* A miniature slide projector attached to a contact lens moves each time the eye moves. As a result, the projected image disappears in a few seconds because it does not move on the retina. *(b)* A similar effect occurs when changes in brightness do not define a distinct edge. In this case, eye movements cannot prevent adaptation. Therefore, if you stare at the dot, the lighter area will disappear. (After Cornsweet, 1970.)

fitting people with a contact lens that has a miniature slide projector attached to it (● Figure 4.32*a*). Because the projector follows the exact movements of the eye, an image can be stabilized on the retina. When this is done, projected geometric designs fade from view within a few seconds (Pritchard, 1961). You can get a similar effect by staring at ● Figure 4.32*b*. Because the lighter circle does not form a distinct edge, the retina adapts to the brightness difference. As it does, the circle gradually disappears.

Selective Attention

As you sit reading this page, receptors for touch and pressure in the seat of your pants are sending nerve impulses to your brain. Although these sensations have been present all along, you were probably not aware of them until just now. This "seat-of-the-pants phenomenon" is an example of **selective attention** (voluntarily focusing on a specific sensory input). We are able to "tune in on" a single sensory message while excluding others. Another familiar example of this is the "cocktail party effect." When you are in a group of people, surrounded by voices, you can still select and attend to the voice of the person you are facing. Or if that person gets dull, you can eavesdrop on conversations all over the room. (Be sure to smile and nod your head occasionally!) Actually, no matter how interesting your companion may be, your attention will probably shift away if you hear your own name spoken somewhere in the room (Conway, Cowan, & Bunting, 2001). We do find what others say about us to be very interesting, don't we?

Sensory Gating

What makes selective attention possible? Selective attention appears to be based on the ability of brain structures to select and divert incoming sensory messages (Sekuler & Blake, 2006). But what about messages that haven't reached the brain? Is it possible that some are blocked while others are allowed to pass? Evidence suggests there are *sensory gates* that control the flow of incoming nerve impulses in just this way. In particular, **sensory gating** refers to facilitating or blocking sensory messages in the spinal cord (Melzack & Katz, 2004; Melzack & Wall, 1996).

Pain Gates

A fascinating example of sensory gating is provided by Ronald Melzack and Patrick Wall (1996), who study "pain gates" in the spinal cord. Melzack and Wall noticed, as you may have, that one type of pain will sometimes cancel another. Their **gate control theory** suggests that pain messages from different nerve fibers pass through the same neural "gate" in the spinal cord. If the gate is "closed" by one pain message, other messages may not be able to pass through (Melzack & Katz, 2004; Melzack & Wall, 1996).

How is the gate closed? Messages carried by large, fast nerve fibers seem to close the spinal pain gate directly. Doing so can prevent slower, "reminding system" pain from reaching the brain. Pain clinics use this effect by applying a mild electrical current to the skin. Such stimulation, felt only as a mild tingling, can greatly reduce more agonizing pain.

Messages from small, slow fibers seem to take a different route. After going through the pain gate, they pass on to a "central biasing system" in the brain. Under some circumstances, the brain then sends a message back down the spinal cord, closing the pain gates (● Figure 4.33). Melzack and Wall believe that gate control theory explains the painkilling effects of *acupuncture*.

Acupuncture is the Chinese medical art of relieving pain and illness by inserting thin needles into the body. As the acupuncturist's needles are twirled, heated, or electrified, they activate small pain fibers. These relay through the biasing system to close the gates to intense or chronic pain (Melzack & Wall, 1996). Studies have shown that acupuncture produces short-term pain relief for 40 to 80 percent of patients tested (Ernst, 1994; Weidenhammer et al., 2007).

Acupuncture has an interesting side effect not predicted by sensory gating. People given acupuncture often report feelings of light-headedness, relaxation, or euphoria. How are these feelings explained? The answer seems to lie in the body's ability to pro-

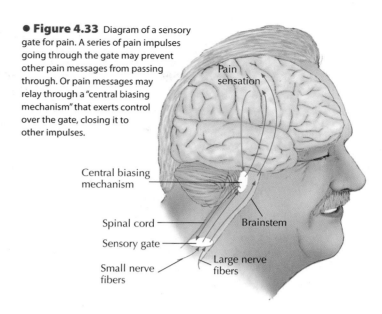

● **Figure 4.33** Diagram of a sensory gate for pain. A series of pain impulses going through the gate may prevent other pain messages from passing through. Or pain messages may relay through a "central biasing mechanism" that exerts control over the gate, closing it to other impulses.

duce opiate-like chemicals. To combat pain, the brain causes the pituitary gland to release a painkilling chemical called **beta-endorphin** (BAY-tah-en-DOR-fin: from *endo*, "within," and *orphin*, "opiate"). Chemically, beta-endorphin is quite similar to morphine.

Such discoveries help explain the painkilling effect of placebos (fake pills or injections), which raise endorphin levels. A release of endorphins also seems to underlie "runner's high," masochism, acupuncture, and the euphoria sometimes associated with childbirth, painful initiation rites, or eating hot chili peppers (Kalat, 2007; Sternberg et al., 1998). In each case, pain and stress cause the release of endorphins. These in turn induce feelings of pleasure or euphoria similar to being "high" on morphine.

The "high" often felt by long-distance runners serves as a good example of the endorphin effect. In one experiment, subjects were tested for pain tolerance. After running 1 mile, each was tested again. In the second test, all could withstand pain about 70 percent longer than before. The runners were then given naloxone, a drug that blocks the effects of endorphins. Following another 1-mile run the subjects were tested again. This time they had lost their earlier protection from pain (Haier et al., 1988). A similar effect occurs with first-time parachute jumpers. After the jump, their endorphin levels increase dramatically and they are much less sensitive to pain (Janssen & Arntz, 2001). Actually, these observa-

Sensory adaptation A decrease in sensory response to an unchanging stimulus.

Selective attention Voluntarily focusing on a specific sensory input.

Sensory gating Alteration of sensory messages in the spinal cord.

Gate control theory Proposes that pain messages pass through neural "gates" in the spinal cord.

Beta-endorphin A natural, painkilling brain chemical similar to morphine.

(left) An acupuncturist's chart. *(right)* Thin stainless steel needles are inserted into areas defined by the chart. Modern research has begun to explain the painkilling effects of acupuncture (see text). Acupuncture's claimed ability to cure diseases is more debatable.

Herve Donnezan/Photo Researchers, Inc.

tions tie in nicely with the idea of pain gates. The central biasing system, which closes pain gates in the spinal cord, is highly sensitive to morphine and other opiate painkillers (Kalat, 2007; Melzack & Wall, 1996). People who say they are "addicted" to running, or bungee jumping, or eating spicy foods may be closer to the truth than they realize. (Can pain gates and endorphins explain every type of pain? See "The Matrix: Do Phantoms Live Here?")

Conclusion and a Look Ahead

The senses supply raw data to the brain, but the information remains mostly meaningless until it is interpreted. It's as if the senses provide only the jumbled pieces of a complex puzzle. In the next chapter we will explore some perceptual processes that help us put the puzzle together.

A variety of psychological factors affect the severity of pain. Because you may not want to try acupuncture or electrical stimulation to control everyday pain, the following discussion describes several practical ways to reduce pain. Before we turn to that useful topic, here's a chance to rehearse what you've learned.

Somesthetic Senses, Adaptation, Attention, and Gating

RECITE
1. Which of the following is a somesthetic sense?
   a. gestation
   b. olfaction
   c. rarefaction
   d. kinesthesis
2. Pain that originates in the internal organs is sometimes felt on the surface of the body as "referred pain." T or F?
3. Warning pain is carried by _____ nerve fibers.
4. An ability to sense the inertia of objects as we move them through space is the basis for _____
   _____.
5. Head movements are detected primarily in the semicircular canals, gravity by the otolith organs. T or F?

6. Sensory conflict theory appears to explain space sickness, but it does not seem to apply to other types of motion sickness. T or F?
7. *Sensory adaptation* refers to an increase in sensory response that accompanies a constant or unchanging stimulus. T or F?
8. The brain-centered ability to influence what sensations we will receive is called
   a. sensory gating
   b. central adaptation
   c. selective attention
   d. sensory biasing
9. The painkilling effects of acupuncture appear to result from _____ _____ and the release of beta-endorphin.

REFLECT
Critical Thinking
10. What special precautions would you have to take to test the ability of acupuncture to reduce pain?
11. In a very real sense, we all live slightly in the past. How could that be true?

Relate
Stand on one foot with your eyes closed. Now touch the tip of your nose with your index finger. Which of the somesthetic senses did you use to perform this feat?

Imagine you are on a boat ride with a friend who starts to feel queasy. Can you explain to your friend what causes motion sickness and what she or he can do to prevent it?

As you sit reading this book, which sensory inputs have undergone adaptation? What new inputs can you become aware of by shifting your focus of attention?

Answers: 1. d **2.** T **3.** large **4.** dynamic touch **5.** T **6.** T **7.** F **8.** c **9.** sensory gating **10.** At the very least, you would have to control for the placebo effect by giving fake acupuncture to control group members. However, a true double-blind study would be difficult to do. Acupuncturists would always know if they were giving a placebo treatment or the real thing, which means they might unconsciously influence subjects. **11.** For all the senses, it takes a split second for sensory receptors to sense a change in external stimuli and for a neural message to arrive at the brain. Therefore, by the time we are aware of an event, such as a very brief flash of light, it is already over.

BRAINWAVES

The Matrix: Do Phantoms Live Here?

In the popular *Matrix* films, Neo, as played by Keanu Reeves, discovers that machines have imprisoned humans in a phantom world called the Matrix, in order to steal human energy for their own use. Actually, the idea of a "matrix" is not totally farfetched. In fact, your own brain may be creating a *neuromatrix* that allows you to perceive your own body.

A person who suffers an amputation doesn't need to believe in the Matrix to encounter phantoms. Most amputees have **phantom limb** sensations, including pain, for months or years after losing a limb (Fraser, 2002; Halbert, Crotty, & Cameron, 2002). Because the phantom limb feels so "real," a patient with a recently amputated leg may inadvertently try to walk on it, risking further injury. Sometimes, phantom limbs feel like they are stuck in awkward positions. For instance, one man can't sleep on his back because his missing arm feels like it is twisted behind him.

What causes phantom limbs? Gate control theory cannot explain phantom limb pain (Hunter, Katz, & Davis, 2003). Because pain can't be coming from the missing limb, it cannot pass through pain gates to the brain (after all, it's missing!). Instead, according to Ronald Melzack (1999; Melzack & Katz, 2006), the brain creates a body image called the *neuromatrix*. This internal model of the body generates our sense of bodily self. Although amputation may remove a limb, as far as the neuromatrix in the brain is concerned, the limb still exists. Functional magnetic resonance imaging (fMRI) confirms that sensory and motor areas of the brain are more active when a person feels a phantom limb (Rosen et al., 2001). Even though pain signals no longer come from the amputated limb, the neuromatrix evidently interprets other sensory experiences as pain from the missing limb.

Sometimes the brain gradually reorganizes to adjust for the sensory loss (Wu & Kaas, 2002). For example, a person who loses an arm may at first have a phantom arm and hand. After many years, the phantom may shrink, until only a hand is felt at the shoulder. Perhaps more vividly than others, people with phantom limbs are reminded that the sensory world we experience is constructed, moment-by-moment, not by some futuristic machines but by our very own neuromatrix in our brains.

PSYCHOLOGY IN ACTION

Controlling Pain—This Won't Hurt a Bit

Gateway Question: How can pain be reduced in everyday situations?

Steve Raymer/National Geographic/Getty Images

In some cultures, people endure tattooing, stretching, cutting, and burning with little apparent pain. How do they do it? Very likely the answer lies in a reliance on psychological factors that anyone can use to reduce pain, such as anxiety reduction, control, attention, and interpretation (Mailis-Gagnon & Israelson, 2005).

Anxiety

The basic sensory message of pain can be separated from emotional reactions to it. Fear or high levels of anxiety almost always increase pain. (**Anxiety** is a feeling of apprehension or uneasiness similar to fear, but based on an unclear threat.) A dramatic reversal of this effect is the surprising lack of pain displayed by soldiers wounded in battle. Being excused from further combat apparently produces a flood of relief. This emotional state leaves many soldiers insensitive to wounds that would agonize a civilian (Melzack & Wall, 1996). In general, unpleasant emotions increase pain and pleasant emotions decrease it (Rainville, 2004).

Control

A moment's reflection should convince you that the most upsetting pain is that over which you have no control. Loss of control seems to increase pain by increasing anxiety and emotional distress. Conversely, if you can regulate a painful stimulus, you have **control** over it. People who are allowed to regulate, avoid, or control a painful stimulus suffer less. In general, the more control you *feel* you have over a painful stimulus, the less pain you will experience. (Vallerand, Saunders, & Anthony, 2007). To apply this principle, you should arrange a signal so your doctor, dentist, or

---

Phantom limb The illusory sensation that a limb still exists after it is lost through accident or amputation.

Anxiety Apprehension, dread, or uneasiness similar to fear but based on an unclear threat.

Control Where pain is concerned, *control* refers to an ability to regulate the pain stimulus.

body piercer will know when to start and stop a painful procedure.

Attention

Distraction can also radically reduce pain. As you'll recall, **attention** refers to voluntarily focusing on a specific sensory input. Pain, even though it is highly persistent, can be selectively "tuned out" (at least partially), just like any other sensation. Children in one experiment tolerated pain better when they were distracted by interacting with a head-mounted audiovisual display (Dahlquist et al., 2007). Similarly, burn patients, who must undergo excruciating pain while their bandages are changed, can be distracted from their pain with video games and virtual reality (Hoffman et al., 2001).

Less dramatically, have you ever temporarily forgotten about a toothache or similar pain while absorbed in a movie or book? As this suggests, concentrating on pleasant, soothing images can be especially helpful. Instead of listening to the whir of a dentist's drill, for example, you might imagine that you are lying in the sun on a beach, listening to the roar of the surf. Or take an iPod along and crank up your favorite MP3s (Bushnell, Villemure, & Duncan, 2004). At home, music can also be a good distractor from chronic pain (Mitchell et al., 2007).

Interpretation

The meaning, or **interpretation,** you give a stimulus also affects pain (Turk & Melzack, 2001). For example, if you give a child a swat on the behind while playing, you'll probably get a burst of laughter. Yet the same swat given as punishment may bring tears. The effects of interpretation are illustrated by a classic experiment in which thinking of pain as pleasurable (denying the pain) greatly increased pain tolerance (Neufeld, 1970). Another study found that people who believe a painful procedure will improve their health feel less pain during the procedure (Staats et al., 1998).

Coping with Pain

How can these facts be applied? In a sense, they already are applied to childbirth. *Prepared childbirth training,* which promotes birth with a minimum of drugs or painkillers, uses all four factors. To prepare for natural childbirth, the expectant mother learns in great detail what to anticipate at each stage

of labor. This greatly relieves her fears and anxieties. During labor, she attends to sensations that mark her progress and she adjusts her breathing accordingly. Her attention is shifted to sensations other than pain, resulting in less discomfort (Leventhal et al., 1989). Also, her positive attitude is maintained by use of the term "contractions" rather than "labor pains." Finally, because of her months of preparation and her active participation, she feels *in control* of the situation.

Natural childbirth techniques reduce pain by an average of about 30 percent. Many women find this reduction quite helpful. However, it is important to remember that labor can produce very severe pain. A woman should not feel guilty if she needs painkillers during labor. Many women who have had prepared childbirth training still end up asking for an epidural block.

For moderate pain, it can make quite a difference to reduce anxiety, redirect attention, and increase control. When you anticipate pain (during a trip to the doctor, dentist, or tattoo parlor), you can lower anxiety by making sure that you are *fully informed.* Be sure that someone explains everything that will happen or could happen to you. Also, be sure to fully discuss any fears you have. If you are physically tense, you can use relaxation exercises to lower your level of arousal. Relaxation methods involve tensing and then releasing muscles in various parts of the body.

> ### bridges
>
> **A typical technique is described in detail in the Psychology in Action section of Chapter 15.** The desensitization procedure described there may also help reduce anxiety.

Distraction and Reinterpretation

Some dentists are now equipped to help you shift attention away from pain. Patients are actively distracted with video games and headphones playing music. In other situations, focusing on some external object may help you shift attention away from pain. Pick a tree outside a window, a design on the wall, or some other stimulus and examine it in great detail. Prior practice in meditation can be a tremendous aid to such attention shifts. Research suggests that dis-

New technologies like this audiovisual headset offer new ways of distracting attention from painful experiences such as visits to the dentist.

traction of this type works best for mild or brief pain. For chronic or strong pain, reinterpretation is more effective (McCaul & Malott, 1984).

Counterirritation

Is there any way to increase control over a painful stimulus? Practically speaking, the choices may be limited. One possibility is related to Ronald Melzack's gate control theory of pain, which suggests that sending *mild* pain messages to the spinal cord and brain may effectively close the neurological gates to more severe or unpredictable pain. Such procedures, known as **counterirritation,** are evident in some of the oldest techniques used to control pain: applying ice packs, hot-water bottles, mustard packs, vibration, or massage to other parts of the body. Pain clinics use counterirritation by applying a mild electrical current to the skin. This causes only a mild tingling, but it can greatly reduce more agonizing pain (Köke et al., 2004). For more extreme pain, the electrical current can be applied directly to the spinal cord (Linderoth & Foreman, 2006).

These facts suggest a way to minimize pain that is based on increased control, counterirritation, and the release of endorphins. If you pinch yourself, you can easily *create and endure* pain equal to that produced by many medical procedures (receiving an injection, having a tooth drilled, and so on). The pain doesn't seem too bad because you have control over it, and it is predictable.

This fact can be used to *mask* one pain with a second painful stimulus that is under your control. For instance, if you are having a tooth filled, try pinching yourself or digging a fingernail into a knuckle while the dentist is working. Focus your attention on the pain

you are creating, and increase its intensity anytime the dentist's work becomes more painful. This strategy may seem strange, but it works. Generations of children have used it to take the edge off a spanking.

KNOWLEDGE BUILDER
Pain Control

RECITE

1. Like heightened anxiety, increased control tends to increase subjective pain. T or F?
2. In one experiment, participants given the task of interacting with a head-mounted audiovisual display experienced less pain than participants who paid attention to the pain stimulus. T or F?
3. Imagining a pleasant experience can be an effective way of reducing pain in some situations. T or F?
4. The concept of counterirritation holds that relaxation and desensitization are key elements of pain control. T or F?

REFLECT

Critical Thinking

5. What measures would you take to ensure that an experiment involving pain is ethical?

Relate

Think about a strategy you have used for reducing pain at the doctor, dentist, or some other painful situation. Did you alter anxiety, control, attention, or interpretation? Can you think of any ways in which you have used counterirritation to lessen pain?

Answers: 1. F **2.** T **3.** T **4.** F **5.** Experiments that cause pain must be handled with care and sensitivity. Participation must be voluntary, the source of pain must be noninjurious, and subjects must be allowed to quit at any time.

---

chapter in review
Gateways to Sensation

The senses act as data reduction systems in order to prevent the brain from being overwhelmed by sensory input.

- Private sensations do not correspond perfectly to external stimuli. Studies in psychophysics relate physical energies to the sensations we experience.
- The sensory organs transduce a limited range of physical energies into nerve impulses.
- The minimum amount of physical energy necessary to produce a sensation defines the absolute threshold. The amount of change necessary to produce a just noticeable difference in a stimulus defines a difference threshold.
- There is evidence that subliminal perception occurs, but subliminal advertising is largely ineffective.
- Sensory analysis and coding influence what we experience.
- Sensory processing is localized in specific parts of the brain.

The visible spectrum is transduced by rods and cones in the retina leading to the construction of visual experience by the brain.

- The visible spectrum consists of electromagnetic radiation in a narrow range.
- The eyes and the brain form a complex system for sensing light. Vision is based on an active, computer-like analysis of light patterns.
- Four common visual defects are myopia (nearsightedness), hyperopia (farsightedness), presbyopia (loss of accommodation), and astigmatism.

- The rods and cones are the eye's photoreceptors in the retina.
- The rods specialize in peripheral vision, night vision, seeing black and white, and detecting movement.
- The cones, found exclusively in the fovea and otherwise toward the middle of the eye, specialize in color vision, acuity, and daylight vision.

Our ability to see colors is explained by the trichromatic theory (in the retina) and by the opponent-process theory (in the visual system beyond the eyes).

- The rods and cones differ in color sensitivity. Yellowish green is brightest for cones, blue-green for the rods (although they will see it as colorless).
- Total color blindness is rare, but 8 percent of males and 1 percent of females are red-green color-weak. Color weakness is a sex-linked trait carried on the X chromosome. The Ishihara test is used to detect color blindness and color weakness.

Attention Voluntarily focusing on a specific sensory input.

Interpretation Where pain is concerned, the meaning given to a stimulus.

Counterirritation Using mild pain to block more intense or long-lasting pain.

- Dark adaptation, an increase in sensitivity to light, is caused mainly by increased concentration of visual pigments in both the rods and the cones but mainly by rhodopsin recombining in the rods. Vitamin A deficiencies may cause night blindness.

Sound waves are transduced by the eardrum, auditory ossicles, oval window, cochlea, and ultimately, hair cells.

- Frequency theory explains how we hear tones up to 4,000 hertz; place theory explains tones above 4,000 hertz.
- Two basic types of hearing loss are conductive hearing loss and sensorineural hearing loss.
- Noise-induced hearing loss is a common form of sensorineural hearing loss caused by exposure to loud noise.

Olfaction (smell) and gustation (taste) are chemical senses responsive to airborne or liquefied molecules.

- It is also suspected that humans are sensitive to pheromones, although the evidence for this sense remains preliminary.
- The lock and key theory of olfaction partially explains smell. In addition, the location of the olfactory receptors in the nose helps identify various scents.
- Sweet and bitter tastes are based on a lock-and-key coding of molecule shapes. Salty and sour tastes are triggered by a direct flow of ions into taste receptors.

The somesthetic senses include the skin senses, kinesthesis, and the vestibular senses.

- The skin senses are touch, pressure, pain, cold, and warmth. Sensitivity to each is related to the number of receptors found in an area of skin.
- Distinctions can be made among various types of pain, including visceral pain, somatic pain, referred pain, warning system pain, and reminding system pain.
- Various forms of motion sickness are related to messages received from the vestibular system, which detects gravity and movement.
- According to sensory conflict theory, motion sickness is caused by a mismatch of visual, kinesthetic, and vestibular sensations. Motion sickness can be avoided by minimizing sensory conflict.

Incoming sensations are affected by sensory adaptation (a reduction in the number of nerve impulses sent), by selective attention (selection and diversion of messages in the brain), and by sensory gating (blocking or alteration of messages flowing toward the brain).

- Selective gating of pain messages apparently takes place in the spinal cord. Gate control theory proposes an explanation for many pain phenomena, except phantom limb pain.

Pain can be reduced or controlled by altering factors that affect pain intensity.

- Pain is greatly affected by anxiety, control over the stimulus, attention, and the interpretation placed on an experience
- Pain can be reduced by controlling these factors through distraction, reinterpretation, counterirritation.

Web Resources

For an up-to-date list of direct links to interesting sites, including those listed here, visit the student companion site for this book at www.cengage.com/psychology/coon

Psychophysics Explore absolute and discrimination thresholds as well as other psychophysics phenomena.

The Joy of Visual Perception An online book about visual perception, including information on the eye.

Virtual Tour of the Ear This site provides educational information about the ear and hearing and provides quick access to ear and hearing Web resources.

Taste and Smell Disorders Read about various disorders of taste and smell and what can be done about them.

American Pain Foundation Find out more about pain and its treatment.

Interactive Learning

Introduction to Psychology: Gateways to Mind and Behavior **Book Companion Website**
www.cengage.com/psychology/coon

Visit your book companion website, where you will find flash cards, practice quizzes, web links, and more to help you study.

CENGAGENOW™ *Just what you need to know NOW!*

Spend time on what you need to master rather than on information you already have learned. Take a pre-test for this chapter, and CengageNOW will generate a personalized study plan based on your results. The study plan will identify the topics you need to review and direct you to online resources to help you master those topics. You can then take a post-test to help you determine the concepts you have mastered and what you will need to work on. Try it out! Go to www.cengage.com/login to sign in with an access code or to purchase access to this product.

CHAPTER 5

Perceiving the World

Gateway Theme

We actively construct our perceptions out of the information provided by our senses and our past experience; the resulting perceptions are not always accurate representations of events.

© 2006 "Pintos" by Bev Doolittle®, courtesy of The Greenwich Workshop, Inc. www.greenwichworkshop.com

Gateway Questions

- In general, how do we construct our perceptions?
- Is perception altered by attention, motives, and emotions?
- What basic principles do we use to group sensations into meaningful patterns?
- What are perceptual constancies, and what is their role in perception?
- How is it possible to see depth and judge distance?
- What effect does learning have on perception?
- To what extent do we see what we expect to see?
- Is extrasensory perception possible?
- How can I learn to perceive events more accurately?

One of your authors was in a supermarket when an 8-year-old girl suddenly came running around a corner. She looked back and screamed, "Stop! Stop! You're killing him! You're killing my father!" Here is your author's account of what followed:

> I retraced the girl's path and saw two men on the floor, struggling violently. The guy on top had his victim by the throat. There was blood everywhere. It was a murder in progress! As a witness, I would have told a jury what I just told you, were it not for an important fact: No murder ever took place that day at the supermarket. When the police arrived, they quickly discovered that the "guy on the bottom" had passed out and hit his head. That caused the cut (actually quite minor) that explained the "blood everywhere." The "guy on top" saw the first man fall and was trying to loosen his collar.

Obviously, the girl had misunderstood what was happening to her father. As a psychologist, I still find it fascinating that her words so dramatically influenced what I *saw*.

In the last chapter we discussed sensation, the process of bringing information into the nervous system. This chapter is about **perception,** or how we assemble sensations into meaningful patterns. As we perceive events, the brain actively selects, organizes, and integrates sensory information to construct a "picture" or model of the world. This process is so automatic that it can take a drastic misperception like that of your author to call attention to it.

Perception creates faces, melodies, works of art, illusions, and on occasion, "murders" out of the raw material of sensation. Let's see how this takes place.

●● Perception: That Extra Step

Gateway Question: In general, how do we construct our perceptions?
You wake up. Without a hint of effort, you see the rising sun.

I see the sunrise because my retinas send information to my brain, right? It may seem as if incoming sensations automatically give rise

"Marilyn Numerisée #420" © Yvaral 1990, Courtesy Circle Gallery

Visual perception involves finding meaningful patterns in complex stimuli. If you look closely at this painting by the artist Yvaral, you will see that it is entirely made up of small, featureless squares. A computer would have no clue what these squares portray. Likewise, an infant or newly sighted person would see only a jumble of meaningless colors. But because the squares form a familiar pattern, you should easily see Marilyn Monroe's face. (Or is that Madonna?).

to your experiences. But they don't. It takes the extra step known as *perception*. Like most experiences, seeing a "sunrise" is a **perceptual construction,** or mental model of an event, that *is actively created by your brain.*

To better understand perception, think again of the eye as being like a digital camera. Both eye and camera focus light on image-capturing surfaces. Both send information onward—your eyes to the brain and the camera first to a memory chip, and from there to your computer. But what happens when your computer receives a digital image? Does the computer recognize that photo of you and your best friend sitting on a beach last summer? Actually, not at all, because computers store photos as lists of numbers. Each number tells the computer what color and brightness to turn on a particular dot (pixel) on the screen. This allows your computer to display the photo, but the computer has no clue about what that photo means.

In sharp contrast, when *you* look at a scene, you don't just mindlessly record the action potentials from your rods and cones. Instead, you *recognize* and *understand* patterns in the messages. This is what creates a perceptual experience, such as seeing a sunrise or a photograph.

It is easy to take perception for granted, but computer scientists have had great difficulty creating even rudimentary artificial vision. For instance, it is not yet possible for video surveillance systems in stores to tell if a robbery is in progress and call the police. And yet, you have had such a system since you were an infant: Your senses send data to your brain, which creates meaningful perceptions of the world around you. If you were in line at a grocery store, you would know in an instant if a robbery were taking place. In other words, current computer systems are great at capturing, storing, and displaying huge volumes of data, but they are not yet very good at recognizing or understanding any of it. In contrast, your brain *is* very good at it. In this chapter we will explore perception, to learn how that extra step takes place.

Bottom-Up and Top-Down Processing

Moment by moment, our perceptions are typically constructed in both *bottom-up* and *top-down* fashion. Think about the process of building a house: Raw materials, such as lumber, doors, tiles, carpets, screws, and nails, must be painstakingly fit together. At the same time, a building plan guides how the raw materials are assembled.

Our brain builds perceptions in similar ways. In **bottom-up processing,** we start constructing at the "bottom," with raw materials. That is, we begin with small sensory units (features), and build upward to a complete perception. The reverse also occurs. In **top-down processing,** preexisting knowledge is used to rapidly organize features into a meaningful whole (Goldstein, 2007). If you put together a picture puzzle you've never seen before, you are relying mainly on bottom-up processing: You must assemble small pieces until a recognizable pattern begins to emerge. Top-down processing is like putting together a puzzle you have solved many times: After only a few pieces are in place, your past experience gives you the plan to rapidly fill in the final picture.

Both types of processing are illustrated by ● Figure 5.1. Also, look ahead to ● Figure 5.6. The first time you see the photo you probably will process it bottom-up, by picking out features. The next time, because of top-down processing, you'll likely recognize the photo instantly. Now that you have the general idea, let's look at perception in more detail.

Art © Estate of Al Held/Licensed by VAGA, NY, NY

● **Figure 5.1** This painting by abstract artist Al Held is 9 feet by 9 feet. If you process the painting "bottom-up," all you will see is two small dark geometric shapes. Would you like to try some top-down processing? Knowing the painting's title will allow you to apply your knowledge and see the painting in an entirely different way. The title? It's *The Big N.* Can you see it now?

●● Perception and Attention— May I Have Your . . . Attention!

Gateway Question: Is perception altered by attention, motives, and emotions?

You are surrounded by sights, sounds, odors, tastes, and touch sensations. Which are you aware of? The first stage of perception is usually attention. As you may recall from Chapter 4, **selective attention** refers to the fact that we give some messages priority and put others on hold (Klein, 2004). (What if you can't easily focus your attention? See "Pay Attention!" to find out.) You might find it helpful to think of selective attention as a *bottleneck,* or narrowing in the information channel linking the senses to perception. When one message enters the bottleneck, it seems to prevent others from passing through (● Figure 5.2). Imagine, for instance, that you are driving a car and approaching an intersection. You need to be sure the traffic light is still green. Just as you are about to check it, your passenger points to a friend at the side of the road. If you then fail to notice the light just changed to red, an accident may be just seconds away.

Have you ever felt overloaded when trying to do several things at once? **Divided attention** arises when you must divide your mental effort among tasks, each of which requires more or less attention. Divided attention is related to our limited *capacity* for storing and thinking about information. For example, when people first learn to drive, almost all their attention is needed to steer,

● **Figure 5.2** The attentional "spotlight" can be widened or narrowed. If you focus on local details in this drawing you will see the letter *A* repeated 13 times. If you broaden your field of attention to encompass the overall pattern, you will see the letter *H.* (After Lamb & Yund, 1996.)

Perception The mental process of organizing sensations into meaningful patterns.

Perceptual construction A meaningful mental model of external events.

Bottom-up processing Organizing perceptions by beginning with low-level features.

Top-down processing Applying higher-level knowledge to rapidly organize sensory information into a meaningful perception.

Selective attention Giving priority to a particular incoming sensory message.

Divided attention Allotting mental space or effort to various tasks or parts of a task.

THE CLINICAL FILE

Pay Attention!

What if you can't? What if your everyday experience is a giant kaleidoscope of rapidly shifting sensory impressions and thoughts? Easily distracted, you may not even notice your teacher exhorting you yet again to "Focus on your work!" Couple that with an inability to sit quietly at your desk and a tendency to say or do the first thing that pops into your mind and you will likely not be teacher's pet or at the top of your class.

People with **attention deficit hyperactivity disorder (ADHD)** have difficulty controlling their attention and are prone to display hyperactive and impulsive behavior (DSM-IV-TR, 2000). According to the National Institute of Mental Health, over two million American children have ADHD and about half will continue to show some symptoms as adults (NIMH, 2008).

The diagnosis of ADHD is very controversial. On the one side are those who insist that ADHD is a biological disorder that is best treated with medications like Ritalin, a stimulant that exerts a curiously calming effect. On the other side are those who insist that ADHD is far too often overdiagnosed or misdiagnosed and that giving millions of young children drugs is inappropriate and wrong (Bratter, 2007). Complicating matters is the fact that boys are over twice as likely to be diagnosed with ADHD than girls (Froehlich et al., 2007), leading some critics to claim that parents and teachers should give their exuberant boys more time to actively play outdoors rather than forcing them to sit still indoors for hours at a time.

Is ADHD a real biological disorder or an unfair label applied to active children? Hopefully further research will answer this important question. Until then, your authors are content to note that this controversy highlights a major theme of this chapter, namely that perception is partly in the eye of the beholder. (You were paying attention, weren't you?)

---

brake, shift, and so forth. However, as a skill becomes more automatic, it requires less attention. In driving, greater skill frees mental capacity for other things, such as tuning the car's radio or carrying on a conversation. Yet even as some driving skills become automated, divided attention can be hazardous (Wester et al., 2008). Many automobile accidents occur when drivers are looking at friends at the side of the road, using cell phones, tending to children, reading maps, touching up their makeup, and the like.

Are some stimuli more attention getting than others? Yes. Very *intense* stimuli usually command attention. Stimuli that are brighter, louder, or larger tend to capture attention: A gunshot in a library would be hard to ignore. If a brightly colored hot-air balloon ever lands at your college campus, it will almost certainly draw a crowd.

Repetitious stimuli, repetitious stimuli, repetitious stimuli, repetitious stimuli, repetitious stimuli, repetitious stimuli are also attention getting. A dripping faucet at night makes little noise by normal standards, but because of repetition, it may become as attention getting as a single sound many times louder. This effect is used repeatedly, so to speak, in television and radio commercials.

ATTENTION IS ALSO **FREQUENTLY** RELATED TO contrast OR *change* IN STIMULATION. The contrasting type styles in the preceding sentence draw attention because they are *unexpected*. Geoffrey Loftus and Norman Mackworth (1978) found that people who look at drawings like ● Figure 5.3 focus first and longest on unexpected objects (the octopus, in this case).

Charles Platiau/Reuters/Corbis

In many sports, experts are much better than beginners at paying attention to key information. Compared with novices, experts scan actions and events more quickly and focus on only the most meaningful information. This allows experts to make decisions and react more quickly (Bard, Fleury, & Goulet, 1994).

● **Figure 5.3** One of the drawings used by Loftus and Mackworth (1978) to investigate attention. Observers attend to unexpected objects longer than they do to expected objects. In this drawing, observers looked longer at the octopus than they did at a tractor placed in the same spot. What do you think would happen if a tractor were shown upside down or on the roof of the barn?

Inattentional Blindness

As we take in information, attention is the key that unlocks the door to perception. In fact, psychologists Arien Mack and Irvin Rock believe that perception cannot occur without attention. Let's say, for example, that you are staring intently at a computer screen, waiting to see if a black cross will appear. The cross flashes on the screen for a split second and you say, "Yes I saw the cross." At the same time, a small blue square is flashed near the cross, also for a split second. Do you see it, too? Amazingly, when people are tested in this way, many never see the blue square. While their attention is intensely focused on one object, they are blind to another—even though it is right in front of their eyes. The image of the blue square falls on the retina, but it might as well be invisible. Mack and Rock call this effect **inattentional blindness** (blindness caused by not attending to a stimulus) (Mack & Rock, 1998). Not seeing something that is plainly before your eyes is most likely to occur when your attention is narrowly focused (Mack, 2002; Most et al., 2005).

Inattentional blindness is vividly illustrated by a study in which participants were shown a film of two basketball teams, one wearing black shirts and the other wearing white. Observers were asked to watch the film closely and count how many times a basketball passed between members of one of the teams, while ignoring the other team. As observers watched and counted, a person wearing a gorilla suit walked into the middle of the basketball game, faced the camera, thumped its chest, and walked out of view. Half the observers failed to notice this rather striking event (Simons & Chabris, 1999). This effect probably explains why fans of opposing sports teams often act as if they had seen two completely different games. In a similar way, using a cell phone while driving can cause inattentional blindness. Instead of ignoring a gorilla, you might miss seeing another car, a motorcyclist, or a pedestrian while your attention is focused on the phone (Bressan & Pizzighello, 2008).

Habituation

Change, contrast, and incongruity are perhaps the most basic sources of attention. We quickly **habituate** (respond less) to predictable and unchanging stimuli. Notice that repetition without variation leads to habituation. Repetition is attention getting when it is irritating or annoying. A dripping faucet varies in timing just enough to gain attention. In contrast, we quickly habituate to the steady tick of a clock.

How does habituation differ from sensory adaptation? As described in Chapter 4, *adaptation* decreases the actual number of sensory messages sent to the brain. When messages do reach the brain, the body has a sort of "What is it?" reaction, known as an *orientation response.* An **orientation response** (OR) prepares us to receive information from a stimulus: The pupils enlarge, brain-wave patterns shift, breathing stops briefly, blood flow to the head increases, and we turn toward the stimulus. Have you ever seen someone stop to take a second look? If so, you have observed an orientation response.

Now, think about what happens when you download some new music for your MP3 player. At first the music holds your attention all the way through. But when the music becomes "old," the song may play without your really attending to it. When a stimulus is repeated *without change,* the OR habituates, or decreases. (Also, see "The 'Boiled Frog Syndrome.'")

Interestingly, creative people habituate *more slowly* than average. We might expect that they would rapidly become bored with a repeated stimulus. Instead, it seems that creative people actively attend to stimuli, even those that are repeated (Colin, Moore, & West, 1996).

Motives, Emotions, and Perception

Our motives and emotions also play a role in shaping our perceptions. For example, if you are hungry, food-related words are more likely to gain your attention than nonfood words (Mogg et al., 1998). Advertisers, of course, know that their pitch will be more effective if it gets your attention. That's why ads are loud, repetitious, and often intentionally irritating. They also take advantage of two motives that are widespread in our society: *anxiety* and *sex.* Everything from mouthwash to automobile tires is merchandised by using sex to gain attention (LaTour & Henthorne, 2003). Other ads combine sex with anxiety. Deodorant, soaps, toothpaste, and countless other articles are pushed in ads that play on desires to be attractive, to have "sex appeal," or to avoid embarrassment.

Our emotions can also influence what we perceive. According to psychologist Barbara Frederickson, negative emotions generally narrow our perceptual focus or "spotlight." This increases the likelihood of inattentional blindness. In contrast, positive emotions can actually broaden the scope of attention (Fredrickson & Branigan, 2005). For example, we are much better at recognizing faces of people from our own race than from others. (This *other-race effect* is discussed in more detail later). But when people are in positive moods, their ability to recognize people from other races improves (Johnson & Fredrickson, 2005).

Attention deficit hyperactivity disorder (ADHD) Disorder usually arising in early childhood characterized by inattention, hyperactivity, and impulsiveness.

Inattentional blindness Failure to perceive a stimulus that is in plain view, but not the focus of attention.

Habituation A decrease in perceptual response to a repeated stimulus.

Orientation response Bodily changes that prepare an organism to receive information from a particular stimulus.

CRITICAL THINKING

The "Boiled Frog Syndrome"

As we have noted, the perceptual system is impressed most by dramatic changes. Humans evolved to detect sharp changes and distinctive events, such as the sudden appearance of a lion, a potential mate, or sources of food. We are far less able to detect gradual changes.

Perceptual capacities that aided survival when humans were hunters and gatherers may now be a handicap. Many of the threats facing civilization develop very slowly. Examples include the stockpiling of nuclear warheads, degradation of the environment, global deforestation, global warming, erosion of the ozone layer, and runaway human population growth.

Robert Ornstein, a psychologist, and Paul Ehrlich, a biologist, believe that many of the large-scale threats we face are similar to the "boiled frog syndrome." Frogs placed in a pan of water that is slowly heated cannot detect the gradual rise in temperature. They will sit still until they die. Like the doomed frogs, many people seem unable to detect gradual but deadly trends in modern civilization (Ornstein & Ehrlich, 1989).

To avoid disasters, it may take a conscious effort by large numbers of people to see the "big picture" and reverse lethal but easily overlooked patterns (O'Neill, 2005). The relatively new field of *community psychology* is dedicated to helping overcome our own narrow perspectives to perceive important larger patterns (Nelson & Prilleltensky, 2005). Understanding how perception shapes "reality" may ultimately prove to be a matter of life or death. Are you paying attention?

Randy Ury/Corbis

---

3. The occurrence of an orientation response shows that habituation is complete. T or F?
4. Changes in brain waves and increased blood flow to the head are part of an OR. T or F?
5. Research shows that positive emotions can broaden the "attentional spotlight." T or F?

REFLECT

Critical Thinking
6. Cigarette advertisements in the United States are required to carry a warning label about the health risks of smoking. How have tobacco companies made these labels less visible?

Relate
Have you ever tried to listen to two people who were talking to you at the same time? What happens to your ability to process information when there's a conflict in selective attention?

You have almost certainly misperceived a situation at some time because of the influence of motives or perceptions. How were your perceptions influenced?

Answers: 1. F 2. a 3. F 4. T 5. T 6. Advertisers place health warnings in the corners of ads, where they attract the least possible attention. Also, the labels are often placed on "busy" backgrounds so that they are partially camouflaged. Finally, the main images in ads are designed to strongly attract attention. This further distracts readers from seeing the warnings.

● Perceptual Organization— Getting It All Together

Gateway Question: What basic principles do we use to group sensations into meaningful patterns?

What would it be like to have your vision restored after a lifetime of blindness? Actually, a first look at the world can be disappointing because your newfound ability to *sense* the world does not guarantee that you can *perceive* it. You may be thrilled by the sheer richness of your newfound visual experience but, like a computer, be unable to *recognize* any of it.

You're kidding, right? Nope. Newly sighted persons must *learn* to recognize objects, to read clocks, numbers, and letters, and to judge sizes and distances (Gregory, 2003). For instance, a cataract patient named Mr. S. B. had been blind since birth. After an operation restored his sight at age 52, Mr. S. B. struggled to use his vision.

Mr. S. B. soon learned to tell time from a large clock and to read block letters he had known only from touch. At a zoo, he recognized an elephant from descriptions he had heard. However, handwriting meant nothing to him for more than a year after he regained sight, and many objects were meaningless until he touched them. Thus, Mr. S. B. slowly learned to organize his *sensations* into meaningful *perceptions*.

Gestalt Principles

How are sensations organized into perceptions? The Gestalt psychologists proposed that the simplest organization is constructed by grouping some sensations into an object, or figure, that stands out on a plainer background (Goldstein, 2007). **Figure-ground organization** is probably inborn, because it is the first perceptual ability to appear after cataract patients regain sight. In normal figure-ground perception, only one figure is seen. In *reversible figures,* however, figure and ground can be switched. In ● Figure 5.4 it is equally possible to see either a wineglass figure on a dark background or two face profiles on a light background. As you shift from one pattern to the other, you should get a clear sense of what figure-ground organization means.

> **bridges**
> See Chapter 1, page 24, for a brief history of Gestalt psychology.

● **Figure 5.4** A reversible figure-ground design. Do you see two faces in profile or a wineglass?

Are there other Gestalt organizing principles? The Gestalt psychologists identified several other principles that bring some order to your perceptions (● Figure 5.5).

1. **Nearness.** All other things being equal, stimuli that are near each other tend to be constructed, or grouped, together (Quinn, Bhatt, & Hayden, 2008). Thus, if three people stand near each other and a fourth person stands 10 feet away, the adjacent three will be seen as a group and the distant person as an outsider (see ● Figure 5.5*a*).

2. **Similarity.** "Birds of a feather flock together," and stimuli that are similar in size, shape, color, or form tend to be grouped together (see ● Figure 5.5*b*). Picture two bands marching side by side. If their uniforms are the same colors, the bands will be seen as one large group, not as two separate groups.

3. **Continuation, or continuity.** Perceptions tend toward simplicity and continuity. In ● Figure 5.5*c* it is easier to visualize a wavy line on a squared-off line than it is to see a complex row of shapes.

4. **Closure.** Closure refers to the tendency to *complete* a figure so that it has a consistent overall form. Each of the drawings in ● Figure 5.5*d* has one or more gaps, yet each is perceived as a recognizable figure. The "shapes" that appear in the two right drawings in ● Figure 5.5*d* are *illusory figures* (implied shapes that are not actually bounded by an edge or an outline). Even young children see these shapes, despite knowing that they are "not really there." Illusory figures reveal that our tendency to form shapes—even with minimal cues—is powerful.

(a) Principle of nearness
Notice how differently a group of six objects can be perceptually organized, depending on their spacing.

(b) Principle of similarity
In these examples, organization depends on similarity of color.

Similarity and nearness can be combined to produce a new organization.

(c) Principle of continuity

This? plus or This?

(d) Principle of closure

(e) Principle of common region

● **Figure 5.5** How we organize perceptions.

Figure-ground organization Part of a stimulus appears to stand out as an object (figure) against a less prominent background (ground).

5. **Contiguity.** A principle that can't be shown in ● Figure 5.5 is contiguity, or nearness in time *and* space. Contiguity is often responsible for the perception that one thing has *caused* another (Buehner & May, 2003). A psychologist friend of ours demonstrates this principle in class by knocking on his head with one hand while knocking on a wooden table (out of sight) with the other. The knocking sound is perfectly timed with the movements of his visible hand. This leads to the irresistible perception that his head is made of wood.

6. **Common region.** As you can see in ● Figure 5.5*e*, stimuli that are found within a common area tend to be seen as a group (Palmer, & Beck, 2007). On the basis of similarity and nearness, the stars in ● Figure 5.5*e* should be one group and the dots another. However, the colored backgrounds define regions that create three groups of objects (four stars, two stars plus two dots, and four dots). Perhaps the principle of common region explains why we tend to mentally group together people from a particular country, state, province, or geographic region.

Clearly, the Gestalt principles offer us some basic "plans" for organizing parts of our day-to-day perceptions in top-down fashion. So too does learning and past experience. Take a moment and look for the camouflaged animal pictured in ● Figure 5.6. (Camouflage patterns break up figure-ground organization). If you had never seen similar animals before, could you have located this one? Mr. S. B. would have been at a total loss to find meaning in such a picture.

In a way, we are all detectives, seeking patterns in what we see. In this sense, a meaningful pattern represents a **perceptual hypothesis,** or initial plan or guess about how to organize sensations. Have you ever seen a "friend" in the distance, only to have the person turn into a stranger as you drew closer? Preexisting ideas and expectations *actively* guide our interpretation of sensations (Most et al., 2005).

The active, constructive nature of perception is perhaps most apparent for *ambiguous stimuli* (patterns allowing more than one interpretation). If you look at a cloud, you may discover dozens of ways to organize its contours into fanciful shapes and scenes. Even clearly defined stimuli may permit more than one interpretation. Look at Necker's cube in ● Figure 5.7 if you doubt that perception is an active process. Visualize the top cube as a wire box. If you stare at the cube, its organization will change. Sometimes it will seem to project upward, like the lower left cube; other times it will project downward. The difference lies in how your brain interprets the same information. In short, we actively *construct* meaningful perceptions; we do not passively record the events and stimuli around us (Coren, Ward, & Enns, 2004).

In some instances, a stimulus may offer such conflicting information that perceptual organization becomes impossible. For example, the tendency to make a three-dimensional object out of a drawing is frustrated by the "three-pronged widget" (● Figure 5.8), an *impossible figure.* Such patterns cannot be organized into stable, consistent, or meaningful perceptions. If you cover either end of the drawing in ● Figure 5.8, it makes sense perceptually. However, a problem arises when you try to organize the entire drawing. Then, conflicting information prevents you from forming a stable perception.

Learning to organize his visual sensations was only one of the hurdles Mr. S. B. faced in learning to see. In the next section, we will consider some others.

● **Figure 5.7** Necker's cube.

● **Figure 5.6** A challenging example of perceptual organization. Once the camouflaged insect (known as a giant walking stick) becomes visible, it is almost impossible to view the picture again without seeing the insect.

E.R. Degginger/Animals Animals

● **Figure 5.8** *(Above)* An impossible figure—the "three-pronged widget." *(Below)* It might seem that including more information in a drawing would make perceptual conflicts impossible. However, Japanese artist Shigeo Fukuda has shown otherwise. ("Disappearing Column" © Shigeo Fukuda, 1985.)

Perceptual Constancies— Taming an Unruly World

Gateway Question: What are perceptual constancies, and what is their role in perception?

When Mr. S. B. first regained his vision, he could only judge distance in familiar situations (Gregory, 1990). One day he was found crawling out of a hospital window to get a closer look at traffic on the street. It's easy to understand his curiosity, but he had to be restrained. His room was on the fourth floor!

Why would Mr. S. B. try to crawl out of a fourth-story window? Couldn't he at least tell distance from the size of the cars? No, you must be visually familiar with objects to use their size to judge distance. Try holding your left hand a few inches in front of your nose and your right hand at arm's length. Your right hand should appear to be about half the size of your left hand. Still, you know your right hand did not suddenly shrink, because you have seen it many times at various distances. We call this **size constancy:** The perceived size of an object remains the same, even though the size of its image on the retina changes.

To perceive your hand accurately, you had to draw on past experience to provide a top-down plan for constructing your perception. Some of these plans are so basic they seem to be *native*

(a)   (b)

● **Figure 5.9** Shape constancy. *(a)* When a door is open, its image actually forms a trapezoid. Shape constancy is indicated by the fact that it is still perceived as a rectangle. *(b)* With great effort you may be able to see this design as a collection of flat shapes. However, if you maintain shape constancy, the distorted squares strongly suggest the surface of a sphere. (From *Spherescapes-1* by Scott Walter and Kevin McMahon, 1983.)

(inborn). An example is the ability to see a line on a piece of paper. Likewise, even newborn babies show some evidence of size constancy (Granrud, 2006; Slater, Mattock, & Brown, 1990). However, many of our perceptions are *empirical,* or based on prior experience. For instance, cars, houses, and people look like toys when seen from a great distance or from an unfamiliar perspective, such as from the top of a skyscraper. This suggests that although some size constancy is innate, it is also affected by learning (Granrud, 2004).

In **shape constancy** the shape of an object remains stable, even though the shape of its retinal image changes. You can demonstrate shape constancy by looking at this page from directly overhead and then from an angle. Obviously, the page is rectangular, but most of the images that reach your eyes are distorted. Yet, though the book's image changes, your perception of its shape remains constant. (For additional examples, see ● Figure 5.9.) On the highway, alcohol intoxication impairs size and shape constancy, adding to the accident rate among drunk drivers (Farrimond, 1990).

Let's say that you are outside in bright sunlight. Beside you, a friend is wearing a gray skirt and a white blouse. Suddenly a cloud shades the sun. It might seem that the blouse would grow dimmer, but it still appears to be bright white. This happens because the blouse continues to reflect a larger *proportion* of light than nearby

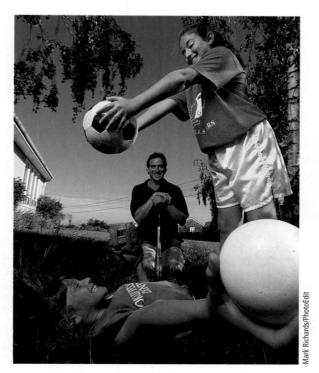

Almost everyone's family album has at least one photo like this. Extreme viewing angles can make maintaining size constancy difficult, even for familiar objects.

Perceptual hypothesis An initial guess regarding how to organize (perceive) a stimulus pattern.

Size constancy The perceived size of an object remains constant, despite changes in its retinal image.

Shape constancy The perceived shape of an object is unaffected by changes in its retinal image.

CRITICAL THINKING

A Bird's-Eye View

Although it is tempting to assume that other animals perceive depth much as we do, this is not the case. Different species actually see the world in rather different ways. Most variations in vision have a purpose. Evolutionary psychologists theorize that human depth perception is an evolutionary holdover—from life in the treetops. The superb depth perception that helped our distant ancestors swing from branch to branch now helps us swing at a softball or avoid erratic drivers in traffic.

It might seem that birds would have acute stereoscopic vision, and some do. But most birds are prey for other animals. When you spend life as a potential meal, it's important to detect approaching predators (Waldvogel, 1990). That's why many birds have an unusually wide field of view (● Figure 5.10a and b). An extreme case is the American woodcock, a bird that can survey a 360-degree panorama without moving its eyes or head. The trade-off for this wide-angle view is a very limited area of *binocular vision*, where depth perception is strongest (● Figure 5.10c). But to the woodcock, an ability to spot hungry predators is probably more valuable than depth perception.

What does the world look like to a woodcock? Computer scientist Ping-Kang Hsiung (1990) used optical ray-tracing to simulate the woodcock's view (● Figure 5.10e and f). As you can see in ● Figure 5.10, even a pretty foxy predator would have trouble sneaking up on a woodcock. When it comes to human vision, perhaps it's too bad that a little of the woodcock's wide-angle vision didn't get thrown in as well.

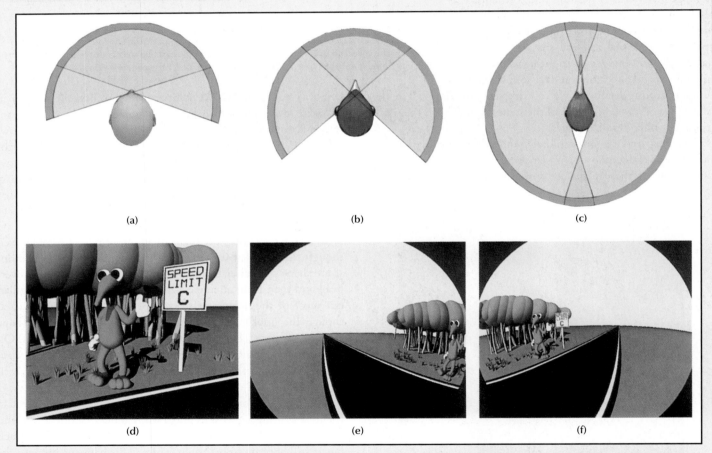

● **Figure 5.10** *(a)* When viewed from above the head, a human's field of view for the right and left eyes contains a large area of overlapping, stereoscopic vision (darker shading). *(b)* The barn swallow's vision, like that of many birds, covers a much wider field of view than ours. Although the swallow's area of binocular vision is smaller than a human's, the swallow has sharper peripheral vision. *(c)* A bird called the American woodcock can see all the way around its head. Binocular vision is limited to a narrow band, but an extremely wide field of view helps the woodcock detect predators. (Adapted from Waldvogel, 1990.) *(d)* This image, created by Ping-Kang Hsiung (1990), shows how an imaginary scene would look to a person standing across the road from a rather strange hitchhiker. *(e, f)* This is what a woodcock's left and right eyes would see if the bird were at the same point as the human in view *d*. (Computer graphics courtesy of Dr. Hsiung.)

objects. **Brightness constancy** refers to the fact that the brightness of objects appears to stay the same as lighting conditions change. However, this holds true only if the blouse and other objects are all illuminated by the same amount of light. You could make an area on your friend's gray skirt look whiter than the shaded blouse by shining a bright spotlight on the skirt.

To summarize, the energy patterns reaching our senses are constantly changing, even when they come from the same object. Size, shape, and brightness constancy rescue us from a confusing world in which objects would seem to shrink and grow, change shape as if made of rubber, and light up or fade like neon lamps.

One of the most amazing perceptual feats is our capacity to construct the experience of three-dimensional space from flat retinal images. We'll explore that topic in a moment, but first here's a chance to rehearse what you've learned.

KNOWLEDGE BUILDER
Gestalt Principles and Perceptual Constancies

RECITE

1. The first and most basic perceptual organization to emerge when sight is restored to a blind person is:
   a. continuity
   b. nearness constancy
   c. recognition of numbers and letters
   d. figure-ground
2. Gestalt principles offer us some basic "plans" for organizing parts of our day-to-day perceptions in top-down fashion. T or F?
3. At times, meaningful perceptual organization represents a _____, or "guess," held until the evidence contradicts it.
4. The design known as Necker's cube is a good example of an impossible figure. T or F?
5. Which among the following are subject to basic perceptual constancy?
   a. figure-ground organization
   b. size
   c. ambiguity
   d. brightness
   e. continuity
   f. closure
   g. shape
   h. nearness

REFLECT

Critical Thinking

6. People who have taken psychedelic drugs, such as LSD or mescaline, often report that the objects and people they see appear to be changing in size, shape, and brightness. This suggests that such drugs disrupt what perceptual process?

Relate

As you look around the area in which you are now, how are the Gestalt principles helping to organize your perceptions? Try to find a specific example for each principle.

If you needed to explain the perceptual constancies to a friend, what would you say? Why are the constancies important for maintaining a stable perceptual world?

Answers: 1. d **2.** T **3.** hypothesis **4.** F **5.** b, d, g **6.** Perceptual constancies (size, shape, and brightness).

Depth Perception—What if the World Were Flat?

Gateway Question: How is it possible to see depth and judge distance?
Close one of your eyes, hold your head very still, and stare at a single point across the room. If you don't move your head or eyes, your surroundings will appear to be almost flat, like a painting or photograph. But even under these conditions you will still have some sense of depth. Now, open both eyes and move your head and eyes as usual. Suddenly, the "3-D" perceptual world returns. How are we able to perceive depth and space?

Depth perception is the ability to see three-dimensional space and to accurately judge distances. Without depth perception, another form of top-down processing, you would be unable to drive a car or ride a bicycle, play catch, shoot baskets, thread a needle, or simply navigate around a room (Howard & Rogers, 2001,a). The world would look like a flat surface. (See "A Bird's-Eye View" on page 158.)

Mr. S. B. had trouble with depth perception after his sight was restored. Is depth perception learned? Some psychologists (nativists) hold that depth perception is inborn. Others (the empiricists) view it as learned. Most likely, depth perception is partly learned and partly innate (Witherington et al., 2005). Some evidence on the issue comes from work with the *visual cliff*. Basically, a visual cliff is a glass-topped table (● Figure 5.11). On one side a checkered surface lies directly beneath the glass. On the other side, the checkered surface is 4 feet below. This makes the glass look like a tabletop on one side and a cliff, or drop-off, on the other.

To test for depth perception, 6- to 14-month-old infants were placed in the middle of the visual cliff. This gave them a choice of crawling to the shallow side or the deep side. (The glass prevented them from doing any "skydiving" if they chose the deep side.) Most infants chose the shallow side. In fact, most refused the deep side even when their mothers tried to call them toward it (Gibson & Walk, 1960).

If the infants were at least 6 months old when they were tested, isn't it possible that they learned to perceive depth? Yes. More recent research has shown that depth perception begins to develop as early as 2 weeks of age (Yonas, Elieff, & Arterberry, 2002). It is very likely that at least a basic level of depth perception is innate. Yet, the development of depth perception is not complete until about 6 months, suggesting that it depends on both brain maturation and individual experience.

Then why do some older babies crawl off tables or beds? As soon as infants become active crawlers, they refuse to cross the deep side of the visual cliff. However, older infants who have just learned to walk must again learn to avoid the "deep" side of the visual cliff

---

Brightness constancy The apparent (or relative) brightness of objects remains the same as long as they are illuminated by the same amount of light.

Depth perception The ability to see three-dimensional space and to accurately judge distances.

● **Figure 5.11** Human infants and newborn animals refuse to go over the edge of the visual cliff.

Glass only

Glass over patterned surface

Deep side

Shallow side

Floor pattern seen through glass

Mark Richards/PhotoEdit

(Witherington et al., 2005). Besides, even babies who perceive depth may not be able to catch themselves if they slip. A lack of coordination—not an inability to see depth—probably explains most "crash landings" after about 4 months of age.

We learn to construct our perception of three-dimensional space by using a variety of *depth cues*. **Depth cues** are features of the environment and messages from the body that supply information about distance and space. Some cues require two eyes (**binocular depth cues**), whereas others will work with just one eye (**monocular depth cues**).

Binocular Depth Cues

The most basic source of depth perception is *retinal disparity* (a discrepancy in the images that reach the right and left eyes). Retinal disparity, which is a binocular cue, is based on the fact that the eyes are about 2.5 inches apart. Because of this, each eye receives a

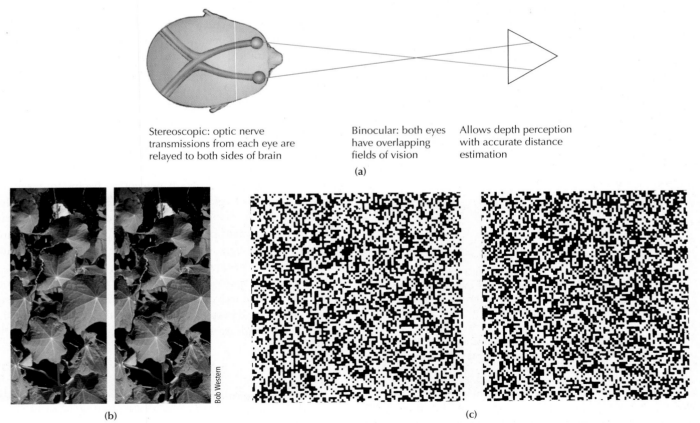

Stereoscopic: optic nerve transmissions from each eye are relayed to both sides of brain

Binocular: both eyes have overlapping fields of vision

Allows depth perception with accurate distance estimation

(a)

Bob Western

(b)

(c)

● **Figure 5.12** *(a)* Stereoscopic vision. *(b)* The photographs show what the right and left eyes would see when viewing a plant. Hold the page about 6 to 8 inches from your eyes. Allow your eyes to cross and focus on the overlapping image between the two photos. Then try to fuse the leaves into one image. If you are successful, the third dimension will appear like magic. *(c)* Now do the same with the random dot stereogram, but with your eyes 10 inches from the page. With luck, you will see a diamond shape hovering over the background. (See text for explanation.) (Julesz, 1971)

● Figure 5.13 This popular style of computer-generated art creates a 3-D illusion by superimposing two patterns. There are mismatches between some areas of the two patterns. This simulates retinal disparity and creates a sensation of depth. To get the 3-D effect, hold the stereogram about 8 inches from the end of your nose. Relax your eyes and look *through* the art, as if you were focusing on something in the distance. If you're patient, you may see a 3-D globe.

slightly different view of the world. Try this: Put a finger in front of your eyes and as close to your nose as you can. First close one eye and then the other, over and over again. You should notice that your finger seems to jump back and forth as you view the different images reaching each eye. However, when the two different images are fused into one overall image, **stereoscopic vision** (three-dimensional sight) occurs (Howard & Rogers, 2001b). The result is a powerful sensation of depth (● Figure 5.12).

Retinal disparity can be used to produce 3-D movies by filming with two cameras separated by several inches. Later, both images are simultaneously projected on a screen. Audience members wear glasses that filter out one of the images to each eye. Because each eye gets a separate image, normal stereoscopic vision is duplicated. Try the following demonstration of retinal disparity and fusion.

Totally Tubular

Roll a piece of paper into a tube. Close your left eye. Hold the tube to your right eye like a telescope. Look through the tube at some object in the distance. Place your left hand against the tube halfway down its length and in front of your left eye. Now open your left eye. You should see a "hole" in your hand. You couldn't expect a professional photographer to do a better job of blending the two images than your visual system does automatically.

How does retinal disparity produce depth? Perceiving depth is more than a simple blending of two "pictures" of the world. In ● Figure 5.12*c* you will find two *random dot stereograms* (patterns of dots that produce an illusion of depth). Notice that they contain no objects, lines, or edges. Just the same, when the stereograms are properly viewed (one to each eye), a center area seems to float above the background. Such designs show that the brain is very sensitive to any *mismatch* of information from the eyes. In ● Figure 5.12*c*, depth comes from shifting dots in the center of one square so that they do not match dots in the other square (Howard & Rogers, 2001a, 2000b; Julesz, 1971). (Also see ● Figure 5.13.)

To a large extent our experience of three-dimensional space is constructed from countless tiny differences between what the right and left eyes see. Direct studies of the brain have shown that visual areas do, in fact, contain cells that detect disparities (Cumming & DeAngelis, 2001).

Convergence is a second binocular depth cue. When you look at a distant object, the lines of vision from your eyes are parallel. You are normally not aware of it, but whenever you estimate a distance under 50 feet (as when you play catch or shoot trash can hoops with the first draft of your essay), you are using convergence. How? Muscles attached to the eyeball feed information on eye position to the brain to help it judge distance (● Figure 5.14).

● Figure 5.14
The eyes must converge, or turn in toward the nose, to focus close objects. The eyes shown are viewed from above the head.

Depth cues Perceptual features that impart information about distance and three-dimensional space.

Binocular depth cues Perceptual features that impart information about distance and three-dimensional space that require two eyes.

Monocular depth cues Perceptual features that impart information about distance and three-dimensional space that require just one eye.

Stereoscopic vision Perception of space and depth caused chiefly by the fact that the eyes receive different images.

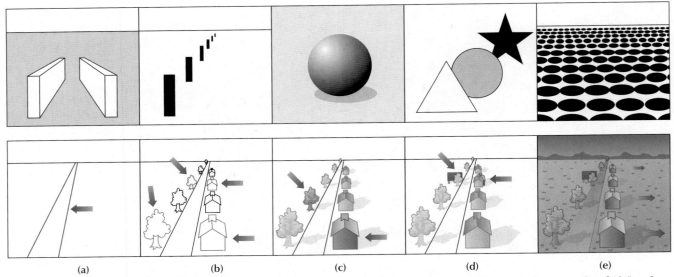

● **Figure 5.15** *(a)* Linear perspective. *(b)* Relative size. *(c)* Light and shadow. *(d)* Overlap. *(e)* Texture gradients. Drawings in the top row show fairly "pure" examples of each of the pictorial depth cues. In the bottom row, the pictorial depth cues are used to assemble a more realistic scene.

You can feel convergence by exaggerating it: Focus on your fingertip and bring it toward your eyes until they almost cross. You can actually feel the muscles that control eye movement working harder and harder as your fingertip gets closer. If you repeat this little exercise with one eye shut, you will feel no increase in muscle tension as your finger gets closer. It takes *both* eyes to converge. This is why we say convergence is also a binocular depth cue.

If disparity and convergence are so important, can a person with one eye perceive depth? Yes, but not as well as a person with two eyes. Overall, stereoscopic vision is 10 times better for judging depth than perception based on just one eye (Rosenberg, 1994). Try driving a car or riding a bicycle with one eye closed. You will find yourself braking too soon or too late, and you will have difficulty estimating your speed. ("But officer, my psychology text said to . . .") Despite this, you will be able to drive, although it will be more difficult than usual. This is possible because your single eye is making use of monocular depth cues.

Monocular Depth Cues

As their name implies, monocular depth cues can be used to construct a three-dimensional perception with information received from just one eye (Sekuler & Blake, 2006). One such cue is *accommodation,* the bending of the lens to focus on nearby objects. Sensations from muscles attached to each lens flow back to the brain. Changes in these sensations help us judge distances within about 4 feet of the eyes. This information is available even if you are just using one eye, so accommodation is a monocular cue. Beyond 4 feet though, accommodation has limited value. Obviously, it is more important to a watchmaker or a person trying to thread a needle than it is to a basketball player or someone driving an automobile.

Other monocular depth cues are also referred to as pictorial depth cues, because a good movie, painting, or photograph can create a convincing sense of depth where none exists.

How is the illusion of depth created on a two-dimensional surface? **Pictorial depth cues** are monocular cues found in paintings, drawings, and photographs that impart information about space, depth, and distance. To understand how these cues work, imagine that you are looking outdoors through a window. If you trace everything you see onto the glass, you will have an excellent drawing, with convincing depth. If you then analyze what is on the glass you will find the following features (● Figure 5.15):

1. **Linear perspective.** This cue is based on the apparent convergence of parallel lines in the environment. If you stand between two railroad tracks, they appear to meet near the horizon, even though they actually remain parallel. Because you know they are parallel, their convergence implies great distance (● Figure 5.15*a*).

2. **Relative size.** If an artist wishes to depict two objects of the same size at different distances, the artist makes the more distant object smaller (● Figure 5.15*b*). Special effects in films create sensational illusions of depth by rapidly changing the image size of planets, airplanes, monsters, or what have you. (Also see ● Figure 5.16.)

Linear perspective is a very powerful cue for depth. Because of the depth cues implied in this drawing, the upper cross on the vertical line appears to be diagonal. It is actually a right angle. The lower cross, which appears to be a right angle, is actually diagonal to the vertical line. (After Enns & Coren, 1995.)

● **Figure 5.16** On a dry lake bed, relative size is just about the only depth cue available for judging the camera's distance from this vintage aircraft. What do you estimate the distance to be? For the answer, look ahead to ● Figure 5.21.

3. **Height in the picture plane.** Objects that are placed higher (closer to the horizon line) in a drawing tend to be perceived as more distant. In the upper frame of ● Figure 5.15*b* the black columns look like they are receding into the distance partly because they become smaller but also because they move higher in the drawing.

4. **Light and shadow.** Most objects are lighted in ways that create clear patterns of light and shadow. Copying such patterns of light and shadow can give a two-dimensional design a three-dimensional appearance (● Figure 5.15*c*). (Also, look ahead to ● Figure 5.17 for more information on light and shadow.)

5. **Overlap.** Overlap (or *interposition*) occurs when one object partially blocks another object. Hold your hands up and ask a friend across the room which is nearer. Relative size will give the answer if one hand is much nearer to your friend than the other. But if one hand is only slightly closer than the other, your friend may not be able to tell—until you slide one hand in front of the other. Overlap then removes any doubt (● Figure 5.15*d*).

6. **Texture gradients.** Changes in texture also contribute to depth perception. If you stand in the middle of a cobblestone street, the street will look coarse near your feet. However, its texture will get smaller and finer if you look into the distance (● Figure 5.15*e*).

7. **Aerial perspective.** Smog, fog, dust, and haze add to the apparent distance of an object. Because of aerial perspective, distant objects tend to be hazy, washed out in color, and lacking in detail. Aerial haze is often most noticeable when it is missing. If you have ever seen a distant mountain range on a crystal-clear day, it might have looked like it was only a few miles away. In reality, you could have been viewing them through 50 miles of crystal-clear air.

8. **Relative motion.** Relative motion, also known as *motion parallax* (PAIR-ah-lax), can be seen by looking out a window and moving your head from side to side. Notice that nearby objects appear to move a sizable distance as your head moves. Trees, houses, and telephone poles that are farther

● **Figure 5.17** *(Above)* When judging depth we usually assume that light comes mainly from one direction, usually from above. Squint a little to blur the image you see here. You should perceive a collection of globes projecting outward. If you turn this page upside down, the globes should become cavities. (After Ramachandran, 1995.) *(Below)* The famed Dutch artist M. C. Escher violated our assumptions about light to create the dramatic illusions of depth found in his 1955 lithograph *Convex and Concave*. In this print, light appears to come from all sides of the scene. (Courtesy of the Collection Haags Gemeente Museum, The Hague. © 1994 M. C. Escher/Cordon Art, Baarn, The Netherlands. All rights reserved.)

away appear to move slightly in relation to the background. Distant objects like hills, mountains, or clouds don't seem to move at all.

When combined, pictorial cues can create a powerful illusion of depth. (See ● Table 5.1 for a summary of all the depth cues we have discussed.)

Is motion parallax really a pictorial cue? Strictly speaking it is not, except in the two-dimensional world of movies, television, or animated cartoons. However, when parallax is present, we almost always perceive depth. Much of the apparent depth of a good movie comes from relative motion captured by the camera.

Pictorial depth cues Features found in paintings, drawings, and photographs that impart information about space, depth, and distance.

Table 5.1 ● Summary of Visual Depth Cues

Binocular Cues		
• Retinal disparity		
• Convergence		
Monocular Cues		
• Accommodation		
• Pictorial depth cues (listed below)		
Linear perspective		
Relative size		
Height in the picture plane		
Light and shadow		
Overlap		
Texture gradients		
Aerial perspective		
Relative motion (motion parallax)		

● **Figure 5.19** A Hudson test picture. Two-dimensional perceivers assume the hunter is trying to spear the distant elephant rather than the nearby antelope. Some acquaintance with conventions for representing depth in pictures and photographs seems necessary. (From "Pictorial Perception and Culture" by J. B. Deregowski. © 1972 Scientific American, Inc. All rights reserved.)

● Figure 5.18 illustrates the defining feature of motion parallax. Imagine that you are in a bus and watching the passing scenery (with your gaze at a right angle to the road). Under these conditions, nearby objects will appear to rush *backward*. Those farther away, such as distant mountains, will seem to move very little or not at all. Objects that are more remote, such as the sun or moon, will appear to move in the *same* direction you are traveling. (That's why the moon appears to "follow" you when you take a stroll at night.)

Are pictorial depth cues universal? Not entirely. Some cultures use only selected pictorial cues to represent depth. People in these cultures may not easily recognize other cues (Deregowski, 1972). For example, researcher William Hudson tested members of remote tribes who do not use relative size to show depth in drawings. These people perceive simplified drawings as flat designs. As you can see in ● Figure 5.19, they do not assume, as we do, that a larger image means that an object is closer. Of course, members of

non-Western cultures can learn to interpret drawings of depth if they are given a chance to practice (Mshelia & Lapidus, 1990).

The Moon Illusion

How do the depth perception cues relate to daily experience? We constantly use both pictorial cues and bodily cues to sense depth and judge distances. Consider an intriguing effect called the **moon illusion** (perceiving the moon as larger when it is low in the sky). When the moon is on the horizon, it tends to look like a silver dollar. When it is directly overhead, it looks more like a dime. Contrary to what some people believe, the moon is not magnified by the atmosphere. But the moon *looks* nearly twice as large when it's low in the sky (Ross & Plug, 2002). This occurs, in part, because the moon's *apparent distance* is greater when it is near the horizon than when it is overhead (Kaufman & Kaufman, 2000).

But if it seems farther away, shouldn't it look smaller? No. When the moon is overhead, few depth cues surround it. In contrast, when you see the moon on the horizon, it is behind houses, trees, telephone poles, and mountains. These objects add numerous depth cues, which cause the horizon to seem more distant than the sky overhead. Picture two balloons, one 10 feet away and the second 20 feet away. Suppose the more distant balloon is inflated until its image matches the image of the nearer balloon. How do we know the more distant balloon is larger? Because its image is the same size as a balloon that is closer. Similarly, the moon makes the same-size image on the horizon as it does overhead. However, the horizon seems more distant because more depth cues are present. As a result, the horizon moon must be perceived as larger (Kaufman & Kaufman, 2000) (● Figure 5.20).

This explanation is known as the **apparent-distance hypothesis** (the horizon seems more distant than the night sky). You can test it by removing depth cues while looking at a horizon moon. Try looking at the moon through a rolled-up paper tube or make your hands into a "telescope" and look at the next large moon you see. It will immediately appear to shrink when viewed without depth cues (Ross & Plug, 2002).

← Direction of travel

● **Figure 5.18** The apparent motion of objects viewed during travel depends on their distance from the observer. Apparent motion can also be influenced by an observer's point of fixation. At middle distances, objects closer than the point of fixation appear to move backward; those beyond the point of fixation appear to move forward. Objects at great distances, such as the sun or moon, always appear to move forward.

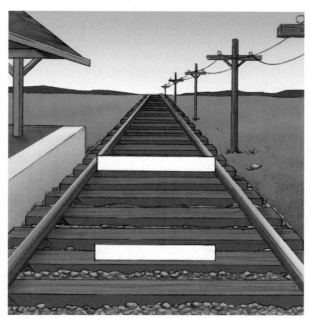

● **Figure 5.20** The Ponzo illusion may help you understand the moon illusion. Picture the two white bars as resting on the railroad tracks. In the drawing, the upper bar is the same length as the lower bar. However, because the upper bar appears to be farther away than the lower bar, we perceive it as longer. The same logic applies to the moon illusion.

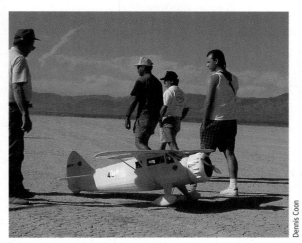

Dennis Coon

● **Figure 5.21** Before you can use familiar size to judge distance, objects must actually be the size you assume they are. Either these men are giants, or the model airplane was closer than you may have thought when you looked at ● Figure 5.16.

To what extent has the apparent-distance hypothesis been confirmed? The father and son team of Lloyd and James Kaufman projected images of the moon on a mirror. This allowed them to superimpose an artificial moon on the sky. In addition, the mirrors were moveable. Volunteer observers reported that as the moon moved closer, it appeared to get smaller. This effect was most dramatic when the moon was near the horizon, where more depth cues are found. This is the strongest confirmation yet of the apparent-distance theory (Kaufman & Kaufman, 2000).

● Perceptual Learning—What if the World Were Upside Down?

Gateway Question: What effect does learning have on perception?

England is one of the few countries in the world where people drive on the left side of the road. Because of this reversal, it is not unusual for visitors to step off curbs in front of cars—after carefully looking for traffic in the *wrong* direction. As this example suggests, learning has a powerful impact on top-down processing in perception.

Moon illusion The apparent change in size that occurs as the moon moves from the horizon (large moon) to overhead (small moon).

Apparent-distance hypothesis An explanation of the moon illusion stating that the horizon seems more distant than the night sky.

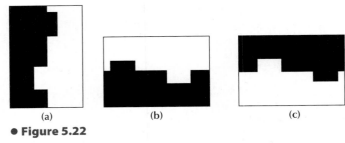

● **Figure 5.22**

How does learning affect perception? The term **perceptual learning** refers to changes in the brain that alter how we construct sensory information into percepts (Fahle & Poggio, 2002). For example, to use a computer, you must learn to pay attention to specific stimuli, such as icons and cursors. We also learn to tell the difference between stimuli that seemed identical at first. An example is the novice chef who discovers how to tell the difference between dried basil, oregano, and tarragon. In other situations, we learn to focus on just one part of a group of stimuli. This saves us from having to process all the stimuli in the group. For instance, a linebacker in football may be able to tell if the next play will be a run or a pass by watching one or two key players, rather than the entire opposing team (Seitz & Watanabe, 2005).

Even something as simple as figure-ground perception is affected by learning. For example, if you cut a shape out of dark paper and place it on a white background, other people are more likely to see it as a figure if it resembles a familiar object. As another example, in ● Figure 5.22*a* you can probably shift between seeing the white shape or the black shape as an object. Now look at ● Figure 5.22*b*. Does the lower black shape seem more like it's the figure than the upper white shape? Next consider ● Figure 5.22*c*. Notice how the white area in ● Figure 5.22*c* seems like it has become the figure. In our daily experience, objects below the horizon are usually closer to us. Also, we typically see more objects below the horizon than above it. Because of such experiences, we are more likely to perceive areas below the "horizon" line in a drawing as objects or figures (Vecera, Vogel, & Woodman, 2002). Does this mean you figure that figures are close to the ground?

Perceptual Habits

In general, learning creates **perceptual habits** (ingrained patterns of organization and attention) that affect our daily experience. Stop for a moment and look at ● Figure 5.23. The left face looks somewhat unusual, to be sure. But the distortion seems mild—until you turn the page upside down. Viewed normally, the face looks quite grotesque. Why is there a difference? Apparently, most people have little experience with upside-down faces. Perceptual learning, therefore, has less impact on our perceptions of an upside-down face. With a face in the normal position, you know what to expect and where to look. Also, you tend to see the entire face as a recognizable pattern. When a face is inverted, we are forced to perceive its individual features separately (Caharel et al., 2006).

Top-down perceptual processing habits can easily lead our perceptions astray. Because we have seen thousands of rooms shaped roughly like a box, we habitually construct perceptions based on this assumption. This need not be true, however. An *Ames room* (named for the man who designed it) is a lopsided space that appears square when viewed from a certain point (● Figure 5.24).

● **Figure 5.23** The effects of prior experience on perception. The doctored face looks far worse when viewed right side up because it can be related to past experience.

● **Figure 5.24** The Ames room. From the front, the room looks normal; actually, the right-hand corner is very short, and the left-hand corner is very tall. In addition, the left side of the room slants away from viewers. The diagram shows the shape of the room and reveals why people appear to get bigger as they cross the room toward the nearer, shorter right corner.

HUMAN DIVERSITY

Do They See What We See?

According to psychologist Richard Nisbett and his colleagues, people from different cultures do, in fact, perceive the world differently. European Americans are individualistic people who tend to focus on themselves and their sense of personal control. In contrast, East Asians are collectivist people who tend to focus on their personal relationships and social responsibilities. As a consequence, European Americans tend to explain actions in terms of internal factors ("she did it because she chose to do it"). In comparison, East Asians tend to explain actions in terms of their social context ("he did it because it was his responsibility to his family") (Norenzayan & Nisbett, 2000).

Do such cultural differences affect our everyday perception of objects and events? Apparently they do. In one study, American and Japanese participants were shown drawings of everyday scenes, such as a farm. Later, they saw a slightly changed version of the scene. Some of the changes were made to the focal point, or figure of the scene. Other changes altered the surrounding context, or ground of the scene. Americans, it turns out, were better at detecting changes in the figure of a scene. Japanese participants were better at finding alterations in the background (Nisbett & Miyamoto, 2005).

To explain this difference, Chua, Boland, and Nisbett (2005) presented American and Chinese participants with pictures of a figure (such as a tiger) placed on a ground (such as a jungle) and monitored their eye-movement patterns. The Americans focused their eye movements on the figure; Chinese participants made more eye movements around the ground. In other words, Westerners have a relatively narrow focus of attention, whereas Easterners have a broader focus of attention. Apparently, the society we live in can, indeed, influence even our most basic perceptual habits.

This illusion is achieved by carefully distorting the proportions of the walls, floor, ceiling, and windows. Because the left corner of the Ames room is farther from a viewer than the right, a person standing in that corner looks very small; one standing in the nearer, shorter right corner looks very large. A person who walks from the left to the right corner, will seem to "magically" grow larger.

Before we continue, read aloud the short phrase in ● Figure 5.25. Did you read, "Paris in the spring"? If so, look again. The word *the* appears twice in the phrase. Because of past experience with the English language, good readers often overlook the repeated word. Again, the effects of perceptual learning are apparent. (Now you know why it is easy to miss spelling mistakes while proofreading your essays.)

As mentioned in Chapter 4, the brain is especially sensitive to **perceptual features** such as lines, shapes, edges, spots, and colors. At least some of this sensitivity appears to be learned. Colin Blakemore and Graham Cooper raised kittens in a room with only vertical stripes on the walls. Another set of kittens saw only horizontal stripes. When returned to normal environments, the "horizontal" cats could easily jump onto a chair, but when walking on the floor, they bumped into chair legs. "Vertical" cats, on the other hand, easily avoided chair legs, but they missed when trying to jump to horizontal surfaces. The cats raised with vertical stripes were "blind" to horizontal lines, and the "horizontal" cats acted as if vertical lines were invisible. In such cases, there is an actual decrease in brain cells tuned to the missing features (Blakemore & Cooper, 1970).

Paris
in the
the spring

● **Figure 5.25**

Perceptual features might seem removed from daily experience. Nevertheless, they can have a profound effect on human behavior. In recognizing faces, for example, a consistent *other-race effect* occurs. This is a sort of "they all look alike to me" bias in perceiving persons from other racial and ethnic groups. In tests of facial recognition, people are much better at recognizing faces of their own race than others. One reason for this difference is that we typically have more experience with people from our own race. As a result, we become very familiar with the features that help us recognize different persons. For other groups, we lack the perceptual expertise needed to accurately separate one face from another (Sporer, 2001). Okay, so maybe members of different races or ethnic groups have developed perceptual habits that lead them to see in-group faces differently, but we all see everything else the same, right? For an answer, see "Do They See What We See?"

Inverted Vision

Would it be possible for an adult to adapt to a completely new perceptual world? An answer comes from an experiment in which a person wore goggles that turned the world upside down and reversed objects from right to left. At first, even the simplest tasks—walking, eating, and so forth—were incredibly difficult. Imagine trying to reach for a door handle and watching your hand shoot off in the wrong direction.

Perceptual learning Changes in how we construct sensory information into percepts that can be attributed to prior experience.

Perceptual habits Well-established patterns of perceptual organization and attention.

Perceptual features Important elements of a stimulus pattern, such as lines, shapes, edges, spots, and colors.

Inverted vision. Adaptation to complete inversion of the visual world is possible, but challenging.

● **Figure 5.26** Are the center dots in both figures the same size?

● **Figure 5.27** Context alters the meaning of the middle figure.

Participants in the experiment also reported that head movements made the world swing violently through space, causing severe headaches and nausea. Yet after several days they began to adapt to inverted vision. Their success, although not complete, was impressive.

Did everything turn upright again for the humans? No. While they wore the goggles, their visual images remained upside down. But in time they learned to perform most routine activities, and their inverted world began to seem relatively normal. In later experiments, some people wearing inverting lenses were able to successfully drive cars. One person even flew an airplane (Kohler, 1962). These feats are like driving or flying upside down, with right and left reversed. Some ride!

Interacting with a new visual world through *active movement* (self-generated action) seems to be a key to rapid adaptation. In one experiment, people wore glasses that grossly distorted vision. Those who walked on their own adapted more quickly than persons pushed around in a wheeled cart (Held, 1971). Why does movement help? Probably because commands sent to the muscles can be related to sensory feedback. Remaining immobile would be like watching a weird movie over which you have no control. There would be less reason for any perceptual learning to occur.

The Context of Perception

The external *context* in which a stimulus is judged is an important factor affecting perception. **Context** refers to information surrounding a stimulus. For example, a man 6 feet in height will look "tall" when surrounded by others of average height, and "short" among a group of professional basketball players. In ● Figure 5.26, the center circle is the same size in both designs. But like the man in different company, context alters the circle's apparent size. The importance of context is also shown by ● Figure 5.27. What do you see in the middle? If you read across, context causes it to be organized as a 13. Reading down makes it a B.

Illusions

Perceptual learning is responsible for a number of *illusions*. In an **illusion,** length, position, motion, curvature, or direction is consistently misjudged. Note that illusions are distorted perceptual constructions of stimuli that actually exist. In a **hallucination,** people perceive objects or events that have no external reality (Lepore, 2002). For example, they hear voices that are not there. (See "Staying in Touch with Reality.") Illusions and hallucinations can be distinguished by *reality testing*.

What do you mean by reality testing? In any situation having an element of doubt or uncertainty, **reality testing** involves obtaining additional information to check your perceptions. If you think you see a 3-foot-tall butterfly, you can confirm you are hallucinating by trying to touch its wings. To detect an illusion, you may have to measure a drawing or apply a straightedge to it. ● Figure 5.28 shows a powerful illusion called Fraser's spiral. What appears to be a spiral is actually made up of a series of closed circles. Most people cannot spontaneously see this reality. Instead, they must carefully trace one of the circles to confirm what is "real" in the design.

THE CLINICAL FILE

Staying in Touch with Reality

Just imagine that often, and without warning, you hear a voice shouting, "Buckets of blood!" or see blood spattering across the walls of your bedroom. Chances are people would think you are mentally disturbed. Hallucinations are a major symptom of psychosis, dementia, epilepsy, migraine headaches, alcohol withdrawal, and drug intoxication (Spence & David, 2004) and are one of the clearest signs that a person has "lost touch with reality."

Yet consider the case of mathematician John Nash (the subject of *A Beautiful Mind*, the winner of the 2002 Oscar for best film).

Even though Nash suffered from schizophrenia, he eventually learned to use his ability to engage in *reality testing* to sort out which of his experiences were perceptions and which were hallucinations. Unlike John Nash, most people who experience full-blown hallucinations also have a limited ability to reality test (Hohwy & Rosenberg, 2005).

Curiously, "sane hallucinations" also occur. *Charles Bonnet syndrome* is a rare condition that afflicts mainly older people who are partially blind but not mentally disturbed. They may "see" people, animals, buildings, plants, and other objects appear

and disappear in front of their eyes. One older man suffering from partial blindness and leukemia complained of seeing animals in his house, including cattle and bears (Jacob et al., 2004). However, people experiencing "sane hallucinations" can more easily tell that their hallucinations aren't real because their capacity to reality test is not impaired.

Such unusual experiences show how powerfully the brain seeks meaningful patterns in sensory input and the role reality testing plays in our normal perceptual experience.

Dennis Coon

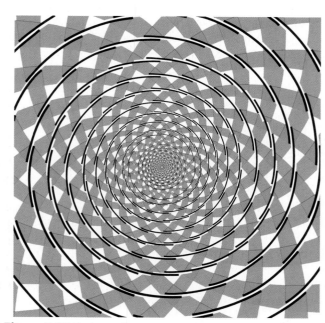

● **Figure 5.28** The limits of pure perception. Even simple designs are easily misperceived. Fraser's spiral is actually a series of concentric circles. The illusion is so powerful that people who try to trace one of the circles sometimes follow the illusory spiral and jump from one circle to the next. (After Seckel, 2000.)

Illusions are a fascinating challenge to our understanding of perception. On occasion, they also have practical uses. An illusion called *stroboscopic* (strobe-oh-SKOP-ik) *movement* puts the "motion" in motion pictures. **Stroboscopic movement** refers to the illusory motion perceived when objects are shown in rapidly changing positions. The strobe lights used on dance floors reverse this illusion. Each time the strobe flashes, it "freezes" dancers in particular positions. However, if the light flashes fast enough, normal motion is seen. In a similar way, movies project a rapid series of "snapshots," so the gaps in motion are imperceptible.

Context Information surrounding a stimulus.

Illusion A misleading or distorted perception.

Hallucination An imaginary sensation, such as seeing, hearing, or smelling something that does not exist in the external world.

Reality testing Obtaining additional information to check on the accuracy of perceptions.

Stroboscopic movement Illusion of movement in which an object is shown in a rapidly changing series of positions.

(a) Which of the horizontal lines is longer?

(b) Is the diagonal a single straight line? Check it with a ruler.

(c) Is this a drawing of a staircase descending from upper left to lower right . . . or is it the view of the underneath of a staircase from lower right to upper left?

(d) Are these lines parallel? Cover some of the slash marks to see.

(e) Which line is longer, horizontal or vertical?

(f) Notice how the background distorts the square.

(g) Which quadrilateral is larger?

(h) Which column is shortest? Which is longest?

● **Figure 5.29** Some interesting perceptual illusions. Such illusions are a normal part of visual perception.

Can other illusions be explained? Not in all cases, or to everyone's satisfaction. Generally speaking, size and shape constancy, habitual eye movements, continuity, and perceptual habits combine in various ways to produce the illusions in ● Figure 5.29. Rather than attempt to explain all the pictured illusions, let's focus on one deceptively simple example.

Consider the drawing in ● Figure 5.29*a*. This is the familiar **Müller-Lyer** (MEOO-ler-LIE-er) **illusion,** in which the horizontal line with arrowheads appears shorter than the line with Vs. A quick measurement will show that they are the same length. How can we explain this illusion? Evidence suggests it is based on a lifetime of experience with the edges and corners of rooms and buildings. Richard Gregory (2000) believes you see the horizontal line with the Vs as if it were the corner of a room viewed from inside (● Figure 5.30). The line with arrowheads, on the other hand, suggests the corner of a room or building seen from outside. In other words, cues that suggest a 3-D space alter our perception of a 2-D design (Enns & Coren, 1995).

● **Figure 5.30** Why does line *(b)* in the Müller-Lyer illusion look longer than line *(a)*? Probably because it looks more like a distant corner than a nearer one. Because the vertical lines form images of the same length, the more "distant" line must be perceived as larger. As you can see in the drawing on the right, additional depth cues accentuate the Müller-Lyer illusion. (After Enns & Coren, 1995.)

(a)   (b)

View I   View II   View III

● **Figure 5.31** "Young woman/old woman" illustrations. As an interesting demonstration of perceptual expectancy, show some of your friends view I and some view II (cover all other views). Next show your friends view III and ask them what they see. Those who saw view I should see the old woman in view III; those who saw view II should see the young woman in view III. Can you see both? (After Leeper, 1935.)

Earlier, to explain the moon illusion, we said that if two objects make images of the same size, the more distant object must be larger. This is known formally as **size-distance invariance** (the size of an object's image is precisely related to its distance from the eyes). Gregory believes the same concept explains the Müller-Lyer illusion. If the V-tipped line looks farther away than the arrowhead-tipped line, you must compensate by seeing the V-tipped line as longer. This explanation presumes that you have had years of experience with straight lines, sharp edges, and corners—a pretty safe assumption in our culture.

Is there any way to show that past experience causes the illusion? If we could test someone who saw only curves and wavy lines as a child, we would know if experience with a "square" culture is important. Fortunately, the Zulus, a group of people in South Africa, live in a "round" culture. In their daily lives, Zulus rarely encounter a straight line: Their houses are shaped like rounded mounds and arranged in a circle, tools and toys are curved, and there are few straight roads or square buildings.

What happens if a Zulu looks at the Müller-Lyer design? The typical Zulu villager does not experience the illusion. At most, she or he sees the V-shaped line as *slightly* longer than the other (Gregory, 1990). This seems to confirm the importance of past experience and perceptual habits in determining our view of the world. But, like many topics in psychology, room for debate remains. The Müller-Lyer illusion also seems to be partly based on directly misperceiving the location of the ends of the lines (Morgan, Hole, & Glennerster, 1990). Thus, it could be that both apparent size and misperception cause the illusion.

What is a perceptual expectancy? A runner in the starting blocks at a track meet is *set* to respond in a certain way. Likewise, past experience, motives, context, or suggestions may create a **perceptual expectancy (or set)** that prepares you to perceive in a certain way. If a car backfires, runners at a track meet may jump the gun. As a matter of fact, we all frequently jump the gun when perceiving. Beginning artists are notoriously bad at drawing faces. Why? When drawing a face, a novice tends to think "nose, mouth, eyes, ears" and tries to draw what he or she *thinks* each of these features looks like, instead of what they *actually* look like (Cohen & Bennett, 1997). In essence, an expectancy is a perceptual hypothesis we are *very likely* to apply to a stimulus—even if applying it is inappropriate.

Perceptual sets often lead us to see what we *expect* to see. For example, let's say you are driving across the desert. You are very low on gas. Finally, you see a sign approaching. On it are the words FUEL AHEAD. You relax, knowing you will not be stranded. But as you draw nearer, the words on the sign become FOOD AHEAD. Most people have had similar experiences in which expectations altered their perceptions. To observe perceptual expectancies first-hand, perform the demonstration described in ● Figure 5.31.

Perceptual expectancies are frequently created by *suggestion*. In one study (wine snobs take note), participants given a taste of a $90 wine reported that it tasted better than a $10 wine. Functional MRI images confirmed that brain areas related to pleasure were indeed more active when participants tasted the more expensive wine (Plassmann et al., 2008). The twist is that exactly the same wine was served in both cases. Merely suggesting that the

●● Perceptual Expectancies— On Your Mark, Get Set

Gateway Question: To what extent do we see what we expect to see?

An excellent example of how top-down processing influences our experiences is found in perceptual expectancies.

Müller-Lyer illusion Two equal-length lines tipped with inward or outward pointing Vs appear to be of different lengths.

Size-distance invariance The strict relationship between the distance an object lies from the eyes and the size of its image.

Perceptual expectancy (or set) A readiness to perceive in a particular manner, induced by strong expectations.

wine was expensive created a perceptual expectancy that it would taste better. And so it did (advertisers also take note).

Does it really make that much difference what you call someone or something? Perceptual categories, especially those defined by labels, do make a difference. This is especially true in perceiving people, where even trained observers may be influenced. For example, in one study, psychotherapists were shown a videotaped interview. Half the therapists were told that the man being interviewed was applying for a job. The rest were told that the man was a mental patient. Therapists who thought the man was a job applicant perceived him as "realistic," "sincere," and "pleasant." Those who thought he was a patient perceived him as "defensive," "dependent," and "impulsive" (Langer & Abelson, 1974).

In the next section, we will go beyond normal perception to ask, "Is extrasensory perception possible?" Before we do that, here's a chance to answer the question, "Is remembering the preceding discussion possible?"

Extrasensory Perception— Do You Believe in Magic?

Gateway Question: Is extrasensory perception possible?

About half the general public believes in the existence of **extrasensory perception** (ESP)—the purported ability to perceive events in ways that cannot be explained by known sensory capacities (Wiseman & Watt, 2006). Actually, it's surprising that even more people aren't believers. ESP and other paranormal events are treated as accepted facts in many movies and television programs. Regardless, very few psychologists share this belief. What is the evidence for and against extrasensory perception?

Parapsychology is the study of ESP and other **psi phenomena** (events that seem to defy accepted scientific laws). (Psi is pronounced like "sigh.") Parapsychologists seek answers to the questions raised by three basic forms that ESP could take. These are:

1. **Telepathy.** The purported ability to communicate directly with another person's mind. When the other person is dead, the communications are called *mediumship*.
2. **Clairvoyance.** The purported ability to perceive events or gain information in ways that appear unaffected by distance or normal physical barriers.
3. **Precognition.** The purported ability to perceive or accurately predict future events. Precognition may take the form of prophetic dreams that foretell the future.

While we are at it, we might as well toss in another purported psi ability:

4. **Psychokinesis.** The purported ability to exert influence over inanimate objects by willpower ("mind over matter"). (Psychokinesis cannot be classed as a type of ESP, but it is frequently studied by parapsychologists.)

The formal investigation of psi events owes much to the late J. B. Rhine, who tried to study ESP objectively. Many of Rhine's experiments made use of **Zener cards** (a deck of 25 cards, each bearing one of five symbols) (● Figure 5.32). In a typical clairvoyance test, people try to guess the symbols on the cards as they are turned up from a shuffled deck. In a typical telepathy test, a *receiver* tries to guess the correct symbol by reading the mind of a *sender* looking at a card. Pure guessing in these tests will produce an average score of 5 "hits" out of 25 cards.

● **Figure 5.32** ESP cards used by J. B. Rhine, an early experimenter in parapsychology.

An Appraisal of ESP

Psychologists as a group are highly skeptical about psi abilities. If you've ever had an apparent clairvoyant or telepathic experience you might be convinced that ESP exists. However, the difficulty of excluding *coincidence* makes such experiences less conclusive than they might seem. Consider a typical "psychic" experience: During the middle of the night, a woman away for a weekend visit suddenly had a strong impulse to return home. When she arrived she found the house on fire with her husband asleep inside (Rhine, 1953). An experience like this is certainly striking, but it does not confirm the reality of ESP. You may not realize it, but such coincidences occur quite often. On any given night, many, many people might act on a "premonition." If, by coincidence, one person's hunch turns out to be correct, it may be *reinterpreted* as precognition or clairvoyance (Marks, 2000; Wiseman & Watt, 2006). In contrast, the vast majority of false premonitions will simply be forgotten.

Fraud and Skepticism

Unfortunately, some of Rhine's most dramatic early experiments used badly printed Zener cards that allowed the symbols to show faintly on the back. It is also very easy to cheat, by marking cards with a fingernail or by noting marks on the cards caused by normal use. Even if this were not the case, there is evidence that early experimenters sometimes unconsciously gave people cues about cards with their eyes, facial gestures, or lip movements. In short, none of the early studies in parapsychology were done in a way that eliminated the possibility of deliberate fraud or the accidental "leakage" of helpful information (Alcock, Burns, & Freeman, 2003).

Modern parapsychologists are now well aware of the need for double-blind experiments, security and accuracy in record keeping, meticulous control, and repeatability of experiments (Milton & Wiseman, 1997; O'Keeffe & Wiseman, 2005). In the last 10 years, hundreds of experiments have been reported in parapsychological journals. Many of them seem to support the existence of psi abilities.

Then why do most psychologists remain skeptical about psi abilities? For one thing, fraud continues to plague the field. The need for skepticism is especially great anytime there's money to be made from purported psychic abilities. For example, the owners of the "Miss Cleo" TV-psychic operation were convicted of felony fraud in 2002. "Miss Cleo," supposedly a Jamaican psychic, was really just an actress from Los Angeles. People who paid $4.99 a minute for a "reading" from "Miss Cleo" actually reached one of several hundred operators. These people were hired through ads that read, "No experience necessary." Despite being entirely faked, the "Miss Cleo" scam brought in more than $1 billion before it was shut down.

Anyone can learn to do "cold readings" (Wood et al., 2003) well enough to produce satisfied customers. *Cold reading* is a set of techniques that are used to lead people to believe in the truth of what a psychic or medium is saying about them. These include a reliance on many of the same techniques used by practitioners of the horoscope, such as uncritical acceptance, positive instances, and the Barnum effect. (Remember Chapter 1, pages 18–19?)

The "psychic" begins a "reading" by making general statements about a person. The "psychic" then plays "hot and cold" by attending to the person's facial expressions, body language, or tone of voice. When the "psychic" is "hot" (on the right track), the "psychic" continues to make similar statements about the person. If the person's reactions signal that the "psychic" is "cold," the psychic drops that topic or line of thought and tries another (Hyman, 2007).

"I see a girl, I see a marriage, I see her not understanding you, I see a beer belly. Do you want me to go on?"

Extrasensory perception The purported ability to perceive events in ways that cannot be explained by known capacities of the sensory organs.

Parapsychology The study of extranormal psychological events, such as extrasensory perception.

Psi phenomena Events that seem to lie outside the realm of accepted scientific laws.

Telepathy The purported ability to directly know another person's thoughts.

Clairvoyance The purported ability to perceive events at a distance or through physical barriers.

Precognition The purported ability to accurately predict future events.

Psychokinesis The purported ability to mentally alter or influence objects or events.

Zener cards A deck of 25 cards bearing various symbols and used in early parapsychological research.

Inconclusive Results, Statistics and Chance

Inconsistency is another major problem in psi research. For every study with positive results, there are many others that fail and are never published (Alcock, 2003). Unfortunately, many of the most spectacular findings in parapsychology simply cannot be **replicated** (reproduced or repeated) (Hyman, 1996a). More important, improved research methods usually result in fewer positive results (Hyman, 1996b; O'Keeffe & Wiseman, 2005).

Even the same researchers using the same experimental subjects typically can't get similar results every time (Schick & Vaughn, 2001). It is rare—in fact, almost unheard of—for a person to maintain psi ability over any sustained period (Alcock, Burns, & Freeman, 2003). ESP researchers believe this "decline effect" shows that parapsychological skills are very fragile. But critics argue that a person who only temporarily scores above chance has just received credit for a **run of luck** (a statistically unusual outcome that could occur by chance alone). When the run is over, it is not fair to assume that ESP is temporarily gone. We must count *all* attempts.

To understand the run-of-luck criticism, imagine that you flip a coin 100 times and record the results. You then flip another coin 100 times, again recording the results. The two lists are compared. For any 10 pairs of flips, we would expect heads or tails to match 5 times. Let's say that you go through the list and find a set of 10 pairs where 9 out of 10 matched. This is far above chance expectation. But does it mean that the first coin "knew" what was going to come up on the second coin? The idea is obviously silly.

Now, what if a person guesses 100 times what will come up on a coin. Again, we might find a set of 10 guesses that matches the results of flipping the coin. Does this mean that the person, for a time, had precognition—then lost it? Parapsychologists tend to believe the answer is yes. Skeptics assume that nothing more than random matching occurred, as in the two-coin example.

Reinterpretation is also a problem in psi experiments. For example, ex-astronaut Edgar Mitchell claimed he did a successful telepathy experiment from space. Yet news accounts never mentioned that on some trials Mitchell's "receivers" scored above chance, whereas on others they scored *below* chance. Although you might assume that below-chance trials were failures to find telepathy, Mitchell reinterpreted them as "successes," claiming that they represented intentional "psi missing." But, as skeptics have noted, if both high scores and low scores count as successes, how can you lose?

Of course, in many ESP tests the outcome is beyond debate. A good example is provided by ESP experiments done through newspapers, radio, and television. In these mass media studies, people attempted to identify ESP targets from a distance. The results of more than 1.5 million ESP trials done through the mass media are easy to summarize: There was no significant ESP effect (Milton & Wiseman, 1999). Zero. Zip. Nada. Clearly, state lottery organizers have nothing to fear!

Stage ESP

If psychic phenomena do occur, they certainly can't be controlled well enough to be used by entertainers. **Stage ESP** simulates ESP for the purpose of entertainment. Like stage magic, it is based on sleight of hand, deception, and patented gadgets (● Figure 5.33). A case in point is self-proclaimed "psychic," Uri Geller, a former nightclub magician who "astounded" audiences—and some scientists—with apparent telepathy, psychokinesis, and precognition.

(a) (b) (c)

● **Figure 5.33** Fake psychokinesis. *(a)* The performer shows an observer several straight keys. While doing so, he bends one of the keys by placing its tip in the slot of another key. Normally, this is done out of sight, behind the "psychic's" hand. It is clearly shown here so that you can see how the deception occurs. *(b)* Next, the "psychic" places the two keys in the observer's hand and closes it. By skillful manipulation, the observer has been kept from seeing the bent key. The performer then "concentrates" on the keys to "bend them with psychic energy." *(c)* The bent key is revealed to the observer. "Miracle" accomplished! (Adapted from Randi, 1997.)

During testing, it seemed that Geller could sense which of 10 film canisters contained a hidden object, he correctly guessed the number that would come up on a die shaken in a closed box, and he reproduced drawings sealed in envelopes.

Was Geller cheating, or was he using some ability beyond normal perception? There is little doubt that Geller was cheating (Randi, 1997). It's now clear that tests of Geller's performance were incredibly sloppy. For instance, Geller reproduced sealed drawings in a room next to the one where the drawings were made. Original reports failed to mention that there was a hole in the wall between the rooms, through which Geller could have heard descriptions of the pictures as they were being drawn. Likewise, in the "die in the box" tests Geller was allowed to hold the box, shake it, and have the honor of opening it.

Why weren't such details reported? Sensational and uncritical reporting of apparent paranormal events is widespread. Hundreds of books, articles, and television programs are produced each year by people who are getting rich by promoting unsupported claims. If a person did have psychic powers, he or she would not have to make a living by entertaining others. A quick trip to a casino would allow the person to retire for life.

Implications

After close to 130 years of investigation, it is still impossible to say conclusively whether psi events occur. As we have seen, a close look at psi experiments often reveals serious problems of evidence, procedure, and scientific rigor (Alcock, Burns, & Freeman, 2003; Hyman, 2007; Stokes, 2001). The more closely psi experiments are examined, the more likely it is that claimed successes will evaporate (Alcock, 2003; Stokes, 2001). As one critic put it, positive ESP results usually mean "Error Some Place" (Marks, 2000).

Yet, being a skeptic does not mean a person is against something. It means that you are unconvinced. The purpose of this discussion, then, has been to counter the *uncritical* acceptance of psi events that is rampant in the media.

What would it take to scientifically demonstrate the existence of ESP? Quite simply, a set of instructions that would allow any competent, unbiased observer to produce a psi event under standardized conditions that rule out any possibility of fraud (Schick & Vaughn, 2001). As we mentioned in Chapter 1, professional magician and skeptic James Randi even offers a $1,000,000 prize to anyone who can demonstrate evidence of psi events under standardized conditions. No one has yet claimed the prize. (You can read all about it if you google the James Randi Educational Foundation.)

Undoubtedly, some intrepid researchers will continue their attempts to supply just that. Others remain skeptics and consider 130 years of inconclusive efforts reason enough to abandon the concept of ESP (Marks, 2000). At the least, it seems essential to be carefully skeptical of evidence reported in the popular press or by researchers who are uncritical "true believers." (But then, you already knew we were going to say that, didn't you!)

A Look Ahead

In this chapter we have moved from basic sensations to the complexities of perceiving people and events. We have also probed some of the controversies concerning ESP. In the Psychology in Action section, we will return to "everyday" perception for a look at perceptual awareness.

KNOWLEDGE BUILDER
Extrasensory Perception

RECITE

1. Four purported psi events investigated by parapsychologists are clairvoyance, telepathy, precognition, and _____.
2. Zener cards were used in early studies of
   a. psi phenomena
   b. inattentional blindness
   c. the Müller-Lyer illusion
   d. top-down processing
3. Natural, or "real-life," occurrences are regarded as the best evidence for the existence of ESP. T or F?
4. Replication rates are very high for ESP experiments. T or F?
5. Skeptics attribute positive results in psi experiments to statistical runs of luck. T or F?

REFLECT

Critical Thinking

6. What would you estimate is the chance that two people will have the same birthday (day and month, but not year) in a group of 30 people?
7. A "psychic" on television offers to fix broken watches for viewers. Moments later, dozens of viewers call the station to say that their watches miraculously started running again. What have they overlooked?

Relate

Let's say that a friend of yours is an avid fan of TV shows that feature paranormal themes. See if you can summarize for her or him what is known about ESP. Be sure to include evidence for and against the existence of ESP and some of the thinking errors associated with nonskeptical belief in the paranormal.

Answers: 1. psychokinesis 2. a 3. F 4. F 5. T 6. Most people assume that this would be a relatively rare event. Actually there is a 71 percent chance that two people will share a birthday in a group of 30. Most people probably underestimate the natural rate of occurrence of many seemingly mysterious coincidences (Alcock, Burns, & Freeman, 2003). 7. When psychologists handled watches awaiting repair at a store, 57 percent began running again, with no help from a "psychic." Believing the "psychic's" claim also overlooks the impact of big numbers: If the show reached a large audience, at least a few "broken" watches would start working merely by chance.

Replicate To reproduce or repeat.

Run of luck A statistically unusual outcome (as in getting five heads in a row when flipping a coin) that could still occur by chance alone.

Stage ESP The simulation of ESP for the purpose of entertainment.

PSYCHOLOGY IN ACTION

Perception and Objectivity—Believing Is Seeing

Gateway Question: How can I learn to perceive events more accurately?

Have you ever seen the sun set? You may think you have. Yet, in reality, we know the sun does not "set." Instead, our viewing angle changes as the earth turns, until the sun is obscured by the horizon. Want to try the alternative? This evening, stand facing the west. With practice, you can learn to feel yourself being swept backward on the rotating surface of the earth as you watch an unmoving sun recede in the distance.

This radical shift in perspective illustrates the limitations of "objective" observation. As we have learned in this chapter, seeing a "sunset" is a *perceptual construction* (mental model) of an external event. As we have seen, perception reflects the needs, expectations, attitudes, values, and beliefs of the perceiver. In this light, the phrase "seeing is believing" must be modified. Clearly, we see what we believe, as well as believe what we see (● Figure 5.34).

In some cases, subjective perception nurtures the personal vision valued in art, music, poetry, and scientific innovation. Often, however, it is a real liability.

"I Saw It with My Own Eyes"

In the courtroom, eyewitness testimony can be a key to proving guilt or innocence. The claim "I saw it with my own eyes" still carries a lot of weight with a jury. Too many jurors (unless they have taken a psychology course) tend to assume that eyewitness testimony is nearly infallible (Durham & Dane, 1999). Even U.S. judges are vulnerable to over-optimism about eyewitness testimony (Wise & Safer, 2004). But, to put it bluntly, eyewitness testimony is frequently wrong (Wells & Olson, 2003). Recall, for instance, that one of your authors would have sworn in court that he had seen a murder taking place at the supermarket—*if* he hadn't received more information to correct his misperceptions.

What about witnesses who are certain that their perceptions were accurate? Should juries believe them? Actually, having confidence in your testimony has almost no bearing on its accuracy (Brewer & Wells, 2006)! Psychologists are gradually convincing lawyers, judges, and police that eyewitness errors are common (Yarmey, 2003). Even so, thousands of people have been wrongfully convicted (Scheck, Neufeld, & Dwyer, 2000).

Unfortunately, perception rarely provides an "instant replay" of events. As stated earlier, impressions formed when a person is surprised, threatened, or under stress are especially prone to distortion (Yuille & Daylen, 1998). In addition, being questioned tends to make witnesses more confident about what they saw, even if they are wrong. Thus, police questioning can actually degrade the value of the testimony witnesses give later, in court (Shaw, 1996).

> ### bridges
> Distortions in memory also affect the accuracy of eyewitness testimony. **See Chapter 8, pages 256–259.**

Because impressions formed when a person is surprised, threatened, or under stress are especially prone to distortion, witnesses to crimes often disagree. As a dramatic demonstration of this problem, a college professor was attacked by an actor in a staged assault. Immediately after the event, 141 witnesses were questioned in detail. Their descriptions were then compared with a videotape made of the staged "crime." The total accuracy score for the group (on features such as appearance, age, weight, and height of the assailant) was only *25 percent* of the maximum possible (Buckhout, 1974). Similarly, a study of real eyewitness cases found that the *wrong person* was chosen from police lineups 25 percent of the time (Levi, 1998).

Wouldn't the victim of a crime remember more than a mere witness? Not necessarily. A revealing study found that eyewitness accuracy is virtually the same for witnessing a crime (seeing a pocket calculator stolen) as it is for being a victim (seeing one's own watch stolen) (Hosch & Cooper, 1982). Placing more weight on the testimony of victims may be a serious mistake. In many crimes, victims fall prey to *weapon focus*. Understandably, they fix their entire attention on the knife, gun, or other weapon used by an attacker. In doing so, they fail to notice details of appear-

● **Figure 5.34** It is difficult to look at this simple drawing without perceiving depth. Yet the drawing is nothing more than a collection of flat shapes. Turn this page counterclockwise 90 degrees and you will see 3 Cs, one within another. When the drawing is turned sideways, it seems nearly flat. However, if you turn the page upright again, a sense of depth will reappear. Clearly, you have used your knowledge and expectations to *construct* an illusion of depth. The drawing itself would only be a flat design if you didn't invest it with meaning.

Even in broad daylight, eyewitness testimony is untrustworthy. In 2001 an American Airlines plane crashed near Kennedy International Airport in New York. Hundreds of people saw the plane go down. Half of them said the plane was on fire. Flight recorders showed there was no fire. One witness in five saw the plane make a right turn. An equal number saw it make a left turn! As one investigator commented, the best witness may be a "kid under 12 years old who doesn't have his parents around." Adults, it seems, are easily swayed by their expectations.

Table 5.2 ● Factors Affecting the Accuracy of Eyewitness Perceptions

Sources of Error	Summary of Findings
1. Wording of questions	An eyewitness's testimony about an event can be affected by how the questions put to that witness are worded.
2. Postevent information	Eyewitness testimony about an event often reflects not only what was actually seen but also information obtained later on.
3. Attitudes, expectations	An eyewitness's perception and memory of an event may be affected by his or her attitudes and expectations.
4. Alcohol intoxication	Alcohol intoxication impairs later ability to recall events.
5. Cross-racial perceptions	Eyewitnesses are better at identifying members of their own race than they are at identifying people of other races.
6. Weapon focus	The presence of a weapon impairs an eyewitness's ability to accurately identify the culprit's face.
7. Accuracy-confidence	An eyewitness's confidence is not a good predictor of his or her accuracy.
8. Exposure time	The less time an eyewitness has to observe an event, the less well she or he will perceive and remember it.
9. Unconscious transference	Eyewitnesses sometimes identify as a culprit someone they have seen in another situation or context.
10. Color perception	Judgments of color made under monochromatic light (such as an orange street light) are highly unreliable.
11. Stress	Very high levels of stress impair the accuracy of eyewitness perceptions.

Adapted from Kassin et al., 2001.

ance, dress, or other clues to identity (Pickel, French, & Betts, 2003). Additional factors that consistently lower eyewitness accuracy are summarized in ● Table 5.2 (Kassin et al., 2001; Wells & Olson, 2003).

Implications

Now that DNA testing is available, more than 200 people who were convicted of murder, rape, and other crimes in the United States have been exonerated. Most of these innocent people were convicted mainly on the basis of eyewitness testimony. Each also spent *years* in prison before being cleared (Foxhall, 2000). How often are everyday perceptions as inaccurate or distorted as those of an emotional eyewitness? The answer we have been moving toward is very frequently. Bearing this in mind may help you be more tolerant of the views of others and more cautious about your own objectivity. It may also encourage more frequent *reality testing* on your part.

Psychologist Sidney Jourard once offered a good example of reality testing. One of Jourard's students believed her roommate was stealing from her. The student gradually became convinced of her roommate's guilt but said nothing. As her distrust and anger grew, their relationship turned cold and distant. Finally, at Jourard's urging, she confronted her roommate. The roommate cleared herself immediately and expressed relief when the puzzling change in their relationship was explained (Jourard, 1974). With their friendship reestablished, the true culprit was soon caught. (The cleaning woman did it!)

If you have ever concluded that someone was angry, upset, or unfriendly without checking the accuracy of your perceptions, you have fallen into a subtle trap. Personal objectivity is an elusive quality, requiring frequent reality testing to maintain. At the very least, it pays to ask a person what she or he is feeling when you are in doubt. Clearly, most of us could learn to be better "eyewitnesses" to daily events.

Positive Psychology: Perceptual Awareness

Do some people perceive things more accurately than others? Humanistic psychologist Abraham Maslow (1969) believed that some people perceive themselves and others with unusual accuracy. Maslow characterized these people as especially alive, open, aware, and mentally healthy. He found that their perceptual styles were marked by immersion in the present; a lack of self-consciousness; freedom from selecting, criticizing, or evaluating; and a general "surrender" to experience. The kind of perception Maslow described is like that of a mother with her newborn infant, a child at Christmas, or two people in love.

The Value of Paying Attention

Whereas the average person has not reached perceptual restriction of the "if you've seen one tree, you've seen them all" variety, the fact remains that most of us tend to look at a tree and classify it into the perceptual category of "trees in general" without really appreciating the miracle standing before us. How, then, can we bring about **dishabituation** (a reversal of habituation) on a day-to-day basis? Does perceptual clarity require years of effort? Fortunately, a more immediate avenue is available. The deceptively simple key to dishabituation is this: Pay attention. The following story summarizes the importance of attention:

> One day a man of the people said to Zen Master Ikkyu: "Master, will you please write for me some maxims of the highest wisdom?"
>
> Ikkyu immediately took his brush and wrote the word "Attention."
>
> "Is that all?" asked the man. "Will you not add something more?"
>
> Ikkyu then wrote twice running: "Attention. Attention."
>
> "Well," remarked the man rather irritably, "I really don't see much depth or subtlety in what you have just written."
>
> Then Ikkyu wrote the same word three times running: "Attention. Attention. Attention." Half angered, the man demanded, "What does that word 'Attention' mean anyway?"
>
> And Ikkyu answered gently: "Attention means attention." (Kapleau, 1966)

To this we can add only one thought, provided by the words of poet William Blake: "If the doors of perception were cleansed, man would see everything as it is, infinite."

Dishabituation A reversal of habituation.

How to Become a Better "Eyewitness" to Life

Here's a summary of ideas from this chapter to help you maintain and enhance perceptual awareness and accuracy.

1. *Remember that perceptions are constructions of reality.* Learn to regularly question your own perceptions. Are they accurate? Could another interpretation fit the facts? What assumptions are you making? Could they be false? How might your assumptions be distorting your perceptions?

2. *Break perceptual habits and interrupt habituation.* Each day, try to get away from habitual, top-down processing and do some activities in new ways. For example, take different routes when you travel to work or school. Do routines, such as brushing your teeth or combing your hair, with your nonpreferred hand. Try to look at friends and family members as if they are persons you just met for the first time.

3. *Seeking out-of-the-ordinary experiences.* The possibilities here range from trying foods you don't normally eat to reading opinions very different from your own. Experiences ranging from a quiet walk in the woods to a trip to an amusement park may be perceptually refreshing.

4. *Beware of perceptual sets.* Anytime you pigeonhole people, objects, or events, there is a danger that your perceptions will be distorted by expectations or pre-existing categories. Be especially wary of labels and stereotypes. Try to see people as individuals and events as unique, one-time occurrences.

5. *Be aware of the ways in which motives and emotions influence perceptions.* It is difficult to avoid being swayed by your own interests, needs, desires, and emotions. But be aware of this trap and actively try to see the world through the eyes of others. Taking the other person's perspective is especially valuable in disputes or arguments. Ask yourself, "How does this look to her or him?"

6. *Make a habit of engaging in reality testing.* Actively look for additional evidence to check the accuracy of your perceptions. Ask questions, seek clarifications, and find alternate channels of information. Remember that perception is not automatically accurate. You could be wrong—we all are frequently.

7. *Pay attention.* Make a conscious effort to pay attention to other people and your surroundings. Don't drift through life in a haze. Listen to others with full concentration. Watch their facial expressions. Make eye contact. Try to get in the habit of approaching perception as if you are going to have to testify later about what you saw and heard.

KNOWLEDGE BUILDER
Perceptual Awareness and Accuracy

RECITE

1. Most perceptions can be described as active constructions of external reality. T or F?
2. Inaccuracies in eyewitness perceptions obviously occur in "real life," but they cannot be reproduced in psychology experiments. T or F?
3. Accuracy scores for facts provided by witnesses to staged crimes may be as low as 25 percent correct. T or F?
4. Victims of crimes are more accurate eyewitnesses than are impartial observers. T or F?
5. A good antidote to perceptual habituation can be found in conscious efforts to
   a. reverse sensory gating
   b. pay attention
   c. achieve visual accommodation
   d. counteract shape constancy

REFLECT
Critical Thinking

6. Return for a moment to the incident described at the beginning of this chapter. What perceptual factors were involved in the first version of the "murder"? How did the girl affect what was seen?

Relate

Because perceptions are constructions or models of external events, we should all engage in more frequent reality testing. Can you think of a recent event when a little reality testing would have saved you from misjudging a situation?

To improve your own perceptual awareness and accuracy, which strategies would you emphasize first?

Answers: 1. T **2.** F **3.** T **4.** F **5.** b **6.** The girl's misperception, communicated so forcefully to one of your authors, created a powerful expectancy that influenced what he perceived. Also, the event happened quickly (the exposure time was brief), and the stressful or emotional nature of the incident encouraged his own misperception.

---

chapter in review   Gateways to Perception

Perception is an active process of constructing sensations into a meaningful mental representation of the world.

- Perceptions are based on simultaneous bottom-up and top-down processing. Complete percepts are assembled out of small sensory features in "bottom-up" fashion guided by preexisting knowledge applied "top-down" to help organize features into a meaningful whole.

Attended sensations become part of the percept; motive and emotions influence attention.

- Attention is selective, and it may be divided among various activities. Attention is closely related to stimulus intensity, repetition, contrast, change, and incongruity.
- The phenomenon called inattentional blindness suggests that there can be no perception without attention.

- Attention is accompanied by an orientation response. When a stimulus is repeated without change, the orientation response undergoes habituation.
- Personal motives and values often alter perceptions by changing the evaluation of what is seen or by altering attention to specific details.

The Gestalt principles of organization bring order to our perceptions.
- Separating figure and ground (object and background) is the most basic perceptual organization.
- The following Gestalt principles also help organize sensations: nearness, similarity, continuity, closure, contiguity, common region, and combinations of the preceding.
- Basic elements of line drawings appear to be universally recognized.
- Perceptual organization shifts for ambiguous stimuli. Impossible figures resist stable organization altogether.
- A perceptual organization may be thought of as a hypothesis held until evidence contradicts it.

Perceptual constancies allow us to find regularity in the constantly changing energy patterns reaching our senses.
- In vision, the image projected on the retina is constantly changing, but the external world appears stable and undistorted because of size, shape, and brightness constancy.

Various visual cues are used to construct the experience of depth.
- A basic, innate capacity for depth perception is present soon after birth.
- Depth perception depends on binocular depth cues of retinal disparity and convergence.
- Stereoscopic vision is created mainly by retinal disparity and the resulting overlap and mismatch of visual sensations.
- Depth perception also depends on the monocular depth cue of accommodation.
- Monocular "pictorial" depth cues also underlie depth perception. They are linear perspective, relative size, height in the picture plane, light and shadow, overlap, texture gradients, aerial haze, and motion parallax.
- The moon illusion can be explained by the apparent-distance hypothesis, which emphasizes that many depth cues are present when the moon is near the horizon, and few are present when it is overhead.

Perceptual learning influences the top-down organization and interpretation of sensations.
- Studies of inverted vision show that even the most basic organization is subject to a degree of change. Active movement speeds adaptation to a new perceptual environment.
- Perceptual judgments are not made in a vacuum. They are almost always related to context.
- One of the most familiar of all illusions, the Müller-Lyer illusion, seems to be related to perceptual learning, linear perspective, size-distance invariance relationships, and mislocating the end points of the figure.

Perceptual sets often lead us to perceive or misperceive what we expect to see.
- Suggestion, motives, emotions, attention, and prior experience combine in various ways to create perceptual sets, or expectancies.

The bulk of the evidence to date is against the existence of ESP.
- Parapsychology is the study of purported psi phenomena, including telepathy (as well as mediumship), clairvoyance, precognition, and psychokinesis.
- Research in parapsychology remains controversial owing to a variety of problems and shortcomings.
- The more carefully controlled an ESP experiment is, the less likely it is to produce evidence that ESP occurs.
- Stage ESP is based on deception and tricks.

Awareness of the factors that can distort perception is the key to improving perceptual accuracy.
- Perception is an active construction of events. This is one reason why eyewitness testimony is surprisingly unreliable. Eyewitness accuracy is further damaged by weapon focus and a number of similar factors.
- Perceptual accuracy is enhanced by reality testing, dishabituation, and conscious efforts to pay attention.
- It is also valuable to break perceptual habits, to beware of perceptual sets, and to be aware of the ways in which motives and emotions influence perceptions.

Web Resources

For an up-to-date list of direct links to interesting sites, including those listed here, visit the student companion site for this book at www.cengage.com/psychology/coon

Figure/Ground in Graphic Design Explore the use of the figure-ground principle in graphic design.

Gallery of Illusions An interesting and fun website that presents illusory stimuli that are fun to view and that provides a basis to learn about sensation and perception.

3-D Stereograms Find the 3-D images hidden in these pictures.

Perceptual Learning Explore an example of perceptual learning through wine tasting.

James Randi Education Foundation Win $1,000,000 for proving, under scientifically controlled conditions, that you have ESP.

The Innocence Project Read about real cases of people convicted through eyewitness testimony but later exonerated by DNA evidence.

Avoiding Habituation Read about how advertisers apply the idea of habituation to the design of advertisements.

Interactive Learning

Introduction to Psychology: Gateways to Mind and Behavior **Book Companion Website**
www.cengage.com/psychology/coon

Visit your book companion website, where you will find flash cards, practice quizzes, web links, and more to help you study.

CENGAGENOW™ *Just what you need to know NOW!*

Spend time on what you need to master rather than on information you already have learned. Take a pre-test for this chapter, and CengageNOW will generate a personalized study plan based on your results. The study plan will identify the topics you need to review and direct you to online resources to help you master those topics. You can then take a post-test to help you determine the concepts you have mastered and what you will need to work on. Try it out! Go to www.cengage.com/login to sign in with an access code or to purchase access to this product.

CHAPTER 6

States of Consciousness

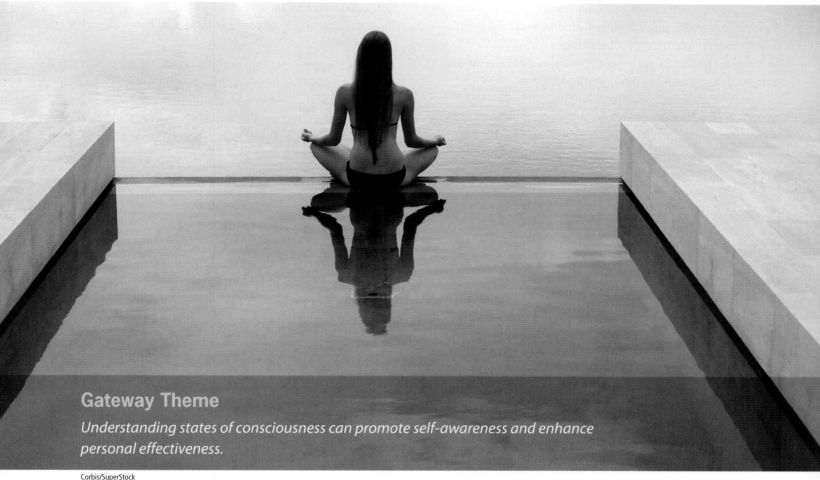

Gateway Theme

Understanding states of consciousness can promote self-awareness and enhance personal effectiveness.

Corbis/SuperStock

Gateway Questions

- *What is an altered state of consciousness?*
- *What are the effects of sleep loss or changes in sleep patterns?*
- *Why do we sleep?*
- *What are some sleep disorders and unusual sleep events?*
- *Do dreams have meaning?*

- *What is hypnosis?*
- *Do meditation and sensory deprivation have any benefits?*
- *What are the effects of the more commonly used psychoactive drugs?*
- *How can dreams be used to promote personal understanding?*

In Los Angeles, California, an aspiring actor consults a hypnotist for help in reducing her stage fright.

In the American Southwest, a Navajo elder gives his congregation peyote tea, a sacrament in the Native American Church, as a drumbeat resounds in the darkness.

In Toronto, Canada, three businesswomen head for a popular tavern after a particularly stressful day.

In Big Bend National Park in southern Texas, a college student spends a day walking through the wilderness, in a quiet state of mindfulness meditation.

In New Zealand, a Maori tohunga (priest) performs a nightlong ritual to talk to the spirits who created the world in the mythical period the Aborigines call Dreamtime.

In Northern Ireland, a nun living in a convent spends an entire week in silent prayer and contemplation.

In Berkeley, California, an artist spends 2 hours in a flotation chamber to clear her head before resuming work on a large painting.

At a park in Amsterdam, a group of street musicians smoke a joint and sing for spare change.

In Tucson, Arizona, one of your authors pours himself another cup of coffee.

Each of these people seeks to alter consciousness—in different ways, to different degrees, and for different reasons. As these examples suggest, consciousness can take many forms. In the discussion that follows, we will begin with the familiar realms of sleep and dreaming and then move to more exotic states of consciousness.

⬤⬤ States of Consciousness—The Many Faces of Awareness

Gateway Question: What is an altered state of consciousness?

To be conscious means to be aware. **Consciousness** consists of all the sensations, perceptions, memories, and feelings you are aware of at any instant (Koch, 2004). (See "What Is It Like to Be a Bat?") We spend most of our lives in **waking consciousness,** a state of clear, organized alertness. In waking consciousness we perceive times, places, and events as real, meaningful, and familiar. But states of consciousness related to fatigue, delirium, hypnosis, drugs, and euphoria may differ markedly from "normal" awareness. Everyone experiences at least some altered states, such as sleep, dreaming, and daydreaming (Blackmore, 2004). In everyday life, changes in consciousness may also accompany long-distance running, listening to music, making love, or other circumstances.

Altered States of Consciousness

How are altered states distinguished from normal awareness? During an **altered state of consciousness (ASC),** changes occur in the quality and pattern of mental activity. Typically there are distinct shifts in our perceptions, emotions, memories, time sense, thoughts, feelings of self-control, and suggestibility (Siegel, 2005). Definitions aside, most people know when they have experienced an ASC.

Are there other causes of ASCs? In addition to the ones mentioned, we could add: sensory overload (a rave, Mardi Gras crowd, or mosh pit), monotonous stimulation (such as "highway hypnotism" on long drives), unusual physical conditions (high fever, hyperventilation, dehydration, sleep loss, near-death experiences), restricted sensory input, and many other possibilities. In some instances, altered states have important cultural meanings. (See "Consciousness and Culture" for more information.)

An unconscious person will die without constant care. Yet as crucial as consciousness is, we can't really explain how it occurs (Robinson, 2008). Nevertheless, it is possible to identify various states of consciousness and to explore the role they play in our lives. Let's begin with a look at the most common altered state, sleep and dreaming.

⬤⬤ Sleep—A Nice Place to Visit

Gateway Question: What are the effects of sleep loss or changes in sleep patterns?

Each of us will spend some 25 years of life asleep. Because sleep is familiar, many people think they know all about it. But many common-sense beliefs about sleep are false. For example, you are not totally unresponsive during sleep. A sleeping mother may ignore a jet thundering overhead but wake at the slightest whimper of her child. Likewise, you are more likely to awaken if you hear your own name spoken, instead of another. It's even possible to do simple tasks while asleep. In one experiment, people learned to avoid an electric shock by touching a switch each time a tone sounded. Eventually, they could do it without waking. (This is much like the basic survival skill of turning off your alarm clock without waking.) Of course, sleep does impose limitations. Don't expect to learn math, a foreign language, or other complex skills while asleep—especially if the snooze takes place in class (Froufe & Schwartz, 2001). But do expect that a good sleep will help you remember what you learned the day before (Fenn, Nusbaum, & Margoliash, 2003; Saxvig et al., 2008).

CRITICAL THINKING

What Is It Like to Be a Bat?

Imagine hurtling through the air on leather wings while shrieking noisily. Suddenly, the faint echo of your own voice draws your attention to a moth that is frantically trying to evade you. You career after it, twisting through the pitch-black jungle. Dodging trees and other bats, you catch the moth and savor your first meal of the still-young night.

In his famous essay, "What Is It Like to Be a Bat?" Thomas Nagel (1974) points out that we can learn a lot about bats from an objec-tive, *third-person* point of view. Scientifically, we know that bats use echolocation (they emit sounds and interpret the echoes) to hunt insects at night. But what does that *feel* like from a subjective, *first-person* point of view? Have you ever been curious about what it is like to be a bat, or a dog, or a cat? What runs through Rover's mind when he sniffs other dogs? Does Fluffy have dreams? Are they as strange as ours? Do cats ever worry about the future? Do they like music? Do animals feel joy?

According to Nagel, we cannot directly know the first-person experience of animals (or even other people, for that matter). The difficulty of knowing other minds is why the early behaviorists distrusted introspection. (Remember Chapter 1?) A key challenge for psychology is to use objective studies of the brain and behavior to help us understand the mind and consciousness, which are basically private phenomena (Koch, 2004; Robinson, 2008).

The Need for Sleep

How strong is the need for sleep? Sleep is an innate **biological rhythm** that can never be entirely ignored (Lavie, 2001; Mistl-berger, 2005). Of course, sleep will give way temporarily, especially at times of great danger. As comedian and filmmaker Woody Allen once put it, "The lion and the lamb shall lie down together, but the lamb will not be very sleepy." However, there are limits to how long humans can go without sleep. A rare disease that prevents sleep always ends with stupor, coma, and death (Dauvilliers et al., 2004) (● Figure 6.1).

How long could a person go without sleep? With few exceptions, 4 days or more without sleep becomes hell for everyone. The world record is held by Randy Gardner, who at age 17 went 264 hours (11 days) without sleep. Surprisingly, Randy needed only 14 hours of sleep to recover. As Randy found, most symptoms of **sleep deprivation** (sleep loss) are reversed by a single night's rest. (In 2007, a man named Tony Wright went 266 hours without

sleep. However, *The Guinness Book of Records* no longer recognizes sleep deprivation competitions because of possible health risks, so Randy still holds the "official" record.)

What are the costs of sleep loss? At various times, Randy's speech was slurred, and he couldn't concentrate, remember clearly, or name common objects (Coren, 1996). Sleep loss also typically causes trembling hands, drooping eyelids, inattention, irritability, staring, increased pain sensitivity, and general discomfort (Doran, Van Dongen, & Dinges, 2001).

Most people experience **hypersomnia** (hi-per-SOM-nee-ah: excessive daytime sleepiness) after even a few hours of sleep loss. Hypersomnia is a common problem during adolescence (Carska-don, Acebo, & Jenni, 2004). Rapid physical changes during puberty increase the need for sleep. However, the quality and quantity of sleep time tends to decrease during the teen years (Fukuda & Ishihara, 2001).

Most people who have not slept for a day or two can still do interesting or complex mental tasks. But they have trouble paying attention, staying alert, and doing simple or boring routines (Belenky et al., 2003). They are also susceptible to **microsleeps,** which are brief shifts in brain activity to the pattern normally recorded during

Timothy Ross/The Image Works

● **Figure 6. 1** Not all animals sleep, but like humans, those that do have power-ful sleep needs. For example, dolphins must voluntarily breathe air, which means they face the choice of staying awake or drowning. The dolphin solves this problem by sleeping on just one side of its brain at a time! The other half of the brain, which remains awake, controls breathing (Jouvet, 1999).

Consciousness Mental awareness of sensations, perceptions, memories, and feelings.

Waking consciousness A state of clear, organized alertness.

Altered state of consciousness (ASC) A condition of awareness distinctly different in quality or pattern from waking consciousness.

Biological rhythm Any repeating cycle of biological activity, such as sleep and waking cycles or changes in body temperature.

Sleep deprivation Being prevented from getting desired or needed amounts of sleep.

Hypersomnia Excessive daytime sleepiness.

Microsleep A brief shift in brain-wave patterns to those of sleep.

HUMAN DIVERSITY

Consciousness and Culture

Throughout history, people have found ways to alter consciousness (Siegel, 2005). A dramatic example is the sweat lodge ceremony of the Sioux Indians. During the ritual, several men sit in total darkness inside a small chamber heated by coals. Cedar smoke, bursts of steam, and sage fill the air. The men chant rhythmically. The heat builds. At last they can stand it no more. The door is thrown open. Cooling night breezes rush in. And then? The cycle begins again—often to be repeated four or five times more.

Like the yoga practices of Hindu mystics or the dances of the Whirling Dervishes of Turkey, the ritual "sweats" of the Sioux are meant to cleanse the mind and body. When they are especially intense, they bring altered awareness and personal revelation.

People seek some altered states for pleasure, as is often true of drug intoxication. Yet as the Sioux illustrate, many cultures regard altered consciousness as a pathway to personal enlightenment. Indeed, all cultures and most religions recognize and accept some alterations of consciousness. However, the meaning given to these states varies greatly—from signs of "madness" and "possession" by spirits, to life-enhancing breakthroughs. Thus, cultural conditioning greatly affects what altered states we recognize, seek, consider normal, and attain (de Rios & Grob, 2005).

In many cultures, rituals of healing, prayer, purification, or personal transformation are accompanied by altered states of consciousness.

---

sleep. Imagine placing an animal on a moving treadmill, over a pool of water. Even under these conditions, animals soon drift into repeated microsleeps. For a pilot or machine operator, this can spell disaster (Hardaway & Gregory, 2005). If a task is monotonous (such as factory work or air traffic control), no amount of sleep loss is safe. In fact, if you lose just 1 hour of sleep a night, it can affect your mood, memory, ability to pay attention, and even your health (Maas, 1999). Sleep helps keep the brain healthy by regulating its temperature, conserving energy, and aiding brain development and repair. Biologically, sleep is a necessity, not a luxury.

When you drive, remember that microsleeps can lead to macro-accidents. Even if your eyes are open, you can fall asleep for a few seconds. A hundred thousand crashes every year are caused by sleepiness (Rau, 2005). Although coffee helps (Kamimori et al., 2005), if you are struggling to stay awake while driving, you should stop, quit fighting it, and take a short nap.

Severe sleep loss can cause a temporary **sleep-deprivation psychosis** (loss of contact with reality). Confusion, disorientation, delusions, and hallucinations are typical of this reaction. Fortunately, such "crazy" behavior is uncommon. Hallucinations and delusions rarely appear before 60 hours of wakefulness (Naitoh, Kelly, & Englund, 1989).

How can I tell how much sleep I really need? Pick a day when you feel well rested. Then sleep that night until you wake without an alarm clock. If you feel rested when you wake up, that's your natural sleep need. If you're sleeping fewer hours than you need, you're building up a sleep debt (Maas, 1999).

Sleep Patterns

Sleep was described as an innate biological rhythm. What does that mean? Daily sleep and waking periods create a variety of **sleep patterns.** Rhythms of sleep and waking are so steady that they continue for many days, even when clocks and light-dark cycles are removed. However, under such conditions, humans eventually shift to a sleep-waking cycle that averages slightly more than 24 hours (Czeisler et al., 1999) (● Figure 6.2). This suggests that external time markers, especially light and dark, help tie our sleep rhythms to days that are exactly 24 hours long. Otherwise, many of us would drift into our own unusual sleep cycles (Duffy & Wright, Jr., 2005).

bridges

Daily sleep cycles can be disrupted by rapid travel across time zones (jet lag) and by shift work. **See Chapter 10, pages 322–323, for more information.**

What is the normal range of sleep? A few rare individuals can get by on an hour or two of sleep a night—and feel perfectly fine. Only a small percentage of the population are *short sleepers,* averaging 5 hours of sleep or less per night. On the other end of the scale we find *long sleepers,* who doze 9 hours or more (Grandner & Kripke, 2004). The majority of us sleep on a familiar 7- to 8-hour-per-night schedule. Urging everyone to sleep 8 hours would be like advising everyone to wear medium-size shoes.

We need less sleep as we get older, right? Yes, total sleep time declines throughout life. Those older than 50 average only 6 hours of sleep a night. In contrast, infants spend up to 20 hours a day sleeping, usually in 2- to 4-hour cycles. As they mature, most children go through a "nap" stage and eventually settle into a steady cycle of sleeping once a day (● Figure 6.3). Perhaps we should all continue to take an afternoon "siesta." Midafternoon sleepiness is a natural part of the sleep cycle. Brief, well-timed naps can help

Time of Day

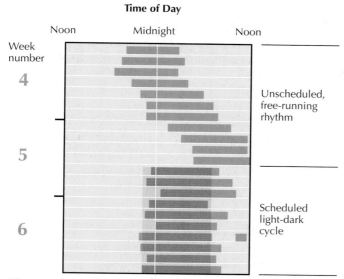

● **Figure 6.2** Sleep rhythms. Bars show periods of sleep during the fourth, fifth, and sixth weeks of an experiment with a human subject. During unscheduled periods, the subject was allowed to select times of sleep and lighting. The result was a sleep rhythm of about 25 hours. Notice how this free-running rhythm began to advance around the clock as they fell asleep later each day. When periods of darkness (shaded area) were imposed during the fifth week, the rhythm quickly resynchronized with 24-hour days. (Adapted from Czeisler et al., 1981.)

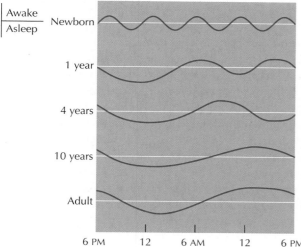

● **Figure 6.3** Development of sleep patterns. Short cycles of sleep and waking gradually become the night-day cycle of an adult. Although most adults don't take naps, midafternoon sleepiness is a natural part of the sleep cycle. (Reprinted from *Electroencephalography & Clinical Neurophysiology*, 17, Williams, Agnew, & Webb et al., Sleep Patterns in young adults: An EEG study, 376-381, 1964, with permission from Elsevier.)

maintain alertness in people like truck drivers and hospital interns, who often must fight to stay alert (Garbarino et al., 2004).

Busy people may be tempted to sleep less. However, people on *shortened* cycles—for example, 3 hours of sleep to 6 hours awake—often can't get to sleep when the cycle calls for it. That's why astronauts continue to sleep on their normal earth schedule while in space. Adapting to *longer*-than-normal days is more promising. Such days can be tailored to match natural sleep patterns, which have a ratio of 2 to 1 between time awake and time asleep

(16 hours awake and 8 hours asleep). For instance, one study showed that 28-hour "days" work for some people. Overall, sleep patterns may be bent and stretched, but they rarely yield entirely to human whims (Åkerstedt, 2007).

●● Stages of Sleep—The Nightly Roller-Coaster

Gateway Question: Why do we sleep?

What causes sleep? Early sleep experts thought that something in the bloodstream must cause sleep. But conjoined twins, whose bodies are joined at birth, show that this is false (● Figure 6.4). During waking hours, a **sleep hormone** (sleep-promoting chemical) collects in the brain and spinal cord, *not* in the blood. If this substance is extracted from one animal and injected into another, the second animal will sleep deeply for many hours (Cravatt et al., 1995). Notice, however, that this explanation is incomplete. For example, why would a well-rested person have to fight to stay awake during a boring midday meeting?

Whether you are awake or asleep right now depends on the *balance* between separate sleep and waking systems. Brain circuits and chemicals in one of the systems promote sleep (Steiger, 2007). A network of brain cells in the other system responds to chemicals that inhibit sleep. The two systems seesaw back and forth, switching the brain between sleep and wakefulness (Lavie, 2001). Note that the brain does not "shut down" during sleep. Rather, the *pattern* of activity changes.

● **Figure 6.4** These conjoined twins share the same blood supply, yet one sleeps while the other is awake. (Photo by Yale Joel, *Life Magazine*. © 1954 Time, Inc.)

Sleep-deprivation psychosis A major disruption of mental and emotional functioning brought about by sleep loss.

Sleep patterns The order and timing of daily sleep and waking periods.

Sleep hormone A sleep-promoting substance found in the brain and spinal cord.

Sleep Stages

How does brain activity change when you fall asleep? Changes in tiny electrical signals (brainwaves) generated by the brain can be amplified and recorded with an **electroencephalograph** (eh-LEK-tro-en-SEF-uh-lo-graf), or **EEG.** When you are awake and alert, the EEG reveals a pattern of small fast waves called **beta waves** (● Figure 6.5). Immediately before sleep, the pattern shifts to larger and slower waves called **alpha waves.** (Alpha waves also occur when you are relaxed and allow your thoughts to drift.) As the eyes close, breathing becomes slow and regular, the pulse rate slows, and body temperature drops. Soon after, we descend into *slow-wave sleep* through four distinct **sleep stages**.

Stage 1

As you enter **light sleep** (stage 1 sleep), your heart rate slows even more. Breathing becomes more irregular. The muscles of your body relax. This may trigger a reflex muscle twitch called a *hypnic*

(a)

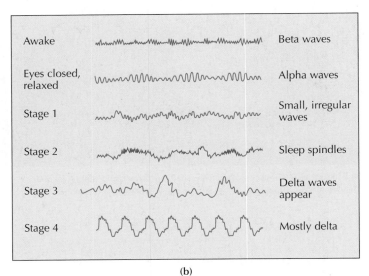

(b)

● **Figure 6.5** *(a)* Photograph of an EEG recording session. The boy in the background is asleep. *(b)* Changes in brain-wave patterns associated with various stages of sleep. Actually, most wave types are present at all times, but they occur more or less frequently in various sleep stages.

(HIP-nik: sleep) *jerk*. (This is quite normal, so have no fear about admitting to your friends that you fell asleep with a hypnic jerk.) In stage 1 sleep the EEG is made up mainly of small, irregular waves with some alpha. Persons awakened at this time may or may not say they were asleep.

Stage 2

As sleep deepens, body temperature drops further. Also, the EEG begins to include **sleep spindles,** which are short bursts of distinctive brain-wave activity (Fogel et al., 2007). Spindles seem to mark the true boundary of sleep. Within 4 minutes after spindles appear, most people will say they were asleep.

Stage 3

In stage 3, a new brainwave called delta begins to appear. **Delta waves** are very large and slow. They signal a move to deeper slow-wave sleep and a further loss of consciousness.

Stage 4

Most people reach **deep sleep** (the deepest level of normal sleep) in about 1 hour. Stage 4 brainwaves are almost pure slow-wave delta, and the sleeper is in a state of oblivion. If you make a loud noise during stage 4, the sleeper will wake up in a state of confusion and may not remember the noise.

The Dual Process Hypothesis of Sleep

There is much more to a night's sleep than a simple descent into stage 4. Fluctuations in other sleep hormones cause recurring cycles of deeper and lighter sleep throughout the night (Steiger, 2007). During these repeated periods of lighter sleep, a curious thing happens: the sleeper's eyes occasionally move under the eyelids. (If you ever get a chance to watch a sleeping child, roommate, or spouse, you may see these eye movements.) **Rapid eye movements,** or **REMs,** are associated with dreaming (● Figure 6.6). In addition to rapid eye movements, **REM sleep** is marked by a return of fast, irregular EEG patterns similar to stage 1 sleep. In fact, the brain is so active during REM sleep that it looks as if the person is awake (Rock, 2004).

The two most basic states of sleep, then, are **non-REM (NREM) sleep** (which occurs during stages 1, 2, 3, and 4) and REM sleep, with its associated dreaming (Rock, 2004). Earlier, we noted some of the biological benefits of sleep. According to the *dual process hypothesis of sleep,* REM and NREM sleep have two added purposes: They help "refresh" the brain and store memories (Ficca & Salzarulob, 2004).

The Function of NREM Sleep

What is the function of NREM sleep? NREM sleep is dream-free about 90 percent of the time and is deepest early in the night during the first few stage 4 periods. Your first period of stage 1 sleep usually lacks REMs and dreams. Later stage 1 periods typically include a shift into REM sleep. Dreamless slow-wave NREM sleep increases after physical exertion and may help us recover from bodily fatigue. It also appears to "calm" the brain during the earlier part of a night's sleep (Tononi & Cirelli, 2003).

According to the dual process hypothesis, we are bombarded by information throughout the day, which causes our neural net-

● **Figure 6.6** *(a)* Average proportion of time adults spend daily in REM sleep and NREM sleep. REM periods add up to about 20 percent of total sleep time. *(b)* Typical changes in stages of sleep during the night. Notice that dreams mostly coincide with REM periods.

works to become more and more active. As a result, your brain requires more and more energy to continue functioning. Slow wave sleep early in the night brings overall brain activation levels back down, allowing a "fresh" approach to the next day.

Consider for a moment the amazing jumble of events that make up a day. Some experiences are worth remembering (like what you are reading right now, of course) and others are not so important (like what you were thinking when you put on your socks). As slow wave sleep reduces overall activation in the brain, less important experiences may fade away and be forgotten. If you wake up feeling clearer about what you studied the previous night, it might be because your brain doesn't "sweat the small stuff"!

The Function of REM Sleep

What then, is the purpose of REM sleep? According to the dual process hypothesis, while NREM sleep "calms" the brain, REM sleep appears to "sharpen" our memories of the previous day's more important experiences (Saxvig et al., 2008). Daytime stress tends to increase REM sleep, which may rise dramatically when there is a death in the family, trouble at work, a marital conflict, or other emotionally charged events. The value of more REM sleep is that it helps us sort and retain memories, especially memories about strategies for solving problems (Walker & Stickgold, 2006). This is why, after studying for a long period, you may remember more if you go to sleep, rather than pulling an all-nighter. (REMember to get some REM!)

Early in life, REM sleep may stimulate the developing brain. Newborn babies have lots of new experiences to process so they spend a hearty 8 or 9 hours a day in REM sleep. That's about 50 percent of their total sleep time.

REM Sleep and Dreaming

Roughly 85 percent of the time, people awakened during REMs report vivid dreams. Some eye movements correspond to dream activities. Dream that you are watching a tennis match, and you will probably move your eyes from side to side. However, people who were born blind still have REMs, so eye movements are not just a result of "watching" dream images (Shafton, 1995). REM sleep is easy to observe in pets, such as dogs and cats. Watch for eye and face movements and irregular breathing. (You can forget about your pet iguana, though. Reptiles show no signs of REM sleep.)

Dreams during REM sleep tend to be longer, clearer, more detailed, more bizarre, and more "dream-like" than thoughts and images that occur in NREM sleep (Hobson, Pace-Schott, & Stickgold, 2000). Also, brain areas associated with imagery and emotion become more active during REM sleep. This may explain why REM dreams tend to be more vivid than NREM dreams (Braun, Balkin, & Herscovitch, 1998; Rock, 2004).

Speaking very loosely, it's as if the dreaming brain were reviewing messages left on a telephone answering machine, to decide which are worth keeping. During the day, when information is streaming in, the brain may be too busy to efficiently select useful memories. When the conscious brain is "off-line," we are better able to build new memories.

What happens to the body when a person dreams? REM sleep is a time of high emotion. The heart beats irregularly. Blood pressure and breathing waver. Both males and females appear to be sexually aroused: Men usually have an erection, and genital blood flow increases in women. This occurs for all REM sleep, so it is not strictly related to erotic dreams (Jouvet, 1999).

Electroencephalograph (EEG) A device designed to detect, amplify, and record electrical activity in the brain.

Beta waves Small, fast brain waves associated with being awake and alert.

Alpha waves Large, slow brain waves associated with relaxation and falling asleep.

Sleep stages Levels of sleep identified by brain-wave patterns and behavioral changes.

Light sleep Stage 1 sleep, marked by small irregular brainwaves and some alpha waves.

Sleep spindles Distinctive bursts of brainwave activity that indicate a person is asleep.

Delta waves Large, slow brainwaves that occur in deeper sleep (stages 3 and 4).

Deep sleep Stage 4 slow-wave sleep; the deepest form of normal sleep.

Rapid eye movements (REMs) Swift eye movements during sleep.

REM sleep Sleep marked by rapid eye movements and a return to stage 1 EEG patterns.

Non-REM (NREM) sleep Non–rapid eye movement sleep characteristic of stages 2, 3, and 4.

CRITICAL THINKING

They Came from Outer Space?

Imagine opening your eyes shortly before dawn, attempting to roll over in your bed, and suddenly realizing that you are entirely paralyzed. While lying helplessly on your back and unable to cry out for help, you become aware of sinister figures lurking in your bedroom. As they move closer to your bed, your heart begins to pound violently and you feel as if you are suffocating. You hear buzzing sounds and feel electrical sensations shooting throughout your body. Within moments, the visions vanish and you can move once again. Terrified, you wonder what has just happened (McNally & Clancy, 2005, p.114).

Sleep paralysis, which normally prevents us from moving during REM sleep, can also occur just as you begin to wake up. During such episodes, people sometimes have

hypnopompic (hip-neh-POM-pik: "upon awakening") hallucinations. According to psychologist Al Cheyne, these hallucinations may include bizarre experiences, such as sensing that an alien being is in your bedroom; feeling something pressing on your chest, suffocating you; or feeling like you are floating out of your body (Cheyne, 2005; Cheyne, Rueffer, & Newby-Clark, 1999).

Although most of us shrug off these weird experiences, some people try to make sense of them. Earlier in history, people interpreted these hallucinated intruders as angels, demons, or witches and believed that their out-of-body experiences were real (Cheyne, Rueffer, & Newby-Clark, 1999). However, as our culture changes so do our interpretations of sleep experiences. Today, for example,

some people who have sleep-related hallucinations believe they have been abducted by space aliens or sexually abused (McNally & Clancy, 2005).

Swiss artist Henry Fuseli drew on hypnopompic imagery as an inspiration for his famous painting, *The Nightmare.*

During REM sleep, your body becomes quite still, as if you were paralyzed. Imagine for a moment the results of acting out some of your recent dreams. Very likely, REM-sleep paralysis prevents some hilarious—and dangerous—nighttime escapades. When it fails, some people thrash violently, leap out of bed, and may attack their bed partners. A lack of muscle paralysis during REM sleep is called *REM behavior disorder* (Ochoa & Pulido, 2005). One patient suffering from the disorder tied himself to his bed every night. That way, he couldn't jump up and crash into furniture or walls (Shafton, 1995). And yet sometimes sleep paralysis can go a little too far. (See "They Came from Outer Space?")

In a moment we will survey some additional sleep problems—if you are still awake. First, here are a few questions to check your memory of our discussion so far.

KNOWLEDGE BUILDER
Altered States and Sleep

RECITE

1. Changes in the quality and pattern of mental activity define
   a. an EEG
   b. an REM
   c. SIDS
   d. an ASC
2. Delusions and hallucinations typically continue for several days after a sleep-deprived individual returns to normal sleep. T or F?
3. Alyssa experiences a microsleep while driving. Most likely, this indicates that she
   a. was producing mostly beta waves
   b. had high levels of sleep hormones in her bloodstream
   c. switched from delta waves to alpha waves
   d. was sleep deprived

4. Older adults, and particularly the elderly, sleep more than children do because the elderly are more easily fatigued. T or F?
5. Alpha waves are to presleep drowsiness as _____ _____ are to stage 4 sleep.
6. Rapid eye movements indicate that a person is in deep sleep. T or F?
7. Which of the following would normally be most incompatible with moving your arms and legs while asleep?
   a. REM sleep
   b. sleep spindles
   c. delta waves
   d. NREM sleep

REFLECT

Critical Thinking

8. Why might it be better for the unscheduled human sleep–waking cycle to average more than 24 hours, instead of less?
9. In addition to helping store memories, what biological advantages might sleeping provide?

Relate

Make a quick list of some altered states of consciousness you have experienced. What do they have in common? How are they different? What conditions caused them?

Imagine that you are a counselor at a sleep clinic. You must explain the basics of sleep and dreaming to a new client who knows little about these topics. Can you do it?

Answers: 1. d 2. F 3. d 4. F 5. delta waves 6. F 7. a 8. Sleep experts theorize that the 25-hour average leaves a little "slack" in the cycle. External time markers can then retard the body cycle slightly to synchronize it with light-dark cycles. If the body cycle were shorter than 24 hours, we all might have to "stretch" every day to adjust. 9. Lowering body activity and metabolism during sleep may help conserve energy and lengthen life. Also, natural selection may have favored sleep because animals that remained active at night probably had a higher chance of being killed. (We'll bet they had more fun, though.)

⬤⬤ Sleep Disturbances—Showing Nightly: Sleep Wars!

Gateway Question: What are some sleep disorders and unusual sleep events?

Sleep quality has taken a beating in North America. Artificial lighting, frenetic schedules, exciting pastimes, smoking, drinking, overstimulation, and many other factors have contributed to a near epidemic of sleep problems. Sleep disturbances are a serious risk to health and happiness. Sleep clinics treat thousands of people each year who suffer from sleep disorders or complaints. These disturbances range from daytime sleep attacks to sleepwalking and terrifying nightmares (● Table 6.1). Let's explore some of the more interesting problems these people face.

Insomnia

Staring at the ceiling at 2 AM is pretty low on most people's list of favorite pastimes. Yet about 60 million Americans have frequent or chronic insomnia (NINDS, 2007). **Insomnia** includes diffi-

culty in going to sleep, frequent nighttime awakenings, waking too early, or a combination of these problems. Insomnia can harm people's work, health, and relationships (Sateia & Nowell, 2004).

Types and Causes of Insomnia

Worry, stress, and excitement can cause *temporary insomnia* and a self-defeating cycle. First, excess mental activity ("I can't stop turning things over in my mind") and heightened arousal block sleep. Then, frustration and anger over not being able to sleep cause more worry and arousal. This further delays sleep, which causes more frustration, and so on (Espie, 2002). A good way to beat this cycle is to avoid fighting it. Get up and do something useful or satisfying when you can't sleep. (Reading a textbook might be a good choice of useful activities.) Return to bed only when you begin to feel that you are struggling to stay awake. If sleeping problems last for more than 3 weeks, then a diagnosis of *chronic insomnia* can be made.

Drug-dependency insomnia (sleep loss caused by withdrawal from sleeping pills) can also occur. There is real irony in the billion dollars a year North Americans spend on sleeping pills. Nonprescription sleeping pills such as Sominex, Nytol, and Sleep-Eze have little sleep-inducing effect. Barbiturates are even worse. These prescription sedatives decrease both stage 4 sleep and REM sleep, drastically lowering sleep quality. In addition, many users become "sleeping-pill junkies" who need an ever-greater number of pills to get to sleep. Victims must be painstakingly weaned from their sleep medicines. Otherwise, terrible nightmares and "rebound insomnia" may drive them back to drug use. It's worth remembering that although alcohol and other depressant drugs may help a person get to sleep, they greatly reduce sleep quality (Nau & Lichstein, 2005). Even newer drugs, such as Ambien and Lunesta, which induce

Table 6.1 ● Sleep Disturbances— Things That Go Wrong in the Night

Hypersomnia	Excessive daytime sleepiness. This can result from depression, insomnia, narcolepsy, sleep apnea, sleep drunkenness, periodic limb movements, drug abuse, and other problems.
Insomnia	Difficulty in getting to sleep or staying asleep; also, not feeling rested after sleeping.
Narcolepsy	Sudden, irresistible, daytime sleep attacks that may last anywhere from a few minutes to a half hour. Victims may fall asleep while standing, talking, or even driving.
Nightmare disorder	Vivid, recurrent nightmares that significantly disturb sleep.
Periodic limb movement syndrome	Muscle twitches (primarily affecting the legs) that occur every 20 to 40 seconds and severely disturb sleep.
REM behavior disorder	A failure of normal muscle paralysis, leading to violent actions during REM sleep.
Restless legs syndrome	An irresistible urge to move the legs to relieve sensations of creeping, tingling, prickling, aching, or tension.
Sleep apnea	During sleep, breathing stops for 20 seconds or more until the person wakes a little, gulps in air, and settles back to sleep; this cycle may be repeated hundreds of times per night.
Sleep drunkenness	A slow transition to clear consciousness after awakening; sometimes associated with irritable or aggressive behavior.
Sleep terror disorder	The repeated occurrence of night terrors that significantly disturb sleep.
Sleep-wake schedule disorder	A mismatch between the sleep-wake schedule demanded by a person's bodily rhythm and that demanded by the environment.
Sleepwalking disorder	Repeated incidents of leaving bed and walking about while asleep.

Bond & Wooten, 1996; DSM-IV-TR, 2000; Hauri & Linde, 1990

"It's only insomnia if there's nothing good on."

Insomnia Difficulty in getting to sleep or staying asleep.

sleep, have drawbacks. Possible side effects include amnesia, impaired judgment, increased appetite, decreased sex drive, depression, and sleepwalking. Rebound insomnia is also a risk, making these drugs at best a temporary remedy for insomnia.

Behavioral Remedies for Insomnia

If sleeping pills are a poor way to treat insomnia, what can be done? Sleep specialists prefer to treat insomnia with lifestyle changes and behavioral techniques (Montgomery & Dennis, 2004). Treatment for chronic insomnia usually begins with a careful analysis of a patient's sleep habits, lifestyle, stress levels, and medical problems. All the approaches discussed in the following list are helpful for treating insomnia (Nau & Lichstein, 2005):

1. **Stimulus control.** Insisting on a regular schedule helps establish a firm body rhythm, greatly improving sleep. This is best achieved by exercising **stimulus control,** which refers to linking a response with specific stimuli. It is important to get up and go to sleep at the same time each day, including weekends (Bootzin & Epstein, 2000). In addition, insomniacs are told to avoid doing anything but sleeping when they are in bed. They are not to study, eat, watch TV, read, pay the bills, worry, or even think in bed. (Lovemaking is okay, however.) In this way, only sleeping and relaxation become associated with going to bed at specific times (Bootzin & Epstein, 2000).

2. **Sleep restriction.** Even if an entire night's sleep is missed, it is important not to sleep late in the morning, nap more than an hour, sleep during the evening, or go to bed early the following night. Instead, restricting sleep to normal bedtime hours avoids fragmenting sleep rhythms (Shneerson, 2005).

3. **Paradoxical intention.** Another helpful approach is to remove the pressures of *trying* to go to sleep. Instead, the goal becomes trying to keep the eyes open (in the dark) and stay awake as long as possible (Nau & Lichstein, 2005). This allows sleep to come unexpectedly and lowers performance anxiety (Espie, 2002).

4. **Relaxation.** Some insomniacs lower their arousal before sleep by using a physical or mental strategy for relaxing, such as progressive muscle relaxation, meditation, or blotting out worries with calming images. It is also helpful to schedule time in the early evening to write down worries or concerns and plan what to do about them the next day, in order to set them aside before going to bed.

> ## bridges
> Learning how to achieve deep relaxation is a highly useful skill. **See Chapter 15, pages 505–507, for more information.**

5. **Exercise.** Strenuous exercise during the day promotes sleep. It is best if done about 6 hours before bedtime (Maas, 1999). However, exercise in the evening is helpful only if it is very light.

6. **Food intake.** What you eat can affect how easily you get to sleep. Eating starchy foods increases the amount of *tryptophan* (TRIP-tuh-fan: an amino acid) reaching the brain. More tryptophan, in turn, increases the amount of serotonin in the brain, which is associated with relaxation, a positive mood, and sleepiness. Thus, to promote sleep, try eating a starchy snack, such as cookies, bread, pasta, oatmeal, pretzels, or dry cereal. If you really want to drop the bomb on insomnia, try eating a baked potato (which may be the world's largest sleeping pill!) (Sahelian, 1998).

7. **Stimulants.** Stimulants, such as coffee and cigarettes, should be avoided. It is also worth remembering that alcohol, although not a stimulant, impairs sleep quality.

Sleepwalking, Sleeptalking, and Sleepsex

Sleepsex? As strange as it may seem, many waking behaviors can be engaged in while asleep, such as driving a car, cooking, playing a musical instrument, and eating (Plazzi et al., 2005). The most famous, sleepwalking, is eerie and fascinating in its own right. **Somnambulists** (som-NAM-bue-lists: those who sleepwalk) avoid obstacles, descend stairways, and on rare occasions may step out of windows or in front of automobiles. Sleepwalkers have been observed jumping into lakes, urinating in garbage pails or closets (phew!), shuffling furniture around, and even brandishing weapons (Schenck & Mahowald, 2005).

The sleepwalker's eyes are usually open, but a blank face and shuffling feet reveal that the person is still asleep. If you find someone sleepwalking, you should gently guide the person back to bed. Awakening a sleepwalker does no harm, but it is not necessary.

Does sleepwalking occur during dreaming? No. Remember that people are normally immobilized during REM sleep. EEG studies have shown that somnambulism occurs during NREM stages 3 and 4 (Stein & Ferber, 2001). Sleeptalking also occurs mostly during NREM sleep. The link with deep sleep explains why sleeptalking makes little sense and why sleepwalkers are confused and remember little when awakened (DSM-IV-TR, 2000).

Oh, yes, you're curious about sleepsex. There is, of course, an official name for it: *sexsomnia* (Shapiro, Trajanovic, & Fedoroff, 2003). Sexsomnia is not as exciting as it might sound: Just imagine being startled wide awake by your bed partner, who is asleep but attempting to have sex with you (Mangan, 2004).

Nightmares and Night Terrors

Stage 4 sleep is also the realm of night terrors. These frightening episodes are quite different from ordinary nightmares (● Table 6.2). A **nightmare** is simply a bad dream that takes place during REM sleep. Frequently occurring nightmares (one a week or more) are associated with higher levels of psychological distress (Levin & Fireman, 2002). During stage 4 **night terrors,** a person suffers total panic and may hallucinate frightening dream images into the bedroom. An attack may last 15 or 20 minutes. When it is over, the person awakens drenched in sweat but only vaguely remembers the terror. Because night terrors occur during NREM sleep (when

Table 6.2 ● Was It a Nightmare or a Night Terror?

	Nightmare	Night Terror
Stage of sleep	REM	NREM
Activity	Slight or no movement	Violent body movement, sits up, cries out, may run
Emotion	Fear or anxiety	Terror and disorganizing panic
Mental state when awakened	Coherent, can be calmed	Incoherent, disoriented, cannot be calmed, may be hallucinating
Physiological changes	No perspiration	Perspires heavily
Recall	Dream activity usually remembered	Amnesia for episode

the body is not immobilized), victims may sit up, scream, get out of bed, or run around the room. Victims remember little afterward. (Other family members, however, may have a story to tell.) Night terrors are most common in childhood, but they continue to plague about 2 out of every 100 adults (Kataria, 2004; Ohayon, Guilleminault, & Priest, 1999).

How to Eliminate a Nightmare

Is there any way to stop a recurring nightmare? A bad nightmare can be worse than any horror movie. It's easy to leave a theater, but we often remain trapped in terrifying dreams. Nevertheless, most nightmares can be banished by following three simple steps. First, write down your nightmare, describing it in detail. Next, change the dream any way you wish, being sure to spell out the details of the new dream. The third step is *imagery rehearsal,* in which you mentally rehearse the changed dream before you fall asleep again (Krakow & Zadra, 2006). Imagery rehearsal may work because it makes upsetting dreams familiar while a person is awake and feeling safe. Or perhaps it mentally "reprograms" future dream content. In any case, the technique has helped many people.

Sleep Apnea

Some sage once said, "Laugh and the whole world laughs with you; snore and you sleep alone." Nightly "wood sawing" is often harmless, but it can signal a serious problem. A person who snores loudly, with short silences and loud gasps or snorts, may suffer from apnea (AP-nee-ah: interrupted breathing). In **sleep apnea,** breathing stops for periods of 20 seconds to 2 minutes. As the need for oxygen becomes intense, the person wakes a little and gulps in air. She or he then settles back to sleep. But soon, breathing stops again. This cycle is repeated hundreds of times a night. As you might guess, apnea victims are extremely sleepy during the day (Collop, 2005).

What causes sleep apnea? Some cases occur because the brain stops sending signals to the diaphragm to maintain breathing. Another cause is blockage of the upper air passages. One of the

most effective treatments is the use of a continuous positive airway pressure (CPAP) mask to aid breathing during sleep. Other treatments include weight loss and surgery for breathing obstructions (Collop, 2005).

SIDS

Sleep apnea is suspected as one cause of **sudden infant death syndrome (SIDS),** or "crib death." Each year 2500 babies are victims of SIDS (NICHD, 2006). In the "typical" crib death, a slightly premature or small baby with some signs of a cold or cough is bundled up and put to bed. A short time later, parents find the child has died. A baby deprived of air will normally struggle to begin breathing again. However, SIDS babies seem to have a weak arousal reflex. This prevents them from changing positions and resuming breathing after an episode of apnea (Horne et al., 2001).

Babies at risk for SIDS must be carefully watched for the first 6 months of life. To aid parents in this task, a special monitor may be used that sounds an alarm when breathing or pulse becomes weak (● Figure 6.7). Babies at risk for SIDS are often premature; have a shrill, high-pitched cry; engage in "snoring," breath-holding, or frequent awakening at night; breathe mainly through an open mouth; or remain passive when their face rolls into a pillow or blanket.

Michael Newman/PhotoEdit

● Figure 6.7 Infants at risk for SIDS are often attached to devices that monitor breathing and heart rate during sleep. An alarm sounds to alert parents if either pulse or respiration falters. SIDS rarely occurs after an infant is 1 year old. Babies at risk for SIDS should be placed on their sides or on their backs.

Stimulus control Linking a particular response with specific stimuli.

Somnambulists People who sleepwalk; occurs during NREM sleep.

Nightmare A bad dream that occurs during REM sleep.

Night terror A state of panic during NREM sleep.

Sleep apnea Repeated interruption of breathing during sleep.

Sudden infant death syndrome (SIDS) The sudden, unexplained death of an apparently healthy infant.

"Back to Sleep"

Sleeping position is another major risk factor for SIDS. Healthy infants are better off sleeping on their backs or sides. (Premature babies, those with respiratory problems, and those who often vomit may need to sleep facedown. Ask a pediatrician for guidance.) Remember, "*back* to sleep" is the safest position for most infants (Hauck et al., 2002). It is also worth eliminating soft objects such as pillows, quilts, comforters, or sheepskins from the baby's bed.

Narcolepsy

One of the most dramatic sleep problems is **narcolepsy** (NAR-koe-lep-see), or sudden, irresistible sleep attacks. These last anywhere from a few minutes to a half hour. Victims may fall asleep while standing, talking, or even driving. Emotional excitement, especially laughter, commonly triggers narcolepsy. (Tell an especially good joke and a narcoleptic may fall asleep.) More than half of all victims also suffer from **cataplexy** (CAT-uh-plex-see), a sudden temporary paralysis of the muscles, leading to complete body collapse. It's easy to understand why narcolepsy can devastate careers and relationships (Thorpy, 2006).

Because sudden paralysis happens during dreaming, is there a connection between narcolepsy and REM sleep? Yes, narcoleptics tend to fall directly into REM sleep. Thus, the narcoleptic's sleep attacks and paralysis appear to occur when REM sleep intrudes into the waking state (Mignot, 2001).

Fortunately, narcolepsy is rare. It runs in families, which suggests that it is hereditary (Chabas et al., 2003). In fact, this has been confirmed by breeding several generations of narcoleptic dogs. (These dogs, by the way, are simply outstanding at learning the trick "Roll over and play dead.") There is no known cure for narcolepsy, but a drug named sodium oxybate reduces the frequency and intensity of attacks (Thorpy, 2006).

● Dreams—A Separate Reality?

Gateway Question: Do dreams have meaning?

When REM sleep was discovered in 1952, it ushered in a "Golden Era" of dream inquiry. To conclude our discussion of sleep, let's consider some age-old questions about dreaming.

Does everyone dream? Do dreams occur in an instant? Most people dream four or five times a night, but not all people remember their dreams. "Nondreamers" are often surprised by their dreams when first awakened during REM sleep. Dreams are usually spaced about 90 minutes apart. The first dream lasts only about 10 minutes; the last averages 30 minutes and may run as long as 50. Dreams, therefore, occur in real time, not as a "flash" (Shafton, 1995).

REM Sleep Revisited

How important is REM sleep? To answer this question, sleep expert William Dement awakened volunteers each time they entered REM sleep. Soon, their need for "dream time" grew more urgent.

By the fifth night, many had to be awakened 20 or 30 times to prevent REM sleep. When the volunteers were finally allowed to sleep undisturbed, they dreamed extra amounts. This effect, called a **REM rebound,** explains why alcoholics have horrible nightmares after they quit drinking. Alcohol reduces sleep quality by suppressing REM sleep, thus setting up a powerful rebound when it is withdrawn (Stein & Friedmann, 2005).

Dement's volunteers complained of memory lapses, poor concentration, and anxiety. For a while, it was thought that people deprived of REM sleep might go crazy. But later experiments showed that missing *any* sleep stage can cause a rebound for that stage. In general, daytime disturbances are related to the *total amount* of sleep lost, not to the *type* of sleep lost (Devoto et al., 1999).

Dream Theories

How meaningful are dreams? Some theorists believe that dreams have deeply hidden meanings. Others regard dreams as nearly meaningless. Yet others hold that dreams reflect our waking thoughts, fantasies, and emotions (Beck, 2004). Let's examine all three views.

Psychodynamic Dream Theory

Psychodynamic theories of dreaming emphasize internal conflicts and unconscious forces. Sigmund Freud's landmark book, *The Interpretation of Dreams* (1900), first advanced the idea that many dreams are based on **wish fulfillment** (an expression of unconscious desires). One of Freud's key proposals was that dreams express unconscious desires and conflicts as disguised **dream symbols** (images that have deeper symbolic meaning). Understanding a dream, then, requires analyzing the dream's **manifest content** (obvious, visible meaning) to uncover its **latent content** (hidden, symbolic meaning).

For instance, a woman who dreams of stealing her best friend's wedding ring and placing it on her own hand may be unwilling to consciously admit that she is sexually attracted to her best friend's husband. Similarly, a journey might symbolize death, and horseback riding or dancing, sexual intercourse.

> bridges
> Interpreting dreams is an important part of Freudian psychoanalysis. **See Chapter 15, pages 498–500.**

Do all dreams have hidden meanings? Probably not. Freud realized that some dreams are trivial "day residues" or carryovers from ordinary waking events. On the other hand, dreams do tend to reflect a person's current concerns, so Freud wasn't entirely wrong.

The Activation-Synthesis Hypothesis

Psychiatrists Allan Hobson and Robert McCarley have a radically different view of dreaming, called the **activation-synthesis hypothesis.** They believe that during REM sleep several lower brain centers are "turned on" *(activated)* in more or less random

According to psychodynamic theory, dream imagery often has symbolic meaning. How would you interpret French artist Henri Rousseau's dreamlike image, titled *The Dream*? The fact that dreams don't have a single unambiguous meaning is one of the shortcomings of Freudian dream theory.

fashion. However, messages from the cells are blocked from reaching the body, so no movement occurs. Nevertheless, the cells continue to tell higher brain areas of their activities. Struggling to interpret this random information, the brain searches through stored memories and manufactures *(synthesizes)* a dream (Hobson, 2000; 2005). However, frontal areas of the cortex, which control higher mental abilities, are mostly shut down during REM sleep. This explains why dreams are more primitive and more bizarre than daytime thoughts (Hobson, 2000).

How does that help explain dream content? According to the activation-synthesis hypothesis, dreams are basically meaningless. Let's use the classic chase dream as an example. In such dreams we feel we are running but not going anywhere. This occurs because the brain is told the body is running, but it gets no feedback from the motionless legs. To try to make sense of this information, the brain creates a chase drama. A similar process probably explains dreams of floating or flying.

So dreams have no meaning? The activation-synthesis hypothesis doesn't rule out the idea that dreams have some meaning. Because dreams are created from memories and past experiences, parts of dreams can sometimes reflect each person's mental life, emotions, and concerns (Hobson, 2000).

Neurocognitive Dream Theory

William Domhoff offers a third view of dreaming. According to his **neurocognitive dream theory,** dreams actually have much in common with waking thoughts and emotions. Most dreams reflect ordinary waking concerns. Domhoff believes this is true because many brain areas that are active when we are awake remain active during dreaming (Domhoff, 2001; 2003; 2005). From this perspective, our dreams are a conscious expression of REM sleep processes that are sorting and storing daily experiences. Thus, we shouldn't be surprised if a student who is angry at a teacher dreams of embarrassing the teacher in class, a lonely person dreams of romance, or a hungry child dreams of food. It is not necessary to seek deep symbolic meanings to understand these dreams.

Dream Worlds

Which dream theory is the most widely accepted? Each theory has strengths and weaknesses. However, studies of dream content do support neurocognitive theory's focus on the continuity between dreams and waking thought. Rather than being exotic or bizarre, most dreams reflect everyday events (Hall, 1966; Pesant & Zadra, 2006). For example, athletes tend to dream about the previous day's athletic activities (Erlacher & Schredl, 2004). In general, the favorite dream setting is a familiar room in a house. Action usually takes place between the dreamer and two or three other emotionally important people—friends, enemies, loved ones, or employers. Dream actions are also mostly familiar: running, jumping, riding, sitting, talking, and watching. About half of all dreams have sexual elements. Dreams of flying, floating, and falling occur less frequently. However, note that such dreams lend some support to the activation-synthesis hypothesis, because they are not everyday events. (Unless you are a trapeze artist.)

Are most dreams happy or sad? If you ask people in the morning what they dreamed about, they mention more unpleasant emotions than pleasant emotions (Merritt et al., 1994). However, it may be that dreams of fear, anger, or sadness are easier to remember. When people are awakened during REM sleep, they report equal numbers of positive and negative emotions (Fosse, Stickgold, & Hobson, 2001).

Even if many dreams can be viewed as just a different form of thought, many psychologists continue to believe that some dreams have deeper meaning (White & Taytroe, 2003; Wilkinson, 2006). There seems to be little doubt that dreams can make a difference in our lives: Veteran sleep researcher William Dement once dreamed that he had lung cancer. In the dream a doctor told Dement he would die soon. At the time, Dement was smoking two packs of cigarettes a day. He says, "I will never

Narcolepsy A sudden, irresistible sleep attack.

Cataplexy A sudden temporary paralysis of the muscles.

REM rebound The occurrence of extra rapid eye movement sleep following REM sleep deprivation.

Psychodynamic theory Any theory of behavior that emphasizes internal conflicts, motives, and unconscious forces.

Wish fulfillment Freudian belief that many dreams express unconscious desires.

Dream symbols Images in dreams that serve as visible signs of hidden ideas, desires, impulses, emotions, relationships, and so forth.

Manifest dream content The surface, "visible" content of a dream; dream images as they are remembered by the dreamer.

Latent dream content The hidden or symbolic meaning of a dream, as revealed by dream interpretation and analysis.

Activation-synthesis hypothesis An attempt to explain how random activity in lower brain centers results in the manufacture of relatively bizarre dreams by higher brain centers.

Neurocognitive dream theory Proposal that dreams reflect everyday waking thoughts and emotions.

forget the surprise, joy, and exquisite relief of waking up. I felt reborn." Dement quit smoking the following day. (For more information about dreaming, see the Psychology in Action section later in this chapter.)

Sleep Disturbances and Dreaming

RECITE

1. Which of the following is *not* a behavioral remedy for insomnia?
   a. daily hypersomnia
   b. stimulus control
   c. progressive relaxation
   d. paradoxical intention
2. Eating a snack that is nearly all starch can promote sleep because it increases _____ in the brain.
   a. beta waves
   b. tryptophan
   c. EEG activity
   d. hypnic cycling
3. Night terrors, sleepwalking, and sleeptalking all occur during stage 1, NREM sleep. T or F?
4. Sleep _____ is suspected as one cause of SIDS.
5. People who suffer from sudden daytime sleep attacks have which sleep disorder?
   a. narcolepsy
   b. REM behavior disorder
   c. somnambulism
   d. sleep spindling
6. According to the activation-synthesis hypothesis of dreaming, dreams are constructed from _____ to explain messages received from nerve cells controlling eye movement, balance, and bodily activity.
7. The favored setting for dreams is
   a. work
   b. school
   c. outdoors or unfamiliar places
   d. familiar rooms
8. Sharpening memories and facilitating their storage is one function of
   a. activation-synthesis cycles
   b. REM sleep
   c. deep sleep
   d. NREM sleep

REFLECT

Critical Thinking

9. Even without being told that somnambulism is an NREM event, you could have predicted that sleepwalking doesn't occur during dreaming. Why?

Relate

Almost everyone suffers from insomnia at least occasionally. Are any of the techniques for combating insomnia similar to strategies you have discovered on your own?

How many sleep disturbances can you name (including those listed in ● Table 6.1)? Are there any that you have experienced? Which do you think would be most disruptive?

Do you think the activation-synthesis hypothesis provides an adequate explanation of your own dreams? Have you had dreams that seem to reflect Freudian wish fulfillment? Do you think your dreams have symbolic meaning or reflect everyday concerns?

Answers: 1. a **2.** b **3.** F **4.** apnea **5.** a **6.** memories **7.** d **8.** b **9.** Because people are immobilized during REM sleep and REM sleep is strongly associated with dreaming. This makes it unlikely that sleepwalkers are acting out dreams.

●● Hypnosis—Look into My Eyes

Gateway Question: What is hypnosis?

"Your body is becoming heavy. You can barely keep your eyes open. You are so tired you can't move. Relax. Let go. Relax. Close your eyes and relax." These are the last words a textbook should ever say to you, and the first a hypnotist might say.

Interest in hypnosis began in the 1700s with Austrian doctor Franz Mesmer, whose name gave us the term *mesmerize* (to hypnotize). Mesmer believed he could cure disease with magnets. Mesmer's strange "treatments" are related to hypnosis because they actually relied on the power of suggestion, not magnetism (Waterfield, 2002). For a time, Mesmer enjoyed quite a following. In the end, however, his theories of "animal magnetism" were rejected and he was branded a fraud.

The term *hypnosis* was later coined by English surgeon James Braid. The Greek word *hypnos* means "sleep," and Braid used it to describe the hypnotic state. Today we know that hypnosis is *not* sleep. Confusion about this point remains because some hypnotists give the suggestion, "Sleep, sleep." However, EEG patterns recorded during hypnosis are different from those observed when a person is asleep or pretending to be hypnotized (Barabasz, 2000).

Theories of Hypnosis

If hypnosis isn't sleep, then what is it? That's a good question. **Hypnosis** is often defined as an altered state of consciousness, characterized by narrowed attention and an increased openness to suggestion (Kallio & Revonsuo, 2003; Kosslyn et al., 2000). Notice that this definition assumes hypnosis is a distinct state of consciousness.

The best-known *state theory* of hypnosis was proposed by Ernest Hilgard (1904–2001), who argued that hypnosis causes a *dissociative state,* or "split" in awareness. To illustrate, he asked hypnotized subjects to plunge one hand into a painful bath of ice water. Subjects told to feel no pain said they felt none. The same subjects were then asked if there was any part of their mind that did feel pain. With their free hand, many wrote, "It hurts," or "Stop it, you're hurting me," while they continued to act pain-free (Hilgard, 1977, 1994). Thus, one part of the hypnotized person says there is no pain and acts as if there is none. Another part, which Hilgard calls the *hidden observer,* is aware of the pain but remains in the background. The **hidden observer** is a detached part of the hypnotized person's awareness that silently observes events.

In contrast, *nonstate theorists* argue that hypnosis is not a distinct state at all. Instead it is merely a blend of conformity, relaxation, imagination, obedience, and role-playing (Kirsch, 2005). For example, many theorists believe that all hypnosis is really self-hypnosis *(autosuggestion)*. From this perspective, a hypnotist merely helps another person to follow a series of suggestions. These suggestions, in turn, alter sensations, perceptions, thoughts, feelings, and behaviors (Lynn & Kirsch, 2006). (See "Swinging Suggestions.")

DISCOVERING PSYCHOLOGY

Swinging Suggestions

Here's a demonstration you can use to gain insight into hypnosis. Tie a short length of string (about 6 inches) to a small, heavy object, such as a ring or a small metal nut. Hold the ring at eye level, about a foot from your face. Concentrate on the ring and notice that it will begin to move, ever so slightly. As it does, focus all your attention on the ring. Narrow your attention to a beam of energy and mentally push the ring away from you. Each time the ring swings away, push on it, using only mental force. Then release it and let it swing back toward you. Continue to mentally push and release the ring until it is swinging freely. For the best results, try this now, before reading more.

Did the ring move? If it did, you used *autosuggestion* to influence your own behavior in a subtle way. Suggestions that the ring would swing caused your hand to make tiny micromuscular movements. These, in turn, caused the ring to move—no special mental powers or supernatural forces are involved.

As is true of hypnotic suggestion, the ring's movement probably seemed to be automatic. Obviously, you could just intentionally swing the ring. However, if you responded to suggestion, the movement seemed to happen without any effort on your part. In the same way, when people are hypnotized, their actions seem to occur without any voluntary intent. Incidentally, autosuggestion likely underlies other phenomena, such as how Ouija boards answer questions without any conscious movements by the person using the pointer.

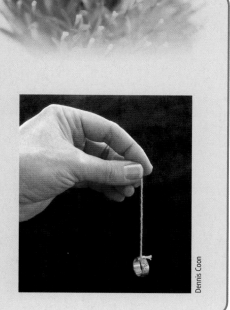
Dennis Coon

Regardless of which theoretical approach finally prevails, both views suggest that hypnosis can be explained by normal principles. It is not mysterious or "magical," despite what stage hypnotists might have you think.

The Reality of Hypnosis

How is hypnosis done? Hypnotists use many different methods. Still, all techniques encourage a person (1) to focus attention on what is being said, (2) to relax and feel tired, (3) to "let go" and accept suggestions easily, and (4) to use vivid imagination (Druckman & Bjork, 1994). Basically, you must cooperate to become hypnotized.

What does it feel like to be hypnotized? You might be surprised at some of your actions during hypnosis. You also might have mild feelings of floating, sinking, anesthesia, or separation from your body. Personal experiences vary widely. A key element in hypnosis is the **basic suggestion effect** (a tendency of hypnotized persons to carry out suggested actions as if they were involuntary). Hypnotized persons feel like their actions and experiences are *automatic*—they seem to happen without effort. Here is how one person described his hypnotic session:

> I felt lethargic, my eyes going out of focus and wanting to close. My hands felt real light. . . . I felt I was sinking deeper into the chair. . . . I felt like I wanted to relax more and more. . . . My responses were more automatic. I didn't have to *wish* to do things so much or *want* to do them. . . . I just did them. . . . I felt floating . . . very close to sleep. (Hilgard, 1968)

Could I be hypnotized against my will? Contrary to the way hypnosis is portrayed in movies, hypnotized people generally remain in control of their behavior and aware of what is going on. For instance, most people will not act out hypnotic suggestions that they consider immoral or repulsive (such as disrobing in public or harming someone) (Kirsch & Lynn, 1995).

Hypnotic Susceptibility

Can everyone be hypnotized? About 8 people out of 10 can be hypnotized, but only 4 out of 10 will be good hypnotic subjects. People who are imaginative and prone to fantasy are often highly responsive to hypnosis (Kallio & Revonsuo, 2003). But people who lack these traits may also be hypnotized. If you are willing to be hypnotized, chances are good that you could be. Hypnosis depends more on the efforts and abilities of the hypnotized person than the skills of the hypnotist. But make no mistake; people who are hypnotized are not merely faking their responses.

Hypnotic susceptibility refers to how easily a person can become hypnotized. It is measured by giving a series of suggestions and counting the number of times a person responds. A typical hypnotic test is the *Stanford Hypnotic Susceptibility Scale*, shown

Hypnosis An altered state of consciousness characterized by narrowed attention and increased suggestibility.

Hidden observer A detached part of the hypnotized person's awareness that silently observes events.

Basic suggestion effect The tendency of hypnotized persons to carry out suggested actions as if they were involuntary.

Hypnotic susceptibility One's capacity for becoming hypnotized.

Table 6.3 ● Stanford Hypnotic Susceptibility Scale

Suggested Behavior	Criterion of Passing
1. Postural sway	Falls without forcing
2. Eye closure	Closes eyes without forcing
3. Hand lowering (left)	Lowers at least 6 inches by end of 10 seconds
4. Immobilization (right arm)	Arm rises less than 1 inch in 10 seconds
5. Finger lock	Incomplete separation of fingers at end of 10 seconds
6. Arm rigidity (left arm)	Less than 2 inches of arm bending in 10 seconds
7. Hands moving together	Hands at least as close as 6 inches after 10 seconds
8. Verbal inhibition (name)	Name unspoken in 10 seconds
9. Hallucination (fly)	Any movement, grimacing, acknowledgment of effect
10. Eye catalepsy	Eyes remain closed at end of 10 seconds
11. Posthypnotic (changes chairs)	Any partial movement response
12. Amnesia test	Three or fewer items recalled

Adapted from Weitzenhoffer & Hilgard, 1959.

in ● Table 6.3. In the test, various suggestions are made, and the person's response is noted. For instance, you might be told that your left arm is becoming more and more rigid and that it will not bend. If you can't bend your arm during the next 10 seconds, you have shown susceptibility to hypnotic suggestions. (Also see ● Figure 6.8.)

● **Figure 6.8** In one test of hypnotizability, subjects attempt to pull their hands apart after hearing suggestions that their fingers are "locked" together.

Effects of Hypnosis

What can (and cannot) be achieved with hypnosis? Many abilities have been tested during hypnosis, leading to the following conclusions (Burgess & Kirsch, 1999; Chaves, 2000):

1. **Superhuman acts of strength.** Hypnosis has no more effect on physical strength than instructions that encourage a person to make his or her best effort.
2. **Memory.** There is some evidence that hypnosis can enhance memory (Wagstaff et al., 2004). However, it frequently increases the number of false memories as well. For this reason, many states now bar persons from testifying in court if they were hypnotized to improve their memory of a crime they witnessed.

> **bridges**
> Should the police use hypnosis to enhance the memories of witnesses? The evidence generally says no. **See Chapter 8, page 258.**

3. **Amnesia.** A person told not to remember something heard during hypnosis may claim not to remember. In some instances this may be nothing more than a deliberate attempt to avoid thinking about specific ideas. However, brief memory loss of this type actually does seem to occur (Barnier, McConkey, & Wright, 2004).
4. **Pain relief.** Hypnosis can relieve pain (Keefe, Abernethy, & Campbell, 2005). It can be especially useful when chemical painkillers are ineffective. For instance, hypnosis can reduce phantom limb pain (Oakley, Whitman, & Halligan, 2002). (As discussed in Chapter 4, amputees sometimes feel phantom pain that seems to come from a missing limb.)
5. **Age regression.** Given the proper suggestions, some hypnotized people appear to "regress" to childhood. However, most theorists now believe that "age-regressed" subjects are only acting out a suggested role.
6. **Sensory changes.** Hypnotic suggestions concerning sensations are among the most effective. Given the proper instructions, a person can be made to smell a small bottle of ammonia and respond as if it were a wonderful perfume. It is also possible to alter color vision, hearing sensitivity, time sense, perception of illusions, and many other sensory responses.

Hypnosis is a valuable tool. It can help people relax, feel less pain, and make better progress in therapy (Chapman, 2006). Generally, hypnosis is more successful at changing subjective experience than it is at modifying behaviors such as smoking or overeating.

Stage Hypnosis

On stage the hypnotist intones, "When I count to three, you will imagine that you are on a train to Disneyland and growing younger and younger as the train approaches." Responding to these suggestions, grown men and women begin to giggle and squirm like children on their way to a circus.

How do stage entertainers use hypnosis to get people to do strange things? They don't. Little or no hypnosis is needed to do a good hypnosis act. **Stage hypnosis** is often merely a simulation of hypnotic effects. Stage hypnotists make use of several features of the stage setting to perform their act (Barber, 2000).

1. **Waking suggestibility.** We are all more or less open to suggestion, but on stage people are unusually cooperative because they don't want to "spoil the act." As a result, they will readily follow almost any instruction given by the entertainer.
2. **Selection of responsive subjects.** Participants in stage hypnotism (all *volunteers*) are first "hypnotized" as a group. Then, anyone who doesn't yield to instructions is eliminated.
3. **The hypnosis label disinhibits.** Once a person has been labeled "hypnotized," she or he can sing, dance, act silly, or whatever, without fear or embarrassment. On stage, being "hypnotized" takes away personal responsibility for one's actions.
4. **The hypnotist as a "director."** After volunteers loosen up and respond to a few suggestions, they find that they are suddenly the stars of the show. Audience response to the antics on stage brings out the "ham" in many people. All the "hypnotist" needs to do is direct the action.
5. **The stage hypnotist uses tricks.** Stage hypnosis is about 50 percent taking advantage of the situation and 50 percent deception. One of the more impressive stage tricks is to rigidly suspend a person between two chairs. This is astounding only because the audience does not question it. Anyone can do it, as is shown in the photographs and instructions in ● Figure 6.9. Try it!

● **Figure 6.9** Arrange three chairs as shown. Have someone recline as shown. Ask him to lift slightly while you remove the middle chair. Accept the applause gracefully! (Concerning hypnosis and similar phenomena, the moral, of course, is, "Suspend judgment until you have something solid to stand on.")

To summarize, hypnosis is real, and it can significantly alter private experience. Hypnosis is a useful tool in a variety of settings. Nightclubs, however, are not one of these settings. Stage "hypnotists" entertain; they rarely hypnotize.

●● Meditation and Sensory Deprivation— Chilling, the Healthy Way

Gateway Question: Do meditation and sensory deprivation have any benefits?

Throughout history, meditation and sensory deprivation have been widely used as a means of altering consciousness through deep relaxation. Let's see what they have in common and how they differ.

Meditation

Meditation is a mental exercise used to alter consciousness. In general, meditation focuses attention and interrupts the typical flow of thoughts, worries, and analysis. People who use meditation to reduce stress often report less daily physical tension and anxiety (Andresen, 2000). Brain scans (positron emission tomography [PET] and functional magnetic resonance imaging [fMRI]) reveal changes in the activity of the frontal lobes during meditation, which suggests that it may be a distinct state of consciousness (Cahn & Polich, 2006; Farb et al., 2007).

Meditation takes two major forms. In **concentrative meditation,** you attend to a single focal point, such as an object, a thought, or your own breathing. In contrast, **mindfulness meditation** is "open," or expansive. In this case, you widen your attention to embrace a total, nonjudgmental awareness of the world (Lazar, 2005). An example is losing all self-consciousness while walking in the wilderness with a quiet and receptive mind. Although it may not seem so, mindfulness meditation is more difficult to attain than concentrative meditation. For this reason, we will discuss concentrative meditation as a practical self-control method.

Performing Concentrative Meditation

How is concentrative meditation done? The basic idea is to sit still and quietly focus on some external object or on a repetitive internal stimulus, such as your own breathing or humming (Blackmore, 2004). As an alternative, you can silently repeat a *mantra* (a word used as the focus of attention in concentrative meditation). Typi-

---

Stage hypnosis Use of hypnosis to entertain; often, merely a simulation of hypnosis for that purpose.

Meditation A mental exercise for producing relaxation or heightened awareness.

Concentrative meditation Mental exercise based on attending to a single object or thought.

Mindfulness meditation Mental exercise based on widening attention to become aware of everything experienced at any given moment.

cal mantras are smooth, flowing sounds that are easily repeated. A widely used mantra is the word "om." A mantra could also be any pleasant word or a phrase from a familiar song, poem, or prayer. If other thoughts arise as you repeat a mantra, just return attention to it as often as necessary to maintain meditation.

The Relaxation Response

The benefits of meditation include lowered heart rate, blood pressure, muscle tension, and other signs of stress (Lazar et al., 2000). Medical researcher Herbert Benson believes that the core of meditation is the **relaxation response**—an innate physiological pattern that opposes your body's fight-or-flight mechanisms. Benson feels, quite simply, that most of us have forgotten how to relax deeply. People in his experiments learned to produce the relaxation response by following these instructions:

> Sit quietly and comfortably. Close your eyes. Relax your muscles, beginning at your feet and progressing up to your head. Relax them deeply. Become aware of breathing through your nose. As you breathe out, say a word like "peace" silently to yourself. Don't worry about how successful you are in relaxing deeply. Just let relaxation happen at its own pace. Don't be surprised by distracting thoughts. When they occur, ignore them and continue repeating "peace." (Adapted from Benson, 1977; Lazar et al., 2000)

As a stress-control technique, meditation may be a good choice for people who find it difficult to "turn off" upsetting thoughts when they need to relax. In one study, a group of college students who received just 90 minutes of training in the relaxation response experienced greatly reduced stress levels (Deckro et al., 2002). The physical benefits of meditation include lowered heart rate, blood pressure, muscle tension, and other signs of stress (Lazar et al., 2000), as well as improved immune system activity (Davidson et al., 2003).

According to Shauna Shapiro and Roger Walsh (2006), meditation has benefits beyond relaxation. Practiced regularly, meditation may foster mental well-being and positive mental skills such as clarity, concentration, and calm. In this sense, meditation may share much in common with psychotherapy. Indeed, research has shown that mindfulness meditation relieves a variety of psychological disorders, from insomnia to anxiety disorders. It can also reduce aggression and the illegal use of psychoactive drugs (Shapiro & Walsh, 2006). Regular meditation may even help people develop self-awareness and maturity (Travis, Arenander, & DuBois, 2004).

Sensory Deprivation

The relaxation response can also be produced by brief sensory deprivation. **Sensory deprivation** (**SD**) refers to any major reduction in the amount or variety of sensory stimulation.

What happens when stimulation is greatly reduced? A hint comes from reports by prisoners in solitary confinement, arctic explorers, high-altitude pilots, long-distance truck drivers, and radar operators. When faced with limited or monotonous stimulation, people sometimes have bizarre sensations, dangerous lapses

● **Figure 6.10** A sensory isolation chamber. Small flotation tanks like the one pictured have been used by psychologists to study the effects of mild sensory deprivation. Subjects float in darkness and silence. The shallow body-temperature water contains hundreds of pounds of Epsom salts so that subjects float near the surface. Mild sensory deprivation produces deep relaxation.

in attention, and wildly distorted perceptions. Intense or prolonged SD is stressful and disorienting. Yet, oddly enough, brief periods of sensory restriction can be very relaxing.

Psychologists have explored the possible benefits of sensory restriction using small isolation tanks like the one pictured in ● Figure 6.10. An hour or two spent in a flotation tank, for instance, causes a large drop in blood pressure, muscle tension, and other signs of stress (van Dierendonck & Te Nijenhuis, 2005). Of course, it could be argued that a warm bath has the same effect. Nevertheless, brief sensory deprivation appears to be one of the surest ways to induce deep relaxation (Suedfeld & Borrie, 1999).

Like meditation, sensory restriction may also help with more than relaxation. Mild sensory deprivation can help people quit smoking, lose weight, and reduce their use of alcohol and drugs (van Dierendonck & Te Nijenhuis, 2005). Psychologist Peter Suedfeld calls such benefits **Restricted Environmental Stimulation Therapy** (**REST**). Deep relaxation makes people more open to suggestion, and sensory restriction interrupts habitual behavior patterns. As a result, REST can "loosen" belief systems and make it easier to change bad habits (Suedfeld & Borrie, 1999).

REST also shows promise as a way to stimulate creative thinking (Norlander, Bergman, & Archer, 1998). Other researchers have reported that REST sessions can enhance performance in skilled sports, such as gymnastics, tennis, basketball, darts, and marksmanship (Druckman & Bjork, 1994; Norlander, Bergman, & Archer, 1999). There is also evidence that REST can relieve chronic pain and reduce stress (Bood et al., 2006). Clearly, there is much yet to be learned from studying "nothingness."

Summary

To summarize, research suggests that meditation and mild sensory deprivation are ways to elicit the relaxation response. For many people, sitting quietly and "resting" can be as effective. Similar stress reduction occurs when people set aside time daily to engage in other restful activities, such as muscle relaxation, positive daydreaming, and even leisure reading. However, if you are the type of person who finds it difficult to ignore upsetting thoughts, then concentrative meditation might be a good way to promote relaxation. Practiced regularly, meditation and REST may even help improve overall mental health—something almost everyone could use in our fast-paced society.

Positive Psychology: Mindfulness and Well-Being

Did you "space out" anytime today? Most of us have occasional moments of reduced awareness. **Mindfulness** is the opposite of such mindless moments: It involves an open, nonjudgmental awareness of current experience. In other words, mindfulness is similar to the state that people who practice receptive meditation are trying to achieve. A person who is mindful is fully present, moment-by-moment. She or he is acutely aware of every thought, emotion, or sensation, but does not judge it or react to it. The person is fully "awake" and attuned to immediate reality.

Psychologists interested in positive mental states have begun to study the effects of mindfulness. For example, cancer patients who are taught mindfulness meditation have lower levels of distress and a greater sense of well-being. Such benefits apply to healthy people, too. In general, mindfulness is associated with self-knowledge and well-being (Brown & Ryan, 2003). Anyone who has a tendency to sleepwalk through life—and that's most of us at times—would be wise to be mindful of the value of mindfulness.

KNOWLEDGE BUILDER
Hypnosis, Meditation, and Sensory Deprivation

RECITE

1. In Ernest Hilgard's dissociative state theory of hypnosis, awareness is split between normal consciousness and
   a. disinhibition
   b. autosuggestion
   c. memory
   d. the hidden observer
2. Tests of hypnotic susceptibility measure a person's tendency to respond to
   a. suggestion
   b. imagery rehearsal
   c. stimulus control techniques
   d. the activation-synthesis effect
3. Which of the following can most definitely be achieved with hypnosis?
   a. unusual strength
   b. pain relief
   c. improved memory
   d. sleep-like brainwaves
4. The focus of attention in concentrative meditation is "open," or expansive. T or F?
5. Mantras are words said silently to oneself to end a session of meditation. T or F?
6. Which terms do not belong together?
   a. concentrative meditation—relaxation response
   b. mindfulness meditation—mantra
   c. sensory deprivation—REST
   d. meditation—alter consciousness
7. The most immediate benefit of meditation appears to be its capacity for producing the relaxation response. T or F?
8. Prolonged periods of extreme sensory deprivation lower anxiety and induce deep relaxation. T or F?

REFLECT

Critical Thinking

9. What kind of control group would you need in order to identify the true effects of hypnosis?

10. Regular meditators report lower levels of stress and a greater sense of well-being. What other explanations must we eliminate before this effect can be regarded as genuine?

Relate

How have your beliefs about hypnosis changed after reading the preceding section? Can you think of specific examples in which hypnosis was misrepresented, such as in high school assemblies, stage acts, movies, or TV dramas?

Various activities can produce the relaxation response. When do you experience states of deep relaxation, coupled with a sense of serene awareness? What similarities do these occurrences have to meditation?

Have you experienced any form of sensory restriction or sensory deprivation? How did you react? Would you be willing to try REST in order to break a bad habit?

Answers: 1. d **2.** a **3.** b **4.** F **5.** F **6.** b **7.** T **8.** F **9.** Most experiments on hypnosis include a control group in which people are asked to simulate being hypnotized. Without such controls, the tendency of subjects to cooperate with experimenters makes it difficult to identify true hypnotic effects. **10.** Studies on the effects of meditation must control for the placebo effect and the fact that those who choose to learn meditation may not be a representative sample of the general population.

⬤ Drug-Altered Consciousness— The High and Low of It

Gateway Question: What are the effects of the more commonly used psychoactive drugs?

The most common way to alter human consciousness is to administer a **psychoactive drug** (a substance capable of altering attention, judgment, memory, time sense, self-control, emotion, or perception). In fact, most Americans regularly use consciousness-altering drugs (don't forget that caffeine, alcohol, and nicotine are mildly psychoactive). Psychoactive drugs alter consciousness by directly influencing brain activity (Julien, 2005). (See "How Psychoactive Drugs Affect the Brain.") Many psychoactive drugs can be placed on a scale ranging from stimulation to depression (● Figure 6.11). A **stimulant** (upper) is a substance that increases activity in the body and nervous system. A **depressant** (downer) does the reverse.

Relaxation response The pattern of internal bodily changes that occurs at times of relaxation.

Sensory deprivation (SD) Any major reduction in the amount or variety of sensory stimulation.

Restricted Environmental Stimulation Therapy (REST) A form of sensory deprivation that results in a variety of psychological benefits.

Mindfulness A state of open, nonjudgmental awareness of current experience.

Psychoactive drug A substance capable of altering attention, memory, judgment, time sense, self-control, mood, or perception.

Stimulant (upper) A substance that increases activity in the body and nervous system.

Depressant (downer) A substance that decreases activity in the body and nervous system.

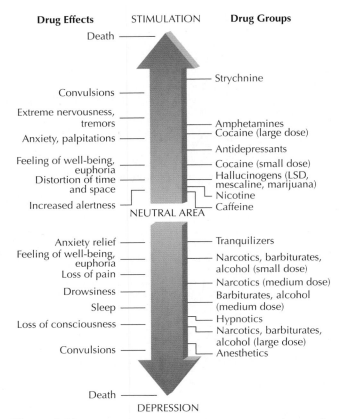

Drug Effects STIMULATION **Drug Groups**

Death ——

—— Strychnine

Convulsions ——

Extreme nervousness, tremors ——
—— Amphetamines
—— Cocaine (large dose)

Anxiety, palpitations ——
—— Antidepressants

Feeling of well-being, euphoria ——
—— Cocaine (small dose)

Distortion of time and space ——
—— Hallucinogens (LSD, mescaline, marijuana)
—— Nicotine

Increased alertness ——
—— Caffeine

NEUTRAL AREA

Anxiety relief ——
—— Tranquilizers

Feeling of well-being, euphoria ——
—— Narcotics, barbiturates, alcohol (small dose)

Loss of pain ——
—— Narcotics (medium dose)

Drowsiness ——
—— Barbiturates, alcohol (medium dose)

Sleep ——
—— Hypnotics

Loss of consciousness ——
—— Narcotics, barbiturates, alcohol (large dose)

Convulsions ——
—— Anesthetics

Death ——

DEPRESSION

● **Figure 6.11** Spectrum and continuum of drug action. Many drugs can be rated on a stimulation-depression scale according to their effects on the central nervous system. Although LSD, mescaline, and marijuana are listed here, the stimulation-depression scale is less relevant to these drugs. The principal characteristic of such hallucinogens is their mind-altering quality.

Because drugs that can ease pain, induce sleep, or end depression have a high potential for abuse, the more powerful psychoactive drugs are controlled substances (Goldberg, 2006). Nevertheless, more than 20 million Americans are currently illicit drug users (SAMHSA, 2005). Drug abuse has been one of the most persistent of all social problems in Western nations.

Why is drug abuse so common? People seek drug experiences for many reasons, ranging from curiosity and a desire to belong to a group, to a search for meaning or an escape from feelings of inadequacy. Many abusers turn to drugs in a self-defeating attempt to cope with life. All the frequently abused drugs produce immediate feelings of pleasure. The negative consequences follow much later. This combination of immediate pleasure and delayed punishment allows abusers to feel good on demand.

In time, of course, most of the pleasure goes out of drug abuse and the abuser's problems get worse. But if an abuser merely feels better (however briefly) after taking a drug, drug taking can become compulsive (Higgins, Heil, & Lussier, 2004). In contrast, people who stop using drugs often say that they quit because the drawbacks had come to exceed the benefits (Toneatto et al., 1999).

The best predictors of adolescent drug use and abuse are drug use by peers, parental drug use, delinquency, parental maladjust-

ment, poor self-esteem, social nonconformity, and stressful life changes. One study found that adolescents who abuse drugs tend to be maladjusted, alienated, impulsive, and emotionally distressed (Masse & Tremblay, 1997). Antisocial behavior, school failure, and risky sexual behavior are also commonly associated with drug abuse (Ary et al., 1999). Such patterns make it clear that taking drugs is a symptom, rather than a cause, of personal and social maladjustment (Ksir, Hart, & Ray, 2006).

Drug Dependence

Another reason why drug abuse is so common is that taking most psychoactive drugs tends to create dependencies. Once you get started, it can be hard to stop. Drug dependence falls into two broad categories. When a person compulsively uses a drug to maintain bodily comfort, a **physical dependence** (addiction) exists (Julien, 2005). Addiction occurs most often with drugs that cause **withdrawal symptoms** (physical illness that follows removal of a drug). Withdrawal from drugs such as alcohol, barbiturates, and opiates can cause violent flu-like symptoms of nausea, vomiting, diarrhea, chills, sweating, and cramps. Addiction is often accompanied by a **drug tolerance** (reduced response to a drug). This leads users to take larger and larger doses to get the desired effect.

Persons who develop a **psychological dependence** feel that a drug is necessary to maintain their comfort or well-being. Usually, they intensely crave the drug and its rewarding qualities (Winger et al., 2005). Psychological dependence can be just as powerful as physical addiction. That's why some psychologists define addiction as any compulsive habit pattern. By this definition, a person who has lost control over drug use, for whatever reason, is addicted. In fact, most people who answer yes to both of the following questions have an alcohol or drug problem and should seek professional help (Brown et al., 1997):

- In the last year, did you ever drink or use drugs more than you meant to?
- Have you felt you wanted or needed to cut down on your drinking or drug use in the last year?

Patterns of Abuse

Some drugs, of course, have a higher potential for abuse than others. Heroin is certainly more dangerous than caffeine. However, this is only one side of the picture. It can be as useful to classify drug-taking *behavior* as it is to rate drugs. For example, some people remain social drinkers for life, whereas others become alcoholics within weeks of taking their first drink (Robinson & Berridge, 2003). In this sense, drug use can be classified as *experimental* (short-term use based on curiosity), *social-recreational* (occasional social use for pleasure or relaxation), *situational* (use to cope with a specific problem, such as needing to stay awake), *intensive* (daily use with elements of dependence), or *compulsive* (intense use and extreme dependence). The last three categories of drug taking tend to be damaging no matter what drug is used.

BRAINWAVES

How Psychoactive Drugs Affect the Brain

Psychoactive drugs influence the activity of brain cells (Kalat, 2007). Typically, drugs imitate or alter the effects of neurotransmitters, the chemicals that carry messages between brain cells. Some drugs, such as Ecstasy, amphetamines, and some antidepressants, cause more neurotransmitters to be released, increasing the activity of brain cells. Other drugs, such as cocaine, slow the removal of neurotransmitters after they are released. This prolongs the action of transmitter chemicals and typically has a stimulating effect. Other drugs, such as nicotine and opiates, directly stimulate brain cells by mimicking neurotransmitters. Another possibility is illustrated by alcohol and tranquilizers. These drugs affect certain types of brain cells that cause relaxation and relieve anxiety. Some drugs fill receptor sites on brain cells and block incoming messages. Other possibilities also exist, which is why drugs can have such a wide variety of effects on the brain (Julien, 2005).

Nearly all addictive drugs stimulate the brain's reward circuitry, producing feelings of pleasure (Kalat, 2007). In particular, addictive drugs stimulate a brain region called the *nucleus accumbens* to release the neurotransmitter dopamine, which results in intensified feelings of pleasure (● Figure 6.12). As one expert put it, addictive drugs fool brain-reward pathways. "As a result, the reward pathway signals, 'That felt good. Let's do it again. Let's remember exactly how we did it.'" This creates a compulsion to repeat the drug experience. It's the hook that eventually snares the addict (Restak, 2001). In the end, the addictive drug physically changes the brain's reward circuitry, making it even harder for the addict to overcome his or her addiction (Robinson & Berridge, 2003). Adolescents are especially susceptible to addiction because brain systems that restrain their risk-taking are not as mature as those that reward pleasure seeking (Chambers, Taylor, & Potenza, 2003).

● **Figure 6.12** Addictive drugs increase dopamine activity in the medial forebrain bundle and the nucleus accumbens, stimulating the frontal cortex and giving rise to intensified feelings of pleasure.

Drugs of Abuse

Note in ● Table 6.4 that the drugs most likely to lead to physical dependence are alcohol, amphetamines, barbiturates, cocaine, codeine, heroin, methadone, morphine, and tobacco (nicotine). Using *any* of the drugs listed in ● Table 6.4 can result in psychological dependence. Note too that people who take drugs intravenously are at high risk for developing hepatitis and AIDS. The discussion that follows focuses on the drugs most often abused by students. A more complete summary of frequently abused psychoactive drugs is given in ● Table 6.4.

> bridges
> See Chapter 11, pages 379–380, for more information about AIDS.

Uppers—Amphetamines, Cocaine, MDMA, Caffeine, Nicotine

Amphetamines are synthetic stimulants. Common street names for amphetamine are "speed," "bennies," "dexies," "go," and "uppers." These drugs were once widely prescribed for weight loss or depression. Today, the main legitimate medical use of amphetamines is to treat childhood hyperactivity and overdoses of depressant drugs. Illicit use of amphetamines is widespread, however, especially by people seeking to stay awake and by those who think drugs can improve mental or physical performance (Iversen, 2006).

Methamphetamine is a more potent variation of amphetamine. It can be snorted, injected, or eaten. Of the various types of amphetamine, methamphetamine has created the largest drug problem. "Bergs," "glass," "meth," or "crystal," as it is known on the street, can be made cheaply in backyard labs and sold for massive profits. In addition to ruining lives through addiction, it has fueled a violent criminal subculture.

Physical dependence (addiction) Physical addiction, as indicated by the presence of drug tolerance and withdrawal symptoms.

Withdrawal symptoms Physical illness and discomfort following the withdrawal of a drug.

Drug tolerance A reduction in the body's response to a drug.

Psychological dependence Drug dependence that is based primarily on emotional or psychological needs.

Table 6.4 ● Comparison of Psychoactive Drugs

Name	Classification	Medical Use	Usual Dose	Duration of Effect
Alcohol	Sedative-hypnotic	Solvent, antiseptic	Varies	1–4 hours
Amphetamines	Stimulant	Relief of mild depression, control of narcolepsy and hyperactivity	2.5–5 milligrams	4 hours
Barbiturates	Sedative-hypnotic	Sedation, relief of high blood pressure, anticonvulsant	50–100 milligrams	4 hours
Benzodiazepines	Anxiolytic (antianxiety drug)	Tranquilizer	2–100 milligrams	10 minutes–8 hours
Caffeine	Stimulant	Counteract depressant drugs, treatment of migraine headaches	Varies	Varies
Cocaine	Stimulant, local anesthetic	Local anesthesia	Varies	Varied, brief periods
Codeine	Narcotic	Ease pain and coughing	30 milligrams	4 hours
GHB	Sedative-hypnotic	Experimental treatment of narcolepsy, alcoholism	1–3 grams (powder)	1–3 hours
Heroin	Narcotic X	Pain relief	Varies	4 hours
LSD	Narcotic	Experimental study of mental function, alcoholism	100–500 milligrams	10 hours
Marijuana (THC)	Relaxant, euphoriant; in high doses, hallucinogen	Treatment of glaucoma and side effects of chemotherapy	1–2 cigarettes	4 hours
MDMA	Stimulant/hallucinogen	None	125 milligrams	4–6 hours
Mescaline	Hallucinogen	None	350 micrograms	12 hours
Methadone	Narcotic	Pain relief	10 milligrams	4–6 hours
Morphine	Narcotic	Pain relief	15 milligrams	6 hours
PCP	Anesthetic	None	2–10 milligrams	4–6 hours, plus 12-hour recovery
Psilocybin	Hallucinogen	None	25 milligrams	6–8 hours
Tobacco (nicotine)	Stimulant	Emetic (nicotine)	Varies	Varies

Question marks indicate conflict of opinion. It should be noted that illicit drugs are frequently adulterated and thus pose unknown hazards to the user.

Amphetamines rapidly produce a drug tolerance. Most abusers end up taking ever-larger doses to get the desired effect. Eventually, some users switch to injecting methamphetamine directly into the bloodstream. True speed freaks typically go on binges lasting several days, after which they "crash" from lack of sleep and food.

Abuse

How dangerous are amphetamines? Amphetamines pose many dangers. Large doses can cause nausea, vomiting, extremely high blood pressure, fatal heart attacks, and disabling strokes. It is important to realize that amphetamines speed up the use of the body's resources; they do not magically supply energy. After an amphetamine binge, people suffer from crippling fatigue, depression, confusion, uncontrolled irritability, and aggression. Repeated amphetamine use damages the brain. Amphetamines can also cause *amphetamine psychosis,* a loss of contact with reality. Affected users have paranoid delusions that someone is out to get them. Acting on these delusions, they may become violent, resulting in suicide, self-injury, or injury to others (Iversen, 2006).

A potent smokable form of crystal methamphetamine has added to the risks of stimulant abuse. This drug, known as "ice" on the street, is highly addictive. Like "crack," the smokable form of cocaine, it produces an intense high. But also like crack (discussed in a moment), crystal methamphetamine leads very rapidly to compulsive abuse and severe drug dependence.

Effects Sought	Long-term Symptoms	Physical Dependence Potential	Psychological Dependence Potential	Organic Damage Potential
Sense alteration, anxiety reduction, sociability	Cirrhosis, toxic psychosis, neurologic damage, addiction	Yes	Yes	Yes
Alertness, activeness	Loss of appetite, delusions, hallucinations, toxic psychosis	Yes	Yes	Yes
Anxiety reduction, euphoria	Addiction with severe withdrawal symptoms, possible convulsions, toxic psychosis	Yes	Yes	Yes
Anxiety relief	Irritability, confusion, depression, sleep disorders	Yes	Yes	No, but can affect fetus
Wakefulness, alertness	Insomnia, heart arrhythmias, high blood pressure	No?	Yes	Yes
Excitation, talkativeness	Depression, convulsions	Yes	Yes	Yes
Euphoria, prevent withdrawal discomfort	Addiction, constipation, loss of appetite	Yes	Yes	No
Intoxication, euphoria, relaxation	Anxiety, confusion, insomnia, hallucinations, seizures	Yes	Yes	No?
Euphoria, prevent withdrawal discomfort	Addiction, constipation, loss of appetite	Yes	Yes	No*
Insightful experiences, exhilaration, distortion of senses	May intensify existing psychosis, panic reactions	No	No?	No?
Relaxation; increased euphoria, perceptions, sociability	Possible lung cancer, other health risks	Yes	Yes	Yes?
Excitation, euphoria	Personality change, hyperthermia, liver damage	No	Yes	Yes
Insightful experiences, exhilaration, distortion of senses	May intensify existing psychosis, panic reactions	No	No?	No?
Prevent withdrawal discomfort	Addiction, constipation, loss of appetite	Yes	Yes	No
Euphoria, prevent withdrawal discomfort	Addiction, constipation, loss of appetite	Yes	Yes	No*
Euphoria	Unpredictable behavior, suspicion, hostility, psychosis	Debated	Yes	Yes
Insightful experiences, exhilaration, distortion of senses	May intensify existing psychosis, panic reactions	No	No?	No?
Alertness, calmness, sociability	Emphysema, lung cancer, mouth and throat cancer, cardiovascular damage, loss of appetite	Yes	Yes	Yes

*Persons who inject drugs under nonsterile conditions run a high risk of contracting AIDS, hepatitis, abscesses, or circulatory disorders.

Cocaine

Cocaine ("coke," "snow," "blow," "snuff") is a powerful central nervous system stimulant extracted from the leaves of the coca plant. Cocaine produces feelings of alertness, euphoria, well-being, power, boundless energy, and pleasure (Julien, 2005). At the turn of the twentieth century, dozens of nonprescription potions and cure-alls contained cocaine. It was during this time that Coca-Cola was indeed the "real thing." From 1886 until 1906, when the U.S. Pure Food and Drug Act was passed, Coca-Cola contained cocaine (which has since been replaced with caffeine).

How does cocaine differ from amphetamines? The two are very much alike in their effects on the central nervous system. The main difference is that amphetamine lasts several hours; cocaine is snorted and quickly metabolized, so its effects last only about 15 to 30 minutes.

Abuse

How dangerous is cocaine? Cocaine's capacity for abuse and social damage rivals that of heroin. When rats and monkeys are given free access to cocaine, they find it irresistible. Many, in fact, end up dying of convulsions from self-administered overdoses of the drug. Even casual or first-time users risk having convulsions, a heart attack, or a stroke (Lacayo, 1995). Cocaine increases the chemical messengers dopamine (DOPE-ah-meen) and noradrenaline (nor-ah-DREN-ah-lin). Noradrenaline arouses the brain, and dopamine produces a "rush" of pleasure. This combination is so power-

National Library of Medicine

Cocaine was the main ingredient in many nonprescription elixirs before the turn of the twentieth century. Today cocaine is recognized as a powerful and dangerous drug. Its high potential for abuse has damaged the lives of countless users.

fully rewarding that cocaine users run a high risk of becoming compulsive abusers (Ridenour et al., 2005).

A person who stops using cocaine does not experience heroin-like withdrawal symptoms. Instead, the brain adapts to cocaine abuse in ways that upset its chemical balance, causing depression when cocaine is withdrawn. First, there is a jarring "crash" of mood and energy. Within a few days, the person enters a long period of fatigue, anxiety, paranoia, boredom, and **anhedonia** (an-he-DAWN-ee-ah: an inability to feel pleasure). Before long, the urge to use cocaine becomes intense. So, although cocaine does not fit the classic pattern of addiction, it is ripe for compulsive abuse. Even a person who gets through withdrawal may crave cocaine months or years later (Withers et al., 1995). If cocaine were cheaper, 9 out of 10 users would progress to compulsive abuse. In fact, rock cocaine ("crack," "rock," or "roca"), which is cheaper, produces very high abuse rates. Here are some signs of cocaine abuse:

- *Compulsive use.* If cocaine is available—say, at a party—you can't say no to it.
- *Loss of control.* Once you have had some cocaine, you will keep using it until you are exhausted or the cocaine is gone.
- *Disregarding consequences.* You don't care if the rent gets paid, your job is endangered, your lover disapproves, or your health is affected, you'll use cocaine anyway.

Anyone who thinks she or he has a cocaine problem should seek advice at a drug clinic or a Cocaine Anonymous meeting. Although quitting cocaine is extremely difficult, three out of four abusers who remain in treatment do succeed in breaking their coke dependence (Simpson et al., 1999; Sinha et al., 2006).

MDMA ("Ecstasy")

The drug MDMA (methylenedioxymethamphetamine, or "Ecstasy") is also chemically similar to amphetamine. In addition to producing a rush of energy, users say it makes them feel closer to others and heightens sensory experiences. Ecstasy causes brain

cells to release extra amounts of serotonin. The physical effects of MDMA include dilated pupils, elevated blood pressure, jaw clenching, loss of appetite, and elevated body temperature (Braun, 2001). Although some users believe that Ecstasy increases sexual pleasure, it *diminishes* sexual performance, impairing erection in 40 percent of men and retarding orgasm in both men and women. (Zemishlany, Aizenberg, & Weizman, 2001).

Abuse

Ecstasy use in North America has declined slightly from a peak around 2002, perhaps because of widespread negative publicity. Regardless, every year more than half a million Americans try Ecstasy for the first time (SAMHSA, 2005). Every year, emergency room doctors see many MDMA cases, including MDMA-related deaths. Some of these incidents are caused by elevated body temperature (hyperthermia) or heart arrhythmias, which can lead to collapse. Ecstasy users at "rave" parties try to prevent overheating by drinking water to cool themselves. This may help to a small degree, but the risk of fatal heat exhaustion is real. MDMA can also cause severe liver damage, which can be fatal (Braun, 2001). In addition, Ecstasy users are more likely to abuse alcohol and other drugs, to neglect studying, to party excessively, and to engage in risky sex (Strote, Lee, & Wechsler, 2002). Ironically, Ecstasy use at "rave" parties actually does intensify the impact of the music. We say ironically because the end result is often overstimulation of the brain, which can result in a "rebound" depression (Michelangelo et al., 2006).

It may take another decade before Ecstasy's full impact on health emerges. For now, we know that repeated use of MDMA damages serotonergic brain cells. This damage lasts for years. It leads to feelings of anxiety or depression that can persist for months after a person stops taking Ecstasy. In addition, heavy users typically do not perform well in tests of learning and memory and show signs of underlying brain damage (Quednow et al., 2006). Despite its street name, Ecstasy may be a ticket to agony for many users (Iversen, 2006; Kuhn & Wilson, 2001).

Caffeine

Caffeine is the most frequently used psychoactive drug in North America. (And that's not counting Seattle!) Caffeine stimulates the brain by blocking chemicals that normally inhibit or slow nerve activity (Julien, 2005). Its effects become apparent with doses as small as 50 milligrams, the amount found in about one-half cup of brewed coffee. Physically, caffeine causes sweating, talkativeness, tinnitus (ringing in the ears), and hand tremors (Nehlig, 2004). Psychologically, caffeine suppresses fatigue or drowsiness and increases feelings of alertness (Wesensten et al., 2002). Some people have a hard time starting a day (or writing another paragraph) without it.

How much caffeine did you consume today? It is common to think of coffee as the major source of caffeine, but there are many others. Caffeine is found in tea, many soft drinks (especially colas), chocolate, and cocoa. More than 2,000 nonprescription drugs also contain caffeine, including stay-awake pills, cold remedies, and many name-brand aspirin products.

Abuse

Are there any serious drawbacks to using caffeine? Overuse of caffeine may result in an unhealthy dependence known as **caffeinism.** Insomnia, irritability, loss of appetite, chills, racing heart, and elevated body temperature are all signs of caffeinism. Many people with these symptoms drink 15 or 20 cups of coffee a day. However, even at lower dosages, caffeine can intensify anxiety and other psychological problems (Hogan, Hornick, & Bouchoux, 2002).

Caffeine poses a variety of health risks. Caffeine encourages the growth of breast cysts in women, and it may contribute to bladder cancer, heart problems, and high blood pressure. Pregnant women should consider giving up caffeine entirely because of a suspected link between caffeine and birth defects. Pregnant women who consume as little as 2 cups coffee a day increase the risk of having a miscarriage (Cnattingius et al., 2000).

It is customary to think that caffeine is not a drug. But as few as 2.5 cups of coffee a day (or the equivalent) can be a problem. People who consume even such modest amounts may experience anxiety, depression, fatigue, headaches, and flu-like symptoms during withdrawal (Juliano & Griffiths, 2004). About half of all caffeine users show some signs of dependence (Hughes et al., 1998). It is wise to remember that caffeine *is* a drug and use it in moderation.

Nicotine

Nicotine is a natural stimulant found mainly in tobacco. Next to caffeine and alcohol, it is the most widely used psychoactive drug (Julien, 2005).

How does nicotine compare with other stimulants? Nicotine is a potent drug. It is so toxic that it is sometimes used to kill insects! In large doses it causes stomach pain, vomiting and diarrhea, cold sweats, dizziness, confusion, and muscle tremors. In very large doses, nicotine may cause convulsions, respiratory failure, and death. For a nonsmoker, 50 to 75 milligrams of nicotine taken in a single dose could be lethal. (Chain-smoking about 17 to 25 cigarettes will produce this dosage.) Most first-time smokers get sick on one or two cigarettes. In contrast, regular smokers build a tolerance for nicotine. A heavy smoker may inhale 40 cigarettes a day without feeling ill.

Abuse

How addictive is nicotine? A vast array of evidence confirms that nicotine is very addictive (Spinella, 2005). The average age of first use is 15, and it takes about a year before dependence sets in (Baker, Brandon, & Chassin, 2004). Among regular smokers who are 15 to 24 years old, 60 percent are addicted (Breslau et al., 2001). For many smokers, withdrawal from nicotine causes headaches, sweating, cramps, insomnia, digestive upset, irritability, and a sharp craving for cigarettes (NIDA, 2006). These symptoms may last from 2 to 6 weeks and may be worse than heroin withdrawal.

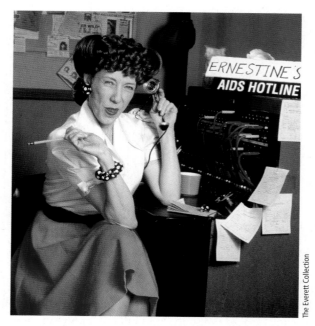

Actress and comedienne Lily Tomlin, here shown portraying one of her comedic characters, Ernestine, once took up smoking for a role in a movie *(Shadows and Fog)* and developed a 4-pack-a-day habit. As Tomlin's experience shows, the best way to avoid developing a nicotine addiction is to not begin smoking in the first place.

Indeed, relapse patterns are nearly identical for alcoholics, heroin addicts, cocaine abusers, and smokers who try to quit (Stolerman & Jarvis, 1995). Up to 90 percent of people who quit smoking relapse within a year, and 20 percent relapse even after 2 years of abstinence (Krall, Garvey, & Garcia, 2002).

Impact on Health

How serious are the health risks of smoking? If you think smoking is harmless, or that there's no connection between smoking and cancer, you're kidding yourself. A burning cigarette releases a large variety of potent *carcinogens* (car-SIN-oh-jins: cancer-causing substances). According to the U.S. Surgeon General (USDHHS, 2004), "smoking harms nearly every organ of the body," leading to an increased risk of many cancers (such as lung cancer), cardiovascular diseases (such as stroke), respiratory diseases (such as chronic bronchitis), and reproductive disorders (such as decreased fertility). Together, these health risks combine to reduce the life expectancy of the average smoker by 10 to 15 years. (Skeptics please note: Wayne McLaren, who portrayed the rugged "Marlboro Man" in cigarette ads, died of lung cancer at age 51.) More people die every year from tobacco use than from motor vehicle injuries, murders, suicides, alcohol use, illegal drug use, and AIDS *combined* (NCCDPHP, 2004).

Anhedonia An inability to feel pleasure.

Caffeinism Excessive consumption of caffeine, leading to dependence and a variety of physical and psychological complaints.

"Not for me thanks, mate - I'm only a passive smoker."

© Clive Goddard/www.CartoonStock.com

By the way, urban cowboys and Skol bandits, the same applies to chewing tobacco and snuff. A 30-minute exposure to one pinch of smokeless tobacco is equivalent to smoking three or four cigarettes. Along with all the health risks of smoking, users of smokeless tobacco also run a higher risk of developing oral cancer (American Lung Association, 2006).

Smokers don't just risk their own health; they also endanger those who live and work nearby. Secondary smoke causes about 3,000 lung cancer deaths and as many as 62,000 heart disease deaths each year in the United States alone. It is particularly irresponsible of smokers to expose young children, who are especially vulnerable, to secondhand smoke (American Lung Association, 2006).

Quitting Smoking

Is it better for a person to quit smoking abruptly or taper down gradually? Most people try to quit by themselves. Some try to quit cold turkey, whereas others try to taper down gradually. Although going cold turkey has its advocates, gradually quitting works better for more people.

Going cold turkey makes quitting an all-or-nothing proposition. Smokers who smoke even one cigarette after "quitting forever" tend to feel they've failed. Many figure they might just as well resume smoking. Those who quit gradually accept that success may take many attempts, spread over several months. If you are going to quit by going cold turkey, you will have a better chance of success if you decide to quit *now* rather than at some time in the future (West & Sohal, 2006).

The best way to taper off is *scheduled gradual reduction* (Riley et al., 2002). There are many ways in which smoking can be gradually reduced. For example, the smoker can (1) delay having a first cigarette in the morning and then try to delay a little longer each day, (2) gradually reduce the total number of cigarettes smoked each day, or (3) quit completely, but for just 1 week, then quit again, a week at a time, for as many times as necessary to make it stick. Deliberately scheduling the gradually stretching of time periods

between cigarettes is a key part of this program. Scheduled smoking apparently helps people learn to cope with the urge to smoke. As a result, people using this method are more likely remain permanent nonsmokers than people using other approaches (Cinciripini, Wetter, & McClure, 1997).

Whatever approach is taken, quitting smoking is not easy (Abrams et al., 2003). Many people find that using nicotine patches or gum helps them get through the withdrawal period (Shiffman et al., 2006). Also, as we have noted, anyone trying to quit should be prepared to make several attempts before succeeding. But the good news is tens of millions of people have quit.

bridges
Behavioral self-management techniques can be very useful for breaking habits such as smoking. **See Chapter 7, pages 247–248, and Chapter 15, pages 522–526.**

⬤⬤ Downers—Sedatives, Tranquilizers, and Alcohol

The most widely used downers, or depressant drugs, are barbiturates, GHB, benzodiazepine (ben-zoe-die-AZ-eh-peen) tranquilizers, and alcohol. These drugs are much alike in their effects. In fact, barbiturates and tranquilizers are sometimes referred to as "solid alcohol." Let's examine the properties of each.

Barbiturates

Barbiturates are sedative drugs that depress brain activity. Common barbiturates include amobarbital, pentobarbital, secobarbital, and Tuinal. On the street they are known as "downers," "blue heavens," "yellow jackets," "lows," "goof balls," "reds," "pink ladies," "rainbows," or "tooies." Medically, barbiturates are used to calm patients or to induce sleep. At mild dosages, barbiturates have an effect similar to alcohol intoxication. Higher dosages can cause severe mental confusion or even hallucinations. Barbiturates are often taken in excess amounts because a first dose may be followed by others, as the user becomes uninhibited or forgetful. Overdoses first cause a loss of consciousness. Then they severely depress brain centers that control heartbeat and breathing. The result is death (McKim, 2007).

GHB

Would you swallow a mixture of degreasing solvent and drain cleaner to get high? Apparently, a lot of people would. A mini-epidemic of GHB (gamma-hydroxybutyrate) use has taken place in recent years, especially at nightclubs and raves. GHB ("goop," "scoop," "max," "Georgia Home Boy") is a central nervous system depressant that relaxes and sedates the body. Users describe its effects as being similar to alcohol. Mild GHB intoxication tends to produce euphoria, a desire to socialize, and a mild loss of inhibitions. GHB's intoxicating effects typically last 3 to 4 hours, depending on the dosage.

Abuse

At lower dosages, GHB can relieve anxiety and produce relaxation. However, as the dose increases, its sedative effects may result in nausea, a loss of muscle control, and either sleep or a loss of consciousness. Potentially fatal doses of GHB are only three times the amount typically taken by users. This narrow margin of safety has led to numerous overdoses, especially when GHB was combined with alcohol. An overdose causes coma, breathing failure, and death. Also, GHB inhibits the gag reflex, so some users choke to death on their own vomit.

In 2000, the U.S. government classified GHB as a controlled substance, making its possession a felony. Clinical evidence increasingly suggests that GHB is addictive and a serious danger to users. Two out of three frequent users have lost consciousness after taking GHB. Heavy users who stop taking GHB have withdrawal symptoms that include anxiety, agitation, tremor, delirium, and hallucinations (Miotto et al., 2001).

As if the preceding weren't enough reason to be leery of GHB, here's one more to consider: GHB is often manufactured in homes with recipes and ingredients purchased on the Internet. As mentioned earlier, it can be produced by combining degreasing solvent with drain cleaner (Falkowski, 2000). If you want to degrease your brain, GHB will do the trick.

Tranquilizers

A **tranquilizer** is a drug that lowers anxiety and reduces tension. Doctors prescribe benzodiazepine tranquilizers to alleviate nervousness and stress. Valium is the best-known drug in this family; others are Xanax, Halcion, and Librium. Even at normal dosages these drugs can cause drowsiness, shakiness, and confusion. When used at too high a dosage or for too long, benzodiazepines are addictive (McKim, 2007).

A drug sold under the trade name Rohypnol (ro-HIP-nol) has added to the problem of tranquilizer abuse. This drug, which is related to Valium, is cheap and 10 times more potent. It lowers inhibitions and produces relaxation or intoxication. Large doses induce short-term amnesia and sleep. "Roofies," as they are known on the street, are odorless and tasteless. They have been used to spike drinks, which are given to the unwary. Victims of this "date rape" drug are then sexually assaulted or raped while they are unconscious. (Be aware, however, that drinking too much alcohol is by far the most common prelude to rape.)

Abuse

Repeated use of barbiturates can cause physical dependence. Some abusers suffer severe emotional depression that may end in suicide. Similarly, when tranquilizers are used at too high a dosage or for too long, addiction can occur. Many people have learned the hard way that their legally prescribed tranquilizers are as dangerous as many illicit drugs (McKim, 2007).

Combining barbiturates or tranquilizers with alcohol is especially risky. When mixed, the effects of both drugs are multiplied by a **drug interaction** (one drug enhances the effect of another). Drug interactions are responsible for many hundreds of fatal drug overdoses every year (Goldberg, 2006). All too often, depressants are gulped down with alcohol or added to a spiked punch bowl. This is the lethal brew that left a young woman named Karen Ann Quinlan in a coma that lasted 10 years, ending with her death. It is no exaggeration to restate that mixing depressants with alcohol can be deadly.

Alcohol

Alcohol is the common name for ethyl alcohol, the intoxicating element in fermented and distilled liquors. Contrary to popular belief, alcohol is not a stimulant. The noisy animation at drinking parties is due to alcohol's effect as a *depressant*. As ● Figure 6.13 shows, small amounts of alcohol reduce inhibitions and produce feelings of relaxation and euphoria. Larger amounts cause ever-greater impairment of the brain until the drinker loses consciousness. Alcohol is also not an aphrodisiac. Rather than enhancing sexual arousal, it usually impairs performance, especially in males. As William Shakespeare observed long ago, drink "provokes the desire, but it takes away the performance."

Some people become aggressive and want to argue or fight when they are drunk. Others become relaxed and friendly. How can the same drug have such different effects? When a person is drunk, thinking and perception become dulled or shortsighted, a condition that has been called **alcohol myopia** (my-OH-pea-ah). Only the most obvious and immediate stimuli catch a drinker's attention. Worries and "second thoughts" that would normally restrain behavior are banished from the drinker's mind. That's why many behaviors become more extreme when a person is drunk. On college campuses, drunken students tend to have accidents, get into fights, sexually assault others, or engage in risky sex. They also destroy property and disrupt the lives of students who are trying to sleep or study (Brower, 2002)

Abuse

Alcohol, the world's favorite depressant, breeds our biggest drug problem. More than 20 million people in the United States and Canada have serious drinking problems. One American dies every 20 minutes in an alcohol-related car crash. The level of alcohol abuse among adolescents and young adults is alarming. Of 18-year-olds, 15 percent are heavy drinkers and 40 percent have engaged in binge drinking (SAMHSA, 2005). **Binge drinking** is

Tranquilizer A drug that lowers anxiety and reduces tension.

Drug interaction A combined effect of two drugs that exceeds the addition of one drug's effects to the other.

Alcohol myopia Shortsighted thinking and perception that occurs during alcohol intoxication.

Binge drinking Consuming five or more drinks in a short time (four drinks for women).

● **Figure 6.13** The behavioral effects of alcohol are related to blood alcohol content and the resulting suppression of higher mental function. Arrows indicate the typical threshold for legal intoxication in the United States. (From Jozef Cohen, *Eyewitness Series in Psychology*, SS 7, p. 44. Copyright © 1970 by Rand McNally and Company. Reprinted by permission of the author's estate.)

Alcohol Consumed	Neural Representation	Behavioral Effect
2 ounces 90 proof whiskey .05% blood alcohol		Affects higher nervous centers; drinker loses inhibitions, forgoes conventions and courtesies, relaxes
6 ounces 90 proof whiskey .15% blood alcohol		Affects deeper motor areas; drinker staggers, has slurred speech, is overconfident, acts on impulse
10 ounces 90 proof whiskey .25% blood alcohol		Affects emotional centers of midbrain; drinker has impaired motor reactions and unsteady gait; sensations are distorted; drinker tends to see double, to fall asleep
16 ounces 90 proof whiskey .4% blood alcohol		Affects sensory area of cerebellum; senses are dulled; drinker is in stupor
24 ounces 90 proof whiskey .6% blood alcohol		Affects perceptual areas; drinker loses consciousness; only functions of breathing and heartbeat remain
32 ounces 90 proof whiskey .8% blood alcohol		Affects entire brain; heartbeat and respiration stop; **death**

defined as downing five or more drinks in a short time (four drinks for women). Apparently, many students think it's entertaining to get completely wasted and throw up on their friends. However, binge drinking is a serious sign of alcohol abuse. It is responsible for 1,400 college student deaths each year and thousands of trips to the ER (Wechsler et al., 2002).

Binge drinking is of special concern because the brain continues to develop into the early 20s. Research has shown that teenagers and young adults who drink too much may lose as much as 10 percent of their brain power—especially their memory capacity (Brown et al., 2000). Such losses can have a long-term impact on a person's chances for success in life. In short, getting drunk is a slow but sure way to get stupid (Wechsler & Wuethrich, 2002).

At Risk

Children of alcoholics and those who have other relatives who abuse alcohol are at greater risk for becoming alcohol abusers themselves. The increased risk appears to be partly genetic. It is based on the fact that some people have stronger cravings for alcohol after they drink (Hutchison et al., 2002). Women also face some special risks. For one thing, alcohol is absorbed faster and metabolized more slowly by women's bodies. As a result, women get intoxicated from less alcohol than men do. Women who drink are also more prone to liver disease, osteoporosis, and depression. As few as three drinks a week may increase a woman's risk of breast cancer by 50 percent.

Positive reinforcement—drinking for pleasure—motivates most people who consume alcohol. What sets alcohol abusers apart is that they also drink to cope with negative emotions, such as anxiety and depression. That's why alcohol abuse increases with the level of stress in people's lives. People who drink to relieve bad feelings are at great risk of becoming alcoholics (Kenneth, Carpenter, & Hasin, 1998).

Recognizing Problem Drinking

What are the signs of alcohol abuse? Because alcohol abuse is such a common problem, it is important to recognize the danger signals. If you can answer yes to even one of the following questions, you may have a problem with drinking (adapted from the College Alcohol Problems Scale, revised; Maddock et al., 2001):

As a Result of Drinking Alcoholic Beverages I . . .

1. engaged in unplanned sexual activity.
2. drove under the influence.
3. did not use protection when engaging in sex.
4. engaged in illegal activities associated with drug use.
5. felt sad, blue, or depressed.
6. was nervous or irritable.
7. felt bad about myself.
8. had problems with appetite or sleeping.

Binge drinking and alcohol abuse have become serious problems among college students. Many alcohol abusers regard themselves as "moderate" drinkers, which suggests that they are in denial about how much they actually drink (Grant & Dawson, 1997).

Table 6.5 ● Drinking in Moderation

Approximate Number of Drinks per Hour to Stay Below 0.05 Blood Alcohol*		
Your Weight (pounds)	**Male**	**Female**
100	0.75	0.60
120	1.00	0.75
140	1.25	0.90
160	1.30	1.00
180	1.50	1.10
200	1.60	1.20
220	1.80	1.35

One drink = 12 ounces beer, 4 ounces wine, 2.5 ounces brandy, or 1.25 ounces 80 proof liquor.

*Table entries are approximate, owing to individual differences in metabolism, recency of meals, and other factors. Estimates are from tables prepared by Vogler and Bartz (1982, 1992).

Perhaps the simplest way to identify problem drinkers is to ask a single question: "When was the last time you had more than five drinks (four for women) in a day?" Eighty-six percent of the people who answer "less than 3 months ago" are alcohol abusers (Williams & Vinson, 2001).

Moderated Drinking

Almost everyone has been to a party spoiled by someone who drank too much too fast. Those who avoid overdrinking have a better time, and so do their friends. But how do you avoid drinking too much? After all, as one wit once observed, "The conscience dissolves in alcohol." Psychologists Roger Vogler and Wayne Bartz (1982, 1992) provide a partial answer.

Vogler and Bartz observe that drinking makes you feel good while blood alcohol is rising and remains below a level of about 0.05. In this range, people feel relaxed, euphoric, and sociable. At higher levels they go from moderately intoxicated to thoroughly drunk. Later, as blood alcohol begins to fall, those who overdrink become sick and miserable. ● Table 6.5 shows the approximate amount per hour that can be consumed without exceeding the 0.05 blood alcohol level. (Even at this level, driving may be impaired.) By pacing themselves, those who choose to drink can remain comfortable, pleasant, and coherent during a long social event. In short, if you drink, it might be wise to learn your "magic" number from ● Table 6.5.

It takes skill to regulate drinking in social situations, where the temptation to drink can be strong. If you choose to drink, here are some guidelines that may be helpful:

Paced Drinking

1. Think about your drinking beforehand and plan how you will manage it.
2. Drink slowly, eat while drinking or drink on a full stomach, and make every other drink (or more) a nonalcoholic beverage.
3. Limit drinking primarily to the first hour of a social event or party. Pace your drinking using the information from ● Table 6.5.
4. Practice how you will politely but firmly refuse drinks.
5. Learn how to relax, meet people, and socialize without relying on alcohol.

Adapted from Miller & Munoz, 2005; Vogler & Bartz, 1992.

Limiting your own drinking may help others as well. When people are tempted to drink too much, their main reason for stopping is that "other people were quitting and deciding they'd had enough" (Johnson, 2002).

Treatment

Treatment for alcohol dependence begins with sobering up the person and cutting off the supply. This phase is referred to as **detoxification** (literally, "to remove poison"). It frequently produces all the symptoms of drug withdrawal and can be extremely unpleasant. The next step is to try to restore the person's health. Heavy abuse of alcohol usually causes severe damage to body organs and the nervous system. After alcoholics have "dried out" and some degree of health has been restored, they may be treated with tranquilizers, antidepressants, or psychotherapy. Unfortunately, the success of these procedures has been limited.

One mutual-help approach that has been fairly successful is Alcoholics Anonymous (AA). AA takes a spiritual approach while acting on the premise that it takes a former alcoholic to understand and help a current alcoholic. Participants at AA meetings admit that they have a problem, share feelings, and resolve to stay "dry" one day at a time. Other group members provide support for those struggling to end dependency. (Other "12-step" programs, such as Cocaine Anonymous and Narcotics Anonymous use the same approach.)

Detoxification In the treatment of alcoholism, the withdrawal of the patient from alcohol.

Eighty percent of those who remain in AA for more than 1 year get through the following year without a drink. However, AA's success rate may simply reflect the fact that members join voluntarily, meaning they have admitted they have a serious problem (Morgenstern et al., 1997). Sadly, it seems that alcohol abusers will often not face their problems until they have "hit rock bottom." If they are willing, though, AA presents a practical approach to the problem (Vaillant, 2005).

Other groups offer a rational, nonspiritual approach to alcohol abuse that better fits the needs of some people. Examples include Rational Recovery and Secular Organizations for Sobriety (SOS). Other alternatives to AA include medical treatment, group therapy, and individual psychotherapy (Buddie, 2004). There is a strong tendency for abusive drinkers to deny they have a problem. The sooner they seek help, the better.

◐ Hallucinogens—Tripping the Light Fantastic

Marijuana is the most popular illicit drug in America (SAMHSA, 2005). The main active chemical in marijuana is tetrahydrocannabinol (tet-rah-hydro-cah-NAB-ih-nol), or THC for short. THC is a mild **hallucinogen** (hal-LU-sin-oh-jin: a substance that alters sensory impressions). Other hallucinogenic drugs include LSD and PCP.

LSD and PCP

The drug LSD (lysergic acid diethylamide, or "acid") is perhaps the best-known hallucinogen. Even when taken in tiny amounts, LSD can produce hallucinations and psychotic-like disturbances in thinking and perception. Two other common hallucinogens are mescaline (peyote) and psilocybin ("magic mushrooms," or "shrooms"). Incidentally, the drug PCP (phencyclidine, or "angel dust") can have hallucinogenic effects. However, PCP, which is an anesthetic, also has stimulant and depressant effects. This potent combination can cause extreme agitation, disorientation, violence—and too often, tragedy. All the hallucinogens, including marijuana, typically affect neurotransmitter systems that carry messages between brain cells (Julien, 2005).

Marijuana

Marijuana and hashish are derived from the hemp plant *Cannabis sativa*. Marijuana ("pot," "grass," "Ganja," "MJ") consists of the dried leaves and flowers of the hemp plant. Hashish is a resinous material scraped from Cannabis leaves. Marijuana's psychological effects include a sense of euphoria or well-being, relaxation, altered time sense, and perceptual distortions. At high dosages, however, paranoia, hallucinations, and delusions can occur (Ksir, Hart, & Ray, 2006). All considered, marijuana intoxication is relatively subtle by comparison to drugs such as LSD or alcohol. Despite this, driving a car while high on marijuana can be extremely hazardous. As a matter of fact, driving under the influence of any intoxicating drug is dangerous.

No overdose deaths from marijuana have been reported. However, marijuana cannot be considered harmless. Particularly worrisome is the fact that THC accumulates in the body's fatty tissues, especially in the brain and reproductive organs. Even if a person smokes marijuana just once a week, the body is never entirely free of THC. Scientists have located a specific receptor site on the surface of brain cells where THC binds to produce its effects (● Figure 6.14).

● **Figure 6.14** This thin slice of a rat's brain has been washed with a radioactive THC-like drug. Yellowish areas show where the brain is rich in THC receptors. In addition to the cortex, or outer layer of the brain, THC receptors are found in abundance in areas involved in the control of coordinated movement. Naturally occurring chemicals similar to THC may help the brain cope with pain and stress. However, when THC is used as a drug, high doses can cause paranoia, hallucinations, and dizziness (Julien, 2005). (From "Marijuana and the Brain," *Science News*, vol. 143.)

Artists have tried at times to capture the effects of hallucinogens. Here, the artist depicts visual experiences he had while under the influence of LSD.

These receptor sites are found in large numbers in the cerebral cortex, which is the seat of human consciousness (Julien, 2005). In addition, THC receptors are found in areas involved in the control of skilled movement. Naturally occurring chemicals similar to THC may help the brain cope with pain and stress. However, when THC is used as a drug, high dosages can cause paranoia, hallucinations, and dizziness.

Dangers of Marijuana Use

Does marijuana produce physical dependence? Yes, according to recent studies (Lichtman & Martin, 2006). Frequent users of marijuana find it very difficult to quit, so dependence is a risk (Budney & Hughes, 2006). But marijuana's potential for abuse lies primarily in the realm of psychological dependence, not physical addiction.

For about a day after a person smokes marijuana, his or her attention, coordination, and short-term memory are impaired (Pope, Gruber, & Yurgelun-Todd, 1995). Frequent marijuana users show small declines in learning, memory, attention, and thinking abilities (Solowij et al., 2002). When surveyed at age 29, nonusers are healthier, earn more, and are more satisfied with their lives than people who smoke marijuana regularly (Ellickson, Martino, & Collins, 2004).

People who smoke five or more joints a week score 4 points lower on IQ tests. This is enough to dull their learning capacity. In fact, many people who have stopped using marijuana say they quit because they were bothered by short-term memory loss and concentration problems. Fortunately, IQ scores and other cognitive measures rebound in about a month after a person quits using marijuana (Grant et al., 2001). In other words, people who smoke dope may act like dopes, but if they quit, there's a good chance they will regain their mental abilities.

An outdated antimarijuana poster demonstrates the kind of misinformation that has long been attached to this drug. Research has finally begun to sort out what risks are associated with use of marijuana.

Long-Term Health Risks

Marijuana's long-term effects include the following health risks:

1. Marijuana smoke contains 50 percent more cancer-causing hydrocarbons and 16 times more tar than tobacco smoke does. Thus, smoking several joints a week may be the equivalent of smoking a dozen cigarettes a day. In regular users, marijuana increases the risk of a variety of cancers, including prostate and cervical cancer (Hashibe, 2005).
2. Marijuana temporarily lowers sperm production in males, and users produce more abnormal sperm. This could be a problem for a man who is marginally fertile and wants to have a family (Schuel et al., 1999).
3. In experiments with female monkeys, THC causes abnormal menstrual cycles and disrupts ovulation. Other animal studies show that THC causes a higher rate of miscarriages and that it can reach the developing fetus. As is true for so many other drugs, it appears that marijuana should be avoided during pregnancy.
4. THC can suppress the body's immune system, increasing the risk of disease.
5. In animals, marijuana causes genetic damage within cells of the body. It is not known to what extent this happens in humans, but it does suggest that marijuana can be detrimental to health.
6. Activity levels in the cerebellum are lower than normal in marijuana abusers. This may explain why chronic marijuana users tend to show some loss of coordination (Volkow et al., 1996).
7. There is some evidence that THC damages parts of the brain important for memory (Chan et al., 1998).
8. Children whose mothers smoked marijuana during pregnancy show lowered ability to succeed in challenging, goal-oriented activities (Fried & Smith, 2001; Noland et al., 2005).

Although much is still unknown, marijuana appears to pose a wide range of health risks. Only future research will tell for sure "what's in the pot."

A Look Ahead

Of the many states of consciousness we have discussed, dreaming remains one of the most familiar—and the most surprising. Are there lessons to be learned from dreams? What personal insights lie hidden in the ebb and flow of your dream images? Let's find out in the upcoming Psychology in Action section.

Hallucinogen A substance that alters or distorts sensory impressions.

KNOWLEDGE BUILDER
Psychoactive Drugs

RECITE

1. Addictive drugs stimulate the brain's reward circuitry by affecting
   a. neurotransmitters
   b. alpha waves
   c. tryptophan levels
   d. delta spindles
2. Which of the drugs listed below are known to cause a physical dependence?
   a. heroin
   b. morphine
   c. codeine
   d. methadone
   e. barbiturates
   f. alcohol
   g. marijuana
   h. amphetamines
   i. nicotine
   j. cocaine
   k. GHB
3. Amphetamine psychosis is similar to extreme _____, in which the individual feels threatened and suffers from delusions.
4. Cocaine is very similar to which of the following in its effects on the central nervous system?
   a. Seconal
   b. codeine
   c. *Cannabis*
   d. amphetamine

5. Drug interaction is a special danger when a person combines
   a. marijuana and amphetamine
   b. barbiturates and alcohol
   c. alcohol and cocaine
   d. marijuana and THC
6. College students may overdrink as they try to keep up with how much they falsely imagine that their peers drink. T or F?
7. Treatment for alcohol dependence begins with sobering up the person and cutting off the supply. This is referred to as
   a. "hitting bottom"
   b. the crucial phase
   c. detoxification
   d. clinical anhedonia

REFLECT

Critical Thinking

8. The U.S. government, which helps fund antismoking campaigns and smoking-related health research, also continues to subsidize tobacco growers. Can you explain this contradiction?
9. Why do you think there is such a contrast between the laws regulating marijuana and those regulating alcohol and tobacco?

Relate

What legal drugs did you use in the last year? Did any have psychoactive properties? How do psychoactive drugs differ from other substances in their potential for abuse?

Answers: 1. a **2.** All of them do **3.** paranoia **4.** d **5.** b **6.** T **7.** c **8.** Neither can we. **9.** Drug laws in Western societies reflect cultural values and historical patterns of use. Inconsistencies in the law often cannot be justified on the basis of pharmacology, health risks, or abuse potential.

PSYCHOLOGY IN ACTION

Exploring and Using Dreams

Gateway Question: How can dreams be used to promote personal understanding?

No matter what theory of dreaming we favor, dreams can be thought of as a message *from* yourself *to* yourself. Thus, the way to understand dreams is to remember them, write them down, look for the messages they contain, and become deeply acquainted with *your own* symbol system. Here's how:

How to Catch a Dream

1. Before going to sleep, plan to remember your dreams. Keep a pen and paper or a recorder beside your bed.
2. If possible, arrange to awaken gradually without an alarm. Natural awakening almost always follows soon after a REM period.
3. If you rarely remember your dreams, you may want to set an alarm clock to go off an hour before you usually awaken.

Although less desirable than awakening naturally, this may let you catch a dream.
4. Upon awakening, lie still and review the dream images with your eyes closed. Try to recall as many details as possible.
5. If you can, make your first dream record (whether by writing or by recording) with your eyes closed. Opening your eyes will disrupt dream recall.
6. Review the dream again and record as many additional details as you can remember. Dream memories disappear quickly. Be sure to describe feelings as well as the plot, characters, and actions of the dream.
7. Put your dreams into a permanent dream diary. Keep dreams in chronological order and review them periodically. This procedure will reveal recurrent themes, conflicts, and emo-

tions. It almost always produces valuable insights.
8. Remember, a number of drugs suppress dreaming by interfering with REM sleep (● Table 6.6).

Dream Work

At one time or another almost everyone has had a dream that seemed to have deep meaning (Rock, 2004). Exploring everyday dream life can be a source of personal enrichment and personal growth (Cartwright & Lamberg, 1992). What strategies do psychologists use to interpret dreams? Let's start with Sigmund Freud's pioneering approach.

To unlock dreams, Freud identified four **dream processes,** or mental filters, that disguise the meanings of dreams. The first is **condensation,** in which several people, objects, or events are combined into a single dream image. A dream character that looks

Table 6.6 ● Effects of Selected Drugs on Dreaming

Drug	Effect on REM Sleep
Alcohol	Decrease
Amphetamines	Decrease
Barbiturates	Decrease
Caffeine	None
Cocaine	Decrease
Ecstasy	Decrease (by interrupting sleep)
LSD	Slight increase
Marijuana	Slight decrease or no effect
Opiates	Decrease
Valium	Decrease

like a teacher, acts like your father, talks like your mother, and is dressed like your employer might be a condensation of authority figures in your life.

Displacement is a second way of disguising dream content. Displacement may cause important emotions or actions of a dream to be redirected toward safe or seemingly unimportant images. Thus, a student angry at his parents might dream of accidentally wrecking their car instead of directly attacking them.

How would you try to find the meaning of this dream? A traditional approach is to look for symbolic messages, as well as literal meanings. If you find yourself wearing a mask in a dream, for instance, it could relate to important roles that you play at school, work, or home. It could also mean that you want to hide or that you are looking forward to a costume party. However, to accurately interpret a dream, it is important to learn your own "vocabulary" of dream images and meanings. Keeping a dream diary is the first step toward gaining valuable insights.

Courtesy of Maryanne Mott

A third dream process is **symbolization.** As mentioned earlier, Freud believed that dreams are often expressed in images that are symbolic rather than literal. That's why it helps to ask what feelings or ideas a dream image might symbolize. Let's say, for example, that a student dreams of coming to class naked. A literal interpretation would be that the student is an exhibitionist. A more likely symbolic meaning is that the student feels vulnerable or unprepared in the class.

Secondary elaboration is the fourth method by which dream meanings are disguised. **Secondary elaboration** is the tendency to make a dream more logical and to add details when remembering it. The fresher a dream memory is, the more useful it is likely to be.

Looking for condensation, displacement, symbolization, and secondary elaboration may help you unlock your dreams. But there are other techniques that may be more effective. Dream theorist Calvin Hall (1974) preferred to think of dreams as plays and the dreamer as a playwright. Although Hall points out that dream images and ideas tend to be more primitive than waking thoughts, much can be learned by simply considering the *setting, cast of characters, plot,* and *emotions* portrayed in a dream.

Another dream theorist, Rosalind Cartwright, suggests that dreams are primarily "feeling statements." According to her, the overall *emotional tone* (underlying mood) of a dream is a major clue to its meaning (Cartwright & Lamberg, 1992). Is the dream comical, threatening, joyous, or depressing? Were you lonely, jealous, frightened, in love, or angry?

Because each dream has several possible meanings or levels of meaning, there is no fixed way to work with it. Telling the dream to others and discussing its meaning can be a good start. Describing it may help you relive some of the feelings in the dream. Also, family members or friends may be able to offer interpretations to which you would be blind. Watch for verbal or visual puns and other playful elements in dreams. For example, if you dream that you are in a wrestling match and your arm is pinned behind your back, it may mean that you feel someone is "twisting your arm" in real life.

The meaning of most dreams will yield to a little detective work. Try asking a series of questions about dreams you would like to understand:

Probing Dreams

1. Who was in the dream? Were there humans, animals, or mythical characters? Do you recognize any of the characters?
2. What social interactions were taking place? Were those interactions friendly? Aggressive? Sexual?
3. What activities were taking place? Were they physical activities or not?
4. Was there striving? Was the striving successful or not?
5. Was the dream about good fortune or misfortune?
6. What emotions were present in the dream? Was there anger, apprehension, confusion, happiness, or sadness?
7. What were the physical surroundings like? What was the setting? Were there any physical objects present? (Adapted from the Hall-Van de Castle system of dream content analysis; Domhoff, 2003.)

If you still have trouble seeing the meaning of a dream, you may find it helpful to use a technique developed by Fritz Perls. Perls, the originator of Gestalt therapy, considered most dreams a special message about what's missing in our lives, what we avoid doing, or feelings that need to be "re-owned." Perls believed that dreams are a way of filling in gaps in personal experience (Perls, 1969).

An approach that Perls found helpful is to "take the part of" or "speak for" each of the characters and objects in the dream. In other words, if you dream about a strange man standing behind a doorway, you would speak aloud to the man, then answer for him. To use Perls' method, you would even speak for the door, perhaps saying something like, "I am a barrier. I keep you safe, but I also keep you locked

Dream processes Mental filters that hide the true meanings of dreams.

Condensation Combining several people, objects, or events into a single dream image.

Displacement Directing emotions or actions toward safe or unimportant dream images.

Symbolization The nonliteral expression of dream content.

Secondary elaboration Making a dream more logical and complete while remembering it.

inside. The stranger has something to tell you. You must risk opening me to learn it."

A particularly interesting dream exercise is to continue a dream as waking fantasy so that it may be concluded or carried on to a more meaningful ending. As the world of dreams and your personal dream language become more familiar, you will doubtless find many answers, paradoxes, intuitions, and insights into your own behavior.

Using Your Dreams

It is possible to learn to use dreams for our own purposes. For example, as mentioned previously, nightmare sufferers can use *imagery rehearsal* to modify their own nightmares (Germain et al., 2004; Krakow & Zadra, 2006). Similarly, it is possible to use your dreams to enhance creativity (Stickgold & Walker, 2004).

Dreams and Creativity

History is full of cases where dreams have been a pathway to creativity and discovery. A striking example is provided by Dr. Otto Loewi, a pharmacologist and winner of a Nobel Prize. Loewi had spent years studying the chemical transmission of nerve impulses. A tremendous breakthrough in his research came when he dreamed of an experiment 3 nights in a row. The first 2 nights he woke up and scribbled the experiment on a pad. But the next morning, he couldn't tell what the notes meant. On the third night, he got up after having the dream. This time, instead of making notes he went straight to his laboratory and performed the crucial experiment. Loewi later said that if the experiment had occurred to him while awake he would have rejected it.

Loewi's experience gives some insight into using dreams to produce creative solutions. Inhibitions are reduced during dreaming, which may be especially useful in solving problems that require a fresh point of view. Even unimaginative people may create amazing worlds each night in their dreams. For many of us, this rich ability to create is lost in the daily rush of sensory input.

Being able to take advantage of dreams for problem solving is improved if you "set" yourself before retiring. Before you go to bed, try to visualize or think intently about a problem you wish to solve. Steep yourself in the problem by stating it clearly and reviewing all relevant information. Then use the suggestions listed previously to catch your dreams. Although this method is not guaranteed to produce a novel solution or a new insight, it is certain to be an adventure. About half of a group of college students using the method for 1 week recalled a dream that helped them solve a personal problem (Barrett, 1993).

Lucid Dreaming

If you would like to press further into the territory of dreams, you may want to learn lucid dreaming, a relatively rare but fascinating experience. During a **lucid dream** a person feels as if she or he is fully awake within the dream world and capable of normal thought and action. If you ask yourself, "Could this be a dream?" and answer "Yes," you are having a lucid dream (LaBerge, 2000; Holzinger, LaBerge, & Levitan, 2006).

Stephen LaBerge and his colleagues at the Stanford University Sleep Research Center have used a unique approach to show that lucid dreams are real and that they occur during REM sleep. In the sleep lab, lucid dreamers agree to make prearranged signals when they become aware they are dreaming. One such signal is to look up abruptly in a dream, causing a distinct upward eye movement. Another signal is to clench the right and left fists (in the dream) in a prearranged pattern. In other words, lucid dreamers can partially overcome REM sleep paralysis. Such signals show very clearly that lucid dreaming and voluntary action in dreams is possible (LaBerge, 2000).

How can a person learn to have lucid dreams? Try following this simple routine: When you awaken spontaneously from a dream, take a few minutes to try to memorize it. Next, engage in 10 to 15 minutes of read-

ing or any other activity requiring full wakefulness. Then while lying in bed and returning to sleep, say to yourself, "Next time I'm dreaming, I want to remember I'm dreaming." Finally, visualize yourself lying in bed asleep while in the dream you just rehearsed. At the same time, picture yourself realizing that you are dreaming. Follow this routine each time you awaken (substitute a dream memory from another occasion if you don't awaken from a dream). Researchers have also found that stimulation from the vestibular system tends to increase lucidity. Thus, sleeping in a hammock, a boat, or on a waterbed might increase the number of lucid dreams you have (Leslie & Ogilvie, 1996).

Why would anyone want to have more lucid dreams? Researchers are interested in lucid dreams because they provide a tool for understanding dreaming (Paulsson & Parker, 2006). Using subjects who can signal while they are dreaming makes it possible to explore dreams with firsthand data from the dreamer's world itself.

On a more personal level, lucid dreaming can convert dreams into a nightly "workshop" for emotional growth. Consider, for example, a recently divorced woman who kept dreaming that she was being swallowed by a giant wave. Rosalind Cartwright asked the woman to try swimming the next time the wave engulfed her. She did, with great determination, and the nightmare lost its terror. More important, her revised dream made her feel that she could cope with life again. For reasons such as this, people who have lucid dreams tend to feel a sense of emotional well-being (Wolpin et al., 1992). Dream expert Allan Hobson believes that learning to voluntarily enter altered states of consciousness (through lucid dreaming or self-hypnosis, for example) has allowed him to have enlightening experiences without the risks of taking mind-altering drugs (Hobson, 2001). So, day or night, don't be afraid to dream a little.

Exploring and Using Dreams

RECITE

1. Which is NOT one of the four dream processes identified by Freud?
   a. condensation
   b. lucidity
   c. displacement
   d. symbolization
2. In secondary elaboration, one dream character stands for several others. T or F?
3. Calvin Hall's approach to dream interpretation emphasizes the setting, cast, plot, and emotions portrayed in a dream. T or F?
4. Rosalind Cartwright stresses that dreaming is a relatively mechanical process having little personal meaning. T or F?
5. Both alcohol and LSD cause a slight increase in dreaming. T or F?
6. "Taking the part of" or "speaking for" dream elements is a dream interpretation technique originated by Fritz Perls. T or F?

7. Recent research shows that lucid dreaming occurs primarily during NREM sleep or micro-awakenings. T or F?

REFLECT

Critical Thinking

8. The possibility of having a lucid dream raises an interesting question: If you were dreaming right now, how could you prove it?

Relate

Some people are very interested in remembering and interpreting their dreams. Others pay little attention to dreaming. What importance do you place on dreams? Do you think dreams and dream interpretation can increase self-awareness?

Answers: 1. b 2. F 3. T 4. T 5. F 6. T 7. F 8. In waking consciousness, our actions have consequences that produce immediate sensory feedback. Dreams lack such external feedback. Thus, trying to walk through a wall or doing similar tests would reveal if you were dreaming.

chapter in review — Gateways to Consciousness

Altered states of consciousness are differentiated from normal waking awareness by changes in the quality and pattern of mental activity.

- Consciousness is a core feature of mental life.
- Cultural conditioning greatly affects what altered states a person recognizes, seeks, considers normal, and attains.

Sleep is necessary for survival. While sleep patterns may be modified, they cannot be disregarded.

- Sleep is an innate biological rhythm essential for survival.
- Moderate sleep loss mainly affects vigilance and performance on routine or boring tasks.
- Higher animals and people deprived of sleep experience involuntary microsleeps.
- Extended sleep loss can (somewhat rarely) produce a temporary sleep-deprivation psychosis.
- Sleep patterns show some flexibility, but 7 to 8 hours remains average. The amount of daily sleep decreases steadily from birth to old age.

According to the dual process hypothesis, sleep "refreshes" the body and brain and helps form lasting memories.

- Sleep occurs in four stages. Stage 1 is light sleep, and stage 4 is deep sleep. The sleeper alternates between stages 1 and 4 (passing through stages 2 and 3) several times each night.
- The two most basic sleep states are rapid eye movement (REM) sleep and non-REM (NREM) sleep. REM sleep is strongly associated with dreaming.
- NREM sleep brings overall brain activation levels down, "calming" the brain.
- REM sleep and dreaming help us store important memories.

Sleep disorders, including insomnia, sleepwalking, nightmares, night terrors, sleep apnea, and narcolepsy are serious health problems that should be corrected when they persist.

- Insomnia may be temporary or chronic. Behavioral approaches to managing insomnia, such as sleep restriction and stimulus control, are quite effective.
- Sleepwalking, sleeptalking, and sleepsex occur during NREM sleep.
- Nightmares occur in REM sleep, whereas night terrors occur in NREM sleep.
- Sleep apnea (interrupted breathing) is one source of insomnia and daytime hypersomnia (sleepiness).
- Apnea is suspected as one cause of sudden infant death syndrome (SIDS). With only a few exceptions, healthy infants should sleep face up or on their sides.
- Narcolepsy (sleep attacks) and cataplexy are caused by a sudden shift to stage 1 REM patterns during normal waking hours.

Dreams are at least as meaningful as waking thoughts. Whether they have deeper, symbolic meaning is still debated.

- REM sleep helps us form memories, and it contributes to general mental effectiveness.
- According to the Freudian (psychodynamic) view, dreams express unconscious wishes through dream symbols.

Lucid dream A dream in which the dreamer feels awake and capable of normal thought and action.

- Many theorists have questioned Freud's view of dreams. For example, the activation-synthesis model portrays dreaming as a random physiological process.
- The neurocognitive view of dreams holds that dreams are continuous with waking thoughts and emotions.
- Most dream content is about familiar settings, people, and actions. Positive and negative emotions occur about equally in dreams.
- The idea that dreams have deep symbolic meaning is debatable.

Hypnosis is an altered state characterized by narrowed attention and increased suggestibility. (Not all psychologists agree that hypnotic effects require an alteration of consciousness.)

- Stage hypnotism takes advantage of typical stage behavior and uses deception to simulate hypnosis.
- Hypnosis appears capable of producing relaxation, controlling pain, and altering perceptions.
- Hypnosis alters perceptions and behavior, but it is more capable of changing subjective experiences than habits, such as smoking.

Meditation and sensory deprivation are beneficial ways to alter consciousness through relaxation.

- Concentrative meditation can be used to focus attention, alter consciousness, and reduce stress. Mindfulness meditation widens attention to achieve similar outcomes.
- Major benefits of meditation are its ability to interrupt anxious thoughts and to elicit the relaxation response.
- Brief exposure to sensory deprivation can also elicit the relaxation response. Under proper conditions, sensory deprivation may help break long-standing habits.

Psychoactive drugs affect the brain in ways that alter consciousness. Most psychoactive drugs can be placed on a scale ranging from stimulation to depression.

- Psychoactive drugs are highly prone to abuse.
- Drug abuse is related to personal maladjustment, the reinforcing qualities of drugs, peer group influences, and expectations about drug effects.
- Drugs may cause a physical dependence (addiction), a psychological dependence, or both. The physically addicting drugs are alcohol, amphetamines, barbiturates, cocaine, codeine, GHB, heroin, marijuana, methadone, morphine, nicotine, and tranquilizers. All psychoactive drugs can lead to psychological dependence.
- Drug use can be classified as experimental, recreational, situational, intensive, and compulsive. Drug abuse is most often associated with the last three.
- Stimulant drugs are readily abused because of the period of depression that often follows stimulation. The greatest risks

are associated with amphetamines (especially methamphetamine), cocaine, MDMA, and nicotine, but even caffeine can be a problem. Nicotine includes the added risk of lung cancer, heart disease, and other health problems.
- Barbiturates and tranquilizers are depressant drugs whose action is similar to that of alcohol.
- The overdose level for barbiturates and GHB is close to the intoxication dosage, making them dangerous drugs. Mixing barbiturates, tranquilizers, or GHB and alcohol may result in a fatal drug interaction.
- Alcohol is the most heavily abused drug in common use today. Binge drinking is a problem among college students. It is possible to pace the consumption of alcohol.
- Marijuana is subject to an abuse pattern similar to alcohol. Studies have linked chronic marijuana use with lung cancer, various mental impairments, and other health problems.

Collecting and interpreting your dreams can promote self-awareness.

- Freud held that the meaning of dreams is hidden by condensation, displacement, symbolization, and secondary elaboration. Hall emphasizes the setting, cast, plot, and emotions of a dream. Cartwright's view of dreams as feeling statements and Perls' technique of speaking for dream elements are also helpful.
- Dreams may be used for creative problem solving, especially when dream awareness is achieved through lucid dreaming.

Web Resources

For an up-to-date list of direct links to interesting sites, including those listed here, visit the student companion site for this book at www.cengage.com/psychology/coon

Sleepless at Stanford What all undergraduates should know about how their sleeping lives affect their waking lives.

Sleep Paralysis Read about hypnopompic and hypnagogic experiences.

Sudden Infant Death and Other Infant Death Information about SIDS, with links to related topics.

Hypnosis and Self-Hypnosis Frequently asked questions; includes a self-hypnosis induction script.

Meditation for Stress Reduction Find out more about how to meditate.

Drugs and Behavior Links Comprehensive links to topics in drugs and behavior.

How to Keep a Diary of Dreams Find out how to keep your own dream diary.

Interactive Learning

Introduction to Psychology: Gateways to Mind and Behavior **Book Companion Website**
www.cengage.com/psychology/coon

Visit your book companion website, where you will find flash cards, practice quizzes, web links, and more to help you study.

CENGAGENOW™ *Just what you need to know NOW!*

Spend time on what you need to master rather than on information you already have learned. Take a pre-test for this chapter, and CengageNOW will generate a personalized study plan based on your results. The study plan will identify the topics you need to review and direct you to online resources to help you master those topics. You can then take a post-test to help you determine the concepts you have mastered and what you will need to work on. Try it out! Go to www.cengage.com/login to sign in with an access code or to purchase access to this product.

CHAPTER 7

Conditioning and Learning

Gateway Theme

The principles of learning can be used to understand and manage behavior.

Dan Barba/Jupiterimages

Gateway Questions

- *What is learning?*
- *How does classical conditioning occur?*
- *Does conditioning affect emotions?*
- *How does operant conditioning occur?*
- *Are there different kinds of operant reinforcement?*

- *How are we influenced by patterns of reward?*
- *What does punishment do to behavior?*
- *What is cognitive learning?*
- *Does learning occur by imitation?*
- *How does conditioning apply to practical problems?*

Larry vividly remembers his mother describing how a rat had terrified her. She gestured excitedly as she relived the horror of seeing the creature scamper out of a camp stove. Although everyone else laughed, 6-year-old Larry shivered as he imagined the attacking rodent. That's the day he learned to fear rats.

Years later, while studying gorillas in Africa, he encountered his first live rat. Larry was shocked by his own reaction. Despite being a respected scientist, he ran away shrieking like a little child. After failing to control his fear a few more times (and being good-naturedly ribbed about it by others), he resolved to conquer it.

Back home, Larry read about irrational fears and realized that a form of learning called *vicarious classical conditioning*

explained how he had come to dread rats. After reading several more books, he returned to the jungle, certain that he could cope with his next close encounter. However, he was shocked to discover that his newfound knowledge was no help at all.

Larry had bumped into a strange truth: All his abstract "book learning," a form of *cognitive learning*, was powerless to protect him in the presence of a rat. Chastened, he went to a therapist who used classical conditioning to help him overcome his fear. Larry eventually came to like rats and now has a pet rat named Einstein. Larry also went on to study how baby gorillas learn by observing others—much as he did when he observed his mother's story about the rat.

Different forms of learning reach into every corner of our lives. Are you ready to learn more? If so, let's begin!

⬤⬤ What Is Learning—Does Practice Make Perfect?

Gateway Question: What is learning?

Almost all human behavior is learned. Imagine if you suddenly lost all you had ever learned. What could you do? You would be unable to read, write, or speak. You couldn't feed yourself, find your way home, and drive a car, play the bassoon, or "party." Needless to say, you would be totally incapacitated. (Dull, too!) **Learning** is a relatively permanent change in behavior due to experience (Domjan, 2006). Notice that this definition excludes both temporary changes and more permanent changes caused by motivation, fatigue, maturation, disease, injury, or drugs. Each of these can alter behavior, but none qualifies as learning.

Types of Learning

As Larry's rat experience illustrates, there are different types of learning. **Associative learning** occurs whenever a person or an animal forms a simple association among various stimuli and/or responses. Humans share the capacity for associative learning with many other species. In a moment, we will explore two types of associative learning called classical conditioning and operant conditioning.

Humans also engage in **cognitive learning,** which refers to understanding, knowing, anticipating, or otherwise making use of information-rich higher mental processes. More complex forms of cognitive learning, such as learning from written language, are unique to humans and are why our species is called *Homo Sapiens* (from the Latin for *man* and *wise*). However, some animals do engage in simpler forms of cognitive learning, which we will describe later in this chapter.

Associative Learning

Isn't learning the result of practice? It depends on what you mean by practice. Merely repeating a response will not necessarily produce learning. You could close your eyes and swing a tennis racket hundreds of times without improving your swing. Reinforcement is the key to associative learning. **Reinforcement** refers to any event that increases the probability that a response will occur again. A response is any identifiable behavior. Responses may be observable actions, such as blinking, eating a piece of candy, or turning a doorknob. They can also be internal, such as having a faster heartbeat.

To teach a dog a trick, we could reinforce correct responses by giving the dog some food each time it sits up. Similarly, you could teach a child to be neat by praising him for picking up his toys. Learning can also occur in other ways. For instance, if a girl gets stung by a bee, she may learn to associate pain with bees and to fear them. In this case, the girl's fear is reinforced by the discomfort she feels immediately after seeing the bee.

Unlocking the secrets of associative learning begins with noting what happens before and after a response. Events that precede a response are **antecedents.** For example, Ashleigh, who is 3, has

---

Learning Any relatively permanent change in behavior that can be attributed to experience.

Associative learning The formation of simple associations between various stimuli and responses.

Cognitive learning Higher-level learning involving thinking, knowing, understanding, and anticipation.

Reinforcement Any event that increases the probability that a particular response will occur.

Antecedents Events that precede a response.

learned that when she hears a truck pull into the driveway, it means that daddy is home. Ashleigh runs to the front door. Effects that follow a response are **consequences.** The hug she gets from her father is what reinforces Ashleigh's tendency to run to the door. As this suggests, paying careful attention to the "before and after" of associative learning is a key to understanding it.

Classical conditioning is based on what happens before we respond. It begins with a stimulus that reliably triggers a response. Imagine, for example, that a puff of air (the stimulus) is aimed at your eye. The air puff will make you blink (a response) every time. The eyeblink is a **reflex** (automatic, nonlearned response). Now, assume that we sound a horn (another stimulus) just before each puff of air hits your eye. If the horn and the air puff occur together many times, what happens? Soon, the horn alone will make you blink. Clearly, you've learned something. Before, the horn didn't make you blink. Now it does.

In **classical conditioning,** an antecedent stimulus that doesn't produce a response is linked with one that does (a horn is associated with a puff of air to the eye, for example). We can say that learning has occurred when the new stimulus will also elicit (bring forth) responses (● Figure 7.1).

In **operant conditioning,** learning is based on the consequences of responding. A response may be followed by a reinforcer (such as food). Or by punishment. Or by nothing. These results determine whether a response is likely to be made again (see ● Figure 7.1). For example, if you wear a particular hat and get lots of compliments (reinforcement), you are likely to wear it more often. If people snicker, insult you, call the police, or scream (punishment), you will probably wear it less often.

Now that you have an idea of what happens in the two basic kinds of associative learning, let's look at classical conditioning in more detail.

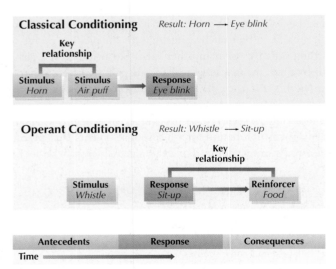

● **Figure 7.1** In classical conditioning, a stimulus that does not produce a response is paired with a stimulus that does elicit a response. After many such pairings, the stimulus that previously had no effect begins to produce a response. In the example shown, a horn precedes a puff of air to the eye. Eventually the horn alone will produce an eye blink. In operant conditioning, a response that is followed by a reinforcing consequence becomes more likely to occur on future occasions. In the example shown, a dog learns to sit up when it hears a whistle.

Classical Conditioning—Does the Name Pavlov Ring a Bell?

Gateway Question: How does classical conditioning occur?

How was classical conditioning discovered? At the beginning of the twentieth century, something happened in the lab of Russian physiologist Ivan Pavlov that brought him the Nobel Prize: Pavlov's subjects drooled at him. Actually, Pavlov was studying digestion. To observe salivation, he placed meat powder or some tidbit on a dog's tongue and measured the resulting flow of saliva. However, after repeating his procedure many times, Pavlov noticed that his dogs were salivating *before* the food reached their mouths (Schultz & Schultz, 2005). Later, the dogs even began to salivate when they saw Pavlov enter the room.

Pavlov knew that salivation is an automatic, inherited reflex. It really shouldn't change from one day to the next. His dogs were *supposed* to salivate when he put food in their mouths, but they were *not supposed* to salivate when they merely saw him. This was a change in behavior due to experience. Pavlov realized that some type of learning had occurred and soon began investigating "conditioning," as he called it (● Figure 7.2). Because of its place in history, this form of learning is now called *classical conditioning* (also known as *Pavlovian conditioning* or *respondent conditioning*) (Mackintosh, 2003).

Pavlov's Experiment

How did Pavlov study conditioning? To begin, he rang a bell. At first, the bell was a neutral stimulus (the dogs did not respond to it by salivating). Immediately after Pavlov rang the bell, he placed meat powder on the dog's tongue, which caused reflex salivation. This sequence was repeated a number of times: bell, meat powder, salivation; bell, meat powder, salivation. Eventually (as conditioning took place), the dogs began to salivate when they heard the bell (● Figure 7.3). By association, the bell, which before had no effect, began to evoke the same response that food did. This was shown by sometimes ringing the bell alone. Then the dog salivated, even though no food had been placed in its mouth.

● **Figure 7.2** An apparatus for Pavlovian conditioning. A tube carries saliva from the dog's mouth to a lever that activates a recording device (far left). During conditioning, various stimuli can be paired with a dish of food placed in front of the dog. The device pictured here is more elaborate than the one Pavlov used in his early experiments.

THE CLINICAL FILE

Coping with Chemo

Our hearts go out to children with cancer. Even the treatment, chemotherapy, makes them miserable because it causes nausea and vomiting. In a cruel twist, after a few treatments, nausea can occur even when no chemotherapy is scheduled. Typically, it is triggered by certain sights or tastes, like the sight of the treatment center or the taste of a food the child ate before an earlier chemotherapy session.

In classical conditioning terms, chemotherapy is a US that leads to nausea, which is a UR. The sight of the treatment center or the taste of food eaten before treatment is initially a neutral stimulus. However, because it is associated with nausea and vomiting, it becomes a CS. These sights or tastes can now elicit anticipatory nausea (a CR) even at times when the child doesn't receive chemotherapy (Chance, 2006).

In nature, many species are *biologically prepared* to associate specific locations and tastes with nausea. If animals eat contaminated food and then get sick and vomit, later the same locations or tastes may trigger anticipatory nausea and vomiting. These reactions discourage animals from eating potentially dangerous food. Unfortunately,

conditioned nausea only complicates treatment for young cancer patients. If Gita eats pepperoni pizza, her favorite meal, before she has a chemotherapy session, the taste of pizza may come to make her feel sick.

Is there any way to prevent conditioned nausea? No, but classical conditioning can provide some relief (Taylor, 2002). Meals eaten before chemotherapy can be strongly flavored with an unusual taste, such as peppermint. The unique flavor *overshadows* other tastes, which don't become linked with nausea (Bovbjerg et al., 1992). In this way, Gita can continue to enjoy her pepperoni pizza.

● **Figure 7.3** The classical conditioning procedure.

Psychologists use several terms to describe these events. The meat powder is an **unconditioned stimulus (US)** (a stimulus innately capable of producing a response; salivation in this case). Notice that the dog did not have to learn to respond to the US. Such stimuli naturally trigger reflexes or emotional reactions. Because a reflex is innate, or "built in," it is called an **unconditioned** (nonlearned) **response (UR).** Reflex salivation was the UR in Pavlov's experiment.

The bell starts out as a **neutral stimulus (NS).** In time, the bell becomes a **conditioned stimulus (CS)** (a stimulus that, because of learning, will elicit a response). When Pavlov's bell also produced salivation, the dog was making a new response. Thus, salivation had also become a **conditioned** (learned) **response (CR).** (See ● Figure 7.3). ● Table 7.1 summarizes the important elements of classical conditioning.

Are all these terms really necessary? Yes, because they help us recognize similarities in various instances of learning. Let's summarize the terms using an earlier example:

Before Conditioning	Example
US → UR	Puff of air → eye blink
NS → no effect	Horn → no effect

After Conditioning	Example
CS → CR	Horn → eye blink

See "Coping with Chemo" for an example of how classical conditioning is used to solve a clinical problem.

Consequences Effects that follow a response.

Reflex An innate, automatic response to a stimulus; for example, an eyeblink.

Classical conditioning A form of learning in which reflex responses are associated with new stimuli.

Operant conditioning Learning based on the consequences of responding.

Unconditioned stimulus (US) A stimulus innately capable of eliciting a response.

Unconditioned response (UR) An innate reflex response elicited by an unconditioned stimulus.

Neutral stimulus (NS) A stimulus that does not evoke a response.

Conditioned stimulus (CS) A stimulus that evokes a response because it has been repeatedly paired with an unconditioned stimulus.

Conditioned response (CR) A learned response elicited by a conditioned stimulus.

Table 7.1 ● Elements of Classical Conditioning

Element	Symbol	Description	Example
Unconditioned stimulus	US	A stimulus innately capable of eliciting a response	Meat powder
Unconditioned response	UR	An innate reflex response elicited by an unconditioned stimulus	Reflex salivation *to the US*
Neutral stimulus	NS	A stimulus that does not evoke the unconditioned response	Bell *before conditioning*
Conditioned stimulus	CS	A stimulus that evokes a response because it has been repeatedly paired with an unconditioned stimulus	Bell *after conditioning*
Conditioned response	CR	A learned response elicited by a conditioned stimulus	Salivation *to the CS*

● **Figure 7.4** Acquisition and extinction of a conditioned response. (After Pavlov, 1927.)

● **Figure 7.5** Higher order conditioning takes place when a well-learned conditioned stimulus is used as if it were an unconditioned stimulus. In this example, a child is first conditioned to salivate to the sound of a bell. In time, the bell will elicit salivation. At that point, you could clap your hands and then ring the bell. Soon, after repeating the procedure, the child would learn to salivate when you clapped your hands.

●● Principles of Classical Conditioning—Here's Johnny

Imagine a boy named Johnny. To observe conditioning, you could ring a bell and squirt lemon juice into Johnny's mouth. By repeating this procedure several times, you could condition Johnny to salivate to the bell. Johnny might then be used to explore other aspects of classical conditioning.

Acquisition

During **acquisition,** or training, a conditioned response must be reinforced (strengthened) (● Figure 7.4). Classical conditioning is *reinforced* when the CS is followed by, or paired with, an unconditioned stimulus. This process is called **respondent reinforcement** because the US brings forth a *response,* which becomes associated with the CS. For Johnny, the bell is the CS, salivating is the UR, and the sour lemon juice is a US. To reinforce salivating to the bell, we must link the bell with the lemon juice. Conditioning will be most rapid if the US (lemon juice) follows *immediately* after the CS (the bell). With most reflexes, the optimal delay between CS and US is from one-half second to about 5 seconds (Chance, 2006).

Higher Order Conditioning

Once a response is learned, it can bring about **higher order conditioning.** In this case, a well-learned CS is used to reinforce further learning (Lefrançois, 2006). That is, the CS has become strong enough to be used like an unconditioned stimulus. Let's illustrate again with our salivating child.

As a result of earlier learning, the bell now makes Johnny salivate. (No lemon juice is needed.) To go a step further, you could clap your hands and then ring the bell. (Again, no lemon juice

would be used.) Through higher order conditioning, Johnny would soon learn to salivate when you clapped your hands (● Figure 7.5). (This little trick could be a real hit with friends and neighbors.)

Higher order conditioning extends learning one or more steps beyond the original conditioned stimulus. Many advertisers use this effect by pairing images that evoke good feelings (such as people smiling and having fun) with pictures of their products. They hope that you will learn, by association, to feel good when you see their products (Priluck & Till, 2004).

Expectancies

Pavlov believed that classical conditioning does not involve any higher mental processes. Today, many psychologists think that classical conditioning does have mental origins because it is related to information that might aid survival. According to this **informational view,** we look for associations among events. Doing so creates new mental **expectancies,** or thoughts about how events are interconnected.

How does classical conditioning alter expectancies? Notice that the conditioned stimulus reliably precedes the unconditioned stimulus. Because it does, the CS *predicts* the US (Rescorla, 1987). During conditioning, the brain learns to *expect* that the US will follow the CS. As a result, the brain prepares the body to respond to the US. Here's an example: When you are about to get a shot with a hypodermic needle, your muscles tighten and there is a catch in your breathing. Why? Because your body is preparing for pain. You have learned to expect that getting poked with a needle will hurt. This expectancy, which was acquired during classical conditioning, changes your behavior.

Extinction and Spontaneous Recovery

Once an association has been classically conditioned will it ever go away? If the US never again follows the CS, conditioning will extinguish, or fade away. Let's return to Johnny. If you ring the bell many times and do not follow it with lemon juice, Johnny's expectancy that "bell precedes lemon juice" will weaken. As it does, he will lose his tendency to salivate when he hears the bell. Thus, we see that classical conditioning can be weakened by removing the connection between the conditioned and unconditioned stimulus (see ● Figure 7.4). This process is called **extinction.**

If conditioning takes a while to build up, shouldn't it take time to reverse? Yes. In fact, it may take several extinction sessions to completely reverse conditioning. Let's say that we ring the bell until Johnny quits responding. It might seem that extinction is complete. However, Johnny will probably respond to the bell again on the following day, at least at first (Rescorla, 2004). The return of a learned response after apparent extinction is called **spontaneous recovery.** It explains why people who have had a car accident may need many slow, calm rides before their fear of driving extinguishes.

Generalization

After conditioning, other stimuli similar to the CS may also trigger a response. This is called **stimulus generalization.** For example, we might find that Johnny salivates to the sound of a ringing telephone or doorbell, even though they were never used as conditioning stimuli.

It is easy to see the value of stimulus generalization. Consider the child who burns her finger while playing with matches. Most likely, lighted matches will become conditioned fear stimuli for her. Because of stimulus generalization, she may also have a healthy fear of flames from lighters, fireplaces, stoves, and so forth. It's fortunate that generalization extends learning to related situations. Otherwise, we would all be far less adaptable.

As you may have guessed, stimulus generalization has limits. As stimuli become less like the original CS, responding decreases. If you condition a person to blink each time you play a particular note on a piano, blinking will decline as you play higher or lower notes. If the notes are *much* higher or lower, the person will not respond at all (● Figure 7.6). Stimulus generalization explains

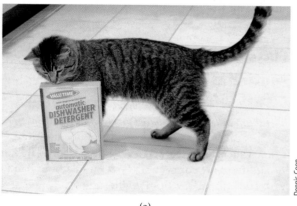

(a)

● **Figure 7.6** *(a)* Stimulus generalization. Stimuli similar to the CS also elicit a response. *(b)* This cat has learned to salivate when it sees a cat food box. Because of stimulus generalization, it also salivates when shown a similar-looking detergent box.

why many stores carry imitations of nationally known products. For many customers, positive attitudes conditioned to the real products tend to generalize to the cheaper knockoffs (Till & Priluck, 2000).

Acquisition The period in conditioning during which a response is reinforced.

Respondent reinforcement Reinforcement that occurs when an unconditioned stimulus closely follows a conditioned stimulus.

Higher order conditioning Classical conditioning in which a conditioned stimulus is used to reinforce further learning; that is, a CS is used as if it were a US.

Informational view Perspective that explains learning in terms of information imparted by events in the environment.

Expectancy An anticipation concerning future events or relationships.

Extinction The weakening of a conditioned response through removal of reinforcement.

Spontaneous recovery The reappearance of a learned response after its apparent extinction.

Stimulus generalization The tendency to respond to stimuli similar to, but not identical to, a conditioned stimulus.

Discrimination

Let's consider one more idea with Johnny (who by now must be ready to hide in the closet). Suppose we again condition Johnny, with a bell as the CS. As an experiment, we occasionally sound a buzzer instead of ringing the bell. However, the buzzer is never followed by the US (lemon juice). At first, Johnny salivates when he hears the buzzer (because of generalization). But after we sound the buzzer several times more, Johnny will stop responding to it. Why? In essence, Johnny's generalized response to the buzzer has extinguished. As a result, he has learned to *discriminate,* or respond differently, to the bell and the buzzer.

Stimulus discrimination is the ability to respond differently to various stimuli. As an example, you might remember the feelings of anxiety or fear you had as a child when your mother's or father's voice changed to the dreaded give-me-that-Wii-controller tone. Most children quickly learn to discriminate voice tones associated with punishment from those associated with praise or affection.

● Classical Conditioning in Humans— An Emotional Topic

Gateway Question: Does conditioning affect emotions?

How much human learning is based on classical conditioning? At its simplest, classical conditioning depends on unconditioned reflex responses. As mentioned earlier, a reflex is a dependable, inborn stimulus-and-response connection. For example, your hand reflexively draws back from pain. Bright light causes the pupil of the eye to narrow. A puff of air directed at your eye will make you blink. Various foods elicit salivation. Any of these reflexes, and others as well, can be associated with a new stimulus. At the very least, you have probably noticed how your mouth waters when you see or smell a bakery. Even pictures of food may make you salivate (a photo of a sliced lemon is great for this).

Conditioned Emotional Responses

More complex *emotional,* or "gut," responses may also be associated with new stimuli. For instance, if your face reddened when you were punished as a child, you may blush now when you are embarrassed or ashamed. Or think about the effects of associating pain with a dentist's office during your first visit. On later visits, did your heart pound and your palms sweat *before* the dentist began?

Many *involuntary,* autonomic nervous system, responses ("fight-or-flight" reflexes) are linked with new stimuli and situations by classical conditioning. For example, learned reactions worsen many cases of hypertension (high blood pressure). Traffic jams, arguments with a spouse, and similar situations can become conditioned stimuli that trigger a dangerous rise in blood pressure (Reiff, Katkin, & Friedman, 1999).

Of course, emotional conditioning also applies to animals. One of the most common mistakes people make with pets (especially dogs) is hitting them if they do not come when called. Calling the animal then becomes a conditioned stimulus for fear and with-

drawal. No wonder the pet disobeys when called on future occasions. Parents who belittle, scream at, or physically abuse their children make the same mistake.

Learned Fears

Some phobias (FOE-bee-ahs) are also based on emotional conditioning. A *phobia* is a fear that persists even when no realistic danger exists. Fears of animals, water, heights, thunder, fire, bugs, elevators, and the like, are common. Psychologists believe that many phobias begin as **conditioned emotional responses (CERs),** or learned emotional reactions to a previously neutral stimulus.

People who have phobias can often trace their fears to a time when they were frightened, injured, or upset by a particular stimulus, especially in childhood (King, Muris, & Ollendick, 2005). Just one bad experience in which you were frightened or disgusted by a spider may condition fears that last for years (de Jong & Muris, 2002). Stimulus generalization and higher order conditioning can spread CERs to other stimuli (Gewirtz & Davis, 1998). As a result, what began as a limited fear may become a disabling phobia (● Figure 7.7).

During a CER, an area of your brain called the amygdala becomes more active and produces feelings of fear. The amygdala is part of the limbic system, which is responsible for other emotions, as well (see Chapter 2). Cognitive learning has little effect on these lower brain areas (Olsson, Nearing, & Phelps, 2007). Perhaps that's why fears and phobias cannot be readily eased by merely reading about how to control fears—as our friend Larry found with his rat phobia. However, conditioned fears do respond to a therapy called **desensitization.** This is done by gradually exposing the phobic person to feared stimuli while she or he remains calm and relaxed. For example, people who fear heights can be slowly taken to ever-higher elevations until their fears extinguish. This therapy even works when computer graphics are used to simulate the experience of heights (Wiederhold & Wiederhold, 2005).

(a)   (b)

(c)   (d)

● **Figure 7.7** Hypothetical example of a CER becoming a phobia. Child approaches dog *(a)* and is frightened by it *(b)*. Fear generalizes to other household pets *(c)* and later to virtually all furry animals *(d)*.

bridges

See Chapter 15, pages 503–509, for more information about therapies based on learning principles.

Undoubtedly, we acquire many of our likes, dislikes, and fears as conditioned emotional responses. As noted before, advertisers try to achieve the same effect by pairing products with pleasant images and music. So do many students on a first date.

Vicarious, or Secondhand, Conditioning

Conditioning can also occur indirectly. Let's say, for example, that you watch another person get an electric shock. Each time, a signal light comes on before the shock is delivered. Even if you don't receive a shock yourself, you will soon develop a CER to the light. Children who learn to fear thunder by watching their parents react to it have undergone similar conditioning. Many Americans were traumatized as a consequence of watching media coverage of the September 11 terrorist attacks in New York and Washington (Blanchard et al., 2004). Similarly, people who counsel traumatized victims of sexual abuse can themselves develop vicarious trauma (Rothschild & Rand, 2006; Way et al., 2004).

Vicarious classical conditioning occurs when we learn to respond emotionally to a stimulus by observing another person's emotional reactions (Olsson, Nearing, & Phelps, 2007). Such "secondhand" learning affects feelings in many situations. Being told that "snakes are dangerous" may not explain the child's *emotional* response. More likely, the child has observed others reacting fearfully to the word *snake* or to snake images on television (King, Muris, & Ollendick, 2005). That is exactly how Larry, the researcher we met at the beginning of this chapter, developed his fear of rats. As children grow up, the emotions of parents, friends, and relatives undoubtedly add to fears of snakes, caves, spiders, heights, and other terrors. Even "horror" movies filled with screaming actors can have a similar effect.

The emotional attitudes we develop toward foods, political parties, ethnic groups, escalators—whatever—are probably conditioned not only by direct experiences but vicariously as well. No one is born prejudiced—all attitudes are learned. Parents may do well to look in a mirror if they wonder how or where a child "picked up" a particular fear or emotional attitude.

KNOWLEDGE BUILDER
Classical Conditioning

RECITE

1. The concept of reinforcement applies to both
   a. antecedents and consequences
   b. neutral stimuli and rewards
   c. classical and operant conditioning
   d. acquisition and spontaneous recovery
2. Classical conditioning, studied by the Russian physiologist _____, is also referred to as _____ conditioning.

3. You smell the odor of cookies being baked and your mouth waters. Apparently, the odor of cookies is a _____ and your salivation is a _____.
   a. CR, CS
   b. CS, CR
   c. consequence, neutral stimulus
   d. reflex, CS
4. The informational view says that classical conditioning is based on changes in mental _____ about the CS and US.
5. After you have acquired a conditioned response, it may be weakened by
   a. spontaneous recovery
   b. stimulus generalization
   c. removing reinforcement
   d. following the CS with a US
6. When a conditioned stimulus is used to reinforce the learning of a second conditioned stimulus, higher order conditioning has occurred. T or F?
7. Psychologists theorize that many phobias begin when a CER generalizes to other, similar situations. T or F?
8. Three-year-old Josh sees his 5-year-old sister get chased by a neighbor's dog. Now Josh is as afraid of the dog as his sister is. Josh's fear is a result of
   a. stimulus discrimination
   b. vicarious conditioning
   c. spontaneous recovery
   d. higher order conditioning

REFLECT
Critical Thinking
9. Lately you have been getting a shock of static electricity every time you touch a door handle. Now there is a hesitation in your door-opening movements. Can you analyze this situation in terms of classical conditioning?

Relate
US, CS, UR, CR—How will you remember these terms? First, you should note that we are interested in either a stimulus (S) or a response (R). What else do we need to know? Each S or R can be either conditioned (C) or unconditioned (U).

Can a stimulus provoke a response before any learning has occurred? If it can, then it's a US. Do you have to learn to respond to the stimulus? Then it's a CS.

Does a response occur without being learned? Then it's a UR. If it has to be learned, then it's a CR.

Answers: 1. c 2. Pavlov, Pavlovian or respondent 3. b 4. expectancies 5. c 6. T 7. T 8. b 9. Door handles have become conditioned stimuli that elicit the reflex withdrawal and muscle tensing that normally follows getting a shock. This conditioned response has also generalized to other handles.

Stimulus discrimination The learned ability to respond differently to similar stimuli.

Conditioned emotional response (CER) An emotional response that has been linked to a previously nonemotional stimulus by classical conditioning.

Desensitization Reducing fear or anxiety by repeatedly exposing a person to emotional stimuli while the person is deeply relaxed.

Vicarious classical conditioning Classical conditioning brought about by observing another person react to a particular stimulus.

Operant Conditioning— Can Pigeons Play Ping-Pong?

Gateway Question: How does operant conditioning occur?

The principles of operant conditioning, another form of associative learning, are among the most powerful tools in psychology. You won't regret learning how to use them. Operant conditioning explains much day-to-day behavior and can be used to alter the behavior of pets, children, other adults, and your own behavior, too.

As stated earlier, in **operant conditioning** (also known as *instrumental learning*) we associate responses with their consequences. The basic principle is simple: Acts that are reinforced tend to be repeated (Mazur, 2006). Pioneer learning theorist Edward L. Thorndike called this the **law of effect:** The probability of a response is altered by the effect it has (Schultz & Schultz, 2005). Learning is strengthened each time a response is followed by a satisfying state of affairs. You are much more likely to keep telling a joke if people laugh at it. If the first three people frown when they hear the joke, you may not tell it again.

In operant conditioning, the learner actively "operates on" the environment. Thus, operant conditioning refers mainly to learning *voluntary* responses. For example, pushing buttons on a TV remote control is a learned operant response. Pushing a particular button is reinforced by gaining the consequence you desire, such as changing channels or muting an obnoxious commercial. In contrast, classical conditioning is passive. It simply "happens to" the learner when a US follows a CS. (See ● Table 7.2 for a further comparison of classical and operant conditioning.)

Positive Reinforcement

The idea that reward affects learning is nothing new to parents (and other trainers of small animals). However, parents, as well as teachers, politicians, supervisors, and even you, may use reward in ways that are inexact or misguided. A case in point is the term *reward*. To be correct, it is better to say *reinforcer*. Why? Because rewards do not always increase responding. If you give chocolate

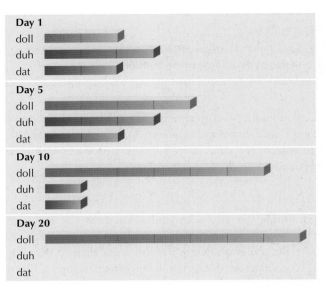

● **Figure 7.8** Assume that a child who is learning to talk points to her favorite doll and says either "doll," "duh," or "dat" when she wants it. Day 1 shows the number of times the child uses each word to ask for the doll (each block represents one request). At first, she uses all three words interchangeably. To hasten learning, her parents decide to give her the doll only when she names it correctly. Notice how the child's behavior shifts as operant reinforcement is applied. By day 20, saying "doll" has become the most probable response.

to a child as a "reward" for good behavior, it will work only if the child likes chocolate. What is reinforcing for one person may not be for another. As a practical rule of thumb, psychologists define an **operant reinforcer** as any event that follows a response and increases its probability of occurring again (● Figure 7.8).

Acquiring an Operant Response

Many studies of operant conditioning in animals make use of an **operant conditioning chamber** (Skinner, 1938). This device is also called a Skinner box, after B. F. Skinner, who invented it (● Figure 7.9). The walls are bare except for a metal lever and a tray into which food pellets can be dispensed. The fact that there's

Table 7.2 ● Comparison of Classical and Operant Conditioning

	Classical Conditioning	Operant Conditioning
Nature of response	Involuntary, reflex	Spontaneous, voluntary
Reinforcement	Occurs *before* response (CS paired with US)	Occurs *after* response (response is followed by reinforcing stimulus or event)
Role of learner	Passive (response is *elicited* by US)	Active (response is emitted)
Nature of learning	Neutral stimulus becomes a CS through association with a US	Probability of making a response is altered by consequences that follow it
Learned expectancy	US will follow CS	Response will have a specific effect

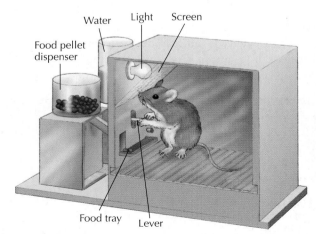

● **Figure 7.9** The Skinner box. This simple device, invented by B. F. Skinner, allows careful study of operant conditioning. When the rat presses the bar, a pellet of food or a drop of water is automatically released.

not much to do in a Skinner box increases the chances that a subject will make the desired response, which is pressing the bar. Also, hunger keeps the animal motivated to seek food and actively *emit*, or freely give off, a variety of responses. A look into a typical Skinner box will clarify the process of operant conditioning.

Einstein Snags a Snack

A smart and hungry rat (yes, it's Larry's rat) is placed in an operant conditioning chamber. For a while our subject walks around, grooms, sniffs at the corners, or stands on his hind legs—all typical rat behaviors. Then it happens. He places his paw on the lever to get a better view of the top of the cage. *Click!* The lever depresses, and a food pellet drops into the tray. The rat scurries to the tray, eats the pellet, and then grooms himself. Up and exploring the cage again, he leans on the lever. *Click!* After a trip to the food tray, he returns to the bar and sniffs it, then puts his foot on it. *Click!* Soon Einstein settles into a smooth pattern of frequent bar pressing.

Notice that the rat did not acquire a new skill in this situation. He was already able to press the bar. Reinforcement only alters how *frequently* he presses the bar. In operant conditioning, new behavior patterns are molded by changing the probability that various responses will be made.

Information and Contingency

Like classical conditioning, we can think of operant learning as being based on information and expectancies (Pierce & Cheney, 2004). In operant conditioning, *we learn to expect that a certain response will have a certain effect at certain times.* That is, we learn that a particular response is associated with reinforcement (Hergenhahn & Olson, 2005). Further, operant reinforcement works best when it is *response contingent* (kon-TIN-jent). That is, it must be given only after a desired response has occurred. From this point of view, a reinforcer tells a person or an animal that a response was "right" and worth repeating.

For example, one severely disturbed 9-year-old child was taught to say "Please," "Thank you," and "You're welcome." During the initial, baseline period, the child rarely used the word "please." Typically, he just grabbed objects and became angry if he couldn't have them. However, when he was consistently reinforced for saying "Please," he soon learned to use the word nearly every time he wanted something. When the child said "Please" he was reinforced in three ways: He received the object he asked for (a crayon, for example); he was given a small food treat, such as a piece of candy, popcorn, or a grape; and he was praised for his good behavior (Matson et al., 1990).

In similar ways, operant principles greatly affect behavior in homes, schools, and businesses. It is always worthwhile to arrange reinforcers so that they encourage productive and responsible behavior.

The Timing of Reinforcement

Operant reinforcement is most effective when it rapidly follows a correct response (Mazur, 2006). For rats in a Skinner box, little or no learning occurs if the delay between bar pressing and receiving food exceeds 50 seconds. (● Figure 7.10). In general, you will be most successful if you present a reinforcer *immediately* after a

● **Figure 7.10** The effect of delay of reinforcement. Notice how rapidly the learning score drops when reward is delayed. Animals learning to press a bar in a Skinner box showed no signs of learning if food reward followed a bar press by more than 100 seconds (Perin, 1943. A quantitative investigation of the delay of reinforcement gradient. *Journal of Experimental Psychology*, 32, 37–51. Copyright © 1943, APA. Reprinted with permission of the publisher.).

response you wish to change. Thus, a child who is helpful or courteous should be immediately praised for her good behavior.

Let's say I work hard all semester in a class to get an A grade. Wouldn't the delay in reinforcement keep me from learning anything? No, for several reasons. First, as a mature human you can anticipate future reward. Second, you get reinforced by quiz and test grades all through the semester. Third, a single reinforcer can often maintain a long response chain (a linked series of actions that lead to reinforcement).

An example of **response chaining** is provided by the sport of dog agility training. Dogs are taught to navigate a variety of obstacles. These include jumping over hurdles, walking over seesaws, climbing up and jumping off inclined walls, and running through tunnels made out of cloth (Helton, 2007). During competitions, a trainer can only reinforce a dog with a snack or a hug after the dog completes the entire response chain. The winning dog is the one who finishes the course with the fewest mistakes and the fastest time. (Good dog!)

Many of the things we do every day involve similar response chains. The long series of events necessary to prepare a meal is rewarded by the final eating. A violinmaker may carry out thousands of steps for the final reward of hearing a first musical note. And as a student, you have built up long response chains for the final reward of getting good grades (right?).

Operant conditioning Learning based on the consequences of responding.

Law of effect Responses that lead to desirable effects are repeated; those that produce undesirable results are not.

Operant reinforcer Any event that reliably increases the probability or frequency of responses it follows.

Operant conditioning chamber (Skinner box) An apparatus designed to study operant conditioning in animals; a Skinner box.

Response chaining The assembly of separate responses into a series of actions that lead to reinforcement.

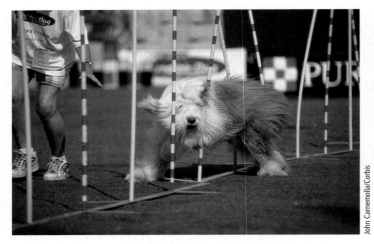

Dogs must build up long response chains to compete in agility training competitions.

John Carnemolla/Corbis

Yale Joel/*Life Magazine*/TimePix/Getty Images

● **Figure 7.11** Operant conditioning principles were used to train these pigeons to play Ping-Pong.

Are You Superstitious?

If a golfer taps her club on the ground three times and then hits a great shot, what happens? The successful shot reinforces not only the correct swing but also the three taps. Reinforcers affect not only the specific response they follow but also other responses that occur shortly before. This helps explain many human superstitions. (During operant training, animals often develop similar unnecessary responses.) If this happens a few times more, the golfer may superstitiously tap her club three times before every shot. Some examples of actual superstitious behaviors of professional baseball players include drawing four lines in the dirt before getting in the batter's box, eating chicken before each game, and always playing in the same athletic supporter—for 4 years (phew!) (Burger & Lynn, 2005).

Superstitious behaviors are repeated because they appear to produce reinforcement, even though they are actually unnecessary (Burger & Lynn, 2005). If you walk under a ladder and then break a leg, you may avoid ladders in the future. Each time you avoid a ladder and nothing bad happens, your superstitious action is reinforced. Belief in magic can also be explained along such lines. Rituals to bring rain, ward off illness, or produce abundant crops very likely earn the faith of participants because they occasionally appear to succeed.

Shaping

How is it possible to reinforce responses that rarely occur? Even in a barren Skinner box, it could take a long time for a rat (even one as smart as Einstein) to accidentally press the bar and get a food pellet. We might wait forever for more complicated responses to occur. For example, you would have to wait a long time for a duck to accidentally walk out of its cage, turn on a light, play a toy piano, turn off the light, and walk back to its cage. If this is what you wanted to reward, you would never get the chance.

Then how are the animals on TV and at amusement parks taught to perform complicated tricks? The answer lies in **shaping,** which is

the gradual molding of responses to a desired pattern. Let's look again at our favorite rat, Einstein.

Einstein Shapes Up

Instead of waiting for Einstein's first accidental bar press, which might have taken a long time, we could have shaped his behavior. Assume that Einstein has not yet learned to press the bar. At first, we settle for just getting him to face the bar. Any time he turns toward the bar, he is reinforced with a bit of food. Soon Einstein spends much of his time facing the bar. Next, we reinforce him every time he takes a step toward the bar. If he turns toward the bar and walks away, nothing happens. But when he faces the bar and takes a step forward, *click!* His responses are being shaped.

By changing the rules about what makes a successful response, we can gradually train the rat to approach the bar and press it. In other words, *successive approximations* (ever-closer matches) to a desired response are reinforced during shaping. B. F. Skinner once taught two pigeons to play Ping-Pong in this way (● Figure 7.11). Shaping applies to humans, too. Let's say you want to study more, clean the house more often, or exercise more. In each case, it would be best to set a series of gradual, daily goals. Then you can reward yourself for small steps in the right direction (Watson & Tharp, 2007).

Operant Extinction

Would a rat stop bar pressing if no more food arrived? Yes, but not immediately. Through **operant extinction,** learned responses that are not reinforced gradually fade away. Just as acquiring an operant response takes time, so does extinction. For example, if a TV program repeatedly bores you, watching the program will likely extinguish over time.

Even after extinction seems complete, the previously reinforced response may return. If a rat is removed from a Skinner box after extinction and given a short rest, the rat will press the bar again when returned to the box. Similarly, a few weeks after they give up on buying state lottery tickets, many people are tempted to try again.

Does extinction take as long the second time? If reinforcement is still withheld, a rat's bar pressing will extinguish again, usually more quickly. The brief return of an operant response after extinction is another example of spontaneous recovery (mentioned earlier regarding classical conditioning). Spontaneous recovery is very adaptive. After a rest period, the rat responds again in a situation that produced food in the past: "Just checking to see if the rules have changed!"

Marked changes in behavior occur when reinforcement and extinction are combined. For example, parents often unknowingly reinforce children for *negative attention seeking* (using misbehavior to gain attention). Children are generally ignored when they are playing quietly. They get attention when they become louder and louder, yell "Hey, Mom!" at the top of their lungs, throw tantrums, show off, or break something. Granted, the attention they get is often a scolding, but attention is a powerful reinforcer, nevertheless. Parents report dramatic improvements when they *ignore* their children's disruptive behavior and praise or attend to a child who is quiet or playing constructively.

Negative Reinforcement

Until now, we have stressed **positive reinforcement,** which occurs when a pleasant or desirable event follows a response. How else could operant learning be reinforced? The time has come to consider **negative reinforcement,** which occurs when making a response removes an unpleasant event. Don't be fooled by the word *negative.* Negative reinforcement also increases responding. However, it does so by ending *(negating)* discomfort.

Let's say that you have a headache and take an aspirin. Your aspirin taking will be negatively reinforced if the headache stops. Likewise, a rat could be taught to press a bar to get food (positive reinforcement), or the rat could be given a continuous mild shock (through the floor of its cage) that is turned off by a bar press (negative reinforcement). Either way, the rat will learn to press the bar more often. Why? Because it leads to a desired state of affairs (food or an end to pain). Here are two additional examples of negative reinforcement:

> While walking outside, your hands get so cold they hurt. You take a pair of gloves out of your backpack and put them on, ending the pain. (Putting on the gloves is negatively reinforced.)
>
> A politician who irritates you is being interviewed on the evening news. You change channels so you won't have to listen to him. (Channel changing is negatively reinforced.)

Punishment

Many people mistake negative reinforcement for punishment. However, **punishment** refers to following a response with an **aversive** (unpleasant) consequence. Punishment *decreases* the likelihood that the response will occur again. As noted, negative reinforcement *increases* responding. The difference can be seen in a hypothetical example. Let's say you live in an apartment and your neighbor's stereo is blasting so loudly that you can't concentrate on reading this book. If you pound on the wall and the volume suddenly drops (negative reinforcement), future wall pounding will be more likely. But if you pound on the wall and the volume

increases (punishment) or if the neighbor comes over and pounds on you (more punishment), wall pounding becomes less likely. Here are two more examples of punishment, in which an unpleasant result follows a response:

> You are driving your car too fast. You are caught in a radar trap and given a speeding ticket. Henceforth, you will be less likely to speed. (Speeding was punished by a fine.)
>
> Every time you give advice to a friend she suddenly turns cold and distant. Lately, you've stopped offering her advice. (Giving advice was punished by rejection.)

Isn't it also punishing to have privileges, money, or other positive things taken away for making a particular response? Yes. Punishment also occurs when a reinforcer or positive state of affairs is removed, such as losing privileges. This second type of punishment is called **response cost.** The best-known form of response cost is *time out,* in which children are removed from situations that normally allow them to gain reinforcement. When your parents put you on time out by sending you to your room, they denied you the reinforcement of being with the rest of your family or hanging out with your friends. Parking tickets and other fines are also based on response cost. For your convenience, ● Table 7.3 summarizes four basic consequences of making a response.

Table 7.3 ● Behavioral Effects of Various Consequences

	Consequence of Making a Response	Example	Effect on Response Probability
Positive reinforcement	Positive event begins	Food given	Increase
Negative reinforcement	Negative event ends	Pain stops	Increase
Punishment	Negative event begins	Pain begins	Decrease
Punishment (response cost)	Positive event ends	Food removed	Decrease
Nonreinforcement	Nothing	—	Decrease

Superstitious behavior A behavior repeated because it seems to produce reinforcement, even though it is actually unnecessary.

Shaping Gradually molding responses to a final desired pattern.

Operant extinction The weakening or disappearance of a nonreinforced operant response.

Positive reinforcement Occurs when a response is followed by a reward or other positive event.

Negative reinforcement Occurs when a response is followed by an end to discomfort or by the removal of an unpleasant event.

Punishment Any event that follows a response and *decreases* its likelihood of occurring again.

Aversive stimulus A stimulus that is painful or uncomfortable.

Response cost Removal of a positive reinforcer after a response is made.

BRAINWAVES

Tickling Your Own Fancy

Suppose you could have an electrode implanted in your brain and connected to an iPod-style controller. Twirl the controller and electrical impulses stimulate one of your brain's "pleasure centers." The very few humans who have ever had a chance to try direct brain stimulation report feeling intense pleasure that is better than food, water, sex, drugs, or any other primary reinforcer (Heath, 1963) (● Figure 7.12).

Most of what we know about intracranial self-stimulation comes from studying rats with similar implants (Olds & Fobes, 1981). A rat "wired for pleasure" can be trained to press the bar in a Skinner box to deliver electrical stimulation to its own limbic system. (Refer back to Figure 2.26.) Some rats will press the bar thousands of times per hour to obtain brain stimulation. After 15 or 20 hours of constant pressing, animals sometimes collapse from exhaustion. When they revive, they begin pressing again. If the reward circuit is not turned off, an animal will ignore food, water, and sex in favor of bar pressing.

> **bridges**
>
> Electrical stimulation is a valuable tool for studying the functions of various brain structures. **See Chapter 2, pages 57–58.**

Many natural primary reinforcers activate the same pleasure pathways in the brain that make ICS so powerful (McBride, Murphy, & Ikemoto, 1999). So do psychoactive drugs, such as alcohol and cocaine (Eisler, Justice, Jr., & Neill, 2004; Rodd et al., 2005). In fact, rats will also self-administer nicotine. When they do, they are even more likely to engage in ICS (Kenny & Markou, 2006). Apparently, nicotine further increases the sensitivity of pleasure pathways in the brain.

One shudders to think what might happen if brain implants were easy and practical to do. (They are not.) Every company from *Playboy* to *Microsoft* would have a device on the market, and we would have to keep a closer watch on politicians than usual!

(a)   (b)

● **Figure 7.12** Humans have been "wired" for brain stimulation, as shown in *(a)*. Occasionally done as an experimental way to restrain uncontrollable outbursts of violence, temporary implants have rarely been done merely to produce pleasure. Most research has been carried out with rats. Using the apparatus shown in *(b)*, the rat can press a bar to deliver mild electric stimulation to a "pleasure center" in the brain.

●● Operant Reinforcers— What's Your Pleasure?

Gateway Question: Are there different kinds of operant reinforcement?

For humans, learning may be reinforced by anything from a candy bar to a word of praise. In categorizing reinforcers, a useful distinction can be made between *primary reinforcers* and *secondary reinforcers*. It is also important to distinguish *reinforcement,* which exerts its effect through associative learning from *feedback,* a key component of cognitive learning. Let's examine reinforcement and feedback in more detail.

Primary Reinforcers

Primary reinforcers produce comfort, end discomfort, or fill an immediate physical need: They are natural, nonlearned, and rooted in biology. Food, water, and sex are obvious examples. Every time you open the refrigerator, walk to a drinking fountain, turn up the heat, or order a double latte, your actions reflect primary reinforcement.

In addition to obvious examples, there are other, less obvious, primary reinforcers, such as psychoactive drugs. One of the most powerful reinforcers is *intracranial self-stimulation* (ICS). ICS involves the direct activation of "pleasure centers" in the brain. (See "Tickling Your Own Fancy.")

Secondary Reinforcers

Much human learning is still strongly tied to food, water, and other primary reinforcers. Regardless, humans also respond to a much broader range of rewards and reinforcers. Money, praise, attention, approval, success, affection, grades, and the like, all serve as learned or **secondary reinforcers.**

How does a secondary reinforcer gain its ability to promote learning? Some secondary reinforcers are simply associated with a primary reinforcer. For example, if you would like to train a dog to follow you ("heel") when you take a walk, you could reward the dog with small food treats for staying near you. If you praise the dog each time you give it a treat, praise will become a secondary reinforcer. In time, you will be able to skip giving treats and simply praise your pup for doing the right thing. The same principle applies to children. One reason that parents' praise becomes a secondary reinforcer is because it is frequently associated with food, candy, hugs, and other primary reinforcers.

Tokens

Secondary reinforcers that can be *exchanged* for primary reinforcers gain their value more directly (Mazur, 2006). Printed money obviously has little or no value of its own. You can't eat it, drink it,

● **Figure 7.13** Poker chips normally have little or no value for chimpanzees, but this chimp will work hard to earn them once he learns that the "Chimp-O-Mat" will dispense food in exchange for them.

● **Figure 7.14** Reinforcement in a token economy. This graph shows the effects of using tokens to reward socially desirable behavior in a mental hospital ward. Desirable behavior was defined as cleaning, making the bed, attending therapy sessions, and so forth. Tokens earned could be exchanged for basic amenities such as meals, snacks, coffee, game-room privileges, or weekend passes. The graph shows more than 24 hours per day because it represents the total number of hours of desirable behavior performed by all patients in the ward. (Adapted from Ayllon & Azrin, 1965.)

or sleep with it. However, it can be exchanged for food, water, lodging, and other necessities.

A **token reinforcer** is a tangible secondary reinforcer, such as money, gold stars, poker chips, and the like. In a series of classic experiments, chimpanzees were taught to work for tokens. The chimps were first trained to put poker chips into a "Chimp-O-Mat" vending machine. Each chip dispensed a few grapes or raisins. Once the animals had learned to exchange tokens for food, they would learn new tasks to earn the chips. To maintain the value of the tokens, the chimps were occasionally allowed to use the "Chimp-O-Mat" (● Figure 7.13) (Cowles, 1937; Wolfe, 1936).

A major advantage of tokens is that they don't lose reinforcing value as quickly as primary reinforcers do. For instance, if you use candy to reinforce a developmentally disabled child for correctly naming things, the child might lose interest once he is satiated (fully satisfied) or no longer hungry. It would be better to use tokens as immediate rewards for learning. Later, the child can exchange his tokens for candy, toys, or other treats.

Tokens have also been used with troubled children and adults in special programs, and even in ordinary elementary school classrooms (Alberto & Troutman, 2006; Spiegler & Guevremont, 2003) (● Figure 7.14). In each case the goal is to provide an immediate reward for learning. Typically, tokens may be exchanged for food, special privileges, or trips to movies, amusement parks, and so forth. Many parents find that tokens greatly reduce discipline problems with younger children. For example, children can earn points or gold stars during the week for good behavior. If they earn enough tokens, they are allowed on Sunday to choose one item out of a "grab bag" of small prizes.

> **bridges**
>
> A *token economy* is a system for managing and altering behavior through reinforcement of selected responses. **See Chapter 15, page 509, for more information on the uses of token economies in behavior therapy.**

Social Reinforcers

As we have noted, learned desires for attention and approval, which are called **social reinforcers,** often influence human behavior. This fact can be used in a classic, if somewhat mischievous, demonstration.

Shaping a Teacher

For this activity, about one half (or more) of the students in a classroom must participate. First, select a target behavior. This should be something like "lecturing from the right side of the room." (Keep it simple, in case

Primary reinforcers Nonlearned reinforcers; usually those that satisfy physiological needs.

Secondary reinforcer A learned reinforcer; often one that gains reinforcing properties by association with a primary reinforcer.

Token reinforcer A tangible secondary reinforcer such as money, gold stars, poker chips, and the like.

Social reinforcer Reinforcement based on receiving attention, approval, or affection from another person.

your teacher is a slow learner.) Begin training in this way: Each time the instructor turns toward the right or takes a step in that direction, participating students should look *really* interested. Also, smile, ask questions, lean forward, and make eye contact. If the teacher turns to the left or takes a step in that direction, participating students should lean back, yawn, check out their split ends, close their eyes, or generally look bored. Soon, without being aware of why, the instructor should be spending most of his or her time each class period lecturing from the right side of the classroom.

This trick has been a favorite of psychology graduate students for decades. For a time, one of your author's professors delivered all her lectures from the right side of the room while toying with the cords on the window shades. (We added the cords the second week!) The point to remember from this example is that attention and approval can change the behavior of children, family members, friends, roommates, and coworkers. Be aware of what you are reinforcing. And be aware that you may be unaware of some of the reinforcers that are changing your own behavior!

Feedback

His eyes, driven and blazing, dart from side to side. His left hand twitches, dances, rises, and strikes, hitting its target again and again. At the same time, his right hand furiously spins in circular motions. Does this describe some strange neurological disorder? Actually, it depicts 10-year-old Vikram as he plays his favorite video game, an animated snowboarding adventure!

How did Vikram learn the complex movements needed to excel at virtual snowboarding? After all, he was not rewarded with food or money. The answer lies in the fact that Vikram's favorite video game provides *feedback,* a key element that underlies learning. **Feedback** (information about the effect a response had) is particularly important in human cognitive learning (Lefrançois, 2006).

Every time a player moves, a video game responds instantly with sounds, animated actions, and a higher or lower score. The machine's responsiveness and the information flow it provides can be very motivating if you want to win. The same principle applies to many other learning situations: If you are trying to learn to use a computer, to play a musical instrument, to cook, or to solve math problems, feedback that you achieved a desired result can be reinforcing in its own right.

The adaptive value of feedback helps explain why much human learning occurs in the absence of obvious reinforcers, such as food or water. Humans readily learn responses that merely have a desired effect or that bring a goal closer. Let's explore this idea further.

Knowledge of Results

Imagine that you are asked to throw darts at a target. Each dart must pass over a screen that prevents you from telling if you hit the target. If you threw 1,000 darts, we would expect little improvement in your performance because no feedback is provided. Vikram's video game did not explicitly reward him for

correct responses. Yet, because it provided feedback, rapid learning took place.

How can feedback be applied? Increased feedback (also called **knowledge of results,** or **KR**) almost always improves learning and performance (Horn et al., 2005). If you want to learn to play a musical instrument, to sing, to speak a second language, or to deliver a speech, recorded feedback can be very helpful. In sports, videos replays are used to provide feedback on everything from tennis serves to pick-off moves in baseball. Whenever you are trying to learn a complex skill, it pays to get more feedback (Wulf et al., 2002). (Also, see "Learning and Conservation.")

Learning Aids

How do these techniques make use of feedback? Feedback is most effective when it is *frequent, immediate,* and *detailed.* **Programmed instruction** teaches students in a format that presents information in small amounts, gives immediate practice, and provides continuous feedback to learners. Frequent feedback keeps learners from practicing errors. It also lets students work at their own pace. (A small sample of programmed instruction is shown in ● Figure 7.15.) Programmed learning can be done in book form, presented on a CD-ROM or through websites (Emurian, 2005; McDonald, Yanchar, & Osguthorpe, 2005).

In *computer-assisted instruction (CAI),* learning is aided by computer-presented information and exercises. In addition to giving learners immediate feedback, the computer can give hints about why an answer was wrong and what is needed to correct it (Timmerman & Kruepke, 2006). Although the final level of skill or knowledge gained is not necessarily higher, CAI can save much time and effort. In addition, people often do better with feedback from a computer because they can freely make mistakes and learn from them (Luyben, Hipworth, & Pappas, 2003; Norton, 2003). For example, CAI can

	Types of Conditioning
classical reflex voluntary	Much _____ conditioning involves involuntary _____ responses. In contrast, operant conditioning affects spontaneous, or _____ , responses.
response CS	Reinforcement occurs before the _____ in classical conditioning as the _____ is paired with the US.
reinforcement after reinforcer	In operant conditioning, _____ occurs _____ the response. In this case, the response is followed by a _____ .
passive elicited	In classical conditioning, the learner is _____ because responses are _____ by the US.
learner emits	In operant conditioning, the _____ actively _____ responses that are affected by reinforcement.

● **Figure 7.15** To sample a programmed instruction format, try covering the terms on the left with a piece of paper. As you fill in the blanks, uncover one new term for each response. In this way, your correct (or incorrect) responses will be followed by immediate feedback. (Actually, this is a somewhat simplified example. In true programmed instruction, new ideas are presented along with opportunities to practice them.)

DISCOVERING PSYCHOLOGY

Learning and Conservation

Psychologists enjoy helping to solve practical problems. One area of behavior very much in need of attention is our "throw-away" society. We burn fossil fuels; destroy forests; use chemical products; and strip, clear, and farm the land. In doing so, we alter the very face of the Earth. What can be done?

One approach involves changing the *consequences* of wasteful energy use, polluting, and the like. For example, energy taxes can be used to increase the cost of using fossil fuels (response cost). On the reinforcement side of the equation, rebates can be offered for installing insulation, or buying energy-efficient appliances or cars, and tax breaks can be given to companies that take steps

to preserve the environment. Recycling is also more effective when entire families participate, with some family members (usually mom, of course) reinforcing the recycling behavior of other family members (Meneses & Beerlipalacio, 2005).

Feedback is also important. For instance, people who set their own goals for recycling materials such as paper, steel, glass, aluminum, and plastic tend to meet them. Likewise, when families, work groups, factories, and dorms receive feedback, on a weekly basis, about how much they recycled, they typically recycle more. New tools, such as *carbon footprint calculators*, make it a lot easier for individuals to get feedback about their

individual resource consumption (Global Footprint Network, 2006).

> **bridges**
> See Chapter 18, pages 597–598, for more information on carbon footprints.

We also know that people are more likely to continue recycling if they feel a sense of satisfaction from helping protect the environment (Ewing, 2001). Is such satisfaction sufficiently reinforcing to encourage more people to reduce, reuse, and recycle? We certainly hope so.

---

give medical students unlimited practice at diagnosing diseases from symptoms (Papa, Aldrich, & Schumacker, 1999).

Some CAI programs, called *serious games,* make use of instructional games in which stories, competition with a partner, sound effects, and game-like graphics increase interest and motivation (Michael & Chen, 2006) (● Figure 7.16). Educational simulations allow students to explore an imaginary situation or "microworld" that simulates real-world problems. By seeing the effects of their choices, students discover basic principles of physics, biology, psychology, or other subjects (Grabe, 2006).

As psychologists fully explore the value and limits of computer-assisted instruction, it seems likely that their efforts will improve not only education but our understanding of human learning as well. Let's pause now for some learning exercises so that you can get some feedback about your mastery of the preceding ideas.

KNOWLEDGE BUILDER
Operant Conditioning

RECITE

1. Responses in operant conditioning are _____ or _____, whereas those in classical conditioning are passive, _____ or _____ responses.
2. Changing the rules in small steps so that an animal (or person) is gradually trained to respond as desired is called _____.
3. Extinction in operant conditioning is also subject to _____ of a response.
   a. successive approximations
   b. shaping
   c. automation
   d. spontaneous recovery
4. Positive reinforcers increase the rate of responding and negative reinforcers decrease it. T or F?
5. Primary reinforcers are those learned through classical conditioning. T or F?

6. Which is a correct match?
   a. social reinforcer–primary reinforcement
   b. token reinforcer–secondary reinforcement
   c. ICS–secondary reinforcement
   d. negative reinforcer–punishment
7. Superstitious responses are those that are
   a. shaped by secondary reinforcement
   b. extinguished
   c. prepotent
   d. unnecessary to obtain reinforcement
8. Knowledge of results, or KR, is also known as _____.

REFLECT

Critical Thinking

9. How might operant conditioning principles be used to encourage people to pick up litter? (What rewards could be offered, and how might the cost of rewards be kept low?)

Relate

Can you explain the difference between positive reinforcement, negative reinforcement, and punishment? Can you give an example of each concept from your own experience?

A friend of yours punishes his dog all the time. What advice would you give him about how to use reinforcement, extinction, and shaping, instead of punishment?

Answers: 1. voluntary or emitted, involuntary or elicited **2.** shaping **3.** d **4.** F **5.** F **6.** b **7.** d **8.** feedback **9.** A strategy that has been used with some success is to hold drawings for various prizes, such as movie or concert passes. Each time a person turns in a specific amount of litter, she or he receives one chance (a token) to enter in the drawing. Giving refunds for cans and bottles is another way to reinforce recycling of litter.

Feedback Information returned to a person about the effects a response has had; also known as knowledge of results.

Knowledge of results (KR) Informational feedback.

Programmed instruction Any learning format that presents information in small amounts, gives immediate practice, and provides continuous feedback to learners.

● **Figure 7.16** Computer-assisted instruction. The screen on the left shows a typical drill-and-practice math problem, in which students must find the hypotenuse of a triangle. The center screen presents the same problem as an instructional game to increase interest and motivation. In the game, a child is asked to set the proper distance on a ray gun in the hovering space ship to "vaporize" an attacker. The screen on the right depicts an educational simulation. Here, students place a "probe" at various spots in a human brain. They then "stimulate," "destroy," or "restore" areas. As each area is altered, it is named on the screen and the effects on behavior are described. This allows students to explore basic brain functions on their own.

◗◗ Partial Reinforcement—Las Vegas, a Human Skinner Box?

Gateway Question: How are we influenced by patterns of reward?

If you would like to influence operant learning, you will need to know how patterns of reinforcement affect behavior. Imagine, for example, that a mother wants to reward her child for turning off the lights when he leaves a room. Contrary to what you might think, it is better to reinforce only some of her son's correct responses. Why should this be so? You'll find the answer in the following discussion.

Until now, we have treated operant reinforcement as if it were continuous. **Continuous reinforcement** means that a reinforcer follows every correct response. At the start, continuous reinforcement is useful for learning new responses (Lefrançois, 2006). To teach your dog to come to you, it is best to reinforce your dog every time it comes when called.

Curiously, once your dog has learned to come when called, it is best to shift to **partial reinforcement,** in which reinforcers do not follow every response. Responses acquired by partial reinforcement are highly resistant to extinction (Svartdal, 2003). For some obscure reason, lost in the lore of psychology, this is called the **partial reinforcement effect.**

How does getting reinforced part of the time make a habit stronger? If you have ever visited a casino, you have probably seen row after row of people playing slot machines. To gain insight into the distinction between continuous and partial reinforcement, imagine that you put a dollar in a slot machine and pull the handle. Ten dollars spills into the tray. Let's say this continues for several minutes. Every pull is followed by a payoff. Because you are being reinforced on a continuous schedule, you quickly "get hooked" (and begin to plan your retirement).

But, alas, suddenly each pull is followed by nothing. Obviously, you would respond several times more before giving up. However, when continuous reinforcement is followed by extinction, the message quickly becomes clear: No more payoffs (or early retirement).

The one-armed bandit (slot machine) is a dispenser of partial reinforcement.

Contrast this with partial reinforcement. This time, imagine that you put a dollar in a slot machine five times without a payoff. You are just about to quit, but decide to play once more. Bingo! The machine returns $20. After this, payoffs continue on a partial schedule; some are large, and some are small. All are unpredictable. Sometimes you hit 2 in a row, and sometimes 20 or 30 pulls go unrewarded.

Now let's say the payoff mechanism is turned off again. How many times do you think you would respond this time before your handle-pulling behavior extinguished? Because you have developed the expectation that any play may be "the one," it will be hard to resist just one more play . . . and one more . . . and one more. Also, because partial reinforcement includes long periods of nonreward, it will be harder to distinguish between periods of reinforcement and extinction. It is no exaggeration to say that the partial reinforcement effect has left many people penniless. Even psychologists visiting a casino may get "cleaned out." (Not your authors, of course!)

To return to our examples, after using continuous reinforcement to teach a child to turn off the lights or a dog to come when called, it is best to shift to partial reinforcement. That way, the new behavior will become more resistant to extinction.

Schedules of Partial Reinforcement

Partial reinforcement can be given in several patterns, or **schedules of reinforcement** (plans for determining which responses will be reinforced) (Domjan, 2006). Let's consider the four most basic, which have some interesting effects on us. Typical responses to each pattern are shown in ● Figure 7.17. Results such as these are obtained when a *cumulative recorder* is connected to a Skinner box. The device consists of a moving strip of paper and a mechanical pen that jumps upward each time a response is made. Rapid responding causes the pen to draw a steep line; a horizontal line indicates no response. Small tick marks on the lines show when a reinforcer was given.

Fixed Ratio (FR)

What would happen if a reinforcer followed only every other response? Or what if we followed every third, fourth, fifth, or other number of responses with reinforcement? Each of these patterns is a **fixed ratio (FR) schedule** (a set number of correct responses must be made to obtain a reinforcer). Notice that in an FR schedule the ratio of reinforcers to responses is fixed: FR-2 means that every other response is rewarded; FR-3 means that every third response is reinforced; in an FR-10 schedule, exactly 10 responses must be made to obtain a reinforcer.

Fixed ratio schedules produce *very high response rates* (● Figure 7.17). A hungry rat on an FR-10 schedule will quickly run off 10 responses, pause to eat, and then run off 10 more. A similar situation occurs when factory or farm workers are paid on a piecework basis. When a fixed number of items must be produced for a set amount of pay, work output is high.

Variable Ratio (VR)

In a **variable ratio (VR) schedule** a varied number of correct responses must be made to get a reinforcer. Instead of reinforcing every fourth response (FR-4), for example, a person or animal on a VR-4 schedule gets rewarded *on the average* every fourth response.

Sometimes 2 responses must be made to obtain a reinforcer; sometimes it's 5; sometimes, 4; and so on. The actual number varies, but it averages out to 4 (in this example). Variable ratio schedules also produce high response rates.

VR schedules seem less predictable than FR. Does that have any effect on extinction? Yes. Because reinforcement is less predictable, VR schedules tend to produce greater resistance to extinction than fixed ratio schedules. Playing a slot machine is an example of behavior maintained by a variable ratio schedule. Another would be our plan to only occasionally reward a child for turning off the lights, once he has learned to do so. Golf, tennis, baseball, and many other sports are also reinforced on a variable ratio basis: Even the best batters in baseball rarely get a hit more than an average of 3 out of every 10 times they are at bat.

Fixed Interval (FI)

In another pattern, reinforcement is given only when a correct response is made after a fixed amount of time has passed. This time interval is measured from the last reinforced response. Responses made during the time interval are not reinforced. In a **fixed interval (FI) schedule** the first correct response made after the time period has passed is reinforced. Thus, a rat on an FI-30-second schedule has to wait 30 seconds after the last reinforced response before a bar press will pay off again. The rat can press the bar as often as it wants during the interval, but it will not be rewarded.

Fixed interval schedules produce *moderate response rates*. Animals working on an FI schedule seem to develop a keen sense of the passage of time (Eckerman, 1999). Few responses occur just after a reinforcement is delivered and a spurt of activity occurs just before the next reinforcement is due. (See "Are Animals Stuck in Time?")

Is getting paid weekly an FI schedule? Pure examples of fixed interval schedules are rare, but getting paid each week at work does come close. Notice, however, that most people do not work faster just before payday, as an FI schedule predicts. A closer parallel would be having a report due every 2 weeks for a class. Right

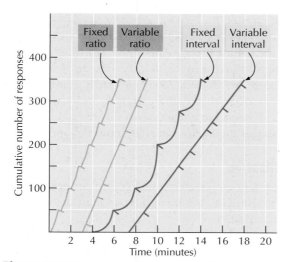

● **Figure 7.17** Typical response patterns for reinforcement schedules.

Continuous reinforcement A schedule in which every correct response is followed by a reinforcer.

Partial reinforcement A pattern in which only a portion of all responses are reinforced.

Partial reinforcement effect Responses acquired with partial reinforcement are more resistant to extinction.

Schedule of reinforcement A rule or plan for determining which responses will be reinforced.

Fixed ratio (FR) schedule A set number of correct responses must be made to get a reinforcer. For example, a reinforcer is given for every four correct responses.

Variable ratio (VR) schedule A varied number of correct responses must be made to get a reinforcer. For example, a reinforcer is given after three to seven correct responses; the actual number changes randomly.

Fixed interval (FI) schedule A reinforcer is given only when a correct response is made after a set amount of time has passed since the last reinforced response. Responses made during the time interval are not reinforced.

CRITICAL THINKING

Are Animals Stuck in Time?

We humans are *cognitive time travelers,* regularly zooming back and forth through time in our minds. You can, for example, think about past events, such as what you had for breakfast this morning. We can also imagine events in the future. Brides-to-be are famous for planning their weddings down to the last detail. But what about animals? Are they cognitive time travelers, or are they less cognitive and hence "stuck in time" (Roberts, 2002; Zentall, 2005)? Do dogs ever think about how hot it was yesterday or what they plan to do tomorrow? To answer such questions, psychologists have used operant conditioning as a research tool.

Conditioning studies have repeatedly shown that animals are sensitive to the passage of time (Zentall, 2005). For example, pigeons and rats reinforced on fixed interval schedules stop responding immediately after they receive a reinforcer and do not start again until just before the next scheduled reinforcement (Roberts, 2002). In one study, pigeons were put in a Skinner box with a pecking key on each wall. They quickly learned to peck only at Key 1 if it was 9:30 in the morning and at Key 3 if it was 4:00 in the afternoon (Saksida & Wilkie, 1994).

Another study focused on scrub jays. These birds are hoarders; they store excess food at different locations and then go back later to eat it. Scrub jays were allowed to hoard some nuts in one location and some worms in another. If they were released 4 hours later, they went directly to the worms. However, if they are released 5 days later, they went straight for the nuts. Worms are a scrub jay's favorite food, which explains their choice after 4 hours. But worms decay after a day or so, while nuts stay edible. It seems that the jays knew exactly where they stored each type of food and how much time had passed (Clayton, Yu, & Dickinson, 2001).

While these studies are suggestive, they are part of an ongoing debate about animal cognition, including whether or not animals are stuck in time (Roberts & Roberts, 2002). Nevertheless, be careful if you forget to feed your beloved dog, Rover, at his usual mealtime. If he has been conditioned to think it's time to eat, he may settle for your favorite flip-flops instead of dog food!

Florida scrub jays are food hoarders. Does their food hoarding behavior prove they are not "trapped in time"?

George McCarthy/NPL/Minden Pictures

---

after turning in a paper, your work would probably drop to zero for a week or more (Chance, 2006).

Variable Interval (VI)

Variable interval (VI) schedules are a variation on fixed intervals. Here, reinforcement is given for the first correct response made after a varied amount of time. On a VI-30-second schedule, reinforcement is available after an interval that *averages* 30 seconds.

VI schedules produce *slow, steady response rates* and tremendous resistance to extinction (Lattal, Reilly, & Kohn, 1998). When you dial a phone number and get a busy signal, reward (getting through) is on a VI schedule. You may have to wait 30 seconds or 30 minutes. If you are like most people, you will doggedly dial over and over again until you get a connection. Success in fishing is also on a VI schedule—which may explain the bulldog tenacity of many anglers (Chance, 2006).

⬤ Stimulus Control—Red Light, Green Light

When you are driving, your behavior at intersections is controlled by the red or green light. In similar fashion, many of the stimuli we encounter each day act like stop or go signals that guide our behavior. To state the idea more formally, stimuli that consistently precede a rewarded response tend to influence when and where the response will occur. This effect is called **stimulus control.** Notice how it works with our friend Einstein.

Lights Out for Einstein

While learning the bar-pressing response, Einstein has been in a Skinner box illuminated by a bright light. During several training sessions, the light is alternately turned on and off. When the light is on, a bar press will produce food. When the light is off, bar pressing goes unrewarded. We soon observe that the rat presses vigorously when the light is on and ignores the bar when the light is off.

In this example, the light signals what consequences will follow if a response is made. Evidence for stimulus control could be shown by turning the food delivery *on* when the light is *off.* A well-trained animal might never discover that the rules had changed (Powell, Symbaluk, & Macdonald, 2005). A similar example of stimulus control would be a child learning to ask for candy when her mother is in a good mood, but not asking at other times. Likewise, we pick up phones that are ringing, but rarely answer phones that are silent.

Generalization

Two important aspects of stimulus control are generalization and discrimination. Let's return to dogs to illustrate these concepts. First, generalization.

Is generalization the same in operant conditioning as it is in classical conditioning? Basically, yes. **Operant stimulus generalization** is the tendency to respond to stimuli similar to those that preceded operant reinforcement. That is, a reinforced response tends to be made again when similar antecedents are present. Assume, for instance, that your dog has begun to jump up at you whenever you are eating dinner at the kitchen table (bad dog!). Mind you, that's because you have been rewarding its behavior with table scraps (bad master!). Now your dog begins to jump any time you sit at the kitchen table. The dog has learned that reinforcement tends to occur when you are at the kitchen table. The dog's behavior has come under stimulus control. Now let's say that there are some other tables in your house. Because they are similar, your dog will likely jump up if you sit at any of them because the jumping response *generalized* to other tables. Similar generalization explains why children may temporarily call all men *daddy*—much to the embarrassment of their parents.

Discrimination

Meanwhile, back at the table. . . . As stated earlier, to discriminate means to respond differently to varied stimuli. Because one table signaled the availability of reinforcement to your dog, it began jumping up while you sat at other tables as well (generalization). If you do not feed your dog while sitting at any other table, the jumping response that originally generalized to them will extinguish because of nonreinforcement. Thus, your dog's jumping response is consistently rewarded in the presence of a specific table. The same response to different tables is extinguished. Through **operant stimulus discrimination,** your dog has learned to differentiate between antecedent stimuli that signal reward and nonreward. As a result, the dog's response pattern will shift to match these **discriminative stimuli** (stimuli that precede reinforced and nonreinforced responses).

A discriminative stimulus that most drivers are familiar with is a police car on the freeway. This stimulus is a clear signal that a specific set of reinforcement contingencies applies. As you have probably observed, the presence of a police car brings about rapid reductions in driving speed, lane changes, and tailgating.

The role of discriminative stimuli may be clarified by an interesting feat achieved by Jack, a psychologist friend of one of your authors. Here is his account of what Jack did:

> Jack decided to teach his cat to say its name. To begin, he gave the cat a pat on the back. If the cat meowed in a way that sounded anything like its name, Jack immediately gave the cat a small amount of food. If the cat made this unusual meow at other times, it received nothing. This process was repeated many times each day.
>
> By gradual shaping, the cat's meow was made to sound very much like its name. Also, this peculiar meow came under stimulus control: When it received a pat on the back, the cat said its name; without the pat, it remained silent or meowed normally.
>
> I should add at this point that I was unaware that Jack had a new cat or that he had trained it. I went to visit him one night and met the cat on the front steps. I gave the cat a pat on the back and said, "Hi kitty, what's your name?" Imagine my surprise when the cat immediately replied, "Ralph"!

Psychologists symbolize a stimulus that precedes reinforced responses as an S+. Discriminative stimuli that precede unrewarded responses are symbolized as S− (Chance, 2006). Thus, • Figure 7.18 summarizes Ralph's training.

Stimulus discrimination is also aptly illustrated by the "sniffer" dogs that locate drugs and explosives at airports and border crossings. Operant discrimination is used to teach these dogs to recognize contraband. During training, they are reinforced only for approaching containers baited with drugs or explosives.

Stimulus discrimination clearly has a tremendous impact on human behavior. Learning to recognize different automobile brands, birds, animals, wines, types of music, and even the answers on psychology tests all depends, in part, on operant discrimination learning.

Antecedent	Response	Consequence
S+ ⟶	"Ralph" ⟶	Food
S− ⟶	"Ralph" ⟶	Nothing
S+ ⟶	"Meow" ⟶	Nothing

• **Figure 7.18** A diagram of Ralph the cat's discrimination training.

Carleton Ray/Photo Researchers, Inc.

Stimulus control. Operant shaping was used to teach this whale to "bow" to an audience. Fish were used as reinforcers. Notice the trainer's hand signal, which serves as a discriminative stimulus to control the performance.

Variable interval (VI) schedule A reinforcer is given for the first correct response made after a varied amount of time has passed since the last reinforced response. Responses made during the time interval are not reinforced.

Stimulus control Stimuli present when an operant response is acquired tend to control when and where the response is made.

Operant stimulus generalization The tendency to respond to stimuli similar to those that preceded operant reinforcement.

Operant stimulus discrimination The tendency to make an operant response when stimuli previously associated with reward are present and to withhold the response when stimuli associated with nonreward are present.

Discriminative stimuli Stimuli that precede rewarded and nonrewarded responses in operant conditioning.

Punishment—Putting the Brakes on Behavior

Gateway Question: What does punishment do to behavior?

Spankings, reprimands, fines, jail sentences, firings, failing grades, and the like, are commonly used to control behavior. Clearly, the story of instrumental learning is unfinished without a return to the topic of punishment. Recall that **punishment** lowers the prob-

Punishers are consequences that lower the probability that a response will be made again. Receiving a traffic citation is directly punishing because the driver is delayed and reprimanded. Paying a fine and higher insurance rates add to the punishment in the form of response cost.

ability that a response will occur again. To be most effective, punishment must be given contingently (only after an undesired response occurs).

Punishers, like reinforcers, are defined by observing their effects on behavior. A **punisher** is any consequence that reduces the frequency of a target behavior. It is not always possible to know ahead of time what will act as a punisher for a particular person. For example, when Jason's mother reprimanded him for throwing toys, he stopped doing it. In this instance, the reprimand was a punisher. However, Chris is starved for attention of any kind from his parents, who both work full-time. For Chris, a reprimand, or even a spanking, might actually reinforce toy throwing. Remember, too, that a punisher can be either the onset of an unpleasant event or the removal of a positive state of affairs (response cost).

Variables Affecting Punishment

How effective is punishment? The effectiveness of punishers depends greatly on their *timing, consistency,* and *intensity.* Punishment works best when it occurs as the response is being made, or *immediately* afterward (timing), and when it is given *each time* a response occurs (consistency). Thus, if simply refusing to feed your dog table scraps is not enough to stop it from jumping at you when you sit at a table, you could effectively (and humanely) punish it by spraying water on its nose each time it jumps up. About 10 to 15 such treatments are usually enough. This would not be the case if you applied punishment haphazardly or long after the jumping stopped. If you discover that your dog dug up a tree and ate it while you were gone, punishing the dog hours later will do little good. Likewise, the commonly heard childhood threat, "Wait 'til your father comes home, then you'll be sorry," just makes the father a feared brute; it doesn't effectively punish an undesirable response.

Severe punishment (following a response with an intensely aversive or unpleasant stimulus) can be extremely effective in stopping behavior. If 3-year-old Beavis sticks his finger in a light socket and gets a shock that may be the last time he *ever* tries it. However, mild punishment only temporarily *suppresses* a response. If the response is still reinforced, punishment may be particularly ineffective.

This fact was demonstrated by slapping rats on the paw as they were bar pressing in a Skinner box. Two groups of well-trained rats were placed on extinction. One group was punished with a slap for each bar press, and the other group was not. It might seem that the slap would cause bar pressing to extinguish more quickly. Yet this was not the case, as you can see in ● Figure 7.19. Punishment tem-

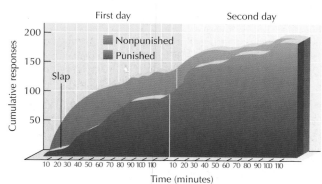

● **Figure 7.19** The effect of punishment on extinction. Immediately after punishment, the rate of bar pressing is suppressed, but by the end of the second day, the effects of punishment have disappeared. (B.F. Skinner, *The Behavior of Organisms*. © 1938. D. Appleton-Century, Co., Inc. Reprinted by permission of Prentice Hall, Inc.)

porarily slowed responding, but it did not cause more rapid extinction. Slapping the paws of rats or children has little permanent effect on a reinforced response.

Similarly, if 7-year-old Alissa sneaks a snack from the refrigerator before dinner and is punished for it, she may pass up snacks for a short time. But because snack sneaking was also rewarded by the sneaked snack, she will probably try sneaky snacking again, sometime later. But seriously, to reiterate, intense punishment may permanently suppress responding, even for actions as basic as eating. Animals severely punished while eating may never eat again (Bertsch, 1976).

The Downside of Punishment

Are there drawbacks to using punishment? There are several, all of which become more of a problem as punishment increases in severity. Basically, punishment is aversive (painful or uncomfortable). As a result, people and situations associated with punishment tend, through classical conditioning, to become feared, resented, or disliked. The aversive nature of punishment makes it especially poor to use when teaching children to eat politely or in toilet training.

Escape and Avoidance

A second major problem is that aversive stimuli encourage escape and avoidance learning (Brennan, Beck, & Servatius, 2003). In **escape learning** we learn to make a response in order to end an aversive stimulus. Escape learning simply reflects the operation of negative reinforcement, as the following example shows.

A dog is placed in a two-compartment cage called a shuttle box. If the dog is shocked while in one of the compartments, it will quickly learn to jump to the other compartment to *escape* the shock. If a buzzer is sounded 10 seconds before each shock begins, the dog will soon learn to associate the buzzer with shock. It will then *avoid* pain by jumping *before* the shock begins (Solomon & Wynne, 1953).

Avoidance learning appears to involve *both* classical and operant conditioning (Levis, 1989). In a shuttle box a dog first learns, through classical conditioning, to fear the buzzer. (The buzzer is a CS, which is followed by shock, a US for pain and fear.) Each time the buzzer sounds, the dog becomes fearful. But by jumping to the "safe" compartment the dog can end the unpleasant fear it feels. Therefore,

learning to jump *before* the onset of the shock is negatively reinforced by fear reduction. This is the operant part of avoidance learning.

Once avoidance is learned it is very persistent. The electric shock in a shuttle box can be turned off, yet the dog will continue to leap from the compartment each time the buzzer sounds. This fact is rather puzzling: If the buzzer is never followed by shock, why doesn't fear of the buzzer extinguish? The dog, it seems, has learned to *expect* that the buzzer will be followed by shock. If the dog leaves before the shock would normally occur, it gets no new information to change the expectancy (Chance, 2006).

Escape and avoidance learning are a regular part of daily experience. For example, if you work with a loud and obnoxious person, you may at first escape from conversations with him to obtain relief. Later you may dodge him altogether. This is an example of **avoidance learning** (making a response to postpone or prevent discomfort). Each time you sidestep him, your avoidance is again reinforced by a sense of relief. In many situations involving frequent punishment, similar desires to escape and avoid are activated. For example, children who run away from punishing parents (escape) may soon learn to lie about their behavior (avoidance) or to spend as much time away from home as possible (also an avoidance response).

Aggression

A third problem with punishment is that it can greatly increase *aggression*. Animals react to pain by attacking whomever or whatever else is around. A common example is the faithful dog that nips its owner during a painful procedure at the veterinarian's office. Likewise, humans who are in pain have a tendency to lash out at others.

We also know that one of the most common responses to frustration is aggression. Generally speaking, punishment is painful, frustrating, or both. Punishment, therefore, sets up a powerful environment for learning aggression. When spanked, a child may feel angry, frustrated, and hostile. What if that child then goes outside and hits a brother, a sister, or a neighbor? The danger is that aggressive acts may feel good because they release anger and frustration. If so, aggression has been rewarded and will tend to occur again in other frustrating situations.

> **bridges**
>
> The connection between frustration and aggression is strong. But does frustration always produce aggression? **For more information, see Chapter 13, pages 435–437, and Chapter 17, pages 567–568.**

Punishment The process of suppressing a response.

Punisher Any event that decreases the probability or frequency of responses it follows.

Escape learning Learning to make a response in order to end an aversive stimulus.

Avoidance learning Learning to make a response in order to postpone or prevent discomfort.

One study found that children who are physically punished are more likely to engage in aggressive, impulsive, antisocial behavior (Thomas, 2004). Similarly, a classic study of angry adolescent boys found that they were severely punished at home. This suppressed their misbehavior at home but made them more aggressive elsewhere. Parents were often surprised to learn that their "good boys" were in trouble for fighting at school (Bandura & Walters, 1959). Fortunately, at least for younger children, if parents change to less punitive parenting, their children's levels of aggression will decline (Thomas, 2004).

In the classroom, physical punishment, yelling, and humiliation are also generally ineffective. Positive reinforcement, in the form of praise, approval, and reward, is much more likely to quell classroom disruptions, defiance, and inattention (Alberto & Troutman, 2006).

> **bridges**
>
> Learning principles are only one element of effective child management. **See Chapter 3, pages 112–115, for additional techniques.**

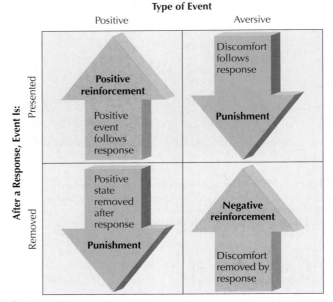

● **Figure 7.20** Types of reinforcement and punishment. The impact of an event depends on whether it is presented or removed after a response is made. Each square defines one possibility: Arrows pointing upward indicate that responding is increased; downward-pointing arrows indicate that responding is decreased.

Using Punishment Wisely

In light of its limitations and drawbacks, should punishment be used to control behavior? Parents, teachers, animal trainers, and the like, have three basic tools to control simple learning: (1) Reinforcement strengthens responses; (2) nonreinforcement causes responses to extinguish; (3) punishment suppresses responses. (Consult ● Figure 7.20 to refresh your memory about the different types of reinforcement and punishment.) These tools work best in combination. It is usually preferable to begin by making liberal use of positive reinforcement, especially praise, to encourage good behavior. Also, try extinction first: See what happens if you ignore a problem behavior, or shift attention to a desirable activity and then reinforce it with praise. Remember, it is much more effective to strengthen and encourage desirable behaviors than it is to punish unwanted behaviors (Gershoff, 2002). When all else fails, it may be necessary to use punishment to help manage the behavior of an animal, child, or even another adult. For those times, here are some tips to keep in mind:

1. *Avoid harsh punishment.* Harsh or excessive punishment has serious negative drawbacks (never slap a child's face, for instance). "Sparing the rod" will not spoil a child. In fact, the reverse is true. As we just discussed, harsh punishment can lead to negative emotional reactions, avoidance and escape behaviors, and increased aggression (Aucoin, Frick, & Bodin, 2006). It can even lead to long-term mental health problems (Afifi et al., 2006).

   What about spanking? Parents should minimize spanking or avoid it entirely (Gershoff, 2002). Although most

children show no signs of long-term damage from spanking if it is backed up by supportive parenting, emotional damage does occur if spankings are severe, frequent, or coupled with harsh parenting (Baumrind, Larzelere, & Cowan, 2002). Like all harsh punishment, frequent spanking tends to increase aggression and leads to more problem behaviors, not fewer (McLoyd & Smith, 2002; Saadeh, Rizzo, & Roberts, 2002). In fact, antispanking laws have been passed in a number of countries around the world.

2. *Use the minimum punishment necessary to suppress misbehavior.* If punishment is used at all, it should be mild. In a situation that poses immediate danger, such as when a child reaches for something hot or a dog runs into the street, mild punishment may prevent disaster. Punishment in such cases works best when it produces actions *incompatible* with the response you want to suppress. Let's say a child reaches toward a stove burner. Would a swat on the bottom serve as an effective punisher? Probably so. It would be better, however, to slap the child's outstretched hand so that it will be *withdrawn* from the source of danger. Taking away privileges or other positive reinforcers (response cost) is usually best for older children and adults. Often, a verbal rebuke or a scolding is enough.

3. *Apply punishment during, or immediately after, misbehavior.* Of course, immediate punishment is not always possible. With older children and adults, you can bridge the delay by clearly stating what act you are punishing. If you cannot punish an animal or young child immediately, wait for the next instance of misbehavior.

4. *Be consistent.* Be very clear about what you regard as misbehavior. Punish every time the misbehavior occurs. Don't punish for something one time and ignore it the next. If you are usually willing to give a child three chances, don't change the rule and explode without warning after a first offense. Both parents should try to punish their children for the same things and in the same way.

5. *Use counter conditioning.* Mild punishment tends to be ineffective if reinforcers are still available in the situation. That's why it is best to also reward an alternate, desired response. For example, a child who has a habit of taking toys from her sister should not just be reprimanded for it. She should be *counter conditioned,* or rewarded for displaying any behavior that is counter to the unacceptable behavior, such as cooperative play or sharing her toys. As desired behaviors become more frequent, undesired behaviors become less frequent. The girl can't very well share her toys and take them from her sister at the same time.

Remember, punishment only tells a person or an animal that a response was "wrong." Punishment does not say what the "right" response is, so it *does not teach new behaviors.* If reinforcement is missing, punishment becomes less effective (Gershoff, 2002).

6. *Expect anger from a punished person.* Briefly acknowledge this anger, but be careful not to reinforce it. Be willing to admit your mistake if you wrongfully punish someone or if you punished too severely.

7. *Punish with kindness and respect.* Avoid punishing when you are angry. It is easy to get carried away and become abusive (Gershoff, 2002). Two-thirds of child abuse cases start out as attempts at physical punishment (Trocmé et al., 2001). One way to guard against doing harm is to punish with kindness and respect. Doing so also allows the punished person to retain self-respect. For instance, do not punish a person in front of others, if possible. A strong, trusting relationship tends to minimize behavior problems. Ideally, others should want to behave well to get your praise, not because they fear punishment.

To summarize, a common error is to over-rely on punishment for training or discipline. Frequent punishment makes a person or an animal unhappy, confused, anxious, aggressive, and fearful (Gershoff, 2002). The overall emotional adjustment of a child or pet disciplined mainly by reward is usually superior to one disciplined mainly by punishment.

Parents and teachers should also be aware that using punishment can be "habit forming." When children are being noisy, messy, disrespectful, or otherwise misbehaving, the temptation to punish them can be strong. The danger is that punishment often works. When it does, a sudden end to the adult's irritation acts as a negative reinforcer. This encourages the adult to use punishment more often in the future (Alberto & Troutman, 2006). Immediate silence may be "golden," but its cost can be very high in terms of a child's emotional health.

KNOWLEDGE BUILDER
Punishment

RECITE
1. Negative reinforcement increases responding; punishment suppresses responding. T or F?
2. Three factors that greatly influence the effects of punishment are timing, consistency, and _____.
3. Mild punishment tends to only temporarily _____ a response that is also reinforced.
   a. enhance
   b. aggravate
   c. replace
   d. suppress
4. Three undesired side effects of punishment are (1) conditioning of fear and resentment, (2) encouragement of aggression, and (3) the learning of escape or _____ responses.
5. Using punishment can be "habit forming" because putting a stop to someone else's irritating behavior can _____ _____ the person who applies the punishment.

REFLECT
Critical Thinking
6. Using the concept of partial reinforcement, can you explain why inconsistent punishment is especially ineffective?
7. Escape and avoidance learning have been applied to encourage automobile seat belt use. Can you explain how?

Relate
Think of how you were punished as a child. Was the punishment immediate? Was it consistent? What effect did these factors have on your behavior? Was the punishment effective? Which of the side effects of punishment have you witnessed or experienced?

Answers: 1. T **2.** intensity **3.** d **4.** avoidance **5.** negatively reinforce **6.** An inconsistently punished response will continue to be reinforced on a partial schedule, which can make it even more resistant to extinction. **7.** Many automobiles have an unpleasant buzzer that sounds if the ignition key is turned before the driver's seat belt is fastened. Most drivers quickly learn to fasten the belt to stop the annoying sound. This is an example of escape conditioning. Avoidance conditioning is evident when a driver learns to buckle up before the buzzer sounds.

Cognitive Learning—Beyond Conditioning

Gateway Question: What is cognitive learning?

Is all learning just an association between stimuli and responses? Much learning can be explained by classical and operant conditioning. But, as we have seen, even basic conditioning has "mental" elements. As a human, you can anticipate future reward or punishment and react accordingly. (You may wonder why this doesn't seem to work when a doctor or dentist says, "This won't hurt a bit." Here's why: They lie!) There is no doubt that human learning includes a large *cognitive,* or mental, dimension (Lefrançois, 2006). As humans, we are greatly affected by information, expectations, perceptions, mental images, and the like.

As we mentioned at the beginning of this chapter, loosely speaking, *cognitive learning* refers to understanding, knowing, anticipating, or otherwise making use of information-rich higher mental processes. Cognitive learning extends beyond basic conditioning into the realms of memory, thinking, problem solving, and language. Because these topics are covered in later chapters, our discussion here is limited to a first look at learning beyond conditioning.

Cognitive Maps

How do you navigate around the town you live in? Have you simply learned to make a series of right and left turns to get from one point to another? More likely, you have an overall mental picture of how the town is laid out. This *cognitive map* acts as a guide even when you must detour or take a new route (Foo et al., 2005). A **cognitive map** is an internal representation of an area, such as a maze, city, or campus. Even the lowly rat—not exactly a mental giant (well, except for Einstein)—learns *where* food is found in a maze, not just which turns to make to reach the food (Tolman, Ritchie, & Kalish, 1946). If you have ever learned your way through some of the levels found in many video games, you will have a good idea of what a cognitive map is. In a sense, cognitive maps also apply to other kinds of knowledge. For instance, it could be said that you have been developing a "map" of psychology while reading this book. That's why students sometimes find

It's easy to get lost when visiting a new city if you don't have a cognitive map of the area. Printed maps help, but they may still leave you puzzled until you begin to form a mental representation of major landmarks and directions.

it helpful to draw pictures or diagrams of how they envision concepts fitting together.

Latent Learning

Cognitive learning is also revealed by latent (hidden) learning. **Latent learning** occurs without obvious reinforcement and remains hidden until reinforcement is provided (Davidson, 2000). Here's an example from a classic animal study: Two groups of rats were allowed to explore a maze. The animals in one group found food at the far end of the maze. Soon, they learned to rapidly make their way through the maze when released. Rats in the second group were unrewarded and showed no signs of learning. But later, when the "uneducated" rats were given food, they ran the maze as quickly as the rewarded group (Tolman & Honzik, 1930). Although there was no outward sign of it, the unrewarded animals had learned their way around the maze. Their learning, therefore, remained latent at first (● Figure 7.21).

How did they learn if there was no reinforcement? Just satisfying curiosity can be enough to reward learning (Harlow & Harlow, 1962). In humans, latent learning is related to higher-level abilities, such as anticipating future reward. For example, if you give an attractive classmate a ride home, you may make mental notes about how to get to his or her house, even if a date is only a remote future possibility.

● **Figure 7.21** Latent learning. *(a)* The maze used by Tolman and Honzik to demonstrate latent learning by rats. *(b)* Results of the experiment. Notice the rapid improvement in performance that occurred when food was made available to the previously unreinforced animals. This indicates that learning had occurred but that it remained hidden or unexpressed. (Adapted from Tolman & Honzik, 1930.)

(a)

(b)

Discovery Learning

Much of what is meant by cognitive learning is summarized by the word "understanding." Each of us has, at times, learned ideas by **rote** (mechanical repetition and memorization). Although rote learning can be efficient, many psychologists believe that learning is more lasting and flexible when people *discover* facts and principles on their own. In **discovery learning,** skills are gained by insight and understanding instead of by rote (Swaak, de Jong, & van Joolingen, 2004).

As long as learning occurs, what difference does it make if it is by discovery or by rote? • Figure 7.22 illustrates the difference. Two groups of students were taught to calculate the area of a parallelogram by multiplying the height by the length of the base. Some were encouraged to see that a "piece" of a parallelogram could be "moved" to create a rectangle. Later, they were better able to solve unusual problems in which the height times base formula didn't seem to work. Students who simply memorized a rule were confused by the similar problems (Wertheimer, 1959). As this implies, discovery can lead to a better understanding of new or unusual problems. When possible, people should try new strategies and discover new solutions during learning. However, this doesn't mean that students are supposed to stumble around and rediscover the principles of math, physics, or chemistry. The best teaching strategies are based on *guided discovery,* in which students are given enough freedom to actively think about problems and enough guidance so that they gain useful knowledge (Mayer, 2004).

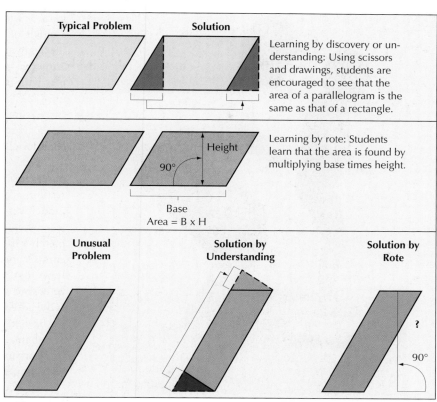

● **Figure 7.22** Learning by understanding and by rote. For some types of learning, understanding may be superior, although both types of learning are useful. (After Wertheimer, 1959.)

Modeling—Do as I Do, Not as I Say

Gateway Question: Does learning occur by imitation?

Many skills are learned by what Albert Bandura (1971) calls *observational learning,* or *modeling.* Watching and imitating the actions of another person or by noting the consequences of the person's actions can lead to **observational learning** (Lefrançois, 2006). We humans share the capacity for observational learning with many mammals, like Larry's beloved gorillas (Meunier, Monfardini, & Boussaoud, 2007).

The value of learning by observation is obvious: Imagine trying to *tell* someone how to tie a shoe, do a dance step, or play a guitar. Bandura believes that anything that can be learned from direct experience can be learned by observation. Often, this allows a person to skip the tedious trial-and-error stage of learning.

Observational Learning

It seems obvious that we learn by observation, but how does it occur? By observing a **model** (someone who serves as an example), a person may (1) learn new responses, (2) learn to carry out or avoid previously learned responses (depending on what happens to the model for doing the same thing), or (3) learn a general rule that can be applied to various situations (Lefrançois, 2006).

For observational learning to occur, several things must take place. First, the learner must pay *attention* to the model and *remember* what was done. (A beginning auto mechanic might be interested enough to watch an entire tune-up, but unable to remember all the steps.) Next, the learner must be able to *reproduce* the modeled behavior. (Sometimes this is a matter of practice, but it may be that the learner will never be able to perform the behavior. We may admire the feats of world-class gymnasts, but most of us could never reproduce them, no matter how

---

Cognitive map Internal images or other mental representations of an area (maze, city, campus, and so forth) that underlie an ability to choose alternative paths to the same goal.

Latent learning Learning that occurs without obvious reinforcement and that remains unexpressed until reinforcement is provided.

Rote learning Learning that takes place mechanically, through repetition and memorization, or by learning rules.

Discovery learning Learning based on insight and understanding.

Observational learning Learning achieved by watching and imitating the actions of another or noting the consequences of those actions.

Model A person who serves as an example in observational learning.

Observational learning often imparts large amounts of information that would be difficult to obtain by reading instructions or memorizing rules.

much we practiced.) If a model is *successful* at a task or *rewarded* for a response, the learner is more likely to imitate the behavior. In general, models who are attractive, trustworthy, capable, admired, powerful, or high in status also tend to be imitated (Brewer & Wann, 1998). Finally, once a new response is tried, *normal reinforcement or feedback determines whether it will be repeated thereafter.* (Notice the similarity to latent learning, described earlier.)

Imitating Models

Modeling has a powerful effect on behavior. In a classic experiment, children watched an adult attack a large blow-up "Bo-Bo the Clown" doll. Some children saw an adult sit on the doll, punch it, hit it with a hammer, and kick it around the room. Others saw a movie of these actions. A third group saw a cartoon version of the aggression. Later, the children were frustrated by having some attractive toys taken away from them. Then, they were allowed to play with the Bo-Bo doll. Most imitated the adult's attack (● Figure 7.23). Some even added new aggressive acts of their own! Interestingly, the cartoon was only slightly less effective in encouraging aggression than the live adult model and the filmed model (Bandura, Ross, & Ross, 1963).

Then do children blindly imitate adults? No. Remember that observational learning only prepares a person to duplicate a response. Whether it is actually imitated depends on whether the model was rewarded or punished for what was done. Nevertheless, when parents tell a child to do one thing but model a completely different response, children tend to imitate what the parents *do,* and *not* what they *say*. Thus, through modeling, children learn not only attitudes, gestures, emotions, and personality traits, but fears, anxieties, and bad habits as well. A good example is the adolescent smoker, who is much more likely to begin smoking if her parents, siblings, and friends smoke (Wilkinson & Abraham, 2004). Tragically, children who witness domestic violence are more likely to commit it themselves (Murrell, Christoff, & Henning, 2007).

Now, consider a typical situation: Little Raymond has just been interrupted at play by his older brother, Robert. Angry and frustrated, he swats Robert. This behavior interrupts his father Frank's TV watching. Father promptly spanks little Raymond, saying, "This will teach you to hit your big brother." And it will. Because of modeling effects, it is unrealistic to expect a child to "Do as I say, not as I do." The message Frank has given the child is clear: "You have frustrated me; therefore, I will hit you." The next time little Raymond is frustrated, it won't be surprising if he imitates his father and hits his brother (so why does everybody love Raymond, anyway?).

Modeling and the Media

Does television promote observational learning? Today's 8- to 18-year-olds spend an average of 44.5 hours a week engaged with various media, including television, video games, movies, the Internet, music, and print media (Roberts, Foehr, & Rideout,

● **Figure 7.23** A nursery school child imitates the aggressive behavior of an adult model he has just seen in a movie.

CRITICAL THINKING

You Mean Video Games Might Be Bad for Me?

Today's kids can experience more gore in a day than most people used to experience in a lifetime, even during military combat. For example, in one video game you can kill an entire marching band with a flamethrower. Some of your victims won't die right away. They will just writhe in pain, begging you to finish them off.

What effects do such experiences have on people who play violent video games? Reviews have concluded that violent video games increase aggressive behavior in children and young adults (Anderson & Bushman, 2001; Anderson, 2004). As with TV, young children are especially susceptible to fantasy violence in video games (Anderson et al., 2003; Bensley & Van Eenwyk, 2001).

One study illustrates the impact of video game violence. First, college students played a violent (Mortal Kombat) or nonviolent (PGA Tournament Golf) video game. Next, they competed with another student (actually an actor) in a task that allowed aggression and retaliation to take place. Students who played Mortal Kombat were much more likely to aggress, by punishing their competitor (Bartholow & Anderson, 2002). (Don't mess with someone who just played Mortal Kombat!)

How does video game violence increase aggressive behavior? One possibility is that repeated exposure to violence desensitizes players, making them less likely to react neg-atively to violence and, hence, more prone to engage in it (Bartholow, Sestir, & Davis, 2005; Funk, 2005). Another possibility is that by practicing violence against other people, players may learn to be aggressive in real life (Unsworth & Ward, 2001).

> **bridges**
> Before you write off video games altogether, read "You Mean Video Games Might Be Good For Me?" in Chapter 9, page 313.

2005). Although overall use is falling, television still consumes the lion's share of media attention, averaging 21 hours every week.

By the time the average person has graduated from high school, she or he will have viewed some 15,000 hours of TV, compared with only 11,000 hours spent in the classroom. In that time, viewers will have seen some 18,000 murders and countless acts of robbery, arson, bombing, torture, and beatings. Even G-rated cartoons average 10 minutes of violence per hour (Yokota & Thompson, 2000). In short, typical TV viewers are exposed to a massive dose of media violence, which tends to promote observational learning of aggression (Bushman & Anderson, 2001).

Televised Aggression

The last finding should come as no surprise. Studies show conclusively that if children watch a great deal of televised violence, they will be more prone to behave aggressively (Anderson et al., 2003; Bushman & Anderson, 2001). In other words, not all children will become more aggressive, but many will. More ominously, the effect can last into early adulthood. A group of primary school students with known television viewing habits were later contacted in early adulthood (Huesmann et al., 2003). Those who watched more violence on television as elementary schoolers were more aggressive as adults 15 years later (● Figure 7.24).

Does the same conclusion apply to video games? Oh, yes. Children tend to imitate what they observe in all media. From professional wrestling (Bernthal, 2003) to rap music (Wingood et al.,

● **Figure 7.24** This graph shows that preschoolers who watched low levels of television violence were less aggressive than average as young adults when contacted 15 years later. In contrast, preschoolers who watched high levels of television violence were more aggressive than average as young adults. The composite aggression score includes measures of indirect aggression (e.g., verbal abusiveness) and direct aggression (physical aggression). (Data adapted from Huesmann et al., 2003.)

Erik S. Lesser/AP/Wide World Photo

TV heroes can act as powerful models for observational learning of aggression.

2003) to video games (Carnagey & Anderson, 2004), children have plenty of opportunity to observe and imitate both the good and the bad. (See "You Mean Video Games Might Be Bad for Me?" for some recent evidence.)

Is it fair to say, then, that media violence causes aggression in consumers, especially children? Media violence can make aggres-

sion more *likely,* but it does not invariably "cause" it to occur for any given child (Kirsh, 2005). Many other factors affect the chances that hostile thoughts will be turned into actions. Youngsters who believe that aggression is an acceptable way to solve problems, who believe that TV violence is realistic, and who identify with TV characters are most likely to copy televised aggression (Huesmann et al., 2003). It is particularly troubling to find media *heroes* behaving aggressively, as well as villains. Younger children, in particular, are more likely to be influenced because they don't fully recognize that media characters and stories are fantasies (McKenna & Ossoff, 1998).

In view of such findings, it is understandable that countries like Canada, Norway, and Switzerland have restricted the amount of permissible violence on television. Should all countries do the same?

A Look Ahead

Conditioning principles are often derived from animal experiments. However, it should be apparent that the same principles apply to human behavior. Perhaps the best way to appreciate this fact is to observe how reinforcement affects your own behavior. With this in mind, the upcoming Psychology in Action section proposes a personal experiment in operant conditioning. Don't miss this coming attraction!

KNOWLEDGE BUILDER
Cognitive Learning and Imitation

RECITE

1. An internal representation of relationships is referred to as a
   _____ _____.
2. Learning that suddenly appears when a reward or incentive for performance is given is called
   a. discovery learning
   b. latent learning
   c. rote learning
   d. reminiscence
3. Psychologists use the term _____ to describe observational learning.
4. If a model is successful, rewarded, attractive, or high in status, his or her behavior is
   a. difficult to reproduce
   b. less likely to be attended to
   c. more likely to be imitated
   d. subject to positive transfer
5. Children who observed a live adult behave aggressively became more aggressive; those who observed movie and cartoon aggression did not. T or F?
6. Children are most likely to imitate TV characters with whom they identify. T or F?
7. Children who watch a great deal of televised violence are more prone to be aggressive, an effect that is best explained by
   a. negative reinforcement
   b. shaping and successive approximations
   c. observational learning
   d. vicarious classical conditioning

REFLECT
Critical Thinking

8. Draw a map of your school's campus as you picture it now. Draw a map of the campus as you pictured it after your first visit. Why do the maps differ?
9. Children who watch many aggressive programs on television tend to be more aggressive than average. Why doesn't this observation prove that televised aggression causes aggressive behavior?

Relate

Try to think of at least one personal example of each of these concepts: cognitive map, latent learning, discovery learning.

Describe a skill you have learned primarily through observational learning. How did modeling help you learn?

What entertainment or sports personalities did you identify with when you were a child? How did it affect your behavior?

Answers: 1. cognitive map **2.** b **3.** modeling **4.** c **5.** F **6.** T **7.** c **8.** Your cognitive map of the campus has undoubtedly become more accurate and intricate over time as you have added details to it. Your drawings should reflect this change. **9.** Because the observation is based on a correlation. Children who are already aggressive may choose to watch more aggressive programs, rather than being made aggressive by them. It took experimental studies to verify that televised aggression promotes aggression by viewers.

PSYCHOLOGY IN ACTION

Behavioral Self-Management—A Rewarding Project

Gateway Question: How does conditioning apply to practical problems?

Would you like to exercise more, attend more classes, cut down on smoking, concentrate longer, or read more books? This is an invitation to carry out a self-management project of your own. As such, this could be the start of one of the most personal applications of psychology in this book.

Self-Managed Behavior

The principles of operant conditioning can be adapted to manage your own behavior (Martin & Pear, 2007; Watson & Tharp, 2007). Here's how:

1. **Choose a target behavior.** Identify the activity you want to change.
2. **Record a baseline.** Record how much time you currently spend performing the target activity or count the number of desired or undesired responses you make each day.
3. **Establish goals.** Remember the principle of shaping and set realistic goals for gradual improvement on each successive week. Also, set daily goals that add up to the weekly goal.
4. **Choose reinforcers.** If you meet your daily goal, what reward will you allow yourself? Daily rewards might be watching television, eating a candy bar, socializing with friends, listening to your iPod, or whatever you enjoy. Also establish a weekly reward. If you reach your weekly goal, what reward will you allow yourself? A movie? A dinner out? Some time playing a game like *Guitar Hero?* A weekend hike?
5. **Record your progress.** Keep accurate records of the amount of time spent each day on the desired activity or the number of times you make the desired response.
6. **Reward successes.** If you meet your daily goal, collect your reward. If you fall short, be honest with yourself and skip the reward. Do the same for your weekly goal.
7. **Adjust your plan as you learn more about your behavior.** Overall progress will reinforce your attempts at self-management.

If you have trouble thinking of rewards, remember that anything done often can serve as reinforcement. This is known as the **Premack principle.** It is named after David Premack, a psychologist who popularized its use. For example, if you like to watch television every night and want to study more, make it a rule not to turn on the set until you have studied for an hour (or whatever length of time you choose). Then lengthen the requirement each week. Here is a sample of one student's plan:

1. *Target behavior:* number of hours spent studying for school.
2. *Recorded baseline:* an average of 25 minutes per day for a weekly total of 3 hours.
3. *Goal for the first week:* an increase in study time to 40 minutes per day; weekly goal of 5 hours total study time. *Goal for second week:* 50 minutes per day and 6 hours per week. *Goal for third week:* 1 hour per day and 7 hours per week. *Ultimate goal:* to reach and maintain 14 hours per week study time.
4. *Daily reward for reaching goal:* 1/2 hour of guitar playing in the evening; no playing if the goal is not met. *Weekly reward for reaching goal:* going to a movie or buying a DVD.

Self-Recording

Even if you find it difficult to give and withhold rewards, **self-recording** (keeping records of response frequencies, a form of feedback) can make a difference all by itself. This is because we tend to react to being observed, even when we are the ones watching our own behavior. In general, when you systematically (and honestly) observe yourself, you are more likely to engage in desired behaviors and less likely to perform undesired behaviors (Fireman, Kose, & Solomon, 2003; Watson & Tharp, 2007).

Keep track of the number of times that you exercise, arrive late to class, eat vegetables, smoke a cigarette, study, watch TV, drink a cappuccino, swear, or whatever you are interested in changing. A simple tally on a piece of paper will do, or you can get a small mechanical counter like those used to keep golf scores or count calories. Record keeping helps break patterns, and the feedback can be motivating as you begin to make progress.

Good Ways to Break Bad Habits

Are there any extra tips for breaking bad habits? By using the methods we have discussed, you can *decrease* unwanted behaviors, such as swearing, biting your nails, criticizing others, smoking, drinking coffee, watching TV too much, or engaging in any other behavior you choose to target. However,

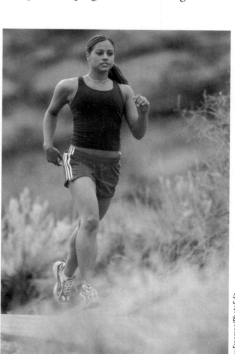

Tony Freeman/PhotoEdit

Premack principle Any high-frequency response can be used to reinforce a low-frequency response.

Self-recording Self-management based on keeping records of response frequencies.

Alternate Responses

A good strategy for change is to try to get the same reinforcement with a new response.

Example: Marta often tells jokes at the expense of others. Her friends sometimes feel hurt by her sharp-edged humor. Marta senses this and wants to change. What can she do? Usually, Marta's joke telling is reinforced by attention and approval. She could just as easily get the same reinforcement by giving other people praise or compliments. Making a change in her behavior should be easy because she will continue to receive the reinforcement she seeks.

Extinction

Try to discover what is reinforcing an unwanted response and remove, avoid, or delay the reinforcement.

Example: Fatima has developed a habit of taking longer and longer "breaks" to watch TV when she should be studying. Obviously, TV watching is reinforcing her break taking. To improve her study habits, Fatima could delay reinforcement by studying at the library or some other location a good distance from her TV.

Response Chains

Break up response chains that precede an undesired behavior; this will help break the bad habit. The key idea is to scramble the chain of events that leads to an undesired response (Watson & Tharp, 2007).

Example: Most nights Ignacio comes home from work, turns on the TV, and eats a whole bag of cookies or chips. He then takes a shower and changes clothes. By dinnertime he has lost his appetite. Ignacio realizes he is substituting junk food for dinner. Ignacio could solve the problem by breaking the response chain that precedes dinner. For instance, he could shower immediately when he gets home, or avoid turning on the television until after dinner.

Cues and Antecedents

Try to avoid, narrow down, or remove stimuli that elicit the bad habit.

Example: Brent wants to cut down on smoking. He can take many smoking cues out of his surroundings by removing ashtrays, matches, and extra cigarettes from his house, car, and office. Drug cravings are strongly related to cues conditioned to the drug, such as the odor of cigarettes (Lazev, Herzog, & Brandon, 1999). Brent can narrow antecedent stimuli even more. He could begin by smoking only in the lounge at work, never in his office or in his car. He could then limit his smoking to home. Then to only one room at home. Then to one chair at home. If he succeeds in getting this far, he may want to limit his smoking to only one unpleasant place, such as a bathroom, basement, or garage (Riley et al., 2002).

Contracting

If you try the techniques described here and have difficulty sticking with them, you may want to try behavioral contracting. In a **behavioral contract,** you state a specific problem behavior you want to control, or a goal you want to achieve. Also state the rewards you will receive, privileges you will forfeit, or punishments you must accept. The contract should be signed by you and a person you trust.

A behavioral contract can be quite motivating, especially when mild punishment is part of the agreement. Here's a classic example reported by Nurnberger and Zimmerman (1970): A student working on his Ph.D. had completed all requirements but his dissertation, yet for 2 years had not written a single page. A contract was drawn up for him in which he agreed to meet weekly deadlines on the number of pages he would complete. To make sure he would meet the deadlines, he wrote postdated checks. These were to be forfeited if he failed to reach his goal for the week. The checks were made out to organizations he despised (the Ku Klux Klan and American Nazi Party). From the time he signed the contract until he finished his degree, the student's work output was greatly improved.

Getting Help

Attempting to manage or alter your own behavior may be more difficult than it sounds. If you feel you need more information, consult the books listed below. You will also find helpful advice in the Psychology in Action section of Chapter 15. If you do try a self-modification project but find it impossible to reach your goals, be aware that professional advice is available.

Where to Obtain More Information

Watson, D. L., & Tharp, R. G. (2007). *Self-directed behavior* (9th ed.). Belmont, CA: Wadsworth.

Martin, G., & Pear, J. (2007). *Behavior modification: What it is and how to do it* (8th ed.). Upper Saddle River, NJ: Prentice-Hall.

KNOWLEDGE BUILDER
Behavioral Self-Management

RECITE

1. After a target behavior has been selected for reinforcement, it's a good idea to record a baseline so that you can set realistic goals for change. T or F?
2. Self-recording, even without the use of extra rewards, can bring about desired changes in target behaviors. T or F?
3. The Premack principle states that behavioral contracting can be used to reinforce changes in behavior. T or F?
4. A self-management plan should make use of the principle of shaping by setting a graduated series of goals. T or F?
5. Eleni ends up playing solitaire on her computer each time she tries to work on a term paper. Eventually she does get to work, but only after a long delay. To break this bad habit Eleni removes the solitaire icon from her computer screen so that she won't see it when she begins work. Eleni has used which strategy for breaking bad habits?
   a. alternative responses
   b. extinction
   c. avoid cues
   d. contracting

REFLECT

Critical Thinking

6. How does setting daily goals in a behavioral self-management program help maximize the effects of reinforcement?

Relate

Even if you don't expect to carry out a self-management project right now, outline a plan for changing your own behavior. Be sure to describe the behavior you want to change, set goals, and identify reinforcers.

Answers: 1. T **2.** T **3.** F **4.** T **5.** c. **6.** Daily performance goals and rewards reduce the delay of reinforcement, which maximizes its impact.

chapter in review

Gateways to Learning and Conditioning

Learning is a relatively permanent change in behavior due to experience.

- Associative learning is a simple type of learning that affects many aspects of daily life.
- Cognitive learning involves making use of information-rich higher mental processes.
- Associative learning depends on reinforcement, which increases the probability that a particular response will occur.
- In classical conditioning, a neutral stimulus is followed by an unconditioned stimulus. With repeated pairings, the neutral stimulus begins to elicit a response.
- In operant conditioning, responses that are followed by reinforcement occur more frequently.

Classical conditioning, studied by Pavlov, occurs when a neutral stimulus (NS) is associated with an unconditioned stimulus (US).

- The US triggers a reflex called the unconditioned response (UR). If the NS is consistently paired with the US, it becomes a conditioned stimulus (CS). After conditioning, a CS is capable of producing a conditioned (learned) response (CR).
- When the conditioned stimulus is followed by the unconditioned stimulus, conditioning is reinforced (strengthened).
- When the CS is repeatedly presented alone, conditioning is extinguished (weakened or inhibited).
- In classical conditioning, the CS creates an expectancy that the US will follow, which alters behavior.
- In higher order conditioning, a well-learned conditioned stimulus is used as if it were an unconditioned stimulus, which leads to further learning.
- Through stimulus generalization, stimuli similar to the conditioned stimulus will also produce a response. Stimulus discrimination occurs when we learn to respond to a particular stimulus, but not to others that are similar.

Conditioning applies to visceral or emotional responses as well as simple reflexes. As a result, conditioned emotional responses (CERs) also occur.

- Irrational fears called phobias may begin as CERs
- Conditioning of emotional responses can occur vicariously (secondhand) as well as directly.

Operant conditioning occurs when a voluntary action is followed by a reinforcer (which increases the frequency of the response) or a punisher (which decreases the frequency of the response).

- Delaying reinforcement greatly reduces its effectiveness, but long chains of responses may be maintained by a single reinforcer.
- Superstitious behaviors often become part of response chains because they *appear* to be associated with reinforcement.

- By rewarding successive approximations to a particular response, behavior can be shaped into desired patterns.
- If an operant response is not reinforced, it may extinguish (disappear). But after extinction seems complete, it may temporarily reappear (spontaneous recovery).
- Both positive reinforcement and negative reinforcement increase the likelihood that a response will be repeated. Punishment decreases the likelihood that the response will occur again.

Operant learning may be based on primary reinforcers (which are rooted in biology), secondary reinforcers (such as tokens and social reinforcers), and feedback (knowledge of results).

- Secondary reinforcers gain their power by association with a primary reinforcer.
- Feedback, or knowledge of results, also aids learning and improves performance.
- Programmed instruction breaks learning into a series of small steps and provides immediate feedback. Computer-assisted instruction (CAI) does the same but has the added advantage of providing alternative exercises and information when needed.

Reward or reinforcement may be given continuously (after every response) or on a schedule of partial reinforcement. Partial reinforcement produces greater resistance to extinction.

- Five basic schedules of reinforcement are continuous, fixed ratio, variable ratio, fixed interval, and variable interval. Each schedule produces a different pattern of responding.
- Stimuli that precede a reinforced response tend to control when and where operant responses occur (stimulus control). Two aspects of stimulus control are generalization and discrimination.
- In generalization, an operant response tends to occur when stimuli similar to those preceding reinforcement are present.
- In discrimination, responses are given in the presence of discriminative stimuli associated with reinforcement (S+) and withheld in the presence of stimuli associated with nonreinforcement (S−).

Punishment decreases response frequency.

- Punishment occurs when a response is followed by the onset of an aversive event or by the removal of a positive event (response cost).

Behavioral contract A formal agreement stating behaviors to be changed and consequences that apply.

- Punishment is most effective when it is immediate, consistent, and intense.
- Although severe punishment can virtually eliminate a particular behavior, mild punishment usually only temporarily suppresses responding. Reinforcement must be used to make lasting changes in the behavior of a person or an animal.
- Punishment tends to produce escape and avoidance learning, and it encourages the learning of aggressive responses.

Cognitive learning involves acquiring higher-level information, rather than just associating stimuli and responses.

- Cognitive learning involves higher mental processes, such as memory, thinking, problem solving, understanding, knowing, and anticipating.
- Even in relatively simple learning situations, animals and people seem to form cognitive maps (internal representations of relationships).
- In latent learning, learning remains hidden or unseen until a reward or incentive for performance is offered.
- Discovery learning emphasizes insight and understanding, in contrast to rote learning.

Learning can occur by merely observing and imitating the actions of another person or by noting the consequences of the person's actions.

- Observational learning is influenced by the personal characteristics of the model and the success or failure of the model's behavior. Aggression is readily learned and released by modeling.
- Media characters can act as powerful models for observational learning. Televised violence increases the likelihood of aggression by viewers.

By applying operant conditioning principles, it is possible to change or manage your own behavior.

- When managing behavior, self-reinforcement, self-recording, feedback, and behavioral contracting are all helpful.
- Four strategies that can help change bad habits are reinforcing alternative responses, promoting extinction, breaking response chains, and avoiding antecedent cues.

Web Resources

For an up-to-date list of direct links to interesting sites, including those listed here, visit the student companion site for this book at www.cengage.com/psychology/coon

Classical Conditioning Experiment Try this demonstration of classical conditioning.

Clicker Training for Animals One approach to using operant conditioning to train animals.

Ten Reasons Not to Hit Your Kids Read more about the limitations of spanking.

Guidelines for Using Time Out with Children and Preteens Read about the use of response cost as an effective form of punishment.

Psychological Self-Tools An online self-help book.

Interactive Learning

Introduction to Psychology: Gateways to Mind and Behavior **Book Companion Website**
www.cengage.com/psychology/coon

Visit your book companion website, where you will find flash cards, practice quizzes, web links, and more to help you study.

CENGAGENOW™ *Just what you need to know NOW!*

Spend time on what you need to master rather than on information you already have learned. Take a pre-test for this chapter, and CengageNOW will generate a personalized study plan based on your results. The study plan will identify the topics you need to review and direct you to online resources to help you master those topics. You can then take a post-test to help you determine the concepts you have mastered and what you will need to work on. Try it out! Go to www.cengage.com/login to sign in with an access code or to purchase access to this product.

CHAPTER 8

Memory

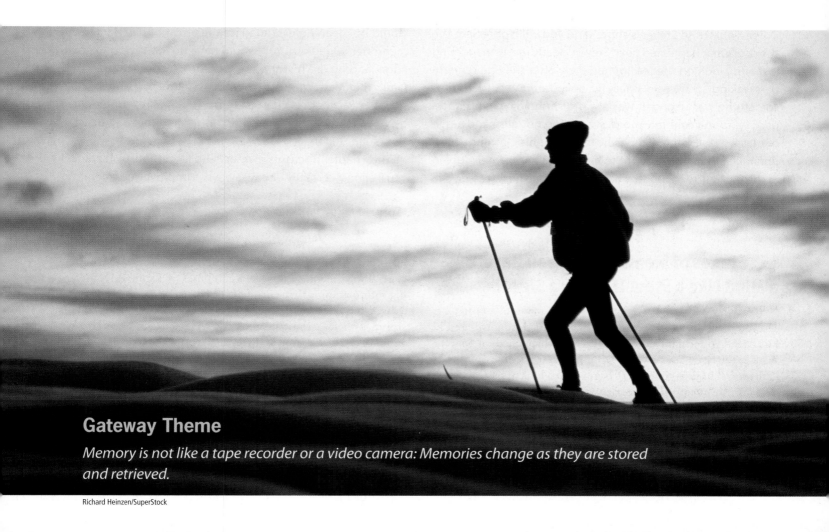

Gateway Theme

Memory is not like a tape recorder or a video camera: Memories change as they are stored and retrieved.

Richard Heinzen/SuperStock

Gateway Questions

- How does memory work?
- *What are the features of short-term memory?*
- *What are the features of long-term memory?*
- *How is memory measured?*
- *Why do we forget?*

- *How does the brain form and store memories?*
- *What are "photographic" memories?*
- *How can I improve my memory?*
- *Are there any tricks to help me with my memory?*

"What the Hell's Going on Here?"

It's February and Steven is cross-country skiing on the ice of Lake Michigan. He realizes he is very cold and decides to turn back. In a few minutes comes a new realization: He is lost. Wandering on the ice, he grows numb and very, very tired.

Put yourself in Steven's shoes, and you will appreciate the shock of what happened next. Steven clearly recalls wandering lost and alone on the ice. Immediately after that, he remembers waking up in a field. But as he looked around, Steven knew something was wrong. It was a warm spring day! In his backpack he found running shoes, swimming goggles, and a pair of glasses—all unfamiliar. As he looked at his clothing—also unfamiliar—Steven thought to himself, "What the hell's going on here?" Fourteen months had passed since he left to go ski-

ing (Loftus & Loftus, 1980). How did he get to the field? Steven couldn't say. He had lost more than a year of his life to total amnesia.

As Steven's amnesia vividly shows, life without memory would be meaningless. Imagine the terror of having all your memories wiped out. You would have no identity, no knowledge, and no life history. You wouldn't recognize friends or family members. When you looked in a mirror, a stranger would stare back at you. In a very real sense, who we are is determined by what we remember *and* what we forget (Behrend, Beike, & Lampinen, 2004).

This chapter discusses memory and forgetting. By reading it you'll almost certainly discover ways to improve your memory.

Stages of Memory—Do You Have a Mind Like a Steel Trap? Or a Sieve?

Gateway Question: How does memory work?

Do you remember what you had for breakfast this morning? The last friend you instant messaged? Or what happened on September 11, 2001? Of course you do. But how is it possible for us to so easily travel back in time? Let's begin with a look at basic memory systems. An interesting series of events must occur before we can say "I remember."

Many people think of memory as "a dusty storehouse of facts." In reality, **memory** is an active system that receives, stores, orga-

nizes, alters, and recovers information (Lieberman, 2004). In some general ways memory acts like a computer (● Figure 8.1). Incoming information is first **encoded,** or changed into a usable form. This step is like typing data into a computer. Next, information is **stored,** or held in the system. (As we will see in a moment, human memory can be pictured as three separate storage systems.) Finally, memories must be **retrieved,** or taken out of storage, to be useful. If you're going to remember all of the 9,856 new terms on your next psychology exam, you must successfully encode, store, and retrieve them.

What are the three separate memory systems just mentioned? To be stored for a long time, information must pass through sensory memory, short-term memory, and long-term memory. These stages are summarized by the Atkinson-Schiffrin model of memory shown in ● Figure 8.2 (Atkinson & Schiffrin, 1968; Goldstein, 2008).

Sensory Memory

Let's say a friend asks you to pick up several things at a market. How will you remember them? Information first enters **sensory memory,** which can hold an exact copy of what you see or hear, for a few seconds or less. We are normally unaware of the functioning of our sensory memories. For instance, look at a flower and then quickly close your eyes. If you are lucky, a fleeting visual image of the flower will persist. **Iconic** (eye-KON-ick) **memories** (sensory images) typically last for about one-half second (Keysers et al., 2005). Similarly, when you hear information, sensory memory stores it as an *echoic memory* for up to 2 seconds (Haenschel et al., 2005). (An **echoic memory** is a brief flurry of activity in the auditory system.) In general, sensory memory holds information just long enough to move it to the second memory system, short-term memory (Neath & Surprenant, 2003).

● **Figure 8.1** In some ways, a computer acts like a mechanical memory system. Both systems process information, and both allow encoding, storage, and retrieval of data.

Retrieval

Storage

Encoding

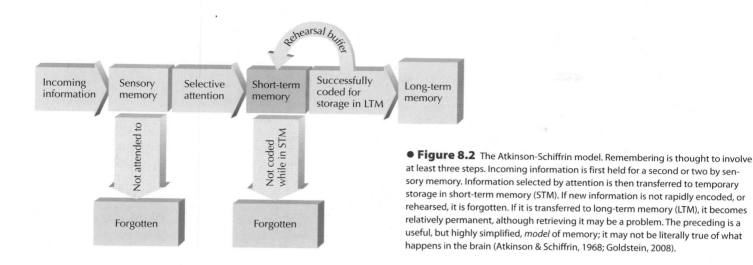

● **Figure 8.2** The Atkinson-Schiffrin model. Remembering is thought to involve at least three steps. Incoming information is first held for a second or two by sensory memory. Information selected by attention is then transferred to temporary storage in short-term memory (STM). If new information is not rapidly encoded, or rehearsed, it is forgotten. If it is transferred to long-term memory (LTM), it becomes relatively permanent, although retrieving it may be a problem. The preceding is a useful, but highly simplified, *model* of memory; it may not be literally true of what happens in the brain (Atkinson & Schiffrin, 1968; Goldstein, 2008).

Short-Term Memory

Not everything we see or hear stays in memory. Imagine that a radio is playing in the background as your friend reads her shopping list. Will you remember what the announcer says, too? Probably not, because *selective attention* (focusing on a selected portion of sensory input) controls what information moves on to short-term memory. **Short-term memory (STM)** holds small amounts of information in conscious awareness for a dozen seconds or so (Jonides et al., 2008). By paying attention to your friend, you will place her shopping list in short-term memory (while you ignore the voice on the radio saying, "Buy Burpo Butter").

How are short-term memories encoded? Short-term memories can be stored as images. But more often they are stored *phonetically* (by sound), especially in recalling words and letters (Page et al., 2007). If you are introduced to Tim at a party and you forget his name, you are more likely to call him by a name that sounds like Tim (Jim, Kim, or Slim, for instance), rather than a name that sounds different, such as Bob or Mike. Your friend with the shopping list may be lucky if you don't bring home jam instead of ham and soap instead of soup!

Short-term memory briefly stores small amounts of information. When you dial a phone number or briefly remember a shopping list, you are using STM. Notice that unless you *rehearse* information (say it over and over to yourself), it is quickly "dumped" from STM and forever lost. Short-term memory prevents our minds from storing useless names, dates, telephone numbers, and other trivia.

As you may have noticed when dialing a telephone, STM is very sensitive to *interruption*, or *interference*. You've probably had something like this happen: Someone leaves a phone number on your answering machine. You repeat the number to yourself as you start to dial. Someone asks you a question. You answer, turn to the phone, and find that you have forgotten the number. Notice again that STM can handle only small amounts of information. It is very difficult to do more than one task at a time in STM (Miyake, 2001; Oberauer & Göthe, 2006).

Working Memory

Short-term memory is often used for more than just storing information. When STM is combined with other mental processes, it acts more like a sort of "mental scratchpad," or **working memory,** where we do much of our thinking. That is, working memory briefly holds the information we need when we are thinking and solving problems (Holmes & Adams, 2006). Whenever you do mental arithmetic, put together a puzzle, plan a meal, follow directions, or read a book, you are using working memory (Baddeley, 2003).

Long-Term Memory

If STM is so limited, how do we remember for longer periods? Information that is important or meaningful is transferred to **long-term memory (LTM),** which acts as a lasting storehouse for knowledge. LTM contains everything you know about the

Memory The mental system for receiving, encoding, storing, organizing, altering, and retrieving information.

Encoding Converting information into a form in which it will be retained in memory.

Storage Holding information in memory for later use.

Retrieval Recovering information from storage in memory.

Sensory memory The first stage of memory, which holds an exact record of incoming information for a few seconds or less.

Iconic memory A mental image or visual representation.

Echoic memory A brief continuation of sensory activity in the auditory system after a sound is heard.

Short-term memory (STM) The memory system used to hold small amounts of information for relatively brief time periods.

Working memory Another name for short-term memory, especially when it is used for thinking and problem solving.

Long-term memory (LTM) The memory system used for relatively permanent storage of meaningful information.

HUMAN DIVERSITY

Cows, Memories, and Culture

If you were on a farm and saw 20 cows walk by, do you think you could remember the age, color, gender, and condition of all of them? Unless you are a dairy farmer, doing so would be quite a feat of memory. As noted, we are most likely to remember information that is personally important or meaningful. However, for a Maasai person from East Africa, it would be easier. Livestock are very important in Maasai culture; a Maasai's wealth is measured by the number of cattle owned. Thus, the Maasai are prepared to encode and store information about cattle that would be difficult for most people in the United States to remember.

Malcolm Linton/Liaison/Getty Images

Culture affects our memories in other interesting ways. For example, American culture emphasizes individuals, whereas Chinese culture emphasizes membership in groups. In one study, European-American and Chinese adults were asked to recall 20 memories from any time in their lives. As expected, American memories tended to be self-centered: Most people remembered surprising events and what they did during the events. Chinese adults, in contrast, remembered important social or historical events and their own interactions with family members, friends, and others (Wang & Conway, 2004). Thus, in the United States, personal memories tend to be about "me"; in China they tend to be about "us."

---

world—from aardvark to zucchini, math to *Desperate Housewives,* facts to fantasy. Yet there appears to be no danger of running out of room. LTM can hold nearly limitless amounts of information. In fact, the more you know, the easier it becomes to add new information to memory. This is the reverse of what we would expect if LTM could be "filled up" (Goldstein, 2008). It is also one of many reasons for getting an education.

Are long-term memories also encoded as sounds? They can be. But typically, long-term memories are stored on the basis of *meaning,* not sound. If you make an error in LTM, it will probably be related to meaning. For example, if you are trying to recall the word "barn" from a memorized list, you are more likely to mistakenly say "shed" or "farm" than "yarn" or "darn." If you can link information in STM to knowledge already stored in LTM, it gains meaning. This makes it easier to remember. As an example, try to memorize this story:

> With hocked gems financing him, our hero bravely defied all scornful laughter. "Your eyes deceive," he had said, "An egg, not a table, correctly typifies this unexplored planet." Now three sturdy sisters sought proof. Forging along, days became weeks as many doubters spread fearful rumors about the edge. At last from nowhere welcome winged creatures appeared, signifying momentous success. (Adapted from Dooling & Lachman, 1971.)

This odd story emphasizes the impact that meaning has on memory. People given the title of the story were able to remember it far better than those not given a title. See if the title helps you as much as it did them: "Columbus Discovers America."

The Relationship Between STM and LTM

Although sensory memory is involved every time we store information, we are most likely to notice STM and LTM. To summarize their connection, picture short-term memory as a small desk at the front of a huge warehouse full of filing cabinets (LTM). As information enters the warehouse, it is first placed on the desk. Because the desk is small, it must be quickly cleared off to make room for new information. Unimportant items are simply tossed away. Meaningful or personally important information is placed in the files (LTM). (See "Cows, Memories, and Culture.") When we want to use knowledge from LTM to answer a question, the information is returned to STM. Or, in our analogy, a folder is taken out of the files (LTM) and moved to the desk (STM), where it can be used.

Now that you have a general picture of memory it is time to explore STM and LTM in more detail. But first, here's a chance to rehearse what you've learned.

KNOWLEDGE BUILDER
Memory Systems

RECITE

Match: **A.** Sensory memory **B.** STM **C.** LTM

1. _____ Information tends to be stored phonetically
2. _____ Holds information for a few seconds or less
3. _____ Stores an iconic memory or echoic memory
4. _____ Permanent, unlimited capacity
5. _____ Temporarily holds small amounts of information
6. _____ Selective attention determines its contents
7. STM is improved by interruption, or interference, because attention is more focused at such times. T or F?

REFLECT

Critical Thinking

8. Why is sensory memory important to filmmakers?

Continued

⬤⬤ Short-Term Memory—Do You Know the Magic Number?

Gateway Question: What are the features of short-term memory?

To make good use of your memory, it is valuable to know more about the quirks and characteristics of both STM and LTM. Let's start with a closer look at STM.

How much information can be held in short-term memory? For an answer, read the following numbers once. Then close the book and write as many as you can in the correct order.

8 5 1 7 4 9 3

This is called a digit-span test. It is a measure of attention and short-term memory. If you were able to correctly repeat 7 digits, you have an average short-term memory. Now try to memorize the following list, again reading it only once:

7 1 8 3 5 4 2 9 1 6 3 4

This series was probably beyond your short-term memory capacity. Psychologist George Miller found that short-term memory is limited to the "magic number" 7 (plus or minus 2) **information bits** (Miller, 1956). A bit is a single meaningful "piece" of information, such as a digit. It is as if short-term memory has 7 "slots" or "bins" into which separate items can be placed. Actually, a few people can remember up to 9 bits, and for some types of information 5 bits is the limit. Thus, an *average* of 7 information bits can be held in short-term memory (Neath & Surprenant, 2003).

When all the "slots" in STM are filled, there is no room for new information. Picture how this works at a party: Let's say your hostess begins introducing everyone who is there, "Chun, Dasia, Sandra, Roseanna, Cholik, Shawn, Kyrene . . ." "Stop," you think to yourself. But she continues, "Nelia, Jay, Frank, Patty, Amit, Ricky." The hostess leaves, satisfied that you have met everyone. And you spend the evening talking with Chun, Dasia, and Ricky, the only people whose names you remember!

Chunking

Before we continue, try your short-term memory again, this time on letters. Read the following letters once, then look away and try to write them in the proper order.

T V I B M U S N Y M C A

Notice that there are 12 letters, or "bits" of information. If you studied the letters one at a time, this should be beyond the 7-item limit of STM. However, you may have noticed that some of the letters can be grouped, or *chunked*, together. For example, you may have noticed that NY is the abbreviation for New York. If so, the two bits N and Y became one chunk. **Information chunks** are made up of bits of information grouped into larger units.

Does chunking make a difference? Yes. Chunking **recodes** (reorganizes) information into units that are already in LTM. In a classic experiment that used lists like this one, people remembered best when the letters were read as familiar meaningful chunks: TV, IBM, USN, YMCA (Bower & Springston, 1970). If you recoded the letters this way, you organized them into four *chunks* of information and probably remembered the entire list. If you didn't, go back and try it again; you'll notice a big difference.

Chunking suggests that STM holds about 5 to 7 of whatever units we are using. A single chunk could be made up of numbers, letters, words, phrases, or familiar sentences. Picture STM as a small desk again. Through chunking, we combine several items into one "stack" of information. This allows us to place 7 stacks on the desk, where before there was only room for 7 separate items. While you are studying, try to find ways to link 2, 3, or more separate facts or ideas into larger chunks, and your short-term memory will improve. Psychologist Nelson Cowan (2005; Jonides et al., 2008) believes that STM may actually hold only 4 items, unless some chunking has occurred. The clear message is that creating information chunks is the key to making good use of your short-term memory (Gobet, 2005).

Rehearsing Information

How long do short-term memories last? They disappear very rapidly. However, you can prolong a memory by silently repeating it, a process called **maintenance rehearsal.** In a sense, rehearsing information allows you to "hear" it many times, not just once (Nairne, 2002). You have probably used maintenance rehearsal to keep a phone number active in your mind while looking at your cell phone and dialing it.

Isn't saying stuff to yourself over and over also a way of studying? It *is* true that the more times a short-term memory is rehearsed,

Information bits Meaningful units of information, such as numbers, letters, words, or phrases.

Information chunks Information bits grouped into larger units.

Recoding Reorganizing or modifying information to assist storage in memory.

Maintenance rehearsal Silently repeating or mentally reviewing information to hold it in short-term memory.

the greater its chances of being stored in LTM (Goldstein, 2008). This is **rote learning** (learning by simple repetition). But rote learning is not a very effective way to study.

Elaborative encoding, which makes information more meaningful, is a far better way to form lasting memories. Elaborative encoding links new information to memories that are already in LTM. When you are studying, you will remember more if you elaborate on the meaning of the information. As you read, try to reflect frequently. Ask yourself "why" questions, such as, "Why would that be true?" (Toyota & Kikuchi, 2005; Willoughby et al., 1997). Also, try to relate new ideas to your own experiences and knowledge (Hartlep & Forsyth, 2000).

What if rehearsal is prevented, so a memory cannot be recycled or moved to LTM? Without maintenance rehearsal, STM is quite brief. In one experiment, subjects heard meaningless syllables like XAR followed by a number like 67. As soon as subjects heard the number, they began counting backward by threes (to prevent them from repeating the syllable). After a delay of between 12 and 18 seconds, their memory for the syllables fell to zero (Peterson & Peterson, 1959).

After *12 to 18 seconds* without rehearsal, the short-term memories were gone forever! Part of this rapid loss can be explained by the testing procedures used (Goldstein, 2008). In daily life, short-term memories usually last longer. Just the same, if you are introduced to someone and the name slips out of STM, it is gone forever. To avoid embarrassment, pay careful attention to the name, repeat it to yourself several times, and try to use it in the next sentence or two—before you lose it (Neath & Surprenant, 2003).

Long-Term Memory—Where the Past Lives

Gateway Question: What are the features of long-term memory?

An electrode touched the patient's brain. Immediately she said, "Yes, sir, I think I heard a mother calling her little boy somewhere. It seemed to be something happening years ago. It was somebody in the neighborhood where I live." A short time later the electrode was applied to the same spot. Again the patient said, "Yes, I hear the same familiar sounds, it seems to be a woman calling, the same lady" (Penfield, 1958). A woman undergoing brain surgery made these statements. There are no pain receptors in the brain, so the patient was awake as her brain was electrically stimulated (● Figure 8.3). When activated, some brain areas seemed to produce vivid memories of long-forgotten events.

Permanence

Are all our experiences permanently recorded in memory? Results like those described led neurosurgeon Wilder Penfield to claim that the brain records the past like a "strip of movie film, complete with sound track" (Penfield, 1957). But as you know, this is an exaggeration. Many events never get past short-term

● **Figure 8.3** Exposed cerebral cortex of a patient undergoing brain surgery. Numbers represent points that reportedly produced "memories" when electrically stimulated. A critical evaluation of such reports suggests that they are more like dreams than memories. This fact raises questions about claims that long-term memories are permanent. (From Penfield, 1958. Courtesy of the author and Charles C Thomas, Publisher, Springfield, Illinois.)

memory. Also, brain stimulation produces memory-like experiences in only about 3 percent of cases. Most reports resemble dreams more than memories, and many are clearly imaginary. Memory experts now believe that long-term memories are only *relatively* permanent (Goldstein, 2008). Perfect, eternal memories are a myth.

Try It Yourself: How's Your Memory?
To better appreciate the next topic, pause for a moment and read the words you see here. Read through the list once. Then continue reading the next section of this chapter.

bed	dream	blanket	doze	pillow	nap
snore	mattress	alarm	clock	rest	slumber
nod	sheet	bunk	cot	cradle	groggy

Constructing Memories

There's another reason for doubting that all our experiences are permanently recorded. As new long-term memories are stored, older memories are often updated, changed, lost, or *revised* (Lieberman, 2004). To illustrate this point, Elizabeth Loftus and John Palmer (1974) showed people a filmed automobile accident. Afterward, some participants were asked to estimate how fast the cars were going when they "smashed" into each other. For others the words "bumped," "contacted," or "hit" replaced "smashed." One week later, each person was asked, "Did you see any broken glass?" Those asked earlier about the cars that "smashed" into each other were more likely to say yes. (No broken glass was shown in

CRITICAL THINKING

Do You Like Jam with Your Memory?

Have you ever wondered why famous companies, which already sell huge amounts of familiar products (such as soft drinks or beer), continue to advertise as heavily as they do? If you believe the point of the advertising is to familiarize people with a product or to inform them about it, this *is* a mystery. But if you think about the constructive nature of memory, the mystery is solved. According to economist Jesse Shapiro (2006), the intent of much advertising is to "jam" your memory with positive impressions of a product.

How does "memory jamming" work? How many times have you had a bottle or can of your favorite beer or soft drink? And how

many commercials for those beverages have you watched? Every extra commercial adds one more positive memory of the beverage to your long-term memory. Here's a typical commercial: Boy goes to cool party, sees a hot girl, flashes favorite beer, gets the girl. (Yes, beer commercials mainly target young men.) Because we cannot always easily tell which recollection is fact and which is fiction, storing enough of these commercials can eventually create "memories" that never happened. For example, you might remember that you enjoyed drinking a particular beverage more than you actually do, in reality.

According to Shapiro (2006), the more positive fictional commercials we see, the less likely we are to remember an actual negative experience with a product. In effect, the positive, fictional memories "jam," or block, our ability to remember actual negative memories when deciding whether to buy a product. Braun-LaTour & LaTour (2004) add that long-term advertising campaigns create a "brand" memory that can be remarkably strong. This appears to be especially true when the ads are first viewed in early childhood. So perhaps you have been having jam with your memories ever since you were a baby.

---

the film.) The new information ("smashed") was included in memories and altered them.

Try It Yourself: Old or New?

Now, without looking back to the list of words you read a few minutes ago, see if you can tell which of the following are "old" words (items from the list you read) and which are "new" words (items that weren't on the list). Mark each of the following words as old or new:

sofa   sleep   lamp   kitchen

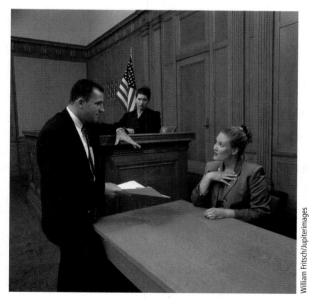

William Fritsch/Jupiterimages

Eyewitness memories are notoriously inaccurate. By the time witnesses are asked to testify in court, information they learned after an incident may blend into their original memories.

Updating memories is called **constructive processing.** Gaps in memory, which are common, may be filled in by logic, guessing, or new information (Schacter, Norman, & Koutstaal, 1998). Indeed, it is possible to have "memories" for things that never happened (such as remembering broken glass at an accident when there was none) (Loftus, 2003a, 2003b). In one study, people who had visited a Disney resort were shown several fake ads for Disney that featured Bugs Bunny. Later, about 16 percent of the people who saw these fake ads claimed that they had met Bugs at Disneyland. This is impossible, of course, because Bugs Bunny is a Warner Brothers character that would never be found at Disneyland (Braun, Ellis, & Loftus, 2002).

In another study, by Sharon Hannigan and Mark Reinitz, college students saw photographs that depicted common activities, such as shopping for groceries or eating at a restaurant. In some cases, the photos showed an unusual event. For example, in one sequence a woman at a grocery store passes a pile of oranges on the floor. Two days later, the students saw the photos again. This time, however, new photos were included that *explained* how the unusual event occurred (● Figure 8.4). For instance, the woman at the market is shown pulling an orange from the bottom of a stack of oranges. Sixty-eight percent of the students were sure they remembered seeing this image (Hannigan & Reinitz, 2001).

Rote learning Learning by simple repetition.

Elaborative encoding Encoding that links new information with existing memories and knowledge.

Constructive processing Reorganizing or updating memories on the basis of logic, reasoning, or the addition of new information.

CRITICAL THINKING

Telling Wrong from Right in Forensic Memory

Imagine that you are a forensic psychologist, investigating a crime. Unfortunately, your witness can't remember much of what happened. As a "memory detective," what can you do to help?

Could hypnosis improve the witness's memory? It might seem so. In one case in California, 26 children were abducted from a school bus and held captive for ransom. Under hypnosis, the bus driver recalled the license plate number of the kidnappers' van. This memory helped break the case. Such successes seem to imply that hypnosis can improve memory. But does it?

Research has shown that hypnosis increases false memories more than it does true ones. Eighty percent of the new memories produced by hypnotized subjects in one classic experiment were *incorrect* (Dywan & Bowers, 1983). This is in part because a hypnotized person is more likely than normal to use imagination to fill in gaps in memory. Also, if a questioner asks misleading or suggestive questions, hypnotized persons tend to weave the information into their memories (Scoboria et al., 2002). To make matters worse, even when a memory is completely false, the hypnotized person's confidence in it can be unshakable (Burgess & Kirsch, 1999). Thus,

hypnosis sometimes uncovers more information, as it did with the bus driver (Schreiber & Schreiber, 1999). However, in the absence of corroborating evidence, there is no sure way to tell which of these memories are false and which are true (Newman & Thompson, 2001).

Is there a better way to improve eyewitness memory? To help police detectives, R. Edward Geiselman and Ron Fisher created the **cognitive interview,** a technique for jogging the memory of eyewitnesses (Fisher & Geiselman, 1987). The key to this approach is recreating the crime scene. Witnesses revisit the scene in their imaginations or in person. That way, aspects of the crime scene, such as sounds, smells, and objects, provide helpful retrieval cues (stimuli associated with a memory). Back in the context of the crime, the witness is encouraged to recall events in different orders and from different viewpoints. Every new memory, no matter how trivial it may seem, can serve as a cue to trigger the retrieval of yet more memories. (Later in this chapter, we will see why such cues are so effective for jogging memories.)

When used properly, the cognitive interview produces 35 percent more correct information than standard questioning (Davis, McMahon, & Greenwood, 2005; Geiselman

et al., 1986). This improvement comes without adding to the number of false memories elicited, as occurs with hypnosis. The result is a procedure that is more effective in actual police work (Ginet & Py, 2001; Kebbell & Wagstaff, 1998) and in different cultures (Stein & Memon, 2006).

Some police detectives, following the advice of psychologists, recreate crime scenes to help witnesses remember what they saw. Typically, people return to the scene at the time of day the crime occurred. They are also asked to wear the same clothing they wore and go through the same motions as they did before the crime. With so many memory cues available, witnesses sometimes remember key items of information they hadn't recalled before.

● **Figure 8.4** Suppose you are shown a series of photographs that depict various scenes related to having lunch at the campus commons. One of the photos shows an unexpected event (the spilled soda). If you were to see all of the photos again a few days later, it's likely that you would "remember" seeing the image on the right, even though it wasn't in the original group of photos. When we see an unexplained event, we are very likely to think about its cause. Later, it is easy to mistake these thoughts for an actual memory (Hannigan & Reinitz, 2001).

Could constructive processing be used to deliberately manipulate memory? Bingo. According to one theory, advertisers do it all the time. See "Do You Like Jam with Your Memory?" on page 257 for more information.

Try It Yourself: And Now, the Results

Return now and look at the labels you wrote on the "old or new" word list. Contrary to what you may think you "remembered," all of the listed words are "new." None was on the original list!

If you thought you "remembered" that "sleep" was on the original list, you had a false memory. The word "sleep" is associated with most of the words on the original list, which creates a strong impression that you saw it before (Roediger & McDermott, 1995).

As the preceding examples show, thoughts, inferences, and mental associations may be mistaken for true memories (Loftus, 2003A, B). People in Elizabeth Loftus's experiments who had these *pseudo-memories* (false memories) were often quite upset to learn they had given false "testimony" (Loftus & Ketcham, 1994).

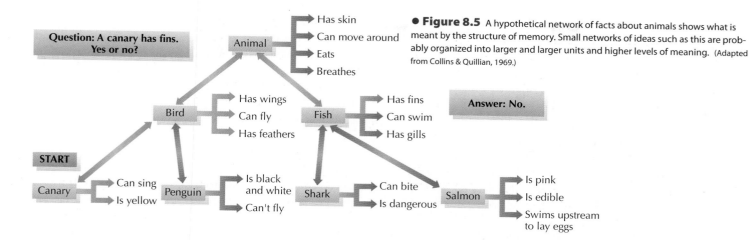

● **Figure 8.5** A hypothetical network of facts about animals shows what is meant by the structure of memory. Small networks of ideas such as this are probably organized into larger and larger units and higher levels of meaning. (Adapted from Collins & Quillian, 1969.)

False long-term memories are a common problem in police work. For example, a witness may select a photo of a suspect from police files or see a photo in the news. Later, the witness identifies the suspect in a lineup or in court. Did the witness really remember the suspect from the scene of the crime? Or was it from the more recently seen photograph?

Does new information "overwrite" existing memories? No, the real problem is that we often can't remember the *source* of a memory (Simons et al, 2004). This can lead witnesses to "remember" a face that they actually saw somewhere other than the crime scene (Ruva, McEvoy, & Bryant, 2007). Many tragic cases of mistaken identity occur this way. One famous example involved memory expert Donald Thomson. After appearing live on Australian television, he was accused of rape. It turns out that the victim was watching him on TV when the actual rapist broke into her apartment (Schacter, 1996, 2001). She correctly remembered his face but attributed it to the wrong source.

Is there any way to avoid such problems? Forensic psychologists have tried a variety of techniques to help improve the memory of witnesses. "Telling Wrong from Right in Forensic Memory" examines research on this important question.

To summarize, forming and using long-term memories is an active, creative, highly personal process. Our memories are colored by emotions, judgments, and quirks of personality. If you and a friend were joined at the hip and you went through life side-by-side, you would still have different memories. What we remember depends on what we pay attention to, what we regard as meaningful or important, and what we feel strongly about (Schacter, 2000).

Organizing Memories

Long-term memory stores huge amounts of information during a lifetime. How are we able to quickly find specific memories? The answer is that each person's "memory index" is highly organized.

Do you mean that information is arranged alphabetically, as in a dictionary? Not a chance! If we ask you to name a black and white animal that lives on ice, is related to a chicken, and cannot fly, you don't have to go from aardvark to zebra to find the answer. You will probably only think of black-and-white birds living in the Antarctic. *Voila,* the answer is a penguin.

Information in LTM may be arranged according to rules, images, categories, symbols, similarity, formal meaning, or personal meaning (Lieberman, 2004). In recent years, psychologists have begun to develop a picture of the *structure,* or organization, of memories. *Memory structure* refers to the pattern of associations among items of information. For example, assume that you are given two statements, to which you must answer yes or no: (1) *A canary is an animal.* (2) *A canary is a bird.* Which do you answer more quickly? Most people can say that *A canary is a bird* faster than they can recognize that *A canary is an animal* (Collins & Quillian, 1969).

Why should this be so? Psychologists believe that a **network model** of memory explains why. According to this view, LTM is organized as a network of linked ideas (● Figure 8.5). When ideas are "farther" apart, it takes a longer chain of associations to connect them. The more two items are separated, the longer it takes to answer. In terms of information links, *canary* is probably "close" to *bird* in your "memory files." *Animal* and *canary* are farther apart. Remember though, this has nothing to do with alphabetical order. We are talking about a system of linked meanings.

Redintegration

Networks of associated memories may also help explain a common experience: Imagine finding a picture taken on your sixth birthday or tenth Christmas. As you look at the photo, one memory leads to another, which leads to another, and another. Soon you have unleashed a flood of seemingly forgotten details. This process is called redintegration (ruh-DIN-tuh-GRAY-shun).

Redintegration seems to spread through the "branches" of memory networks. Many people find that redintegration can also

Cognitive interview Use of various cues and strategies to improve the memory of eyewitnesses.

Network model A model of memory that views it as an organized system of linked information.

Redintegration Process by which memories are reconstructed or expanded by starting with one memory and then following chains of association to other, related memories.

be touched off by distinctive odors out of the past—from a farm visited in childhood, Grandma's kitchen, the seashore, a doctor's office, the perfume or aftershave of a former lover, and so on. The key idea in redintegration is that one memory serves as a cue to trigger another. As a result, an entire past experience may be reconstructed from one small recollection.

Skill Memory and Fact Memory

How many types of long-term memory are there? It is becoming clear that more than one type of long-term memory exists. For example, a curious thing happens to many people who develop amnesia. Amnesic patients may be unable to learn a telephone number, an address, or a person's name. Yet the same patients can learn to solve complex puzzles in a normal amount of time (Cavaco et al., 2004) (● Figure 8.6). These and other observations have led many psychologists to conclude that long-term memories fall into at least two categories. One is called *procedural memory* (or skill memory). The other is *declarative memory* (also sometimes called fact memory).

Skills

Procedural memory includes basic conditioned responses and learned actions, such as those involved in typing, driving, or swinging a golf club. Memories such as these can be fully expressed only as actions (or "know-how"). It is likely that skill memories register in "lower" brain areas, especially the cerebellum. They represent the more basic "automatic" elements of conditioning, learning, and memory (Hermann et al., 2004).

Facts

Declarative memory stores specific factual information, such as names, faces, words, dates, and ideas. Declarative memories are expressed as words or symbols. For example, knowing that Peter Jackson directed both the *Lord of the Rings* trilogy and the latest remake of *King Kong* is a declarative memory. This is the type of memory that a person with amnesia lacks and that most of us take for granted. Declarative memory can be further divided into *semantic memory* and *episodic memory* (Tulving, 2002).

● **Figure 8.6** The tower puzzle. In this puzzle, all the colored disks must be moved to another post without ever placing a larger disk on a smaller one. Only one disk may be moved at a time, and a disk must always be moved from one post to another (it cannot be held aside). An amnesic patient learned to solve the puzzle in 31 moves, the minimum possible. Even so, each time he began, he protested that he did not remember ever solving the puzzle before and that he did not know how to begin. Evidence like this suggests that memories for skills are distinct from memories for facts.

Semantic Memory

Most of our basic factual knowledge about the world is almost totally immune to forgetting. The names of objects, the days of the week or months of the year, simple math skills, the seasons, words and language, and other general facts are all quite lasting. Such impersonal facts make up a part of LTM called **semantic memory.** Semantic memory serves as a mental dictionary or encyclopedia of basic knowledge.

Episodic Memory

Semantic memory has no connection to times or places. It would be rare, for instance, to remember when and where you first learned the names of the seasons. In contrast, **episodic** (ep-ih-SOD-ik) **memory** is an "autobiographical" record of personal experiences. It stores life events (or "episodes") day after day, year after year. Can you remember your seventh birthday? Your first date? An accident you witnessed? What you did yesterday? All are episodic memories. Note that episodic memories are about the "what," "where," and "when" of our lives. More than a simple ability to store information, they make it possible for us to mentally travel back in time and *re-experience* events (Tulving, 2002).

Are episodic memories as lasting as semantic memories? In general, episodic memories are more easily forgotten than semantic memories. In fact, it is the forgetting of episodic information that results in the formation of semantic memories. At first, you remembered when and where you were when you learned the names of the seasons. Over time you forgot the episodic details but will likely remember the names for the rest of your life.

How Many Types of Memory?

In answer to the question posed at the beginning of this section, it is very likely that three kinds of long-term memories exist: procedural memory and two types of declarative memory, semantic and episodic (● Figure 8.7).

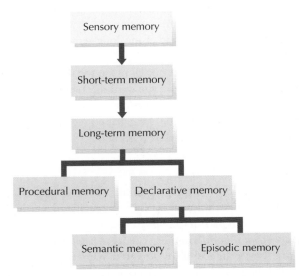

● **Figure 8.7** In the model shown here, long-term memory is divided into procedural memory (learned actions and skills) and declarative memory (stored facts). Declarative memories can be either semantic (impersonal knowledge) or episodic (personal experiences associated with specific times and places).

KNOWLEDGE BUILDER
STM and LTM

RECITE

1. Information is best transferred from STM to LTM when a person engages in
   a. maintenance chunking
   b. maintenance recoding
   c. elaborative networking
   d. elaborative encoding
2. Constructive processing is often responsible for creating pseudo-memories. T or F?
3. Electrical stimulation of the brain has shown conclusively that all memories are stored permanently, but not all memories can be retrieved. T or F?
4. Memories elicited under hypnosis are more vivid, complete, and reliable than normal. T or F?
5. The existence of redintegration is best explained by _____ models of memory.
   a. network
   b. integrative
   c. implicit
   d. chunking
6. Which of the following is a synonym for skill memory?
   a. semantic memory
   b. declarative memory
   c. episodic memory
   d. procedural memory

REFLECT

Critical Thinking

7. Parents sometimes warn children not to read comic books, fearing that they will learn less in school if they "fill their heads up with junk." Why is this warning unnecessary?

Relate

Telephone numbers are divided into an area code (3 digits) and a 7-digit number that is divided into 3 digits, plus 4 more. Can you relate this practice to STM? How about to chunking and recoding?

Think about how you've used your memory in the last hour. See if you can identify an example of each of the following: a procedural memory, a declarative memory, a semantic memory, and an episodic memory.

Answers: 1. d 2. T 3. F 4. F 5. a 6. d 7. Because the more information you have in long-term memory, the greater the possibilities for linking new information to it. Generally, the more you know, the more you can learn—even if some of what you know is "junk."

and last letter and the number of syllables of the word they were seeking. They also gave words that sounded like or meant the same thing as the defined word (Brown & McNeill, 1966). In another study, people listened to theme music from popular TV shows. They then tried to name the program the tune came from. This produced TOT experiences for about 1 out of 5 tunes (Riefer, Keveri, & Kramer, 1995).

The items listed next may induce the TOT state. See if you can name the defined words. (*Answers are below.)

What's on the Tip of Your Tongue?

1. To officially renounce a throne
2. A nylon strip surfaced with tiny hooks that fasten to another strip surfaced with uncut pile
3. Produced by humans rather than natural
4. The pictorial system of writing used in ancient Egypt
5. A small fish that attaches itself to a shark

Closely related to the TOT state is the fact that people can often tell beforehand if they are likely to remember something. This is called the **feeling of knowing** (Widner, Jr., Otani, & Winkelman, 2005). Feeling-of-knowing reactions are easy to observe on TV game shows, where they occur just before contestants are allowed to answer.

Déjà vu is the illusion that you have already experienced a new situation that you are actually seeing for the first time. Most likely, saying to yourself, "I feel like I've seen it before," is another example of partial retrieval. Déjà vu occurs when a new experience triggers vague memories of a past experience, without yielding any details (Brown, 2004). The new experience seems familiar even though the older memory is too weak to rise to the level of awareness.

Because memory is not an all-or-nothing event, there are several ways of measuring it. Three commonly used **memory tasks** (tests of memory) are recall, recognition, and relearning. Let's see how they differ.

*1. abdicate 2. Velcro 3. artificial 4. hieroglyphics 5. Remora

Measuring Memory—The Answer Is on the Tip of My Tongue

Gateway Question: How is memory measured?

You either remember something or you don't, right? Wrong. Partial memories are common. For instance, have you ever tried to remember something only to find yourself stuck in a **tip-of-the-tongue (TOT) state?** This is the feeling that a memory is available but not quite retrievable (Schwartz, 2002). It is as if an answer or a memory is just out of reach—on the "tip of your tongue." In a classic TOT study, university students read the definitions of words such as *sextant, sampan,* and *ambergris.* Students who "drew a blank" and couldn't name a defined word were asked to give any other information they could. Often, they could guess the first

Procedural memory Long-term memories of conditioned responses and learned skills.

Declarative memory That part of long-term memory containing specific factual information.

Semantic memory A subpart of declarative memory that records impersonal knowledge about the world.

Episodic memory A subpart of declarative memory that records personal experiences that are linked with specific times and places.

Tip-of-the-tongue (TOT) state The feeling that a memory is available but not quite retrievable.

Feeling of knowing A feeling that allows people to predict beforehand whether they will be able to remember something.

Memory task Any task designed to test or assess memory.

Recalling Information

What is the name of the first song on your favorite CD? Who won the World Series last year? Who wrote *Hamlet*? If you can answer these questions, you are using **recall**, a direct retrieval of facts or information. Tests of recall often require *verbatim* (word-for-word) memory. If you study a poem until you can recite it without looking at it, you are recalling it. If you complete a fill-in-the-blank question, you are using recall. When you answer an essay question by providing facts and ideas, you are also using recall, even though you didn't learn your essay verbatim.

The order in which information is memorized has an interesting effect on recall. To experience it, try to memorize the following list, reading it only once:

> bread, apples, soda, ham, cookies, rice, lettuce, beets, mustard, cheese, oranges, ice cream, crackers, flour, eggs

If you are like most people, it will be hardest for you to recall items from the middle of the list. ● Figure 8.8 shows the results of a similar test. Notice that most errors occur with middle items of an ordered list. This is the **serial position effect.** You can remember the last items on a list because they are still in STM. The first items are also remembered well because they entered an "empty" short-term memory. This allows you to rehearse the items so they move into long-term memory (Addis & Kahana, 2004). The middle items are neither held in short-term memory nor moved to long-term memory, so they are often lost.

Recognizing Information

Try to write down everything you can remember learning from a class you took last year. If you actually did this, you might conclude that you had learned very little. However, a more sensitive test based on recognition could be used. In **recognition memory,** previously learned material is correctly identified. For instance, you could take a multiple-choice test on facts and ideas from the course. Because you would only have to recognize correct answers, you would probably find that you had learned a lot.

Recognition memory can be amazingly accurate for pictures and photographs (Whitehouse, Mayberry, & Durkin, 2006). In one classic study, the investigator showed people 2,560 photographs at a rate of one every 10 seconds. Each person was then shown 280 pairs of photographs. Each pair included an "old" picture (from the first set of photos) and a similar "new" image. Subjects could tell 85 to 95 percent of the time which photograph they had seen before (Haber, 1970). This finding may explain why we rarely need to see our friends' vacation photos more than once.

Recognition is usually superior to recall. That's why people so often say, "I may forget a name, but I never forget a face." (You recall the name but recognize the face.) That's also why police departments use photographs or a lineup to identify criminal suspects. Witnesses who disagree when they try to recall a suspect's height, weight, age, or eye color often agree completely when they merely need to recognize the person.

Is recognition always superior? It depends greatly on the kind of *distractors* used (Flowe & Ebbese, 2007). These are false items included with an item to be recognized. If distractors are very similar to the correct item, memory may be poor. A reverse problem occurs when only one choice looks like it could be correct. This can produce a *false positive,* or false sense of recognition, like the false memory you had earlier when you thought you remembered seeing the word *sleep.*

There have been instances in which witnesses described a criminal as black, tall, or young. Then a lineup was held in which a suspect was the only African American among whites, the only tall suspect, or the only young person. In such cases a false identification is very likely. A better method is to have *all* the distractors look like the person witnesses described. Also, to reduce false positives, witnesses should be warned that the culprit *may not be present.* Many hundreds of people have been put in jail on the basis of mistaken eyewitness memories (Wells, Memon, & Penrod, 2006). To avoid tragic mistakes, it's far better to show witnesses one photo at a time (a sequential lineup). For each photo, the witness must decide whether the person is the culprit before another photo is shown (Wells, 2001; Wells & Olsen, 2003).

● **Figure 8.8** The serial position effect. The graph shows the percentage of subjects correctly recalling each item in a 15-item list. Recall is best for the first and last items. (Data from Craik, 1970.)

Police lineups make use of the sensitivity of recognition memory. However, unless great care is taken, false identifications are still possible (Wells, 2001).

Relearning Information

In another classic experiment, a psychologist read a short passage in Greek to his son every day when the boy was between 15 months and 3 years of age. At age 8, the boy was asked if he remembered the Greek passage. He showed no evidence of recall. He was then shown selections from the passage he heard and selections from other Greek passages. Could he recognize the one he heard as an infant? "It's all Greek to me!" he said, indicating a lack of recognition (and drawing a frown from everyone in the room).

Had the psychologist stopped, he might have concluded that no memory of the Greek remained. However, the child was then asked to memorize the original quotation and others of equal difficulty. This time his earlier learning became evident. The boy memorized the passage he had heard in childhood 25 percent faster than the others (Burtt, 1941). As this experiment suggests, **relearning** is typically the most sensitive measure of memory.

When a person is tested by relearning, how do we know a memory still exists? As with the boy described, relearning is measured by a *savings score* (the amount of time saved when relearning information). Let's say it takes you 1 hour to memorize all the names in a telephone book. (It's a small town.) Two years later you relearn them in 45 minutes. Because you "saved" 15 minutes, your savings score would be 25 percent (15 divided by 60 times 100). Savings of this type are a good reason for studying a wide range of subjects. It may seem that learning algebra, history, or a foreign language is wasted if you don't use the knowledge immediately. But when you do need such information, you will be able to relearn it quickly.

Implicit and Explicit Memories

Many memories remain outside of conscious awareness. For example, if you know how to type, it is apparent that you know where the letters are on the keyboard. But how many typists could correctly label blank keys in a drawing of a keyboard? Many people find that they cannot directly remember such information, even though they "know" it.

Who were the last three presidents of the United States? What did you have for breakfast today? What is the title of the Black Eyed Peas' latest album? Explicit memory is used in answering each of these questions. **Explicit memories** are past experiences that are consciously brought to mind. Recall, recognition, and the tests you take in school rely on explicit memories. In contrast, **implicit memories** lie outside of awareness (Roediger & Amir, 2005). That is, we are not aware that a memory exists. Neverthe-

less, implicit memories—such as unconsciously knowing where the letters are on a keyboard—greatly influence our behavior (Neath & Surprenant, 2003).

Priming

How is it possible to show that a memory exists if it lies outside of awareness? Psychologists first noticed implicit memory while studying memory loss caused by brain injuries. Let's say, for example, that a patient is shown a list of common words, such as *chair, tree, lamp, table,* and so on. A few minutes later, the patient is asked to recall words from the list. Sadly, he has no memory of the words.

Now, instead of asking the patient to explicitly recall the list, we could "prime" his memory by giving him the first two letters of each word. "We'd like you to say a word that begins with these letters," we tell him. "Just say whatever comes to mind." Of course, many words could be made from each pair of letters. For example, the first item (from chair) would be the letters CH. The patient could say "child," "chalk," "chain," "check," or many other words. Instead, he says "chair," a word from the original list. The patient is not aware that he is remembering the list, but as he gives a word for each letter pair, almost all are from the list. Apparently, the letters **primed** (activated) hidden memories, which then influenced his answers.

Similar effects have been found for people with normal memories. As the preceding example implies, implicit memories are often revealed by giving a person limited cues, such as the first letter of words or partial drawings of objects. Typically, the person believes that he or she is just saying whatever comes to mind. Nevertheless, information previously seen or heard affects his or her answers (Rueckl & Galantucci, 2005).

> **KNOWLEDGE BUILDER**
> ## Measuring Memory
> **RECITE**
> 1. Four techniques for measuring or demonstrating memory are
> _____, _____, _____
> _____.
> 2. Essay tests require _____ of facts or ideas.
>
> *Continued*

Recall To supply or reproduce memorized information with a minimum of external cues.

Serial position effect The tendency to make the most errors in remembering the middle items of an ordered list.

Recognition memory An ability to correctly identify previously learned information.

Relearning Learning again something that was previously learned. Used to measure memory of prior learning.

Explicit memory A memory that a person is aware of having; a memory that is consciously retrieved.

Implicit memory A memory that a person does not know exists; a memory that is retrieved unconsciously.

Priming Facilitating the retrieval of an implicit memory by using cues to activate hidden memories.

Can you label the letter keys on this blank keyboard? If you can, you probably used implicit memory to do it.

3. As a measure of memory, a savings score is associated with
   a. recognition
   b. eidetic images
   c. relearning
   d. reconstruction
4. The two most sensitive tests of memory are
   a. recall and redintegration
   b. recall and relearning
   c. recognition and relearning
   d. recognition and digit-span
5. Priming is used to reveal which type of memories?
   a. explicit
   b. sensory
   c. skill
   d. implicit

REFLECT

Critical Thinking

6. When asked to explain why they may have failed to recall some information, people often claim it must be because the information is no longer in their memory. Why does the existence of implicit memories challenge this explanation?

Relate

Have you experienced a TOT state recently? Were you able to retrieve the word you were searching for? If not, what could you remember about it?

Do you prefer tests based primarily on recall or recognition? Have you observed a savings effect while relearning information you studied in the past (such as in high school)?

Can you think of things you do that are based on implicit memories? For instance, how do you know which way to turn various handles in your house, apartment, or dorm? Do you have to explicitly think, "Turn it to the right," before you act?

What kinds of information are you good at remembering? Why do you think your memory is better for those topics?

Answers: 1. recall, recognition, relearning, priming **2.** recall **3.** c **4.** c **5.** d **6.** It is possible to have an implicit memory that cannot be consciously recalled. Memories like these (*available*) in memory even though they are not consciously *accessible*) show that failing to recall something does not mean it is no longer in memory (Allik, 2000).

⬤⬤ Forgetting in LTM—Why We, uh, Let's See; Why We, uh ... Forget!

Gateway Question: Why do we forget?

We don't expect sensory memories and short-term memories to remain with us for long. But when you deliberately encode and store information in long-term memory you want it to stay there (it is, after all, *long*-term). For example, when you study for an exam you count on your long-term memory to retain the information at least until you take your exam. Why do we forget long-term memories? The more you know about how we "lose" memories, the better you will be able to hang on to them.

Most forgetting tends to occur immediately after memorization. Herman Ebbinghaus (1885) famously tested his own memory at various intervals after learning. To be sure he would not be swayed by prior learning, he memorized *nonsense syllables*. These are meaningless three-letter words such as CEF, WOL, and GEX. The importance of using meaningless words is shown by the fact

that VEL, FAB, and DUZ are no longer used on memory tests. People who recognize these words as detergent names find them very easy to remember. This is another reminder that relating new information to what you already know can improve memory.

By waiting various lengths of time before testing himself, Ebbinghaus plotted a **curve of forgetting**. This graph shows the amount of information remembered after varying lengths of time (● Figure 8.9). Notice that forgetting is rapid at first and is then followed by a slow decline (Hintzman, 2005). The same applies to meaningful information, but the forgetting curve is stretched over a longer time. As you might expect, recent events are recalled more accurately than those from the remote past (O'Connor et al., 2000). Thus, you are more likely to remember that *No Country for Old Men* won the "Best Picture" Academy Award for 2007 than you are to remember that *Chicago* was the 2002 winner.

As a student, you should note that a short delay between studying and taking a test minimizes forgetting. However, this is no reason for cramming. Most students make the error of *only* cramming. If you cram, you don't have to remember for very long, but you may not learn enough in the first place. If you use short, daily study sessions *and* review intensely before a test, you will get the benefit of good preparation and a minimum time lapse.

The Ebbinghaus curve shows less than 30 percent remembered after only 2 days have passed. Is forgetting really that rapid? No, not always. Meaningful information is not lost nearly as quickly as nonsense syllables. After 3 years, students who took a university psychology course had forgotten about 30 percent of the facts they learned. After that, little more forgetting occurred (Conway, Cohen, & Stanhope, 1992). Actually, as learning grows stronger, some knowledge may become nearly permanent (Berntsen & Thomsen, 2005).

While the Ebbinghaus curve gives a general picture of forgetting from long-term memory, it doesn't explain it. For explanations we must search further. (Before we do, look at "Card Magic!" where you will find an interesting demonstration.) Earlier in this chapter we pointed out that three processes are involved in suc-

● **Figure 8.9** The curve of forgetting. This graph shows the amount remembered (measured by relearning) after varying lengths of time. Notice how rapidly forgetting occurs. The material learned was nonsense syllables. Forgetting curves for meaningful information also show early losses followed by a long, gradual decline, but overall, forgetting occurs much more slowly. (After Ebbinghaus, 1885.)

DISCOVERING PSYCHOLOGY

Card Magic!

● **Figure 8.10**

Pick a card from the six shown in ● Figure 8.10 above. Look at it closely and be sure you can remember which card is yours. Now, snap your fingers and look at the cards in ● Figure 8.11 below.

Poof! Only five cards remain, and the card you chose has disappeared. Obviously, you could have selected any one of the six cards in ● Figure 8.10. How did we know which one to remove?

This trick is based entirely on an illusion of memory. Recall that you were asked to concentrate on one card among the six cards in ● Figure 8.10. That prevented you from paying attention to the other cards, so they weren't stored in your memory (Mangels, Picton, & Craik, 2001; Naveh-

Benjamin, Guez, & Sorek, 2007). The five cards you see below are all new (none is shown in ● Figure 8.10). Because you couldn't find your card in the "remaining five," your card seemed to disappear. What looked like "card magic" is actually memory magic. Now return to "When Encoding Fails" and continue reading to learn more about forgetting.

● **Figure 8.11**

● **Figure 8.12** Some of the distractor items used in a study of recognition memory and encoding failure. Penny A is correct but was seldom recognized. Pennies G and J were popular wrong answers. (Adapted from Nickerson & Adams, 1979.)

cessfully remembering: encoding, storage, and retrieval. Conversely, forgetting can be due to the failure of any one of these three processes.

When Encoding Fails

Whose head is on a U.S. penny? Which way is it facing? What is written at the top of a penny? Can you accurately draw and label a penny? In an interesting experiment, Ray Nickerson and Marilyn Adams (1979) asked a large group of students to draw a penny. Few could. In fact, few could even recognize a drawing of a real penny among fakes (● Figure 8.12).

The most obvious reason for forgetting is also the most commonly overlooked. Obviously, few of us ever encode the details of a penny. Similarly, we may not encode the details of what we are reading in a book or studying for an exam. In such cases, we "forget" because of **encoding failure.** That is, a memory was never formed in the first place (the card trick you just saw is another example). If you are bothered by frequent forgetting or absentmindedness, it is wise to ask yourself, "Have I been storing the information in the first place?" (Schacter, 2001). By the way, if you like to study while watching television or instant messaging,

beware. Dividing your attention between studying and other activities can also lead to encoding failure (Naveh-Benjamin, Guez, & Sorek, 2007).

Actively thinking about the information you are learning (elaborative encoding) is a good way to prevent encoding failure (Hall et al., 2007). You'll find more memory strategies in The Psychology of Studying (at the beginning of this book). Check it out, if you haven't already.

Curve of forgetting A graph that shows the amount of memorized information remembered after varying lengths of time.

Encoding failure Failure to store sufficient information to form a useful memory.

College Students: They're All Alike!

Encoding failures also affect our memories of people. Imagine yourself in this situation: As you are walking on campus, a young man, who looks like a college student, approaches you and asks for directions. While you are talking, two workers carrying a door pass between you and the young man. While your view is blocked by the door, another man takes the place of the first. Now you are facing a different person than the one who was there just seconds earlier. If this happened to you, do you think you would notice the change? Remarkably, only half the people tested in this way noticed the switch (Simons & Levin, 1998)!

How could anyone fail to notice that one stranger had been replaced by another? The people who didn't remember the first man were all older adults. College students weren't fooled by the switch. Apparently, older adults encoded the first man in very general terms as a "college student." As a result, that's all they remembered about him. Because his replacement also looked like a college student, they thought he was the same person (Simons & Levin, 1998).

Actually, we all tend to categorize strangers in general terms: Is the person young or old, male or female, a member of my ethnic group or another? This tendency is one reason why eyewitnesses are better at identifying members of their own ethnic group than persons from other groups (Burgess & Weaver, 2003; Michel, Caldara, & Rossion, 2006). It may seem harsh to say so, but during brief social contacts, people really do act as if members of other ethnic groups "all look alike." Of course, this bias disappears when people get acquainted and learn more about one another as individuals. (McKone et al., 2007).

When Memory Storage Fails

One view of forgetting holds that **memory traces** (changes in nerve cells or brain activity) decay (fade or weaken) over time. **Memory decay** appears to be a factor in the loss of sensory memories. Such fading also applies to short-term memory. Information stored in STM seems to initiate a brief flurry of activity in the brain that quickly dies out. Short-term memory therefore operates like a "leaky bucket": New information constantly pours in, but it rapidly fades away and is replaced by still newer information. Let's say that you are trying to remember a short list of letters, numbers, or words after seeing or hearing them once. If it takes you more than 4 to 6 seconds to repeat the list, you will forget some of the items (Dosher & Ma, 1998).

Disuse

Does decay also occur in long-term memory? There is evidence that memories not retrieved and "used" or rehearsed become weaker over time (Schacter, 2001). That is, some long-term memory traces may fade from **disuse** (infrequent retrieval) and eventually become too weak to retrieve. However, disuse alone cannot fully explain forgetting.

Disuse doesn't seem to account for our ability to recover seemingly forgotten memories through redintegration, relearning, and priming. It also fails to explain why some unused memories fade, whereas others are carried for life. A third contradiction will be recognized by anyone who has spent time with the elderly. People growing senile may become so forgetful that they can't remember what happened a week ago. Yet at the same time your Uncle Oscar's recent memories are fading, he may have vivid memories of trivial and long-forgotten events from the past. "Why, I remember it as clearly as if it were yesterday," he will say, forgetting that the story he is about to tell is one he told earlier the same day. In short, disuse offers no more than a partial explanation of long-term forgetting.

When Retrieval Fails

If decay and disuse don't fully explain forgetting from long-term memory, what does? If you have encoded and stored information, that leaves retrieval as a likely cause of forgetting. Even if memories are **available** (stored in your memory), you still have to be able to **access** them (locate or retrieve them) in order to remember. For example, you've probably had the experience of knowing you know the answer to an exam question (you knew it was available), but being unable to retrieve it during the exam (it was inaccessible). You know what happens next, right? As you leave the exam, the answer "pops" into your head!

Cue-Dependent Forgetting

One reason retrieval may fail is because **memory cues** (stimuli associated with a memory) are missing when the time comes to retrieve information. For instance, if you were asked, "What were you doing on Monday afternoon of the third week in May 2 years ago?" your reply might be, "Come on, how should I know?" How-

External cues like those found in a photograph, in a scrapbook, or during a walk through an old neighborhood often aid recall of seemingly lost memories. For many veterans, finding a familiar name engraved in the Vietnam Veterans Memorial unleashes a flood of memories.

ever, if you were reminded, "That was the day the courthouse burned," or "That was the day Stacy had her automobile accident," you might remember immediately.

The presence of appropriate cues almost always enhances memory (Nairne, 2002). For example, memory will tend to be better if you study in the same room where you will be tested. Because this is often impossible, when you study, try to visualize the room where you will be tested. Doing so can enhance memory later (Jerabek & Standing, 1992). Similarly, people remember better if the same odor (such as lemon or lavender) is present when they study and are tested (Parker, Ngu, & Cassaday, 2001). If you wear a particular perfume or cologne while you prepare for a test, it might be wise to wear it when you take the test.

State-Dependent Learning

Have you heard the one about the drunk who misplaced his wallet and had to get drunk again to find it? Actually, this is not too farfetched. The bodily state that exists during learning can be a strong retrieval cue for later memory, an effect known as **state-dependent learning** (Neath & Surprenant, 2003). Being very thirsty, for instance, might prompt you to remember events that took place on another occasion when you were thirsty. Because of such effects, information learned under the influence of a drug is best remembered when the drugged state occurs again (Slot & Colpaert, 1999). Here's a better idea: Study with a clear mind in the first place.

A similar effect applies to emotional states (Wessel & Wright, 2004). For instance, Gordon Bower (1981) found that people who learned a list of words while in a happy mood recalled them better when they were again happy. People who learned while they felt sad remembered best when they were sad (● Figure 8.13). Similarly, if you are in a happy mood, you are more likely to remember recent happy events. If you are in a bad mood, you will tend to have unpleasant memories. Such links between emotional cues and memory could explain why couples who quarrel often end up remembering—and rehashing—old arguments.

How could anyone lose something as large as a car? If you park your car in a different place every day, you may have experienced forgetting caused by interference. Today's memory about your car's location is easily confused with memories from yesterday, and the day before, and the day before that.

Interference

Further insight into forgetting comes from a classic experiment in which college students learned lists of nonsense syllables. After studying, students in one group slept for 8 hours and were then tested for memory of the lists. A second group stayed awake for 8 hours and went about business as usual. When members of the second group were tested, they remembered *less* than the group that slept (● Figure 8.14). This difference is based on the fact that new learning can interfere with the ability to retrieve previous learning. **Interference** refers to the tendency for new memories to impair retrieval of older memories (and the reverse). It seems to apply to both short-term and long-term memory (Lustig, May, & Hasher, 2001; Nairne, 2002).

● **Figure 8.13** The effect of mood on memory. Subjects best remembered a list of words when their mood during testing was the same as their mood was when they learned the list. (Adapted from Bower, 1981.)

Memory traces Physical changes in nerve cells or brain activity that take place when memories are stored.

Memory decay The fading or weakening of memories assumed to occur when memory traces become weaker.

Disuse Theory that memory traces weaken when memories are not periodically used or retrieved.

Availability (in memory) Memories currently stored.

Accessibility (in memory) Memories currently stored that can be retrieved when necessary.

Memory cue Any stimulus associated with a particular memory. Memory cues usually enhance retrieval.

State-dependent learning Memory influenced by one's bodily state at the time of learning and at the time of retrieval. Improved memory occurs when the bodily states match.

Interference The tendency for new memories to impair retrieval of older memories, and the reverse.

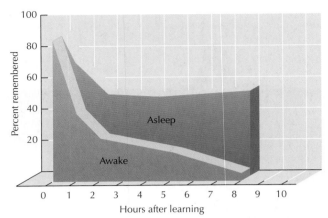

● **Figure 8.14** The amount of forgetting after a period of sleep or of being awake. Notice that sleep causes less memory loss than activity that occurs while one is awake. (After Jenkins & Dallenbach, 1924.)

bridges

Sleep can improve memory in another way: REM sleep and dreaming appear to help us form certain types of memories. **See Chapter 6, pages 187–188.**

It is not completely clear if new memories alter existing memory traces or if they make it harder to retrieve earlier memories. In any case, there is no doubt that interference is a major cause of forgetting (Neath & Surprenant, 2003). College students who memorized 20 lists of words (one list each day) were able to recall only 15 percent of the last list. Students who learned only one list remembered 80 percent (Underwood, 1957) (● Figure 8.15).

The sleeping college students remembered more because retroactive (RET-ro-AK-tiv) interference was held to a minimum. **Retroactive interference** refers to the tendency for new learning to inhibit retrieval of old learning. Avoiding new learning prevents retroactive interference. This doesn't exactly mean you should hide in a closet after you study for an exam. However, you should avoid studying other subjects until the exam. Sleeping after study can help you retain memories, and reading, writing, or even watching TV may cause interference.

● **Figure 8.15** Effects of interference on memory. A graph of the approximate relationship between percentage recalled and number of different word lists memorized. (Adapted from Underwood, 1957.)

Retroactive interference is easily demonstrated in the laboratory by this arrangement:

Experimental group:	Learn A	Learn B	Test A
Control group:	Learn A	Rest	Test A

Imagine yourself as a member of the experimental group. In task A, you learn a list of telephone numbers. In task B, you learn a list of Social Security numbers. How do you score on a test of task A (the telephone numbers)? If you do not remember as much as the control group that learns *only* task A, then retroactive interference has occurred. The second thing learned interfered with memory of the first thing learned; the interference went "backward," or was "retroactive" (● Figure 8.16).

Proactive (pro-AK-tiv) interference is the second type of interference. **Proactive interference** occurs when prior learning inhibits recall of later learning. A test for proactive interference would take this form:

Experimental group:	Learn A	Learn B	Test B
Control group:	Rest	Learn B	Test B

Let's assume that the experimental group remembers less than the control group on a test of task B. In that case, learning task A interfered with memory for task B.

Then proactive interference goes "forward"? Yes. For instance, if you cram for a psychology exam and then later the same night cram for a history exam, your memory for the second subject studied (history) will be less accurate than if you had studied only history. (Because of retroactive interference, your memory for psychology would

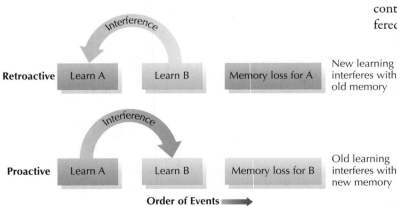

● **Figure 8.16** Retroactive and proactive interference. The order of learning and testing shows whether interference is retroactive (backward) or proactive (forward).

THE CLINICAL FILE

The Recovered Memory/False Memory Debate

Many sexually abused children develop problems that persist into adulthood. In some instances, they repress all memory of the abuse. According to some psychologists, uncovering these hidden memories can be an important step toward regaining emotional health (Palm & Gibson, 1998).

Although the preceding may be true, the search for repressed memories of sexual abuse has itself been a problem. Families have been torn apart by accusations of sexual abuse that later turned out to be completely false (Porter et al., 2003). For example, Gary Ramona lost his marriage and his $400,000-a-year job when his daughter Holly alleged that he molested her throughout her childhood. To prove to Holly that her memories were true, the therapists gave her the drug Amytal, and told her that it was a "truth drug." (Amytal is a hypnotic drug that induces a twilight state of consciousness. People do not automatically tell the truth while under its influence.) Ramona sued Holly's therapists, claiming that they had been irresponsible. After reviewing the evidence, a jury awarded Gary Ramona $500,000 in damages. In a way, Gary Ramona was lucky. Most people who are falsely accused have no way to prove their innocence (Loftus & Ketcham, 1994).

Why would anyone have false memories about such disturbing events? Several popular books and a few misguided therapists have actively encouraged people to find repressed memories of abuse. Hypnosis, guided visualization, suggestion, age regression, and similar techniques can elicit fantasies that are mistaken for real memories. As we saw earlier, it is easy to create false memories, especially by using hypnosis (Loftus, 2003b; Loftus & Bernstein, 2005).

In an effort to illustrate how easy it is to create false memories, and to publicize *false memory syndrome,* memory expert Elizabeth Loftus once deliberately implanted a false memory in actor Alan Alda. As the host of the television series *Scientific American Frontiers,* he was scheduled to interview Loftus. Before the interview, Alda was asked to fill out a questionnaire about his tastes in food. When he arrived, Loftus told Alda that his answers revealed that he must once have gotten sick after eating hard-boiled eggs (which was false). Later that day, at a picnic, Alda would not eat hard-boiled eggs (Loftus, 2003a).

Certainly, some memories of abuse that return to awareness are genuine and must be dealt with. However, there is little doubt that some "recovered" memories are pure fantasy.

No matter how real a recovered memory may seem, it could be false, unless it can be verified by others or by court or medical records (Olio, 2004). The saddest thing about such claims is that they deaden public sensitivity to actual abuse. Childhood sexual abuse is widespread. Awareness of its existence must not be repressed.

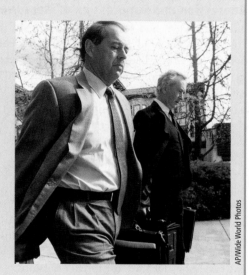

Gary Ramona's life was shattered by "recovered" memories that turned out to be false.

probably also suffer.) The greater the similarity in the two subjects studied, the more interference takes place. The moral, of course, is don't procrastinate in preparing for exams. The more you can avoid storing competing information, the more likely you are to recall what you want to remember (Anderson & Bell, 2001; Wixted, 2004).

The interference effects we have described apply primarily to memories of verbal information, such as the contents of this chapter. When you are learning a skill, similarity can sometimes be beneficial, rather than disruptive. The next section explains how this occurs.

Transfer of Training

Two people begin mandolin lessons. One already plays the violin. The other is a trumpet player. All other things being equal, which person will initially do better in learning the mandolin? If you chose the violin player, you have an intuitive grasp of what positive transfer is. (The strings on a mandolin are tuned the same as a violin.) **Positive transfer** takes place when mastery of one task aids mastery of a second task. Another example would be learning to

balance and turn on a bicycle before learning to ride a motorcycle or motor scooter. Likewise, surfing and skateboarding skills transfer to snowboarding.

Is there such a thing as negative transfer? There is indeed. In **negative transfer,** skills developed in one situation conflict with those required to master a new task. Learning to back a car with a trailer attached to it is a good example. Normally, when you are backing a car, the steering wheel is turned in the direction you want to go, the same as when moving forward. However, when

Retroactive interference The tendency for new memories to interfere with the retrieval of old memories.

Proactive interference The tendency for old memories to interfere with the retrieval of newer memories.

Positive transfer Mastery of one task aids learning or performing another.

Negative transfer Mastery of one task conflicts with learning or performing another.

backing a trailer, you must turn the steering wheel *away* from the direction you want the trailer to go. This situation results in negative transfer, and often creates comical scenes at campgrounds and boat launching ramps.

On a more serious note, many tragic crashes caused by negative transfer finally led to greater standardization of airplane cockpits. Fortunately, negative transfer is usually brief, and it occurs less often than positive transfer. Negative transfer is most likely to occur when a new response must be made to an old stimulus (Besnard & Cacitti, 2005). If you have ever encountered a pull-type handle on a door that must be pushed open, you will appreciate this point.

Repression and Suppression of Memories

Take a moment and scan over the events of the last few years of your life. What kinds of things most easily come to mind? Many people remember happy, positive events better than disappointments and irritations (Moore & Zoellner, 2007). This tendency is called **repression,** or motivated forgetting. Through repression, painful, threatening, or embarrassing memories are held out of consciousness (Anderson et al., 2004). An example is provided by soldiers who have repressed some of the horrors they saw during combat (Karon & Widener, 1997).

The forgetting of past failures, upsetting childhood events, the names of people you dislike, or appointments you don't want to keep may reveal repression. People prone to repression tend to be extremely sensitive to emotional events. As a result, they use repression to protect themselves from threatening thoughts (McNally, Clancy, & Barrett, 2004). See "The Recovered Memory/ False Memory Debate" for further cautions.

If I try to forget a test I failed, am I repressing it? No. Repression can be distinguished from **suppression,** an active, conscious attempt to put something out of mind. By not thinking about the test, you have merely suppressed a memory. If you choose to, you can remember the test. Clinicians consider true repression an *unconscious* event. When a memory is repressed we may be unaware that forgetting has even occurred.

> **bridges**
> Clinical psychologists regard repression as one of the major psychological defenses we use against emotional threats. **See Chapter 13, pages 441–442, for details.**

Although some psychologists have questioned whether repression exists (Court & Court, 2001), evidence suggests that we can choose to actively suppress upsetting memories (Anderson, 2001). If you have experienced a painful emotional event, you will probably avoid all thoughts associated with it. This tends to keep cues out of mind that could trigger a painful memory. In time, your active suppression of the memory may become true repression (Anderson & Green, 2001).

Memory and the Brain—Some "Shocking" Findings

Gateway Question: How does the brain form and store memories?

One possibility overlooked in our discussion of forgetting is that memories may be lost as they are being formed (Papanicolaou, 2006). For example, a head injury may cause a "gap" in memories preceding the accident. *Retrograde amnesia,* as this is called, involves forgetting events that occurred before an injury or trauma. In contrast, *anterograde amnesia* involves forgetting events that follow an injury or trauma (Behrend, Beike, & Lampinen, 2004). (We will discuss an example of this type of amnesia in a moment.)

Consolidation

We can explain retrograde amnesia by assuming that it takes time to form a lasting memory, a process called **consolidation** (Vogel, Woodman, & Luck, 2006). You can think of consolidation as being somewhat like writing your name in wet concrete. Once the concrete is set, the information (your name) is fairly lasting. But while it is setting, it can be wiped out (amnesia) or scribbled over (interference).

Consider a classic experiment on consolidation, in which a rat is placed on a small platform. The rat steps down to the floor and receives a painful electric shock. After one shock, the rat can be returned to the platform repeatedly, but it will not step down. Obviously, the rat remembers the shock. Would it remember if consolidation were disturbed?

Interestingly, one way to prevent consolidation is to give a different kind of shock called **electroconvulsive shock (ECS).** ECS is a mild electric shock to the brain. It does not harm the animal, but it does destroy any memory that is being formed. If each painful shock (the one the animal remembers) is followed by ECS (which wipes out memories during consolidation), the rat will step down over and over. Each time, ECS will erase the memory of the painful shock.

> **bridges**
> ECS has been used with humans as a psychiatric treatment for severe depression. Used in this way, electroshock therapy also causes memory loss. **See Chapter 15, page 519.**

What would happen if ECS were given several hours after the learning? Recent memories are more easily disrupted than older memories. If enough time is allowed to pass between learning and ECS, the memory will be unaffected because consolidation is already complete. That's why people with mild head injuries lose only memories from just before the accident, while older memories remain intact (Lieberman, 2004). Likewise, you would forget more if you studied, stayed awake 8 hours, and then slept 8 hours than you would if you studied, slept 8 hours, and were awake for 8 hours. Either way, 16 hours would pass. However, less forgetting would occur in the second instance because more consolidation would occur before interference begins (Wixted, 2005).

Where does consolidation take place in the brain? Actually, many parts of the brain are responsible for memory, but the **hippocampus** is particularly important (Sutherland et al., 2006). The hippocampus acts as a sort of "switching station" between short-term and long-term memory (Squire, 2004). The hippocampus does this, in part, by growing new neurons (nerve cells) and by making new connections within the brain (Eichenbaum & Fortin, 2005).

If the hippocampus is damaged, patients usually develop anterograde amnesia, and show a striking inability to consolidate new memories (Zola & Squire, 2001). A man described by Brenda Milner provides a dramatic example. Two years after an operation damaged his hippocampus, the 29-year-old patient continued to give his age as 27. He also reported that it seemed as if the operation had just taken place (Milner, 1965). His memory of events before the operation remained clear, but he found forming new long-term memories almost impossible. When his parents moved to a new house a few blocks away on the same street, he could not remember the new address. Month after month, he read the same magazines over and over without finding them familiar. If you were to meet this man, he would seem fairly normal because he still has short-term memory. But if you were to leave the room and return 15 minutes later, he would act as if he had never seen you before. Years ago his favorite uncle died, but he suffers the same grief anew each time he is told of the death. Lacking the ability to form new lasting memories, he lives eternally in the present (Corkin, 2002).

Memory and Emotion

Do you remember when you first learned about the terrorist attacks on New York City's World Trade Center in 2001? Can you recall lots of detail, including how you reacted? If so, you have a **flashbulb memory** for 9/11. A flashbulb memory is an especially vivid image that seems to be frozen in memory at times of personal tragedy, accident, or other emotionally significant events. Depending on your age, you may also have a "flashbulb" memory for the assassinations of John F. Kennedy and Martin Luther King, the *Challenger* or *Columbia* space shuttle disasters, or the death of Princess Diana (Curci & Luminet, 2006; Sharot et al., 2007).

Are flashbulb memories handled differently by the brain? Powerful experiences activate the limbic system, a part of the brain that processes emotions. Heightened activity in the limbic system, in turn, appears to intensify memory consolidation (LaBar, 2007; Kensinger, 2007). As a result, flashbulb memories tend to form at times of intense emotion.

Flashbulb memories are often related to public tragedies, but memories of both positive and negative events can have "flashbulb" clarity (Paradis et al., 2004; Rubin, 1985). Would you consider any of the following to be a flashbulb memory? Your first kiss, a special date, or your prom night? How about a time you had to speak in front of a large audience? A car accident you were in or witnessed?

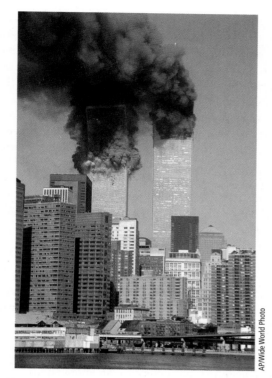

It is highly likely that you have a flashbulb memory about where you were when you first learned about the terrorist attack on the World Trade Center in New York. If someone alerted you about the news, you will remember that person's call and you will have clear memories about how you reacted to seeing the collapse of the towers.

Some memories go beyond flashbulb clarity and become so intense that they may haunt a person for years. Extremely traumatic experiences, such as military combat, can produce so much limbic system activation that the resulting memories and "flashbacks" leave a person emotionally handicapped (Nemeroff et al., 2006).

bridges
To read more about posttraumatic stress disorder, see Chapter 14, page 483.

Repression Unconsciously pushing unwanted memories out of awareness.

Suppression A conscious effort to put something out of mind or to keep it from awareness.

Consolidation Process by which relatively permanent memories are formed in the brain.

Electroconvulsive shock (ECS) An electric current passed directly through the brain, producing a convulsion.

Hippocampus A brain structure associated with emotion and the transfer of information from short-term memory to long-term memory.

Flashbulb memories Memories created at times of high emotion that seem especially vivid.

The term *flashbulb memories* was first used to describe recollections that seemed to be unusually vivid and permanent (Brown & Kulik, 1977). It has become clear, however, that flashbulb memories are not always accurate (Greenberg, 2004; Kensinger, 2007). More than anything else, what sets flashbulb memories apart is that we tend to place great *confidence* in them—even when they are wrong (Niedzwienska, 2004). Perhaps that's because we review emotionally charged events over and over and tell others about them. Also, public events such as wars, earthquakes, and assassinations reappear many times in the news, which highlights them in memory. Over time, flashbulb memories tend to crystallize into consistent, if not entirely accurate, landmarks in our lives (Schmolck, Buffalo, & Squire, 2000).

Long-Term Memory and the Brain

Somewhere within the 3-pound mass of the human brain lies all we know: ZIP codes, faces of loved ones, history, favorite melodies, the taste of an apple, and much, much more. Where is this information? According to neuroscientist Richard Thompson (2005), many parts of the brain become active when we form long-term memories, but some areas are more important for each type of memory. For example, patterns of blood flow in the cerebral cortex (the wrinkled outer layer of the brain) can be used to map brain activity. ● Figure 8.17 shows the results of measuring blood flow while people were thinking about a semantic memory *(a)* or an episodic memory *(b)*. In the map, green indicates areas that are more active during semantic thinking. Reds show areas of greater activity during episodic thinking. The brain in view *c* shows the difference in activity between views *a* and *b*. The resulting pattern indicates that we use the front of the cortex for episodic memory. Back areas are more associated with semantic memory (Tulving, 2002).

Let's summarize (and simplify greatly). Earlier we noted that the hippocampus handles memory consolidation (Zola & Squire, 2001). Once declarative long-term memories are formed, they appear to be stored in the cortex of the brain (episodic in the front, semantic in the back) (Squire, 2004). Long-term procedural (skill) memories are stored in the cerebellum, a part of the brain that is also responsible for muscular coordination (Hermann et al., 2004).

How are memories recorded in the brain? Scientists are beginning to identify the exact ways in which nerve cells record information. For example, Eric Kandel and his colleagues have studied learning in the marine snail *aplysia* (ah-PLEEZ-yah). Kandel found that learning in *aplysia* occurs when certain nerve cells in a circuit alter the amount of transmitter chemicals they release (Bailey & Kandel, 2004). Learning also alters the activity, structure, and chemistry of brain cells. Such changes determine which connections get stronger and which become weaker. This "reprograms" the brain and records information (Abraham, 2006; Squire, 2004).

Jeffrey L. Rotman/Corbis

An *aplysia*. The relatively simple nervous system of this sea animal allows scientists to study memory as it occurs in single nerve cells.

Scientists continue to study various chemicals, especially neurotransmitters, that affect memory. Their research may eventually help the millions of persons who suffer from memory impairment (Elli & Nathan, 2001). (See "The Long-Term Potential of a Memory Pill.")

KNOWLEDGE BUILDER

Forgetting

RECITE

1. According to the Ebbinghaus curve of forgetting, we forget slowly at first and then a rapid decline occurs. T or F?
2. Which explanation seems to account for the loss of short-term memories?
   a. decay
   b. disuse
   c. repression
   d. interference
3. When memories are available but not accessible, forgetting may be cue dependent. T or F?
4. When learning one thing makes it more difficult to recall another, forgetting may be caused by _____.
5. You are asked to memorize long lists of telephone numbers. You learn a new list each day for 10 days. When tested on list three, you remember less than a person who only learned the first three lists. Your larger memory loss is probably caused by
   a. disuse
   b. retroactive interference
   c. regression
   d. proactive interference

Continued

(a)   (b)   (c)

© Tulving, E. (1989). Remembering and knowing the past. *American Scientist, 77*(4), 361–367.

● **Figure 8.17** Patterns of blood flow in the cerebral cortex (wrinkled outer layer of the brain) change as areas become more or less active. Thus, blood flow can be used to draw "maps" of brain activity. This drawing, which views the brain from the top, shows the results of measuring cerebral blood flow while people were thinking about a semantic memory *(a)* or an episodic memory *(b)*. In the map, green indicates areas that are more active during semantic thinking. Reds show areas of greater activity during episodic thinking. The brain in view *c* shows the difference in activity between views *a* and *b*. The resulting pattern suggests that the front of the cortex is related to episodic memory. Areas toward the back and sides of the brain, especially the temporal lobes, are more associated with semantic memory (Gabrieli, 1998; Tulving, 1989, 2002).

BRAINWAVES

The Long-Term Potential of a Memory Pill

At long last, scientists may have found the chemical "signature" that records memories in everything from snails to rats to humans. If two or more interconnected brain cells become more active at the same time, the connections between them grow stronger (Squire & Kandel, 2000). This process is called *long-term potentiation*. After it occurs, an affected brain cell will respond more strongly to messages from the other cells. The brain appears to use this mechanism to form lasting memories (García-Junco-Clemente, Linares-Clemente, & Fernández-Chacón, 2005).

How has that been demonstrated? Electrically stimulating parts of the brain involved in memory, such as the hippocampus, can decrease long-term potentiation (Ivanco & Racine, 2000). As we saw earlier, using electroconvulsive shock to overstimulate memory areas in the brains of rats interferes with long-term potentiation (Trepel & Racine, 1999). It also causes memory loss—just as it does when humans are given ECS for depression.

Will researchers ever produce a "memory pill" for people with normal memory? It's a growing possibility. Drugs that *increase* long-term potentiation also tend to improve memory (Shakesby, Anwyl, & Rowan, 2002). For example, rats administered such drugs could remember the correct path through a maze better than rats not given the drug (Service, 1994). Such findings suggest that memory can be and will be artificially enhanced (Schacter, 2000). However, the possibility of something like a "physics pill" or a "math pill" still seems remote.

---

6. If you consciously succeed at putting a painful memory out of mind, you have used
   a. redintegration
   b. suppression
   c. negative rehearsal
   d. repression
7. Retrograde amnesia results when consolidation is speeded up. T or F?

REFLECT

Critical Thinking

8. Based on state-dependent learning, why do you think that music often strongly evokes memories?
9. You must study French, Spanish, psychology, and biology in one evening. What do you think would be the best order in which to study these subjects so as to minimize interference?

Relate

Which of the following concepts best explain why you have missed some answers on psychology tests: encoding failure, decay, disuse, memory cues, interference?

Do you know someone whose name you have a hard time remembering? Do you like or dislike that person? Do you think your difficulty is an instance of repression? Suppression? Interference? Encoding failure?

Have you had a flashbulb memory? How vivid is the memory today? How accurate do you think it is?

Answers: 1. F **2.** a and d **3.** T **4.** interference **5.** b **6.** b **7.** F **8.** Music tends to affect the mood that a person is in, and moods tend to affect memory (Miranda & Kihlstrom, 2005). **9.** Any order that separates French from Spanish and psychology from biology would be better (for instance: French, psychology, Spanish, biology).

Exceptional Memory— Wizards of Recall

Gateway Question: What are "photographic" memories?

In this section we will explore exceptional memories. Is superior memory a biological gift, such as having a "photographic" memory? Or do excellent memorizers merely make better-than-average use of normal memory capacities?

Can you remember how many doors there are in your house or apartment? To answer a question like this, many people form **mental images** (mental pictures) of each room and count the doorways they visualize. As this example implies, many memories are stored as mental images (Roeckelein, 2004).

Stephen Kosslyn, Thomas Ball, and Brian Reiser (1978) found an interesting way to show that memories do exist as images. Participants first memorized a sort of treasure map similar to the one shown in ● Figure 8.18*a*. They were then asked to picture a black dot moving from one object, such as one of the trees, to another, such as the hut at the top of the island. Did people really form an image to do this task? It seems they did. As shown in ● Figure 8.18*b*, the time it took to "move" the dot was directly related to actual distances on the map.

Is the "treasure map" task an example of photographic memory? In some ways, internal memory images do have "photographic" qualities. However, the term "photographic memory" is more often used to describe a memory ability called eidetic imagery.

Eidetic Imagery

Eidetic (eye-DET-ik) **imagery** occurs when a person has visual images clear enough to be "scanned" or retained for at least 30 seconds. Internal memory images can be "viewed" mentally with the eyes closed. In contrast, eidetic images are "projected" out in front of a person. That is, they are best "seen" on a plain surface, such as a blank piece of paper. In this respect, eidetic images are somewhat like the afterimages you might have after looking at a flashbulb or a brightly lit neon sign (Haber & Haber, 2000).

Mental images Internal images or visual depictions used in memory and thinking.

Eidetic imagery The ability to retain a "projected" mental image long enough to use it as a source of information.

● **Figure 8.18** (a) "Treasure map" similar to the one used by Kosslyn, Ball, and Reiser (1978) to study images in memory. (b) This graph shows how long it took subjects to move a visualized spot various distances on their mental images of the map. (See text for explanation.)

(a)

(b)

Eidetic memory is more common in childhood, with about 8 children in 100 having eidetic images. In one series of tests, children were shown a picture from *Alice's Adventures in Wonderland* (● Figure 8.19). To test your eidetic imagery, look at the picture and read the instructions there.

Now, let's see how much you remember. Can you say (without looking again) which of Alice's apron strings is longer? Are the

● **Figure 8.19** A test picture like that used to identify children with eidetic imagery. To test your eidetic imagery, look at the picture for 30 seconds. Then look at a blank surface and try to "project" the picture onto it. If you have good eidetic imagery, you will be able to see the picture in detail. Return now to the text and try to answer the questions there. (Redrawn from an illustration in Lewis Carroll's *Alice's Adventures in Wonderland*.)

cat's front paws crossed? How many stripes are on the cat's tail? After the picture was removed from view, one 10-year-old boy was asked what he saw. He replied, "I see the tree, gray tree with three limbs. I see the cat with stripes around its tail." Asked to count the stripes, the boy replied, "There are about 16" (a correct count!). The boy then went on to describe the remainder of the picture in striking detail (Haber, 1969).

Don't be disappointed if you didn't do too well when you tried your eidetic skills. Most eidetic imagery disappears during adolescence and becomes rare by adulthood (Haber & Haber, 2000).

A Case of Photographic Memory

Let's return now to the concept of mental images. In rare instances, such images may be so vivid that it is reasonable to say that a person has "photographic memory." A notable example was reported by Aleksandr Luria (1968) in his book, *The Mind of a Mnemonist*. Luria studied a man he called Mr. S who had practically unlimited memory for visual images. Mr. S could remember almost everything that ever happened to him with incredible accuracy. Luria tried to test Mr. S's memory by using longer and longer lists of words or numbers. However, he soon discovered that no matter how long the list, Mr. S was able to recall it without error. Mr. S could memorize, with equal ease, strings of digits, meaningless consonants, mathematical formulas, and poems in foreign languages. His memory was so powerful that he had to devise ways to *forget*—such as writing information on a piece of paper and then burning it.

Don't be too quick to envy Mr. S's abilities, however. He remembered so much that he couldn't separate important facts from trivia or facts from fantasy (Neath & Surprenant, 2003). For instance, if you asked him to read this chapter, he might remember every word. Yet he might also recall all the images each word made him think of and all the sights, sounds, and feelings that occurred as he was reading. Therefore, finding the answer for a specific question, writing a logical essay, or even understanding a single sentence was very difficult for him. If you didn't have selective memory, you would recall all the ingredients on your cereal box, every street number you've seen, and countless other scraps of information.

Few people in history have possessed memory abilities like Mr. S's. Instead most people with good memories have learned effective strategies for remembering. Let's investigate further.

Strategies for Remembering

At first, a student volunteer named Steve could remember 7 digits—a typical score for a college student. Could he improve with practice? For 20 months Steve practiced memorizing ever-longer lists of digits. Ultimately, he was able to memorize approximately 80 digits, like this sample:

928420480508422689539901902529128079997066065747173106010805
85269726026357332135

How did Steve do it? Basically, he worked by chunking digits into meaningful groups containing 3 or 4 digits each. Steve's avid interest in long-distance running helped greatly. For instance, to him the first 3 digits above represented 9 minutes and 28 seconds, a good time for a 2-mile run. When running times wouldn't work, Steve used other associations, such as ages or dates, to chunk digits (Ericsson & Chase, 1982). It seems apparent that Steve's success was based on learned strategies. By using similar memory systems, other people have trained themselves to equal Steve's feat (Bellezza, Six, & Phillips, 1992). In fact, the ability to organize information into chunks underlies expertise in many fields (Gobet, 2005).

Psychologist Anders Ericsson believes that most exceptional memory is merely a learned extension of normal memory (Ericsson et al., 2004). As evidence, he notes that Steve's short-term memory did not improve during months of practice. For example, Steve could still memorize only 7 consonants. Steve's phenomenal memory for numbers grew as he figured out new ways to chunk digits as he encoded them and stored them in LTM.

Researchers studying Rajan Mahadevan have drawn similar conclusions about his spectacular memory for long strings of digits. In 1981 Rajan earned a place in the *Guinness Book of World Records* by reciting the first 31,811 digits of *pi!* Yet, like Steve, Rajan's memory for most other types of information is average. His exceptional memory seems to be based on highly practiced strategies for encoding and storing digits (Thompson, Cowan, & Frieman, 1993). By using similar memory systems, college students have even managed to duplicate some of Mr. S's feats, such as memorizing a 50-digit matrix in 3 minutes (Higbee, 1997).

Steve and Rajan began with normal memory for digits. Both extended their memory abilities by diligent practice. Clearly, exceptional memory can be learned (Ericsson et al., 2004). However, we still have to wonder, do some people have naturally superior memories?

Memory Champions

Each year the World Memory Championship is held in England. Contestants must rapidly memorize daunting amounts of information, such as long lists of unrelated words and numbers. Psychologists John Wilding and Elizabeth Valentine saw this event as an opportunity to study exceptional memory and persuaded the

This number matrix is similar to the ones contestants in the World Memory Championship had to memorize. To be scored as correct, digits had to be recalled in their proper positions (Wilding & Valentine, 1994a. Memory champions. *British Journal of Psychology*, 85(2), 231-244.)

```
8 7 3 7 9 2 6 8
2 0 1 1 7 4 9 5
0 1 7 5 8 7 8 3
1 9 4 7 6 0 6 9
3 6 1 6 8 1 5 4
4 5 2 4 0 2 9 7
```

contestants to take some additional memory tests. These ranged from ordinary (recall a story), to challenging (recall the telephone numbers of 6 different people), to diabolical (recall 48 numerals arranged in rows and columns; recognize 14 previously seen pictures of snowflakes among 70 new photos) (Maguire et al., 2003; Wilding & Valentine, 1994).

Exceptional memorizers were found to:

- Use memory strategies and techniques
- Have specialized interests and knowledge that make certain types of information easier to encode and recall
- Have naturally superior memory abilities, often including vivid mental images
- Not have superior intellectual abilities or different brains

The first two points confirm what we learned from Steve's acquired memory ability. Many of the contestants, for example, actively used memory strategies, including special memory "tricks" called *mnemonics* (nee-MON-iks). Specialized interests and knowledge also helped for some tasks. For example, one contestant, who is a mathematician, was exceedingly good at memorizing numbers (Wilding & Valentine, 1994).

Several of the memory contestants were able to excel on tasks that prevented the use of learned strategies and techniques. This observation implies that superior memory ability can be a "gift" as well as a learned skill. Wilding and Valentine conclude that exceptional memory may be based on either natural ability or learned strategies. Usually it requires both.

Improving Memory—Keys to the Memory Bank

Gateway Question: How can I improve my memory?

Let's see how you can improve your memory. To begin, there is very little you can do to improve your brain's ability to store long-term memories. The jury is still out on the use of herbs (such as Ginkgo) and vitamins (such as vitamin E) to improve human memory (McDaniel, Maier, & Einstein, 2002). However, until there's a memory pill, you can immediately use learned strategies to improve memory encoding and memory retrieval. Most super memorizers use these strategies to augment whatever natural talents they have. Some of their strategies are described in the remainder of this section. Later, mnemonics are explored in this chapter's Psychology in Action section. Please do remember to read it.

Encoding Strategies

One way to improve your memory is to be sure to fully encode information. That way you can avoid forgetting due to encoding failure. Here are some steps you can take to become a better encoder:

Rehearsal

The more you *rehearse* (mentally review) information as you read, the better you will remember it. But remember that maintenance rehearsal alone is not very effective. Elaborative encoding, in which you look for connections to existing knowledge, is far better. Thinking about facts helps link them together in memory. To learn college-level information, you must make active use of more reflective rehearsal strategies (Santrock & Halonen, 2007).

Selection

The Dutch scholar Erasmus said that a good memory should be like a fish net: It should keep all the big fish and let the little ones escape. If you boil down the paragraphs in most textbooks to one or two important terms or ideas, your memory chores will be more manageable. Practice very selective marking in your texts and use marginal notes to further summarize ideas. Most students mark their texts too much instead of too little. If everything is underlined, you haven't been selective. And, very likely, you didn't pay much attention in the first place (Peterson, 1992).

Organization

Assume that you must memorize the following list of words: north, man, red, spring, woman, east, autumn, yellow, summer, boy, blue, west, winter, girl, green, south. This rather difficult list could be reorganized into *chunks* as follows: north-east-south-west, spring-summer-autumn-winter, red-yellow-green-blue, man-woman-boy-girl. Organizing class notes and summarizing chapters can be quite helpful (Hettich, 2005). You may even want to summarize your summaries, so that the overall network of ideas becomes clearer and simpler. Summaries improve memory by encouraging better encoding of information (Hadwin, Kirby, & Woodhouse, 1999).

Whole Versus Part Learning

If you have to memorize a speech, is it better to try to learn it from beginning to end? Or in smaller parts like paragraphs? Generally it is better to practice whole packages of information rather than smaller parts *(whole learning)*. This is especially true for fairly short, organized information. An exception is that learning parts may be better for extremely long, complicated information. In *part learning,* subparts of a larger body of information are studied (such as sections of a textbook chapter). To decide which approach to use, remember to study the *largest meaningful amount of information* you can at one time.

For very long or complex material, try the *progressive-part method,* by breaking a learning task into a series of short sections. At first, you study part A until it is mastered. Next, you study parts A and B; then A, B, and C; and so forth. This is a good way to learn the lines of a play, a long piece of music, or a poem (Ash & Holding, 1990). After the material is learned, you should also practice by starting at points other than A (at C, D, or B, for example). This helps prevent getting "lost" or going blank in the middle of a performance.

Serial Position

Whenever you must learn something in order, be aware of the serial position effect. As you will recall, this is the tendency to make the most errors in remembering the middle of a list. If you are introduced to a long line of people, the names you are likely to forget will be those in the middle, so you should make an extra effort to attend to them. You should also give extra practice to the middle of a list, poem, or speech. Try to break long lists of information into short sublists, and make the middle sublists the shortest of all.

Cues

The best *memory cues* (stimuli that aid retrieval) are those that were present during encoding (Anderson, 2005). For example, students in one study had the daunting task of trying to recall a list of 600 words. As they read the list (which they did not know they would be tested on), the students gave three other words closely related in meaning to each listed word. In a test given later, the words each student supplied were used as cues to jog memory. The students recalled an astounding 90 percent of the original word list (Mantyla, 1986).

Now read the following sentence:

The fish bit the swimmer.

If you were tested a week from now, you would be more likely to recall the sentence if you were given a memory cue. And, surprisingly, the word "shark" would work better as a reminder than "fish" would. The reason for this is that most people think of a shark when they read the sentence. As a result, "shark" becomes a potent memory cue (Schacter, 2000).

The preceding example shows, once again, that it often helps to *elaborate* information as you learn. When you study, try to use new names, ideas, or terms in several sentences. Also, form images that include the new information and relate it to knowledge you already have. Your goal should be to knit meaningful cues into your memory code to help you retrieve information when you need it (● Figure 8.20).

Overlearning

Numerous studies have shown that memory is greatly improved when you **overlearn** or continue to study beyond bare mastery. After you have learned material well enough to remember it once without error, you should continue studying. Overlearning is your best insurance against going blank on a test because of being nervous.

● **Figure 8.20** Actors can remember large amounts of complex information for many months, even when learning new roles in between. During testing, they remember their lines best when they are allowed to move and gesture as they would when performing. Apparently their movements supply cues that aid recall (Noice & Noice, 1999).

Spaced Practice

To keep boredom and fatigue to a minimum, try alternating short study sessions with brief rest periods. This pattern, called **spaced practice,** is generally superior to **massed practice,** in which little or no rest is given between learning sessions. By improving attention and consolidation, three 20-minute study sessions can produce more learning than 1 hour of continuous study. There's an old joke that goes, "How do you get to Carnegie Hall?" The answer is, "Practice, practice, practice." A better answer would be "Practice, wait awhile, practice, wait awhile, practice" (Neath & Surprenant, 2003).

Perhaps the best way to make use of spaced practice is to *schedule* your time. To make an effective schedule, designate times during the week before, after, and between classes when you will study particular subjects. Then treat these times just as if they are classes you have to attend.

Retrieval Strategies

Once you have successfully encoded information, you still have to retrieve it. Here are some strategies to help you avoid retrieval failure.

Recitation

Learning proceeds best when feedback, or *knowledge of results,* allows you to check your progress. Feedback can help you identify ideas that need extra practice. In addition, knowing that you have remembered or answered correctly is rewarding. A prime way to provide feedback for yourself while studying is *recitation.* If you are going to remember something, eventually

you will have to retrieve it. *Recitation* refers to summarizing aloud while you are learning. Recitation forces you to practice retrieving information. When you are reading a text, you should stop frequently and try to remember what you have just read by restating it in your own words. In one classic experiment, the best memory score was earned by a group of students who spent 80 percent of their time reciting and only 20 percent reading (Gates, 1958). Maybe students who talk to themselves aren't crazy after all.

Review

If you have spaced your practice and overlearned, retrieval practice in the form of review will be like icing on your study cake. Reviewing shortly before an exam cuts down the time during which you must remember details that may be important for the test. When reviewing, hold the amount of new information you try to memorize to a minimum. It may be realistic to take what you have actually learned and add a little more to it at the last minute by cramming. But remember that more than a little new learning may interfere with what you already know.

Using a Strategy to Aid Recall

Successful retrieval is usually the result of a planned *search* of memory (Herrmann et al., 2006). For example, one study found that students were most likely to recall names that eluded them if they made use of partial information (Reed & Bruce, 1982). The students were trying to answer questions such as, "He is best remembered as the scarecrow in the Judy Garland movie *The Wizard of Oz.*" (The answer is Ray Bolger.) Partial information that helped students remember included impressions about the length of the name, letter sounds within the name, similar names, and related information (such as the names of other characters in the movie). A similar helpful strategy is to go through the alphabet, trying each letter as the first sound of a name or word you are seeking.

The *cognitive interview* described earlier in this chapter (see "Telling Wrong from Right in Forensic Memory") offers some further hints for recapturing context and jogging memories:

1. Say or write down *everything* you can remember that relates to the information you are seeking. Don't worry about how trivial any of it seems; each bit of information you remember can serve as a cue to bring back others.
2. Try to recall events or information in different orders. Let your memories flow out backward or out of order, or start with whatever impressed you the most.

Overlearning Continuing to study beyond the point of bare mastery of facts.

Spaced practice A practice schedule that alternates study periods with brief rests.

Massed practice A practice schedule in which studying continues for long periods, without interruption.

3. Recall from different viewpoints. Review events by mentally standing in a different place. Or try to view information as another person would remember it. When taking a test, for instance, ask yourself what other students or your professor would remember about the topic.

4. Mentally put yourself back in the situation where you learned the information. Try to mentally recreate the learning environment or relive the event. As you do, include sounds, smells, details of weather, nearby objects, other people present, what you said or thought, and how you felt as you learned the information (Fisher & Geiselman, 1987; Milne & Bull, 2002).

Extend How Long You Remember

When you are learning new information, practice retrieval repeatedly. As you do, gradually lengthen the amount of time that passes before you test yourself again. For example, if you are studying German words on flash cards, look at the first card and then move it a few cards back in the stack. Do the same with the next few cards. When you get to the first "old" card, test yourself on it and check the answer. Then, move it farther back in the stack. Do the same with other "old" cards as they come up. When "old" cards come up for the third time, put them clear to the back of the stack (Cull, Shaughnessy, & Zechmeister, 1996).

Sleep and Memory

Remember that sleeping after study reduces interference. However, unless you are a "night person," late evening may not be a very efficient time for you to study. Also, you obviously can't sleep after every study session or study everything just before you sleep. That's why your study schedule should include ample breaks between subjects as described earlier. (See "Spaced Practice.") The breaks and free time in your schedule are as important as your study periods.

Hunger and Memory

People who are hungry almost always score lower on memory tests. So mother was right, it's a good idea to make sure you've had a good breakfast or lunch before you take tests at school (Smith, Clark, & Gallagher, 1999). And a cup of coffee won't hurt your test performance, either (Smith, 2005).

A Look Ahead

Psychologists still have much to learn about the nature of memory and how to improve it. For now, one thing stands out clearly: People who have good memories excel at organizing information and making it meaningful. Sometimes, however, you are faced with the need to memorize information without much inherent meaning. For example, a shopping list is just a list of more or less unrelated items. There isn't much of a meaningful relationship between carrots, rolls of toilet paper, TV dinners, and Twinkies except that you need more of them. With this in mind, the Psychology in Action discussion for this chapter tells how you can use mnemonics to better memorize when meaning-based memory strategies, like those described in this section, are not helpful.

KNOWLEDGE BUILDER
Improving Memory

RECITE

1. Children with eidetic imagery typically have no better than average long-term memory. T or F?
2. For most people, having an especially good memory is based on
   a. maintenance rehearsal
   b. constructive processing
   c. phonetic imagery
   d. learned strategies
3. As new information is encoded it is helpful to elaborate on its meaning and connect it to other information. T or F?
4. Organizing information while studying has little effect on memory because long-term memory is already highly organized. T or F?
5. The progressive part method of study is best suited to long and complex learning tasks. T or F?
6. To improve memory, it is reasonable to spend as much or more time reciting as reading. T or F?
7. The cognitive interview helps people remember more by providing
   a. memory cues
   b. a serial position effect
   c. phonetic priming
   d. massed practice

REFLECT

Critical Thinking

8. Mr. S had great difficulty remembering faces. Can you guess why?
9. What advantages would there be to taking notes as you read a textbook, as opposed to underlining words in the text?

Relate

What kinds of information are you good at remembering? Why do you think your memory is better for those topics?

Return to the topic headings in the preceding pages that list techniques for improving memory. Place a checkmark next to those that you have used recently. Review any you didn't mark and think of a specific example of how you could use each technique at school, at home, or at work.

Answers: 1. T **2.** d **3.** T **4.** F **5.** T **6.** T **7.** a **8.** Mr. S's memory was so specific that faces seemed different and unfamiliar if he saw them from a new angle or if a face had a different expression on it than when Mr. S last saw it. **9.** Note-taking is a form of elaborative encoding and recitation; it encourages elaborative rehearsal and facilitates the organization and selection of important ideas, and your notes can be used for review.

PSYCHOLOGY IN ACTION

Mnemonics—Memory Magic

Gateway Question: Are there any tricks to help me with my memory?

Just imagine the poor biology or psychology student who is required to learn the names of the 12 cranial nerves (in order, of course). Although the spinal nerves connect the brain to the body through the spinal cord, the cranial nerves do so directly. Just in case you wanted to know, the names of the 12 cranial nerves are: olfactory, optic, oculomotor, trochlear, trigeminal, abducens, facial, vestibulocochlear, glossopharyngeal, vagus, spinal accessory, and hypoglossal.

As you might imagine, most of us find it difficult to successfully encode this list. In the absence of any obvious meaningful relationship among these terms, many students find it difficult to apply the memory strategies we discussed earlier in the chapter and instead turn to *rote* learning (learning by simple repetition). Fortunately, there *is* an alternative: mnemonics (nee-MON-iks) (Lieberman, 2004; Neath & Surprenant, 2003). A **mnemonic** is any kind of memory system or aid. The superiority of mnemonic learning as opposed to rote learning has been demonstrated many times (Carney & Levin, 2003; Manalo, 2002).

Some mnemonic systems are so common that almost everyone knows them. If you are trying to remember how many days there are in a month, you may find the answer by reciting, "Thirty days hath September . . ." Physics teachers often help students remember the colors of the spectrum by giving them the mnemonic "Roy G. Biv": **R**ed, **O**range, **Y**ellow, **G**reen, **B**lue, **I**ndigo, **V**iolet. The budding sailor who has trouble telling port from starboard may remember that port and left both have four letters or may remind herself, "I *left* port." And what beginning musician hasn't remembered the notes represented by the lines and spaces of the musical staff by learning "F-A-C-E" and "**E**very **G**ood **B**oy **D**oes **F**ine"?

Generations of students have learned the names of the spinal nerves by memorizing the sentence "**O**n **O**ld **O**lympus' **T**owering **T**op **A** **F**amous **V**ocal **G**erman **V**iewed **S**ome **H**ops. This mnemonic, which uses the first letter of each of the cranial nerves to generate a nonsense sentence, indeed produces better recall of the cranial nerves. Such *acrostics* are even more effective if you make up your own (Bloom & Lamkin, 2006). By practicing mnemonics you should be able to greatly improve your memory with little effort.

Here, then, are some basic principles of mnemonics:

1. **Make things meaningful.** In general, transferring information from short-term memory to long-term memory is aided by making it meaningful. If you encounter technical terms that have little or no immediate meaning for you, *give* them meaning, even if you have to stretch the term to do so. (This point is clarified by the examples following this list.)

2. **Make information familiar.** Another way to get information into long-term memory is to connect it to information already stored there. If some facts or ideas in a chapter seem to stay in your memory easily, associate other more difficult facts with them.

3. **Use mental pictures.** Visual pictures, or images, are generally easier to remember than words. Turning information into mental pictures is therefore very helpful. Make these images as vivid as possible (Neath & Surprenant, 2003).

4. **Form bizarre, unusual, or exaggerated mental associations.** Forming images that make sense is better in most situations. However, when associating two ideas, terms, or especially mental images, you may find that the more outrageous and exaggerated the association, the more likely you are to remember. Bizarre images make stored information more *distinctive* and therefore easier to retrieve (Worthen & Marshall, 1996). Imagine, for example, that you have just been introduced to Mr. Rehkop. To remember his name, you could picture him wearing a police uniform. Then replace his nose with a ray gun. This bizarre image will

Mnemonics can be an aid in preparing for tests. However, because mnemonics help most in the initial stages of storing information, it is important to follow through with other elaborative learning strategies.

provide two hints when you want to remember Mr. Rehkop's name: *ray* and *cop*. This technique works for other kinds of information, too. College students who used exaggerated mental associations to remember the names of unfamiliar animals outperformed students who just used rote memory (Carney & Levin, 2001). Bizarre images mainly help improve immediate memory, and they work best for fairly simple information (Fritz et al., 2007; Robinson-Riegler & McDaniel, 1994). Nevertheless, they can be a first step toward learning.

A sampling of typical applications of mnemonics should make these four points clearer to you.

Example 1

Let's say you have 30 new vocabulary words to memorize in Spanish. You can proceed by rote memorization (repeat them over and over until you begin to get them), or you can learn them with little effort by using the key-

Mnemonic Any kind of memory system or aid.

word method (Fritz et al., 2007; Pressley, 1987). In the **keyword method** a familiar word or image is used to link two other words or items. To remember that the word *pajaro* (pronounced PAH-hah-ro) means bird, you can link it to a "key" word in English: *Pajaro* sounds a bit like "parked car-o." Therefore, to remember that *pajaro* means bird, you might visualize a parked car jam-packed full of birds. You should try to make this image as vivid and exaggerated as possible, with birds flapping and chirping and feathers flying everywhere. Similarly, for the word *carta* (which means "letter"), you might imagine a shopping *cart* filled with postal letters.

If you link similar keywords and images for the rest of the list, you may not remember them all, but you will get most without any more practice. As a matter of fact, if you have formed the *pajaro* and *carta* images just now, it is going to be almost impossible for you to ever see these words again without remembering what they mean. The keyword method is also superior when you want to work "backward" from an English word to a foreign vocabulary word (Hogben & Lawson, 1992).

What about a year from now? How long do keyword memories last? Mnemonic memories work best in the short run. Later, they may be more fragile than conventional memories. That's why it's usually best to use mnemonics during the initial stages of learning (Carney & Levin, 2003). To create more lasting memories, you'll need to use the techniques discussed earlier in this chapter.

Example 2

Let's say you have to learn the names of all the bones and muscles in the human body for biology. You are trying to remember that the jawbone is the *mandible*. This one is easy because you can associate it to a *man nibbling,* or maybe you can picture a *man dribbling* a basketball with his jaw (make this image as ridiculous as possible). If the muscle name *latissimus dorsi* gives you trouble, familiarize it by turning it into *"the ladder misses the door, sigh."* Then picture a ladder glued to your back where the muscle is found. Pic-

ture the ladder leading up to a small door at your shoulder. Picture the ladder missing the door. Picture the ladder sighing like an animated character in a cartoon.

This seems like more to remember, not less; and it seems like it would cause you to misspell things. Mnemonics are not a complete substitute for normal memory; they are an aid to normal memory. Mnemonics are not likely to be helpful unless you make extensive use of *images* (Willoughby et al., 1997). Your mental pictures will come back to you easily. As for misspellings, mnemonics can be thought of as a built-in hint in your memory. Often, when taking a test, you will find that the slightest hint is all you need to remember correctly. A mnemonic image is like having someone leaning over your shoulder who says, "Psst, the name of that muscle sounds like 'ladder misses the door, sigh.'" If misspelling continues to be a problem, try to create memory aids for spelling, too.

Here are two more examples to help you appreciate the flexibility of a mnemonic approach to studying.

Example 3

Your art history teacher expects you to be able to name the artist when you are shown slides as part of exams. You have seen many of the slides only once before in class. How will you remember them? As the slides are shown in class, make each artist's name into an object or image. Then picture the object *in* the paintings done by the artist. For example, you can picture Van Gogh as a *van* (automobile) *going* through the middle of each Van Gogh painting. Picture the van running over things and knocking things over. Or, if you remember that Van Gogh cut off his ear, picture a giant bloody ear in each of his paintings.

Example 4

If you have trouble remembering history, try to avoid thinking of it as something from the dim past. Picture each historical personality as a person you know right now (a friend, teacher, parent, and so on). Then picture these people doing whatever the historical figures did. Also, try visualizing battles or other events as if they were happening in your town or make parks and schools into countries. Use your imagination.

Exaggerated mental images can link two words or ideas in ways that aid memory. Here, the keyword method is used to link the English word "letter" with the Spanish word *carta*.

How can mnemonics be used to remember things in order? Here are three techniques that are helpful:

1. **Form a story or a chain.** To remember lists of ideas, objects, or words in order, try forming an exaggerated association (mental image) connecting the first item to the second, then the second to the third, and so on. To remember the following short list in order—elephant, doorknob, string, watch, rifle, oranges—picture a full-size *elephant* balanced on a *doorknob* playing with a *string* tied to him. Picture a *watch* tied to the string, and a *rifle* shooting *oranges* at the watch. This technique can be used quite successfully for lists of 20 or more items. In one test, people who used a linking mnemonic did much better at remembering lists of 15 and 22 errands (Higbee et al., 1990). Try it next time you go shopping and leave your list at home. Another helpful strategy is to make up a short story that links all the items on a list you want to remember (McNamara & Scott, 2001).

2. **Take a mental walk.** Ancient Greek orators had an interesting way to remember ideas in order when giving a speech. Their method was to take a mental walk along a familiar path. As they did, they associated topics with the images of statues found along the walk. You can do the same thing by "placing" objects or ideas along the way as you mentally take a familiar walk (Neath & Surprenant, 2003).

3. **Use a system.** As we have already seen, many times the first letters or syllables of words or ideas can be formed into another word that will serve as a reminder of order. "Roy G. Biv" is an example. As an alternative, learn the following: 1 is a bun, 2 is a shoe, 3 is a tree, 4 is a door, 5 is a hive, 6 is sticks, 7 is heaven, 8 is a gate, 9 is a line, 10 is a hen. To remember a list in order, form an image associating bun with the first item on your list. For example, if the first item is *frog*, picture a "frog-burger" on a bun to remember it. Then, associate shoe with the second item, and so on.

If you have never used mnemonics, you may still be skeptical, but give this approach a fair trial. Most people find they can greatly extend their memory through the use of mnemonics. But remember, like most things worthwhile, remembering takes effort.

KNOWLEDGE BUILDER
Mnemonics

RECITE

1. Memory systems and aids are referred to as _____.
2. Which of the following is least likely to improve memory?
   a. using exaggerated mental images
   b. forming a chain of associations
   c. turning visual information into verbal information
   d. associating new information to information that is already known or familiar
3. Bizarre images make stored information more distinctive and therefore easier to retrieve. T or F?
4. In general, mnemonics only improve memory for related words or ideas. T or F?
5. The keyword method is a commonly used
   a. cognitive interviewing technique
   b. massed practice strategy
   c. mnemonic technique
   d. first step in the progressive-part method

REFLECT

Critical Thinking

6. How are elaborative encoding and mnemonics alike?

Relate

The best mnemonics are your own. As an exercise, see if you can create a better acrostic for the 12 cranial nerves. One student generated **O**ld **O**tto **O**ctavius **T**ried **T**rigonometry **A**fter **F**acing **V**ery **G**rim **V**irgin's **S**ad **H**usbands (Bloom & Lamkin, 2006).

Come up with mnemonics for the words *iconic memory, implicit memory,* and *mnemonic*. Here is an example to help you get started. An iconic memory is a visual image: Picture an *eye* in a *can* to remember that iconic memories store visual information.

Now, go through the glossary items in this chapter and make up mnemonics for any terms you have difficulty remembering.

Answers: 1. mnemonics **2.** c **3.** T **4.** F **5.** c **6.** Both attempt to relate new information to information stored in LTM that is familiar or already easy to retrieve.

chapter in review — Gateways to Memory

Remembering is an active process. Memories are frequently lost, altered, revised, or distorted.

- Memory systems allow us to encode, store, and retrieve information.
- The three stages of memory (sensory memory, short-term memory, and long-term memory) hold information for increasingly longer periods.
- The best way to remember depends, to an extent, on which memory system you are using.
- Sensory memories are encoded as iconic memories or echoic memories. Short-term memories tend to be encoded by sound, and long-term memories by meaning.

Short-term memory holds small amounts of information in conscious awareness for brief intervals.

- Selective attention determines what information moves from sensory memory, which is exact but very brief, on to STM.
- STM has a capacity of about 5 to 7 bits of information, but this limit can be extended by chunking.
- Short-term memories are brief and very sensitive to interruption or interference. However, they can be kept alive by maintenance rehearsal.

Long-term memory stores large amounts of meaningful information for long periods of time.

- LTM serves as a general storehouse for meaningful information. Elaborative encoding helps us form lasting, long-term memories.
- Long-term memories are relatively permanent. LTM seems to have an almost unlimited storage capacity.

- Constructive processing tends to alter memories. Remembering is an active process. Our memories are frequently lost, altered, revised, or distorted.
- LTM is highly organized. The structure of memory networks is the subject of current research.
- In redintegration, memories are reconstructed, as one bit of information leads to others, which then serve as cues for further recall.
- LTM contains procedural (skill) and declarative (fact) memories. Declarative memories can be semantic or episodic.

Memories may be revealed by recall, recognition, relearning, or priming.

- The tip-of-the-tongue state shows that memory is not an all-or-nothing event.
- In recall, memories are retrieved without explicit cues, as in an essay exam. Recall of listed information often reveals a serial position effect.
- A common test of recognition is the multiple-choice question.
- In relearning, material that seems to be forgotten is learned again, and memory is revealed by a savings score.

Keyword method As an aid to memory, using a familiar word or image to link two items.

- Recall, recognition, and relearning mainly measure explicit memories. Other techniques, such as priming, are necessary to reveal implicit memories.

Forgetting can occur because of failures of encoding, of storage, or of retrieval.

- Herman Ebbinghaus found that forgetting is most rapid immediately after learning, as shown by the curve of forgetting.
- Failure to encode information is a common cause of "forgetting."
- Forgetting in sensory memory and STM is due to a failure of storage through a weakening (decay) of memory traces. Decay of memory traces may also explain some LTM losses.
- Failures of retrieval occur when information that resides in memory is nevertheless not retrieved.
- A lack of memory cues can produce retrieval failure. State-dependent learning is related to the effects of memory cues.
- Much forgetting in STM and LTM is caused by interference. In retroactive interference, new learning interferes with the ability to retrieve earlier learning. Proactive interference occurs when old learning interferes with the retrieval of new learning.
- Memories can be consciously suppressed and they may be unconsciously repressed.
- Extreme caution is warranted when "recovered" memories are the only basis for believing that a person was sexually abused during childhood.

Lasting memories are recorded by changes in the activity, structure, and chemistry of brain cells.

- It takes time to consolidate memories. In the brain, memory consolidation takes place in the hippocampus.
- Intensely emotional experiences can result in flashbulb memories.
- After memories have been consolidated, they appear to be stored in the cortex of the brain.

"Photographic" memory (eidetic imagery) occurs when a person is able to project an image onto a blank surface.

- Although it's true that some people have naturally superior memories, everyone can learn to improve his or her memory.
- Eidetic imagery is rarely found in adults. However, many adults have internal memory images, which can be very vivid.
- Exceptional memory may be based on natural ability or learned strategies. Usually it involves both.

Excellent memory abilities are based on using strategies and techniques that make learning efficient and that compensate for natural weaknesses in human memory.

- Some people have naturally superior memories, but even they find it beneficial to use memory strategies.
- Memory can be improved by using feedback, recitation, and rehearsal, by selecting and organizing information, and by using the progressive part method, spaced practice, overlearning, and active search strategies.
- When you are studying or memorizing, you should also keep in mind the effects of serial position, sleep, review, cues, and elaboration.

Memory systems (mnemonics) greatly improve immediate memory.

- Memory systems (mnemonics) greatly improve immediate memory. However, conventional learning tends to create the most lasting memories.
- Mnemonic systems use mental images and unusual associations to link new information with familiar memories already stored in LTM.
- Effective mnemonics tend to rely on mental images and bizarre or exaggerated mental associations.

Web Resources

For an up-to-date list of direct links to interesting sites, including those listed here, visit the student companion site for this book at www.cengage.com/psychology/coon

Playing Games with Memory Try some activities to test your memory.

The Atkinson-Schiffrin Model Further explore the three-store model of memory.

The Magical Number Seven, Plus or Minus Two Read George Miller's original paper on capacity limits in short-term memory.

Questions and Answers about Memories of Childhood Abuse Read a summary of the repressed memory issue from the American Psychological Association.

Free Recall Test Test your free recall ability.

Memory Strategies Read about a useful list of memory strategies for studying.

Memory Techniques and Mnemonics Follow links to information on mnemonics.

Interactive Learning

Introduction to Psychology: Gateways to Mind and Behavior Book Companion Website
www.cengage.com/psychology/coon

Visit your book companion website, where you will find flash cards, practice quizzes, web links, and more to help you study.

CENGAGENOW™ *Just what you need to know NOW!*

Spend time on what you need to master rather than on information you already have learned. Take a pre-test for this chapter, and CengageNOW will generate a personalized study plan based on your results. The study plan will identify the topics you need to review and direct you to online resources to help you master those topics. You can then take a post-test to help you determine the concepts you have mastered and what you will need to work on. Try it out! Go to www.cengage.com/login to sign in with an access code or to purchase access to this product.

CHAPTER 9

Cognition, Language, Creativity, and Intelligence

Gateway Theme

Thinking, language, problem solving, and creativity underlie intelligent behavior. Measuring intelligence is worthwhile, but tests provide limited definitions of intelligent behavior.

Manahem Kahana/AFP/Getty Images

Gateway Questions

- *What is the nature of thought?*
- *In what ways are images related to thinking?*
- *What are concepts?*
- *What is the role of language in thinking?*
- *What do we know about problem solving?*
- *What is creative thinking?*

- *How accurate is intuition?*
- *How is human intelligence defined and measured?*
- *How much does intelligence vary from person to person?*
- *What are some controversies in the study of intelligence?*
- *Are IQ tests fair to all cultural and racial groups?*

He can't walk or talk. When he was 13, Lou Gehrig's disease began to slowly destroy nerve cells in his spinal cord, short-circuiting messages between his brain and muscles. Today, he is confined to a wheelchair and "speaks" by manually controlling a speech synthesizer.

Yet despite his severe disabilities, Steven Hawking can still *think*. His brain is unaffected by the disease and remains fiercely active. Steven is a theoretical physicist and one of the best-known scientific minds of modern times. With courage and determination, he has used his intellect to advance our understanding of the universe.

Our species is called *Homo Sapiens* (from the Latin for *man* and *wise*). But what exactly is wisdom? How do we think? How are we able to solve problems? How do people like Steven Hawking create works of science, art, and literature? What is intelligence? Is it all in our genes? For some preliminary answers, we will investigate thinking, problem solving, language, creativity, and intelligence in the following pages.

What Is Thinking?—Brains over Brawn

Gateway Question: What is the nature of thought?

Humans are highly adaptable creatures. We live in deserts, jungles, mountains, frenzied cities, placid retreats, and space stations. Unlike other species, our success owes more to thinking abilities and intelligence than it does to physical strength or speed (Goldstein, 2008). Let's see how concepts, language, and mental images make abstract thinking possible.

Cognition refers to mentally processing information. Our thoughts take many forms, including daydreaming, problem solving, and reasoning (to name but a few). Although thinking is not limited to humans, imagine trying to teach an animal to match the feats of Shakuntala Devi, who once set a "world's record" for mental calculation by multiplying two randomly chosen 13-digit numbers (7,686,369,774,870 times 2,465,099,745,779) in her head, giving the answer in 28 seconds. (That's 18,947,668,104,042,434, 089,403,730 if you haven't already figured it out.)

Some Basic Units of Thought

At its most basic, thinking is an *internal representation* (mental expression) of a problem or situation. Picture a chess player who mentally tries out several moves before actually touching a chess piece. By *planning* her moves, she can avoid many mistakes. Imagine planning what to study for an exam, what to say at a job interview, or how to get to your spring break hotel. In each of these cases, imagine what might happen if you couldn't plan at all.

The power of being able to mentally represent problems and plan is dramatically illustrated by chess grand master Miguel Najdorf, who once simultaneously played 45 chess games while blindfolded. How did Najdorf do it? Like most people, he used the basic units of thought: images, concepts, and language (or symbols). **Images** are picture-like mental representations. **Concepts** are ideas that represent categories of objects or events. **Language** consists of words or symbols, and rules for combining them. Thinking often involves all three units. For example, blindfolded chess players rely on visual images, concepts ("Game 2 begins with a strategy called an English opening"), and the notational system, or "language," of chess.

In a moment we will delve further into imagery, concepts, and language. Be aware, however, that thinking involves attention, pattern recognition, memory, decision-making, intuition, knowledge, and more. The rest of this section is just a sample of what cognitive psychology is about.

Mental Imagery—Does a Frog Have Lips?

Gateway Question: In what ways are images related to thinking?

Almost everyone has visual and auditory images. More than half of us have imagery for movement, touch, taste, smell, and pain. Thus, mental images are sometimes more than just "pictures." For example, your image of a bakery may also include its delicious odor. Some people have a rare form of imagery called *synaesthesia* (sin-es-THEE-zyah). For these individuals, images cross normal sensory barriers (Kadosh & Henik, 2007). For one such person, spiced chicken tastes "pointy"; for another, pain is the color orange; and for a third, human voices unleash a flood of colors and tastes (Dixon, Smilek, & Merikle, 2004; Robertson & Sagiv, 2005). Despite such variations, most of us use images to think, remember, and solve problems. For instance, we may use mental images to:

- Make a decision or solve a problem (choosing what clothes to wear; figuring out how to arrange furniture in a room).
- Change feelings (thinking of pleasant images to get out of a bad mood; imagining yourself as thin to stay on a diet).
- Improve a skill or prepare for some action (using images to improve a tennis stroke; mentally rehearsing how you will ask for a raise).
- Aid memory (picturing Mr. Cook wearing a chef's hat, so you can remember his name).

The Nature of Mental Images

Mental images are not flat, like photographs. Researcher Stephen Kosslyn showed this by asking people, "Does a frog have lips and a stubby tail?" Unless you often kiss frogs, you will probably tackle this question by using mental images. Most people picture a frog, "look" at its mouth, and then mentally "rotate" the frog in mental space to check its tail (Kosslyn, 1983). Mental rotation is partly based on imagined movements (● Figure 9.1). That is, we mentally "pick up" an object and turn it around (Wraga et al., 2005).

"Reverse Vision"

What happens in the brain when a person has visual images? Seeing something in your "mind's eye" is similar to seeing real objects. Information from the eyes normally activates the brain's primary visual area, creating an image (● Figure 9.2). Other brain areas then help us recognize the image by relating it to stored knowledge. When you form a mental image, the system works in reverse. Brain areas where memories are stored send signals back to the visual cortex, where once again, an image is created (Ganis, Thompson, & Kosslyn, 2004; Kosslyn, 2005). For example, if you visualize a friend's face right now, the area of your brain that specializes in perceiving faces will become more active (O'Craven & Kanwisher, 2000).

Using Mental Images

How are images used to solve problems? We use *stored images* (information from memory) to apply past experiences to problem solving. Let's say you are asked, "How many ways can you use an empty egg carton?" You might begin by picturing uses you have already seen, such as sorting buttons into a carton. To give more original answers, you will probably need to use *created* images, which are assembled or invented, rather than simply remembered. Thus, an artist may completely picture a proposed sculpture before beginning work. People with good imaging abilities tend to score higher on tests of creativity (Morrison & Wallace, 2001). In fact, Albert Einstein, Thomas Edi-

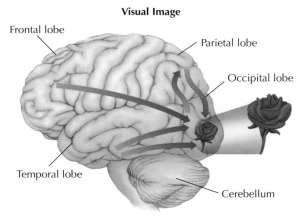

● **Figure 9.2** When you see a flower, its image is represented by activity in the primary visual area of the cortex, at the back of the brain. Information about the flower is also relayed to other brain areas. If you form a mental image of a flower, information follows a reverse path. The result, once again, is activation of the primary visual area.

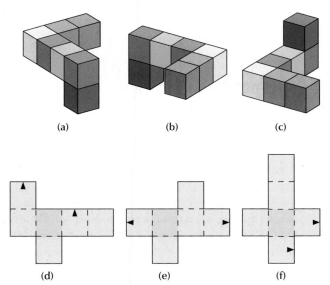

● **Figure 9.1** Imagery in thinking. *(Top)* Subjects were shown a drawing similar to *(a)* and drawings of how *(a)* would look in other positions, such as *(b)* and *(c)*. Subjects could recognize *(a)* after it had been "rotated" from its original position. However, the more *(a)* was rotated in space, the longer it took to recognize it. This result suggests that people actually formed a three-dimensional image of *(a)* and rotated the image to see if it matched (Shepard, 1975. Form, formation, and transformation of internal representations. In R.L. Solso (Ed.), Information processing and cognition: The Loyola Symposium. Hillsdale, NJ: Erlbaum.). *(Bottom)* Try your ability to manipulate mental images: Picture each of these shapes as a piece of paper that can be folded to make a cube. After they have been folded, on which cubes do the arrow tips meet (Kosslyn, 1983. Stalking the mental image. *Psychology Today,* May 23-28. Reprinted with permission from Psychology Today Magazine, Copyright © 1983 Sussex Publishers, LLC.)

Cognition The process of thinking or mentally processing information (images, concepts, words, rules, and symbols).

Image Most often, a mental representation that has picture-like qualities; an icon.

Concept A generalized idea representing a category of related objects or events.

Language Words or symbols, and rules for combining them, that are used for thinking and communication.

The Guggenheim Museum in Bilbao, Spain, was designed by architect Frank Gehry. Could a person lacking mental imagery design such a masterpiece? Three people out of 100 find it impossible to produce mental images, and 3 out of 100 have very strong imagery. Most artists, architects, designers, sculptors, and filmmakers have excellent visual imagery.

son, Lewis Carroll, and many other of history's most original intellects relied heavily on imagery (West, 1991).

Does the "size" of a mental image affect thinking? To find out, first picture a cat sitting beside a housefly. Now try to "zoom in" on the cat's ears so you see them clearly. Next, picture a rabbit sitting beside an elephant. How quickly can you "see" the rabbit's front feet? Did it take longer than picturing the cat's ears?

When a rabbit is pictured with an elephant, the rabbit's image must be small because the elephant is large. Using such tasks, Stephen Kosslyn found that the smaller an image is, the harder it is to "see" its details. To put this finding to use, try forming oversize images of things you want to think about. For example, to understand electricity, picture the wires as large pipes with electrons the size of golf balls moving through them; to understand the human ear, explore it (in your mind's eye) like a large cave; and so forth.

Kinesthetic Imagery

Do muscular responses relate to thinking? In a sense, we think with our bodies as well as our heads. *Kinesthetic images* are created from muscular sensations (Holmes & Collins, 2001). Such images help us think about movements and actions. As you think and talk, kinesthetic sensations can guide the flow of ideas. For example, if you try to tell a friend how to make bread, you may move your hands as if kneading the dough. Or, try answering this question: Which direction do you turn the hot-water handle in your kitchen to shut off the water? Most people haven't simply memorized the words "Turn it clockwise" or "Turn it counterclockwise." Instead you will probably "turn" the faucet in your imagination before answering. You may even make a turning motion with your hand before answering.

Kinesthetic images are especially important in music, sports, dance, skateboarding, martial arts, and other movement-oriented skills. People with good kinesthetic imagery (or high *bodily-kinesthetic intelligence*) learn such skills faster than those with poor imagery (Glisky, Williams, & Kihlstrom, 1996).

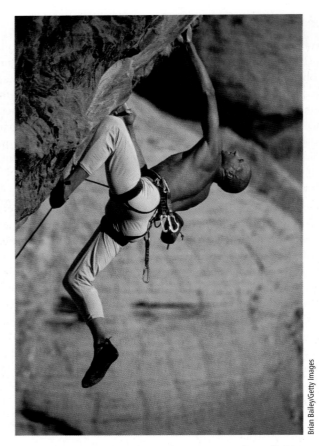

A study found that rock climbers use kinesthetic imagery to learn climbing routes and to plan their next few moves (Smyth & Waller, 1998).

Concepts—I'm Positive, It's a Whatchamacallit

Gateway Question: What are concepts?

A *concept* is an idea that represents a category of objects or events. Concepts help us identify important features of the world. That's why experts in various areas of knowledge are good at classifying objects. Bird watchers, tropical fish fanciers, 5-year-old dinosaur enthusiasts, and other experts all learn to look for identifying details that beginners tend to miss. If you are knowledgeable about a topic, such as horses, flowers, or football, you literally see things differently than less well-informed people do (Johnson & Mervis, 1997; Ross, 2006).

Forming Concepts

How are concepts learned? **Concept formation** is the process of classifying information into meaningful categories (Ashby & Maddox, 2005). At its most basic, concept formation is based on experience with *positive* and *negative instances* (examples that belong, or do not belong, to the concept class). Concept formation is not as simple as it might seem. Imagine a child learning the concept of *dog:*

Dog Daze

A child and her father go for a walk. At a neighbor's house, they see a medium-size dog. The father says, "See the dog." As they pass the next yard, the child sees a cat and says, "Dog!" Her father corrects her, "No, that's a *cat*." The child now thinks, "Aha, dogs are large and cats are small." In the next yard, she sees a Pekingese and says, "Cat!" "No, that's a dog," replies her father.

The child's confusion is understandable. At first she might even mistake a Pekingese for a dust mop. However, with more positive and negative instances, the child will eventually recognize everything from Great Danes to Chihuahuas as members of the same category—dogs.

As adults, we often acquire concepts by learning or forming rules. A *conceptual rule* is a guideline for deciding whether objects or events belong to a concept class. For example, a triangle must be a closed shape with three sides made of straight lines. Rules are an efficient way to learn concepts, but examples remain important. It's unlikely that memorizing rules would allow a new listener to accurately categorize *punk, hip-hop, fusion, salsa, metal, country,* and *rap* music.

Types of Concepts

Are there different kinds of concepts? Yes, **conjunctive concepts,** or "and concepts," are defined by the presence of two or more features (Reed, 2007). In other words, an item must have "this feature *and* this feature *and* this feature." For example, a *motorcycle* must have two wheels *and* an engine *and* handlebars.

Relational concepts are based on how an object relates to something else, or how its features relate to one another. All of the following are relational concepts: *larger, above, left, north,* and *upside down.* Another example is *brother,* which is defined as "a male considered in his relation to another person having the same parents."

Disjunctive concepts have at *least one* of several possible features. These are "either/or" concepts. To belong to the category, an item must have "this feature *or* that feature *or* another feature." For example, in baseball, a *strike* is *either* a swing and a miss *or* a pitch over the plate *or* a foul ball. The either/or quality of disjunctive concepts makes them hard to learn.

Prototypes

When you think of the concept *bird,* do you mentally list the features that birds have? Probably not. In addition to rules and features, we use **prototypes,** or ideal models, to identify concepts (Burnett et al., 2005; Rosch, 1977). A robin, for example, is a prototypical bird; an ostrich is not. In other words, some items are better examples of a concept than others. Which of the drawings in ● Figure 9.3 best represents a cup? At some point, as a cup grows taller or wider, it becomes a vase or a bowl. How do we know when the line is crossed? Probably, we mentally compare objects to an "ideal" cup, like number 5. That's why it's hard to identify concepts when we can't come up with relevant prototypes. What, for example, are the objects shown in ● Figure 9.4? As you can see, prototypes are especially helpful when we try to categorize complex stimuli (Minda & Smith, 2001).

● **Figure 9.3** When does a cup become a bowl or a vase? Deciding if an object belongs to a conceptual class is aided by relating it to a prototype, or ideal example. Subjects in one experiment chose number 5 as the "best" cup. (Copyright 1973 by Georgetown University Press. "The Boundaries of Words and Their Meanings" by William Labov. From *New Ways of Analyzing Variation in English,* Charles-James N. Bailey and Roger W. Shuy, Editors, p. 354. Reprinted with permission. www.press.georgetown.edu.)

● **Figure 9.4** Use of prototypes in concept identification. Even though its shape is unusual, item *(a)* can be related to a model (an ordinary set of pliers) and thus recognized. But what are items *(b)* and *(c)*? If you don't recognize them, look ahead to ● Figure 9.6. (Bransford & McCarrell, 1977. A sketch of cognitive approach to comprehension: Some thoughts about understanding what it means to comprehend. In P. N. Johnson-Laird & P. C. Wason (Eds.), *Thinking: Readings in cognitive science.* Cambridge: Cambridge University Press.)

Faulty Concepts

Using inaccurate concepts often leads to thinking errors. For example, *social stereotypes* are oversimplified concepts of groups of people. Stereotypes about men, African Americans, women, conservatives, liberals, police officers, or other groups often muddle thinking about members of the group. A related problem is *all-or-nothing thinking* (one-dimensional thought). In this case, we classify things as absolutely right or wrong, good or bad, fair or unfair,

Concept formation The process of classifying information into meaningful categories.

Conjunctive concept A class of objects that have two or more features in common. (For example, to qualify as an example of the concept an object must be both red *and* triangular.)

Relational concept A concept defined by the relationship between features of an object or between an object and its surroundings (for example, "greater than," "lopsided").

Disjunctive concept A concept defined by the presence of at least one of several possible features. (For example, to qualify an object must be either blue *or* circular.)

Prototype An ideal model used as a prime example of a particular concept.

black or white, honest or dishonest. Thinking this way prevents us from appreciating the subtleties of most life problems (Bastian & Haslam, 2006).

Stereotypes have a major impact on social behavior by contributing to prejudice and discrimination. **See Chapter 17, pages 573–576, for more information.**

Connotative Meaning

Generally speaking, concepts have two types of meaning. The **denotative meaning** of a word or concept is its exact definition. The **connotative meaning** is its emotional or personal meaning. The denotative meaning of the word "naked" (having no clothes) is the same for a nudist as it is for a movie censor, but we could expect their connotations to differ. Connotative differences can influence how we think about important issues. For example, the term "enhanced radiation device" has a more positive connotation than "neutron bomb" does (Gruner & Tighe, 1995).

Can you clarify what a connotative meaning is? Yes, connotative meaning can be measured with a technique called the *semantic differential,* as shown in ● Figure 9.5. When we rate words or concepts, most of their connotative meaning boils down to the dimensions *good/bad, strong/weak,* and *active/passive.* These dimensions give words very different connotations, even when their denotative meanings are similar. For example, I am *conscientious;* you are *careful;* he is *nitpicky!* Because we are conscientious (not nitpicky, right?), let's further explore language.

Rate this word: JAZZ

Rounded		Angular
Strong		Weak
Smooth		Rough
Passive		Active
Large		Small
Hot		Cold
Bad		Good
Relaxed		Tense
Dry		Wet
Stale		Fresh

● **Figure 9.5** This is an example of Osgood's semantic differential. The connotative meaning of the word *jazz* can be established by rating it on the scales. Mark your own rating by placing dots or Xs in the spaces. Connect the marks with a line; then have a friend rate the word and compare your responses. It might be interesting to do the same for "rock and roll," "classical," and "rap." You also might want to try the word "psychology." (From C.E. Osgood. The nature and measurement of meaning. *Psychology Bulletin,* 49, 197-237. Copyright © 1952 APA. Reprinted with permission of the publisher.)

● **Figure 9.6** Context can substitute for a lack of appropriate prototypes in concept identification.

◖◗ Language—Don't Leave Home without It

Gateway Question: What is the role of language in thinking?

As we have seen, thinking may occur without language. Everyone has searched for a word to express an idea that exists as a vague image or feeling. Nevertheless, most thinking relies heavily on language, because words *encode* (translate) the world into mental symbols that are easy to manipulate (● Figure 9.7).

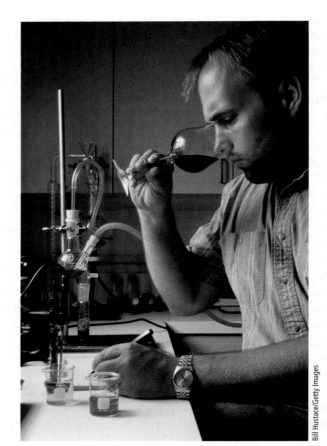

● **Figure 9.7** Wine tasting illustrates the encoding function of language. To communicate their experiences to others, wine connoisseurs must put taste sensations into words. The wine you see here is "Marked by deeply concentrated nuances of plum, blackberry, and currant, with a nice balance of tannins and acid, building to a spicy oak finish." (Don't try this with a Pop-tart!)

HUMAN DIVERSITY

Bilingualism—*Si o No, Oui ou Non,* Yes or No?

Are there advantages to being able to speak more than one language? Definitely. **Bilingualism** is the ability to speak two languages. Studies have found that students who learn to speak two languages well have better mental flexibility, general language skills, control of attention, and problem-solving abilities (Bialystok, 2001; Craik & Bialystok, 2005; Cromdal, 1999).

Unfortunately, millions of minority American children who do not speak English at home experience *subtractive bilingualism.* Immersed in English-only classrooms, where they are expected to "sink or swim," they usually end up losing some of their native language skills. Such children risk becoming less than fully competent in *both* their first and second languages. In addition, they tend to fall behind educationally. As they struggle with English, their grasp of arithmetic, social studies, science, and other subjects may also suffer. In short, English-only instruction can

leave them poorly prepared to succeed in the majority culture (Genesee, Paradis, & Crago, 2004; Matthews & Matthews, 2004).

For the majority of children who speak English at home the picture can be quite different, because learning a second language is almost always beneficial. It poses no threat to the child's home language and improves a variety of cognitive skills. This has been called *additive bilingualism* because learning a second language adds to a child's overall competence (Hinkel, 2005).

An approach called **two-way bilingual education** can help children benefit from bilingualism and avoid its drawbacks (Lessow-Hurley, 2005). In such programs, majority group children and children with limited English skills are taught part of the day in English and part in a second language. Both majority and minority language speakers become fluent in two languages, and they perform as well or better than single-

language students in English and general academic abilities.

Then why isn't two-way bilingual education more widely used? Bilingual education tends to be politically unpopular among majority language speakers. Language is an important sign of group membership. Even where the majority culture is highly dominant, some of its members may feel that recent immigrants and "foreign languages" are eroding their culture. Regardless, an ability to think and communicate in a second language is a wonderful gift.

Although minority children are certainly at a disadvantage if they do not become proficient in English, native English speakers may be shortchanged by English-only schools as well. Given the cognitive benefits, fostering bilingualism may turn out to be one of the best ways to improve competitiveness in our rapidly globalizing information economy.

The study of meaning in words and language is known as **semantics.** It is here that the link between words and thinking becomes most evident. Suppose, on an intelligence test, you were asked to circle the word that does not belong in this series:

| SKYSCRAPER | CATHEDRAL | TEMPLE | PRAYER |

If you circled *prayer,* you answered as most people do. Now try another problem, again circling the odd item:

| CATHEDRAL | PRAYER | TEMPLE | SKYSCRAPER |

Did you circle *skyscraper* this time? The new order subtly alters the meaning of the last word (Mayer, 1995). This occurs because words get much of their meaning from *context.* For example, the word "shot" means different things when we are thinking of marksmanship, bartending, medicine, photography, or golf (Carroll, 2008; Miller, 1999).

Likewise, the words we use can greatly affect our thinking: Has one country's army "invaded" another or "effected a protective incursion"? Is the martini "half full" or "half empty"? Would you rather eat "rare prime beef" or "bloody slab of dead cow"? More subtle effects also occur. For example, most people have difficulty quickly naming the color of the ink used to print the words in the bottom two rows of ● Figure 9.8. The word meanings are just too strong to ignore.

Language also plays a major role in defining ethnic communities and other social groups. Thus, language can be a bridge or a

PURPLE	BLUE	GREEN	GREEN
RED	PURPLE	RED	GREEN

● **Figure 9.8** The Stroop interference task. Test yourself by naming the colors in the top two rows as quickly as you can. Then name the colors of the *ink* used to print the words in the bottom two rows (do not read the words themselves). Was it harder to name the ink colors in the bottom rows? (Adapted from MacLeod, 2005.)

barrier between cultures. Translating languages can cause a rash of semantic problems. Perhaps the San Jose, California, public library can be excused for once displaying a large banner that was supposed to say "You are welcome" in a native Philippine language.

Denotative meaning The exact dictionary definition of a word or concept; its objective meaning.

Connotative meaning The subjective, personal, or emotional meaning of a word or concept.

Bilingualism An ability to speak two languages.

Two-way bilingual education A program in which English-speaking children and children with limited English proficiency are taught half the day in English and half in a second language.

Semantics The study of meanings in words and language.

The banner actually said "You are circumcised." However, in more important situations, such as in international business and diplomacy, avoiding semantic confusion may be vital. (See "Bilingualism—*Si o No, Oui ou Non,* Yes or No?")

The Structure of Language

What does it take to make a language? First, a language must provide *symbols* that stand for objects and ideas (Jay, 2003). The symbols we call words are built out of **phonemes** (FOE-neems: basic speech sounds) and **morphemes** (MOR-feems: speech sounds collected into meaningful units, such as syllables or words). For instance, in English the sounds *m, b, w,* and *a* cannot form a syllable *mbwa.* In Swahili, they can. (Also, see ● Figure 9.9.)

Next, a language must have a **grammar,** or set of rules for making sounds into words and words into sentences (Reed, 2007). One part of grammar, known as **syntax,** concerns rules for word order. Syntax is important because rearranging words almost always changes the meaning of a sentence: "Dog bites man" versus "Man bites dog."

Traditional grammar is concerned with "surface" language—the sentences we actually speak. Linguist Noam Chomsky has focused instead on the unspoken rules we use to change core ideas into various sentences. Chomsky (1986) believes that we do not learn all the sentences we might ever say. Rather, we actively *create* them by applying **transformation rules** to universal, core patterns. We use these rules to change a simple declarative sentence to other voices or forms (past tense, passive voice, and so forth). For example, the core sentence "Dog bites man" can be transformed to these patterns (and others as well):

Past: The dog bit the man.
Passive: The man was bitten by the dog.
Negative: The dog did not bite the man.
Question: Did the dog bite the man?

Children seem to be using transformation rules when they say things such as "I runned home." That is, the child applied the normal past tense rule to the irregular verb *to run.*

A true language is also *productive*—it can generate new thoughts or ideas. In fact, words can be rearranged to produce a nearly infinite number of sentences. Some are silly: "Please don't feed me to the goldfish." Some are profound: "We hold these truths to be self-evident, that all men are created equal." In either case, the productive quality of language makes it a powerful tool for thinking.

Gestural Languages

Contrary to common belief, language is not limited to speech. Consider the case of Ildefonso, a young man who was born deaf. At age 24, Ildefonso had never communicated with another human, except by mime. Then at last, Ildefonso had a breakthrough: After much hard work with a sign language teacher, he understood the link between a cat and the gesture for it. At that magic moment, he grasped the idea that "cat" could be communicated to another person, just by signing the word.

American Sign Language (ASL), a gestural language, made Ildefonso's long-awaited breakthrough possible. ASL is not pantomime or a code. It is a true language, like German, Spanish, or Japanese (Liddell, 2003). In fact, those who use other gestural languages, such as French Sign, Chinese Sign, or Old Kentish Sign, do not understand ASL.

Although ASL has a *spatial* grammar, syntax, and semantics all its own (● Figure 9.10), both speech and signing follow similar universal language patterns. Signing children pass through the

Look at   **Stare**

● **Figure 9.10** ASL has only 3,000 root signs, compared with roughly 600,000 words in English. However, variations in signs make ASL a highly expressive language. For example, the sign LOOK-AT can be varied in ways to make it mean look at me, look at her, look at each, stare at, gaze, watch, look for a long time, look at again and again, reminisce, sightsee, look forward to, predict, anticipate, browse, and many more variations.

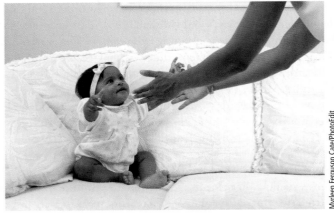

Infants can express the idea "pick me up" in gestures before they can make the same request in words. Their progression from gestures to speech may mirror the evolution of human language abilities (Stokoe, 2001).

Albanian	mak, mak
Chinese	gua, gua
Dutch	rap, rap
English	quack, quack
French	coin, coin
Italian	qua, qua
Spanish	cuá, cuá
Swedish	kvack, kvack
Turkish	vak, vak

Guy Edwardes/Getty Images

● **Figure 9.9** Animals around the world make pretty much the same sounds. Notice, however, how various languages use slightly different phonemes to express the sound a duck makes.

Nouns		Verbs		Concepts Conditionals		Adjectives (Colors)	
Sarah	Chocolate	Is	Give	Same	Different	Red	Yellow

● **Figure 9.11** Here is a sample of some of the word-symbols that Sarah the chimpanzee used to communicate with humans. (Premack & Premack, 1972. Teaching language to an ape. *Scientific American*, Oct., 92-99. Copyright © 1972 by Scientific American. All rights reserved. Reproduced by permission.)

stages of language development at about the same age as speaking children do. Some psychologists now believe that speech evolved from gestures, far back in human history (Corballis, 2002). Gestures help us string words together as we speak (Morsella & Krauss, 2004). Some people would have difficulty speaking with their hands tied to their sides. Do you ever make hand gestures when you are speaking on the phone? If so, you may be displaying a remnant of the gestural origins of language. Perhaps that's also why the same brain areas become more active when a person speaks or signs (Emmorey et al., 2003).

Sign languages naturally arise out of a need to communicate visually. But they also embody a personal identity and define a distinct community. Those who "speak" sign share not just a language, but a rich culture as well (Singleton & Newport, 2004).

The Animal Language Debate

Do animals use language? Animals do communicate. The cries, gestures, and mating calls of animals have broad meanings immediately understood by other animals of the same species (Searcy & Nowicki, 2005). For the most part, however, natural animal communication is quite limited. Even apes and monkeys make only a few dozen distinct cries, which carry messages such as "attack," "flee," or "food here." More important, animal communication lacks the productive quality of human language. For example, when a monkey gives an "eagle distress call," it means something like, "I see an eagle." The monkey has no way of saying, "I don't see an eagle," or "Thank heavens that wasn't an eagle," or "That sucker I saw yesterday was some huge eagle" (Pinker & Jackendoff, 2005). Let's consider some of psychology's successes and failures in trying to teach animals to use language.

Talking Chimps

Early attempts to teach chimps to talk were a dismal failure. The world record was held by Viki, a chimp who could say only four words ("mama," "papa," "cup," and "up") after 6 years of intensive training (Fleming, 1974; Hayes, 1951). (Actually, all four words sounded something like a belch.) Then there was a breakthrough. Beatrix and Allen Gardner used operant conditioning and imitation to teach a female chimp named Washoe to use American Sign Language. Washoe was soon able to put together primitive sentence strings like "Come-gimme sweet," "Out please," "Gimme tickle," and "Open food drink." At her peak, Washoe could construct 6-word sentences and use about 240 signs (Gardner & Gardner, 1989).

A chimp named Sarah was another well-known pupil of human language. David Premack taught Sarah to use 130 "words" consisting of plastic chips arranged on a magnetized board (● Figure 9.11). From the beginning of her training, Sarah was required to use proper word order. She learned to answer questions; to label things "same" or "different"; to classify objects by color, shape, and size; and to form compound sentences (Premack & Premack, 1983). One of Sarah's top achievements was her use of conditional sentences. A *conditional statement* contains a qualification, often in the if/then form: "If Sarah take apple, then Mary give Sarah chocolate." "If Sarah take banana, then Mary no give Sarah chocolate" (● Figure 9.12).

Can it be said with certainty that the chimps understand such interchanges? Most researchers working with chimps believe that

● **Figure 9.12** After reading the message "Sarah insert apple pail banana dish" on the magnetic board, Sarah performed the actions as directed. (From "Teaching Language to an Ape," by Ann J. Premack and David Premack. Copyright © 1972 Scientific American, Inc. Reprinted by permission of Eric Mose, Jr.)

Phonemes The basic speech sounds of a language.

Morphemes The smallest meaningful units in a language, such as syllables or words.

Grammar A set of rules for combining language units into meaningful speech or writing.

Syntax Rules for ordering words when forming sentences.

Transformation rules Rules by which a simple declarative sentence may be changed to other voices or forms (past tense, passive voice, and so forth).

they have indeed communicated with them. Especially striking are the chimps' spontaneous responses. Washoe once "wet" on psychologist Roger Fouts's back while riding on his shoulders. When Fouts asked, with some annoyance, why she had done it, Washoe signed, "It's funny!"

Criticisms

Such interchanges are impressive. But communication and real language usage are different things. Even untrained chimps use simple gestures to communicate with humans. For example, a chimp will point at a banana that is out of reach, while glancing back and forth between the banana and a person standing nearby (Leavens & Hopkins, 1998). (The meaning of the gesture is clear. The meaning of the exasperated look on the chimp's face is less certain, but it probably means, "Give me the banana, you idiot.")

Also, problems with syntax (word order) have plagued almost all animal language studies. For example, when a chimp named Nim Chimpsky (no relation to Noam Chomsky) wanted an orange, he would typically signal a grammarless string of words: "Give orange me give eat orange me eat orange give me eat orange give me you." This might be communication, but it is not language.

Lexigrams

More recently, Kanzi, a pygmy chimpanzee studied by Duane Rumbaugh and Sue Savage-Rumbaugh, has learned to communicate by pushing buttons on a computer keyboard. Each of the 250 buttons is marked with a *lexigram,* or geometric word-symbol (● Figure 9.13). Using the lexigrams, Kanzi can create primitive sentences several words long. He can also understand about 650 spoken sentences. During testing, Kanzi hears spoken words over headphones, so his caretakers cannot visually prompt him (Savage-Rumbaugh & Lewin, 1996; Savage-Rumbaugh, Shanker, & Taylor, 1998).

Kanzi's sentences consistently follow correct word order. Like a child learning language, Kanzi picked up some rules from his caregivers (Segerdahl, Fields, & Savage-Rumbaugh, 2005). However,

● **Figure 9.13** Kanzi's language learning has been impressive. He can comprehend spoken English words. He can identify lexigram symbols when he hears corresponding words. He can use lexigrams when the objects they refer to are absent, and he can, if asked, lead someone to the object. All these skills were acquired through observation, not conditioning (Savage-Rumbaugh et al., 1990).

The Great Ape Trust of Iowa

he has developed other patterns on his own. For example, Kanzi usually places action symbols in the order he wants to carry them out, such as "chase tickle" or "chase hide." In this respect, Kanzi's grammar is on a par with that of a 2-year-old child (Savage-Rumbaugh et al., 1993).

Kanzi's ability to invent a simple grammar may help us better understand the roots of human language. It is certainly the strongest answer yet to critics (Benson et al., 2002). On the other hand, Chomsky insists that if chimps were biologically capable of language they would use it on their own. Although the issue is far from resolved, such research may unravel the mysteries of language learning.

KNOWLEDGE BUILDER
Imagery, Concepts, and Language

RECITE

1. List three primary units of thought: _____ _____ _____

2. Our reliance on imagery in thinking means that problem solving is impaired by the use of language or symbols. T or F?

3. A person doing mental rotation would need to use which basic unit of thought?
   a. concepts
   b. language
   c. images
   d. symbols

4. Our ability to think about movements and actions is aided by
   a. kinesthetic imagery
   b. rotational concepts
   c. mental calculation
   d. relational concepts

5. A *mup* is defined as anything that is small, blue, and hairy. *Mup* is a _____ concept.

6. The connotative meaning of the word "naked" is "having no clothes." T or F?

7. The basic speech sounds are called _____; the smallest meaningful units of speech are called _____.

8. Noam Chomsky believes that we use _____ to change core declarative sentences into other voices and forms.
   a. phonemes
   b. transformation rules
   c. conditional statements
   d. conjunctive encoding

REFLECT

Critical Thinking

9. A Democrat and a Republican are asked to rate the word "democratic" on the semantic differential. Under what conditions would their ratings be most alike?

10. Chimpanzees and other apes are intelligent and entertaining animals. If you were doing language research with a chimp, what major problem would you have to guard against?

Relate

Name some ways in which you have used imagery in the thinking you have done today.

Write a conceptual rule for the following idea: *unicycle.* Were you able to define the concept with a rule? Would positive and negative instances help make the concept clearer for others?

A true sports car has two seats, a powerful engine, good brakes, and excellent handling. What kind of a concept is the term *sports car?* What do you think of as a prototypical sports car?

Continued

You must learn to communicate with an alien life form whose language cannot be reproduced by the human voice. Do you think it would be better to use a gestural language or lexigrams? Why?

(rotated text, upside down:) researchers spend many hours "conversing" with chimps. ing human characteristics to animals) is especially difficult to avoid when cal party or a candidate. **10.** The problem of anthropomorphizing (ascribing) they both assume the word refers to a form of government, not a political listed. **2.** F **3.** c **4.** a **5.** conjunctive **6.** F **7.** phonemes, morphemes **8.** b **9.** If **Answers: 1.** images, concepts, language or symbols (others could be

⬤ Problem Solving—Getting an Answer in Sight

Gateway Question: What do we know about problem solving?

We all solve many problems every day. Problem solving can be as commonplace as figuring out how to make a nonpoisonous meal out of leftovers or as significant as developing a cure for cancer. How do we solve such problems? A good way to start a discussion of problem solving is to solve a problem. Give this one a try.

> A famous ocean liner (the *Queen Latifah*) is steaming toward port at 20 miles per hour. The ocean liner is 50 miles from shore when a seagull takes off from its deck and flies toward port. At the same instant, a speedboat leaves port at 30 miles per hour. The bird flies back and forth between the speedboat and the *Queen Latifah* at a speed of 40 miles per hour. How far will the bird have flown when the two boats pass?

If you don't immediately see the answer to this problem, read it again. (The answer is revealed in the "Insightful Solutions" section.)

Mechanical Solutions

For routine problems, a **mechanical solution** may be adequate. Mechanical solutions are achieved by trial and error or by rote. If you forget the combination to your bike lock, you may be able to discover it by trial and error. In an era of high-speed computers, many trial-and-error solutions are best left to machines. A computer could generate all possible combinations of the five numbers on the lock in a split second. (Of course, it would take a long time to try them all.) When a problem is solved by *rote,* thinking is guided by an **algorithm,** or learned set of rules that always leads to a correct solution. A simple example of an algorithm is the steps needed to divide one number into another (by doing arithmetic, not by using a calculator).

If you have a good background in math, you may have solved the problem of the bird and the boats by rote. (Your authors hope you didn't. There is an easier solution.)

Solutions by Understanding

Many problems cannot be solved mechanically. In that case, **understanding** (deeper comprehension of a problem) is necessary. Try this problem:

> A person has an inoperable stomach tumor. A device is available that produces rays that at high intensity will destroy tissue (both healthy and dis-

eased). How can the tumor be destroyed without damaging surrounding tissue? (Also see the sketch in ⬤ Figure 9.14.)

What does this problem show about problem solving? German psychologist Karl Duncker gave college students this problem in a classic series of studies. Duncker asked them to think aloud as they worked. He found that successful students first had to discover the *general properties* of a correct solution. A **general solution** defines the requirements for success but not in enough detail to guide further action. This phase was complete when students realized that the intensity of the rays had to be lowered on their way to the tumor. Then, in the second phase, they proposed a number of **functional** (workable) **solutions** and selected the best one (Duncker, 1945). (One solution is to focus weak rays on the tumor from several angles. Another is to rotate the person's body, to minimize exposure of healthy tissue.)

It might help to summarize with a more familiar example. Almost everyone who has tried to play a poker game like Texas Hold 'Em begins at the mechanical, *trial-and-error level.* If you want to take the easy, *rote,* route, printed odds tables are available for every stage of play. In time, those who persist begin to *understand* the *general properties* of the game. After that, they can play fast enough to keep up with other players.

Heuristics

"You can't get there from here," or so it often seems when facing a problem. Solving problems often requires a strategy. If the number of alternatives is small, a **random search strategy** may work. This is another example of trial-and-error thinking in which all possibilities are tried, more or less randomly. Imagine that you are traveling and decide to look up an old friend, Janet Smith, in a city you are visiting. You open the phone book and find 47 J. Smiths listed. Of course, you could dial each number until you find the right one. "Forget it," you say to yourself. "Is there any way I can

⬤ **Figure 9.14** A schematic representation of Duncker's tumor problem. The dark spot represents a tumor surrounded by healthy tissue. How can the tumor be destroyed without injuring surrounding tissue? (Duncker, 1945. On problem solving. *Psychological Monographs,* 58(270). Copyright © 1945 APA. Reprinted with permission of the publisher.)

Mechanical solution A problem solution achieved by trial and error or by a fixed procedure based on learned rules.

Algorithm A learned set of rules that always leads to the correct solution of a problem.

Understanding In problem solving, a deeper comprehension of the nature of the problem.

General solution A solution that correctly states the requirements for success but not in enough detail for further action.

Functional solution A detailed, practical, and workable solution.

Random search strategy Trying possible solutions to a problem in a more or less random order.

narrow the search?" "Oh, yeah! I remember hearing that Janet lives by the beach." Then you take out a map and call only the numbers with addresses near the waterfront (Hunt & Ellis, 2004).

The approach used in this example is a **heuristic** (hew-RIS-tik: a strategy for identifying and evaluating problem solutions). Typically, a heuristic is a "rule of thumb" that *reduces the number of alternatives* thinkers must consider (Solso, MacLin, & MacLin, 2008). Although this raises the odds of success, it does not guarantee a solution. Here are some heuristic strategies that often work:

- Try to identify how the current state of affairs differs from the desired goal. Then find steps that will reduce the difference.
- Try working backward from the desired goal to the starting point or current state.
- If you can't reach the goal directly, try to identify an intermediate goal or subproblem that at least gets you closer.
- Represent the problem in other ways, with graphs, diagrams, or analogies, for instance.
- Generate a possible solution and test it. Doing so may eliminate many alternatives, or it may clarify what is needed for a solution.

Experts and Novices

Research has shown that expert skills are based on *acquired strategies* (learned heuristics) and specific *organized knowledge* (systematic information). Experts are better able to see the true nature of problems and to define them in terms of general principles (Anderson, 2005). For example, chess experts are much more likely than novices to have heuristics available for solving problems. However, what really sets master players apart is their ability to intuitively recognize *patterns* that suggest what lines of play should be explored next. This helps eliminate a large number of possible moves. The chess master, therefore, does not waste time exploring unproductive pathways (Ross, 2006).

In other words, becoming a star performer does not come from some general strengthening of the mind. Master chess players don't necessarily have better memories than beginners (except for realistic chess positions) (Gobet & Simon, 1996; Solso, MacLin, & MacLin, 2008) (● Figure 9.15). And, typically, they don't explore more moves ahead than lesser players.

Expertise also allows more *automatic processing,* or fast, fairly effortless thinking based on experience with similar problems. Automatic processing frees "space" in short-term memory, making it easier to work on the problem. At the highest skill levels, expert performers tend to rise above rules and plans. Their decisions, thinking, and actions become rapid and fluid. Thus, when a chess master recognizes a pattern on the chessboard, the most desirable tactic comes to mind almost immediately.

Mind you, this capacity comes at a price. Expert chess players can automatically recognize 50,000 to 100,000 patterns, a level of skill that takes about 10 years to build up (Ross, 2006). Many other kinds of expertise take about 10 years to develop, suggesting that American inventor Thomas Edison was right when he said, "Genius is one percent inspiration and ninety-nine percent perspiration."

Real Game **Random Placement**

Black

White

● **Figure 9.15** The left chessboard shows a realistic game. The right chessboard is a random arrangement of pieces. Expert chess players can memorize the left board at a glance, yet they are no better than beginners at memorizing the random board (Ross, 2006). Expert performance at most thinking tasks is based on acquired strategies and knowledge. If you would like to excel at a profession or a mental skill, plan on adding to your knowledge every day (Goldstein, 2008). (Solso, MacLin, & MacLin, 2005. *Cognitive Psychology* (7th ed.) Boston: Allyn & Bacon.)

Insightful Solutions

A thinker who suddenly solves a problem has experienced **insight.** Insight is so rapid and clear that we may wonder why we didn't see the solution sooner (Schilling, 2005). Insights are usually based on reorganizing a problem. This allows us to see problems in new ways and makes their solutions seem obvious (Robertson, 2001).

Let's return now to the problem of the boats and the bird. The best way to solve it is by insight. Because the boats will cover the 50-mile distance in exactly 1 hour, and the bird flies 40 miles per hour, the bird will have flown 40 miles when the boats meet. Very little math is necessary if you have insight into this problem. ● Figure 9.16 lists some additional insight problems you may want to try. (The answers can be found in ● Table 9.1.)

The Nature of Insight

Psychologists Robert Sternberg and Janet Davidson (1982) believe that insight involves three abilities. The first is *selective encoding,* which refers to selecting information that is relevant to a problem, while ignoring distractions. For example, consider the following problem:

If you have white socks and black socks in your drawer, mixed in the ratio of 4 to 5, how many socks will you have to take out to ensure you have a pair of the same color?

A person who recognizes that "mixed in a ratio of 4 to 5" is irrelevant will be more likely to come up with the correct answer of 3 socks.

Insight also relies on *selective combination,* or bringing together seemingly unrelated bits of useful information. Try this sample problem:

With a 7-minute hourglass and an 11-minute hourglass, what is the simplest way to time the boiling of an egg for 15 minutes?

Water lilies

Problem: Water lilies growing in a pond double in area every 24 hours. On the first day of spring, only one lily pad is on the surface of the pond. Sixty days later, the pond is entirely covered. On what day is the pond half-covered?

Twenty dollars

Problem: Jessica and Blair both have the same amount of money. How much must Jessica give Blair so that Blair has $20 more than Jessica?

How many pets?

Problem: How many pets do you have if all of them are birds except two, all of them are cats except two, and all of them are dogs except two?

Between 2 and 3

Problem: What one mathematical symbol can you place between 2 and 3 that results in a number greater than 2 and less than 3?

One word

Problem: Rearrange the letters NEWDOOR to make one word.

● **Figure 9.16**

Table 9.1 ● Solutions to Insight Problems

Water lilies: Day 59
Twenty dollars: $10
How many pets: Three (one bird, one cat, and one dog)
Between 2 and 3: A decimal point
One word: ONE WORD (You may object that the answer is two words, but the problem called for the answer to be "one word," and it is.)

The answer requires using both hourglasses in combination. First, the 7-minute and the 11-minute hourglasses are started. When the 7-minute hourglass runs out, it's time to begin boiling the egg. At this point, 4 minutes remain on the 11-minute hourglass. Thus, when it runs out it is simply turned over. When it runs out again, 15 minutes will have passed.

A third source of insights is *selective comparison.* This is the ability to compare new problems with old information or with problems already solved. A good example is the hat rack problem, in which subjects must build a structure that can support an overcoat in the middle of a room. Each person is given only two long sticks and a C-clamp to work with. The solution, shown in ● Figure 9.17, is to clamp the two sticks together so that they are wedged between the floor and ceiling. If you were given this problem, you would be more likely to solve it if you first thought of how pole lamps are wedged between floor and ceiling. (See "How to Weigh an Elephant.")

Fixations

One of the most important barriers to problem solving is **fixation,** the tendency to get "hung up" on wrong solutions or to become blind to alternatives. Usually this occurs when we place unnecessary restric-

● **Figure 9.17** A solution to the hat rack problem.

tions on our thinking (German & Barrett, 2005). How, for example, could you plant four small trees so that each is an equal distance from all the others? (The answer is shown in ● Figure 9.18.)

A prime example of restricted thinking is **functional fixedness.** This is an inability to see new uses (functions) for familiar objects or for things that were used in a particular way (German & Barrett, 2005). If you have ever used a dime as a screwdriver, you've overcome functional fixedness.

Heuristic Any strategy or technique that aids problem solving, especially by limiting the number of possible solutions to be tried.

Insight A sudden mental reorganization of a problem that makes the solution obvious.

Fixation The tendency to repeat wrong solutions or faulty responses, especially as a result of becoming blind to alternatives.

Functional fixedness A rigidity in problem solving caused by an inability to see new uses for familiar objects.

HUMAN DIVERSITY

How to Weigh an Elephant

Does the culture we grow up in affect our ability to use selective comparison to solve problems? See if you can solve this problem:

A treasure hunter wanted to explore a cave, but he was afraid that he might get lost. Obviously, he did not have a map of the cave; all that he had with him were some common items such as a flashlight and a bag. What could he do to make sure he did not get lost trying to get back out of the cave later? (Adapted from Chen, Mo, & Honomichl, 2004.)

To solve his problem, the man could leave a trail of small objects, such as pebbles or sand, while traveling through the cave, and then follow this trail out to exit.

Seventy-five percent of American college students, but only 25 percent of Chinese students, were able to solve the cave problem. Why was there such a difference in the two groups? It seems that American students benefited from having heard the story of Hansel

and Gretel when they were growing up. As you may recall, Hansel and Gretel were able to find their way out of the woods because Hansel made a trail of breadcrumbs that led back home (Chen, Mo, & Honomichl, 2004). Now try this problem:

In a village by a river, the chief of a tribe guards a sacred stone statue. Every year, the chief goes downriver to the next village to collect taxes. There, he places the statue in a tub at one end of a hanging balance. To pay their taxes, the villagers have to fill a tub at the other end of the scale with gold coins until the scale balances. This year, the chief forgot to bring his balance scale. How can he figure out how much gold to collect to match the statue's weight? (Adapted from Chen, Mo, & Honomichl, 2004.)

To solve this problem, the chief could put a tub in the river, and place the statue in the tub. Then he could mark the water level on

the outside of the tub. To pay their taxes, the villagers would have to put gold coins in the tub until it sank to the same level as it did when the statue was in it.

Sixty-nine percent of Chinese students, but only 8 percent of American students, were able to solve this problem. Again, it seems that being exposed to a similar problem in the past was helpful. Most Chinese are familiar with a traditional tale about weighing an elephant that is too big to put on a scale. In the story, the elephant is placed in a boat and the water level is marked. After the elephant is removed, the boat is filled with small stones until the water again reaches the mark. Then, each of the stones is weighed on a small scale and the total weight of the elephant is calculated (Chen, Mo, & Honomichl, 2004).

Every culture prepares its members to solve some types of problems more easily than others. As a result, learning about other cultures can make us more flexible and resourceful thinkers—and that's no fairy tale.

● **Figure 9.18** Four trees can be placed equidistant from one another by piling dirt into a mound. Three of the trees are planted equal distances apart around the base of the mound. The fourth tree is planted on the top of the mound. If you were fixated on arrangements that involve level ground, you may have been blind to this three-dimensional solution.

(a) (b) (c)

● **Figure 9.19** Materials for solving the candle problem were given to subjects in boxes *(a)* or separately *(b)*. Functional fixedness caused by condition *(a)* interfered with solving the problem. The solution to the problem is shown in *(c)*.

How does functional fixedness affect problem solving? Karl Duncker illustrated the effects of functional fixedness by asking students to mount a candle on a vertical board so the candle could burn normally. Duncker gave each student three candles, some matches, some cardboard boxes, some thumbtacks, and other items. Half of Duncker's subjects received these items *inside* the cardboard boxes. The others were given all the items, including the boxes, spread out on a tabletop.

Duncker found that when the items were in the boxes, solving the problem was very difficult. Why? If students saw the boxes as

containers, they didn't realize the boxes might be part of the solution. (If you haven't guessed the solution, check ● Figure 9.19.) Undoubtedly, we could avoid many fixations by being more flexible in categorizing the world (Langer, 2000). For instance, creative thinking could be facilitated in the container problem by saying "This *could be* a box," instead of "This *is* a box." When tested with the candle problem, 5-year-old children show no signs of functional fixedness. Apparently, this is because they have had less experience with the use of various objects. It is sometimes said that to be more creative, you should try to see the world without preconceptions, as if through the eyes of a child. In the case of functional fixedness that may actually be true (German & Defeyter, 2000).

Common Barriers to Problem Solving

Functional fixedness is just one of the mental blocks that prevent insight. Here's an example of another: A $5 bill is placed on a table, and a stack of objects is balanced precariously on top of the bill. How can the bill be removed without touching or moving the objects? A good answer is to split the bill on one of its edges. Gently pulling from opposite ends will tear the bill in half and remove it without toppling the objects. Many people fail to see this solution because they have learned not to destroy money (Adams, 1988). Notice again the impact of placing something in a category, in this case, "things of value" (which should not be destroyed). Other common mental blocks can hinder problem solving, too, as listed here.

1. **Emotional barriers:** inhibition and fear of making a fool of oneself, fear of making a mistake, inability to tolerate ambiguity, excessive self-criticism
   Example: An architect is afraid to try an unconventional design because she fears that other architects will think it is frivolous.
2. **Cultural barriers:** values that hold that fantasy is a waste of time; that playfulness is for children only; that reason, logic, and numbers are good; that feelings, intuitions, pleasure, and humor are bad or have no value in the serious business of problem solving
   Example: A corporate manager wants to solve a business problem but becomes stern and angry when members of his marketing team joke playfully about possible solutions.
3. **Learned barriers:** conventions about uses (functional fixedness), meanings, possibilities, taboos.
   Example: A cook doesn't have any clean mixing bowls and fails to see that he could use a frying pan as a bowl.
4. **Perceptual barriers:** habits leading to a failure to identify important elements of a problem
   Example: A beginning artist concentrates on drawing a vase of flowers without seeing that the "empty" spaces around the vase are part of the composition, too.

KNOWLEDGE BUILDER
Problem Solving
RECITE
1. Insight refers to rote, or trial-and-error, problem solving. T or F?
2. After you find a general solution to a problem you must usually also find a
   a. heuristic
   b. search strategy
   c. fixation
   d. functional solution
3. Problem-solving strategies that guide the search for solutions are called _____.

4. A common element underlying insight is that information is encoded, combined, and compared
   a. mechanically
   b. by rote
   c. functionally
   d. selectively
5. Functional fixedness is a major barrier to
   a. insightful problem solving
   b. using random search strategies
   c. mechanical problem solving
   d. achieving fixations through problem solving
6. Organized knowledge, acquired heuristics, and the ability to recognize patterns are all characteristics of human expertise. T or F?

REFLECT
Critical Thinking
7. Do you think that it is true that "a problem clearly defined is a problem half solved"?
8. Sea otters select suitably sized rocks and use them to hammer shellfish loose for eating. They then use the rock to open the shell. Does this qualify as thinking?

Relate
Identify at least one problem you have solved mechanically or by rote. Now identify a problem you solved by understanding. Did the second problem involve finding a general solution or a functional solution? Or both? What heuristics did you use to solve the problem?

What is the best insightful solution you've ever come up with? Did it involve selective encoding, combination, or comparison?

Can you think of a time when you overcame functional fixedness to solve a problem?

Answers: 1. F **2.** d **3.** heuristics **4.** d **5.** a **6.** T **7.** Although this might be an overstatement, it is true that clearly defining a starting point and the desired goal can serve as a heuristic in problem solving. **8.** Psychologist Donald Griffin (1992) believes it does because thinking is implied by actions that appear to be planned with an awareness of likely results.

🔴 Creative Thinking—Down Roads Less Traveled

Gateway Question: What is creative thinking?

Original ideas have changed the course of human history. Much of what we now take for granted in art, medicine, music, technology, and science was once regarded as radical or impossible. How do creative thinkers like Steven Hawking achieve the breakthroughs that advance us into new realms? Creativity is elusive. Nevertheless, psychologists have learned a great deal about how creativity occurs and how to promote it, as you will soon learn.

We have seen that problem solving may be mechanical, insightful, or based on understanding. To this we can add that thinking may be **inductive** (going from specific facts or observations to

Inductive thought Thinking in which a general rule or principle is gathered from a series of specific examples; for instance, inferring the laws of gravity by observing many falling objects.

general principles) or **deductive** (going from general principles to specific situations). Thinking may also be **logical** (proceeding from given information to new conclusions on the basis of explicit rules) or **illogical** (intuitive, associative, or personal).

What distinguishes creative thinking from more routine problem solving? Creative thinking involves all these thinking styles, plus *fluency, flexibility,* and *originality.* Let's say that you would like to find creative uses for the billions of plastic containers discarded each year. The creativity of your suggestions could be rated in this way: **Fluency** is defined as the total number of suggestions you are able to make. **Flexibility** is the number of times you shift from one class of possible uses to another. **Originality** refers to how novel or unusual your ideas are. By counting the number of times you showed fluency, flexibility, and originality, we could rate your creativity, or capacity for *divergent thinking* (Baer, 1993; Runco, 2004).

In routine problem solving or thinking, there is one correct answer, and the problem is to find it (Cropley, 2006). This leads to **convergent thinking** (lines of thought converge on the answer). **Divergent thinking** is the reverse, in which many possibilities are developed from one starting point (Baer, 1993). (See ● Table 9.2 for some examples.) Rather than repeating learned solutions, cre-

Table 9.2 ● Convergent and Divergent Problems

Convergent Problems
- What is the area of a triangle that is 3 feet wide at the base and 2 feet tall?
- Erica is shorter than Zoey but taller than Carlo, and Carlo is taller than Jared. Who is the second tallest?
- If you simultaneously drop a baseball and a bowling ball from a tall building, which will hit the ground first?

Divergent Problems
- What objects can you think of that begin with the letters BR?
- How could discarded aluminum cans be put to use?
- Write a poem about fire and ice.

The first paper clip was patented in 1899. Competition for sales, combined with divergent thinking, has resulted in a remarkable array of alternative designs. These are drawings of just a few of the variations that have appeared over the years. (Adapted from Kim, 2000.)

ative thinking produces new answers, ideas, or patterns (Davidovitch & Milgram, 2006).

Tests of Creativity

Divergent thinking can be measured in several ways. In the *Unusual Uses Test,* you would be asked to think of as many uses as possible for some object, such as the plastic containers mentioned earlier. In the *Consequences Test,* you would list the consequences that would follow a basic change in the world. For example, you might be asked, "What would happen if everyone suddenly lost their sense of balance and could no longer stay upright?" People try to list as many reactions as possible. If you were to take the *Anagrams Test,* you would be given a word such as "creativity" and asked to make as many new words as possible by rearranging the letters. Each of these tests can be scored for fluency, flexibility, and originality. (For an example of other tests of divergent thinking, see ● Figure 9.20.) Tests of divergent thinking seem to tap something quite different from intelligence. Generally, there is little correlation between creativity tests and IQ test scores (Preckel, Holling, & Wiese, 2006).

Creativity tests have been useful, but they are not the whole story. If you want to predict whether a person will be creative in the future, it helps to look at two more kinds of information (Feldhusen & Goh, 1995):

- The *products* of creative thinking (such as essays, poems, drawings, or constructed objects) are often more informative than test results. When creative people are asked to actually produce something, others tend to judge their work as creative.
- A simple listing of a person's *past creative activities and achievements* is an excellent guide to the likelihood that she or he will be creative in the future.

Isn't creativity more than divergent thought? What if a person comes up with a large number of useless answers to a problem? A good question. Divergent thinking is an important part of creativ-

Fluency is an important part of creative thinking. Mozart produced more than 600 pieces of music. Shakespeare wrote 154 sonnets. Salvador Dali (shown here) created more than 1,500 paintings, as well as sculptures, drawings, illustrations, books, and even an animated cartoon. Not all these works were masterpieces. However, a fluent outpouring of ideas fed the creative efforts of each of these geniuses.

John Bryson/Sygma/Corbis

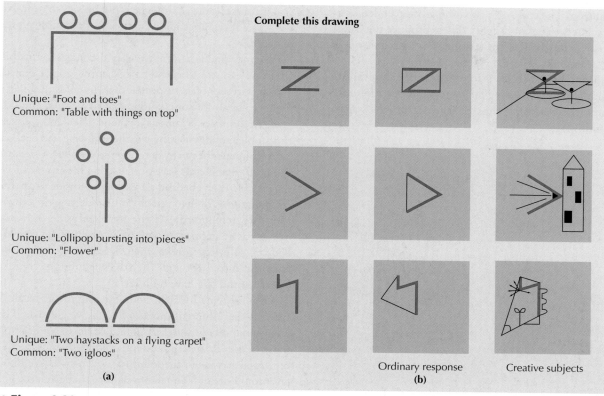

Complete this drawing

Unique: "Foot and toes"
Common: "Table with things on top"

Unique: "Lollipop bursting into pieces"
Common: "Flower"

Unique: "Two haystacks on a flying carpet"
Common: "Two igloos"

(a)

Ordinary response   Creative subjects
(b)

● **Figure 9.20** Some tests of divergent thinking. Creative responses are more original and more complex. ((*a*) Adapted from Wallach & Kogan, 1965; (*b*) adapted from Barron, 1958.)

Hat-tipping device. According to the patent, it is for "automatically effecting polite salutations by the elevation and rotation of the hat on the head of the saluting party when said person bows to the person or persons saluted." In addition to being original or novel, a creative solution must fit the demands of the problem. Is this a creative solution to the "problem" of hat tipping? (U.S. Patent No. 556,248. From *Absolutely Mad Inventions,* by A. E. Brown and H. A. Jefcott, Jr., Dover, 1970.)

ity, but there is more to it. To be creative, the solution to a problem must be more than novel, unusual, or original. It must also be *practical* if it is an invention and *sensible* if it is an idea. This is the dividing line between a "harebrained scheme" and a "stroke of genius." In other words, the creative person brings reasoning and critical thinking to bear on new ideas once they are produced (Runco, 2003).

Stages of Creative Thought

Is there any pattern to creative thinking? Typically, five stages occur during creative problem solving:

1. **Orientation.** As a first step, the person defines the problem and identifies its most important dimensions.

2. **Preparation.** In the second stage, creative thinkers saturate themselves with as much information about the problem as possible.

3. **Incubation.** Most major problems produce a period during which all attempted solutions will be futile. At this point, problem solving may proceed on a subconscious level: Although the problem seems to have been set aside, it is still "cooking" in the background.

Deductive thought Thought that applies a general set of rules to specific situations; for example, using the laws of gravity to predict the behavior of a single falling object.

Logical thought Drawing conclusions on the basis of formal principles of reasoning.

Illogical thought Thought that is intuitive, haphazard, or irrational.

Fluency In tests of creativity, fluency refers to the total number of solutions produced.

Flexibility In tests of creativity, flexibility is indicated by the number of different types of solutions produced.

Originality In tests of creativity, originality refers to how novel or unusual solutions are.

Convergent thinking Thinking directed toward discovery of a single established correct answer; conventional thinking.

Divergent thinking Thinking that produces many ideas or alternatives; a major element in original or creative thought.

4. **Illumination.** The stage of incubation is often ended by a rapid insight or series of insights. These produce the "Aha!" experience, often depicted in cartoons as a light bulb appearing over the thinker's head.

5. **Verification.** The final step is to test and critically evaluate the solution obtained during the stage of illumination. If the solution proves faulty, the thinker reverts to the stage of incubation.

The development of modern aircraft has been highly creative and quite rapid. Even so, it has been marked more by continuous incremental progress than by dramatic breakthroughs.

Of course, creative thought is not always so neat. Nevertheless, the stages listed are a good summary of the most typical sequence of events.

You may find it helpful to relate the stages to the following true (more or less) story. Legend has it that the king of Syracuse (a city in ancient Greece) once suspected that his goldsmith had substituted cheaper metals for some of the gold in a crown and kept the extra gold. Archimedes, a famous mathematician and thinker, was given the problem of discovering whether the king had been cheated.

Archimedes began by defining the problem *(orientation)*: "How can I tell what metals have been used in the crown without damaging it?" He then checked all known methods of analyzing metals *(preparation)*. All involved cutting or melting the crown, so he was forced to temporarily set the problem aside *(incubation)*. Then one day as he stepped into his bath, Archimedes suddenly knew he had the solution *(illumination)*. He was so excited he is said to have run naked through the streets shouting, "Eureka, eureka!" (I have found it, I have found it!).

On observing his own body floating in the bath, Archimedes realized that different metals of equal weight would displace different amounts of water. A pound of brass, for example, occupies more space than a pound of gold, which is denser. All that remained was to test the solution *(verification)*. Archimedes placed an amount of gold (equal in weight to that given the goldsmith) in a tub of water. He marked the water level and removed the gold. He then placed the crown in the water. Was the crown pure gold? If it was, it would raise the water to exactly the same level. Unfortunately, the purity of the crown and the fate of the goldsmith are to this day unknown! (Too bad Archimedes didn't grow up in China. If he had heard the "weighing-the-elephant" tale, he might have quickly solved the crown problem.)

The preceding account is a good general description of creative thinking. However, rather than springing from sudden insights, much creative problem solving is incremental. That is, it is the end result of many small steps. This is certainly true of many inventions, which build on earlier ideas. Some authors believe that truly exceptional creativity requires a rare combination of thinking skills, personality, and a supportive social environment. This mix, they believe, accounts for creative giants such as Edison, Freud, Mozart, Picasso, and others (Runco, 2004; Tardif & Sternberg, 1988).

Positive Psychology: The Creative Personality

What makes a person creative? According to the popular stereotype, highly creative people are eccentric, introverted, neurotic, socially inept, unbalanced in their interests, and on the edge of madness. Although some artists and musicians cultivate this public image, there is little truth in it. Direct studies of creative individuals paint a very different picture (Winner, 2003):

1. There is a small positive correlation between creativity and IQ. In other words, smarter people have a slight tendency to be more creative. But, for the most part, at any given level of IQ, some people are creative and some are not (Preckel, Holling, & Wiese, 2006).

2. Creative people usually have a greater-than-average range of knowledge and interests, and they are more fluent in combining ideas from various sources. They are also good at using mental images and metaphors in thinking (Riquelme, 2002).

3. Creative people are open to a wide variety of experiences. They accept irrational thoughts and are uninhibited about their feelings and fantasies. They tend to use broad categories, to question assumptions, to break mental sets, and they find order in chaos. They also experience more unusual states of consciousness, such as vivid dreams and mystical experiences (Ayers, Beaton, & Hunt, 1999).

4. Creative people enjoy symbolic thought, ideas, concepts, and possibilities. They tend to be interested in truth, form, and beauty, rather than in fame or success. Their creative work is an end in itself (Sternberg & Lubart, 1995).

5. Creative people value their independence and prefer complexity. However, they are unconventional and nonconforming primarily in their work; otherwise they do not have unusual, outlandish, or bizarre personalities.

> ### bridges
> For more information about how dreams can contribute to creative problem solving, see Chapter 6, page 214.

Living More Creatively

Can creativity be learned? It is beginning to look as if some creative thinking skills can be learned. In particular, you can become more creative by practicing divergent thinking and by taking risks, analyzing ideas, and seeking unusual connections between ideas (Baer, 1993; Sternberg, 2001). Psychologist Mihalyi Csikszentmihalyi (sik-sent-me-HALE-yee) (1997) makes these recommendations about how to become more creative:

- Find something that surprises you every day.
- Try to surprise at least one person every day.
- If something sparks your interest, follow it.
- Make a commitment to doing things well.
- Seek challenges.
- Take time for thinking and relaxing.
- Start doing more of what you really enjoy, less of what you dislike.
- Try to look at problems from as many viewpoints as you can.

Even if you don't become more creative by following these suggestions, they are still good advice. Life is not a standardized test with a single set of correct answers. It is more like a blank canvas on which you can create designs that uniquely express your talents and interests. To live more creatively, you must be ready to seek new ways of doing things. Try to surprise at least one person today—yourself, if no one else.

> ### bridges
> Humanistic psychologist Abraham Maslow believed that we must live honestly and creatively to make full use our potentials. **See Chapter 12, pages 408–410, for a discussion of self-actualization.**

⬤⬤ Intuitive Thought—Mental Shortcut? Or Dangerous Detour?

Gateway Question: How accurate is intuition?

At the same time that irrational, intuitive thought may contribute to creative problem solving, it can also lead to thinking errors. To see how this can happen, try the following problems:

Problem 1 An epidemic breaks out, and 600 people are about to die. Doctors have two choices. If they give drug A, 200 lives will be saved. If they give drug B, there is a one-third chance that 600 people will be saved and a two-thirds chance that none will be saved. Which drug should they choose?

Problem 2 Again, 600 people are about to die, and doctors must make a choice. If they give drug A, 400 people will die. If they give drug B, there is a one-third chance that no one will die and a two-thirds chance that 600 will die. Which drug should they choose?

Most people choose drug A for the first problem and drug B for the second. This is fascinating because the two problems are identical. The only difference is that the first is stated in terms of lives saved, the second in terms of lives lost. Yet, even people who realize that their answers are contradictory find it difficult to change them (Kahneman & Tversky, 1972, 1973).

Intuition

As the example shows, we often make decisions intuitively, rather than logically or rationally. **Intuition** is quick, impulsive thought. It may provide fast answers, but it can also be misleading and sometimes disastrous. (But see "Have You Ever Thin Sliced Your Teacher?")

Two noted psychologists, Daniel Kahneman (KON-eh-man) and Amos Tversky (tuh-VER-ski) (1937–1996), studied how we make decisions in the face of uncertainty. They found that human judgment is often seriously flawed (Kahneman, 2003; Kahneman, Slovic, & Tversky, 1982). Let's explore some common intuitive thinking errors, so you will be better prepared to avoid them.

Intuition Quick, impulsive thought that does not make use of formal logic or clear reasoning.

CRITICAL THINKING

Have You Ever Thin Sliced Your Teacher?

Think back to your least favorite teacher (not your current one, of course!). How long did it take you to figure out that he or she wasn't going to make your list of star teachers?

In an intriguing study, psychologist Nalini Ambady asked people to watch video clips of teachers they did not know. After watching three 10-second segments, participants were asked to rate the teachers. Amazingly, their ratings correlated highly with year-end course evaluations made by actual students (Ambady & Rosenthal, 1993). Ambady obtained the same result when she presented

an even thinner "slice" of teaching behavior, just three 2-second clips. A mere 6 seconds is all that participants needed to form intuitive judgments of the instructors' teaching!

In his book *Blink*, Malcolm Gladwell (2005) argues that this was not a case of hurried irrationality. Instead, it was "thin-slicing," or quickly making sense of thin slivers of experience. According to Gladwell, these immediate, intuitive reactions can sometimes form the basis of more carefully reasoned judgments. They are a testament to the power of the *cognitive unconscious*, which is a part of

the brain that does automatic, unconscious processing (Wilson, 2002). Far from being irrational, intuition may be an important part of how we think.

The trick, of course, is figuring out when thin slicing can be trusted and when it can't. After all, first impressions aren't always right. For example, have you ever had a teacher you came to appreciate only after classes were well under way or only after the course was over? In many circumstances, quick impressions are most valuable when you take the time to verify them through further observation.

Representativeness

One very common pitfall in judgment is illustrated by this question: Which is more probable?

A. Tiger Woods will not be in the lead after the first round of golf of a tournament but will win the tournament.

B. Tiger Woods will not be in the lead after the first round of golf of a tournament.

Tversky and Kahneman (1982) found that most people regard statements like A as more probable than B. However, this intuitive answer overlooks an important fact: The likelihood of two events occurring together is lower than the probability of either one alone. (For example, the probability of getting one head when flipping a coin is one half, or 0.5. The probability of getting two heads when flipping two coins is one fourth, or 0.25.) Therefore, A is less likely to be true than B.

According to Tversky and Kahneman, such faulty conclusions are based on the **representativeness heuristic.** That is, we tend to give a choice greater weight if it seems to be representative of what we already know. Thus, you probably compared the information about Tiger Woods with your mental model of what a golf pro's behavior should be like. Answer A seems to better represent the model. Therefore, it seems more likely than answer B, even though it isn't. In courtrooms, jurors are more likely to think a defendant is guilty if the person appears to fit the profile of a person likely to commit a crime (Davis & Follette, 2002). For example, a young single male from a poor neighborhood would be more likely to be judged guilty of theft than a middle-aged married father from an affluent suburb.

Emotion

Feelings also tend to affect good judgment. When we must make a choice, our emotional reactions to various alternatives can determine what intuitively seems to be the right answer. Emotions such

as fear, hope, anxiety, liking, or disgust can eliminate possibilities from consideration or promote them to the top of the list (Kahneman, 2003). For many people, choosing which political candidate to vote for is a good example of how emotions can cloud clear thinking. Rather than comparing candidates' records and policies, it is tempting to vote for the person we like, rather than the person who is most qualified for the job.

Underlying Odds

Another common error in judgment involves ignoring the **base rate,** or underlying probability of an event. People in one experiment were told that they would be given descriptions of 100 people—70 lawyers and 30 engineers. Subjects were then asked to guess, without knowing anything about a person, whether she or he was an engineer or a lawyer. All correctly stated the probabilities as 70 percent for lawyer and 30 percent for engineer. Participants were then given this description:

> Eric is a 30-year-old man. He is married with no children. A man of high ability and high motivation, he promises to be quite successful in his field. He is well liked by his colleagues.

Notice that the description gives no new information about Eric's occupation. He could still be either an engineer or a lawyer. Therefore, the odds should again be estimated as 70-30. However, most people changed the odds to 50-50. Intuitively it seems that Eric has an equal chance of being either an engineer or a lawyer. But this guess completely ignores the underlying odds.

Perhaps it is fortunate that we do at times ignore underlying odds. Were this not the case, how many people would get married in the face of a 50 percent divorce rate? Or how many would start high-risk businesses? On the other hand, people who smoke, drink and then drive, or skip wearing auto seat belts ignore rather high odds of injury or illness. In many high-risk situations, ignoring base rates is the same as thinking you are an exception to the rule.

Framing

The most general conclusion about intuition is that the way a problem is stated, or **framed,** affects decisions (Tversky & Kahneman, 1981). As the first example in this discussion revealed, people often give different answers to the same problem if it is stated in slightly different ways. To gain some added insight into framing, try another thinking problem:

> A couple are divorcing. Both parents seek custody of their only child, but custody can be granted to just one parent. If you had to make a decision based on the following information, to which parent would you award custody of the child?
>
> **Parent A:** average income, average health, average working hours, reasonable rapport with the child, relatively stable social life.
>
> **Parent B:** above-average income, minor health problems, lots of work-related travel, very close relationship with the child, extremely active social life.

Most people choose to award custody to Parent B, the parent who has some drawbacks but also several advantages (such as above-average income). That's because people tend to look for *positive qualities* that can be *awarded* to the child. However, how would you choose if you were asked this question: Which parent should be denied custody? In this case, most people choose to deny custody to Parent B. Why is Parent B a good choice one moment and a poor choice the next? It's because the second question asked who should be *denied* custody. To answer this question, people tend to look for *negative qualities* that would *disqualify* a parent. As you can see, the way a question is framed can channel us down a narrow path so we attend to only part of the information provided, rather than weighing all the pros and cons (Shafir, 1993).

Usually, the *broadest* way of framing or stating a problem produces the best decisions. However, people often state problems in increasingly narrow terms until a single, seemingly "obvious" answer emerges. For example, to select a career, it would be wise to consider pay, working conditions, job satisfaction, needed skills, future employment outlook, and many other factors. Instead, such decisions are often narrowed to thoughts such as, "I like to write, so I'll be a journalist," "I want to make good money and law pays well," or "I can be creative in photography." Framing decisions so narrowly greatly increases the risk of making a poor choice. If you would like to think more critically and analytically, it is important to pay attention to how you are defining problems before you try to solve them. Remember, shortcuts to answers often short-circuit clear thinking.

Wisdom

People can be intelligent without being wise. For example, a person who does well in school and on IQ tests may make a total mess of her life. Likewise, people can be intelligent without being creative, and clear, rational thinking can lead to correct, but uninspired, answers (Solomon, Marshall, & Gardner, 2005). In many areas of human life, wisdom represents a mixture of convergent thinking, intelligence, and reason, spiced with creativity and originality. People who are wise approach life with openness and tolerance (Helson & Srivastava, 2002).

Representativeness heuristic A tendency to select wrong answers because they seem to match preexisting mental categories.

Base rate The basic rate at which an event occurs over time; the basic probability of an event.

Framing In thought, the terms in which a problem is stated or the way that it is structured.

HUMAN DIVERSITY

Intelligence—How Would a Fool Do It?

You have been asked to sort some objects into categories. Wouldn't it be smart to put the clothes, containers, implements, and foods in separate piles? Not necessarily. When members of the Kpelle culture in Liberia were asked to sort objects, they grouped them together by function. For example, a potato (food) would be placed together with a knife (implement). When the Kpelle were asked why they grouped the objects this way, they often said that's how a wise man would do it. The researchers finally asked the Kpelle, "How

would a fool do it?" Only then did the Kpelle sort the objects into the nice, neat categories we Westerners prefer.

This anecdote, related by cultural psychologist Patricia Greenfield (1997), raises serious questions about general definitions of intelligence. For example, among the Cree of Northern Canada, "smart" people are the ones who have visual skills needed to find food on the frozen tundra (Darou, 1992). For the Puluwat people in the South Pacific, being smart means having oceangoing navi-

gation skills necessary to get from island to island (Sternberg, 2004). And so it goes, as each culture teaches its children the kinds of "intelligence" valued in that culture—how the wise man would do it, not a fool (Correa-Chávez, Rogoff, & Arauz, 2005).

In view of such differences, psychologists have tried to create "culture-fair" intelligence tests. Some have even questioned the value of intelligence testing itself. We'll discuss both these ideas in this chapter's Psychology in Action section.

⬤⬤ Human Intelligence—The IQ and You

Gateway Question: How is human intelligence defined and measured?

What do we mean when we say that a person like Steven Hawking is "smart" or "intelligent"? Can intelligence be measured? Can intelligence tests predict success in life? What are the consequences of having extremely high or low intelligence? These questions and others concerning intelligence have fascinated psychologists for more than 100 years (Flynn, 2007). Let's see what has been learned and what issues are still debated.

Like many important concepts in psychology, intelligence cannot be observed directly. Nevertheless, we feel certain it exists. Let's compare two children:

> When she was 14 months old, Anne H. wrote her own name. She taught herself to read at age 2. At age 5, she astounded her kindergarten teacher by bringing a notebook computer to class—on which she was reading an encyclopedia. At 10 she breezed through an entire high school algebra course in 12 hours.
>
> Billy A., who is 10 years old, can write his name and can count, but he has trouble with simple addition and subtraction problems and finds multiplication impossible. He has been held back in school twice and is still incapable of doing the work his 8-year-old classmates find easy.

Anne is considered a genius; Billy, a slow learner. There seems little doubt that they differ in intelligence.

Wait! Anne's ability is obvious, but how do we know that Billy isn't just lazy? This is the same question that Alfred Binet faced in 1904 (Jarvin & Sternberg, 2003). The minister of education in Paris had asked Binet to find a way to distinguish slower students from the more capable (or the capable but lazy). In a flash of brilliance, Binet and an associate created a test made up of "intellectual" questions and problems. Next, they learned which questions an average child could answer at each age. By giving children the test, they could tell if a child was performing up to his or her potential (Kaufman, 2000).

Binet's approach gave rise to modern intelligence tests. At the same time, it launched nearly 100 years of heated debate. Part of the debate is related to the basic difficulty of defining intelligence (Sternberg, Grigorenko, & Kidd, 2005).

Defining Intelligence

Isn't there an accepted definition of intelligence? Yes, **intelligence** is the global capacity to act purposefully, to think rationally, and to deal effectively with the environment. The core of intelligence consists of *general mental abilities* (called the **g-factor**) in the areas of reasoning, problem solving, knowledge, memory, and successful adaptation to one's surroundings (Sternberg, 2004). Beyond this, however, there is much disagreement. In fact, many psychologists simply accept an *operational definition* of intelligence by spelling out the procedures they use to measure it. Thus, by selecting items for an intelligence test, a psychologist is saying in a very direct way, "This is what I mean by intelligence." A test that measures memory, reasoning, and verbal fluency offers a very different

Modern intelligence tests are widely used to measure intellectual abilities. When properly administered, such tests provide an operational definition of intelligence.

definition of intelligence than one that measures strength of grip, shoe size, length of the nose, or the person's best *Too Human* video game score. (For a glimpse at how other cultures define "intelligent" behavior, see "Intelligence—How Would a Fool Do It?")

Intelligence Tests

American psychologists quickly saw the value of Alfred Binet's test. In 1916, Lewis Terman and others at Stanford University revised it for use in North America. After more revisions, the *Stanford-Binet Intelligence Scales, Fifth Edition* continues to be widely used. The original Stanford-Binet assumed that a child's intellectual abilities improve with each passing year. Today's Stanford-Binet (or SB5) is still primarily made up of age-ranked questions. Naturally, these questions get a little harder at each age level. The SB5 is appropriate for people from age 2 to 85+ years (Roid, 2003).

The SB5 measures five cognitive factors (types of mental abilities) that make up general intelligence. These are *fluid reasoning, knowledge, quantitative reasoning, visual-spatial processing,* and *working memory*. Each factor is measured with verbal questions (those involving words and numbers) and nonverbal questions (items that use pictures and objects). Let's see what each factor looks like.

Fluid Reasoning

Fluid Reasoning tests reasoning ability with questions like the following:

> How are an apple, a plum, and a banana different from a beet?
> An apprentice is to a master as a novice is to an _____.
> "I knew my bag was going to be in the last place I looked, so I looked there first." What is silly or impossible about that?

Other items ask people to fill in the missing shape in a group of shapes and to tell a story that explains what's going on in a series of pictures.

Knowledge

The Knowledge factor assesses the person's knowledge about a wide range of topics.

> Why is yeast added to bread dough?
> What does cryptic mean?
> What is silly or impossible about this picture? (For example, a bicycle has square wheels.)

Quantitative Reasoning

Test items for Quantitative Reasoning measure a person's ability to solve problems involving numbers. Here are some samples:

> If I have six marbles and you give me another one, how many marbles will I have?
> Given the numbers 3, 6, 9, 12, what number would come next?
> If a shirt is being sold for 50 percent of the normal price, and the price tag is $60, what is the cost of the shirt?

Visual-Spatial Processing

People who have visual-spatial skills are good at putting picture puzzles together and copying geometric shapes (such as triangles, rectangles, and circles). Visual-Spatial Processing questions ask test takers to reproduce patterns of blocks and choose pictures that show how a piece of paper would look if it were folded or cut. Verbal questions can also require visual-spatial abilities:

> Suppose that you are going east, then turn right, then turn right again, then turn left. In what direction are you facing now?

Working Memory

The Working Memory part of the SB5 measures the ability to use short-term memory. Some typical memory tasks include the following:

> Correctly remember the order of colored beads on a stick.
> After hearing several sentences, name the last word from each sentence.
> Repeat a series of digits (forward or backward) after hearing them once.

If you were to take the SB5, it would yield a score for your general intelligence, verbal intelligence, nonverbal intelligence, and each of the five cognitive factors (Bain & Allin, 2005).

Intelligence Quotients

Imagine that a child named Yuan can answer questions that an average 7-year-old can answer. How smart is she? Actually, we can't say yet, because we don't know how old Yuan is. If she is 10, she's not very smart. If she's 5, she is very bright. Thus, to estimate a child's intelligence we need to know both her **mental age** (average intellectual performance) and her **chronological age** (age in years).

Mental age is based on the level of age-ranked questions a person can answer. For example, at ages 8 or 9, very few children can define the word "connection." At age 10, 10 percent can. At age 13, 60 percent can. Thus, a 13-year-old of average ability can define "connection." If we had only this one item to test children with, those who answered correctly would be given a mental age of 13. When scores from many such items are combined, a child's overall mental age can be found. ● Table 9.3 is a sample of items that persons of average intelligence can answer at various ages.

Intelligence An overall capacity to think rationally, act purposefully, and deal effectively with the environment.

g-factor A general ability factor or core of general intellectual ability that involves reasoning, problem-solving ability, knowledge, memory, and successful adaptation to one's surroundings.

Mental age The average mental ability people display at a given age.

Chronological age A person's age in years.

Table 9.3 ● Sample Items from the Stanford-Binet Intelligence Scale

Age	Item
2 years old	On a large paper doll, points out the hair, mouth, feet, ears, nose, hands, and eyes. When shown a tower built of four blocks, builds one like it.
3 years old	When shown a bridge built of three blocks, builds one like it. When shown a drawing of a circle, copies it with a pencil.
4 years old	Fills in the missing word when asked, "Brother is a boy; sister is a _____." "In daytime it is light; at night it is _____." Answers correctly when asked, "Why do we have houses?" "Why do we have books?"
5 years old	Defines *ball*, *hat*, and *stove*. When shown a drawing of a square, copies it with a pencil.
9 years old	Answers correctly when examiner says, "In an old graveyard in Spain they have discovered a small skull which they believe to be that of Christopher Columbus when he was about 10 years old. What is foolish about that?" Answers correctly when asked, "Tell me the name of a color that rhymes with head." "Tell me a number that rhymes with tree."
Adult	Can describe the difference between laziness and idleness, poverty and misery, character and reputation. Answers correctly when asked, "Which direction would you have to face so your right hand would be toward the north?"

L. Terman & M. Merrill, *Stanford-Binet Intelligence Scale*, 1937. Revised edition, 1960b. Houghton Mifflin, Co.

● **Figure 9.21** With a score of 230, Marilyn vos Savant has the highest IQ ever officially recorded. When she was only 7 years and 9 months old, vos Savant could answer questions that the average 13-year-old can answer. At ages 8, 9, and 10, she got perfect scores on the Stanford-Binet scale. Now in her 60s, she is a well-published author and recently became the host of an *Ask Marilyn* segment for CBS TV News.

Mental age is a good measure of actual ability. But mental age says nothing about whether overall intelligence is high or low compared with other people of the same age. To find out what a particular mental age means, we must relate mental age to actual age. This yields an **intelligence quotient**, or **IQ.** A quotient results from dividing one number into another. When the Stanford-Binet was first used, IQ was defined as mental age (MA) divided by chronological age (CA) and multiplied by 100. (Multiplying by 100 changes the IQ into a whole number, rather than a decimal.)

$$\frac{MA}{CA} \times 100 = IQ$$

An advantage of the original IQ calculation was that intelligence could be compared among children with different chronological and mental ages. For instance, 10-year-old Justin has a mental age of 12. Thus, his IQ is 120:

$$\frac{(MA)\ 12}{(CA)\ 10} \times 100 = 120\ (IQ)$$

Justin's friend Suke also has a mental age of 12. However, Suke's chronological age is 12, so his IQ is 100:

$$\frac{(MA)\ 12}{(CA)\ 12} \times 100 = 100\ (IQ)$$

The IQ shows that 10-year-old Justin is brighter than his 12-year-old friend Suke, even though their intellectual skills are about the same. Notice that a person's IQ will be 100 when mental age equals chronological age. An IQ score of 100 is therefore defined as average intelligence.

Then does a person with an IQ score below 100 have below average intelligence? Not unless the IQ is well below 100. An IQ of 100 is the *mathematical* average (or mean) for such scores. However, average intelligence is usually defined as any score from 90 to 109. The important point is that IQ scores will be over 100 when mental age is higher than age in years (● Figure 9.21). IQ scores below 100 occur when a person's age in years exceeds his or her mental age. An example of the second situation would be a 15-year-old with an MA of 12:

$$\frac{12}{15} \times 100 = 80\ (IQ)$$

Deviation IQs

The preceding examples may give you insight into IQ scores. However, it's no longer necessary to directly calculate IQs. Instead, modern tests use **deviation IQs.** These scores are based on a person's relative standing in his or her age group. That is, they tell how far above or below average the person's score falls. (For more information, see the Statistics appendix near the end of this book.) Tables supplied with the test are then used to convert a person's relative standing in the group to an IQ score. For example, if you score at the fiftieth percentile, half the people your age who take the test score higher than you and half score lower. In this case, your IQ score is 100. If you score at the eighty-fourth percentile, your IQ score is 115. If you score at the ninety-seventh percentile, your IQ score is 130.

Table 9.4 ● **Sample Items Similar to Those Used on the WAIS-III**

Verbal Subtests	Sample Items
Information	How many wings does a bird have? Who wrote *Paradise Lost*?
Digit span	Repeat from memory a series of digits, such as 3 1 0 6 7 4 2 5, after hearing it once.
General comprehension	What is the advantage of keeping money in the bank? Why is copper often used in electrical wires?
Arithmetic	Three men divided 18 golf balls equally among themselves. How many golf balls did each man receive? If 2 apples cost 15¢, what will be the cost of a dozen apples?
Similarities	In what way are a lion and a tiger alike and/or unalike? In what way are a saw and a hammer alike and/or unalike?
Vocabulary	What is a guitar? What does "robin" mean?
Letter-number sequencing	Repeat a list of mixed numbers and letters, numbers first, in numerical order, and letters second, in alphabetical order.
Performance Subtests	**Description of Item**
Picture arrangement	Arrange a series of cartoon panels to make a meaningful story.
Picture completion	What is missing from these pictures?
Block design	Copy designs with blocks.
Object assembly	Put together a jigsaw puzzle.
Digit symbol	Fill in the symbols.
Matrix reasoning	Select the item that completes the matrix.
Symbol search	Match symbols appearing in separate groups.

Courtesy of the Psychological Corporation.

The Wechsler Tests

Is the Stanford-Binet the only intelligence test? A widely used alternative is the *Wechsler Adult Intelligence Scale–Third Edition* (WAIS-III). A version for children is called the *Wechsler Intelligence Scale for Children–Fourth Edition* (WISC-IV) (Baron, 2005).

The Wechsler tests are similar to the Stanford-Binet but differ in important ways. For one thing, the WAIS-III was specifically designed to test adult intelligence. The original Stanford-Binet was better suited for children and adolescents. The latest Stanford-Binet (the SB5) can now be used for all ages, but the WAIS was the first "adult" IQ test. Like the Stanford-Binet, the Wechsler tests yield a single overall IQ. In addition, the WAIS and WISC give separate scores for **performance** (nonverbal) **intelligence** and **verbal** (language- or symbol-oriented) **intelligence**. (Note that this feature was also recently added to the SB5.) The abilities measured by the Wechsler tests and some sample test items are listed in ● Table 9.4.

Group Tests

The SB5 and the Wechsler tests are **individual intelligence tests,** which must be given to a single person by a trained specialist. In contrast, **group intelligence tests** can be given to large groups of people with minimal supervision. Group tests usually require people to read, to follow instructions, and to solve problems of logic, reasoning, mathematics, or spatial skills. If you're wondering if you have ever taken an intelligence test, the answer is probably yes. The well-known *SAT Reasoning Test* measures aptitudes for language, math, and reasoning. The SAT is designed to predict your chances for success in college. Because it measures a number of different mental aptitudes, it can also be used to estimate general intelligence (Frey & Detterman, 2004).

Intelligence quotient (IQ) An index of intelligence defined as a person's mental age divided by his or her chronological age and multiplied by 100.

Deviation IQ An IQ obtained statistically from a person's relative standing in his or her age group; that is, how far above or below average the person's score was relative to other scores.

Performance intelligence Intelligence measured by solving puzzles, assembling objects, completing pictures, and other nonverbal tasks.

Verbal intelligence Intelligence measured by answering questions involving vocabulary, general information, arithmetic, and other language- or symbol-oriented tasks.

Individual intelligence test A test of intelligence designed to be given to a single individual by a trained specialist.

Group intelligence test Any intelligence test that can be administered to a group of people with minimal supervision.

Variations in Intelligence— Curved Like a Bell

Gateway Question: How much does intelligence vary from person to person?

IQ scores are classified as shown in ● Table 9.5. A look at the percentages reveals a definite pattern. The distribution (or scattering) of IQ scores approximates a **normal** (bell-shaped) **curve.** That is, most scores fall close to the average and very few are found at the extremes. ● Figure 9.22 shows this characteristic of measured intelligence.

The Mentally Gifted

How high is the IQ of a genius? Only 2 people out of 100 score above 130 on IQ tests. These bright individuals are usually described as "gifted." Less than one-half of 1 percent of the population scores above 140. These people are certainly gifted or perhaps even "geniuses." However, some psychologists reserve the term "genius" for people with even higher IQs or those who are exceptionally creative (Hallahan & Kauffman, 2006).

Gifted Children

Do high IQ scores in childhood predict later ability? To directly answer this question, Lewis Terman selected 1,500 children with IQs of 140 or more. Terman followed this gifted group (the "Ter-

Table 9.5 ● Distribution of Adult IQ Scores on WAIS-III

IQ	Description	Percent
Above 130	Very superior	2.2
120–129	Superior	6.7
110–119	Bright normal	16.1
90–109	Average	50.0
80–89	Dull normal	16.1
70–79	Borderline	6.7
Below 70	Intellectual disabled	2.2

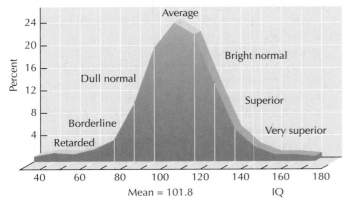

● **Figure 9.22** Distribution of Stanford-Binet Intelligence Test scores for 3,184 children. (Adapted from Terman & Merrill, 1960.)

mites" as he called them) into adulthood and found that most were quite successful. A majority finished college, earned advanced degrees, or held professional positions, and many had written books or scientific articles (Terman & Oden, 1959).

In general, the correlation between IQ scores and school grades is 0.50, a sizable association. The link would be even stronger, but motivation, special talents, off-campus learning, and many other factors also affect grades. The same is true of "real-world" success beyond school. IQ is not at all good at predicting success in art, music, writing, dramatics, science, and leadership. Creativity is much more strongly related to doing well in these areas (Preckel, Holling, & Wiese, 2006; Runco, 2004). Regardless, when people score in the gifted range, their chances for high achievement do seem to rise (Shurkin, 1992).

Were all the gifted children superior as adults? No. Although most were mentally healthy and successful, some had committed crimes, were unemployable, or were emotionally troubled. Remember that a high IQ reveals *potential.* It does not guarantee success. Marilyn vos Savant, with an IQ of 230, has contributed little to science, literature, or art. Nobel prize–winning physicist Richard Feynman, whom many regarded as a genius, had an IQ of 122 (Michalko, 1998).

How did Terman's more successful Termites differ from the less successful? Most of them had educated parents who taught them to value learning. They also had *intellectual determination,* which is a desire to know, to excel, and to persevere (Winner, 2003). Thus, successful gifted persons tend to be *persistent* and *motivated* to learn. No one is paid to sit around being *capable* of achievement. What you do is always more important than what you should be able to do. That's why a child's talents are most likely to blossom when they are nurtured with support, encouragement, education, and effort (Callahan, 2006).

Identifying Gifted Children

How might a parent spot an unusually bright child? Early signs of giftedness are not always purely "intellectual." **Giftedness** can be either the possession of a high IQ or special talents or aptitudes, such as creativity.

The following signs may reveal that a child is gifted: A tendency to seek out older children and adults; an early fascination with explanations and problem solving; talking in complete sentences as early as 2 or 3 years of age; an unusually good memory; precocious talent in art, music, or number skills; an early interest in books, along with early reading (often by age 3); showing of kindness, understanding, and cooperation toward others (Alvino & Editors, 1996; Distin, 2006).

Notice that this list goes beyond straight g-factor, or general "academic" intelligence. In fact, if artistic talent, mechanical aptitude, musical aptitude, athletic potential, and so on are considered, many children have a special "gift" of one kind or another. Limiting giftedness to high IQ can shortchange children with special talents. This is especially true of ethnic minority children, who may be the victims of subtle biases in standardized intelligence tests. These children, as well as children with physical dis-

THE CLINICAL FILE

Meet the Rain Man

Richard Green

Once, four months after reading a Tom Clancy novel, *The Hunt for Red October,* Kim was asked about a character, a Russian radio operator. He immediately named the character, gave the page number on which a description appeared, and accurately recited several paragraphs about the character (Treffert & Christensen, 2005).

Meet Kim Peek, the model for Dustin Hoffman's character in the Academy Award–winning movie *Rain Man.* Kim began memorizing books at 18 months of age. Today, he can recite from memory more than 9,000 books. He knows all the zip codes and area codes in America and can give accurate travel directions between any two major U.S. cities. He can also discuss hundreds of pieces of classical music in detail and is even learning to play all that music. Amazingly, though, for someone with such skills, Kim has difficulty with abstract thinking and tests of general intelligence. He is poorly coordinated and cannot button his own clothes (Treffert & Christensen, 2005).

Kim Peek has *savant syndrome,* in which a person of limited intelligence shows exceptional mental ability in one or more narrow areas, such as mental arithmetic, calendar calculations, art, or music (Young, 2005).

Do savants have special mental powers not shared by most people? According to one theory, many savants have suffered some form of damage to their left hemispheres, freeing them from the "distractions" of language, concepts, and higher-level thought. This allows them to focus with crystal clarity on music, drawing, prime numbers, license plates, TV commercials, and other specific information (Young, 2005). Another theory holds that the performances of many savants result from intense practice (Miller, 1999). Perhaps each of us harbors embers of mental brilliance that intense practice could fan into full flame (Snyder et al., 2006).

Although savant syndrome hasn't been fully explained, it shows that extraordinary abilities can exist apart from general intelligence.

Dan McCoy/Rainbow

Christiana Dittmann/Rainbow

It is wise to remember that there are many ways in which a child may be gifted. Many schools now offer Gifted and Talented Education programs for students with a variety of special abilities—not just for those who score well on IQ tests.

Intellectual Disability

A person with mental abilities far below average is termed **intellectually disabled** (a related term, **mentally retarded,** is seen by many as offensive). Intellectual disability begins at an IQ of approximately 70 or below. However, a person's ability to perform *adaptive behaviors* (basic skills such as dressing, eating, communicating, shopping, and working) also figures into evaluating this disability (DSM-IV-TR, 2000; Hallahan & Kauffman, 2006) (● Table 9.6).

It's important to realize that intellectually disabled persons have no handicap where feelings are concerned. They are easily hurt by rejection, teasing, or ridicule. Likewise, they respond warmly to love and acceptance. They have a right to self-respect and a place in the community (AAIDD, 2004). This is especially

abilities, are less likely to be recognized as gifted (Ford & Moore, 2006; Robinson & Clinkenbeard, 1998).

In the next section, we will discuss intellectual disability. Before you begin, take a few moments to read "Meet the Rain Man," where you will find information about a strange mixture of brilliance and mental disability.

Normal curve A bell-shaped curve characterized by a large number of scores in a middle area, tapering to very few extremely high and low scores.

Giftedness The possession of a high IQ or special talents or aptitudes.

Intellectual disability (formerly **mental retardation**) The presence of a developmental disability, a formal IQ score below 70, or a significant impairment of adaptive behavior.

Table 9.6 ● Levels of Intellectual Disability

IQ Range	Degree of Intellectual Disability	Educational Classification	Required Level of Support
50–55 to 70	Mild	Educable	Intermittent
35–40 to 50–55	Moderate	Trainable	Limited
20–25 to 35–40	Severe	Dependent	Extensive
Below 20–25	Profound	Life support	Pervasive

DSM-IV-TR, 2000; Hodapp, 1994.

These youngsters are participants in the Special Olympics—an athletic event for the intellectually disabled. It is often said of the Special Olympics that "everyone is a winner—participants, coaches, and spectators."

Stan Godlewski/Getty Images

important during childhood, when support from others adds greatly to the person's chances of becoming a well-adjusted member of society.

Causes of Intellectual Disability

What causes intellectual disability? About half of all cases of intellectual disability are *organic,* or related to physical disorders (Das, 2000). These include *fetal damage* (prenatal damage from teratogens such as disease, infection, or drugs) and *birth injuries* (such as lack of oxygen during delivery). *Metabolic disorders,* which affect energy production and use in the body, also cause intellectual disability. Some forms of intellectual disability are linked to *genetic abnormalities,* such as missing genes, extra genes, or defective genes. Malnutrition and exposure to lead, PCBs, and other toxins early in childhood can also cause organic intellectual disability (Beirne-Smith, Patton, & Shannon, 2006).

In 30 to 40 percent of cases, no known biological problem can be identified. In many such instances, the degree of intellectual disability is mild, in the 50 to 70 IQ range. Often, other family members are also mildly intellectually disabled. *Familial intellectual disability,* as this is called, occurs mostly in very poor households where nutrition, intellectual stimulation, medical care, and emotional support may be inadequate. This suggests that familial

intellectual disability is based largely on an impoverished environment. Thus, better nutrition, education, and early childhood enrichment programs could prevent many cases of intellectual disability (Beirne-Smith, Patton, & Shannon, 2006).

> **bridges**
>
> All children benefit from enriched environments. **For a discussion of enrichment and some guidelines for parents, see Chapter 3, pages 83–84.**

●● Questioning Intelligence—How Intelligent Are Intelligence Tests?

Gateway Question: What are some controversies in the study of intelligence?

Defining intelligence as a g-factor (general ability) has been controversial. As we noted earlier in our discussion of "intelligent" behavior in other cultures, there are many ways to be smart. For example, consider William, a grade-school student 2 years behind in reading, who shows his teacher how to solve a difficult computer-programming problem. Or what about his classmate, Malika, who performs poorly in math but plays intricate pieces of piano music? Both these children show clear signs of intelligence. And yet, each might score below average on a traditional IQ test. And, as we have seen, savants like Kim Peek have even more extreme intellectual strengths and weaknesses. Such observations have convinced many psychologists that it is time to forge new, broader definitions of intelligence. Their basic goal is to better predict "real-world" success—not just the likelihood of success in school (Sternberg & Grigorenko, 2006).

Multiple Intelligences

One such psychologist is Howard Gardner of Harvard University. Gardner (2003, 2004) theorizes that there are actually eight distinctly different kinds of intelligence. These are different mental "languages" that people use for thinking. Each is listed below, with examples of pursuits that make use of them.

1. *Language* (linguistic abilities)—writer, lawyer, comedian
2. *Logic and math* (numeric abilities)—scientist, accountant, programmer
3. *Visual and spatial* (pictorial abilities)—engineer, inventor, artist
4. *Music* (musical abilities)—composer, musician, music critic
5. *Bodily-kinesthetic* (physical abilities)—dancer, athlete, surgeon
6. *Intrapersonal* (self-knowledge)—poet, actor, minister
7. *Interpersonal* (social abilities)—psychologist, teacher, politician
8. *Naturalist* (an ability to understand the natural environment)—biologist, medicine man, organic farmer

Two composers. The one on the left was a genius who wrote sublime, multi-voiced harmonies. The one on the right has created reasonably good, if uninspired, music. Computer models of thought can approximate intelligent human behavior. However, rule-based computer "thinking" still lacks the flexibility, creativity, and common sense of human intelligence.

According to Howard Gardner's theory, bodily-kinesthetic skills reflect one of eight distinct types of intelligence.

To simplify a great deal, people can be "word smart," "number smart," "picture smart," "musically smart," "body smart," "self smart," "people smart," and/or "nature smart."

Most of us are probably strong in only a few types of intelligence. In contrast, geniuses like Albert Einstein seem to be able to use nearly all of the intelligences, as needed, to solve problems.

If Gardner's theory of **multiple intelligences** is correct, traditional IQ tests measure only a part of real-world intelligence—namely, linguistic, logical-mathematical, and spatial abilities. A further implication is that our schools may be wasting a lot of human potential (Campbell, Campbell, & Dickinson, 2003). For example, some children might find it easier to learn math or reading if these topics were tied into art, music, dance, drama, and so on. Already, many schools are using Gardner's theory to cultivate a wider range of skills and talents (Campbell, Campbell, & Dickinson, 2003; Kornhaber & Gardner, 2006). Before we return to human intelligence, let's see what we can learn from some smart machines.

Artificial Intelligence: I Compute, Therefore I Am

How smart are computers and robots? Just as savants like Kim Peek challenge our understanding of general intelligence, so too does the prospect of creating intelligent machines. Let's say you are exchanging instant messages over the Internet with someone you don't know. You are allowed to make any comments and ask any questions you like, for as long as you like. In reality, the "person" you are communicating with is a computer. Do you think a computer could fool you into believing it was human? If it did,

wouldn't that qualify it as "intelligent"? You may be surprised to learn that, to date, no machine has come close to passing this test (Moor, 2003).

The problem computers face is that we humans can mentally "shift gears" from one topic to another with incredible flexibility. In contrast, machine "intelligence" is currently "blind" outside its underlying set of rules. As a tiny example, u cann understnd wrds thet ar mizpeld. Computers are very literal and easily stymied by such errors.

Regardless, artificial intelligence has been successful at very specific tasks. **Artificial intelligence (AI)** usually refers to computer programs capable of doing things that require intelligence when done by people (Russell & Norvig, 2003). For example, listeners sometimes mistake music created by Kemal Ebcioglu for that written by Johann Sebastian Bach, the eighteenth-century German composer. Ebcioglu wrote a computer program that creates harmonies remarkably similar to Bach's. By analyzing Bach's music, Ebcioglu came up with 350 rules that govern harmonization. The result is a program that displays artificial intelligence in a specific area.

Much of current artificial intelligence is based on the fact that many tasks—from harmonizing music to diagnosing disease—can be reduced to a set of rules applied to a collection of information. AI is valuable in situations where speed, vast memory, and persistence are required. In fact, AI programs are better at some tasks than humans are. An example is world chess champion Garry Kasparov's loss, in 1997, to a computer called Deep Blue.

Multiple intelligences Howard Gardner's theory that there are several specialized types of intellectual ability.

Artificial intelligence (AI) Any artificial system (often a computer program) that is capable of human-like problem solving or intelligent responding.

AI and Cognition

Although AI is a long way from duplicating general human intelligence, artificial intelligence offers a way to probe some of our specific cognitive skills, or intelligences. For instance, computer simulations and expert systems provide good examples of how AI is being used as a research tool.

Computer simulations are programs that attempt to duplicate specific human behaviors, especially thinking, decision making, or problem solving. Here, the computer acts as a "laboratory" for testing models of cognition. If a computer program behaves as humans do (including making the same errors), then the program may be a good model of how we think.

Expert systems are computer programs that respond as a human expert would (Giarratano & Riley, 2005). They have demystified some human abilities by converting complex skills into clearly stated rules a computer can follow. Expert systems can predict the weather, analyze geological formations, diagnose disease, play chess, read, tell when to buy or sell stocks, and perform many other tasks.

Eventually, AI will almost certainly lead to robots that recognize voices and that speak and act "intelligently" in specific areas of ability. To achieve this, should intelligence be directly programmed into computers? Or should computers be designed to learn from experience, like the human brain does (McClelland & Rogers, 2003)? Only time will tell. For now, it's interesting to note that these questions mirror another area of controversy—whether human intelligence is inherited or learned from experience.

Heredity, Environment, and Intelligence

Is intelligence inherited? Most people are aware that there is a moderate similarity in the intelligence of parents and their children, or between brothers and sisters. As ● Figure 9.23 shows, the similarity in IQ scores among relatives grows in proportion to how close they are on the family tree.

Does this indicate that intelligence is hereditary? Not necessarily. Brothers, sisters, and parents share similar environments as well as similar heredity. To separate nature and nurture, **twin studies** may be done. Such studies compare the IQs of twins who were raised

together or separated at birth. This allows us to estimate how much heredity and environment affect intelligence.

Twin Studies

Notice in ● Figure 9.23 that the IQs of fraternal twins are more alike than the IQs of ordinary siblings. *Fraternal twins* come from two separate eggs fertilized at the same time. Genetically, they are no more alike than ordinary siblings. Why, then, should the twins' IQs be more similar? The reason may be environmental: Parents treat twins more alike than ordinary siblings, resulting in a closer match in IQs.

More striking similarities are observed with *identical twins,* who develop from a single egg and have identical genes. At the top of ● Figure 9.23 you can see that identical twins who grow up in the same family have highly correlated IQs. This is what we would expect with identical heredity and very similar environments. Now, let's consider what happens when identical twins are reared apart. As you can see, the correlation drops, but only from 0.86 to 0.72. Psychologists who emphasize genetics believe these figures show that adult intelligence is roughly 50 percent hereditary (Grigorenko & Sternberg, 2003).

> **bridges**
> Identical twins also tend to have similar personality traits. This suggests that heredity contributes to personality, as well as intelligence. **See Chapter 12, pages 390–391.**

How do environmentalists interpret the figures? They point out that the IQs of some separated twins differ by as much as 20 points. Such IQ gaps occur when the twins grow up with big educational and environmental differences. It is more common for separated twins to be placed in homes socially and educationally similar to their biological parents. This fact would tend to inflate apparent genetic effects by making the separated twins' IQs more alike. Another frequently overlooked fact is that twins grow up in the same environment *before birth* (in the womb). If we take such environmental similarities into account, intelligence would seem to be less than 50 percent hereditary (Devlin, Daniels, & Roeder, 1997; Turkheimer et al., 2003).

IQ and Environment

How much can environment alter intelligence? Strong evidence for an environmental view of intelligence comes from adoption studies. Consider families having one adopted child and one biological child. As ● Figure 9.24 shows, parents contribute genes *and* environment to their biological child. With an adopted child they contribute only environment. If intelligence is highly genetic, the IQs of biological children should be more like their parents' IQs than are the IQs of adopted children. However, one study found that children reared by the same mother tend to resemble her IQ to the same degree. It does not matter whether or not they share her genes (Kamin, 1981; Weinberg, 1989).

In another study, striking increases in IQ occurred in 25 children who were moved from an orphanage and were eventually adopted

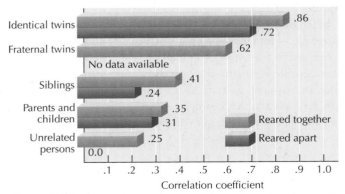

● **Figure 9.23** Approximate correlations between IQ scores for persons with varying degrees of genetic and environmental similarity. Notice that the correlations grow smaller as the degree of genetic similarity declines. Also note that a shared environment increases the correlation in all cases. (Estimates from Bouchard, 1983; Henderson, 1982.)

CRITICAL THINKING

You Mean Video Games Might Be Good for Me?

Although rapidly rising Western IQ scores suggest that environmental factors influence intelligence (Flynn, 2007; Schooler, 1998), we are left with the question, Which factors? Writer Steven Johnson (2005) believes that popular culture is responsible. Although he agrees that much popular media content is too violent or sexual in nature, he points out that video games, the Internet, and even television are becoming more complex. As a result, they demand ever-greater cognitive effort from us. In other words, it is as important to understand *how* we experience the environment as it is to understand *what* we experience.

For example, early video games, such as *Pong* or *Pac Man,* offered simple, repetitive visual experiences. In contrast, today's popular games, such as *The World of Warcraft* or *Second Life,* offer rich, complicated experiences that can take many hours of intense problem solving to complete. Furthermore, players must usually figure out the rules by themselves. Instructions that fans have written for popular games are typically much longer than chapters in this book. Only a complex and engaging game would prompt players to use such instructions, much less write them for others to use (Johnson, 2005).

According to Johnson, other forms of popular culture have also become more complex, including the Internet, computer software, and even popular television. For example, compared with television dramas of the past, modern dramas weave plot lines and characters through an entire season of programs. In the end, popular culture may well be inviting us to read, reflect, and problem-solve more than ever before (Jaeggi et al., 2008).

> **bridges**
> Before you uncritically embrace video games, read "You Mean Video Games Might Be Bad for Me?" in Chapter 7, page 245.

● **Figure 9.24** Comparison of an adopted child and a biological child reared in the same family. (Adapted from Kamin, 1981.)

by parents who gave them love, a family, and a stimulating home environment. Once considered intellectually disabled and unadoptable, the children gained an average of 29 IQ points. A second group of initially less "intellectually disabled" children, who stayed in the orphanage, *lost* an average of 26 IQ points (Skeels, 1966)!

A particularly dramatic environmental effect is the fact that Westernized nations have shown average IQ gains of 15 points during the last 30 years (Dickens & Flynn, 2001). These IQ boosts occurred in far too short a time for genetics to explain them. It is more likely that the gains reflect environmental forces, such as improved education and nutrition and living in a technologically complex society (Johnson, 2005). If you've ever tried to play a computer game or set up a wireless network in your home, you'll understand why people may be getting better at answering IQ test questions. (See "You Mean Video Games Might Be Good for Me?")

Summary

In the final analysis, intelligence reflects development as well as potential, nurture as well as nature (Grigorenko, 2005). Moreover, the fact that intelligence is partly determined by heredity tells us little of any real value. Genes are fixed at birth. Improving the environments in which children learn and grow is the main way in which we can ensure that they reach their full potential (Grigorenko & Sternberg, 2003; White, 2006).

KNOWLEDGE BUILDER
Intelligence
RECITE
1. Which modern intelligence test originated with attempts to measure the mental abilities of children in Paris?
   a. SB5
   b. WAIS
   c. SAT
   d. WISC
2. If we define intelligence by writing a test, we are using a(n) _____ definition.
3. By definition, a person has average intelligence when
   a. MA = CA
   b. CA = 100
   c. MA = 100
   d. MA × CA = 100
4. The WAIS-III is a group intelligence test. T or F
5. The distribution of IQs approximates a _____ (bell-shaped) curve.
6. One thing that the mentally gifted and the intellectually disabled have in common is that both have
   a. a tendency to suffer from metabolic disorders
   b. to be tested with the WAIS, rather than the SB5
   c. MAs that are higher than their CAs
   d. extreme IQ scores
7. Many cases of intellectual disability without known organic causes appear to be _____.

Continued

Twin study A comparison of the characteristics of twins who were raised together or separated at birth; used to identify the relative impact of heredity and environment.

8. From a practical point of view, intelligence can most readily be increased by
   a. genetics
   b. teaching adaptive behaviors
   c. stimulating environments
   d. applying deviation IQs

REFLECT

Critical Thinking

9. Is it ever accurate to describe a machine as "intelligent"?
10. Some people treat IQ as if it were a fixed number, permanently stamped on the forehead of each child. Why is this view in error?

Relate

If you were going to write an intelligence test, what kinds of questions would you include? How much would they resemble the questions found on the SB5, the WAIS-III, or culture-fair tests?

How has your understanding of the following concepts changed: IQ, giftedness, intellectual disability?

A friend says to you, "I think intelligence is entirely inherited from parents." What could you tell your friend to make sure she or he is better informed?

Answers: 1. a **2.** operational **3.** a **4.** F **5.** normal **6.** d **7.** familial **8.** c **9.** Rule-driven expert systems may appear "intelligent" within a narrow range of problem solving. However, they are "stone stupid" at everything else. This is usually not what we have in mind when discussing human intelligence. **10.** Because one's IQ depends on the intelligence test used to measure it: Change the test and you will change the score. Also, heredity establishes a range of possibilities; it does not automatically preordain a person's intellectual capacities.

PSYCHOLOGY IN ACTION

Culture, Race, IQ, and You

Gateway Question: Are IQ tests fair to all cultural and racial groups?

Do you consider yourself intelligent? Okay, then give the Dove Test a try.

If you scored 14 on this exam, your IQ is approximately 100, indicating average intelligence. If you scored 10 or less, you are intellectually disabled. With luck and the help of a special educational program, you may be able to learn a few simple skills!

Isn't the Dove Test a little unfair? No, it's *very* unfair. It was written in 1971 by African-American sociologist Adrian Dove as "a half serious attempt to show that we're just not talking the same language." Dove tried to slant his test as much in favor of urban African-American culture as he believes typical IQ tests are biased toward a white middle-class background (Jones, 2003). (Because of its age, the test is probably now also unfair for African Americans under 40.)

Dove's test is a thought-provoking reply to the fact that African-American children score an average of about 15 points lower on standardized IQ tests than European-American children. By reversing the bias, Dove has shown that intelligence tests are not equally valid for all groups. As psychologist Jerome Kagan once said, "If the Wechsler and Binet scales were translated into Spanish, Swahili, and Chinese and given to every 10-year-old in Latin America, East Africa, and China, the majority would obtain IQ scores in the intellectually disabled range."

Culture-Fair Testing

Certainly we cannot believe that children of other cultures are all intellectually disabled. The fault must lie with the test (White, 2006). As noted earlier, cultural values, knowledge, language patterns, and traditions can greatly affect performance on tests designed for Western cultures (Neisser et al., 1996; Sternberg & Grigorenko, 2005). To avoid this problem, some psychologists have tried to develop culture-fair tests that do not disadvantage certain groups. A **culture-fair test** is designed to minimize the importance of skills and knowledge that may be more common in some cultures than in others. (For a sample of culture-fair test items, see ● Figure 9.25.)

● **Figure 9.25** Sample items from a culture-fair test. **1.** Which pattern is different from the remaining four? (Number 3.) **2.** Which of the five figures on the right would properly continue the three on the left—that is, fill the blank? (Number 5.) **3.** Which of the figures on the right should go in the square on the left to make it look right? (Number 2.) **4.** At left, the dot is outside the square and inside the circle. In which of the figures on the right could you put a dot outside the square and inside the circle? (Number 3.) (Courtesy of R.B. Cattell.)

Culture-fair tests attempt to measure intelligence without, as much as possible, being influenced by a person's verbal skills, cultural background, and educational level. Their value lies not just in testing people from other cultures. They are also useful for testing children in the United States who come from poor communities, rural areas, or ethnic minority families (Stephens et al., 1999). However, no intelligence test can be entirely free of cultural influences. For instance, our culture is very "visual," because children are constantly exposed to television, movies, video games, and the like. Thus, compared with children in developing countries,

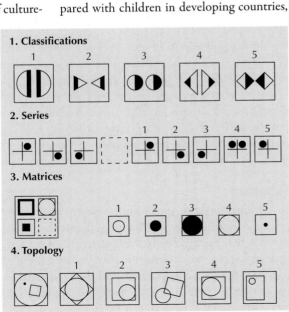

Dove Counterbalance Intelligence Test

Time limit: 5 minutes.
Circle the correct answer.

1. T-bone Walker got famous for playing what?
   a. trombone
   b. piano
   c. T-flute
   d. guitar
   e. "hambone"

2. A "gas head" is a person who has a
   a. fast-moving car
   b. stable of "lace"
   c. "process"
   d. habit of stealing cars
   e. long jail record for arson

3. If you throw the dice and 7 is showing on the top, what is facing down?
   a. 7
   b. snake eyes
   c. boxcars
   d. little joes
   e. 11

4. Cheap chitlings (not the kind you purchase at a frozen-food counter) will taste rubbery unless they are cooked long enough. How soon can you quit cooking them to eat and enjoy them?
   a. 45 minutes
   b. 2 hours
   c. 24 hours
   d. 1 week (on a low flame)
   e. 1 hour

5. Bird or Yardbird was the jacket jazz lovers from coast to coast hung on
   a. Lester Young
   b. Peggy Lee
   c. Benny Goodman
   d. Charlie Parker
   e. Birdman of Alcatraz

6. A "handkerchief head" is
   a. a cool cat   b. a porter
   c. an Uncle Tom   d. a hoddi
   e. a preacher

7. Jet is
   a. an East Oakland motorcycle club
   b. one of the gangs in West Side Story
   c. a news and gossip magazine
   d. a way of life for the very rich

8. "Bo Diddley" is a
   a. game for children
   b. down-home cheap wine
   c. down-home singer
   d. new dance
   e. Moejoe call

9. Which word is most out of place here?
   a. splib   b. blood
   c. gray   d. spook
   e. black

10. If a pimp is uptight with a woman who gets state aid, what does he mean when he talks about "Mother's Day"?
    a. second Sunday in May
    b. third Sunday in June
    c. first of every month
    d. none of these
    e. first and fifteenth of every month

11. Many people say that "Juneteenth" (June 10) should be made a legal holiday because this was the day when
    a. the slaves were freed in the United States
    b. the slaves were freed in Texas
    c. the slaves were freed in Jamaica
    d. the slaves were freed in California
    e. Martin Luther King was born
    f. Booker T. Washington died

12. If a man is called a "blood," then he is a
    a. fighter
    b. Mexican-American
    c. Black
    d. hungry hemophile
    e. red man or Indian

13. What are the Dixie Hummingbirds?
    a. a part of the KKK
    b. a swamp disease
    c. a modern gospel group
    d. a Mississippi Negro paramilitary strike force
    e. deacons

14. The opposite of square is
    a. round.
    b. up
    c. down
    d. hip
    e. lame

Answers: 1. d 2. c 3. a 4. c 5. d 6. c 7. c 8. c 9. c 10. c 11. b 12. c 13. c 14. d

a child who grows up in the United States may be better prepared to take *both* nonverbal tests and traditional IQ tests.

Because the concept of intelligence exhibits such diversity across cultures, many psychologists have begun to stress the need to rethink the concept of intelligence itself (Greenfield, 1997; Sternberg & Grigorenko, 2005). If we are to find a truly culture-fair way to measure intelligence, we first need to identify those core cognitive skills, or multiple intelligences, that lie at the heart of human intelligence the world around (Sternberg & Grigorenko, 2006).

The Politics of Race, Culture, and IQ

Biased tests are not the only IQ issue African Americans have confronted. One persistent claim is that African Americans score below average in IQ because of their "genetic heritage" and that they are genetically incapable of climbing out of poverty (Hernstein & Murray, 1994; Rushton & Jensen, 2005). Psychologists

have responded to such claims with a number of counterarguments.

First, it is no secret that as a group African Americans are more likely than European Americans to live in environments that are physically, educationally, and intellectually impoverished. As we saw earlier in this chapter, when unequal education is part of the equation, IQs tell us little about how heredity affects intelligence (Sternberg, Grigorenko, & Kidd, 2005; Suzuki & Aronson, 2005). Indeed, one study found that placing poor African-American children into better-off European-American adoptive families increased the children's IQs by an average of 13 points, bringing them into line with those of European-American children (Nisbett, 2005). That is, providing African-American children with the same environmental experiences available to European-American children erased IQ differences.

Second, the point made by the Dove Test is often overlooked. The assumptions, biases, and content of standard IQ tests do not always

allow meaningful comparisons between ethnic, cultural, or racial groups (Fagan & Holland, 2007; Suzuki & Aronson, 2005). As Leon Kamin (1981) says, "The important fact is that we cannot say which sex (or race) might be more intelligent, because we have no way of measuring 'intelligence.' We have only IQ tests." Kamin's point is that the makers of IQ tests decided in advance to use test items that would give men and women equal IQ scores. It would be just as easy to put together an IQ test that would give African Americans and European Americans equal scores. Differences in IQ scores are not a fact of nature, but a decision by the test makers. That's why European Americans do better on IQ tests written by European Americans, and African Americans do better on IQ tests devised by African Americans.

Culture-fair test A test (such as an intelligence test) designed to minimize the importance of skills and knowledge that may be more common in some cultures than in others.

Third, although IQ predicts school performance, it does not predict later career success (McClelland, 1994). In this regard, "street smarts," or what psychologist Robert Sternberg calls *practical intelligence* (Stemler & Sternberg, 2006), may be seen by minority cultures as more important than "book learning," or what Sternberg calls *analytic intelligence* (Sankofa et al., 2005).

Most psychologists have concluded there is no scientific evidence that group differences in average IQ are based on genetics. In fact, studies that used actual blood group testing found no significant correlations between ethnic ancestry and IQ scores. This is because it does not even make genetic sense to talk about "races" at all because obvious external markers, like skin color, have little to do with underlying genetic differences (Bonham et al., 2005; Sternberg, 2007). Group differences in IQ scores are based on cultural and environmental diversity, as much as on heredity (Neisser et al., 1996; Nisbett, 2005). To conclude otherwise reflects political beliefs and biases, not scientific facts.

Thinking Beyond the Numbers Game

African Americans are not the only segment of the population with reason to question the validity of intelligence testing and the role of heredity in determining intelligence. The clarifications they have won extend to others as well.

Consider the 9-year-old child confronted with this question on an intelligence test:

"Which of the following does not belong with the others? Roller skates, airplane, train, bicycle." If the child fails to answer "airplane," does it reveal a lack of intelligence? It can be argued that an intelligent choice could be based on any of these alternatives: Roller skates are not typically used for transportation; an airplane is the only nonland item; a train can't be steered; a bicycle is the only item with just two wheels. The parents of a child who misses this question may have reason to be angry because educational systems tend to classify children and then make the label stick.

In response to such concerns, court decisions have led some states to outlaw the use of intelligence tests in public schools.

High-Stakes Testing

Widespread reliance on standardized intelligence tests and aptitude tests has raised questions about the relative good and harm they do. On the positive side, tests can open opportunities as well as close them. A high test score may allow a disadvantaged youth to enter college, or it may identify a child who is bright but emotionally disturbed. Test scores may also be fairer and more objective than arbitrary judgments made by admissions officers or employment interviewers. Also, tests *do* accurately predict academic performance. The fact that academic performance *does not* predict later success may call for an overhaul of college course work, not an end to testing.

On the negative side, mass testing can sometimes exclude people of obvious ability. Other complaints relate to the frequent appearance of bad or ambiguous questions on standardized tests, overuse of class time to prepare students for the tests (instead of teaching general skills), and in the case of intelligence tests, the charge that tests are often biased. Also, most standardized tests demand passive recognition of facts, assessed with a multiple-choice format. They do not, for the most part, test a person's ability to think critically or creatively or to apply knowledge to solve problems.

Conclusion

An application of the preceding discussion to your personal understanding of intelligence can be summarized in this way: Intelligence tests are a double-edged sword; we have learned much from their use, yet they have the potential to do great harm. In the final analysis, it is important to remember—as Howard Gardner has pointed out—that creativity, motivation, physical health, mechanical aptitude, artistic ability, and numerous other qualities not measured by intelligence tests contribute to the achievement of life goals. Also remember that IQ is not intelligence. IQ is an *index* of intelligence (as narrowly defined by a particular test). Change the test and you change the score. An IQ is not some permanent number stamped on your forehead (or the foreheads of your friends and classmates) that forever determines your potential. The real issue is what skills people have and how they apply them, not what their test scores are (White, 2006).

---

chapter in review

Gateways to Cognition, Language, Creativity and Intelligence

Thinking is an internal representation of external stimuli or situations.
- Three basic units of thought are images, concepts, and language (or symbols).

Mental images may be retrieved from memory or created to solve problems.
- Images can be three-dimensional, they can be rotated in space, and their size may change.
- Kinesthetic images are used to represent movements and actions. Kinesthetic sensations help structure the flow of thoughts for many people.

A concept is a generalized idea of a class of objects or events.
- Concept formation may be based on positive and negative instances or rule learning.
- Concept identification frequently makes use of prototypes, or ideal models.
- Concepts may be conjunctive ("and" concepts), disjunctive ("either/or" concepts), or relational.
- The denotative meaning of a word or concept is its dictionary definition. Connotative meaning is personal or emotional.

Language is an especially powerful way to encode information and manipulate ideas.
- Language encodes events as symbols, for easy mental manipulation. The study of meaning in language is called *semantics.*
- Bilingualism is a valuable ability. Two-way bilingual education allows children to develop additive bilingualism while in school.
- Language carries meaning by combining a set of symbols according to a set of rules (grammar), which includes rules about word order (syntax).
- True languages are productive and can be used to generate new ideas or possibilities.
- Complex gestural systems, such as American Sign Language, are true languages.
- Chimpanzees and other primates have been taught American Sign Language and similar systems. This suggests to some that primates are capable of very basic language use. Others question this conclusion.

Expert problem solving is based on learned mental heuristics and highly organized knowledge.
- The solution to a problem may be arrived at mechanically (by trial and error or by rote application of rules), but mechanical solutions are often inefficient.
- Solutions by understanding usually begin with discovery of the general properties of an answer, followed by a functional solution.

- Problem solving is aided by heuristics, which narrow the search for solutions.
- Experts are not naturally smarter than novices.
- When understanding leads to a rapid solution, insight has occurred. Three elements of insight are selective encoding, selective combination, and selective comparison.
- Insight can be blocked by fixations. Functional fixedness is a common fixation, but emotional blocks, cultural values, learned conventions, and perceptual habits are also problems.

Creative thinking is novel, divergent, and tempered with a dash of practicality.
- To be creative, a solution must be practical and sensible as well as original. Creative thinking requires divergent thought, characterized by fluency, flexibility, and originality. Tests of creativity measure these qualities. Creativity can be enhanced by strategies that promote divergent thinking.
- Five stages often seen in creative problem solving are orientation, preparation, incubation, illumination, and verification. Not all creative thinking fits this pattern.
- Studies suggest that the creative personality has a number of characteristics, most of which contradict popular stereotypes. There is only a very small correlation between IQ and creativity.
- Some creative thinking skills can be learned.

Some common thinking errors can be avoided if you know the pitfalls of intuitive thought.
- Intuitive thinking often leads to errors. Wrong conclusions may be drawn when an answer seems highly representative of what we already believe is true.
- Emotions also lead to intuitive thinking and poor choices.
- Another problem is ignoring the base rate (or underlying probability) of an event.
- Clear thinking is usually aided by stating or framing a problem in broad terms.

Intelligence refers to the general capacity (or g-factor) to act purposefully, think rationally, and deal effectively with the environment.
- In practice, intelligence is operationally defined by intelligence tests, which provide a useful but narrow estimate of real-world intelligence.
- The first intelligence test was assembled by Alfred Binet. A modern version of Binet's test is the *Stanford-Binet Intelligence Scale.*
- Intelligence is expressed as an intelligence quotient (IQ), defined as mental age divided by chronological age and then multiplied by 100. The distribution of IQ scores approximates a normal curve.

- Another major intelligence test is the *Wechsler Adult Intelligence Scale* (WAIS). The WAIS measures both verbal and performance intelligence. Group intelligence tests are also available.

There is a wide range of mental abilities. Everyone has special aptitudes (talents and potentials).

- Most people score in the mid-range on intelligence tests. Only a small percentage of people have exceptionally high and low IQ scores.
- People with IQs in the gifted or "genius" range of above 140 tend to be superior in many respects. A high IQ does not automatically lead to high achievement. A high IQ reveals potential, but it does not guarantee success.
- The term *intellectually disabled* is applied to those whose IQ falls below 70 or who lack various adaptive behaviors. About 50 percent of the cases of intellectual disability are organic. The remaining cases are of undetermined cause. Many of these cases are thought to reflect familial intellectual disability.
- The majority of people who are intellectually disabled can master basic adaptive behaviors and with support they can find a place in the community.

The definition of intelligence and the assumption that intelligence is mainly inherited have been called into question.

- Traditional IQ tests measure linguistic, logical-mathematical, and spatial abilities. It is likely that we all use other types of intelligence in daily life.
- Many psychologists have begun to forge new, broader definitions of intelligence. Howard Gardner's theory of multiple intelligences is a good example.
- Real-world intelligence combines a fast nervous system with learned knowledge and skills and an acquired ability to manage one's own thinking and problem solving.
- *Artificial intelligence* refers to any artificial system that can perform tasks that require intelligence when done by people. Two principal areas of artificial intelligence research on particular human skills are computer simulations and expert systems.
- Intelligence is partially determined by heredity. However, environment is also important, as revealed by IQ increases induced by education and stimulating environments.

Traditional IQ tests are not universally valid for all cultural groups.

- Traditional IQ tests often suffer from a degree of cultural bias. For this and other reasons, it is wise to remember that IQ is merely an index of intelligence and that intelligence is narrowly defined by most tests.

- IQ is related to achievement in school, but many other factors are also important. Outside school, the connection between IQ and achievement is even weaker.
- The use of standard IQ tests for educational placement of students (especially into special education classes) has been prohibited by law in some states.

Web Resources

For an up-to-date list of direct links to interesting sites, including those listed here, visit the student companion site for this book at www.cengage.com/psychology/coon

Amoeba Web Psychology Resources: Cognitive Psychology Go to the "Cognitive Psychology" link on this web page and you will find numerous other links to articles/information on many areas of cognitive psychology.

Koko.org View the sign language (and art!) of Koko, the gorilla.

Functional Fixedness Read about tool use and functional fixedness.

Creativity Web Multiple links to resources on creativity.

Multiple Intelligences in Education Learn more about Gardner's theory of multiple intelligences and how it is being applied in education.

The Knowns and Unknowns of Intelligence From the APA, what is known about intelligence and intelligence tests.

Interactive Learning

Introduction to Psychology: Gateways to Mind and Behavior Book Companion Website
www.cengage.com/psychology/coon

Visit your book companion website, where you will find flash cards, practice quizzes, web links, and more to help you study.

CENGAGENOW™ *Just what you need to know NOW!*

Spend time on what you need to master rather than on information you already have learned. Take a pre-test for this chapter, and CengageNOW will generate a personalized study plan based on your results. The study plan will identify the topics you need to review and direct you to online resources to help you master those topics. You can then take a post-test to help you determine the concepts you have mastered and what you will need to work on. Try it out! Go to www.cengage.com/login to sign in with an access code or to purchase access to this product.

CHAPTER 10

Motivation and Emotion

Gateway Theme

Our behavior is energized and directed by motives and emotions.

Camay Sungu/AP/Wide World Photo

Gateway Questions

- *What is motivation? Are there different types of motives?*

- *What causes hunger? Overeating? Eating disorders?*

- *Is there more than one type of thirst? In what ways are pain avoidance and the sex drive unusual?*

- *How does arousal relate to motivation?*

- *What are learned motives? Social motives? Why are they important?*

- *Are some motives more basic than others?*

- *What happens during emotion?*

- *What physiological changes underlie emotion? Can "lie detectors" really detect lies?*

- *How accurately are emotions expressed by the face and "body language"?*

- *How do psychologists explain emotions?*

- *What does it mean to have "emotional intelligence"?*

Robert was in his doctor's waiting room when he suffered a "strange attack." Robert recalls that the "atmosphere changed, the walls seemed to close in, and the voices of other patients became a buzz." However, months of therapy were no help because Robert simply couldn't talk about his feelings. When asked how he felt, Robert might reply "Fine" or "I don't know." Or he might describe a bodily sensation by replying, "My stomach hurts" (Lumley, 2004). The scientific name for Robert's problem is *alexithymia* (a-LEX-ih-THIGH-me-ah), from the Latin for "can't name emotions."

In a sense, you could say that emotion is the "music" that enriches the rhythms of our lives. Sadly, Robert is not moved by the music of life as intensely as most of us are. Not only is Robert unable to name his emotions, he is only vaguely aware of them in the first place. As you might suspect, people like Robert find it hard to form close relationships because they cannot easily empathize with the feelings of others. This lack of inner awareness can also lead to health problems, such as depression or addictive behaviors (Lumley, 2004).

In this chapter you will learn how motives provide the drumbeat of human behavior and emotions color its rhythms. The words "motivation" and "emotion" both derive from the Latin word *movere* (to move). As we will see, both play complex roles in our daily lives. Even "simple" motivated activities, such as eating, are not solely under the control of the body. In many instances, external cues, expectations, learning, cultural values, and other factors influence our motives and emotions (Beck, 2004).

Let's begin with basic motives, such as hunger and thirst, and end by exploring how emotions affect us. Although emotions can be the music of life, they are sometimes the music of death as well. Read on to find out why.

Motivation—Forces That Push and Pull

Gateway Questions: What is motivation? Are there different types of motives?

What do you plan to do today? What are your goals? Why do you pursue them? How vigorously do you try to reach them? When are you satisfied? When do you give up? These are all questions about motivation, or why we act as we do. Let's begin with a basic model of motivation and an overview of types of motives. **Motivation** refers to the dynamics of behavior—the ways in which our actions are *initiated, sustained, directed,* and *terminated* (Franken, 2007).

Can you clarify that? Yes. Imagine that Kayleigh is studying biology in the library. Her stomach begins to growl and she can't concentrate. She grows restless and decides to buy an apple from a vending machine. The machine is empty, so she goes to the cafeteria. Closed. Kayleigh drives home, where she cooks a meal and eats it. At last her hunger is satisfied, and she resumes studying. Notice how Kayleigh's food seeking was *initiated* by a bodily need. Her search was *sustained* because her need was not immediately met, and her actions were *directed* by possible sources of food. Finally, achieving her goal *terminated* her food seeking.

A Model of Motivation

Many motivated activities begin with a **need**, or internal deficiency. The need that initiated Kayleigh's search was a shortage of key substances in her body. Needs cause a **drive** (an energized motivational state) to develop. The drive was hunger, in Kayleigh's case. Drives activate a **response** (an action or series of actions) designed to attain a **goal** (the "target" of motivated behavior). Reaching a goal that satisfies the need will end the chain of events. Thus, a simple model of motivation can be shown in this way:

NEED ⟶ DRIVE ⟶ RESPONSE ⟶ GOAL ⟶ (NEED REDUCTION)

Aren't needs and drives the same thing? No, because the strength of needs and drives can differ (Franken, 2007). If you begin fasting today, your bodily need for food will increase every day. However, you would probably feel less "hungry" on the seventh day of fasting than you did on the first. Whereas your need for food steadily increases, the hunger drive comes and goes.

Now let's observe Kayleigh again. It's Saturday night: For dinner, Kayleigh has soup, salad, a large steak, a baked potato, four pieces of bread, two pieces of cheesecake, and three cups of coffee. After dinner, she complains that she is "too full to move." Soon after, Kayleigh's roommate arrives with a strawberry pie. Kayleigh exclaims that strawberry pie is her favorite dessert and eats three large pieces! Is this hunger? Certainly, Kayleigh's dinner satisfied her biological needs for food.

How does that change the model of motivation? Kayleigh's "pie lust" illustrates that motivated behavior can be energized by the "pull" of external stimuli, as well as by the "push" of internal needs.

Incentives

The "pull" of a goal is called its **incentive value** (the goal's appeal beyond its ability to fill a need). Some goals are so desirable (strawberry pie, for example) that they can motivate behavior in the absence of an internal need. Other goals are so low in incentive value that they may be rejected even if they meet the internal need. Fresh, live grub worms, for instance, are highly nutritious. However, it is doubtful that you would eat one no matter how hungry you might be.

(a) High-incentive value goal

(b) Low-incentive value goal

David Austen/Woodfin Camp & Associates

● **Figure 10.1** Needs and incentives interact to determine drive strength *(top)*. *(a)* Moderate need combined with a high-incentive goal produces a strong drive. *(b)* Even when a strong need exists, drive strength may be moderate if a goal's incentive value is low. It is important to remember, however, that incentive value lies "in the eye of the beholder" *(photo)*. No matter how hungry, few people would be able to eat the pictured grub worms.

Usually, our actions are energized by a mixture of internal needs *and* external incentives. That's why a strong need may change an unpleasant incentive into a desired goal. Perhaps you've never eaten a grub worm, but we'll bet you've eaten some pretty horrible leftovers when the refrigerator was bare. The incentive value of goals also helps explain motives that don't seem to come from internal needs, such as drives for success, status, or approval (● Figure 10.1).

Types of Motives

For our purposes, motives can be divided into three major categories:

1. **Biological motives** are based on biological needs that must be met for survival. The most important biological motives are hunger, thirst, pain avoidance, and needs for air, sleep, elimination of wastes, and regulation of body temperature. Biological motives are innate.
2. **Stimulus motives** express our needs for stimulation and information. Examples include activity, curiosity, exploration, manipulation, and physical contact. Although such motives also appear to be innate, they are not strictly necessary for survival.
3. **Learned motives** are based on learned needs, drives, and goals. Learned motives help explain many human activities, such as standing for election, blogging, or auditioning for *American Idol*. Many learned motives are related to learned needs for power, affiliation (the need to be with others), approval, status, security, and achievement. Fear and aggression also appear to be greatly affected by learning.

Biological Motives and Homeostasis

How important is air in your life? Water? Sleep? Food? Temperature regulation? Finding a public restroom? For most of us, satisfying biological needs is so routine that we tend to overlook how

Motivation Internal processes that initiate, sustain, and direct activities.

Need An internal deficiency that may energize behavior.

Drive The psychological expression of internal needs or valued goals. For example, hunger, thirst, or a drive for success.

Response Any action, glandular activity, or other identifiable behavior.

Goal The target or objective of motivated behavior.

Incentive value The value of a goal above and beyond its ability to fill a need.

Biological motives Innate motives based on biological needs.

Stimulus motives Innate needs for stimulation and information.

Learned motives Motives based on learned needs, drives, and goals.

much of our behavior they direct. But exaggerate any of these needs through famine, shipwreck, poverty, near drowning, bitter cold, or drinking 10 cups of coffee, and their powerful grip on behavior becomes evident. We are, after all, still animals in many ways.

Biological drives are essential because they maintain **homeostasis** (HOE-me-oh-STAY-sis), or bodily equilibrium (Cannon, 1932).

What is homeostasis? The term "homeostasis" means "standing steady," or "steady state." Optimal levels exist for body temperature, for chemicals in the blood, for blood pressure, and so forth (Levin, 2006). When the body deviates from these "ideal" levels, automatic reactions begin to restore equilibrium (Deckers, 2005). Thus, it might help to think of homeostasis as being similar to a thermostat set at a particular temperature.

A (Very) Short Course on Thermostats

The thermostat in your house constantly compares the actual room temperature to a *set point,* or ideal temperature, which you can control. When room temperature falls below the set point, the heat is automatically turned on to warm the room. When the heat equals or slightly exceeds the set point, it is automatically turned off or the air conditioning is turned on. In this way room temperature is kept in a state of equilibrium hovering around the set point.

The first reactions to disequilibrium in the human body are also automatic. For example, if you become too hot, more blood will flow through your skin and you will begin to perspire, thus lowering body temperature. We are not usually aware of such changes, unless continued disequilibrium drives us to seek shade, warmth, food, or water.

Circadian Rhythms

Our needs and drives can change from moment to moment. After eating, our motivation to eat more food tends to diminish, and a few minutes in the hot sun can leave us feeling thirsty. But our motivation can also vary over longer cycles. Scientists have long known that body activity is guided by internal "biological clocks." Every 24 hours, your body undergoes a cycle of changes called **circadian** (SUR-kay-dee-AN) **rhythms** (*circa:* about; *diem:* a day) (Beersma & Gordijn, 2007). Throughout the day, activities in the liver, kidneys, and endocrine glands undergo large changes. Body temperature, blood pressure, and amino acid levels also shift from hour to hour. These activities, and many others, peak once a day (● Figure 10.2). People are usually more motivated and alert at the high point of their circadian rhythms (Antle & Mistlberger, 2005).

People with early peaks in their circadian rhythms are "day people," who wake up alert, are energetic early in the day, and fall asleep early in the evening. People with later peaks are "night people," who wake up groggy, are lively in the afternoon or early evening, and stay up late (Duffy, Rimmer, & Czeisler, 2001). Such differences are so basic that when a day person rooms with a night person, both are more likely to give their relationship a negative rating (Carey, Stanley, & Biggers, 1988). This is easy to under-

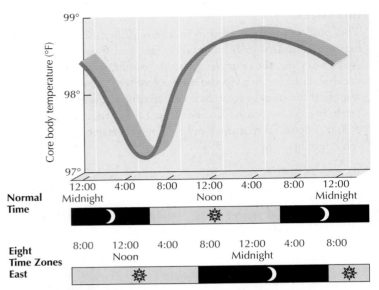

● **Figure 10.2** Core body temperature is a good indicator of a person's circadian rhythm. Most people reach a low point two to three hours before their normal waking time. It's no wonder that both the Chernobyl and Three Mile Island nuclear power plant accidents occurred around 4 AM. Rapid travel to a different time zone, shift work, depression, and illness can throw sleep and waking patterns out of synchronization with the body's core rhythm. Mismatches of this kind are very disruptive (Hauri & Linde, 1990).

stand: What could be worse than having someone bounding around cheerily when you're half asleep, or the reverse?

Shift Work and Jet Lag

Circadian rhythms are most noticeable after a major change in time schedules. Businesspersons, athletes, and other time zone travelers tend to perform poorly when their body rhythms are disturbed. If you travel great distances east or west, the peaks and valleys of your circadian rhythms will be out of phase with the sun and clocks. For example, you might be wide awake at midnight and feel like you're sleepwalking during the day. (Return to ● Figure 10.2.) Shift work has the same effect, causing fatigue, irritability, upset stomach, and depression (Garbarino, 2002; Shen et al., 2006).

How fast do people adapt to rhythm changes? For major time zone shifts (5 hours or more) it can take up to 2 weeks to resynchronize. The *direction* of travel also affects adaptation (Herxheimer & Waterhouse, 2003). If you fly west, adapting is relatively easy; if you fly east, adapting takes much longer (● Figure 10.3). When you fly east, the sun comes up *earlier* relative to your "home" time. Let's say that you live in Seattle and fly to Miami. If you get up at 7 AM in Miami, it's 4 AM back in Seattle—and your body knows it. If you fly west, the sun comes up later. In this case, it is easier for people to "advance" (stay up later and sleep in) than it is to shift backward.

Adjusting to jet lag is slowest when you stay indoors, where you can sleep and eat on "home time." Getting outdoors speeds adapta-

● **Figure 10.3** Time required to adjust to air travel across six time zones. The time it took individuals to resynchronize was, on average, shorter for westbound travel than for eastbound flights. (Data from Beljan et al., 1972; cited by Moore-Ede, Sulzman, & Fuller, 1982.)

tion. A few intermittent 5-minute periods of exposure to bright light early in the morning are also helpful for resetting your circadian rhythm (Duffy & Wright, Jr., 2005). Bright light affects the timing of body rhythms by reducing the amount of a brain chemical called melatonin produced by the pineal gland. When melatonin levels rise late in the evening, it's bedtime as far as the brain is concerned.

How does this affect those of us who are not world travelers? There are few college students who have not at one time or another "burned the midnight oil," especially for final exams. At such times it is wise to remember that departing from your regular schedule usually costs more than it's worth. You may be motivated to do as much during 1 hour in the morning as you could have done in 3 hours of work after midnight. You might just as well go to sleep 2 hours earlier.

In general, if you can anticipate an upcoming body rhythm change, it is best to preadapt to your new schedule. Preadaptation refers to gradually matching your sleep–waking cycle to a new time schedule. Before traveling, for instance, you should go to sleep 1 hour later (or earlier) each day until your sleep cycle matches the time at your destination.

To reset the body's clock in a new time zone, a small amount of melatonin can be taken about an hour before bedtime. This dose is continued for as many days as necessary to ease jet lag. The same treatment can be used for rotating work shifts (Comperatore et al, 1996; Sharkey & Eastman, 2002).

> ### bridges
> Changes in melatonin levels are thought to partly explain winter depressions that occur when people endure several months of long, dark days. **See Chapter 14, page 479.**

KNOWLEDGE BUILDER
Overview of Motivation

RECITE
Classify the following needs or motives by placing the correct letter in the blank.
A. Biological motive **B.** Stimulus motive **C.** Learned motive

1. _____ curiosity   4. _____ thirst
2. _____ status   5. _____ achievement
3. _____ sleep   6. _____ physical contact
7. Motives _____, sustain, and _____ activities.
8. The maintenance of bodily equilibrium is called thermostasis. T or F?
9. Desirable goals are motivating because they are high in
   a. secondary value
   b. stimulus value
   c. homeostatic value
   d. incentive value
10. The term "jet lag" is commonly used to refer to disruptions of
    a. the inverted U function
    b. circadian rhythms
    c. any of the episodic drives
    d. the body's set point

REFLECT

Critical Thinking
11. Many people mistakenly believe that they suffer from "hypoglycemia" (low blood sugar), which is often blamed for fatigue, difficulty concentrating, irritability, and other symptoms. Why is it unlikely that many people actually have hypoglycemia?

Relate
Motives help explain why we do what we do. See if you can think of something you do that illustrates the concepts of need, drive, response, and goal. Does the goal in your example vary in incentive value? What effects do high- and low-incentive-value goals have on your behavior?

Mentally list some biological motives you have satisfied today. Some stimulus motives. Some learned motives. How did each influence your behavior?

Answers: 1. b **2.** c **3.** a **4.** a **5.** c **6.** b **7.** initiate, direct **8.** F **9.** d **10.** b **11.** Because of homeostasis: Blood sugar is normally maintained within narrow bounds. While blood sugar levels fluctuate enough to affect hunger, true hypoglycemia is an infrequent medical problem.

Homeostasis A steady state of bodily equilibrium.

Circadian rhythms Cyclical changes in bodily functions and arousal levels that vary on a schedule approximating a 24-hour day.

⬤⬤ Hunger—Pardon Me, My Hypothalamus Is Growling

Gateway Questions: What causes hunger? Overeating? Eating disorders?

You get hungry, you find food, and you eat: Hunger might seem like a "simple" motive, but we have only recently begun to understand it. Hunger provides a good model of how internal and external factors direct our behavior. And, as we will see later, many of the principles that explain hunger also apply to thirst. Like almost every other human motive, our hunger levels are affected by both internal bodily factors and external environmental and social ones. To understand how this works, let's begin with a survey of some of the internal factors controlling our hunger.

Internal Factors in Hunger

Don't feelings of hunger originate in the stomach? To find out, Walter Cannon and A. L. Washburn (1912) decided to see if stomach contractions cause hunger. In an early study, Washburn trained himself to swallow a balloon, which could be inflated through an attached tube. This allowed Cannon to record the movements of Washburn's stomach (⬤ Figure 10.4). When Washburn's stomach contracted, he reported that he felt "hunger pangs." In view of this, the two scientists concluded that hunger is nothing more than the contractions of an empty stomach. (However, this proved to be an inflated conclusion.)

For many people, hunger produces an overall feeling of weakness or shakiness, rather than a "growling" stomach. Of course, eating *does* slow when the stomach is stretched or distended (full). (Remember last Thanksgiving?) However, we now know that the stomach is not essential for feeling hunger. Even people who have had their stomachs removed for medical reasons continue to feel hungry and eat regularly (Woods et al., 2000).

Then what does cause hunger? Many different factors combine to promote and suppress hunger. The brain receives many signals from parts of the digestive system, ranging from the tongue and stomach to the intestines and the liver.

The liver? Yes, as the levels of blood sugar (glucose) drop, the liver responds by sending nerve impulses to the brain. These "messages" contribute to a desire to eat (Woods et al., 2000).

Brain Mechanisms

What part of the brain controls hunger? When you are hungry, many parts of the brain are affected, so no single "hunger thermostat" exists. However, a small area called the **hypothalamus** (HI-po-THAL-ah-mus) is especially important because it regulates many motives, including hunger, thirst, and the sex drive (⬤ Figure 10.5).

> ### bridges
> For more information about the role of the hypothalamus in controlling behavior, see Chapter 2, pages 68–69.

⬤ **Figure 10.4** In Cannon's early study of hunger, a simple apparatus was used to simultaneously record hunger pangs and stomach contractions. (After Cannon, 1934.)

⬤ **Figure 10.5** Location of the hypothalamus in the human brain.

The hypothalamus is sensitive to levels of sugar in the blood (and other substances described in a moment). It also receives neural messages from the liver and stomach. When combined, these signals determine if you are hungry or not (Woods et al., 2000).

One part of the hypothalamus acts as a *feeding system* that initiates eating. If the *lateral hypothalamus* is "turned on" with an electrified probe, even a well-fed animal will immediately begin eating. (The term "lateral" simply refers to the sides of the hypothalamus. (● Figure 10.6). If the same area is destroyed, the animal may never eat again.

The lateral hypothalamus is normally activated in a variety of ways. For example, when you are hungry your stomach lining produces ghrelin (GREL-in), a hormone that activates your lateral hypothalamus (Olszewski et al., 2003). (If your stomach is growlin', it's probably releasing ghrelin.) Ghrelin also activates parts of your brain involved in learning. This means you should consider studying before you eat, not immediately afterward (Diano et al., 2006).

A second area in the hypothalamus is part of a *satiety system,* or "stop mechanism" for eating. If the *ventromedial hypothalamus* (VENT-ro-MEE-dee-al) is destroyed, dramatic overeating results. (Ventromedial refers to the bottom middle of the hypothalamus.) Rats with such damage will eat until they balloon up to weights of 1,000 grams or more (● Figure 10.7). A normal rat weighs about 180 grams. To put this weight gain in human terms, picture someone you know who weighs 180 pounds growing to a weight of 1,000 pounds.

The *paraventricular* (PAIR-uh-ven-TRICK-you-ler) *nucleus* of the hypothalamus also affects hunger. (See ● Figure 10.6.) This area helps keep blood sugar levels steady by both starting and stopping eating. The paraventricular nucleus is sensitive to a substance called *neuropeptide Y* (NPY). If NPY is present in large amounts, an animal will eat until it cannot hold another bite (Williams et al., 2004). Incidentally, the hypothalamus also responds to a chemical in marijuana, which can produce intense hunger (the "munchies") (Di Marzo et al., 2001).

How do we know when to stop eating? A chemical called glucagon-like peptide 1 (GLP-1) causes eating to cease. After you eat a meal, GLP-1 is released by the intestines. From there, it travels in the bloodstream to the brain. When enough GLP-1 arrives, your desire to eat ends (Nori, 1998). As you might imagine, GLP-1 pills show promise in the treatment of obesity (Raun et al., 2007). By the way, it takes at least 10 minutes for the hypothalamus to respond after you begin eating. That's why you are less likely to overeat if you eat slowly, which gives your brain time to get the message that you've had enough (Liu et al., 2000).

In addition to knowing when to start eating and when meals are over, your brain also controls your weight over longer periods of time. (See "Your Brain's 'Fat Point.' ")

● **Figure 10.7** Damage to the hunger satiety system in the hypothalamus can produce a very fat rat, a condition called hypothalamic *hyperphagia* (hi-per-FAGE-yah: overeating). This rat weighs 1,080 grams. (The pointer has gone completely around the dial and beyond.) (Courtesy of Neal E. Miller. Rockefeller University.)

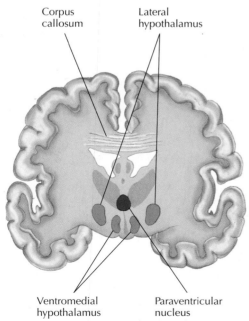

Corpus callosum   Lateral hypothalamus

Ventromedial hypothalamus   Paraventricular nucleus

● **Figure 10.6** This is a cross section through the middle of the brain (viewed from the front of the brain). Indicated areas of the hypothalamus are associated with hunger and the regulation of body weight.

Hypothalamus A small area at the base of the brain that regulates many aspects of motivation and emotion, especially hunger, thirst, and sexual behavior.

BRAINWAVES

Your Brain's "Fat Point"

A thermostat set to, say, 72 degrees will constantly turn the heat and/or air conditioning on and off to maintain the temperature at that set point. Like a thermostat, your brain maintains a **set point** in order to control your weight over the long term. It does this by monitoring the amount of fat stored in your body in specialized *fat cells* (Ahima & Osei, 2004).

Your set point is the weight you maintain when you are making no effort to gain or lose weight. When your body weight goes below its set point, you will feel hungry most of the time. On the other hand, fat cells release a substance called *leptin* when your "spare tire" is well inflated. Leptin is carried in the bloodstream to the hypothalamus, where it tells us to eat less (Williams et al., 2004).

Can you change your fat set point? Good question. Your leptin levels are partly under genetic control. In rare cases mice (and we humans) inherit a genetic defect that reduces leptin levels in the body, leading to obesity. In such cases, the administration of leptin can help (Williamson et al., 2005).

For the rest of us, the news is not so encouraging because there is currently no known way to lower your set point for fat. Since the body replaces fat cells at roughly the rate they are lost, the number of fat cells remains unchanged throughout adult life (Spalding et al., 2008). To make matters worse, radical diets do not help. (But you knew that already, didn't you?) They may even raise the set point for fat, resulting in *diet-induced obesity* (Ahima & Osei, 2004). You may not be able to lose weight by resetting your hypothalamus, but psychologists have studied other approaches to weight loss. We will examine some later in this section.

The mouse on the left has a genetic defect that prevents its fat cells from producing normal amounts of leptin. Without this chemical signal, the mouse's body acts as if its set point for fat storage is, shall we say, rather high.

The substances we have reviewed are only some of the chemical signals that start and stop eating (Geary, 2004). Others continue to be discovered. In time, they may make it possible to artificially control hunger. If so, better treatments for extreme obesity and self-starvation could follow (Batterham et al., 2003).

External Factors in Hunger and Obesity

As we have seen, "hunger" is affected by more than just our biological needs for food. In fact, if internal needs alone controlled eating, fewer people would overeat. Nevertheless, roughly 65 percent of adults in the United States are overweight (● Figure 10.8). In 2006, more than one-third were obese (Ogden et al., 2007). (See "What's Your BMI?") Let's consider some external influences on hunger and their role in obesity, a major health risk and, for many, a source of social stigma and low self-esteem. As a result, obesity is overtaking smoking as a cause of needless deaths (Murray, 2001).

External Eating Cues

Most of us are sensitive to *external eating cues*. These are signs and signals linked with food. For example, do you tend to eat more when food is highly visible and easy to get? If so, then external cues affect your food intake. In cultures like ours, where food is plentiful, eating cues add greatly to the risk of overeating (Woods et al., 2000). Many college freshmen gain weight rapidly during their first 3 months on campus (the famous "Frosh 15"). All-you-can-eat dining halls in the dorms and nighttime snacking appear to be the culprits (Levitsky et al., 2003). The presence of others can also affect whether people overeat (or undereat) depending on how much everyone else is eating and how important it is to impress them (Pliner & Mann, 2004).

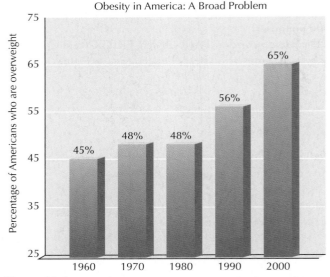

● **Figure 10.8** A near epidemic of obesity has occurred in the United States during the last 20 years, with 65 percent of all Americans now classified as overweight (Ogden et al., 2007).

Taste

The availability of a variety of tasty foods can also lead to overeating and obesity in societies where such foods are plentiful. Normally, tastes for foods vary considerably. For example, if you are well fed, leptin dulls the tongue's sensitivity to sweet tastes (Kawai et al., 2000). If you have noticed that you lose your "sweet tooth" when you are full, you may have observed this effect. Actually, if you eat too much of any particular food, it will become less appealing. This

DISCOVERING PSYCHOLOGY

What's Your BMI? (We've Got Your Number)

From the standpoint of fashion, you may already have an opinion about whether you are overweight. But how do you rate from a medical perspective? Obesity is directly linked to heart disease, high blood pressure, stroke, diabetes, and premature death. But how heavy do you have to be to endanger your health? A measure called the *body mass index* (BMI) can be used to assess where you stand on the weight scale (so to speak). You can calculate your BMI by using the following formula:

$$BMI = \frac{(\text{your weight in pounds})}{(\text{height in inches})\,(\text{height in inches})} \times 703$$

To use the formula, take your height in inches and multiply that number by itself

(square the number). Then divide the result into your weight in pounds. Multiply the resulting number by 703 to obtain your BMI. For example, a person who weighs 220 pounds and is 6 feet 3 inches tall has a BMI of 27.5.

$$\frac{(220 \text{ pounds})}{(75 \text{ inches})\,(75 \text{ inches})} \times 703 = 27.5$$

Now, compare your BMI to the following scale:

Underweight	less than 18.5
Normal weight	18.5 to 24.9
Overweight	25 to 29.9
Obesity	30 or greater

If your BMI is greater than 25, you should be concerned. If it is greater than 30, your weight may be a serious health risk. (There are two exceptions: The BMI may overestimate body fat if you have a muscular build, and it may underestimate body fat in older persons who have lost muscle mass.) Losing weight and keeping it off can be very challenging. However, if you're overweight, lowering your BMI is well worth the effort. In the long run, it could save your life.

---

probably helps us maintain variety in our diets. However, it also encourages obesity. If you overdose on fried chicken or French fries, moving on to some cookies or chocolate cheesecake certainly won't do your body much good (Pinel, Assanand, & Lehman, 2000).

It is easy to acquire a **taste aversion,** or active dislike, for a particular food. This can happen if a food causes sickness or if it is merely associated with nausea (Jacobsen et al., 1993). Not only do we learn to avoid such foods, but they too can become nauseating. A friend of one of your authors once became ill after eating a cheese Danish (well, actually, *several*) and has never again been able to come face to face with this delightful pastry.

If you like animals, you will be interested in an imaginative approach to an age-old problem. In many rural areas, predators are poisoned, trapped, or shot by ranchers. These practices have nearly wiped out the timber wolf, and in some areas the coyote faces a similar end. How might the coyote be saved without a costly loss of livestock?

In a classic experiment, coyotes were given lamb tainted with lithium chloride. Coyotes who took the bait became nauseated and vomited. After one or two such treatments, they developed **bait shyness**—a lasting distaste for the tainted food (Gustavson & Garcia, 1974). If applied consistently, taste aversion conditioning might solve many predator–livestock problems.

If getting sick occurs long after eating, how does it become associated with a particular food? A good question. Taste aversions are a type of classical conditioning. As stated in Chapter 7, a long delay between the conditioned stimulus (CS) and the unconditioned stimulus (US) usually prevents conditioning. However, psychologists theorize that we have a biological tendency to associate an upset stomach with foods eaten earlier. Such learning is usually protective. Yet, as we saw previously (in Chapter 7), many cancer patients suffer taste aversions long after the nausea of their drug treatments has passed (Chance, 2006; Stockhorst, Klosterhalfen, & Steingrueber, 1998).

Taste aversions may also help people avoid severe nutritional imbalances. For example, if you go on a fad diet and eat only grapefruit, you will eventually begin to feel ill. In time, associating your discomfort with grapefruit may create an aversion to it and restore some balance to your diet.

Emotional Eating

Is it true that people also overeat when they are emotionally upset? Yes. People with weight problems are prone to overeat when they are anxious, angry, or sad (Geliebter & Aversa, 2003). Furthermore, obese individuals are often unhappy in our fat-conscious culture. The result is overeating that leads to emotional distress

---

bridges

Bait shyness is similar to human aversion conditioning, which is used to help people control bad habits, such as smoking, drinking, or nail biting. **See Chapter 15, page 504, to explore this connection.**

Set point The proportion of body fat that tends to be maintained by changes in hunger and eating.

Taste aversion An active dislike for a particular food.

Bait shyness An unwillingness or hesitation on the part of animals to eat a particular food.

and still more overeating. This makes weight control extremely difficult (Rutledge & Linden, 1998).

Cultural Factors

Learning to think of some foods as desirable and others as revolting has a large impact on what we eat. In North America we would never consider eating the eyes out of the steamed head of a monkey, but in some parts of the world they are considered a delicacy. By the same token, vegans and vegetarians think it is barbaric to eat any kind of meat. In short, cultural values greatly affect the *incentive value* of foods.

Dieting

A diet is not just a way to lose weight. Your current diet is defined by the types and amounts of food you regularly eat. Some diets actually encourage overeating. For instance, placing animals on a "supermarket" diet leads to gross obesity. In one classic experiment, rats were given meals of chocolate chip cookies, salami, cheese, bananas, marshmallows, milk chocolate, peanut butter, and fat. These pampered rodents overate, gaining almost three times as much weight as rats that ate only laboratory chow (Sclafani & Springer, 1976). (Rat chow is a dry mixture of several bland grains. If you were a rat, you'd probably eat more cookies than rat chow, too.)

People are also sensitive to dietary content. In general, *sweetness,* high *fat content,* and *variety* tend to encourage overeating (Lucas & Sclafani, 1990). Unfortunately, North American culture provides the worst kinds of foods for people who suffer from obesity. For example, restaurant and fast food tends to be higher in fat and calories than meals made at home (Brownell, 2003). "Supersized" meals are another problem. Food portions at restaurants in the United States are 25 percent larger, or more, than they are in France. Far fewer people are obese in France, most likely because they simply eat less. The French also take longer to eat a meal, which discourages overeating (Rozin et al., 2003).

An added problem faced by people who want to control their weight concerns "yo-yo" dieting.

The Paradox of Yo-Yo Dieting

If dieting works, why are hundreds of "new" diets published each year? The answer is that although dieters do lose weight, most regain it soon after they stop dieting. In fact, many people end up weighing even more than before. Why should this be so? Dieting (starving) slows the body's rate of metabolism (the rate at which energy is used up). In effect, a dieter's body becomes highly efficient at *conserving* calories and storing them as fat (Pinel, Assanand, & Lehman, 2000).

Apparently, evolution prepared us to save energy when food is scarce and to stock up on fat when food is plentiful. Briefly starving yourself, therefore, may have little lasting effect on weight. "Yo-yo dieting," or repeatedly losing and gaining weight, is especially dangerous. Frequent changes in weight can dramatically slow the body's metabolic rate. As noted earlier, this may raise the body's set point for fat and makes it harder to lose weight each time a person diets and easier to regain weight when the diet ends. Frequent weight changes also increase the risk of heart disease and premature death (Wang & Brownell, 2005). To avoid bouncing between feast and famine requires a permanent change in eating habits and exercise.

To summarize, eating and overeating are related to internal and external influences, diet, emotions, genetics, exercise, and many other factors. People become obese in different ways and for different reasons. We live in a culture that provides inexpensive, good-tasting food everywhere, and have a brain that evolved to say "Eat whenever food is available." Clearly, scientists are still a long way from winning the "battle of the bulge." Nevertheless, many people have learned to take control of eating by applying psychological principles. (See "Behavioral Dieting.")

Eating Disorders

Under the sheets of her hospital bed Krystal looks like a skeleton. If her **anorexia nervosa** (AN-uh-REK-see-yah ner-VOH-sah: self-starvation) cannot be stopped, Krystal may die of malnutrition.

"Supersized" portions contribute to overeating. A fast-food meal consisting of a hamburger, medium fries, and a medium soda averages 1,200 calories, which is over half the daily caloric need for an adult. Make that a double burger, add cheese, and supersize the fries and the drink and you will consume two thirds of the food you need in a day in just one meal. Notice, too, that people tend to eat all the food they have paid for, even if it is more than they need.

Actress Valerie Bertinelli has been a lifelong yo-yo dieter who tried many different diets. As a spokeswoman for a national weight-loss program, Valerie lost about 40 pounds. Will she maintain her weight loss after she reaches her target weight?

DISCOVERING PSYCHOLOGY

Behavioral Dieting

As we have noted, dieting is usually followed by rapid weight gain. If you really want to lose weight, you must overhaul your eating habits, an approach called **behavioral dieting.** Here are some helpful behavioral techniques:

1. **Get yourself committed to weight loss.** Involve other people in your efforts. Programs such as Overeaters Anonymous or Take Off Pounds Sensibly can be a good source of social support.

2. **Exercise.** No diet can succeed for long without an increase in exercise, because exercise burns calories. To lose weight, you must use more calories than you take in. Burning just 200 extra calories a day can help prevent rebound weight gains. Add activity to your routine in every way you can think of. Stop saving steps and riding elevators. Buy a *step counter* to track the number of steps you take every day. Walking 10,000 steps per day will burn between 2,000 and 3,500 calories a week (depending on your weight). The more frequently and vigorously you exercise, the more weight you will lose (Jeffery & Wing, 2001).

3. **Learn your eating habits by observing yourself and keeping a "diet diary."** Begin by making a complete, 2-week record of when and where you eat, what you eat, and the feelings and events that occur just before and after eating. Is a roommate, relative, or spouse encouraging you to overeat? What are your most "dangerous" times and places for overeating?

4. **Learn to weaken your personal eating cues.** When you have learned when and where you do most of your eating, avoid these situations. Try to restrict your eating to one room, and do not read, watch TV, study, or talk on the phone while eating. Require yourself to interrupt what you are doing in order to eat.

5. **Count calories, but don't starve yourself.** To lose weight, you must eat less, and counting calories allows you to keep a record of your food intake. If you have trouble eating less every day, try dieting 4 days a week. People who diet intensely every other day lose as much as those who diet moderately every day (Viegener et al., 1990).

6. **Develop techniques to control the act of eating.** Whenever you can, check for nutritional information and buy groceries and meals lower in calories and fats. Also begin to take smaller portions. Carry to the table only what you plan to eat. Put all other food away before leaving the kitchen. Eat slowly, sip water between bites of food, leave food on your plate, and stop eating before you are completely full. Be especially wary of the extra-large servings at fast-food restaurants. Saying "supersize me" too often can, indeed, leave you super sized (Murray, 2001).

7. **Avoid snacks.** It is generally better to eat more small meals a day than fewer large ones because more calories are burned (Assanand, Pinel, & Lehman, 1998). However, high-calorie snacks tend to be eaten *in addition to* meals. If you have an impulse to snack, set a timer for 20 minutes and see if you are still hungry then. Delay the impulse to snack several times if possible. Dull your appetite by filling up on raw carrots, bouillon, water, coffee, or tea.

8. **Chart your daily progress.** Record your weight, the number of calories eaten, and whether you met your daily goal. Set realistic goals by cutting down calories gradually. Losing about a pound per week is realistic, but remember, you are changing habits, not just dieting. Diets don't work!

9. **Set a "threshold" for weight control.** Maintaining weight loss can be even more challenging than losing weight. It is easier to maintain weight loss if you set a regain limit of 3 pounds or less. In other words, if you gain more than 2 or 3 pounds, you immediately begin to make corrections in your eating habits and amount of exercise (Brownell, 2003).

Be patient with this program. It takes years to develop eating habits. You can expect it to take at least several months to change them. If you are unsuccessful at losing weight with these techniques, you might find it helpful to seek the aid of a psychologist familiar with behavioral weight-loss techniques.

AN OPTIMIST'S RESPONSE TO A STALLED DIET.

OH WELL, I'LL JUST HAVE TO EAT NOTHING BUT PIZZA AND DOUGHNUTS FOR A WHILE UNTIL I CAN GET BACK TO WHERE I CAN START LOSING WEIGHT AGAIN.

BRIAN BASSET 5-24
© 2003 UNIVERSAL PRESS SYNDICATE

WWW.UCOMICS.COM

Victims of anorexia, who are mostly adolescent females, suffer devastating weight losses from severe, self-inflicted dieting (Cooper, 2005).

Do anorexics lose their appetite? Although the compulsive attempt to lose weight causes them to not seek or desire food, they often still feel physical hunger. Often, anorexia starts with "normal" dieting that slowly begins to dominate the person's life. In

Anorexia nervosa Active self-starvation or a sustained loss of appetite that has psychological origins.

Behavioral dieting Weight reduction based on changing exercise and eating habits, rather than temporary self-starvation.

Table 10.1 ● Recognizing Eating Disorders

Anorexia Nervosa
- Body weight below 85 percent of normal for one's height and age.
- Refusal to maintain body weight in normal range.
- Intense fear of becoming fat or gaining weight, even though underweight.
- Disturbance in one's body image or perceived weight.
- Self-evaluation is unduly influenced by body weight.
- Denial of seriousness of abnormally low body weight.
- Absence of menstrual periods.
- Purging behavior (vomiting or misuse of laxatives or diuretics).

Bulimia Nervosa
- Normal or above-normal weight.
- Recurring binge eating.
- Eating within an hour or two an amount of food that is much larger than most people would consume.
- Feeling a lack of control over eating.
- Purging behavior (vomiting or misuse of laxatives or diuretics).
- Excessive exercise to prevent weight gain.
- Fasting to prevent weight gain.
- Self-evaluation is unduly influenced by body weight.

DSM-IV-TR, 2000.

Anorexia nervosa is far more dangerous than many people realize. This haunting Italian anti-anorexia poster shows 68-pound model Isabelle Caro, who has struggled with anorexia for 15 years. Many celebrities have struggled with eating disorders, including Karen Carpenter (who died of starvation-induced heart failure), Paula Abdul, Kirstie Alley, Fiona Apple, Victoria Beckham (Posh Spice), Princess Diana, Tracey Gold, Janet Jackson, and Mary-Kate Olsen.

Pascal Le Segretain/Getty Images

time, anorexics suffer debilitating health problems. From 5 to 8 percent (more than 1 in 20) die of malnutrition (Polivy & Herman, 2002). ● Table 10.1 lists the symptoms of anorexia nervosa.

Bulimia nervosa (bue-LIHM-ee-yah) is a second major eating disorder. Bulimic persons gorge on food, then vomit or take laxatives to avoid gaining weight. (See ● Table 10.1.) Like anorexia, most victims of bulimia are girls or women. Approximately 5 percent of college women are bulimic, and as many as 60 percent have milder eating problems. Bingeing and purging can seriously damage health. Typical risks include sore throat, hair loss, muscle spasms, kidney damage, dehydration, tooth erosion, swollen salivary glands, menstrual irregularities, loss of sex drive, and even heart attack.

Men and Eating Disorders

Eating disorders are on the rise among men. Currently, one third of men say they want less body fat and another third want more muscles (McCabe & Ricciardelli, 2004). As a result, many men are altering what they eat and exercising excessively. Some are going too far: About 10 percent of anorexics and 25 percent of bulimics are now males (Weltzin et al., 2005).

Causes

What causes anorexia and bulimia? Women and men who suffer from eating disorders are extremely dissatisfied with their bodies (Crisp et al., 2006). Usually, they have distorted views of themselves, exaggerated fears of becoming fat, and low self-esteem. Many overestimate their body size by 25 percent or more. As a result, they think they are disgustingly "fat" when they are actually wasting away (● Figure 10.9) (Polivy & Herman, 2002).

Many of these problems are related to the idealized body images presented in the media (Levine & Harrison, 2004). Some websites even go so far as to endorse anorexia and bulimia (referred to by "fans" as "Ana" and "Mia") (Tierney, 2008). Girls who spend a lot of time reading fashion magazines or visiting

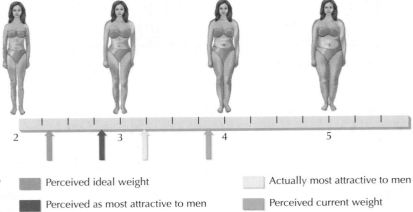

● Figure 10.9 Women with abnormal eating habits were asked to rate their body shape on a scale similar to the one you see here. As a group, they chose ideal figures much thinner than what they thought their current weights were. (Most women say they want to be thinner than they currently are, but to a lesser degree than women with eating problems.) Notice that the women with eating problems chose an ideal weight that was even thinner than what they thought men prefer. This is not typical of most women. In this study, only women with eating problems wanted to be thinner than what they thought men find attractive (Zellner, D. A., Harner, D. E., & Adler, R. L. (1989). Effects of eating abnormalities and gender on perceptions of desirable body shape. *Journal of Abnormal Psychology*, 98(1), 93-96. Copyright © 1989 APA. Reprinted with permission of the publisher.).

■ Perceived ideal weight
■ Perceived as most attractive to men
□ Actually most attractive to men
■ Perceived current weight

these websites are more likely to have distorted body images and unrealistic ideas about how they compare with others (Martinez-Gonzalez et al., 2003).

The popularity of fitness, exercise, and sports has also contributed to eating disorders. Today, more people are changing their diets in search of a lean, muscular look. People engaged in sports that require low body fat or extreme weight loss (such as wrestling, gymnastics, pole vaulting, high jumping, and even cycling) are particularly likely to develop eating disorders (Weltzin et al., 2005).

People with eating disorders appear to be trying to gain some measure of control. Anorexic teen girls are usually described as "perfect" daughters—helpful, considerate, conforming, and obedient. They seem to be seeking perfect control in their lives by being perfectly slim (Castro et al., 2004). People suffering from bulimia are also concerned with control. Typically they are obsessed with thoughts of weight, food, eating, and ridding themselves of food. As a result, they feel guilt, shame, self-contempt, and anxiety. Vomiting reduces their anxiety, which makes purging highly reinforcing (Powell & Thelen, 1996).

Treatment

Most people suffering from eating disorders will not seek help on their own. This is especially true for men, because eating disorders are still widely perceived to be a female problem (Weltzin et al., 2005). Typically, it takes strong urging by family or friends to get victims into treatment.

Treatment for anorexia usually begins with giving drugs to relieve obsessive fears of gaining weight. Then a medical diet is used to restore weight and health. Next, a counselor may help patients work on the emotional conflicts that led to weight loss. For bulimia, behavioral counseling may include self-monitoring of food intake. A related cognitive-behavioral approach focuses on changing the thinking patterns and beliefs about weight and body shape that perpetuate eating disorders (Byrne & McLean, 2002; Cooper, 2005).

Culture, Ethnicity, and Dieting

Women with eating disorders are not alone in having body image problems. In Western cultures, many women learn to see themselves as "objects" that are evaluated by others. As a result, they try to shape their bodies to the cultural ideal of slimness through dieting (Fredrickson et al., 1998).

Just looking at a fashion magazine tends to leave women less satisfied with their weight and anxious to be thinner (Simpson, 2002). However, women from some cultural backgrounds appear to be less susceptible to the glorification of slimness. For example, Asian-American college students are only half as likely to diet as other college women are (Tsai, Hoerr, & Song, 1998). Within the African-American and Pacific-Islander communities there is a general preference for a fuller and shapelier figure. In these groups a larger body size is associated with high social status, health, and beauty (Flynn & Fitzgibbon, 1998; Ofosu, Lafreniere, & Senn, 1998). Clearly, what constitutes an attractive body style is a matter of opinion.

Biological Motives Revisited— Thirst, Sex, and Pain

Gateway Questions: Is there more than one type of thirst? In what ways are pain avoidance and the sex drive unusual?

Most biological motives work in ways that are similar to hunger. For example, thirst is only partially controlled by dryness of the mouth. If you were to take a drug that made your mouth constantly wet, or dry, your water intake would remain normal. Like hunger, thirst is regulated by separate *thirst* and *thirst satiety* systems in the hypothalamus. Also like hunger, thirst is strongly affected by learning and cultural values.

Thirst

You may not have noticed, but there are actually two kinds of thirst. **Extracellular thirst** occurs when water is lost from the fluids surrounding the cells of your body. Bleeding, vomiting, diarrhea, sweating, and drinking alcohol cause this type of thirst (Franken, 2007). When a person loses both water and minerals in any of these ways—especially by perspiration—a slightly salty liquid may be more satisfying than plain water.

Why would a thirsty person want to drink salty water? The reason is that before the body can retain water, minerals lost through perspiration (mainly salt) must be replaced. In lab tests, animals greatly prefer saltwater after salt levels in their bodies are lowered (Strickler & Verbalis, 1988). Similarly, some nomadic peoples of the Sahara Desert prize blood as a beverage, probably because of its saltiness. (Maybe they should try Gatorade?)

A second type of thirst occurs when you eat a salty meal. In this instance your body does not lose fluid. Instead, excess salt causes fluid to be drawn out of cells. As the cells "shrink," **intracellular thirst** is triggered. Thirst of this type is best quenched by plain water.

The drives for food, water, air, sleep, and elimination are all similar in that they are generated by a combination of activities in the body and the brain, and they are influenced by various external factors. However, the drive to avoid pain and the sex drive are more unusual.

Pain

How is the drive to avoid pain different? Hunger, thirst, and sleepiness come and go in a fairly regular cycle each day. Pain avoidance, by contrast, is an **episodic drive** (ep-ih-SOD-ik). That is, it occurs

Bulimia nervosa Excessive eating (gorging) usually followed by self-induced vomiting and/or taking laxatives.

Extracellular thirst Thirst caused by a reduction in the volume of fluids found between body cells.

Intracellular thirst Thirst triggered when fluid is drawn out of cells due to an increased concentration of salts and minerals outside the cell.

Episodic drive A drive that occurs in distinct episodes.

Alain Evrard/Photo Researchers.

Tolerance for pain and the strength of a person's motivation to avoid discomfort are greatly affected by cultural practices and beliefs.

in distinct episodes when bodily damage takes place or is about to occur. Most drives prompt us to actively seek a desired goal (food, drink, warmth, and so forth). Pain prompts us to *avoid* or *eliminate* sources of discomfort.

Some people feel they must be "tough" and not show any distress. Others complain loudly at the smallest ache or pain. The first attitude raises pain tolerance, and the second lowers it. As this suggests, the drive to avoid pain is partly learned. That's why members of some societies endure cutting, burning, whipping, tattooing, and piercing of the skin that would agonize most people (but apparently not devotees of piercing and "body art"). In general, we learn how to react to pain by observing family members, friends, and other role models (McMahon & Koltzenburg, 2005).

The Sex Drive

Sex is unlike other biological motives because sex (contrary to anything your personal experience might suggest) is not necessary for *individual* survival. It is necessary, of course, for *group* survival.

The term **sex drive** refers to the strength of one's motivation to engage in sexual behavior. In lower animals the sex drive is directly related to hormones. Female mammals (other than humans) are interested in mating only when their fertility cycles are in the stage of **estrus,** or "heat." Estrus is caused by a release of **estrogen** (a female sex hormone) into the bloodstream. Hormones are important in males as well. In most animals, castration will abolish the sex drive. But in contrast to females, the normal male animal is almost always ready to mate. His sex drive is primarily aroused by the behavior and scent of a receptive female. Therefore, in many species mating is closely tied to female fertility cycles.

How much do hormones affect human sex drives? Hormones affect the human sex drive, but not as directly as in animals

(Crooks & Baur, 2008). The sex drive in men is related to the amount of **androgens** (male hormones such as testosterone) provided by the testes. When the supply of androgens dramatically increases at puberty, so does the male sex drive. Likewise, the sex drive in women is related to their estrogen levels (Hyde & DeLamater, 2006). However, "male" hormones also affect the female sex drive. In addition to estrogen, a woman's body produces small amounts of androgens. When their androgen levels increase, many women experience a corresponding increase in sex drive (Van Goozen et al., 1995). Testosterone levels decline with age, and various medical problems can lower sexual desire. In some instances, taking testosterone supplements can restore the sex drive in both men and women (Crooks & Baur, 2008).

Human sexual behavior and attitudes are discussed in detail in Chapter 11. For now it is enough to note that the sex drive is largely **non-homeostatic** (relatively independent of bodily need states). In humans, the sex drive can be aroused at virtually any time by almost anything. It therefore shows no clear relationship to deprivation (the amount of time since the drive was last satisfied). Certainly, an increase in desire may occur as time passes. But recent sexual activity does not prevent sexual desire from occurring again. Notice, too, that people may seek to arouse the sex drive as well as to reduce it. This unusual quality makes the sex drive capable of motivating a wide range of behaviors. It also explains why sex is used to sell almost everything imaginable.

The non-homeostatic quality of the sex drive can be shown in this way: A male animal is allowed to copulate until it seems to have no further interest in sexual behavior. Then a new sexual partner is provided. Immediately the animal resumes sexual activity. This pattern is called the *Coolidge effect* after former U.S. president Calvin Coolidge. What, you might ask, does Calvin Coolidge have to do with the sex drive? The answer is found in the following story.

While touring an experimental farm, Coolidge's wife reportedly asked if a rooster mated just once a day. "No ma'am," she was told, "he mates dozens of times each day." "Tell that to the president," she said, with a faraway look in her eyes. When President Coolidge reached the same part of the tour, his wife's message was given to him. His reaction was to ask if the dozens of matings were with the same hen. No, he was told, different hens were involved. "Tell *that* to Mrs. Coolidge," the president is said to have replied.

KNOWLEDGE BUILDER
Hunger, Thirst, Pain, and Sex
RECITE
1. The hunger satiety system in the hypothalamus signals the body to start eating when it receives signals from the liver or detects changes in blood sugar. T or F?
2. Maintaining your body's set point for fat is closely linked with the amount of _____ in the bloodstream.
   a. hypothalamic factor-1
   b. ventromedial peptide-1
   c. NPY
   d. leptin

Continued

3. People who frequently diet tend to benefit from practice: They lose weight more quickly each time they diet. T or F?
4. Bingeing and purging are most characteristic of people who have
   a. taste aversions
   b. anorexia
   c. bulimia
   d. strong sensitivity to external eating cues
5. In addition to changing eating habits, a key element of behavioral dieting is
   a. exercise
   b. well-timed snacking
   c. better eating cues
   d. commitment to "starving" every day
6. A cancer patient has little appetite for food several weeks after the nausea caused by chemotherapy has ended. Her loss of appetite is probably best explained by
   a. increased NPY in the brain
   b. a conditioned taste aversion
   c. the aftereffects of yo-yo dieting
   d. a loss of extracellular hunger
7. Thirst may be either intracellular or _____.
8. Pain avoidance is an _____ drive.
9. Sexual behavior in animals is largely controlled by estrogen levels in the female and the occurrence of estrus in the male. T or F?

REFLECT

Critical Thinking

10. Kim, who is overweight, is highly sensitive to external eating cues. How might her wristwatch contribute to her overeating?

Relate

Think of the last meal you ate. What caused you to feel hungry? What internal signals told your body to stop eating? How sensitive are you to external eating cues? How were you influenced by portion size? Have you developed any taste aversions?

A friend of yours seems to be engaging in yo-yo dieting. Can you explain to her or him why such dieting is ineffective? Can you summarize how behavioral dieting is done?

If you wanted to provoke extracellular thirst in yourself, what would you do? How could you make intracellular thirst occur?

Answers: 1. F **2.** d **3.** F **4.** c **5.** a **6.** b **7.** extracellular **8.** episodic **9.** F **10.** The time of day can influence eating, especially for externally cued eaters, who tend to get hungry at mealtimes, irrespective of their internal needs for food.

🔵🔵 Stimulus Drives—Skydiving, Horror Movies, and the Fun Zone

Gateway Question: How does arousal relate to motivation?

Are you full of energy right now? Are you feeling tired? Clearly, the level of arousal you are experiencing is closely linked with your motivation. Are there ideal levels of arousal for different people and different activities? Let's find out.

Most people enjoy a steady "diet" of new movies, novels, tunes, fashions, games, news, websites, and adventures. Yet **stimulus drives,** which reflect needs for information, exploration, manipulation, and sensory input, go beyond mere entertainment. Stimulus drives also help us survive. As we scan our surroundings, we constantly identify sources of food, danger, shelter, and other key

● **Figure 10.10** Monkeys happily open locks that are placed in their cage. Because no reward is given for this activity, it provides evidence for the existence of stimulus needs. (Courtesy of Harry F. Harlow.)

details. The drive for stimulation is already present during infancy. By the time a child can walk, there are few things in the home that have not been tasted, touched, viewed, handled, or, in the case of toys, destroyed!

Stimulus drives are readily apparent in animals as well as humans. For example, monkeys will quickly learn to solve a mechanical puzzle made up of interlocking metal pins, hooks, and latches (Butler, 1954) (● Figure 10.10). No food treats or other external rewards are needed to get them to explore and manipulate their surroundings. The monkeys seem to work for the sheer fun of it.

Arousal Theory

Are stimulus drives homeostatic? Yes. According to **arousal theory** we try to keep arousal at an optimal level (Franken, 2007; Hancock & Ganey, 2003). In other words, when your level of arousal is too low or too high, you will seek ways to raise or lower it.

What do you mean by arousal? Arousal refers to activation of the body and the nervous system. Arousal is zero at death; it is low

---

Sex drive The strength of one's motivation to engage in sexual behavior.

Estrus Changes in the sexual drives of animals that create a desire for mating; particularly used to refer to females in heat.

Estrogen Any of a number of female sex hormones.

Androgen Any of a number of male sex hormones, especially testosterone.

Non-homeostatic drive A drive that is relatively independent of physical deprivation cycles or bodily need states.

Stimulus drives Drives based on needs for exploration, manipulation, curiosity, and stimulation.

Arousal theory Assumes that people prefer to maintain ideal, or comfortable, levels of arousal.

HUMAN DIVERSITY

Xtreme!

Where would you prefer to go on your next summer vacation? How about a week with your best friends at a cottage on a nearby lake? Or a shopping and museum trip to New York City? Better yet, how about cage diving with great white sharks in South Africa? If the shark adventure attracts you, you are probably high in sensation seeking and would be interested in a vacation that includes activi-

Thrill seeking is an element of the sensation-seeking personality.

Jeffrey L. Rotman/Corbis

ties like bungee jumping, scuba diving, skiing, surfing, skydiving, or whitewater rafting (Pizam et al., 2004).

Marvin Zuckerman (1990, 2000) has devised a test to measure differences in sensation seeking. His *Sensation-Seeking Scale* (SSS) includes statements like the samples shown here (from Zuckerman, 1996):

Thrill and adventure seeking
- I would like to try parachute jumping.
- I think I would enjoy the sensations of skiing very fast down a high mountain slope.

Experience seeking
- I like to explore a strange city or section of town myself, even if it means getting lost.
- I like to try new foods that I have never tasted before.

Disinhibition
- I like wild, "uninhibited" parties.
- I often like to get high (drinking liquor or smoking marijuana).

Boredom susceptibility
- I can't stand watching a movie that I've seen before.
- I like people who are sharp and witty, even if they do sometimes insult others.

So who are the potential cage divers? Perhaps it's not surprising that SSS scores tend to be higher among men and younger people (Butkovic & Bratko, 2003; Roberti, 2004). SSS scores also vary across cultures. In one study of 11 different cultures, people from America, Israel, and Ireland scored higher on the SSS than people from South Africa, Slovakia, Sicily, or Gabon (Pizam et al., 2004).

Exciting lives aside, there is a dark side to sensation seeking as well. High sensation seekers are also more likely to engage in high-risk behaviors such as substance abuse (Horvath et al., 2004) and casual unprotected sex (Gullette & Lyons, 2005).

---

during sleep; it is moderate during normal daily activities; and it is high at times of excitement, emotion, or panic. Arousal theory assumes that we become uncomfortable when arousal is too low ("I'm bored") or when it is too high, as in fear, anxiety, or panic ("The dentist will see you now"). Most adults vary their activities to maintain a comfortable level of activation. Music, parties, sports, conversation, sleep, surfing the web, and the like are combined to keep arousal at moderate levels. The right mix of activities prevents boredom *and* overstimulation (Csikszentmihalyi, Abuhamdeh, & Nakamura, 2005).

Sensation Seekers

Do people vary in their needs for stimulation? Picture a city dweller who is visiting the country. Before long, she begins to complain that it is "too quiet" and seeks some "action." Now imagine a country dweller who is visiting the city. Very soon, she finds the city "overwhelming" and seeks peace and quiet. These examples are extremes, but arousal theory also suggests that people learn to seek particular levels of arousal.

Sensation seeking is a trait of people who prefer high levels of stimulation (Gray & Wilson, 2007). Whether you are high or low in sensation seeking is probably based on how your body responds to new, unusual, or intense stimulation (Zuckerman, 2002). People high in sensation seeking tend to be bold and independent, and they value change. They also report more sexual partners than

low scorers, they are more likely to smoke, and they prefer spicy, sour, and crunchy foods over bland foods. Low sensation seekers are orderly, nurturant, and giving, and they enjoy the company of others. Which are you? (Most people fall somewhere between the extremes. See "Xtreme!")

Levels of Arousal

Is there an ideal level of arousal for peak performance? If we set aside individual differences, most people perform best when their arousal level is *moderate*. Let's say that you have to take an essay exam. If you are feeling sleepy or lazy (arousal level too low), your performance will suffer. If you are in a state of anxiety or panic about the test (arousal level too high), you will also perform below par. Thus, the relationship between arousal and performance forms an *inverted U function* (a curve in the shape of an upside-down U) (● Figure 10.11) (Hancock & Ganey, 2003).

The inverted U tells us that at very low levels of arousal you're not sufficiently energized to perform well. Performance will improve as your arousal level increases, up to the middle of the curve. Then it begins to drop off, as you become emotional, frenzied, or disorganized. For example, imagine trying to start a car stalled on a railroad track, with a speeding train bearing down on you. That's what the high-arousal end of the curve feels like.

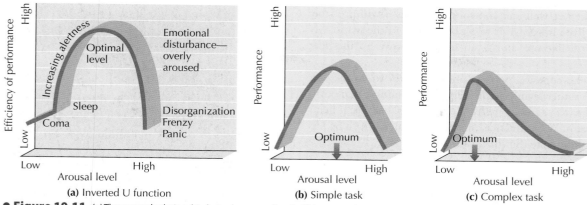

● **Figure 10.11** *(a)* The general relationship between arousal and efficiency can be described by an inverted U curve. The optimal level of arousal or motivation is higher for a simple task *(b)* than for a complex task *(c)*.

Is performance always best at moderate levels of arousal? No, the ideal level of arousal depends on the complexity of a task. If a task is relatively simple, it is best for arousal to be high. When a task is more complex, your best performance will occur at lower levels of arousal. This relationship is called the **Yerkes-Dodson law.** (See ● Figure 10.11.) It applies to a wide variety of tasks and to measures of motivation other than arousal.

For example, at a track meet, it is almost impossible for sprinters to get too aroused for a race. The task is direct and simple: Run as fast as you can for a short distance. On the other hand, a golfer making a tournament-deciding putt faces a more sensitive and complex task. Excessive arousal is almost certain to hurt his or her performance. In school, most students have had experience with "test anxiety," a familiar example of how too much arousal can lower performance.

> **bridges**
> One of the best ways to avoid test anxiety is to improve your study skills. **If test anxiety is a problem for you, it would be wise to return to the Introduction in this text and review the learning and test-taking skills described there.**

Coping with Test Anxiety

Then is it true that by learning to calm down, a person would do better on tests? Usually, but not always. To begin with, some arousal is healthy; it focuses us on the task at hand. It is only when arousal interferes with performance that we refer to anxiety. **Test anxiety** is a mixture of *heightened physiological arousal* (nervousness, sweating, pounding heart) and *excessive worry*. This combination—arousal plus worry—tends to distract students with a rush of upsetting thoughts and feelings (Stipek, 2001).

Also, studies show that students are typically most anxious when they don't know the material (Cassady, 2004). If this is the case, calming down simply means you will remain calm while failing. Here are some suggestions for coping with test anxiety:

Preparation

Hard work is the most direct antidote for test anxiety. Many anxious students simply study too little, too late. That's why improving your study skills is a good way to reduce test anxiety (Cassady, 2004). The best solution is to *overprepare* by studying long before the "big day." Well-prepared students score higher, worry less, and are less likely to panic (Zohar, 1998).

Relaxation

Learning to relax is another way to lower test anxiety (Ricketts & Galloway, 1984). You can learn self-relaxation skills by looking at Chapter 13, where a relaxation technique is described. Emotional support also helps (Stöber, 2004). If you are test anxious, discuss the problem with your professors or study for tests with a supportive classmate.

Rehearsal

To reduce nervousness, rehearse how you will cope with upsetting events. Before taking a test, imagine yourself going blank, running out of time, or feeling panicked. Then calmly plan how you will handle each situation—by keeping your attention on the task, by focusing on one question at a time, and so forth (Watson & Tharp, 2007).

Restructuring Thoughts

Another helpful strategy involves listing the upsetting thoughts you have during exams. Then you can learn to combat these worries with calming, rational replies (Jones & Petruzzi, 1995). (These are called *coping statements;* see Chapter 13 for more information.) Let's say you think, "I'm going to fail this test and everybody will think I'm stupid." A good reply to this upsetting thought would be

Yerkes-Dodson law A summary of the relationships among arousal, task complexity, and performance.

Test anxiety High levels of arousal and worry that seriously impair test performance.

to say, "If I prepare well and control my worries, I will probably pass the test. Even if I don't, it won't be the end of the world. My friends will still like me, and I can try to improve on the next test."

Students who cope well with exams usually try to do the best they can, even under trying circumstances. Becoming a more confident test taker can actually increase your scores, because it helps you remain calm. With practice, most people can learn to be less testy at test-taking time (Smith, 2002).

Learned Motives—The Pursuit of Excellence

Gateway Questions: What are learned motives? Social motives? Why are they important?

Many motives are acquired directly. It is easy enough to see that praise, money, success, pleasure, and similar reinforcers affect our goals and desires. But how do people learn to enjoy activities that are at first painful or frightening? Why do people climb rocks, jump out of airplanes, run marathons, take sauna baths, or swim in frozen lakes? For an answer, let's examine a related situation.

When a person first tries a drug such as heroin, he or she feels a "rush" of pleasure. However, as the drug wears off, discomfort and craving occurs. The easiest way to end the discomfort is to take another dose—as most drug users quickly learn. But in time, habituation takes place; the drug stops producing pleasure, although it will end discomfort. At the same time, the aftereffects of the drug grow more painful. At this point, the drug user has acquired a powerful new motive. In a vicious cycle, heroin relieves discomfort, but it guarantees that withdrawal will occur again in a few hours.

Opponent-Process Theory

Psychologist Richard L. Solomon (1980) offers an intriguing explanation for drug addiction and other learned motives. According to his **opponent-process theory,** if a stimulus causes a strong emotion, such as fear or pleasure, an opposite emotion tends to occur when the stimulus ends. For example, if you are in pain, and the pain ends, you will feel a pleasant sense of relief. If a person feels pleasure, as in the case of drug use, and the pleasure ends, it will be followed by craving or discomfort. If you are in love and feel good when you are with your lover, you will be uncomfortable when she or he is absent.

What happens if the stimulus is repeated? Solomon assumes that when a stimulus is repeated, our response to it habituates, or gets weaker. First-time skydivers, for instance, are almost always terrified. But with repeated jumps, fear decreases, until finally the skydiver feels a "thrill" instead of terror (Roth et al., 1996). In contrast, emotional after effects get stronger with repetition. After a first jump, beginners feel a brief but exhilarating sense of relief. After many such experiences, seasoned skydivers can get a "rush" of euphoria that lasts for hours after a jump (● Figure 10.12).

● **Figure 10.12** A skydiver takes the plunge. The typical emotional sequence for a first jump is anxiety before, terror during, and relief after the jump. After many jumps the emotional sequence becomes eagerness before, a thrill during, and exhilaration after a jump. The new sequence strongly reinforces skydiving.

With repetition, the pleasurable aftereffect gets stronger and the initial "cost" (pain or fear) gets weaker. The opponent-process theory thus explains how skydiving, rock climbing, ski jumping, and other hazardous pursuits become reinforcing. If you are a fan of horror movies, carnival rides, or bungee jumping, your motives may be based on the same effect. (Notice, too, the strong link between motivation and emotion in such examples. We will return to this idea later.)

Social Motives

Some of your friends are more interested than others in success, achievement, competition, money, possessions, status, love, approval, grades, dominance, power, or belonging to groups—all of which are *social motives* or goals. We acquire **social motives** in complex ways, through socialization and cultural conditioning (Franken, 2007). The behavior of outstanding artists, scientists, athletes, educators, and leaders is best understood in terms of such learned needs, particularly the need for achievement.

The Need for Achievement

To many people, being "motivated" means being interested in achievement (Wigfield & Eccles, 2002). In a later chapter we will investigate aggression, helping, affiliation, seeking approval, and other social motives. For now, let us focus on the **need for achievement (nAch),** which is a desire to meet an internal standard of excellence (McClelland, 1961). People with a high need for achievement strive to do well any time they are evaluated.

Is that like the aggressive businessperson who strives for success? Not necessarily. Needs for achievement may lead to wealth and prestige, but people who are high achievers in art, music, science, or amateur sports may excel without seeking riches. Such people typically enjoy challenges and they relish a chance to test their abilities (Puca & Schmalt, 1999).

Power

The need for achievement differs from the **need for power,** which is a desire to have impact or control over others (McClelland, 1975). People with strong needs for power want their importance to be visible: They buy expensive possessions, wear prestigious clothes, and exploit relationships. In some ways the pursuit of power and financial success is the dark side of the American dream. People whose main goal in life is to make lots of money tend to be poorly adjusted and unhappy (Kasser & Ryan, 1993).

Characteristics of Achievers

Using a simple measure, David McClelland (1917–1998) found that he could predict the behavior of high and low achievers. For instance, McClelland compared people's occupations with scores on an achievement test they took as college sophomores. Fourteen years later, those who scored high in nAch tended to have jobs that involved risk and responsibility (McClelland, 1965).

Here's a test: In front of you are five targets. Each is placed at an increasing distance from where you are standing. You are given a beanbag to toss at the target of your choice. Target A, anyone can

hit; target B, most people can hit; target C, some people can hit; target D, very few people can hit; target E is rarely if ever hit. If you hit A, you will receive $2; B, $4; C, $8; D, $16; and E, $32. You get only one toss. Which one would you choose? McClelland's research suggests that if you have a high need for achievement, you will select C or perhaps D. Those high in nAch are *moderate* risk takers. When faced with a problem or a challenge, persons high in nAch avoid goals that are too easy.

Why do they pass up sure success? They do it because easy goals offer no sense of satisfaction. They also avoid long shots because there is either no hope of success, or "winning" will be due to luck rather than skill. Persons low in nAch select sure things or impossible goals. Either way, they don't have to take any responsibility for failure.

Desires for achievement and calculated risk taking lead to success in many situations. People high in nAch complete difficult tasks, they earn better grades, and they tend to excel in their occupations. College students high in nAch attribute success to their own ability, and failure to insufficient effort. Thus, high nAch students are more likely to renew their efforts when they perform poorly. When the going gets tough, high achievers get going.

The Key to Success?

What does it take to achieve extraordinary success? Psychologist Benjamin Bloom studied America's top concert pianists, Olympic swimmers, sculptors, tennis players, mathematicians, and research neurologists. Bloom (1985) found that drive and determination, not great natural talent, led to exceptional success.

The first steps toward high achievement began when parents exposed their children to music, swimming, scientific ideas, and so forth, "just for fun." At first, many of the children had very ordinary skills. One Olympic swimmer, for instance, remembers repeatedly losing races as a 10-year-old. At some point, however, the children began to actively cultivate their abilities. Before long, parents noticed the child's rapid progress and found an expert instructor or coach. After more successes, the youngsters began "living" for their talent and practiced many hours daily. This continued for many years before they reached truly outstanding heights of achievement.

The upshot of Bloom's work is that talent is nurtured by dedication and hard work (R. C. Beck, 2004). It is most likely to blossom when parents actively support a child's special interest and

Kevin Lamarque/Reuters/Corbis

The person with high needs for achievement strives to do well in any situation in which evaluation takes place.

Opponent-process theory States that strong emotions tend to be followed by an opposite emotional state; also the strength of both emotional states changes over time.

Social motives Learned motives acquired as part of growing up in a particular society or culture.

Need for achievement (nAch) The desire to excel or meet some internalized standard of excellence.

Need for power The desire to have social impact and control over others.

emphasize doing one's best at all times. Studies of child prodigies and eminent adults also show that intensive practice and expert coaching are common ingredients of high achievement. Elite performance in music, sports, chess, the arts, and many other pursuits typically requires at least 10 years of dedicated practice (Ericsson & Charness, 1994; Ross, 2006). The belief that talent will magically surface on its own is largely a myth. This is especially true for talented women, who face a wide variety of social obstacles to exceptional achievement (Noble, Subotnik, & Arnold, 1996).

Self-Confidence

Achieving elite performance may be reserved for the dedicated few. Nevertheless, like elite athletes, you may be able to improve your motivation by increasing your self-confidence (Hanton, Mellalieu, & Hall, 2004). People with self-confidence believe they can successfully carry out an activity or reach a goal. To enhance self-confidence, it is wise to do the following (Druckman & Bjork, 1994):

- Set goals that are specific and challenging, but attainable.
- Visualize the steps you need to take to reach your goal.
- Advance in small steps.
- When you first acquire a skill, your goal should be to make progress in learning. Later, you can concentrate on improving your performance, compared with other people.
- Get expert instruction that helps you master the skill.
- Find a skilled model (someone good at the skill) to emulate.
- Get support and encouragement from an observer.
- If you fail, regard it as a sign that you need to try harder, not that you lack ability.

Self-confidence affects motivation by influencing the challenges you will undertake, the effort you will make, and how long you will persist when things don't go well. You can be confident that self-confidence is worth cultivating.

influence your own behavior. Which seem strongest? Which do you spend the most time and energy satisfying? Now look at Maslow's hierarchy (● Figure 10.13).

Note that physiological needs are at the base of the pyramid. Because these needs must be met if we are to survive, they tend to be *prepotent,* or dominant over the higher needs. That's why, when you are really hungry, you can think of little else but food. Maslow believed that higher, more fragile needs are expressed only after we satisfy our physiological needs. This is also true of needs for safety and security. Until they are met, we may have little interest in higher pursuits. For instance, a person who is feeling threatened might have little interest in writing poetry or even talking with friends. For this reason, Maslow described the first four levels of the hierarchy as **basic needs.** Other basic needs include love and belonging (family, friendship, caring), and needs for esteem and self-esteem (recognition and self-respect).

All the basic needs are *deficiency* motives. That is, they are activated by a *lack* of food, water, security, love, esteem, or other basic needs. At the top of the hierarchy we find **growth needs,** which are expressed as a need for self-actualization. The need for self-actualization is not based on deficiencies. Rather, it is a positive, life-enhancing force for personal growth (Reiss & Havercamp, 2005). Like other humanistic psychologists, Maslow believed that people are basically good. If our basic needs are met, he said, we will tend to move on to actualizing our potentials.

How are needs for self-actualization expressed? Maslow called the less powerful but humanly important actualization motives **meta-needs** (Maslow, 1970). Meta-needs are an expression of tendencies to fully develop your personal potentials. The meta-needs are:

1. Wholeness (unity)
2. Perfection (balance and harmony)
3. Completion (ending)
4. Justice (fairness)
5. Richness (complexity)

●● Motives in Perspective— A View from the Pyramid

Gateway Question: Are some motives more basic than others?

As you may recall from Chapter 1, Abraham Maslow called the full use of personal potential *self-actualization.* Maslow also described a **hierarchy of human needs,** in which some needs are more basic or powerful than others. Think about the needs that

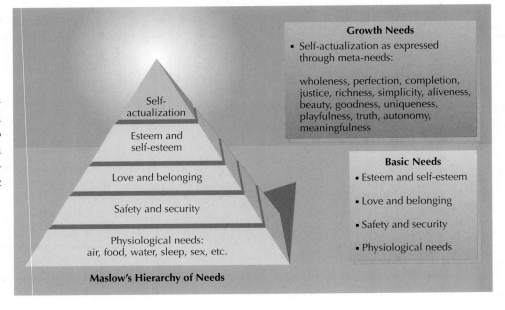

● **Figure 10.13** Maslow believed that lower needs in the hierarchy are dominant. Basic needs must be satisfied before growth motives are fully expressed. Desires for self-actualization are reflected in various meta-needs (see text).

Growth Needs
- Self-actualization as expressed through meta-needs:

  wholeness, perfection, completion, justice, richness, simplicity, aliveness, beauty, goodness, uniqueness, playfulness, truth, autonomy, meaningfulness

Basic Needs
- Esteem and self-esteem
- Love and belonging
- Safety and security
- Physiological needs

Self-actualization

Esteem and self-esteem

Love and belonging

Safety and security

Physiological needs: air, food, water, sleep, sex, etc.

Maslow's Hierarchy of Needs

Wheelchair athletes engage in vigorous competition. Maslow considered such behavior an expression of the need for self-actualization.

6. Simplicity (essence)
7. Aliveness (spontaneity)
8. Beauty (rightness of form)
9. Goodness (benevolence)
10. Uniqueness (individuality)
11. Playfulness (ease)
12. Truth (reality)
13. Autonomy (self-sufficiency)
14. Meaningfulness (values)

According to Maslow, we tend to move up through the hierarchy of needs, toward the meta-needs. When the meta-needs are unfulfilled, people fall into a "syndrome of decay" marked by despair, apathy, and alienation.

bridges
Maslow provided few guidelines for promoting self-actualization. However, some suggestions can be gleaned from his writings. **See Chapter 12, pages 409–410, for more about self-actualization.**

Maslow's point is that mere survival or comfort is usually not enough to make a full and satisfying life. It's interesting to note, in this regard, that college students who are primarily concerned with money, personal appearance, and social recognition score lower than average in vitality, self-actualization, and general well-being (Kasser & Ryan, 1996).

Maslow's hierarchy is not well documented by research, and parts of it are questionable. How, for instance, do we explain the actions of a person who fasts as part of a social protest? How can the meta-need for justice overcome the more basic need for food? (Perhaps the answer is that fasting is temporary and self-imposed.) Despite such objections, Maslow's views are a good way to understand and appreciate the rich interplay of human motives.

Are many people motivated by meta-needs? Maslow estimated that few people are primarily motivated by needs for self-actualization.

Most of us are more concerned with esteem, love, or security. Perhaps this is because rewards in our society tend to encourage conformity, uniformity, and security in schools, jobs, and relationships. When was the last time you met a meta-need?

Intrinsic and Extrinsic Motivation

Some people cook for a living and consider it hard work. Others cook for pleasure and dream of opening a restaurant. For some people, mountain biking, gardening, writing, photography, or jewelry making is fun. For others the same activities are drudgery they must be paid to do. How can the same activity be "work" for one person and "play" for another?

When you do something for enjoyment or to improve your abilities, your motivation is usually *intrinsic*. **Intrinsic motivation** occurs when we act without any obvious external rewards. We simply enjoy an activity or see it as an opportunity to explore, learn, and actualize our potentials. In contrast, **extrinsic motivation** stems from external factors, such as pay, grades, rewards, obligations, and approval. Most of the activities we think of as "work" are extrinsically rewarded (Baard, Deci, & Ryan, 2004; Ryan & Deci, 2000).

Turning Play into Work

Don't extrinsic incentives strengthen motivation? Yes they can, but not always. In fact, *excessive* rewards can decrease intrinsic motivation and spontaneous interest. For instance, in one classic study, children who were lavishly rewarded for drawing with felt-tip pens later showed little interest in playing with the pens again (Greene & Lepper, 1974). Apparently, "play" can be turned into "work" by *requiring* people to do something they would otherwise enjoy. When we are coerced or "bribed" to act, we tend to feel as if we are "faking it." Employees who lack initiative and teenagers who reject school and learning are good examples of such reactions (Ryan & Deci, 2000).

Creativity

People are more likely to be creative when they are intrinsically motivated. On the job, for instance, salaries and bonuses may increase the amount of work done. However, work *quality* is

Hierarchy of human needs Abraham Maslow's ordering of needs, based on their presumed strength or potency.

Basic needs The first four levels of needs in Maslow's hierarchy; lower needs tend to be more potent than higher needs.

Growth needs In Maslow's hierarchy, the higher-level needs associated with self-actualization.

Meta-needs In Maslow's hierarchy, needs associated with impulses for self-actualization.

Intrinsic motivation Motivation that comes from within, rather than from external rewards; motivation based on personal enjoyment of a task or activity.

Extrinsic motivation Motivation based on obvious external rewards, obligations, or similar factors.

affected more by intrinsic factors, such as personal interest and freedom of choice (Nakamura & Csikszentmihalyi, 2003). People who are intrinsically motivated usually get personally involved in tasks, which leads to greater creativity (Ruscio, Whitney, & Amabile, 1998). Psychologist Teresa Amabile lists the following as "creativity killers" on the job:

- Working under surveillance
- Having your choices restricted by rules
- Working primarily to get a good evaluation (or avoid a bad one)
- Working mainly to get more money

Time pressure also kills creativity. Employees are less likely to solve tricky problems and come up with innovative ideas when they work "under the gun." When a person is intrinsically motivated, a certain amount of challenge, surprise, and complexity makes a task rewarding. When extrinsic motivation is stressed, people are less likely to solve tricky problems and come up with innovative ideas (Amabile, Hadley, & Kramer, 2002).

Should extrinsic motivation always be avoided? No, but extrinsic motivation shouldn't be overused, especially with children. In general, (1) if there's no intrinsic interest in an activity to begin with, you have nothing to lose by using extrinsic rewards; (2) if basic skills are lacking, extrinsic rewards may be necessary at first; (3) extrinsic rewards can focus attention on an activity so real interest will develop; and (4) if extrinsic rewards are used, they should be small and phased out as soon as possible (Cameron & Pierce, 2002; Greene & Lepper, 1974). It also helps to tell children they seem to be *really interested* in drawing, playing the piano, learning a language, or whatever activity you are rewarding (Cialdini et al., 1998).

At work, it is valuable for managers to find out what each employee's interests and career goals are. People are not solely motivated by money. A chance to do challenging, interesting, and intrinsically rewarding work is often just as important. In many situations it is important to encourage intrinsic motivation, especially when children are learning new skills.

KNOWLEDGE BUILDER
Stimulus Drives, Learned Motives, Maslow, and Intrinsic Motivation

RECITE

1. Exploration, manipulation, and curiosity provide evidence for the existence of _____ drives.
2. People who score high on the SSS tend to be extroverted, independent, and individuals who value change. T or F?
3. Complex tasks, such as taking a classroom test, tend to be disrupted by high levels of arousal, an effect predicted by
   a. the Sensation-Seeking Scale
   b. the Yerkes-Dodson law
   c. studies of circadian arousal patterns
   d. studies of the need for achievement
4. Two key elements of test anxiety that must be controlled are _____ and excessive _____.
5. People high in nAch
   a. prefer long shots
   b. prefer sure things
   c. are moderate risk takers
   d. prefer change and high levels of stimulation
6. The highest level of Maslow's hierarchy of motives involves
   a. meta-needs
   b. needs for safety and security
   c. needs for love and belonging
   d. extrinsic needs
7. Intrinsic motivation is often undermined in situations in which obvious external rewards are applied to a naturally enjoyable activity. T or F?
8. Which of the following is *not* a characteristic of people who score high on the Sensation-Seeking Scale?
   a. boredom susceptibility
   b. experience seeking
   c. inhibition
   d. thrill seeking

REFLECT

Critical Thinking

9. Many U.S. college freshmen say that "being well-off financially" is an essential life goal and that "making more money" was a very important factor in their decision to attend college. Which meta-needs are fulfilled by "making more money"?

Continued

People who are intrinsically motivated feel free to explore creative solutions to problems. *(Left)* Dean Kaman, inventor of the Segway personal transportation device. *(Right)* "Kinetic Koffee," an entrant in The Great Arcata to Ferndale World Championship Cross Country Kinetic Sculpture Race.

Rick Friedman/Corbis

Gregory A. Beaumont/® The Great Arcata to Ferndale World Championship Cross Country Kinetic Sculpture Race

Inside an Emotion—How Do You Feel?

Gateway Question: What happens during emotion?

Picture the faces of terrified people fleeing a school shooter like the one at Virginia Tech and it's easy to see that motivation and emotion are closely related. Emotions shape our relationships and color our daily activities. **Emotion** is characterized by physiological arousal, and changes in facial expressions, gestures, posture, and subjective feelings. As mentioned earlier, the word "emotion" derives from the Latin word meaning "to move."

What "moves" during an emotion? First of all, your body is physically aroused during emotion. Such bodily stirrings are what cause us to say we were "moved" by a play, a funeral, or an act of kindness. Second, we are often motivated, or moved to take action, by emotions such as fear, anger, or joy. Many of the goals we seek make us feel good. Many of the activities we avoid make us feel bad. We feel happy when we succeed and sad when we fail (Kalat & Shiota, 2007).

Emotions are linked to many basic **adaptive behaviors,** such as attacking, fleeing, seeking comfort, helping others, and reproducing. Such behaviors help us survive and adjust to changing conditions (Plutchik, 2003). However, it is also apparent that emotions can have negative effects. Stage fright or "choking" in sports can spoil performances. Hate, anger, contempt, disgust, and fear disrupt behavior and relationships. But more often, emotions aid survival. As social animals, it would be impossible for humans to live in groups, cooperate in raising children, and defend one another without positive emotional bonds of love, caring, and friendship (Buss, 2000).

A pounding heart, sweating palms, "butterflies" in the stomach, and other bodily reactions are a major element of fear, anger, joy, and other emotions. Typical **physiological changes** include changes in heart rate, blood pressure, perspiration, and other bodily stirrings. Most are caused by activity in the sympathetic nervous system and by the hormone **adrenaline,** which the adrenal glands release into the bloodstream.

Emotional expressions, or outward signs of what a person is feeling, are another ingredient of emotion. For example, when you are intensely afraid, your hands tremble, your face contorts, your posture becomes tense and defensive, and your voice changes. In general, these expressions serve to tell others what emotions we are experiencing (Hortman, 2003).

Emotional feelings (a person's private emotional experience) are a final major element of emotion. This is the part of emotion with which we are usually most familiar.

Primary Emotions

Are some emotions more basic than others? Yes. Robert Plutchik (2003) has identified eight **primary emotions.** These are fear, surprise, sadness, disgust, anger, anticipation, joy, and trust (acceptance). If the list seems too short, it's because each emotion can vary in *intensity*. When you're angry, for instance, you may feel anything from rage to simple annoyance (● Figure 10.14).

As shown in ● Figure 10.14, each pair of adjacent primary emotions can be mixed to yield a third, more complex emotion. Other mixtures are also possible. For example, 5-year-old Tupac feels both joy and fear as he eats a cookie he stole from mom's cookie jar. The result? Guilt—as you may recall from your own childhood. Likewise, jealousy could be a mixture of love, anger, and fear.

A *mood* is the mildest form of emotion (● Figure 10.15). **Moods** are low intensity emotional states that can last for many hours, or even days. Moods often affect day-to-day behavior by preparing us to act in certain ways. For example, when your neighbor Roseanne is in an irritable mood she may react angrily to almost anything you say. When she is in a happy mood, she can easily laugh off an insult. Happy, positive moods tend to make us more adaptable in several ways. For example, when you are in a good mood, you are likely to make better decisions and you will be more helpful, efficient, creative, and peaceful (Compton, 2005).

Like our motives, our moods are closely tied to circadian rhythms. When your body temperature is at its daily low point, you are more likely to feel "down" emotionally. When body temperature is at its peak, your mood is likely to be positive—even if you missed a night of sleep (Boivin, Czeisler, & Waterhouse, 1997).

Emotion A state characterized by physiological arousal, changes in facial expression, gestures, posture, and subjective feelings.

Adaptive behaviors Actions that aid attempts to survive and adapt to changing conditions.

Physiological changes (in emotion) Alterations in heart rate, blood pressure, perspiration, and other involuntary responses.

Adrenaline A hormone produced by the adrenal glands that tends to arouse the body.

Emotional expression Outward signs that an emotion is occurring.

Emotional feelings The private, subjective experience of having an emotion.

Primary emotions According to Robert Plutchik's theory, the most basic emotions are fear, surprise, sadness, disgust, anger, anticipation, joy, and acceptance.

Mood A low-intensity, long-lasting emotional state.

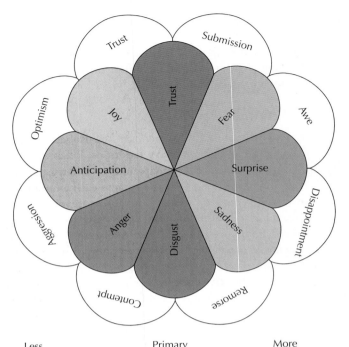

Less intense	Primary emotion	More intense
Interest	Anticipation	Vigilance
Serenity	Joy	Ecstasy
Acceptance	Trust	Admiration
Apprehension	Fear	Terror
Distraction	Surprise	Amazement
Pensiveness	Sadness	Grief
Boredom	Disgust	Loathing
Annoyance	Anger	Rage

● **Figure 10.14** Primary and mixed emotions. In Robert Plutchik's model there are eight primary emotions, as listed in the inner areas. Adjacent emotions may combine to give the emotions listed around the perimeter. Mixtures involving more widely separated emotions are also possible. For example, fear plus anticipation produces anxiety. (Adapted from Plutchik, 2003.)

Emotion and the Brain

Emotions can be either positive or negative. Ordinarily, we might think that positive and negative emotions are mutually exclusive. But this is not the case. As Tupac's "cookie guilt" implies, you can have positive and negative emotions at the same time. How is that possible? In the brain, positive emotions are processed mainly in the left hemisphere. In contrast, negative emotions are processed in the right hemisphere. The fact that positive and negative emotions are based on different brain areas helps explain why we can feel happy and sad at the same time (Canli et al., 1998). It also explains why your right foot is more ticklish than your left foot! The left hemisphere controls the right side of the body and processes positive emotions (Smith & Cahusac, 2001). Thus, most people are more ticklish on their right side. If you really want to tickle someone, be sure to "do it right."

Scientists used to think that all emotions are processed by the cerebral cortex. However, this is not always the case. Imagine this

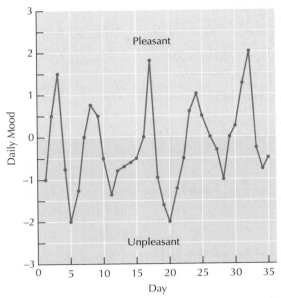

● **Figure 10.15** Folklore holds that people who work or attend school on a weekly schedule experience their lowest moods on "Blue Monday." Actually, moods tend to be generally lower for *most* weekdays than they are on weekends. The graph shown here plots the average daily mood ratings made by a group of college students over a 5-week period. As you can see, many people find that their moods rise and fall on a 7-day cycle. For most students, a low point tends to occur around Monday or Tuesday and a peak on Friday or Saturday. In other words, moods are often entrained (pulled along) by weekly schedules. (Adapted from Larsen & Kasimatis, 1990.)

test of willpower: Go to a zoo and place your face close to the glass in front of a rattlesnake display. Suddenly, the rattlesnake strikes at your face. Do you flinch? Even though you know you are safe, Joseph LeDoux predicts that you will recoil from the snake's attack (LeDoux, 2000).

LeDoux and other researchers have found that an area of the brain called the **amygdala** (ah-MIG-duh-la) specializes in producing fear (● Figure 10.16). (See Chapter 2 for more information.) The amygdala receives sensory information very directly and quickly, bypassing the cortex. As a result, it allows us to respond to potential danger before we really know what's happening. This primitive fear response is not under the control of higher brain centers. The role of the amygdala in emotion may explain why people who suffer from phobias and disabling anxiety often feel afraid without knowing why (Fellous & Ledoux, 2005).

People who suffer damage to the amygdala become "blind" to emotion. An armed robber could hold a gun to the person's

● **Figure 10.16** An amygdala can be found buried within the temporal lobes on each side of the brain (see Chapter 2). The amygdala appears to provide "quick and dirty" processing of emotional stimuli that allows us to react involuntarily to danger.

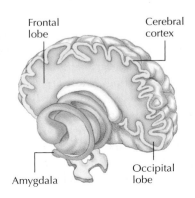

head and the person wouldn't feel fear. Such people are also unable to "read" or understand other people's emotions. Like Robert, who you met at the beginning of this chapter, many lose their ability to relate normally to friends, family, and coworkers (Goleman, 1995).

Later we will attempt to put all the elements of emotion together into a single picture. But first, we need to look more closely at bodily arousal and emotional expressions.

⬤⬤ Physiology and Emotion—Arousal, Sudden Death, and Lying

Gateway Questions: What physiological changes underlie emotion? Can "lie detectors" really detect lies?

An African Bushman frightened by a lion and a city dweller frightened by a prowler will react in much the same way. Such encounters usually produce muscle tension, a pounding heart, irritability, dryness of the throat and mouth, sweating, butterflies in the stomach, frequent urination, trembling, restlessness, sensitivity to loud noises, and numerous other body changes. These reactions are nearly universal because they are innate. Specifically, they are caused by the **autonomic nervous system (ANS)** (the neural system that connects the brain with internal organs and glands). As you may recall from Chapter 2, activity of the ANS is *automatic,* rather than voluntary (Kalat & Shiota, 2007).

Fight or Flight

The ANS has two divisions, the sympathetic branch and the parasympathetic branch. The two branches are active at all times. Whether you are relaxed or aroused at any moment depends on the combined activity of both branches.

What does the ANS do during emotion? In general, the **sympathetic branch** activates the body for emergency action—for "fighting or fleeing." It does this by arousing some body systems and inhibiting others (⬤ Figure 10.17). Sugar is released into the bloodstream for quick energy, the heart beats faster to supply blood to the muscles, digestion is temporarily slowed, blood flow in the skin is restricted to reduce bleeding, and so forth. Such reactions improve the chances of surviving an emergency.

The **parasympathetic branch** reverses emotional arousal. This calms and relaxes the body. After a period of high emotion, the heart is slowed, the pupils return to normal size, blood pressure drops, and so forth. In addition to restoring balance, the parasympathetic system helps build up and conserve the body's energy.

The parasympathetic system responds much more slowly than the sympathetic system. That's why a pounding heart, muscle tension, and other signs of arousal don't fade for 20 or 30 minutes after you feel an intense emotion, such as fear. Moreover, after a strong emotional shock, the parasympathetic system may overreact and lower blood pressure too much. This can cause you to become dizzy or faint after seeing something shocking, such as a horrifying accident.

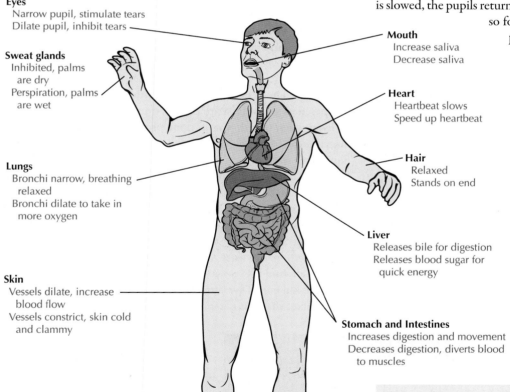

Eyes
Narrow pupil, stimulate tears
Dilate pupil, inhibit tears

Sweat glands
Inhibited, palms are dry
Perspiration, palms are wet

Lungs
Bronchi narrow, breathing relaxed
Bronchi dilate to take in more oxygen

Skin
Vessels dilate, increase blood flow
Vessels constrict, skin cold and clammy

Mouth
Increase saliva
Decrease saliva

Heart
Heartbeat slows
Speed up heartbeat

Hair
Relaxed
Stands on end

Liver
Releases bile for digestion
Releases blood sugar for quick energy

Stomach and Intestines
Increases digestion and movement
Decreases digestion, diverts blood to muscles

⬤ Parasympathetic
⬤ Sympathetic

● **Figure 10.17** The parasympathetic branch of the ANS calms and quiets the body. The sympathetic branch arouses the body and prepares it for emergency action.

Amygdala A part of the limbic system (within the brain) that produces fear responses.

Autonomic nervous system (ANS) The system of nerves that connects the brain with the internal organs and glands.

Sympathetic branch A part of the ANS that activates the body at times of stress.

Parasympathetic branch A part of the autonomic system that quiets the body and conserves energy.

Sudden Death

An overreaction to intense emotion is called a **parasympathetic rebound.** If the rebound is severe, it can sometimes cause death. In times of war, for instance, combat can be so savage that some soldiers literally die of fear (Moritz & Zamchech, 1946). Apparently, such deaths occur because the parasympathetic nervous system slows the heart to a stop. Even in civilian life this is possible. In one case, a terrified young woman was admitted to a hospital because she felt she was going to die. A backwoods midwife had predicted that the woman's two sisters would die before their 16th and 21st birthdays. Both died as predicted. The midwife also predicted that this woman would die before her 23rd birthday. She was found dead in her hospital bed the day after she was admitted. It was 2 days before her 23rd birthday (Seligman, 1989). The woman was an apparent victim of her own terror.

Is the parasympathetic nervous system always responsible for such deaths? Probably not. For older persons or those with heart problems, stress-related sympathetic effects may be enough to bring about heart attack and collapse. For example, five times more people than usual died of heart attacks on the day of a major 1994 earthquake in Los Angeles (Leor, Poole, & Kloner, 1996). In Asia, the number 4 is considered unlucky, and more heart patients die on the fourth day of the month than any other day. Because they fear they will die on an "unlucky day," their chance of dying actually increases (Phillips et al., 2001).

Lie Detectors

We know that people are not always truthful. In addition to the many instances in which people lie to avoid arrest, as many as 25 percent of all wrongful convictions include false confessions as evidence (Kassin, 2005). If you can't count on someone's word, what can you trust? The most popular method for detecting falsehoods measures the bodily changes that accompany emotion. However, the accuracy of "lie detector" tests is doubtful, and they can be a serious invasion of privacy (Lykken, 2001; National Academy of Sciences, 2002).

What is a lie detector? Do lie detectors really detect lies? The lie detector is more accurately called a *polygraph,* a word that means "many writings" (● Figure 10.18). The polygraph was invented in 1915 by psychologist William Marston. He also created the comic book character *Wonder Woman,* a superhero whose "magic lasso" could force people to tell the truth (Grubin & Madsen, 2005).

Although the polygraph is popularly known as a lie detector because the police use it for that purpose, in reality the polygraph is not a lie detector at all (Bunn, 2007). The device only records *general emotional arousal*—it can't tell the difference between lying and fear, anxiety or excitement (Lykken, 2001).

A typical **polygraph** records changes in heart rate, blood pressure, breathing, and the **galvanic skin response (GSR).** The GSR is recorded from the hand by electrodes that measure skin conductance or, more simply, sweating.

When trying to detect a lie, the polygraph operator begins by asking irrelevant (neutral, non-emotional) questions, such as, "Is your name (person's name)?" "Did you eat lunch today?" and so forth. This establishes a "baseline" for normal emotional responses. Then the examiner asks relevant questions: "Did you murder Hensley?" Presumably, only a guilty person will become anxious or emotional if they lie when answering relevant questions.

Wouldn't a person be nervous just from being questioned? Yes, but to minimize this problem, skilled polygraph examiners ask a *series* of questions with critical items mixed among them. An innocent person may respond emotionally to the whole procedure, but only a guilty person is supposed to respond more to key questions. For example, a suspected bank robber might be shown several pictures and asked, "Was the teller who was robbed this person? Was it this person?"

As an alternative, subjects may be asked **control questions,** which are designed to make almost anyone anxious: "Have you ever stolen anything from your place of work?" Typically, such questions are very difficult to answer truthfully with an unqualified no. In theory they show how a person reacts to doubt or misgivings. The person's reaction to critical questions can then be compared with responses to control questions.

Even when questioning is done properly, lie detection may be inaccurate (Grubin & Madsen, 2005). For example, a man named Floyd Fay was convicted of murdering his friend Fred Ery. To prove his innocence, Fay volunteered to take a lie detector test, which he failed. Fay spent 2 years in prison before the real killer confessed to the crime. Psychologist David Lykken (1998, 2001) has documented many cases in which innocent people were jailed after being convicted on the basis of polygraph evidence.

If Floyd Fay was innocent, why did he fail the test? Put yourself in his place, and it's easy to see why. Imagine the examiner asking, "Did you kill Fred?" Because you knew Fred, and you are a suspect, it's no secret that this is a critical question. What would happen to

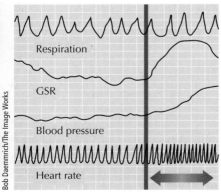

● **Figure 10.18** *(Left)* A typical polygraph includes devices for measuring heart rate, blood pressure, respiration, and galvanic skin response. Pens mounted on the top of the machine make a record of bodily responses on a moving strip of paper. *(Right)* Changes in the area marked by the arrow indicate emotional arousal. If such responses appear when a person answers a question, he or she may be lying, but other causes of arousal are also possible.

Respiration

GSR

Blood pressure

Heart rate

Bob Daemmrich/The Image Works

CRITICAL THINKING

To Catch a Terrorist

An airport check-in agent asks a passenger if he packed his own luggage. He says he did, but he is sitting in a booth that records infrared images of the heat patterns on his face. The images reveal stress, suggesting that he is lying. His luggage is searched and an otherwise undetectable explosive device is confiscated, averting a potential disaster.

Although the above scenario is not yet a reality, it is not as far-fetched as you might think. The growing realization that polygraph tests are not very accurate could not have come at a worse time for national security

(Knight, 2005). The infrared scanner is just one alternative currently under development. Preliminary research indicates that infrared face scans are at least as accurate as polygraphs at detecting lying (Pavlidis, Eberhardt, & Levine, 2002).

Other new techniques look directly at brain activity, thus bypassing the traditional approach of measuring indirect signs of emotional arousal. For example, researchers have found that different brain areas are involved in telling a lie (Abe et al., 2007). Psychiatrist Daniel Langleben theorizes that

a liar must inhibit telling the truth in order to lie (Langleben et al., 2002; Langleben, 2008). Thus, extra brain areas must be activated to tell a lie, which can be seen in fMRI brain images when people are lying. (See Chapter 2, page 59.)

Even if new methods are used, the key problem remains: How can we avoid falsely classifying liars as truth tellers and truth tellers as liars? Until that can be done with acceptable accuracy, the new techniques may have no more value than the polygraph does.

your heart rate, blood pressure, breathing, and perspiration under such circumstances?

Proponents of lie detection claim it is 95 percent accurate. But in one study, accuracy was dramatically lowered when people thought about past emotional experiences as they answered irrelevant questions (Ben-Shakhar & Dolev, 1996). Similarly, the polygraph may be thrown off by self-inflicted pain, by tranquilizing drugs, or by people who can lie without anxiety (Waid & Orne, 1982). Worst of all, the test is much more likely to label an innocent person guilty, rather than a guilty person innocent. In studies involving real crimes, an average of one innocent person in five was rated as guilty by the lie detector (Lykken, 2001). For such reasons, the National Academy of Sciences recently concluded that polygraph tests should not be used to screen employees (National Academy of Sciences, 2002).

Despite the lie detector's flaws, you may be tested for employment or for other reasons. Should this occur, the best advice is to remain calm; then actively challenge the results if the machine wrongly questions your honesty. And beware; newer, possibly more accurate, methods of detecting lies are under development. (See "To Catch a Terrorist.")

KNOWLEDGE BUILDER
Emotion and Physiological Arousal

RECITE

1. Many of the physiological changes associated with emotion are caused by secretion of the hormone
   a. atropine
   b. adrenaline
   c. attributine
   d. amoduline
2. Emotional _____ often serve to communicate a person's emotional state to others.
3. Awe, remorse, and disappointment are among the primary emotions listed by Robert Plutchik. T or F?

4. Emotional arousal is closely related to activity of the _____ nervous system.
5. Preparing the body for "fighting or fleeing" is largely the job of the
   a. paraventricular nucleus
   b. sympathetic branch
   c. GSR
   d. left hemisphere
6. The parasympathetic system inhibits digestion and raises blood pressure and heart rate. T or F?
7. What body changes are measured by a polygraph?

REFLECT

Critical Thinking

8. Can you explain why people "cursed" by shamans or "witch doctors" sometimes actually die?

Relate

How did your most emotional moment of the past week affect your behavior, expressions, feelings, and bodily state? Could you detect both sympathetic and parasympathetic effects?

Make a list of the emotions you consider to be most basic. To what extent do they agree with Plutchik's list?

What did you think about the lie detectors before reading this chapter? What do you think now?

Answers: 1. b **2.** expressions **3.** F **4.** autonomic **5.** b **6.** F **7.** heart rate, blood pressure, breathing rate, galvanic skin response **8.** In cultures where there is deep belief in magic or voodoo, a person who thinks that she or he has been cursed may become uncontrollably emotional. After several days of intense terror, a parasympathetic rebound is likely. If the rebound is severe enough, it can lead to physical collapse and "voodoo death."

Parasympathetic rebound Excess activity in the parasympathetic nervous system following a period of intense emotion.

Polygraph A device for recording heart rate, blood pressure, respiration, and galvanic skin response; commonly called a "lie detector."

Galvanic skin response (GSR) A change in the electrical resistance (or inversely, the conductance) of the skin, due to sweating.

Control questions In a polygraph exam, questions that almost always provoke anxiety.

● **Figure 10.19** Is anger expressed the same way in different cultures? Masks that are meant to be frightening or threatening are strikingly similar around the world. Most have an open, downward-curved mouth and diagonal or triangular eyes, eyebrows, nose, cheeks, and chin. (Keep this list in mind next Halloween.) Obviously, the pictured mask is not meant to be warm and cuddly. Your ability to "read" its emotional message suggests that basic emotional expressions have universal biological roots (Aronoff et al., 1988; Smith et al., 2005).

Angry   Sad   Happy   Scheming   Neutral

Gary Conner/PhotoEdit

Expressing Emotions—Making Faces and Talking Bodies

Gateway Question: How accurately are emotions expressed by the face and "body language"?

Next to our own feelings, the expressions of others are the most familiar part of emotion. Are emotional expressions a carryover from human evolution? Charles Darwin thought so. Darwin (1872) observed that angry tigers, monkeys, dogs, and humans all bare their teeth in the same way. Psychologists believe that emotional expressions evolved to communicate our feelings to others, which aids survival. Such messages give valuable hints about what other people are likely to do next (Kalat & Shiota, 2007). For instance, in one study, people were able to detect angry and scheming faces faster than happy, sad, or neutral faces (● Figure 10.19). Presumably, we are especially sensitive to threatening faces because they warn us of possible harm (Tipples, Atkinson, & Young, 2002.)

Facial Expressions

Are emotional expressions the same for all people? Basic expressions appear to be fairly universal (● Figure 10.20). Facial expressions of *fear, anger, disgust, sadness, surprise,* and *happiness* (enjoyment) are recognized around the world (Smith et al., 2005). *Contempt* and *interest* may also be universal, but researchers are less certain of these expressions (Ekman, 1993). Notice that this list covers most of the primary emotions described earlier. Children who are born blind have little opportunity to learn emotional expressions from others. Even so, they also display basic expressions in the same way sighted people do (Galati, Scherer, & Ricci-Bitti, 1997). It's also nice to note that a smile is the most universal and easily recognized facial expression of emotion.

● **Figure 10.20** When shown groups of simplified faces (without labels), the angry and scheming faces "jumped out" at people faster than sad, happy, or neutral faces. An ability to rapidly detect threatening expressions probably helped our ancestors survive. (Adapted from Tipples, Atkinson, & Young, 2002.)

Gary Conner/PhotoEdit

There are more than a few facial expressions, aren't there? Yes. Your face can produce some 20,000 different expressions, which makes it the most expressive part of your body. Most of these are *facial blends* (a mixture of two or more basic expressions). Imagine, for example, that you just received an F on an unfair test. Quite likely, your eyes, eyebrows, and forehead would reveal anger, while your mouth would be turned downward in a sad frown.

Most of us believe we can fairly accurately tell what others are feeling by observing their facial expressions. If thousands of facial blends occur, how do we make such judgments? The answer is that facial expressions can be boiled down to three basic dimensions: *pleasantness–unpleasantness, attention–rejection,* and *activation* (or arousal) (Schlosberg, 1954). By smiling when you give a friend a hard time, you add an emotional message of acceptance to the verbal insult, which changes its meaning. As they say in movie Westerns, it makes a big difference to "Smile when you say that, partner."

Some facial expressions are shaped by learning and may be found only in specific cultures. Among the Chinese, for example, sticking out the tongue is a gesture of surprise, not of disrespect or teasing. If a person comes from another culture, it is wise to remember that you may easily misunderstand his or her expressions. At such times, knowing the social *context* in which an expression occurs helps clarify its meaning (Carroll & Russell, 1996; Kalat & Shiota, 2007). (Also, see "Crow's-Feet and Smiles Sweet.")

Cultural Differences in Emotion

How many times have you been angry this week? If it was more than once, you're not unusual. Anger is a very common emotion in Western cultures. Very likely this is because our culture emphasizes personal independence and a free expression of individual rights and needs. In North America, anger is widely viewed as a "natural" reaction to feeling that you have been treated unfairly.

In contrast, many Asian cultures place a high value on group harmony. In Asia, expressing anger in public is less common and anger is regarded as less "natural." The reason for this is that anger tends to separate people. Thus, being angry is at odds with a culture that values cooperation.

Culture also influences positive emotions. In America, we tend to have positive feelings such as pride, happiness, and superiority, which emphasize our role as *individuals*. In Japan, positive feelings are more often linked with membership in groups (friendly feelings, closeness to others, and respect) (Kitayama et al., 2000; Markus et al., 2006). It is common to think of emotion as an individual event. However, as you can see, emotion is shaped by cultural ideas, values, and practices (Mesquita & Markus, 2004).

CRITICAL THINKING

Crow's-Feet and Smiles Sweet

The next time you see an athletic contest or a beauty pageant on television, look closely at the winner's smile and the smile of the runner-up. Although both people will be smiling, it is likely that the winner's smile will be authentic and the loser's smile will be forced.

We smile for many reasons: to be polite or because of embarrassment, or sometimes to deceive (Frank, 2002; Frank & Ekman, 2004). These "social smiles" are often intentional or forced, and they only involve lifting the corners of the mouth. What does a genuine smile look like? A real smile involves not only the mouth, but also the small muscles around the eyes. These muscles lift the cheeks and make crow's-feet or crinkles in the outside corners of the eyes.

Authentic smiles are called *Duchenne smiles* (after Guilluame Duchenne, a French scientist who studied facial muscles). The muscles around the eyes are very difficult to tighten on command. Hence, to tell if a smile in authentic, or merely posed, look at the corners of a person's eyes, not the mouth (Williams et al., 2001). To put it another way, crow's-feet mean a smile is sweet.

Duchenne smiles signal genuine happiness and enjoyment (Soussignan, 2002). In a recent study, women who had authentic smiles in their college yearbook photos were contacted 6, 22, and 31 years later. At each interval, real smiles in college were associated with more positive emotions and a greater sense of competence. We can only speculate about why this is the case. However, it is likely that smiling signals that a person is helpful or nurturing. This leads to more supportive social relationships and, in a self-fulfilling manner, to greater happiness (Gladstone & Parker, 2002).

Dennis Coon

The face on the left shows a social smile; the one on the right is an authentic, or Duchenne, smile.

Gender and Emotion

Women have a reputation for being "more emotional" than men. Are they? Compared with women, men in Western cultures are more likely to have difficulty expressing their emotions. According to

Sergei Karpukhgin/Reuters/Corbis

The expression of emotion is strongly influenced by learning. As you have no doubt observed, women cry more often, longer, and more intensely than men do. Men begin learning early in childhood to suppress crying—possibly to the detriment of their emotional health (Levant, 2003). Many men are especially unwilling to engage in public displays of emotion, in contrast to these women, who are grieving for the victims of a 2004 school siege in Beslan, Russia, which left nearly 200 children dead.

psychologist Ronald Levant, although male babies start out life more emotionally expressive than female babies, little boys soon learn to "toughen up," beginning in early childhood (Levant et al., 2006). As a result, men have learned to curtail the expression of most of their emotions, although not to the extent of Robert, the alexithymic man we met at the beginning of the chapter. While girls are encouraged to express sadness, fear, shame, and guilt, boys are more likely to be allowed to express only anger and hostility (Fischer et al., 2004).

But does this mean that men experience emotions less than women? Ronald Levant believes that men who fail to express emotions become less aware of their own emotions. For many men, an inability to express feelings or to even be aware of them is a major barrier to having close, satisfying relationships with others (Levant, 2003). Blunted emotions may even contribute to tragedies like the mass murders at Columbine High School in Littleton, Colorado. For many young males, anger is the only emotion they can freely feel and express.

Body Language

If a friend walked up to you and said, "Hey, ugly, what are you doing?" would you be offended? Probably not, because such remarks are usually delivered with a big grin. The facial and bodily would predict, then, that if you met a bear, you would be aroused. If the bear seemed unfriendly, you would interpret your arousal as fear, and if the bear offered to shake your "paw," you would be happy, amazed, and relieved!

Misattribution

We now move from slapstick movies and fear of bear bodies to an appreciation of bare bodies. There is no guarantee that we always make the correct attributions about our emotions. For example, Valins (1966) showed male college students a series of photographs of nude females. While watching the photographs, each student heard an amplified heartbeat that he believed was his own. In reality, students were listening to a recorded heartbeat carefully designed to beat *louder* and *stronger* when some (but not all) of the slides were shown.

After watching the slides, each student was asked to say which was most attractive. Students who heard the false heartbeat consistently rated slides paired with a "pounding heart" as the most attractive. In other words, when a student saw a slide and heard his heart beat louder, he attributed his "emotion" to the slide. His attribution seems to have been, "Now that one I like!" His next reaction, perhaps, was "But why?" Later research suggests that subjects persuaded themselves that the slide really was more attractive in order to explain their apparent arousal (Truax, 1983).

That seems somewhat artificial. Does it really make any difference what arousal is attributed to? Yes. To illustrate attribution in the "real world," consider what happens when parents interfere with the budding romance of a son or daughter. Often, trying to separate a young couple *intensifies* their feelings. Meddling parents add frustration, anger, and fear or excitement (as in seeing each other "on the sly") to the couple's feelings. Because they already care for each other, they are likely to attribute all this added emotion to "true love" (Walster, 1971).

Attribution theory predicts that you are most likely to "love" someone who gets you stirred up emotionally (Foster et al., 1998). This is true even when fear, anger, frustration, or rejection is part of the formula. Thus, if you want to successfully propose marriage, take your intended to the middle of a narrow, windswept suspension bridge over a deep chasm and look deeply into his or her eyes. As your beloved's heart pounds wildly (from being on the bridge, not from your irresistible charms), say, "I love you." Attribution theory predicts that your companion will conclude, "Oh wow, I must love you too."

The preceding is not as farfetched as it may seem. In an ingenious study, a female psychologist interviewed men in a park. Some were on a swaying suspension bridge 230 feet above a river. The rest were on a solid wooden bridge just 10 feet above the ground. After the interview, the psychologist gave each man her telephone number, so he could "find out about the results" of the study. Men interviewed on the suspension bridge were much more likely to give the "lady from the park" a call (Dutton & Aron, 1974). Apparently, these men experienced heightened arousal, which they misinterpreted as attraction to the experimenter—a clear case of love at first fright!

bridges

Love is one basis for interpersonal attraction, but there are others, such as similarity and proximity. **To learn more about what brings people together, see Chapter 17, pages 561–563.**

Emotional Appraisal

According to Richard Lazarus (1991a, b), the role of cognition in experiencing emotions is not restricted to making attributions about arousal *after* it has occurred. Rather, emotions you experience are greatly influenced by how you think about an event *in the first place*. **Emotional appraisal** refers to evaluating the personal meaning of a stimulus: Is it good/bad, threatening/supportive, relevant/irrelevant, and so on. Some examples of emotional appraisals and the emotions they give rise to can be found in
● Table 10.2.

bridges

Emotional appraisals have a major impact on the ability to cope with threats and stress, which may ultimately affect your health. **See Chapter 13, pages 433–434.**

The Facial Feedback Hypothesis

Schachter and Lazarus added thinking and interpretation (cognition) to our view of emotion, but the picture still seems incomplete. What about expressions? How do they influence emotion? As Charles Darwin observed, the face is very central to emotion— perhaps it is more than just an "emotional billboard."

Table 10.2 ● Appraisals and Corresponding Emotions

Appraisal	Emotion
You have been slighted or demeaned	Anger
You feel threatened	Anxiety
You have experienced a loss	Sadness
You have broken a moral rule	Guilt
You have not lived up to your ideals	Shame
You desire something another has	Envy
You are near something repulsive	Disgust
You fear the worst but yearn for better	Hope
You are moving toward a desired goal	Happiness
You are linked with a valued object or accomplishment	Pride
You have been treated well by another	Gratitude
You desire affection from another person	Love
You are moved by someone's suffering	Compassion

Adapted from Lazarus, 1991b.

THE CLINICAL FILE

Suppressing Emotion—Don't Turn Off the Music

According to popular media, we are supposed to be happy all the time (Hecht, 2007). Thus, while sharing a beautiful day with friends, you can freely express your happiness. Yet real emotional life has its ups and downs. Often we try to appear less emotional than we really are, especially when we are feeling negative emotions. Have you ever been angry with a friend in public? Embarrassed by someone's behavior at a party? Disgusted by someone's table manners? In such circumstances, people are quite good at suppressing outward signs of emotion.

However, restraining emotion can actually increase activity in the sympathetic nervous system. In other words, hiding emotion requires a lot of effort. Suppressing emotions can also impair thinking and memory, as you devote energy to self-control. Thus, while suppressing emotion allows us to appear calm and collected on the outside, this cool appearance comes at a high cost (Richards & Gross, 2000). People who constantly suppress their emotions cope poorly with life and are prone to depression and other problems (Lynch et al., 2001).

Conversely, people who express their emotions generally experience better emotional and physical health (Lumley, 2004; Pennebaker, 2004). Paying attention to our negative emotions can also lead us to think more clearly about the positive *and* the negative. The end result is better decision making, which can increase our overall happiness in the long run (Norem, 2002). Usually, it's better to manage emotions than it is to suppress them. You will find some suggestions for managing emotions in the upcoming Psychology in Action section.

● **Figure 10.22** Facial feedback and emotion. Participants in Ekman's study formed facial expressions like those normally observed during emotion. When they did this, emotion-like changes took place in their body activity. (Adapted from Ekman, Levenson, & Friesen, 1983.)

Dennis Coon

Psychologist Carrol Izard (1977, 1990) was among the first to suggest that the face does, indeed, affect emotion. According to Izard, emotions cause innately programmed changes in facial expression. Sensations from the face then provide cues to the brain that help us determine what emotion we are feeling. This idea is known as the **facial feedback hypothesis** (Soussignan, 2002). Stated another way, it says that having facial expressions and becoming aware of them is what influences our private emotional experience. Exercise, for instance, arouses the body, but we don't experience this arousal as emotion because it does not trigger emotional expressions.

Psychologist Paul Ekman takes this idea one step further. He believes that "making faces" can actually cause emotion (Ekman, 1993). In one study, participants were guided as they arranged their faces, muscle by muscle, into expressions of surprise, disgust, sadness, anger, fear, and happiness (● Figure 10.22). At the same time, each person's bodily reactions were monitored.

Contrary to what you might expect, "making faces" can affect the autonomic nervous system, as shown by changes in heart rate and skin temperature. In addition, each facial expression produces a different pattern of activity. An angry face, for instance, raises heart rate and skin temperature, whereas disgust lowers both (Ekman et al., 1983). Other studies have confirmed that posed expressions alter emotions and bodily activity (Duclos & Laird, 2001; Soussignan, 2002).

In a fascinating experiment on facial feedback, people rated how funny they thought cartoons were while holding a pen crosswise in their mouths. Those who held the pen in their teeth thought the cartoons were funnier than did people who held the pen in their lips. Can you guess why? The answer is that if you hold a pen with your teeth, you are forced to form a smile. Holding it with the lips makes a frown. As predicted by the facial feedback hypothesis, emotional experiences were influenced by the facial expressions that people made (Strack, Martin, & Stepper, 1988). Next time you're feeling sad, bite a pen!

It appears, then, that not only do emotions influence expressions, but expressions influence emotions, as shown here (Duclos & Laird, 2001):

Contracted Facial Muscles	Felt Emotion
Forehead	Surprise
Brow	Anger
Mouth (down)	Sadness
Mouth (smile)	Joy

Emotional appraisal Evaluating the personal meaning of a stimulus or situation.

Facial feedback hypothesis States that sensations from facial expressions help define what emotion a person feels.

This could explain an interesting effect you have probably observed. When you are feeling "down," forcing yourself to smile will sometimes be followed by an actual improvement in your mood (Kleinke, Peterson, & Rutledge, 1998).

If smiling can improve a person's mood, is it a good idea to inhibit negative emotions? For an answer, see "Suppressing Emotion—Don't Turn Off the Music."

A Contemporary Model of Emotion

To summarize, James and Lange were right that feedback from arousal and behavior adds to our emotional experiences. Cannon and Bard were right about the timing of events. Schachter showed us that cognition is important. In fact, psychologists are increasingly aware that how you *appraise* a situation greatly affects your emotions (Strongman, 2003). Richard Lazarus stressed the importance of emotional appraisal. Let's put these ideas together in a single model of emotion (● Figure 10.23).

Imagine that a large snarling dog lunges at you with its teeth bared. A modern view of your emotional reactions goes something like this: An *emotional stimulus* (the dog) is *appraised* (judged) as a threat or other cause for emotion. (You think to yourself, "Uh oh, big trouble!") Your appraisal gives rise to *ANS arousal* (your heart pounds, and your body becomes stirred up) and *cognitive labeling*. The appraisal also releases *innate emotional expressions* (your face twists into a mask of fear, and your posture becomes tense). At the same time, your appraisal leads to *adaptive behavior* (you run from the dog). It also causes a change in consciousness that you recognize as the subjective experience of fear. (The intensity of this *emotional feeling* is directly related to the amount of ANS arousal taking place in your body.)

Each element of emotion—ANS arousal, labeling, adaptive behavior, subjective experience, and your emotional expressions—may further alter your emotional appraisal of the situation, as well as your

thoughts, judgments, and perceptions. Thus, according to the facial feedback hypothesis, your facial expression will further influence your emotion. Such changes affect each of the other reactions, which again alters your appraisal and interpretation of events. Thus, emotion may blossom, change course, or diminish as it proceeds. Note too that the original emotional stimulus can be external, like the attacking dog, or internal, such as a memory of being chased by a dog, rejected by a lover, or praised by a friend. That's why mere thoughts and memories can make us fearful, sad, or happy (Strongman, 2003).

Our discussion suggests that emotion is greatly influenced by how you think about an event. For example, if another driver "cuts you off" on the highway, you could become very angry. But if you do, you will add 15 minutes of emotional upset to your day. By changing your appraisal, you could just as easily choose to laugh at the other driver's childish behavior—and minimize the emotional wear-and-tear (Gross, 2001).

A Look Ahead

In the Psychology in Action section of this chapter we will look further at the impact of emotional appraisals through an examination of *emotional intelligence*. Before we continue, you might want to appraise your learning with the exercises that follow.

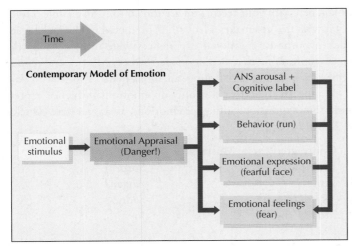

● **Figure 10.23** A contemporary model of emotion. Appraisal gives rise to arousal and cognitive labeling, behavior, facial/postural expressions, and emotional feelings. Arousal, attribution, behavior, and expressions add to emotional feelings. Emotional feelings influence appraisal, which further affects arousal, behavior, expressions, and feelings.

KNOWLEDGE BUILDER
Emotional Expression and Theories of Emotion

RECITE
1. Charles Darwin held that emotional expressions aid survival for animals. T or F?
2. A formal term for "body language" is _____.
3. Which three dimensions of emotion are communicated by facial expressions?
   a. pleasantness–unpleasantness
   b. complexity
   c. attention–rejection
   d. anger
   e. curiosity–disinterest
   f. activation
4. According to the James-Lange theory, emotional experience precedes physical arousal and emotional behavior. (We see a bear, are frightened, and run.) T or F?
5. The Cannon-Bard theory of emotion says that bodily arousal and emotional experience occur _____.
6. The idea that making attributions to label arousal helps define what emotions we experience is associated with
   a. the James-Lange theory
   b. Schachter's cognitive theory
   c. the Cannon-Bard theory
   d. Darwin's theory of innate emotional expressions
7. Subjects in Valins's false heart rate study attributed increases in their heart rate to the action of a placebo. T or F?
8. As you try to wiggle your ears, you keep pulling the corners of your mouth back into a smile. Each time you do, you find yourself giggling. Which of the following provides the best explanation for this reaction?
   a. attribution
   b. the Cannon-Bard theory
   c. appraisal
   d. facial feedback

Continued

PSYCHOLOGY IN ACTION

Emotional Intelligence—The Fine Art of Self-Control

Gateway Question: What does it mean to have "emotional intelligence"?

The Greek philosopher Aristotle had a recipe for handling relationships smoothly: "Be angry with the right person, to the right degree, at the right time, for the right purpose, and in the right way." Psychologists Peter Salovey and John Mayer call such self-control **emotional intelligence,** the ability to perceive, use, understand, and manage emotions (Salovey & Mayer, 1997). In general, being emotionally intelligent means accepting that emotions are an essential part of who we are and how we survive. Being emotionally skilled can make us more flexible, adaptable, and emotionally mature (Bonanno et al., 2004).

People who excel in life tend to be emotionally intelligent (Mehrabian, 2000). If our emotions are the music of life, then emotionally intelligent people are good musicians. They do not stifle their emotions or overindulge in them. Instead, they compose them into sustaining life rhythms that mesh well with other people. They are more *agreeable* than people with low emotional skills (Haas et al., 2007).

Indeed, the costs of poor emotional skills can be high. They range from problems in marriage and parenting to poor physical health. A lack of emotional intelligence can ruin careers and sabotage achievement. Perhaps the greatest toll falls on children and teenagers. For them, having poor emotional

skills can contribute to depression, eating disorders, unwanted pregnancy, aggression, violent crime, and poor academic performance (Parker, 2005). Thus, in many life circumstances emotional intelligence is as important as IQ (Dulewicz & Higgs, 2000).

Are there specific skills that make up emotional intelligence? Many elements contribute to emotional intelligence (Larsen & Prizmic, 2004; Mayer et al., 2001). A description of some of the most important skills follows:

Perceiving emotions The foundation of emotional intelligence is the ability to perceive emotions in yourself and others. Emotionally intelligent people are tuned in to their own feelings, unlike alexithy-

Peter Beavis/Getty Images

mic people such as Robert (Taylor & Taylor-Allan, 2007). For example, they are able to recognize quickly if they are angry, or envious, or feeling guilty, or depressed. This is valuable because many people have disruptive emotions without being able to pinpoint why they are uncomfortable. At the same time, emotionally intelligent people have *empathy*. They accurately perceive emotions in others and sense what others are feeling. They are good at "reading" facial expressions, tone of voice, and other signs of emotion.

Using Emotions People who are emotionally intelligent use their feelings to enhance thinking and decision-making. For example, if you can remember how you reacted emotionally in the past, it can help you react better to new situations. You can also use emotions to promote personal growth and improve relationships with others. For instance, you may have noticed that helping someone else makes you feel better, too. Likewise, when good fortune comes their way, people who are emotionally smart share the news with others. Almost always, doing so

Emotional intelligence The ability to perceive, use, understand, and manage emotions.

strengthens relationships and increases emotional well-being (Gable et al., 2004).

Understanding Emotions Emotions contain useful information. For instance, anger is a cue that something is wrong; anxiety indicates uncertainty; embarrassment communicates shame; depression means we feel helpless; enthusiasm tells us we're excited. People who are emotionally intelligent know what causes various emotions, what they mean, and how they affect behavior.

Managing Emotions Emotional intelligence involves an ability to manage your own emotions and those of others. For example, you know how to calm down when you are angry and you also know how to calm others. As Aristotle noted so long ago, people who are emotionally intelligent have an ability to amplify or restrain emotions, depending on the situation (Bonanno et al., 2004).

Positive Psychology and Positive Emotions

It's obvious that joy, interest, contentment, love, and similar emotions are pleasant and rewarding. There is a natural tendency to enjoy positive emotions while treating negative emotions as unwelcome misery. However, as psychologist Barbara Fredrickson has pointed out, both negative and positive emotions have other benefits.

Negative emotions are associated with actions that probably helped our ancestors save their skins: escaping, attacking, expelling poison, and the like. As useful as these reactions may be, they tend to narrow our focus of attention and limit our ideas about possible actions. Make no mistake, though. Negative emotions can also be valuable and constructive. For example, persistent distress may motivate a person to seek help, mend a relationship, or find a new direction in life (Plutchik, 2003).

In contrast, positive emotions tend to broaden our focus (Fredrickson & Branigan, 2005). This opens up new possibilities and builds up our personal resources. For instance, emotions such as joy, interest, and contentment create an urge to play, to be creative, to explore, to savor life, to seek new experiences, to integrate, and to grow.

In short, positive emotions are not just a pleasant side effect of happy circumstances. They also encourage personal growth and social connection. Happiness can be culti-

vated by using the strengths we already possess—including kindness, originality, humor, optimism, and generosity. Such strengths are natural buffers against misfortune, and they can help people live more positive, genuinely happy lives (Seligman, 2002). A capacity for having positive emotions is a basic human strength, and cultivating good feelings is a part of emotional intelligence (Fredrickson, 2003).

Becoming Emotionally Smart

How would a person learn the skills that make up emotional intelligence? Psychologists are still unsure how to teach emotional intelligence. Nevertheless, it's clear that emotional skills can be learned. Accepting that emotions are valuable is an important first step. There are many valuable lessons to learn from paying close attention to your emotions and the emotions of others. It's a good bet that many of the people you admire the most are not just smart, but also emotionally smart. They are people who know how to offer a toast at a wedding, tell a joke at a roast, comfort the bereaved at a funeral, add to the fun at a party, or calm a frightened child. These are skills worth cultivating.

---

chapter in review

Gateways to Motivation and Emotion

Motivation refers to the dynamics of behavior. Three principal types of motives are primary motives, stimulus motives, and secondary motives.

- Motives initiate, sustain, and direct activities. Motivation typically involves this sequence: need, drive, goal, and goal attainment (need reduction).
- Behavior can be activated either by needs (push) or by goals (pull). The attractiveness of a goal and its ability to initiate action are related to its incentive value.
- Most primary motives operate to maintain homeostasis.
- Circadian rhythms of bodily activity are closely tied to sleep, activity, and energy cycles. Time zone travel and shift work can seriously disrupt sleep and bodily rhythms.

Hunger, overeating, and eating disorders are complexly determined.

- Hunger is influenced by a complex interplay between fullness of the stomach, blood sugar levels, metabolism in the liver, and fat stores in the body.
- The most direct control of eating is effected by the hypothalamus, which has areas that act like feeding and satiety systems. The hypothalamus is sensitive to both neural and chemical messages, which affect eating.
- Other factors influencing hunger are the body's set point, external eating cues, the attractiveness and variety of diet, emotions, learned taste preferences and taste aversions, and cultural values.
- Obesity is the result of a complex interplay of internal and external influences, diet, emotions, genetics, and exercise.
- The most effective way to lose weight is behavioral dieting, which is based on techniques that change eating patterns and exercise habits.
- Anorexia nervosa and bulimia nervosa are two prominent eating disorders. Both tend to involve conflicts about self-image, self-control, and anxiety.

Both intracellular and extracellular thirst are homeostatic, pain avoidance is episodic, and the sex drive is non-homeostatic.

- Like hunger, thirst and other basic motives are affected by a number of bodily factors but are primarily under the central control of the hypothalamus.
- Pain avoidance is unusual because it is episodic as opposed to cyclic. Pain avoidance and pain tolerance are partially learned.
- The sex drive is also unusual in that it is non-homeostatic.

Many activities are related to needs for stimulation and our efforts to maintain desired levels of arousal.

- Drives for stimulation are partially explained by arousal theory, which states that an ideal level of bodily arousal will be maintained if possible. The desired level of arousal or stimulation varies from person to person, as measured by the *Sensation-Seeking Scale.*
- Optimal performance on a task usually occurs at *moderate* levels of arousal. This relationship is described by an inverted U function. The Yerkes-Dodson law further states that for simple tasks the ideal arousal level is higher, and for complex tasks it is lower.

Learned motives, including social motives, account for much of the diversity of human motivation.

- Opponent-process theory explains the operation of some acquired motives.
- Social motives are acquired in complex ways, through socialization and cultural conditioning.
- Self-confidence greatly affects motivation in everyday life.

Maslow's hierarchy of motives categorizes needs as basic and growth oriented.

- Lower needs in the hierarchy are assumed to be prepotent (dominant) over higher needs. Self-actualization, the highest and most fragile need, is reflected in meta-needs.
- Meta-needs are closely related to intrinsic motivation. In some situations, external rewards can undermine intrinsic motivation, enjoyment, and creativity.

An emotion consists of physiological changes, adaptive behavior, emotional expressions, and emotional feelings.

- Emotions can be disruptive, but overall they help us to adapt and survive.
- The primary emotions of fear, surprise, sadness, disgust, anger, anticipation, joy, and acceptance can be mixed to produce more complex emotional experiences.
- The left hemisphere of the brain primarily processes positive emotions. Negative emotions are processed in the right hemisphere.
- The amygdala provides a "quick and dirty" pathway for the arousal of fear that bypasses the cerebral cortex.
- Body changes that occur during emotion are caused by the hormone adrenaline and by activity in the autonomic nervous system (ANS).
- The sympathetic branch of the ANS is primarily responsible for arousing the body, the parasympathetic branch for quieting it.

Autonomic nervous system arousal underlies emotion and is all that "lie detectors" can detect.

- Emotional arousal involves changes in heart rate, blood pressure, breathing rate, and the galvanic skin response (GSR).
- The polygraph, or "lie detector," measures emotional arousal (rather than lying).
- Under some circumstances, the accuracy of the lie detector can be quite low.

Basic facial expressions of fear, anger, disgust, sadness, and happiness are universally recognized.

- Contempt, surprise, and interest may be universal as well.
- Body gestures and movements (body language) express general emotional tone rather than specific universal messages.
- Facial expressions reveal pleasantness versus unpleasantness, attention versus rejection, and a person's degree of emotional activation. Body positioning expresses relaxation or tension and liking or disliking.
- Lying can sometimes be detected from changes in illustrators or emblems and from signs of general arousal.

A variety of theories have been proposed to explain emotions.

- The James-Lange theory says that emotional experience follows bodily reactions. In contrast, the Cannon-Bard theory says that bodily reactions and emotional experiences occur at the same time.
- Schachter's cognitive theory emphasizes that labeling bodily arousal can determine what emotion you feel. Appropriate labels are chosen by attribution (ascribing arousal to a particular source).
- The facial feedback hypothesis holds that facial expressions help define the emotions we feel.
- Contemporary views of emotion place greater emphasis on the effects of cognitive appraisals. Also, our feelings and actions change as each element of emotion interacts with others. One of the best ways to manage emotion is to change your emotional appraisal of a situation.

Emotional intelligence is the ability to consciously make your emotions work for you in a wide variety of life circumstances.

- People who are "smart" emotionally are self-aware, empathetic, know how to use emotions to enhance thinking, decision-making, and relationships, and have an ability to understand and manage emotions.
- Positive emotions are valuable because they tend to broaden our focus and they encourage personal growth and social connection.

Web Resources

For an up-to-date list of direct links to interesting sites, including those listed here, visit the student companion site for this book at www.cengage.com/psychology/coon

Theories of Motivation Because no single theory can account for all aspects of biological aspects of motivation, this site examines the major approaches to understanding motivation and includes discussions of both the strengths and weaknesses of each theory.

Eating Disorders Website Home page of a self-help group for those afflicted with eating disorders.

Healthy Dieting Find your body mass index as you learn more about healthy dieting.

Sensation-Seeking Scale Find out if you are high or low in sensation seeking.

The Affective System An overview of the affective system that provides information about how particular parts of the brain are associated with different aspects of emotion, a classification of basic emotions, and an explanation of how emotions impact our behavior.

When a Patient Has No Story To Tell Read the case histories of several people with alexithymia.

Emotional IQ Test Measure your emotional intelligence.

Interactive Learning

Introduction to Psychology: Gateways to Mind and Behavior **Book Companion Website**
www.cengage.com/psychology/coon

Visit your Book Companion Website, where you will find flash cards, practice quizzes, web links, and more to help you study.

CENGAGENOW™ *Just what you need to know NOW!*

Spend time on what you need to master rather than on information you already have learned. Take a pre-test for this chapter, and CengageNOW will generate a personalized study plan based on your results. The study plan will identify the topics you need to review and direct you to online resources to help you master those topics. You can then take a post-test to help you determine the concepts you have mastered and what you will need to work on. Try it out! Go to www.cengage.com/login to sign in with an access code or to purchase access to this product.

CHAPTER 11

Gender and Sexuality

Gateway Theme

The sexes are more alike than different. Sexuality is a normal and healthy part of human behavior.

Peter Bános/Alamy Images

Gateway Questions

- *What are the basic dimensions of sex?*

- *What is sexual orientation?*

- *How does one's sense of maleness or femaleness develop?*

- *What is psychological androgyny (and is it contagious)?*

- *What are the most typical patterns of human sexual behavior?*

- *To what extent do females and males differ in sexual response?*

- *What are the most common sexual disorders?*

- *Have recent changes in attitudes affected sexual behavior?*

- *What impacts have sexually transmitted diseases had on sexual behavior?*

- *How can couples keep their relationship exciting? What are the most common sexual adjustment problems?*

Pink and Blue

Girls are girls and boys are boys, right? Wrong. Even something as basic as biological sex is many-sided and far from black and white (pink and blue?).

The complexity of sexual identity is hinted at by Michelle's journey from her early life as a man to her current life as a woman. Michelle is a transsexual who acted on her deeply held desire to change her sex, biologically, psychologically, and socially. About her transition, Michelle remarked, "Whatever it takes to create a foundation, I am happy for. It was hard for them (her parents) to have a gay boy, and then a gay boy into a girl, and then a gay girl who is dating a girl who is actually a boy. I think it has been about a year now that she (her mother) has been using, 'I love you'" (Kaufmann, 2007, p. 6).

Genetically Michelle is still male, but psychologically she is female, she has female genitals, and she functions socially as a female (Hyde & DeLamater, 2006). Is Michelle, then, female or male? You might view Michelle as an unfair example because transsexuals seek to alter their "natural" sex. For most people, the indicators of maleness or femaleness are in agreement. Nevertheless, it is not unusual to find ambiguities among various aspects of a person's sex.

One thing we never forget about a person is his or her sex. Considering the number of activities, relationships, conflicts, and choices influenced by sex, it is no wonder that we pay such close attention to it (Hyde & DeLamater, 2006).

⬤⬤ Sexual Development— Circle One: XX or XY?

Gateway Question: What are the basic dimensions of sex?

The term **sex** refers to whether you are biologically female or male. In contrast, **gender** refers to all the psychological and social traits associated with being male or female (Crooks & Baur, 2008). In other words, after we establish that you are male or female, gender tells us if you are masculine or feminine (as defined by the culture in which you live). Two important aspects of gender are *gender roles* and *gender identity,* which we will discuss later in this chapter. As Michelle's story so clearly illustrates, biological sex does not always align with psychological and social gender. In **transsexuals,** a person's biological sex conflicts with his or her preferred psychological and social gender roles. For the moment, let's focus on the biology of what it means to be female or male.

Dimensions of Sex

What causes the development of sex differences? At the very least, classifying a person as female or male must take into account the following biological factors: (1) **genetic sex** (*XX* or *XY* chromosomes), (2) **hormonal sex** (predominance of androgens or estrogens), (3) **gonadal sex** (ovaries or testes), (4) **genital sex** (clitoris and vagina in females, penis and scrotum in males). To see why sex must be defined along these four dimensions, let's trace the events involved in becoming female or male.

Genetic Sex

Becoming male or female starts simply enough. Genetic sex is determined at the instant of conception: Two *X* **chromosomes** initiate female development; an *X* chromosome plus a *Y* **chromo-**

some produces a male. A woman's ovum always provides an *X* chromosome, because she has two *X*'s in her own genetic makeup. In contrast, one half of the male's sperm carry *X* chromosomes and the other half *Y*'s.

Even at conception, variations may occur because some individuals begin life with too many or too few sex chromosomes (Crooks & Baur, 2008). For example, in *Klinefelter's syndrome* a boy is born XXY, with an extra *X* chromosome. As a result, when he matures he may appear feminine, have undersized sexual organs, and be infertile. In *Turner's syndrome*, a girl is born with only one *X* chromosome and no *Y* chromosome. As an adolescent, she may appear boyish, and she will also be infertile.

Hormonal and Gonadal Sex

While genetic sex stays the same throughout life, it alone does not determine biological sex. In general, sexual characteristics are also related to the effects of sex hormones before birth. (Hormones are chemical substances secreted by endocrine glands.) The **gonads** (or sex glands) affect sexual development and behavior by secreting **estrogens** (female hormones) and **androgens** (male hormones). The gonads in the male are the testes; female gonads are the ovaries. The adrenal glands (located above the kidneys) also supply sex hormones.

Interestingly, everyone normally produces both estrogens and androgens. Sex differences are related to the *proportion* of these hormones found in the body. In fact, prenatal development of male or female anatomy is largely due to the presence or absence of **testosterone** (tes-TOSS-teh-rone: one of the androgens, secreted mainly by the testes) (LeVay & Valente, 2006). For the first 6 weeks of prenatal growth, genetically female and male embryos look identical. However, if a *Y* chromosome is present, testes develop in the embryo and supply testosterone (Knickmeyer & Baron-Cohen, 2006). This stimulates growth of the penis and other male structures (● Figure 11.1). In the absence of testosterone, the embryo will develop female reproductive organs and genitals, regardless of genetic sex (LeVay & Valente, 2006). It might be said, then, that nature's primary impulse is to make a female. Without testosterone, we would all be women.

(a) Undifferentiated

(b) Female _XX_ Chromosomes

(c) Male _XY_ Chromosomes

● **Figure 11.1** Prenatal development of the reproductive organs. Early development of ovaries or testes affects hormonal balance and alters sexual anatomy. *(a)* At first the sex organs are the same in the human female and male. *(b)* When androgens are absent, female structures develop. *(c)* Male sex organs are produced when androgens are present.

Prenatal growth does not always match genetic sex. A genetic male won't develop male genitals if too little testosterone is available. Even if testosterone is present, an inherited *androgen insensitivity* (unresponsiveness to testosterone) may exist. Again, the result is female development (LeVay & Valente, 2006).

Similarly, androgens must be at low levels or absent for an *XX* embryo to develop as a female. Thus, for both genetic females and males, hormonal problems before birth may produce an **intersexual person** (one who has ambiguous sexual anatomy). For instance, a developing female may be masculinized by the anti-miscarriage drug progestin, or by a problem known as *androgenital syndrome* (an-dro-JEN-ih-tal). In androgenital syndrome, the child's body produces estrogen, but a genetic abnormality causes the adrenal glands to release too much androgen. In such cases, a female child may be born with genitals that are more male than female.

Can sex be assigned? For a variety of reasons, including transsexuality and intersexuality, it may make sense to reassign the sex of an individual. Surgery can reconfigure the external appearance of the genitals, hormone treatments can shift the chemical balance in the body, and a deliberate effort can be made to transform the person's sense of sexual identity. However, experts are divided about the success of such measures. (See "Bruce or Brenda—Can Sex Be Assigned?")

Sex One's biological classification as female or male.

Gender Psychological and social characteristics associated with being male or female; defined especially by one's gender identity and learned gender roles.

Transsexual A person with a deep conflict between his or her biological sex and preferred psychological and social gender roles.

Genetic sex Sex as indicated by the presence of *XX* (female) or *XY* (male) chromosomes.

Hormonal sex Sex as indicated by a preponderance of estrogens (female) or androgens (male) in the body.

Gonadal sex Sex as indicated by the presence of ovaries (female) or testes (male).

Genital sex Sex as indicated by the presence of male or female genitals.

X **chromosome** The female chromosome contributed by the mother; produces a female when paired with another *X* chromosome, and a male when paired with a *Y* chromosome.

Y **chromosome** The male chromosome contributed by the father; produces a male when paired with an *X* chromosome. Fathers may give either an *X* or a *Y* chromosome to their offspring.

Gonads The primary sex glands—the testes in males and ovaries in females.

Estrogen Any of a number of female sex hormones.

Androgen Any of a number of male sex hormones, especially testosterone.

Testosterone A male sex hormone, secreted mainly by the testes and responsible for the development of many male sexual characteristics.

Intersexual person A person who has genitals suggestive of both sexes.

THE CLINICAL FILE

Bruce or Brenda—Can Sex Be Assigned?

Just after Bruce was born, disaster struck. A normally routine circumcision destroyed his penis. Doctors suggested to his parents that Bruce should be sexually reassigned to become Brenda, a girl. With multiple surgeries and hormone treatments, the doctors said, Brenda would turn out just fine. Following their advice, Brenda wasn't told about the "accident" and she was raised as a girl. For many years, her case was considered a prime example of successful sex reassignment.

However, by puberty Brenda was miserable and suicidal, never quite fitting in with the other girls. In desperation, her parents told her the truth. Initially, Brenda was relieved. She opted for surgical reconstruction as a boy and took the name David. In 2000, he helped author John Colapinto tell his story in *As Nature Made Him* (Colapinto, 2000). After some initial successes as a man, David's mar-

riage and finances failed. Tragically, he committed suicide in 2004.

Although many cases of sexual reassignment are successful, David's case is not unique. Of course, David was neither a transsexual nor an intersexual person. But even some intersexual children whose sex is changed have similar experiences. If their "secret" is revealed, intersexual people may feel damaged—that their bodies were surgically altered without their permission (Cull, 2002). Also like David, an intersexual child who is biologically male but raised as a girl may continue to feel that she is a boy, especially at puberty when "she" may begin growing a beard.

As this discussion implies, a heated controversy exists about the treatment of sex and gender issues in young children (Williams, 2002). Supporters of early sex assignment

argue that the benefits usually outweigh the long-term psychological costs (Slijper et al., 2000). Critics believe that it is better for individuals to accept who they are and to realize that some bodies do not neatly fit into the categories of male and female (Holmes, 2002). Rather than impose the choice on them as children, they argue it is better to wait until adulthood, when transsexual and intersexual individuals can choose for themselves whether or not to have surgery and whether to live as a man or a woman (Thyen, et al., 2005).

Only time will tell which approach is more successful, and for which particular transsexual and intersex conditions. Because sex and gender are complex, the best course of treatment may prove to be different for different people (Rathus, Nevid, & Fichner-Rathus, 2005).

Genital Sex

Mature males and females also differ in both *primary* and *secondary* sexual characteristics. **Primary sexual characteristics** refer to the sexual and reproductive organs themselves: the vagina, ovaries, and uterus in females and the penis, testes, and scrotum in males (● Figure 11.2 and ● Figure 11.3; ● Table 11.1). **Secondary sexual characteristics** are more superficial physical features that appear at puberty. These features develop in response to hormonal signals from the pituitary gland. In females, secondary sexual char-

acteristics include breast development, broadening of the hips, and other changes in body shape. Males grow facial and body hair, and the voice deepens. These changes signal that a person is biologically ready to reproduce. Reproductive maturity is especially evident in the female *menarche* (MEN-are-kee: the onset of menstruation). Soon after menarche, monthly ovulation begins. *Ovulation* refers to the release of ova (eggs) from the ovaries. From the first ovulation until *menopause* (the end of regular monthly fertility cycles in the late 40s or early 50s), women can bear children.

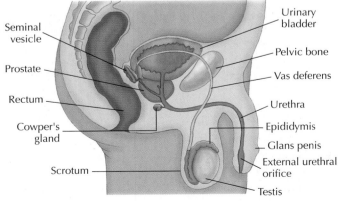

● **Figure 11.2** Cutaway view of internal and external male reproductive structures.

● **Figure 11.3** Cutaway view of internal and external female reproductive structures.

Table 11.1 ● Female and Male Sexual Anatomy

Female Reproductive Structures

Cervix (SER-vix) The lower end of the uterus that projects into the vagina.

Clitoris (KLIT-er-iss) Small, sensitive organ made up of erectile tissue; located above the vaginal opening.

Fallopian tube (feh-LOPE-ee-en) One of two tubes that carry eggs from the ovaries to the uterus.

Labia majora (LAY-bee-ah mah-JOR-ah) The larger outer lips of the vulva.

Labia minora (LAY-bee-ah mih-NOR-ah) Inner lips of the vulva, surrounding the vaginal opening.

Ovary (OH-vah-ree) One of the two female reproductive glands; ovaries are the source of hormones and eggs.

Uterus (YOO-ter-us) The pear-shaped muscular organ in which the fetus develops during pregnancy; also known as the womb.

Vagina (vah-JINE-ah) Tube-like structure connecting the external female genitalia with the uterus.

Male Reproductive Structures

Cowper's glands Two small glands that secrete a clear fluid into the urethra during sexual excitement.

Epididymis (ep-ih-DID-ih-mus) A coiled structure at the top of the testes in which sperm are stored.

External urethral orifice (yoo-REE-thral OR-ih-fis) The opening at the tip of the penis through which urine and semen pass.

Glans penis (glanz PEA-nis) The tip of the penis.

Prostate (PROSS-tate) A gland located at the base of the urinary bladder that supplies most of the fluid that makes up semen.

Scrotum (SKROE-tehm) The sac-like pouch that holds the testes.

Seminal vesicles (SEM-in-uhl VES-ih-kuhlz) These two small organs (one on each side of the prostate) supply fluid that becomes part of semen.

Testis (TES-tis, singular; testes, plural) One of the two male reproductive glands; the testes are a source of hormones and sperm.

Vas deferens (vaz DEH-fur-enz) The duct that carries sperm from the testes to the urethra.

Related Structures

Pelvic bone One of the bones at the front of the pelvis (the pelvis connects the spine with the legs).

Rectum The lowest section of the large intestine.

Urethra (yoo-REE-thra) The tube through which urine drains as it leaves the body. In males, semen also passes through the urethra.

Urinary bladder The sac that collects urine before it is eliminated from the body.

●● Sexual Orientation—Who Do You Love?

Gateway Question: What is sexual orientation?

Yet another aspect of sexuality is **sexual orientation,** your degree of emotional and erotic attraction to members of the same sex, opposite sex, or both sexes. **Heterosexual** people are romantically and erotically attracted to members of the opposite sex. Those who are **homosexual** are attracted to people whose sex matches their own. A person who is **bisexual** is attracted to both men and women. In short, sexual orientation answers these questions: Who are you attracted to? Who do you

have erotic fantasies about? Do you love men, or women, or both (Garnets, 2002)?

Sexual orientation is a deep part of personal identity. Starting with their earliest erotic feelings, most people remember being attracted to either the opposite sex or the same sex. The chances are practically nil of an exclusively heterosexual or homosexual person being "converted" from one orientation to the other. If you are heterosexual, you are probably certain that nothing could ever make you have homoerotic feelings. If so, then you know how homosexual persons feel about the prospects for changing *their* sexual orientation (Seligman, 1994).

But what about people who have had both heterosexual and homosexual relationships? The fact that sexual orientation is usually quite stable doesn't rule out the possibility that for some people erotic feelings may change during the course of a lifetime. However, many such instances involve homosexual people who date or marry members of the opposite sex because of pressures to fit into heterosexual society. When these people realize they are being untrue to themselves, their identity and relationships may shift. Other apparent shifts in orientation probably involve people who are basically bisexual.

What determines a person's sexual orientation? Research suggests that hereditary, biological, social, cultural, and psychological influences combine to produce one's sexual orientation (Carroll, 2007; Garnets, 2002). "Genes, the Brain, and Sexual Orientation" summarizes some interesting findings about the origins of sexual orientation.

Homosexuality

As the preceding discussion implies, homosexuality is part of the normal range of variations in sexual orientation (Garnets, 2002). Based on a national survey, it is estimated that about 4 percent of all adults regard themselves as homosexual or bisexual (Mosher, Chandra, & Jones, 2005). Here are the figures:

	Men	Women
Heterosexual	90.2%	90.3%
Homosexual	2.3%	1.3%
Bisexual	1.8%	2.8%

Primary sexual characteristics Sex as defined by the genitals and internal reproductive organs.

Secondary sexual characteristics Sexual features other than the genitals and reproductive organs—breasts, body shape, facial hair, and so forth.

Sexual orientation One's degree of emotional and erotic attraction to members of the same sex, opposite sex, or both sexes.

Heterosexual A person romantically and erotically attracted to members of the opposite sex.

Homosexual A person romantically and erotically attracted to same-sex persons.

Bisexual A person romantically and erotically attracted to both men and women.

BRAINWAVES

Genes, the Brain, and Sexual Orientation

Why are some people attracted to the opposite sex whereas others prefer members of the same sex? Available evidence suggests that sexual orientation is at least partly hereditary (LeVay & Valente, 2006). One study found that if one identical twin is homosexual or bisexual, there is a 50 percent chance that the other twin is too. Similar findings lead some researchers to estimate that sexual orientation is 30 to 70 percent genetic (Mustanski, Chivers, & Bailey, 2002).

How could genes affect sexual orientation? Possibly, heredity shapes areas of the brain that orchestrate sexual behavior. Support for this idea comes from the work of neuroscientists who have shown that various brain structures (LeVay, 1993) and brain chemicals (Kinnunen et al., 2004) do indeed differ in heterosexuals and homosexuals. Other research suggests that sexual orientation is influenced by a gene or genes found on the *X* chromosome. Thus, genetic tendencies for homosexuality may be passed from mothers to their children (Hu et al., 1995; Rahman & Wilson, 2003). During human evolution, homosexuality may have developed to reduce competi-

tion between males for a limited number of potential female mates (Schuiling, 2004).

The most popular theory holds that genes affect hormone levels in the developing fetus (LeVay & Valente, 2005). According to the *prenatal hormonal theory of homosexuality*, some male fetuses are exposed to too little testosterone. Similarly, some female fetuses are exposed to too much testosterone. These differences, in turn, can impact sexual orientation (Mustanski, Chivers, & Bailey, 2002). Incidentally, many people mistakenly believe that homosexuality is caused by a hormone imbalance in adulthood. However, it is highly unlikely that adult hormone levels affect sexual orientation because the hormone levels of most gay men and lesbians are within the normal range (Banks & Gartrell, 1995).

Hormonal differences during pregnancy may alter areas of the brain that orchestrate sexual behavior. Support for this idea comes from the finding that parts of the hypothalamus, which is connected with sexual activity, differ in size in heterosexuals and homosexuals (Kinnunen et al., 2004; LeVay, 1993). Furthermore, differences in neurotransmitter

levels have been detected in the hypothalamus in homosexual and heterosexual persons (Kinnunen et al., 2004).

Consistent with the biological view of sexual orientation, it is unlikely that parenting makes children homosexual. There is little difference between the development of children with gay or lesbian parents and those who have heterosexual parents (Patterson, 2002; Wainwright, Russell, & Patterson, 2004). Most lesbians and gay men were raised by heterosexual parents, and most children raised by gay or lesbian parents become heterosexual (Garnets, 2002).

All these findings tend to discredit myths about parents making children homosexual or claims that homosexuality is merely a choice. Although learning contributes to one's sexual orientation, it appears that nature strongly prepares people to be either homosexual or heterosexual (LeVay, 1993). In view of this, discriminating against homosexuals is much like rejecting a person for being blue-eyed or left-handed (Rathus, Nevid, & Fichner-Rathus, 2005).

This means about 12 million people in the United States alone are gay, lesbian, or bisexual. Millions of others have a family member who is homosexual. Historically, homosexuality has been a part of human sexuality since the dawn of time.

In contrast to heterosexuals, homosexual persons tend to discover their sexual orientation at a fairly late date—often not until early adolescence. Very likely, this is because they are surrounded by powerful cultural images that contradict their natural feelings. However, most homosexual persons begin to sense that they are different in childhood. By early adolescence, gay men and lesbians begin to feel an attraction to members of the same sex. Gradually, this leads them to question their sexual identity and accept their same-sex orientation (Diamond, 1998).

The problems faced by lesbians and gay men tend to be related to rejection by family and discrimination in hiring and housing. It is important to note that gay men, lesbians, and bisexuals encounter hostility because they are members of minority groups, not because there is anything inherently wrong with them (APA, 2004; Balsam & Mohr, 2007). Such unfair treatment is based on homophobia and heterosexism in our society (Balsam & Mohr, 2007; Cowan et al., 2005). *Homophobia* refers to prejudice, fear, and dislike directed at homosexuals. *Heterosex-*

ism is the belief that heterosexuality is better or more natural than homosexuality.

Understandably, social rejection tends to produce higher rates of anxiety, depression, and suicidal thinking among gay and lesbian people (Cochran, 2001; Gilman et al., 2001; Lester, 2006). However, anyone facing discrimination and stigma would react in much the same way (Jorm et al., 2002). When such stresses are factored out, homosexual persons are no more likely to have emotional problems than heterosexual people are (Goldfried, 2001).

Most homosexual people have at one time or another suffered verbal abuse—or worse—because of their sexual orientation (Balsam & Mohr, 2007; Cochran, 2001). Much of this rejection is based on false stereotypes about gay and lesbian people. The following points are a partial reply to such stereotypes. Gay and lesbian people

- Do not try to convert others to homosexuality.
- Do not molest children.
- Are not mentally ill.
- Do not hate persons of the opposite sex.
- Do not, as parents, make their own children gay.
- Do have long-term, caring, monogamous relationships.
- Are no less able to contribute to society than heterosexuals.

Contrary to the common stereotype, many lesbian and homosexual couples are in long-term committed relationships.

Homosexual people are found in all walks of life, at all social and economic levels, and in all cultural groups. They are as diverse in terms of race, ethnicity, age, parenthood, relationships, careers, health, education, politics, and sexual behavior as the heterosexual community (Garnets, 2002). Perhaps as more people come to see gay and lesbian people in terms of their humanity, rather than their sexuality, the prejudices they have faced will wane.

KNOWLEDGE BUILDER
Sexual Development and Sexual Orientation

RECITE

1. The four basic dimensions of biological sex are:
_____, _____, _____, and _____.
2. All individuals normally produce both androgens and estrogens, although the proportions differ in females and males. T or F?
3. In females, intersexual anatomy may result from
   a. an androgen insensitivity
   b. androgenital syndrome
   c. excessive estrogen
   d. all of these
4. _____ sexual characteristics refer to the sexual and reproductive organs; _____ sexual characteristics refer to other bodily changes that take place at puberty.
5. Research suggests that homosexuality is closely related to hormonal imbalances found in roughly 4 percent of all adults. T or F?
6. Whether a person has erotic fantasies about women or men is a strong indicator of his or her sexual orientation. T or F?

REFLECT

Critical Thinking

7. Why might reaching puberty be a mixed blessing for some adolescents?

Relate

In 2007 the American Medical Association changed its antidiscrimination policies to include transsexual people. This means, for example, that doctors can no longer refuse medical treatment to transsexual patients. Do you agree or disagree with this change?

Which of your prior beliefs about sexual orientation are true? Which are false?

Answers: 1. genetic sex, gonadal sex, hormonal sex, genital sex **2.** T **3.** b **4.** Primary, secondary **5.** F **6.** T **7.** When girls reach puberty early, they may experience heightened social anxiety about their new bodies and increased sexual pressure (Deardorff et al., 2007). When boys reach it late, they may also experience social anxiety.

●● Gender Development—Circle One: Masculine or Feminine

Gateway Question: How does one's sense of maleness or femaleness develop?

Another important part of a person's sexual makeup is his or her gender, as expressed in **gender identity** (one's subjective sense of being male or female as expressed in appearance, behavior, and attitudes).

Is your gender identity biologically determined or is it learned? That's a good question. In animals, clear links exist between prenatal hormones and male or female behaviors. In humans prenatal androgens and estrogens also subtly influence development of the body, nervous system, and later behavior patterns. Sex hormones may "sex-type" the brain before birth, altering the chances of developing feminine or masculine traits (LeVay & Valente, 2006). Evidence for this idea is provided by females exposed to androgens before birth. After birth, their hormones shift to female, and they are raised as girls. Nevertheless, the prenatal exposure to male hormones has a masculinizing effect. During childhood, such girls are typically "tomboys" who prefer the company of boys to girls.

Although it would be a mistake to ignore this **biological biasing effect,** most human sex-linked behaviors are influenced much more by learning than is the case for animals (Helgeson, 2005). For example, after adolescence the tomboyism of masculinized girls usually gives way to female interests and gender characteristics. Cases like these make it clear that both prenatal hormones and later social factors contribute to adult sexual identity (Breedlove, Cooke, & Jordan, 1999).

Let's consider the belief that the biological biasing effect imparts different thinking abilities in women and men. Women, it is said, are more often "left-brained," and men, "right-brained." The left brain, you may recall, is largely responsible for language and rote

Gender identity One's personal, private sense of maleness or femaleness as expressed in appearance, behavior, and attitudes.

Biological biasing effect Hypothesized effect that prenatal exposure to sex hormones has on development of the body, nervous system, and later behavior patterns.

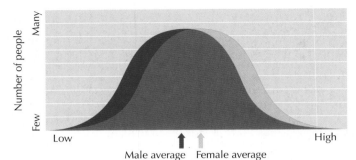

• **Figure 11.4** Recorded differences in various abilities that exist between women and men are based on *averages*. For example, if we were to record the number of men and women who have low, medium, or high scores on tests of language ability, we might obtain graphs like those shown. For other abilities, men would have a higher average. However, such average differences are typically small. As a result, the overlap in female abilities and male abilities is very large (LeVay & Valente, 2005).

learning. The right brain is superior at spatial reasoning. Thus, some psychologists think that biological differences explain why men (as a group) do slightly better on spatial tasks and math and why women are slightly better at language skills (Clements et al., 2006; Hiscock, Perachio, & Inch, 2001).

> **bridges**
>
> Differences in male and female brains may affect the chances of retaining language abilities after a person suffers a stroke or brain injury. **See "His and Hers Brains?" in Chapter 2, page 66.**

Others, however, reject this theory, claiming it is based on shaky evidence and sexist thinking. The most telling evidence on this point may be that female and male scores on the Scholastic Reasoning Test (SAT) are rapidly becoming more alike. The same applies to tests of math ability (Halpern, 2001). The narrowing gap is probably explained by a growing similarity in male and female interests, experiences, and educational goals.

Note also that the differences that do exist between women and men are based on *averages* (• Figure 11.4). Many women are better at math than most men are. Likewise, many men are better at verbal skills than most women are. Scores for women and men overlap so much that it is impossible to predict if any one person will be good or bad at math or language skills simply from knowing his or her sex. There is no biological basis for the unequal treatment women have faced at work, school, and elsewhere. Most male–female performance gaps can be traced to *social* differences in the power and opportunities given to men and women. Unequal power tends to exaggerate differences between men and women, and then makes these artificial differences appear to be real (Goodwin & Fiske, 2001).

Gender Identity

As stated earlier, gender identity, your personal, private sense of being female or male, is at least partly learned.

How is gender identity acquired? Obviously, it begins with *labeling* ("It's a girl," "It's a boy") (Eagly, 2001). Thereafter it is shaped by **gender role socialization** (the process of learning gender behaviors regarded as appropriate for one's sex in a given culture). Gender role socialization reflects all the subtle pressures from parents, peers, and cultural forces that urge boys to "act like boys" and girls to "act like girls." By the time they are just 2 years of age, children are aware of gender role differences (Witt, 1997). At 3 or 4 years of age, gender identity is usually well formed.

Gender Roles

Gender roles probably have as big an influence on sexual behavior as chromosomal, genital, or hormonal factors do. A **gender role** is the favored pattern of behavior expected of each sex. In our culture, boys are encouraged to be strong, fast, aggressive, dominant, and achieving. Traditional females are expected to be sensitive, intuitive, passive, emotional, and "naturally" interested in child rearing. This often leads to stereotyped thinking, as illustrated by the following riddle:

Question: How many men does it take to change a light bulb?
Answer: None. Real men aren't afraid of the dark.

This joke pokes fun at the North American stereotype of manhood. Despite much progress in the last 20 years, gender role stereotypes continue to have a major impact on women and men. **Gender role stereotypes** are oversimplified beliefs about what men and women are actually like. (See "High Test.")

Gender roles influence how we act. Gender role stereotypes, in contrast, turn gender roles into false beliefs about what men and women can and can't do. Are women suited to be fighter pilots,

HUMAN DIVERSITY

High Test

A common gender stereotype holds that men are vulnerable to thinking with their, well, . . . gonads. Actually, there's a bit of truth to the stereotype and more to the story, as well. Recent research confirms that men may make poorer decisions about sexual behavior when they are "turned on" (Ariely & Loewenstein, 2006). Compared with unaroused men, those who are sexually

excited are more willing to press women to have sex. They are also more likely to engage in risky sexual behavior. When unaroused men were asked if they thought being sexually aroused might influence their sexual choices, they predicted that arousal would have little effect. (Wrong!)

Of course, women are not immune to having their heads turned by sexual passion.

However, many people see male sexual irresponsibility as part of a larger pattern that includes aggression. Some go so far as to say that men suffer from "testosterone poisoning" because men are responsible for most violence. Again, there is an element of truth to this stereotype. Men who have high testosterone levels, and who are sexually aroused, are more likely to make poor decisions about sexual behavior (Van den Bergh & Dewitte, 2006). They are also more likely to become aggressive (Millet & Dewitte, 2007).

Then are high testosterone levels a problem? Not always. For example, men with low testosterone levels may have difficulty thinking and concentrating. In such cases, testosterone supplements can actually help them think more clearly, rather than less. Furthermore, older men and women with too little testosterone tend to have memory problems and a greater risk of developing Alzheimer's disease (Janowsky, 2006).

Before we leave this topic, let's remember that we have been discussing a gender stereotype, albeit one with some truth to it. Most men, including those with high testosterone levels, manage to keep their sexual impulses and aggressiveness within acceptable limits.

The character of Charlie Harper (played by actor Martin Sheen), from the comedy series *Two and a Half Men*, has fun with the stereotype of a man who thinks with his gonads.

Warner Bros. TV/Chuck Lorre Prod./The Kobal Collection

corporate presidents, military commanders, or racecar drivers? A person with strong gender role stereotypes might say, "No, because women are not sufficiently aggressive, dominant, or mechanically inclined for such roles." Yet today's women have performed successfully in virtually all realms. Nevertheless, gender role stereotypes persist. For example, the United States has never had a woman president.

Gender role stereotypes can be a major career obstacle. For many jobs, your chances of being hired could be reduced by your sex, be it male or female. Unequal pay for comparable work and experience is also a major problem for women. In the professions, women earn only about 76 cents for every dollar earned by men (NAFE, 2004). The rate for women of color is worse—65 cents for African American women and a measly 55 cents for Latinas. The male-female pay difference is even found in colleges, where greater awareness of gender fairness should prevail (Kite et al., 2001).

Like all stereotypes, those based on gender roles ignore the wonderful diversity of humanity. Fortunately, extreme gender stereotyping has declined somewhat in the last 20 years (Helwig,

1998; Kite et al., 2001). Just the same, in business, academia, medicine, law, sports, and politics, women continue to earn less money and achieve lower status than men. In other words, many women are still "running in place," hobbled by gender stereotyping (DeArmond et al., 2006).

Culture

A look at other cultures shows that our gender roles are by no means "natural" or universal. For example, in many cultures women do the heavy work because men are considered too weak for it (Best, 2002). In Russia, roughly 75 percent of all medical doctors are women, and women make up a large portion of the workforce.

Gender role socialization The process of learning gender behaviors considered appropriate for one's sex in a given culture.

Gender role The pattern of behaviors that are regarded as "male" or "female" by one's culture; sometimes also referred to as a sex role.

Gender role stereotypes Oversimplified and widely held beliefs about the basic characteristics of men and women.

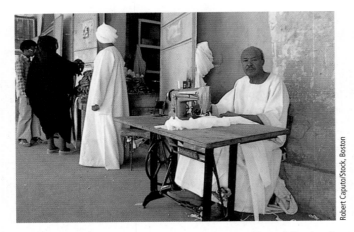

Is this man less of a man because he sews? Behaviors that are considered typical and appropriate for each sex (gender roles) vary a great deal from culture to culture. Undoubtedly some cultures magnify sex differences more than others (Carroll, 2007).

● **Figure 11.5** One study found that the mothers interacted differently with their infant sons and daughters as they played with gender-neutral toys. Mothers of girls asked more questions and engaged in more conversation, whereas mothers of boys made more directive comments and offered more instructions without expecting a response (Clearfield & Nelson, 2006).

Many more examples could be cited, but one of the most interesting is anthropologist Margaret Mead's (1935) classic observations of the Tchambuli people of New Guinea.

Gender roles for the Tchambuli are a nearly perfect reversal of North American stereotypes. Tchambuli women do the fishing and manufacturing, and they control the power and economic life of the community. Women also take the initiative in courting and sexual relations. Tchambuli men, on the other hand, are expected to be dependent, flirtatious, and concerned with their appearance. Art, games, and theatrics occupy most of the Tchambuli males' time, and men are particularly fond of adorning themselves with flowers and jewelry.

As the Tchambuli show, men and women are expected to act in quite different ways in various cultures. The arbitrary nature of gender roles is also apparent. A man is no less a man if he cooks, sews, or cares for children. A woman is no less a woman if she excels in sports, succeeds in business, or works as an auto mechanic. Still, adult personality and gender identity are closely tied to cultural definitions of "masculinity" and "femininity."

Gender Role Socialization

How are gender differences created? Learning gender roles begins immediately. Infant girls are held more gently and treated more tenderly than boys. Both parents play more roughly with sons than with daughters (who are presumed to be more "delicate"). Later, boys are allowed to roam over a wider area without special permission. They are also expected to run errands earlier than girls. Daughters are told that they are pretty and that "nice girls don't fight." Boys are told to be strong and that "tough guys don't cry." Sons are more often urged to control their emotions, except for anger and aggression, which parents tolerate more in boys than in girls.

Toys are strongly sex typed: Parents buy dolls for girls; trucks, tools, and sports equipment for boys. Fathers, especially, tend to encourage their children to play with "appropriate" sex-typed toys (Raag & Rackliff, 1998) (● Figure 11.5). By the time children

reach kindergarten they have learned to think that doctors, firefighters, and pilots are men and that nurses, secretaries, and hairdressers are women (Eagly, 2000). And why not? The workforce is still highly segregated by sex, and children learn from what they observe. Stereotyped gender roles are even the norm in TV commercials, children's picture books, and video games (Browne, 1998; Oppliger, 2007)!

"Male" and "Female" Behavior

Overall, parents tend to encourage their sons to engage in **instrumental** (goal-directed) **behaviors,** to control their emotions, and to prepare for the world of work. Daughters, on the other hand, are encouraged in **expressive** (emotion-oriented) **behaviors** and, to a lesser degree, are socialized for motherhood.

When parents are told they treat boys and girls differently, many explain that the sexes are just "naturally" different. But what comes first, "natural differences" or the gender-based expectations that create them? In our culture, "male" seems—for many—to be defined as "not female." That is, parents often have a vague fear of expressive and emotional behavior in male children. To them, such behavior implies that a boy is effeminate or a sissy. Many parents who would not be troubled if their daughters engaged in "masculine" play might be upset if their sons played with dolls or imitated "female" mannerisms.

Differences between boys and girls are magnified by sex-segregated play. Beginning around age 3, boys start to play mostly with boys and girls play with girls. And how do they play? Girls tend to play indoors and near adults. They like to cooperate by playing house and other games that require lots of verbal give-and-take. Boys prefer superhero games and rough-and-tumble play outdoors. They tend to be concerned with dominance or who's the boss. Thus, from an early age males and females tend to grow up in different, gender-defined cultures (Martin & Fabes, 2001; Oppliger, 2007).

To summarize, gender role socialization in our society prepares children for a world in which men are expected to be instrumental, conquering, controlling, and unemotional. Women, in contrast, are expected to be expressive, emotional, passive, and dependent. Thus, gender role socialization teaches us to be highly competent in some respects and handicapped in others (Levant, 1996, 2003).

> **bridges**
>
> In males, a restricted ability to express emotion is one of the costs of adopting a masculine gender role, at least as it is defined in North America. **See Chapter 10, page 347.**

Of course, many people find traditional gender roles acceptable and comfortable. It seems evident, however, that many more will benefit when the more stereotyped and burdensome aspects of gender roles are set aside. The next section explains why.

Androgyny—Are You Masculine, Feminine, or Androgynous?

Gateway Question: What is psychological androgyny (and is it contagious)?

Are you aggressive, ambitious, analytical, assertive, athletic, competitive, decisive, dominant, forceful, independent, individualistic, self-reliant, and willing to take risks? If so, you are quite "masculine." Are you affectionate, cheerful, childlike, compassionate, flatterable, gentle, gullible, loyal, sensitive, shy, soft-spoken, sympathetic, tender, understanding, warm, and yielding? If so, then you are quite "feminine." What if you have traits from both lists? In that case, you may be *androgynous* (an-DROJ-ih-nus).

The two lists you just read are from the seminal work of psychologist Sandra Bem (1974). By combining 20 traditionally "masculine" traits (self-reliant, assertive, and so forth), 20 traditionally "feminine" traits (affectionate, gentle), and 20 neutral traits (truthful, friendly) Bem created the *Bem Sex Role Inventory* (BSRI). (Some psychologists prefer to use the term *sex role* instead of gender role.) Next, she and her associates gave the BSRI to thousands of people, asking them to say whether each trait applied to them. Of those surveyed, 50 percent fell into traditional feminine or masculine categories, 15 percent scored higher on traits of the opposite sex, and 35 percent were androgynous, getting high scores on both feminine and masculine items.

Psychological Androgyny

The word **androgyny** (an-DROJ-ih-nee) literally means "man-woman" and refers to having both masculine and feminine traits (Helgeson, 2005). Bem is convinced that our complex society requires flexibility with respect to gender roles. She believes that it is necessary for men to also be gentle, compassionate, sensitive, and yielding and for women to also be forceful, self-reliant, independent, and ambitious—*as the situation requires.* In short, Bem feels that more people should be androgynous.

Adaptability

Bem has shown that androgynous individuals are more adaptable. They seem especially to be less hindered by images of "feminine" or "masculine" behavior. In contrast, rigid gender stereotypes and gender roles can seriously restrict behavior.

For example, in one study people were given the choice of doing either a "masculine" activity (oil a hinge, nail boards together, and so forth) or a "feminine" activity (prepare a baby bottle, wind yarn into a ball, and so on). Masculine men and feminine women consistently chose to do gender-appropriate activities, even when the opposite choice paid more!

Bem has concluded that masculine males have great difficulty expressing warmth, playfulness, and concern—even when they are appropriate (Bem, 1975, 1981). Masculine men, it seems, tend to

Kevin Fitzgerald/Getty Images

Vario Press/Imapress/The Image Works

Androgynous individuals adapt more easily to both traditionally "feminine" and "masculine" situations.

Instrumental behaviors Behaviors directed toward the achievement of some goal; behaviors that are instrumental in producing some effect.

Expressive behaviors Behaviors that express or communicate emotion or personal feelings.

Androgyny The presence of both "masculine" and "feminine" traits in a single person (as masculinity and femininity are defined within one's culture).

view such feelings as unacceptably "feminine." Masculine men (let's call them "manly men") also find it hard to accept emotional support from others, particularly from women (Levant, 2001, 2003). They tend to be interested in sports, have mostly male friends, dislike feminists, and sit with their knees wide apart (really!).

Problems faced by highly feminine women are the reverse of those faced by masculine men. Such women have trouble being independent and assertive, even when these qualities are desirable. In contrast, more androgynous individuals are higher in emotional intelligence (remember Chapter 10?) (Guastello & Guastello, 2003).

Over the years androgyny has been variously supported, attacked, and debated. Now, as the dust begins to settle, the picture looks like this:

- Having "masculine" traits primarily means that a person is independent and assertive. Scoring high in "masculinity," therefore, is related to high self-esteem and to success in many situations (Long, 1989).
- Having "feminine" traits primarily means that a person is nurturing and interpersonally oriented. People who score high in "femininity," therefore, are more likely to seek and receive social support. They tend to experience greater social closeness with others and more happiness in marriage (Reevy & Maslach, 2001).

In sum, there are advantages to possessing both "feminine" and "masculine" traits (Guastello & Guastello, 2003; Lefkowitz & Zeldow, 2006). In general, androgynous persons are more flexible when it comes to coping with difficult situations (Crooks & Baur, 2008; Woodhill & Samuels, 2004) (● Figure 11.6). Androgynous persons also tend to be more satisfied with their lives. Apparently, they can use both instrumental and emotionally expressive capacities to enhance their lives and relationships (Lefkowitz & Zeldow, 2006).

Interestingly, some men appear to be moving toward more balanced definitions of manhood. For instance, more Mexican-American men than European-American men are androgynous (Sugihara & Warner, 1999). Along the same lines, some Asian-American men, especially those who were born in the United States, appear to be creating a more flexible masculinity free from male dominance. These men link their masculinity with a capacity for caring, and they are not afraid of doing "feminine tasks," such as cooking or housework (Chua & Fujino, 1999).

It is worth saying again that many people remain comfortable with traditional views of gender. Nevertheless, "feminine" traits and "masculine" traits can exist in the same person, and androgyny can be a highly adaptive balance.

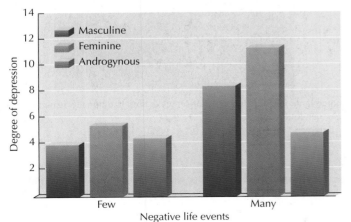

● **Figure 11.6** Another indication of the possible benefits of androgyny is found in a study of reactions to stress. When confronted with an onslaught of negative events, strongly masculine or feminine persons become more depressed than androgynous individuals do. (Adapted from Roos & Cohen, 1987.)

KNOWLEDGE BUILDER
Gender Development and Androgyny

RECITE

1. For humans, the biological biasing effect of prenatal hormones tends to override all other influences. T or F?
2. One's private sense of maleness or femaleness is referred to as
   _____ _____.
3. Traditional gender role socialization encourages _____ behavior in males.
   a. instrumental
   b. emotional
   c. expressive
   d. dependent
4. A person who is androgynous is one who scores high on ratings of traits usually possessed by the opposite sex. T or F?
5. For both women and men, having masculine traits is associated with greater happiness in marriage. T or F?

REFLECT

Critical Thinking

6. As children are growing up, the male emphasis on instrumental behavior comes into conflict with the female emphasis on expressive behavior. At what age do you think such conflicts become prominent?
7. Could a person be androgynous in a culture where "masculine" and "feminine" traits differ greatly from those on Bem's list?

Relate

Can you remember an example of gender role socialization you experienced as a child? Do you think you were encouraged to engage more in instrumental behaviors or expressive behaviors?

Mentally change your male friends to females and your female friends to males. Can you separate the "human being" or "core person" from your friends' normal gender identities and gender roles?

Think of three people you know, one who is androgynous, one who is traditionally feminine, and one who is traditionally masculine. What advantages and disadvantages do you see in each collection of traits? How do you think you would be classified if you took the BSRI?

Answers: 1. F 2. gender identity 3. a 4. F 5. F 6. Children segregate themselves into same-sex groups during much of childhood, which limits conflicts between male and female patterns of behavior. However, as children move into adolescence they begin to spend more time with members of the opposite sex. This brings the dominant, competitive style of boys into conflict with the nurturing, expressive style of girls, often placing girls at a disadvantage (Maccoby, 1990). 7. Yes. Being androgynous means having both masculine and feminine traits as they are defined within one's culture.

Sexual Behavior—Mapping the Erogenous Zones

Gateway Question: What are the most typical patterns of human sexual behavior?

Sexuality is a natural part of being human. A capacity for sexual arousal is apparent at birth or soon after. Researcher Alfred Kinsey verified instances of orgasm in boys as young as 5 months old and girls as young as 4 months (Kinsey, Pomeroy, & Martin, 1948, 1953). Kinsey also found that 2- to 5-year-old children spontaneously touch and exhibit their genitals.

Various sexual behaviors continue throughout childhood. But as a child matures, cultural norms place greater restrictions on sexual activities. Still, many females and males engage in preadolescent sex play. In adulthood, norms continue to shape sexual activity along socially approved lines. In our culture, for example, sex between children, incest (sex between close relatives), prostitution, and extramarital sex are all discouraged.

As was true of gender roles, it's apparent that such restrictions are somewhat arbitrary. Sexual activities of all kinds are more common in cultures that place fewer restrictions on sexual behavior. Apart from cultural norms, it can be said that any sexual act engaged in by consenting adults is "normal" if it does not hurt anyone. (Atypical sexual behavior is discussed later in this chapter.)

Sexual Arousal

Human sexual arousal is complex. It may, of course, be produced by direct stimulation of the body's **erogenous zones** (eh-ROJ-eh-nus: productive of pleasure or erotic desire). Human erogenous zones include the genitals, mouth, breasts, ears, anus, and to a lesser degree, the entire surface of the body. It is clear, however, that more than physical contact is involved: A urological or gynecological exam rarely results in any sexual arousal. Likewise, an unwanted sexual advance may produce only revulsion. Human sexual arousal obviously includes a large mental element.

Sexual Scripts

In a restaurant we commonly expect certain things to occur. It could even be said that each of us has a restaurant "script" that defines a plot (eating dinner outside of the home), the dialogue (ordering from the menu), and actions that should take place (paying for the dinner before leaving). We also learn a variety of **sexual scripts,** or unspoken mental plans that guide our sexual behavior. Such scripts determine when and where we are likely to express sexual feelings, and with whom (Lenton & Bryan, 2005). They provide a "plot" for the order of events in lovemaking, and they outline "approved" actions, motives, and outcomes.

When two people follow markedly different scripts, misunderstandings are almost sure to occur. Consider, for instance, what happens when a woman acting out a "friendly-first-date" script is paired with a man following a "seduction" script: The result is

often anger, hurt feelings, or worse (Schleicher & Gilbert, 2005). A tip for females: If you initiate the first date, your male companion may well assume that you have more than kissing in mind (Morr Serewicz & Gale, 2008). Even newlyweds may find that their sexual "agendas" differ. In such cases, considerable "rewriting" of scripts is often needed for sexual compatibility. For humans the mind (or brain) is the ultimate erogenous zone.

Are men more easily sexually aroused than women? Overall, women and men have equal potential for sexual arousal and women are no less *physically* responsive than men. However, women tend to place more emphasis on emotional closeness with a lover than men do (Basson et al., 2005; Peplau, 2003).

In one study women watched excerpts from two erotic films. One was made by a man for male viewers. The other was directed by a woman and presented from a female point of view. Although women's physical arousal was nearly identical for both films, as measured by a medical recording device, their subjective experiences differed greatly. Many women reported being repulsed, disgusted, and decidedly not aroused by the male-oriented film. When they watched the film made for women, subjects reported more subjective feelings of sexual arousal, more positive emotions, and more interest in the film (Laan et al., 1994).

Why did the women respond so differently? Basically, the male-centered film was a macho fantasy in which the woman was little more than a sexual prop—her pleasure and fulfillment were portrayed as largely unimportant. In the woman-made film, the female character took the initiative in lovemaking and obviously enjoyed it. Clearly, a woman's subjective feelings of arousal tend to be more closely tied to her emotional response to erotic cues. It would appear that many women want to be active partners in lovemaking and they want their needs and preferences to be acknowledged.

Based on the frequency of orgasm (from masturbation or intercourse), the peak of male sexual activity is at age 18. The peak rate of female sexual activity appears to occur a little later (Janus & Janus, 1993). However, male and female sexual patterns are rapidly becoming more alike. ● Figure 11.7 presents some of the data on sexual behavior from a major national health survey of American men and women ages 25 to 44. As you can see, in any given year men and women do not differ in their average number of opposite-sex partners or in their overall pattern of sexual activity (Mosher, Chandra, & Jones, 2005). Exaggerating the differences between male and female sexuality is not only inaccurate, it can also create artificial barriers to sexual satisfaction (Wiederman, 2001). For example, assuming that men should always initiate sex denies the fact that women have comparable sexual interests and needs.

Erogenous zones Areas of the body that produce pleasure and/or provoke erotic desire.

Sexual script An unspoken mental plan that defines a "plot," dialogue, and actions expected to take place in a sexual encounter.

No partners   One partner   Two partners   Three or more partners

(a)

Any opposite sex contact   Vaginal intercourse   Oral sex with opposite sex
Anal sex with opposite sex   Same-sex contact

(b)

● **Figure 11.7** These graphs show the pattern of sexual behavior for American adults. *(a)* Men and women do not differ in their average number of sexual partners or *(b)* in their overall pattern of sexual activity. (Adapted from Mosher, Chandra, & Jones, 2005.)

Sex Drive

What causes differences in sex drive? The term **sex drive** refers to the strength of one's motivation to engage in sexual behavior. Attitudes toward sex, sexual experience, and recency of sexual activity are all important, but physical factors also play a role. As discussed in Chapter 10, a man's sex drive is related to the amount of androgens (especially testosterone) supplied by the testes (Crooks & Baur, 2008). The connection can be very direct: When a man chats with a woman he finds attractive, his testosterone levels actually increase (Roney, 2003). Likewise, the sex drive in women is related to estrogen levels (Graziottin, 1998). As you may recall, testosterone also plays a role in female sexuality. A woman's sex drive is closely related to the testosterone level in her bloodstream. Of course, women produce much smaller amounts of testosterone than men do. But that doesn't mean their sex drive is weaker. Women's bodies are more sensitive to testosterone, and their sex drive is comparable to males.

Does alcohol increase the sex drive? In general, no. Alcohol is a *depressant.* As such, it may, in small doses, stimulate erotic desire by lowering inhibitions. This effect no doubt accounts for alcohol's reputation as an aid to seduction. (Humorist Ogden Nash once summarized this bit of folklore by saying "Candy is dandy, but liquor is quicker.") However, in larger doses alcohol suppresses orgasm in women and erection in men. Getting drunk *decreases* sexual desire, arousal, pleasure, and performance (McKay, 2005).

Numerous other drugs are reputed to be *aphrodisiacs* (af-ruh-DEEZ-ee-aks: substances that increase sexual desire or pleasure). However, like alcohol, many other drugs actually impair sexual response, rather than enhance it (McKay, 2005). Some examples are amphetamines, amyl nitrite, barbiturates, cocaine, Ecstasy, LSD, and marijuana. In the end, love is the best aphrodisiac (Crooks & Baur, 2008).

Does removal of the testes or ovaries abolish the sex drive? In lower animals, **castration** (surgical removal of the testicles or ovaries) tends to abolish sexual activity in *inexperienced* animals. In humans, the effects of male and female castration vary. At first, some people experience a loss of sex drive; in others there is no change. (That's why castration of sex offenders is not likely to curb their behavior.) However, after several years almost all subjects report a decrease in sex drive unless they take hormone supplements.

The preceding observations have nothing to do with **sterilization** (surgery to make a man or woman infertile). The vast majority of women and men who choose surgical birth control (such as a tubal ligation or a vasectomy) do not lose interest in sex. If anything, they may become more sexually active when pregnancy is no longer a concern.

What happens to the sex drive in old age? A natural decline in sex drive typically accompanies aging. As noted earlier, this is related to a reduced output of sex hormones, especially testosterone (Crooks & Baur, 2008) (● Figure 11.8). However, sexual activity need not come to an end. Some people in their 80s and 90s continue to have active sex lives. The crucial factor for an extended sex life appears to be regularity and opportunity. ("Use it or lose it.") People who fairly regularly engage in intercourse have less diffi-

● **Figure 11.8** Average frequency of sexual intercourse per week for adults in the United States. Average intervals for intercourse decline from once every 4 to 5 days in young adulthood, to once every 16 days for people in their 60s. Remember that averages such as these are lowered by the inclusion of people who are abstinent or who do not have sexual partners (such as many widowed persons). However, the age declines noted here also show up for people who are married, ranging from an average rate of intercourse of twice a week for couples under 30 to once every 3 weeks for those over 70. This suggests that the average frequency of intercourse does decline with advancing age (Smith, T. W. (1990). Adult sexual behavior in 1989: Number of partners, frequency, and risk. Paper presented to the American Association for the Advancement of Science, February, 1990, New Orleans).

culty in later years (Janus & Janus, 1993). Also, in some instances, testosterone supplements can restore the sex drive in both men and women (Crooks & Baur, 2008).

Masturbation

One of the most basic sexual behaviors is **masturbation** (self-stimulation that causes sexual pleasure or orgasm). Self-stimulation has been observed in infants under 1 year of age. In adulthood, female masturbation most often involves rubbing the clitoris or areas near it. Male masturbation usually takes the form of rubbing or stroking the penis.

Do more men masturbate than women? Yes. Of the women who took part in a national survey, 89 percent reported that they had masturbated at some time. Of the males, 95 percent reported that they had masturbated. (Some cynics add, "And the other 5 percent lied!") As ● Figure 11.9 shows, masturbation is a regular feature of the sex lives of many people (Janus & Janus, 1993).

What purpose does masturbation serve? Through masturbation, people discover what pleases them sexually. Masturbation is an important part of the psychosexual development of most adolescents. Among other things, it provides a healthy substitute for sexual involvement at a time when young people are maturing emotionally.

Is it immature for masturbation to continue after marriage? If it is, there are many "immature" people around! Approximately 70 percent of married women and men masturbate at least occasionally. Generally speaking, masturbation is valid at any age and usually has no effect on marital relationships. Contrary to popular myths, people are not always compelled to masturbate because they lack a sexual partner (Das, 2007). Masturbation is often just "one more item on the menu" for people with active sex lives (Laumann et al., 1994).

Is there any way in which masturbation can cause harm? Fifty years ago, a child might have been told that masturbation would cause insanity, acne, sterility, or other such nonsense. "Self-abuse," as it was then called, has enjoyed a long and unfortunate history of religious and medical disapproval. The modern view is that masturbation is a normal sexual behavior (Bockting & Coleman, 2003). Enlightened parents are well aware of this fact. Still, many

children are punished or made to feel guilty for touching their genitals. This is unfortunate because masturbation itself is harmless. Typically, its only negative effects are feelings of fear, guilt, or anxiety that arise from learning to think of masturbation as "bad" or "wrong." In an age when people are urged to practice "safer sex," masturbation remains the safest sex of all.

●● Human Sexual Response— Sexual Interactions

Gateway Question: To what extent do females and males differ in sexual response?

The pioneering work of gynecologist William Masters and psychologist Virginia Johnson greatly expanded our understanding of sexual response (Masters & Johnson, 1966, 1970). In a series of experiments, interviews, and controlled observations, Masters and Johnson directly studied sexual intercourse and masturbation in nearly 700 males and females. This objective information has given us a much clearer picture of human sexuality.

According to Masters and Johnson, sexual response can be divided into four phases: (1) *excitement,* (2) *plateau,* (3) *orgasm,* and (4) *resolution* (● Figure 11.10 and ● Figure 11.11). These four

● **Figure 11.10** Female sexual response cycle. The green line shows that sexual arousal rises through the excitement phase and levels off for a time during the plateau phase. Arousal peaks during orgasm and then returns to pre-excitement levels. In pattern A, arousal rises from excitement, through the plateau phase, and peaks in orgasm. Resolution may be immediate, or it may first include a return to the plateau phase and a second orgasm (dotted line). In pattern B, arousal is sustained at the plateau phase and slowly resolved without sexual climax. Pattern C shows a fairly rapid rise in arousal to orgasm. Little time is spent in the plateau phase and resolution is fairly rapid. (Reproduced by permission from Frank A. Beach [ed.] [1965]. *Sex and Behavior,* New York: John Wiley & Sons, Inc.)

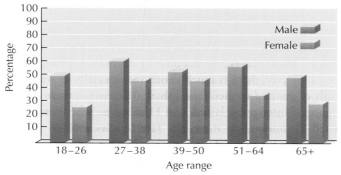

● **Figure 11.9** Percentage of women and men who masturbate. (Data from Janus & Janus, 1993. Janus, S. S., & Janus, C. L. (1993). *The Janus report.* New York: Wiley.)

Sex drive The strength of one's motivation to engage in sexual behavior.

Castration Surgical removal of the testicles or ovaries.

Sterilization Medical procedures such as vasectomy or tubal ligation that make a man or a woman infertile.

Masturbation Self-stimulation that causes sexual pleasure or orgasm.

CRITICAL THINKING

Are We Oversexualizing Young Girls?

As the sexual double standard continues to fade, women feel freer to express their sexuality. But there is a negative side: Many experts now fear that young girls are being oversexualized by influences such as beauty pageants for very young girls, the public antics of female role models, such as Paris Hilton and Brittany Spears, and the availability of consumer goods such as padded bras for girls as young as six (Durham, 2008). Greater sexual freedom is a positive development only for those ready for it (APA, 2007).

According to a recent American Psychological Association Task Force, unhealthy sexualization can be distinguished from healthy sexuality when one or more of the following conditions occurs (APA, 2007):

- A person is valued solely due to sexual appearance or behavior and not other characteristics.

- A person is led to narrowly equate sexual attractiveness with being "sexy."
- A person is objectified sexually (treated as an object for the gratification of other people).
- A person is inappropriately used sexually by another person.

From media images to popular fashions, young girls are more likely to be oversexualized than are young boys (APA, 2007). Oversexualization leads young girls to see themselves as having value only as sexual objects. This results in low self-esteem, eating disorders, depression, and feelings of shame (Ward, 2004). Some studies have even shown that sexualized girls perform more poorly on intellectual activities (Hebl, King, & Lin, 2004). Most worrisome is an increasing tendency for young girls to engage in risky sexual behaviors, such as unprotected oral sex (Atwood, 2006; Prinstein, Meade, & Cohen, 2003).

According to the APA Task Force, parents, educators, and others should encourage young girls to develop relationships based on their personalities and interests, rather than on how they look (APA, 2007).

Karen Kasmauski/Corbis

What messages do beauty pageants send to these young girls?

Slow Death of the Double Standard

A good summary of one major change that has occurred in sexual behavior is found in the phrase "the slow death of the double standard." The **double standard** refers to using different rules to judge the appropriateness of male and female sexual behavior.

In past decades, for example, males were largely forgiven for engaging in premarital sex. Young males who "sowed some wild oats" were widely tolerated. In fact, many were tacitly encouraged to seek casual sex as a step toward manhood. On the other hand, women who were sexually active before marriage ran the risk of being labeled "easy," "bad," or "promiscuous." Similar differences pervade sexual mores and frequently place women in a "separate but not equal" position with regard to sexual behavior (Sprecher & Hatfield, 1996). However, as the gap between female and male sexual patterns continues to close, it is increasingly likely that an end to the double standard is in sight (Schleicher & Gilbert, 2005).

Sexuality Worldwide

Our discussion has focused on sexuality in the United States and Canada. What about the rest of the world? A survey of 59 nations found that a "sexual revolution" has not occurred in most other countries (Wellings et al., 2006). People from the United States and other industrialized nations are more likely to have had two or more recent sexual partners; most people from developing countries have had only one recent sexual partner. On average, teenagers around the world have their first sexual experience at the same age as American teenagers. One finding of particular note concerns Africa, the epicenter of the AIDS epidemic. Contrary to popular opinion elsewhere, Africans are not promiscuous. They report fewer sexual partners than their counterparts in developed countries. Instead, it's likely that high rates of venereal disease in Africa result from a lack of knowledge and access to condoms.

Choices

A more comfortable acceptance of human sexuality is the positive side of changing sexual attitudes and values. The negative side is revealed by the plight of people who are not ready for, or interested in, greater sexual freedom. (See "Are We Oversexualizing Young Girls?") Apparently, some individuals feel pressured into sexual behavior because it is "expected." Six percent of first sexual intercourse experiences are against the person's will (Bajracharya, Sarvela, & Isberner, 1995).

CRITICAL THINKING

Gender Role Stereotyping and Rape

Rape is related to traditional gender role socialization. Traditional feminine stereotypes include the idea that women should not show direct interest in sex. Traditional masculine stereotypes, on the other hand, include the ideas that a man should take the initiative and persist in attempts at sexual intimacy—even when the woman says no (Locke & Mahalik, 2005).

Psychologists James Check and Neil Malamuth (1983) believe that such attitudes create a "rape-supportive culture." In their view, rape is only an extreme expression of a system that condones coercive (forced) sexual intimacy. They point out, for instance, that the most used cries of rapists to their victims are "You know you want it," and afterward, "There now, you really enjoyed it, didn't you?"

In general, research has confirmed a link between acceptance of rape myths and sexual violence toward women (Forbes, Adams-Curtis, & White, 2004). In a classic experimental confirmation of the hypothesis that stereotyped images contribute to rape, male college students were classified as either high or low in gender role stereotyping. Each student then read one of three stories: The first described voluntary intercourse; the second depicted stranger rape; and the third described date rape.

As predicted, college males high in gender role stereotyping were more aroused by the rape stories. Their arousal patterns, in fact, were similar to those found among actual rapists. Moreover, a chilling 44 percent of those tested indicated they would consider rape—especially if they could be sure of not being caught (Check & Malamuth, 1983).

In view of such findings—and the continuing widespread belief that when a woman says no she means yes—it is little wonder that rape occurs every 6 minutes in the United States. Perhaps the time has come for our culture to make it clear that no means no. Educating men about rape myths has been one of the most successful ways of preventing sexual assault (King, 2005; Reppucci, Woolard, & Fried, 1999).

Pressures to engage in sex probably come as much from the individual as from others. For a greater acceptance of sexuality to be constructive, people must feel that they have the right to say no, as well as the right to choose when, where, how, and with whom they will express their sexuality. As is true elsewhere, freedom must be combined with responsibility, commitment, and caring if it is to have meaning.

The Crime of Rape

Many women feel confident that their chances of being raped are low. But the facts tell a different story (CDC, 2007; FVPF, 2007):

- At least 1 woman in 7 will be raped in her lifetime. Because only 1 rape in 5 is reported, the true figure is much higher.
- Pregnancy is one result of rape in 32,000 cases every year.
- Four to 30 percent of rape victims contract sexually transmitted diseases.

Although it is commonly believed that rapists are usually strangers to the women they rape, nothing could be further from the truth. Seventy-six percent of American women who have been sexually or physically assaulted reported that the perpetrator was a husband, intimate partner, or acquaintance (FVPF, 2007). From 10 to 14 percent of all married women have experienced *marital rape,* which usually includes being beaten by their husbands (Martin, Taft, & Resick, 2007). Similarly, 5 to 15 percent of all female college students report having been raped. Roughly one half of these rapes were **acquaintance (date) rapes** (forced intercourse that occurs in the context of a date or other voluntary encounter). In other words, they were carried out by first dates, casual dates, or romantic acquaintances (Fisher, Cullen, & Daigle, 2005; Koss, 2000).

Men who commit marital or date rape often believe they have done nothing wrong. A typical explanation is, "Her words were saying no, but her body was saying yes." (See "Gender Role Stereotyping and Rape.") But forced sex is rape, even if the rapist doesn't use a knife or become violent. The effects of rape by someone familiar are no less devastating than those of rape committed by a stranger.

Rape Myths

A study of college men found that many tend to blame *women* for date rape. According to them, women who are raped by an acquaintance actually wanted to have sex. This is just one of several widely held beliefs that qualify as **rape myths** (Forbes, Adams-Curtis, & White, 2004; Jones, Russell, & Bryant, 1998). All these statements are myths:

- A woman who appears alone in public and dresses attractively is "asking for it."
- When a woman says no she really means yes.
- Many women who are raped actually enjoy it.
- If a woman goes home with a man on a first date, she is interested in sex.
- If a woman is sexually active, she is probably lying if she says she was raped.

Double standard Applying different standards for judging the appropriateness of male and female sexual behavior.

Acquaintance (date) rape Forced intercourse that occurs in the context of a date or other voluntary encounter.

Rape myths False beliefs about rape that tend to blame the victim and increase the likelihood that some men will think that rape is justified.

Men who believe rape myths are more likely to misread a woman's resistance to unwanted sexual advances, assuming that she really means yes when she says no (Forbes, Adams-Curtis, & White, 2004). Add some alcohol to the situation and the risk of sexual assault is even greater: Men who believe rape myths and who have been drinking are especially likely to ignore signals that a woman wants sexual advances to stop (Bernat, Calhoun, & Stolp, 1998; Marx, Gross, & Adams, 1999).

Forcible Rape

Date rape is coercive, but not necessarily violent. **Forcible rape,** which is distressingly common, is carried out under the threat of bodily injury. Rapists often inflict more violence on their victims than is necessary to achieve their goal.

Most psychologists no longer think of forcible rape as a primarily sexual act. Rather, it is an act of brutality or aggression based on the need to debase others. Many rapists impulsively take what they want without concern for the feelings of the victim or guilt about their deed. Others harbor deep-seated resentment or outright hatred of women.

Typical after-effects for the victim include rage, guilt, depression, loss of self-esteem, shame, sexual adjustment problems, and, in many cases, a lasting mistrust of male–female relationships. The impact is so great that most women continue to report fear, anxiety, and sexual dysfunction a year or two after being raped. Even years later, rape survivors are more likely to suffer from depression, alcohol or drug abuse, and other emotional problems.

It is also important to be aware that men can also be the victims of rape, especially homosexual rape (Davies & McCartney, 2003). Any man who doubts the seriousness of rape should imagine him-self mistakenly placed in jail, where he is violently raped (sodomized) by other inmates. There is no pleasure in rape for victims of either sex. It is truly a despicable crime.

STDs and Safer Sex—Choice, Risk, and Responsibility

Gateway Question: What impacts have sexually transmitted diseases had on sexual behavior?

In general, most adults favor greater freedom of choice for themselves, including choice about sexual behavior. Yet, as noted, there is some ambivalence toward greater sexual freedom. As the upcoming discussion of AIDS suggests, there are new and compelling reasons for caution in sexual behavior.

A **sexually transmitted disease (STD)** is an infection passed from one person to another by intimate physical contact. Sexually active people run a higher risk of getting chlamydia (klah-MID-ee-ah), gonorrhea, hepatitis B, herpes, genital warts, syphilis, and other STDs (● Table 11.2). Many people who carry STDs remain *asymptomatic* (a-SIMP-teh-mat-ik: lacking obvious symptoms). It is easy to have an infection without knowing it. Likewise, it is often impossible to tell if a sexual partner is infectious. Thus, risky sex is a serious hazard. A recent study of sexually active teenage girls engaging in risky sex is a case in point. Nearly 90 percent of the girls thought that they had virtually no chance of getting an STD. In reality, over the next 18 months one in four got chlamydia or gonorrhea (Ethier et al., 2003).

A major problem is the fact that people who are sexually active may have indirect contact with many other people. A recent study

Table 11.2 ● Common Sexually Transmitted Diseases

STD	Male Symptoms	Female Symptoms	Prevention	Treatment
Gonorrhea	Milky discharge from urethra; painful, frequent urination	Vaginal discharge and inflammation, painful urination	Condom/safer sex practices	Antibiotics
Chlamydia	Painful urination, discharge from urethra	Painful urination, discharge from vagina, abdominal pain	Condom/safer sex practices	Antibiotics
Syphilis	Painless sores on genitals, rectum, tongue, or lips; skin rash, fever, headache, aching bones and joints	Same	Condom/safer sex practices	Antibiotics
Genital herpes	Pain or itching on the penis; water blisters or open sores	Pain or itching in the genital area; water blisters or open sores	Condom/safer sex practices	Symptoms can be treated but not cured
Genital warts	Warty growths on genitals	Same	Condom/safer sex practices	Removal by surgery or laser
HIV/AIDS	Prolonged fatigue, swollen lymph nodes, fever lasting more than 10 days, night sweats, unexplained weight loss, purplish lesions on skin, persistent cough or sore throat, persistent colds, persistent diarrhea, easy bruising or unexplained bleeding	Same	Condom/safer sex practices	Can be treated with various drugs but cannot be cured
Hepatitis B	Mild cases may have no symptoms, but infection can cause chronic liver disease, cirrhosis of the liver, or liver cancer	Same	Vaccination	None available
Pelvic inflammatory disease	Does not apply	Intense pain in lower back and/or abdomen, fever	Condom/safer sex practices	Antibiotics

of sexual relationships at a high school in a Midwestern city found long chains of sexual contact between students. Thus, a student at the end of the chain might have had sex with only one person, but in reality she or he had indirect contact with dozens or even hundreds of others (Bearman, Moody, & Stovel, 2004).

For many sexually active people, the human immunodeficiency virus (HIV) has added a new threat. HIV is a sexually transmitted disease that disables the immune system. Whereas most STDs are treatable, HIV infections can be lethal. Check your knowledge about HIV against the following summary.

HIV/AIDS

Acquired immunodeficiency syndrome (AIDS) is caused by an HIV infection. As the immune system weakens, other "opportunistic" diseases invade the body. Most people with AIDS eventually die of multiple infections (although newer multidrug therapies have greatly improved the odds of survival). The first symptoms of AIDS may show up as little as 2 months after infection, but they typically don't appear for 10 years. Because of this long incubation period, infected persons often pass HIV on to others without knowing it. Medical tests can detect an HIV infec-

The AIDS Memorial Quilt was begun in 1985 to commemorate those who have died from AIDS. The photo is of the last public display of the complete quilt, in 1996. Today, the quilt has grown to immense size, symbolizing the extent of the AIDS epidemic. Originally the quilt memorialized only homosexual victims. It now includes heterosexual men, women, and children, signifying that AIDS respects no boundaries.

tion. However, for at least the first 6 months after becoming infected, a person can test negative while carrying the virus. A negative test result, therefore, is no guarantee that someone is a "safe" sex partner.

HIV infections are spread by direct contact with body fluids—especially blood, semen, and vaginal secretions. HIV cannot be transmitted by casual contact. People do not get AIDS from shaking hands, touching or using objects touched by a person who has AIDS, eating food prepared by an infected person, social kissing, sweat or tears, sharing drinking glasses, sharing towels, and so forth.

HIV can be spread by all forms of sexual intercourse, and it has affected persons of all sexual orientations. Recently, the AIDS epidemic has spread more quickly among heterosexuals, women, African Americans, Hispanics, and children (Taylor-Seehafer & Rew, 2000). Around the world, almost half of all HIV cases are female (UNAIDS, 2006). HIV infection is the leading cause of death among women and men between the ages of 25 and 44 (Gayle, 2000). Worldwide, 2.9 million people die each year from HIV/AIDS and 4.3 million new infections occur (UNAIDS, 2006).

Populations at Risk

In North America, those who are at greatest risk for HIV infection remain men who have had sex with other men (homosexual and bisexual men), people who have shared needles (for tattoos or for intravenous drug use), hemophiliacs (who require frequent blood transfusions), sexual partners of people in the preceding groups, and heterosexuals with a history of multiple partners. Thus, the vast majority of people are not at high risk of HIV infection. Still, 1.4 million people in North America are now infected with HIV, of whom 26 percent are women. Each year, over 40,000 more people in the United States become infected (UNAIDS, 2006). In short, people who engage in unsafe sex are gambling with their lives—at very poor odds.

Behavioral Risk Factors

Sexually active people can do much to protect their own health. The behaviors listed here are risky when performed with an infected person:

Risky Behaviors
- Sharing drug needles and syringes
- Anal sex, with or without a condom
- Vaginal or oral sex with someone who injects drugs or engages in anal sex
- Sex with someone you don't know well, or with someone you know has several partners
- Unprotected sex (without a condom) with an infected partner
- Having two or more sex partners (additional partners further increase the risk)

Forcible rape Sexual intercourse carried out against the victim's will, under the threat of violence or bodily injury.

Sexually transmitted disease (STD) A disease that is typically passed from one person to the next by intimate physical contact; a venereal disease.

In the United States, between 2 and 4 of every 100 adults put themselves at high risk by engaging in the behaviors just listed (Gayle, 2000). It's important to remember that you can't tell from appearance if a person is infected. Many people would be surprised to learn that their partners have engaged in behavior that places them both at risk.

The preceding high-risk behaviors can be contrasted with the following list of safer sexual practices. Note, however, that unless a person completely abstains, sex can be made safer, but not risk-free.

Safer Sex Practices
- Not having sex
- Sex with one mutually faithful, uninfected partner
- Not injecting drugs
- Discussing contraception with partner
- Being selective regarding sexual partners
- Reducing the number of sexual partners
- Discussing partner's sexual health prior to engaging in sex
- Not engaging in sex while intoxicated
- Using a condom

Sexually active persons should practice safer sex until their partner's sexual history and/or health has been clearly established. And remember, a condom offers little or no protection if it is misused. Sadly, one of three sexually active teens don't know how to use a condom correctly (and virgins of both sexes are even more clueless) (Crosby & Yarber, 2001).

HIV and AIDS initially had a strong impact on sexual behavior in some groups. Among gay men there was a sharp decrease in risky sex and an increase in monogamous relationships. Unfortunately, this trend has recently reversed. Once again, STD rates are rising dramatically among gay men. In part, this may be due to the fact that new medical treatments are helping people with HIV live longer. Many victims simply do not look or act sick. This gives a false impression about the dangers of HIV infection and encourages foolish risk taking (Handsfield, 2001).

Other groups are also not getting the message. The AIDS epidemic has thus far had little impact on the willingness of high school and college age students to engage in risky behavior (casual sex) or to use condoms (Bauman, Karasz, & Hamilton, 2007). A study of heterosexual adults found that the majority did not practice safer sex with their last partner. Most of these "gamblers" knew too little about their partners to be sure they were not taking a big risk. For many people, drinking alcohol greatly increases the likelihood of taking sexual risks (Corbin & Fromme, 2002).

Apparently, heterosexual people still don't feel that they are truly at risk. However, *75 percent* of people with HIV were infected through heterosexual sex. Over the next 20 to 30 years, heterosexual transmission is expected to become the primary means of spreading HIV. Over the next 15 years, 65 million more people will die of AIDS unless prevention efforts are greatly expanded (Altman, 2002).

Risk and Responsibility

The threat of HIV/AIDS has forced many people to face new issues of risk and responsibility. Those who do not ensure their own safety are playing Russian roulette with their health. One chilling study of HIV patients—who knew they were infectious—found that 41 percent of those who were sexually active did not always use condoms (Sobel et al., 1996)! Thus, responsibility for "safer sex" rests with each sexually active individual. It is unwise to count on a sexual partner for protection against HIV infection.

A special risk that befalls people in committed relationships is that they often interpret practicing safer sex as a sign of mistrust. Taking precautions could, instead, be defined as a way of showing that you really care about the welfare of your partner (Hammer et al., 1996). Likewise, dating couples who have high levels of emotional, social, and intellectual intimacy are more likely to use contraceptives (Davis & Bibace, 1999).

The sexual revolution was fueled, in part, by "the pill" and other birth control methods. Will the threat of AIDS reverse the tide of changes that occurred in previous decades? Will STD come to mean Sudden Total Disinterest in sex? The answers may depend on how quickly people learn to respect HIV and whether its prevention or cure can be achieved.

KNOWLEDGE BUILDER
Sexual Behavior, Response, and Attitudes

RECITE
1. Areas of the body that produce erotic pleasure are called _____ zones.
2. When exposed to erotic stimuli, men and women vary in their most common emotional reactions, but there appears to be no difference in their levels of physical arousal. T or F?
3. There is some evidence to suggest that sexual activity and sex drives peak later for males than they do for females. T or F?
4. More males than females report that they masturbate. T or F?
5. List the four phases of sexual response identified by Masters and Johnson:
_____, _____, _____, _____
6. Males typically experience _____ after ejaculation.
   a. an increased potential for orgasm
   b. a short refractory period
   c. the excitement phase
   d. muscular contractions of the uterus
7. During lovemaking, 10 to 20 minutes is often required for a woman to go from excitement to orgasm, whereas a male may experience all four stages of sexual response in as little as 3 minutes. T or F?
8. Recent research shows that more liberal views regarding sexual behavior have erased the traditional values that link sexual involvement with committed relationships. T or F?
9. The term _____ describes the tendency for the sexual behavior of women and men to be judged differently.
10. One woman in 70 will be raped in her lifetime and chances are greater than 50 percent that the rapist will be a friend or acquaintance. T or F?
11. Because AIDS is spread by direct contact with body fluids, it can be transmitted by social kissing or contact with food or dishes handled by an AIDS patient. T or F?

Continued

ual partner (because it deprives the partner of satisfaction) to the suggestion that most early male sexual experiences tend to encourage rapid climax (such as those taking place in the backseat of a car and masturbation). H. S. Kaplan (1974) adds that excessive arousal and anxiety over performance are usually present. Also, some men simply engage in techniques that maximize sensation and make rapid orgasm inevitable.

Ejaculation is a reflex. To control it, a man must learn to recognize the physical signals that it is about to occur. Some men have simply never learned to be aware of these signals. Whatever the causes, premature ejaculation can be a serious difficulty, especially in the context of long-term relationships (King, 2005).

Treatment

Treatment for premature ejaculation is highly successful and relatively simple. The most common treatment is a "stop-start" procedure called the **squeeze technique** (Grenier & Byers, 1995). The man's sexual partner stimulates him manually until he signals that ejaculation is about to occur. The man's partner then firmly squeezes the tip of his penis to inhibit orgasm.

When the man feels he has control, stimulation is repeated. Later the squeeze technique is used during lovemaking. Gradually, the man acquires the ability to delay orgasm sufficiently for mutually satisfactory lovemaking. During treatment, skills that improve communication between partners are developed, along with a better understanding of the male's sexual response cues (McCarthy & Fucito, 2005).

Sexual Pain Disorders

Pain in the genitals before, during, or after sexual intercourse is called **dyspareunia** (DIS-pah-ROO-nee-ah) (Binik, 2005). Both females and males can experience dyspareunia. However, this problem is actually rare in males. In women, dyspareunia is often related to **vaginismus** (VAJ-ih-NIS-mus), a condition in which muscle spasms of the vagina prevent intercourse (*DSM-IV-TR*, 2000).

Vaginismus is often accompanied by obvious fears of intercourse, and where fear is absent, high levels of anxiety are present (Reissing et al., 2004). Vaginismus therefore appears to be a phobic response to intercourse. Predictably, its causes include experiences of painful intercourse, rape or other

brutal and frightening sexual encounters, fear of men and of penetration, misinformation about sex (belief that it is injurious), fear of pregnancy, and fear of the specific male partner (Read, 1995; Reissing et al., 2003).

Treatment

Treatment of vaginismus is similar to what might be done for a nonsexual phobia. It includes extinction of conditioned muscle spasms by progressive relaxation of the vagina, desensitization of fears of intercourse, and masturbation or manual stimulation to associate pleasure with sexual approach by the woman's partner (Bergeron & Lord, 2003). Hypnosis has also been used successfully in some cases.

Summary

Solving sexual problems can be difficult. The problems described here are rarely solved without professional help (a possible exception is premature ejaculation). If a serious sexual difficulty is not resolved in a reasonable amount of time, the aid of an appropriately trained psychologist, physician, or counselor should be sought. The longer the problem is ignored, the more difficult it is to solve. But professional help is available.

KNOWLEDGE BUILDER
Sexual Problems

RECITE

1. Sexual adjustment is best viewed as a relationship issue, not just one partner's problem. T or F?
2. The term "gunnysacking" refers to the constructive practice of hiding anger until it is appropriate to express it. T or F?
3. Males suffering from primary erectile dysfunction have never been able to have or maintain an erection. T or F?
4. According to the latest figures, most erectile disorders are caused by castration fears. T or F?
5. Sensate focus is the most common treatment for premature ejaculation. T or F?
6. Premature ejaculation is considered the rarest of the male sexual adjustment problems. T or F?
7. As it is for female sexual arousal disorder, the sensate focus technique is a primary treatment mode for male sexual arousal disorder. T or F?
8. Vaginismus, which appears to be a phobic response to sexual intercourse, can also cause dyspareunia. T or F?

REFLECT

Critical Thinking

9. Who would you expect to have the most frequent sex and the most satisfying sex, married couples or single persons?

Relate

We all make mistakes in relationships. Using the discussion in the Psychology in Action as a guide, which mistakes have you avoided? Which would you like to avoid or correct?

In plain language, sexual disorders can be summarized this way: The person doesn't want to do it. The person wants to do it but can't get aroused. The person wants to do it, gets aroused, but has problems with orgasm. The person wants to do it and gets aroused, but lovemaking is uncomfortable. What are the formal terms for each of these possibilities?

Answers: 1. T **2.** F **3.** T **4.** F **5.** F **6.** F **7.** T **8.** T **9.** Contrary to mass media portrayals of sexy singles, married couples have the most sex and are most likely to have orgasms when they do. Greater opportunity, plus familiarity with a partner's needs and preferences probably account for these findings (Laumann et al., 1994).

Sensate focus A form of therapy that directs a couple's attention to natural sensations of sexual pleasure.

Female sexual arousal disorder A lack of physical arousal to sexual stimulation.

Female orgasmic disorder A persistent inability to reach orgasm during lovemaking.

Male orgasmic disorder A persistent inability to reach orgasm during lovemaking.

Premature ejaculation Ejaculation that consistently occurs before the man and his partner want it to occur.

Squeeze technique A method for inhibiting ejaculation by compressing the tip of the penis.

Dyspareunia Genital pain before, during, or after sexual intercourse.

Vaginismus Muscle spasms of the vagina.

chapter in review   Gateways to Gender and Sexuality

Male and female are not simple either/or categories. Sexual identity is complex, multifaceted, and influenced by biology, socialization, and learning.

- Biological sex consists of genetic sex, gonadal sex, hormonal sex, and genital sex.
- Sexual development begins with genetic sex (*XX* or *XY* chromosomes) and is then influenced by prenatal hormone levels.
- Androgen insensitivity, exposure to progestin, the androgenital syndrome, and similar problems can cause a person to be born with an intersexual condition.
- Estrogens (female sex hormones) and androgens (male sex hormones) influence the development of different primary and secondary sexual characteristics in males and females.

Sexual orientation refers to one's degree of emotional and erotic attraction to members of the same sex, opposite sex, or both sexes. A person may be heterosexual, homosexual, or bisexual.

- Similar factors (heredity, biology, and socialization) underlie all sexual orientations.
- As a group, homosexual men and women do not differ psychologically from heterosexuals.
- All three sexual orientations (heterosexual, homosexual, bisexual) are part of the normal range of sexual behavior.

Male and female behavior patterns are related to learned gender identity and gender role socialization.

- Many researchers believe that prenatal hormones exert a biological biasing effect that combines with social factors to influence psychosexual development.
- On most psychological dimensions, women and men are more alike than they are different.
- Gender identity usually becomes stable by age 3 or 4 years.
- Gender role socialization seems to account for most observed female–male gender differences. Parents tend to encourage boys in instrumental behaviors and girls in expressive behaviors.
- Gender role stereotypes often distort perceptions about the kinds activities for which men and women are suited.

People who possess both masculine and feminine traits are androgynous (and it is isn't contagious).

- Roughly one third of all persons are androgynous. Approximately 50 percent are traditionally feminine or masculine.
- Psychological androgyny is related to greater behavioral adaptability and flexibility.

While "normal" sexual behavior is defined differently by various cultures, adults typically engage in a wide variety of sexual behaviors. However, coercive and/or compulsive sexual behaviors are emotionally unhealthy.

- Sexual arousal is related to the body's erogenous zones, but mental and emotional reactions are the ultimate source of sexual responsiveness.
- Evidence indicates that the sex drive peaks at a later age for females than it does for males, although this difference is diminishing.
- Castration may or may not influence sex drive in humans. Sterilization does not alter the sex drive.
- Frequency of sexual intercourse gradually declines with increasing age. However, many elderly persons remain sexually active, and large variations exist at all ages.
- Masturbation is a common, normal, and completely acceptable behavior.

The similarities between female and male sexual responses far outweigh the differences.

- Sexual response can be divided into four phases: excitement, plateau, orgasm, and resolution.
- There do not appear to be any differences between "vaginal orgasms" and "clitoral orgasms." Fifteen percent of women are consistently multi-orgasmic, and at least 50 percent are capable of multiple orgasm.
- Males experience a refractory period after orgasm, and only 5 percent of men are multi-orgasmic.
- Mutual orgasm has been abandoned by most sex counselors as the ideal in lovemaking.

The most common sexual disorders are pedophilia and exhibitionism.

- Compulsive sexual behaviors (paraphilias) tend to emotionally handicap people.
- The paraphilias include pedophilia, exhibitionism, voyeurism, frotteurism, fetishism, sexual masochism, sexual sadism, and transvestic fetishism.
- The effects of child molestation vary greatly, depending on the severity of the molestation and the child's relationship to the molester.
- Exhibitionists are usually not dangerous but can escalate their sexual aggression. They can best be characterized as sexually inhibited and immature.

In the United States, a liberalization of attitudes toward sex has been paralleled by a gradual increase in sexual behavior over the last 50 years.

- Adolescents and young adults engage in more frequent sexual activity than they did 50 years ago.
- In recent years there has been a greater acceptance of female sexuality and a narrowing of differences in female and male patterns of sexual behavior.
- Forcible rape, acquaintance rape, and rape-supportive attitudes and beliefs are major problems in North America.

Each person must now take responsibility for practicing safer sex and for choosing when, where, and with whom to express his or her sexuality.

- During the last 20 years the incidence of sexually transmitted diseases has steadily increased.
- STDs and the spread of HIV/AIDS have had a sizable impact on patterns of sexual behavior, including some curtailment of risk taking.
- Many sexually active people continue to take unnecessary risks with their health by failing to follow safer sex practices.

Although solutions exist for many sexual adjustment problems, good communication and a healthy relationship are the real keys to sexual satisfaction.

- Communication skills that foster and maintain intimacy are the key to successful relationships.
- Most sexual adjustment problems are closely linked to the general health of a couple's relationship.
- Problems with sexual function can involve desire, arousal, orgasm, or pain.
- Behavioral methods and counseling techniques have been developed to alleviate many sexual problems.

Web Resources

For an up-to-date list of direct links to interesting sites, including those listed here, visit the student companion site for this book at www.cengage.com/psychology/coon

Sex and Gender Read an article about the difference between sex and gender.

My Life as an Intersexual Read the story of one person's life as an intersexual.

Simon LeVay's Home Page Read about the biology of sexual orientation.

Facts about Sexual Orientation Read about sexual prejudice in our society.

Sexual Response Explore the sexual response cycle.

Paraphilias and Sexual Disorders Read more about sexual disorders.

Sexuality and Intimacy Read a series of articles on the role of intimacy in sexuality.

Interactive Learning

Introduction to Psychology: Gateways to Mind and Behavior **Book Companion Website**
www.cengage.com/psychology/coon

Visit your Book Companion Website, where you will find flash cards, practice quizzes, web links, and more to help you study.

CENGAGENOW™ *Just what you need to know NOW!*

Spend time on what you need to master rather than on information you already have learned. Take a pre-test for this chapter, and CengageNOW will generate a personalized study plan based on your results. The study plan will identify the topics you need to review and direct you to online resources to help you master those topics. You can then take a post-test to help you determine the concepts you have mastered and what you will need to work on. Try it out! Go to www.cengage.com/login to sign in with an access code or to purchase access to this product.

CHAPTER 12

Personality

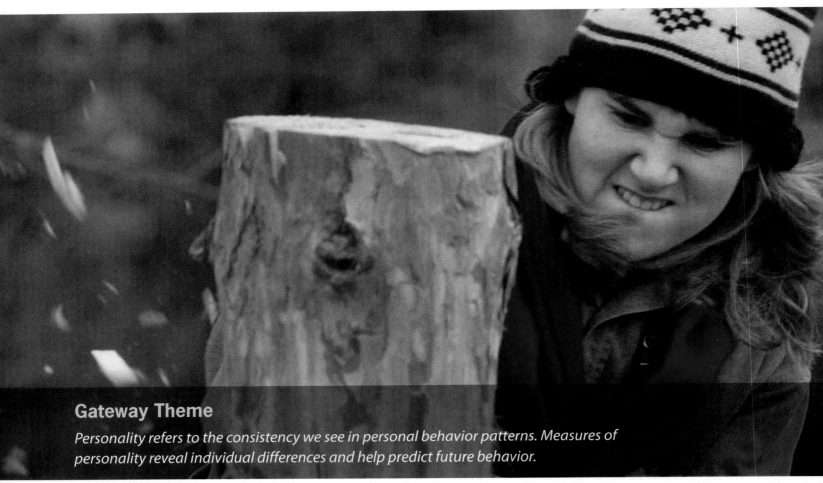

Gateway Theme

Personality refers to the consistency we see in personal behavior patterns. Measures of personality reveal individual differences and help predict future behavior.

Andre Forget/AP/Wide World Photo

Gateway Questions

- *How do psychologists use the term "personality"?*
- *Are some personality traits more basic or important than others?*
- *How do psychodynamic theories explain personality?*
- *What do behaviorists emphasize in their approach to personality?*
- *How do humanistic theories differ from other perspectives?*
- *How do psychologists measure personality?*
- *What causes shyness? What can be done about it?*

Rural Colorado. The car banged over one last, brain-jarring rut and lurched toward the dilapidated farmhouse. Annette, a friend of one of your authors, was on the porch, hooting and whooping and obviously happy to see old friends arrive.

If anyone was suited for a move to the "wilds" of Colorado, it was Annette, a strong and resourceful woman. Still, it was hard to imagine a more radical change. After separating from her husband, she had traded a comfortable life in the city for rough times in the high country. Annette was working as a ranch hand and a lumberjack (lumberjill?), trying to make it through some hard winters.

So radical were the changes in Annette's life, we worried that she might be entirely different. She was, on the contrary, more her "old self" than ever.

Perhaps you have had a similar experience. After several years of separation, it is always intriguing to see an old friend. At first you may be struck by how the person has changed. ("Where did you get that haircut!?") Soon, however, you will probably be delighted to discover that the semi-stranger before you is still the person you once knew. It is exactly this core of consistency that psychologists have in mind when they use the term "personality."

Without doubt, personality touches our daily lives. Falling in love, choosing friends, getting along with co-workers, voting for a president, or coping with your zaniest relatives all raise questions about personality.

What is personality? How does it differ from temperament, character, or attitudes? Is it possible to measure personality? Can we change our personality? We'll address these questions and more in this chapter.

The Psychology of Personality— Do You Have Personality?

Gateway Question: How do psychologists use the term "personality"?

"Annette has a very optimistic personality." "Ramiro's not handsome, but he has a great personality." "My father's business friends think he's a nice guy. They should see him at home where his real personality comes out." "It's hard to believe Tanya and Nikki are sisters. They have such opposite personalities." It's obvious that we all frequently use the term "personality." But if you think that personality means "charm," "charisma," or "style," you have misused the term. Psychologists regard **personality** as a person's unique long-term pattern of thinking, emotions, and behavior (Burger, 2008; Mischel, 2004). In other words, personality refers to the consistency in who you are, have been, and will become. It also refers to the special blend of talents, values, hopes, loves, hates, and habits that makes each of us a unique person.

Many people also confuse personality with the term **character,** which implies that a person has been evaluated, not just described (Skipton, 1997). If, by saying someone has "personality," you mean the person is friendly, outgoing, and attractive, you are describing what we regard as good character in our culture. But in some cultures it is deemed good for people to be fierce, warlike, and cruel. So, whereas everyone in a particular culture has personality, not everyone has character—or at least not good character. (Do you know any good characters?)

Personality is also distinct from *temperament,* the "raw material" from which personalities are formed. **Temperament** refers to the hereditary aspects of your personality, such as your sensitivity, irritability, distractibility, and typical mood (Rothbart, 2007).

Matthew Mendelsohn/Corbis

Does this man have personality? Do you?

Personality A person's unique and relatively stable behavior patterns.

Character Personal characteristics that have been judged or evaluated; a person's desirable or undesirable qualities.

Temperament The hereditary aspects of personality, including sensitivity, activity levels, prevailing mood, irritability, and adaptability.

Judging from Annette's adult personality, you might guess that she was an active, happy baby.

bridges

Even newborn babies differ in temperament, which implies that it is hereditary. Temperament has a large impact on how infants interact with their parents. **See Chapter 3, page 84.**

Psychologists use a large number of models and concepts to explain personality. It might be wise, therefore, to start with a few key concepts. These ideas should help you keep your bearings as you read this chapter.

Traits

We use the idea of traits every day to talk about personality. For instance, Dan is *sociable, orderly,* and *intelligent.* His sister Kayla is *shy, sensitive,* and *creative.* As we observed in our reunion with Annette, personality traits like these can be quite stable (Gustavsson et al., 1997; Hergenhahn & Olson, 2007). Think about how little the traits of your best friends have changed in the last 5 years. It would be strange indeed to feel like you were talking with a different person every time you met a friend or an acquaintance. In general, then, **personality traits** like these are stable qualities that a person shows in most situations (Matthews, Deary, & Whiteman, 2003). Traits even influence our health as well as our marital and occupational success (Roberts et al., 2007). For example, who do you think would be more successful in her career: Jane, who is conscientious, or Sally, who is not (Chamorro-Premuzic & Furnham, 2003)?

Typically, traits are inferred from behavior. If you see Dan talking to strangers—first at a supermarket and later at a party—you might deduce that he is "sociable." Once personality traits are

identified, they can be used to predict future behavior. For example, noting that Dan is outgoing might lead you to predict that he will be sociable at school or at work. In fact, such consistencies can span many years. A study of women who appeared to be happy in their college yearbook photos (they had genuine smiles) found that most were still happy people 30 years later (Harker & Keltner, 2001).

At what age are personality traits firmly established? Personality starts to stabilize at around age 3 and continues to "harden" through age 50 (Caspi, Roberts, & Shiner, 2005). However, personality slowly matures during old age as most people continue to become more conscientious, agreeable, and emotionally stable (Roberts & Mroczek, 2008). It appears that stereotypes of the "grumpy old man" and "cranky old woman" are largely unfounded.

Do We Inherit Personality?

Does the stability of personality traits mean that they are affected by heredity? Some breeds of dogs have reputations for being friendly, aggressive, intelligent, calm, or emotional. Such differences fall in the realm of **behavioral genetics,** the study of inherited behavioral traits. We know that facial features, eye color, body type, and many other physical characteristics are inherited. So are many of our behavioral tendencies (Bouchard, 2004; Kalat, 2007). Genetic studies have shown that intelligence, some mental disorders, temperament, and other complex qualities are influenced by heredity. In view of such findings, it wouldn't be a surprise to find that genes affect personality as well (Nettle, 2006).

bridges

Behavioral genetic research has helped us better understand the hereditary origins of intelligence and psychological disorders. **See Chapter 9, pages 312–313, and Chapter 14, page 473.**

Wouldn't comparing the personalities of identical twins help answer the question? It would indeed—especially if the twins were separated at birth or soon after.

Twins and Traits

For several decades, psychologists at the University of Minnesota have been studying identical twins who grew up in different homes. Medical and psychological tests reveal that reunited twins are very much alike, even when they are reared apart (Figure 12.5) (Bouchard, 2004; Bouchard et al., 1990). They may even be similar in appearance, voice quality, facial gestures, hand movements, and nervous tics, such as nail biting. Separated twins also tend to have similar talents. If one twin excels at art, music, dance, drama, or athletics, the other is likely to as well—despite wide differences in childhood environment. However, as "The Amazing Twins" explains, it's wise to be cautious about some reports of extraordinary similarities in reunited twins.

Bill Bachman/PhotoEdit

Psychologists and employers are especially interested in the personality traits of individuals who hold high-risk, high-stress positions involving public safety, such as police, air traffic controllers, and nuclear power plant employees.

CRITICAL THINKING

The Amazing Twins

Many reunited twins in the Minnesota study (the Minnesota Twins?) have displayed similarities far beyond what would be expected on the basis of heredity. The "Jim twins," James Lewis and James Springer, are one famous example. Both Jims had married and divorced women named Linda. Both had undergone police training. One named his firstborn son James Allan, the other named *his* firstborn son James Alan. Both drove Chevrolets and vacationed at the same beach each summer. Both listed carpentry and mechanical drawing among their hobbies. Both had built benches around trees in their yards. And so forth (Holden, 1980).

Are all identical twins so, well, identical? No, they aren't. Consider identical twins Carolyn Spiro and Pamela Spiro Wagner who, unlike the "Jim Twins," lived together throughout their childhood. While in sixth grade, they found out that President Kennedy had been assassinated. Carolyn wasn't sure why everyone was so upset. Pamela heard voices announcing that she was responsible for his death. After years of hiding her voices from everyone, Pamela tried to commit suicide while the twins were attending Brown University. She was diagnosed with schizophrenia. Never to be cured, she has gone on to write award-winning poetry. Carolyn eventually became a Harvard psychiatrist (Spiro Wagner & Spiro, 2005). Some twins

reared apart appear very similar; some reared together appear rather different.

So why are some identical twins, like the Jim Twins, so much alike even if they were reared apart? Although genetics is important, it is preposterous to suggest that there are child-naming genes and bench-building genes. How, then, do we explain the eerie similarities in some separated twins' lives? Imagine that you were separated at birth from a twin brother or sister. If you were

Identical twins Pam (left) and Carolyn (right) were raised together. Regardless, Carolyn became a psychiatrist while Pamela developed schizophrenia and went on to become an award-winning poet (Spiro Wagner & Spiro, 2005). Their story illustrates the complex interplay of forces that shape our adult personalities.

Courtesy of Pam Wagner

reunited with your twin today, what would you do? Quite likely, you would spend the next several days comparing every imaginable detail of your lives. Under such circumstances it is virtually certain that you and your twin would notice and compile a long list of similarities. ("Wow! I use the same brand of toothpaste you do!") Yet, two unrelated persons of the same age, sex, and race could probably rival your list—*if* they were as motivated to find similarities.

In fact, one study compared twins to unrelated pairs of students. The unrelated pairs, who were the same age and sex, were almost as alike as the twins. They had highly similar political beliefs, musical interests, religious preferences, job histories, hobbies, favorite foods, and so on (Wyatt et al., 1984). Why were the unrelated students so similar? Basically, it's because people of the same age and sex live in the same historical times and select from similar societal options. As just one example, in nearly every elementary school classroom you will find several children with the same first name.

It appears then that many of the seemingly "astounding" coincidences shared by reunited twins may be a special case of the fallacy of positive instances (described in Chapter 1, pages 18–19). Reunited twins tend to notice the similarities and ignore the differences.

Summary

Studies of twins make it clear that heredity has a sizable effect on each of us. All told, it seems reasonable to conclude that heredity is responsible for about 25 to 50 percent of the variation in many personality traits (Caspi, Roberts, & Shiner, 2005; Loehlin et al., 1998). Notice, however, that the same figures imply that personality is shaped as much, or more, by environment as it is by heredity.

Each personality, then, is a unique blend of heredity and environment, biology and culture. We are not—thank goodness—genetically programmed robots whose behavior and personality traits are "wired in" for life. Where you go in life is the result of the choices you make. Although these choices are influenced by inherited tendencies, they are not merely a product of your genes (Funder, 2006).

Types

Have you ever asked the question, "What type of person is she (or he)?" A **personality type** refers to people who have *several traits in common* (Larsen & Buss, 2005). Informally, your own thinking might include categories such as the executive type, the

Personality trait A stable, enduring quality that a person shows in most situations.

Behavioral genetics The study of inherited behavioral traits and tendencies.

Personality type A style of personality defined by a group of related traits.

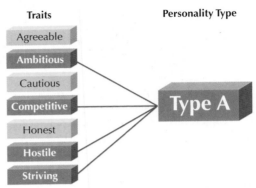

Traits   **Personality Type**

- Agreeable
- Ambitious
- Cautious
- Competitive   **Type A**
- Honest
- Hostile
- Striving

● **Figure 12.1** Personality types are defined by the presence of several specific traits. For example, several possible personality traits are shown in the left column. A person who has a Type A personality typically possesses all or most of the highlighted traits. Type A persons are especially prone to heart disease. (See Chapter 13.)

athletic type, the motherly type, the hip-hop type, the techno geek, and so forth. If you tried to define these informal types, you would probably list a different collection of traits for each one.

How valid is it to speak of personality "types"? Over the years, psychologists have proposed many ways to categorize personalities into types. For example, Swiss psychiatrist Carl Jung (yoong) proposed that people are either *introverts* or *extroverts*. An **introvert** is a shy, reserved person whose attention is focused inward. An **extrovert** is a bold, outgoing person whose attention is directed outward. These terms are so widely used that you may think of yourself and your friends as being one type or the other. However, the wildest, wittiest, most party-loving "extrovert" you know is introverted at times. Likewise, extremely introverted persons are assertive and sociable in some situations. In short, two categories (or even several) are often inadequate to fully capture differences in personality. That's why rating people on a list of traits tends to be more informative than classifying them into two or three types.

Even though types tend to oversimplify personality, they do have value. Most often, types are a shorthand way of labeling people who have several key traits in common. For example, in the next chapter we will discuss Type A and Type B personalities. Type A's are people who have personality traits that increase their chance of suffering a heart attack; Type B's take a more laid-back approach to life (● Figure 12.1). Similarly, you will read in Chapter 14 about unhealthy personality types such as the paranoid personality, the dependent personality, and the antisocial personality. Each problem type is defined by a specific collection of maladaptive traits.

Self-Concept

Self-concepts provide another way of understanding personality. The rough outlines of your self-concept could be revealed by this request: "Please tell us about yourself." In other words, your **self-concept** consists of all your ideas, perceptions, stories, and feelings about who you are. It is the mental "picture" you have of your own personality (Swann, Chang-Schneider, & Larsen McClarty, 2007).

We creatively build our self-concepts out of daily experiences. Then we slowly revise them as we have new experiences. Once a stable self-concept exists, it tends to guide what we pay attention

Matt Cardy/Getty Images

Self-concepts can be remarkably consistent. In an interesting study, old people were asked how they had changed over the years. Almost all thought they were essentially the same person they were when they were young (Troll & Skaff, 1997). Mick Jagger, for example, has been the charismatic and passionate lead singer of the Rolling Stones for over 40 years.

to, remember, and think about. Because of this, self-concepts can greatly affect our behavior and personal adjustment—especially when they are inaccurate (Ryckman, 2008). For instance, Alesha is a student who thinks she is stupid, worthless, and a failure, despite getting good grades. With such an inaccurate self-concept, she tends to be depressed regardless of how well she does.

Self-Esteem

Note that in addition to having a faulty self-concept, Alesha has low **self-esteem** (a negative self-evaluation). A person with high self-esteem is confident, proud, and self-respecting. One who has low self-esteem is insecure, lacking in confidence, and self-critical. Like Alesha, people with low self-esteem are usually anxious and unhappy.

Self-esteem tends to rise when we experience success or praise. A person who is competent and effective and who is loved, admired, and respected by others will almost always have high self-esteem (Baumeister et al., 2003). (The reasons for having high self-esteem can vary in different cultures. See "Self-Esteem and Culture" for more information.)

People who have low self-esteem typically also suffer from poor self-knowledge. Like Alesha, their self-concepts are inconsistent, inaccurate, and confused. Problems of this type are explored later in this chapter.

HUMAN DIVERSITY

Self-Esteem and Culture—Hotshot or Team Player?

You and some friends are playing soccer. Your team wins, in part because you make some good plays. After the game, you bask in the glow of having performed well. You don't want to brag about being a hotshot, but your self-esteem gets a boost from your personal success.

In Japan, Shinobu and some of his friends are playing soccer. His team wins, in part because he makes some good plays. After the game Shinobu is happy because his team did well. However, Shinobu also dwells on the ways in which he let his team down. He thinks about how he could improve, and he resolves to be a better team player.

These sketches illustrate a basic difference in Eastern and Western psychology. In individualistic cultures such as the United States, self-esteem is based on personal success and outstanding performance (Lay & Verkuyten, 1999). For us, the path to higher self-esteem lies in self-enhancement. We are pumped up by our successes and tend to downplay our faults and failures (Ross et al., 2005).

Japanese and other Asian cultures place a greater emphasis on collectivism, or interdependence among people. For them, self-esteem is based on a secure sense of belonging to social groups. As a result,

people in Asian cultures are more apt to engage in self-criticism (Ross et al., 2005). By correcting personal faults, they add to the well-being of the group (Kitayama, Markus, & Kurokawa, 2000). And, when the *group* succeeds, individual members feel better about themselves, which raises their self-esteem.

Perhaps self-esteem is still based on success in both Eastern and Western cultures. However, it is fascinating that cultures define success in such different ways (Schmitt & Allik, 2005). The North American emphasis on winning is not the only way to feel good about yourself.

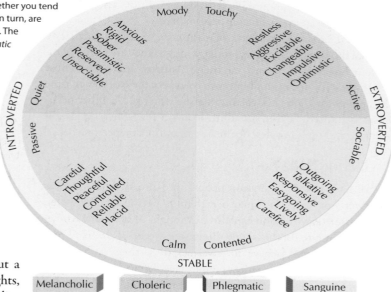

● **Figure 12.2** English psychologist Hans Eysenck (1916–1997) believed that many personality traits are related to whether you are mainly introverted or extroverted and whether you tend to be emotionally stable or unstable (highly emotional). These characteristics, in turn, are related to four basic types of temperament first recognized by the early Greeks. The types are: *melancholic* (sad, gloomy), *choleric* (hot-tempered, irritable), *phlegmatic* (sluggish, calm), and *sanguine* (cheerful, hopeful). (Adapted from Eysenck, 1981.)

What if you "think you're hot," but you're not? Genuine self-esteem is based on an accurate appraisal of your strengths and weaknesses. A positive self-evaluation that is bestowed too easily may not be healthy (Twenge & Campbell, 2001). People who think very highly of themselves (and let others know it) may at first seem confident, but their arrogance quickly turns off other people (Paulhus, 1998).

Personality Theories

As you can already see, it would be easy to get lost without a framework for understanding personality. How do our thoughts, actions, and feelings relate to one another? How does personality develop? Why do some people suffer from psychological problems? How can they be helped? To answer such questions, psychologists have created a dazzling array of theories. A **personality theory** is a system of concepts, assumptions, ideas, and principles proposed to explain personality (● Figure 12.2). In this chapter, we can only explore a few of the many personality theories. These are the four major perspectives we will consider:

1. **Trait theories** attempt to learn what traits make up personality and how they relate to actual behavior.
2. **Psychodynamic theories** focus on the inner workings of personality, especially internal conflicts and struggles.

Introvert A person whose attention is focused inward; a shy, reserved, self-centered person.

Extrovert A person whose attention is directed outward; a bold, outgoing person.

Self-concept A person's perception of his or her own personality traits.

Self-esteem Regarding oneself as a worthwhile person; a positive evaluation of oneself.

Personality theory A system of concepts, assumptions, ideas, and principles used to understand and explain personality.

3. **Behavioristic and social learning theories** place importance on the external environment and on the effects of conditioning and learning. Social learning theories attribute differences in personality to socialization, expectations, and mental processes.

4. **Humanistic theories** stress private, subjective experience, and personal growth.

With these broad perspectives in mind, let's take a deeper look at personality.

⬤⬤ The Trait Approach—Describe Yourself in 18,000 Words or Less

Gateway Question: Are some personality traits more basic or important than others?

The trait approach is currently the dominant method for studying personality. Psychologists seek to describe personality with a small number of key traits or factors. How many words can you think of to describe the personality of a close friend? Your list might be long: More than 18,000 English words refer to personal characteristics. As we have noted, traits are stable qualities that a person shows in most situations (Matthews, Deary, & Whiteman, 2003). For example, if you are usually friendly, optimistic, and cautious, these qualities are traits of your personality.

What if I am also sometimes shy, pessimistic, or uninhibited? The original three qualities are still traits as long as they are most *typical* of your behavior. Let's say our friend Annette approaches most situations with optimism, but tends to expect the worst each time she applies for a job and worries that she won't get it. If her pessimism is limited to this situation or just a few others, it is still accurate and useful to describe her as an optimistic person.

Predicting Behavior

As we have noted, separating people into broad types, such as "introvert" or "extrovert," may oversimplify personality. However, introversion/extroversion can also be thought of as a trait. Knowing how you rate on this single dimension would allow us to predict how you will behave in a variety of settings. Where, for example, do you prefer to meet people, face-to-face or through the Internet? Researchers have found that students high in the trait of introversion are more likely to prefer the Internet because they find it easier to talk with people online (Koch & Pratarelli, 2004). (Other interesting links exist between traits and behavior. See "What's Your Musical Personality?")

Describing People

In general, psychologists try to identify traits that best describe a person. Take a moment to check the traits in ⬤ Table 12.1 that describe your personality. Are the traits you checked of equal importance? Are some stronger or more basic than others? Do any overlap? For example, if you checked "dominant," did you also check "confident" and "bold"? Answers to these questions would

Table 12.1 ● Adjective Checklist

Check the traits you feel are characteristic of your personality. Are some more basic than others?			
aggressive	organized	ambitious	clever
confident	loyal	generous	calm
warm	bold	cautious	reliable
sensitive	mature	talented	jealous
sociable	honest	funny	religious
dominant	dull	accurate	nervous
humble	uninhibited	visionary	cheerful
thoughtful	serious	helpful	emotional
orderly	anxious	conforming	good-natured
liberal	curious	optimistic	kind
meek	neighborly	passionate	compulsive

interest a trait theorist. To better understand personality, **trait theorists** attempt to analyze, classify, and interrelate traits.

Classifying Traits

Are there different types of traits? Yes, psychologist Gordon Allport (1961) identified several kinds. **Common traits** are characteristics shared by most members of a culture. Common traits tell us how people from a particular nation or culture are similar, or which traits a culture emphasizes. In America, for example, competitiveness is a fairly common trait. Among the Hopi of Northern Arizona, however, it is relatively rare.

Of course, common traits don't tell us much about individuals. Although many people are competitive in American culture, various people you know may rate high, medium, or low in this trait. Usually we are also interested in **individual traits,** which describe a person's unique qualities.

Here's an analogy to help you separate common traits from individual traits: If you decide to buy a pet dog, you will want to know the general characteristics of the dog's breed (its common traits). In addition, you will want to know about the "personality" of a specific dog (its individual traits) before you decide to take it home.

Allport also made distinctions between *cardinal traits, central traits,* and *secondary traits.* **Cardinal traits** are so basic that all of a person's activities can be traced to the trait. For instance, compassion was an overriding trait of Mother Teresa's personality. Likewise, Abraham Lincoln's personality was dominated by the cardinal trait of honesty. According to Allport, few people have cardinal traits.

Central Traits

How do central and secondary traits differ from cardinal traits? **Central traits** are the basic building blocks of personality. A surprisingly small number of central traits can capture the essence of a person. For instance, just six traits would provide a good descrip-

DISCOVERING PSYCHOLOGY

What's Your Musical Personality?

Even if you like all kinds of music, you probably prefer some styles to others. Of the styles listed here, which three do you enjoy the most? (Circle your choices.)

blues jazz classical folk rock alternative heavy metal country soundtrack religious pop rap/hip-hop soul/funk electronic/dance

In one study, Peter Rentfrow and Samuel Gosling found that the types of music people prefer tend to be associated with their personality characteristics (Rentfrow & Gosling,

2003). See if your musical tastes match their findings (Rentfrow & Gosling, 2007):

- People who value aesthetic experiences, have good verbal abilities, are liberal, and tolerant of others tend to like music that is reflective and complex (blues, jazz, classical, and folk music).
- People who are curious about new experiences, enjoy taking risks, and are physically active prefer intense, rebellious music (rock, alternative, and heavy metal music).

- People who are cheerful, conventional, extroverted, reliable, helpful, and conservative tend to enjoy upbeat conventional music (country, soundtrack, religious, and pop music).
- People who are talkative, full of energy, forgiving, and physically attractive, and who reject conservative ideals tend to prefer energetic, rhythmic music (rap/hip-hop, soul/funk, and electronic/dance music).

Unmistakably, personality traits affect our everyday behavior.

---

tion of Annette's personality: dominant, sociable, honest, cheerful, intelligent, and optimistic. When college students were asked to describe someone they knew well, they mentioned an average of seven central traits (Allport, 1961).

Secondary traits are more superficial personal qualities, such as food preferences, attitudes, political opinions, musical tastes, and so forth. In Allport's terms, a personality description might therefore include the following items:

Name: Jane Doe
Age: 22
Cardinal traits: None
Central traits: Possessive, autonomous, artistic, dramatic, self-centered, trusting
Secondary traits: Prefers colorful clothes, likes to work alone, politically liberal, always late

Source Traits

How can you tell if a personality trait is central or secondary? Raymond B. Cattell (1906–1998) tried to answer this question by directly studying the traits of a large number of people. Cattell began by measuring visible features of personality, which he called **surface traits.** Soon, Cattell noticed that these surface traits often appeared together in groups. In fact, some traits clustered together so often that they seemed to represent a single more basic trait. Cattell called these deeper characteristics, or dimensions, **source traits** (Cattell, 1965). They are the core of each individual's personality.

How do source traits differ from Allport's central traits? Allport classified traits subjectively, and it's possible that he was wrong at times. To look for connections among traits, Cattell used **factor analysis,** a statistical technique used to correlate multiple measurements and identify general underlying factors. For example, he found that imaginative people are almost always *inventive, origi-*

nal, curious, creative, innovative, and *ingenious.* If you are an imaginative person, we automatically know that you have several other traits, too. Thus, *imaginative* is a source trait. (Source traits are also called factors.)

Cattell identified 16 source traits. According to him, all 16 are needed to fully describe a personality. Source traits are measured by a test called the *Sixteen Personality Factor Questionnaire* (often referred to as the 16 PF). Like many personality tests, the 16 PF can be used to produce a **trait profile,** or graph of a person's score on each trait. Trait profiles draw a "picture" of individual personalities, which makes it easier to compare them (● Figure 12.3).

Trait theorist A psychologist interested in classifying, analyzing, and interrelating traits to understand personality.

Common traits Personality traits that are shared by most members of a particular culture.

Individual traits Personality traits that define a person's unique individual qualities.

Cardinal trait A personality trait so basic that all of a person's activities relate to it.

Central traits The core traits that characterize an individual personality.

Secondary traits Traits that are inconsistent or relatively superficial.

Surface traits The visible or observable traits of one's personality.

Source traits Basic underlying traits, or dimensions, of personality; each source trait is reflected in a number of surface traits.

Factor analysis A statistical technique used to correlate multiple measurements and identify general underlying factors.

Trait profile A graph of the scores obtained on several personality traits.

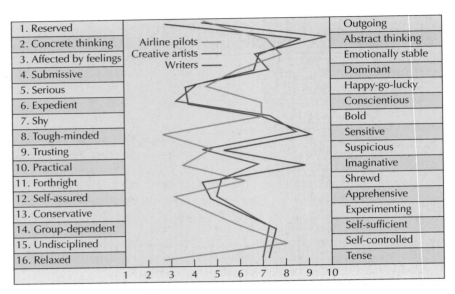

● **Figure 12.3** The 16 source traits measured by Cattell's 16 PF are listed beside the graph. Scores can be plotted as a profile for an individual or a group. The profiles shown here are group averages for airline pilots, creative artists, and writers. Notice the similarity between artists and writers and the difference between these two groups and pilots. (After R. B. Cattell, "Personality Pinned Down," 1973. Reprinted by permission of Dr. R. B. Cattell.)

The Big Five

Noel is outgoing and friendly, conscientious, even-tempered, and curious. His brother Joel is reserved, hostile, irresponsible, temperamental, and disinterested in ideas. You will be spending a week in a space capsule with either Noel or Joel. Who would you choose? If the answer seems obvious, it's because Noel and Joel were described with the **five-factor model,** a system that identifies the five most basic dimensions of personality.

The "Big Five" factors listed in ● Figure 12.4 attempt to further reduce Cattell's 16 factors to just five universal dimensions, or source traits (Costa & McCrae, 2006). The Big Five may be the best answer of all to the question, What is the essence of human personality (McCrae & Terracciano, 2005)?

Five Key Dimensions

If you would like to compare the personalities of two people, try rating them informally on the five dimensions shown in ● Figure 12.4. For factor 1, *extroversion,* rate how introverted or extroverted each person is. Factor 2, *agreeableness,* refers to how friendly, nurturant, and caring a person is, as opposed to cold, indifferent, self-centered, or spiteful. A person who is *conscientious* (factor 3) is self-disciplined, responsible, and achieving. People low on this factor are irresponsible, careless, and undependable. Factor 4, *neuroticism,* refers to negative, upsetting emotions. People who are high in neuroticism tend to be anxious, emotionally "sour," irritable, and unhappy. Finally, people who rate high on factor 5, *openness to experience,* are intelligent and open to new ideas (McCrae & Costa, 2001).

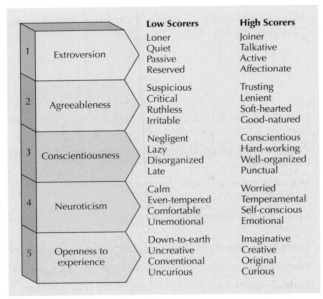

● **Figure 12.4** The Big Five. According to the five-factor model, basic differences in personality can be "boiled down" to the dimensions shown here. The five-factor model answers these essential questions about a person: Is she/he extroverted or introverted? Agreeable or difficult? Conscientious or irresponsible? Emotionally stable or unstable? Smart or unintelligent? These questions cover a large measure of what we might want to know about someone's personality. (Trait descriptions adapted from McCrae & Costa, 2001.)

Knowing where a person stands on the "Big Five" personality factors helps predict his or her behavior. For example, people who score low on conscientiousness tend to be unsafe drivers who are more likely to have automobile accidents (Arthur & Doverspike, 2001).

THE CLINICAL FILE

Perfectly Miserable

Up to a point, conscientiousness is associated with high achievement. However, having impossibly high standards, a trait called *perfectionism*, can be a problem. As you might expect, college students who are perfectionists tend to get good grades. Yet some students cross the line into maladaptive perfectionism, which typically *lowers* performance at school and elsewhere (Accordino, Accordino, & Slaney, 2000).

People who suffer from unhealthy perfectionism set unattainably high standards for themselves. This causes them to feel as if they are always failing. Perfectionistic students are self-critical, terrified of making mistakes, and often seriously depressed (Grzegorek et al., 2004; Sumi & Kanda, 2002).

For many students, maladaptive perfectionism begins with harsh, perfectionistic parenting. There's nothing wrong with having parents who expect a lot of you—if they are also emotionally supportive. However, parents who are demanding and highly critical may leave a student feeling that nothing she or he does is ever quite good enough. As already noted, this is a recipe for self-doubt and depression.

Authentic Navajo rugs always have a flaw in their intricate designs. Navajo weavers intentionally make a "mistake" in each rug as a reminder that humans are not perfect. There is a lesson in this: It is not always necessary, or even desirable, to be "perfect." To learn from your experiences you must feel free to make mistakes (Castro & Rice, 2003). Success, in the long run, is more often based on seeking "excellence," rather than "perfection" (Enns, Cox, & Clara, 2005).

The beauty of the Big-Five model is that almost any trait you can name will be related to one of the five factors. If you were selecting a college roommate, hiring an employee, or answering a singles ad, you would probably like to know all the personal dimensions covered by the Big Five.

The Big Five traits have been related to different brain systems and chemicals (Ashton, 2007; Nettle, 2008). They also predict how people will act in various circumstances. For example, people who score high in conscientiousness tend to perform well at work, do well in school, and rarely have automobile accidents (Arthur & Doverspike, 2001; Barrick, Moun, & Judge, 2001; Chamorro-Premuzic & Furnham, 2003). They even live longer (Martin, Friedman, & Schwartz, 2007). (Is it possible to be too conscientious? See "Perfectly Miserable" for an answer.)

Before you read the next section, take a moment to answer the questions that follow. Doing so will add to your understanding of a long-running controversy in the psychology of personality.

Rate Yourself: How Do You View Personality?

1. My friends' actions are fairly consistent from day to day and in different situations. T or F?
2. Whether a person is honest or dishonest, kind or cruel, a hero or a coward depends mainly on circumstances. T or F?
3. Most people I have known for several years have pretty much the same personalities now as they did when I first met them. T or F?
4. The reason people in some professions (such as teachers, lawyers, or doctors) seem so much alike is because their work requires that they act in particular ways. T or F?
5. One of the first things I would want to know about a potential roommate is what the person's personality is like. T or F?
6. I believe that immediate circumstances usually determine how people act at any given time. T or F?
7. To be comfortable in a particular job, a person's personality must match the nature of the work. T or F?
8. Almost anyone would be polite at a wedding reception; it doesn't matter what kind of personality the person has. T or F?

Now count the number of times you marked true for the odd-numbered items. Do the same for the even-numbered items. If you agreed with most of the odd-numbered items, you tend to view behavior as strongly influenced by personality traits or lasting personal dispositions. If you agreed with most of the even-numbered items, you view behavior as strongly influenced by external situations and circumstances.

What if I answered true about equally for odd and even items? Then you place equal weight on traits and situations as ways to explain behavior. This is the view now held by many personality psychologists (Funder, 2006; Mischel & Shoda, 1998).

Traits, Consistency, and Situations

Does that mean that to predict how a person will act, it is better to focus on both personality traits and external circumstances? Yes, it's best to take both into account. Personality traits are quite consistent. Also, they can predict such things as job performance, dangerous driving, or a successful marriage (Funder, 2006). Yet, *situations* also greatly influence our behavior. For instance, it would be unusual for you to dance at a movie or read a book at a football game. Likewise, few people sleep in roller coasters or tell off-color jokes at funerals. However, your personality traits may predict whether you choose to read a book, go to a movie, or attend a football game in the first place. Typically, traits *interact* with situations to determine how we will act (Mischel, 2004).

Five-factor model Proposes that there are five universal dimensions of personality.

In a **trait-situation interaction,** external circumstances influence the expression of a personality trait. For instance, imagine what would happen if you moved from a church to a classroom to a party to a football game. As the setting changed, you would probably become louder and more boisterous. This change would show situational effects on behavior. At the same time, your personality traits would also be apparent: If you were quieter than average in church and class, you would probably be quieter than average in the other settings, too.

KNOWLEDGE BUILDER
Personality and Trait Theories

RECITE

1. When someone's personality has been evaluated, we are making a judgment about his or her
   a. temperament
   b. character
   c. extroversion
   d. self-esteem
2. A personality type is usually defined by the presence of
   a. all five personality dimensions
   b. a stable self concept
   c. several specific traits
   d. a source trait
3. The research methods of _____ have been used to study the extent to which we inherit personality characteristics.
   a. behavioral genetics
   b. social learning theory
   c. factor analysis
   d. trait profiling
4. Central traits are those shared by most members of a culture. T or F?
5. Cattell believes that clusters of _____ traits reveal the presence of underlying _____ traits.
6. Which of the following is *not* one of the Big Five personality factors?
   a. submissiveness
   b. agreeableness
   c. extroversion
   d. neuroticism
7. To understand personality, it is wise to remember that traits and situations _____ to determine our behavior.

RELFECT

Critical Thinking

8. In what way would memory contribute to the formation of an accurate or inaccurate self-image?
9. Are situations equally powerful in their impact on behavior?

Relate

See if you can define or describe the following terms in your own words: personality, character, temperament, trait, type, self-concept, self-esteem.

List six or seven traits that best describe your personality. Which system of traits seems to best match your list, Allport's, Cattell's, or the Big Five?

Choose a prominent trait from your list. Does its expression seem to be influenced by specific situations? Do you think that heredity contributed to the trait?

be of greater importance.

matter what their personality traits may be. In other situations, traits may

weak influence. In some situations, almost everyone will act the same, no

moldability of self-concept. **9.** No. Circumstances can have a strong or

ries are often distorted by recent information. Such properties add to the

cussed in Chapter 8, memory is highly selective, and long-term memo-

Answers: 1. b **2.** c **3.** a **4.** F **5.** surface, source **6.** a **7.** interact **8.** As dis-

---

● ● Psychoanalytic Theory—
Id Came to Me in a Dream

Gateway Question: How do psychodynamic theories explain personality?

Psychodynamic theorists are not content with studying traits. Instead, they try to probe under the surface of personality—to learn what drives, conflicts, and energies animate us. Psychodynamic theorists believe that many of our actions are based on hidden, or unconscious, thoughts, needs, and emotions.

Psychoanalytic theory, the best-known psychodynamic approach, grew out of the work of Sigmund Freud, a Viennese physician. As a doctor, Freud was fascinated by patients whose problems seemed to be more emotional than physical. From about 1890 until he died in 1939, Freud evolved a theory of personality that deeply influenced modern thought (Jacobs, 2003; Schultz & Schultz, 2005). Let's consider some of its main features.

The Structure of Personality

How did Freud view personality? Freud's model portrays personality as a dynamic system directed by three mental structures, the **id,** the **ego,** and the **superego.** According to Freud, most behavior involves activity of all three systems. (Freud's theory includes a large number of concepts. For your convenience, they are defined in ● Table 12.2 rather than in glossary boxes.)

The Id

The id is made up of innate biological instincts and urges. It is self-serving, irrational, impulsive, and totally unconscious. The id operates on the **pleasure principle.** That is, it seeks to freely express pleasure-seeking urges of all kinds. If we were solely under control of the id, the world would be chaotic beyond belief.

The id acts as a well of energy for the entire **psyche** (sigh-KEY), or personality. This energy, called **libido** (lih-BEE-doe), flows from the **life instincts** (or **Eros**). According to Freud, libido underlies our efforts to survive, as well as our sexual desires and pleasure seeking. Freud also described a **death instinct. Thanatos,** as he called it, produces aggressive and destructive urges. Freud offered humanity's long history of wars and violence as evidence of such urges. Most id energies, then, are aimed at discharging tensions related to sex and aggression.

The Ego

The ego is sometimes described as the "executive," because it directs energies supplied by the id. The id is like a blind king or queen whose power is awesome but who must rely on others to carry out orders. The id can only form mental images of things it desires. The ego wins power to direct behavior by relating the desires of the id to external reality.

Are there other differences between the ego and the id? Yes. Recall that the id operates on the pleasure principle. The ego, in contrast,

"All is Vanity" courtesy of Illusions, Park Ridge, IL.

Freud considered personality an expression of two conflicting forces, life instincts and the death instinct. Both are symbolized in this drawing by Allan Gilbert. (If you don't immediately see the death symbolism, stand farther from the drawing.)

is guided by the **reality principle.** The ego is the system of thinking, planning, problem solving, and deciding. It is in conscious control of the personality and often delays action until it is practical or appropriate.

The Superego

What is the role of the superego? The superego acts as a judge or censor for the thoughts and actions of the ego. One part of the superego, called the **conscience,** reflects actions for which a person has been punished. When standards of the conscience are not met, you are punished internally by *guilt* feelings.

A second part of the superego is the **ego ideal.** The ego ideal reflects all behavior one's parents approved of or rewarded. The ego ideal is a source of goals and aspirations. When its standards are met, we feel *pride.*

The superego acts as an "internalized parent" to bring behavior under control. In Freudian terms, a person with a weak superego will be a delinquent, criminal, or antisocial personality. In contrast, an overly strict or harsh superego may cause inhibition, rigidity, or unbearable guilt.

The Dynamics of Personality

How do the id, ego, and superego interact? Freud didn't picture the id, ego, and superego as parts of the brain or as "little people" running the human psyche. Instead, they are conflicting mental processes. Freud theorized a delicate balance of power among the three. For example, the id's demands for immediate pleasure often

Table 12.2 ● Key Freudian Concepts

Anal stage The psychosexual stage corresponding roughly to the period of toilet training (ages 1 to 3).

Anal-expulsive personality A disorderly, destructive, cruel, or messy person.

Anal-retentive personality A person who is obstinate, stingy, or compulsive, and who generally has difficulty "letting go."

Conscience The part of the superego that causes guilt when its standards are not met.

Conscious The region of the mind that includes all mental contents a person is aware of at any given moment.

Ego The executive part of personality that directs rational behavior.

Ego ideal The part of the superego representing ideal behavior; a source of pride when its standards are met.

Electra conflict A girl's sexual attraction to her father and feelings of rivalry with her mother.

Erogenous zone Any body area that produces pleasurable sensations.

Eros Freud's name for the "life instincts."

Fixation A lasting conflict developed as a result of frustration or overindulgence.

Genital stage Period of full psychosexual development, marked by the attainment of mature adult sexuality.

Id The primitive part of personality that remains unconscious, supplies energy, and demands pleasure.

Latency According to Freud, a period in childhood when psychosexual development is more or less interrupted.

Libido In Freudian theory, the force, primarily pleasure oriented, that energizes the personality.

Moral anxiety Apprehension felt when thoughts, impulses, or actions conflict with the superego's standards.

Neurotic anxiety Apprehension felt when the ego struggles to control id impulses.

Oedipus conflict A boy's sexual attraction to his mother, and feelings of rivalry with his father.

Oral stage The period when infants are preoccupied with the mouth as a source of pleasure and means of expression.

Oral-aggressive personality A person who uses the mouth to express hostility by shouting, cursing, biting, and so forth. Also, one who actively exploits others.

Oral-dependent personality A person who wants to passively receive attention, gifts, love, and so forth.

Phallic personality A person who is vain, exhibitionistic, sensitive, and narcissistic.

Phallic stage The psychosexual stage (roughly ages 3 to 6) when a child is preoccupied with the genitals.

Pleasure principle A desire for immediate satisfaction of wishes, desires, or needs.

Preconscious An area of the mind containing information that can be voluntarily brought to awareness.

Psyche The mind, mental life, and personality as a whole.

Psychosexual stages The oral, anal, phallic, and genital stages, during which various personality traits are formed.

Reality principle Delaying action (or pleasure) until it is appropriate.

Superego A judge or censor for thoughts and actions.

Thanatos The death instinct postulated by Freud.

Unconscious The region of the mind that is beyond awareness, especially impulses and desires not directly known to a person.

Trait-situation interaction The influence that external settings or circumstances have on the expression of personality traits.

Psychoanalytic theory Freudian theory of personality that emphasizes unconscious forces and conflicts.

clash with the superego's moral restrictions. Perhaps an example will help clarify the role of each part of the personality.

Freud in a Nutshell

Let's say you are sexually attracted to an acquaintance. The id clamors for immediate satisfaction of its sexual desires but is opposed by the superego (which finds the very thought of sex shocking). The id says, "Go for it!" The superego icily replies, "Never even think that again!" And what does the ego say? The ego says, "I have a plan!"

Of course, this is a drastic simplification, but it does capture the core of Freudian thinking. To reduce tension, the ego could begin actions leading to friendship, romance, courtship, and marriage. If the id is unusually powerful, the ego may give in and attempt a seduction. If the superego prevails, the ego may be forced to *displace* or *sublimate* sexual energies to other activities (sports, music, dancing, push-ups, cold showers). According to Freud, internal struggles and rechanneled energies typify most personality functioning.

Is the ego always caught in the middle? Basically yes, and the pressures on it can be intense. In addition to meeting the conflicting demands of the id and superego, the overworked ego must deal with external reality.

According to Freud, you feel anxiety when your ego is threatened or overwhelmed. Impulses from the id cause **neurotic anxiety** when the ego can barely keep them under control. Threats of punishment from the superego cause **moral anxiety.** Each person develops habitual ways of calming these anxieties, and many resort to using *ego-defense mechanisms* to lessen internal conflicts. Defense mechanisms are mental processes that deny, distort, or otherwise block out sources of threat and anxiety.

> ### bridges
> The ego-defense mechanisms that Freud identified are used as a form of protection against stress, anxiety, and threatening events. **See Chapter 13, pages 440–442.**

© Sidney Harris/www.CartoonStock.com

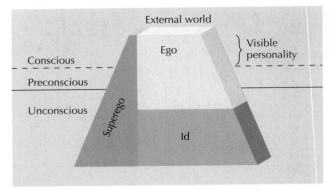

● **Figure 12.5** The approximate relationship between the id, ego, and superego, and the levels of awareness.

Levels of Awareness

Like other psychodynamic theorists, Freud believed that our behavior often expresses unconscious (or hidden) forces. The **unconscious** holds repressed memories and emotions, plus the instinctual drives of the id. Interestingly, modern scientists have found that the brain's limbic system does, in fact, seem to process unconscious emotions and memories (LeDoux, 2000).

Even though they are beyond awareness, unconscious thoughts, feelings, or urges may slip into behavior in disguised or symbolic form. For example, if you meet someone you would like to know better, you may unconsciously leave a book or a jacket at that person's house to ensure another meeting.

Are the actions of the ego and superego also unconscious, like the id? At times, yes, but they also operate on two other levels of awareness (● Figure 12.5). The **conscious** level includes everything you are aware of at a given moment, including thoughts, perceptions, feelings, and memories. The **preconscious** contains material that can be easily brought to awareness. If you stop to think about a time when you felt angry or rejected, you will be moving this memory from the preconscious to the conscious level of awareness.

The superego's activities also reveal differing levels of awareness. At times we consciously try to live up to moral codes or standards. Yet at other times a person may feel guilty without knowing why. Psychoanalytic theory credits such guilt to unconscious workings of the superego. Indeed, Freud believed that the unconscious origins of many feelings cannot be easily brought to awareness.

Personality Development

How does psychoanalytic theory explain personality development? Freud theorized that the core of personality is formed before age 6 in a series of **psychosexual stages.** Freud believed that erotic urges in childhood have lasting effects on development. As you might expect, this is a controversial idea. However, Freud used the terms "sex" and "erotic" very broadly to refer to many physical sources of pleasure.

A Freudian Fable?

Freud identified four psychosexual stages, the **oral, anal, phallic,** and **genital.** (He also described a period of "latency" between the phallic and genital stages. Latency is explained in a moment.) At each stage, a different part of the body becomes a child's primary **erogenous zone** (an area capable of producing pleasure). Each area then serves as the main source of pleasure, frustration, and self-expression. Freud believed that many adult personality traits can be traced to **fixations** in one or more of the stages.

What is a fixation? A fixation is an unresolved conflict or emotional hangup caused by overindulgence or by frustration. As we describe the psychosexual stages you'll see why Freud considered fixations important.

The Oral Stage

During the first year of life, most of an infant's pleasure comes from stimulation of the mouth. If a child is overfed or frustrated, oral traits may be created. Adult expressions of oral needs include gum chewing, nail biting, smoking, kissing, overeating, and alcoholism.

What if there is an oral fixation? Fixation early in the oral stage produces an **oral-dependent personality.** Oral-dependent persons are gullible (they swallow things easily!) and passive and need lots of attention (they want to be mothered and showered with gifts). Frustrations later in the oral stage may cause aggression, often in the form of biting. Fixations here create cynical, **oral-aggressive** adults who exploit others. They also like to argue. ("Biting sarcasm" is their forte!)

Bettmann/Corbis

Was Freud's ever-present cigar a sign of an oral fixation? Was it a phallic symbol? Was it both? Or was it neither? Once, when he was asked, Freud apparently replied, "Sometimes a cigar is just a cigar." An inability to say for sure is one of the shortcomings of psychoanalytic theory.

The Anal Stage

Between the ages of 1 and 3, the child's attention shifts to the process of elimination. When parents attempt toilet training, the child can gain approval or express rebellion or aggression by "holding on" or by "letting go." Therefore, harsh or lenient toilet training can cause an anal fixation that may lock such responses into personality. Freud described the **anal-retentive** (holding-on) **personality** as obstinate, stingy, orderly, and compulsively clean. The **anal-expulsive** (letting-go) **personality** is disorderly, destructive, cruel, or messy.

The Phallic Stage

Adult traits of the **phallic personality** are vanity, exhibitionism, sensitive pride, and narcissism (self-love). Freud theorized that phallic fixations develop between the ages of 3 and 6. At this time, increased sexual interest causes the child to be physically attracted to the parent of the opposite sex. In males this attraction leads to an **Oedipus conflict.** In it, the boy feels a rivalry with his father for the affection of his mother. Freud believed that the male child feels threatened by the father (specifically, the boy fears castration). To ease his anxieties, the boy must **identify** with the father. Their rivalry ends when the boy seeks to become more like his father. As he does, he begins to accept the father's values and forms a conscience.

What about the female child? Girls experience an **Electra conflict.** In this case, the girl loves her father and competes with her mother. However, according to Freud, the girl identifies with the mother more gradually.

Freud believed that females already feel castrated. Because of this, they are less driven to identify with their mothers than boys are with their fathers. This, he said, is less effective in creating a conscience. This particular part of Freudian thought has been thoroughly (and rightfully) rejected by modern experts in the psychology of women. It is better understood as a reflection of the male-dominated times in which Freud lived.

Latency

According to Freud there is a period of **latency** from age 6 to puberty. Latency is not so much a stage as it is a quiet time during which psychosexual development is dormant. Freud's belief that psychosexual development is "on hold" at this time is hard to accept. Nevertheless, Freud saw latency as a relatively quiet time compared with the stormy first 6 years of life.

The Genital Stage

At puberty an upswing in sexual energies activates all the unresolved conflicts of earlier years. This upsurge, according to Freud, is the reason why adolescence can be filled with emotion and turmoil. The **genital stage** begins at puberty. It is marked, during

Identification Feeling emotionally connected to a person and seeing oneself as like him or her.

adolescence, by a growing capacity for responsible social–sexual relationships. The genital stage ends with a mature capacity for love and the realization of full adult sexuality.

Critical Comments

As bizarre as Freud's theory might seem, it has been influential for several reasons. First, it pioneered the idea that the first years of life help shape adult personality. Second, it identified feeding, toilet training, and early sexual experiences as critical events in personality formation. Third, Freud was among the first to propose that development proceeds through a series of stages.

---

bridges

Erik Erikson's psycho*social* stages, which cover development from birth to old age, are a modern offshoot of Freudian thinking. **See Chapter 3, pages 106–108.**

Is the Freudian view of development widely accepted? Few psychologists wholeheartedly embrace Freud's theory today. In some cases Freud was clearly wrong. His portrayal of the elementary school years (latency) as free from sexuality and unimportant for personality development is hard to believe. His idea of the role of a stern or threatening father in the development of a strong conscience in males has also been challenged. Studies show that a son is more likely to develop a strong conscience if his father is affectionate and accepting, rather than stern and punishing. Freud also overemphasized sexuality in personality development. Other motives and cognitive factors are of equal importance.

Freud has been criticized for his views of patients who believed they were sexually molested as children. Freud assumed that such events were merely childhood fantasies. This view led to a long-standing tendency to disbelieve children who have been molested and women who have been raped (Brannon, 1996).

Another important criticism is that Freud's concepts are almost impossible to verify scientifically. The theory provides numerous ways to explain almost any thought, action, or feeling *after* it has occurred. However, it leads to few predictions, which makes its claims difficult to test. Although more criticisms of Freud could be listed, the fact remains that there is an element of truth to much of what he said (Jacob, 2003). Because of this, some clinical psychologists continue to regard Freudian theory as a useful way to think about human problems.

The Neo-Freudians

Freud's ideas quickly attracted a brilliant following. Just as rapidly, the importance Freud placed on instinctual drives and sexuality caused many to disagree with him. Those who stayed close to the core of Freud's thinking are called *neo-Freudians* (*neo* means "new"). **Neo-Freudians** accepted the broad features of Freud's theory but revised

parts of it. Some of the better-known neo-Freudians are Karen Horney, Anna Freud (Freud's daughter), Otto Rank, and Erich Fromm. Other early followers broke away more completely from Freud and created their own opposing theories. This group includes people such as Alfred Adler, Harry Sullivan, and Carl Jung.

The full story of other psychodynamic theories must await your first course in personality. For now, let's sample three views. The first represents an early rejection of Freud's thinking (Adler). The second embraces most but not all of Freud's theory (Horney). The third involves a carryover of Freudian ideas into a related but unique theory (Jung).

Alfred Adler (1870–1937)

Adler broke away from Freud because he disagreed with Freud's emphasis on the unconscious, on instinctual drives, and on the importance of sexuality. Adler believed that we are social creatures governed by social urges, not by biological instincts (Shulman, 2004). In Adler's view, the main driving force in personality is a **striving for superiority**. This striving, he said, is a struggle to overcome imperfections, an upward drive for competence, completion, and mastery of shortcomings.

What motivates "striving for superiority"? Adler believed that everyone experiences feelings of inferiority. This occurs mainly because we begin life as small, weak, and relatively powerless children surrounded by larger and more powerful adults. Feelings of inferiority may also come from our personal limitations. The struggle for superiority arises from such feelings.

Although everyone strives for superiority, each person tries to **compensate** for different limitations, and each chooses a different pathway to superiority. Adler believed that this situation creates a unique **style of life** (or personality pattern) for each individual. According to Adler the core of each person's style of life is formed by age 5. (Adler also believed that valuable clues to a person's style of life are revealed by the earliest memory that can be recalled. You might find it interesting to search back to your earliest memory and contemplate what it tells you.) However, later in his life Adler began to emphasize the existence of a **creative self**. By this he meant that humans create their personalities through choices and experiences.

Karen Horney (1885–1952)

Karen Horney (HORN-eye) remained faithful to most of Freud's theory, but she resisted his more mechanistic, biological, and instinctive ideas. For example, as a woman, Horney rejected Freud's claim that "anatomy is destiny." This view, woven into Freudian psychology, held that males are dominant or superior to females. Horney was among the first to challenge the obvious male bias in Freud's thinking (Eckardt, 2005).

Horney also disagreed with Freud about the causes of neurosis. Freud held that neurotic (anxiety-ridden) individuals are struggling with forbidden id drives that they fear they cannot control. Horney's view was that a core of **basic anxiety** occurs when people feel isolated and helpless in a hostile world. These feelings, she believed, are rooted in childhood. Trouble occurs when an individual tries to control basic anxiety by exaggerating a single mode of interacting with others.

What do you mean by "mode of interacting"? According to Horney, each of us can move *toward* others (by depending on them for love, support, or friendship), we can move *away* from others (by withdrawing, acting like a "loner," or being "strong" and independent), or we can move *against* others (by attacking, competing with, or seeking power over them). Horney believed that emotional health reflects a balance in moving toward, away from, and against others. In her view, emotional problems tend to lock people into overuse of one of the three modes—an insight that remains valuable today.

Carl Jung (1875–1961)

Carl Jung was a student of Freud's, but the two parted ways as Jung began to develop his own ideas. Like Freud, Jung called the conscious part of the personality the ego. However, he further noted that a *persona*, or "mask" exists between the ego and the outside world. The **persona** is the "public self" presented to others. It is most apparent when we adopt particular roles or hide our deeper feelings. As mentioned earlier, Jung believed that actions of the ego may reflect attitudes of **introversion** (in which energy is mainly directed inward), or of **extroversion** (in which energy is mainly directed outward).

Was Jung's view of the unconscious the same as Freud's? Jung used the term *personal unconscious* to refer to what Freud simply called the unconscious (Mayer, 2002). The **personal unconscious** is a mental storehouse for a single individual's experiences, feelings, and memories. But Jung also described a deeper **collective unconscious,** or mental storehouse for unconscious ideas and images shared by all humans. Jung believed that, from the beginning of time, all humans have had experiences with birth, death, power, god figures, mother and father figures, animals, the earth, energy, evil, rebirth, and so on. According to Jung, such universals create **archetypes** (ARE-keh-types: original ideas, images, or patterns).

Archetypes, found in the collective unconscious, are unconscious images that cause us to respond emotionally to symbols of birth, death, energy, animals, evil, and the like (Maloney, 1999). Jung believed that he detected symbols of such archetypes in the art, religion, myths, and dreams of every culture and age. Let us say, for instance, that a man dreams of dancing with his sister. To Freud this would probably be a sign of hidden incestuous feelings. To Jung the image of the sister might represent an unexpressed feminine side of the man's personality and the dream might represent the cosmic dance that intertwines "maleness" and "femaleness" in all lives.

Are some archetypes more important than others? Two particularly important archetypes are the **anima** (female principle) and the **animus** (male principle). In men, the anima is an unconscious, idealized image of women. This image is based, in part, on real experiences with women (the man's mother, sister, friends). How-

Digital Vision/Alamy

Jung regarded circular designs as symbols of the self-archetype and representations of unity, balance, and completion within the personality.

ever, the experiences men have had with women throughout history form the true core of the anima. The reverse is true of women, who possess an animus or idealized image of men. The anima in males and the animus in females enable us to relate to members of the opposite sex. The anima and animus also make it possible for

Neo-Freudian A theorist who has revised Freud's theory, while still accepting some of its basic concepts.

Striving for superiority According to Adler, this basic drive propels us toward perfection.

Compensation Any attempt to overcome feelings of inadequacy or inferiority.

Style of life The pattern of personality and behavior that defines the pathway each person takes through life.

Creative self The "artist" in each of us that creates a unique identity and style of life

Basic anxiety A primary form of anxiety that arises from living in a hostile world.

Persona The "mask" or public self presented to others.

Introversion Ego attitude in which in which energy is mainly directed inward.

Extroversion Ego attitude in which in which energy is mainly directed outward.

Personal unconscious A mental storehouse for a single individual's unconscious thoughts.

Collective unconscious A mental storehouse for unconscious ideas and images shared by all humans.

Archetype A universal idea, image, or pattern, found in the collective unconscious.

Anima An archetype representing the female principle.

Animus An archetype representing the male principle.

people to learn to express both "masculine" and "feminine" sides of their personalities.

Jung regarded the *self archetype* as the most important of all. The **self archetype** represents unity. Its existence causes a gradual movement toward balance, wholeness, and harmony within the personality. Jung felt that we become richer and more completely human when a balance is achieved between the conscious and unconscious, the anima and animus, thinking and feeling, sensing and intuiting, the persona and the ego, introversion and extroversion.

Was Jung talking about self-actualization? Essentially he was. Jung was the first to use the term *self-actualization* to describe a striving for completion and unity. He believed that the self archetype is symbolized in every culture by **mandalas** (magic circles) of one kind or another.

Jung's theory may not be scientific, but clearly he was a man of genius and vision. If you would like to know more about Jung and his ideas, a good starting place is his autobiography, *Memories, Dreams, Reflections* (Jung, 1961).

KNOWLEDGE BUILDER
Psychodynamic Theories

RECITE

1. List the three divisions of personality postulated by Freud.
   _____, _____, _____
2. Which division is totally unconscious? _____
3. Which division is responsible for moral anxiety?
   _____
4. Freud proposed the existence of a life instinct known as Thanatos. T or F?
5. Freud's view of personality development is based on the concept of _____ stages.
6. Arrange these stages in the proper order: phallic, anal, genital, oral.
   _____, _____, _____, _____
7. Freud considered the anal-retentive personality to be obstinate and stingy. T or F?
8. Karen Horney theorized that people control basic anxiety by moving toward, away from, and _____ others.
9. Carl Jung's theory states that archetypes, which are found in the personal unconscious, exert an influence on behavior. T or F?

REFLECT

Critical Thinking
10. Many adults would find it embarrassing or humiliating to drink from a baby bottle. Can you explain why?

Relate
Try to think of at least one time when your thoughts, feelings, or actions seemed to reflect the workings of each of the following: the id, the ego, and the superego.

Do you know anyone who seems to have oral, anal, or phallic personality traits? Do you think Freud's concept of fixation explains their characteristics?

Do any of your personal experiences support the existence of an Oedipus conflict or an Electra conflict? If not, is it possible that you have repressed feelings related to these conflicts?

If you had to summarize your style of life in one sentence, what would it be?

Which of Horney's three modes of interacting do you think you rely on the most? Do you overuse one of the modes?

Think of the images you have seen in art, mythology, movies, and popular culture. Do any seem to represent Jungian archetypes—especially the self archetype?

Answers: 1. id, ego, superego **2.** id **3.** superego **4.** F **5.** psychosexual **6.** oral, anal, phallic, genital **7.** T **8.** against **9.** F **10.** A psychoanalytic theorist would say that it is because the bottle rekindles oral conflicts and feelings of vulnerability and dependence.

● ● Learning Theories of Personality— Habit I Seen You Before?

Gateway Question: What do behaviorists emphasize in their approach to personality?

After exploring psychodynamic theories, you might be relieved to know that behavioral theorists explain personality through straightforward concepts, such as learning, reinforcement, and imitation. Behavioral and social learning theories are based on scientific research, which makes them powerful ways of looking at personality.

How do behaviorists approach personality? According to some critics, as if people are robots. Actually, the behaviorist position is not nearly that mechanistic, and its value is well established. Behaviorists have shown repeatedly that children can *learn* things like kindness, hostility, generosity, or destructiveness. What does this have to do with personality? Everything, according to the behavioral viewpoint.

Behavioral personality theories emphasize that personality is no more (or less) than a collection of learned behavior patterns. Personality, like other learned behavior, is acquired through classical and operant conditioning, observational learning, reinforcement, extinction, generalization, and discrimination. When Mother says, "It's not nice to make mud pies with Mommy's

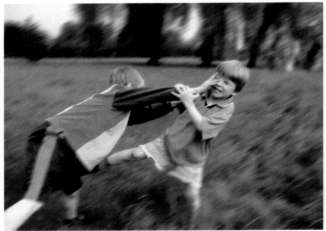

Freud believed that aggressive urges are "instinctual." In contrast, behavioral theories assume that personal characteristics such as aggressiveness are learned. Is this boy's aggression the result of observational learning, harsh punishment, or prior reinforcement?

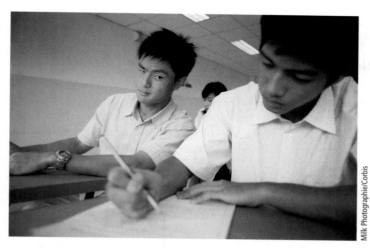

Seventy-five percent of American college students admit that they have been academically dishonest in one way or another. What can be done about these high rates of dishonesty? The behavioral perspective holds that honesty is determined as much by circumstances as it is by personality. In line with this, simple measures like announcing in classes that integrity codes will be enforced can significantly reduce cheating. Using multiple forms of exams and web-based plagiarism software and educating students about plagiarism also tend to deter dishonesty (Altschuler, 2001; McKeever, 2006).

blender. If we want to grow up to be a big girl, we won't do it again, will we?" she serves as a model and in other ways shapes her daughter's personality.

Strict learning theorists reject the idea that personality is made up of traits. They would assert, for instance, that there is no such thing as a trait of "honesty" (Mischel, 2004).

Certainly some people are honest and others are not. How can honesty not be a trait? Learning theorists recognize that some people are honest *more often* than others. But knowing this does not allow us to predict whether a person will be honest in a specific situation. It would not be unusual, for example, to find that a person honored for returning a lost wallet had cheated on a test, bought a term paper, or broken the speed limit. If you were to ask a learning theorist, "Are you an honest person?" the reply might be, "In what situation?"

As you can see, learning theorists are interested in the **situational determinants** (external causes) of our actions. A good example of how situations can influence behavior is a study in which people were intentionally overpaid for doing an assigned task. Under normal circumstances, 80 percent kept the extra money without mentioning it. But as few as 17 percent were dishonest if the situation was altered. For instance, if people thought the money was coming out of the pocket of the person doing the study, far fewer were dishonest (Bersoff, 1999). Thus, situations always interact with our prior learning to activate behavior.

How Situations Affect Behavior

Situations vary greatly in their impact. Some are powerful. Others are trivial and have little effect on behavior. The more powerful the situation, the easier it is to see what is meant by *situational determinants*. For example, each of the following situations would

undoubtedly have a strong influence on your behavior: an armed person walks into your classroom; you accidentally sit on a lighted cigarette; you find your lover in bed with your best friend. Yet even these situations could provoke very different reactions from different personalities. That's why behavior is always a product of both prior learning and the situations in which we find ourselves (Mischel, Shoda, & Smith, 2004).

Ultimately, what is predictable about personality is that we respond in consistent ways to certain *types of situations*. Consider, for example, two people who are easily angered: One person might get angry when she is delayed (for example, in traffic or a checkout line) but not when she misplaces something at home; the other person might get angry whenever she misplaces things but not when she is delayed. Overall, the two women are equally prone to anger, but their anger tends to occur in different patterns and different types of situations (Mischel, 2004).

Personality = Behavior

How do learning theorists view the structure of personality? The behavioral view of personality can be illustrated with an early theory proposed by John Dollard and Neal Miller (1950). In their view, **habits** (learned behavior patterns) make up the structure of personality. As for the dynamics of personality, habits are governed by four elements of learning: *drive, cue, response,* and *reward*. A **drive** is any stimulus strong enough to goad a person to action (such as hunger, pain, lust, frustration, or fear). **Cues** are signals from the environment. These signals guide **responses** (actions) so that they are most likely to bring about **reward** (positive reinforcement).

How does that relate to personality? Let's say a child named Amina is frustrated by her older brother Kelvin, who takes a toy from her. Amina could respond in several ways: She could throw a temper tantrum, hit Kelvin, tell Mother, and so forth. The response she chooses is guided by available cues and the previous effects of each response. If telling Mother has paid off in the past, and the mother is present, telling again may be her immediate response. If a different set of cues exists (if Mother is absent or if Kelvin looks

---

Self archetype An unconscious image representing, unity, wholeness, completion, and balance.

Mandala A circular design representing balance, unity, and completion.

Behavioral personality theory Any model of personality that emphasizes learning and observable behavior.

Situational determinants External conditions that strongly influence behavior.

Habit A deeply ingrained, learned pattern of behavior.

Drive Any stimulus (especially an internal stimulus such as hunger) strong enough to goad a person to action.

Cue External stimuli that guide responses, especially by signaling the presence or absence of reinforcement.

Response Any behavior, either observable or internal.

Reward Anything that produces pleasure or satisfaction; a positive reinforcer.

particularly menacing), Amina may select some other response. To an outside observer, Amina's actions seem to reflect her personality. To a learning theorist, they simply express the combined effects of drive, cue, response, and reward.

> bridges
>
> Behavioral theories have contributed greatly to the creation of therapies for various psychological problems and disorders.
>
> **See the discussion of behavior therapy in Chapter 15, pages 503–507.**

Doesn't this analysis leave out a lot? Yes. Learning theorists first set out to provide a simple, clear model of personality. But in recent years they have had to face a fact that they originally tended to overlook: People think. The new breed of behavioral psychologists—whose views include perception, thinking, expectations, and other mental events—are called social learning theorists. Learning principles, modeling, thought patterns, perceptions, expectations, beliefs, goals, emotions, and social relationships are combined in **social learning theory** to explain personality (Mischel, Shoda, & Smith, 2004).

Social Learning Theory

The "cognitive behaviorism" of social learning theory can be illustrated by three concepts proposed by Julian Rotter: the psychological situation, expectancy, and reinforcement value (Rotter & Hochreich, 1975). Let's examine each.

Someone trips you. How do you respond? Your reaction probably depends on whether you think it was planned or an accident. It is not enough to know the setting in which a person responds. We also need to know the person's **psychological situation** (how the person interprets or defines the situation). As another example, let's say you score low on an exam. Do you consider it a challenge to work harder, a sign that you should drop the class, or an excuse to get drunk? Again, your interpretation is important.

Our actions are affected by an **expectancy,** or anticipation, that making a response will lead to reinforcement. To continue the example, if working harder has paid off in the past, it is a likely reaction to a low test score. But to predict your response, we would also have to know if you *expect* your efforts to pay off in the present situation. In fact, expected reinforcement may be more important than actual past reinforcement. And what about the *value* you attach to grades, school success, or personal ability? The third concept, **reinforcement value,** states that we attach different subjective values to various activities or rewards. You will likely choose to study harder if passing your courses and obtaining a degree is highly valued. This, too, must be taken into account to understand personality.

Self-Efficacy

An ability to control your own life is the essence of what it means to be human. Because of this, Albert Bandura believes that one of the most important expectancies we develop concerns **self-**efficacy (EF-uh-keh-see: a capacity for producing a desired result). You're attracted to someone in your anthropology class. Will you ask him or her out? You're thinking about learning to snowboard. Will you try it this winter? You're beginning to consider a career in psychology. Will you take the courses you need to get into graduate school? You'd like to exercise more on the weekends. Will you join a hiking club? In these and countless other situations, efficacy beliefs play a key role in shaping our lives by influencing the activities and environments we choose (Bandura, 2001; Schultz & Schultz, 2005).

Self-Reinforcement

One more idea deserves mention. At times, we all evaluate our actions and may reward ourselves with special privileges or treats for "good behavior." With this in mind, social learning theory adds the concept of self-reinforcement to the behavioristic view. **Self-reinforcement** refers to praising or rewarding yourself for having made a particular response (such as completing a school assignment). Thus, habits of self-praise and self-blame become an important part of personality (Schultz & Schultz, 2005). In fact, self-reinforcement can be thought of as the social learning theorist's counterpart to the superego.

Rate Yourself: Self-Reinforcement

Check the statements in the list that apply to you.

___ I often think positive thoughts about myself.

___ I frequently meet standards that I set for myself.

___ I try not to blame myself when things go wrong.

___ I usually don't get upset when I make mistakes because I learn from them.

___ I can get satisfaction out of what I do even if it's not perfect.

___ When I make mistakes I take time to reassure myself.

___ I don't think talking about what you've done right is too boastful.

Through self-reinforcement we reward ourselves for personal achievements and other "good" behavior.

© Vic Lee. Reprinted with special permission of King Features Syndicate.

___ Praising yourself is healthy and normal.

___ I don't think I have to be upset every time I make a mistake.

___ My feelings of self-confidence and self-esteem stay pretty steady.

People who agree with most of these statements tend to have high rates of self-reinforcement (Heiby, 1983).

Self-reinforcement is closely related to high self-esteem. The reverse is also true: Mildly depressed college students tend to have low rates of self-reinforcement. It is not known if low self-reinforcement leads to depression, or the reverse. In either case, higher rates of self-reinforcement are associated with less depression and greater life satisfaction (Seybolt & Wagner, 1997). From a behavioral viewpoint, there is value in learning to be "good to yourself."

Behavioristic View of Development

How do learning theorists account for personality development? Many of Freud's ideas can be restated in terms of learning theory. Dollard and Miller (1950) agree with Freud that the first 6 years are crucial for personality development, but for different reasons. Rather than thinking in terms of psychosexual urges and fixations, they ask, "What makes early learning experiences so lasting in their effects?" Their answer is that childhood is a time of urgent drives, powerful rewards and punishments, and crushing frustrations. Also important is **social reinforcement,** which is based on praise, attention, or approval from others. These forces combine to shape the core of personality.

Critical Situations

Dollard and Miller believe that during childhood four **critical situations** are capable of leaving a lasting imprint on personality. These are (1) feeding, (2) toilet or cleanliness training, (3) sex training, and (4) learning to express anger or aggression.

Why are these of special importance? Feeding serves as an illustration. If children are fed when they cry, it encourages them to actively manipulate their parents. The child allowed to cry without being fed learns to be passive. Thus, a basic active or passive orientation toward the world may be created by early feeding experiences. Feeding can also affect later social relationships because the child learns to associate people with pleasure or with frustration and discomfort.

Toilet and cleanliness training can be a particularly strong source of emotion for both parents and children. Rashad's parents were aghast the day they found him smearing feces about with joyful abandon. They reacted with sharp punishment, which frustrated and confused Rashad. Many attitudes toward cleanliness, conformity, and bodily functions are formed at such times. Studies have also long shown that severe, punishing, or frustrating toilet training can have undesirable effects on personality development (Christophersen & Mortweet, 2003). Because of this, toilet and cleanliness training demand patience and a sense of humor.

What about sex and anger? When, where, and how a child learns to express anger and sexual feelings can leave an imprint on personality. Specifically, permissiveness for sexual and aggressive behavior in childhood is linked to adult needs for power (McClelland & Pilon, 1983). This link probably occurs because permitting such behaviors allows children to get pleasure from asserting themselves. As we saw in the last chapter, sex training also involves learning socially defined "male" and "female" gender roles—which also affect personality (Pervin, Cervone, & John, 2005).

Personality and Gender

From birth onward, children are labeled as boys or girls and encouraged to learn sex-appropriate behavior (Denmark, Rabinowitz, & Sechzer, 2005).

Social learning theory An explanation of personality that combines learning principles, cognition, and the effects of social relationships.

Psychological situation A situation as it is perceived and interpreted by an individual, not as it exists objectively.

Expectancy Anticipation about the effect a response will have, especially regarding reinforcement.

Reinforcement value The subjective value a person attaches to a particular activity or reinforcer.

Self-efficacy Belief in your capacity to produce a desired result.

Self-reinforcement Praising or rewarding oneself for having made a particular response (such as completing a school assignment).

Social reinforcement Praise, attention, approval, and/or affection from others.

Critical situations Situations during childhood that are capable of leaving a lasting imprint on personality.

What does it mean to have a "masculine" or "feminine" personality? According to social learning theory, identification and imitation contribute greatly to personality development and to sex training. Through identification children become emotionally attached to admired adults, especially those who provide love and care. Identification typically encourages **imitation,** a desire to act like the admired person. Many "male" or "female" traits come from children's attempts to imitate a same-sex parent with whom they identify.

If children are around parents of both sexes, why don't they imitate behavior typical of the opposite sex as well as of the same sex? You may recall from Chapter 7 that learning takes place vicariously as well as directly. This means that we can learn without direct reward by observing and remembering the actions of others. But the actions we choose to imitate depend on their outcomes. For example, boys and girls have equal chances to observe adults and other children acting aggressively. However, girls are less likely than boys to imitate directly aggressive behavior (shouting at or hitting another person). Instead, girls are more likely to rely on indirectly aggressive behavior (excluding others from friendship, spreading rumors). This may well be because the expression of direct aggression is thought to be inappropriate for girls. As a consequence, girls rarely see direct female aggression rewarded or approved (Richardson & Green, 1999). In others words, "girl-fighting" is likely a culturally reinforced pattern (Brown, 2005). Intriguingly, over the last few years, girls have become more willing to engage in direct aggression as popular culture presents more and more images of directly aggressive women (Artz, 2005).

Laura Dwight/PhotoEdit

Adult personality is influenced by identification with parents.

We have considered only a few examples of the links between social learning and personality. Nevertheless, the connection is unmistakable. When parents accept their children and give them affection, the children become sociable, positive, and emotionally stable, and they have high self-esteem. When parents are rejecting, punishing, sarcastic, humiliating, or neglectful, their children become hostile, unresponsive, unstable, and dependent and have impaired self-esteem (Triandis & Suh, 2002).

KNOWLEDGE BUILDER

Behavioral and Social Learning Theories

RECITE

1. Learning theorists believe that personality "traits" really are _____ acquired through prior learning. They also emphasize _____ determinants of behavior.
2. Dollard and Miller consider cues the basic structure of personality. T or F?
3. To explain behavior, social learning theorists include mental elements, such as _____ (the anticipation that a response will lead to reinforcement).
4. Self-reinforcement is to behavioristic theory as superego is to psychoanalytic theory. T or F?
5. Which of the following is *not* a "critical situation" in the behaviorist theory of personality development?
   a. feeding
   b. sex training
   c. language training
   d. anger training
6. In addition to basic rewards and punishments, a child's personality is also shaped by _____ reinforcement.
7. Social learning theories of development emphasize the impact of identification and _____.

REFLECT

Critical Thinking

8. The concept of *reinforcement value* is closely related to a motivational principle discussed in Chapter 10. Can you name it?

Relate

What is your favorite style of food? Can you relate Dollard and Miller's concepts of habit, drive, cue, response, and reward to explain your preference?

Some people love to shop. Others hate it. How have the psychological situation, expectancy, and reinforcement value affected your willingness to "shop 'til you drop"?

Who did you identify with as a child? What aspects of that person's behavior did you imitate?

Answers: 1. habits, situational **2.** F **3.** expectancies **4.** T **5.** c **6.** social **7.** imitation **8.** Incentive value.

⬤◐ Humanistic Theory—Peak Experiences and Personal Growth

Gateway Question: How do humanistic theories differ from other perspectives?

At the beginning of this chapter you met Annette. A few years ago, Annette and her husband spent a year riding mules across the country as a unique way to see America and get to know themselves better. Where do such desires for personal growth come from? Humanistic theories pay special attention to the fuller use of human potentials and they help bring balance to our overall views of personality.

Humanism focuses on human experience, problems, potentials, and ideals. It is a reaction to the rigidity of traits, the pessimism of psychoanalytic theory, and the mechanical nature of learning theory. At its core is a positive image of what it means to be human. Humanists reject the Freudian view of personality as a battleground for instincts and unconscious forces. Instead, they view human nature as inherently good. (**Human nature** consists of the traits, qualities, potentials, and behavior patterns most characteristic of the human species.) Humanists also oppose the machine-like overtones of behaviorism. We are not, they say, merely a bundle of moldable responses. Rather, we are creative beings capable of *free choice* (an ability to choose that is not determined by genetics, learning, or unconscious forces). In short, humanists seek ways to encourage our potentials to blossom.

To a humanist the person you are today is largely the product of all the choices you have made. Humanists also emphasize immediate **subjective experience** (private perceptions of reality), rather than prior learning. They believe that there are as many "real worlds" as there are people. To understand behavior, we must learn how a person subjectively views the world—what is "real" for her or him.

Who are the major humanistic theorists? Many psychologists have added to the humanistic tradition. Of these, the best known are Abraham Maslow (1908–1970) and Carl Rogers (1902–1987). Because Maslow's idea of self-actualization was introduced in Chapter 1, let's begin with a more detailed look at this facet of his thinking.

Maslow and Self-Actualization

Abraham Maslow became interested in people who were living unusually effective lives. How were they different? To find an answer, Maslow began by studying the lives of great men and women from history, such as Albert Einstein, William James, Jane Addams, Eleanor Roosevelt, Abraham Lincoln, John Muir, and Walt Whitman. From there he moved on to directly study living artists, writers, poets, and other creative individuals.

Along the way, Maslow's thinking changed radically. At first he studied only people of obvious creativity or high achievement. However, it eventually became clear that a housewife, clerk, student, or someone like our friend Annette could live a rich, creative, and satisfying life. Maslow referred to the process of fully developing personal potentials as **self-actualization** (Maslow, 1954). The heart of self-actualization is a continuous search for personal fulfillment (Ewen, 2003; Reiss & Havercamp, 2005).

Characteristics of Self-Actualizers

A self-actualizer is a person who is living creatively and fully using his or her potentials. In his studies, Maslow found that self-actualizers share many similarities. Whether famous or unknown,

well-schooled or uneducated, rich or poor, self-actualizers tend to fit the following profile:

1. **Efficient perceptions of reality.** Self-actualizers are able to judge situations correctly and honestly. They are very sensitive to the fake and dishonest.
2. **Comfortable acceptance of self, others, nature.** Self-actualizers accept their own human nature with all its flaws. The shortcomings of others and the contradictions of the human condition are accepted with humor and tolerance.
3. **Spontaneity.** Maslow's subjects extended their creativity into everyday activities. Actualizers tend to be unusually alive, engaged, and spontaneous.
4. **Task centering.** Most of Maslow's subjects had a mission to fulfill in life or some task or problem outside of themselves to pursue. Humanitarians such as Albert Schweitzer and Mother Teresa represent this quality.
5. **Autonomy.** Self-actualizers are free from reliance on external authorities or other people. They tend to be resourceful and independent.
6. **Continued freshness of appreciation.** The self-actualizer seems to constantly renew appreciation of life's basic goods. A sunset or a flower will be experienced as intensely time after time as it was at first. There is an "innocence of vision," like that of an artist or child.
7. **Fellowship with humanity.** Maslow's subjects felt a deep identification with others and the human situation in general.
8. **Profound interpersonal relationships.** The interpersonal relationships of self-actualizers are marked by deep, loving bonds (Hanley & Abell, 2002).
9. **Comfort with solitude.** Despite their satisfying relationships with others, self-actualizing persons value solitude and are comfortable being alone (Sumerlin & Bundrick, 1996).
10. **Nonhostile sense of humor.** This refers to the wonderful capacity to laugh at oneself. It also describes the kind of humor a man like Abraham Lincoln had. Lincoln probably never made a joke that hurt anybody. His wry comments were a gentle prodding of human shortcomings.
11. **Peak experiences.** All of Maslow's subjects reported the frequent occurrence of **peak experiences** (temporary moments of self-actualization). These occasions were marked by feel-

Imitation An attempt to match one's own behavior to another person's behavior.

Humanism An approach that focuses on human experience, problems, potentials, and ideals.

Human nature Those traits, qualities, potentials, and behavior patterns most characteristic of the human species.

Subjective experience Reality as it is perceived and interpreted, not as it exists objectively.

Self-actualization The process of fully developing personal potentials.

Peak experiences Temporary moments of self-actualization.

ings of ecstasy, harmony, and deep meaning. Self-actualizers reported feeling at one with the universe, stronger and calmer than ever before, filled with light, beautiful and good, and so forth.

In summary, self-actualizers feel safe, nonanxious, accepted, loved, loving, and alive.

Maslow's choice of people for study seems pretty subjective. Do they really provide a fair representation of self-actualization? Although Maslow tried to investigate self-actualization empirically, his choice of people for study *was* subjective. Undoubtedly there are many ways to make full use of personal potential. Maslow's primary contribution was to draw our attention to the possibility of lifelong personal growth.

What steps can be taken to promote self-actualization? Maslow made few specific recommendations about how to proceed. There is no magic formula for leading a more creative life. Self-actualization is primarily a *process,* not a goal or an end point. As such, it requires hard work, patience, and commitment. Nevertheless, some helpful suggestions can be gleaned from his writings (Maslow, 1954, 1967, 1971). Here are some ways to begin:

1. **Be willing to change.** Begin by asking yourself, "Am I living in a way that is deeply satisfying to me and that truly expresses me?" If not, be prepared to make changes in your life. Indeed, ask yourself this question often and accept the need for continual change.
2. **Take responsibility.** You can become an architect of self by acting as if you are personally responsible for every aspect of your life. Shouldering responsibility in this way helps end the habit of blaming others for your own shortcomings.
3. **Examine your motives.** Self-discovery involves an element of risk. If your behavior is restricted by a desire for safety or security, it may be time to test some limits. Try to make each life decision a choice for growth, not a response to fear or anxiety.
4. **Experience honestly and directly.** Wishful thinking is another barrier to personal growth. Self-actualizers trust themselves enough to accept all kinds of information without distorting it to fit their fears and desires. Try to see yourself as others do. Be willing to admit, "I was wrong," or, "I failed because I was irresponsible."
5. **Make use of positive experiences.** Maslow considered peak experiences temporary moments of self-actualization. Therefore, you might actively repeat activities that have caused feelings of awe, amazement, exaltation, renewal, reverence, humility, fulfillment, or joy.
6. **Be prepared to be different.** Maslow felt that everyone has a potential for "greatness," but most fear becoming what they might. As part of personal growth, be prepared to trust your own impulses and feelings; don't automatically judge yourself by the standards of others. Accept your uniqueness.
7. **Get involved.** With few exceptions, self-actualizers tend to have a mission or "calling" in life. For these people, "work" is not done just to fill deficiency needs, but to satisfy higher yearnings for truth, beauty, community, and meaning. Get personally involved and committed. Turn your attention to problems outside yourself.
8. **Assess your progress.** There is no final point at which one becomes self-actualized. It's important to gauge your progress frequently and to renew your efforts. If you feel bored at school, at a job, or in a relationship, consider it a challenge. Have you been taking responsibility for your own personal growth? Almost any activity can be used as a chance for self-enhancement if it is approached creatively.

Positive Psychology: Positive Personality Traits

It could be said that self-actualizing people are thriving, not just surviving. In recent years, proponents of positive psychology have tried to scientifically study positive personality traits that contribute to happiness and well-being (Keyes & Haidt, 2003; Seligman, 2003). Although their work does not fall within the humanistic tradition, their findings are relevant here.

Martin Seligman, Christopher Peterson, and others have identified six human strengths that contribute to well-being and life satisfaction. Each strength is expressed by the positive personality traits listed here (Peterson & Seligman, 2004).

- **Wisdom and knowledge:** Creativity, curiosity, open-mindedness, love of learning, perspective
- **Courage:** Bravery, persistence, integrity, vitality
- **Humanity:** Love, kindness, social intelligence
- **Justice:** Citizenship, fairness, leadership
- **Temperance:** Forgiveness, humility, prudence, self-control
- **Transcendence:** Appreciation of beauty and excellence, gratitude, hope, humor, spirituality

Which of the positive personality traits are most closely related to happiness? A recent study found that traits of hope, vitality, gratitude, love, and curiosity are strongly associated with life satisfaction (Park, Peterson, & Seligman, 2004). These characteristics, in combination with Maslow's descriptions of self-actualizers, provide a good guide to the characteristics that help people live happy, meaningful lives.

Carl Rogers' Self Theory

Carl Rogers, another well-known humanist, also emphasized the human capacity for inner peace and happiness. The **fully functioning person**, he said, lives in harmony with his or her deepest feelings and impulses. Such people are open to their experiences and they trust their inner urges and intuitions (Rogers, 1961). Rogers believed that this attitude is most likely to occur when a person receives ample amounts of love and acceptance from others.

Personality Structure and Dynamics

Rogers' theory emphasizes the **self,** a flexible and changing perception of personal identity. Much behavior can be understood as an attempt to maintain consistency between our *self-image* and our actions. (Your **self-image** is a total subjective perception of your

Humanists consider self-image a central determinant of behavior and personal adjustment.

Photolibrary/PictureQuest

body and personality.) For example, people who think of themselves as kind tend to be considerate in most situations.

Let's say I know a person who thinks she is kind, but she really isn't. How does that fit Rogers' theory? According to Rogers, we allow experiences that match our self-image into awareness, where they gradually change the self. Information or feelings inconsistent with the self-image are said to be *incongruent*. Thus, a person who thinks she is kind, but really isn't, is in a state of **incongruence**. In other words, there is a discrepancy between her experiences and her self-image. As another example, it would be incongruent to believe that you are a person who "never gets angry," if you spend much of each day seething inside.

Experiences seriously incongruent with the self-image can be threatening and are often distorted or denied conscious recognition. Blocking, denying, or distorting experiences prevents the self from changing. This creates a gulf between the self-image and reality. As the self-image grows more unrealistic, the incongruent person becomes confused, vulnerable, dissatisfied, or seriously maladjusted (● Figure 12.6). In line with Rogers's observations, a

study of college students confirmed that being *authentic* is vital for healthy functioning. That is, we need to feel that our behavior accurately expresses who we are (Sheldon et al., 1997). Please note, however, that being authentic doesn't mean you can do whatever you want. Being true to yourself is no excuse for acting irresponsibly or ignoring the feelings of others.

When your self-image is consistent with what you really think, feel, do, and experience, you are best able to actualize your potentials. Rogers also considered it essential to have congruence between the self-image and the **ideal self**. The ideal self is similar to Freud's ego ideal. It is an image of the person you would most like to be.

> **bridges**
> Rogers and other humanistic theorists believe that some psychological disorders are caused a faulty or incongruent self-image. **See Chapter 14, page 486.**

Is it really incongruent not to live up to your ideal self? Rogers was aware that we never fully attain our ideals. Nevertheless, the greater the gap between the way you see yourself and the way you would like to be, the more tension and anxiety you will experience.

Rogers emphasized that to maximize our potentials, we must accept information about ourselves as honestly as possible. In accord with his thinking, researchers have found that people with a close match between their self-image and ideal self tend to be socially poised, confident, and resourceful. Those with a poor match tend to be depressed, anxious, and insecure (Boldero et al., 2005).

According to psychologists Hazel Markus and Paula Nurius (1986), our ideal self is only one of a number of **possible selves** (persons we could become or are afraid of becoming). Annette, who was described earlier, is an interesting personality, to say the least. Annette is one of those people who seems to have lived many lives in the time that most of us manage only one. Like Annette, you may have pondered many possible personal identities. (See "Telling Stories about Ourselves.")

Possible selves translate our hopes, fears, fantasies, and goals into specific images of who we *could* be. Thus, a beginning law

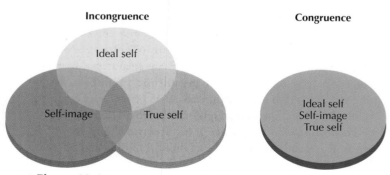

Incongruence   Congruence

● **Figure 12.6** Incongruence occurs when there is a mismatch between any of these three entities: the ideal self (the person you would like to be), your self-image (the person you think you are), and the true self (the person you actually are). Self-esteem suffers when there is a large difference between one's ideal self and self-image. Anxiety and defensiveness are common when the self-image does not match the true self.

Fully functioning person A person living in harmony with her or his deepest feelings, impulses, and intuitions.

Self A continuously evolving conception of one's personal identity.

Self-image Total subjective perception of one's body and personality (another term for self-concept).

Incongruence State that exists when there is a discrepancy between one's experiences and self-image or between one's self-image and ideal self.

Ideal self An idealized image of oneself (the person one would like to be).

Possible self A collection of thoughts, beliefs, feelings, and images concerning the person one could become.

THE CLINICAL FILE

Telling Stories About Ourselves

You know these two student types: the carefree party animal and the conscientious bookworm. Perhaps you even think of yourself as one or the other. Is there any truth to these (stereo)types? Can you change your type?

There is little doubt that college life creates a conflict between new opportunities for fun with friends and the need to study hard. In general, our personality traits are relatively stable lifelong characteristics (McAdams & Pals, 2006). As a result, a person high in the Big Five traits of extraversion and agreeableness will tend to embrace a carefree college lifestyle. In comparison, someone high in conscientiousness will find it easier to hit the books (McGregor, McAdams, & Little, 2006).

Does that mean a partier can't become a bookworm (or vice versa)? It depends: Do you mean over a week? Or a lifetime? As we saw earlier, personality traits do slowly change as we age. In particular, we tend to become more agreeable, conscientious, and emo-tionally stable as we grow older (Roberts & Mroczek, 2008).

Oh, you need to change by the end of the semester? That's a taller order. One promising approach is to tell yourself stories about possible selves you could become. The *narrative approach* to personality asserts that our personalities are shaped by the stories we tell about ourselves (Pals, 2006). In other words, alternate life stories are not just fantasies or daydreams. They actually influence who we are and who we become. Narratives may even underlie successful psychotherapy. Rather than trying to change personality traits, effective therapists help clients tell better stories about their lives (McAdams & Pals, 2006).

So, if you feel that you are being too careless and carefree at school, start imagining yourself studying more, getting to classes on time, and getting good grades. Listen to the stories of successful students and use them to revise your own story. Visit your campus counseling center to learn more about how to succeed at school. In other words, imagine yourself as a bit more of a bookworm. (Don't worry, your carefree nature won't desert you!)

If you feel you are too conscientious and working too hard, imagine yourself going out to socialize more often. Listen to the stories of your extraverted friends. Imagine the benefits of balancing work and play in your life. If you are shy or perfectionistic, visit your campus counseling center to learn how to become more social or relaxed. And, again, don't worry: Having more fun doesn't mean you will suddenly become irresponsible.

Whatever possible self you choose to pursue, you are more likely to become what you imagine if you elaborate your story, making it more detailed and "real" as you gradually adopt new patterns. You *can* create a new narrative identity for yourself (Bauer, McAdams, & Pals, 2008).

---

student might picture herself as a successful attorney, an enterprising college student might imagine himself as an Internet entrepreneur, and a person on a diet might imagine both slim and grossly obese possible selves. Such images tend to direct our future behavior (Oyserman et al., 2004).

Of course, almost everyone over age 30 has probably felt the anguish of realizing that some cherished possible selves will never be realized. Nevertheless, there is value in asking yourself not just "Who am I?" but also "Who would I like to become?" As you do, remember Maslow's advice that everyone has a potential for "greatness," but most fear becoming what they might.

Humanistic View of Development

Why do mirrors, photographs, video cameras, and the reactions of others hold such fascination and threat for many people? Carl Rogers's theory suggests it is because they provide information about one's self. The development of a self-image depends greatly on information from the environment. It begins with a sorting of perceptions and feelings: my body, my toes, my nose, I want, I like, I am, and so on. Soon, it expands to include self-evaluation: I am a good person, I did something bad just now, and so forth.

How does development of the self contribute to later personality functioning? Rogers believed that positive and negative evaluations by others cause children to develop internal standards of evaluation called **conditions of worth.** In other words, we learn that some actions win our parents' love and approval whereas others are rejected. More important, parents may label some *feelings* as bad or wrong. For example, a child might be told that it is wrong to feel angry toward a brother or sister—even when anger is justified. Likewise, a little boy might be told that he must not cry or show fear, two very normal emotions.

Learning to evaluate some experiences or feelings as "good" and others as "bad" is directly related to a later capacity for self-esteem, positive self-evaluation, or **positive self-regard,** to use Rogers' term. To think of yourself as a good, lovable, worthwhile person, your behavior and experiences must match your internal conditions of worth. The problem is that this can cause incongruence by leading to the denial of many true feelings and experiences.

To put it simply, Rogers blamed many adult emotional problems on attempts to live by the standards of others. He believed that congruence and self-actualization are encouraged by replacing conditions of worth with **organismic valuing** (a natural, undistorted, full-body reaction to an experience). Organismic valuing is a direct, gut-level response to life that avoids the filtering and distortion of incongruence. It involves trusting one's own feelings and perceptions. Organismic valuing is most likely to develop, Rogers felt, when children (or adults) receive **unconditional positive regard** (unshakable love and approval) from others. That is, when they are "prized" as worthwhile human beings, just for being themselves, without any conditions or strings attached. Although this may be a luxury few people enjoy, we are more likely to move toward our ideal selves if we receive affirmation and support from a close partner (Drigotas et al., 1999).

Humanistic Theory

RECITE

1. Humanists view human nature as basically good, and they emphasize the effects of subjective learning and unconscious choice. T or F?
2. Maslow used the term _____ to describe the tendency of certain individuals to fully use their talents and potentials.
3. According to Rogers, a close match between the self-image and the ideal self creates a condition called incongruence. T or F?
4. Markus and Nurius describe alternative self-concepts that a person may have as "possible selves." T or F?
5. Carl Rogers believed that personal growth is encouraged when conditions of worth are replaced by
   a. self-efficacy
   b. instrumental worth
   c. latency
   d. organismic valuing
6. According to Maslow, a preoccupation with one's own thoughts, feelings, and needs is characteristic of self-actualizing individuals. T or F?
7. Maslow thought of peak experiences as temporary moments of
   a. congruence
   b. positive self-regard
   c. self-actualization
   d. self-reinforcement
8. Which of the following is *not* one of the six human strengths identified by positive psychologists?
   a. congruence
   b. courage
   c. justice
   d. transcendence

REFLECT

Critical Thinking

8. What role would "possible selves" have in the choice of a college major?

Relate

How do your views of human nature and free choice compare with those of the humanists?

Do you know anyone who seems to be making especially good use of his or her personal potentials? Does that person fit Maslow's profile of a self-actualizer?

How much difference do you think there is between your self-image, your ideal self, and your true self? Do you think Rogers is right about the effects of applying conditions of worth to your perceptions and feelings?

Answers: 1. F **2.** self-actualization **3.** F **4.** T **5.** d **6.** F **7.** c **8.** a **9.** Career decisions almost always involve, in part, picturing oneself occupying various occupational roles.

Personality Theories—Overview and Comparison

Which personality theory is right? Each theory has added to our understanding by organizing observations of human behavior. Nevertheless, theories can't be fully proved or disproved. We can only ask, "Does the evidence tend to support this theory or disconfirm it?" Yet although theories are neither true nor false, their implications or predictions may be. The best way to judge a theory,

then, is in terms of its *usefulness*. Does the theory adequately explain behavior? Does it stimulate new research? Does it suggest how to treat psychological disorders? Each theory has fared differently in these areas (Pervin, Cervone, & John, 2005).

Trait Theories

Traits are very useful for describing and comparing personalities. Many of the personality tests used by clinical psychologists are based on trait theories. However, trait theories tend to have a circular quality. For example, how do we know that a young woman named Carrie has the trait of shyness? Because we frequently observe Carrie avoiding conversations with others. And why doesn't Carrie socialize with others? Because shyness is a trait of her personality. And how do we know she has the trait of shyness? Because we observe that she avoids socializing with others. And so on.

Psychoanalytic Theory

By present standards, psychoanalytic theory seems to exaggerate the impact of sexuality and biological instincts. These distortions were corrected somewhat by the neo-Freudians, but problems remain. One of the most telling criticisms of Freudian theory is that it can explain any psychological event *after* it has occurred. But beforehand it offers little help in predicting future behavior. For this reason, many psychoanalytic concepts are difficult or impossible to test scientifically (Schick & Vaughn, 1995).

Behavioristic and Social Learning Theories

Learning theories have provided a good framework for personality research. Of the major perspectives, the behaviorists have made the best effort to rigorously test and verify their ideas. They have, however, been criticized for understating the impact that temperament, emotion, thinking, and subjective experience have on personality. Social learning theory answers some of these criticisms, but it may still understate the importance of private experience.

Humanistic Theory

A great strength of the humanists is the attention they have given to positive dimensions of personality. As Maslow (1968) put it, "Human nature is not nearly as bad as it has been thought to be. It is as if Freud supplied us with the sick half of psychology and we must now fill it out with the healthy half." Despite their contribu-

Conditions of worth Internal standards used to judge the value of one's thoughts, actions, feelings, or experiences.

Positive self-regard Thinking of oneself as a good, lovable, worthwhile person.

Organismic valuing A natural, undistorted, full-body reaction to an experience.

Unconditional positive regard Unshakable love and approval given without qualification.

Table 12.3 ● Comparison of Personality Theories

	Trait Theories	Psychoanalytic Theory	Behavioristic and Social Learning Theories	Humanistic Theory
View of human nature	Neutral	Negative	Neutral	Positive
Is behavior free or determined?	Determined	Determined	Determined	Free choice
Principal motives	Depends on one's traits	Sex and aggression	Drives of all kinds	Self-actualization
Personality structure	Traits	Id, ego, superego	Habits, expectancies	Self
Role of unconscious	Minimized	Maximized	Practically nonexistent	Minimized
Conception of conscience	Traits of honesty, etc.	Superego	Self-reinforcement, punishment history	Ideal self, valuing process
Developmental emphasis	Combined effects of heredity and environment	Psychosexual stages	Critical learning situations, identification, and imitation	Development of self-image
Barriers to personal growth	Unhealthy traits	Unconscious conflicts, fixations	Maladaptive habits, unhealthy environment	Conditions of worth, incongruence

tions, humanists can be criticized for using "fuzzy" concepts that are difficult to measure and study objectively. Even so, humanistic thought has encouraged many people to seek greater self-awareness and personal growth. Also, humanistic concepts have been very useful in counseling and psychotherapy.

In the final analysis, we need all four major perspectives to explain personality. Each provides a sort of lens through which human behavior can be viewed. In many instances, a balanced picture emerges only when each theory is considered. ● Table 12.3 provides a final overview of the principal approaches to personality.

●● Personality Assessment— Psychological Yardsticks

Gateway Question: How do psychologists measure personality?

Measuring personality can help predict how people will behave at work, at school, and in therapy. However, painting a detailed picture can be a challenge. In many instances, it requires several of the techniques described in this unit. To capture a personality as unique as Annette's, it might take all of them!

How is personality "measured"? Psychologists use interviews, observation, questionnaires, and projective tests to assess personality (Burger, 2008). Each method has strengths and limitations. For this reason, they are often used in combination.

Formal personality measures are refinements of more casual ways of judging a person. At one time or another, you have probably "sized up" a potential date, friend, or roommate by engaging in conversation (interview). Perhaps you have asked a friend, "When I am delayed I get angry. Do you?" (questionnaire). Maybe you watch your professors when they are angry or embarrassed to learn what they are "really" like when they're caught off-guard (observation). Or possibly you have noticed that when you say, "I think people feel . . . ," you may be expressing your own feelings (projection). Let's see how psychologists apply each of these methods to probe personality.

The Interview

In an **interview,** direct questioning is used to learn about a person's life history, personality traits, or current mental state (Sommers-Flanagan & Sommers-Flanagan, 2002). In an *unstructured interview,* conversation is informal and topics are taken up freely as they arise. In a *structured interview,* information is gathered by asking a planned series of questions.

How are interviews used? Interviews are used to identify personality disturbances; to select people for jobs, college, or special programs; and to study the dynamics of personality. Interviews also provide information for counseling or therapy. For instance, a counselor might ask a depressed person, "Have you ever contemplated suicide? What were the circumstances?" The counselor might then follow by asking, "How did you feel about it?" or, "How is what you are now feeling different from what you felt then?"

In addition to providing information, interviews make it possible to observe a person's tone of voice, hand gestures, posture, and facial expressions. Such "body language" cues are important because they may radically alter the message sent, as when a person claims to be "completely calm" but trembles uncontrollably.

Computerized Interviews

If you were distressed and went to a psychologist or psychiatrist, what is the first thing she or he might do? Typically, a *diagnostic interview* is used to find out how a person is feeling and what complaints or symptoms he or she has. In many cases, such interviews are based on a specific series of questions. Because the questions are always the same, some researchers have begun to wonder, "Why not let a computer ask them?"

The results of computerized interviews have been promising. In one study, people were interviewed by both a computer and a psychiatrist. Eighty-five percent of these people thought the computer did an acceptable interview (Dignon, 1996). Another study found that a computerized interview was highly accurate at identifying psychiatric disorders and symptoms. It also closely agreed with diagnoses made by psychiatrists (Marion, Shayka, & Marcus, 1996). Thus, it may soon become common for people to "Tell it to the computer," at least in the first stages of seeking help (Peters, Clark, & Carroll, 1998).

Limitations

Interviews give rapid insight into personality, but they have limitations. For one thing, interviewers can be swayed by preconceptions. A person identified as a "housewife," "college student," "high school athlete," "punk," "geek," or "ski bum" may be misjudged because of an interviewer's personal biases. Second, an interviewer's own personality, or even gender, may influence a client's behavior. When this occurs, it can accentuate or distort the person's apparent traits (Pollner, 1998). A third problem is that people sometimes try to deceive interviewers. For example, a person accused of a crime might try to avoid punishment by pretending to be mentally disabled.

A fourth problem is the **halo effect,** which is the tendency to generalize a favorable (or unfavorable) impression to an entire personality (Lance, LaPointe, & Stewart, 1994). Because of the halo effect, a person who is likable or physically attractive may be rated more mature, intelligent, or mentally healthy than she or he actually is. The halo effect is something to keep in mind at job interviews. First impressions do make a difference (Lance, LaPointe, & Stewart, 1994).

Even with their limitations, interviews are a respected method of assessment. In many cases, interviews are the first step in evaluating personality and an essential prelude to therapy. Nevertheless, interviews are usually not enough and must be supplemented by other measures and tests (Meyer et al., 2001).

Direct Observation and Rating Scales

Are you fascinated by airports, bus depots, parks, taverns, subway stations, or other public places? Many people relish a chance to observe the actions of others. When used for assessment, **direct observation** (looking at behavior) is a simple extension of this natural interest in "people watching." For instance, a psychologist might arrange to observe a disturbed child as she plays with other children. Is the child withdrawn? Does she become hostile or aggressive without warning? By careful observation, the psychologist can identify the girl's personality traits and clarify the nature of her problems.

Wouldn't observation be subject to the same problems of misperception as an interview? Yes. Misperceptions can be a difficulty, which is why rating scales are sometimes used (● Figure 12.7). A **rating scale** is a list of personality traits or aspects of behavior that can be used to evaluate a person. Rating scales limit the chance that some traits will be overlooked while others are exaggerated (Synhorst et al., 2005). Perhaps they should be a standard procedure for choosing a roommate, spouse, or lover!

An alternative approach is to do a **behavioral assessment** by counting the frequency of specific behaviors. In this case, observers record *actions,* not what traits they think a person has (Ramsay, Reynolds, & Kamphaus, 2002). For example, a psychologist working with hospitalized mental patients might note the frequency of a patient's aggression, self-care, speech, and unusual behaviors. Behavioral assessments can also be used to probe thought processes. In one study, for example, couples were assessed while talking with each other about their sexuality. Couples with sexual difficulties were less likely to be receptive to discussing their sexuality and more likely to blame each other than were couples with no sexual difficulties (Kelly, Strassberg, & Turner, 2006).

Situational Testing

In **situational testing,** real-life conditions are simulated so that a person's spontaneous reactions can be observed. Such tests assume that the best way to learn how people react is to put them in realis-

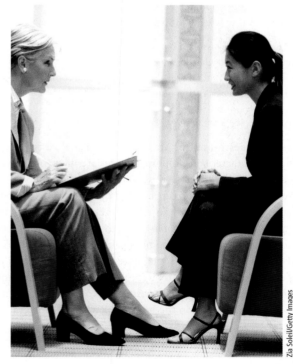

What is your initial impression of the person wearing the black suit? If you think that she looks friendly, attractive, or neat, your subsequent perceptions might be altered by a positive first impression. Interviewers are often influenced by the halo effect (see text).

Zia Soleil/Getty Images

Interview (personality) A face-to-face meeting held for the purpose of gaining information about an individual's personal history, personality traits, current psychological state, and so forth.

Halo effect The tendency to generalize a favorable or unfavorable first impression to unrelated details of personality.

Direct observation Assessing behavior through direct surveillance.

Rating scale A list of personality traits or aspects of behavior on which a person is rated.

Behavioral assessment Recording the frequency of various behaviors.

Situational test Simulating real-life conditions so that a person's reactions may be directly observed.

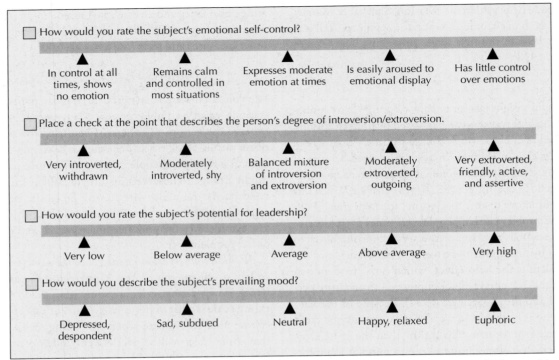

●Figure 12.7 Sample rating scale items. To understand how the scale works, imagine someone you know well. Where would you place checkmarks on each of the scales to rate that person's characteristics?

tic situations and watch what happens. Situational tests expose people to frustration, temptation, pressure, boredom, or other conditions capable of revealing personality characteristics (Olson-Buchanan & Drasgow, 2006; Weekley & Jones, 1997). Some popular "reality TV" programs, such as *American Idol, Survivor,* and *The Amazing Race,* bear some similarity to situational tests—which may account for their ability to attract millions of viewers.

How are situational tests done? An interesting example of situational testing is the judgmental firearms training provided by many police departments. At times, police officers must make split-second decisions about using their weapons. A mistake could be fatal. In a typical shoot/don't-shoot test, actors play the part of armed criminals. As various high-risk scenes are acted out live, on videotape, or by computer, officers must decide to shoot or hold fire. A newspaper reporter who once took the test (and failed it) gives this account (Gersh, 1982):

> I judged wrong. I was killed by a man in a closet, a man with a hostage, a woman interrupted when kissing her lover, and a man I thought was cleaning a shotgun. . . . I shot a drunk who reached for a comb, and a teenager who pulled out a black water pistol. Looked real to me.

Personality Questionnaires

Personality questionnaires are paper-and-pencil tests that reveal personality characteristics. Questionnaires are more objective than interviews or observation. (An **objective test** gives the same score when different people correct it.) Questions, administration, and scoring are all standardized so that scores are unaffected by any biases an examiner may have. However, this is not enough to ensure accuracy. A good test must also be reliable and valid. A test is **reliable** if it yields close to the same score each time it is given to the same person. A test has **validity** if it measures what it claims to measure. Unfortunately, many personality tests you will encounter, such as those in magazines or on the Internet, have little or no validity.

David McNew/Newsmakers/Getty Images

A police officer undergoes judgmental firearms training. Variations on this test are used by many police departments. All officers must score a passing grade.

> **bridges**
> Reliability and validity are important characteristics of all psychological tests, especially intelligence and aptitude tests. **See Chapter 9, pages 314–316.**

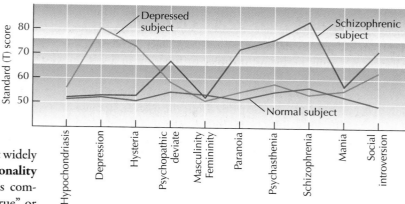

● Figure 12.8 An MMPI-2 profile showing hypothetical scores indicating normality, depression, and psychosis. High scores begin at 66 and very high scores at 76. An unusually low score (40 and below) may also reveal personality characteristics or problems.

Dozens of personality tests are available, including the *Guilford-Zimmerman Temperament Survey,* the *California Psychological Inventory,* the *Allport-Vernon Study of Values,* the *16 PF,* and many more. One of the best-known and most widely used objective tests is the **Minnesota Multiphasic Personality Inventory-2 (MMPI-2)** (Butcher, 2005). The MMPI-2 is composed of 567 items to which a test taker must respond "true" or "false." Items include statements such as the following:

Everything tastes the same.
I am very normal, sexually.
I like birds.
I usually daydream in the afternoon.
Mostly I stay away from other people.
Someone has been trying to hurt me.
Sometimes I think strange thoughts.*

How can these items show anything about personality? For instance, what if a person has a cold so that "everything tastes the same"? For an answer (and a little bit of fun), read the following items. Answer "Yes," "No," or "Don't bother me, I can't cope!"

I would enjoy the work of a chicken flicker.
My eyes are always cold.
Frantic screaming makes me nervous.
I believe I smell as good as most people.
I use shoe polish to excess.
The sight of blood no longer excites me.
As an infant I had very few hobbies.
Dirty stories make me think about sex.
I stay in the bathtub until I look like a raisin.
I salivate at the sight of mittens.
I never finish what I†

These items were written by humorist Art Buchwald (1965) to satirize personality questionnaires. Such questions may seem ridiculous, but they are not very different from the real thing. How, then, do the items on tests such as the MMPI-2 reveal anything about personality? The answer is that a single item tells little about personality. For example, a person who agrees that "Everything tastes the same" might simply have a cold. It is only through *patterns* of response that personality dimensions are revealed.

Items on the MMPI-2 were selected for their ability to correctly identify persons with particular psychological problems (Butcher, 2005). For instance, if depressed persons consistently answer a series of items in a particular way, it is assumed that others who answer the same way are also prone to depression. As silly as

the gag items in the preceding lists may seem, it is possible that some could actually work in a legitimate test. But before an item could be part of a test, it would have to be shown to correlate highly with some trait or dimension of personality.

The MMPI-2 measures 10 major aspects of personality (listed in ● Table 12.4). After the MMPI-2 is scored, results are charted graphically as an **MMPI-2 profile** (● Figure 12.8). By comparing a person's profile to scores produced by typical, normal adults, a

Table 12.4 ● MMPI-2 Basic Clinical Subscales

1. **Hypochondriasis** (HI-po-kon-DRY-uh-sis). Exaggerated concern about one's physical health.
2. **Depression.** Feelings of worthlessness, hopelessness, and pessimism.
3. **Hysteria.** The presence of physical complaints for which no physical basis can be established.
4. **Psychopathic deviate.** Emotional shallowness in relationships and a disregard for social and moral standards.
5. **Masculinity/femininity.** One's degree of traditional "masculine" aggressiveness or "feminine" sensitivity.
6. **Paranoia.** Extreme suspiciousness and feelings of persecution.
7. **Psychasthenia** (sike-as-THEE-nee-ah). The presence of obsessive worries, irrational fears (phobias), and compulsive (ritualistic) actions.
8. **Schizophrenia.** Emotional withdrawal and unusual or bizarre thinking and actions.
9. **Mania.** Emotional excitability, manic moods or behavior, and excessive activity.
10. **Social introversion.** One's tendency to be socially withdrawn.

Personality questionnaire A paper-and-pencil test consisting of questions that reveal aspects of personality.

Objective test A test that gives the same score when different people correct it.

Reliability The ability of a test to yield nearly the same score each time it is given to the same person.

Validity The ability of a test to measure what it purports to measure.

Minnesota Multiphasic Personality Inventory-2 (MMPI-2) One of the best-known and most widely used objective personality questionnaires.

MMPI-2 profile A graphic representation of an individual's scores on each of the primary scales of the MMPI-2.

*MMPI-2 statements themselves cannot be reproduced to protect the validity of the test.
†Art Buchwald quotation courtesy of Art Buchwald, *Washington Post.*

psychologist can identify various personality disorders. Additional scales can identify substance abuse, eating disorders, Type A (heart-attack prone) behavior, repression, anger, cynicism, low self-esteem, family problems, inability to function in a job, and other problems (Butcher, 2005).

How accurate is the MMPI-2? Personality questionnaires are only accurate if people tell the truth about themselves. Because of this, the MMPI-2 has additional **validity scales** that reveal whether a person's scores should be discarded. The validity scales detect attempts by test takers to "fake good" (make themselves look good) or "fake bad" (make it look like they have problems). Other scales uncover defensiveness or tendencies to exaggerate shortcomings and troubles. When taking the MMPI-2, it is best to answer honestly, without trying to second-guess the test.

A clinical psychologist trying to decide if a person has emotional problems would be wise to take more than the MMPI-2 into account. Test scores are informative, but they can incorrectly label some people (Urbina, 2004). Fortunately, clinical judgments usually rely on information from interviews, tests, and other sources. Also, despite their limitations, it is reassuring to note that psychological assessments are at least as accurate as commonly used medical tests (Meyer et al., 2001).

Projective Tests of Personality— Inkblots and Hidden Plots

Projective tests take a different approach to personality. Interviews, observation, rating scales, and inventories try to directly identify overt, observable traits (Leichtman, 2004). By contrast, projective tests seek to uncover deeply hidden or *unconscious* wishes, thoughts, and needs.

As a child you may have delighted in finding faces and objects in cloud formations. Or perhaps you have learned something about your friends' personalities from their reactions to movies or paintings. If so, you will have some insight into the rationale for projective tests. In a **projective test**, a person is asked to describe ambiguous stimuli or make up stories about them. Describing an unambiguous stimulus (a picture of an automobile, for example) tells little about your personality. But when you are faced with an unstructured stimulus, you must organize what you see in terms of your own life experiences. Everyone sees something different in a projective test, and what is perceived can reveal the inner workings of personality.

Projective tests have no right or wrong answers, which makes them difficult to fake (Leichtman, 2004). Moreover, projective tests can be a rich source of information, because responses are not restricted to simple true/false or yes/no answers.

The Rorschach Inkblot Test

Is the inkblot test a projective technique? The inkblot test, or **Rorschach** (ROAR-shock) **Technique**, is one of the oldest and most widely used projective tests. Developed by Swiss psychologist Hermann Rorschach in the 1920s, it consists of 10 standardized inkblots. These vary in color, shading, form, and complexity.

How does the test work? First, a person is shown each blot and asked to describe what she or he sees in it (● Figure 12.9). Later the psychologist may return to a blot, asking the person to identify specific sections of it, to expand previous descriptions, or to give new impressions about what it contains. Obvious differences in content—such as "blood dripping from a dagger" versus "flowers blooming in a basket"—are important for identifying personal conflicts and fantasies. But surprisingly, content is less important than what parts of the inkblot are used to organize images. These factors allow psychologists to detect emotional disturbances by observing how a person perceives the world (Hilsenroth, 2000).

> ### bridges
> Schizophrenia and other psychotic disorders are associated with severe disturbances in thinking and perception. Such disturbances are usually readily apparent during projective testing. **See Chapter 14, pages 467–468.**

The Thematic Apperception Test

Another popular projective test is the **Thematic Apperception Test (TAT)** developed by personality theorist Henry Murray (1893–1988).

● **Figure 12.9** Inkblots similar to those used on the Rorschach. What do you see?

How does the TAT differ from the Rorschach? The TAT consists of 20 sketches depicting various scenes and life situations (● Figure 12.10). During testing, a person is shown each sketch and asked to make up a story about the people in it. Later, the person looks at each sketch a second or a third time and elaborates on previous stories or creates new stories.

To score the TAT, a psychologist analyzes the content of the stories. Interpretations focus on how people feel, how they interact, what events led up to the incidents depicted in the sketch, and how the story will end. For example, TAT stories told by bereaved college students typically include themes of death, grief, and coping with loss (Balk et al., 1998).

A psychologist might also count the number of times the central figure in a TAT story is angry, overlooked, apathetic, jealous, or threatened. Here is a story written by a student to describe ● Figure 12.10:

> The girl has been seeing this guy her mother doesn't like. The mother is telling her that she better not see him again. The mother says, "He's just like your father." The mother and father are divorced. The mother is smiling because she thinks she is right. But she doesn't really know what the girl wants. The girl is going to see the guy again, anyway.

As this example implies, the TAT is especially good at revealing feelings about a person's social relationships (Alvarado, 1994; Aronow, Altman Weiss, & Reznikoff, 2001).

Limitations of Projective Testing

Although projective tests have been popular, their validity is considered lowest among tests of personality (Lilienfeld, 1999; Wood et al., 2003). Objectivity and reliability (consistency) are also low for different users of the TAT and Rorschach. Note that after a person interprets an ambiguous stimulus, the scorer must interpret the person's (sometimes) ambiguous responses. In a sense, the

● **Figure 12.10** This is a picture like those used for the Thematic Apperception Test. If you wish to simulate the test, tell a story that explains what led up to the pictured situation, what is happening now, and how the action will end.

interpretation of a projective test may be a projective test for the scorer!

Despite their drawbacks, projective tests still have value (Hilsenroth, 2000). This is especially true when they are used as part of a *test battery* (collection of assessment devices and interviews). In the hands of a skilled clinician, projective tests can be a good way to detect major conflicts, to get clients to talk about upsetting topics, and to set goals for therapy (O'Roark, 2001).

●● Sudden Murderers— A Research Example

Personality assessments provide us with clues to some of the most perplexing human events. Consider Fred Cowan, a model student in school and described by those who knew him as quiet, gentle, and a man who loved children. Despite his size (6 feet tall, 250 pounds), Fred was described by a co-worker as "someone you could easily push around."

Fred Cowan represents a puzzling phenomenon: We occasionally read in the news about sudden murderers—gentle, quiet, shy, good-natured people who explode without warning into violence (Cartwright, 2002a; Lee, Zimbardo, & Bertholf, 1977). Two weeks after he was suspended from his job, Fred returned to work determined to get even with his supervisor. Unable to find the man, he killed four co-workers and a policeman before taking his own life.

Isn't such behavior contrary to the idea of personality traits? It might seem that sudden murderers are newsworthy simply because they are unlikely candidates for violence. On the contrary, research conducted by Melvin Lee, Philip Zimbardo, and Minerva Bertholf suggests that sudden murderers explode into violence *because* they are shy, restrained, and inexpressive, not in spite of it. These researchers studied prisoners at a California prison. Ten were inmates whose homicide was an unexpected first offense. Nine were criminals with a record of habitual violence prior to murder. Sixteen were inmates convicted of nonviolent crimes.

Did the inmates differ in personality makeup? Each of the inmates took a battery of tests, including the MMPI, a measure of shyness, and an *adjective checklist* (in which inmates described themselves by selecting relevant adjectives from a list of adjectives used to describe people). Personal interviews were also done with each inmate. As expected, the sudden murderers were passive, shy, and overcontrolled (restrained) individuals. The habitually violent inmates were "masculine" (aggressive), undercontrolled

Validity scales Scales that tell whether test scores should be invalidated for lying, inconsistency, or "faking good."

Projective tests Psychological tests making use of ambiguous or unstructured stimuli.

Rorschach Technique A projective test comprised of 10 standardized inkblots.

Thematic Apperception Test (TAT) A projective test consisting of 20 different scenes and life situations about which respondents make up stories.

(impulsive), and less likely to view themselves as shy than the inmates convicted of nonviolent crimes (Lee, Zimbardo, & Bertholf, 1977).

Psychologists have learned that quiet, overcontrolled individuals are likely to be especially violent if they ever lose control. Their attacks are usually triggered by a minor irritation or frustration, but the attack reflects years of unexpressed feelings of anger and belittlement. When sudden murderers finally release the strict controls they have maintained on their overcontrolled behavior, a furious and frenzied attack ensues (Cartwright, 2002b). Usually it is totally out of proportion to the offense against them and many have amnesia for their violent actions.

In comparison, the previously violent murderers showed very different reactions. Although they killed, their violence was moderate—usually only enough to do the necessary damage. Typically, they felt they had been cheated or betrayed and that they were doing what was necessary to remedy the situation or maintain their manhood (Lee, Zimbardo, & Bertholf, 1977).

A Look Ahead

The preceding example illustrates how some of the concepts and techniques discussed in this chapter can be applied to further our understanding. The Psychology in Action section that follows should add balance to your view of personality. Don't be shy. Read on!

KNOWLEDGE BUILDER
Personality Assessment

RECITE

1. The halo effect can be a serious problem in accurate personality assessment that is based on
   a. projective testing
   b. behavioral recording
   c. interviewing
   d. the TAT
2. Situational testing allows direct _____ of personality characteristics.
3. A psychotic person would probably score highest on which MMPI-2 scale?
   a. depression
   b. hysteria
   c. schizophrenia
   d. mania
4. The use of ambiguous stimuli is most characteristic of
   a. interviews
   b. projective tests
   c. personality inventories
   d. direct observation
5. The content of one's responses to the MMPI-2 is considered an indication of unconscious wishes, thoughts, and needs. T or F?
6. Doing a behavioral assessment requires direct observation of the person's actions or a direct report of the person's thoughts. T or F?

7. Which of the following items *does not* belong with the others?
   a. Rorschach Technique
   b. TAT
   c. MMPI-2
   d. projective testing
8. A surprising finding is that sudden murderers are usually undercontrolled, very masculine, and more impulsive than average. T or F?
9. A test is considered valid if it consistently yields the same score when the same person takes it on different occasions. T or F?

REFLECT

Critical Thinking

10. Can you think of one more reason why personality traits may not be accurately revealed by interviews?
11. Projective testing would be of greatest interest to which type of personality theorist?

Relate

How do *you* assess personality? Do you informally make use of any of the methods described in this chapter?

You are a candidate for a desirable job. Your personality is going to be assessed by a psychologist. What method (or methods) would you prefer that she or he use? Why?

Answers: 1. c 2. observation 3. c 4. b 5. F 6. T 7. c 8. F 9. F 10. Because of trait-situation interactions, a person may not behave in a normal fashion while being evaluated in an interview. 11. Psychodynamic, because projective testing is designed to uncover unconscious thoughts, feelings, and conflicts.

PSYCHOLOGY IN ACTION

Barriers and Bridges—Understanding Shyness

Gateway Questions: What causes shyness? What can be done about it?

Do you

• Find it hard to talk to strangers?
• Lack confidence with people?
• Feel uncomfortable in social situations?
• Feel nervous with people who are not close friends?

As a personality trait, **shyness** refers to a tendency to avoid others, as well as feelings of anxiety, preoccupation, and social inhibition (uneasiness and strain when socializing) (Bruch, 2001). Shy persons fail to make eye contact, retreat when spoken to, speak too quietly, and display little interest or animation

in conversations. Mild shyness may be no more than a nuisance. However, extreme shyness (which may be diagnosed as *social anxiety disorder*) is often associated with depression, loneliness, fearfulness, social anxiety, inhibition, and low self-esteem (Derlega, Winstead, & Jones, 2005; Stein & Stein, 2008).

Elements of Shyness

What causes shyness? To begin with, shy persons often lack *social skills* (proficiency at interacting with others). Many simply have not learned how to meet people or how to start a conversation and keep it going. **Social anxiety** (a feeling of apprehension in the presence of others) is also a factor in shyness. Almost everyone feels nervous in some social situations (such as meeting an attractive stranger). Typically, this is a reaction to evaluation fears (fears of being inadequate, embarrassed, ridiculed, or rejected). Although fears of rejection are common, they are much more frequent or intense for shy persons (Bradshaw, 2006; Jackson, Towson, & Narduzzi, 1997). A third problem for shy persons is a *self-defeating bias* (distortion) in their thinking. Specifically, shy persons almost always blame themselves when a social encounter doesn't go well. They are unnecessarily self-critical in social situations (Lundh et al., 2002).

Situational Causes of Shyness

Shyness is most often triggered by *novel* or *unfamiliar* social situations. A person who does fine with family or close friends may become shy and awkward when meeting a stranger. Shyness is also magnified by formality, meeting someone of higher status, being noticeably different from others, or being the focus of attention (as in giving a speech) (Larsen & Buss, 2005).

Don't most people become cautious and inhibited in such circumstances? Yes. That's why we need to see how the personalities of shy and not-shy persons differ.

Dynamics of the Shy Personality

There is a tendency to think that shy persons are wrapped up in their own feelings and thoughts. But surprisingly, researchers Jona-

Michelle D. Birdwell/PhotoEdit

than Cheek and Arnold Buss (1979) found no connection between shyness and **private self-consciousness** (attention to inner feelings, thoughts, and fantasies). Instead, they discovered that shyness is linked to **public self-consciousness** (acute awareness of oneself as a social object).

Persons who rate high in public self-consciousness are intensely concerned about what others think of them (Cowden, 2005). They worry about saying the wrong thing or appearing foolish. In public, they may feel "naked" or as if others can "see through them." Such feelings trigger anxiety or outright fear during social encounters, leading to awkwardness and inhibition (Cowden, 2005). The shy person's anxiety, in turn, often causes her or him to misperceive others in social situations (Schroeder, 1995).

As mentioned, almost everyone feels anxious in at least some social situations. But there is a key difference in the way shy and not-shy persons *label* this anxiety. Shy persons tend to consider their social anxiety a *lasting personality trait*. Shyness, in other words, becomes part of their self-concept. In contrast, not-shy persons believe that *external situations* cause their occasional feelings of shyness. When not-shy persons feel anxiety or "stage fright," they assume that almost anyone would feel as they do under the same circumstances (Zimbardo, Pilkonis, & Norwood, 1978).

Labeling is important because it affects *self-esteem*. In general, not-shy persons tend to have higher self-esteem than shy persons. This is because not-shy persons give themselves credit for their social successes and they recognize that failures are often due to circumstances. In contrast, shy people blame themselves for social failures, never give themselves credit for successes, and expect to be rejected (Jackson et al., 2002).

Shy Beliefs

What can be done to reduce shyness? Shyness is often maintained by unrealistic or self-defeating beliefs (Antony, 2004; Butler, 2001). Here's a sample of such beliefs:

1. *If you wait around long enough at a social gathering, something will happen.*
   Comment: This is really a cover-up for fear of starting a conversation. For two people to meet, at least one has to make an effort, and it might as well be you.

2. *Other people who are popular are just lucky when it comes to being invited to social events or asked out.*
   Comment: Except for times when a person is formally introduced to someone new, this is false. People who are more active socially typically make an effort to meet and spend time with others. They join clubs, invite others to do things, strike up conversations, and generally leave little to luck.

3. *The odds of meeting someone interested in socializing are always the same, no matter where I am.*
   Comment: This is another excuse for inaction. It pays to seek out situations that have a higher probability of leading to social contact, such as clubs, teams, and school events.

4. *If someone doesn't seem to like you right away, they really don't like you and never will.*
   Comment: This belief leads to much needless shyness. Even when a person doesn't show immediate interest, it doesn't mean the person dislikes you. Liking takes time and opportunity to develop.

Unproductive beliefs like the preceding can be replaced with statements such as the following:

1. I've got to be active in social situations.
2. I can't wait until I'm completely relaxed or comfortable before taking a social risk.
3. I don't need to pretend to be someone I'm not; it just makes me more anxious.
4. I may think other people are harshly evaluating me, but actually I'm being too hard on myself.
5. I can set reasonable goals for expanding my social experience and skills.
6. Even people who are very socially skillful are never successful 100 percent of the time. I shouldn't get so upset when an encounter goes badly. (Adapted from Antony, 2004; Butler, 2001.)

Shyness A tendency to avoid others plus uneasiness and strain when socializing.

Social anxiety A feeling of apprehension in the presence of others.

Private self-consciousness Preoccupation with inner feelings, thoughts, and fantasies.

Public self-consciousness Intense awareness of oneself as a social object.

Social Skills

Learning social skills takes practice (Carducci & Fields, 2007). There is nothing "innate" about knowing how to meet people or start a conversation. Social skills can be directly practiced in a variety of ways. It can be helpful, for instance, to get a tape recorder and listen to several of your conversations. You may be surprised by the way you pause, interrupt, miss cues, or seem disinterested. Similarly, it can be useful to look at yourself in a mirror and exaggerate facial expressions of surprise, interest, dislike, pleasure, and so forth. By such methods, most people can learn to put more animation and skill into their self-presentation. (For a discussion of related skills, see the section on self-assertion in Chapter 16.)

Conversation

One of the simplest ways to make better conversation is by learning to ask questions. A good series of questions shifts attention to the other person and shows you are interested. Nothing fancy is needed. You can do fine with questions such as, "Where do you (work, study, live)? Do you like (dancing, travel, music)? How long have you (been at this school, worked here, lived here)?" After you've broken the ice, the best questions are often those that are *open ended* (they can't be answered yes or no):

"What parts of the country have you seen?" (as opposed to, "Have you ever been to Florida?")

"What's it like living on the West Side?" (as opposed to, "Do you like living on the West Side?")

"What kinds of food do you like?" (as opposed to, "Do you like Chinese cooking?")

It's easy to see why open-ended questions are helpful. In replying to open-ended questions, people often give "free information" about themselves. This extra information can be used to ask other questions or to lead into other topics of conversation.

This brief sampling of ideas is no substitute for actual practice. Overcoming shyness requires a real effort to learn new skills and test old beliefs and attitudes. It may even require the help of a counselor or therapist. At the very least, a shy person must be willing to take social risks. Breaking down the barriers of shyness will always include some awkward or unsuccessful encounters. Nevertheless, the rewards are powerful: human companionship and personal freedom.

KNOWLEDGE BUILDER
Understanding Shyness

RECITE

1. Shy people do not have self-defeating biases in their thinking. T or F?
2. Social anxiety and evaluation fears are seen almost exclusively in shy individuals; the not shy rarely have such experiences. T or F?
3. Unfamiliar people and situations most often trigger shyness. T or F?
4. Contrary to what many people think, shyness is *not* related to
   a. private self-consciousness
   b. social anxiety
   c. self-esteem
   d. blaming oneself for social failures
5. Shy persons tend to consider their social anxiety to be a
   a. situational reaction
   b. personality trait
   c. public efficacy
   d. habit
6. Changing personal beliefs and practicing social skills can be helpful in overcoming shyness. T or F?

REFLECT

Critical Thinking

7. Shyness is a trait of Vonda's personality. Like most shy people, Vonda is most likely to feel shy in unfamiliar social settings. Vonda's shy behavior demonstrates that the expression of traits is governed by what concept?

Relate

If you are shy, see if you can summarize how social skills, social anxiety, evaluation fears, self-defeating thoughts, and public self-consciousness contribute to your social inhibition. If you're not shy, imagine how you would explain these concepts to a shy friend.

Answers: 1. F **2.** F **3.** T **4.** a **5.** b **6.** T **7.** trait-situation interactions (again)

---

chapter in review · Gateways to Personality

Personality refers to a person's consistent and unique patterns of thinking, emotion, and behavior

- Character is personality evaluated, or the possession of desirable qualities.
- Temperament refers to the hereditary aspects of one's emotional nature.
- Traits are lasting personal qualities that are inferred from behavior.

- Behavioral genetics and studies of identical twins show that heredity contributes significantly to personality traits.
- Personality types group people into categories on the basis of shared traits.
- Behavior is influenced by self-concept and self-esteem.
- Personality theories combine interrelated assumptions, ideas, and principles to explain personality.

Allport made distinctions between common traits and individual traits and among cardinal, central, and secondary traits.

- Trait theories identify lasting and consistent personal characteristics.
- Cattell's theory attributes visible surface traits to the existence of 16 underlying source traits.
- The five-factor model identifies the following five universal dimensions of personality: extroversion, agreeableness, conscientiousness, neuroticism, and openness to experience.
- Traits and situations interact to determine how we behave.

Psychodynamic theories emphasize internal (and often unconscious) forces and mental activities.

- According to Sigmund Freud's psychoanalytic theory, personality consists of three mental systems: the id, the ego, and the superego.
- Libido, derived from the life instincts, is the primary source of energy within the personality.
- Internal conflicts may cause neurotic anxiety or moral anxiety and lead to the use of ego-defense mechanisms.
- Personal awareness operates on three levels: conscious, preconscious, and unconscious.
- According to Freud, personality development occurs in four psychosexual stages: oral, anal, phallic, and genital.
- Fixation at any stage of psychosexual development can leave a lasting imprint on adult personality.
- Neo-Freudian theorists accepted the broad features of Freudian psychology, but developed their own views. Three representative neo-Freudians are Alfred Adler, Karen Horney, and Carl Jung.

Behavioral theories of personality emphasize learning, conditioning, and the situational determinants of behavior.

- Learning theorists John Dollard and Neal Miller consider habits the basic core of personality. Habits express the combined effects of drive, cue, response, and reward.
- To explain personality, social learning theory combines learning with thinking, expectations, and other mental processes.
- Social learning theory is exemplified by Julian Rotter's concepts of the psychological situation, expectancies, and reinforcement value.
- The behavioristic view of personality development holds that social reinforcement in four situations is critical. The critical situations are feeding, toilet or cleanliness training, sex training, and anger or aggression training.
- Identification and imitation are of particular importance in learning to be "male" or "female."

Humanistic theories stress subjective experience, free choice, self-actualization, and positive models of human nature.

- Abraham Maslow's study of self-actualizers showed that they share traits that range from efficient perceptions of reality to frequent peak experiences.
- Carl Rogers's theory views the self as an entity that emerges from personal experience. Experiences that match the self-image are symbolized (admitted to consciousness), whereas those that are incongruent are excluded.
- The incongruent person has a highly unrealistic self-image and/or a mismatch between the self-image and the ideal self. The congruent or fully functioning person is flexible and open to experiences and feelings.
- In the development of personality, humanists are primarily interested in the emergence of a self-image and in self-evaluations.
- As parents apply conditions of worth to children's behavior, thoughts, and feelings, children begin to do the same. Internalized conditions of worth then contribute to incongruence and disrupt the organismic valuing process.

Psychologists use interviews, direct observation, questionnaires, and projective tests to measure and assess personality.

- Structured and unstructured interviews provide much information, but they are subject to interviewer bias, misperceptions, and the halo effect.
- Direct observation, sometimes involving situational tests, behavioral assessment, or rating scales, allows psychologists to evaluate a person's actual behavior.
- Personality questionnaires, such as the *Minnesota Multiphasic Personality Inventory-2* (MMPI-2), are objective and reliable, but their validity is open to question.
- Projective tests ask a person to project thoughts or feelings to an ambiguous stimulus or unstructured situation.
- The *Rorschach Technique,* or inkblot test, is a well-known projective technique. A second is the *Thematic Apperception Test* (TAT).
- Projective tests are low in validity and objectivity. Nevertheless, they are considered useful by many clinicians.

Shyness is related to public self-consciousness and other psychological factors that can be altered, thereby helping some people overcome shyness.

- Shyness typically involves social anxiety, evaluation fears, self-defeating thoughts, public self-consciousness, and a lack of social skills.
- Shyness is marked by heightened public self-consciousness and a tendency to regard one's shyness as a lasting trait.
- Shyness can be reduced by replacing self-defeating beliefs with more supportive thoughts and by learning social skills.

Web Resources

For an up-to-date list of direct links to interesting sites, including those listed here, visit the student companion site for this book at www.cengage.com/psychology/coon

Personality Theories Explore an electronic textbook about personality theories.

Internet Personality Inventory Test yourself on the Big Five.

Psychodynamic and Neo-Freudian Theories Freud's followers did not always agree with his views. Read about their views on personality.

Information on Self-Efficacy Read about Albert Bandura and the idea of self-efficacy.

Maslow's Hierarchy of Needs Read more about Maslow's hierarchy of needs and self-actualization.

MMPI Explore a research project about the MMPI.

The Classical Rorschach Explore Hermann Rorschach and his famous inkblot test.

The Shyness Home Page Try several shyness surveys.

Interactive Learning

Introduction to Psychology: Gateways to Mind and Behavior **Book Companion Website**
www.cengage.com/psychology/coon

Visit your book companion website, where you will find flash cards, practice quizzes, web links, and more to help you study.

CENGAGENOW™ *Just what you need to know NOW!*

Spend time on what you need to master rather than on information you already have learned. Take a pre-test for this chapter, and CengageNOW will generate a personalized study plan based on your results. The study plan will identify the topics you need to review and direct you to online resources to help you master those topics. You can then take a post-test to help you determine the concepts you have mastered and what you will need to work on. Try it out! Go to www.cengage.com/login to sign in with an access code or to purchase access to this product.

CHAPTER 13

Health, Stress, and Coping

Gateway Theme

Health is affected greatly by lifestyle and behavior patterns, especially those related to stress.

Greg Epperson/Photolibrary

Gateway Questions

- *What is health psychology? How does behavior affect health?*
- *What is stress?*
- *What causes frustration, and what are typical reactions to it?*
- *Are there different types of conflict?*

- *What are defense mechanisms?*
- *What do we know about coping with feelings of helplessness and depression?*
- *How is stress related to health and disease?*
- *What are the best strategies for managing stress?*

Somehow, Jennifer had managed to survive the rush of make-or-break term papers, projects, and classroom speeches. Then it was on to the last leg of her race to the end of term: finals. Perfectly timed to inflict as much suffering as possible, her two hardest exams fell on the same day! Great.

On the last day of finals, Jennifer got caught in a traffic jam on her way to school. Two drivers cut her off, and another gave her a one-finger salute. When Jennifer finally got to campus the parking lot was swarming with frantic students. Most of them, like her, were within minutes of missing a final exam. At last, Jennifer spied an empty space. As she started toward it, a Mini Cooper darted around the corner and into "her" place. The driver of the car behind her began to honk impatiently. For a moment, Jennifer was seized by a colossal desire to run over anything in sight.

Finally, after a week and a half of stress, pressure, and frustration, Jennifer had crossed the finish line. Sleep deprivation,

gallons of coffee, junk food, and equal portions of cramming and complaining had carried her through finals. She was off for a summer of rock climbing. At last, she could kick back, relax, and have some fun. Or could she? Just 4 days after the end of school, Jennifer got a bad cold, followed by bronchitis that lasted for nearly a month.

Jennifer's experience illustrates what happens when stress, emotion, personal habits, and health collide. Though the timing of her cold might have been a coincidence, odds are it wasn't. Periods of stress are frequently followed by illness.

In the first part of this chapter we will explore a variety of behavioral health risks. Then we will look more closely at what stress is and how it affects us. After that, we will emphasize ways of coping with stress, so you can do a better job of staying healthy than Jennifer did.

⬤⬤ Health Psychology—Here's to Your Good Health

Gateway Questions: What is health psychology? How does behavior affect health?

Most of us agree that our health is priceless. Yet many diseases and half of all deaths in North America can be traced to our unhealthy behaviors (Mokdad et al., 2004). **Health psychology** aims to use behavioral principles to prevent illness and death and to promote health. Psychologists working in the allied field of **behavioral medicine** apply psychology to manage medical problems, such as diabetes or asthma. Their interests include pain control, helping people cope with chronic illness, stress-related diseases, self-screening for diseases (such as breast cancer), and similar topics (Brannon & Feist, 2007).

Behavioral Risk Factors

A century ago, people primarily died from infectious diseases and accidents. Today, people generally die from **lifestyle diseases,** which are related to health-damaging personal habits (Mokdad et al., 2004). Examples include heart disease, stroke, and lung cancer (⬤ Figure 13.1). Clearly, some lifestyles promote health, whereas others lead to illness and death. As one observer put it, "If you don't take care of yourself, the undertaker will overtake that responsibility for you."

What are some unhealthy behaviors? Some causes of illness are beyond our control, but many behavioral risks can be reduced. **Behavioral risk factors** are actions that increase the chances of disease, injury, or early death. For example, approximately 440,000

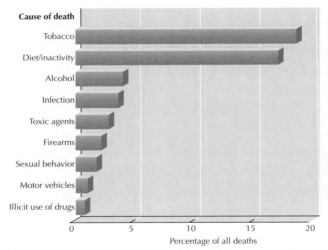

● **Figure 13.1** The nine leading causes of death in the United States are shown in this graph. As you can see, eight of the top nine causes are directly related to behavioral risk factors (infection is the exception). At least 45 percent of all deaths can be traced to unhealthful behavior. The percentage of day-to-day health problems related to unhealthful behavior is even higher. (Data from Mokdad et al., 2004)

people die every year from smoking-related diseases (CDC, 2005). Similarly, being overweight *doubles* the chance of dying from cancer or heart disease. Roughly 65 percent of all American adults are overweight (CDC, 2003). As a result, obesity may soon overtake smoking as the main cause of preventable deaths. Being fat is not just a matter of fashion—in the long run it could kill you. A person who is overweight at age 20 can expect to lose 5 to 20 years of life expectancy (Fontaine et al., 2003).

Each of the following factors is a major behavioral risk (Baum & Posluszny, 1999): high levels of stress, untreated high blood pressure, cigarette smoking, abuse of alcohol or other drugs, overeating, inadequate exercise, unsafe sexual behavior, exposure to toxic substances, violence, excess sun exposure, reckless driving, and disregarding personal safety (avoidable accidents). Seventy percent of all medical costs are related to just six of the listed factors—smoking, alcohol and drug abuse, poor diet, insufficient exercise, and risky sexual practices (Orleans, Gruman, & Hollendonner, 1999).

The personal habits you have by the time you are 18 or 19 greatly affect your health, happiness, and life expectancy years later (Gurung, 2006; Vaillant & Mukamal, 2001). ● Table 13.1 shows how many American high school students engage in various kinds of risky behaviors.

Specific risk factors are not the only concern. Some people have a general **disease-prone personality** that leaves them depressed, anxious, hostile, and . . . frequently ill. In contrast, people who are intellectually resourceful, compassionate, optimistic, and non-hostile tend to enjoy good health (Taylor, 2006; Taylor et al., 2000). Depression, in particular, is likely to damage health (Allgower, Wardle, & Steptoe, 2001; Luppa et al., 2007). People who are depressed eat poorly, sleep poorly, rarely exercise, fail to use seat belts in cars, smoke more, and so on.

Lifestyle

In your mind's eye, fast-forward an imaginary film of your life all the way to old age. Do it twice—once with a lifestyle including a large number of behavioral risk factors, and again without them. It should be obvious that many small risks can add up, dramatically raising the chance of illness. If stress is a frequent part of your life, visualize your body seething with emotion, day after day. If you smoke, picture a lifetime's worth of cigarette smoke blown through your lungs in a week. If you drink, take a lifetime of alcohol's assaults on the brain, stomach, and liver and squeeze them into a month: Your body would be poisoned, ravaged, and soon dead. If

In the long run, behavioral risk factors and lifestyles do make a difference in health and life expectancy.

you eat a high-fat, high-cholesterol diet, fast-forward a lifetime of heart-killing plaque clogging your arteries.

We don't mean to sermonize. We just want to remind you that risk factors make a difference. To make matters worse, unhealthy lifestyles almost always create multiple risks. That is, people who smoke are also likely to drink excessively. Those who overeat usually do not get enough exercise, and so on (Straub, 2006). Even infectious diseases are often linked to behavioral risks. For example, pneumonia and other infections occur at higher rates in people who have cancer, heart disease, lung disease, or liver disease. Thus, many deaths attributed to infections can actually be traced to smoking, poor diet, or alcohol abuse (Mokdad et al., 2004).

Health-Promoting Behaviors

To prevent disease, health psychologists first try to remove behavioral risk factors. All the medicine in the world may not be enough to restore health without changes in behavior. We all know someone who has had a heart attack or lung disease who couldn't change the habits that led to his or her illness.

Table 13.1 ● Percentage of U.S. High School Students Who Engaged in Health-Endangering Behaviors

Risky Behavior	Percentage
Rode with drinking driver	30
Were in a physical fight	33
Carried a weapon	17
Drank alcohol	45
Used marijuana	22
Engaged in sexual intercourse	47
Did not use condom during last sexual intercourse	37
Smoked cigarettes	22
Did not eat enough fruits and vegetables	78
Did not get enough physical exercise	33

Source: Grunbaum et al., 2004.

Health psychology Study of the ways in which behavioral principles can be used to prevent illness and promote health.

Behavioral medicine The study of behavioral factors in medicine, physical illness, and medical treatment.

Lifestyle disease A disease related to health-damaging personal habits.

Behavioral risk factors Behaviors that increase the chances of disease, injury, or premature death.

Disease-prone personality A personality type associated with poor health; marked by persistent negative emotions, including anxiety, depression, and hostility.

RODNEY KICKED OFF HIS NEW FITNESS REGIME BY BUYING A HEAVIER REMOTE CONTROL ...THIS WAS NOT ENOUGH!

© Fran/www.CartoonStock.

Table 13.2 ● Major Health-Promoting Behaviors

	Source	Desirable Behaviors
	Nutrition	Eating a balanced, low-fat diet; appropriate caloric intake; maintenance of healthy body weight
	Exercise	At least 30 minutes of aerobic exercise, 5 days per week
	Blood pressure	Lower blood pressure with diet and exercise, or medicine if necessary
	Alcohol and drugs	No more than two drinks per day; abstain from using drugs
	Tobacco	Do not smoke; do not use smokeless tobacco
	Sleep and relaxation	Avoid sleep deprivation; provide for periods of relaxation every day
	Sex	Practice safer sex; avoid unplanned pregnancy
	Injury	Curb dangerous driving habits, use seat belts; minimize sun exposure; forgo dangerous activities
	Stress	Learn stress management; lower hostility

In some cases, lifestyle diseases can be treated or prevented by making specific, minor changes in behavior. For example, hypertension (high blood pressure) can be deadly. Yet, consuming less sodium (salt) can help fend off this "silent killer." (Losing weight, using alcohol sparingly, and getting more exercise will also help [Georgiades et al., 2000].)

In addition to removing specific risk factors, psychologists are interested in getting people to increase behaviors that promote health. Health-promoting behaviors include such obvious practices as getting regular exercise, controlling smoking and alcohol use, maintaining a balanced diet, getting good medical care, and managing stress (Zarcadoolas, Pleasant, & Greer, 2006). In one study, the risk of dying was cut by 65 percent during a 10-year period for adults who were careful about diet, alcohol, exercise, and smoking (Knoops et al., 2004).

Health-promoting behaviors don't have to be restrictive or burdensome. For instance, maintaining a healthy diet doesn't mean surviving on tofu and wheatgrass. The healthiest people in the study just described ate a tasty "Mediterranean diet" high in fruit, vegetables, and fish and low in red meat and dairy products. Like-

wise, you don't need to exercise like an Olympic athlete to benefit from physical activity. All you need is 30 minutes of exercise (the equivalent of a brisk walk) three or four times a week. Almost everyone can fit such "lifestyle physical activity" into his or her schedule (Pescatello, 2001).

What about alcohol? Moderation in drinking doesn't mean that you must be a teetotaler. Consuming one or two alcoholic drinks per day is generally safe for most people, especially if you remain alcohol free 2 or 3 days a week. A glass of red wine daily may even be healthy (Anekonda, 2006). However, having three or more drinks a day greatly increases the risk of stroke, cirrhosis of the liver, cancer, high blood pressure, heart disorders, and other diseases (Knoops et al., 2004).

To summarize, a small number of behavioral patterns accounts for many common health problems (Grunbaum et al., 2004). ● Table 13.2 lists several major ways to promote good health. (To explore an interesting social factor underlying common health problems see "Unhealthy Birds of a Feather.")

DISCOVERING PSYCHOLOGY

Unhealthy Birds of a Feather

Would you like to eat better or exercise more, or would you like to quit smoking? Researchers Nicholas Christakis and James Fowler believe they know why it can be difficult to alter unhealthy behaviors. Often, social factors are a barrier to change. If you are a smoker, do your friends also smoke? Are your family members fast-food junkies just like you? Unhealthy behaviors such as overeating or smoking seem to spread almost like a "mental virus."

One study of social contagion found that people were 57 percent more likely to become obese if they had a friend who became fat first (Christakis & Fowler, 2007). Another study noted that smokers tend to "hang out" with other smokers (Christakis & Fowler, 2008). Apparently, we tend to flock together with like-minded people and adopt many of their habits.

Does that mean I am doomed to be unhealthy if my family and friends have unhealthy habits? Not necessarily. Social networks can also spread healthful behaviors. If one smoker in a group of smokers quits, others are more likely to follow suit. If your spouse quits smoking, you are 67 percent more likely to quit. If a good friend quits smoking, your chances of abandoning tobacco go up by 36 percent (Christakis & Fowler, 2008). The growing social unpopularity of smoking may explain why American adults who still smoke (now only 19 percent) are becoming an endangered species (Schroeder, 2008).

The implication? Don't wait for your friends or family to adopt healthier habits. Take the lead and get them to join you. Failing that, start hanging out with a healthier crowd. You might catch something healthy.

Early Prevention

Of the behavioral risks we have discussed, smoking is the largest preventable cause of death and the single most lethal factor (Mokdad et al., 2004). As such, it illustrates the prospect for preventing illness.

What have health psychologists done to lessen the risks of smoking? Attempts to "immunize" youths against pressures to start smoking are a good example. When humorist Mark Twain said, "Giving up smoking is the easiest thing in the world. I know because I've done it thousands of times," he stated a basic truth—only 1 smoker in 10 has long-term success at quitting. Thus, the best way to deal with smoking is to prevent it before it becomes a lifelong habit. For example, prevention programs in schools discourage smoking with quizzes about smoking, antismoking art contests, poster and T-shirt giveaways, antismoking pamphlets for parents, and questions for students to ask their parents (Zarcadoolas, Pleasant, & Greer, 2006). Such efforts are designed to persuade kids that smoking is dangerous and "uncool." Apparently, many teens are getting the message, as attitudes toward smoking are now more negative than they were 20 years ago (Chassin et al., 2003).

Some antismoking programs include **refusal skills training.** In this case, youths learn to resist pressures to begin smoking (or using other drugs). For example, junior high students can role-play ways to resist smoking pressures from peers, adults, and cigarette ads. Similar methods can be applied to other health risks, such as sexually transmitted diseases and teen pregnancy (Wandersman & Florin, 2003).

Many health programs also teach students general life skills. The idea is to give kids skills that will help them cope with day-to-day stresses. That way, they will be less tempted to escape problems through drug use or other destructive behaviors. **Life skills training** includes practice in stress reduction, self-protection, decision making, goal setting, self-control, and social skills (Tobler et al., 2000).

Reuters/Corbis

Celebrities can also help persuade young people to not start smoking in the first place.

Refusal skills training Program that teaches youths how to resist pressures to begin smoking. (Can also be applied to other drugs and health risks.)

Life skills training A program that teaches stress reduction, self-protection, decision making, self-control, and social skills.

Community Health

In addition to early prevention, health psychologists have had some success with **community health campaigns.** These are community-wide education projects designed to lessen major risk factors. Health campaigns inform people of risks such as stress, alcohol abuse, high blood pressure, high cholesterol, smoking, sexually transmitted diseases, or excessive sun exposure. This is followed by efforts to motivate people to change their behavior. Campaigns sometimes provide *role models* (positive examples) who show people how to improve their own health. They also direct people to services for health screening, advice, and treatment. Health campaigns may reach people through the mass media, public schools, health fairs, worksites, or self-help programs. Such programs are increasingly successful in helping people make healthful changes in their behavior (Orleans, 2000).

Positive Psychology: Wellness

Health is not just an absence of disease (Allen, Carlson, & Ham, 2007). People who are truly healthy enjoy a positive state of **wellness** or well-being. Maintaining wellness is a lifelong pursuit and, hopefully, a labor of love. People who attain optimal wellness are both physically and psychologically healthy. They are happy, optimistic, self-confident individuals who can bounce back emotionally from adversity (Tugade, Fredrickson, & Barrett, 2004).

People who enjoy a sense of well-being also have supportive relationships with others, they do meaningful work, and they live in a clean environment. Many of these aspects of wellness are addressed elsewhere in this book. In this chapter we will give special attention to the effect that stress has on health and sickness. Understanding stress and learning to control it can improve not only your health, but the quality of your life as well (Suinn, 2001). For these reasons, a discussion of stress and stress management follows.

KNOWLEDGE BUILDER
Health Psychology

RECITE

1. Adjustment to chronic illness and the control of pain are topics that would more likely be of interest to a specialist in

   _____

   rather than to a health psychologist.
2. With respect to health, which of the following is *not* a major behavioral risk factor?
   a. over-exercise
   b. cigarette smoking
   c. stress
   d. high blood pressure
3. Lifestyle diseases related to just six behaviors account for 70 percent of all medical costs. The behaviors are smoking, alcohol and drug abuse, poor diet, insufficient exercise, and
   a. driving too fast
   b. excessive sun exposure
   c. unsafe sex
   d. exposure to toxins

4. Health promoting behaviors that combat hypertension include the following: lose weight, consume less sodium, use alcohol sparingly, and get more
   a. sleep
   b. exercise
   c. carbohydrates
   d. cholesterol
5. Health psychologists tend to prefer _____ rather than modifying habits (like smoking) that become difficult to break once they are established.
6. The disease-prone personality is marked by _____, anxiety, and hostility.

REFLECT

Critical Thinking

7. The general public is increasingly well informed about health risks and healthful behavior. Can you apply the concept of reinforcement to explain why so many people fail to act on this information?

Relate

If you were to work as a health psychologist, would you be more interested in preventing disease or managing it?

Make a list of the major behavioral risk factors that apply to you. Are you laying the foundation for a lifestyle disease?

Which of the health-promoting behaviors listed in ● Table 13.2 would you like to increase?

If you were designing a community health campaign, who would you use as role models of healthful behavior?

Answers: 1. behavioral medicine **2.** a **3.** c **4.** b **5.** prevention **6.** depression **7.** Many of the health payoffs are delayed by months or years, greatly lessening the immediate rewards for healthful behavior.

● Stress—Thrill or Threat?

Gateway Question: What is stress?

Stress can be can be a major behavioral risk factor if it is prolonged or severe, but it isn't always bad. As Canadian stress research pioneer Hans Selye (SEL-yay) (1976) observed, "To be totally without stress is to be dead." That's because **stress** is the mental and physical condition that occurs when we adjust or adapt to the environment. Unpleasant events such as work pressures, marital problems, or financial woes naturally produce stress. But so do travel, sports, a new job, rock climbing, dating, and other positive activities. Even if you aren't a thrill seeker, a healthy lifestyle may include a fair amount of *eustress* (good stress). Activities that provoke "good stress" are usually challenging, rewarding, and energizing.

It might seem that stressful events "happen to" people. Although this is sometimes the case, more often stress is a matter of how we perceive events and react to them. Because of this, stress can often be managed or controlled. Let's explore how stress occurs and typical reactions to it.

A **stress reaction** begins with the same autonomic nervous system arousal that occurs during emotion. Imagine you are standing at the top of a wind-whipped ski jump for the first time. Internally, you would experience a rapid surge in your heart rate, blood pressure, respiration, muscle tension, and other ANS responses. *Short-term* stresses of this kind can be uncomfortable, but they rarely do any damage. (Your landing might, however.) *Long-term* stresses are another matter entirely (Sternberg, 2000).

General Adaptation Syndrome

The impact of long-term stresses can be understood by examining the body's defenses against stress, a pattern known as the general adaptation syndrome.

The **general adaptation syndrome (GAS)** is a series of bodily reactions to prolonged stress. Selye (1976) noticed that the first symptoms of almost any disease or trauma (poisoning, infection, injury, or stress) are almost identical. The body responds in the same way to any stress, be it infection, failure, embarrassment, a new job, trouble at school, or a stormy romance.

How does the body respond to stress? The GAS consists of three stages: an alarm reaction, a stage of resistance, and a stage of exhaustion (● Figure 13.2) (Selye, 1976).

In the **alarm reaction,** your body mobilizes its resources to cope with added stress. The pituitary gland signals the adrenal glands to produce more adrenaline, noradrenaline, and cortisol. As these stress hormones are dumped into the bloodstream, some bodily processes are speeded up and others are slowed. This allows bodily resources to be applied where they are needed (Lyons & Chamberlain, 2006).

We should all be thankful that our bodies automatically respond to emergencies. But brilliant as this emergency system is, it can also cause problems. In the first phase of the alarm reaction, people have such symptoms as headache, fever, fatigue, sore muscles, shortness of breath, diarrhea, upset stomach, loss of appetite, and a lack of energy. Notice that these are also the symptoms of being sick, of stressful travel, of high-altitude sickness, of final exams week, and (possibly) of falling in love!

During the **stage of resistance,** bodily adjustments to stress stabilize. As the body's defenses come into balance, symptoms of the alarm reaction disappear. Outwardly, everything seems normal. However, this appearance of normality comes at a high cost. The body is better able to cope with the original stressor, but its resistance to other stresses is lowered. For example, animals placed

in extreme cold become more resistant to the cold but more susceptible to infection. It is during the stage of resistance that the first signs of psychosomatic disorders (physical disorders triggered by psychological factors) begin to appear.

Continued stress leads to the **stage of exhaustion,** in which the body's resources are drained and stress hormones are depleted. Some of the typical signs or symptoms of impending exhaustion include the following (Friedman, 2002):

Emotional signs: Anxiety, apathy, irritability, mental fatigue
Behavioral signs: Avoidance of responsibilities and relationships, extreme or self-destructive behavior, self-neglect, poor judgment
Physical signs: Excessive worry about illness, frequent illness, exhaustion, overuse of medicines, physical ailments and complaints

The GAS may sound melodramatic if you are young and healthy or if you've never endured prolonged stress. However, you should not take stress lightly. Unless a way of relieving stress is found, the result will be a psychosomatic disease, a serious loss of health, or complete collapse. When Selye examined animals in the later stages of the GAS, he found that their adrenal glands were enlarged and discolored. There was intense shrinkage of internal organs, such as the thymus, spleen, and lymph nodes, and many animals had stomach ulcers. In addition to such direct effects, stress can disrupt the body's immune system, as described next.

Stress, Illness, and Your Immune System

How can prolonged stress result in a physical illness? An answer can be found in your body's *immune system,* which mobilizes defenses (such as white blood cells) against invading microbes and other disease agents. The immune system is regulated, in part, by the brain. Because of this link, stress and upsetting emotions can affect

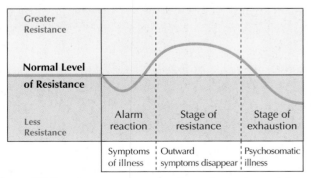

● **Figure 13.2** The General Adaptation Syndrome. During the initial alarm reaction to stress, resistance falls below normal. It rises again as bodily resources are mobilized, and it remains high during the stage of resistance. Eventually, resistance falls again as the stage of exhaustion is reached. (From *The Stress of Life* by Hans Selye. Copyright © 1978 by Hans Selye. Used by permission of McGraw-Hill Book Company.)

Community health campaign A community-wide education program that provides information about how to lessen risk factors and promote health.

Wellness A positive state of good health; more than the absence of disease.

Stress The mental and physical condition that occurs when a person must adjust or adapt to the environment.

Stress reaction The physical response to stress, consisting mainly of bodily changes related to autonomic nervous system arousal.

General adaptation syndrome (GAS) A series of bodily reactions to prolonged stress; occurs in three stages: alarm, resistance, and exhaustion.

Alarm reaction First stage of the GAS, during which bodily resources are mobilized to cope with a stressor.

Stage of resistance Second stage of the GAS, during which bodily adjustments to stress stabilize, but at a high physical cost.

Stage of exhaustion Third stage of the GAS, at which time the body's resources are exhausted and serious health consequences occur.

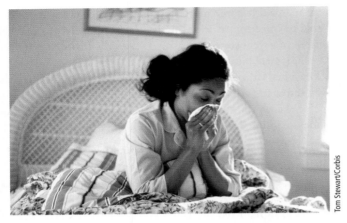

Stress and negative emotions lower immune system activity and increase inflammation. This, in turn, raises our vulnerability to infection, worsens illness, and delays recovery.

the immune system in ways that increase susceptibility to disease (Miller, Cohen, & Ritchey, 2002). By the way, the study of links among behavior, stress, disease, and the immune system is called **psychoneuroimmunology** (Daruna, 2004). (Try dropping that into a conversation sometime if you want to see a stress reaction!)

Studies show that the immune system is weakened in students during major exam times, as Jennifer found out during her mad dash to the end of term. Immunity is also lowered by divorce, bereavement, a troubled marriage, job loss, poor sleep, depression, and similar stresses (Deinzer et al., 2000; Motivala & Irwin, 2007; Segerstrom & Miller, 2004). Lowered immunity explains why the "double whammy" of getting sick when you are trying to cope with prolonged or severe stress is so common (Lyons & Chamberlain, 2006). Stress causes the body to release substances that increase inflammation. This is part of the body's self-protective response to threats, but it can prolong infections and delay healing (Kiecolt-Glaser et al., 2002; Wargo, 2007). It's also worth noting again the value of positive emotions. Happiness, laughter, and delight tend to strengthen immune system response. Doing things that make you happy can also protect your health (Rosenkranz et al., 2003).

Could reducing stress help prevent illness? Yes. Various psychological approaches, such as support groups, relaxation exercises, guided imagery, and stress management training, can actually boost immune system functioning (Dougall & Baum, 2003). By doing so, they help promote and restore health. For example, stress management reduced the severity of cold and flu symptoms in a group of university students (Reid, Mackinnon, & Drummond, 2001).

There is even evidence that stress management can improve the chances of survival in people with life-threatening diseases, such as cancer, heart disease, and human immunodeficiency virus/acquired immunodeficiency syndrome (HIV/AIDS) (Schneiderman et al., 2001). With some successes to encourage them, psychologists are now searching for the best combination of treatments to help people resist disease (Miller & Cohen, 2001).

When Is Stress a Strain?

It goes almost without saying that some events are more likely to cause stress than others. A **stressor** is a condition or event that challenges or threatens a person. Police officers, for instance, suffer from a high rate of stress-related diseases. The threat of injury or death, plus occasional confrontations with angry, drunk, or hostile citizens, takes a toll. A major factor is the *unpredictable* nature of police work. An officer who stops a car to issue a traffic ticket never knows if a cooperative citizen or an armed gang member is waiting inside.

A revealing study shows how unpredictability adds to stress. In a series of 1-minute trials, college students breathed air through a mask. In some trials, the air contained 20 percent more carbon dioxide (CO_2) than normal. If you were to inhale this air, you would feel anxious, stressed, and a little like you were suffocating. Students tested this way hated the "surprise" doses of CO_2. They found it much less stressful to be told in advance which trials would include a choking whiff of CO_2 (Lejuez et al., 2000).

Pressure is another element of stress, especially job stress. **Pressure** occurs when a person must meet *urgent* external demands or expectations (Weiten, 1998). For example, we feel pressured when activities must be speeded up, when deadlines must be met, when extra work is added, or when we must work near maximum capacity for long periods. Most students who have survived final exams are familiar with the effects of pressure.

What if I set deadlines for myself? Does it make a difference where the pressure comes from? Yes. People generally feel more stress in situations over which they have little or no control (Taris et al., 2005). In one study, nurses with a high sense of control (e.g., over the pacing of work and the physical arrangement of the working environment) were less likely to get sick, both physically and men-

Air traffic control is stressful work. Employees must pay intense attention for long periods, they have little control over the pace of work, and the consequences of making a mistake can be dire.

THE CLINICAL FILE

Burnout—The High Cost of Caring

Margo, a young nurse, realizes with dismay that she has "lost all patience with her patients" and wishes they would "go somewhere else to be sick." Margo's feelings are a clear sign of job **burnout,** a condition in which workers are physically, mentally, and emotionally drained (Greenglass, Burke, & Moore, 2003). Burnout has three aspects (Maslach, Schaufeli, & Leiter, 2001):

- **Emotional exhaustion:** Affected persons are fatigued, tense, apathetic, and suffer from physical ailments. They feel "used up" and "empty."
- **Cynicism or detachment:** Burned-out workers have an "I don't give a damn anymore" attitude and they treat clients coldly, as if they were objects.
- **Feelings of reduced personal accomplishment:** Burned-out workers do poor work and feel helpless, hopeless, or angry.

Burnout may occur in any job, but it is a special problem in emotionally demanding helping professions, such as nursing, teaching, social work, child care, counseling, or police work. Often, the most idealistic and caring workers are the ones who burn out. As some say, "You have to be on fire to burn out" (Maslach, Schaufeli, & Leiter, 2001).

If we wish to keep caring people in the helping professions, it may be necessary to adjust workloads, rewards, and the amount of control people have in their jobs (Leiter & Maslach, 2005). In general, social support helps people from many cultures resist burnout (Pines et al., 2002). For example, support groups at work help caregivers deal with stress by allowing them to talk about their feelings and problems at work (Greenglass, Burke, & Konarski, 1998).

Can college students experience burnout? Yes, they can. If you have a negative attitude toward your studies and feel that your col-

lege workload is too heavy, you may be vulnerable to burnout (Jacobs & Dodd, 2003). On the other hand, if you have a positive attitude toward your studies, participate in extracurricular activities, and enjoy good social support from your friends, rock on!

The helping professions require empathy, caring, and emotional involvement. As a result, caregivers risk depleting their emotional resources and ability to cope. Over time, this can lead to burnout.

---

tally, than were nurses with a low sense of control (Ganster, Fox, & Dwyer, 2001).

To summarize, when emotional "shocks" are *intense* or *repeated, unpredictable, uncontrollable,* and linked to *pressure,* stress will be magnified and damage is more likely to result. At work, people face many of these sources of stress every day (See ● Table 13.3 for a list of the most common sources of stress at work.) In fact, chronic job stress sometimes results in *burnout,* a pattern of emotional exhaustion. (See "Burnout—The High Cost of Caring.")

Table 13.3 ● The Top 10 Work Stresses

Work Stress	Rank
Workload	1
Feeling undervalued	2
Deadlines	3
Type of work people have to do	4
Having to take on other people's work	5
Lack of job satisfaction	6
Lack of control over the working day	7
Having to work long hours	8
Frustration with the working environment	9
Performance targets	10

Source: Data from Skillsoft, 2006.

Appraising Stressors

Our reactions to stressful events are greatly affected by how we appraise situations. That's why some people are distressed by events that others view as a thrill or a challenge (eustress). Ultimately, stress depends on how you perceive a situation. Our friend Akihito would find it stressful to listen to five of his son's hip-hop CDs in a row. His son Takashi would find it stressful to listen to *one* of his father's opera CDs. To know if you are stressed, we must know what meaning you place on events. As we will see in a moment, whenever a stressor is appraised as a *threat* (potentially harmful), a powerful stress reaction follows (Folkman & Moskowitz, 2004; Lazarus, 1991a).

bridges

See Chapter 10, page 350, for a discussion of how appraisal influences emotions.

Psychoneuroimmunology Study of the links among behavior, stress, disease, and the immune system.

Stressor A specific condition or event in the environment that challenges or threatens a person.

Pressure A stressful condition that occurs when a person must meet urgent external demands or expectations.

Burnout A job-related condition of mental, physical, and emotional exhaustion.

"Am I Okay or in Trouble?"

You have been selected to give a speech to 300 people. Or a doctor tells you that you must undergo a dangerous and painful operation. Or the one true love of your life walks out the door. What would your emotional response to these events be? How do you cope with a threat?

According to Richard Lazarus (1991a), there are two important steps in managing a threat. The first is a **primary appraisal,** in which you decide if a situation is relevant or irrelevant, positive or threatening. In essence, this step answers the question, "Am I okay or in trouble?" Then you make a **secondary appraisal,** in which you assess your resources and choose a way to meet the threat or challenge. ("What can I do about this situation?") Thus, the way a situation is "sized up" greatly affects our ability to cope with it (● Figure 13.3). Public speaking, for instance, can be appraised as an intense threat or as a chance to perform. Emphasizing the threat—by imagining failure, rejection, or embarrassment— obviously invites disaster (Strongman, 2003).

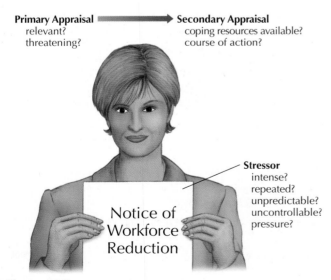

Primary Appraisal → Secondary Appraisal
relevant?   coping resources available?
threatening?   course of action?

Stressor
intense?
repeated?
unpredictable?
uncontrollable?
pressure?

Notice of Workforce Reduction

● **Figure 13.3** Stress is the product of an interchange between a person and the environment.

The Nature of Threat

What does it mean to feel threatened by a stressor? Certainly in most day-to-day situations it doesn't mean you think your life is in danger. (Unless, of course, you owe money to "Eddie the Enforcer.") Threat has more to do with the idea of control. We are particularly prone to feel stressed when we can't—or think we can't—control our immediate environment. In short, a *perceived* lack of control is just as threatening as an actual lack of control. For example, college students who feel overloaded experience stress even though their workload may not actually be heavier than that of their classmates (Jacobs & Dodd, 2003).

A sense of control also comes from believing you can reach desired goals. It is threatening to feel that we lack *competence* to cope with life's demands (Bandura, 2001). Because of this, the intensity of your body's stress reaction often depends on what you think and tell yourself about a stressor. That's why it's valuable to learn to think in ways that ward off the body's stress response. (Some strategies for controlling upsetting thoughts are described in the Psychology in Action section of this chapter.)

Coping with Threat

You have appraised a situation as threatening. What will you do next? You have two major choices. Both involve thinking and acting in ways that help us handle stressors. In **emotion-focused coping,** we try to control our emotional reactions to the situation. For example, a distressed person may distract herself by listening to music, taking a walk to relax, or seeking emotional support from others. In contrast, **problem-focused coping** is aimed at managing or correcting the distressing situation itself. Some examples are making a plan of action or concentrating on your next step (Folkman & Moskowitz, 2004).

Couldn't both types of coping occur together? Yes. Sometimes the two types of coping aid one another. For instance, quieting your emotions may make it easier for you to find a way to solve a problem. Say, for example, that a woman feels anxious as she steps to the podium to give a speech. If she does some deep breathing to reduce her anxiety (emotion-focused coping), she will be better able to glance over her notes to improve her delivery (problem-focused coping).

It is also possible for coping efforts to clash. For instance, if you have to make a difficult decision, you may suffer intense emotional distress. In such circumstances there is a temptation to make a quick, ill-advised choice, just to end the suffering. Doing so may allow you to cope with your emotions, but it shortchanges problem-focused coping.

In general, problem-focused coping tends to be especially useful when you are facing a controllable stressor—that is, a situation you can actually do something about. Emotion-focused efforts are best suited to managing your reaction to stressors you cannot control (Folkman & Moskowitz, 2004). To improve your chances of coping effectively, the stress-fighting strategies described in this chapter include a mixture of both techniques.

THE CLINICAL FILE

Coping with Traumatic Stress

Traumatic experiences produce psychological injury or intense emotional pain. Victims of **traumatic stresses,** such as war, torture, rape, assassination, plane crashes, natural disasters, or street violence, may suffer from nightmares, flashbacks, insomnia, irritability, nervousness, grief, emotional numbing, and depression. There is little doubt that the 2008 earthquake in Sichuan, China, caused these effects for those people living or working in the quake zone. Like most traumatic stresses, the impact was, and continues to be, overwhelming.

People who personally witness or survive a disaster are most affected by traumatic stress.

With a death toll of more than 60,000 victims, there can be little doubt that the 2008 earthquake in China was a traumatically stressful event. Even people who merely witnessed the aftermath of the disaster on television may suffer from stress symptoms.

Lui Jin/AFP/Getty Images

Twenty percent of the people who lived close to the World Trade Center in New York City suffered serious stress disorders after the 9/11 terrorist attack (Galea et al., 2002). Yet even those who experience horror at a distance may be traumatized (Galea & Resnick, 2005). Forty-four percent of U.S. adults who only saw the 9/11 attacks on television had at least some stress symptoms (Schuster et al., 2001). For example, Americans faced elevated risks of hypertension and heart problems for three years after 9/11 (Holman et al., 2008). Indirect exposure to such terrorist attacks, coupled with the ongoing risk of more attacks, has ensured that many people will suffer ongoing stress into the foreseeable future (Marshall et al., 2007).

Traumatic stress produces feelings of helplessness and vulnerability (Fields & Margolin, 2001). Victims realize that disaster could strike again without warning. In addition to feeling threatened, many victims sense that they are losing control of their lives (Scurfield, 2002).

What can people do about such reactions? Psychologists recommend the following:

- Identify what you are feeling and talk to others about your fears and concerns.
- Think about the skills that have helped you overcome adversity in the past and apply them to the present situation.
- Continue to do the things that you enjoy and that make life meaningful (LeDoux & Gorman, 2001).
- Get support from others. This is a major element in recovery from all traumatic events.
- Give yourself time to heal. Fortunately, most people are more resilient than they think.

When traumatic stresses are severe or repeated, some people have even more serious symptoms. They suffer from crippling anxiety or become emotionally numb. Typically, they can't stop thinking about the disturbing event, they anxiously avoid anything associated with the event, and they are constantly fearful or nervous. (These are the symptoms of *stress disorders,* which are discussed in Chapter 14, page 483.) Such reactions can leave victims emotionally handicapped for months or years after a disaster. The consequences can last a lifetime for children who are the victims of trauma (Gillespie & Nemeroff, 2007). If you feel that you are having trouble coping with a severe emotional shock, consider seeking help from a psychologist or other professional (Bisson et al., 2007).

So far, our discussion has focused on everyday stresses. How do people react to the extreme stresses imposed by war, violence, or disaster? "Coping with Traumatic Stress" discusses this important topic.

Frustration—Blind Alleys and Lead Balloons

Gateway Question: What causes frustration, and what are typical reactions to it?

Do you remember how frustrated Jennifer was when she couldn't find a parking place? **Frustration** is a negative emotional state that occurs when people are prevented from reaching desired goals. In Jennifer's case, the goal of finding a parking space was blocked by another car.

Obstacles of many kinds cause frustration. A useful distinction can be made between external and personal sources of frustration.

External frustration is based on conditions outside a person that impede progress toward a goal. All the following are external frustrations: getting stuck with a flat tire; having a marriage proposal rejected; finding the cupboard bare when you go to get your poor

---

Primary appraisal Deciding if a situation is relevant to oneself and if it is a threat.

Secondary appraisal Deciding how to cope with a threat or challenge.

Emotion-focused coping Managing or controlling one's emotional reaction to a stressful or threatening situation.

Problem-focused coping Directly managing or remedying a stressful or threatening situation.

Traumatic stresses Extreme events that cause psychological injury or intense emotional pain.

Frustration A negative emotional state that occurs when one is prevented from reaching a goal.

dog a bone; finding the refrigerator bare when you go to get your poor tummy a T-bone; finding the refrigerator gone when you return home; being chased out of the house by your starving dog. In other words, external frustrations are based on *delays, failure, rejection, loss,* and other direct blocking of motivated behavior.

Notice that external obstacles can be either *social* (slow drivers, tall people in theaters, people who cut into lines) or *nonsocial* (stuck doors, a dead battery, rain on the day of the game). If you ask your friends what has frustrated them recently, most will probably mention someone's behavior ("My sister wore one of my dresses when I wanted to wear it," "My supervisor is unfair," "My history teacher grades too hard"). As social animals, we humans are highly sensitive to social sources of frustration (Taylor, 2006). That's probably why unfair treatment associated with racial or ethnic prejudice is a major source of frustration and stress in the lives of many African Americans and other minority group members (Clark et al., 1999; Gurung, 2006).

Frustration usually increases as the *strength, urgency,* or *importance* of a blocked motive increases. Jennifer was especially frustrated in the parking lot because she was late for an exam. Likewise, an escape artist submerged in a tank of water and bound with 200 pounds of chain would become *quite* frustrated if a trick lock jammed. Remember, too, that motivation becomes stronger as we near a goal. As a result, frustration is more intense when a person runs into an obstacle very close to a goal. If you've ever missed an A grade by 5 points, you were probably very frustrated. If you've missed an A by 1 point—well, frustration builds character, right?

A final factor affecting frustration is summarized by the old phrase "the straw that broke the camel's back." The effects of *repeated* frustrations can accumulate until a small irritation sets off an unexpectedly violent response. A case in point is the fact that people with long daily commutes are more likely to display "road rage" (angry, aggressive driving) (Harding et al., 1998).

Personal frustrations are based on personal characteristics. If you are 4 feet tall and aspire to be a professional basketball player, you very likely will be frustrated. If you want to go to medical school but can earn only D grades, you will likewise be frustrated. In both examples, frustration is actually based on personal limitations. Yet failure may be *perceived* as externally caused. We will return to this point in a discussion of stress management. In the meantime, let's look at some typical reactions to frustration.

Reactions to Frustration

Aggression is any response made with the intent of harming a person or an object. It is one of the most persistent and frequent responses to frustration (Anderson & Bushman, 2002). The frustration–aggression link is so common, in fact, that experiments are hardly necessary to show it. A glance at almost any newspaper will provide examples like the one that follows.

Justifiable Autocide

Burien, Washington (AP)—Barbara Smith committed the assault, but police aren't likely to press charges. Her victim was an old Oldsmobile, which failed once too often to start.

When Officer Jim Fuda arrived at the scene, he found one beat-up car, a broken baseball bat and a satisfied 23-year-old Seattle woman.

"I feel good," Ms. Smith reportedly told the officer. "That car's been giving me misery for years and I killed it."

Does frustration always cause aggression? Aren't there other reactions? Although the connection is strong, frustration does not always incite aggression. More often, frustration is met first with *persistence,* often in the form of more vigorous efforts and varied responses (● Figure 13.4). For example, if you put your last quarter in a vending machine and pressing the button has no effect, you will probably press harder and faster (vigorous effort). Then you will press all the other buttons (varied response). Persistence may help you reach your goal by getting *around* a barrier. However, if the machine *still* refuses to deliver, or return your quarter, you may become aggressive and kick the machine (or at least tell it what you think of it).

Persistence can be very adaptive. Overcoming a barrier ends the frustration and allows the need or motive to be satisfied. The same is true of aggression that removes or destroys a barrier. Picture a small band of nomadic humans, parched by thirst but separated from a water hole by a menacing animal. It is easy to see that attacking the animal may ensure their survival. In modern society such direct aggression is seldom acceptable. If you find a long line at the drinking fountain, aggression is hardly appropriate. Because direct aggression is discouraged, it is frequently *displaced.*

How is aggression displaced? Directing aggression toward a source of frustration may be impossible, or it may be too dangerous. If you are frustrated by your boss at work or by a teacher at school, the cost of direct aggression may be too high (losing your job or failing

● **Figure 13.4** Frustration and common reactions to it.

a class). Instead, the aggression may be displaced, or redirected, toward whomever or whatever is available. Targets of **displaced aggression** tend to be safer, or less likely to retaliate, than the original source of frustration. At one time or another, you have probably lashed out at a friend or relative who was not the real cause of your annoyance. As this suggests, excessive anger over a minor irritation is a common form of displaced aggression (Miller et al., 2003).

Psychologists attribute much hostility to displaced aggression. A disturbing example is the finding that unemployment and divorce are associated with increased child abuse (Weissman, Jogerst, & Dawson, 2003). In a pattern known as **scapegoating,** a person or a group is blamed for conditions not of their making. A *scapegoat* is a person who has become a habitual target of displaced aggression. Despite recent progress, many minority groups continue to face hostility based on scapegoating. Think, for example, about the hostility expressed toward illegal immigrants during times of economic hardship. In many communities, layoffs and job losses are closely linked to increased violence (Catalano, Novaco, & McConnell, 1997). Or think about the hostility expressed toward anyone in the United States who looked even vaguely "foreign" right after the 9/11 terrorist attacks.

I have a friend who dropped out of school to hitchhike around the country. He seemed very frustrated before he quit. What type of response to frustration is that? Another major reaction to frustration is escape, or withdrawal. It is stressful and unpleasant to be frustrated. If other reactions do not reduce frustration, a person may try to escape. **Escape** may mean actually leaving a source of frustration (dropping out of school, quitting a job, leaving an unhappy marriage), or it may mean psychologically escaping. Two common forms of psychological escape are feigned apathy (pretending not to care) and the use of drugs such as cocaine, alcohol, marijuana, or narcotics. (Notice that these are examples of *ineffective* emotion-focused coping.) (See ● Figure 13.4 for a summary of common reactions to frustration.)

Paintball seems to bring out aggressive impulses in many players. Wild shootouts are part of the fun, but are some players displacing aggressive urges related to frustration in other areas of their lives?

Steve Nagy/Photolibrary

Coping with Frustration

In a classic experiment, a psychologist studying frustration placed rats on a small platform at the top of a tall pole. Then he forced them to jump off the platform toward two elevated doors, one locked and the other unlocked. If the rat chose the correct door, it swung open and the rat landed safely on another platform. Rats who chose the locked door bounced off it and fell into a net far below.

The problem of choosing the open door was made unsolvable and very frustrating by randomly alternating which door was locked. After a time, most rats adopted a stereotyped response. That is, they chose the same door every time. This door was then permanently locked. All the rat had to do was to jump to the other door to avoid a fall, but time after time the rat bounced off the locked door (Maier, 1949).

Isn't that an example of persistence? No. Persistence that is *inflexible* can turn into "stupid," stereotyped behavior like that of a rat on a jumping platform. When dealing with frustration, you must know when to quit and establish a new direction. Here are some suggestions to help you avoid needless frustration:

1. Try to identify the source of your frustration. Is it external or personal?
2. Is the source of frustration something that can be changed? How hard would you have to work to change it? Is it under your control at all?
3. If the source of your frustration can be changed or removed, are the necessary efforts worth it?

The answers to these questions help determine if persistence will be futile. There is value in learning to accept gracefully those things that cannot be changed.

It is also important to distinguish between *real* barriers and *imagined* barriers. All too often we create our own imaginary barriers. For example, Corazon wants a part-time job to earn extra money. At the first place she applied, she was told that she didn't have enough "experience." Now she complains of being frustrated because she wants to work but cannot. She needs "experience" to work, but can't get experience without working. She has quit looking for a job.

Is Corazon's need for experience a real barrier? Unless she applies for *many* jobs it is impossible to tell if she has overestimated its importance. For her the barrier is real enough to prevent further efforts, but with persistence she might locate an "unlocked door." If a reasonable amount of effort does show that experience is essential, it might be obtained in other ways—through temporary volunteer work, for instance.

Aggression Any response made with the intent of causing harm.

Displaced aggression Redirecting aggression to a target other than the actual source of one's frustration.

Scapegoating Blaming a person or a group of people for conditions not of their making.

Escape Reducing discomfort by leaving frustrating situations or by psychologically withdrawing from them.

⬤⬤ Conflict—Yes, No, Yes, No, Yes, No, Well, Maybe

Gateway Question: Are there different types of conflict?

Conflict occurs whenever a person must choose between contradictory needs, desires, motives, or demands. Choosing between college and work, marriage and single life, or study and failure are common conflicts. There are four basic forms of conflict. As we will see, each has its own properties (● Figure 13.5 and ● Figure 13.6).

Approach-Approach Conflicts

A simple **approach-approach conflict** comes from having to choose between two positive, or desirable, alternatives. Choosing between tutti-frutti–coconut–mocha–champagne ice and orange marmalade–peanut butter–coffee swirl at the ice cream parlor may throw you into a temporary conflict. However, if you really like both choices, your decision will be quickly made. Even when more important decisions are at stake, approach-approach conflicts tend to be the easiest to resolve. The old fable about the mule

● **Figure 13.5** Three basic forms of conflict. For this woman, choosing between pie and ice cream is a minor approach-approach conflict; deciding whether to take a job that will require weekend work is an approach-avoidance conflict; and choosing between paying higher rent and moving is an avoidance-avoidance conflict.

that died of thirst and starvation while standing between a bucket of water and a bucket of oats is obviously unrealistic. When both options are positive, the scales of decision are easily tipped one direction or the other.

Avoidance-Avoidance Conflicts

Being forced to choose between two negative, or undesirable, alternatives creates an **avoidance-avoidance conflict.** A person in an avoidance conflict is caught between "the devil and the deep blue sea," "the frying pan and the fire," or "a rock and a hard place." In real life, double-avoidance conflicts involve dilemmas such as choosing between unwanted pregnancy and abortion, the dentist and tooth decay, a monotonous job and poverty, or dorm food and starvation.

Suppose I don't object to abortion. Or suppose that I consider any pregnancy sacred and not to be tampered with? Like many other stressful situations, these examples can be defined as conflicts only on the basis of personal needs and values. If a woman wants to end a pregnancy and does not object to abortion, she experiences no conflict. If she would not consider abortion under any circumstances, there is also no conflict.

Avoidance conflicts often have a "damned if you do, damned if you don't" quality. In other words, both choices are negative, but *not choosing* may be impossible or equally undesirable. To illustrate, imagine the plight of a person trapped in a hotel fire 20 stories from the ground. Should she jump from the window and almost surely die on the pavement? Or should she try to dash through the flames and almost surely die of smoke inhalation and burns? When faced with a choice such as this, it is easy to see why people often *freeze,* finding it impossible to decide or take action. In actual disasters of this sort, people are often found dead in their rooms, victims of an inability to take action.

Indecision, inaction, and freezing are not the only reactions to double-avoidance conflicts. Because avoidance conflicts are stressful and difficult to solve, people sometimes pull out of them entirely. This reaction, called *leaving the field,* is another form of escape. It may explain the behavior of a student who could not attend school unless he worked. However, if he worked he could

● **Figure 13.6** Conflict diagrams. As shown by the colored areas in the graphs, desires to approach and to avoid increase near a goal. The effects of these tendencies are depicted below each graph. The "behavior" of the ball in each example illustrates the nature of the conflict above it. An approach conflict *(left)* is easily decided. Moving toward one goal will increase its attraction *(graph)* and will lead to a rapid resolution. (If the ball moves in either direction, it will go all the way to one of the goals.) In an avoidance conflict *(center)*, tendencies to avoid are deadlocked, resulting in inaction. In an approach-avoidance conflict *(right)*, approach proceeds to the point where desires to approach and avoid cancel each other. Again, these tendencies are depicted *(below)* by the action of the ball. (Graphs after Miller, 1944.)

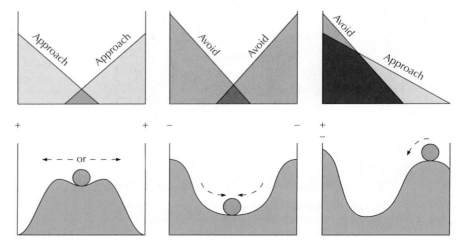

not earn passing grades. His solution after much conflict and indecision? He joined the navy.

Approach-Avoidance Conflicts

Approach-avoidance conflicts are also difficult to resolve. In some ways they are more troublesome than avoidance conflicts because people seldom escape them. A person in an **approach-avoidance conflict** is "caught" by being attracted to, and repelled by, the same goal or activity. Attraction keeps the person in the situation, but its negative aspects cause turmoil and distress. For example, a high school student arrives to pick up his date for the first time. He is met at the door by her father, who is a professional wrestler—7 feet tall, 300 pounds, and entirely covered with hair. The father gives the boy a crushing handshake and growls that he will break him in half if the girl is not home on time. The student considers the girl attractive and has a good time. But does he ask her out again? It depends on the relative strength of his attraction and his fear. Almost certainly he will feel *ambivalent* about asking her out again, knowing that another encounter with her father awaits him.

Ambivalence (mixed positive and negative feelings) is a central characteristic of approach-avoidance conflicts. Ambivalence is usually translated into *partial approach* (Miller, 1944). Because our student is still attracted to the girl, he may spend time with her at school and elsewhere. But he may not actually date her again. Some more realistic examples of approach-avoidance conflicts are planning to marry someone your parents strongly disapprove of, wanting to be in a play but suffering stage fright, wanting to buy a car but not wanting to make monthly payments, and wanting to eat when you're already overweight. Many of life's important decisions have approach-avoidance dimensions.

Multiple Conflicts

Aren't real-life conflicts more complex than the ones described here? Yes. Conflicts are rarely as clear-cut as those described. People in conflict are usually faced with several dilemmas at once, so several types of conflict may be intermingled. The fourth type of conflict moves us closer to reality. In a **double approach-avoidance conflict** each alternative has both positive and negative qualities. For example, you are offered two jobs: One has good pay but poor hours and dull work; the second has interesting work and excellent hours, but low pay. Which do you select? This situation is more typical of the choices we must usually make. It offers neither completely positive nor completely negative options.

As with single approach-avoidance conflicts, people faced with double approach-avoidance conflicts feel ambivalent about each choice. This causes them to *vacillate*, or waver between the alternatives. Just as you are about to choose one such alternative, its undesirable aspects tend to loom large. So, what do you do? You swing back toward the other choice. If you have ever been romantically attracted to two people at once—each having qualities you like and dislike—then you have probably experienced vacillation. Another example that may be familiar is trying to decide between two college majors, each with advantages and disadvantages.

In real life it is common to face **multiple approach-avoidance conflicts** in which several alternatives each have positive and negative features. An example would be trying to choose which automobile to buy among several brands. When multiple approach-avoidance conflicts involve major life decisions, such as choosing a career, a school, a mate, or a job, they can add greatly to the amount of stress we experience.

Managing Conflicts

How can I handle conflicts more effectively? Most of the suggestions made earlier concerning frustration also apply to conflicts. However, here are some additional things to remember when you are in conflict or must make a difficult decision:

1. Don't be hasty when making important decisions. Hasty decisions are often regretted. Even if you do make a faulty decision, it will trouble you less if you know that you did everything possible to avoid a mistake.
2. Try out important decisions *partially* when possible. If you are thinking about moving to a new town, try to spend a few days there first. If you are choosing between colleges, do the same. If classes are in progress, sit in on some. If you want to learn to scuba dive, rent equipment for a reasonable length of time before buying.
3. Look for workable compromises. Again, it is important to get all available information. If you think that you have only one or two alternatives and they are undesirable or unbearable, seek the aid of a teacher, counselor, minister, or social service agency. You may be overlooking possible alternatives these people will know about.
4. When all else fails, make a decision and live with it. Indecision and conflict exact a high cost. Sometimes it is best to select a course of action and stick with it unless it is very obviously wrong after you have taken it.

Conflicts are a normal part of life. With practice you can learn to manage many of the conflicts you will face.

Conflict A stressful condition that occurs when a person must choose between incompatible or contradictory alternatives.

Approach-approach conflict Choosing between two positive, or desirable, alternatives.

Avoidance-avoidance conflict Choosing between two negative, undesirable, alternatives.

Approach-avoidance conflict Being attracted to and repelled by the same goal or activity.

Ambivalence Mixed positive and negative feelings or simultaneous attraction and repulsion.

Double approach-avoidance conflict Being simultaneously attracted to and repelled by each of two alternatives.

Multiple approach-avoidance conflict Being simultaneously attracted to and repelled by each of several alternatives.

Stress, Frustration, and Conflict

RECITE

1. The first signs of psychosomatic disorders begin to appear during the stage of
   a. alarm
   b. exhaustion
   c. resistance
   d. appraisal
2. Students taking stressful final exams are more susceptible to the cold virus, a pattern best explained by
   a. the disease-prone personality
   b. psychoneuroimmunology
   c. emotion-focused coping
   d. reaction formation
3. Whereas stressful incidents suppress the immune system, stress management techniques have almost no effect on immune system functioning. T or F?
4. Emotional exhaustion, cynicism, and reduced accomplishment are characteristics of job _____.
5. Stress tends to be greatest when a situation is appraised as a _____ and a person does not feel _____ to cope with the situation.
6. According to Richard Lazarus, choosing a way to meet a threat or challenge takes place during the
   a. primary stress reaction
   b. secondary stress reaction
   c. primary appraisal
   d. secondary appraisal
7. Which of the following is *not* a common reaction to frustration?
   a. ambivalence
   b. aggression
   c. displaced aggression
   d. persistence
8. Displaced aggression is closely related to the pattern of behavior known as
   a. scapegoating
   b. leaving the field
   c. stereotyped responding
   d. burnout
9. You would be most likely to experience vacillation if you found yourself in
   a. an approach-approach conflict
   b. an avoidance-avoidance conflict
   c. a double approach-avoidance conflict
   d. the condition called emotion-focused coping

REFLECT

Critical Thinking

10. Which do you think would produce more stress: (a) Appraising a situation as mildly threatening but feeling like you are totally incompetent to cope with it? Or (b) appraising a situation as very threatening but feeling that you have the resources and skills to cope with it?
11. Being frustrated is unpleasant. If some action, including aggression, ends frustration, why might we expect the action to be repeated on other occasions?

Relate

What impact did pressure, control, predictability, repetition, and intensity have on your last stress reaction?

What type of coping do you tend to use when you face a stressor such as public speaking or taking an important exam?

Think of a time when you were frustrated. What was your goal? What prevented you from reaching it? Was your frustration external or personal?

Have you ever displaced aggression? Why did you choose another target for your hostility?

Review the major types of conflict and think of a conflict you have faced that illustrates each type. Did your reactions match those described in the text?

11. If a response ends discomfort, the response has been negatively reinforced. This makes the response more likely to occur in the future.
10. There is no correct answer here because individual stress reactions vary greatly. However, the secondary appraisal of a situation often determines just how stressful it is. Feeling incapable of coping is very threatening.

Answers: 1. c 2. b 3. F 4. burnout 5. threat, competent 6. d 7. a 8. a 9. c

◉ Psychological Defense— Mental Karate?

Gateway Question: What are defense mechanisms?

Threatening situations tend to produce **anxiety.** When you are anxious you feel tense, uneasy, apprehensive, worried, and vulnerable. This unpleasant state can lead to emotion-focused coping that is *defensive* in nature (Lazarus, 1991b). Psychodynamic psychologists have identified various defense mechanisms that allow us to reduce anxiety caused by stressful situations or our own shortcomings.

> **bridges**
> Severe anxiety can be extremely disruptive. It is the basis for some of the most common psychological disorders. **See Chapter 14, page 480.**

What are psychological defense mechanisms and how do they reduce anxiety? A **defense mechanism** is any mental process used to avoid, deny, or distort sources of threat or anxiety, especially threats to one's self-image. Many of the defenses were first identified by Sigmund Freud, who assumed they operate *unconsciously.* Often, defense mechanisms create large blind spots in awareness. For instance, you might know an extremely stingy person who is completely unaware that he is a tightwad. Everyone has at one time or another used defense mechanisms. Let's consider some of the most common. (A more complete listing is given in ● Table 13.4.)

Denial

One of the most basic defenses is **denial** (protecting oneself from an unpleasant reality by refusing to accept it or believe it). We are prone to deny death, illness, and similar painful and threatening events. For instance, if you were told that you had only 3 months to live, how would you react? Your first thoughts might be, "Aw, come on, someone must have mixed up the X-rays," or, "The doctor must be mistaken," or simply, "It can't be true!" Similar denial and disbelief are common reactions to the unexpected death of a friend or relative: "It's just not real. I just don't believe it!"

Table 13.4 ● Psychological Defense Mechanisms

Compensation Counteracting a real or imagined weakness by emphasizing desirable traits or seeking to excel in the area of weakness or in other areas.

Denial Protecting oneself from an unpleasant reality by refusing to perceive it.

Fantasy Fulfilling unmet desires in imagined achievements or activities.

Identification Taking on some of the characteristics of an admired person, usually as a way of compensating for perceived personal weaknesses or faults.

Intellectualization Separating emotion from a threatening or anxiety-provoking situation by talking or thinking about it in impersonal "intellectual" terms.

Isolation Separating contradictory thoughts or feelings into "logic-tight" mental compartments so that they do not come into conflict.

Projection Attributing one's own feelings, shortcomings, or unacceptable impulses to others.

Rationalization Justifying your behavior by giving reasonable and "rational," but false, reasons for it.

Reaction formation Preventing dangerous impulses from being expressed in behavior by exaggerating opposite behavior.

Regression Retreating to an earlier level of development or to earlier, less demanding habits or situations.

Repression Unconsciously preventing painful or dangerous thoughts from entering awareness.

Sublimation Working off unmet desires, or unacceptable impulses, in activities that are constructive.

Repression

Freud noticed that his patients had tremendous difficulty recalling shocking or traumatic events from childhood. It seemed that powerful forces were holding these painful memories from awareness. Freud called this **repression,** and said we use it to protect ourselves by blocking out threatening thoughts and impulses. Feelings of hostility toward a family member, the names of people we dislike, and past failures are common targets of repression. Research suggests that you are most likely to repress information that threatens your self-image (Mendolia, 2002).

Reaction Formation

In a **reaction formation,** impulses are not just repressed; they are also held in check by exaggerating opposite behavior. For example, a mother who unconsciously resents her children may, through reaction formation, become absurdly overprotective and overindulgent. Her real thoughts of "I hate them" and "I wish they were gone" are replaced by "I love them" and "I don't know what I would do without them." The mother's hostile impulses are traded for "smother" love, so that she won't have to admit she hates her children. Thus, the basic idea in a reaction formation is that the individual acts out an opposite behavior to block threatening impulses or feelings.

Regression

In its broadest meaning, **regression** refers to any return to earlier, less demanding situations or habits. Most parents who have a second child have to put up with at least some regression by the older child. Threatened by a new rival for affection, an older child may regress to childish speech, bed-wetting, or infantile play after the new baby arrives. If you've ever seen a child get homesick at summer camp or on a vacation, you've observed regression. The child wants to go home, where it's "safe." An adult who throws a temper tantrum or a married adult who "goes home to mother" is also regressing.

Projection

Projection is an unconscious process that protects us from the anxiety we would feel if we were to discern our faults. A person who is projecting tends to see his or her own feelings, shortcomings, or unacceptable impulses in others. **Projection** lowers anxiety by exaggerating negative traits in others. This justifies one's own actions and directs attention away from personal failings.

One of your authors once worked for a greedy shop owner who cheated many of his customers. This same man considered himself a pillar of the community and very moral and religious. How did he justify to himself his greed and dishonesty? He believed that everyone who entered his store was bent on cheating *him* any way they could. In reality, few, if any, of his customers shared his motives, but he projected his own greed and dishonesty onto them.

Rationalization

Every teacher is familiar with this strange phenomenon: On the day of an exam, an incredible wave of student disasters sweeps through the city. Mothers, fathers, sisters, brothers, aunts, uncles, grandparents, friends, relatives, and pets of students become ill or die. Motors suddenly fall out of cars. Books are lost or stolen. Alarm clocks go belly-up and ring no more. All manner of computer equipment malfunctions.

The making of excuses comes from a natural tendency to explain our behavior. **Rationalization** refers to justifying personal actions by giving "rational" but false reasons for them. When the explanation you give for your behavior is reasonable and convincing—but not the real reason—you are *rationalizing.* For example, Jennifer failed to turn in an assignment made at the beginning of the semester in one of her classes. Here's the explanation she gave her professor:

My car broke down 2 days ago, and I couldn't get to the library until yesterday. Then I couldn't get all the books I needed because some were checked out, but I wrote what I could. Then last night, as the last straw, the ink car-

Anxiety Apprehension, dread, or uneasiness similar to fear but based on an unclear threat.

Defense mechanism A habitual and often unconscious psychological process used to reduce anxiety.

tridge in my printer ran out, and since all the stores were closed, I couldn't finish the paper on time.

When asked why she left the assignment until the last minute (the real reason it was late), Jennifer offered another set of rationalizations. Like many people, Jennifer had difficulty seeing herself without the protection of her rationalizations.

All the defense mechanisms described seem pretty undesirable. Do they have a positive side? People who overuse defense mechanisms become less adaptable, because they consume great amounts of emotional energy to control anxiety and maintain an unrealistic self-image. Defense mechanisms do have value, though. Often, they help keep us from being overwhelmed by immediate threats. This can provide time for a person to learn to cope in a more effective, problem-focused manner. If you recognize some of your own behavior in the descriptions here, it is hardly a sign that you are hopelessly defensive. As noted earlier, most people occasionally use defense mechanisms.

Two defense mechanisms that have a decidedly more positive quality are compensation and sublimation.

Compensation

Compensatory reactions are defenses against feelings of inferiority. A person who has a defect or weakness (real or imagined) may go to unusual lengths to overcome the weakness or to *compensate* for it by excelling in other areas. One of the pioneers of "pumping iron" is Jack LaLanne, who opened the first modern health club in America. LaLanne made a successful career out of bodybuilding in spite of the fact that he was thin and sickly as a young man. Or perhaps it would be more accurate to say *because* he was thin and sickly. You can find dozens of examples of **compensation** at work. A childhood stutterer may excel in debate at college. As a child, Helen Keller was unable to see or hear, but she became an outstanding thinker and writer. Perhaps Ray Charles, Stevie Wonder, Andrea Bocelli, and other blind entertainers were drawn to music because of their handicap.

Sublimation

The defense called **sublimation** (sub-lih-MAY-shun) is defined as working off frustrated desires (especially sexual desires) through socially acceptable activities. Freud believed that art, music, dance, poetry, scientific investigation, and other creative activities could serve to rechannel sexual energies into productive behavior. Freud also felt that almost any strong desire could be sublimated. For example, a very aggressive person may find social acceptance as a professional soldier, boxer, or football player. Greed may be refined into a successful business career. Lying may be sublimated into storytelling, creative writing, or politics.

Sexual motives appear to be the most easily and widely sublimated (Jacobs, 2003). Freud would have had a field day with such modern pastimes as surfing, motorcycle riding, drag racing, and dancing to or playing rock music, to name but a few. People enjoy each of these activities for a multitude of reasons, but it is hard to overlook the rich sexual symbolism apparent in each.

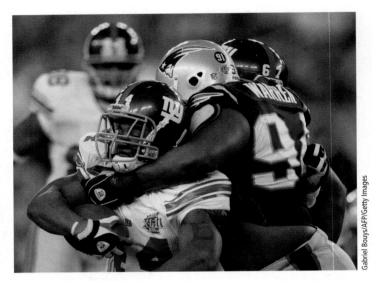

For some players—and fans—football probably allows sublimation of aggressive urges. *Grand Theft Auto* and similar computer games may serve the same purpose.

Learned Helplessness—Is There Hope?

Gateway Question: What do we know about coping with feelings of helplessness and depression?

What would happen if a person's defenses failed or if the person appraised a threatening situation as hopeless? Martin Seligman studied the case of a young marine who seemed to have adapted to the stresses of being held prisoner during the Vietnam War. The marine's health was related to a promise made by his captors: If he cooperated, they said, he would be released on a certain date. As the date approached, his spirits soared. Then came a devastating blow. He had been deceived. His captors had no intention of ever releasing him. He immediately lapsed into a deep depression, refused to eat or drink, and died shortly thereafter.

That seems like an extreme example. Does anything similar occur outside of concentration camps? Apparently so. For example, researchers in San Antonio, Texas, asked older people if they were hopeful about the future. Those who answered "No" died at elevated rates (Stern, Dhanda, & Hazuda, 2001).

To explain such patterns psychologists have focused on the concept of **learned helplessness,** an acquired inability to overcome obstacles and avoid aversive stimuli (Seligman, 1989). To observe learned helplessness, let's see what happens when animals are tested in a shuttle box (● Figure 13.7). If placed in one side of a divided box, dogs will quickly learn to leap to the other side to escape an electric shock. If they are given a warning before the shock occurs (for example, a light that dims), most dogs learn to avoid the shock by leaping the barrier before the shock arrives. This is true of most dogs, but not those who have learned to feel helpless (Overmier & LoLordo, 1998).

How is a dog made to feel helpless? Before being tested in the shuttle box, a dog can be placed in a harness (from which the dog

• **Figure 13.7** In the normal course of escape and avoidance learning, a light dims shortly before the floor is electrified *(a)*. Because the light does not yet have meaning for the dog, the dog receives a shock (noninjurious, by the way) and leaps the barrier *(b)*. Dogs soon learn to watch for the dimming of the light *(c)* and to jump before receiving a shock *(d)*. Dogs made to feel "helpless" rarely even learn to escape shock, much less to avoid it.

cannot escape) and then given several painful shocks. The animal is helpless to prevent these shocks. When placed in the shuttle box, dogs prepared this way react to the first shock by crouching, howling, and whining. None of them try to escape. They helplessly resign themselves to their fate. After all, they have already learned that there is nothing they can do about shock.

As the shuttle box experiments suggest, helplessness is a psychological state that occurs when events *appear to be uncontrollable* (Seligman, 1989). Helplessness also afflicts humans. It is a common reaction to repeated failure and to unpredictable or unavoidable punishment. A prime example is college students who feel helpless about their schoolwork. Such students tend to procrastinate, give up easily, and drop out of school (Perry, 2003).

Where humans are concerned, attributions (discussed in Chapter 10, pages 349–350) have a large effect on helplessness. Persons who are made to feel helpless in one situation are more likely to act helpless in other situations if they attribute their failure to *lasting, general* factors. An example would be concluding, "I must be stupid," after doing poorly on a test in a biology class. In contrast, attributing a low score to specific factors in the situation ("I'm not too good at the type of test my biology professor uses" or "I'm not very interested in biology") tends to prevent learned helplessness from spreading (Peterson & Vaidya, 2001).

Depression

Seligman and others have pointed out the similarities between learned helplessness and **depression.** Both are marked by feelings of despondency, powerlessness, and hopelessness. "Helpless" animals display decreased activity, lowered aggression, blunted appetite, and a loss of sex drive. Humans suffer from similar effects and also tend to see themselves as failing, even when they're not (LoLordo, 2001; Seligman, 1989).

Depression is one of the most widespread emotional problems, and it undoubtedly has many causes. However, learned helplessness seems to explain many cases of depression and hopelessness. For example, Seligman (1972) describes the fate of Archie, a 15-year-old boy. For Archie, school is an unending series of shocks and failures. Other students treat him as if he's stupid; in class he rarely answers questions because he doesn't know some of the words. He feels knocked down everywhere he turns. These may not be electric shocks, but they are certainly emotional "shocks," and Archie has learned to feel helpless to prevent them. When he leaves school his chances of success will be poor. He has learned to passively endure whatever shocks life has in store for him. Archie is not alone in this regard. Hopelessness is almost always a major element of depression (Ciarrochi, Dean, & Anderson, 2002).

> **bridges**
>
> Depression is a complex problem that takes many forms and has many causes. **See Chapter 14, pages 476–479.**

Hope

Does Seligman's research give any clues about how to "unlearn" helplessness? With dogs, an effective technique is to forcibly drag them away from shock into the "safe" compartment. After this is done

Learned helplessness A learned inability to overcome obstacles or to avoid punishment; learned passivity and inaction to aversive stimuli.

Depression A state of despondency marked by feelings of powerlessness and hopelessness.

Mastery training can occur informally when people learn to cope with challenges. For example, 18- to 21-year-old trainees on a transatlantic sailing voyage showed marked improvements in their ability to cope with stress (Norris & Weinman, 1996).

several times, the animals regain "hope" and feelings of control over the environment. Just how this can be done with humans is a question psychologists are exploring. It seems obvious, for instance, that someone like Archie would benefit from an educational program that would allow him to "succeed" repeatedly.

In **mastery training,** responses are reinforced that lead to mastery of a threat or control over one's environment. Animals who undergo such training become more resistant to learned helplessness (Volpicelli et al., 1983). For example, animals that first learn to escape shock become more persistent in trying to flee inescapable shock. In effect, they won't give up, even when the situation really is "hopeless."

Such findings suggest that we might be able to "immunize" people against helplessness and depression by allowing them to master difficult challenges. The Outward Bound schools, in which people pit themselves against the rigors of mountaineering, whitewater canoeing, and wilderness survival, might serve as a model for such a program.

The value of hope should not be overlooked. As fragile as this emotion seems to be, it is a powerful antidote to depression and helplessness. As an individual, you may find hope in religion, nature, human companionship, or even technology. Wherever you find it, remember its value: Hope is among the most important of all human emotions. Having positive beliefs, such as optimism, hope, and a sense of meaning and control, is closely related to overall well-being (Taylor et al., 2000, 2003).

Depression: Why Students Get the Blues

During the school year, many college students suffer some symptoms of depression, which can exert a toll on academic performance. In one study, students diagnosed with depression scored half a grade point below nondepressed students (Hysenbegasi, Hass, & Rowland,

2005). Why do students get "blue"? Various problems contribute to depressive feelings. Here are some of the most common:

1. Stresses from college work and pressures to choose a career can leave students feeling that they are missing out on fun or that all their hard work is meaningless.
2. Isolation and loneliness are common when students leave their support groups behind. In the past, family, a circle of high school friends, and often a boyfriend or girlfriend could be counted on for support and encouragement.
3. Problems with studying and grades frequently trigger depression. Many students start college with high aspirations and little prior experience with failure. At the same time, many lack basic skills necessary for academic success and are afraid of failure (Martin & Marsh, 2003).
4. Depression can be triggered by the breakup of an intimate relationship, either with a former boyfriend or girlfriend or with a newly formed college romance.
5. Students who find it difficult to live up to their idealized images of themselves are especially prone to depression (Scott & O'Hara, 1993).
6. An added danger is that depressed students are more likely to abuse alcohol, which is a depressant (Weitzman, 2004).

Recognizing Depression

Most people know, obviously enough, when they are "down." Aaron Beck, an authority on depression, suggests you should assume that more than a minor fluctuation in mood is involved when five conditions exist (Beck & Greenberg, 1974):

1. You have a consistently negative opinion of yourself.
2. You engage in frequent self-criticism and self-blame.
3. You place negative interpretations on events that usually wouldn't bother you.
4. The future looks bleak and negative.
5. You feel that your responsibilities are overwhelming.

What can be done to combat depression? Bouts of the college blues are closely related to stressful events. Learning to manage college work and to challenge self-critical thinking can help alleviate mild school-related depression.

In a survey, college students reported that they were depressed from one to two times a month. These episodes lasted from a few hours to several days.

Attacks of the college blues are common and should be distinguished from more serious cases of depression. Severe depression is a serious problem that can lead to suicide or a major impairment of emotional functioning. In such cases it would be wise to seek professional help.

Coping with Depression

If you don't do well on a test or a class assignment, how do you react? If you see it as a small, isolated setback, you probably won't feel too bad. However, if you feel like you have "blown it" in a big way, depression may follow. Students who strongly link everyday events to long-term goals (such as a successful career or high income) tend to overreact to day-to-day disappointments (McIntosh, Harlow, & Martin, 1995).

What does the preceding tell us about the college blues? The implication is that it's important to take daily tasks one step at a time and chip away at them. That way, you are less likely to feel overwhelmed, helpless, or hopeless. One classic suggestion comes from Aaron Beck and Ruth Greenberg (1974): When you feel "blue," you should make a *daily schedule* for yourself. Try to schedule activities to fill up every hour during the day. It is best to start with easy activities and progress to more difficult tasks. Check off each item as it is completed. That way, you will begin to break the self-defeating cycle of feeling helpless and falling further behind. (Depressed students spend much of their time sleeping.) A series of small accomplishments, successes, or pleasures may be all that you need to get going again. However, if you are lacking skills needed for success in college, ask for help in getting them. Don't remain "helpless."

Feelings of worthlessness and hopelessness are usually supported by self-critical or negative thoughts. Beck and Greenberg recommend writing down such thoughts as they occur, especially those that immediately precede feelings of sadness. After you have collected these thoughts, write a rational answer to each. For example, the thought "No one loves me" should be answered with a list of those who do care. (See Chapter 15 for more information.) One more point to keep in mind is this: When events begin to improve, try to accept it as a sign that better times lie ahead. Positive events are most likely to end depression if you view them as stable and continuing, rather than temporary and fragile (Needles & Abramson, 1990).

KNOWLEDGE BUILDER
Defense Mechanisms, Helplessness, and Depression

RECITE

1. The psychological defense known as denial refers to the natural tendency to explain or justify one's actions. T or F?
2. Fulfilling frustrated desires in imaginary achievements or activities defines the defense mechanism of
   a. compensation
   b. isolation
   c. fantasy
   d. sublimation

3. In compensation, one's own undesirable characteristics or motives are attributed to others. T or F?
4. Of the defense mechanisms, two that are considered relatively constructive are
   a. compensation
   b. denial
   c. isolation
   d. projection
   e. regression
   f. rationalization
   g. sublimation
5. Depression in humans is similar to _____ _____ observed in animal experiments.
6. Learned helplessness tends to occur when events appear to be
   a. frustrating
   b. in conflict
   c. uncontrollable
   d. problem-focused
7. At any given time, more than half the college student population suffers symptoms of depression. T or F?
8. Frequent self-criticism and self-blame are a natural consequence of doing college work. T or F?

REFLECT

Critical Thinking

9. Learned helplessness is most closely related to which of the factors that determine the severity of stress?

Relate

We tend to be blind to our own reliance on defense mechanisms. Return to the definitions in ● Table 13.4 and see if you can think of one example of each defense that you have observed someone else using.

Have you ever felt helpless in a particular situation? What caused you to feel that way? Does any part of Seligman's description of learned helplessness match your own experience?

Imagine that a friend of yours is suffering from the college blues. What advice would you give your friend?

Answers: 1. F **2.** c **3.** F **4.** a, g **5.** learned helplessness **6.** c **7.** F **8.** F **9.** Feelings of incompetence and lack of control.

●● Stress and Health—Unmasking a Hidden Killer

Gateway Question: How is stress related to health and disease?

At the beginning of this chapter you read about Jennifer, our intrepid student who became ill after a stressful final exam period. Was Jennifer's illness a coincidence? Psychologists have now firmly established that stress affects our health. Let's see how this occurs. We will also explore some factors that limit the health risks we face. Because we live in a fast-paced and often stressful society, these are topics worth stressing.

Disaster, depression, and sorrow often precede illness (Brannon & Feist, 2007). As Jennifer learned after finals week, stressful events reduce the body's natural defenses against disease. More

---

Mastery training Reinforcement of responses that lead to mastery of a threat or control over one's environment.

Table 13.5 ● Social Readjustment Rating Scale

Rank	Life Event	Life Change Units
1	Death of spouse or child	119
2	Divorce	98
3	Death of close family member	92
4	Marital separation	79
5	Fired from work	79
6	Major personal injury or illness	77
7	Jail term	75
8	Death of close friend	70
9	Pregnancy	66
10	Major business readjustment	62
11	Foreclosure on a mortgage or loan	61
12	Gain of new family member	57
13	Marital reconciliation	57
14	Change in health or behavior of family member	56
15	Change in financial state	56
16	Retirement	54
17	Change to different line of work	51
18	Change in number of arguments with spouse	51
19	Marriage	50
20	Spouse begins or ends work	46
21	Sexual difficulties	45
22	Child leaving home	44
23	Mortgage or loan greater than $10,000	44
24	Change in responsibilities at work	43
25	Change in living conditions	42
26	Change in residence	41
27	Begin or end school	38
28	Trouble with in-laws	38
29	Outstanding personal achievement	37
30	Change in work hours or conditions	36
31	Change in schools	35
32	Christmas	30
33	Trouble with boss	29
34	Change in recreation	29
35	Mortgage or loan less than $10,000	28
36	Change in personal habits	27
37	Change in eating habits	27
38	Change in social activities	27
39	Change in number of family get-togethers	26
40	Change in sleeping habits	26
41	Vacation	25
42	Change in church activities	22
43	Minor violations of the law	22

Source: Reprinted from *Journal of Psychosomatic Research*, Vol. 43, No. 3.

surprising is the finding that *life changes*—both good and bad—can increase susceptibility to accidents or illness. Major changes in our surroundings or routines require us to be vigilant, on guard, and ready to react. Over long periods, this can be quite stressful (Sternberg, 2000).

Life Events and Stress

How can I tell if I am subjecting myself to too much stress? Psychiatrist Thomas Holmes and graduate student Richard Rahe developed the first rating scale to estimate the health hazards we face when stresses add up (Holmes & Rahe, 1967). Still widely used today, a version of the **Social Readjustment Rating Scale (SRRS)** is reprinted in ● Table 13.5 (Scully, Tosi, & Banning, 2000). Notice that the impact of life events is expressed in *life change units (LCUs)* (numerical values assigned to each life event).

As you read the scale, note again that positive life events may be as costly as disasters. Marriage rates 50 life change units, even though it is usually a happy event. You'll also see many items that read "Change in . . ." This means that an improvement in life conditions can be as costly as a decline. A stressful adjustment may be required in either case.

To use the scale shown in Table 13.5, add up the LCUs for all life events you have experienced during the last year and compare the total to the following standards:

0–150:	No significant problems
150–199:	Mild life crisis (33 percent chance of illness)
200–299:	Moderate life crisis (50 percent chance of illness)
300 or more:	Major life crisis (80 percent chance of illness)

According to Holmes, there is a high chance of illness or accident when your LCU total exceeds 300 points. A more conservative rating of stress can be obtained by totaling LCU points for only the previous 6 months.

Many of the listed life changes don't seem relevant to young adults or college students. Does the SRRS apply to them? The SRRS tends to be more appropriate for older, more established adults. The health of college students is also affected by stressful events, such as entering college, changing majors, or the breakup of a steady relationship. (Look ahead to Table 13.8 for more information.)

Evaluation

People differ greatly in their reactions to the same event. For such reasons, the SRRS is at best a rough index of stress. Nevertheless, it's hard to ignore a classic study in which people were deliberately exposed to the virus that causes common colds. The results were nothing to sneeze at: If a person had a high stress score, she or he was much more likely to actually get a cold (Cohen, Waltzman, & Fisher, 1993). In view of such findings, a high LCU score should be taken seriously. If your score goes much over 300, an adjustment in your activities or lifestyle may be needed. Remember, "To be forewarned is to be forearmed."

Marriage is usually a positive life event. Nevertheless, the many changes it brings can be stressful.

The Hazards of Hassles

There must be more to stress than major life changes. Isn't there a link between ongoing stresses and health? In addition to having a direct impact, major life events spawn countless daily frustrations and irritations (Pillow, Zautra, & Sandler, 1996). Also, many of us face ongoing stresses at work or at home that do not involve major life changes (Pett & Johnson, 2005). Such minor but frequent stresses are called **hassles,** or **microstressors.** (See ● Table 13.6 for some examples of hassles faced by college students.)

Table 13.6 ● Examples of Common Hassles Faced by College Students

Too many things to do
Not enough money for housing
Feeling discriminated against
People making gender jokes
Communication problems with friends
Driving to school
People making fun of my religion
Fear of losing valuables
Work schedule
Getting into shape
Parents' expectations

Source: Pett & Johnson, 2005.

In a yearlong study, 100 men and women recorded the hassles they endured. Participants also reported on their physical and mental health. Frequent and severe hassles turned out to be better predictors of day-to-day health than major life events were. However, major life events did predict changes in health 1 or 2 years after the events took place. It appears that daily hassles are closely linked to immediate health and psychological well-being (Crowther et al., 2001). Major life changes have more of a long-term impact.

One way to guarantee that you will experience a large number of life changes and hassles is to live in a foreign culture. "Acculturative Stress—Stranger in a Strange Land" offers a brief glimpse into some of the consequences of culture shock.

What can be done about a high LCU score or feeling excessively hassled? A good response is to use stress management skills. For serious problems, stress management should be learned directly from a therapist or a stress clinic. When ordinary stresses are involved, there is much you can do on your own. An upcoming discussion of stress management will give you a start. In the meantime, take it easy!

Psychosomatic Disorders

As we have seen, chronic or repeated stress can damage physical health, as well as upset emotional well-being. Prolonged stress reactions are closely related to a large number of psychosomatic (SIKE-oh-so-MAT-ik) illnesses. In **psychosomatic disorders** (*psyche:* mind; *soma:* body), psychological factors contribute to actual bodily damage or to damaging changes in bodily functioning (Asmundson & Taylor, 2005). Psychosomatic problems, therefore, are *not* the same as hypochondria. **Hypochondriacs** (HI-po-KON-dree-aks) imagine that they have diseases. There is nothing imaginary about asthma, a migraine headache, or high blood pressure. Severe psychosomatic disorders can be fatal. The person who says, "Oh it's *just* psychosomatic" doesn't understand how serious stress-related diseases really are. (See "It's All in Your Mind.")

The most common psychosomatic problems are gastrointestinal and respiratory (stomach pain and asthma, for example), but many others exist. Typical problems include eczema (skin rash), hives, migraine headaches, rheumatoid arthritis, hypertension (high blood pressure), colitis (ulceration of the colon), and heart disease. Actually, these are only the major problems. Many lesser

Social Readjustment Rating Scale (SRRS) A scale that rates the impact of various life events on the likelihood of illness.

Hassle (microstressor) Any distressing, day-to-day annoyance.

Psychosomatic disorders Illnesses in which psychological factors contribute to bodily damage or to damaging changes in bodily functioning.

Hypochondriac A person who complains about illnesses that appear to be imaginary.

HUMAN DIVERSITY

Acculturative Stress—Stranger in a Strange Land

Around the world, an increasing number of emigrants and refugees must adapt to dramatic changes in language, dress, values, and social customs. For many, the result is a period of culture shock or **acculturative stress** (stress caused by adapting to a foreign culture). Typical reactions to acculturative stress are anxiety, hostility, depression, alienation, physical illness, or identity confusion (Rummens, Beiser, & Noh, 2003). For many young immigrants, acculturative stress is a major source of mental health problems (Yeh, 2003).

Morton Beebe/Corbis

One of the best antidotes for acculturative stress is a society that tolerates or even celebrates ethnic diversity. Although some people find it hard to accept new immigrants, the fact is, nearly everyone's family tree includes people who were once strangers in a strange land.

The severity of acculturative stress is related, in part, to how a person adapts to a new culture. There are four main patterns of adaptation (Berry, 1990; Berry et al., 2005):

Integration—maintain your old cultural identity but participate in the new culture

Separation—maintain your old cultural identity and avoid contact with the new culture

Assimilation—adopt the new culture as your own and have contact with its members

Marginalization—reject your old culture but suffer rejection by members of the new culture

To illustrate each pattern, let's consider a family that has immigrated to the United States from the imaginary country of Farlandia:

The father favors integration. He is learning English and wants to get involved in American life. At the same time, he is a leader in the Farlandian-American community and spends much of his leisure time with other Farlandian-Americans. His level of acculturative stress is low.

The mother only speaks Farlandish and only interacts with other Farlandian-Americans. She remains almost completely separate from American society. Her stress level is high.

The teenage daughter is annoyed by hearing Farlandish spoken at home, by her mother's serving only Farlandian food, and by having to spend her leisure time with her extended Farlandian family. She would prefer to speak English and to be with her American friends. Her desire to assimilate creates moderate stress.

The son doesn't particularly value his Farlandian heritage, yet his schoolmates reject him because he speaks with a Farlandian accent. He feels trapped between two cultures. His position is marginal and his stress level is high.

To summarize, those who feel marginalized tend to be highly stressed; those who seek to remain separate are also highly stressed; those who pursue integration into their new culture are minimally stressed; and those who assimilate are moderately stressed. As you can see, integration and assimilation are the best options. However, a big benefit of assimilating is that people who embrace their new culture experience fewer social difficulties. For many, this justifies the stress of adopting new customs and cultural values (Gurung, 2006; Ward & Rana-Deuba, 1999).

---

health complaints are also stress related. Typical examples include sore muscles, headaches, neck aches, backaches, indigestion, constipation, chronic diarrhea, fatigue, insomnia, premenstrual problems, and sexual dysfunctions (Taylor, 2006). For some of these problems biofeedback may be helpful. The next section explains how.

Biofeedback

Psychologists have discovered that people can learn to control bodily activities once thought to be involuntary. This is done by applying informational feedback to bodily control, a process called **biofeedback.** If I were to say to you, "Raise the temperature of your right hand," you probably couldn't, because you wouldn't know if you were succeeding. To make your task easier, we could attach a sensitive thermometer to your hand. The thermometer could be wired so that an increase in temperature would activate a

signal light. Then all you would have to do is try to keep the light on as much as possible. With practice and the help of biofeedback, you could learn to raise your hand temperature at will.

Biofeedback holds promise as a way to treat some psychosomatic problems (● Figure 13.8). For instance, people have been trained to prevent migraine headaches with biofeedback. Sensors are taped to patients' hands and foreheads. Patients then learn to redirect blood flow away from the head to their extremities. Because migraine headaches involve excessive blood flow to the head, biofeedback helps patients reduce the frequency of their headaches (Andrasik, 2003; Larsson et al., 2005).

Early successes led many to predict that biofeedback would offer a cure for psychosomatic illnesses, anxiety, phobias, drug abuse, and a long list of other problems. In reality, biofeedback has proved helpful but not an instant cure (Schwartz & Andrasik, 2003). Biofeedback can help relieve muscle-tension headaches, migraine headaches, and chronic pain (Middaugh & Pawlick,

CRITICAL THINKING

It's All in Your Mind

Have you ever had someone dismiss a health concern by saying, "Its all in your mind," as if your problem might be imaginary? For centuries the *medical model* has dominated Western thinking. From this perspective, health is an absence of illness and your body is a complex biological machine that can break down and become ill. Sometimes, you inflict the damage yourself through poor lifestyle choices, such as smoking or overeating. Sometimes, an external cause, such as a virus, is the culprit. In either event, the problem is physical and your mind has little to do with it. Moreover, physical problems call for physical treatments ("Take your medicine"), so your mind has little to do with your recovery. In the medical model, *any* impact of the mind on health was dismissed as a mere placebo effect.

> ### bridges
>
> **To remind yourself about placebo effects see Chapter 1, page 35.**

Over the last 50 years, the medical model has slowly given way to the *biopsychosocial model*. This view states that diseases are caused by a combination of biological, psychological, and social factors. Most important, the biopsychosocial model defines health as a state of well-being that we can *actively* attain and maintain (Oakley, 2004). Instead of passively getting treatments from a doctor, this model says that you play a role in fostering your own health. Thus, it may no longer be inaccurate to say, "It's all in your mind," *if* you mean that a person's beliefs—which affect behavior—can have a dramatic impact on health. Even the term "placebo effect" is being replaced with the term "meaning response" to better reflect our new understanding that medicine works best when doctors help people *make sense* of their medical condition to maximize healing (Moerman, 2002). So, as you take responsibility for your own well-being, remember that in some ways health *is* all in your mind!

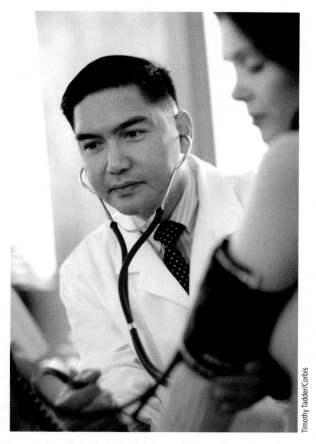

It is estimated that at least half of all patients who see a doctor have a psychosomatic disorder or an illness that is complicated by psychosomatic symptoms.

Timothy Tadder/Corbis

2002). It shows promise for lowering blood pressure and controlling heart rhythms (Rau, Bührer, & Weitkunat, 2003). The technique has been used with some success to control epileptic seizures and hyperactivity in children (Demos, 2005). Insomnia also responds to biofeedback therapy (Gathchel & Oordt, 2003).

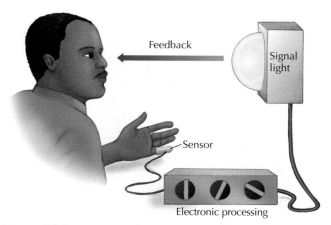

● **Figure 13.8** In biofeedback training bodily processes are monitored and processed electronically. A signal is then routed back to the patient through headphones, signal lights, or other means. This information helps the patient alter bodily activities not normally under voluntary control.

Acculturative stress Stress caused by the many changes and adaptations required when a person moves to a foreign culture.

Biofeedback Information given to a person about his or her ongoing bodily activities; aids voluntary regulation of bodily states.

How does biofeedback help? Some researchers believe that many of its benefits arise from *general relaxation.* Others stress that there is no magic in biofeedback itself. The method simply acts as a "mirror" to help a person perform tasks involving *self-regulation.* Just as a mirror does not comb your hair, biofeedback does not do anything by itself. It can, however, help people make desired changes in their behavior (Weems, 1998).

The Cardiac Personality

It would be a mistake to assume that stress is the sole cause of psychosomatic diseases. Genetic differences, organ weaknesses, and learned reactions to stress combine to do damage. Personality also enters the picture. As mentioned earlier, a general disease-prone personality type exists. To a degree, there are also "headache personalities," "asthma personalities," and so on. The best documented of such patterns is the "cardiac personality"—a person at high risk for heart disease.

Two cardiologists, Meyer Friedman and Ray Rosenman, offer a glimpse at how some people create stress for themselves. In a landmark study of heart problems, Friedman and Rosenman (1983) classified people as either **Type A personalities** (those who run a high risk of heart attack) or **Type B personalities** (those who are unlikely to have a heart attack). Then they did an 8-year follow-up, finding more than twice the rate of heart disease in Type As than in Type Bs (Rosenman et al., 1975).

Type A

What is the Type A personality like? Type A people are hard driving, ambitious, highly competitive, achievement oriented, and striving. Type A people believe that with enough effort they can overcome any obstacle, and they "push" themselves accordingly.

Individuals with Type A personalities feel a continuous sense of anger, irritation, and hostility.

Perhaps the most telltale signs of a Type A personality are *time urgency* and chronic *anger* or *hostility.* Type As seem to chafe at the normal pace of events. They hurry from one activity to another, racing the clock in self-imposed urgency. As they do, they feel a constant sense of frustration and anger. Feelings of anger and hostility, in particular, are strongly related to increased risk of heart attack (Boyle et al., 2004; Bunde & Suls, 2006). One study found that 15 percent of a group of 25-year-old doctors and lawyers who scored high on a hostility test were dead by age 50. The most damaging pattern may occur in hostile persons who keep their anger "bottled up." Such people seethe with anger, but don't express it outwardly. This increases their pulse rate and blood pressure and puts a tremendous strain on the heart (Bongard, al'Absi, & Lovallo, 1998).

To summarize, there is growing evidence that anger or hostility may be the core lethal factor of Type A behavior (Krantz & McCeney, 2002; Niaura et al., 2002). To date, hundreds of studies have supported the validity of the Type A concept. In view of this, Type As would be wise to take their increased health risks seriously.

How are Type A people identified? Characteristics of Type A people are summarized in the short self-identification test presented in ● Table 13.7. If most of the list applies to you, you might be a Type A. However, confirmation of your type would require more powerful testing methods. Also, remember that the original definition of Type A behavior was probably too broad. The key

Table 13.7 ● Characteristics of the Type A Person

Check the items that apply to you. Do you	
_____	Have a habit of explosively accentuating various key words in ordinary speech even when there is no need for such accentuation (I HATE it when you do THAT!)?
_____	Finish other persons' sentences for them?
_____	*Always* move, walk, and eat rapidly?
_____	Quickly skim reading material and prefer summaries or condensations of books?
_____	Become easily angered by slow-moving lines or traffic?
_____	Feel an impatience with the rate at which most events take place?
_____	Tend to be unaware of the details or beauty of your surroundings?
_____	Frequently strive to think of or do two or more things simultaneously?
_____	Almost always feel vaguely guilty when you relax, vacation, or do absolutely nothing for several days?
_____	Tend to evaluate your worth in quantitative terms (number of A's earned, amount of income, number of games won, and so forth)?
_____	Have nervous gestures or muscle twitches, such as grinding your teeth, clenching your fists, or drumming your fingers?
_____	Attempt to schedule more and more activities into less time and in so doing make fewer allowances for unforeseen problems?
_____	Frequently think about other things while talking to someone?
_____	Repeatedly take on more responsibilities than you can comfortably handle?

Source: Shortened and adapted from Friedman and Rosenman, *Type A Behavior and Your Heart,* Alfred A. Knopf, Inc., © 1983. Reprinted with permission.

psychological factors that increase heart disease risk appear to be anger, hostility, and mistrust (Krantz & McCeney, 2002; Smith et al., 2004). Also, although Type A behavior appears to promote heart disease, depression or distress may be what finally triggers a heart attack (Denollet & Van Heck, 2001; Dinan, 2001).

Because our society places a premium on achievement, competition, and mastery, it is not surprising that many people develop Type A personalities. The best way to avoid the self-made stress this causes is to adopt behavior that is the opposite of that listed in ● Table 13.7 (Williams, Barefoot, & Schneiderman, 2003). It is entirely possible to succeed in life without sacrificing your health or happiness in the process. People who frequently feel angry and hostile toward others may benefit from the advice of Redford Williams, a physician interested in Type A behavior.

Strategies for Reducing Hostility

According to Redford Williams, reducing hostility involves three goals. First, you must stop mistrusting the motives of others. Second, you must find ways to reduce how often you feel anger, indignation, irritation, and rage. Third, you must learn to be kinder and more considerate. Based on his clinical experience, Williams (1989) recommends 12 strategies for reducing hostility and increasing trust:

1. Become aware of your angry, hostile, and cynical thoughts by logging them in a notebook. Record what happened, what you thought and felt, and what actions you took. Review your hostility log at the end of each week.
2. Admit to yourself and to someone you trust that you have a problem with excessive anger and hostility.
3. Interrupt hostile, cynical thoughts whenever they occur.

> **bridges**
>
> The Psychology in Action section of Chapter 15, pages 522–526, explains a thought-stopping method you can use for this step.

4. When you have an angry, hostile, or cynical thought about someone, silently look for the ways in which it is irrational or unreasonable.
5. When you are angry, try to mentally put yourself in the other person's shoes.
6. Learn to laugh at yourself, and use humor to defuse your anger.
7. Learn reliable ways to relax.

> **bridges**
>
> Two methods are described in this chapter's Psychology in Action section, pages 453–457. Another can be found in the Psychology in Action discussion in Chapter 15, pages 522–526.

8. Practice trusting others more. Begin with situations where no great harm will be done if the person lets you down.
9. Make an effort to listen more to others and to really understand what they are saying.
10. Learn to be assertive, rather than aggressive, in upsetting situations.

> **bridges**
>
> See Chapter 16, pages 551–553, for information about self-assertion skills.

11. Rise above small irritations by pretending that today is the last day of your life.
12. Rather than blaming people for mistreating you, and becoming angry over it, try to forgive them. We all have shortcomings.

Hardy Personality

How do Type A people who do not develop heart disease differ from those who do? Psychologist Salvatore Maddi has studied people who have a **hardy personality.** Such people seem to be unusually resistant to stress. The first study of hardiness began with two groups of managers at a large utility company. All the managers held high-stress positions. Yet some tended to get sick after stressful events, whereas others were rarely ill. How did the people who were thriving differ from their "stressed-out" colleagues? Both groups seemed to have traits typical of the Type A personality, so that wasn't the explanation. They were also quite similar in most other respects. The main difference was that the hardy group seemed to hold a worldview that consisted of three traits (Maddi, 2006):

1. They had a sense of personal *commitment* to self, work, family, and other stabilizing values.
2. They felt that they had *control* over their lives and their work.
3. They had a tendency to see life as a series of *challenges,* rather than as a series of threats or problems.

How do such traits protect people from the effects of stress? Persons strong in *commitment* find ways of turning whatever they are doing into something that seems interesting and important. They tend to get involved rather than feeling alienated.

Persons strong in *control* believe that they can more often than not influence the course of events around them. This prevents them from passively seeing themselves as victims of circumstance.

Type A personality A personality type with an elevated risk of heart disease; characterized by time urgency, anger, and hostility.

Type B personality All personality types other than Type A; a low cardiac-risk personality.

Hardy personality A personality style associated with superior stress resistance.

DISCOVERING PSYCHOLOGY

Feeling Stressed? You've Got a Friend

Here's an interesting exercise to try: Briefly answer the following four questions about a specific person you are currently close to—someone you can turn to when you need help, advice, or encouragement:

1. What do you value or appreciate most about this person?
2. What does this person value or appreciate most about you?
3. What does this person do for you that is supportive or helpful?
4. How do you feel about this person after being away from her or him for a few hours or a few days? (Adapted from Smith, Ruiz, & Uchino, 2004.)

Do you feel more relaxed and at ease after answering these questions? In a recent study, the questions were used to get people to think about a close, supportive person for a few minutes. After that, subjects had to give a stressful speech. For some participants, thinking about a supportive person helped lower their stress levels (Smith, Ruiz, & Uchino, 2004).

The preceding study suggests that you may be able to reduce the stress you feel in difficult situations by thinking about a person who supports and encourages you. If that doesn't help, and you own a pet, there may be a good alternative strategy. Many people view their pets as loving, supportive com-

panions who are better, in some ways, than humans. In another study, some people were asked to do stressful tasks alone, whereas others had a friend, a spouse, or a pet present. Under these conditions, the greatest amount of stress relief occurred when a pet (dog or cat) was present (Allen, Blascovich, & Mendes, 2002). Thus, if you have a pet, you might find it helpful to imagine the animal by your side when you face a stressful situation. Silently talking to your furry friend can be quite calming. In any case, whether your comfort comes from a human or an animal companion, it's valuable to remind yourself that "you've got a friend."

Finally, people strong in *challenge* find fulfillment in continual growth. They seek to learn from their experiences, rather than accepting easy comfort, security, and routine (Maddi, 2006). Indeed, many "negative" experiences can actually enhance personal growth—if you have support from others and the skills needed to cope with challenge (Armeli, Gunthert, & Cohen, 2001).

Positive Psychology: Hardiness, Optimism, and Happiness

Good and bad events occur in all lives. What separates happy people from those who are unhappy is largely a matter of attitude. Happy people tend to see their lives in more positive terms, even when trouble comes their way. For example, happier people tend to find humor in disappointments. They look at setbacks as challenges. They are strengthened by losses (Lyubomirsky & Tucker, 1998). In short, happiness tends to be related to hardiness (Maddi, 2006). Why is there a connection? As psychologist Barbara Fredrickson has pointed out, positive emotions tend to broaden our mental focus. Emotions such as joy, interest, and contentment create an urge to play, to be creative, to explore, to savor life, to seek new experiences, to integrate, and to grow. When you are stressed, experiencing positive emotions can make it more likely that you will find creative solutions to your problems. Positive emotions also tend to reduce the bodily arousal that occurs when we are stressed, possibly limiting stress-related damage (Fredrickson, 2003).

Elsewhere in this chapter, we have noted the value of optimism, which goes hand in hand with hardiness and happiness. Optimists tend to expect that things will turn out well. This motivates them to actively cope with adversity. They are less likely to be stopped by temporary setbacks, and more likely to deal with problems head-on. Pessimists are more likely to ignore or deny problems.

The result of such differences is that optimists are less stressed and anxious than pessimists. They are also in better health than pessimists. In general, optimists tend to take better care of themselves because they believe that their efforts to stay healthy will succeed (Peterson & Chang, 2003).

The Value of Social Support

Social support (close, positive relationships with others) provides one more important antidote to stress. People with close, supportive relationships tend to be happy, hardy, optimistic, and healthy (Kiecolt-Glaser et al., 2002). Apparently, support from family and friends serves as a buffer to cushion the impact of stressful events. (See "Feeling Stressed? You've Got a Friend.")

Support from family and friends acts as a major buffer against stress.

Tim Pannell/Corbis

Women tend to make better use of social support than men do. Women who are stressed seek support and they nurture others. Men are more likely to become aggressive or to withdraw emotionally (Taylor et al., 2000). This may be why "manly men" won't ask for help, whereas women in trouble call their friends! Where stress is concerned, many men could benefit from adopting women's tendency to tend to and befriend others.

How else might social support help? Most people share positive events, such as marriages, births, graduations, and birthdays, with others. When things go well, we like to tell others about them. Sharing such events tends to amplify positive emotions and

to further increase social support. In many ways, the sharing of good news is an important means by which positive events contribute to individual well-being (Gable et al., 2004).

A Look Ahead

The work we have reviewed here has drawn new attention to the fact that each of us has a personal responsibility for maintaining and promoting health. In the Psychology in Action section that follows, we will look at what you can do to better cope with stress and the health risks that it entails. But first, the following questions may help you maintain a healthy grade on your next psychology test.

KNOWLEDGE BUILDER
Stress and Health

RECITE

1. Ratings on the SRRS are based on the total number of _____ a person experienced in the preceding year.
   a. hassles
   b. LCUs
   c. STDs
   d. psychosomatic illnesses
2. The SRRS appears to predict long-range changes in health, whereas the frequency and severity of daily microstressors is closely related to immediate ratings of health. T or F?
3. Ulcers, migraine headaches, and hypochondria are all frequently psychosomatic disorders. T or F?
4. Which of the following is *not* classified as a psychosomatic disorder?
   a. hypertension
   b. colitis
   c. eczema
   d. thymus
5. Two major elements of biofeedback training appear to be relaxation and self-regulation. T or F?
6. Anger, hostility, and mistrust appear to be the core lethal factors in
   a. hypochondria
   b. learned helplessness
   c. the GAS
   d. Type A behavior
7. A sense of commitment, challenge, and control characterizes the hardy personality. T or F?
8. Research shows that social support from family and friends has little effect on the health consequences of stress. T or F?

REFLECT
Critical Thinking
9. People with a hardy personality type appear to be especially resistant to which of the problems discussed earlier in this chapter?

Relate
Pick a year from your life that was unusually stressful. Use the SRRS to find your LCU score for that year. Do you think there was a connection between your LCU score and your health? Or have you observed more of a connection between microstressors and your health?

Mindy complains about her health all the time, but she actually seems to be just fine. An acquaintance of Mindy's dismisses her problems by saying, "Oh, she's not really sick. It's just psychosomatic." What's wrong with this use of the term "psychosomatic"?

Do you think you are basically a Type A or a Type B personality? To what extent do you possess traits of the hardy personality?

Answers: 1. b 2. T 3. F 4. d 5. T 6. d 7. T 8. F 9. Learned helplessness.

PSYCHOLOGY IN ACTION

Stress Management

Gateway Question: What are the best strategies for managing stress?

Stress management is the use of cognitive and behavioral strategies to reduce stress and improve coping skills. As promised, this section describes strategies for managing stress.

Before you continue reading, you may want to assess your level of stress again, this time using a scale developed for undergraduate students (● Table 13.8). Like the SRRS, high scores on the *College Life Stress Inventory* suggest that you have been exposed to health-

Social support Close, positive relationships with other people.

Stress management The application of cognitive and behavioral strategies to reduce stress and improve coping skills.

Table 13.8 ● College Life Stress Inventory

Circle the "stress rating" number for any item that has happened to you in the last year, then add them.

Event	Stress Rating	Event	Stress Rating
Being raped	100	Lack of sleep	69
Finding out that you are HIV-positive	100	Change in housing situation (hassles, moves)	69
Being accused of rape	98	Competing or performing in public	69
Death of a close friend	97	Getting in a physical fight	66
Death of a close family member	96	Difficulties with a roommate	66
Contracting a sexually transmitted disease (other than AIDS)	94	Job changes (applying, new job, work hassles)	65
Concerns about being pregnant	91	Declaring a major or concerns about future plans	65
Finals week	90	A class you hate	62
Concerns about your partner being pregnant	90	Drinking or use of drugs	61
Oversleeping for an exam	89	Confrontations with professors	60
Flunking a class	89	Starting a new semester	58
Having a boyfriend or girlfriend cheat on you	85	Going on a first date	57
Ending a steady dating relationship	85	Registration	55
Serious illness in a close friend or family member	85	Maintaining a steady dating relationship	55
Financial difficulties	84	Commuting to campus or work, or both	54
Writing a major term paper	83	Peer pressures	53
Being caught cheating on a test	83	Being away from home for the first time	53
Drunk driving	82	Getting sick	52
Sense of overload in school or work	82	Concerns about your appearance	52
Two exams in one day	80	Getting straight A's	51
Cheating on your boyfriend or girlfriend	77	A difficult class that you love	48
Getting married	76	Making new friends; getting along with friends	47
Negative consequences of drinking or drug use	75	Fraternity or sorority rush	47
Depression or crisis in your best friend	73	Falling asleep in class	40
Difficulties with parents	73	Attending an athletic event (e.g., football game)	20
Talking in front of a class	72		

Source: "Teaching of Psychology" by Michael J. Renner and R. S. Mackin, © 1998 Lawrence Erlbaum Associates and the authors. Reprinted by permission.

threatening levels of stress (Renner & Mackin, 1998).

The *College Life Stress Inventory* is scored by adding the ratings for all the items that have happened to you in the last year. The following scale is an approximate guide to the meaning of your score. But remember, stress is an internal state. If you are good at coping with stressors, a high score may not be a problem for you.

0–150:	Very low
151–590:	Low
591–1030:	Below average
1031–1470:	Average
1471–1910:	High
1911–2350:	Very high
2351 or more:	Extremely high

Now that you have a picture of your current level of stress, what can you do about it?

The simplest way of coping with stress is to modify or remove its source—by leaving a stressful job, for example. Obviously this is often impossible, which is why learning to manage stress is so important.

As shown in ● Figure 13.9, stress triggers *bodily effects, upsetting thoughts,* and *ineffective behavior.* Also shown is the fact that each element worsens the others in a vicious cycle. Indeed, the basic idea of the "Stress Game" is that once it begins, *you lose*—unless you take action to break the cycle. The information that follows tells how.

Managing Bodily Reactions

Much of the immediate discomfort of stress is caused by fight-or-flight emotional responses. The body is ready to act, with tight muscles and a pounding heart. If action is prevented,

we merely remain "uptight." A sensible remedy is to learn a reliable, drug-free way of relaxing.

Exercise

Stress-based arousal can be dissipated by using the body. Any full-body exercise can be effective. Our intrepid student, Jennifer, enjoys rock climbing. Swimming, dancing, jumping rope, yoga, most sports, and especially walking are valuable outlets. Regular exercise alters hormones, circulation, muscle tone, and a number of other aspects of physical functioning. Together, such changes can reduce anxiety and lower the risks for disease (Linden, 2005; Salmon, 2001).

Be sure to choose activities that are vigorous enough to relieve tension, yet enjoyable enough to be done repeatedly. Exercising for stress management is most effective when it is

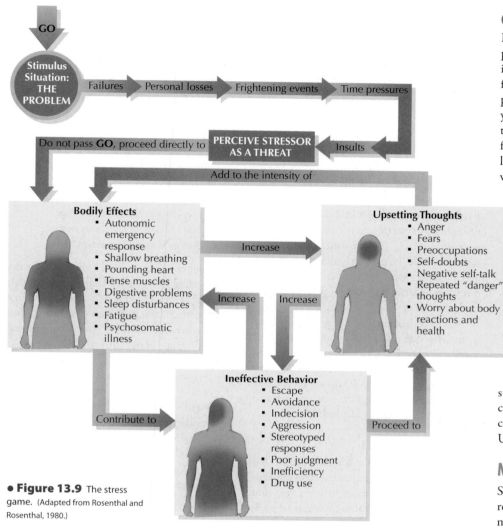

• **Figure 13.9** The stress game. (Adapted from Rosenthal and Rosenthal, 1980.)

done daily. As little as 30 minutes of total exercise per day, even if it occurs in short 10- to 20-minute sessions, can improve mood and energy (Hansen, Stevens, & Coast, 2001).

Meditation

Many stress counselors recommend *meditation* for quieting the body and promoting relaxation. For now, it is enough to state that meditation is easy to learn—taking an expensive commercial course is unnecessary.

> **bridges**
> To learn more about meditation and its effects, read Chapter 6, pages 197–198.

Meditation is one of the most effective ways to relax (Deckro et al., 2002). But be aware that listening to or playing music, taking nature walks, enjoying hobbies, and the

like can be meditations of sorts. Anything that reliably interrupts upsetting thoughts and promotes relaxation can be helpful.

Progressive Relaxation

It is possible to relax systematically, completely, and by choice. The basic idea of **progressive relaxation** is to tighten all the muscles in a given area of your body (the arms, for instance) and then voluntarily relax them. By first tensing and relaxing each area of the body, you can learn what muscle tension feels like. Then when each area is relaxed, the change is more noticeable and more controllable. In this way it is possible, with practice, to greatly reduce tension.

> **bridges**
> To learn the details of how this is done, consult Chapter 15, page 506.

Guided Imagery

In a technique called **guided imagery,** people visualize images that are calming, relaxing, or beneficial in other ways. Relaxation, for instance, can be promoted by visualizing peaceful scenes. Pick several places where you feel safe, calm, and at ease. Typical locations might be a beach or lake, the woods, floating on an air mattress in a warm pool, or lying in the sun at a quiet park. To relax, vividly imagine yourself in one of these locations. In the visualized scene, you should be alone and in a comfortable position. It is important to visualize the scene as realistically as possible. Try to feel, taste, smell, hear, and see what you would actually experience in the calming scene. Practice forming such images several times a day for about 5 minutes each time. When your scenes become familiar and detailed they can be used to reduce anxiety and encourage relaxation (Rosenthal, 1993).

Remember, too, that imagining that a supportive friend or a loving pet is nearby can reduce tension and anxiety (Allen, Blascovich, & Mendes, 2002; Smith, Ruiz, & Uchino, 2004).

Modifying Ineffective Behavior

Stress is often made worse by our misguided responses to it. The following suggestions may help you deal with stress more effectively.

Slow Down

Remember that stress can be self-generated. Try to deliberately do things at a slower pace—especially if your pace has speeded up over the years. Tell yourself, "What counts most is not if I get there first, but if I get there at all," or "My goal is distance, not speed."

Organize

Disorganization creates stress. Try to take a fresh look at your situation and get organized. Setting priorities can be a real stress fighter. Ask yourself what's really important

Progressive relaxation A method for producing deep relaxation of all parts of the body.

Guided imagery Intentional visualization of images that are calming, relaxing, or beneficial in other ways.

and concentrate on the things that count. Learn to let go of trivial but upsetting irritations. And above all, when you are feeling stressed, remember to KIS: **K**eep **I**t **S**imple. (Some people prefer KISS: Keep It Simple, Stupid.)

Strike a Balance

Work, school, family, friends, interests, hobbies, recreation, community, church—there are many important elements in a satisfying life. Damaging stress often comes from letting one element—especially work or school—get blown out of proportion. Your goal should be quality in life, not quantity. Try to strike a balance between challenging "good stress" and relaxation. Remember, when you are "doing nothing" you are actually doing something very important: Set aside time for "me acts" such as loafing, browsing, puttering, playing, and napping.

Recognize and Accept Your Limits

Many of us set unrealistic and perfectionist goals. Given that no one can ever be perfect, this attitude leaves many people feeling inadequate, no matter how well they have performed. Set gradual, achievable goals for yourself. Also, set realistic limits on what you try to do on any given day. Learn to say no to added demands or responsibilities.

Write About Your Feelings

If you don't have someone you can talk to about stressful events, you might try expressing your thoughts and feelings in writing. Several studies have found that students who write about their upsetting experiences, thoughts, and feelings are better able to cope with stress. They also experience fewer illnesses, and they get better grades (Esterling et al., 1999; Pennebaker, 2004). Writing about your feelings tends to leave your mind clearer. This makes it easier to pay attention to life's challenges and come up with effective coping strategies (Klein & Boals, 2001a, 2001b). Thus, after you write about your feelings, it helps to make specific plans for coping with upsetting experiences (Pennebaker & Chung, 2007).

As an alternative, you might want to try writing about positive experiences. In one study, college students who wrote about intensely positive experiences had fewer illnesses over the next 3 months. Writing just 20 minutes a day for 3 days improved the students' moods and had a surprisingly long-lasting effect on their health (Burton & King, 2004).

Avoiding Upsetting Thoughts

Assume you are taking a test. Suddenly you realize that you are running short of time. If you say to yourself, "Oh no, this is terrible, I've blown it now," your body's response will probably be sweating, tenseness, and a knot in your stomach. On the other hand, if you say, "I should have watched the time, but getting upset won't help, I'll just take one question at a time," your stress level will be much lower.

As stated earlier, stress is greatly affected by the views we take of events. Physical symptoms and a tendency to make poor decisions are increased by negative thoughts or "self-talk." In many cases what you say to yourself can be the difference between coping and collapsing (Matheny et al., 1996).

Coping Statements

Psychologist Donald Meichenbaum has popularized a technique called **stress inoculation.** In it, clients learn to fight fear and anxiety with an internal monologue of positive coping statements. First, clients learn to identify and monitor **negative self-statements** (self-critical thoughts that increase anxiety). Negative thoughts are a problem because they tend to directly elevate physical arousal. To counter this effect, clients learn to replace negative statements with coping statements from a supplied list. Eventually they are encouraged to make their own lists (Saunders et al., 1996).

How are coping statements applied? **Coping statements** are reassuring and self-enhancing. They are used to block out, or counteract, negative self-talk in stressful situations. Before giving a short speech, for instance, you would replace "I'm scared," "I can't do this," "My mind will go blank and I'll panic," or "I'll sound stupid and boring" with "I'll give my speech on something I like," or "I'll breathe deeply before I start my speech," or "My pounding heart just means I'm psyched up to do my best." Additional examples of coping statements follow.

Preparing for Stressful Situation
I'll just take things one step at a time.
If I get nervous, I'll just pause a moment.
Tomorrow I'll be through it.
I've managed to do this before.
What exactly do I have to do?

Confronting the Stressful Situation
Relax now, this can't really hurt me.
Stay organized, focus on the task.
There's no hurry. Take it step by step.
Nobody's perfect, I'll just do my best.
It will be over soon, just be calm.

Meichenbaum cautions that saying the "right" things to yourself may not be enough to improve stress tolerance. You must practice this approach in actual stress situations. Also, it is important to develop your own personal list of coping statements by finding what works for you. Ultimately, the value of learning this and other stress management skills ties back into the idea that much stress is self-generated. Knowing that you can manage a demanding situation is in itself a major antidote for stress. In a recent study, college students who learned stress inoculation not only had less anxiety and depression, but better self-esteem as well (Schiraldi & Brown, 2001).

Lighten Up

Humor is worth cultivating as a way to reduce stress. A good sense of humor can lower your distress/stress reaction to difficult events (Lefcourt, 2003). In addition, an ability to laugh at life's ups and downs is associated with better immunity to disease (McClelland & Cheriff, 1997). Don't be afraid to laugh at yourself and at the many ways in which we humans make things difficult for ourselves. You've probably heard the following advice about everyday stresses: "Don't sweat the small stuff," and "It's all small stuff." Humor is one of the best antidotes for anxiety and emotional distress because it helps put things into perspective (Henman, 2001; Szabo, 2003). The vast majority of events are only as stressful as you allow them to be. Have some fun. It's perfectly healthy.

Coping with Stress

RECITE

1. Exercise, meditation, and progressive relaxation are considered effective ways of countering negative self-statements. T or F?
2. A person using progressive relaxation for stress management is most likely trying to control which component of stress?
   a. bodily reactions
   b. upsetting thoughts
   c. ineffective behavior
   d. the primary appraisal
3. Exercise, meditation, progressive relaxation, and guided imagery would be least likely to help a person who is in the GAS stage of
   a. alarm
   b. resistance
   c. exhaustion
   d. adaptation

4. While taking a stressful classroom test you say to yourself, "Stay organized, focus on the task." It's obvious that you are using
   a. guided imagery
   b. coping statements
   c. LCUs
   d. guided relaxation

REFLECT

Critical Thinking

5. Stefan always feels extremely pressured when the due date arrives for his major term papers. How could he reduce stress in such instances?

Relate

If you were going to put together a "tool kit" for stress management, what items would you include?

Answers: 1. F **2.** a **3.** c **4.** b **5.** The stress associated with doing term papers can be almost completely eliminated by breaking up a long-term assignment into many small daily or weekly assignments. Students who habitually procrastinate are often amazed at how pleasant college work can be once they renounce "brinkmanship."

chapter in review

Gateways to Health, Stress, and Coping

Health psychology studies how personal habits and behavior patterns can lead to illness and death or can promote health.

- Studies of health and illness have identified a number of behavioral risk factors and health-promoting behaviors.
- Health psychologists have pioneered efforts to prevent the development of unhealthy habits and to improve well-being through community health campaigns.
- Maintaining good health is a personal responsibility, not a matter of luck. Wellness is based on minimizing risk factors and engaging in health-promoting behaviors.

Stress occurs when demands are placed on an organism to adjust or adapt.

- Stress is a normal part of life; however, it is also a major risk factor for illness and disease.
- Although some events are more stressful than others, stress always represents an interaction between people and the environments in which they live.
- The body reacts to stress in a series of stages called the general adaptation syndrome (GAS).
- The stages of the GAS are alarm, resistance, and exhaustion. Bodily reactions in the GAS follow the pattern observed in the development of psychosomatic disorders.
- Studies of psychoneuroimmunology show that stress lowers the body's resistance to disease by weakening the immune system.

- Events tend to be more stressful when they involve pressure, a lack of control, unpredictability, and intense or repeated emotional shocks.
- Stress is intensified when a situation is perceived as a threat and when a person does not feel competent to cope with it.
- In work settings, prolonged stress can lead to burnout.
- Making a primary appraisal greatly affects our emotional responses to a situation.
- Stress reactions, in particular, are related to an appraisal of threat.
- During a secondary appraisal we select problem-focused coping or emotion-focused coping (or both) as a way of managing stress.

Frustration, a negative emotional state that occurs when we are prevented from reaching desired goals, becomes more intense as the strength, urgency, or importance of a blocked motive increases.

- Major behavioral reactions to frustration include persistence, more vigorous responding, circumvention, direct aggression, displaced aggression (including scapegoating), and escape or withdrawal.

Stress inoculation Use of positive coping statements to control fear and anxiety.

Negative self-statements Self-critical thoughts that increase anxiety and lower performance.

Coping statements Reassuring, self-enhancing statements that are used to stop self-critical thinking.

Four major types of conflict are approach-approach, avoidance-avoidance, approach-avoidance, and multiple conflicts (double approach-avoidance and multiple approach-avoidance).

- Contradictory needs, desires, motives, or demands create psychological conflicts.
- Approach-approach conflicts are usually the easiest to resolve.
- Avoidance conflicts are difficult to resolve and are characterized by inaction, indecision, freezing, and a desire to escape (called leaving the field).
- People usually remain in approach-avoidance conflicts, but fail to fully resolve them. Approach-avoidance conflicts are associated with ambivalence and partial approach.
- Vacillation is a common reaction to double and multiple approach-avoidance conflicts.

Defense mechanisms are mental processes used to avoid, deny, or distort sources of threat or anxiety, including threats to one's self-image.

- Overuse of defense mechanisms makes people less adaptable.
- A large number of defense mechanisms have been identified, including compensation, denial, fantasy, intellectualization, isolation, projection, rationalization, reaction formation, regression, repression, and sublimation.

Learned helplessness can be used as a model for understanding depression. Mastery training, optimism, and hope all act as antidotes for learned helplessness.

- Depression is a major, and surprisingly common, emotional problem. Actions and thoughts that counter feelings of helplessness tend to reduce depression.
- The college blues are a relatively mild form of depression. Learning to manage college work and to challenge self-critical thinking can help alleviate the college blues.

The body's reactions to stress can directly damage internal organs, and stress impairs the body's immune system, increasing susceptibility to disease.

- The *Social Readjustment Rating Scale* rates the impact of life changes on long-range susceptibility to accident or illness.
- Immediate psychological and mental health is more closely related to the intensity and severity of daily hassles or microstressors.
- Intense or prolonged stress may cause damage in the form of psychosomatic problems.
- During biofeedback training, bodily processes are monitored and converted to a signal that tells what the body is doing. Biofeedback allows people to alleviate some psychosomatic illnesses by altering bodily activities.
- Personality characteristics affect the amount of stress a person experiences and the subsequent risk of illness.
- People with Type A personalities are competitive, striving, hostile, impatient, and prone to having heart attacks.
- People who have traits of the hardy personality seem to be resistant to stress, even if they also have Type A traits.
- Optimism, positive emotions, and social support tend to buffer stress.

The damaging effects of stress can be reduced with cognitive and behavioral stress management techniques.

- All of the following are good ways to manage bodily reactions to stress: exercise, meditation, progressive relaxation, and guided imagery.
- To minimize ineffective behavior when you are stressed you can slow down, get organized, balance work and relaxation, accept your limits, and write about your feelings.
- Learning to use coping statements is a good way to combat upsetting thoughts.

Web Resources

For an up-to-date list of direct links to interesting sites, including those listed here, visit the student companion site for this book at www.cengage.com/psychology/coon

The Longevity Game Find out how long you might live; explore your options.

Defense Mechanisms Try to role play various defense mechanisms.

Depression and Control Explore the relationship between learned helplessness and depression.

SRRS Fill out an online version of the Social Readjustment Rating Scale.

Stress, Anxiety, Fears, and Psychosomatic Disorders A comprehensive source on stress, anxiety, and related disorders.

Type A Behavior Describes Type A behavior, with links to an online test and related sites.

Self-Growth.Com Explore a self-improvement and personal growth website that provides many links to stress management resources, including online articles and information on related topics such as biofeedback and stress.

Stress Management Resources A site that helps you deal with job-related stress.

Interactive Learning

Introduction to Psychology: Gateways to Mind and Behavior **Book Companion Website**
www.cengage.com/psychology/coon

Visit your book companion website, where you will find flash cards, practice quizzes, web links, and more to help you study.

CENGAGENOW™ *Just what you need to know NOW!*

Spend time on what you need to master rather than on information you already have learned. Take a pre-test for this chapter, and CengageNOW will generate a personalized study plan based on your results. The study plan will identify the topics you need to review and direct you to online resources to help you master those topics. You can then take a post-test to help you determine the concepts you have mastered and what you will need to work on. Try it out! Go to www.cengage.com/login to sign in with an access code or to purchase access to this product.

CHAPTER 14

Psychological Disorders

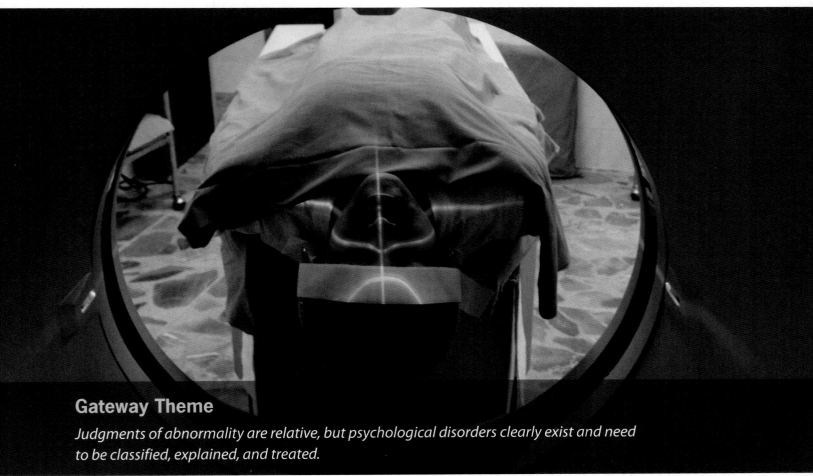

Gateway Theme

Judgments of abnormality are relative, but psychological disorders clearly exist and need to be classified, explained, and treated.

Gabriel M. Covian/Getty Images

Gateway Questions

- *How is abnormality defined?*
- *What are the major psychological disorders?*
- *What are the general characteristics of psychotic disorders?*
- *What is the nature of a delusional disorder?*
- *What forms does schizophrenia take? What causes it?*

- *What are mood disorders? What causes them?*
- *What problems result when a person suffers high levels of anxiety?*
- *How do psychologists explain anxiety-based disorders?*
- *What is a personality disorder?*
- *Why do people commit suicide? Can suicide be prevented?*

Beware the Helicopters

"The helicopters. Oh no, not the helicopters. Have come to tear the feathers out of my frontal lobes. Help me, nurse, help me, can't you hear them? Gotta get back into my body to save it. . . . The doctor is thinking I would make good glue."

These are the words of Carol North, a psychiatrist who survived schizophrenia. In addition to being plagued by hallucinated helicopters, Carol heard voices that said: "Be good," "Do bad," "Stand up," "Sit down," "Collide with the other world," "Do you want a cigar?" (North, 1987).

Carol North's painful journey into the shadows of madness left her incapacitated for nearly 20 years. Wonderfully, she has since forged her career as an eminent psychiatrist concerned with helping others escape the maze of mental illness (see, for example, North et al., 2008). Her case is but one hint of the magnitude of mental health problems. Here are some facts on psychological disorders (NIMH, 2006b):

- 1 in 4 American adults suffers from a diagnosable mental disorder in any given year.
- Mental disorders are the leading cause of disability for Americans and Canadians ages 15 to 44.
- Anxiety disorders are often accompanied by depression and/or substance abuse.
- In 2002, almost 32,000 Americans committed suicide.
- More than 20,000,000 Americans suffer from mood disorders in any given year.

What does it mean to be "crazy"? A hundred years ago, doctors and nonprofessionals alike used terms such as "crazy," "insane," "cracked," and "lunatic" quite freely. The "insane" were thought of as bizarre and definitely different from the rest of us. Today, our understanding of psychological disorders is more sophisticated. To draw the line between normal and abnormal, we must weigh some complex issues. We'll explore some of them in this chapter, as well as an array of psychological problems.

Normality—What's Normal?

Gateway Question: How is abnormality defined?

"That guy is really wacko. His porch lights are dimming." "Yeah, the butter's sliding off his waffle. He's ready to go postal." Informally, it's tempting to make such snap judgments about mental health. But deciding if a person's behavior is abnormal is harder than it might seem. To seriously classify people as psychologically unhealthy raises complex and age-old issues. The conservative, churchgoing housewife down the street might be flagrantly psychotic and a lethal danger to her children. The reclusive eccentric who hangs out at the park could be the sanest person in town. Let's begin our discussion with some basic factors that affect judgments of normality.

The scientific study of mental, emotional, and behavioral disorders is known as **psychopathology.** The term also refers to mental disorders themselves, such as schizophrenia or depression, and to behavior patterns that make people unhappy and impair their personal growth (Butcher, Mineka, & Hooley, 2007).

Defining abnormality can be tricky. We might begin by saying that psychopathology is characterized by *subjective discomfort* (private feelings of pain, unhappiness, or emotional distress) like Carol North endured.

But couldn't a person be seriously disturbed without feeling discomfort? Yes. Psychopathology doesn't always cause personal anguish. A person suffering from mania might feel elated and "on top of the world." Also, a *lack* of discomfort may reveal a problem. For example, if you showed no signs of grief after the death of a close friend, we might suspect psychopathology. In practice, subjective discomfort explains most instances in which people voluntarily seek professional help.

Some psychologists use statistics to define normality more objectively. **Statistical abnormality** refers to scoring very high or low on some dimension, such as intelligence, anxiety, or depression. Anxiety, for example, is a feature of several psychological disorders. To measure it, we could create a test to learn how many people show low, medium, or high levels of anxiety. Usually, the results of such tests will form a *normal* (bell-shaped) *curve.* (*Normal* in this case refers only to the *shape* of the curve.) Notice that most people score near the middle of a normal curve; very few have extremely high and low scores (● Figure 14.1). A person who deviates from the average by being anxious all the time (high anxiety) might be abnormal. So, too, might a person who never feels anxiety.

Then statistical abnormality tells us nothing about the meaning of deviations from the norm? Right. It is as statistically "abnormal" (unusual) for a person to score above 145 on an IQ test as it is to score below 55. However, only the lower score is regarded as "abnormal" or undesirable. In the same sense, it is unusual for a person to speak four languages or to win an event at the Olympics, but these are desirable, if rare, accomplishments.

Statistical definitions also can't tell us *where to draw the line* between normality and abnormality. To take a new example, we could obtain the average frequency of sexual intercourse for persons of a particular age, sex, sexual orientation, and marital status.

DISCOVERING PSYCHOLOGY

Crazy for a Day

Performing a mildly abnormal behavior is a good way to get a sense of how social norms define "normality" in daily life. Here's your assignment: Do something strange in public and observe how people react to you. (Please don't do anything dangerous, harmful, or offensive—and don't get arrested!) Here are some deviant behaviors that other students have staged:

- Sit in the dining area of a fast-food restaurant and loudly carry on a conversation with an imaginary companion.

- Stand in a busy hallway on campus and adopt a Kung Fu stance. Remain in that position for 10 minutes.
- Walk around campus on a sunny day while wearing a raincoat and carrying an open umbrella. Keep the umbrella over your head when you are inside buildings.
- Stick one finger in your nose and another in your ear. Walk through a busy shopping mall.
- Cover your head with aluminum foil for a day.

Does the idea of performing any of these actions make you uncomfortable? If so, you may not need to do anything more to appreciate how powerfully social norms constrain our actions. As we have noted, social nonconformity is just one facet of abnormal behavior. Nevertheless, actions that are regarded as "strange" within a particular culture are often the first sign to others that a person has a problem.

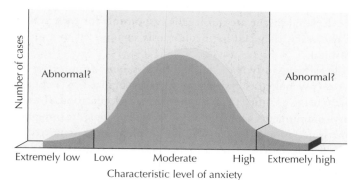

● **Figure 14.1** The number of people displaying a personality characteristic may help define what is statistically abnormal.

Rick Friedman/Corbis

Social nonconformity does not automatically indicate psychopathology.

Clearly, a person who feels driven to have sex dozens of times a day has a problem. But as we move back toward the norm we face the problem of drawing lines. How often does a normal behavior have to occur before it becomes abnormal? As you can see, statistical boundary lines tend to be somewhat arbitrary (Comer, 2005).

Atypical behavior or nonconformity may underlie some disorders. **Social nonconformity** refers to disobeying public standards for acceptable conduct. Extreme nonconformity can lead to destructive or self-destructive behavior. (Think, for instance, of a drug abuser or a prostitute.) However, we must be careful to separate unhealthy nonconformity from creative lifestyles. Many eccentric "characters" are charming and emotionally stable. Note, too, that strictly following social norms is no guarantee of mental health. In some cases, psychopathology involves rigid conformity. (See "Crazy for a Day.")

A young woman ties a thick rubber cord around her ankles, screams hysterically, and jumps headfirst off a bridge. Thirty years ago, the woman's behavior might have seemed completely crazy. Today, it is a routine form of entertainment (called "bungee jumping"). Before any behavior can be defined as abnormal, we must consider the *situational context* (social situation, behavioral setting, or general circumstances) in which it occurs. Is it normal to stand outside and water a lawn with a hose? It depends on whether it is raining. Is it abnormal for a grown man to remove his pants and expose himself to another man or woman in a place of business? It depends on whether the other person is a bank clerk or a doctor!

Almost any imaginable behavior can be considered normal in some contexts. In 1972, an airplane carrying a rugby team crashed in the snow-capped Andes of South America. Incredibly, 16 of the 45 people onboard survived 73 days in deep snow and subfreezing temperatures. They were forced to use extremely grim measures to do so—they ate the bodies of those who died in the crash.

Psychopathology The scientific study of mental, emotional, and behavioral disorders; also, abnormal or maladaptive behavior.

Statistical abnormality Abnormality defined on the basis of an extreme score on some dimension, such as IQ or anxiety.

Social nonconformity Failure to conform to societal norms or the usual minimum standards for social conduct.

As implied by our earlier discussion of social norms, culture is one of the most influential contexts in which any behavior is judged (Fabrega, 2004). In some cultures it is considered normal to defecate or urinate in public or to appear naked in public. In our culture such behaviors would be considered unusual or abnormal. In Muslim cultures, women who remain completely housebound are considered normal or even virtuous. In Western cultures they might be diagnosed as suffering from a disorder called agoraphobia. (Agoraphobia is described later in this chapter.)

Thus, *cultural relativity* (the idea that judgments are made relative to the values of one's culture) can affect the diagnosis of psychological disorders. Still, *all* cultures classify people as abnormal if they fail to communicate with others or are consistently unpredictable in their actions.

Core Features of Disordered Behavior

If abnormality is so hard to define, how are judgments of psychopathology made? Although the standards we have discussed are *relative*, abnormal behavior does have two core features. First, it is **maladaptive.** Rather than helping people cope successfully, abnormal behavior makes it more difficult for them to meet the demands of day-to-day life. Second, people suffering from psychological disorders *lose the ability to control* their thoughts, behaviors, or feelings adequately. For example, gambling is not a problem if people bet for entertainment and can maintain self-control. However, compulsive gambling is a sign of psychopathology. The voices that Carol North kept hearing are a prime example of what it means to lose control of one's thoughts. In the most extreme cases, people become a danger to themselves or others, which is clearly maladaptive (Hansell, 2007).

Various levels of functioning—from superior to severely disturbed—are described in ● Table 14.1. Note that the bottom of the scale reads, "Persistent danger of hurting self or others." Obviously, behavior at that level is maladaptive and involves a serious loss of control.

In practice, deciding that a person needs help usually occurs when the person *does something* (hits a person, hallucinates, stares into space, collects rolls of toilet paper, and so forth) that *annoys* or *gains the attention* of a person in a *position of power* in the person's life (an employer, teacher, parent, spouse, or the person himself or herself). That person then *does something* about it. (A police officer may be called, the person may be urged to see a psychologist, a relative may start commitment proceedings, or the person may voluntarily seek help.)

Insanity

Commitment proceedings may result in the finding of **insanity,** which is a *legal* term. It refers to an inability to manage one's affairs or foresee the consequences of one's actions. People who are declared insane are not legally responsible for their actions. If necessary, they can be involuntarily committed to a mental hospital.

Legally, insanity is established by testimony from *expert witnesses* (psychologists and psychiatrists) recognized by a court of law as being qualified to give opinions on a specific topic. Involuntary commitments happen most often when people are brought to emergency rooms. People who are involuntarily committed are usually judged to be a danger to themselves or to others, or they are severely mentally disabled (Luchins et al., 2004).

Table 14.1 ● Levels of Functioning

Scale	Level of Functioning	Examples
100	Superior functioning in a wide range of activities. No symptoms.	Life's problems never seem to get out of hand. Person is sought by others because of his or her many positive qualities.
90	Absent or minimal symptoms, functioning well in all areas, no more than everyday problems.	Has mild anxiety before exams, occasional arguments with family members.
80	If symptoms are present, they are brief and common reactions to stressors. No more than slight impairment in relationships, work, or school.	Has difficulty concentrating after family arguments, is falling behind in schoolwork.
70	Some mild symptoms, or some difficulty with relationships, work, or school.	Mood is depressed and has mild insomnia. Has been truant at school and has stolen things at home.
60	Moderate symptoms or moderate problems with relationships, work, or school.	Emotions are blunted, speech evasive, occasional panic attacks, no friends, unable to keep a job.
50	Serious symptoms or any serious impairments in relationships, work, or school.	Person has suicidal thoughts, engages in obsessional rituals, shoplifts, has no friends, is unable to keep a job.
40	Some impairment in grasp of reality or in communication, plus major impairments in work or school relationships, judgment, thinking, or mood.	Speech is illogical, obscure, or irrelevant. Person is depressed and avoids friends, neglects family, and is unable to work.
30	Behavior is considerably affected by delusions or hallucinations; or, person is seriously impaired in communication or judgment; or, is unable to function in almost all areas.	Person is sometimes incoherent; acts grossly inappropriately; is preoccupied with suicide; stays in bed all day; has no job, home, or friends.
20	Some danger of hurting self or others; or, occasionally fails to maintain minimal personal hygiene; or, communication is grossly impaired.	Person makes tentative suicide attempts, is frequently violent and manically excited, smears own feces; is either incoherent or mute.
10	Persistent danger of severely hurting self or others; or, persistent inability to maintain minimal personal hygiene; or, serious suicidal acts.	Repeatedly violent, maintains almost no personal hygiene, has made potentially lethal suicide attempts.

Adapted from "Global Assessment of Functioning Scale," *DSM-IV*, 1994.

Table 14.2 ● Major *DSM-IV-TR* Categories

Disorders Usually First Diagnosed in Infancy, Childhood, or Adolescence	**Mood Disorders**
Mental retardation	**Depressive disorders**
Example: Mild mental retardation	Example: Major depressive disorder
Learning disorders	**Bipolar disorders**
Example: Reading disorder	Example: Bipolar I disorder
Motor skills disorder	**Mood disorder due to a general medical condition**
Example: Developmental coordination disorder	**Substance-induced mood disorder**
Communication disorders	**Mood disorder not otherwise specified**
Example: Stuttering	
Pervasive developmental disorders	**Anxiety Disorders**
Example: Autistic disorder	Example: Panic disorder
Attention-deficit and disruptive behavior disorders	
Example: Attention-deficit/hyperactivity disorder	**Somatoform Disorders**
Feeding and eating disorders of infancy or early childhood	Example: Conversion disorder
Example: Pica (eating inedible substances)	
Tic disorders	**Factitious Disorders (Faked Disability or Illness)**
Example: Tourette's disorder	Example: Factitious disorder
Elimination disorders	
Example: Enuresis (bedwetting)	**Dissociative Disorders**
Other disorders of infancy, childhood, or adolescence	Example: Dissociative identity disorder
Example: Separation anxiety disorder	
	Sexual and Gender Identity Disorders
Delirium, Dementia, Amnestic, and Other Cognitive Disorders	**Sexual dysfunctions**
Delirium	Example: Sexual arousal disorders
Example: Delirium due to a general medical condition	**Paraphilias**
Dementia	Example: Voyeurism
Example: Dementia of the Alzheimer's type	**Sexual disorder not otherwise specified**
Amnestic disorders (memory loss)	**Gender identity disorders**
Example: Amnestic disorder due to a general medical condition	Example: Gender identity disorder
Cognitive disorder not otherwise specified	
	Eating Disorders
Mental Disorders Due to a General Medical Condition Not Elsewhere Classified	Example: Anorexia nervosa
Catatonic disorder due to a general medical condition	**Sleep Disorders**
Personality change due to a general medical condition	**Primary sleep disorders**
Mental disorder not otherwise specified due to a general medical condition	**Dyssomnias**
	Example: Primary insomnia
Substance-Related Disorders	**Parasomnias**
Example: Cocaine use disorders	Example: Sleep terror disorder
	Sleep disorders related to another mental disorder
Schizophrenia and Other Psychotic Disorders	Example: Insomnia related to posttraumatic stress disorder
Schizophrenia	**Other sleep disorders**
Example: Schizophrenia, paranoid type	Example: Substance-induced sleep disorder
Schizophreniform disorder	
Schizoaffective disorder	**Impulse Control Disorders Not Elsewhere Classified**
Delusional disorder	Example: Kleptomania
Example: Delusional disorder, grandiose type	
Brief psychotic disorder	**Adjustment Disorders**
Shared psychotic disorder (folie a deux)	Example: Adjustment disorder
Psychotic disorder due to a general medical condition	
Substance-induced psychotic disorder	**Personality Disorders**
Psychotic disorder not otherwise specified	Example: Antisocial personality disorder

●● Classifying Mental Disorders— Problems by the Book

Gateway Question: What are the major psychological disorders?

Psychological problems are classified by using the *Diagnostic and Statistical Manual of Mental Disorders* (*DSM-IV-TR,* 2000). The DSM helps psychologists correctly identify mental disorders and select the best therapies to treat them (First & Pincus, 2002).

A **mental disorder** is a significant impairment in psychological functioning. If you were to glance through the *DSM-IV-TR,* you

would see many disorders described, including those in ● Table 14.2. (The "IV-TR" in DSM-IV-TR means fourth version, text revision.) It's impossible here to discuss all these problems. Major disorders are listed in the table so you can see the types of problems found in the

Maladaptive behavior Behavior that makes it difficult to adapt to the environment and meet the demands of day-to-day life.

Insanity A legal term that refers to a mental inability to manage one's affairs or to be aware of the consequences of one's actions.

Mental disorder A significant impairment in psychological functioning.

DSM-IV-TR is not the only system for classifying mental disorders. Nevertheless, most activities in mental health settings—from diagnosis to therapy to billing of insurance companies—are influenced by the *DSM*. *DSM-IV-TR* is both a scientific document and a social one. Major disorders are well-documented problems. Some problems, however, have little to do with "mental illness." Instead, they are primarily socially disapproved behaviors. (Reprinted with permission from the *Diagnostic and Statistical Manual of Mental Disorders, Fourth Edition, Text Revision,* © 2000 American Psychiatric Association.)

● **Figure 14.2** This MRI scan of a human brain (viewed from the top) reveals a tumor (dark spot). Mental disorders sometimes have organic causes of this sort. However, in many instances no organic damage can be found.

DSM. (You don't need to memorize all of them.) The descriptions that follow will give you an overview of some selected problems.

An Overview of Psychological Disorders

People suffering from **psychotic disorders** have "retreated from reality." That is, they suffer from hallucinations and delusions and are socially withdrawn. Psychotic disorders are severely disabling and often lead to hospitalization. Typically, psychotic patients cannot control their thoughts and actions. For example, David often heard the voice of his Uncle Bill: "He told me to turn off the TV. He said, 'It's too damn loud, turn it down, turn it down.' Other times he talks about fishing. 'Good day for fishing. Got to go fishing' " (Durand & Barlow, 2006). Psychotic symptoms occur in schizophrenia, delusional disorders, and some mood disorders.

Also, psychosis may be related to medical problems, drug abuse, and other conditions. (● Table 14.3 provides a simplified list of major disorders.)

Organic mental disorders are problems caused by brain pathology; that is, by drug damage, diseases of the brain, injuries, poisons, and so on (● Figure 14.2). A person with an organic disorder may have severe emotional disturbances, impaired thinking, memory loss, personality changes, delirium, or psychotic symptoms (Nolen-Hoeksema, 2007).

In reality, almost all mental disorders are partly biological (Hansell, 2007). That's why *DSM-IV-TR* does not list "organic

Table 14.3 ● Some Selected Categories of Psychopathology

Problem	Primary Symptom	Typical Signs of Trouble
Psychotic disorders	Loss of contact with reality	You hear or see things that others don't; your mind has been playing tricks on you
Mood disorders	Mania or depression	You feel sad and hopeless; or you talk too loud and too fast and have a rush of ideas and feelings that others think are unreasonable
Anxiety disorders	High anxiety or anxiety-based distortions of behavior	You have anxiety attacks and feel like you are going to die; or you are afraid to do things that most people can do; or you spend unusual amounts of time doing things like washing your hands or counting your heartbeats
Somatoform disorders	Bodily complaints without an organic (physical) basis	You feel physically sick, but your doctor says nothing is wrong with you; or you suffer from pain that has no physical basis; or you are preoccupied with thoughts about being sick
Dissociative disorders	Amnesia, feelings of unreality, multiple identities	There are major gaps in your memory of events; you feel like you are a robot or a stranger to yourself; others tell you that you have done things that you don't remember doing
Personality disorders	Unhealthy personality patterns	Your behavior patterns repeatedly cause problems at work, at school, and in your relationships with others
Sexual and gender identity disorders	Disturbed gender identity, deviant sexual behavior, problems in sexual adjustment	You feel that you are a man trapped in a woman's body (or the reverse); or you can only gain sexual satisfaction by engaging in highly atypical sexual behavior; or you have problems with sexual desire, arousal, or performance
Substance-related disorders	Disturbances related to drug abuse or dependence	You have been drinking too much, using illegal drugs, or taking prescription drugs more often than you should

The self-portraits shown here were painted by Andy Wilf during a 4-year period. At that time, Wilf is said to have increasingly abused drugs and alcohol. This dramatic series of images is a record of his self-destructive descent into a private hell. The third painting shows a shrouded skull—and foretells the artist's fate. Wilf died of a drug overdose. Drug abuse is but one of the many psychopathologies, or "problems in living," psychologists seek to alleviate.

Courtesy of Ulrike Kantor Gallery

mental disorders" as a separate category. Nevertheless, all the following problems are closely associated with organic damage: delirium, dementia, amnesia, and other cognitive disorders; mental disorders due to a general medical condition; and substance-related disorders (drug abuse).

Mood disorders are primarily defined by the presence of extreme, intense, and long-lasting emotions. Afflicted persons may be *manic,* meaning agitated, elated, and hyperactive, or they may be *depressed.* Some people with mood disorders alternate between mania and depression, and they may have psychotic symptoms as well.

Anxiety disorders are marked by fear or anxiety and by distorted behavior. Some anxiety disorders involve feelings of panic. Others take the form of phobias (irrational fears) or just overwhelming anxiety and nervousness. Two additional anxiety disorders are posttraumatic stress disorder and acute stress disorder. Obsessive-compulsive behavior patterns are also associated with high anxiety. (These problems are described later in this chapter.)

A person with a **dissociative disorder** may have temporary amnesia or multiple personalities. Also included in this category are frightening episodes of depersonalization, in which people feel like they are outside their bodies, are behaving like robots, or are lost in a dream world.

Somatoform (so-MAT-oh-form) **disorders** occur when a person has physical symptoms that mimic disease or injury (paralysis, blindness, illness, or chronic pain, for example), for which there is no identifiable physical cause. In such cases, psychological factors appear to explain the symptoms.

Personality disorders are deeply ingrained, unhealthy personality patterns. Such patterns usually appear in adolescence and continue through much of adult life. They include paranoid (overly suspicious), narcissistic (self-loving), dependent, borderline, and antisocial personality types, as well as others.

Sexual and gender identity disorders include any of a wide range of difficulties with sexual identity, deviant sexual behavior, or sexual adjustment. In gender identity disorders, sexual identity does not match a person's physical sex and the person may seek a sex-change operation. Deviations in sexual behavior known as *paraphilias* include exhibitionism, fetishism, voyeurism, and so on.

Also found in this category are a variety of *sexual dysfunctions* (problems in sexual desire, arousal, or response).

> **bridges**
> Sexual dysfunctions are discussed in Chapter 11, pages 382–385.

Substance-related disorders involve abuse of, or dependence on, psychoactive drugs. Typical culprits include alcohol, barbiturates, opiates, cocaine, amphetamines, hallucinogens, marijuana, and nicotine. A person with a substance-related disorder cannot stop using the drug and may also suffer from withdrawal symptoms, delirium, dementia, amnesia, psychosis, emotional outbursts, sexual problems, and sleep disturbances.

> **bridges**
> Problems with drug abuse and dependence are discussed in Chapter 6. See pages 199–201.

Psychotic disorder A severe mental disorder characterized by a retreat from reality, by hallucinations and delusions, and by social withdrawal.

Organic mental disorder A mental or emotional problem caused by brain diseases or injuries.

Mood disorder A major disturbance in mood or emotion, such as depression or mania.

Anxiety disorder Disruptive feelings of fear, apprehension, or anxiety, or distortions in behavior that are anxiety related.

Dissociative disorder Temporary amnesia, multiple personality, or depersonalization.

Somatoform disorder Physical symptoms that mimic disease or injury for which there is no identifiable physical cause.

Personality disorder A maladaptive personality pattern.

Sexual and gender identity disorders Any of a wide range of difficulties with sexual identity, deviant sexual behavior, or sexual adjustment.

Substance-related disorder Abuse of or dependence on a mood- or behavior-altering drug.

HUMAN DIVERSITY

Running Amok with Cultural Maladies

Every culture recognizes the existence of psychopathology, and most have at least a few folk names for afflictions you won't find in the *DSM-IV-TR*. Called *culture-bound syndromes*, here are some examples from around the world (Durand & Barlow, 2006; López & Guarnaccia, 2000; Sumathipala, Siribaddana, & Bhugra, 2004):

- **Amok** Men in Malaysia, Laos, the Philippines, and Polynesia who believe they have been insulted are sometimes known to go amok. After a period of brooding they erupt into an outburst of violent, aggressive, or homicidal behavior randomly directed at people and objects.
- **Susto** Among Latin Americans, the symptoms of *susto* include insomnia, irritability, phobias, and an increase in sweating and heart rate. Susto can result if someone is badly frightened by a black magic curse. In extreme cases, *voodoo death* can result, as the person is literally scared to death.
- **Ghost sickness** Among many American Indian tribes, people who become preoc-

cupied with death and the deceased are said to suffer from ghost sickness. The symptoms of ghost sickness include bad dreams, weakness, loss of appetite, fainting, dizziness, fear, anxiety, hallucinations, loss of consciousness, confusion, feelings of futility, and a sense of suffocation.

- **Koro** In south and east Asia, a man may experience sudden and intense anxiety that his penis (or, in females, the vulva and nipples) will recede into the body. In addition to the terror this incites, victims also believe that advanced cases of *koro* can cause death. A similar fear of shrinking genitals has also been reported from West Africa (Dzokoto, & Adams, 2005).
- **Zar** In North African and Middle Eastern societies, *zar* is said to occur when spirits possess an individual. *Zar* is marked by shouting, laughing, hitting the head against a wall, singing, or weeping. Victims may become apathetic or withdrawn and they may refuse to eat or carry out daily tasks.

- **Dhat** In Indian society, *dhat* is the fear of the loss of semen during nocturnal emissions. A man suffering from *dhat* will feel anxious and perhaps also guilty. He may also experience fatigue, loss of appetite, weakness, anxiety, and sexual dysfunction.

It's clear that people have a need to label and categorize disturbed behavior. As you can see, however, folk terminology tends to be vague. The terms listed here provide little guidance about the true nature of a person's problems or the best ways to treat them. That's why the DSM is based on empirical data and clinical observations. Otherwise, psychologists and psychiatrists would be no better than folk healers when making diagnoses (Ancis, Chen, & Schultz, 2004).

By the way, culture-bound disorders occur in all societies. For example, American psychologists Pamela Keel and Kelly Klump believe that the eating disorder bulimia is primarily a syndrome of Western cultures, including the United States (Keel & Klump, 2003).

Shouldn't neurosis be listed here? Neurosis was once a recognized mental disorder. However, it is no longer included in the DSM because the term "neurosis" is too imprecise. Behavior that psychologists used to refer to as "neurotic" is now part of anxiety, somatoform, or dissociative disorders. Even though **neurosis** is an outdated term, you may hear it used to loosely refer to problems involving excessive anxiety.

In addition to the formal mental disorders we have reviewed, many cultures have names for "unofficial" psychological "disorders." See "Running Amok with Cultural Maladies" for some examples.

General Risk Factors

What causes psychological disorders like those listed in ● *Table 14.3?* We will soon explore the causes of some specific problems. For now, here are some general risk factors that contribute to psychopathology, including the following factors:

- **Biological/physical factors:** genetic defects or inherited vulnerabilities, poor prenatal care, very low birth weight, chronic physical illness or disability, exposure to toxic chemicals or drugs, head injuries
- **Psychological factors:** stress, low intelligence, learning disorders, lack of control or mastery

- **Family factors:** parents who are immature, mentally disturbed, criminal, or abusive; severe marital strife; extremely poor child discipline; disordered family communication patterns
- **Social conditions:** poverty, stressful living conditions, homelessness, social disorganization, overcrowding

Ethnic Group Membership

Culture also influences our susceptibility to various psychological disorders. For example, a recent study found that some disorders are less common in three ethnic groups than they are among European Americans (Zhang & Snowden, 1999):

- Compared with European Americans, African Americans are less likely to suffer from depression, obsessive-compulsive disorder, substance abuse, antisocial personality disorder, and anorexia nervosa.
- Compared with European Americans, Asian Americans are less likely to suffer from schizophrenia, mania or bipolar disorders, panic, somatization, substance abuse, and antisocial personality.
- Hispanic Americans have lower rates of schizophrenia, obsessive-compulsive disorder, panic, and substance abuse than European Americans do.

It is probably fair to say that the social world and the psychological world interact on an equal footing with biological factors to produce human behavior. For this reason, cultural factors can influence the expression of psychological disorders. Different values, support networks, stress levels, behavior patterns, family ties, and cultural beliefs can have a big impact on overall mental health (López & Guarnaccia, 2000).

An Important Note—You're Okay, Really!

In upcoming sections we will explore some selected problems in more detail, beginning with psychotic disorders. As your authors, we hope that you will not fall prey to "medical student's disease." Medical students, it seems, have a predictable tendency to notice in themselves the symptoms of each dreaded disease they study. As a psychology student you may notice what seem to be abnormal tendencies in your own behavior. If so, don't panic. In most instances, this only shows that pathological behavior is an *exaggeration* of normal defenses and reactions, not that your behavior is abnormal.

KNOWLEDGE BUILDER
Normality and Psychopathology

RECITE

1. The core feature of abnormal behavior is that it is
   a. statistically unusual
   b. maladaptive
   c. socially nonconforming
   d. a source of subjective discomfort
2. One of the most powerful contexts in which judgments of normality and abnormality are made is
   a. the family
   b. occupational settings
   c. religious systems
   d. culture
3. Which of the following is a *legal* concept?
   a. neurosis
   b. psychosis
   c. culture-bound syndrome
   d. insanity
4. Amnesia, multiple identities, and depersonalization are possible problems in
   a. mood disorders
   b. somatoform disorders
   c. psychosis
   d. dissociative disorders
5. Which among the following is *not* a major psychological problem listed in *DSM-IV-TR*?
   a. mood disorders
   b. personality disorders
   c. insanity
   d. anxiety disorders
6. People are said to have "retreated from reality" when they suffer from
   a. psychotic disorders
   b. mood disorders
   c. somatoform disorders
   d. personality disorders
7. Koro and dhat are
   a. somatoform disorders
   b. forms of psychosis
   c. folk terminology
   d. organic mental disorders

8. Someone who engages in one of the paraphilias has what type of disorder?
   a. dissociative
   b. somatoform
   c. substance
   d. sexual

REFLECT

Critical Thinking

9. Brian, a fan of grunge rock, occasionally wears a skirt in public. Does Brian's cross-dressing indicate that he has a mental disorder?
10. Many states began to restrict use of the insanity defense after John Hinkley Jr., who tried to murder former U.S. President Ronald Reagan, was acquitted by reason of insanity. What does this trend reveal about insanity?

Relate

Think of an instance of abnormal behavior you have witnessed. By what formal standards would the behavior be regarded as abnormal? In what way was the behavior maladaptive?

What disorders would the following sentences help you remember? An anxious psychotic in a bad mood asked for an organic substance. "First you have to fill out a somato form and tell us what sex or gender you are," he was told. "Don't diss my personality," he replied.

Answers: 1. b **2.** d **3.** d **4.** d **5.** c **6.** a **7.** c **8.** d **9.** Probably not. Undoubtedly, many people socially disapprove of Brian's cross-dressing. Nevertheless, to be classified as a mental disorder it must cause him to feel disabling shame, guilt, depression, or anxiety. The cultural relativity of behavior like Brian's is revealed by the fact that it is fashionable and acceptable for women to wear men's clothing. **10.** It emphasizes that insanity is a legal concept, not a psychiatric diagnosis. Laws reflect community standards. When those standards change, lawmakers may seek to alter definitions of legal responsibility.

● Psychotic Disorders—The Dark Side of the Moon

Gateway Question: What are the general characteristics of psychotic disorders?

Psychotic disorders are among the most dramatic and serious of all mental problems. Imagine that a member of your family (Floyd?) has been hearing voices, is talking strangely, has covered his head with aluminum foil, and believes that houseflies are speaking to him in code. If you observed such symptoms, would you be concerned? Of course you would, and rightly so.

A person who is psychotic undergoes a number of striking changes in thinking, behavior, and emotion. Basic to all these changes is the fact that **psychosis** reflects a loss of contact with shared views of reality (psycho*sis,* singular; psycho*ses,* plural). The following comments, made by a psychotic patient, illustrate

---

Neurosis An outdated term once used to refer, as a group, to anxiety disorders, somatoform disorders, dissociative disorders, and some forms of depression.

Psychosis A withdrawal from reality marked by hallucinations and delusions, disturbed thought and emotions, and personality disorganization.

what is meant by a "split" from reality (Durand & Barlow, 2006):

> When you do the 25 of the clock, it means that you leave the house 25 after 1 to mail letters so they can check on you . . . and they know where you're at. That's the Eagle.

The Nature of Psychosis

What are the major features of psychotic disorders? Delusions and hallucinations are core features, but there are others as well.

People who suffer from **delusions** hold false beliefs that they insist are true, regardless of how much the facts contradict them. An example is a 43-year-old schizophrenic man who was convinced he was pregnant (Mansouri & Adityanjee, 1995).

Are there different types of delusions? Yes, some common types of delusions are (1) *depressive* delusions, in which people feel that they have committed horrible crimes or sinful deeds; (2) *somatic* delusions, such as believing your body is "rotting away" or that it is emitting foul odors; (3) delusions of *grandeur,* in which people think they are extremely important; (4) delusions of *influence,* in which people feel they are being controlled or influenced by others or by unseen forces; (5) delusions of *persecution,* in which people believe that others are "out to get them"; and (6) delusions of *reference,* in which people give great personal meaning to unrelated events. For instance, delusional people sometimes think that television programs are giving them a special personal message (*DSM-IV-TR,* 2000).

Hallucinations are imaginary sensations, such as seeing, hearing, or smelling things that don't exist in the real world. The most common psychotic hallucination is hearing voices, like the voice that told Carol North to "Collide with the other world." Sometimes these voices command patients to hurt themselves. Unfortunately, sometimes people obey (Barrowcliff & Haddock, 2006). More rarely, psychotic people may feel "insects crawling under their skin," taste "poisons" in their food, or smell "gas" their "enemies" are using to "get" them. Sensory changes, such as anesthesia (numbness, or a loss of sensation) or extreme sensitivity to heat, cold, pain, or touch, can also occur.

During a psychotic episode, emotions are often severely disturbed. For instance, the psychotic person may be wildly elated, depressed, hyperemotional, or apathetic. Sometimes psychotic patients display *flat affect,* a condition in which the face is frozen in a blank expression. Brain images from psychotic patients with "frozen faces" reveal that their brains process emotions abnormally (Fahim et al., 2005).

Some psychotic symptoms can be thought of as a primitive type of communication. That is, many patients can only use their actions to say, "I need help," or "I can't handle it anymore." Disturbed verbal communication is a nearly universal symptom of psychosis. In fact, psychotic speech tends to be so garbled and chaotic that it sometimes sounds like a "word salad."

Major disturbances such as those just described—as well as added problems with thinking, memory, and attention—bring about personality disintegration and a break with reality. *Personality disintegration* occurs when a person's thoughts, actions, and emotions are no longer coordinated. When psychotic disturbances and a fragmented personality are evident for weeks or months, the person has suffered a psychosis (*DSM-IV-TR,* 2000) (● Table 14.4).

Organic Psychosis

In a sense, all psychoses are partly organic, involving physical changes in the brain. However, the general term *organic psychosis* is usually reserved for problems involving clear-cut brain injuries or diseases. For example, poisoning by lead or mercury can damage the brain and cause hallucinations, delusions, and a loss of emotional control (● Figure 14.3). A particularly dangerous situation is found in old buildings that contain leaded paints. Lead tastes sweet. Thus, young children may be tempted to eat leaded paint flakes as if they were candy. Children who eat leaded paint can become psychotic or intellectually disabled (Mielke, 1999).

Table 14.4 ● Warning Signs of Psychotic Disorders and Major Mood Disorders

- You express bizarre thoughts or beliefs that defy reality.
- You have withdrawn from family members and other relationships.
- You hear unreal voices or sees things others don't.
- You are extremely sad, persistently despondent, or suicidal.
- You are excessively energetic and have little need for sleep.
- You lose your appetite, sleep excessively, and have no energy.
- You exhibit extreme mood swings.
- You believe someone is trying to get you.
- You have engaged in antisocial, destructive, or self-destructive behavior.

Harvey et al., 1996; Sheehy & Cournos, 1992.

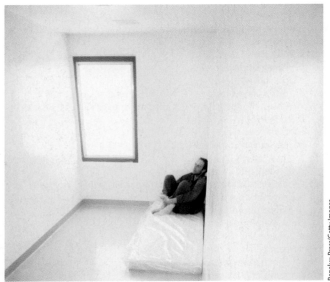

A psychotic individual in a state mental hospital.

Benelux Press/Getty Images

● **Figure 14.3** The Mad Hatter, from Lewis Carroll's *Alice's Adventures in Wonderland.* History provides numerous examples of psychosis caused by toxic chemicals. Carroll's Mad Hatter character is modeled after an occupational disease of the eighteenth and nineteenth centuries. In that era, hat makers were heavily exposed to mercury used in the preparation of felt. Consequently, many suffered brain damage and became psychotic, or "mad" (Kety, 1979).

Former U.S. President Ronald Reagan was diagnosed with Alzheimer's disease in 1995. Like many Alzheimer's victims, Reagan slipped into a slow mental decline. He died in 2004.

Leaded paints also release powdered lead into the air. Children may breathe the powder or eat it after handling contaminated toys. Other sources of lead are soldered water pipes, old lead-lined drinking fountains, lead-glazed pottery, and lead deposited years ago from automobile exhaust. Children with higher levels of lead in their blood are more likely to be arrested as adults for criminal offenses (Wright et al., 2008). On a much larger scale, "poisoning" of another type, in the form of drug abuse, can also produce deviant behavior and psychotic symptoms (*DSM-IV-TR,* 2000).

The most common organic problem is **dementia** (duh-MEN-sha), a serious mental impairment in old age caused by deterioration of the brain (Gatz, 2007). In dementia, we see major disturbances in memory, reasoning, judgment, impulse control, and personality. This combination usually leaves people confused, suspicious, apathetic, or withdrawn. Some common causes of

dementia are circulatory problems, repeated strokes, or general shrinkage and atrophy of the brain. The majority of people who suffer from dementia slowly lose their mental abilities without becoming psychotic. However, some do develop delusions and lose contact with reality.

The most common cause of dementia is **Alzheimer's disease** (ALLS-hi-merz), one of the most fearsome problems of aging. Alzheimer's victims slowly lose the ability to work, cook, drive, read, write, or do arithmetic. Eventually they are mute and bed-ridden. Alzheimer's disease appears to be caused by unusual webs and tangles in the brain that damage areas important for memory and learning (Ingram, 2003). Genetic factors can increase the risk of developing this devastating disease (Gatz, 2007). Understandably, efforts to find a cure for Alzheimer's disease are expanding. For some of us, such efforts may be a race against time.

Are there specific kinds of psychotic disorders? Two major types of psychosis are *delusional disorders* and *schizophrenia.* As you will recall, mood disorders mainly involve emotional extremes. Nevertheless, psychotic symptoms can also occur in some mood disorders. You'll find information on each of these problems in upcoming discussions.

The soil and dust in cities and near busy streets is often heavily contaminated with lead. This lead came from automobile exhaust before leaded gasoline was banned. Young children frequently put objects and their hands in their mouths. This, then, is a major source of lead poisoning for many children. Paving play areas or covering them with clean soil can greatly reduce lead exposure (Mielke, 1999).

Delusion A false belief held against all contrary evidence.

Hallucination An imaginary sensation, such as seeing, hearing, or smelling things that don't exist in the real world.

Dementia A serious mental impairment in old age caused by physical deterioration of the brain.

Alzheimer's disease An age-related disease characterized by memory loss, mental confusion, and, in its later stages, a nearly total loss of mental abilities.

⬤⬤ Delusional Disorders—An Enemy Behind Every Tree

Gateway Question: What is the nature of a delusional disorder?

People with delusional disorders usually do not suffer from hallucinations, emotional excesses, or personality disintegration. Even so, their break with reality is unmistakable. The main feature of **delusional disorders** is the presence of deeply held false beliefs, which may take the following forms (*DSM-IV-TR*, 2000):

- **Erotomanic type:** In this disorder, people have erotic delusions that they are loved by another person, especially by someone famous or of higher status. As you might imagine, some celebrity stalkers suffer from erotomania.
- **Grandiose type:** In this case, people suffer from the delusion that they have some great, unrecognized talent, knowledge, or insight. They may also believe that they have a special relationship with an important person or with God or that they are a famous person. (If the famous person is alive, the deluded person regards her or him as an imposter.)
- **Jealous type:** An example of this type of delusion would be having an all-consuming, but unfounded, belief that your spouse or lover is unfaithful.
- **Persecutory type:** Delusions of persecution involve belief that you are being conspired against, cheated, spied on, followed, poisoned, maligned, or harassed.
- **Somatic type:** People suffering from somatic delusions typically believe that their bodies are diseased or rotting, or infested with insects or parasites, or that parts of their bodies are defective.

Although they are false, and sometimes far-fetched, all these delusions are about experiences that could occur in real life (Manschreck, 1996). In other types of psychosis, delusions tend to be more bizarre. For example, a person with schizophrenia might believe that space aliens have replaced all his internal organs with electronic monitoring devices. In contrast, people with ordinary delusions merely believe that someone is trying to steal their money, that they are being deceived by a lover, that the FBI is watching them, and the like (*DSM-IV-TR*, 2000).

Paranoid Psychosis

The most common delusional disorder, often called **paranoid psychosis,** centers on delusions of persecution. Many self-styled reformers, crank letter writers, conspiracy theorists, "UFO abductees," and the like suffer paranoid delusions. Paranoid individuals often believe that they are being cheated, spied on, followed, poisoned, harassed, or plotted against. Usually they are intensely suspicious, believing they must be on guard at all times.

The evidence such people find to support their beliefs usually fails to persuade others. Every detail of the paranoid person's existence is woven into a private version of "what's really going on." Buzzing during a telephone conversation may be interpreted as "someone listening"; a stranger who comes to the door asking for directions may be seen as "really trying to get information"; and so forth.

It is difficult to treat people suffering from paranoid delusions because it is almost impossible for them to accept that they need help. Anyone who suggests that they have a problem simply becomes part of the "conspiracy" to "persecute" them. Consequently, paranoid people frequently lead lonely, isolated, and humorless lives dominated by constant suspicion and hostility.

Although they are not necessarily dangerous to others, they can be. People who believe that the Mafia, "government agents," terrorists, or a street gang is slowly closing in on them may be moved to violence by their irrational fears. Imagine that a stranger comes to the door to ask a paranoid person for directions. If the stranger has his hand in his coat pocket, he could become the target of a paranoid attempt at "self-defense."

Delusional disorders are rare. By far, the most common form of psychosis is schizophrenia. Let's explore schizophrenia in more detail and see how it differs from a delusional disorder.

⬤⬤ Schizophrenia—Shattered Reality

Gateway Questions: What forms does schizophrenia take? What causes it?

Schizophrenia (SKIT-soh-FREN-ee-uh) is marked by delusions, hallucinations, apathy, thinking abnormalities, and a "split" between thought and emotion. In schizophrenia, emotions may become blunted or very inappropriate. For example, if a person with schizophrenia is told his mother just died, he might smile, or giggle, or show no emotion at all. Schizophrenic delusions may include the idea that the person's thoughts and actions are being controlled, that thoughts are being broadcast (so others can hear them), that thoughts have been "inserted" into the person's mind, or that thoughts have been removed. In addition, schizophrenia involves withdrawal from contact with others, a loss of interest in external activities, a breakdown of personal habits, and an inability to deal with daily events (Neufeld et al., 2003). One person in 100 has schizophrenia in any given year (NIMH, 2006b).

Many schizophrenic symptoms appear to be related to problems with *selective attention*. In other words, it is hard for people with schizophrenia to focus on one item of information at a time. Having an impaired "sensory filter" in their brains may be why they are overwhelmed by a jumble of thoughts, sensations, images, and feelings (Heinrichs, 2001).

Do people with schizophrenia have two personalities? No. How many times have you heard people say something like, "David was so warm and friendly yesterday, but today he's as cold as ice. He's so schizophrenic that I don't know how to react." Such statements show how often the term "schizophrenic" is misused. As we will see later on in this chapter, a person who displays two or more personalities has a dissociative disorder and is not "schizophrenic." Neither, of course, is a person like David, whose behavior is merely inconsistent.

Is there more than one type of schizophrenia? Schizophrenia appears to be a group of related disturbances. It has four major subtypes:

- **Disorganized type:** Schizophrenia marked by incoherence, grossly disorganized behavior, bizarre thinking, and flat or grossly inappropriate emotions.
- **Catatonic type:** Schizophrenia marked by stupor; rigidity; unresponsiveness; posturing; mutism; and, sometimes, agitated, purposeless behavior.
- **Paranoid type:** Schizophrenia marked by a preoccupation with delusions or by frequent auditory hallucinations related to a single theme, especially grandeur or persecution.
- **Undifferentiated type:** Schizophrenia in which there are prominent psychotic symptoms, but none of the specific features of catatonic, disorganized, or paranoid types.

Disorganized Schizophrenia

The disorder known as disorganized schizophrenia (sometimes called hebephrenic schizophrenia) comes close to matching the stereotyped images of "madness" seen in movies. In **disorganized schizophrenia,** personality disintegration is almost complete: Emotions, speech, and behavior are all highly disorganized. The result is silliness, laughter, and bizarre or obscene behavior, as shown by this intake interview of a patient named Edna:

Dr. I am Dr. _____. I would like to know something more about you.
Patient You have a nasty mind. Lord! Lord! Cats in a cradle.
Dr. Tell me, how do you feel?
Patient London's bell is a long, long dock. Hee! Hee! (Giggles uncontrollably.)
Dr. Do you know where you are now?
Patient D_____n! S_____t on you all who rip into my internals! The grudgerometer will take care of you all! (Shouting) I am the Queen, see my magic, I shall turn you all into smidgelings forever!
Dr. Your husband is concerned about you. Do you know his name?
Patient (Stands, walks to and faces the wall) Who am I, who are we, who are you, who are they, (turns)
I...I...I...I! (Makes grotesque faces.)
Edna was placed in the women's ward where she proceeded to masturbate. Occasionally, she would scream or shout obscenities. At other times she giggled to herself. She was known to attack other patients. She began to complain that her uterus was attached to a "pipeline to the Kremlin" and that she was being "infernally invaded" by Communism. (Suinn, 1975*)

Disorganized schizophrenia typically develops in adolescence or young adulthood. Chances of improvement are limited, and social impairment is usually extreme (*DSM-IV-TR*, 2000).

Catatonic Schizophrenia

The catatonic person seems to be in a state of total panic (Fink & Taylor, 2003). **Catatonic schizophrenia** brings about a stuporous condition in which odd positions may be held for hours or even

In disorganized schizophrenia, behavior is marked by silliness, laughter, and bizarre or obscene behavior.

Peter Granser/Laif/Aurora Photos

days. These periods of rigidity may be similar to the tendency to "freeze" at times of great emergency or panic. Catatonic individuals appear to be struggling desperately to control their inner turmoil. One sign of this is the fact that stupor may occasionally give way to agitated outbursts or violent behavior. The following excerpt describes a catatonic episode:

Manuel appeared to be physically healthy upon examination. Yet he did not regain his awareness of his surroundings. He remained motionless, speechless, and seemingly unconscious. One evening an aide turned him on his side to straighten out the sheet, was called away to tend another patient, and forgot to return. Manuel was found the next morning, still on his side, his arm tucked under his body, as he had been left the night before. His arm was turning blue from lack of circulation, but he seemed to be experiencing no discomfort. (Suinn, 1975)

Notice that Manuel did not speak. *Mutism,* along with a marked decrease in responsiveness to the environment, makes patients with catatonic schizophrenia difficult to "reach." Fortu-

Delusional disorder A psychosis marked by severe delusions of grandeur, jealousy, persecution, or similar preoccupations.

Paranoid psychosis A delusional disorder centered especially on delusions of persecution.

Schizophrenia A psychosis characterized by delusions, hallucinations, apathy, and a "split" between thought and emotion.

Disorganized schizophrenia Schizophrenia marked by incoherence, grossly disorganized behavior, bizarre thinking, and flat or grossly inappropriate emotions.

Catatonic schizophrenia Schizophrenia marked by stupor, rigidity, unresponsiveness, posturing, mutism, and, sometimes, agitated, purposeless behavior.

---

*All Suinn quotes in this chapter are from *Fundamentals of Behavior Pathology* by R. M. Suinn. Copyright © 1975. Reprinted by permission of John Wiley & Sons, Inc.

Can the catatonic's rigid postures and stupor be understood in terms of abnormal body chemistry? Environment? Heredity? As is true of other forms of schizophrenia, the answer appears to be all three factors.

nately, this bizarre disorder has become rare in Europe and North America (*DSM-IV-TR*, 2000).

Paranoid Schizophrenia

Paranoid schizophrenia is the most common schizophrenic disorder. As in paranoid delusional disorders, **paranoid schizophrenia** centers on delusions of grandeur and persecution. However, paranoid schizophrenics also hallucinate, and their delusions are more bizarre and unconvincing than those in a delusional disorder (Freeman & Garety, 2004).

Thinking that God, the government, or "cosmic rays from space" are controlling their minds or that someone is trying to poison them, people suffering from paranoid schizophrenia may feel forced into violence to "protect" themselves. An example is James Huberty, who brutally murdered 21 people at a McDonald's restaurant in San Ysidro, California. Huberty, who had paranoid schizophrenia, felt persecuted and cheated by life. Shortly before he announced to his wife that he was "going hunting humans," Huberty had been hearing hallucinated voices. ● Figure 14.4 outlines the case of Theodore Kaczynski.

How dangerous are the mentally ill? Horrific crimes, like the San Ysidro murders, lead many people to believe that the mentally ill are dangerous. Is that true? You might be surprised by the answer, found in "Are the Mentally Ill Prone to Violence?"

Undifferentiated Schizophrenia

The three types of schizophrenia just described occur most often in textbooks. In reality, patients may shift from one pattern to another at different times. Many patients, therefore, are simply classified as suffering from **undifferentiated schizophrenia,** in which the specific features of catatonic, disorganized, or paranoid types are missing. Diagnosing schizophrenia is fairly subjective.

● **Figure 14.4** Over a period of years, Theodore Kaczynski mailed bombs to unsuspecting victims, many of whom were maimed or killed. As a young adult, Kaczynski was a brilliant mathematician. At the time of his arrest, he had become the Unabomber—a reclusive "loner" who deeply mistrusted other people and modern technology. After his arrest, Kaczynski was judged to be suffering from paranoid schizophrenia.

All things considered, however, there is no doubt that schizophrenia is real or that its treatment is a major challenge.

The Causes of Schizophrenia

Former British Prime Minister Winston Churchill once described a question that perplexed him as "a riddle wrapped in a mystery inside an enigma." The same words might describe the causes of schizophrenia.

Environment

What causes schizophrenia? An increased risk of developing schizophrenia may begin at birth or even before. Women who are exposed to the influenza (flu) virus or to rubella (German measles) during the middle of pregnancy have children who are more likely to become schizophrenic (Brown et al., 2001). Malnutrition during pregnancy and complications at the time of birth can have a similar impact. Possibly, such events disturb brain development, leaving people more vulnerable to a psychotic break with reality (Walker et al., 2004).

Early **psychological trauma** (a psychological injury or shock) may also add to the risk. Often, the victims of schizophrenia were exposed to violence, sexual abuse, death, divorce, separation, or other stresses in childhood (Walker et al., 2004). Living in a troubled family is a related risk factor. In a disturbed family environment, stressful relationships, communication patterns, and negative emotions prevail. Deviant communication patterns cause anxiety, confusion, anger, conflict, and turmoil. Typically, disturbed families interact in ways that are laden with guilt, prying, criticism, negativity, and emotional attacks (Bressi, Albonetti, & Razzoli, 1998; Davison & Neale, 2006).

Although they are attractive, environmental explanations alone are not enough to account for schizophrenia. For example, when the children of schizophrenic parents are raised away from their chaotic home environment, they are still more likely to become psychotic (Walker et al., 2004).

CRITICAL THINKING

Are the Mentally Ill Prone to Violence?

News reports and television programs tend to exaggerate the connection between mental illness and violence. Such media reports both create and reflect deeply held beliefs about mental disorders in our society. Such beliefs are important because they affect laws and personal attitudes toward the mentally ill. For example, people who strongly believe that the mentally ill are prone to violence are typically afraid to have former mental patients as neighbors, co-workers, or friends (Corrigan & Watson, 2005).

The reality is just the opposite. According to the largest study ever conducted on this question, mentally ill individuals who are not also substance abusers are no more prone to violence than are normal individuals (Monahan et al., 2001). There are only a few exceptions to this conclusion, and in those cases the risk is not very large (Lidz et al., 2007; Rice, 1997):

- Only persons who are also involved with *substance abuse* are more prone to violence than nonpatients.
- Only persons who are *actively psychotic* are more violence prone than non-patients. That is, if a person is experienc-

ing delusions and hallucinations, the risk of violence is elevated. Other mental problems are unrelated to violence.

- Only persons *currently* experiencing psychotic symptoms are at increased risk for violence. Violent behavior is not related to having been a mental patient in the past or having had psychotic symptoms in the past.

Thus, most news stories give a false impression. Only a small minority of the actively mentally ill poses an increased risk. Even when we consider people who are actively psychotic, we find that the vast majority are not violent. Former mental patients, in particular, are no more likely to be violent than people in general. No matter how disturbed a person may have been, she or he merits respect and compassion.

The risk of violence from mental patients is actually many times lower than that from persons who have the following attributes: young, male, poor, and intoxicated (Corrigan & Watson, 2005). Remember, people who are not mentally ill commit the overwhelming majority of violent crimes.

Many news stories give the impression that the mentally ill are dangerous. Consider, for example, the ghastly case of Jeffrey Dahmer, who killed, sexually molested, and then ate his victims. Like Dahmer, most of the mentally disordered persons who make the evening news have committed murder or some other horrible crime. This tends to give the impression that the mentally ill are violent and dangerous. Yet in reality, only a tiny percentage of all mentally disordered persons are more violent than average. (Dahmer was killed in prison by another inmate in 1994.)

Curt Borgwardt/Corbis Sygma

Heredity

Does that mean that heredity affects the risk of developing schizophrenia? There is now little doubt that heredity is a factor in schizophrenia. It appears that some individuals inherit a *potential* for developing schizophrenia. They are, in other words, more *vulnerable* to the disorder (Harrison & Weinberger, 2005; Walker et al., 2004).

How has that been shown? If one identical twin becomes schizophrenic (remember, identical twins have identical genes), then the other twin has a *48 percent* chance of also becoming schizophrenic (Lenzenweger & Gottesman, 1994). The figure for twins can be compared with the risk of schizophrenia for the population in general, which is 1 percent. (See ● Figure 14.5 for other relationships.) In general, schizophrenia is clearly more common among close relatives and it tends to run in families. There's even a case on record of *four* identical quadruplets *all* developing schizophrenia (Mirsky et al., 2000). In light of such evidence, researchers are now beginning to search for specific genes related to schizophrenia.

A problem exists with current genetic explanations of schizophrenia: Very few people with schizophrenia have children. How could a genetic defect be passed from one generation to the next if

afflicted people don't reproduce? One possible answer is suggested by the fact that the older a man is (even if he doesn't suffer from schizophrenia) when he fathers a child, the more likely it is that the child will develop schizophrenia. Apparently, genetic mutations occur in aging male reproductive cells and increase the risk of schizophrenia (as well as other medical problems) (Malaspina et al., 2005; Sipos et al., 2004).

Brain Chemistry

Amphetamine, LSD, PCP ("angel dust"), and similar drugs produce effects that partially mimic the symptoms of schizophrenia. Also, the same drugs (phenothiazines) used to treat LSD over-

Paranoid schizophrenia Schizophrenia marked by a preoccupation with delusions or by frequent auditory hallucinations related to a single theme, especially grandeur or persecution.

Undifferentiated schizophrenia Schizophrenia lacking the specific features of catatonic, disorganized, or paranoid types.

Psychological trauma A psychological injury or shock, such as that caused by violence, abuse, neglect, separation, and so forth.

● **Figure 14.5** Lifetime risk of developing schizophrenia is associated with how closely a person is genetically related to a schizophrenic person. A shared environment also increases the risk. (Estimates from Lenzenweger & Gottesman, 1994.)

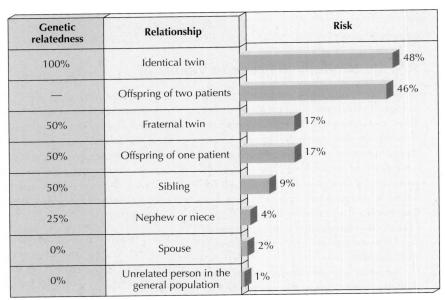

Genetic relatedness	Relationship	Risk
100%	Identical twin	48%
—	Offspring of two patients	46%
50%	Fraternal twin	17%
50%	Offspring of one patient	17%
50%	Sibling	9%
25%	Nephew or niece	4%
0%	Spouse	2%
0%	Unrelated person in the general population	1%

doses tend to alleviate psychotic symptoms. Facts such as these suggest that biochemical abnormalities (disturbances in brain chemicals or neurotransmitters) may occur in schizophrenic people. It is possible that the schizophrenic brain produces some substance similar to a *psychedelic* (mind-altering) drug. At present, one likely candidate is dopamine (DOPE-ah-meen), an important chemical messenger found in the brain.

Many researchers believe that schizophrenia is related to overactivity in brain dopamine systems (Durand & Barlow, 2006; Kapur & Lecrubier, 2003). Another possibility is that dopamine receptors become super-responsive to normal amounts of dopamine. Dopamine appears to trigger a flood of unrelated thoughts, feelings, and perceptions, which may account for the voices, hallucinations, and delusions of schizophrenia. The implication is that schizophrenic people may be on a sort of drug trip caused by their own bodies (● Figure 14.6).

Dopamine is not the only brain chemical that has caught scientists' attention. The neurotransmitter glutamate also appears to be related to schizophrenia (van Elst et al., 2005). People who take the hallucinogenic drug PCP, which affects glutamate, have symptoms that closely mimic schizophrenia (Murray, 2002). This occurs because glutamate influences brain activity in areas that control emotions and sensory information (Tsai & Coyle, 2002). Another tantalizing connection is the fact that stress alters glutamate levels, which in turn alter dopamine systems (Moghaddam, 2002). The story is far from complete, but it appears that dopamine, glutamate, and other brain chemicals partly explain the devastating symptoms of schizophrenia (Walker et al., 2004). (See "The Schizophrenic Brain.")

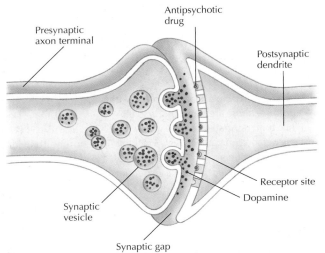

● **Figure 14.6** Dopamine normally crosses the synapse between two neurons, activating the second cell. Antipsychotic drugs bind to the same receptor sites as dopamine does, blocking its action. In people suffering from schizophrenia, a reduction in dopamine activity can quiet a person's agitation and psychotic symptoms.

Derik Bayes/Courtesy Guttman-Maclay *Life* Picture Service

This series of paintings by Louis Wain reflects a troubled personality. Wain was a British illustrator who became schizophrenic in middle age. As Wain's psychosis progressed, his cat paintings became highly abstract and fragmented. In many ways, Wain's paintings resemble the perceptual changes caused by psychedelic drugs such as mescaline and LSD. Recent research suggests that psychosis may, in fact, be the result of mind-altering changes in brain chemistry.

BRAINWAVES

The Schizophrenic Brain

Several brain imaging methods (remember Chapter 2?) have made it possible to directly observe the living schizophrenic brain. CT scans and MRI scans, which can reveal brain structure, suggest that the brains of schizophrenics have shrunk (atrophied). For example, ● Figure 14.7 shows a *CT scan* (*CT* stands for computed tomography, or computer-enhanced X-ray images) of the brain of John Hinkley Jr., who shot former U.S. President Ronald Reagan and three other men in 1981. In the ensuing trial, Hinkley was declared insane. As you can see, his brain had wider-than-normal surface fissuring.

Similarly, *MRI* (magnetic resonance imaging) *scans* indicate that schizophrenic people tend to have enlarged ventricles (fluid-filled spaces within the brain), again suggesting that surrounding brain tissue has withered (Barkataki et al., 2006). One possible explanation is that the schizophrenic brain may be unable to continually create new neurons to replace old ones that have died (Toro & Deakin, 2007). Normal brains continue to produce new neurons (a process referred to as *neurogenesis*) throughout life (Toro & Deakin, 2007). It is telling that the affected areas are crucial for regulating motivation, emotion, perception, actions, and attention (Gur et al., 1998; Walker et al., 2004).

Other methods provide images of brain activity, including PET scans. To make a *PET* (positron emission tomography) *scan*, a radioactive sugar solution is injected into a vein. When the sugar reaches the brain, an electronic device measures how much is used in each area. These data are then translated into a color map, or scan, of brain activity (● Figure 14.8).Researchers are finding patterns in such scans that are consistently linked with schizophrenia, affective disorders, and other problems. For instance, activity tends to be abnormally low in the frontal lobes of the schizophrenic brain (Durand & Barlow, 2006; Velakoulis & Pantelis, 1996). In the future, PET scans may be used to accurately diagnose schizophrenia. For now, such scans show that there is a clear difference in schizophrenic brain activity.

Dennis Brack/Black Star

● **Figure 14.7** *(Left)* CT scan of would-be presidential assassin John Hinkley Jr., taken when he was 25. The X-ray image shows widened fissures in the wrinkled surface of Hinkley's brain. *(Right)* CT scan of a normal 25-year-old's brain. In most young adults the surface folds of the brain are pressed together too tightly to be seen. As a person ages, surface folds of the brain normally become more visible. Pronounced brain fissuring in young adults may be a sign of schizophrenia, chronic alcoholism, or other problems.

> **bridges**
> Brain scans have provided valuable new insights into brain structures and activities. **See Chapter 2, pages 56–59.**

The Brookhaven National Laboratory

NORMAL   SCHIZOPHRENIC   MANIC-DEPRESSIVE

● **Figure 14.8** Positron emission tomography produces PET scans of the human brain. In the scans shown here, red, pink, and orange indicate lower levels of brain activity; white and blue indicate higher activity levels. Notice that activity in the schizophrenic brain is quite low in the frontal lobes (top area of each scan) (Velakoulis & Pantelis, 1996). Activity in the manic-depressive brain is low in the left brain hemisphere and high in the right brain hemisphere. The reverse is more often true of the schizophrenic brain. Researchers are trying to identify consistent patterns like these to aid diagnosis of mental disorders.

Implications

In summary, the emerging picture of psychotic disorders such as schizophrenia takes this form: Anyone subjected to enough stress may be pushed to a psychotic break. (Battlefield psychosis is an example.) However, some people inherit a difference in brain chemistry or brain structure that makes them more susceptible—even to normal life stresses.

Thus, the right mix of inherited potential and environmental stress brings about mind-altering changes in brain chemicals and brain structure. This explanation is called a **stress-vulnerability model**. It attributes psychotic disorders to a blend of environmental stress and inherited susceptibility (Walker et al., 2004). The model seems to apply to other forms of psychopathology as well, such as depression (● Figure 14.9).

Despite advances in our understanding, psychosis remains "a riddle wrapped in a mystery inside an enigma." Let us hope that recent progress toward a cure for schizophrenia will continue.

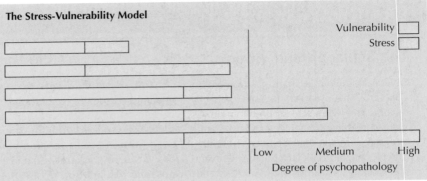

The Stress-Vulnerability Model

Vulnerability ▢
Stress ▢

Low   Medium   High
Degree of psychopathology

● **Figure 14.9** Various combinations of vulnerability and stress may produce psychological problems. The top bar shows low vulnerability and low stress. The result? No problem. The same is true of the next bar down, where low vulnerability is combined with moderate stress. Even high vulnerability (third bar) may not lead to problems if stress levels remain low. However, when high vulnerability combines with moderate or high stress (bottom two bars) the person "crosses the line" and suffers from psychopathology.

KNOWLEDGE BUILDER
Psychosis, Delusional Disorders, and Schizophrenia

RECITE

1. Carol wrongly believes that her body is "rotting away." She is suffering from
   a. depressive hallucinations
   b. a delusion
   c. flat affect
   d. Alzheimer's disease
2. Colin, who has suffered a psychotic break, is hearing voices. This symptom is referred to as
   a. flat affect
   b. hallucination
   c. a word salad
   d. organic delusions
3. A psychosis caused by lead poisoning would be regarded as an organic disorder. T or F?
4. Hallucinations and personality disintegration are the principal features of paranoid psychosis. T or F?
5. Which of the following is *not* one of the subtypes of schizophrenia?
   a. erotomanic type
   b. catatonic type
   c. paranoid type
   d. disorganized type
6. Environmental explanations of schizophrenia emphasize emotional trauma and
   a. manic parents
   b. schizoaffective interactions
   c. psychedelic interactions
   d. disturbed family relationships
7. The _____ _____ of a schizophrenic person runs a 48 percent chance of also becoming psychotic.
8. Biochemical explanations of schizophrenia have focused on excessive amounts of _____ in the brain.
   a. radioactive sugar
   b. webs and tangles
   c. PCP
   d. dopamine and glutamate

9. The stress-vulnerability model of psychosis explains mental disorders as a product of environmental stresses and
   a. psychological trauma
   b. deviant communication
   c. exposure to the flu virus during pregnancy
   d. heredity

REFLECT

Critical Thinking

10. Researchers have found nearly double the normal number of dopamine receptor sites in the brains of schizophrenics. Why might that be important?
11. Enlarged surface fissures and ventricles are frequently found in the brains of chronic schizophrenics. Why is it a mistake to conclude that such features cause schizophrenia?

Relate

What did you think psychosis was like before you read about it? How has your understanding changed? If you were writing a "recipe" for psychosis, what would the main "ingredients" be?

If you were asked to play the role of a paranoid person for a theater production, what symptoms would you emphasize?

You have been asked to explain the causes of schizophrenia to the parents of a schizophrenic teenager. What would you tell them?

Answers: 1. b **2.** b **3.** T **4.** F **5.** a **6.** d **7.** identical twin **8.** d **9.** d **10.** Because of the extra receptors, schizophrenics may get psychedelic effects from normal levels of dopamine in the brain. **11.** Because correlation does not confirm causation. Structural brain abnormalities are merely correlated with schizophrenia. They could be additional symptoms, rather than causes, of the disorder.

⬤ Mood Disorders—Peaks and Valleys

Gateway Questions: What are mood disorders? What causes them?

For some people, minor bouts of depression are as common as colds. But extreme swings of mood can be as disabling as a serious physical illness. In fact, depression can be deadly, because depressed persons may be suicidal. It is difficult to imagine how bleak and hopeless the world looks to a person who is deeply depressed, or how "crazy" it can be to ride a wave of mania. Let's explore mood disorders and their causes.

Table 14.5 ● *DSM-IV-TR* Classification of Mood Disorders

Problem	Primary Symptom	Typical Signs of Trouble
Depressive Disorders		
Major depressive disorder	Extreme emotional depression for at least 2 weeks	You feel extremely sad, worthless, fatigued, and empty; you are unable to feel pleasure; you are having thoughts of suicide.
Dysthymic disorder	Moderately depressed mood on most days during the last 2 years	You feel down and depressed more days than not; your self-esteem and energy levels have been low for many months.
Bipolar Disorders		
Bipolar I disorder	Extreme mania and depression	At times you have little need for sleep, can't stop talking, your mind races, and everything you do is of immense importance; at other times you feel extremely sad, worthless, and empty.
Bipolar II disorder	Emotional depression and at least one episode of mild mania	Most of the time you feel extremely sad, worthless, fatigued, and empty; however, at times you feel unusually good, cheerful, energetic, or "high."
Cyclothymic disorder	Periods of moderate depression and moderate mania for at least 2 years	You have been experiencing upsetting emotional ups and downs for many months.

Nobody loves you when you're down and out—or so it seems. Psychologists have come to realize that **mood disorders** (major disturbances in emotion) are among the most serious of all psychological conditions. In any given year, roughly 9.5 percent of the U. S. population suffers from a mood disorder (NIMH, 2006b).

Two general types of mood disorder are depressive disorders and bipolar disorders (Nevid & Greene, 2005). (See ● Table 14.5.) In **depressive disorders,** sadness and despondency are exaggerated, prolonged, or unreasonable. Signs of a depressive disorder are dejection, hopelessness, and an inability to feel pleasure or to take interest in anything. Other common symptoms are fatigue, disturbed sleep and eating patterns, feelings of worthlessness, a very negative self-image, and thoughts of suicide. In **bipolar disorders,** people go both "up" and "down" emotionally (*DSM-IV-TR,* 2000).

Some mood disorders are long-lasting but relatively moderate problems. If a person is mildly depressed for at least 2 years, the problem is called a **dysthymic disorder** (dis-THY-mik). If depression alternates with periods when the person's mood is cheerful, expansive, or irritable, the problem is a **cyclothymic disorder** (SIKE-lo-THY-mik). Even at this level, mood disorders can be debilitating. However, major mood disorders are much more damaging.

Major Mood Disorders

Major mood disorders are characterized by emotional extremes. The person who only goes "down" emotionally suffers from a **major depressive disorder.** During major depressive episodes everything looks bleak and hopeless. The person has feelings of failure, worthlessness, and total despair. Suffering is intense, and the person may become extremely subdued, withdrawn, or intensely suicidal. Suicide attempted during a major depression is rarely a "plea for help." Usually, the person intends to succeed and may give no prior warning.

In a **bipolar I disorder,** people experience both extreme mania and deep depression. During manic episodes, the person is loud, elated, hyperactive, grandiose, and energetic. Manic patients may go bankrupt in a matter of days, get arrested, or go on a binge of promiscuous sex. During periods of depression, the person is deeply despondent and possibly suicidal.

In a **bipolar II disorder** the person is mostly sad and guilt ridden, but has had one or more mildly manic episodes (called *hypomania*). That is, in a bipolar II disorder both elation and depression occur, but the person's mania is not as extreme as in a bipolar I disorder. Bipolar II patients who are hypomanic usually just manage to irritate everyone around them. They are excessively cheerful, aggressive, or irritable, and they may brag, talk too fast, interrupt conversations, or spend too much money (Nolen-Hoeksema, 2007).

In serious cases of depression it is impossible for a person to function at work or at school. Sometimes, depressed individuals cannot even feed or dress themselves. In cases of depression and/or mania that are even more severe, the person may also lose touch with reality and display psychotic symptoms.

Stress-vulnerability model Attributes mental disorders such as psychosis to a combination of environmental stress and inherited susceptibility.

Mood disorder Major disturbances in mood or emotion, such as depression or mania.

Depressive disorders Emotional disorders primarily involving sadness, despondency, and depression.

Bipolar disorders Emotional disorders involving both depression and mania or hypomania.

Dysthymic disorder Moderate depression that persists for 2 years or more.

Cyclothymic disorder Moderate manic and depressive behavior that persists for 2 years or more.

Major mood disorders Disorders marked by lasting extremes of mood or emotion and sometimes accompanied by psychotic symptoms.

Major depressive disorder A mood disorder in which the person has suffered one or more intense episodes of depression.

Bipolar I disorder A mood disorder in which a person has episodes of mania (excited, hyperactive, energetic, grandiose behavior) and also periods of deep depression.

Bipolar II disorder A mood disorder in which a person is mostly depressed (sad, despondent, guilt ridden) but has also had one or more episodes of mild mania (hypomania).

Darren Robb/Getty Images

In major depressive disorders, suicidal impulses can be intense and despair total.

How do major mood disorders differ from dysthymic and cyclothymic disorders? As mentioned, the major mood disorders involve more severe emotional changes. Also, major mood disorders more often appear to be **endogenous** (en-DODGE-eh-nus: produced from within) rather than a reaction to external events.

What Causes Mood Disorders?

Depression and other mood disorders have resisted adequate explanation and treatment. Some scientists are focusing on the biology of mood changes. They are interested in brain chemicals and transmitter substances, especially serotonin, noradrenaline, and dopamine levels. Their findings are incomplete, but progress has been made. For example, the chemical *lithium carbonate* can be effective for treating some cases of bipolar depression.

Other researchers seek psychological explanations. Psychoanalytic theory, for instance, holds that depression is caused by repressed anger. This rage is displaced and turned inward as self-blame and self-hate. As discussed in Chapter 13, behavioral theories of depression emphasize learned helplessness (LoLordo, 2001; Seligman, 1989). Cognitive psychologists believe that self-criticism and negative, distorted, or self-defeating thoughts underlie many cases of depression. (This view is discussed in Chapter 15.) Clearly, life stresses trigger many mood disorders (Maier, 2001). This is especially true for people who have personality traits and thinking patterns that make them vulnerable to depression (Dozois & Dobson, 2002).

Gender and Depression

Overall, women are twice as likely as men to experience depression (Kuehner, 2003). Researchers believe that social and environmental conditions are the main reason for this difference (Winstead & Sanchez, 2005). Factors that contribute to women's greater risk of depression include conflicts about birth control and pregnancy, work and parenting, and the strain of providing emotional support for others. Marital strife, sexual and physical abuse, and poverty are also factors. Nationwide, women and children are most likely to live in poverty. As a result, poor women frequently suffer the stresses associated with single parenthood, loss of control over their lives, poor housing, and dangerous neighborhoods (Stoppard & McMullen, 2003). One study found that women in the United States were most likely to be depressed if they lacked education, were unmarried, were Latina, had high stress levels, and experienced feelings of hopelessness (Myers et al., 2002).

Postpartum Depression

One source of women's depression is fairly easy to identify. After pregnancy and childbirth, many women face a high risk of becoming depressed.

Two weeks after her child was born, Makemba realized something was wrong. She could no longer ignore that she was extremely irritable, fatigued, tearful, and depressed. "Shouldn't I be happy?" she wondered. "What's wrong with me?"

Many women are surprised to learn that they face a risk of depression after giving birth. The two most common forms of the problem are maternity blues and postpartum depression. (The term *postpartum* refers to the time following childbirth.)

An estimated 25 to 50 percent of all women experience *maternity blues,* a mild depression that usually lasts from 1 to 2 days after childbirth. These "third-day blues" are marked by crying, fitful sleep, tension, anger, and irritability. For most women, such reactions are a normal part of adjusting to childbirth. The depression is usually brief and not too severe.

For some women, maternity blues can be the beginning of a serious depression. Roughly 13 percent of all women who give birth develop **postpartum depression,** a moderately severe depression that begins within 3 months following childbirth. Typical signs of postpartum depression are mood swings, despondency, feelings of inadequacy, and an inability to cope with the new baby. Unlike other types of depression, postpartum depression also features unusually high levels of restlessness and difficulty concentrating (Bernstein et al., 1998). Depression of this kind may last anywhere from 2 months to about a year. Women are not the only ones to suffer when postpartum depression strikes. A depressed mother can seriously retard her child's rate of development (Cooper & Murray, 2001).

Stress and anxiety before birth and negative attitudes toward child rearing increase the risk of postpartum depression. A troubled marriage and lack of support from the father are also danger signs. Part of the problem may be hormonal: After a woman gives birth, her estrogen levels can drop, altering her mood (Bloch, Daly, & Rubinow, 2003).

Women who become depressed tend to see their husbands as unsupportive. Therefore, educating new parents about the importance of supporting one another may reduce the risk of depression. Groups where new mothers can discuss their feelings are also helpful. If depression is severe or long lasting, new mothers should seek professional help.

Biology and Depression

Does the fact that major mood disorders appear to be endogenous imply that heredity is involved? Yes, especially in bipolar disorders (McGuffin et al., 2003). As a case in point, if one identical twin is depressed, the other has a 67 percent chance of suffering depression, too. For fraternal twins the probability is 19 percent. This difference may be related to the recent finding that people who have a particular version of a gene are more likely to become depressed when they are stressed (Caspi et al., 2003). As we have noted, psychological causes are important in many cases of depression. But for major mood disorders, biological factors seem to play a larger role. Surprisingly, one additional source of depression is related to the seasons.

Seasonal Affective Disorder

Unless you have experienced a winter of "cabin fever" in the far north, you may be surprised to learn that the rhythms of the seasons underlie **seasonal affective disorder (SAD),** or depression that only occurs during the fall and winter months. Almost anyone can get a little depressed when days are short, dark, and cold. But when a person's symptoms are lasting and disabling, the problem may be SAD. Here are some of the major symptoms of SAD, according to Swedish psychiatrist Åsa Westrin and Canadian neuroscientist Raymond Lam (Westrin & Lam, 2007a):

- **Fatigue:** You feel too tired to maintain a normal routine.
- **Oversleeping and difficulty staying awake:** Your sleep patterns may be disturbed, and waking very early in the morning is common.
- **Craving:** You hunger for carbohydrates and sweets, leading to overeating and weight gain.
- **Inability to cope:** You feel irritable and stressed.
- **Social withdrawal:** You become unsocial in the winter but are socially active during other seasons.

Starting in the fall, people with SAD sleep longer but more poorly. During the day they feel tired and drowsy, and they tend to overeat. With each passing day they become more sad, anxious, irritable, and socially withdrawn.

Although their depressions are usually not severe, many victims of SAD face each winter with a sense of foreboding. SAD is especially prevalent in northern latitudes (think of countries like Sweden and Canada), where days are very short during the winter (Michalak & Lam, 2002) (● Figure 14.10). For instance, one study found that 13 percent of college students living in northern New England showed signs of suffering from SAD (Low & Feiss-

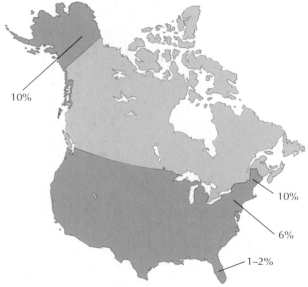

Rates of seasonal affective disorder, by latitude

● **Figure 14.10** Seasonal affective disorder appears to be related to reduced exposure to daylight during the winter. SAD affects 1 to 2 percent of Florida's population, about 6 percent of the people living in Maryland and New York City, and nearly 10 percent of the residents of New Hampshire and Alaska (Booker & Hellekson, 1992).

ner, 1998). The students most likely to be affected were those who had moved from the South to attend college!

Seasonal depressions are related to the release of more melatonin during the winter. This hormone, which is secreted by the pineal gland in the brain, regulates the body's response to changing light conditions (Wehr et al., 2001). That's why 80 percent of SAD patients can be helped by extra doses of bright light, a remedy called phototherapy (● Figure 14.11). **Phototherapy** involves exposing SAD patients to one or more hours of very bright fluorescent light each day (Neumeister, 2004; Westrin & Lam, 2007b). This is best done early in the morning, where it simulates dawn in the summer (Avery et al., 2001). For many SAD sufferers a hearty dose of morning "sunshine" appears to be the next best thing to vacationing in the tropics.

> **bridges**
> In addition to its role in producing SAD, melatonin regulates normal circadian rhythms. **See Chapter 10, page 322–323.**

Endogenous depression Depression that appears to be produced from within (perhaps by chemical imbalances in the brain), rather than as a reaction to life events.

Postpartum depression A mild to moderately severe depression that begins within 3 months following childbirth.

Seasonal affective disorder (SAD) Depression that occurs only during fall and winter; presumably related to decreased exposure to sunlight.

Phototherapy A treatment for seasonal affective disorder that involves exposure to bright, full-spectrum light.

Science Museum/SSPL/The Image Works

● **Figure 14.11** An hour or more of bright light a day can dramatically reduce the symptoms of seasonal affective disorder. Treatment is usually necessary from fall through spring. Light therapy typically works best when it is used early in the morning (Lewy et al., 1998).

KNOWLEDGE BUILDER
Mood Disorders

RECITE

1. Dysthymic disorder is to depression as cyclothymic disorder is to manic-depression. T or F?
2. Major mood disorders, especially bipolar disorders, often appear to be endogenous. T or F?
3. Learned helplessness is emphasized by _____ theories of depression.
   a. humanistic
   b. biological
   c. behaviorist
   d. psychoanalytic
4. Women are more likely than men to become depressed because of _____ conditions.
   a. social and environmental
   b. existential
   c. biological
   d. postpartum
5. Roughly 13 percent of all new mothers experience the maternity blues, which are the first stage of postpartum depression. T or F?
6. Depression that occurs only in the winter is likely to be classified as
   a. SAD
   b. PTSD
   c. bipolar
   d. endogenous

REFLECT

Critical Thinking

7. How might relationships contribute to the higher rates of depression experienced by women?

●● Anxiety-Based Disorders— When Anxiety Rules

Gateway Question: What problems result when a person suffers high levels of anxiety?

Anxiety refers to feelings of apprehension, dread, or uneasiness. We all feel anxiety, but anxiety that is out of proportion to a situation may reveal a problem. An example is a college student named Jian, who became unbearably anxious when he took exams. By the time Jian went to see a counselor, he had skipped several tests and was in danger of dropping out of school. In general, people with anxiety-related problems like Jian's display the following characteristics:

● High levels of anxiety and/or restrictive, self-defeating behavior patterns
● A tendency to use elaborate defense mechanisms or avoidance responses to get through the day
● Pervasive feelings of stress, insecurity, inferiority, and dissatisfaction with life

People with anxiety-related problems feel threatened and often can't do anything constructive about it. They struggle to control themselves, but they remain ineffective and unhappy (Rachman, 2004). In any given year, roughly 18 percent of the adult population suffers from an anxiety disorder (NIMH, 2006b).

If anxiety is a normal emotion, when does it signify a problem? A problem exists when intense anxiety prevents people from doing what they want or need to do. Also, their anxieties are out of control—they simply cannot stop worrying.

> **bridges**
> Excessive use of psychological defense mechanisms is a feature of many anxiety disorders. **See Chapter 13, pages 440–442.**

Adjustment Disorders

Do such problems cause a "nervous breakdown"? People suffering from anxiety-based problems may be miserable, but they rarely experience a "breakdown." Actually, the term "nervous break-down" has no formal meaning. Nevertheless, a problem known as an *adjustment disorder* does come close to being something of a "breakdown."

Adjustment disorders occur when ordinary stresses push people beyond their ability to cope with life. Examples of such stresses are losing a job, intense marital strife, and chronic physical illness. People suffering from an adjustment disorder may be extremely irritable, anxious, apathetic, or depressed. They also have trouble sleeping, lose their appetite, and suffer from various physical complaints. Often, their problems can be relieved by rest, sedation, supportive counseling, and a chance to "talk through" their fears and anxieties (*DSM-IV-TR*, 2000).

How is an adjustment disorder different from an anxiety disorder? The outward symptoms are similar. However, adjustment disorders disappear when a person's life circumstances improve (Jones, Yates, & Zhou, 2002). People suffering from anxiety disorders seem to generate their own misery, regardless of what's happening around them. They feel that they must be on guard against *future* threats that *could happen* at any time (Barlow, 2000).

Anxiety Disorders

In most anxiety disorders, distress seems greatly out of proportion to a person's circumstances. For example, consider the following description of Adrian H:

> She becomes very anxious that her children "might have been hurt or killed if they were out of the neighborhood playing and she hadn't heard from them in a couple of hours." She also worries all the time about her job performance and her relationships with men. Adrian believes that men rarely call back after a date or two because "They can sense I'm not a fun person." She never really relaxes, has difficulty focusing at work, has frequent headaches, and suffers from insomnia. (Adapted from Brown & Barlow, 2007.)

Distress like Adrian H's is a key ingredient in anxiety disorders. It also may underlie dissociative and somatoform disorders, where maladaptive behavior serves to reduce anxiety and discomfort. To deepen your understanding, let's first examine the anxiety disorders themselves (● Table 14.6). Then we will see how anxiety contributes to other problems.

Generalized Anxiety Disorder

A person with a **generalized anxiety disorder** has been extremely anxious and worried for at least 6 months. Sufferers typically complain of sweating, a racing heart, clammy hands, dizziness, upset stomach, rapid breathing, irritability, and poor concentration. Overall, more women than men have these symptoms (Brown & Barlow, 2007).

Was Adrian H's problem a generalized anxiety disorder? Yes. However, if she also experienced *anxiety attacks,* then she would likely be diagnosed with panic disorder.

Panic Disorder (Without Agoraphobia)

In a **panic disorder (without agoraphobia)** people are highly anxious and also feel sudden, intense, unexpected panic. During a panic attack, victims experience chest pain, a racing heart, dizziness, choking, feelings of unreality, trembling, or fears of losing

Table 14.6 ● Anxiety Disorders

Type of Disorder	Typical Signs of Trouble
Generalized anxiety disorder	You have been extremely anxious or worried for 6 months.
Panic disorder (without agoraphobia)	You are anxious much of the time and have sudden panic attacks.
Panic disorder (with agoraphobia)	You have panic attacks and are afraid that they might occur in public places, so you rarely leave home.
Agoraphobia (without a history of panic disorder)	You fear that something extremely embarrassing will happen if you leave home (but you don't have panic attacks).
Specific phobia	You have an intense fear of specific objects, activities, or locations.
Social phobia	You fear social situations where people can watch, criticize, embarrass, or humiliate you.
Obsessive-compulsive disorder	Your thoughts make you extremely nervous and compel you to rigidly repeat certain actions or routines.
Acute stress disorder	You are tormented for less than a month by the emotional aftereffects of horrible events you have experienced.
Posttraumatic stress disorder	You are tormented for more than a month by the emotional aftereffects of horrible events you have experienced.

DSM-IV-TR, 2000.

control. Many believe that they are having a heart attack, are going insane, or are about to die. Needless to say, this pattern leaves victims unhappy and uncomfortable much of the time. Again, the majority of people who suffer from panic disorder are women (Foot & Koszycki, 2004).

To get an idea of how a panic attack feels, imagine that you are trapped in your stateroom on a sinking ocean liner (the *Titanic*?). The room fills with water. When only a small air space remains near the ceiling and you are gasping for air, you'll know what a panic attack feels like.

Panic Disorder (with Agoraphobia)

In a **panic disorder (with agoraphobia)** people suffer from chronic anxiety and sudden panic. In addition, they have agoraphobia (ah-go-rah-FOBE-ee-ah), which is an intense *fear that a panic attack*

Adjustment disorder An emotional disturbance caused by ongoing stressors within the range of common experience.

Generalized anxiety disorder A chronic state of tension and worries about work, relationships, ability, or impending disaster.

Panic disorder (without agoraphobia) A chronic state of anxiety and also has brief moments of sudden, intense, unexpected panic.

Panic disorder (with agoraphobia) A chronic state of anxiety and brief moments of sudden panic. The person fears that these panic attacks will occur in public places or unfamiliar situations.

will occur in a public place or unfamiliar situation. That is, agoraphobics intensely fear leaving their home and familiar surroundings. Typically, they find ways of avoiding places that frighten them—such as crowds, open roads, supermarkets, automobiles, and so on. As a result, some agoraphobics are prisoners in their own homes (*DSM-IV-TR,* 2000).

Agoraphobia

The problem known as **agoraphobia** can also occur without panic. In this case, people *fear that something extremely embarrassing will happen* if they leave home or enter an unfamiliar situation. For example, an agoraphobic person may refuse to go outside because he or she fears having a sudden attack of dizziness, or diarrhea, or shortness of breath. Going outside the home alone, being in a crowd, standing in line, crossing a bridge, or riding in a car can be impossible for an agoraphobic person (*DSM-IV-TR,* 2000). About 4.2 percent of all adults suffer from agoraphobia (with or without panic) during their lifetime (Grant et al., 2006).

Specific Phobia

As we noted earlier, phobias are intense, irrational fears that a person cannot shake off, even when there is no real danger. In a **specific phobia,** the person's fear, anxiety, and avoidance are focused on particular objects, activities, or situations. People affected by phobias recognize that their fears are unreasonable, but they cannot control them. For example, a person with a spider phobia would find it impossible to ignore a *picture* of a spider, even though a photograph can't bite anyone (Miltner et al., 2004). Specific phobias can be linked to nearly any object or situation. In descending order of prevalence, the most common specific phobias among Americans are (Stinson et al., 2007):

Fear of insects, birds, snakes, or other animals (including, of course, arachnophobia, the fear of spiders and zoophobia, fear of animals)
Acrophobia—fear of heights
Astraphobia—fear of storms, thunder, lightning
Aquaphobia—fear of being on or in water
Aviophobia—fear of airplanes
Claustrophobia—fear of closed spaces
Agoraphobia—fear of crowds

By combining the appropriate root word with the word "phobia," any number of fears can be named. Some are triskaidekaphobia, fear of the number 13; xenophobia, fear of strangers; and hematophobia, fear of blood. One of your authors' favorites is coulrophobia, fear of clowns. Another is arachibutyrophobia, fear of peanut butter sticking to the roof of the mouth.

Almost everyone has a few mild phobias, such as fearing heights, closed spaces, or bugs and crawly things. A phobic disorder differs from such garden-variety fears in that it produces overwhelming fear. True phobias may lead to vomiting, wild climbing and running, or fainting. For a phobic disorder to exist, the person's fear must disrupt his or her daily life. Phobic persons are so threatened that they will go to almost any length to avoid the

For a person with a strong fear of snakes (ophidiophobia), merely looking at this picture may be unsettling.

feared object or situation, such as driving 50 miles out of the way to avoid crossing a bridge. About 8 percent of all adults have phobic disorders during their lifetime (NIMH, 2006a).

Social Phobia

In a **social phobia,** people fear situations in which they can be observed, evaluated, embarrassed, or humiliated by others. This leads them to avoid certain social situations, such as eating, writing, using the rest room, or speaking in public. When such situations cannot be avoided, people endure them with intense anxiety or distress. It is common for them to have uncomfortable physical symptoms, such as a pounding heart, shaking hands, sweating, diarrhea, mental confusion, and blushing. Social phobias greatly impair a person's ability to work, attend school, and form personal relationships (*DSM-IV-TR,* 2000). About 7 percent of all adults are affected by social phobias in a given year (NIMH, 2006b).

Obsessive-Compulsive Disorder

People who suffer from **obsessive-compulsive disorder** are preoccupied with certain distressing thoughts and feel compelled to perform certain behaviors. You have probably experienced a mild obsessional thought, such as a song or stupid commercial jingle that repeats over and over in your mind. This may be irritating, but it's usually not terribly disturbing. True obsessions are images or thoughts that force their way into awareness against a person's will. They are so disturbing that they cause intense anxiety. The most common obsessions are about violence or harm (such as one's spouse being poisoned or being hit by a car), about being "dirty" or "unclean," about whether one has performed some action (such as locking the door), and about committing immoral acts (Grabill et al., 2008).

Obsessions usually give rise to compulsions. These are irrational acts that a person feels driven to repeat. Often, compulsive acts

Bettmann/Corbis

Dennis Coon

The severe obsessions and compulsions of billionaire Howard Hughes led him to live as a recluse for more than 20 years. Hughes had an intense fear of contamination. To avoid infection, he constructed sterile, isolated environments in which his contact with people and objects was strictly limited by complicated rituals. Before handling a spoon, for instance, Hughes had his attendants wrap the handle in tissue paper and seal it with tape. A second piece of tissue was then wrapped around the first before he would touch it (Hodgson & Miller, 1982). A spoon prepared as Hughes required is shown at right.

Brandi Simons/Getty Images

The 2008 U.S. tornado season killed many people and upset the lives of many more. In the aftermath of such disasters, many survivors suffer from acute stress reactions. For some, the flare-up of anxiety and distress occurs months or years after the stressful event, an example of a posttraumatic stress reaction.

help control or block out anxiety caused by an obsession. For example, a minister who finds profanities popping into her mind might start compulsively counting her heartbeat. Doing this would prevent her from thinking "dirty" words.

Many compulsive people are *checkers* or *cleaners*. For instance, a young mother who repeatedly pictures a knife plunging into her baby might check once an hour to make sure all the knives in her house are locked away. Doing so may reduce her anxieties, but it will probably also take over her life. Likewise, a person who feels "contaminated" from touching ordinary objects because "germs are everywhere" may be driven to wash his hands hundreds of times a day.

Of course, not all obsessive-compulsive disorders are so dramatic. Many simply involve extreme orderliness and rigid routine. Compulsive attention to detail and rigidly following rules helps keep activities totally under control and makes the highly anxious person feel more secure. (If such patterns are long-standing, but less intense, they are classified as personality disorders, which we will discuss later in more detail.)

Stress Disorders

Stress disorders occur when people experience stresses outside the range of normal human experience, such as floods, tornadoes, earthquakes, or horrible accidents. They affect many political hostages; combat veterans; prisoners of war; victims of terrorism, torture, violent crime, child molestation, rape, or domestic violence; or people who have witnessed a death or serious injury (Brown & Barlow, 2007).

Symptoms of stress disorders include repeatedly reliving the traumatic event, avoiding reminders of the event, and blunted emotions. Also common are insomnia, nightmares, wariness, poor concentration, irritability, and explosive anger or aggression. If

such reactions last *less* than a month after a traumatic event, the problem is called an **acute stress disorder.** If they last *more* than a month, the person is suffering from **posttraumatic stress disorder** (**PTSD**) (Nemeroff et al., 2006).

If a situation causes distress, anxiety, or fear, we tend to avoid it in the future. This is a normal survival instinct. However, victims of PTSD fail to recover from these reactions. Military combat accounts for more than a quarter of the cases of PTSD among American men (Prigerson, Maciejewski, & Rosenheck, 2002). The constant threat of death and the gruesome sights and sounds of war take a terrible toll. Psychologists are already seeing high rates of PTSD among soldiers involved in combat in Iraq (Hoge et al., 2004). Sadly, 8 percent of military veterans still suffer from PTSD decades after they were in combat (Dirkzwager, Bramsen, & Van Der Ploeg, 2001). About 3.5 percent of adults suffer from posttraumatic stress in any given year (NIMH, 2006b).

Agoraphobia (without panic) The fear that something extremely embarrassing will happen if one leaves the house or enter unfamiliar situations.

Specific phobia An intense, irrational fear of specific objects, activities, or situations.

Social phobia An intense, irrational fear of being observed, evaluated, embarrassed, or humiliated by others in social situations.

Obsessive-compulsive disorder An extreme preoccupation with certain thoughts and compulsive performance of certain behaviors.

Stress disorder A significant emotional disturbance caused by stresses outside the range of normal human experience.

Acute stress disorder A psychological disturbance lasting up to 1 month following stresses that would produce anxiety in anyone who experienced them.

Posttraumatic stress disorder (PTSD) A psychological disturbance lasting more than 1 month following stresses that would produce anxiety in anyone who experienced them.

THE CLINICAL FILE

Sick of Being Sick

At 14, Ben was in the hospital again for his sinus problem. He had already undergone 40 surgeries since the age of 8. In addition, he had been diagnosed at various times with bipolar disorder, oppositional defiant disorder, and attention deficit disorder. Ben was taking 19 different medications, and his mother said she desperately wanted him to be "healed." She sought numerous tests and never missed an appointment. But at long last, it became clear that there was nothing wrong with Ben. Left alone with doctors, Ben revealed that he was "sick of being sick."

In reality, it was Ben's mother who was sick. She was eventually diagnosed as suffer-ing from **Munchausen syndrome by proxy** (Awadallah et al., 2005). This is a pattern in which a person fakes the medical problems of someone in his or her care. (In **Munchausen syndrome,** the person fakes his or her own medical problems.) As in Ben's case, most people with the syndrome are mothers who fabricate their children's illnesses. Sometimes they even deliberately harm their children. For example, one mother injected her son with 7-Up (Reisner, 2006).

But why? People who suffer from Munchausen syndrome and Munchausen by proxy appear to have a pathological need to seek attention and sympathy from medi-cal professionals. They may also win praise for being health conscious or a good parent (*DSM-IV-TR*, 2000).

This case illustrates another point about psychological disorders: Sam's mother was eventually diagnosed with several disorders, including Munchausen by proxy, schizo-affective disorder, and borderline personality disorder. As this suggests, many disturbed people are *comorbid*. That is, they suffer from more than one disorder at a time. Not only does comorbidity increase their misery, it makes it more difficult for health care provid-ers to diagnose and treat them.

Dissociative Disorders

In dissociative reactions we see striking episodes of *amnesia, fugue,* or *multiple identity*. **Dissociative amnesia** is an inability to recall one's name, address, or past. **Dissociative fugue** (FEWG) involves sudden, unplanned travel away from home and confusion about personal identity. Dissociations are often triggered by highly trau-matic events (McLewin & Muller, 2006). In such cases, forgetting personal identity and fleeing unpleasant situations appear to be defenses against intolerable anxiety.

A person suffering from a **dissociative identity disorder** has two or more separate identities or personality states. (Don't forget that identity disorders are not the same as schizophrenia. Schizo-phrenia, which is a psychotic disorder, was discussed earlier in this chapter.) One famous and dramatic example of multiple identities is described in the book *Sybil* (Schreiber, 1973). Sybil reportedly had 16 different personality states. Each identity had a distinct voice, vocabulary, and posture. One personality could play the piano (not Sybil), but the others could not.

When an identity other than Sybil was in control, Sybil experi-enced a "time lapse," or memory blackout. Sybil's amnesia and alternate identities first appeared during childhood. As a girl she was beaten, locked in closets, perversely tortured, sexually abused, and almost killed. Sybil's first dissociations allowed her to escape by creating another person who would suffer torture in her place. Identity disorders often begin with unbearable childhood experi-ences, like Sybil endured. A history of childhood trauma, espe-cially sexual abuse, is found in a high percentage of persons whose personalities split into multiple identities (McLewin & Muller, 2006; Simeon et al., 2002).

Flamboyant cases like Sybil's have led some experts to question the existence of multiple personalities (Casey, 2001). However, a majority of psychologists continue to believe that multiple iden-tity is a real, if rare, problem (Cormier & Thelen, 1998).

Therapy for dissociative identity disorders may make use of hypnosis, which allows contact with the various personality states. The goal of therapy is *integration* and *fusion* of the identities into a single, balanced personality. Fortunately, multiple identity disor-ders are far rarer in real life than they are in TV dramas!

Somatoform Disorders

Have you ever known someone who appeared to be healthy but seemed to constantly worry about disease? These people are pre-occupied with bodily functions, such as their heartbeat or breath-ing or digestion. Minor physical problems—even a small sore or an occasional cough—may convince them that they have cancer or some other dreaded disease. Typically, they can't give up their fears of illness, even if doctors can find no medical basis for their com-plaints (Korol, Craig, & Firestone, 2003).

Are you describing hypochondria? Yes. In **hypochondriasis** (HI-po-kon-DRY-uh-sis), people interpret normal bodily sensations as proof that they have a terrible disease. (See "Sick of Being Sick" for a related disorder with a curious twist). In a problem called **soma-tization disorder** (som-ah-tuh-ZAY-shun), people express their anxieties through various bodily complaints. That is, they suffer from problems such as vomiting or nausea, shortness of breath, dif-ficulty swallowing, or painful menstrual periods. Typically, the person feels ill much of the time and visits doctors repeatedly. Most sufferers take medicines or other treatments, but no physical cause can be found for their distress. Similarly, a person with **pain disor-der** is disabled by pain that has no identifiable physical basis.

A rarer somatoform disorder ("body-form" disorder) is called a *conversion reaction*. In a **conversion disorder,** severe emotional

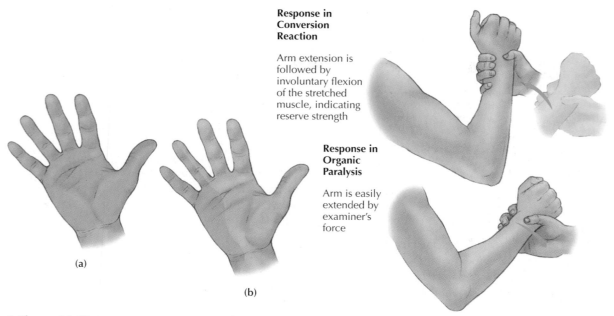

Response in Conversion Reaction

Arm extension is followed by involuntary flexion of the stretched muscle, indicating reserve strength

Response in Organic Paralysis

Arm is easily extended by examiner's force

(a)

(b)

● **Figure 14.12** *(Left)* "Glove anesthesia" is a conversion reaction involving loss of feeling in areas of the hand that would be covered by a glove *(a)*. If the anesthesia were physically caused, it would follow the pattern shown in *(b)*. *(Right)* To test for organic paralysis of the arm, an examiner can suddenly extend the arm, stretching the muscles. A conversion reaction is indicated if the arm pulls back involuntarily. (Adapted from Weintraub, 1983.)

Adam Barnes/Getty Images

Uncontrollable sneezing, which may continue for days or weeks, is often a conversion disorder. In such cases, sneezing is atypical in rate and rhythm. In addition, the person's eyes do not close during a sneeze and sneezing does not occur during sleep. (A normal sneeze is shown here.) All these signs suggest that the cause of the sneezing is psychological, not physical (Fochtmann, 1995).

conflicts are "converted" into symptoms that actually disturb physical functioning or closely resemble a physical disability. For instance, a soldier might become deaf or lame or develop "glove anesthesia" just before a battle.

What is "glove anesthesia"? "Glove anesthesia" is a loss of sensitivity in the areas of the skin that would normally be covered by a glove. Glove anesthesia shows that conversion symptoms often contradict known medical facts. The system of nerves in the hands does not form a glove-like pattern and could not cause such symptoms (● Figure 14.12).

If symptoms disappear when a victim is asleep, hypnotized, or anesthetized, a conversion reaction must be suspected (Russo et al., 1998). Another sign to watch for is that victims of conversion reactions are strangely unconcerned about suddenly being disabled.

Munchausen syndrome by proxy An affected person fakes the medical problems of someone in his or her care in order to gain attention.

Munchausen syndrome An affected person fakes his or her own medical problems in order to gain attention.

Dissociative amnesia Loss of memory (partial or complete) for important information related to personal identity.

Dissociative fugue Sudden travel away from home, plus confusion about one's personal identity.

Dissociative identity disorder The presence of two or more distinct personalities (multiple personality).

Hypochondriasis A preoccupation with fears of having a serious disease. Ordinary physical signs are interpreted as proof that the person has a disease, but no physical disorder can be found.

Somatization disorder Afflicted persons have numerous physical complaints. Typically, they have consulted many doctors, but no organic cause for their distress can be identified.

Pain disorder Pain that has no identifiable physical cause and appears to be of psychological origin.

Conversion disorder A bodily symptom that mimics a physical disability but is actually caused by anxiety or emotional distress.

bridges
Don't confuse somatoform disorders with psychosomatic illnesses, which occur when stress causes real physical damage to the body. **See Chapter 13, pages 431–433.**

Anxiety and Disorder—Four Pathways to Trouble

Gateway Question: How do psychologists explain anxiety-based disorders?

What causes anxiety disorders? Susceptibility to anxiety-based disorders appears to be partly inherited (Rachman, 2004). Studies show that being high strung, nervous, or emotional runs in families. For example, 60 percent of children born to parents suffering from panic disorder have a fearful, inhibited temperament. Such children are irritable and wary as infants, shy and fearful as toddlers, and quiet and cautious introverts in elementary school. By the time they reach adulthood, they are at high risk for anxiety problems, such as panic attacks (Barlow, 2000; Durand & Barlow, 2006).

At least four major psychological perspectives on the causes of dissociative, anxiety-based, and somatoform disorders exist. These are (1) the *psychodynamic* approach, (2) the *humanistic-existential* approach, (3) the *behavioral* approach, and (4) the *cognitive* approach.

Psychodynamic Approach

The term *psychodynamic* refers to internal motives, conflicts, unconscious forces, and other dynamics of mental life. Freud was the first to propose a psychodynamic explanation for what he called "neurosis." According to Freud, disturbances like those we have described represent a raging conflict among subparts of the personality—the id, ego, and superego.

Freud emphasized that intense anxiety can be caused by forbidden id impulses for sex or aggression that threaten to break through into behavior. The person constantly fears doing something "crazy" or forbidden. She or he may also be tortured by guilt, which the superego uses to suppress forbidden impulses. Caught in the middle, the ego is eventually overwhelmed. This forces the person to use rigid defense mechanisms and misguided, inflexible behavior to prevent a disastrous loss of control. (See Chapter 12, pages 398–402, for more information).

Humanistic-Existential Approaches

Humanistic theories emphasize subjective experience, human problems, and personal potentials. Humanistic psychologist Carl Rogers regarded emotional disorders as the end product of a faulty self-image or self-concept (Rogers, 1959). Rogers believed that anxious individuals have built up unrealistic mental images of themselves. This leaves them vulnerable to contradictory informa-

tion. Let's say, for example, that an essential part of Cheyenne's self-image is the idea that she is highly intelligent. If Cheyenne does poorly in school, she may deny or distort her perceptions of herself and the situation. Should Cheyenne's anxiety become severe, she may resort to using defense mechanisms. A conversion reaction, anxiety attacks, or similar symptoms could also result from threats to her self-image. These symptoms, in turn, would become new threats that provoke further distortions. Soon, she would fall into a vicious cycle of maladjustment and anxiety that feeds on itself once started.

Existentialism focuses on the elemental problems of existence, such as death, meaning, choice, and responsibility. Psychologists who take a more existential view stress that unhealthy anxiety reflects a loss of *meaning* in one's life. According to them, we must show *courage* and *responsibility* in our choices if life is to have meaning. Too often, they say, we give in to "existential anxiety" and back away from life-enhancing choices. Existential anxiety is the unavoidable anguish that comes from knowing we are personally responsible for our lives. Hence, we have a crushing need to choose wisely and courageously as we face life's empty and impersonal void. Adolescents may experience considerable existential anxiety as they develop their identity (Berman, Weems, & Stickle, 2006).

From the existential view, people who are anxious are living in "bad faith." That is, they have collapsed in the face of the awesome responsibility to choose a meaningful existence. In short, they have lost their way in life. From this point of view, making choices that don't truly reflect what you value, feel, and believe can make you sick.

Behavioral Approach

Behaviorist approaches emphasize overt, observable behavior and the effects of learning and conditioning. Behaviorists assume that the "symptoms" we have discussed are learned, just as other behaviors are. You might recall from Chapter 7, for instance, that phobias can be acquired through classical conditioning. Similarly, anxiety attacks may reflect conditioned emotional responses that generalize to new situations and the hypochondriac's "sickness behavior" may be reinforced by the sympathy and attention he or she gets.

One point that all theorists agree on is that disordered behavior is ultimately self-defeating because it makes the person more miserable in the long run, even though it temporarily lowers anxiety.

But if the person becomes more miserable in the long run, how does the pattern get started? The behavioral explanation is that self-defeating behavior begins with avoidance learning (described in Chapter 7). Avoidance learning occurs when making a response delays or prevents the onset of a painful or unpleasant stimulus. Here's a quick review to refresh your memory:

An animal is placed in a special cage. After a few minutes a light comes on, followed a moment later by a painful shock. Quickly, the animal escapes into a second chamber. After a few minutes, a light comes on in this chamber, and the shock is repeated. Soon the animal learns to avoid pain by moving before the shock occurs. Once an animal learns to avoid the shock, it can be turned off altogether. A well-trained animal may avoid the nonexistent shock indefinitely.

The same analysis can be applied to human behavior. A behaviorist would say that the powerful reward of immediate relief from anxiety keeps self-defeating avoidance behaviors alive. This view, known as the **anxiety reduction hypothesis,** seems to explain why the behavior patterns we have discussed often look very "stupid" to outside observers.

Cognitive Approach

The cognitive view is that distorted thinking causes people to magnify ordinary threats and failures, which leads to distress (Provencher, Dugas, & Ladouceur, 2004). For example, Bonnie, who is socially phobic, constantly has upsetting thoughts about being evaluated at school. One reason for this is that people with social phobias tend to be perfectionists. Like other social phobics, Bonnie is excessively concerned about making mistakes. She also perceives criticism where none exists. If Bonnie expects that a social situation will focus too much attention on her, she avoids it (Brown & Barlow, 2007). Even when socially phobic persons are successful, distorted thoughts lead them to believe they have failed (Barlow, 2002). In short, changing the thinking patterns of anxious individuals like Bonnie can greatly lessen their fears (Hall, 2006).

Implications

All four psychological explanations probably contain a core of truth. For this reason, understanding anxiety-based disorders may be aided by combining parts of each perspective. Each viewpoint also suggests a different approach to treatment. Because many possibilities exist, therapy is discussed later, in Chapter 15.

⬤⬤ Personality Disorders—Blueprints for Maladjustment

Gateway Question: What is a personality disorder?

"Get out of here and leave me alone so I can die in peace," Judy screamed at her nurses in the seclusion room of the psychiatric hospital. On one of her arms, long dark red marks mingled with the scars of previous suicide attempts. Judy once bragged that her record was 67 stitches. Today, the nurses had to strap her into restraints to keep her from gouging her own eyes. She was given a sedative and slept for 12 hours. She woke calmly and asked for her therapist—even though her latest outburst began when he canceled a morning appointment and changed it to afternoon.

Judy has a condition called *borderline personality disorder.* Although she is capable of working, Judy has repeatedly lost jobs because of her turbulent relationships with other people. At times she can be friendly and a real charmer. At other times she is extremely unpredictable, moody, and even suicidal. Being a friend to Judy can be a fearsome challenge. Canceling an appointment,

forgetting a special date, a wrong turn of phrase—these and similar small incidents may trigger Judy's rage or a suicide attempt. Like other people with borderline personality disorder, Judy is extremely sensitive to ordinary criticism, which leaves her feeling rejected and abandoned. Typically, she reacts with anger, self-hatred, and impulsive behavior. These "emotional storms" damage her personal relationships and leave her confused about who she is (Siever & Koenigsberg, 2000).

Maladaptive Personality Patterns

As stated earlier, a person with a personality disorder has maladaptive personality traits. For example, people with a paranoid personality disorder are suspicious, hypersensitive, and wary of others. Narcissistic persons need constant admiration, and they are lost in fantasies of power, wealth, brilliance, beauty, or love. Celebrities appear to more likely to be narcissistic than noncelebrities, perhaps because they receive so much attention (Young & Pinsky, 2006). The dependent personality suffers from extremely low self-confidence. Dependent persons allow others to run their lives, and they place everyone else's needs ahead of their own. People with a histrionic personality disorder constantly seek attention by dramatizing their emotions and actions.

Typically, patterns such as the ones just described begin during adolescence or even childhood. Thus, personality disorders are deeply rooted and usually span many years. The list of personality disorders is long (● Table 14.7), so let us focus on a single frequently misunderstood problem, the antisocial personality.

> ### bridges
> Personality patterns begin to stabilize by age 3. This makes personality disorders difficult to treat. **See Chapter 12, page 390.**

Antisocial Personality

What are the characteristics of an antisocial personality? A person with an **antisocial personality** lacks a conscience. Such people are impulsive, selfish, dishonest, emotionally shallow, and manipulative. Antisocial persons, who are sometimes called *sociopaths* or *psychopaths,* are poorly socialized and seem to be incapable of feeling guilt, shame, fear, loyalty, or love (*DSM-IV-TR,* 2000).

Are sociopaths dangerous? Sociopaths tend to have a long history of conflict with society. Many are delinquents or criminals who may be a threat to the general public (Ogloff, 2006). However, sociopaths are rarely the crazed murderers you may have seen por-

Anxiety reduction hypothesis Explains the self-defeating nature of avoidance responses as a result of the reinforcing effects of relief from anxiety.

Antisocial personality A person who lacks a conscience; is emotionally shallow, impulsive, and selfish; and tends to manipulate others.

Table 14.7 ● Personality Disorders and Typical Degree of Impairment

Moderate Impairment	
Dependent	You lack confidence and you are extremely submissive and dependent on others (clinging).
Histrionic	You are dramatic and flamboyant; you exaggerate your emotions to get attention from others.
Narcissistic	You think you are wonderful, brilliant, important, and worthy of constant admiration.
Antisocial	You are irresponsible, lack guilt or remorse, and engage in antisocial behavior, such as aggression, deceit, or recklessness.
High Impairment	
Obsessive-compulsive	You demand order, perfection, control, and rigid routine at all times.
Schizoid	You feel very little emotion and can't form close personal relationships with others.
Avoidant	You are timid, uncomfortable in social situations, and fear evaluation.
Severe Impairment	
Borderline	Your self-image, moods, and impulses are erratic, and you are extremely sensitive to any hint of criticism, rejection, or abandonment by others.
Paranoid	You deeply distrust others and are suspicious of their motives, which you perceive as insulting or threatening.
Schizotypal	You are a loner, you engage in extremely odd behavior, and your thought patterns are bizarre, but you are not actively psychotic.

DSM-IV-TR, 2000; Millon, 1981.

More than 65 percent of all persons with antisocial personalities have been arrested, usually for crimes such as robbery, vandalism, or rape.

trayed on TV and in movies. In fact, many sociopaths are "charming" at first. Their "friends" only gradually become aware of the sociopath's lying and self-serving manipulation. One study found that psychopaths are "blind" to signs of disgust in others. This may add to their capacity for cruelty and their ability to use others (Kosson et al., 2002). Many successful businesspersons, entertainers, politicians, and other seemingly normal people have psychopathic leanings. Basically, antisocial persons coldly use others and cheat their way through life (Ogloff, 2006).

Causes

What causes sociopathy? Typically, people with antisocial personalities showed similar problems in childhood (Burt et al., 2007). Many were emotionally deprived and physically abused as children (Pollock et al., 1990). Adult sociopaths also display subtle neurological problems (● Figure 14.13). For example, they have unusual brain-wave patterns that suggest underarousal of the brain. This may explain why sociopaths tend to be thrill seekers. Quite likely, they are searching for stimulation strong enough to overcome their chronic underarousal and feelings of "boredom" (Hare, 2006).

In a revealing study, psychopaths were shown extremely grisly and unpleasant photographs of mutilations. The photos were so upsetting that they visibly startled normal people. The psychopaths, however, showed no startle response to the photos (Levenston et al., 2000). (They didn't "bat an eyelash.") Those with antisocial personalities might therefore be described as *emotionally cold.* They simply do not feel normal pangs of conscience, guilt, or anxiety (Blair et al., 2006). Again, this coldness seems to account for an unusual ability to calmly lie, cheat, steal, or take advantage of others.

Can sociopathy be treated? Antisocial personality disorders are rarely treated with success (Hare, 2006). All too often, sociopaths manipulate therapy, just like any other situation. If it is to their advantage to act "cured," they will do so. However, they return to their former behavior patterns as soon as possible. On a more positive note, antisocial behavior does tend to decline somewhat

● **Figure 14.13** Using PET scans, Canadian psychologist Robert Hare found that the normally functioning brain *(left)* lights up with activity when a person sees emotion-laden words such as "maggot" or "cancer." But the brain of a psychopath *(right)* remains inactive, especially in areas associated with feelings and self-control. When Dr. Hare showed the right image to several neurologists, one asked, "Is this person from Mars?"

CRITICAL THINKING

A Disease Called Freedom

The year is 1840. You are a slave who has tried repeatedly to escape from a cruel and abusive master. You want to be free. An expert is consulted about your "abnormal" behavior. His conclusion? You are suffering from "drapetomania," a mental "disorder" that causes slaves to run away (Wakefield, 1992). Your "cure"? The expert will cut off your toes.

As this example suggests, psychiatric terms are easily abused. Historically, some have been applied to culturally disapproved behaviors that are not really disorders. Another of our personal favorites is the long-outdated diagnosis of "anarchia," a form of insanity that leads one to seek a more democratic society (Brown, 1990).

All of the following were also once considered disorders: childhood masturbation, lack of vaginal orgasm, self-defeating personality (applied mainly to women), homosexuality, and nymphomania (a woman with a healthy sexual appetite) (Wakefield, 1992). Even today, race, gender, and social class continue to affect the diagnosis of various disorders (Durand & Barlow, 2006; Poland & Caplan, 2004).

Gender is probably the most common source of bias in judging normality because standards tend to be based on males (Nolen-Hoeksema, 2007; Widiger, 2005). According to psychologist Paula Caplan (1995) and others, women are penalized both for conforming to female stereotypes and for ignoring them. If a woman is independent, aggressive, and unemotional, she may be considered "unhealthy." Yet at the same time, a woman who is vain, emotional, irrational, and dependent on others (all "feminine" traits in our culture) may be classified as having a personality disorder (Bornstein, 1996). Indeed, a majority of persons classified as having dependent personality disorder are women. In view of this, Paula Caplan asks, why isn't there a category called "delusional dominating personality disorder" for obnoxious men (Caplan, 1995)?

Because biases can influence perceptions of disorder and normality, it is worth being cautious before you leap to conclusions about the mental health of others (*DSM-IV-TR*, 2000). (They might be doing an assignment for their psychology class!)

---

after age 40, even without treatment, because people tend to become more "mellow" as they age (Laub & Sampson, 2003).

Disorders in Perspective— Psychiatric Labeling

As we conclude our survey of psychological disorders, a caution is in order. The terms we have reviewed in this chapter are meant to aid communication about human problems. But if used maliciously or carelessly, they can hurt people. (See "A Disease Called Freedom.") Everyone has felt or acted "crazy" during brief periods of stress or high emotion. People with psychological disorders have problems that are more severe or long lasting than most of us experience. Otherwise, they may not be that different from you or me.

A fascinating classic study carried out by psychologist David Rosenhan illustrates the impact of psychiatric labeling. Rosenhan and several colleagues had themselves committed to mental hospitals with a diagnosis of "schizophrenia" (Rosenhan, 1973). After being admitted, each of these "pseudo-patients" dropped all pretense of mental illness. Yet even though they acted completely normal, none of the researchers was ever recognized by hospital *staff* as a phony patient. Real patients were not so easily fooled. It was not unusual for a patient to say to one of the researchers, "You're not crazy, you're checking up on the hospital!" or, "You're a journalist."

To record his observations, Rosenhan took notes by carefully jotting things on a small piece of paper hidden in his hand. However, he soon learned that stealth was totally unnecessary. Rosen-

han simply walked around with a clipboard, recording observations. No one questioned this behavior. Rosenhan's note taking was just regarded as a symptom of his "illness." This observation clarifies why staff members failed to detect the fake patients. Because they were in a mental ward, and because they had been *labeled* schizophrenic, anything the pseudo-patients did was seen as a symptom of psychopathology.

As Rosenhan's study shows, it is far better to label *problems* than to label people. Think of the difference in impact between saying, "You are experiencing a serious psychological disorder," and saying, "You're a schizophrenic." Which statement would you prefer to have said about yourself?

> **bridges**
> Labels and categories greatly influence our perceptions in many circumstances. See Chapter 5, pages 171–172.

Social Stigma

An added problem with psychiatric labeling is that it frequently leads to prejudice and discrimination. That is, the mentally ill in our culture are often *stigmatized* (rejected and disgraced). People who have been labeled mentally ill (at any time in their lives) are less likely to be hired. They also tend to be denied housing, and they are more likely to be falsely accused of crimes. Thus, people who are grappling with mental illness may be harmed as much by social stigma as they are by their immediate psychological problems (Corrigan & Penn, 1999).

A Look Ahead

Treatments for psychological problems range from counseling and psychotherapy to mental hospitalization and drug therapy. Because they vary greatly, a complete discussion of therapies is found in the next chapter. For now, it's worth noting that many milder mental disorders can treated successfully. Even major disorders may respond well to drugs and other techniques. It is wrong to fear "former mental patients" or to exclude them from work, friend-ships, and other social situations. A struggle with major depression or a psychotic episode does not inevitably lead to lifelong dysfunction. Too often, however, it does lead to unnecessary rejection based on groundless fears (Sarason & Sarason, 2005).

Let's conclude with a look at a widely misunderstood problem: By the time you finish reading this page, someone in the United States will have attempted suicide. What can be done about suicide? The upcoming Psychology in Action provides some answers.

KNOWLEDGE BUILDER
Anxiety-Based Disorders and Personality Disorders

RECITE

1. When prolonged unemployment, a bad marriage, or physical illness pushes a person beyond his or her ability to cope, it is most likely that which of the following problems will occur?
   a. a dissociative disorder
   b. agoraphobia
   c. an adjustment disorder
   d. a conversion disorder
2. Panic disorder can occur with or without agoraphobia, but agora-phobia cannot occur alone, without the presence of a panic disorder. T or F?
3. Alice has a phobic fear of heights. What is the formal term for her fear?
   a. nyctophobia
   b. acrophobia
   c. pathophobia
   d. pyrophobia
4. A person who intensely fears eating, writing, or speaking in public suffers from _____ _____.
5. "Checkers" and "cleaners" suffer from which disorder?
   a. acarophobia
   b. panic disorder with agoraphobia
   c. generalized anxiety disorder
   d. obsessive-compulsive disorder
6. The symptoms of acute stress disorders last less than 1 month; post-traumatic stress disorders last more than 1 month. T or F?
7. Which of the following is *not* a dissociative disorder?
   a. fugue
   b. amnesia
   c. conversion reaction
   d. multiple identity
8. According to the _____ view, anxiety disorders are the end result of a faulty self-image.
   a. psychodynamic
   b. humanistic
   c. behaviorist
   d. cognitive

9. Which of the following personality disorders is associated with an inflated sense of self-importance and a constant need for attention and admiration?
   a. narcissistic
   b. antisocial
   c. paranoid
   d. manipulative
10. Antisocial personality disorders are difficult to treat, but there is typi-cally a decline in antisocial behavior a year or two after adolescence. T or F?

REFLECT

Critical Thinking

11. Many of the physical complaints associated with anxiety disorders are closely related to activity of what part of the nervous system?
12. How could someone get away with Munchausen syndrome by proxy? Wouldn't doctors figure out that something was fishy with Ben long before he had 40 surgeries for a faked sinus disorder? (See "Sick of Being Sick.")

Relate

Which of the anxiety disorders would you *least* want to suffer from? Why? What minor obsessions or compulsions have you experienced?

What is the key difference between a stress disorder and an adjust-ment disorder? (Review both discussions if you don't immediately know the answer.)

Which of the four psychological explanations of anxiety-based disor-ders do you find most convincing?

Many of the qualities that define personality disorders exist to a minor degree in normal personalities. Try to think of a person you know who has some of the characteristics described for each type of personal-ity disorder.

Answers: 1. c 2. F 3. b 4. social phobia 5. d 6. T 7. c 8. b 9. a 10. F 11. The autonomic nervous system (ANS), especially the sympathetic branch of the ANS. 12. No one doctor tolerates false symptoms for long. Once a doctor refuses further treatment, the Munchausen suf-ferer will move on to another. Also, sometimes more than one doctor is being seen at one time.

PSYCHOLOGY IN ACTION

Suicide—Lives on the Brink

Gateway Questions: Why do people commit suicide? Can suicide be prevented?

"Suicide: A permanent solution to a tempo-rary problem."

We tend to be very concerned about the high rates of murder in North America. Yet for every 3 people who die by homicide, 5 will kill themselves. And there may be as many as 25 attempts for every "successful" suicide (NIMH, 2003). Sooner or later you are likely to be affected by the suicide attempt of some-one you know.

Images/SuperStock

What factors affect suicide rates? Suicide rates vary greatly, but some general patterns do emerge.

Gender

Men are "better" at suicide than women. Four times as many men *complete* suicide, but women make more attempts (NIMH, 2006b). Male suicide attempts are more lethal because men typically use a gun or an equally fatal method (Garland & Zigler, 1993). Women most often attempt a drug overdose, so there's a better chance of help arriving before death occurs. Sadly, women are beginning to use more deadly methods and may soon equal men in their likelihood of death by suicide.

Ethnicity

Suicide rates vary dramatically from country to country. The rate in the United States is almost 10 times higher than the rate in Azer-

baijan and, in turn, the rate in Hungary is more than 3 times the U.S. rate (Lester & Yang, 2005). Within the United States, Caucasians generally have higher suicide rates than do non-Caucasians (● Figure 14.14). Sadly, the suicide rate among Native Americans is by far the highest in the country (suicide rates are equally high among the aboriginal peoples of Australia and New Zealand) (Goldson et al., 2008; McKenzie, Serfaty, & Crawford, 2003).

Age

Suicide rates increase with advancing age. More than half of all suicide victims are over 45 years old. (See ● Figure 14.14.) White males 65 years and older are particularly at risk. Of special concern is the rate of suicide among younger people. Between 1950 and 1990, suicide rates for adolescents and young adults doubled (Durand & Barlow, 2006). Among college students, suicide is the third leading cause of death (Jamison, 2001). School is a factor in some suicides, but only in the sense that suicidal students were not living up to their own extremely high standards. Many were good students. Other important factors in student suicide are cocaine or alcohol use (Garlow, Purselle, & Heninger, 2007), chronic health problems (real or imagined), and interpersonal difficulties (some who commit suicide are rejected lovers, but others are simply withdrawn and friendless people).

Marital Status

Marriage (when successful) may be the best natural guard against suicidal impulses. Married individuals have lower rates than the divorced, the widowed, and single persons (Yip & Thorburn, 2004).

Immediate Causes of Suicide

Why do people try to kill themselves? The best explanation for suicide may simply come from a look at the conditions that precede it. A diagnosable mental disorder (usually depression or substance abuse disorder) is a factor in 90 percent of all suicides (NIMH, 2006b). Suicidal people usually have a history of trouble with family, a lover, or a spouse. Often they have drinking or drug abuse problems, sexual adjustment problems, or job difficulties.

The following are all major *risk factors* for suicide (NIMH, 2003; Rudd, Joiner Jr., & Rajab, 2001): Drug or alcohol abuse; a prior suicide attempt; depression or other mood disorder; feelings of hopelessness or worthlessness; antisocial, impulsive, or aggressive behavior; severe anxiety; panic attacks; a family history of suicidal behavior; shame, humiliation, failure, or rejection; and the availability of a firearm. Among ethnic adolescents, loss of face, acculturative stress, racism, and discrimination have been identified as additional risk factors (Goldston et al., 2008).

Typically, suicidal people isolate themselves from others; feel worthless, helpless, and misunderstood; and want to die. An extremely negative self-image and severe feelings of *hopelessness* are warnings that the risk of suicide is very high (Beck et al., 1990; Heisel, Flett, & Hewitt, 2003). However, a long history of such conditions is not always necessary to produce a desire for suicide. Anyone may temporarily reach a state of depression severe enough to attempt suicide. Most dangerous for the average person are times of divorce, separation, rejection, failure, and bereavement. Each situation can seem intolerable and motivate an intense desire to die, to escape, or to obtain relief (Boergers, Spirito, & Donaldson, 1998). For young people, feelings of anger and hostility add to the danger. When the impulse to harm others is turned inward, the risk of suicide increases dramatically (Jamison, 2001).

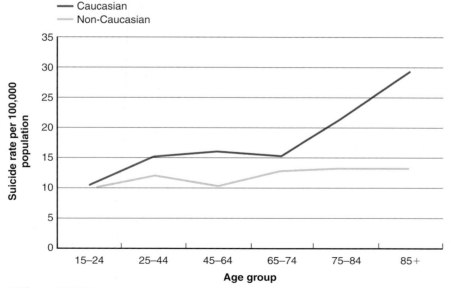

● **Figure 14.14** In the United States, suicide rates for Caucasians are higher than those for non-Caucasians. Also, older people have higher suicide rates than younger people (CDC, 2003).

Preventing Suicide

Is it true that people who talk about or threaten suicide are rarely the ones who try it? No, this is a major fallacy. Of every 10 potential suicides, 8 give warning beforehand. A person who threatens suicide should be taken seriously (● Figure 14.15). A suicidal person may say nothing more than, "I feel sometimes like I'd be better off dead." Warnings may also come indirectly. If a friend gives you a favorite ring and says, "Here, I won't be needing this anymore," or comments, "I guess I won't get my watch fixed—it doesn't matter anyway," it may be a plea for help. The warning signs in the list that follows—especially if they are observed in combination—can signal an impending suicide attempt (Leenaars, Lester, & Wenckstern, 2005; Slaby, Garfinkel, & Garfinkel, 1994).

- Withdrawal from contact with others
- Sudden swings in mood
- Recent occurrence of life crisis or emotional shock
- Personality change
- Gift giving of prized possessions
- Depression/hopelessness
- Aggression and/or risk taking
- Single-car accident
- Preoccupation with death
- Drug use
- Death imagery in art
- Direct threats to commit suicide

Is it true that suicide can't be prevented, that the person will find a way to do it anyway? No. Suicide attempts usually come when a person is alone, depressed, and unable to view matters objectively. You *should* intervene if someone seems to be threatening suicide.

It is estimated that about two thirds of all suicide attempts are made by people who do not really want to die. Almost a third more are *ambivalent* or undecided about dying.

Only 3 to 5 percent of suicide cases involve people who really want to die. Most people, therefore, are relieved when someone comes to their aid. Remember that suicide is almost always a cry for help and that you *can* help. As

suicide expert Edwin Shneidman (1987a) puts it, "Suicidal behavior is often a form of communication, a cry for help born out of pain, with clues and messages of suffering and anguish and pleas for response."

How to Help

What is the best thing to do if someone hints they are thinking about suicide? It helps to know some of the common characteristics of suicidal thoughts and feelings (Leenaars, Lester, & Wenckstern, 2005; Shneidman, 1987b):

1. **Escape.** At times, everyone feels like running away from an upsetting situation. Running away from home, quitting school, abandoning a marriage—these are all departures. Suicide, of course, is the ultimate escape. It helps when suicidal persons see that the natural wish for escape doesn't have to be expressed by ending it all.
2. **Unbearable psychological pain.** Emotional pain is what the suicidal person is seeking to escape. A goal of anyone hoping to prevent suicide should be to reduce the pain in any way possible. Ask the person, "Where does it hurt?" Suicide occurs when pain exceeds a person's resources for coping with pain.
3. **Frustrated psychological needs.** Often, suicide can be prevented if a distressed person's frustrated needs can be identified and eased. Is the person deeply frustrated in his or her search for love, achievement, trust, security, or friendship?
4. **Constriction of options.** The suicidal person feels helpless and decides that death is the *only* solution. The person has narrowed all his or her options solely to death. The rescuer's goal, then, is to help broaden the person's perspective. Even when all the choices are unpleasant, suicidal persons can usually be made to see that their *least unpleasant option* is better than death.

Knowing these patterns will give some guidance in talking to a suicidal person. In

addition, your most important task may be to establish *rapport* (a harmonious connection) with the person. You should offer support, acceptance, and legitimate caring.

Remember that a suicidal person feels misunderstood. Try to accept and understand the feelings the person is expressing. Acceptance should also extend to the idea of suicide itself. It is completely acceptable to ask, "Are you thinking of suicide?"

Establishing communication with suicidal persons may be enough to carry them through a difficult time. You may also find it helpful to get day-by-day commitments from them to meet for lunch, share a ride, and the like. Let the person know you *expect* her or him to be there. Such commitments, even though small, can be enough to tip the scales when a person is alone and thinking about suicide.

Don't end your efforts too soon. A dangerous time for suicide is when a person suddenly seems to get better after a severe depression. This often means the person has finally decided to end it all. The improvement in mood is deceptive because it comes from an anticipation that suffering is about to end.

Crisis Intervention

Most cities have mental health crisis intervention teams or centers for suicide prevention. Both have staff members trained to talk with suicidal persons over the phone. Give a person who seems to be suicidal the number of one of these services. Urge the person to call you or the other number if she or he becomes frightened or impulsive. Or better yet, help the person make an appointment to get psychological treatment (Weishaar, 2006).

The preceding applies mainly to persons who are having mild suicidal thoughts. If a person actually threatens suicide, or if a suicide attempt seems to be imminent, don't worry about overreacting. Immediately seek professional assistance by calling the police, crisis intervention, or a rescue unit. If that is infeasible, ask how the person plans to carry out the suicide. A person who has a *specific, workable plan* and the means to carry it out should be asked to accompany you to the emergency ward of a hospital.

Needless to say, you should call immediately if a person is in the act of attempting suicide or if a drug has already been taken. The majority of suicide attempts come at temporary low points in a person's life and may never be repeated. Get involved—you may save a life!

● **Figure 14.15** Suicidal behavior usually progresses from suicidal thoughts, to threats, to attempts. A person is unlikely to make an attempt without first making threats. Thus, suicide threats should be taken seriously (Garland & Zigler, 1993).

Suicide and Suicide Prevention

RECITE

1. More women than men use guns in their suicide attempts. T or F?
2. Although the overall suicide rate has remained about the same, there has been a decrease in adolescent suicides. T or F?
3. Suicide is equally a problem in all countries. T or F?
4. Higher suicide rates are found among the divorced. T or F?
5. The majority (two thirds) of suicide attempts are made by people who do not really want to die. T or F?
6. The risk that a person may attempt suicide is greatest if the person has
   a. a concrete, workable plan
   b. had a recent life crisis
   c. withdrawn from contact with others
   d. frustrated psychological needs

REFLECT

Critical Thinking

7. If you follow the history of popular music, see if you can answer this question: What two major risk factors contributed to the 1994 suicide of Kurt Cobain, lead singer for the rock group Nirvana?

Relate

You're working a suicide hotline and you take a call from a very distressed young man. What risk factors will you look for as he tells you about his anguish?

What are the common warning signs of impending suicide? If a friend of yours were to show any of these signs, how would you respond?

Answers: 1. F **2.** F **3.** F **4.** T **5.** T **6.** a **7.** Drug or alcohol abuse and availability of a firearm.

chapter in review — Gateways to Psychological Disorders

Two key elements of mental disorder are that abnormal behavior is maladaptive and it involves a loss of self-control.

- Psychopathology refers to maladaptive behavior and to the scientific study of mental disorders.
- Factors that typically affect judgments of abnormality include subjective discomfort, statistical abnormality, nonconformity, context, and culture.
- "Insanity" is a legal term defining whether a person may be held responsible for his or her actions. Sanity is determined in court on the basis of testimony by expert witnesses.

Major mental problems include psychotic disorders, organic disorders, mood disorders, anxiety disorders, somatoform disorders, dissociative disorders, personality disorders, sexual or gender identity disorders, and substance-related disorders.

- Psychological problems are classified by using the *Diagnostic and Statistical Manual of Mental Disorders*.

Psychosis is a break in contact with reality that is marked by delusions, hallucinations, sensory changes, disturbed emotions, disturbed communication, and personality disintegration.

- An organic psychosis is based on known injuries or diseases of the brain.
- Some common causes of organic psychosis are poisoning, drug abuse, and dementia (especially Alzheimer's disease).

Delusional disorders are almost totally based on the presence of deeply held false beliefs of grandeur, persecution, infidelity, romantic attraction, or physical disease.

- The most common delusional disorder is paranoid psychosis. Paranoid persons may be violent if they believe they are threatened.

The varieties of schizophrenia all involve delusions, hallucinations, communication difficulties, and a split between thought and emotion. Current explanations of schizophrenia emphasize a combination of prenatal injuries, early trauma, environmental stress, inherited susceptibility, and abnormalities in the brain.

- Disorganized schizophrenia is marked by extreme personality disintegration and silly, bizarre, or obscene behavior.
- Catatonic schizophrenia is associated with stupor, mutism, and odd postures. Sometimes violent and agitated behavior also occurs.
- In paranoid schizophrenia (the most common type), outlandish delusions of grandeur and persecution are coupled with psychotic symptoms and personality breakdown.
- Environmental factors that increase the risk of schizophrenia include viral infection or malnutrition during the mother's pregnancy, birth complications, early psychological trauma, and a disturbed family environment.
- Heredity is a major factor in schizophrenia.
- Recent biochemical studies have focused on the brain transmitter dopamine and its receptor sites.
- The dominant explanation of schizophrenia, and other problems as well, is the stress-vulnerability model.

Mood disorders primarily involve disturbances of mood or emotion, producing manic or depressive states. Severe mood disorders may include psychotic features. Major mood disorders are partially explained by genetic vulnerability and changes in brain chemistry. Other important factors are loss, anger, learned helplessness, stress, and self-defeating thinking patterns.

- In a dysthymic disorder, depression is long lasting, though moderate. In a cyclothymic disorder, people suffer from long-lasting, though moderate, swings between depression and elation.

- Bipolar disorders combine mania and depression. In a bipolar I disorder the person swings between severe mania and severe depression. In a bipolar II disorder the person is mostly depressed but has had periods of mild mania.
- A major depressive disorder involves extreme sadness and despondency but no signs of mania.
- Many women experience a brief period of depression, called the maternity blues, shortly after giving birth. Some women suffer from a more serious and lasting condition called postpartum depression.
- Seasonal affective disorder (SAD), which occurs during the winter months, is another common form of depression. SAD is typically treated with phototherapy.

Anxiety disorders, dissociative disorders, and somatoform disorders are characterized by high levels of anxiety, rigid defense mechanisms, and self-defeating behavior patterns.

- In an adjustment disorder, ordinary stresses push people beyond their ability to cope with life.
- Anxiety disorders include generalized anxiety disorder, panic disorder (with or without agoraphobia), agoraphobia, specific phobias, social phobia, obsessive-compulsive disorder, post-traumatic stress disorder, and acute stress disorder.
- Dissociative disorders may take the form of amnesia, fugue, or multiple identities.
- Somatoform disorders center on physical complaints that mimic disease or disability. Four examples of somatoform disorders are hypochondriasis, somatization disorder, somatoform pain disorder, and conversion disorders.

Psychodynamic, humanistic, behavioristic and cognitive approaches offer explanations of anxiety-based disorders.

- The psychodynamic approach emphasizes unconscious conflicts as the cause of disabling anxiety.
- The humanistic approach emphasizes the effects of a faulty self-image.
- The behaviorists emphasize the effects of previous learning, particularly avoidance learning.
- Cognitive theories of anxiety focus on distorted thinking, judgment, and attention.

Personality disorders are persistent, maladaptive personality patterns.

- Sociopathy is a common personality disorder. Antisocial persons lack a conscience, and they are emotionally cold, manipulative, shallow, and dishonest.

Suicide is a relatively common cause of death that can, in many cases, be prevented.

- Suicide is statistically related to such factors as age, gender, and marital status.
- In individual cases, the potential for suicide is best identified by a desire to escape, unbearable psychological pain, and frustrated psychological needs.

- People contemplating suicide narrow their options until death seems like the only way out.
- The impulse to attempt suicide is usually temporary. Efforts to prevent suicide are worthwhile.

Web Resources

For an up-to-date list of direct links to interesting sites, including those listed here, visit the student companion site for this book at www.cengage.com/psychology/coon

Against All Odds Read an article about Carol North, the psychiatrist who overcame schizophrenia.

Psychiatric Disorders Explore a complete listing of the *DSM-IV-TR* diagnostic categories.

Famous People with Phobias Find out more about famous phobias and how to live with them.

Psychotic Disorders Read more about the psychotic disorders.

William Utermohlen's Self-Portraits View these remarkable paintings by a man descending into Alzheimer's disease.

Schizophrenia Explore this extensive website, which includes brain images and videos about schizophrenia.

Depression Take a depression test and find out more about depression.

Are You Worried About a Friend or Loved One? Visit this website if you are worried about someone near to you committing suicide.

Interactive Learning

Introduction to Psychology: Gateways to Mind and Behavior **Book Companion Website**
www.cengage.com/psychology/coon

Visit your book companion website, where you will find flash cards, practice quizzes, web links, and more to help you study.

CENGAGENOW™ *Just what you need to know NOW!*

Spend time on what you need to master rather than on information you already have learned. Take a pre-test for this chapter, and CengageNOW will generate a personalized study plan based on your results. The study plan will identify the topics you need to review and direct you to online resources to help you master those topics. You can then take a post-test to help you determine the concepts you have mastered and what you will need to work on. Try it out! Go to www.cengage.com/login to sign in with an access code or to purchase access to this product.

CHAPTER 15

Therapies

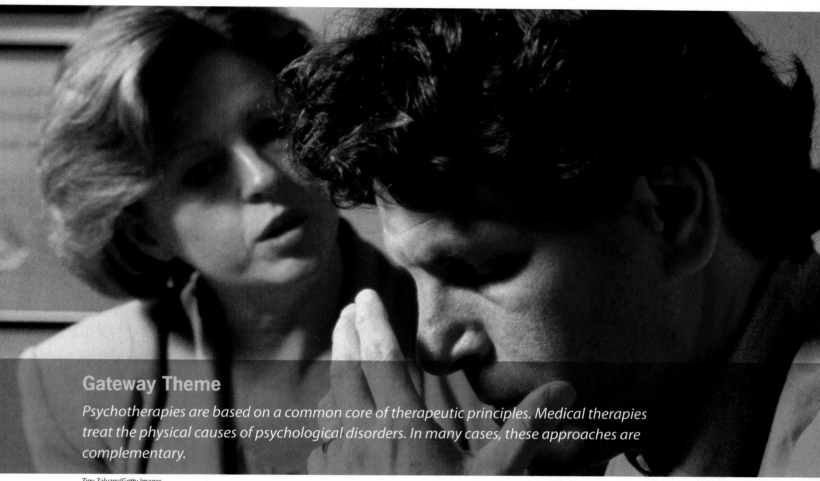

Gateway Theme

Psychotherapies are based on a common core of therapeutic principles. Medical therapies treat the physical causes of psychological disorders. In many cases, these approaches are complementary.

Zigy Zaluzny/Getty Images

Gateway Questions

- How do psychotherapies differ?
- How did psychotherapy originate?
- Is Freudian psychoanalysis still used?
- What are the major humanistic therapies?
- Can therapy be conducted at a distance?
- What is behavior therapy?
- What role do operant principles play in behavior therapy?

- Can therapy change thoughts and emotions?
- Can psychotherapy be done with groups of people?
- What do various therapies have in common?
- How do psychiatrists treat psychological disorders?
- How are behavioral principles applied to everyday problems? How could a person find professional help?

The Duck Syndrome

Outside, some ducks quacked as they explored the campus pond. Susan's psychology professor could hear them between Susan's frightened sobs. As psychologists, we meet many students with personal problems. Still, Susan's teacher was surprised to see her at his office door. Her excellent work in class and her healthy, casual appearance left him unprepared for her first words. "I feel like I'm losing my mind," she said. "Can I talk to you?"

In the next hour, Susan described her own personal hell. In a sense, she was like the ducks outside, appearing peaceful on the surface, but madly paddling underneath. She was working hard to hide a world of crippling fear, anxiety, and depression. At work, she was deathly afraid of talking to co-workers and customers. Her social phobia led to frequent absenteeism and embarrassing behavior. At each job she held, it was only a matter of time until she got fired.

At school Susan felt "different" and was sure that other students could tell she was "weird." Several disastrous romances

had left her terrified of men. Lately she had been so depressed that she thought of suicide. Often, she became terrified for no apparent reason. Each time, her heart pounded wildly and she felt that she was about to completely lose control.

Susan's request for help was an important turning point. Emotional conflicts had made her existence a nightmare. At a time when she was becoming her own worst enemy, Susan realized she needed help from another person. In Susan's case, that person was a talented psychologist to whom her teacher referred her. With psychotherapy, the psychologist was able to help Susan come to grips with her emotions and regain her balance.

This chapter discusses methods used to alleviate problems like Susan's. First, we will describe therapies that emphasize the value of gaining *insight* into personal problems. Then, we will focus on *behavior therapies* and *cognitive therapies,* which directly change troublesome actions and thoughts. Later, we will conclude with *medical therapies,* which are based on psychiatric drugs and other physical treatments.

⬤⬤ Psychotherapy—The Talking Cure

Gateway Question: How do psychotherapies differ?

Psychotherapy refers to any psychological technique that can bring about positive changes in personality, behavior, or personal adjustment. Psychotherapy is usually based on a dialogue between therapists and their clients, although some therapists also use learning principles to directly alter troublesome behaviors.

Therapists have many approaches to choose from: psychoanalysis, client-centered therapy, Gestalt therapy, behavior therapy, and cognitive therapy—to name but a few. As we will see, each therapy emphasizes different concepts and methods. For this reason, the best approach for a particular person or problem may vary (Trull, 2005).

Dimensions of Therapy

The terms in the list that follows describe basic aspects of various therapies (Sharf, 2008). Notice that more than one term may apply to a particular therapy. For example, it is possible to have a directive, action-oriented group therapy or a nondirective, individual, insight-oriented therapy:

- **Individual therapy:** A therapy involving only one client and one therapist.
- **Group therapy:** A therapy session in which several clients participate at the same time.
- **Insight therapy:** Any psychotherapy whose goal is to lead clients to a deeper understanding of their thoughts, emotions, and behavior.

- **Action therapy:** Any therapy designed to bring about direct changes in troublesome thoughts, habits, feelings, or behavior, without seeking insight into their origins or meanings.
- **Directive therapy:** Any approach in which the therapist provides strong guidance.
- **Nondirective therapy:** A style of therapy in which clients assume responsibility for solving their own problems; the therapist assists, but does not guide or give advice.
- **Time-limited therapy:** Any therapy begun with the expectation that it will last only a limited number of sessions.
- **Supportive therapy:** An approach in which the therapist's goal is to offer support, rather than to promote personal change. A person trying to get through an emotional crisis or one who wants to solve day-to-day problems may benefit from supportive therapy.
- **Positive therapy:** Techniques designed to enhance personal strengths, rather than "fix" weaknesses.

Myths

Psychotherapy has been depicted as a complete personal transformation—a sort of "major overhaul" of the psyche. But therapy is *not* equally effective for all problems. Chances of improvement are fairly good for phobias, low self-esteem, some sexual problems, and marital conflicts. More complex problems can be difficult to solve. For many people, the major benefit of therapy is that it provides comfort, support, and a way to make constructive changes (Bloch, 2006; Hellerstein et al., 1998).

Table 15.1 ● Elements of Positive Mental Health

- Personal autonomy and independence
- A sense of identity
- Feelings of personal worth
- Skilled interpersonal communication
- Sensitivity, nurturance, and trust
- Genuine and honest with self and others
- Self-control and personal responsibility
- Committed and loving personal relationships
- Capacity to forgive others and oneself
- Personal values and a purpose in life
- Self-awareness and motivation for personal growth
- Adaptive coping strategies for managing stresses and crises
- Fulfillment and satisfaction in work
- Good habits of physical health

Adapted from Bergin, 1991.

● **Figure 15.1** Primitive "treatment" for mental disorders sometimes took the form of boring a hole in the skull. This example shows signs of healing, which means the patient survived the treatment. Many didn't.

In short, it is often unrealistic to expect psychotherapy to undo a person's entire past. Yet even when problems are severe, therapy may help a person gain a new perspective or learn behaviors to better cope with life. Psychotherapy can be hard work for both clients and therapists, but when it succeeds, few activities are more worthwhile.

It's also a mistake to think that psychotherapy is only used to solve problems or end a crisis. Even if a person is already doing well, therapy can be a way to promote personal growth (Bloch, 2006). Therapists in the positive psychology movement are developing ways to help people make use of their personal strengths. Rather than trying to fix what is "wrong" with a person, they seek to nurture positive traits and actively solve problems (Compton, 2005). ● Table 15.1 lists some of the elements of positive mental health that therapists seek to restore or promote.

⬤⬤ Origins of Therapy—Bored Out of Your Skull

Gateway Question: How did psychotherapy originate?

Early treatments for mental problems give good reasons to appreciate modern therapies (Sharf, 2008). Archaeological findings dating to the Stone Age suggest that most primitive approaches were marked by fear and superstitious belief in demons, witchcraft, and magic. One of the more dramatic "cures" practiced by primitive "therapists" was a process called *trepanning* (treh-PAN-ing), also sometimes spelled *trephining* (Terry, 2006). In modern usage, trepanning is any surgical procedure in which a hole is bored in the skull. In the hands of primitive therapists it meant boring, chipping, or bashing holes into a patient's head. Presumably this was done to relieve pressure or release evil spirits. Surprisingly, some "patients" actually survived the "treatment" (● Figure 15.1).

During the Middle Ages, treatments for mental illness in Europe focused on **demonology,** the study of demons and persons plagued by spirits. Medieval "therapists" commonly blamed abnormal behavior on supernatural forces, such as possession by the devil, or on curses from witches and wizards. As a cure, they used exorcism to "cast out evil spirits." For the fortunate, exorcism was a religious ritual. More often, physical torture was used to make the body an inhospitable place for the devil to reside. Modern analyses of "demonic possession" suggest that many victims were suffering from epilepsy, schizophrenia (Mirsky & Duncan, 2005), dissociative disorders (van der Hart, Lierens, & Goodwin, 1996), and depression (Thase, 2006).

One reason for the rise of demonology may lie in *ergotism* (AIR-got-ism), a psychotic-like condition caused by ergot poisoning. In the Middle Ages, rye (grain) fields were often infested with ergot fungus. Ergot, we now know, is a natural source of LSD and other mind-altering chemicals. Eating tainted bread could have caused symptoms that were easily mistaken for bewitchment or madness. Pinching sensations, muscle twitches, facial spasms, delirium, and hallucinations are all signs of ergot poisoning (Matossian, 1982). Thus, many people "treated" by demonologists may have been doubly victimized.

It wasn't until 1793 that the emotionally disturbed were regarded as "mentally ill" and given compassionate treatment. That was the year a French doctor named Philippe Pinel changed the Bicêtre Asylum in Paris from a squalid "madhouse" into a mental hospital by unchaining the inmates (Harris, 2003). Although it has been

Psychotherapy Any psychological technique used to facilitate positive changes in a person's personality, behavior, or adjustment.

Demonology In medieval Europe, the study of demons and the treatment of persons "possessed" by demons.

(Left) Many early asylums were no more than prisons with inmates held in chains. *(Right)* One late-nineteenth-century "treatment" was based on swinging the patient in a harness—presumably to calm the patient's nerves.

more than 200 years since Pinel began humane treatment, the process of improving care continues today.

When was psychotherapy developed? The first true psychotherapy was created by Sigmund Freud little more than 100 years ago (Jacobs, 2003). As a physician in Vienna, Freud was intrigued by cases of *hysteria*. People suffering from hysteria have physical symptoms (such as paralysis or numbness) for which no physical causes can be found. (Such problems are now called somatoform disorders, as discussed in Chapter 14, pages 484–485.) Slowly, Freud became convinced that hysteria was related to deeply hidden unconscious conflicts. Based on this insight, Freud developed a therapy called *psychoanalysis.* Because it is the "granddaddy" of more modern therapies, let us examine psychoanalysis in some detail.

⬤⬤ Psychoanalysis—Expedition into the Unconscious

Gateway Question: Is Freudian psychoanalysis still used?

Isn't psychoanalysis the therapy where the patient lies on a couch? Freud's patients usually reclined on a couch during therapy, while Freud sat out of sight taking notes and offering interpretations. This procedure was supposed to encourage a free flow of thoughts and images from the unconscious. However, it is the least important element of psychoanalysis and many modern analysts have abandoned it.

How did Freud treat emotional problems? Freud's theory stressed that "neurosis" and "hysteria" are caused by repressed memories, motives, and conflicts—particularly those stemming from instinctual drives for sex and aggression. Although they are hidden, these forces remain active in the personality and cause some people to

develop rigid ego-defenses and compulsive, self-defeating behavior. Thus, the main goal of **psychoanalysis** is to reduce internal conflicts that lead to emotional suffering (Marcus, 2002).

Freud developed four basic techniques to uncover the unconscious roots of neurosis (Freud, 1949). These are *free association, dream analysis, analysis of resistance,* and *analysis of transference.*

Free Association

Saying whatever comes to mind is the basis for **free association.** Patients must speak without worrying whether ideas are painful, embarrassing, or illogical. Thoughts are simply allowed to move freely from one idea to the next, without self-censorship. The purpose of free association is to lower defenses so that unconscious thoughts and feelings can emerge (Hoffer & Youngren, 2004).

Dream Analysis

Freud believed that dreams provide a "royal road to the unconscious," which disguises consciously unacceptable feelings and forbidden desires in dream form (Rock, 2004). The job of the psychoanalyst is to help the patient work past the obvious, visible meaning of the dream *(manifest content)* to uncover the hidden, symbolic meaning *(latent content).* This is achieved by analyzing *dream symbols* (images that have personal or emotional meanings).

Suppose a young man dreams of pulling a pistol from his waistband and aiming at a target while his wife watches. The pistol repeatedly fails to discharge, and the man's wife laughs at him. Freud might have seen this as an indication of repressed

Pioneering psychotherapist Sigmund Freud's famous couch.

feelings of sexual impotence, with the gun serving as a disguised image of the penis.

bridges
See Chapter 6, pages 192 and pages 212–214, for more information on Freudian dream theory.

Analysis of Resistance

When free associating or describing dreams, patients may *resist* talking about or thinking about certain topics. Such **resistances** (blockages in the flow of ideas) reveal particularly important unconscious conflicts. As analysts become aware of resistances, they bring them to the patient's awareness so the patient can deal with them realistically. Rather than being roadblocks in therapy, resistances can be challenges and guides (Engle & Arkowitz, 2006).

Analysis of Transference

Transference is the tendency to "transfer" feelings to a therapist similar to those the patient had for important persons in his or her past. At times, the patient may act as if the analyst is a rejecting father, an unloving or overprotective mother, or a former lover, for example. As the patient re-experiences repressed emotions, the therapist can help the patient recognize and understand them. Troubled persons often provoke anger, rejection, boredom, criticism, and other negative reactions from others. Effective therapists learn to avoid reacting as others do and playing the patient's habitual resistance and transference "games." This, too, contributes to therapeutic change (Marcus, 2002).

Psychoanalysis Today

What is the status of psychoanalysis today? Traditional psychoanalysis called for three to five therapy sessions a week, often for many years. Today, most patients are only seen once or twice per week, but treatment may still go on for years (Friedman et al., 1998). Because of the huge amounts of time and money this requires, psychoanalysts have become relatively rare. Nevertheless, psychoanalysis made a major contribution to modern therapies by highlighting the importance of unconscious conflicts (Friedman, 2006).

Many therapists have switched to doing **brief psychodynamic therapy,** which uses direct questioning to reveal unconscious conflicts (Binder, 2004). Modern therapists also actively provoke emotional reactions that will lower defenses and provide insights. Interestingly, brief therapy appears to accelerate recovery. Patients seem to realize that they need to get to the heart of their problems quickly (Messer & Kaplan, 2004).

Interpersonal Psychotherapy

One example of a brief dynamic therapy is **interpersonal psychotherapy (IPT),** which was first developed to help depressed people improve their relationships with others (Trull, 2005). Research

has confirmed that IPT is effective for depressive disorders, as well as eating disorders, substance abuse, social phobias, and personality disorders (Fiore et al., 2008; Hoffart, 2005; Talbot & Gamble, 2008; Trull, 2005).

Liona's therapy is a good example of IPT (Brown & Barlow, 2007). Liona was suffering from depression that a therapist helped her trace to a conflict with her parents. When her father was absent, Liona adopted the role of her mother's protector and friend. However, when her father was home she was expected to resume her role as a daughter. She was angry at her father for frequently abandoning her mother and upset about having to switch roles so often. Liona's IPT sessions (which sometimes included her mother) focused on clarifying Liona's family roles. Her mood improved a lot after her mother urged her to "stick to being herself."

Is Traditional Psychoanalysis Effective?

The development of newer, more streamlined dynamic therapies is in part due to questions about whether traditional psychoanalysis "works." In a classic criticism, Hans Eysenck (1994) suggested that psychoanalysis simply takes so long that patients experience a *spontaneous remission* of symptoms (improvement due to the mere passage of time).

How seriously should the possibility of spontaneous remission be taken? It's true that problems ranging from hyperactivity to anxiety do improve with the passage of time. Regardless, researchers have confirmed that psychoanalysis does, in fact, produce improvement in a majority of patients (Doidge, 1997).

The real value of Eysenck's critique is that it encouraged psychologists to try new ideas and techniques. Researchers began to ask, "When psychoanalysis works, why does it work? Which parts of it are essential and which are unnecessary?" Modern therapists have given surprisingly varied answers to these questions. Upcoming sections will acquaint you with some of the therapies currently in use.

Psychoanalysis A Freudian therapy that emphasizes the use of free association, dream interpretation, resistances, and transference to uncover unconscious conflicts.

Free association In psychoanalysis, the technique of having a client say anything that comes to mind, regardless of how embarrassing or unimportant it may seem.

Resistance A blockage in the flow of free association; topics the client resists thinking or talking about.

Transference The tendency of patients to transfer feelings to a therapist that correspond to those the patient had for important persons in his or her past.

Brief psychodynamic therapy A modern therapy based on psychoanalytic theory but designed to produce insights more quickly.

Interpersonal psychotherapy (IPT) A brief dynamic psychotherapy designed to help people by improving their relationships with other people.

Psychotherapy and Psychoanalysis

RECITE

Match:

_____ 1. Directive therapies   **A.** Change behavior
_____ 2. Action therapies   **B.** Place responsibility on the client
_____ 3. Insight therapies   **C.** The client is guided strongly
_____ 4. Nondirective therapies   **D.** Seek understanding

5. An approach that is incompatible with insight therapy is
   a. individual therapy
   b. action therapy
   c. nondirective therapy
   d. interpersonal psychotherapy
6. A scientific explanation of medieval "possessions" by "demons" is related to the effects of
   a. ergot poisoning
   b. trepanning
   c. exorcism
   d. unconscious transference
7. Pinel is famous for his use of exorcism. T or F?
8. In psychoanalysis, an emotional attachment to the therapist is called
   a. free association
   b. manifest association
   c. resistance
   d. transference

REFLECT

Critical Thinking

9. According to Freud's concept of *transference,* patients "transferred" their feelings onto the psychoanalyst. In light of this idea, to what might the term *countertransference* refer?

Relate

Make a list describing what you think it means to be mentally healthy. How well does your list match the items in ● Table 15.1?

The use of trepanning, demonology, and exorcism all implied that the mentally ill are "cursed." To what extent are the mentally ill rejected and stigmatized today?

Try to free associate (aloud) for 10 minutes. How difficult was it? Did anything interesting surface?

Can you explain, in your own words, the role of dream analysis, resistances, and transference in psychoanalysis?

Answers: 1. C 2. A 3. D 4. B 5. b 6. a 7. F 8. d 9. Psychoanalysts (and therapists in general) are also human. They may transfer their own unresolved, unconscious feelings onto their patients. This sometimes hampers the effectiveness of therapy.

●● Humanistic Therapies—Restoring Human Potential

Gateway Question: What are the major humanistic therapies?

When most people picture clinical psychologists at work, they probably imagine them doing insight therapy. As stated earlier, insight therapists help clients gain a deeper understanding of their thoughts, emotions, and behavior. Let's sample a variety of insight-oriented approaches, including therapies done at a distance (by telephone or over the Internet).

Better self-knowledge was the goal of traditional psychoanalysis. However, Freud claimed that his patients could expect only to change their "hysterical misery into common unhappiness"! Humanistic therapists are more optimistic, believing that humans have a natural urge to seek health and self-growth. Most assume that it is possible for people to use their potentials fully and live rich, rewarding lives.

Client-Centered Therapy

What is client-centered therapy? How is it different from psychoanalysis? Psychoanalysts delve into the unconscious. Psychologist Carl Rogers (1902–1987) found it more beneficial to explore *conscious* thoughts and feelings. The psychoanalyst tends to take a position of authority, stating what dreams, thoughts, or memories "mean." In contrast, Rogers believed that what is right or valuable for the therapist may be wrong for the client. (Rogers preferred the term "client" to "patient" because "patient" implies that a person is "sick" and needs to be "cured.") Consequently, the client determines what will be discussed during each session. Thus, **client-centered therapy** (also called **person-centered therapy**) is nondirective and based on insights from conscious thoughts and feelings (Brodley, 2006; Schneider, 2002).

If the client runs things, what does the therapist do? The therapist cannot "fix" the client (Whitton, 2003). Instead, the therapist's job is to create a safe "atmosphere of growth." The therapist provides opportunities for change, but the client must actively seek to solve his or her problems.

Health-Promoting Conditions

Rogers believed that effective therapists maintain four basic conditions. First, the therapist offers the client **unconditional positive regard** (unshakable personal acceptance). The therapist refuses to react with shock, dismay, or disapproval to anything the client says or feels. Total acceptance by the therapist is the first step to self-acceptance by the client.

Second, the therapist attempts to achieve genuine **empathy** by trying to see the world through the client's eyes and feeling some part of what the client is feeling.

As a third essential condition, the therapist strives to be **authentic** (genuine and honest). The therapist must not hide behind a professional role. Rogers believed that phony fronts destroy the growth atmosphere sought in client-centered therapy.

Psychotherapist Carl Rogers, who originated client-centered therapy.

Fourth, the therapist does not make interpretations, propose solutions, or offer advice. Instead, the therapist **reflects** (rephrases, summarizes, or repeats) the client's thoughts and feelings. This enables the therapist to act as a psychological "mirror" so clients can see themselves more clearly. Rogers theorized that a person armed with a realistic self-image and greater self-acceptance will gradually discover solutions to life's problems.

Existential Therapy

According to the existentialists, "being in the world" (existence) creates deep anxiety. Each of us must deal with the realities of death. We must face the fact that we create our private world by making choices. We must overcome isolation on a vast and indifferent planet. Most of all, we must confront feelings of meaninglessness.

What do these concerns have to do with psychotherapy? **Existential therapy** focuses on the problems of existence, such as meaning, choice, and responsibility. Like client-centered therapy, it promotes self-knowledge. However, there are important differences. Client-centered therapy seeks to uncover a "true self" hidden behind a screen of defenses. In contrast, existential therapy emphasizes free will, the human ability to make choices. Accordingly, existential therapists believe you can *choose to become* the person you want to be.

Existential therapists try to give clients the *courage* to make rewarding and socially constructive choices. Typically, therapy focuses on *death, freedom, isolation,* and *meaninglessness,* the "ultimate concerns" of existence (van Deurzen & Kenward, 2005). These universal human challenges include an awareness of one's mortality, the responsibility that comes with freedom to choose, being alone in your own private world, and the need to create meaning in your life.

One example of existential therapy is Victor Frankl's *logotherapy,* which emphasizes the need to find and maintain meaning in life. Frankl (1904–1997) based his approach on experiences he had as a prisoner in a Nazi concentration camp. In the camp, Frankl saw countless prisoners break down as they were stripped of all hope and human dignity (Frankl, 1955). Those who survived with their sanity did so because they managed to hang on to a sense of meaning *(logos).* Even in less dire circumstances, a sense of purpose in life adds greatly to psychological well-being (Prochaska & Norcross, 2007).

What does the existential therapist do? The therapist helps clients discover self-imposed limitations in personal identity. To be successful, the client must fully accept the challenge of changing his or her life (Bretherton & Orner, 2004). Interestingly, Buddhists seek a similar state that they call "radical acceptance" (Brach, 2003).

A key aspect of existential therapy is *confrontation,* in which clients are challenged to examine their values and choices and to take responsibility for the quality of their existence (Gerwood, 1998). An important part of confrontation is the unique, intense, here-and-now *encounter* between two human beings. When existential therapy is successful, it brings about a renewed sense of purpose and a reappraisal of what's important in life. Some clients even experience an emotional rebirth, as if they had survived a close brush with death. As Marcel Proust wrote, "The real voyage of discovery consists not in seeing new landscapes but in having new eyes."

Gestalt Therapy

Gestalt therapy is based on the idea that perception, or *awareness,* is disjointed and incomplete in maladjusted persons. The German word *Gestalt* means "whole," or "complete." **Gestalt therapy** helps people rebuild thinking, feeling, and acting into connected wholes. This is achieved by expanding personal awareness; by accepting responsibility for one's thoughts, feelings, and actions; and by filling in gaps in experience (Joyce & Sills, 2001).

What are "gaps in experience?" Gestalt therapists believe that we often shy away from expressing or "owning" upsetting feelings. This creates a gap in self-awareness that may become a barrier to personal growth. For example, a person who feels anger after the death of a parent might go for years without fully expressing it. This and similar threatening gaps may impair emotional health.

The Gestalt approach is more directive than client-centered or existential therapy and it emphasizes immediate experience. Working either one-to-one or in a group setting, the Gestalt therapist encourages clients to become more aware of their moment-to-moment thoughts, perceptions, and emotions (Staemmler, 2004). Rather than discussing *why* clients feel guilt, anger, fear, or boredom, they are encouraged to have these feelings in the "here and now" and become fully aware of them. The therapist promotes awareness by drawing attention to a client's posture, voice, eye movements, and hand gestures. Clients may also be asked to exaggerate vague feelings until they become clear. Gestalt therapists believe that expressing such feelings allows people to "take care of unfinished business" and break through emotional impasses (O'Leary, 2006).

Client-centered (or person-centered) therapy A nondirective therapy based on insights gained from conscious thoughts and feelings; emphasizes accepting one's true self.

Unconditional positive regard An unqualified, unshakable acceptance of another person.

Empathy A capacity for taking another's point of view; the ability to feel what another is feeling.

Authenticity In Carl Rogers's terms, the ability of a therapist to be genuine and honest about his or her own feelings.

Reflection In client-centered therapy, the process of rephrasing or repeating thoughts and feelings expressed by clients so they can become aware of what they are saying.

Existential therapy An insight therapy that focuses on the elemental problems of existence, such as death, meaning, choice, and responsibility; emphasizes making courageous life choices.

Gestalt therapy An approach that focuses on immediate experience and awareness to help clients rebuild thinking, feeling, and acting into connected wholes; emphasizes the integration of fragmented experiences.

Gestalt therapy is often associated with the work of Fritz Perls (1969). According to Perls, emotional health comes from knowing what you *want* to do, not dwelling on what you *should* do, *ought* to do, or *should want* to do (Rosenberg & Lynch, 2002). In other words, emotional health comes from taking full responsibility for one's feelings and actions. For example, it means changing "I can't" to "I won't," or "I must" to "I choose to."

How does Gestalt therapy help people discover their real wants? Above all else, Gestalt therapy emphasizes *present* experience. Clients are urged to stop intellectualizing and talking *about* feelings. Instead, they learn to live now; live here; stop imagining; experience the real; stop unnecessary thinking; taste and see; express rather than explain, justify, or judge; give in to unpleasantness and pain just as to pleasure; and surrender to being as you are. Gestalt therapists believe that, paradoxically, the best way to change is to become who you really are (Joyce & Sills, 2001).

Because of their emphasis on verbal interaction, insight therapies may be conducted at a distance, by telephone, e-mail, or videoconferencing. Let's investigate this possibility.

● Therapy at a Distance—Psych Jockeys and Cybertherapy

Gateway Question: Can therapy be conducted at a distance?

How valid are psychological services offered at a distance? For better or worse, high-tech psychotherapy and counseling are rapidly becoming commonplace (Ormay, 2006). Today, psychological services are available through radio, telephone, e-mail, Internet chat rooms, and videoconferencing (Maheu et al., 2004). What are the advantages and disadvantages of getting help at a distance?

Media Psychologists

By now you have probably heard a phone-in radio psychologist or watched one on television. On a typical program, participants describe problems arising from child abuse, loneliness, love affairs, phobias, sexual adjustment, or depression. The media psychologist then offers reassurance, advice, or suggestions for getting help. Such talk-radio and television programs may seem harmless, but they raise some important questions. For instance, is it reasonable to give advice without knowing anything about a person's background? Could the advice do harm? What good can a psychologist do in 3 minutes or even an hour?

In their own defense, media psychologists point out that listeners and viewers may learn solutions to their problems by hearing others talk. Many also stress that their work is educational, not therapeutic. The well-known media psychologist Dr. Phil McGraw has even been awarded a President's Citation from the American Psychological Association for his work in publicizing mental health issues (Meyers, 2006).

Nevertheless, the question arises: When does advice become therapy? The American Psychological Association urges media psychologists to discuss problems only of a general nature, instead

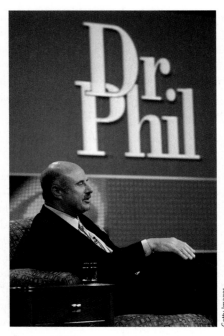

Media psychologists have been urged to educate without actually doing therapy. Some overstep this boundary, however. Do you think popular TV psychologist Dr. Phil sometimes goes too far?

of actually counseling anyone. For example, if a caller complains about insomnia, the radio psychologist should talk about insomnia in general, not probe the caller's personal life. A good guide for anyone tempted to call a radio psychologist or accept advice from a TV psychologist might be "let the consumer beware."

Telephone Therapists

The same caution applies to commercial telephone therapists, who can be reached through 900-number services for $3 to $4 per minute. To date, there is little evidence that commercial telephone counseling is generally effective.

A key feature of successful face-to-face therapy is the establishment of a continuing *relationship* between two people. In this regard, telephone therapy is seriously limited by a lack of visual cues, such as facial expressions and body language. Regardless, under the right circumstances, telephone therapy can be as successful as face-to-face therapy (Day & Schneider, 2002). For example, in one study, telephone counseling helped improve success rates for smokers who wanted to quit (Rabius et al., 2004). Other studies have shown that depressed people benefit from telephone therapy (Mohr et al., 2005; Simon et al., 2004).

It is also important to note that legitimate therapists may use the phone to calm, console, or advise their clients between therapy sessions. Others are experimenting with actually doing therapy by telephone. For example, after the attack on the World Trade Center towers, many rescue personnel needed counseling. To fill the need, a phone network was created to link emergency workers with psychologists all over the country (Murray, 2001; Shore, 2003).

Internet Therapy

The ever-evolving Internet has provided new communication tools that blend voice, text, graphics, and video. Psychological advice, support groups, self-help magazines, and even online therapy are available via the Internet. Some services, such as support groups, are free while online counseling or advice is typically offered for a fee. Some online therapists will "discuss" problems with you through e-mail messages (Chester & Glass, 2006). Others merely answer questions or give advice concerning specific problems.

Online counseling and advice services do have some advantages. For one thing, clients can remain anonymous. Thus, a person who might hesitate to see a psychologist can seek help privately, online. Likewise, the Internet can link people who live in rural areas with psychologists living in large cities. And, compared with traditional office visits, Internet therapy is less expensive.

As with radio talk shows and telephone counselors, many concerns can be raised about online psychological services. Clearly, brief e-mail messages are no way to make a diagnosis. And forget about facial expressions or body language—not even tone of voice reaches the online therapist. Typing emotional icons (called *emoticons*) like little smiley faces (☺) or frowns (☹) is a poor substitute for real human interaction.

Another problem is that e-mail counseling may not be completely confidential and could be intercepted and misused. Of special concern is the fact that "cybershrinks" may or may not be trained professionals (Bloom, 1998). And even if they are, questions exist about whether a psychologist licensed in one state can legally do therapy in another state via the Internet. Despite such objections, psychologists have demonstrated some success providing therapy over the Internet, at least for certain types of problems (Carlbring et al., 2007; Klein, Richards, & Austin, 2006).

Many of the drawbacks we have discussed can be solved with videoconferencing. A two-way audio-video link allows the client and therapist to see one another on computer monitors and to talk via speakerphones. Doing therapy this way still lacks the close personal contact of face-to-face interaction. However, it does remove many of the objections to doing therapy at a distance. It's very likely that distance services will continue to evolve (Riva & Wiederhold, 2006) and become a major source of mental health care in coming years (Schopp, Demiris, & Glueckauf, 2006).

Implications

As you can see, psychological services that rely on electronic communication may serve some useful purposes. However, the value of therapy offered by commercial telephone "counselors" and Internet "therapists" remains open to question. The very best advice given by media psychologists, telephone "counselors," or Internet "therapists" may be, "If at all possible, you should consider discussing this problem with a psychologist or counselor in your own community."

Behavior Therapy—Healing by Learning

Gateway Question: What is behavior therapy?

Jay repeatedly and vividly imagined himself going into a store to steal something. He then pictured himself being caught and turned over to the police, who handcuffed him and hauled him off to jail. Once there, he imagined calling his wife to tell her he had been arrested for shoplifting. He became very distressed as he faced her anger and his son's disappointment (Kohn & Antonuccio, 2002).

Why would anyone imagine such a thing? Jay's behavior is not as strange as it may seem. His goal was self-control: Jay is a *kleptomaniac* (a compulsive thief). The method he chose (called *covert sensitization*) is a form of behavior therapy (Corsini, 2001). **Behavior therapy** is the use of learning principles to make constructive changes in behavior.

In general, how does behavior therapy work? Behavior therapists believe that deep insight into one's problems is often unnecessary for improvement. Instead, they try to directly alter troublesome thoughts and actions. Jay didn't need to probe into his past or his emotions and conflicts; he simply wanted to break his shoplifting habit.

Behavior therapists assume that people have *learned* to be the way they are. If they have learned responses that cause problems, then they can change them by *relearning* more appropriate behaviors. Broadly speaking, **behavior modification** refers to any use of classical or operant conditioning to directly alter human behavior (Miltenberger, 2008; Spiegler & Guevremont, 2003). (Some therapists prefer to call this approach *applied behavior analysis.*) Behavioral approaches include aversion therapy, desensitization, token economies, and other techniques (Forsyth & Savsevitz, 2002).

How does classical conditioning work? I'm not sure I remember. Classical conditioning is a form of learning in which simple responses (especially reflexes) are associated with new stimuli. Perhaps a brief review would be helpful. In classical conditioning, a neutral stimulus is followed by an *unconditioned stimulus* (US) that consistently produces an unlearned reaction, called the *unconditioned response* (UR). Eventually, the previously neutral stimulus begins to produce this response directly. The response is then called a *conditioned response* (CR), and the stimulus becomes a *conditioned stimulus* (CS). Thus, for a child the sight of a hypodermic needle (CS) is followed by an injection (US), which causes anxiety or fear (UR). Eventually the sight of a hypodermic (the conditioned stimulus) may produce anxiety or fear (a conditioned response) *before* the child gets an injection.

> **bridges**
>
> For a more thorough review of classical conditioning, return to Chapter 7, pages 220–225.

What does classical conditioning have to do with behavior modification? Classical conditioning can be used to associate discomfort with a bad habit, as Jay did. More powerful versions of this approach are called aversion therapy.

Aversion Therapy

Imagine that you are eating an apple. Suddenly you discover that you just bit a large green worm in half. You vomit. Months later you cannot eat an apple again without feeling ill. It's apparent that you have developed a conditioned aversion to apples. (A *conditioned aversion* is a learned dislike or negative emotional response to some stimulus.)

How are conditioned aversions used in therapy? In **aversion therapy,** an individual learns to associate a strong aversion to an undesirable habit such as smoking, drinking, or gambling. Aversion therapy has been used to cure hiccups, sneezing, stuttering, vomiting, nail-biting, bed-wetting, compulsive hair-pulling, alcoholism, and the smoking of tobacco, marijuana, or crack cocaine. Actually, aversive conditioning happens every day. For example, not many physicians who treat lung cancer patients are smokers, nor do many emergency room doctors drive without using their seat belts (Eifert & Lejuez, 2000).

Puffing Up an Aversion

The fact that nicotine is toxic makes it easy to create an aversion that helps people give up smoking. Behavior therapists have found that electric shock, nauseating drugs, and similar aversive stimuli are not required to make smokers uncomfortable. All that is needed is for the smoker to smoke—rapidly, for a long time, at a forced pace. During rapid smoking, clients are told to smoke continuously, taking a puff every 6 to 8 seconds. Rapid smoking continues until the smoker is miserable and can stand it no more. By then, most people are thinking, "I never want to see another cigarette for the rest of my life."

Rapid smoking has long been known as an effective behavior therapy for smoking (McRobbie & Hajek, 2007). Nevertheless, anyone tempted to try rapid smoking should realize that it is very unpleasant. Without the help of a therapist, most people quit too soon for the procedure to succeed. In addition, rapid smoking can be dangerous. It should only be done with professional supervision. (An alternative method that is more practical is described in the Psychology in Action section of this chapter.)

Aversive Therapy for Drinking

Another excellent example of aversion therapy was pioneered by Roger Vogler and his associates (1977). Vogler worked with alcoholics who were unable to stop drinking and for whom aversion therapy was a last chance. While drinking an alcoholic beverage, clients receive a painful (although not injurious) electric shock to the hand. Most of the time, these shocks occur as the client is beginning to take a drink of alcohol.

These *response-contingent shocks* (shocks that are linked to a response) obviously take the pleasure out of drinking. Shocks also cause the alcohol abuser to develop a conditioned aversion to drinking. Normally, the misery caused by alcohol abuse comes long after the act of drinking—too late to have much effect. But if alcohol can be linked with *immediate* discomfort, then drinking will begin to make the individual very uncomfortable.

Is it really acceptable to treat clients this way? People are often disturbed (shocked?) by such methods. However, clients usually *volunteer* for aversion therapy because it helps them overcome a destructive habit. Indeed, commercial aversion programs for overeating, smoking, and alcohol abuse have attracted many willing customers. More important, aversion therapy can be justified by its long-term benefits. As behaviorist Donald Baer put it, "A small number of brief, painful experiences is a reasonable exchange for the interminable pain of a lifelong maladjustment."

Desensitization

How is behavior therapy used to treat phobias, fears, and anxieties? Assume that you are a swimming instructor who wants to help a child named Janice overcome fear of the high diving board. How might you proceed? Directly forcing Janice off the high board could be a psychological disaster. Obviously, a better approach would be to begin by teaching her to dive off the edge of the pool. Then she could be taught to dive off the low board, followed by a platform 6 feet above the water and then an 8-foot platform. As a last step, Janice could try the high board.

Who's Afraid of a Hierarchy?

This rank-ordered series of steps (called a **hierarchy**) allows Janice to undergo *adaptation*. Gradually, she adapts to the high dive and overcomes her fear. When Janice has conquered her fear, we can say that *desensitization* (dee-SEN-sih-tih-ZAY-shun) has occurred (Spiegler & Guevremont, 2003).

Desensitization is also based on **reciprocal inhibition** (using one emotional state to block another) (Heriot & Pritchard, 2004). For instance, it is impossible to be anxious and relaxed at the same time. If we can get Janice onto the high board in a relaxed state, her anxiety and fear will be inhibited. Repeated visits to the high board should cause fear to disappear in this situation. Again we would say that Janice has been desensitized. Typically, **systematic desensitization** (a guided reduction in fear, anxiety, or aversion) is attained by gradually approaching a feared stimulus while maintaining relaxation.

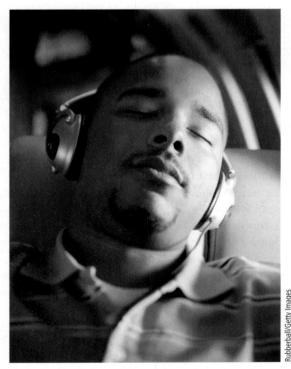

Programs for treating fears of flying combine relaxation, systematic desensitization, group support, and lots of direct and indirect exposure to airliners. Many such programs conclude with a brief flight, so that participants can "test their wings."

What is desensitization used for? Desensitization is primarily used to help people unlearn phobias (intense, unrealistic fears) or strong anxieties. For example, each of these people might be a candidate for desensitization: a teacher with stage fright, a student with test anxiety, a salesperson who fears people, or a newlywed with an aversion to sexual intimacy.

Performing Desensitization

How is desensitization done? First, the client and the therapist *construct a hierarchy*. This is a list of fear-provoking situations, arranged from least disturbing to most frightening. Second, the client is taught *exercises that produce deep relaxation*. (See "Feeling a Little Tense? Relax!") Once the client is relaxed, she or he proceeds to the third step by trying to *perform the least disturbing item* on the list. For a fear of heights (acrophobia), this might be: "(1) Stand on a chair." The first item is repeated until no anxiety is felt. Any change from complete relaxation is a signal that clients must relax again before continuing. Slowly, clients move up the hierarchy: "(2) Climb to the top of a small stepladder"; "(3) Look down a flight of stairs"; and so on, until the last item is performed without fear: "(20) Fly in an airplane."

For many phobias, desensitization works best when people are directly exposed to the stimuli and situations they fear (Bourne, 2005). For something like a simple spider phobia, this exposure can even be done in groups. Also, for some fears (such as fear of riding an elevator) desensitization may be completed in a single session (Sturges & Sturges, 1998).

Vicarious Desensitization

I understand how some fears could be desensitized by gradual approach—as in the case of the child on the high dive. But what if it's not practical to directly act out the steps of a hierarchy? For a fear of heights, the steps of the hierarchy might be acted out. However, if this is impractical the problem can be handled by having clients observe *models* who are performing the feared behavior (● Figure 15.2) (Eifert & Lejuez, 2000). A model is a person (either live or filmed) who serves as an example for observational

Behavior therapy Any therapy designed to actively change behavior.

Behavior modification The application of learning principles to change human behavior, especially maladaptive behavior.

Aversion therapy Suppressing an undesirable response by associating it with aversive (painful or uncomfortable) stimuli.

Hierarchy A rank-ordered series of higher and lower amounts, levels, degrees, or steps.

Reciprocal inhibition The presence of one emotional state can inhibit the occurrence of another, such as joy preventing fear or anxiety inhibiting pleasure.

Systematic desensitization A reduction in fear, anxiety, or aversion brought about by planned exposure to aversive stimuli.

DISCOVERING PSYCHOLOGY

Feeling a Little Tense? Relax!

The key to desensitization is relaxation. To inhibit fear, you must *learn* to relax. One way to voluntarily relax is by using the **tension-release method.** To achieve deep muscle relaxation, try the following exercise:

Tense the muscles in your right arm until they tremble. Hold them tight as you slowly count to 10 and then let go. Allow your hand and arm to go limp and to relax completely. Repeat the procedure. Releasing tension two or three times will allow you to feel whether or not your arm muscles have relaxed. Repeat the tension-release procedure with your left arm. Compare it with your right arm. Repeat until the left arm is equally relaxed. Apply the tension-release technique to your right leg; to your left leg; to your abdomen; to your chest and shoulders. Clench and release your chin, neck, and throat. Wrinkle and release your forehead and scalp. Tighten and release your mouth and face muscles. As a last step, curl your toes and tense your feet. Then release.

If you carried out these instructions, you should be noticeably more relaxed than you were before you began. Practice the tension-release method until you can achieve complete relaxation quickly (5 to 10 minutes). After you have practiced relaxation once a day for a week or two, you will begin to be able to tell when your body (or a group of muscles) is tense. Also, you will begin to be able to relax on command. This is a valuable skill that you can apply in any situation that makes you feel tense or anxious.

● **Figure 15.2** Treatment of a snake phobia by vicarious desensitization. These classic photographs show models interacting with snakes. To overcome their own fears, phobic subjects observed the models. (Bandura, Blanchard, & Ritter, 1969. Photos courtesy of Albert Bandura.)

Albert Bandura

learning. If such **vicarious desensitization** (second-hand learning) can't be used, there is yet another option. Fortunately, desensitization works almost as well when a person *vividly imagines* each step in the hierarchy (Yahnke, Sheikh, & Beckman, 2003). If the steps can be visualized without anxiety, fear in the actual situation is reduced. Because imagining feared stimuli can be done at a therapist's office, it is the most common way of doing desensitization.

Virtual Reality Exposure

Desensitization is an *exposure therapy*. Like other such therapies, it involves exposing people to feared stimuli until their fears extinguish. In an important new development, psychologists are using virtual reality to treat phobias. Virtual reality is a computer-generated, three-dimensional "world" that viewers enter by wearing a head-mounted video display. **Virtual reality exposure** presents computerized fear stimuli to clients in a realistic, yet carefully controlled fashion (Wiederhold & Wiederhold, 2005). It has already been used to treat fears of flying, driving, and public speaking as well as acrophobia (fear of heights), claustrophobia, and spider phobias (Arbona et al., 2004; Giuseppe, 2005; Hoffman et al., 2003; Lee et al., 2002; Wald and Taylor, 2000) (● Figure 15.3).

Desensitization has been one of the most successful behavior therapies. A second new technique may provide yet another way to lower fears, anxieties, and psychological pain.

Eye Movement Desensitization

Traumatic events produce painful memories. Disturbing flashbacks often haunts victims of accidents, disasters, molestations, muggings, rapes, or emotional abuse. Recently, Dr. Francine Shapiro developed **eye movement desensitization and reprocessing (EMDR)** to help ease traumatic memories and posttraumatic stress.

In a typical EMDR session, the client is asked to visualize the images that most upset her or him. At the same time, a pencil (or other object) is moved rapidly from side to side in front of the person's eyes. Watching the moving object causes the person's eyes to dart swiftly back and forth. After about 30 seconds, clients describe any memories, feelings, and thoughts that emerged and discuss them with the therapist. These steps are repeated until troubling thoughts and emotions no longer surface (Shapiro, 2001; Shapiro & Forrest, 2004).

● **Figure 15.3** *(Top)* Dr. Larry Hodges (in the head-mounted display) and Dr. Page Anderson show how a virtual reality system is used to expose people to feared stimuli. *(Bottom)* A computer image from a virtual Iraq. Iraq veterans suffering from post-traumatic stress disorder (PTSD) can re-experience their traumas. For example, someone whose Humvee was destroyed by an improvised explosive device can relive that moment complete with sights, sounds, vibrations, and even smells. Successive exposures result in a reduction of PTSD symptoms (Gerardi et al., 2008). (Images courtesy of Virtually Better.)

(side) Images courtesy of Virtually Better

A number of studies suggest that EMDR lowers anxieties and takes the pain out of traumatic memories (Seidler & Wagner, 2006; Silver et al., 2005). However, EMDR is highly controversial. Some studies, for example, have found that eye movements add nothing to the treatment. The apparent success of EMDR may simply be based on gradual exposure to upsetting stimuli, as in other forms of desensitization (Cahill, Carrigan, & Frueh, 1999; Davidson & Parker, 2001). On the other hand, some researchers continue to find that EMDR is superior to traditional therapies (Greenwald, 2006; Rogers & Silver, 2002).

Is EMDR a breakthrough? Given the frequency of traumas in modern society, it shouldn't be long before we find out.

Tension-release method A procedure for systematically achieving deep relaxation of the body.

Vicarious desensitization A reduction in fear or anxiety that takes place vicariously ("secondhand") when a client watches models perform the feared behavior.

Virtual reality exposure Use of computer-generated images to present fear stimuli. The virtual environment responds to a viewer's head movements and other inputs.

Eye movement desensitization and reprocessing (EMDR) A technique for reducing fear or anxiety; based on holding upsetting thoughts in mind while rapidly moving the eyes from side to side.

Operant Therapies—All the World Is a Skinner Box?

Gateway Question: What role do operant principles play in behavior therapy?

Aversion therapy and desensitization are based on classical conditioning. Where does operant conditioning fit in? As you may recall, operant conditioning refers to learning based on the consequences of making a response. The operant principles most often used by behavior therapists to deal with human behavior are:

1. **Positive reinforcement.** Responses that are followed by reward tend to occur more frequently. If children whine and get attention, they will whine more frequently. If you get As in your psychology class, you may become a psychology major.

2. **Nonreinforcement.** A response that is not followed by reward will occur less frequently.

3. **Extinction.** If a response is not followed by reward after it has been repeated many times, it will go away. After winning three times, you pull the handle on a slot machine 30 times more without a payoff. What do you do? You go away. So does the response of handle pulling (for that particular machine, at any rate).

4. **Punishment.** If a response is followed by discomfort or an undesirable effect, the response will be suppressed (but not necessarily extinguished).

5. **Shaping.** Shaping means rewarding actions that are closer and closer approximations to a desired response. For example, to reward an intellectually disabled child for saying "ball," you might begin by rewarding the child for saying anything that starts with a *b* sound.

6. **Stimulus control.** Responses tend to come under the control of the situation in which they occur. If you set your clock 10 minutes fast, it may be easier to leave the house on time in the morning. Your departure is under the stimulus control of the clock, even though you know it is fast.

7. **Time out.** A time-out procedure usually involves removing the individual from a situation in which reinforcement occurs. Time out is a variation of response cost: It prevents reward from following an undesirable response. For example, children who fight with each other can be sent to separate rooms and allowed out only when they are able to behave more calmly.

> bridges
> **For a more thorough review of operant learning, return to Chapter 7, pages 226–241.**

As simple as these principles may seem, they have been used very effectively to overcome difficulties in work, home, school, and industrial settings. Let's see how.

Nonreinforcement and Extinction

An extremely overweight mental patient had a persistent and disturbing habit: She stole food from other patients. No one could persuade her to stop stealing or to diet. For the sake of her health, a behavior therapist assigned her a special table in the ward dining room. If she approached any other table, she was immediately removed from the dining room. Because her attempts to steal food went unrewarded, they rapidly disappeared. Additionally, any attempt to steal from others caused the patient to miss her own meal (Ayllon, 1963).

What operant principles did the therapist in this example use? The therapist used *nonreward* to produce *extinction*. The most frequently occurring human behaviors lead to some form of reward. An undesirable response can be eliminated by *identifying* and *removing* the rewards that maintain it. But people don't always do things for food, money, or other obvious rewards. Most of the rewards maintaining human behavior are subtler. *Attention, approval,* and *concern* are common yet powerful reinforcers for humans (● Figure 15.4).

Nonreward and extinction can eliminate many problem behaviors, especially in schools, hospitals, and institutions. Often, difficulties center around a limited number of particularly disturbing responses. Time out is a good way to remove such responses, usually by refusing to pay attention to a person who is misbehaving. For example, 14-year-old Terrel periodically appeared in the nude in the activity room of a training center for disturbed adolescents. This behavior always generated a great deal of attention from staff and other patients. As an experiment, the next time he appeared nude, counselors and other staff members greeted him normally

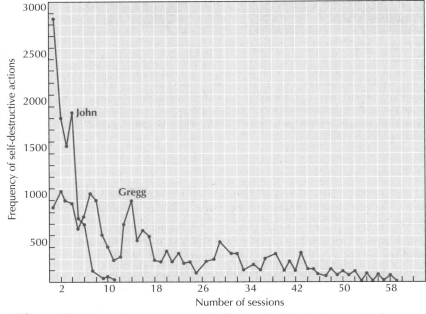

● **Figure 15.4** This graph shows extinction of self-destructive behavior in two autistic boys. Before extinction began, the boys received attention and concern from adults for injuring themselves. During extinction, the adults were taught to ignore the boys' self-damaging behavior. As you can see, the number of times that the boys tried to injure themselves declined rapidly. (Adapted from Lovaas & Simmons, 1969.)

and then ignored him. Attention from other patients rapidly subsided. Sheepishly he returned to his room and dressed.

Reinforcement and Token Economies

A distressing problem therapists sometimes face is how to break through to severely disturbed patients who won't talk. Conventional psychotherapy offers little hope of improvement for such patients.

What can be done for them? One widely used approach is based on *tokens* (symbolic rewards that can be exchanged for real rewards). Tokens may be printed slips of paper, check marks, points, or gold stars. Whatever form they take, tokens serve as rewards because they may be exchanged for candy, food, cigarettes, recreation, or privileges, such as private time with a therapist, outings, or watching TV. Tokens are used in mental hospitals, halfway houses, schools for the intellectually disabled, programs for delinquents, and ordinary classrooms. They usually produce improvements in behavior (Dickerson, Tenhula, & Green-Paden, 2005; Reitman et al., 2004).

Credit Card

OXNARD DAY TREATMENT CENTER CREDIT INCENTIVE SYSTEM

EARN CREDITS BY		SPEND CREDITS FOR	
MONITOR DAILY	15	COFFEE	5
MENU PLANNING CHAIRMAN	50	LUNCH	10
PARTICIPATE	5	EXCEPT THURSDAY	15
BUY FOOD AT STORE	10	BUS TRIP	5
COOK FOR/PREPARE LUNCH	5	BOWLING	8
WIPE OFF KITCHEN TABLE	3	GROUP THERAPY	5
WASH DISHES	5-10	PRIVATE STAFF TIME	5
DRY AND PUT AWAY DISHES	5	DAY OFF	5-20
MAKE COFFEE AND CLEAN URN	15	WINDOW SHOPPING	5
CLEAN REFRIGERATOR	20	REVIEW WITH DR.	10
ATTEND PLANNING CONFERENCE	1	DOING OWN THING	1
OT PREPARATION	1-5	LATE 1 PER EVERY 10 MIN	
COMPLETE OT PROJECT	5	PRESCRIPTION FROM DR.	10
RETURN OT PROJECT	2		
DUST AND POLISH TABLES	5		
PUT AWAY GROCERIES	3		
CLEAN TABLE	5		
CLEAN 6 ASH TRAYS	2		
CLEAN SINK	5		
CARRY OUT CUPS & BOTTLES	5		
CLEAN CHAIRS	5		
CLEAN KITCHEN CUPBOARDS	5		
ASSIST STAFF	5		
ARRANGE MAGAZINES NEATLY	3		
BEING ON TIME	5		
MONITOR-ANN			

● **Figure 15.5** Shown here is a token used in one token economy system. In this instance the token is a card that records the number of credits earned by a patient. Also pictured is a list of credit values for various activities. Tokens may be exchanged for items or for privileges listed on the board. (Adapted from photographs by Robert P. Liberman.)

> **bridges**
> Tokens provide an effective way to change behavior because they are secondary reinforcers. **See Chapter 7, pages 230–231.**

By using tokens, a therapist can *immediately reward* positive responses. For maximum impact, therapists select specific *target behaviors* (actions or other behaviors the therapist seeks to modify). Target behaviors are then reinforced with tokens. For example, a mute mental patient might first be given a token each time he or she says a word. Next, tokens may be given for speaking a complete sentence. Later, the patient could gradually be required to speak more often, then to answer questions, and eventually to carry on a short conversation in order to receive tokens. In this way, deeply withdrawn patients have been returned to the world of normal communication.

Full-scale use of tokens in an institutional setting produces a *token economy*. In a **token economy,** patients are rewarded with tokens for a wide range of socially desirable or productive activities (Spiegler & Guevremont, 2003). They must *pay* tokens for privileges and for engaging in problem behaviors (● Figure 15.5). For example, tokens are given to patients who get out of bed, dress themselves, take required medication, arrive for meals

on time, and so on. Constructive activities, such as gardening, cooking, or cleaning, may also earn tokens. Patients must *exchange* tokens for meals and private rooms, movies, passes, off-ward activities, and other privileges. They are *charged* tokens for staying in bed, disrobing in public, talking to themselves, fighting, crying, and similar target behaviors (Morisse et al., 1996).

Token economies can radically change a patient's overall adjustment and morale. Patients are given an incentive to change, and they are held responsible for their actions. The use of tokens may seem manipulative, but it actually empowers patients. Many "hopelessly" intellectually disabled, mentally ill, and delinquent people have been returned to productive lives by means of token economies (Field et al., 2004). By the time they are ready to leave, patients may be earning tokens on a weekly basis for maintaining sane, responsible, and productive behavior (Miltenberger, 2008). Typically, the most effective token economies are those that gradually switch from tokens to *social rewards* such as praise, recognition, and approval. Such rewards are what patients will receive when they return to family, friends, and community.

Token economy A therapeutic program in which desirable behaviors are reinforced with tokens that can be exchanged for goods, services, activities, and privileges.

●● Cognitive Therapy—Think Positive!

Gateway Question: Can therapy change thoughts and emotions?

How would a behavior therapist treat a problem like depression? None of the techniques described seem to apply. As we have discussed, behavior therapists usually try to change troublesome actions. However, in recent years cognitive therapists have become interested in what people think, believe, and feel, as well as how they act. In general, **cognitive therapy** helps clients change thinking patterns that lead to troublesome emotions or behaviors (Hall, 2006). For example, compulsive hand-washing can be greatly reduced by changing a client's thoughts and beliefs about dirt and contamination (Jones & Menzies, 1998). Cognitive therapy has been used as a remedy for many problems, but it has been especially successful in treating depression (Chambless & Ollendick, 2001; Hollon, Stewart, & Strunk, 2006).

Cognitive Therapy for Depression

As you may recall from Chapter 13, cognitive psychologists believe that negative, self-defeating thoughts underlie depression. According to Aaron Beck (1991), depressed persons see themselves, the world, and the future in negative terms. Beck believes this occurs because of major distortions in thinking. The first is **selective perception,** which refers to perceiving only certain stimuli in a larger array. If five good things and three bad things happen during the day, depressed people focus only on the bad. A second thinking error in depression is **overgeneralization,** the tendency to think that an upsetting event applies to other, unrelated situations. An example would be considering yourself a total failure, or completely worthless, if you were to lose a part-time job or fail a test. To complete the picture, depressed persons tend to magnify the importance of undesirable events by engaging in **all-or-nothing thinking.** That is, they see events as completely good or bad, right or wrong, and themselves as either successful or failing miserably (Beck, 2002; Gilbert, 2001).

How do cognitive therapists alter such patterns? Cognitive therapists make a step-by-step effort to correct negative thoughts that lead to depression or similar problems. At first, clients are taught to recognize and keep track of their own thoughts. The client and therapist then look for ideas and beliefs that cause depression, anger, and avoidance. For example, here's how a therapist might challenge all-or-nothing thinking (Burns & Persons, 1982):

> *Client:* I'm feeling even more depressed. No one wants to hire me, and I can't even clean up my apartment. I feel completely incompetent!
>
> *Therapist:* I see. The fact that you are unemployed and have a messy apartment proves that you are completely incompetent?
>
> *Client:* Well . . . I can see that doesn't add up.

Next, clients are asked to gather information to test their beliefs. For instance, a depressed person might list his or her activities for a week. The list is then used to challenge all-or-nothing thoughts, such as "I had a terrible week" or "I'm a complete failure." With more coaching, clients learn to alter their thoughts in ways that improve their moods, actions, and relationships.

Cognitive therapy is as effective as drugs for treating many cases of depression. More important, people who have adopted new thinking patterns are less likely to become depressed again—a benefit that drugs can't impart (Dozois & Dobson, 2004; Hollon, Stewart, & Strunk, 2006).

In an alternate approach, cognitive therapists look for an *absence* of effective coping skills and thinking patterns, not for the *presence* of self-defeating thoughts (Dobson, Backs-Dermott, & Dozois, 2000). The aim is to teach clients how to cope with anger, depression, shyness, stress, and similar problems. Stress inoculation, which was described in Chapter 13, is a good example of this approach.

Cognitive therapy is a rapidly expanding specialty. Before we leave the topic, let's explore another widely used cognitive therapy.

Rational-Emotive Behavior Therapy

Rational-emotive behavior therapy (REBT) attempts to change irrational beliefs that cause emotional problems. According to Albert Ellis (1913–2007), the basic idea of REBT is as easy as A-B-C (Ellis, 1995, 2004). Ellis assumes that people become unhappy and develop self-defeating habits because they have unrealistic or faulty *beliefs.*

How are beliefs important? Ellis analyzes problems in this way: The letter A stands for an *activating experience,* which the person assumes to be the cause of C, an *emotional consequence.* For instance, a person who is rejected (the activating experience) feels depressed, threatened, or hurt (the consequence). Rational-emotive behavior therapy shows the client that the real problem is what comes between A and C: In between is B, the client's irrational and unrealistic *beliefs.* In this example, an unrealistic belief leading to unnecessary suffering is, "I must be loved and approved by everyone at all times." REBT holds that events do not *cause* us to have feelings. We feel as we do because of our beliefs (Kottler, 2004). (For some examples, see "Ten Irrational Beliefs—Which Do You Hold?")

> **bridges**
>
> The REBT explanation of emotional distress is related to the effects of emotional appraisals. **See Chapter 10, page 350.**

Ellis (1979, 2004) says that most irrational beliefs come from three core ideas, each of which is unrealistic:

1. I *must* perform well and be approved of by significant others. If I don't, then it is awful, I cannot stand it, and I am a rotten person.
2. You *must* treat me fairly. When you don't, it is horrible, and I cannot bear it.
3. Conditions *must* be the way I want them to be. It is terrible when they are not, and I cannot stand living in such an awful world.

It's easy to see that such beliefs can lead to much grief and needless suffering in a less than perfect world. Rational-emotive behavior therapists are very directive in their attempts to change a client's irrational beliefs and "self-talk." The therapist may directly attack clients' logic, challenge their thinking, confront them with evidence contrary to their beliefs, and even assign "homework." Here,

DISCOVERING PSYCHOLOGY

Ten Irrational Beliefs—Which Do You Hold?

Rational-emotive behavior therapists have identified numerous beliefs that commonly lead to emotional upsets and conflicts. See if you recognize any of the following irrational beliefs:

1. I must be loved and approved by almost every significant person in my life or it's awful and I'm worthless.
   Example: "One of my roommates doesn't seem to like me. I must be a total zero."
2. I should be completely competent and achieving in all ways to be a worthwhile person.
   Example: "I don't understand my chemistry class. I guess I really am a stupid person."
3. Certain people I must deal with are thoroughly bad and should be severely blamed and punished for it.
   Example: "The old man next door is such a pain. I'm going to play my stereo

even louder the next time he complains."
4. It is awful and upsetting when things are not the way I would very much like them to be.
   Example: "I should have gotten a B in that class. The teacher is unfair."
5. My unhappiness is always caused by external events; I cannot control my emotional reactions.
   Example: "You make me feel awful. I would be happy if it weren't for you."
6. If something unpleasant might happen, I should keep dwelling on it.
   Example: "I'll never forget the time my boss insulted me. I think about it every day at work."
7. It is easier to avoid difficulties and responsibilities than to face them.
   Example: "I don't know why my wife seems angry. Maybe it will just pass if I ignore it."

8. I should depend on others who are stronger than I am.
   Example: "I couldn't survive if he left me."
9. Because something once strongly affected my life, it will do so indefinitely.
   Example: "My girlfriend dumped me during my junior year in college. I don't know if I can ever trust a woman again."
10. There is always a perfect solution to human problems and it is awful if this solution is not found.
    Example: "I'm so depressed about politics in this country. It all seems hopeless."

If any of the listed beliefs sound familiar, you may be creating unnecessary emotional distress for yourself by holding on to unrealistic expectations.

*Adapted from Beck, 2002; Ellis, 2004; Rohsenow & Smith, 1982.

for instance, are some examples of statements that dispute irrational beliefs (after Kottler, 2004):

- "Where is the evidence that you are a loser just because you didn't do well this one time?"
- "Who said the world should be fair? That's your rule."
- "What are you telling yourself to make yourself feel so upset?"
- "Is it really terrible that things aren't working out as you would like? Or is it just inconvenient?"

Many of us would probably do well to give up our irrational beliefs. Improved self-acceptance and a better tolerance of daily annoyances are the benefits of doing so. (See "Overcoming the Gambler's Fallacy" on the next page.)

The value of cognitive approaches is further illustrated by three techniques (*covert sensitization, thought stopping,* and *covert reinforcement*) described in this chapter's Psychology in Action section. A little later you can see what you think of them.

KNOWLEDGE BUILDER
Operant Therapies and Cognitive Therapies

RECITE
1. Behavior modification programs aimed at extinction of an undesirable behavior typically make use of what operant principles?
   a. punishment and stimulus control
   b. punishment and shaping
   c. nonreinforcement and time out
   d. stimulus control and time out

2. Attention can be a powerful _____ for humans.
3. Token economies depend on the time-out procedure. T or F?
4. Tokens basically allow the operant shaping of desired responses or "target behaviors." T or F?
5. According to Beck, selective perception, overgeneralization, and _____ thinking are cognitive habits that underlie depression.
6. The B in the A-B-C of REBT stands for
   a. behavior
   b. belief
   c. being
   d. Beck
7. REBT teaches people to change the antecedents of irrational behavior. T or F?

Continued

Cognitive therapy A therapy directed at changing the maladaptive thoughts, beliefs, and feelings that underlie emotional and behavioral problems.

Selective perception Perceiving only certain stimuli among a larger array of possibilities.

Overgeneralization Blowing a single event out of proportion by extending it to a large number of unrelated situations.

All-or-nothing thinking Classifying objects or events as absolutely right or wrong, good or bad, acceptable or unacceptable, and so forth.

Rational-emotive behavior therapy (REBT) An approach that states that irrational beliefs cause many emotional problems and that such beliefs must be changed or abandoned.

THE CLINICAL FILE

Overcoming the Gambler's Fallacy

Seventeen-year-old Jonathan just lost his shirt again. This time he did it playing online Blackjack. Jonathan started out making $5 bets and then doubled his bet over and over. Surely, he thought, his luck would eventually change. However, he ran out of money after just eight hands, having lost more than $1,000. Last week he lost a lot of money playing Texas Hold 'Em. Now Jonathan is in tears—he has lost most of his summer earnings, and he is worried about having to drop out of school and tell his parents about his losses. Jonathan has had to admit that he is part of the growing ranks of underage gambling addicts (LaBrie & Shaffer, 2007; Wilber & Potenza, 2006).

Like many problem gamblers, Jonathan suffers from several cognitive distortions

related to gambling. Here are some of his mistaken beliefs (adapted from Toneatto, 2002):

Magnified gambling skill: Your self-confidence is exaggerated, despite the fact that you lose persistently.

Attribution errors: You ascribe you wins to skill but blame losses on bad luck.

Gambler's fallacy: You believe that a string of losses soon must be followed by wins.

Selective memory: You remember your wins but forget your losses.

Overinterpretation of cues: You put too much faith in irrelevant cues such as bodily sensations or a feeling that your next bet will be a winner.

Luck as a trait: You believe that you are a "lucky" person in general.

Probability biases: You have incorrect beliefs about randomness and chance events.

Do you have any of these mistaken beliefs? Taken together, Jonathan's cognitive distortions created an illusion of control. That is, he believed that if he worked hard enough, he could figure out how to win. Fortunately, a cognitive therapist helped Jonathan *cognitively restructure* his beliefs. He now no longer believes he can control chance events. Jonathan still gambles a bit, but he only does so recreationally, keeping his losses within his budget and enjoying himself in the process.

Group Therapy—People Who Need People

Gateway Question: Can psychotherapy be done with groups of people?

To complete our discussion of psychotherapies, we will begin with a brief look at group therapy. Group therapy has certain advantages, not the least of which is reduced cost. After that, we will try to identify the core features and helping skills that make psychotherapy "work."

Group therapy is psychotherapy done with more than one person. Most of the therapies we have discussed can be adapted for use in groups (Corey, 2008). Psychologists first tried working with groups because there was a shortage of therapists. Surprisingly, group therapy has turned out to be just as effective as individual therapy, and it has some special advantages (Burlingame, Fuhriman, & Mosier, 2003).

What are the advantages? In group therapy, a person can *act out* or directly experience problems. Doing so often produces insights that might not occur from merely talking about an issue. In addition, other group members with similar problems can offer support and useful input. Group therapy is especially good for helping people understand their personal relationships (McCluskey, 2002). For reasons such as these, a number of specialized groups have emerged. Because they range from Alcoholics Anonymous to Marriage Encounter, we will sample only a few examples.

Psychodrama

One of the first group therapies was developed by Jacob L. Moreno (1953), who called his technique psychodrama. In **psychodrama,** clients act out personal conflicts with others who play supporting roles (Blatner, 2006). Through role-playing, the client re-enacts incidents that cause problems in real life. For example, Don, a disturbed teenager, might act out a typical family fight, with the therapist playing his father and with other clients playing his mother, brothers, and sisters. Moreno believed that insights gained in this way transfer to real-life situations.

Therapists using psychodrama often find that role reversals are helpful. A **role reversal** involves taking the part of another person

A group therapy session. Group members offer mutual support while sharing problems and insights.

to learn how he or she feels. For instance, Don might role-play his father or mother, to better understand their feelings. A related method is the **mirror technique,** in which clients observe another person re-enact their behavior. Thus, Don might briefly join the audience and watch as another group member plays his role. This would allow him to see himself as others do. Later, the group may summarize what happened and reflect on its meaning (Turner, 1997).

Family and Couples Therapy

Family relationships are the source of great pleasure and, all too often, of great pain. In **family therapy,** husband, wife, and children work as a group to resolve the problems of each family member. This is also called *couples therapy* when children are not involved (Scheinkman, 2008). Family and couples therapy tends to be brief and focused on specific problems, such as frequent fights or a depressed teenager. For some types of problems, family therapy may be superior to other approaches (Capuzzi, 2003; Eisler et al., 2007).

Family therapists believe that a problem experienced by one family member is really the whole family's problem. If the entire pattern of behavior in a family doesn't change, improvements in any single family member may not last. Thus, family members work together to improve communication, to change destructive patterns, and to see themselves and each other in new ways. This helps them reshape distorted perceptions and interactions directly with the very persons with whom they have troubled relationships (Goldenberg & Goldenberg, 2004).

Does the therapist work with the whole family at once? Family therapists treat the family as a unit, but they may not meet with the entire family at each session (Eisler et al., 2007). If a family crisis is at hand, the therapist may first try to identify the most resourceful family members, who can help solve the immediate problem. The therapist and family members may then work on resolving more basic conflicts and on improving family relationships (Griffin, 2002).

Group Awareness Training

During the 1960s and 1970s, the human potential movement led many people to seek personal growth experiences. Often, their interest was expressed by participation in sensitivity training or encounter groups.

What is the difference between sensitivity and encounter groups? Sensitivity groups tend to be less confrontational than encounter groups. Participants in **sensitivity groups** take part in exercises that gently enlarge self-awareness and sensitivity to others. For example, in a "trust walk," participants expand their confidence in others by allowing themselves to be led around while blindfolded.

Encounter groups are based on an honest expression of feelings, and intensely personal communication may take place. Typically, the emphasis is on tearing down defenses and false fronts. Because there is a danger of hostile confrontation, participation is safest when members are carefully screened and a trained leader guides the group. Encounter group "casualties" are rare, but they do occur (Shaffer & Galinsky, 1989).

In business settings, psychologists still use the basic principles of sensitivity and encounter groups—truth, self-awareness, and self-determination—to improve employee relationships. Specially designed encounter groups for married couples are also widely held (Harway, 2004).

There has also been much public interest in various forms of large-group awareness training. **Large-group awareness training** refers to programs that claim to increase self-awareness and facilitate constructive personal change. The Garden Company, Lifespring, the Forum, the Hoffman Quadrinity Process, and similar commercial programs are examples. Like the smaller groups

Group therapy Psychotherapy conducted in a group setting to make therapeutic use of group dynamics.

Psychodrama A therapy in which clients act out personal conflicts and feelings in the presence of others who play supporting roles.

Role reversal Taking the role of another person to learn how one's own behavior appears from the other person's perspective.

Mirror technique Observing another person re-enact one's own behavior, like a character in a play; designed to help persons see themselves more clearly.

Family therapy Technique in which all family members participate, both individually and as a group, to change destructive relationships and communication patterns.

Sensitivity group A group experience consisting of exercises designed to increase self-awareness and sensitivity to others.

Encounter group A group experience that emphasizes intensely honest interchanges among participants regarding feelings and reactions to one another.

Large-group awareness training Any of a number of programs (many of them commercialized) that claim to increase self-awareness and facilitate constructive personal change.

CRITICAL THINKING

How Do We Know Therapy Actually Works?

Why is it risky to believe people who say their therapy was effective? An old joke among doctors is that a cold lasts a week without treatment and seven days with it. Perhaps the same is true of therapy. Someone who feels better after 6 months of therapy may have experienced a spontaneous remission—they just feel better because so much time has passed. Or perhaps the crisis that triggered the therapy is now nearly forgotten. Or maybe some sort of therapy placebo effect has occurred. Also, it's possible that the person has received help from other people, such as family, friends, or clergy.

In order to rule out similar explanations, we need to use some of the research methods described in Chapter 1. Ideally, we would randomly divide a group of clients into an experimental group that receives therapy and a control group that does not. When this is done, it is not unusual for the control group to show some improvement, even without receiving therapy (Lambert & Ogles, 2002). Thus, the therapy can be deemed effective only if the experimental group shows *more* improvement than the control group.

But isn't it unethical to withhold treatment from someone who really needs therapy?

That's right. One way to deal with this is to use a *waiting-list control group* consisting of individuals who are waiting to see a therapist and who will eventually also receive therapy.

When the results of many experiments are combined, the effectiveness of therapy becomes clear (Lipsey & Wilson, 1993). Recently, studies have shown that some therapies are most effective for specific disorders (Bradley et al., 2005; Eddy et al., 2004). For example, behavioral, cognitive-behavioral, and drug therapies are particularly helpful in treating obsessive-compulsive disorder.

---

that preceded them, large-group training combines psychological exercises, confrontation, new viewpoints, and group dynamics to promote personal change.

Are sensitivity, encounter, and awareness groups really psychotherapies? These experiences tend to be positive, but they produce only moderate benefits (Faith, Wong, & Carpenter, 1995). Moreover, many of the claimed benefits may simply result from a kind of **therapy placebo effect,** in which improvement is based on a client's belief that therapy will help. Positive expectations, a break in daily routine, and an excuse to act differently can have quite an impact. Also, less ambitious goals may be easier to attain. For example, one program succeeded in teaching stress-management techniques in a large group setting (Timmerman, Emmelkamp, & Sanderman, 1998). Because of their versatility, groups undoubtedly will continue to be a major tool for solving problems and improving lives (Corey, 2008).

● Psychotherapy—An Overview

Gateway Question: What do various therapies have in common?

How effective is psychotherapy? Judging the outcome of therapy is tricky. In a national survey, nearly 9 out of 10 people who have sought mental health care say their lives improved as a result of the treatment (Kotkin, Daviet, & Gurin, 1996). Unfortunately you can't just take people's word for it. (See "How Do We Know Therapy Actually Works?") Fortunately, there is direct evidence that therapy is beneficial. Hundreds of studies show a strong pattern of positive effects for psychotherapy, counseling, and other psychological treatments (Barlow, 2004; Lambert & Cattani-Thompson, 1996).

In general, then, psychotherapy works (Moras, 2002). Of course, results vary in individual cases. For some people therapy is immensely helpful; for others it is unsuccessful; overall it is effective for more

people than not. Speaking more subjectively, a real success, in which a person's life is changed for the better, can be worth the frustration of several cases in which little progress is made.

Although it is common to think of therapy as a long, slow process, this is not normally the case (Shapiro et al., 2003). Research shows that about 50 percent of all clients feel better after between 13 and 18 weekly 1-hour therapy sessions (Howard et al., 1986). This means that the majority of clients improve after 6 months of therapy. Such rapid improvement is impressive in view of the fact that people often suffer for several years before seeking help. Unfortunately, because of high costs and limited insurance coverage, the average client receives only 5 therapy sessions, after which only 20 percent of patients feel better (Hansen, Lambert, & Forman, 2002).

Core Features of Psychotherapy

What do psychotherapies have in common? We have sampled only a few of the many therapies in use today. For a summary of major differences among psychotherapies, see ● Table 15.2. To add to your understanding, let us briefly summarize what all techniques have in common.

Psychotherapies of various types share all or most of these goals: restoring hope, courage, and optimism; gaining insight; resolving conflicts; improving one's sense of self; changing unacceptable patterns of behavior; finding purpose; mending interpersonal relations; and learning to approach problems rationally (Frank & Frank, 2004; Seligman, 1998). To accomplish these goals, psychotherapies offer the following:

1. Therapy provides a *caring relationship* between the client and therapist, called a **therapeutic alliance.** Emotional rapport, warmth, friendship, understanding, acceptance, and empathy are the basis for this relationship. The therapeutic alliance unites the client and therapist as they work together to solve

Table 15.2 ● Comparison of Psychotherapies

	Insight or Action?	Directive or Nondirective?	Individual or Group?	Therapy's Strength*
Psychoanalysis	Insight	Directive	Individual	Searching honesty
Brief psychodynamic therapy	Insight	Directive	Individual	Productive use of conflict
Client-centered therapy	Insight	Nondirective	Both	Acceptance, empathy
Existential therapy	Insight	Both	Individual	Personal empowerment
Gestalt therapy	Insight	Directive	Both	Focus on immediate awareness
Behavior therapy	Action	Directive	Both	Observable changes in behavior
Cognitive therapy	Action	Directive	Individual	Constructive guidance
Rational-emotive behavior therapy	Action	Directive	Individual	Clarity of thinking and goals
Psychodrama	Insight	Directive	Group	Constructive re-enactments
Family therapy	Both	Directive	Group	Shared responsibility for problems

*This column based in part on Andrews (1989).

the client's problems. The strength of this alliance has a major impact on whether therapy succeeds (Kozart, 2002; Meier et al., 2006).

2. Therapy offers a *protected setting* in which emotional *catharsis* (release) can take place. Therapy is a sanctuary in which the client is free to express fears, anxieties, and personal secrets without fearing rejection or loss of confidentiality.

3. All therapies to some extent offer an *explanation* or *rationale* for the client's suffering. Additionally, they propose a line of action that will end this suffering.

4. Therapy provides clients with a *new perspective* about themselves and their situations and a chance to practice *new behaviors* (Crencavage & Norcross, 1990; Prochaska & Norcross, 2007). Insights gained during therapy can bring about lasting changes in clients' lives (Grande et al., 2003).

If you recall that our discussion began with trepanning and demonology, it is clear that psychotherapy has come a long way. Still, the search for ways to improve psychotherapy remains an urgent challenge for those who devote their lives to helping others.

Master Therapists

Because therapies have much in common, a majority of psychologists have become *eclectic* in their work (Kopta et al., 1999). Eclectic therapists use whatever methods best fit a particular problem (Norcross, 2005). In addition, some seek to combine the best elements of various therapies to broaden their effectiveness.

What do the most capable therapists have in common? One study of master therapists found that they share several characteristics (Jennings & Skovholt, 1999). The most effective therapists:

- Are enthusiastic learners
- Draw on their experience with similar problems
- Value complexity and ambiguity
- Are emotionally open
- Are mentally healthy and mature
- Nurture their own emotional well-being

- Realize that their emotional health affects their work
- Have strong social skills
- Cultivate a working alliance
- Expertly use their social skills in therapy

Notice that this list also could describe the kind of person most of us would want to talk to when facing a life crisis.

The Future of Psychotherapy

What will psychotherapy look like in the future? A group of experts predicted the following (Norcross, Hedges, & Prochaska, 2002):

- There will be an increase in the use of short-term therapy and solution-focused, problem-solving approaches.
- More therapy will be provided by master's-level practitioners (counselors, social workers, and psychiatric nurses).
- The use of lower-cost Internet services, telephone counseling, paraprofessionals, and self-help groups will grow.
- The use of psychiatrists and psychoanalysis will decrease.

As you might guess, many of these predicted changes are based on pressures to reduce the cost of mental health services. Another interesting cost-saving measure is the idea that computers may be able to treat some relatively minor problems. In a recent study, clients worked through ten computer-guided sessions that helped them identify a problem, form a plan of action, and work through carrying out the plan. Most were satisfied with the help they received (Jacobs et al., 2001).

In another major development, psychologists are making progress in identifying "empirically supported" (or "evidence-based") therapies (Westen & Bradley, 2005). Rather than just relying on

Therapy placebo effect Improvement caused not by the actual process of therapy but by a client's expectation that therapy will help.

Therapeutic alliance A caring relationship that unites a therapist and a client in working to solve the client's problems.

intuition, clinicians are seeking guidance from research experiments and guidelines developed through clinical practice (Carroll & Rounsaville, 2007; Miller & Binder, 2002). The end result is a better understanding of which therapies "work" best for specific types of problems. This trend is also helping to weed out fringe "therapies" that have little or no value.

Basic Counseling Skills

A number of general helping skills can be distilled from the various approaches to therapy. These are points to keep in mind if you would like to comfort a person in distress, such as a troubled friend or relative (● Table 15.3).

Active Listening

People frequently talk "at" each other without really listening. A person with problems needs to be heard. Make a sincere effort to listen to and understand the person. Try to accept the person's message without judging it or leaping to conclusions. Let the person know you are listening, through eye contact, posture, your tone of voice, and your replies (Kottler, 2004).

Reflect Thoughts and Feelings

One of the best things you can do when offering support to another person is to give feedback by simply restating what is said. This is also a good way to encourage a person to talk. If your friend seems to be at a loss for words, *restate* or *paraphrase* his or her last sentence. Here's an example:

> *Friend:* I'm really down about school. I can't get interested in any of my classes. I flunked my Spanish test, and somebody stole my notebook for psychology.
> *You:* You're really upset about school, aren't you?
> *Friend:* Yeah, and my parents are hassling me about my grades again.
> *You:* You're feeling pressured by your parents?
> *Friend:* Yeah, damn.
> *You:* It must make you angry to be pressured by them.

Table 15.3 ● Helping Behaviors

To help another person gain insight into a personal problem it is valuable to keep the following comparison in mind.	
Behaviors That Help	**Behaviors That Hinder**
Active listening	Probing painful topics
Acceptance	Judging/moralizing
Reflecting feelings	Criticism
Open-ended questioning	Threats
Supportive statements	Rejection
Respect	Ridicule/sarcasm
Patience	Impatience
Genuineness	Placing blame
Paraphrasing	Opinionated statements

Adapted from Kottler, 2004.

As simple as this sounds, it is very helpful to someone trying to sort out feelings. Try it. If nothing else, you'll develop a reputation as a fantastic conversationalist!

Silence

Counselors tend to wait longer before responding than do people in everyday conversations. Pauses of 5 seconds or more are not unusual, and interrupting is rare. Listening patiently lets the person feel unhurried and encourages her or him to speak freely.

Questions

Because your goal is to encourage free expression, *open-ended questions* tend to be the most helpful. A *closed question* is one that can be answered yes or no. Open-ended questions call for an open-ended reply. Say, for example, that a friend tells you, "I feel like my boss has it in for me at work." A closed question would be, "Oh yeah? So, are you going to quit?" Open-ended questions, such as, "Do you want to talk about it?" or "How do you feel about it?" are more likely to be helpful.

> **bridges**
> Open-ended questions are an effective way to begin and sustain a conversation. **See Chapter 12, page 422.**

Clarify the Problem

People who have a clear idea of what is wrong in their lives are more likely to discover solutions. Try to understand the problem from the person's point of view. As you do, check your understanding often. For example, you might ask, "Are you saying that you feel depressed just at school? Or in general?" Remember, a problem well defined is often half solved.

Focus on Feelings

Feelings are neither right nor wrong. By focusing on feelings you can encourage the outpouring of emotion that is the basis for catharsis. Passing judgment on what is said just makes people defensive. For example, a friend confides that he has failed a test. Perhaps you know that he studies very little. If you say, "Just study more and you will do better," he will probably become defensive or hostile. Much more can be accomplished by saying, "You must feel very frustrated" or simply, "How do you feel about it?"

Avoid Giving Advice

Many people mistakenly think that they must solve problems for others. Remember that your goal is to provide understanding and support, not solutions. Of course, it is reasonable to give advice when you are asked for it, but beware of the trap of the "Why don't you . . . ? Yes, but . . ." game. According to psychotherapist Eric Berne (1964), this "game" follows a pattern: Someone says, "I have this problem." You say, "Why don't you do

Therapy and Culture—A Bad Case of "Ifufunyane"

At the age of 23, the patient was clearly suffering from "ifufunyane," a form of bewitchment common in the Xhosa culture of South Africa. However, he was treated at a local hospital by psychiatrists, who said he had schizophrenia and gave him antipsychotic drugs. The drugs helped, but his family shunned his fancy medical treatment and took him to a traditional healer who gave him herbs for his ifufunyane. Unfortunately, he got worse and was readmitted to the hospital. This time, the psychiatrists included the patient's family in his treatment. Together, they agreed to treat him with a combination of antipsychotic drugs *and* traditional herbs. This time, the patient got much better and his ifufunyane was alleviated, too (Niehaus et al., 2005).

As this example illustrates, **culturally skilled therapists** are trained to work with clients from various cultural backgrounds. To be culturally skilled, a counselor must be able to do all of the following (APA, 2003; Draguns, Gielen, & Fish, 2004; Fowers & Davidov, 2006):

- Adapt traditional theories and techniques to meet the needs of clients from non-European ethnic or racial groups
- Be aware of his or her own cultural values and biases
- Establish rapport with a person from a different cultural background
- Be open to cultural differences without resorting to stereotypes

- Treat members of racial or ethnic communities as individuals
- Be aware of a client's ethnic identity and degree of acculturation to the majority society
- Use existing helping resources within a cultural group to support efforts to resolve problems

Cultural awareness has helped broaden our ideas about mental health and optimal development (Draguns, Gielen, & Fish, 2004). It is also worth remembering that cultural barriers apply to communication in all areas of life, not just therapy. Although such differences can be challenging, they are also frequently enriching (Uwe et al., 2006).

Gilles Mingasson/Getty Images

Teams of psychologists and counselors are often assembled to provide support to victims of major accidents and natural disasters. Because their work is stressful and often heart wrenching, relief workers also benefit from on-site counseling. Expressing emotions and talking about feelings are major elements of disaster counseling.

thus and so?" The person replies, "Yes, but . . ." and then tells you why your suggestion won't work. If you make a new suggestion the reply will once again be, "Yes, but . . ." Obviously, the person either knows more about his or her personal situation than you do or he or she has reasons for avoiding your advice. The student described earlier knows he needs to study. His problem is to understand why he doesn't *want* to study.

Accept the Person's Frame of Reference

W. I. Thomas said, "Things perceived as real are real in their effects." Try to resist imposing your views on the problems of others. Because we all live in different psychological worlds, there is no "correct" view of a life situation. A person who feels that his or her viewpoint has been understood feels freer to examine it objectively and to question it. Understanding another person's perspective is especially important when cultural differences may create a barrier between a client and therapist (Draguns, Gielen, & Fish, 2004). (See "Therapy and Culture—A Bad Case of 'Ifufunyane.'")

Maintain Confidentiality

Your efforts to help will be wasted if you fail to respect the privacy of someone who has confided in you. Put yourself in the person's place. Don't gossip.

These guidelines are not an invitation to play "junior therapist." Professional therapists are trained to approach serious problems with skills far exceeding those described here. However, the points made help define the qualities of a therapeutic relationship. They also emphasize that each of us can supply two of the greatest mental health resources available at any cost: friendship and honest communication.

Culturally skilled therapist A therapist who has the awareness, knowledge, and skills necessary to treat clients from diverse cultural backgrounds.

Medical Therapies—Psychiatric Care

Gateway Question: How do psychiatrists treat psychological disorders?

Psychotherapy may be applied to anything from a brief crisis to a full-scale psychosis. However, most psychotherapists *do not* treat patients with major depressive disorders, schizophrenia, or other severe conditions. Major mental disorders are more often treated medically (Julien, 2004).

Three main types of **somatic** (bodily) **therapy** are *pharmacotherapy, electrical stimulation therapy,* and *psychosurgery.* Somatic therapy is often done in the context of psychiatric hospitalization. All the somatic approaches have a strong medical slant, and they are typically administered by psychiatrists.

Drug Therapies

The atmosphere in psychiatric wards and mental hospitals changed radically in the mid-1950s with the widespread adoption of **pharmacotherapy** (FAR-meh-koe-THER-eh-pea), the use of drugs to treat psychopathology. Drugs may relieve the anxiety attacks and other discomforts of milder psychological disorders. More often, however, they are used to combat schizophrenia and major mood disorders.

What sort of drugs are used in pharmacotherapy? Three major types of drugs are used. All achieve their effects by influencing the activity of different brain neurotransmitters. **Anxiolytics** (such as Valium) produce relaxation or reduce anxiety. **Antidepressants** are mood-elevating drugs that combat depression. **Antipsychotics** (also called **major tranquilizers**) have tranquilizing effects and, in addition, reduce hallucinations and delusions. (See ● Table 15.4 for examples of each class of drugs.)

Are drugs a valid approach to treatment? Drugs have shortened hospital stays, and they have greatly improved the chances that people will recover from major psychological disorders. Drug therapy has also made it possible for many people to return to the community, where they can be treated on an outpatient basis.

Limitations of Drug Therapy

Although few experts would argue for a return to the conditions that existed before pharmacotherapy became available, all drugs involve a trade-off between benefits and risks. For example, 15 percent of patients taking major tranquilizers for long periods develop a neurological disorder that causes rhythmic facial and mouth movements (Chakos et al., 1996). Similarly, the drug clo-

Rodger Casier

The work of artist Rodger Casier illustrates the value of psychiatric care. Despite having a form of schizophrenia, Casier produces artwork that has received public acclaim and has been featured in professional journals.

zapine (Clozaril) can relieve the symptoms of schizophrenia in some previously "hopeless" cases. But Clozaril is also dangerous: 2 out of 100 patients taking the drug suffer from a potentially fatal blood disease (Ginsberg, 2006).

Is the risk worth it? Many experts think it is, because chronic schizophrenia robs people of almost everything that makes life worth living. It's possible, of course, that newer drugs will improve the risk/benefit ratio in the treatment of severe problems like schizophrenia. For example, the drug risperidone (Risperdal) appears to be as effective as Clozaril, without the same degree of lethal risk. But even the best new drugs are not cure-alls. They help some people and relieve some problems, but not all. It is noteworthy that for serious mental disorders a combination of medication and psychotherapy almost always works better than drugs

Table 15.4 ● Commonly Prescribed Psychiatric Drugs

Class	Examples (Trade Names)	Effects
Antiolytics (minor tranquilizers)	Ativan, Halcion, Librium, Restoril, Valium, Xanax (antianxiety drugs)	Reduce anxiety, tension, fear
Antidepressants	Anafranil, Elavil, Nardil, Norpramin, Parnate, Paxil, Prozac, Tofranil, Zoloft	Counteract depression
Antipsychotics (major tranquilizers)	Clozaril, Haldol, Mellaril, Navane, Risperdal, Thorazine	Reduce agitation, delusions, hallucinations, thought disorders

alone (Manber et al., 2008). Nevertheless, where schizophrenia and major mood disorders are concerned, drugs will undoubtedly remain the primary mode of treatment (Vasa, Carlino, & Pine, 2006; Walker et al., 2004).

Electrical Stimulation Therapy

In contrast to drug therapies, electrical stimulation therapies achieve their effects by altering the electrical activity of the brain. Electroconvulsive therapy is the first, and most dramatic, of these therapies. Widely used since the 1940s, it remains controversial to this day (Hirshbein & Sarvananda, 2008).

Electroshock

In **electroconvulsive therapy (ECT)** a 150-volt electrical current is passed through the brain for slightly less than a second. This rather drastic medical treatment for depression triggers a convulsion and causes the patient to lose consciousness for a short time. Muscle relaxants and sedative drugs are given before ECT to soften its impact. Treatments are given in a series of six to eight sessions spread over 3 to 4 weeks.

How does shock help? Actually, it is the seizure activity that is believed to be helpful. Proponents of ECT claim that shock-induced seizures alter (reboot?) the biochemical and hormonal balance in the brain and body, bringing an end to severe depression and suicidal behavior (Fink, 2000), as well as improving long-term quality of life (McCall et al., 2006). Others have charged that ECT works only by confusing patients so they can't remember why they were depressed.

Not all professionals support the use of ECT. However, most experts seem to agree on the following: (1) At best, ECT produces only temporary improvement—it gets the patient out of a bad spot, but it must be combined with other treatments; (2) ECT can cause memory losses in some patients; (3) ECT should be used only after other treatments have failed; and (4) to lower the chance of a relapse, ECT should be followed by antidepressant drugs (Sackeim et al., 2001). All told, ECT is considered by many to be a valid treatment for selected cases of depression—especially when it rapidly ends wildly self-destructive or suicidal behavior (Pagnin et al., 2004). It's interesting to note that most ECT patients feel that the treatment helped them. Most, in fact, would have it done again (Bernstein et al., 1998).

Implanted Electrodes

Unlike ECT, implanting electrodes requires surgery but allows for electrical stimulation of targeted brain regions. In one study, depressed patients who hadn't benefited from drug therapy and ECT improved when a specific brain region was stimulated (Mayberg et al., 2005). Stimulating pleasure centers in the brains of another group of patients also relieved depression (Schlaepfer et al., 2008). Unlike ECT, implanted electrodes can be used to treat disorders other than depression, such as obsessive-compulsive disorder (Nuttin et al., 1999).

> **bridges**
> Electrical stimulation of the brain is one of several methods used to investigate the brain's inner workings. **For more information, see Chapter 2, pages 56–59.**

Psychosurgery

Psychosurgery (any surgical alteration of the brain) is the most extreme medical treatment. The oldest and most radical psychosurgery is the lobotomy. In *prefrontal lobotomy* the frontal lobes are surgically disconnected from other brain areas. This procedure was supposed to calm persons who didn't respond to any other type of treatment.

When the lobotomy was first introduced in the 1940s, there were enthusiastic claims for its success. But later studies suggested that some patients were calmed, some showed no change, and

Will & Deni McIntyre/Photo Researchers, Inc.

In electroconvulsive therapy, electrodes are attached to the head and a brief electrical current is passed through the brain. ECT is used in the treatment of severe depression.

Somatic therapy Any bodily therapy, such as drug therapy, electroconvulsive therapy, or psychosurgery.

Pharmacotherapy The use of drugs to treat psychopathology.

Anxiolytics Drugs (such as Valium) that produce relaxation or reduce anxiety.

Antidepressants Mood-elevating drugs.

Antipsychotics Drugs that, in addition to having tranquilizing effects, also tend to reduce hallucinations and delusional thinking. (Also called **major tranquilizers.**)

Electroconvulsive therapy (ECT) A treatment for severe depression, consisting of an electric shock passed directly through the brain, which induces a convulsion.

Psychosurgery Any surgical alteration of the brain designed to bring about desirable behavioral or emotional changes.

some became mental "vegetables." Lobotomies also produced a high rate of undesirable side effects, such as seizures, blunted emotions, major personality changes, and stupor. At about the same time that such problems became apparent, the first antipsychotic drugs became available. Soon after, the lobotomy was abandoned (Mashour, Walker, & Martuza, 2005).

To what extent is psychosurgery used now? Psychosurgery is still considered valid by many neurosurgeons. However, most now use *deep lesioning,* in which small target areas are destroyed in the brain's interior. The appeal of deep lesioning is that it can have value as a remedy for some very specific disorders (Mashour, Walker, & Martuza, 2005). For instance, patients suffering from a severe type of obsessive-compulsive disorder may be helped by psychosurgery (Dougherty et al., 2002).

> **bridges**
>
> Deep lesioning is another method used to study the brain. **See Chapter 2, page 58.**

Depending on the quality of the institution, hospitalization may be a refuge or a brutalizing experience. Many state "asylums" or mental hospitals are antiquated and in need of drastic improvement.

It is worth remembering that psychosurgery cannot be reversed. Whereas a drug can be given or taken away and electrical stimulation can be turned off, you can't take back psychosurgery. Critics argue that psychosurgery should be banned altogether; others continue to report success with brain surgery. All things considered, it is perhaps most accurate, even after decades of use, to describe psychosurgery as an experimental technique. Nevertheless, it may have value as a remedy for some very specific disorders (Fenton, 1998; Mashour, Walker, & Martuza, 2005).

Hospitalization

Mental hospitalization for major mental disorders involves placing a person in a protected setting where medical therapy is provided. Hospitalization, by itself, can be a form of treatment. Staying in a hospital takes patients out of situations that may be sustaining their problems. For example, people with drug addictions may find it nearly impossible to resist the temptations for drug abuse in their daily lives. Hospitalization can help them make a clean break from their self-destructive behavior patterns (André et al., 2003).

At their best, hospitals are sanctuaries that provide diagnosis, support, refuge, and therapy. This is frequently true of psychiatric units in general hospitals and private psychiatric hospitals. At worst, confinement to an institution can be a brutal experience that leaves people less prepared to face the world than when they arrived. This is more often the case in large state mental hospitals (Gorman, 1996).

In most instances, hospitals are best used as a last resort, after other forms of treatment within the community have been exhausted. Actually, most psychiatric patients do as well with short-term hospitalization as they do with longer periods. For this

reason, the average stay in psychiatric hospitals is now just 20 days, rather than 3 to 4 months, as it was 20 years ago.

Another trend in treatment is **partial hospitalization.** In this approach, some patients spend their days in the hospital, but go home at night. Others attend therapy sessions during the evening. A major advantage of partial hospitalization is that patients can go home and practice what they've been learning. Eventually, most return to normal life. Overall, partial hospitalization can be just as effective as full hospitalization (Kiser, Heston, & Paavola, 2006).

Deinstitutionalization

In the last 50 years the population in large mental hospitals has dropped by two thirds. This is largely a result of **deinstitutionalization,** or reduced use of full-time commitment to mental institutions. Long-term "institutionalization" can lead to dependency, isolation, and continued emotional disturbance (Chamberlin & Rogers, 1990). Deinstitutionalization was meant to remedy this problem

How successful has deinstitutionalization been? In truth, its success has been limited (Talbott, 2004). Many states reduced mental hospital populations primarily as a way to save money. The upsetting result is that many chronic patients have been discharged to hostile communities without adequate care. Many former patients have joined the ranks of the homeless. Others are repeatedly jailed for minor crimes. Sadly, patients who trade hospitalization for unemployment, homelessness, and social isolation all too often end up rehospitalized or in jail (Goldman, 1998).

Large mental hospitals may no longer be warehouses for society's unwanted, but many former patients are no better off in bleak nursing homes, single-room hotels, board-and-care homes, shelters, or jails. One in five of the 2 million Americans who are in jail

A well-run halfway house can be a humane and cost-effective way to ease former mental patients back into the community (Soyez & Broekaert, 2003).

or prison are mentally ill—three times the number who are in mental hospitals (Human Rights Watch, 2003). These figures suggest that jails are replacing mental hospitals as our society's "solution" for mental illness. Yet, ironically, high-quality care is available in almost every community. As much as anything, a simple lack of money prevents large numbers of people from getting the help they need (Torrey, 1996).

Halfway houses may be a better way to ease a patient's return to the community (Soyez & Broekaert, 2003). **Halfway houses** are short-term group living facilities for people making the transition from an institution (mental hospital, prison, and so forth) to independent living. Typically, they offer supervision and support, without being as restricted and medically oriented as hospitals. They also keep people near their families. Most important, halfway houses can reduce a person's chances of being readmitted to a hospital (Coursey, Ward-Alexander, & Katz, 1990).

Community Mental Health Programs

Community mental health centers are a bright spot in the area of mental health care. **Community mental health centers** offer a wide range of mental health services and psychiatric care. Such centers try to help people avoid hospitalization and find answers to mental health problems (Burns, 2004). Typically, they do this by providing short-term treatment, counseling, outpatient care, emergency services, and suicide prevention.

If it is like most, the primary aim of the mental health center in your community is to directly aid troubled citizens. Its second goal is likely to be *prevention*. Consultation, education, and **crisis intervention** (skilled management of a psychological emergency) are used to prevent problems before they become serious. Also, some centers attempt to raise the general level of mental health in a community by combating unemployment, delinquency, and drug abuse (Tausig, Michello, & Subedi, 2004).

Have community mental health centers succeeded in meeting their goals? In practice, they have concentrated much more on providing clinical services than they have on preventing problems. This

appears to be primarily the result of wavering government support (translation: money). Overall, community mental health centers have succeeded in making psychological services more accessible than ever before. Many of their programs rely on **paraprofessionals** (individuals who work in a near-professional capacity under the supervision of more highly trained staff). Some paraprofessionals are ex-addicts, ex-alcoholics, or ex-patients who have "been there." Many more are persons (paid or volunteer) who have skills in tutoring, crafts, or counseling or who are simply warm, understanding, and skilled at communication. Often, paraprofessionals are more approachable than "doctors." This encourages people to seek mental health services that they might otherwise be reluctant to use (Everly, 2002).

A Look Ahead

In the Psychology in Action section that follows we will return briefly to behavioral approaches. There you will find a number of useful techniques that you may be able to apply to your own behavior. You'll also find a discussion of when to seek professional help and how to find it. Here's your authors' professional advice: This is information you won't want to skip.

KNOWLEDGE BUILDER
Group Therapy, Helping Skills, and Medical Therapies

RECITE
1. In psychodrama, people attempt to form meaningful wholes out of disjointed thoughts, feelings, and actions. T or F?
2. Most large-group awareness trainings make use of Gestalt therapy. T or F?
3. The mirror technique is frequently used in
   a. exposure therapy
   b. psychodrama
   c. family therapy
   d. ECT

Continued

Mental hospitalization Placing a person in a protected, therapeutic environment staffed by mental health professionals.

Partial hospitalization An approach in which patients receive treatment at a hospital during the day but return home at night.

Deinstitutionalization Reduced use of full-time commitment to mental institutions to treat mental disorders.

Halfway house A community-based facility for individuals making the transition from an institution (mental hospital, prison, and so forth) to independent living.

Community mental health center A facility offering a wide range of mental health services, such as prevention, counseling, consultation, and crisis intervention.

Crisis intervention Skilled management of a psychological emergency.

Paraprofessional An individual who works in a near-professional capacity under the supervision of a more highly trained person.

4. Research shows that about half of all patients feel better after their first _____ therapy sessions.
   a. 8
   b. 16
   c. 24
   d. 26
5. Emotional rapport, warmth, understanding, acceptance, and empathy are the core of
   a. the therapeutic alliance
   b. large-group awareness training
   c. role reversals
   d. action therapy
6. Culturally skilled therapists do all but one of the following; which does *not* apply?
   a. Are aware of the client's degree of acculturation
   b. Use helping resources within the client's cultural group
   c. Adapt standard techniques to match cultural stereotypes
   d. Are aware of their own cultural values
7. ECT is a modern form of pharmacotherapy. T or F?
8. Currently, the frontal lobotomy is the most widely used form of psychosurgery. T or F?
9. Major tranquilizers are also known as
   a. anxiolytics
   b. antipsychotics
   c. antidepressants
   d. prefrontal sedatives
10. Deinstitutionalization is an advanced form of partial hospitalization. T or F?

REFLECT

Critical Thinking

11. In your opinion, do psychologists have a duty to protect others who may be harmed by their clients? For example, if a patient has homicidal fantasies about his ex-wife, should she be informed?
12. Residents of Berkeley, California, once voted on a referendum to ban the use of ECT within city limits. Do you think that the use of certain psychiatric treatments should be controlled by law?

Relate

Would you rather participate in individual therapy or group therapy? What advantages and disadvantages do you think each has?

Based on your own experience, how valid do you think it is to say that within families "a problem for one is a problem for all"?

What lies at the "heart" of psychotherapy? How would you describe it to a friend?

Which of the basic counseling skills do you already use? Which would improve your ability to help a person in distress?

If a family member of yours became severely depressed, what therapies would be available to him or her? What are the pros and cons of each choice?

Answers: 1. F **2.** b **3.** b **4.** a **5.** a **6.** c **7.** F **8.** F **9.** b **10.** F **11.** According to the law, there is a duty to protect others when a therapist could, with little effort, prevent serious harm. However, this duty can conflict with a client's rights to confidentiality and with client–therapist trust. Therapists often must make difficult choices in such situations. **12.** The question of who can prescribe drugs, perform surgery, and administer ECT is controlled by law. However, psychiatrists strongly object to residents, city councils, or government agencies making *medical* decisions.

PSYCHOLOGY IN ACTION

Self-Management and Finding Professional Help

Gateway Questions: How are behavioral principles applied to everyday problems? How could a person find professional help?

Behavior therapy is not a cure-all. Its use is often quite complicated and requires a great deal of expertise. Still, behavior therapy offers a straightforward solution to many problems.

Covert Reward and Punishment—Boosting Your "Willpower"

As mentioned elsewhere in this book, you should seek professional help when a significant problem exists. For lesser difficulties you may want to try applying behavioral principles yourself (Watson & Tharp, 2007). Let us see how this might be done:

Therapist: "Have you ever decided to quit smoking cigarettes, watching television too much, eating too much, drinking too much, or driving too fast?"

Client: "Well, one of those applies. I have decided several times to quit smoking."

Therapist: "When have you decided?"

Client: "Usually after I am reminded of how dangerous smoking is—like when I heard that my uncle had died of lung cancer. He smoked constantly."

Therapist: "If you have decided to quit 'several times,' I assume you haven't succeeded."

Client: "No, the usual pattern is for me to become upset about smoking and then to cut down for a day or two."

Therapist: "You forget the disturbing image of your uncle's death, or whatever, and start smoking again."

Client: "Yes. I suppose if I had an uncle die every day or so, I might actually quit!"

The use of intensive behavioral principles, such as electric shock, to condition an aversion seems remote from everyday problems. Even naturally aversive actions are difficult to apply to personal behavior. As mentioned earlier, for instance, rapid smoking is difficult for most smokers to carry out on their own. And what about a problem like overeating? It would be difficult indeed to eat enough to create a lasting aversion to over-

Sheila Terry/Photo Researchers, Inc.

eating. (Although it's sometimes tempting to try.)

In view of such limitations, psychologists have developed an alternative procedure that can be used to curb smoking, overeating, and other habits (Cautela & Kearney, 1986; Watson & Tharp, 2007).

Covert Sensitization

In **covert sensitization,** aversive imagery is used to reduce the occurrence of an undesired response. Here's how it's done: Obtain six 3-by-5 cards and on each write a brief description of a scene related to the habit you wish to control. The scene should be so *disturbing* or *disgusting* that thinking about it would temporarily make you very uncomfortable about indulging in the habit. For smoking, the cards might read:

- "I am in a doctor's office. The doctor looks at some reports and tells me I have lung cancer. She says a lung will have to be removed and schedules the operation for next week."
- "I am in bed under an oxygen tent. My chest feels caved in. There is a tube in my throat. I can barely breathe."
- "I wake up in the morning and smoke a cigarette. I begin coughing up blood."
- "My lover won't even kiss me because my breath smells bad."

Other cards would continue along the same line.

For overeating the cards might read like this:

- I am at the beach. I get up to go for a swim and I overhear people whispering to each other, "Isn't that fat disgusting?"
- I am at a store buying clothes. I try on several things that are too small. The only things that fit look like rumpled sacks. Salespeople are staring at me.
- I can't fit into my seat at the movies.

The trick is to get yourself to imagine or picture vividly each of these disturbing scenes *several times* a day. Imagining the scenes can be accomplished by placing them under *stimulus control.* Simply choose something you do *frequently* each day (such as getting a cup of coffee or getting up from your chair). Next make a rule: Before you can get a cup of coffee or get up from your chair, or whatever you have selected as a cue, you must take out your cards and *vividly picture* yourself engaging in the action you wish to curb (eating or smok-

ing, for example). Then *vividly picture* the scene described on the top card. Imagine the scene for 30 seconds.

After visualizing the top card, move it to the bottom so the cards are rotated. Make up new cards each week. The scenes can be made much more upsetting than the samples given here, which are toned down to keep you from being "grossed out."

Covert sensitization can also be used directly in situations that test your self-control. If you are trying to lose weight, for instance, you might be able to turn down a tempting dessert in this way: As you look at the dessert, visualize maggots crawling all over it. If you make this image as vivid and nauseating as possible, losing your appetite is almost a certainty. If you want to apply this technique to other situations, be aware that vomiting scenes are especially effective. Covert sensitization may sound as if you are "playing games with yourself," but it can be a great help if you want to cut down on a bad habit (Cautela & Kearney, 1986). Try it!

Thought Stopping

As discussed earlier, behavior therapists accept that thoughts, like visible responses, can also cause trouble. Think of times when you have repeatedly "put yourself down" mentally or when you have been preoccupied by needless worries, fears, or other negative and upsetting thoughts. If you would like to gain control over such thoughts, thought stopping may help you do it.

In **thought stopping,** aversive stimuli are used to interrupt or prevent upsetting thoughts. The simplest thought-stopping technique makes use of mild punishment to suppress upsetting mental images and internal "talk." Simply place a large, flat rubber band around your wrist. As you go through the day apply this rule: Each time you catch yourself thinking the upsetting image or thought, pull the rubber band away from your wrist and snap it. You need not make this terribly painful. Its value lies in drawing your attention to how often you form negative thoughts and in interrupting the flow of thoughts.

A second thought-stopping procedure requires only that you interrupt upsetting thoughts each time they occur. Begin by setting aside time each day during which you will deliberately think the unwanted thought. As you begin to form the thought, shout "Stop!" aloud, with conviction. (Obviously,

you should choose a private spot for this part of the procedure!)

Repeat the thought-stopping procedure 10 to 20 times for the first 2 or 3 days. Then switch to shouting "Stop!" covertly (to yourself) rather than aloud. Thereafter, thought stopping can be carried out throughout the day, whenever upsetting thoughts occur (Williams & Long, 1991). After several days of practice, you should be able to stop unwanted thoughts whenever they occur.

Covert Reinforcement

Earlier we discussed how punishing images can be used to decrease undesirable responses, such as smoking or overeating. Many people also find it helpful to covertly *reinforce* desired actions. **Covert reinforcement** is the use of positive imagery to reinforce desired behavior. For example, suppose your target behavior is, once again, not eating dessert. If this were the case, you could do the following (Cautela & Kearney, 1986; Watson & Tharp, 2007):

> Imagine that you are standing at the dessert table with your friends. As dessert is passed, you politely refuse and feel good about staying on your diet.

These images would then be followed by imagining a pleasant, reinforcing scene:

> Imagine that you are your ideal weight. You look really slim in your favorite color and style. Someone you really like says to you, "Gee, you've lost weight. I've never seen you look so good."

For many people, of course, actual direct reinforcement (as described in the Psychology in Action section of Chapter 7, pages 247–248) is the best way to alter behavior. Nevertheless, covert or "visualized" reinforcement can have similar effects. To make use of covert reinforcement, choose one or more target behaviors and rehearse them mentally. Then

Covert sensitization Use of aversive imagery to reduce the occurrence of an undesired response.

Thought stopping Use of aversive stimuli to interrupt or prevent upsetting thoughts.

Covert reinforcement Using positive imagery to reinforce desired behavior.

follow each rehearsal with a vivid, rewarding image.

Self-Directed Desensitization — Overcoming Common Fears

You have prepared for 2 weeks to give a speech in a large class. As your turn approaches, your hands begin to tremble. Your heart pounds, and you find it difficult to breathe. You say to your body, "Relax!" What happens? Nothing! That's why the first step in desensitization is learning to relax voluntarily, by using the tension-release method described earlier in this chapter. As an alternative, you might want to try imagining a very safe, pleasant, and relaxing scene. Some people find such images as relaxing as the tension-release method (Rosenthal, 1993). Another helpful technique is to do some deep breathing. Typically, a person who is breathing deeply is relaxed. Shallow breathing involves little movement of the diaphragm. If you place your hand on your abdomen, it will move up and down if you are breathing deeply.

Once you have learned to relax, the next step is to identify the fear you would like to control and construct a hierarchy.

Procedure for Constructing a Hierarchy

Make a list of situations (related to the fear) that make you anxious. Try to list at least 10 situations. Some should be very frightening and others only mildly frightening. Write a short description of each situation on a separate 3-by-5 card. Place the cards in order from the least disturbing situation to the most disturbing. Here is a sample hierarchy for a student afraid of public speaking:

1. Being given an assignment to speak in class
2. Thinking about the topic and the date the speech must be given
3. Writing the speech; thinking about delivering the speech
4. Watching other students speak in class the week before the speech date
5. Rehearsing the speech alone; pretending to give it to the class
6. Delivering the speech to my roommate; pretending my roommate is the teacher
7. Reviewing the speech on the day it is to be presented
8. Entering the classroom; waiting and thinking about the speech
9. Being called; standing up; facing the audience
10. Delivering the speech

Using the Hierarchy

When you have mastered the relaxation exercises and have the hierarchy constructed, set aside time each day to work on reducing your fear. Begin by performing the relaxation exercises. When you are completely relaxed, visualize the scene on the first card (the least frightening scene). If you can *vividly* picture and imagine yourself in the first situation twice *without a noticeable increase in muscle tension,* proceed to the next card. Also, as you progress, relax yourself between cards.

Each day, stop when you reach a card that you cannot visualize without becoming tense in three attempts. Each day, begin one or two cards before the one on which you stopped the previous day. Continue to work with the cards until you can visualize the last situation without experiencing tension (techniques are based on Wolpe, 1974).

By using this approach you should be able to reduce the fear or anxiety associated with things such as public speaking, entering darkened rooms, asking questions in large classes, heights, talking to members of the opposite sex, and taking tests (Watson & Tharp, 2007). Even if you are not always able to reduce a fear, you will have learned to place relaxation under voluntary control. This alone is valuable because controlling unnecessary tension can increase energy and efficiency.

Seeking Professional Help — When, Where, and How?

Chances are good that at some point you or someone in your family will benefit from mental health services of one kind or another. In one survey, half of all American households included someone who received mental health treatment during the preceding year (Chamberlin, 2004).

How would I know if I should seek professional help at some point in my life? Although there is no simple answer to this question, the following guidelines may be helpful:

1. If your level of psychological discomfort (unhappiness, anxiety, or depression, for example) is comparable to a level of physical discomfort that would cause you to see a doctor or dentist, you should consider seeing a psychologist or a psychiatrist.
2. Another signal to watch for is significant changes in behavior, such as the quality of your work (or schoolwork), your rate of absenteeism, your use of drugs (including alcohol), or your relationships with others.
3. Perhaps you have urged a friend or relative to seek professional help and were dismayed because he or she refused to do so. If *you* find friends or relatives making a similar suggestion, recognize that they may be seeing things more clearly than you are.
4. If you have persistent or disturbing suicidal thoughts or impulses, you should seek help immediately.

Locating a Therapist

If I wanted to talk to a therapist, how would I find one? Here are some suggestions that could help you get started:

1. **Colleges and universities.** If you are a student, don't overlook counseling services offered by a student health center or special student counseling facilities.
2. **Workplaces.** If you have a job, check with your employer. Some employers have employee assistance programs that offer confidential free or low-cost therapy for employees.
3. **The Yellow Pages.** Psychologists are listed in the telephone book or on the Internet under "Psychologist," or in some cases under "Counseling Services." Psychiatrists are generally listed as a subheading under "Physicians." Counselors are usually found under the heading "Marriage and Family Counselors." These listings will usually put you in touch with individuals in private practice.
4. **Community or county mental health centers.** Most counties and many cities offer public mental health services. (These are listed in the phone book.) Public mental health centers usually provide counseling and therapy services directly, and they can refer you to private therapists.
5. **Mental health associations.** Many cities

have mental health associations organized by concerned citizens. Groups such as these usually keep listings of qualified therapists and other services and programs in the community.

6. **Newspaper and online advertisements.** Some psychologists advertise their services in newspapers and/or online. Also, low-cost "outreach" clinics often try to make their presence known to the public by advertising. In either case, you should carefully inquire into a therapist's training and qualifications. Without the benefit of a referral from a trusted person, it is wise to be cautious.

7. **Crisis hotlines.** The typical crisis hotline is a telephone service staffed by community volunteers. These people are trained to provide information concerning a wide range of mental health problems. They also have lists of organizations, services, and other resources in the community where you can go for help.

● Table 15.5 summarizes all the sources for psychotherapy, counseling, and referrals we have discussed, as well as some additional possibilities.

Options *How would I know what kind of a therapist to see? How would I pick one?* The choice between a psychiatrist and a psychologist is somewhat arbitrary. Both are trained to do psy-

Table 15.5 ● Mental Health Resources

- Family doctors (for referrals to mental health professionals)
- Mental health specialists, such as psychiatrists, psychologists, social workers, or mental health counselors
- Religious leaders/counselors
- Health maintenance organizations (HMOs)
- Community mental health centers
- Hospital psychiatry departments and outpatient clinics
- University– or medical school–affiliated programs
- State hospital outpatient clinics
- Social service agencies
- Private clinics and facilities
- Employee assistance programs
- Local medical and/or psychiatric societies

NIMH, 2005.

chotherapy and can be equally effective as therapists (Seligman, 1995). Although a psychiatrist can administer somatic therapy and prescribe drugs, so can psychologists in New Mexico and Louisiana (Munsey, 2006). Besides, a psychologist can work in conjunction with a physician if such services are needed.

Fees for psychiatrists are usually higher, averaging about $160 to $200 an hour. Psychologists average about $100 an hour. Counselors and social workers typically charge about $80 per hour. Group therapy averages only about $40 an hour because the therapist's fee is divided among several people.

Be aware that most health insurance plans will pay for psychological services. If fees are a problem, keep in mind that many therapists charge on a sliding scale, or ability-to-pay basis, and that community mental health centers almost always charge on a sliding scale. In one way or another, help is almost always available for anyone who needs it.

Some communities and college campuses have counseling services staffed by sympathetic paraprofessionals or peer counselors. These services are free or very low cost. As mentioned earlier, paraprofessionals are people who work in a near-professional capacity under professional supervision. **Peer counselors** are nonprofessional persons who have learned basic counseling skills. There is a natural tendency, perhaps, to doubt the abilities of paraprofessionals. However, many studies have shown that paraprofessional counselors are often as effective as professionals (Christensen & Jacobson, 1994).

Also, don't overlook self-help groups, which can add valuable support to professional treatment. Members of a self-help group typically share a particular type of problem, such as eating disorders or coping with an alcoholic parent. **Self-help groups** offer members mutual support and a chance to discuss problems. In many instances helping others also serves as therapy for those who give help (Burlingame & Davies, 2002). For some problems, self-help groups may be the best choice of all (Fobair, 1997; Galanter et al., 2005).

Qualifications You can usually find out about a therapist's qualifications simply by asking. A reputable therapist will be glad to reveal his or her background. If you have any doubts, credentials may be checked and other help-

ful information can be obtained from local branches of any of the following organizations. You can also browse the websites listed here:

> American Association for Marriage and Family Therapy (www.aamft.org)
> American Family Therapy Association (www.afta.org)
> American Psychiatric Association (www.psych.org)
> American Psychological Association (www.apa.org)
> Association of Humanistic Psychology (www.ahpweb.org)
> Canadian Psychiatric Association (www.cpa-apc.org)
> Canadian Psychological Association (www.cpa.ca)
> National Mental Health Association (www.nmha.org)

The question of how to pick a particular therapist remains. The best way is to start with a short consultation with a respected psychiatrist, psychologist, or counselor. This will allow the person you consult to evaluate your difficulty and recommend a type of therapy or a therapist who is likely to be helpful. As an alternative you might ask the person teaching this course for a referral.

Evaluating a Therapist *How would I know whether or not to quit or ignore a therapist?* A balanced look at psychotherapies suggests that all techniques can be successful (Wampold et al., 1997). However, all *therapists* are not equally successful. Far more important than the approach used are the therapist's personal qualities (Okiishi et al., 2003; Prochaska & Norcross, 2007). The most consistently successful therapists are those who are willing to use whatever method seems most helpful for a client. They are also marked by personal characteristics of warmth, integrity, sincerity, and empathy. Former clients consistently rate the person doing the therapy as more important than the type of therapy used (Elliott & Williams, 2003).

Peer counselor A nonprofessional person who has learned basic counseling skills.

Self-help group A group of people who share a particular type of problem and provide mutual support to one another.

It is perhaps most accurate to say that at this stage of development, psychotherapy is an art, not a science. The *relationship* between a client and therapist is the therapist's most basic tool (Hubble, Duncan, & Miller, 1999; Prochaska & Norcross, 2007). This is why you must trust and easily relate to a therapist for therapy to be effective. Here are some danger signals to watch for in psychotherapy:

- Sexual advances by therapist
- Therapist makes repeated verbal threats or is physically aggressive
- Therapist is excessively blaming, belittling, hostile, or controlling
- Therapist makes excessive small talk; talks repeatedly about his or her own problems

- Therapist encourages prolonged dependence on him or her
- Therapist demands absolute trust or tells client not to discuss therapy with anyone else

Clients who like their therapist are generally more successful in therapy (Talley, Strupp, & Morey, 1990). An especially important part of the therapeutic alliance is agreement about the goals of therapy (Meier et al., 2006). It is therefore a good idea to think about what you would like to accomplish by entering therapy. Write down your goals and discuss them with your therapist during the first session. Your first meeting with a therapist should also answer all the following questions (Somberg, Stone, & Claiborn, 1993):

- Will the information I reveal in therapy remain completely confidential?
- What risks do I face if I begin therapy?
- How long do you expect treatment to last?
- What form of treatment do you expect to use?
- Are there alternatives to therapy that might help me as much or more?

It's always tempting to avoid facing up to personal problems. With this in mind, you should give a therapist a fair chance and not give up too easily. But don't hesitate to change therapists or to terminate therapy if you lose confidence in the therapist or if you don't relate well to the therapist as a person.

KNOWLEDGE BUILDER
Self-Management and Finding Professional Help

RECITE

1. Covert sensitization and thought stopping combine aversion therapy and cognitive therapy. T or F?
2. Like covert aversion conditioning, covert reinforcement of desired responses is also possible. T or F?
3. The tension-release method is an important part of
   a. covert reinforcement
   b. thought stopping
   c. desensitization
   d. REBT
4. Items in a desensitization hierarchy should be placed in order from the least disturbing to the most disturbing. T or F?
5. The first step in desensitization is to place the visualization of disturbing images under stimulus control. T or F?
6. Persistent emotional discomfort is a clear sign that professional psychological counseling should be sought. T or F?
7. Community mental health centers rarely offer counseling or therapy themselves; they only do referrals. T or F?
8. In many instances, a therapist's personal qualities have more of an effect on the outcome of therapy than does the type of therapy used. T or F?

REFLECT

Critical Thinking

9. Would it be acceptable for a therapist to urge a client to break all ties with a troublesome family member?

Relate

How could you use covert sensitization, thought stopping, and covert reinforcement to change your behavior? Try to apply each technique to a specific example.

Just for practice, make a fear hierarchy for a situation you find frightening. Does vividly picturing items in the hierarchy make you tense or anxious? If so, can you intentionally relax using the tension-release method?

Assume that you want to seek help from a psychologist or other mental health professional. How would you proceed? Take some time to actually find out what mental health services are available to you.

Answers: 1. T **2.** T **3.** c **4.** T **5.** F **6.** T **7.** F **8.** T **9.** Such decisions must be made by clients themselves. Therapists can help clients evaluate important decisions and feelings about significant persons in their lives. However, actively urging a client to sever a relationship borders on unethical behavior.

---

chapter in review   Gateways to Therapy

Psychotherapies may be classified as insight, action, directive, nondirective, or supportive therapies, and combinations of these.

- Psychotherapy facilitates positive changes in personality, behavior, or adjustment.
- Therapies may be conducted either individually or in groups, and they may be time limited.

Early approaches to mental illness were dominated by superstition and moral condemnation.

- Demonology attributed mental disturbance to supernatural forces, such as demonic possession, and prescribed exorcism as the cure.
- In some instances, the actual cause of bizarre behavior may have been ergot poisoning.

- More humane treatment began in 1793 with the work of Philippe Pinel in Paris.

Psychoanalysts have become relatively rare because psychoanalysis is expensive and time-intensive. However, as the first true psychotherapy, Freud's psychoanalysis gave rise to modern psychodynamic therapies.

- Psychoanalysis seeks to reveal unconscious thoughts, emotions, and conflicts.
- The psychoanalyst uses free association, dream analysis, and analysis of resistance and transference to reveal health-producing insights.
- Some critics argue that traditional psychoanalysis receives credit for spontaneous remissions of symptoms. However, psychoanalysis is successful for many patients.
- Brief psychodynamic therapy (which relies on psychoanalytic theory but is brief and focused) is as effective as other major therapies. One example is interpersonal psychotherapy.

The major humanistic therapies are client-centered (or person-centered) therapy, existential therapy, and gestalt therapy.

- Client-centered (or person-centered) therapy is nondirective, based on insights gained from conscious thoughts and feelings, and dedicated to creating an atmosphere of growth.
- Unconditional positive regard, empathy, authenticity, and reflection are combined to give the client a chance to solve his or her own problems.
- Existential therapies focus on the end result of the choices one makes in life. Clients are encouraged through confrontation and encounter to exercise free will and to take responsibility for their choices.
- Gestalt therapy emphasizes immediate awareness of thoughts and feelings. Its goal is to rebuild thinking, feeling, and acting into connected wholes and to help clients break through emotional blockages.

Therapy may be conducted through the media, the telephone, and the Internet.

- Media psychologists, telephone counselors, and cybertherapists may, on occasion, do some good. However, each has serious drawbacks, and the effectiveness of telephone counseling and cybertherapy has not been established.
- Therapy by videoconferencing shows more promise as a way to provide mental health services at a distance.

Behavior therapists use the learning principles of classical or operant conditioning to directly change human behavior.

- In aversion therapy, classical conditioning is used to associate maladaptive behavior (such as smoking or drinking) with pain or other aversive events in order to inhibit undesirable responses.
- In desensitization, gradual adaptation and reciprocal inhibition break the link between fear and particular situations.
- Typical steps in desensitization are: Construct a fear hierarchy, learn to produce total relaxation, and perform items on the hierarchy (from least to most disturbing).

- Desensitization may be carried out in real settings or it may be done by vividly imagining the fear hierarchy or by watching models perform the feared responses.
- In some cases, virtual reality exposure can be used to present fear stimuli in a controlled manner.
- A new technique called eye movement desensitization and reprocessing (EMDR) shows promise as a treatment for traumatic memories and stress disorders. At present, however, EMDR is highly controversial.

Operant principles, such as positive reinforcement, nonreinforcement, extinction, punishment, shaping, stimulus control, and time out, are used to extinguish undesirable responses and to promote constructive behavior.

- Nonreward can extinguish troublesome behaviors. Often this is done by simply identifying and eliminating reinforcers, particularly attention and social approval.
- To apply positive reinforcement and operant shaping, tokens are often used to reinforce selected target behaviors.
- Full-scale use of tokens in an institutional setting produces a token economy. Toward the end of a token economy program, patients are shifted to social rewards such as recognition and approval.

Cognitive therapy emphasizes changing thought patterns that underlie emotional or behavioral problems. Its goals are to correct distorted thinking and/or teach improved coping skills.

- Irrational beliefs are the core of many maladaptive thinking patterns. Changing such beliefs can have a positive impact on emotions and behavior.
- In a variation of cognitive therapy called rational-emotive behavior therapy (REBT), clients learn to recognize and challenge their own irrational beliefs.

Therapy can be done with groups of people based on a simple extension of individual methods or based on techniques developed specifically for groups.

- In psychodrama, individuals enact roles and incidents resembling their real-life problems. In family therapy, the family group is treated as a unit.
- Sensitivity and encounter groups encourage positive personality change. Large-group awareness training attempts to do the same, but the benefits of such programs are questionable.

Effective psychotherapies are based on the therapeutic alliance, a protected setting, catharsis, insights, new perspectives, and a chance to practice new behaviors.

- Psychotherapy is generally effective, although no single form of therapy is superior to others.
- All of the following are helping skills that can be learned: active listening, acceptance, reflection, open-ended questioning, support, respect, patience, genuineness, and paraphrasing.
- The culturally skilled counselor must be able to establish rapport with a person from a different cultural background and adapt traditional theories and techniques to meet the needs of clients from non-European ethnic groups.

Medical approaches to mental disorders, such as drugs, surgery, and hospitalization, are similar to medical treatments for physical ailments.

- All medical treatments for psychological disorders have pros and cons. Overall, however, their effectiveness is improving.
- Three medical, or somatic, approaches to treatment are pharmacotherapy, electrical stimulation therapy (including ECT), and psychosurgery.
- Community mental health centers seek to avoid or minimize mental hospitalization. They also seek to prevent mental health problems through education, consultation, and crisis intervention.

Some personal problems can be successfully treated with self-management techniques. Everyone should know how to obtain high-quality mental health care in his or her community.

- Cognitive techniques can be an aid to managing personal behavior.
- In covert sensitization, aversive images are used to discourage unwanted behavior.
- Thought stopping uses mild punishment to prevent upsetting thoughts.
- Covert reinforcement is a way to encourage desired responses by mental rehearsal.
- Desensitization pairs relaxation with a hierarchy of upsetting images in order to lessen fears.
- In most communities, a competent and reputable therapist can be located with public sources of information or through a referral.
- Practical considerations such as cost and qualifications enter into choosing a therapist. However, the therapist's personal characteristics are of equal importance.

Web Resources

For an up-to-date list of direct links to interesting sites, including those listed here, visit the student companion site for this book at www.cengage.com/psychology/coon

Pre-Columbian Trephination Read about the first psychosurgery as a treatment for mental illness.

Dr. Phil See for yourself how Dr. Phil publicizes mental health issues.

Aversion therapy Read more about aversion therapy.

Systematic Desensitization Explore this self-administered procedure.

American Self-Help Group Clearinghouse Explore this database of more than 1,000 self-help groups.

Lobotomy Read a case study of lobotomy and the history of the transorbital lobotomy procedure.

Finding a Therapist in Your Hometown Use the Internet to locate a local therapist.

Interactive Learning

Introduction to Psychology: Gateways to Mind and Behavior **Book Companion Website**
www.cengage.com/psychology/coon

Visit your book companion website, where you will find flash cards, practice quizzes, web links, and more to help you study.

CENGAGENOW™ *Just what you need to know NOW!*

Spend time on what you need to master rather than on information you already have learned. Take a pre-test for this chapter, and CengageNOW will generate a personalized study plan based on your results. The study plan will identify the topics you need to review and direct you to online resources to help you master those topics. You can then take a post-test to help you determine the concepts you have mastered and what you will need to work on. Try it out! Go to www.cengage.com/login to sign in with an access code or to purchase access to this product.

CHAPTER 16

Social Thinking and Social Influence

Gateway Theme

Humans are social animals. We live in a social world in which our thoughts, feelings, and behavior are profoundly influenced by the presence of others.

Paul Chesley/Getty Images

Gateway Questions

- *How does group membership affect individual behavior?*
- *How do we perceive the motives of others and the causes of our own behavior?*
- *What are attitudes? How are they acquired?*
- *Under what conditions is persuasion most effective? What is cognitive dissonance?*
- *What is social influence and social power?*
- *How does the mere presence of others affect behavior?*

- *What have social psychologists learned about conformity?*
- *What factors lead to increased compliance?*
- *Can people be too obedient?*
- *Is brainwashing actually possible? How are people converted to cult membership?*
- *How does self-assertion differ from aggression?*

"No man is an island, entire of itself."
—John Donne

Here's your assignment: You have been given a message and the name, address, and occupation of the person who should receive it. The "target person" lives somewhere else on earth. You can move the message by e-mail, but you may send it only to a first-name acquaintance. That person, in turn, must forward the message to a first-name acquaintance. The message is to be moved in this fashion until it reaches the target person, whom the previous person must know by name.

Sound impossible? Following up on the pioneering work of social psychologist Stanley Milgram (1967), sociologist Duncan Watts asked more than 60,000 senders to use this method to forward e-mails to 18 target recipients in 13 countries. Like Milgram before him, Watts found that the average number of intermediaries was six (Dodds, Muhamad, & Watts, 2003).

How is that possible? Each of us is part of a rich tapestry of social relationships. You probably know at least dozens of people by name. Each of them knows dozens more people, who each know still more people, and so on. Thus, each social relationship connects with many others. By following all the social links, you could reach millions of people just six "layers" out. With the recent explosion in popularity of social networking sites like Blogger, Facebook, Friendster, and MySpace, our social worlds will undoubtedly expand even more.

Our social networks strongly influence our behavior, which is probably why we spend so much time thinking about them. These topics have been the target of an immense amount of study—too much, in fact, for us to cover in detail. Therefore, this chapter is a social psychology "sampler." We will look some ways we think about social situations and the various ways in which we influence others. We hope that you will find the topics interesting and thought provoking.

◑ Humans in a Social Context—People, People, Everywhere

Gateway Question: How does group membership affect individual behavior?

Families, teams, crowds, tribes, companies, parties, troops, bands, sects, gangs, crews, clans, communities, and nations. Participation in various groups is a basic fact of social life. How do groups influence our behavior? Because you are a member of a group called "psychology class," it would be wise to find out.

Social psychology is the scientific study of how individuals behave, think, and feel in social situations (that is, in the presence, actual or implied, of others) (Baron, Byrne, & Branscombe, 2007). Every day, there is a fascinating interplay between our own behavior and that of people around us. We are born into an organized society. Established values, expectations, and behavior patterns are present when we arrive. So too is **culture,** an ongoing pattern of life that is passed from one generation to the next. To appreciate the impact of culture, think about how you have been affected by language, marriage customs, concepts of ownership, and sex roles.

Roles

We all belong to many overlapping social groups, and in each we occupy a *position* in the *structure* of the group. **Social roles** are patterns of behavior expected of persons in various social positions (Breckler, Olson, & Wiggins, 2006). For instance, playing the role of mother, boss, or student involves different sets of behaviors and expectations. Some roles are *ascribed* (they are assigned to a person or are not under personal control): male or female, son, adolescent, inmate. *Achieved roles* are voluntarily attained by special effort: spouse, teacher, scientist, bandleader, criminal.

What effect does role-playing have on behavior? Roles streamline daily interactions by allowing us to anticipate what others will do. When a person is acting as a doctor, mother, clerk, or police officer, we expect certain behaviors. However, roles have a negative side, too. Many people experience **role conflicts,** in which two or more roles make conflicting demands on them. Consider, for example, a teacher who must flunk a close friend's daughter; a

Roles have a powerful impact on social behavior. What kinds of behavior do you expect from your teachers? What behaviors do they expect from you? What happens if either of you fails to match the other's expectations?

mother who has a full-time job; and a soccer coach whose son is on the team but isn't a very good athlete. Likewise, the clashing demands of work, family, and school create role conflicts for many students (Hammer, Grigsby, & Woods, 1998; Senécal, Julien, & Guay, 2003). Role conflicts at work (such as being a good team player versus being a strong manager) lead to job burnout (Jawahar, Stone, & Kisamore, 2007) and negative health outcomes (Pomaki, Supeli, & Verhoeven, 2007).

Survivor and other "reality" television programs have offered an interesting, if voyeuristic, look at some of the best and worst aspects of human behavior. However, such programs have nothing over the most revealing experiments in social psychology. For example, a classic study done by Phil Zimbardo and his students at Stanford University showed dramatically how social settings influence our behavior.

In the study, normal healthy male college students were paid to serve as "inmates" and "guards" in a simulated prison (Zimbardo, Haney, & Banks, 1973). After just 2 days in "jail," the inmates grew restless and defiant. When they staged a disturbance, the guards unmercifully suppressed the rebellion. Over the next few days, the guards clamped down with increasing brutality. In a surprisingly short time, the fake convicts looked like real prisoners: They were dejected, traumatized, passive, and dehumanized. Four of them had to be released because they were crying, confused, or severely depressed. Each day, the guards tormented the prisoners with more commands, insults, and demeaning tasks. After 6 days the experiment had to be halted.

What had happened? Apparently, the assigned social roles—prisoner and guard—were so powerful that in just a few days the experiment became "reality" for those involved. Afterward, it was difficult for many of the guards to believe their own behavior. As one recalls, "I was surprised at myself. I made them call each other names and clean toilets out with their bare hands. I practically considered the prisoners cattle" (Zimbardo, Haney, & Banks, 1973). We tend to think of people as inherently good or bad. But students in the Stanford prison study were randomly assigned to be prisoners or guards. Clearly, the origins of many destructive human relationships can be found in destructive roles.

Group Structure and Cohesion

Are there other dimensions of group membership? Two important dimensions of any group are its structure and cohesiveness (Forsyth, 2006). **Group structure** consists of the network of roles, communication pathways, and power in a group. Organized groups such as an army or an athletic team have a high degree of structure. Informal friendship groups may or may not be very structured.

Group cohesiveness refers to the degree of attraction among group members or the strength of their desire to remain in the group. Members of cohesive groups literally stick together: They tend to stand or sit close together, they pay more attention to one another, and they show more signs of mutual affection. Also, their behavior tends to be closely coordinated (Chansler, Swamidass, &

Cammann, 2003). Cohesiveness is the basis for much of the power that groups exert over us. Therapy groups, businesses, sports teams, and the like seek to increase cohesion because it helps people work together better (Craig & Kelly, 1999; Marmarosh, Holtz, & Schottenbauer, 2005).

In-groups

Cohesiveness is particularly strong for **in-groups** (groups with which a person mainly identifies). Very likely, your own in-groups are defined by a combination of prominent social dimensions, such as nationality, ethnicity, age, education, religion, income, political values, gender, sexual orientation, and so forth. In-group membership helps define who we are socially. Predictably, we tend to attribute positive characteristics to our in-group and negative qualities to **out-groups** (groups with which we do not identify). We also tend to exaggerate differences between members of out-groups and our own groups. This sort of "us-and-them" thinking seems to be a basic fact of social life. It also sets the stage for conflict between groups and for racial and ethnic prejudice—topics we will explore in the next chapter.

Status

In addition to defining roles, a person's social position within groups determines his or her **status**, or level of social power and importance. Higher status bestows special privileges and respect. For example, in one experiment, a man walked into a number of bakeries and asked for a croissant while claiming he did not have enough money to pay for it. Half the time he was well dressed and half the time he was poorly dressed. If the man was polite when he asked, he was equally likely to be given a free croissant no matter how he was dressed (95 versus 90 percent). But if he was impolite when he asked, he was much less likely to get a croissant if he was poorly dressed than if he was well dressed (75 versus 20 percent) (Guéguen & Pascual, 2003).

Social psychology The scientific study of how individuals behave, think, and feel in social situations.

Culture An ongoing pattern of life, characterizing a society at a given point in history.

Social role Expected behavior patterns associated with particular social positions (such as daughter, worker, student).

Role conflict Trying to occupy two or more roles that make conflicting demands on behavior.

Group structure The network of roles, communication pathways, and power in a group.

Group cohesiveness The degree of attraction among group members or their commitment to remaining in the group.

In-group A group with which a person identifies.

Out-group A group with which a person does not identify.

Status An individual's position in a social structure, especially with respect to power, privilege, or importance.

CRITICAL THINKING

Touch and Status

Pause for a moment and think about who you touch during a typical day. Do you think that social status affects your patterns of touching and being touched by others?

It would be surprising if touching weren't affected by status. Touch is one of the most basic forms of communication. Its message can be one of warmth, friendship, caring, nurturance, or sexual interest. Touching is also a "privilege" of power and high status (Guéguen, 2002). Older persons, for instance, are more likely to touch younger persons than the reverse. Likewise, people of high socioeconomic status are more likely to touch those of lower status.

Even in situations where persons touch each other equal amounts, there is an important difference. When a person of higher status touches one of lower status, the contact is more likely to be "personal" or familiar. When lower-status persons touch those of higher status, it is more likely to be formal or impersonal, such as a handshake (Hall, 1996; Hall, Coats, & LeBeau, 2005).

There is another difference worth noting. Men, by virtue of their higher status and greater power in society, are more likely to touch women than women are to touch men (Major, Schmidlin, & Williams, 1990). This difference is highly visible in most work settings: Picture a male boss touching his female secretary on the shoulder or arm to get her attention; she, in turn, never touches him. Although women have moved toward equal status with men, patterns of social touching suggest that subtle inequalities in power and dominance persist.

You don't have to be in a bakery for this to work. In most situations, we are more likely to comply with a request made by a high-status (well-dressed) person (Guéguen, 2002). Perhaps the better treatment given "higher status" persons, even when they are impolite, explains some of our society's preoccupation with expensive clothes, cars, and other status symbols. (For more, see "Touch and Status.")

Norms

We are also greatly affected by group norms. A **norm** is a widely accepted (but often unspoken) standard for appropriate behavior. If you have the slightest doubt about the power of norms, try this test: Walk into a crowded supermarket, get in a checkout line, and begin singing loudly in your fullest voice. Are you the 1 person in 100 who could actually carry out these instructions?

The impact of norms is shown by an interesting study of littering. The question was, Does the amount of trash in an area affect littering? To find out, people were given flyers as they walked into a public parking garage. As you can see in ● Figure 16.1, the more litter there was on the floor, the more likely people were to add to it by dropping their flyer. Apparently, seeing that others had already littered implied a lax norm about whether littering is acceptable. The moral? The cleaner a public area is kept, the less likely people are to "trash" it (Cialdini, Reno, & Kallgren, 1990).

How are norms formed? One early study of group norms made use of a striking illusion called the **autokinetic effect.** In a completely darkened room, a stationary pinpoint of light will appear to drift or move about. (The light is therefore *autokinetic,* or "self-moving.") Muzafer Sherif (1906–1988) found that people give very different estimates of how far the light moves. However, when two or more people announce their estimates at the same time, their judgments rapidly converge. This is an example of *social influence,* in which one person's behavior is changed by the actions of others (Brehm, & Kassin, & Fein, 2005). We will return to social influence later. For now, it is enough to note that a conver-

● **Figure 16.1** Results of an experiment on norms concerning littering. The prior existence of litter in a public setting implies that littering is acceptable. This encourages others to "trash" the area. (From Cialdini, Reno, & Kallgren, 1990.)

gence of attitudes, beliefs, and behaviors tends to take place in many groups (Crano, 2000).

Norms are often based on our *perceptions* of what others think and do. For example, a majority of college students believe that they are more troubled about excessive drinking on campus than other students are. Apparently, many students are fooled by this false norm. Ironically, they help create this false impression by not speaking up. If disapproving students actually outnumber "party animals," then campus norms for acceptable drinking should be fairly conservative, which is usually not the case (Prentice & Miller, 1993).

Despite the fact that we are immersed in social relationships with other people all the time and can freely *observe* their behavior, figuring out *why* they behave the way they do is another matter entirely. In the next section we will consider a kind of impromptu detective work that we engage in as we try to guess the motives of others and the causes of their actions. Let's see how this is done.

Social Cognition—Behind the Mask

Gateway Question: How do we perceive the motives of others and the causes of our own behavior?

Every day we must guess how people will act, often from small shreds of evidence. We do this through a form of social cognition called **attribution.** As we observe others, we make inferences about them. Vonda just insulted Sutchai. But why? Why did Nick change his college major? Why does Kirti talk so fast when she's around men? In answering such questions we *attribute* people's behavior to various causes. Whether we are right or wrong about the causes of their behavior, our conclusions affect how *we* act. To learn how we fill in the "person behind the mask," let's explore the making of attributions.

Attribution Theory

Two people enter a restaurant and order different meals. Nell tastes her food, then salts it. Bert salts his food before he tastes it. How would you explain their behavior? In Nell's case, you might assume that the *food* needed salt. If so, you have attributed her actions to an **external cause** (one that lies outside a person). With Bert, you might be more inclined to conclude that he must really *like* salt. If so, the cause of his behavior is internal. **Internal causes,** such as needs, personality traits, and Bert's taste for salt, lie within the person.

> ### bridges
> Attributing bodily arousal to various sources can also have a large impact on emotions. **See Chapter 10, page 350.**

AFP/Getty Images

In 2005, in the aftermath of hurricane Katrina, many celebrities, including actor Sean Penn, went to New Orleans to help hurricane victims. As you watched these events, did you attribute the celebrities' actions to selfless concern for the suffering in New Orleans? Or were the celebrities motivated by a selfish desire to hog the limelight? Such attributions greatly affect how we perceive and respond to the social behavior of others.

What effects do such interpretations have? It is difficult to fully understand social behavior without considering the attributions that we make. For instance, let's say that Tam, who is in one of your classes, seems to avoid you. You see Tam at a market. Do you say hello to him? It could depend on how you have explained Tam's actions to yourself. Have you assumed his avoidance is caused by shyness? Coincidence? Dislike? Many factors affect such judgments. Let's examine a few.

Making Attributions

According to Harold Kelley (1921–2003), one of the originators of attribution theory, when we make attributions we are sensitive to how *consistent* and *distinctive* a person's behavior is (Kelley, 1967). A person's behavior is *consistent* if it changes very little when we observe it on many different occasions. The first time that Tam avoided you he might have just been in a bad mood. However, if Tam has consistently avoided you, it's not likely that he was in a bad mood every time. That rules out coincidence. Still, Tam's avoidance could mean he is shy, not that he dislikes you. That's why distinctiveness is also important. When we watch other people, *distinctiveness* refers to noting that their behavior occurs only under specific circumstances. If you notice that Tam seems to avoid other people too, you may conclude that he is shy or unfriendly. If his avoidance is consistently and distinctively linked only with you, you will probably assume he dislikes you. You could be wrong, of course, but your behavior toward him will change just the same.

To deduce causes, we typically take into account the behavior of the *actor* (the person of interest), the *object* the person's action is directed toward, and the *setting* (social or physical environment) in which the action occurs (Kelley, 1967). Imagine for example, that someone compliments you on your taste in clothes. If you are at a picnic, you may attribute this compliment to what you are wearing (the "object"), unless, of course, you're wearing your worst "grubbies." If you are, you may simply assume that the person (or "actor") is friendly or tactful. However, if you are in a clothing store and a salesperson compliments you, you will probably attribute the compliment to the setting. It's still possible that the salesperson actually likes what you are wearing. Nevertheless, when we make attributions we are very sensitive to the *situational demands* affecting other people's behavior. **Situational demands** are pres-

Norm A widely accepted (but often unspoken) standard of conduct for appropriate behavior.

Autokinetic effect The apparent movement of a stationary pinpoint of light displayed in a darkened room.

Attribution The process of making inferences about the causes of one's own behavior, and that of others.

External cause A cause of behavior that is assumed to lie outside a person.

Internal cause A cause of behavior assumed to lie within a person—for instance, a need, preference, or personality trait.

Situational demands Unstated expectations that define desirable or appropriate behavior in various settings and social situations.

THE CLINICAL FILE

Self-Handicapping—Smoke Screen for Failure

Have you ever known someone who got drunk before taking an exam or making a speech? Why would a person risk failure in this way? Often, the reason lies in **self-handicapping** (arranging to perform under conditions that impair performance). By providing an excuse for poor performance, self-handicapping makes people feel better in situations where they might fail (Kimble & Hirt, 2005).

What if a person succeeds while "handicapped"? Well, then, so much the better. The person's self-image then gets a boost because she or he succeeded under conditions that normally lower performance (Murray & Warden, 1992).

Do you believe that "you either have it or you don't" where ability is concerned? If so, you may be particularly prone to self-handicapping. By working with a handicap,

people can avoid any chance of discovering that they "don't have it" (Rhodewalt, 1994)! For instance, college athletes often protect their self-esteem by practicing *less* before important games or events (Bailis, 2001; Kuczka & Treasure, 2005). That way, if they don't do well, they have an excuse for their poor performance.

Drinking alcohol is one of the most popular—and dangerous—self-handicapping strategies. A person who is drunk can attribute failure to being "loaded," while accepting success if it occurs. Examples of using alcohol for self-handicapping include being drunk for school exams, job interviews, or an important first date. A person who gets drunk at such times should be aware that coping with anxiety in this way can lead to serious alcohol abuse (Zuckerman & Tsai, 2005).

Any time you set up excuses for a poor performance, you are self-handicapping. Other examples of self-handicapping include making a half-hearted effort, claiming to be ill, and procrastinating (Urdan & Midgley, 2001). Incidentally, men are more likely than women to self-handicap (Kimble & Hirt, 2005).

Most of us have used self-handicapping at times. Indeed, life would be harsh if we didn't sometimes give ourselves a break from accepting full responsibility for success or failure. Self-handicapping is mainly a problem when it becomes habitual. When it does, it typically leads to lower self-esteem, poor adjustment, and poor health (Zuckerman, Kieffer, & Knee, 1998; Zuckerman & Tsai, 2005). So, watch out for self-handicapping, but try not to be too hard on yourself.

---

sures to behave in certain ways in particular settings and social situations. If you see Tam at a funeral and he is quiet and polite, it will tell you little about his motives and personality traits. The situation demands such behavior.

When situational demands are strong, we tend to *discount* (downgrade) internal causes as a way of explaining a person's behavior. Actually, this is true anytime strong external causes for behavior are present. For example, you have probably discounted the motives of professional athletes who praise shaving creams, hair tonics, deodorants, and the like. Obviously, the large sums of money they receive fully explain their endorsements. It's not necessary to assume they actually *like* the potions they sell. ("Self-Handicapping—Smoke Screen for Failure" discusses a related phenomenon.)

Yet another factor affecting attribution is *consensus* (or agreement). When many people act alike (there is a consensus in their behavior), it implies that their behavior is externally caused. For example, if millions of people go to see the latest Hollywood blockbuster, we tend to say *the movie* is good. If someone you know goes to see a movie six times, when others are staying away in droves, the tendency is to assume that *the person* likes "that type of movie."

Actor and Observer

Let's say that at the last five parties you've been to, you've seen a woman named Macy. Based on this, you assume that Macy likes to socialize. You see Macy at yet another gathering and mention that

she seems to like parties. She says, "Actually, I hate these parties, but I get invited to play my tuba at them. My music teacher says I need to practice in front of an audience, so I keep attending these dumb events. Want to hear a Sousa march?"

We seldom know the real reasons for others' actions. That is why we tend to infer causes from *circumstances*. However, in doing so, we often make mistakes like the one with Macy. The most com-

Forest Whitaker won an Academy Award for his portrayal of dictator Idi Amin in the film *The Last King of Scotland*. Is Forest Whitaker a ruthless person, or did he portray ruthlessness as a part of his role? According to Tal-Or and Papirman (2007), we are prone to attribute actors' screen actions to their personalities rather than to the personalities of the roles they are playing. Why do you think this occurs?

mon error is to attribute the actions of others to internal causes (Follett & Hess, 2002; Jones & Nisbett, 1971). This mistake is called the **fundamental attribution error.** We tend to think the actions of others have internal causes even if they are actually caused by external forces or circumstances. One amusing example of this error is the tendency of people to attribute the actions of actors in television programs to the personality of the actor rather than the obvious external cause (that they are playing a character) (Tal-Or & Papirman, 2007).

Where our own behavior is concerned, we are more likely to think that external causes explain our actions. In other words, there is an **actor–observer bias** in how we explain behavior. As *observers,* we attribute the behavior of others to their wants, motives, and personality traits (this is the fundamental attribution error). As *actors,* we tend to find external explanations for our own behavior (Gordon & Kaplar, 2002). No doubt you chose your major in school because of what it has to offer. Other students choose *their* majors because of the kind of people they are. Other people who don't leave tips in restaurants are cheapskates. If you don't leave a tip, it's because the service was bad. And, of course, other people are always late because they are irresponsible. You are late because you were held up by events beyond your control.

As you can see, attribution theory summarizes how we think about ourselves and others, including the errors we tend to make.

KNOWLEDGE BUILDER
Social Behavior and Attribution

RECITE

1. Research has shown that the number of first-name acquaintances needed to interconnect two widely separated strangers averages about six people. T or F?
2. Social psychology is the study of how people behave in _____.
3. Male, female, and adolescent are examples of _____ roles.
4. The Stanford prison experiment demonstrated the powerful influence of the autokinetic effect on behavior. T or F?
5. Status refers to a set of expected behaviors associated with a social position. T or F?
6. When situational demands are weak, we tend to attribute a person's actions to internal causes. T or F?
7. The fundamental attribution error is to attribute the actions of others to internal causes. T or F?

REFLECT

Critical Thinking

8. The Stanford prison experiment also illustrates a major concept of personality theory (Chapter 12), especially social learning theory. Can you name it?
9. How could the autokinetic effect contribute to UFO sightings?

Relate

What are the most prominent roles you play? Which are achieved and which are ascribed? How do they affect your behavior? What conflicts do they create?

Think of a time when your attributions were affected by consistency and distinctiveness. Did situational demands also affect your judgments?

Have you ever engaged in self-handicapping? Try to relate the concept to a specific example.

How often do you commit the fundamental attribution error? Again, try to think of a specific personal example that illustrates the concept.

Answers: 1. T **2.** social situations or the presence of others **3.** ascribed **4.** F **5.** F **6.** T **7.** T **8.** It is the idea that behavior is often strongly influenced by situations rather than by personal traits. **9.** Any point of light in the night sky may appear to move because of the autokinetic effect. This could cause a stationary light to look like it is flying or changing direction rapidly.

●● Attitudes—Belief + Emotion + Action

Gateway Questions: What are attitudes? How are they acquired?

What is your attitude toward affirmative action, euthanasia, environmental groups, the death penalty, legalized abortion, junk food, psychology? Your answers, which are often influenced by social situations, can have far-reaching effects on your behavior. Attitudes are intimately woven into our actions and views of the world. Our tastes, friendships, votes, preferences, goals, and behavior in many other situations are all touched by attitudes (Baumeister & Bushman, 2008). Let's see how attitudes are formed and changed.

What specifically is an attitude? An **attitude** is a mixture of belief and emotion that predisposes a person to respond to other people, objects, or institutions in a positive or negative way. Attitudes summarize your *evaluation* of objects (Oskamp & Schultz, 2005). As a result, they predict or direct future actions.

For example, an approach known as the *misdirected letter technique* shows how actions are closely linked to attitudes. During a period of violence in Northern Ireland, attitudes toward the Irish were measured in a sample of English households. Later, wrongly addressed letters were sent to the same households. Each letter had either an English name or an Irish name on it. The question was: Would the "Irish" letters be returned to the post office or thrown away? As predicted, letters were more often thrown away by people living in households where anti-Irish attitudes had been measured earlier (Howitt et al., 1977).

"Your attitude is showing," is sometimes said. Actually, attitudes are expressed through beliefs, emotions, and actions. The **belief component** of an attitude is what you believe about a par-

---

Self-handicapping Arranging to perform under conditions that usually impair performance, so as to have an excuse for a poor showing.

Fundamental attribution error The tendency to attribute the behavior of others to internal causes (personality, likes, and so forth).

Actor–observer bias The tendency to attribute the behavior of others to internal causes while attributing one's own behavior to external causes (situations and circumstances).

Attitude A learned tendency to respond to people, objects, or institutions in a positive or negative way.

Belief component What a person thinks or believes about the object of an attitude.

● **Figure 16.2** Elements of positive and negative attitudes toward affirmative action.

ticular object or issue. The **emotional component** consists of your feelings toward the attitudinal object. The **action component** refers to your actions toward various people, objects, or institutions. Consider, for example, your attitude toward gun control. You will have beliefs about whether gun control would affect rates of crime or violence. You will respond emotionally to guns, finding them either attractive and desirable or threatening and destructive. And you will have a tendency to seek out or avoid gun ownership. The action component of your attitude may well include support of organizations that urge or oppose gun control. As you can see, attitudes orient us to the social world. In doing so, they prepare us to act in certain ways (Albarracín, Johnson, & Zanna, 2005). (For another example, see ● Figure 16.2.)

Forming Attitudes

How do people acquire attitudes? Attitudes are acquired in several basic ways. Sometimes, attitudes come from *direct contact* (personal experience) with the object of the attitude—such as opposing pollution when a nearby factory ruins your favorite river (Ajzen, 2005). Some attitudes are simply formed through chance

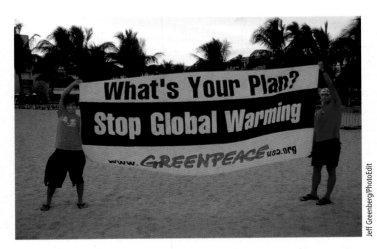

Attitudes are an important dimension of social behavior. They are often greatly influenced by the groups to which we belong.

conditioning (learning that takes place by chance or coincidence) (Olson & Zanna, 1993). Let's say, for instance, that you have had three encounters in your lifetime with psychologists. If all three were negative, you might take an unduly dim view of psychology. In the same way, people often develop strong attitudes toward cities, foods, or parts of the country on the basis of one or two unusually good or bad experiences.

Attitudes are also learned through *interaction with others*; that is, through discussion with people holding a particular attitude. For instance, if three of your good friends are volunteers at a local recycling center and you talk with them about their beliefs, you may well come to favor recycling, too. More generally, there is little doubt that many of our attitudes are influenced by *group membership*. In most groups, pressures to conform shape our attitudes, just as they do our behavior. *Child rearing* (the effects of parental values, beliefs, and practices) also affects attitudes (Bartram, 2006). For example, if both parents belong to the same political party, chances are that their children will belong to that party as adults.

Finally, there can be no doubt that attitudes are influenced by the media, such as newspapers, television, and the Internet. Every day we are coaxed, persuaded, and skillfully manipulated by messages in mass media. Consider, for example, the impact of television. Ninety-nine percent of North American homes have a television set, which is on an average of more than 7 hours a day (Steuer & Hustedt, 2002). The information thus channeled into homes has a powerful impact. For instance, frequent viewers mistrust others and overestimate their own chances of being harmed. This suggests that a steady diet of TV violence leads some people to develop a *mean worldview,* in which they regard the world as a dangerous and threatening place (Eschholz, Chiricos, & Gertz, 2003).

Attitudes and Behavior

Why are some attitudes acted on, whereas others are not? To answer this question, let's consider an example. Assume that a woman named Lorraine knows that automobiles are expensive to operate and add to air pollution, and she hates smog. Why would Lorraine continue to drive to work every day? Probably it is because the *immediate consequences* of our actions weigh heavily on the choices we make. No matter what Lorraine's attitude may be, it is difficult for her to resist the immediate convenience of driving. Our expectations of how *others will evaluate* our actions are also important. Lorraine may resist taking public transit to work for fear that her coworkers will be critical of her environmental stand. By taking this factor into account, researchers have been able to predict family planning choices, alcohol use by teenagers, re-enlistment in the National Guard, voting on a nuclear power plant initiative, and so forth (Cialdini, 2001). Finally, we must not overlook the effects of long-standing *habits* (Oskamp & Schultz, 2005). Let's say that after years of driving to work Lorraine finally vows to shift to public transit. Two months later it would not be unusual if she found herself driving again because of habit despite her good intentions.

In short, there are often large differences between attitudes and behavior—particularly between privately held attitudes and public behavior. However, barriers to action typically fall when a person holds an attitude with *conviction*. If you have **conviction** about an issue, it evokes strong feelings, you think about it and discuss it often, and you are knowledgeable about it. Attitudes held with passionate conviction often lead to major changes in personal behavior (Oskamp & Schultz, 2005).

Attitude Measurement

How are attitudes measured? Attitudes can be measured several ways. In an **open-ended interview,** people are asked to freely express their attitudes toward a particular issue. For example, a person might be asked, "What do you think about freedom of speech on college campuses?" Attitudes toward social groups can be measured with a **social distance scale.** On such scales people say how willing they are to admit members of a group to various levels

of social closeness. These levels range from "would exclude from my country" to "would admit to marriage in my family." If a person is prejudiced toward a group, she or he will prefer to remain socially distant from members of the group (Cover, 1995).

Attitude scales are a widely used measure. **Attitude scales** consist of statements expressing various possible views on an issue (for example, "Socialized medicine would destroy health care in this country," or "This country needs a national health care program"). People typically respond to such statements on a 5-point scale, ranking it from "strongly agree" to "strongly disagree." By combining scores on all items, we can learn if a person accepts or rejects a particular issue. When used in public polls, attitude scales provide useful information about the feelings of large segments of the population.

●● Attitude Change—Why the Seekers Went Public

Gateway Questions: Under what conditions is persuasion most effective? What is cognitive dissonance?

Although attitudes are fairly stable, they do change. Some attitude change can be understood in terms of **reference groups** (any group an individual uses as a standard for social comparison). It is not necessary to have face-to-face contact with other people for them to be a reference group. It depends instead on whom you identify with or whose attitudes and values you care about (Ajzen, 2005).

In the 1930s, Theodore Newcomb studied real-life attitude change among students at Bennington College (Alwin, Cohen, & Newcomb, 1991). Most students came from conservative homes, but Bennington was a very liberal school. Newcomb found that most students shifted significantly toward more liberal attitudes during their 4 years at Bennington. Those who didn't change kept their parents and hometown friends as primary reference groups. This is typified by a student who said, "I decided I'd rather stick to my father's ideas." Those who did change identified primarily with the campus community. Notice that all students could count the

Emotional component One's feelings toward the object of an attitude.

Action component How one tends to act toward the object of an attitude.

Conviction Beliefs that are important to a person and that evoke strong emotion.

Open-ended interview An interview in which persons are allowed to freely state their views.

Social distance scale A rating of the degree to which a person would be willing to have contact with a member of another group.

Attitude scale A collection of attitudinal statements with which respondents indicate agreement or disagreement.

Reference group Any group that an individual identifies with and uses as a standard for social comparison.

Do you exercise regularly? Like students in the Bennington study, your intentions to exercise are probably influenced by the exercise habits of your reference groups (Terry & Hogg, 1996).

Bob Llewellen/Pictor International Ltd./Jupiterimages

college and their families as *membership* groups. However, one group or the other tended to become their point of reference.

Persuasion

What about advertising and other direct attempts to change attitudes? Are they effective? **Persuasion** is any deliberate attempt to change attitudes or beliefs through information and arguments (Brock & Green, 2005). Businesses, politicians, and others who seek to persuade us obviously believe that attitudes can be changed. More than a hundred billion dollars are spent yearly on television advertising in the United States and Canada alone. Persuasion can range from the daily blitz of media commercials to personal discussion among friends. In most cases, the success or failure of persuasion can be understood if we consider the *communicator,* the *message,* and the *audience.*

At a community meeting, let's say you have a chance to promote an issue important to you (for or against building a new mall

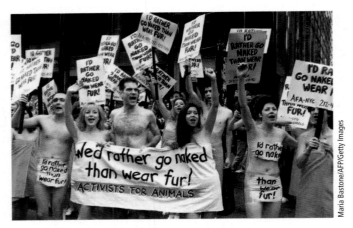

Persuasion. Would you be likely to be swayed by this group's message? Successful persuasion is related to characteristics of the communicator, the message, and the audience.

Maria Bastone/AFP/Getty Images

nearby, for instance). Whom should you choose to make the presentation, and how should that person present it? Research suggests that attitude change is encouraged when the following conditions are met. You should have little trouble seeing how these principles are applied to sell everything from underarm deodorants to presidents:

1. The communicator is likable, expressive, trustworthy, an expert on the topic, and similar to the audience in some respect.
2. The communicator appears to have nothing to gain if the audience accepts the message.
3. The message appeals to emotions, particularly to fear or anxiety.
4. The message also provides a clear course of action that will, if followed, reduce fear or produce personally desirable results.
5. The message states clear-cut conclusions.
6. The message is backed up by facts and statistics.
7. The message is repeated as frequently as possible
8. Both sides of the argument are presented in the case of a well-informed audience.
9. Only one side of the argument is presented in the case of a poorly informed audience.

(Aronson, 1992; Oskamp & Schultz, 2005).

As we have just seen, we sometimes change our attitudes in response to external persuasion (Gass & Seiter, 2007). Sometimes, however, the internal process of *cognitive dissonance* can also lead to attitude change.

Cognitive Dissonance Theory

What happens if people act in ways that are inconsistent with their attitudes or self-images? Cognitions are thoughts. Dissonance means clashing. The influential theory of **cognitive dissonance** states that contradicting or clashing thoughts cause discomfort. That is, we have a need for *consistency* in our thoughts, perceptions, and images of ourselves (Cooper, Mirabile, & Scher, 2005; Festinger, 1957). Inconsistency, then, can motivate people to make their thoughts or attitudes agree with their actions (Oskamp & Schultz, 2005).

For example, smokers are told on every pack that cigarettes endanger their lives. They light up and smoke anyway. How do they resolve the tension between this information and their actions? They could quit smoking, but it may be easier to convince themselves that smoking is not really so dangerous. To do this, a smoker might seek examples of heavy smokers who have lived long lives, spend time with other smokers, and avoid information about the link between smoking and cancer. According to cognitive dissonance theory, we also tend to reject new information that contradicts ideas we already hold. We're all guilty of this "don't bother me with the facts, my mind is made up" strategy at times.

A famous example of cognitive dissonance in action involves a woman named Mrs. Keech, who claimed she was in communication with beings on a planet called Clarion (Festinger, 1957). The messages foretold the destruction of North America. Mrs. Keech and her followers, the Seekers, were to be rescued by a flying saucer. The news media became involved and reported on the proceedings. When nothing happened, the Seekers suffered a bitter and embarrassing disappointment.

Did the group break up then? Amazingly, instead of breaking up, the Seekers became *more* convinced than ever before that they were right. Mrs. Keech announced that she had received a new message explaining that the Seekers had saved the world. Before, the Seekers were uninterested in persuading other people that the world was coming to an end. Now they called newspapers and radio stations to convince others of their accomplishment.

Why did their belief in Mrs. Keech's messages *increase* after the world failed to end? Why did the group suddenly become interested in convincing others that they were right? Cognitive dissonance theory explains that after publicly committing themselves to their beliefs, they had a strong need to maintain consistency (Tavris & Aronson, 2007). In effect, convincing others was a way of adding proof that they were correct (● Table 16.1).

Cognitive dissonance also underlies attempts to convince *ourselves* that we've done the right thing. Here's an example you may recognize: As romantic partners become better acquainted, they sooner or later begin to notice things they don't like about each other. How do they reduce the cognitive dissonance and doubts caused by their partners' shortcomings? Basically, they create stories that change their partners' faults into virtues: He seems cheap, but he's really frugal; she seems egotistical, but she's really self-confident; he's not stubborn, he just has integrity;

● **Figure 16.3** Summary of the Festinger and Carlsmith (1959) study from the viewpoint of a person experiencing cognitive dissonance.

she's not undependable, she's a free spirit; and so on (Murray & Holmes, 1993).

Making choices often causes dissonance. This is especially true if a rejected alternative seems better than the one selected. To minimize such dissonance, we tend to emphasize positive aspects of what we choose, while downgrading other alternatives. Thus, college students are more likely to think their courses will be good *after* they have registered than they did before making a commitment (Rosenfeld, Giacalone, & Tedeschi, 1983).

Acting contrary to one's attitudes doesn't always bring about change. How does cognitive dissonance explain that? The amount of justification for acting contrary to your attitudes and beliefs affects how much dissonance you feel. (*Justification* is the degree to which a person's actions are explained by rewards or other circumstances.) In a classic study, college students did an extremely boring task (turning wooden pegs on a board) for a *long* time. Afterward, they were asked to help lure others into the experiment by pretending that the task was interesting and enjoyable. Students paid $20 for lying to others did not change their own negative opinion of the task: "That was *really* boring!" Those who were paid only $1 later rated the task as "pleasant" and "interesting." How can we explain these results? Apparently, students paid $20 experienced no dissonance. These students could reassure themselves that anybody would tell a little white lie for $20. Those paid $1 were faced with the conflicting thoughts: "I lied" and " I had no good reason to do it." Rather than admit to themselves that they had lied, these students changed their attitude toward what they had done (Festinger & Carlsmith, 1959) (● Figure 16.3).

Table 16.1 ● Strategies for Reducing Cognitive Dissonance

LeShawn, who is a college student, has always thought of himself as an environmental activist. Recently, LeShawn "inherited" a car from his parents, who were replacing the family "barge." In the past, LeShawn biked or used public transportation to get around. His parents' old car is an antiquated gas-guzzler, but he has begun to drive it every day. How might LeShawn reduce the cognitive dissonance created by the clash between his environmentalism and his use of an inefficient automobile?

Strategy	Example
Change your attitude	"Cars are not really a major environmental problem."
Add consonant thoughts	"This is an old car, so keeping it on the road makes good use of the resources consumed when it was manufactured."
Change the importance of the dissonant thoughts	"It's more important for me to support the environmental movement politically than it is to worry about how I get to school and work."
Reduce the amount of perceived choice	"My schedule has become too hectic. I really can't afford to bike or take the bus anymore."
Change your behavior	"I'm only going to use the car when it's impossible to bike or take the bus."

After Franzoi, 2002.

Persuasion A deliberate attempt to change attitudes or beliefs with information and arguments.

Cognitive dissonance An uncomfortable clash between self-image, thoughts, beliefs, attitudes, or perceptions and one's behavior.

Attitudes and Attitude Change

RECITE

1. Attitudes have three parts, a _____ component, an _____ component, and an _____ component.

2. Which of the following is associated with attitude formation?
   a. group membership
   b. mass media
   c. chance conditioning
   d. child rearing
   e. all of the preceding
   f. a and d only

3. Because of the immediate consequences of actions, behavior contrary to one's stated attitudes is often enacted. T or F?

4. Items such as "would exclude from my country" or "would admit to marriage in my family" are found in which attitude measure?
   a. a reference group scale
   b. a social distance scale
   c. an attitude scale
   d. an open-ended interview

5. In presenting a persuasive message, it is best to give both sides of the argument if the audience is already well informed on the topic. T or F?

6. Much attitude change is related to a desire to avoid clashing or contradictory thoughts, an idea summarized by _____ _____ theory.

REFLECT

Critical Thinking

7. Students entering a college gym are asked to sign a banner promoting water conservation. Later, the students shower at the gym. What effect would you expect signing the banner to have on how long students stay in the showers?

Relate

Describe an attitude that is important to you. What are its three components?

Which of the various sources of attitudes best explain your own attitudes?

Who belongs to your most important reference group?

Imagine that you would like to persuade voters to support an initiative to preserve a small wilderness area by converting it to a park. Using research on persuasion as a guide, what could you do to be more effective?

How would you explain cognitive dissonance theory to a person who knows nothing about it?

Answers: 1. belief, emotional, action **2.** e **3.** T **4.** b **5.** T **6.** cognitive dissonance **7.** Cognitive dissonance theory predicts that students who sign the banner will take shorter showers, to be consistent with their publicly expressed support of water conservation. This is exactly the result observed in a study done by social psychologist Elliot Aronson.

◖◗ Social Influence—Follow the Leader

Gateway Question: What is social influence and social power?

No topic lies nearer the heart of social psychology than **social influence** (changes in behavior induced by the actions of others). When people interact, they almost always affect one another's behavior (Crano, 2000; Kassin, Fein, & Markus, 2008). For example, in a sidewalk experiment, various numbers of people stood on a busy New York City street. On cue they all looked at a sixth-floor window across the street. A camera recorded how many passersby also stopped to stare. The larger the influencing group, the more people were swayed to join in staring at the window (Milgram, Bickman, & Berkowitz, 1969).

Are there different kinds of social influence? Social influence ranges from milder to stronger. The gentlest form of social influence is *mere presence* (changing behavior just because other people are nearby). We *conform* when we spontaneously change our behavior to bring it into agreement with others. Compliance is a more directed form of social influence. We *comply* when we change our behavior in response to another person who has little or no social power, or authority. Obedience is an even stronger form of social influence. We *obey* when we change our behavior in direct response to the demands of an authority. The strongest form of social influence is *coercion* (changing behavior because you are forced to). Daily behavior is probably most influenced by group pressures for conformity (Baron, Byrne, & Branscombe, 2007).

Social Power

The people we encounter on any given day vary in their power to influence us. Here's something to think about: Strength is a quality possessed by individuals; power is always social—it arises when people come together and disappears when they disperse. In trying to understand the ways in which people are able to influence each other, it is helpful to distinguish among five types of **social power** (the capacity to control, alter, or influence the behavior of another person) (Raven, 1974):

Reward power lies in the ability to reward a person for complying with desired behavior. Teachers try to exert reward power over students with grades. Employers command reward power by their control of wages and bonuses.

Coercive power is based on an ability to punish a person for failure to comply. Coercive power is the basis for most laws, in that fines or imprisonment are used to control behavior.

Legitimate power comes from accepting a person as an agent of an established social order. For example, elected leaders and supervisors have legitimate power. So does a teacher in the classroom. Outside the classroom that power would have to come from another source.

Referent power is based on respect for or identification with a person or a group. The person "refers to" the source of referent power for direction. Referent power is responsible for much of the conformity we see in groups.

Expert power is based on recognition that another person has knowledge necessary for achieving a goal. We allow teachers, lawyers, and other experts to guide behavior because of their ability to produce desired results. Physicians, psychologists, programmers, and plumbers have expert power.

A person who has power in one situation may have very little in another. In those situations where a person has power, she or he is described as an *authority*. Regardless of whether or not the people around you are authorities, friends, or strangers, their mere presence is likely to influence your behavior.

⬤⬤ Mere Presence—Just Because You Are There

Gateway Question: How does the mere presence of others affect behavior?

Suppose you just happened to be alone in a room, picking your nose. (We know, none of us would do that, right?) Would you continue if a stranger entered the room? **Mere presence** refers to the tendency for people to change their behavior just because of the presence of other people. Let's explore some of the ways mere presence can induce us to modify our behavior.

Social Facilitation and Loafing

Imagine you are out riding your mountain bike when another rider pulls up beside you. Will you pick up your pace? Slow down? Completely ignore the other rider? In 1898, psychologist Norman Triplett's investigation of just such a social situation was the first published social psychology experiment (Strubbe, 2005). According to Triplett, you are more likely to speed up. This is **social facilitation,** the tendency to perform better when in the presence of others.

Does mere presence always improve performance? No. If you are confident in your abilities, your behavior will most likely be facilitated in the presence of others. If you are not, then your performance is more likely to be impaired (Uziel, 2007). Another classic study focused on college students shooting pool at a student union. Good players who were confident (sharks?) normally made 71% of their shots. Their accuracy improved to 80% when they were being watched by others. Less confident, average players (marks?) who normally made 36% of their shots dropped to 25% accuracy when someone was watching them (Michaels et al., 1982).

Social loafing is another consequence of having other people nearby. People tend to work less hard (loaf) when they are part of a group than they do when they are solely responsible for their work. In one study, people playing tug-of-war while blindfolded pulled harder if they thought they were competing alone. When they thought others were on their team, they made less of an effort (Ingham et al., 1974).

Personal Space

The next time you are talking with an acquaintance, move in closer and watch the reaction. Most people show signs of discomfort and step back to re-establish their original distance. Those who hold their ground may turn to the side, look away, or position an arm in front of themselves as a barrier. If you persistently edge toward your subjects, it should be easy to move them back several feet.

In this case, your mere (and close) presence amounted to an invasion of that person's **personal space,** an area surrounding the body that is regarded as private and subject to personal control. Basically, personal space extends "I" or "me" boundaries past the skin to the immediate environment. Personal space is

The use of space in public places is governed by unspoken norms, or "rules," about what is appropriate.

also illustrated by the fact that many train commuters prefer to stand up if it means they can avoid sitting too close to strangers (Evans & Wener, 2007). The systematic study of norms concerning the use of personal space is called **proxemics** (prok-SEE-miks) (Harrigan, 2005). Such norms may explain why people who feel offended by another person sometimes say, "Get out of my face.

Would approaching "too close" work with a good friend? Possibly not. Norms governing comfortable or acceptable distances vary according to relationships as well as activities. Hall (1966) identified four basic zones: *intimate, personal, social,* and *public* distance (● Figure 16.4).

Social influence Changes in a person's behavior induced by the presence or actions of others.

Social power The capacity to control, alter, or influence the behavior of another person.

Reward power Social power based on the capacity to reward a person for acting as desired.

Coercive power Social power based on the ability to punish others.

Legitimate power Social power based on a person's position as an agent of an accepted social order.

Referent power Social power gained when one is used as a point of reference by others.

Expert power Social power derived from possession of knowledge or expertise.

Mere presence The tendency for people to change their behavior just because of the presence of other people.

Social facilitation The tendency to perform better when in the presence of others.

Social loafing The tendency of people to work less hard when part of a group than when they are solely responsible for their work.

Personal space An area surrounding the body that is regarded as private and subject to personal control.

Proxemics Systematic study of the human use of space, particularly in social settings.

Intimate (0–1.5) Personal (1.5–4) Social (4–12) Public (12+)

● **Figure 16.4** Typical spatial zones (in feet) for face-to-face interactions in North America. Often, we must stand within intimate distance of others in crowds, buses, subways, elevators, and other public places. At such times, privacy is maintained by avoiding eye contact, by standing shoulder-to-shoulder or back-to-back, and by positioning a purse, bag, package, or coat as a barrier to spatial intrusions.

Spatial Norms

Cultural differences also affect spatial norms. In many Middle Eastern countries, people hold their faces only inches apart while talking. In Western Europe, the English sit closer together when conversing than the French do. The Dutch, on the other hand, sit farther apart than the French (Remland, Jones, & Brinkman, 1991). In many parts of the world, merely crossing a border can dramatically change spatial behavior (Beaulieu, 2004). The distances listed below apply to face-to-face interactions in North America:

1. **Intimate distance.** For the majority of people, the most private and exclusive space extends about 18 inches out from the skin. Entry within this space (face to face) is reserved for special people or special circumstances. Lovemaking, comforting others, and cuddling children all take place within this space.
2. **Personal distance.** This is the distance maintained in comfortable interaction with friends. It extends from about 18 inches to 4 feet from the body. Personal distance basically keeps people within "arm's reach" of each other.
3. **Social distance.** Impersonal business and casual social gatherings take place in a range of about 4 to 12 feet. This distance eliminates most touching, and it formalizes conversation by requiring greater voice projection. "Important people" in many business offices use the imposing width of their desks to maintain social distance. A big smelly cigar helps, too.
4. **Public distance.** This is the distance at which formal interactions occur (about 12 feet or more from the body). When separated by more than 12 feet, people look "flat" and they must raise their voices to speak to one another. Formal speeches, lectures, business meetings, and the like are conducted at public distance.

Because spatial behavior is very consistent, you can learn about your relationship to others by observing the distance you comfortably hold between yourselves. But remember to be aware of cultural differences. When two people of different nationalities have different norms for personal space, both are likely to be uncomfortable when talking, as one tries to move closer and the other

keeps moving back. This can lead to misunderstandings in which one person feels that the other is being too familiar at the same time as the person moving closer feels rejected (Beaulieu, 2004).

Whereas mere presence can influence our behavior in a variety of ways, conformity involves a more specific response to the presence of others.

◑ Conformity—Don't Stand Out

Gateway Question: What have social psychologists learned about conformity?

We **conform** when we bring our behavior into agreement with the actions, norms, or values of others in the absence of any direct pressure. When Harry met Sally they fell in love and were not shy about expressing themselves around campus. Some students in Harry's classes advised him to be a bit more discreet. Increasingly, Sally noticed other students staring at her and Harry when they were, well, expressing their love. Although they never made a conscious decision to conform, in another week their publicly intimate moments were a thing of the past.

As mentioned earlier, all groups have unspoken rules of conduct called *norms*. The broadest norms, defined by society as a whole,

Conformity is a subtle dimension of daily life. Notice the similarities in the clothing worn by this group of friends.

CRITICAL THINKING

Groupthink—Agreement at Any Cost

As we write this, debate continues about the Iraq war. Why, for example, were no weapons of mass destruction found, even though their existence was the major justification for the war in the first place? Was the decision to invade Iraq made by a small group of policymakers with little tolerance for dissenting views? Already, it has been suggested that this war may have been a result of **groupthink**—an urge by decision makers to maintain each other's approval, even at the cost of critical thinking (Singer, 2005).

Yale psychologist Irving Janis (1918–1990) first proposed the concept of groupthink in an attempt to understand a series of disastrous decisions made by government officials and determine what happens when people in positions of power fall prey to pressures for conformity (Janis, 1989). The core of groupthink is misguided loyalty. Group members are hesitant to "rock the boat," question sloppy thinking, or tolerate alternative views. This self-censorship leads people to believe they agree more than they actually do (Henningsen et al., 2006; Whyte, 2000).

Other crises have also been blamed on groupthink, such as the *Columbia* space shuttle disaster in 2003, and the loss, in 1999, of the $165 million *Mars Climate Orbiter*. In both cases, groupthink contributed to the overlooking of crucial technical flaws that were later found to have caused the disasters. One analysis of 19 international crises found that groupthink contributed to most (Schafer & Crichlow, 1996).

To prevent groupthink, group leaders should take the following steps:

- Define each group member's role as a "critical evaluator."
- Avoid revealing any personal preferences in the beginning.
- State the problem factually, without bias.
- Invite a group member or outside person to play devil's advocate.
- Make it clear that group members will be held accountable for decisions.
- Encourage open inquiry and a search for alternate solutions (Baron, 2005; Chen et al., 1996).

In addition, Janis suggested that there should be a "second-chance" meeting to re-evaluate important decisions. That is, each decision should be reached twice.

In fairness to our decision makers, it is worth noting that the presence of too many alternatives can lead to *deadlock*, in which an inability to make a choice can delay taking necessary action (Kowert, 2002). Regardless, in an age clouded by the threat of war, energy and food shortages, global warming, and terrorism, even stronger solutions to the problem of groupthink would be welcome. Perhaps we should form a group to think about it!

---

establish "normal" or acceptable behavior in most situations. Comparing hairstyles, habits of speech, dress, eating habits, and social customs in two or more cultures makes it clear that we all conform to social norms. In fact, a degree of uniformity is necessary if we are to interact comfortably. Imagine being totally unable to anticipate the actions of others. In stores, schools, and homes this would be frustrating and disturbing. On the highways it would be lethal.

The Asch Experiment

How strong are group pressures for conformity? One of the first experiments on conformity was staged by Solomon Asch (1907–1996). To fully appreciate it, imagine yourself as a subject. Assume that you are seated at a table with six other students. Your task is actually quite simple: You are shown three lines on a card and you must select the line that matches a "standard" line (● Figure 16.5).

As the testing begins, each person announces an answer for the first card. When your turn comes, you agree with the others. "This isn't hard at all," you say to yourself. For several more trials your answers agree with those of the group. Then comes a shock. All six people announce that line 1 matches the standard, and you were about to say line 2 matches. Suddenly you feel alone and upset. You nervously look at the lines again. The room falls silent. Everyone seems to be staring at you. The experimenter awaits your answer. Do you yield to the group?

In this study the other "students" were all actors who gave the wrong answer on about a third of the trials to create group pressure (Asch, 1956). Real students conformed to the group on about one third of the critical trials. Of those tested, 75 percent yielded at least once. People who were tested alone erred in less than 1 percent of their judgments. Clearly, those who yielded to group pressures were denying what their eyes told them.

(a)	(1) (2) (3)
Standard Line	**Comparison Lines**

● **Figure 16.5** Stimuli used in Solomon Asch's conformity experiments.

Intimate distance The most private space immediately surrounding the body (up to about 18 inches from the skin).

Personal distance The distance maintained when interacting with close friends (about 18 inches to 4 feet from the body).

Social distance Distance at which impersonal interaction takes place (about 4 to 12 feet from the body).

Public distance Distance at which formal interactions, such as giving a speech, occur (about 12 feet or more from the body).

Conformity Bringing one's behavior into agreement or harmony with norms or with the behavior of others in a group.

Groupthink A compulsion by members of decision-making groups to maintain agreement, even at the cost of critical thinking.

Are some people more susceptible to group pressures than others? People with high needs for structure or certainty are more likely to conform. So are people who are anxious, low in self-confidence, or concerned with the approval of others. People who live in cultures that emphasize group cooperation (such as many Asian cultures) are also more likely to conform (Bond & Smith, 1996; Fu et al., 2007).

In addition to personal characteristics, certain situations tend to encourage conformity—sometimes with disastrous results. "Groupthink—Agreement at Any Cost" offers a prime example.

Group Factors in Conformity

How do groups enforce norms? In most groups, we have been rewarded with acceptance and approval for conformity and threatened with rejection or ridicule for nonconformity. These reactions are called **group sanctions**. Negative sanctions range from laughter, staring, or social disapproval to complete rejection or formal exclusion. If you've ever felt the sudden chill of disapproval by others, as Harry and Sally did, you will understand the power of group sanctions.

Wouldn't the effectiveness of group sanctions depend on the importance of the group? Yes. The more important group membership is to a person, the more he or she will be influenced by other group members. The risk of being rejected can be a threat to our sense of personal identity (Crano, 2000). That's why the Asch experiments are impressive. Because these were only temporary groups, sanctions were informal and rejection had no lasting importance. Just the same, the power of the group was evident.

What other factors, besides importance of the group, affect the degree of conformity? In the sidewalk experiment described earlier, we noted that large groups had more influence. In Asch's face-to-face groups the size of the majority also made a difference, but a surprisingly small one. In other studies, the number of people who conformed increased dramatically as the majority grew from two to three people. However, a majority of three produced about as much yielding as a majority of eight. The next time you want to talk someone into (or out of) something, take two friends along and see what a difference it makes! (Sometimes it helps if the two are large and mean looking.)

Even more important than the size of the majority is its *unanimity* (total agreement). Having at least one person in your corner can greatly reduce pressures to conform. When Asch gave subjects an ally (who also opposed the majority by giving the correct answer), conformity was lessened. In terms of numbers, a unanimous majority of three is more powerful than a majority of eight with one dissenting. Perhaps this accounts for the rich diversity of human attitudes, beliefs, opinions, and lifestyles. If you can find at least one other person who sees things as you do (no matter how weird), you can be relatively secure in your opposition to other viewpoints. Incidentally, the Internet now makes it much easier to find that other like-minded person.

Compliance—A Foot in the Door

Gateway Question: What factors lead to increased compliance?

Pressures to "fit in" and conform are usually indirect. In contrast, the term **compliance** refers to situations in which one person bends to the requests of another person who has little or no authority. These more direct pressures to comply are quite common. For example, a stranger might ask to borrow your cell phone so he can make a call; a saleswoman might suggest that you buy a more expensive watch than you had planned on; or a co-worker might ask you for money to buy a cappuccino.

What determines whether a person will comply with a request? Many factors could be listed, but three stand out as especially interesting.

The Foot-in-the-Door Effect

People who sell door to door have long recognized that once they get a foot in the door, a sale is almost a sure thing. To state the **foot-in-the-door effect** more formally, a person who first agrees to a small request is later more likely to comply with a larger demand (Pascual & Guéguen, 2005). For instance, if someone asked you to put a large, ugly sign in your front yard to promote safe driving, you would probably refuse. If, however, you had first agreed to put a small sign in your window, you would later be much more likely to allow the big sign in your yard.

Apparently, the foot-in-the-door effect is based on observing one's own behavior. Seeing yourself agree to a small request helps convince you that you didn't mind doing what was asked. After that, you are more likely to comply with a larger request (Pascual & Guéguen, 2005).

The Door-in-the-Face Effect

Let's say that a neighbor comes to your door and asks you to feed his dogs, water his plants, and mow his yard while he is out of town for a month. This is quite a major request—one that most people would probably turn down. Feeling only slightly guilty, you tell your neighbor that you're sorry but you can't help him. Now, what if the same neighbor returns the next day and asks if you would at least pick up his mail while he is gone. Chances are very good that you would honor this request, even if you might have originally turned it down, too.

Psychologist Robert Cialdini coined the term **door-in-the-face effect** to describe the tendency for a person who has refused a major request to agree to a smaller request. In other words, after a person has turned down a major request ("slammed the door in your face"), he or she may be more willing to comply with a lesser demand. This strategy works because a person who abandons a large request appears to have given up something. In response, many people feel that they must repay her or him by giving in to the smaller request (Cialdini & Goldstein, 2004). In fact, a good way to get another person to comply with a request is to first do a small favor for the person.

The Lowball Technique

Anyone who has purchased an automobile will recognize a third way of inducing compliance. Automobile dealers are notorious for convincing customers to buy cars by offering "lowball" prices that undercut the competition. The dealer first gets the customer to agree to buy at an attractively low price. Then, once the customer is committed, various techniques are used to bump the price up before the sale is concluded.

The **lowball technique** consists of getting a person committed to act and then making the terms of acting less desirable (Guéguen, Pascual, & Dagot, 2002). Here's another example: A fellow student asks to borrow $25 for a day. This seems reasonable and you agree. However, once you have given your classmate the money, he explains that it would be easier to repay you after pay-

day, in 2 weeks. If you agree, you've succumbed to the lowball technique. Here's another example: Let's say you ask someone to give you a ride to school in the morning. Only after the person has agreed do you tell her that you have to be there at 6 AM.

Gaining Compliance

To summarize, there are three basic ways to get people to voluntarily comply with a request:

- You can start with a small request that is easy for the person to agree to, and then make a bigger request. (This is the foot-in-the-door strategy.)
- You can make a major request that you know the person will turn down, and then make a smaller request (the one you actually wanted the person to comply with in the first place). (This is the door-in-the-face strategy.)
- You can make a request and get the person to agree to it. Then change the requirements for fulfilling the request to something the person probably wouldn't have otherwise agreed to do. (This is the lowball technique.)

One of the main benefits of knowing these strategies is that you can protect yourself from being manipulated by people using them. For example, "How to Drive a Hard Bargain" explains how car salespersons use compliance techniques on customers.

Passive Compliance

Complying with requests is a normal part of daily social life. At times, however, a willingness to comply can exceed what is reasonable. Researcher Thomas Moriarty (1975) has observed that many

---

Group sanctions Rewards and punishments (such as approval or disapproval) administered by groups to enforce conformity among members.

Compliance Bending to the requests of a person who has little or no authority or other form of social power.

Foot-in-the-door effect The tendency for a person who has first complied with a small request to be more likely later to fulfill a larger request.

Door-in-the-face effect The tendency for a person who has refused a major request to subsequently be more likely to comply with a minor request.

Lowball technique A strategy in which commitment is gained first to reasonable or desirable terms, which are then made less reasonable or desirable.

CRITICAL THINKING

How to Drive a Hard Bargain

Your local car lot is a good place to study compliance. Automobile salespersons play the compliance game daily and get very good at it. If you understand what they are up to, and you are able to critically evaluate their tactics, you will have a far better chance of resisting their sales pressure (Cialdini, 2001; Cialdini & Goldstein, 2004).

A Foot in the Door

The salesperson offers you a test drive. If you accept, you will have made a small commitment of time to a particular car and to the salesperson. The salesperson will then ask you to go to an office and fill out some papers, "just to see what kind of a price" she or he can offer. If you go along, you will be further committed.

The Lowball Technique

To get things under way the salesperson will offer you a very good price for your trade-in or will ask you to make an offer on the new car, "any offer, no matter how low." The salesperson will then ask if you will buy the car if she or he can sell it for the price you state. If you say yes, you have virtually bought the car. Most people find it very difficult to walk away once bargaining has reached this stage.

The Hook Is Set

Once buyers are "hooked" by a lowball offer, the salesperson goes to the manager to have the sale "approved." On returning, the salesperson will tell you with great disappointment that the dealership would lose money on the deal. "Couldn't you just take a little less for the trade-in or pay a little more for the car?" the salesperson will ask. At this point many people hesitate and grumble, but most

give in and accept some "compromise" price or trade-in amount.

Evening the Odds

To combat all of the preceding, you must arm yourself with accurate information. In the past, salespeople had a great advantage in negotiating because they knew exactly how much the dealership paid for each car. Now, you can obtain detailed automobile pricing information on the Internet. With such information in hand, you will find it easier to challenge a salesperson's manipulative tactics.

After you've negotiated a final "best offer," get it in writing. Then walk out. Go to another dealer and see if the salesperson will better the price, in writing. When he or she does, return to the first dealership and negotiate for an even better price. Then decide where to buy. Now that you know some of the rules of the "car game," you might even enjoy playing it.

---

people will put up with almost anything to avoid a confrontation. As a consequence, they are prone to **passively comply,** which refers to quietly bending to unreasonable demands or unacceptable conditions.

In one experiment, two people (one was actually an accomplice) were seated back-to-back and left alone to work in a small room. As soon as the experimenter left, the phony participant cranked up some music. The accomplice was instructed to turn the music off only after a third request. In this particular experiment, 80 percent of the subjects said nothing, although they glared, covered their ears, stopped work, and so forth. An interview later showed that most were angry or annoyed but were afraid to tell the other person to be quiet.

> bridges
>
> For some people, passive compliance may be an expression of learned helplessness. **See Chapter 13, pages 442–443.**

Similarly, when loud conversations were staged behind theater patrons or people studying in a library, very few protested. Also, people were accosted in phone booths. The experimenter explained that he had left a ring in the booth and asked if the person had found it. When subjects said no, the experimenter demanded that they empty their pockets. Most did.

In these and similar situations, people passively accepted having their personal rights trampled, even when objecting presented no threat to their safety (● Figure 16.6).

In the next section we will investigate **obedience,** a special type of conformity to the demands of an authority. You've probably seen a bumper sticker that says "Question authority." Actually,

● **Figure 16.6** In an experiment done at an airport, a smoker intentionally sat or stood near nonsmokers. Only 9 percent of the nonsmokers asked the smoker to stop smoking, even when no-smoking signs were clearly visible nearby (Gibson & Werner, 1994).

• **Figure 16.7** Scenes from Stanley Milgram's study of obedience: the "shock generator," strapping a "learner" into his chair, and a "teacher" being told to administer a severe shock to the learner.

that's not bad advice if it means "Think critically." However, obedience to authority is a normal part of social life. But what are the limits of obedience? When is it appropriate to resist authority? These are essential questions about how we are affected by social influence based on authority.

Obedience—Would You Electrocute a Stranger?

Gateway Question: Can people be too obedient?

The question is this: If ordered to do so, would you shock a man with a heart condition who is screaming and asking to be released? Certainly, few people would obey. Or would they? In Nazi Germany, obedient soldiers (once average citizens) helped slaughter more than 6 million people in concentration camps. Do such inhumane acts reflect deep character flaws? Are they the acts of heartless psychopaths or crazed killers? Or are they simply the result of obedience to authority? These are questions that puzzled social psychologist Stanley Milgram (1965) when he began a provocative series of studies on obedience.

How did Milgram study obedience? As was true of the Asch experiments, Milgram's research is best appreciated by imagining yourself as a subject. Place yourself in the following situation.

Milgram's Obedience Studies

Imagine answering a newspaper ad to take part in a "learning" experiment at Yale University. When you arrive, a coin is flipped and a second subject, a pleasant-looking man in his fifties, is designated the "learner." By chance you have become the "teacher."

Your task is to read a list of word pairs. The learner's task is to memorize them. You are to punish him with an electric shock each time he makes a mistake. The learner is taken to an adjacent room, and you watch as he is seated in an "electric chair" apparatus. Electrodes are attached to his wrists. You are then escorted to your position in front of a "shock generator." On this device is a row of 30 switches marked from 15 to 450 volts. Corresponding labels range from "Slight Shock" to "Extreme Intensity Shock" and finally "Danger: Severe Shock." Your instructions are to shock the learner each time he makes a mistake. You are to begin with 15 volts

and then move one switch (15 volts) higher for each additional mistake (• Figure 16.7).

The experiment begins, and the learner soon makes his first error. You flip a switch. More mistakes. Rapidly you reach the 75-volt level. The learner moans after each shock. At 100 volts he complains that he has a heart condition. At 150 volts he says he no longer wants to continue and demands to be released. At 300 volts he screams and says he can no longer give answers.

At some point, you begin to protest to the experimenter. "That man has a heart condition," you say; "I'm not going to kill that man." The experimenter says, "Please continue." Another shock and another scream from the learner and you say, "You mean I've got to keep going up the scale? No, sir. I'm not going to give him 450 volts!" The experimenter says, "The experiment requires that you continue." For a time the learner refuses to answer any more questions and screams with each shock (Milgram, 1965). Then he falls chillingly silent for the rest of the experiment.

It's hard to believe many people would do this. What happened? Milgram also doubted that many people would obey his orders. When he polled a group of psychiatrists before the experiment, they predicted that less than 1 percent of those tested would obey. The astounding fact is that 65 percent obeyed completely by going all the way to the 450-volt level. Virtually no one stopped short of 300 volts ("Severe Shock") (• Figure 16.8).

Was the learner injured? The "learner" was actually an actor who turned a tape recorder on and off in the shock room. No shocks were ever administered, but the dilemma for the "teacher" was quite real. Subjects protested, sweated, trembled, stuttered, bit their lips, and laughed nervously. Clearly they were disturbed by what they were doing. Nevertheless, most obeyed the experimenter's orders.

Milgram's Follow-Up

Why did so many people obey? Some have suggested that the prestige of Yale University added to subjects' willingness to obey. Could it be that they assumed the professor running the experi-

Passive compliance Passively bending to unreasonable demands or circumstances.

Obedience Conformity to the demands of an authority.

DISCOVERING PSYCHOLOGY

Quack Like a Duck

Imagine your response to the following events. On the first day of class, your psychology professor begins to establish the basic rules of behavior for the course. Draw a line under the first instruction you think you would refuse to carry out:

1. Seats are assigned and you are told to move to a new location.
2. You are told not to talk during class.
3. Your professor tells you that you must have permission to leave early.

4. You are told to bring your textbook to class at all times.
5. Your professor tells you to use only a pencil for taking notes.
6. You are directed to take off your watch.
7. The professor tells you to keep both hands on your desktop at all times.
8. You are instructed to keep both your feet flat on the floor.
9. You are told to stand up and clap your hands three times.

10. Your professor says, "Stick two fingers up your nose and quack like a duck."

At what point would you stop obeying such orders? In reality, you might find yourself obeying a legitimate authority long after that person's demands had become unreasonable (Aronson, Wilson, & Akert, 2007). What would happen, though, if a few students resisted orders early in the sequence? Would that help free others to disobey? For an answer, return to the discussion of Milgram's experiment for some final remarks.

Shock level

• **Figure 16.8** Results of Milgram's obedience experiment. Only a minority of subjects refused to provide shocks, even at the most extreme intensities. The first substantial drop in obedience occurred at the 300-volt level (Milgram, 1963).

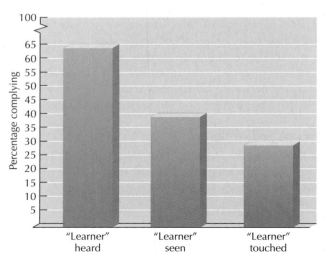

• **Figure 16.9** Physical distance from the "learner" had a significant effect on the percentage of subjects obeying orders.

ment would not really allow anyone to be hurt? To test this possibility, the study was rerun in a shabby office building in nearby Bridgeport, Connecticut. Under these conditions fewer people obeyed (48 percent), but the reduction was minor.

Milgram was disturbed by the willingness of people to knuckle under to authority and senselessly shock someone. In later experiments, he tried to reduce obedience. He found that the distance between the teacher and the learner was important. When subjects were in the *same room* as the learner, only 40 percent fully obeyed. When they were *face-to-face* with the learner and required to force his hand down on a simulated "shock plate," only 30 percent obeyed (• Figure 16.9). Distance from the authority also had an effect. When the experimenter gave his orders over the phone, only 22 percent obeyed. You may doubt that Milgram's study of obedience applies to you. If so, take a moment to read "Quack Like a Duck."

Implications

Milgram's research raises nagging questions about our willingness to commit antisocial or inhumane acts commanded by a "legitimate authority." The excuse so often given by war criminals—"I was only following orders"—takes on new meaning in this light. Milgram suggested that when directions come from an authority, people rationalize that they are not personally responsible for their actions. In locales as diverse as Cambodia, Rwanda, Bosnia, Vietnam, Darfur, Sri Lanka, and Iraq, the tragic result has been "sanctioned massacres" of chilling proportions. Even in everyday life, crimes of obedience are common (Zimbardo, 2007). In order to keep their jobs, many people obey orders to do things that they know are dishonest, unethical, or harmful (Hamilton & Sanders, 1995).

Isn't that an overly negative view of obedience? Obedience to authority is obviously necessary and desirable in many circumstances. Just the same, it is probably true, as C. P. Snow (1961) observed, "When you think of the long and gloomy history of

Obedience to authority is often necessary and reasonable; however, it can also be destructive.

man, you will find more hideous crimes have been committed in the name of obedience than in the name of rebellion." With this in mind, let us end on a more positive note. In one of his experiments, Milgram found that group support can greatly reduce destructive obedience. When real subjects saw two other "teachers" (both actors) resist orders and walk out of the experiment, only 10 percent continued to obey. Thus, a personal act of courage or moral fortitude by one or two members of a group may free others to disobey misguided or unjust authority.

Coercion—Brainwashing and Cults

Gateway Questions: Is brainwashing actually possible? How are people converted to cult membership?

We close this section on social influence by examining some forms of *coercion,* the most extreme type of social influence. You are being **coerced** if you are forced to change your beliefs or your behavior against your will.

If you're a history enthusiast, you may associate *brainwashing* with techniques used by the Communist Chinese on prisoners during the Korean War (Jowett, 2006). Through various types of "thought reform," the Chinese were able to coerce some of these prisoners to sign false confessions. More recently, the mass murder/suicide at Jonestown, the Branch Davidian tragedy at Waco, the Heaven's Gate group suicide in San Diego, and Osama bin Laden's al-Qaeda movement have heightened public interest in coerced attitude and behavior change.

How does brainwashing differ from other persuasive techniques? As we have noted, advertisers, politicians, educators, religious organizations, and others actively seek to alter attitudes and opinions. To an extent, their persuasive efforts resemble brainwashing, but there is an important difference: **Brainwashing,** or forced attitude change, requires a captive audience. If you are offended by a television commercial, you can tune it out. Prisoners are completely at the mercy of their captors. Complete control over the environment allows a degree of psychological manipulation that would be impossible in a normal setting.

Brainwashing

How does captivity facilitate coercion? Brainwashing typically begins by making the target person feel completely helpless. Physical and psychological abuse, lack of sleep, humiliation, and isolation serve to *unfreeze,* or loosen, former values and beliefs. When exhaustion, pressure, and fear become unbearable, *change* occurs as the person begins to abandon former beliefs. Prisoners who reach the breaking point may sign a false confession or cooperate to gain relief. When they do, they are suddenly rewarded with praise, privileges, food, or rest. From that point on, a mixture of hope and fear, plus pressures to conform, serves to *refreeze* (solidify) new attitudes (Taylor, 2004).

How permanent are changes coerced by brainwashing? In most cases, the dramatic shift in attitudes brought about by brainwashing is temporary. Most "converted" prisoners who returned to the United States after the Korean War eventually reverted to their original beliefs. Nevertheless, brainwashing can be powerful, as shown by the success of cults in recruiting new members.

Cults

Exhorted by their leader, some 900 members of the Reverend Jim Jones's People's Temple picked up paper cups and drank purple Kool-Aid laced with the deadly poison cyanide. Psychologically the mass suicide at Jonestown in 1978 is not so incredible as it might seem (Dein & Littlewood, 2005). The inhabitants of Jonestown were isolated in the jungles of Guyana, intimidated by guards, and lulled with sedatives. They were also cut off from friends and relatives and totally accustomed to obeying rigid rules of conduct, which primed them for Jones's final "loyalty test." Of greater psychological interest is the question of how people reach such a state of commitment and dependency

Why do people join groups such as the People's Temple? The People's Temple was a classic example of a **cult,** an authoritarian group in which the leader's personality is more important than the beliefs she or he preaches. Cult members give their allegiance to this person, who is regarded as infallible, and they follow his or her dictates without question. Almost always, cult members are victimized by their leaders in one way or another.

For example, in April 1993, David Koresh and members of his Branch Davidian group perished in a fire at their Waco, Texas, compound. Like Jim Jones had done years before in Jonestown, Koresh took nearly total control of his followers' lives. He told them what to eat, dictated sexual mores, and had errant followers paddled. Followers were persuaded to surrender money, property,

Coercion Being forced to change your beliefs or your behavior against your will.

Brainwashing Engineered or forced attitude change involving a captive audience.

Cult A group that professes great devotion to some person and follows that person almost without question; cult members are typically victimized by their leaders in various ways.

In April 1993, David Koresh and members of his Branch Davidian group perished in an inferno at their Waco, Texas, compound. Authorities believe the fire was set by a cult member, under the direction of Koresh. Like Jim Jones had done years before in Jonestown, Koresh took nearly total control of his followers' lives.

and even their children and wives. Like Jones, Koresh also took mistresses and had children out of wedlock. And like other cult leaders, Jones and Koresh demanded absolute loyalty and obedience to themselves and to their cult, with tragic results (Dein & Littlewood, 2005; Reiterman, 1993).

Psychologist and pioneering brainwashing expert Margaret Singer (1921–2003) studied and aided hundreds of former cult members. Her interviews reveal that in recruiting new members, cults use a powerful blend of guilt, manipulation, isolation, deception, fear, and escalating commitment. In this respect, cults employ high-pressure indoctrination techniques not unlike those used in brainwashing (Singer, 2003; Singer & Addis, 1992). In the United States alone, an estimated 2 to 5 million people have succumbed to the lure of cults (Robinson, Frye, & Bradley, 1997).

Recruitment

Some people studied by Singer were seriously distressed when they joined a cult. Most, however, were simply undergoing a period of mild depression, indecision, or alienation from family and friends (Hunter, 1998). Cult members try to catch potential converts at a time of need—especially when a sense of belonging will be attractive to converts. For instance, many people were approached just after a romance had broken up, or when they were struggling with exams, or were trying to become independent from their families (Sirkin, 1990). At such times, people are easily persuaded that joining the group is all they need to do to be happy again (Hunter, 1998). Adolescents are especially vulnerable to recruitment into cults because they may be seeking a cause to conform to as a replacement for the parental authority they are rebelling against (Richmond, 2004).

bridges
People suffering from identity confusion, which is common during adolescence, are more susceptible to recruitment by coercive groups. **See Chapter 3, pages 102–104.**

Conversion

How is conversion achieved? Often it begins with intense displays of affection and understanding ("love bombing"). Next comes isolation from non–cult members and drills, discipline, and rituals (all-night meditation or continuous chanting, for instance). These rituals wear down physical and emotional resistance, discourage critical thinking, and generate feelings of commitment (Langone, 2002).

Many cults make clever use of the foot-in-the-door technique (described previously). At first, recruits make small commitments (to stay after a meeting, for example). Then, larger commitments are encouraged (to stay an extra day, to call in sick at work, and so forth). Making a major commitment is usually the final step. The new devotee signs over a bank account or property to the group, moves in with the group, and so forth. Making such major public commitments creates a powerful cognitive dissonance effect. Before long, it becomes virtually impossible for converts to admit they have made a mistake.

Once in the group, members are cut off from family and friends (former reference groups), and the cult can control the flow and interpretation of information to them. Members are isolated from their former value systems and social structures. Conversion is complete when they come to think of themselves more as group members than as individuals. At this point obedience is nearly total (Wexler, 1995).

Why do people stay in cults? Most former members mention guilt and fear as the main reasons for not leaving when they wished they could. Most had been reduced to childlike dependency on the group for meeting all their daily needs (Singer, 2003). After they leave, many former cult members suffer from anxiety, panic attacks, and emotional disturbances much like posttraumatic stress disorder (West, 1993).

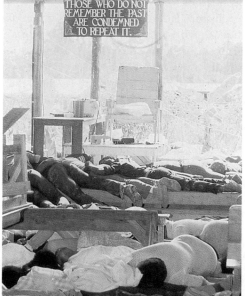

Aftermath of the mass suicide at Jonestown. How do cult-like groups recruit new devotees?

Implications

Behind the "throne" from which Jim Jones ruled Jonestown was a sign bearing these words: "Those who do not remember the past are condemned to repeat it." Sadly, another cult-related tragedy occurred in 2001. The terrorist attacks on the United States were carried out by followers of cult leader Osama bin Laden. At his direction, they learned hatred and contempt for everyone outside their band of true believers. If there is a lesson to be learned from such destructive cults, it is this: All true spiritual leaders have taught love and compassion. They also encourage followers to question their beliefs and to reach their own conclusions about how to live. In contrast, destructive cults show how dangerous it is to trade personal independence and critical thinking for security (Goldberg, 2001).

A Look Ahead

In the upcoming discussion of Psychology in Action, we will return to the problem of passive behavior to learn how you can better handle difficult social situations. Be assertive, and read on.

KNOWLEDGE BUILDER
Obedience, Compliance, and Coercion

RECITE

1. An ability to punish others for failure to obey is the basis for
   a. referent power
   b. legitimate power
   c. expert power
   d. coercive power
2. The term *compliance* refers to situations in which a person complies with commands made by a person who has authority. T or F?
3. Obedience in Milgram's experiments was related to
   a. distance between learner and teacher
   b. distance between experimenter and teacher
   c. obedience of other teachers
   d. all of these
4. Obedience is conformity to the commands of an _____.
5. By repeating his obedience experiment in a downtown office building, Milgram demonstrated that the prestige of Yale University was the main reason for subjects' willingness to obey in the original experiment. T or F?
6. Brainwashing differs from other persuasive attempts in that brainwashing requires a _____.
7. Which statement about brainwashing is *false*?
   a. The target person is isolated from others.
   b. Attitude changes brought about by brainwashing are usually permanent.
   c. The first step is unfreezing former values and beliefs.
   d. Cooperation with the indoctrinating agent is rewarded.

REFLECT

Critical Thinking

8. Modern warfare allows killing to take place impersonally and at a distance. How does this relate to Milgram's experiments?
9. Cognitive dissonance theory predicts that false confessions obtained during brainwashing are not likely to bring about lasting changes in attitudes. Why?

Relate

Return to the description of various types of social power. Can you think of a setting in which you have (to a greater or lesser degree) each type of power?

You would like to persuade people to donate to a deserving charity. How, specifically, could you use compliance techniques to get people to donate?

Are you surprised that so many people obeyed orders in Milgram's experiments? Do you think you would have obeyed? How actively do you question authority?

To what extent are governments entitled to use coercion to modify the attitudes or behavior of individuals?

Answers: 1. d **2.** F **3.** d **4.** authority **5.** F **6.** captive audience **7.** b **8.** There is a big difference between killing someone in hand-to-hand combat and killing someone by lining up images on a video screen. Milgram's research suggests that it is easier for a person to follow orders to kill another human when the victim is at a distance and removed from personal contact. **9.** Because there is strong justification for such actions. As a result, little cognitive dissonance is created when a prisoner makes statements that contradict his or her beliefs.

PSYCHOLOGY IN ACTION

Assertiveness Training—Standing Up for Your Rights

Gateway Question: How does self-assertion differ from aggression?

Most of us have been rewarded, first as children and later as adults, for compliant, obedient, or "good" behavior. Perhaps this is why so many people find it difficult to assert themselves. Or perhaps not asserting yourself is related to anxiety about "making a scene" or feeling disliked by others. Whatever the causes, some people suffer tremendous anguish in any situation requiring poise, self-

confidence, or self-assertion. Have you ever done any of the following?

- Hesitated to question an error on a restaurant bill because you were afraid of making a scene?
- Backed out of asking for a raise or a change in working conditions?
- Said yes when you wanted to say no?
- Been afraid to question a grade that seemed unfair?

If you have ever had difficulty asserting yourself in similar situations, behavior therapist Joseph Wolpe (1974) has a solution for you: a technique called **assertiveness training** (instruction in how to be self-assertive).

What is done in assertiveness training? Assertiveness training is a very direct proce-

Assertiveness training Instruction in how to be self-assertive.

dure. By using group exercises, videotapes, mirrors, and staged conflicts, the instructor teaches assertive behavior. People learn to practice honesty, disagreeing, questioning authority, and assertive postures and gestures. As their self-confidence improves, nonassertive clients are taken on "field trips" to shops and restaurants where they practice what they have learned.

Nonassertion requiring therapy is unusual. Nevertheless, many people become tense or upset in at least some situations in which they must stand up for their rights. For this reason, many people have found the techniques and exercises of assertiveness training helpful. If you have ever eaten a carbonized steak when you ordered it rare or stood in silent rage as a clerk ignored you, the following discussion will be of interest.

Self-Assertion

The first step in assertiveness training is to convince yourself of three basic rights: You have the right to refuse, to request, and to right a wrong. **Self-assertion** involves standing up for these rights by speaking out in your own behalf.

Is self-assertion just getting things your own way? Not at all. A basic distinction can be made between *self-assertion* and *aggressive* behavior. Self-assertion is a direct, honest expression of feelings and desires. It is not exclusively self-serving. People who are nonassertive are usually patient to a fault. Sometimes their pent-up anger explodes with unexpected fury, which can damage relationships. In contrast to assertive behavior, **aggression** involves hurting another person

or achieving one's goals at the expense of another. Aggression does not take into account the feelings or rights of others. It is an attempt to get one's own way no matter what. Assertion techniques emphasize firmness, not attack (● Table 16.2).

Assertiveness Training

The basic idea in assertiveness training is that each assertive action is practiced until it can be repeated even under stress. For example, let's say it really angers you when a store clerk waits on several people who arrived after you did. To improve your assertiveness in this situation, you would begin by *rehearsing* the dialogue, posture, and gestures you would use to confront the clerk or the other customer. Working in front of a mirror can be very helpful. If possible, you should *role-play* the scene with a friend. Be sure to have your friend take the part of a really aggressive or irresponsible clerk, as well as a cooperative one. Rehearsal and role-playing should also be used when you expect a possible confrontation with someone—for example, if you are going to ask for a raise, challenge a grade, or confront a landlord.

Is that all there is to it? No. Another important principle is **overlearning** (practice that continues after initial mastery of a skill). When you rehearse or role-play assertive behavior, it is essential to continue to practice until your responses become almost automatic. This helps prevent you from getting flustered in the actual situation.

One more technique you may find useful is the **broken record.** This is a self-assertion technique involving repeating a request until it is acknowledged. (In ancient times, when people played phonograph records, the needle sometimes got "stuck in a groove." When

this happened, part of a song might repeat over and over. Hence, the term *broken record* refers to repeating yourself.) Repetition is also a good way to prevent assertion from becoming aggression.

As an illustration, let's say you are returning a pair of shoes to a store. After two wearings the shoes fell apart, but you bought them 2 months ago and no longer have a receipt. The broken record could sound something like this:

> *Customer:* I would like to have these shoes replaced.
> *Clerk:* Do you have a receipt?
> *Customer:* No, but I bought them here, and since they are defective, I would like to have you replace them.
> *Clerk:* I can't do that without a receipt.
> *Customer:* I understand that, but I want them replaced.
> *Clerk:* Well, come back this afternoon and talk to the manager.
> *Customer:* I've brought these shoes in because they are defective.
> *Clerk:* Well, I'm not authorized to replace them.
> *Customer:* Yes, well, if you'll replace these, I'll be on my way.

Notice that the customer did not attack the clerk or create an angry confrontation. Simple persistence is often all that is necessary for successful self-assertion.

How would I respond assertively to a put-down? Responding assertively to verbal aggression (a "put-down") is a real challenge. The tendency is to respond aggressively, which usually makes things worse. A good way to respond to a put-down uses the following steps: (1) If you are wrong, admit it; (2) acknowledge the person's feelings; (3) assert yourself about the other person's aggression; (4) briskly end the interchange.

Jeff Widener/AP/Wide World Photo

Associated Press photographer Jeff Widener snapped this timeless photo of a lone protester literally standing up on his own behalf while he halted a column of tanks during the 1989 pro-democracy rallies in Tiananmen Square in Beijing, China. How many of us would find the courage to assert ourselves against such direct expressions of authority?

Table 16.2 ● Comparison of Assertive, Aggressive, and Nonassertive Behavior

	Actor	Receiver of Behavior
Nonassertive behavior	Self-denying, inhibited, hurt, and anxious; lets others make choices; goals not achieved	Feels sympathy, guilt, or contempt for actor; achieves goals at actor's expense
Aggressive behavior	Achieves goals at others' expense; expresses feelings, but hurts others; chooses for others or puts them down	Feels hurt, defensive, humiliated, or taken advantage of; does not meet own needs
Assertive behavior	Self-enhancing; acts in own best interests; expresses feelings; respects rights of others; goals usually achieved; self-respect maintained	Needs respected and feelings expressed; may achieve goal; self-worth maintained

Psychologists Robert Alberti and Michael Emmons (2001) offer an example of how to use the four steps. Let's say you accidentally bump into someone. The person responds angrily, "Damn it! Why don't you watch where you're going! You fool, you could have hurt me!" A good response would be to say, "I'm sorry I bumped you. I didn't do it intentionally. It's obvious you're upset, but I don't like your calling me names or yelling. I can get your point without that."

Now, what if someone insults you indirectly? ("I love your taste in clothes, it's so 'folksy.'") Alberti and Emmons suggest you ask for a clarification. ("What are you trying to say?") This will force the person to take responsibility for the aggression. It can also provide an opportunity to change the way the person interacts with you: "If you really don't like what I'm wearing, I'd like to know it. I'm not always sure I like the things I buy, and I value your opinion."

To summarize, self-assertion does not supply instant poise, confidence, or self-assurance. However, it is a way of combating anxieties associated with life in an impersonal and sometimes intimidating society. If you are interested in more information, you can consult a book titled *Your Perfect Right* by Alberti and Emmons (2001).

KNOWLEDGE BUILDER
Assertiveness Training

RECITE

1. In assertiveness training, people learn techniques for getting their way in social situations and angry interchanges. T or F?
2. Nonassertive behavior causes hurt, anxiety, and self-denial in the actor and sympathy, guilt, or contempt in the receiver. T or F?
3. Overlearning should be avoided when rehearsing assertive behaviors. T or F?
4. The "broken record" must be avoided because it is nonassertive behavior. T or F?

REFLECT

Critical Thinking

5. When practicing self-assertion, do you think it would be better to improvise your own responses or imitate those of a person skilled in self-assertion?

Relate

Pick a specific instance when you could have been more assertive. How would you handle the situation if it occurs again?

Think of a specific instance when you were angry and acted aggressively. How could you have handled the situation through self-assertion, instead of aggression?

Answers: 1. F 2. T 3. F 4. F 5. One study found that imitating an assertive model is more effective than improvising your own responses (Kipper, 1992). If you know an assertive and self-assured person, you can learn a lot by watching how he or she handles difficult situations.

chapter in review   Gateways to Social Thinking and Social Influence

Membership in groups, and social situations in general, strongly influence how people behave, think, and feel.

- Social psychology studies humans as social animals enmeshed in complex networks of social relationships.
- Culture provides a broad social context for our behavior.
- One's position in groups defines a variety of roles to be played.
- Social roles, which may be achieved or ascribed, are particular behavior patterns associated with social positions. When two or more contradictory roles are held, role conflict may occur. The Stanford prison experiment showed that destructive roles may override individual motives for behavior.
- Positions within groups typically carry higher or lower levels of status. High status is associated with special privileges and respect.
- Group structure refers to the organization of roles, communication pathways, and power within a group. Group

cohesiveness is basically the degree of attraction among group members.
- Norms are standards of conduct enforced (formally or informally) by groups. The autokinetic effect has been used to demonstrate that norms rapidly form even in temporary groups.

Self-assertion A direct, honest expression of feelings and desires.

Aggression Hurting another person or achieving one's goals at the expense of another person.

Overlearning Learning or practice that continues after initial mastery of a skill.

Broken record A self-assertion technique involving repeating a request until it is acknowledged.

Social behavior cannot be fully understood unless we know what causes people attribute their behavior to and how they explain the behavior of others.

- Attribution theory is concerned with how we make inferences about behavior. A variety of factors affect attribution, including consistency, distinctiveness, situational demands, and consensus.
- The fundamental attribution error is to ascribe the actions of others to internal causes. Because of actor–observer differences, we tend to attribute our own behavior to external causes.
- Self-handicapping involves arranging excuses for poor performance as a way to protect one's self-image or self-esteem.

Attitudes are learned dispositions formed by direct contact, interaction with others, child-rearing practices, and group pressures.

- Attitudes subtly affect nearly all aspects of social behavior.
- Attitudes are made up of a belief component, an emotional component, and an action component.
- Peer-group influences, the mass media, and chance conditioning also appear to be important in attitude formation.
- Attitudes are typically measured by use of techniques such as open-ended interviews, social distance scales, and attitude scales. Attitudes expressed in these ways do not always correspond to actual behavior.

Effective persuasion occurs when characteristics of the communicator, the message, and the audience are well matched. Cognitive dissonance occurs when there is a clash between thoughts or between thoughts and actions.

- Attitude change is related to reference group membership, to deliberate persuasion, and to significant personal experiences (which may be engineered through role-playing).
- In general, a likable and believable communicator who repeats a credible message that arouses emotion in the audience and states clear-cut conclusions will be persuasive.
- The maintenance and change of attitudes is closely related to needs for consistency in thoughts and actions. Cognitive dissonance theory explains the dynamics of such needs.
- The amount of reward or justification for one's actions influences whether dissonance occurs. We are motivated to reduce dissonance when it occurs, often by changing beliefs or attitudes.

Social influence refers to alterations in behavior brought about by the behavior of others, and social power refers to the ability of people to exert social influence.

- A major fact of social life is that our behavior is influenced in numerous ways by the actions of other people.
- Social influence ranges from mild (mere influence, conformity, and compliance) to strong (obedience and coercion). Conformity to group pressure is a familiar example of social influence.
- Social influence is also related to five types of social power: reward power, coercive power, legitimate power, referent power, and expert power.

The presence of others may facilitate (or inhibit) performance.

- People may also engage in social loafing, working less hard when they are part of a group.
- The study of personal space is called proxemics. Four basic spatial zones around each person's body are intimate distance (0–18 inches), personal distance (1½–4 feet), social distance (4–12 feet), and public distance (12 feet or more).
- The nature of many relationships is revealed by the distance you are comfortable maintaining between yourself and another person.

Virtually everyone conforms to a variety of broad social and cultural norms. Conformity pressures also exist within smaller groups.

- The famous Asch experiments demonstrated that various group sanctions encourage conformity.
- Groupthink refers to compulsive conformity in group decision making. Victims of groupthink seek to maintain each other's approval, even at the cost of critical thinking.

Three strategies for inducing compliance are the foot-in-the-door technique, the door-in-the-face approach, and the lowball technique.

- Compliance with direct requests is another means by which behavior is influenced.

Research suggests that in addition to excessive obedience to authority, many people show a surprising passive compliance to unreasonable requests.

- Obedience to authority has been investigated in a variety of experiments, particularly those by Milgram. Obedience in Milgram's studies decreased when the victim was in the same room, when the victim and subject were face to face, when the authority figure was absent, and when others refused to obey.

Brainwashing is possible and depends on control of the target person's total environment. Forced attitude change (brainwashing) is sometimes used by cults and other coercive groups.

- Coercion involves forcing people to change their beliefs or behavior against their will.
- Brainwashing is a form of forced attitude change. Three steps in brainwashing are unfreezing, changing, and refreezing attitudes and beliefs.
- Many cults recruit new members with high-pressure indoctrination techniques resembling brainwashing. Such groups attempt to catch people when they are vulnerable. Then they combine isolation, displays of affection, discipline and rituals, intimidation, and escalating commitment to bring about conversion.

Self-assertion involves standing up for yourself, whereas aggression involves achieving your goals at the expense of another.

- Assertiveness is a valuable alternative to becoming aggressive or being victimized in social situations.
- Self-assertion, as opposed to aggression, involves clearly stating one's wants and needs to others. Learning to be assertive is accomplished by role-playing, rehearsing assertive actions,

overlearning, and use of specific techniques, such as the "broken record."

- Everyone is affected by pressures to conform, comply, and obey. There are times when it is valuable to know how to recognize and resist such pressures.

Web Resources

.....r an up-to-date list of direct links to interesting sites, including those listed here, visit the student companion site for this book at www.cengage.com/psychology/coon

World Project Join Duncan Watt's online experiment to see if we are really all connected through six degrees of separation.

Social Psychology Network Explore this massive website devoted to social psychology.

Stanford Prison Study Explore Phil Zimbardo's classic study of the power of social roles.

The Two Step Dig down deeper into the foot-in-the-door and door-in-the-face compliance techniques.

Milgram's Study of Obedience Listen to audio clips of this infamous experiment.

Assertiveness Access a collection on virtual pamphlets on assertiveness.

Interactive Learning

Introduction to Psychology: Gateways to Mind and Behavior **Book Companion Website**
www.cengage.com/psychology/coon

Visit your book companion website, where you will find flash cards, practice quizzes, web links, and more to help you study.

CENGAGENOW™ *Just what you need to know NOW!*

Spend time on what you need to master rather than on information you already have learned. Take a pre-test for this chapter, and CengageNOW will generate a personalized study plan based on your results. The study plan will identify the topics you need to review and direct you to online resources to help you master those topics. You can then take a post-test to help you determine the concepts you have mastered and what you will need to work on. Try it out! Go to www.cengage.com/login to sign in with an access code or to purchase access to this product.

CHAPTER 17

Prosocial and Antisocial Behavior

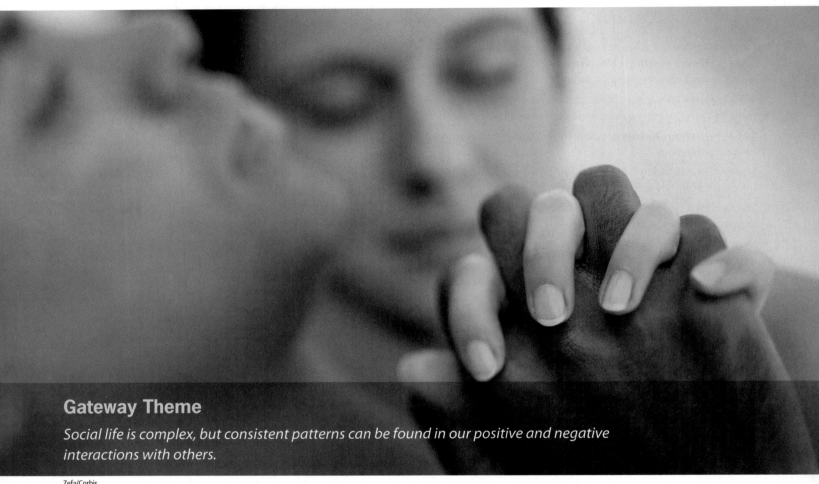

Gateway Theme

Social life is complex, but consistent patterns can be found in our positive and negative interactions with others.

Zefa/Corbis

Gateway Questions

- *Why do people affiliate?*
- *What factors influence interpersonal attraction?*
- *How do liking and loving differ?*
- *Why are bystanders so often unwilling to help in an emergency?*
- *How do psychologists explain human aggression?*

- *What causes prejudice?*
- *What can be done about prejudice and intergroup conflict?*
- *How can we promote multiculturalism and social harmony?*

Jasmine and Osama are moving to Europe. As Jasmine wryly comments, "We were naive and thought we could win this fight but we can't. So we have to go abroad and start a new life." The fight they lost was another round in the universal struggle between love and hate. You see, Jasmine is a Jewish Israeli and Osama is Palestinian Muslim. They met, fell in love, and were married. Since then they have been endlessly harassed by the hatred built up during the Palestinian–Israeli conflict. Both sides are hostile to the love Jasmine and Osama have for each other. The Middle East is no place for them to live anymore (Price, 2007).

Jasmine and Osama are not alone. Prejudice and hatred between various groups around the world, from Catholics and Protestants in Northern Ireland and Hutus and Tutsis in Rwanda to African Americans and European Americans right here in the United States has produced countless tragic stories like that of Jasmine and Osama. These two, at least, can be thankful they escaped with their lives.

In this chapter we will explore the social psychology of both love and hate. Various forms of love affect other people positively. Broadly speaking, **prosocial behavior** is any behavior that has a positive impact on other people. In contrast, **antisocial behavior** is any behavior that has a negative impact on other people. Let's start on a positive note with a look at what brings people together.

◖◗ The Need for Affiliation— Come Together

Gateway Question: Why do people affiliate?

Why do people choose to congregate with others? Hanging out with other people is the most basic form of prosocial behavior. We are social beings with a **need to affiliate** (a desire to associate with other people) based on basic human desires for approval, support, friendship, and information (Baumeister & Bushman, 2008). We also seek the company of others to alleviate fear or anxiety. This point is illustrated by a classic experiment in which college women were threatened with electric shock.

Zilstein's Shock Emporium

A man introduced as Dr. Gregor Zilstein ominously explained to arriving participants, "We would like to give each of you a series of electric shocks . . . these shocks will hurt, they will be painful." In the room was a frightening electrical device that seemed to verify Zilstein's plans. While waiting to be shocked, each woman was given a choice of waiting alone or with other participants. Women frightened in this way more often chose to wait with others; those who expected the shock to be "a mild tickle or tingle" were more willing to wait alone. (Schachter, 1959)

Apparently, the frightened women found it comforting to be with others. Should we conclude that "misery loves company"? Actually, that's not entirely correct. In a later experiment, women who expected to be shocked were given the choice of waiting with other future shock recipients, with women waiting to see their college advisers, or alone. Most women chose to wait with other future "victims." In short, misery seems to love miserable company! In general, we prefer to be with people in circumstances similar to our own (Gump & Kulik, 1997).

Is there a reason for that? Yes. Other people provide information that helps us evaluate our own reactions. When a situation is threatening or unfamiliar, or when we are in doubt, *social comparisons* tend to guide our behavior (Kulik, Mahler, & Moore, 2003).

Social Comparison Theory

If you want to know how heavy you are, you simply get on a scale. But how do you know if you are a good athlete, worker, parent, or friend? How do you know if your views on politics, religion, or

High-school class reunions are notorious for the rampant social comparison they often encourage. Apparently it's hard to resist comparing yourself to former classmates to see how you are doing in life.

Prosocial behavior Any behavior that has a positive impact on other people.

Antisocial behavior Any behavior that has a negative impact on other people.

Need to affiliate The desire to associate with other people.

hip-hop are unusual or widely shared? When there are no objective standards, the only available yardstick is provided by comparing yourself with others (Miller, 2006).

Social psychologist Leon Festinger (1919–1989) theorized that group membership fills needs for **social comparison** (comparing your own actions, feelings, opinions, or abilities to those of others). Have you ever "compared notes" with other students after taking an exam? ("How did you do?" "Wasn't that last question hard?") If you have, you were satisfying needs for social comparison (Festinger, 1957).

Typically, we don't make social comparisons randomly or on some absolute scale. Meaningful evaluations are based on comparing yourself with people of similar backgrounds, abilities, and circumstances (Stapel & Marx, 2007). To illustrate, let's ask a student named Wendy if she is a good tennis player. If Wendy compares herself with a professional, the answer will be no. But this tells us little about her *relative* ability. Within her tennis group, Wendy is regarded as an excellent player. On a fair scale of comparison, Wendy knows she is good and she takes pride in her tennis skills. In the same way, thinking of yourself as successful, talented, responsible, or fairly paid depends entirely on whom you choose for comparison. Thus, a desire for social comparison provides a motive for associating with others and influences which groups we join (Franzoi & Klaiber, 2007).

In addition to providing information, social comparisons may, at times, be made in ways that reflect desires for self-protection or self-enhancement (Schwinghammer, Stapel, & Blanton, 2006). If you feel threatened, you may make a **downward comparison** by contrasting yourself with a person who ranks lower on some dimension (Gibbons et al., 2002). For example, if you have a part-time job and your employer cuts your hours, you may comfort yourself by thinking about a friend who just lost a job.

What about upward comparisons? Do they occur, too? As Wendy's tennis playing suggests, comparing yourself with people of much higher ability will probably just make you feel bad (Tyler & Feldman, 2006). However, **upward comparisons,** in which we compare ourselves to a person who ranks higher on some dimension, are sometimes used for self-improvement. One way that Wendy can learn to improve her tennis skills is to compare herself with players who are only a little better than she is (Huguet et al., 2001).

In general, social comparison theory holds that desires for self-evaluation, self-protection, and self-enhancement provide motives for associating with others. In doing so, they influence which groups we join.

Don't people also affiliate out of attraction for one another? They do, of course. The next section tells why.

⬤⬤ Interpersonal Attraction— Social Magnetism?

Gateway Question: What factors influence interpersonal attraction?

"Birds of a feather flock together." "Familiarity breeds contempt." "Opposites attract." "Absence makes the heart grow fonder." Are these statements true? Actually, the folklore about friendship is, at best, a mixture of fact and fiction.

What does attract people to each other? **Interpersonal attraction** (affinity to another person) is the basis for most voluntary social relationships (Berscheid & Regan, 2005). As you might expect, we look for friends and lovers who are kind and understanding, who have attractive personalities, and who like us in return (Sprecher, 1998). Deciding whether you would like to know another person can happen very quickly, sometimes within just minutes of meeting (Sunnafrank, Ramirez, & Metts, 2004). In addition, several less obvious factors influence attraction.

Physical Proximity

Our choice of friends (and even lovers) is based more on *physical proximity* (nearness) than we might care to believe. For example, the closer people live to each other, the more likely they are to become friends. Likewise, lovers like to think they have found the "one and only" person in the universe for them. In reality, they have probably found the best match in a 5-mile radius (Buss, 1985)! Marriages are not made in heaven—they are made in local schools, businesses, churches, bars, clubs, and neighborhoods.

Proximity promotes attraction by increasing the *frequency of contact* between people. In general, we are attracted to people we see often. (That's one reason why actors costarring in movies together often become romantically involved.) In short, there does seem to be a "boy-next-door" or "girl-next-door" effect in romantic attraction, and a "folks-next-door" effect in friendship. Notice, however, that the Internet is making it increasingly easier to stay in constant "virtual contact," which is leading to more and more long-distance friendships and romances (Lawson & Leck, 2006; Ridings & Gefen, 2004).

What attracts people to each other? Proximity and frequency of contact have a surprisingly large impact.

Physical Attractiveness

People who are *physically attractive* are regarded as good-looking by others. Beautiful people are generally rated as more appealing than average. This is due, in part, to the *halo effect,* a tendency to generalize a favorable impression to unrelated personal characteristics. Because of it, we assume that attractive people are also likable, intelligent, warm, witty, mentally healthy, and socially skilled (Feingold, 1992). Basically, we act as if "what is beautiful is good." Even characters in Hollywood movies tend to be portrayed more favorably if they are beautiful (Smith, McIntosh, & Bazzini, 1999).

There are limits to the traits we associate with beauty. For instance, we do not expect beautiful people to be more honest or concerned about others (Johnson, 1991)! And in reality, physical attractiveness has almost *no* connection to intelligence, talents, or abilities (Feingold, 1992).

Being physically attractive can be an advantage for both males and females (Mehrabian & Blum, 2003). Good-looking people are less lonely, less socially anxious, more popular, more socially skilled, and more sexually experienced than unattractive people (Feingold, 1992). Where romance is concerned, physical attractiveness has more influence on a woman's fate than on a man's (Feingold, 1990). For instance, there is a strong relationship between a woman's physical beauty and her frequency of dating. For men, looks are unrelated to dating frequency. When men and women first meet, beauty affects attractiveness more for women and personality more for men (Berry & Miller, 2001).

Do these findings seem shallow and sexist? If so, it may be reassuring to know that beauty is a factor mainly in initial acquaintance (Keller & Young, 1996). Later, more meaningful qualities gain in importance (Berscheid, 2000; Miller, Perlman, & Brehm, 2007). As you discover that someone has a good personality, he or she will even start looking more attractive to you (Lewandowski, Aron, & Gee, 2007). It takes more than appearance to make a lasting relationship.

Competence

People who are *competent* have knowledge, ability, or proficiency. All other things being equal, we are more attracted to people who are talented or competent. However, there's an interesting twist to this. In a revealing classic study, college students listened to audiotapes of candidates for a "college quiz bowl." Two of the candidates seemed to be highly intelligent. The other two were of average ability. In addition, one "intelligent" candidate and one "average" candidate could be heard to clumsily spill coffee on themselves. Later, students rated the intelligent candidate who blundered as *most* attractive. In contrast, the average person who blundered was rated *least* attractive (Aronson, 1969). Thus, the superior but clumsy person was more attractive than the person who was only superior. Apparently, we like people who are competent but imperfect—which makes them more "human."

Similarity

Take a moment to make a list of your closest friends. What do they have in common (other than the joy of knowing you)? It is likely that their ages are similar to yours and you are of the same sex and ethnicity. There will be exceptions, of course. But similarity on these three dimensions is the general rule for friendships.

Similarity refers to how alike you are to another person in background, age, interests, attitudes, beliefs, and so forth. In everything from casual acquaintance to marriage, similar people are attracted to each other (Figueredo, Sefcek, & Jones, 2006; Miller, Perlman, & Brehm, 2007). And why not? It's reinforcing to see our beliefs and attitudes shared by others. It shows we are "right" and reveals that they are clever people as well!

So similarity also influences mate selection? Yes, in choosing a mate we tend to marry someone who is like us in almost every way, a pattern called **homogamy** (huh-MOG-ah-me) (Blackwell & Lichter, 2004). Studies show that married couples are highly similar in age, education, ethnicity, and religion. To a lesser degree, they are also similar in attitudes and opinions, mental abilities, status, height, weight, and eye color. In case you're wondering, homogamy also applies to unmarried couples who are living together (Blackwell & Lichter, 2004). Homogamy is probably a good thing. The risk of divorce is highest among couples with sizable differences in age and education (Tzeng, 1992).

Image Source/SuperStock

Physical beauty can be socially advantageous because of the widespread belief that "what is beautiful is good." However, physical beauty is generally unrelated to actual personal traits and talents.

Social comparison Making judgments about ourselves through comparison with others.

Downward comparison Comparing yourself with a person who ranks lower than you on some dimension.

Upward comparison Comparing yourself with a person who ranks higher than you on some dimension.

Interpersonal attraction Social attraction to another person.

Homogamy Marriage of two people who are similar to one another.

Self-Disclosure

How do people who are not yet friends learn if they are similar? To get acquainted you must be willing to talk about more than just the weather, sports, or nuclear physics. At some point you must begin to share private thoughts and feelings and reveal yourself to others. This process, which is called **self-disclosure,** is essential for developing close relationships. In general, as friends talk, they gradually deepen the level of liking, trust, and self-disclosure (Levesque, Steciuk, & Ledley, 2002).

We more often reveal ourselves to persons we like than to those we find unattractive. Disclosure also requires a degree of trust. Many people play it safe, or "close to the vest," with people they do not know well. Indeed, self-disclosure is governed by unspoken rules about what's acceptable. Moderate self-disclosure leads to *reciprocity* (a return in kind). In contrast, *overdisclosure* exceeds what is appropriate for a relationship or social situation, giving rise to suspicion and reducing attraction. For example, imagine standing in line at a store and having the stranger in front of you say, "Lately I've been thinking about how I really feel about myself. I think I'm pretty well adjusted, but I occasionally have some questions about my sexual adequacy."

When self-disclosure proceeds at a moderate pace, it builds trust, intimacy, reciprocity, and positive feelings. When it is too rapid or inappropriate, we are likely to "back off" and wonder about the person's motives. It's interesting to note that on the Internet (and especially on social networking websites like Facebook and MySpace) people often feel freer to express their true feelings, which can lead to genuine, face-to-face friendships (Bargh, McKenna, & Fitzsimons, 2002). However, it can also lead to some very dramatic overdisclosure (George, 2006).

Is self-disclosure similar for men and women? Women and men display an interesting difference in patterns of self-disclosure, as described next.

Excessive self-disclosure is a staple of many television talk shows. Guests frequently reveal intimate details about their personal lives, including private family matters, sex and dating, physical or sexual abuse, major embarrassments, and criminal activities. Viewers probably find such intimate disclosures entertaining, rather than threatening, because they don't have to reciprocate.

Gendered Friendships

Two male friends share lunch at a restaurant. In the next hour they talk about sports, cars, sports cars, the *Sports Illustrated* swimsuit edition, sports, cars, and golf. (Did we mention sports and cars?) Janis, who was at a nearby table, overheard the entire conversation. Here's her summary of what the men said to each other: "Absolutely nothing!"

In North American culture most male friendships are *activity based.* That is, men tend to do things together—a pattern that provides companionship without closeness.

The friendships of women are more often based on *shared feelings and confidences.* If two female friends spent an afternoon together and did not reveal problems, private thoughts, and feelings to one another, they would assume that something was wrong. For women, friendship is a matter of talking about shared concerns and intimate matters.

Actually, the differences between male and female friendships are smaller than implied here. Men do know *something* about the private thoughts and feelings of their friends. Nevertheless, most contemporary men do not form close friendships with other men. Many could probably learn something from female friendships: Men live their friendships side by side; women live them face-to-face (Bank & Hansford, 2000).

Social Exchange Theory

Self-disclosure involves an exchange of personal information, but other exchanges also occur. In fact, many relationships can be understood as an ongoing series of **social exchanges** (transfers of attention, information, affection, favors, and the like between two people). In many social exchanges, people try to maximize their rewards while minimizing their "costs." When a friendship or love relationship ceases to be attractive, people often say, "I'm not getting anything out of it anymore." Actually, they probably are, but their costs—in terms of effort, irritation, or lowered self-esteem—have exceeded their rewards.

According to **social exchange theory,** we unconsciously weigh social rewards and costs. For a relationship to last, it must be *profitable* (its rewards must exceed its costs) for both parties. For instance, Troy and Helen have been dating for 2 years. Although they still have fun at times, they also frequently argue and bicker. If the friction in their relationship gets much stronger, it will exceed the rewards of staying together. When that happens they will probably split up (Gottman, 1994).

Actually, just being profitable is not the whole story. It is more accurate to say that a relationship needs to be *profitable enough.* Generally, the balance between rewards and costs is judged in comparison with what we have come to expect from past experience. The personal standard a person uses to evaluate rewards and costs is called the **comparison level.** The comparison level is high for people with histories of satisfying and rewarding relationships. It is lower for someone whose relationships have been unsatisfying. Thus, the decision to continue a relationship is affected by your personal comparison level. A lonely person, or one whose friendships have been marginal, might stay in a relationship that you would consider unacceptable.

Liking and Loving—Dating, Rating, Mating

Gateway Question: How do liking and loving differ?

How does love differ from interpersonal attraction? It depends on what you mean by the word "love." **Romantic love**, for example, is based on interpersonal attraction, but it also involves high levels of passion: emotional arousal and/or sexual desire (Berscheid & Regan, 2005; Miller, Perlman, & Brehm, 2007).

To get another (tri?)angle on love, psychologist Robert Sternberg (1988) created his influential *triangular theory of love*. According to Sternberg, different forms of love arise from different combinations of three basic components (● Figure 17.1). **Intimacy** refers to feelings of connectedness and affection. **Passion** refers to deep emotional and/or sexual feelings. **Commitment** involves the determination to stay in a long-term relationship with another person.

How does this work? Try it for yourself. Think of a person you love. Now read ● Table 17.1 as you ask yourself three yes/no questions: Do I feel intimate with this person; do I feel passion for this person; am I committed to this person? (● Table 17.1.) Find the kind of love that fits your answers. For example, if you answered *yes* to intimacy but *no* to passion and commitment, you **like** that person; you are friends. Alternately, if you answered *yes* to intimacy and commitment but *no* to passion, then you are feeling **companionate love**. This form of love is more common among couples who have been together for a long time.

Does that mean the most complete form of love is consummate love? You've got it! We experience **consummate love** when we feel intimacy with, passion for, *and* commitment to another person.

Table 17.1 ● Sternberg's Triangular Theory of Love

Combinations of intimacy, passion, and commitment			
Type of love	**Intimacy**	**Passion**	**Commitment**
Nonlove			
Liking	Yes		
Infatuated love		Yes	
Empty love			Yes
Romantic love	Yes	Yes	
Companionate love	Yes		Yes
Fatuous love		Yes	Yes
Consummate love	Yes	Yes	Yes

Sternberg, 1988.

Romantic love differs from friendship in another interesting way. In contrast to simple liking, romantic love usually involves deep **mutual absorption.** In other words, lovers (unlike friends) attend almost exclusively to one another.

What do lovers see when they gaze into each other's eyes? A final interesting characteristic of romantic love is lovers' ability to see their partners in idealized ways. Nobody's perfect, of course. That's why it's no surprise that relationships are most likely to persist when lovers idealize one another. Doing so doesn't just blind them to their partner's faults, it actually helps them create the relationship they wish for (Murray, Holmes, & Griffin, 1996, 2003).

● **Figure 17.1** The Triangle of Love. Each of the three basic components of love (intimacy, passion, and commitment) appears at one corner of the triangle and is associated with a form of love. Pairs of components and their associated form of love appear on lines of the triangle. Consummate love, which involves all three components, is pictured at the center of the triangle. (Adapted from Sternberg, 1988.)

Self-disclosure The process of revealing private thoughts, feelings, and one's personal history to others.

Social exchange Any exchange between two people of attention, information, affection, favors, or the like.

Social exchange theory Theory stating that rewards must exceed costs for relationships to endure.

Comparison level A personal standard used to evaluate rewards and costs in a social exchange.

Romantic love Love that is associated with high levels of interpersonal attraction, heightened arousal, mutual absorption, and sexual desire.

Intimacy Feelings of connectedness and affection for another person.

Passion Deep emotional and/or sexual feelings for another person.

Commitment The determination to stay in a long-term relationship with another person.

Liking A relationship based on intimacy, but lacking passion and commitment.

Companionate love Form of love characterized by intimacy and commitment but not passion.

Consummate love Form of love characterized by intimacy, passion, *and* commitment.

Mutual absorption With regard to romantic love, the nearly exclusive attention lovers give to one another.

Love and Attachment

Sheela has been dating Paul for over a year. Although they have had some rough spots, Sheela is comfortable, secure, and trusting in her love for Paul. Charlene, in contrast, has had a long series of unhappy romances with men. She is basically a loner who has difficulty trusting others. Like Sheela, Eduardo has been dating the same person for a year. However, his relationship with Tanya has been stormy and troubled. Eduardo is strongly attracted to Tanya. Yet he is also in a constant state of anxiety over whether she really loves him.

Sheela, Charlene, and Eduardo might be surprised to learn that the roots of their romantic relationships may lie in childhood. There is growing evidence that early attachments to caregivers can have a lasting impact on how we relate to others (Fraley, 2002; Fraley & Shaver, 2000).

> **bridges**
> Forming a secure attachment to a caregiver is a major event in early child development. **See Chapter 3, pages 89–90.**

For example, studies of dating couples have identified secure, avoidant, and ambivalent attachment patterns similar to those seen in early child development (Mikulincer & Nachshon, 1991). Nationally, about 59 percent of all adults have a secure attachment style, 25 percent are avoidant, and 11 percent have anxious attachment styles (Mickelson, Kessler, & Shaver, 1997).

Secure attachment is a stable and positive emotional bond. A secure attachment style like Sheela's is marked by caring, intimacy, supportiveness, and understanding in love relationships. Secure persons regard themselves as friendly, good natured, and likable. They think of others as generally well intentioned, reliable, and trustworthy. People with a secure attachment style find it relatively easy to get close to others. They are comfortable depending on others and having others depend on them. In general, they don't worry too much about being abandoned or about having someone become too emotionally close to them. Most people prefer to have a secure partner, whatever their own style might be (Latty-Mann & Davis, 1996).

Charlene's **avoidant attachment** style reflects a fear of intimacy and a tendency to resist commitment to others. Avoidant persons tend to pull back when things don't go well in a relationship. The avoidant person is suspicious, aloof, and skeptical about love. She or he tends to see others as either unreliable or overly eager to commit to a relationship. As a result, avoidant persons find it hard to completely trust and depend on others. Avoidant persons get nervous when anyone gets too close emotionally. Basically, they avoid intimacy (Tidwell, Reis, & Shaver, 1996).

Persons like Eduardo have an **ambivalent attachment** style, marked by mixed emotions about relationships. Conflicting feelings of affection, anger, emotional turmoil, physical attraction, and doubt leave them in an unsettled, ambivalent state.

Often, ambivalent persons regard themselves as misunderstood and unappreciated. They tend to see their friends and lovers as unreliable and unable or unwilling to commit themselves to lasting relationships. Ambivalent persons worry that their romantic partners don't really love them or may leave them. Although they want to be extremely close to their partners, they are also preoccupied with doubts about the partner's dependability and trustworthiness.

How could emotional attachments early in life affect adult relationships? It appears that we use early attachment experiences to build mental models about affectionate relationships. Later, we use these models as a sort of blueprint for forming, maintaining, and breaking bonds of love and affection (Sroufe et al., 2005). Thus, the quality of childhood bonds to parents or other caregivers may hold a key to understanding how we approach romantic relationships (Fraley & Shaver, 2000). Maybe it's no accident that persons who are romantically available are often described as "unattached."

It is fascinating to think that our relationships may be influenced by events early in childhood. Could the source of adult mating patterns reach even further back? The next section explores that possibility.

Evolution and Mate Selection

Evolutionary psychology is the study of the evolutionary origins of human behavior patterns. Many psychologists believe that evolution left an imprint on men and women that influences everything from sexual attraction and infidelity to jealousy and divorce. According to David Buss, the key to understanding human mating patterns is to understand how evolved behavior patterns guide our choices (Buss, 2004, 2007).

In a study of 37 cultures on six continents, Buss found the following patterns: Compared with women, men are more interested in casual sex; they prefer younger, more physically attractive partners; and they get more jealous over real or imagined sexual infidelities than they do over a loss of emotional commitment. Compared with men, women prefer slightly older partners who appear to be industrious, higher in status, or economically successful; women are more upset by a partner who becomes emotionally involved with someone else, rather than one who is sexually unfaithful (Buss, 2000; Regan et al., 2000) (● Figure 17.2).

Why do such differences exist? Buss and others believe that mating preferences evolved in response to the differing reproductive challenges faced by men and women. As a rule, women must invest more time and energy in reproduction and nurturing the young than men do. Consequently, women evolved an interest in whether their partners will stay with them and whether their mates have the resources to provide for their children (Buss, 2004, 2007; Regan et al., 2000).

In contrast, the reproductive success of men depends on their mates' fertility. Men, therefore, tend to look for health, youth, and beauty in a prospective mate, as signs of suitability for reproduction (Buss, 2007). This preference, perhaps, is why some older men abandon their first wives in favor of young, beautiful "trophy wives."

Evolutionary theory further proposes that the male emphasis on their mates' sexual fidelity is based on concerns about the paternity of offspring. From a biological perspective, men do not benefit from investing resources in children they did not sire (Buller, 2005).

Although some evidence supports the evolutionary view of mating, it is important to remember that evolved mating tendencies are subtle at best and easily overruled by other factors. Some mating patterns may simply reflect the fact that men still tend to control the power and resources in most societies (Feingold, 1992). Also, early research may be misleading because women tend to give "polite" answers to questions about jealousy. Privately, they may be just as furious about a mate's sexual infidelity as any man would be (Harris, 2004).

Whatever the outcome of the debate about evolution and mate selection, it is important to remember this: Potential mates are rated as most attractive if they are kind, secure, intelligent, and supportive (Klohnen & Luo, 2003; Regan et al., 2000). These qualities are love's greatest allies.

While every society places high value on friendship and love, all would agree that the ultimate prosocial act is helping another human being, especially if he or she is a stranger in need. In the next section, we turn our attention to helping others. Before we do, here are some questions to help you help yourself.

● **Figure 17.2** What do people look for when considering potential dating partners? Here are the results of a study in which personal ads were placed in newspapers. As you can see, men were more influenced by looks, and women by success (Goode, 1996).

Bill Bachmann/PhotoEdit

According to evolutionary psychologists, women tend to be concerned with whether mates will devote time and resources to a relationship. Men place more emphasis on physical attractiveness and sexual fidelity.

KNOWLEDGE BUILDER
Affiliation, Attraction, Liking, and Loving
RECITE

1. Women threatened with electric shock in an experiment generally chose to wait alone or with other women not taking part in the experiment. T or F?
2. The need to affiliate is related to interest in social comparison. T or F?
3. Social comparisons are made pretty much at random. T or F?
4. Interpersonal attraction is increased by all but one of the following. (Which does not fit?)
   a. physical proximity
   b. competence
   c. similarity
   d. social costs
5. High levels of self-disclosure are reciprocated in most social encounters. T or F?
6. In Sternberg's triangular theory, infatuated love involves commitment but not passion or intimacy. T or F?
7. The most striking finding about marriage patterns is that most people choose mates whose personalities are quite unlike their own. T or F?
8. Both ambivalent and avoidant attachment patterns are associated with difficulties in trusting a romantic partner. T or F?
9. Compared with men, women tend to be more upset by sexual infidelity than by a loss of emotional commitment on the part of their mates. T or F?

REFLECT

Critical Thinking

10. How has the Internet altered the effects of proximity on interpersonal attraction?

Continued

Secure attachment A stable and positive emotional bond.

Avoidant attachment An emotional bond marked by a tendency to resist commitment to others.

Ambivalent attachment An emotional bond marked by conflicting feelings of affection, anger, and emotional turmoil.

Evolutionary psychology Study of the evolutionary origins of human behavior patterns.

Robert Brenner/PhotoEdit, Inc.

Does the person lying on the ground need help? What factors determine whether a person in trouble will receive help in an emergency? Surprisingly, more potential helpers tend to lower the chances that help will be given.

●● Helping Others—The Good Samaritan

Gateway Question: Why are bystanders so often unwilling to help in an emergency?

Let's begin our exploration of helping behavior by first exploring why people sometimes do *not* help. That will make it clearer just how remarkable it is when people *do* help others.

Late one night, tenants of a Queens, New York, apartment building watched and listened in horror as a young woman named Kitty Genovese was murdered on the sidewalk outside. From the safety of their rooms, no fewer than 38 people heard the agonized screams as her assailant stabbed her, was frightened off, and returned to stab her again.

Kitty Genovese's murder took more than 30 minutes, but none of her neighbors tried to help. None even called the police until after the attack had ended. Perhaps it is understandable that no one wanted to get involved. After all, it could have been a violent lovers' quarrel. Or helping might have meant risking personal injury. But what prevented these people from at least calling the police? Although many details of the Kitty Genovese murder have been called into question, the episode was instrumental in launching research into *bystander apathy* (Manning, Levine, & Collins, 2007).

Isn't this an example of the alienation of city life? News reports treated this incident as evidence of a breakdown in social ties caused by the impersonality of the city. Although it is true that urban living can be dehumanizing, this does not fully explain such **bystander apathy** (the unwillingness of bystanders to offer help during emergencies is also referred to as the *bystander effect*). According to landmark work by psychologists John Darley and Bibb Latané (1968), failure to help is related to the number of people present. Over the years many studies have shown that the *more* potential helpers present, the *less* likely people are to help (Latané, Nida, & Wilson, 1981; Miller, 2006).

Why would people be less willing to help when others are present? In Kitty Genovese's case, the answer is that everyone thought *someone else* would help. The

dynamics of this effect are easily illustrated: Suppose that two motorists have stalled at the roadside, one on a sparsely traveled country road and the other on a busy freeway. Who gets help first?

On the freeway, where hundreds of cars pass every minute, each driver can assume that someone else will help. Personal responsibility for helping is spread so thin that no one takes action. On the country road, one of the first few people to arrive will probably stop, because the responsibility is clearly theirs. In general, Latané and Darley assume that bystanders are not apathetic or uncaring; they are inhibited by the presence of others.

Bystander Intervention

People must pass through four decision points before giving help. First they must notice that something is happening. Next they must define the event as an emergency. Then they must take responsibility. Finally, they must select a course of action (● Figure 17.3). Laboratory experiments have shown that each step can be influenced by the presence of other people.

Noticing

What would happen if you fainted and collapsed on the sidewalk? Would someone stop to help? Would people think you were drunk? Would they even notice you? Latané and Darley sug-

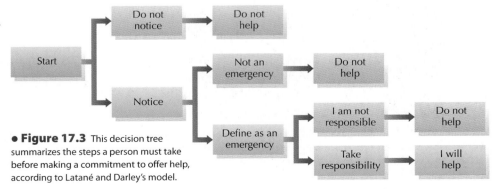

● **Figure 17.3** This decision tree summarizes the steps a person must take before making a commitment to offer help, according to Latané and Darley's model.

gest that if the sidewalk is crowded, few people will even see you. This has nothing to do with people blocking each other's vision. Instead, it is related to widely accepted norms against staring at others in public. People in crowds typically "keep their eyes to themselves."

Is there any way to show that this is a factor in bystander apathy? To test this idea, students were asked to fill out a questionnaire either alone or in a room full of people. While the students worked, a thick cloud of smoke was blown into the room through a vent.

Most students left alone in the room noticed the smoke immediately. Few of the people in groups noticed the smoke until it actually became difficult to see through it. Subjects working in groups politely kept their eyes on their papers and avoided looking at others (or the smoke). In contrast, those who were alone scanned the room from time to time.

Defining an Emergency

The smoke-filled room also shows the influence others have on defining a situation as an emergency. When subjects in groups finally noticed the smoke, they cast sidelong glances at others in the room. Apparently, they were searching for clues to help interpret what was happening. No one wanted to overreact or act like a fool if there was no emergency. However, as subjects coolly surveyed the reactions of others, they were themselves being watched. In real emergencies, people sometimes "fake each other out" and underestimate the need for action because each person attempts to appear calm. In short, until someone acts, no one acts.

Taking Responsibility

Perhaps the most crucial step in helping is assuming responsibility. In this case, groups limit helping by causing a **diffusion of responsibility** (spreading responsibility among several people).

Is that like the unwillingness of drivers to offer help on a crowded freeway? Exactly. It is the feeling that no one is personally responsible for helping. This problem was demonstrated in an experiment in which students took part in a group discussion over an intercom system. Actually, there was only one real subject in each group; the others were tape-recorded actors. Each subject was placed in a separate room (supposedly to maintain confidentiality), and discussions of college life were begun. During the discussion, one of the "students" simulated an epileptic-like seizure and called out for help. In some cases, subjects thought they were alone with the seizure victim. Others believed they were members of three- or six-person groups.

People who thought they were alone with the "victim" of this staged emergency reported it immediately or tried to help. Some subjects in the three-person groups failed to respond, and those who did were slower. In the six-person groups, over a third of the subjects took no action at all. People in this experiment were obviously faced with a conflict like that in many real emergencies: Should they be helpful and responsible, or should they mind their own business? Many were influenced toward inaction by the presence of others.

People do help in some emergencies. How are these different? It is not always clear what makes the difference. Helping behavior is complex and influenced by many variables. One naturalistic experiment staged in a New York City subway gives a hint of the kinds of things that may be important. When a "victim" (actor) "passed out" in a subway car, he received more help when carrying a cane than when carrying a liquor bottle. More important, however, was the fact that most people were willing to help in either case (Piliavin, Rodin, & Piliavin, 1969).

To better answer the question we need to consider some factors not included in Latané and Darley's account of helping.

Who Will Help Whom?

Many studies suggest that when we see a person in trouble, it tends to cause *heightened arousal* (Dovidio et al., 2006). This aroused, keyed-up feeling can motivate us to give aid, but only if the rewards of helping outweigh the costs. Higher costs (such as great effort, personal risk, or possible embarrassment) almost always decrease helping. In addition to general arousal, potential helpers may also feel **empathic arousal.** This means they empathize with the person in need or feel some of the person's pain, fear, or anguish. Helping is much more likely when we are able to take the perspective of others and feel sympathy for their plight (Batson & Powell, 2003).

If people feel sad or distressed when another person is in trouble, couldn't it be that they help just to make themselves feel better? It is certainly possible that some helping is actually "selfish." But research has shown that empathy (empathic arousal) really does unleash altruistic motivation based on sympathy and compassion. Most helping, including such altruistic acts as making donations or being kind, is motivated by a true desire to relieve the distress of others (Dovidio, Allen, & Schroeder, 1990).

Empathic arousal is especially likely to motivate helping when the person in need seems to be similar to ourselves (Batson & Powell, 2003). In fact, a feeling of connection to the victim may be one of the most important factors in helping. This, perhaps, is why being in a good mood also increases helping. When we are feeling successful, happy, or fortunate, we may also feel more connected to others (Dovidio & Penner, 2001). In summary, there is a strong **empathy-helping relationship:** We are most likely to help someone in need when we "feel for" that person and experience emotions such as empathy, sympathy, and compassion (Batson, 2006).

Bystander apathy Unwillingness of bystanders to offer help during emergencies or to become involved in others' problems.

Diffusion of responsibility Spreading the responsibility to act among several people; reduces the likelihood that help will be given to a person in need.

Empathic arousal Emotional arousal that occurs when you feel some of another person's pain, fear, or anguish.

Empathy-helping relationship Observation that we are most likely to help someone else when we feel emotions such as empathy and compassion.

Is there anything that can be done to encourage prosocial behavior? People who see others helping are more likely to offer help themselves. Also, persons who give help in one situation tend to perceive themselves as helpful people. This change in self-image encourages them to help in other situations. One more point is that norms of fairness encourage us to help others who have helped us (Dovidio & Penner, 2001). For all these reasons, helping others not only assists them directly, it encourages others to help too.

"De-victimize" Yourself

If you should find yourself in need of help during an emergency, what can you do to avoid being a victim of bystander apathy? The work we have reviewed here suggests that you should make sure that you are noticed, that people realize there's an emergency, and that they need to take action. Being noticed can be promoted in some situations by shouting "Fire!" Bystanders who might run away from a robbery or an assault may rush to see where the fire is. At the very least, remember to not just scream. Instead, you should call out, "Help," or, "I need help right now." Whenever possible, define your situation for bystanders. Say, for instance, "I'm being attacked, call the police." Or, "Stop that man, he has my purse." You can also directly assign responsibility to a bystander by pointing to someone and saying, "You, call the police," or, "I'm injured, I need you to call an ambulance" (Cummins, 1995).

Positive Psychology: Everyday Heroes

Every year awards are given to people who risk their lives while saving the lives of others. These heroes are typically honored for saving people from fires, drowning, animal attacks, electrocution, and suffocation. The majority of people who perform such heroic acts are men, perhaps because of the physical dangers involved. However, there are other heroic, prosocial acts that save lives and involve personal risk. Examples are kidney donors, Peace Corp volunteers, and Doctors of the World volunteers. In such endeavors, we find as many women as men, and often more. It is important to remember, perhaps, that sensational and highly visible acts of heroism are only one of many ways in which people engage in selfless, altruistic behavior (Becker & Eagly, 2004). People who serve as community volunteers, tutors, coaches, blood donors, and the like don't just help others. Often, their efforts contribute to personal growth and make them healthier and happier. Thus, it can be said, "We do well by doing good" (Piliavin, 2003).

Despite the many instances of prosocial behavior that occur every day, people in need are sometimes mugged or exploited, rather than aided. Bluntly put, we humans are capable of cruelty as well as love. In the next few sections we will turn our attention to the dark side of social behavior. To reiterate, **antisocial behavior** is any behavior that has a negative impact on other people. Aggression, prejudice, and intergroup conflict are all examples.

●● Aggression—The World's Most Dangerous Animal

Gateway Question: How do psychologists explain human aggression?
"I know not with what weapons World War III will be fought, but World War IV will be fought with sticks and stones."
Albert Einstein

Aggression is a human tragedy. Helping others is a source of hope. It might seem that the horrors of war would lead to a worldwide revulsion for killing. In reality, homicide rates have increased in many countries in recent years. What causes aggression? Can violence be reduced? Can we promote prosocial behavior? More than ever, these are pressing questions.

For a time, the City Zoo of Los Angeles, California, had on display two examples of the world's most dangerous animal—the only animal capable of destroying the earth and all other animal species. Perhaps you have already guessed which animal it was. In the cage were two college students, representing the species *Homo sapiens!*

The human capacity for aggression is staggering. It has been estimated that 58 million humans were killed by other humans (an average of nearly one person per minute) during the 125-year period ending with World War II. Murder now ranks as a major cause of death in the United States. One American kills another every half hour—making the United States one of the world's most violent nations. War, homicide, riots, family violence, assassination, rape, assault, forcible robbery, and other violent acts offer sad testimony to the realities of human aggression.

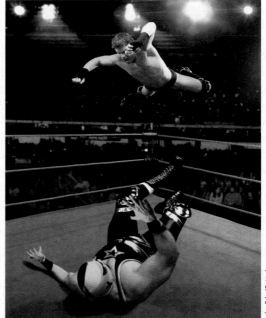

John Eder/Getty Images

Ritualized human aggression. Violent and aggressive behavior is so commonplace it may be viewed as entertainment. How "natural" is aggressive behavior?

What causes aggression? **Aggression** refers to any action carried out with the intention of harming another person. Aggression has many potential causes. Brief descriptions of some of the major possibilities follow.

Instincts

Some theorists argue we are naturally aggressive creatures, having inherited a "killer instinct" from our animal ancestors. Ethologists theorize that aggression is a biologically rooted behavior observed in all animals, including humans (Blanchard & Blanchard, 2003). (An **ethologist** is a person who studies the natural behavior patterns of animals.) Noted ethologist Konrad Lorenz (1966, 1974) also believed that humans lack certain innate patterns that inhibit aggression in animals. For example, in a dispute over territory, two wolves may growl, lunge, bare their teeth, and fiercely threaten each other. In most instances, though, neither is killed or even wounded. One wolf, recognizing the dominance of the other, will typically bare its throat in a gesture of submission. The dominant wolf could kill in an instant, but it is inhibited by the other wolf's submissive gesture. In contrast, human confrontations of equal intensity almost always end in injury or death.

The idea that humans are "naturally" aggressive has an intuitive appeal, but many psychologists question it. Many of Lorenz's "explanations" of aggression are little more than loose comparisons between human and animal behavior. Just labeling a behavior as "instinctive" does little to explain it. More important, we are left with the question of why some individuals or human cultures (the Arapesh, the Senoi, the Navajo, the Eskimo, and others) show little hostility or aggression. And, thankfully, the vast majority of humans *do not* kill or harm others.

Biology

Despite problems with the instinctive view, aggression may have biological roots. Physiological studies have shown that some brain areas are capable of triggering or ending aggressive behavior. Also, researchers have found a relationship between aggression and such physical factors as hypoglycemia (low blood sugar), allergy, and specific brain injuries and diseases. For both men and women, higher levels of the hormone testosterone may be associated with more aggressive behavior (Harris et al., 1996; McDermott et al., 2007). Perhaps because of their higher testosterone levels, men are more likely to engage in physical aggression than women (Anderson & Bushman, 2002). However, none of these biological factors can be considered a direct *cause* of aggression (Moore, 2001; Popma et al., 2007). Instead, they probably lower the threshold for aggression, making hostile behavior more likely to occur.

The effects of alcohol and other drugs provide another indication of the role of the brain and biology in violence and aggression. A variety of studies show that alcohol is involved in large percentages of murders and violent crimes. Intoxicating drugs also seem to lower inhibitions to act aggressively—often with tragic results (Anderson & Bushman, 2002; Quigley & Leonard, 2000).

To summarize, the fact that we are biologically *capable* of aggression does not mean that aggression is inevitable or "part of human nature." Twenty eminent scientists who studied the question concluded that "Biology does not condemn humanity to war. . . . Violence is neither in our evolutionary legacy nor in our genes. The same species that invented war is capable of inventing peace" (Scott & Ginsburg, 1994; UNESCO, 1990). Humans are fully capable of learning to inhibit aggression. For example, American Quakers and Amish, who live in this country's increasingly violent culture, adopt nonviolence as a way of life (Bandura, 2001).

Frustration

Step on a dog's tail and you may get nipped. Frustrate a human and you may get insulted. The **frustration-aggression hypothesis** states that frustration tends to lead to aggression.

Does frustration always produce aggression? Although the connection is strong, a moment's thought will show that frustration

Road rage and some freeway shootings may be a reaction to the frustration of traffic congestion. The fact that automobiles provide anonymity, or a loss of personal identity, may also encourage aggressive actions that would not otherwise occur.

Antisocial behavior Any behavior that has a negative impact on other people.

Aggression Any action carried out with the intention of harming another person.

Ethologist A person who studies the natural behavior patterns of animals.

Frustration-aggression hypothesis States that frustration tends to lead to aggression.

does not *always* lead to aggression. Frustration, for instance, may lead to stereotyped responding or perhaps to a state of "learned helplessness." (See Chapter 13, pages 442–443.) Also, aggression can occur in the absence of frustration. This possibility is illustrated by sports spectators who start fights, throw bottles, tear down goalposts, and so forth after their team has *won*.

Aversive Stimuli

Frustration probably encourages aggression because it is uncomfortable. Various *aversive stimuli,* which produce discomfort or displeasure, can heighten hostility and aggression (Anderson, Anderson, & Deuser, 1996; Morgan, 2005) (● Figure 17.4). Examples include insults, high temperatures, pain, and even disgusting scenes or odors. Such stimuli probably raise overall arousal levels so that we become more sensitive to **aggression cues** (signals that are associated with aggression) (Carlson, Marcus-Newhall, & Miller, 1990). Aversive stimuli also tend to activate ideas, memories, and expressions associated with anger and aggression (Morgan, 2005).

Some cues for aggression are internal (angry thoughts, for instance). Many are external: Certain words, actions, and gestures made by others are strongly associated with aggressive responses. A raised middle finger, for instance, is an almost universal invitation to aggression in North America. Weapons serve as particularly strong cues for aggressive behavior (Morgan, 2005). The implication of this **weapons effect** seems to be that the symbols and trappings of aggression encourage aggression. A prime example is the fact that murders are more likely to occur in homes where guns are kept (Miller, Hemenway, & Azraela, 2007). Nearly 80 percent of the victims in such homes are killed by a family member or acquaintance. Only 4 percent are murdered by strangers (Kellermann et al., 1993).

● **Figure 17.4** Personal discomfort caused by aversive (unpleasant) stimuli can make aggressive behavior more likely. For example, studies of crime rates show that the incidence of highly aggressive behavior, such as murder, rape, and assault, rises as the air temperature goes from warm to hot to sweltering (Anderson, 1989). The results you see here further confirm the heat-aggression link. The graph shows that there is a strong association between the temperatures at major league baseball games and the number of batters hit by a pitch during those games. When the temperature exceeds 90°, watch out for that fastball (Reifman, Larrick, & Fein, 1991)!

Social Learning

One of the most widely accepted explanations of aggression is also the simplest. Social learning theory holds that we learn to be aggressive by observing aggression in others (Bandura, 2001). To explain behavior, **social learning theory** combines learning principles with cognitive processes, socialization, and modeling. According to this view, there is no instinctive human programming for fist fighting, pipe-bombing, knife wielding, gun loading, 95-mile-an-hour "bean balls," or other violent or aggressive actions. Hence, aggression must be learned (● Figure 17.5). Is it any wonder that people who were the victims of violence during childhood are likely to become violent themselves (Murrell, Christoff, & Henning, 2007)?

Aggressive Models

Social learning theorists predict that people growing up in nonaggressive cultures will themselves be nonaggressive. Those raised in a culture with aggressive models and heroes will learn aggressive responses (Bandura, 2001). Considered in such terms, it is no wonder that America has become one of the most violent of all countries. A violent crime occurred every 23 seconds in the United States during 2005 (FBI, 2005). Approximately 40 percent of the population owns firearms. Nationally, 70 percent agree that "When a boy is growing up, it is very important for him to have a few fistfights." Children and adults are treated to an almost nonstop parade of aggressive models, in the media as well as in actual behavior. We are, without a doubt, an aggressive culture. (See "Pornography and Aggression Against Women.")

The World According to TV

Did you know that the world is populated primarily by males, professionals, European Americans, and members of the middle class? Did you know that women make up only 28 percent of the population; that one half of all women are teenagers or in their early twenties; that more than one third are unemployed or have no purpose beyond offering emotional support to men or serving as objects of sexual desire? That minorities are generally service workers, criminals, victims, or students? That over one half of all villains have accents? That most victims are single women, young boys, or people of color? If you watch much TV, these are the impressions you get daily on the tube.

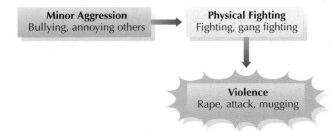

● **Figure 17.5** Violent behavior among delinquent boys doesn't appear overnight. Usually, their capacity for violence develops slowly, as they move from minor aggression to increasingly brutal acts. Overall aggression increases dramatically in early adolescence as boys gain physical strength and more access to weapons (Loeber & Hay, 1997).

CRITICAL THINKING

Pornography and Aggression Against Women—Is There a Link?

A heated debate has raged for years about the effects of pornography. Early studies suggested that viewing pornography has no major adverse effects. This conclusion appears to remain valid for stimuli that can be described as merely erotic or sexual in content (Malamuth, Addison, & Koss, 2000). However, in recent years there has been a dramatic increase in aggressive-pornographic images in the mass media. **Aggressive pornography** refers to depictions in which violence, threats, or obvious power differences are used to force someone (usually a woman) to engage in sex (Davis et al., 2006).

The main finding of studies on aggressive-pornographic stimuli is that they do increase aggression against females in men who are prone to sexual violence (Malamuth, Addison, & Koss, 2000). As researchers Neil Malamuth and Ed Donnerstein (1982) concluded, "Exposure to mass media stimuli that have violent *and* sexual content increases the audience's aggressive-sexual fantasies, beliefs in rape myths, and aggressive behavior." Donnerstein and Daniel Linz (1986) add that media *violence* is most damaging. As they put it, "Violent images, rather than sexual ones, are most responsible for people's attitudes about women and rape." The problem, then, extends far beyond X-rated films and books. Mainstream movies, magazines, music videos, and television programs are equally to blame for reinforcing the myth that women find force or aggression pleasurable (Donnerstein, 2001). It is telling that rapists are sexually aroused by both sexual and nonsexual violence. Clearly, violence is a major dimension of rape and sexual aggression (Forbes & Adams-Curtis, 2001).

Media Violence

Every day, mainstream media provide an endless stream of bad models, especially concerning violence. TV, movies, computer games, and even music lyrics all contain violence. According to the organization Adults and Children Against Violence Together, young children spend about 35 hours a week in front of TV or computer screens. By the end of elementary school, children will have seen about 8,000 murders and 100,000 other violent acts depicted on TV. Eighty percent of popular video games contain violent content. Many popular toys are also linked to violent media (ACT Against Violence, 2005a). And, of course, teenagers and young people are also chronically exposed to violence in the media.

How much does TV violence affect children? As Albert Bandura showed in his studies of imitation (see Chapter 7, pages 244–246) children may learn new aggressive actions by watching violent or aggressive behavior, or they may learn that violence is "okay." Either way, they are more likely to act aggressively. Heroes on TV are as violent as the villains, and they usually receive praise for their violence. There is now little doubt that widespread exposure to media violence contributes to aggression (Anderson et al., 2003; DeGaetano, 2005). Boys and girls who watch a lot of violence on TV are much more likely to be aggressive as adults (Huesmann et al., 2003). Violent video games are at least as problematic (Bartholow, Bushman, & Sestir, 2006), and even violent song lyrics increase aggressive tendencies (Anderson, Carnagey, & Eubanks, 2003).

In addition to teaching new antisocial actions, media such as TV and video games may disinhibit dangerous impulses that viewers already have. **Disinhibition** (the removal of inhibition) results in acting out behavior that normally would be restrained. For example, many TV programs give the message that violence is acceptable behavior that leads to success and popularity. For some people, this message can lower inhibitions against acting out hostile feelings (Anderson et al., 2003).

Another effect of media violence is that it tends to lower sensitivity to violent acts (Funk, 2005). As anyone who has seen a street fight or a mugging can tell you, TV violence is sanitized and unrealistic. The real thing is gross, ugly, and gut wrenching. Even when media violence is graphic, as it is in many video games, it is experienced in the relaxed and familiar setting of the home. For at least some viewers, this combination diminishes emotional reactions to violent scenes (Carnagey, Anderson, & Bushman, 2007). More than 30 years ago, when Victor Cline and his associates showed a bloody fight film to a group of boys, they found that heavy TV viewers (averaging 42 hours a week) showed much less emotion than those who watched little or no TV (Cline, Croft, & Courrier, 1972). Media, it seems, can cause

bridges

Modeling and observational learning explain much of television's impact on our behavior. **See Chapter 7, pages 243–246.**

Aggression cues Stimuli or signals that are associated with aggression and that tend to elicit it.

Weapons effect The observation that weapons serve as strong cues for aggressive behavior.

Social learning theory Combines learning principles with cognitive processes, socialization, and modeling, to explain behavior.

Aggressive pornography Media depictions of sexual violence or of forced participation in sexual activity.

Disinhibition The removal of inhibition; results in acting out behavior that normally would be restrained.

a **desensitization** (reduced emotional sensitivity) to violence (Huesmann et al., 2003).

Preventing Aggression

What can be done about aggression? Social learning theory implies that "aggression begets aggression." For example, children who are physically abused at home, those who suffer severe physical punishment, and those who merely witness violence in the community are more likely to be involved in fighting, aggressive play, and anti-social behavior at school (Bartholow, Sestir, & Davis, 2005; Margolin & Gordis, 2000).

According to social learning theorists, watching a prizefight, sporting event, or violent television program may increase aggression, rather than drain off aggressive urges. A case in point is provided by psychologist Leonard Eron, who spent 22 years following over 600 children into adulthood. Eron (1987) observes, "Among the most influential models for children were those observed on television. One of the best predictors of how aggressive a young man would be at age 19 was the violence of the television programs he preferred when he was 8 years old" (● Figure 17.6). According to Eron, children learn aggressive strategies and actions from TV violence. Because of this, they are more prone to aggress when they face frustrating situations or cues. Others have found that viewers who experience violent media have more aggressive thoughts. As we have noted, violent thoughts often precede violent actions (Anderson, Carnagey, & Eubanks, 2003). Thus, the spiral of aggression might be broken if we did not so often portray it, reward it, and glorify it (Hughes & Hasbrouck, 1996).

Parents as Media Guides

As the preceding studies show, reducing exposure to violent media is one way to lower aggression. However, other than pulling the plug, what can parents do about media's negative effects on children? Actually, quite a lot. Parents can make a big difference if they do the following (ACT Against Violence, 2005b; Frydman, 1999):

1. Start by creating a safe, warm environment at home and school and by modeling positive ways of getting along in the world. Children typically model parents' behavior, including their media viewing habits, and they are guided by parents' reactions to media.
2. Limit total media time so that TV and computer games do not dominate your child's view of the world. If necessary, set schedules for when watching TV or playing video games is allowed. Don't use media as a babysitter.
3. Closely monitor what your child does experience. Change channels or turn off the TV if you object to a program. Be prepared to offer games and activities that stimulate your child's imagination and creativity.
4. Actively seek media your child will enjoy, especially those that model positive behavior and social attitudes.
5. Explore media with your child so that you can counter what is shown. Help your child distinguish between reality and fantasy in media. Reply to distortions and stereotypes as they appear on screen.
6. Discuss the social conflicts and violent solutions shown in media. Ask your child in what ways the situations are unrealistic and why the violence shown would not work in the real world. Encourage the child to propose more mature, realistic, and positive responses to situations.
7. Show by your own disapproval that violent TV and computer game heroes are not the ones to emulate. Remember, children who identify with media characters are more likely to be influenced by media aggression.

By following these guidelines you can help children learn to enjoy television without being overly influenced by programs and advertisers. A recent study found that elementary school children become less aggressive when they decrease the amount of time they spend watching TV and playing video games (Robinson et al., 2001).

TV as a Positive Model

Couldn't TV's impact also be used constructively? There is no denying TV's tremendous power to inform and to entertain. When these features are combined, the effect can be quite constructive. Perhaps the best examples of TV as a positive social force are educational programs such as *Barney and Friends, Sesame Street,* and *Mr. Rogers' Neighborhood.* Numerous research reports have found that the impact of these programs is positive. Clearly, television can teach children while holding their interest and attention.

As a model for positive attitudes and responses, TV could be used to promote helping, cooperation, charity, and brotherhood in the same way that it has tended to stereotype and encourage aggression (Penner et al., 2005). Over 200 studies have shown that prosocial behavior on TV increases prosocial behavior by viewers (Hearold, 1987).

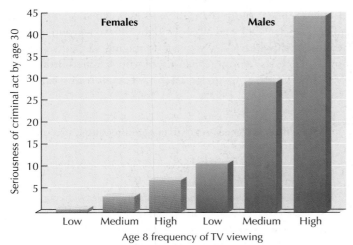

● **Figure 17.6** Although TV violence does not cause aggression, it can encourage it. The likelihood of committing criminal acts by age 30 is related to the amount of TV watching a person did when she or he was a child (Eron, 1987). (Copyright © 1987 by the American Psychological Association, Inc. Reprinted by permission of the author.)

The Photo Works/Photo Researchers, Inc.

A study by Jerome and Dorothy Singer found that preschoolers who watch *Barney and Friends* show improved cognitive skills and knowledge—such as knowing colors and shapes, numbers, vocabulary, good manners, and facts about nature and health (deGroot, 1994).

Anger Control

On a personal level, psychologists have succeeded in teaching some people to control their anger and aggressive impulses. **Anger control** refers to personal strategies for reducing or curbing anger. The key to remaining calm is to define upsetting situations as *problems to be solved.* Therefore, to limit anger, people are taught to do the following:

1. Define the problem as precisely as possible.
2. Make a list of possible solutions.
3. Rank the likely success of each solution.
4. Choose a solution and try it.
5. Assess how successful the solution was, and make adjustments if necessary.

Taking these steps has helped many people to lessen tendencies toward child abuse, family violence, and other destructive outbursts (Meichenbaum, Henshaw, & Himel, 1982).

Beyond this, the question remains: How shall we tame the world's most dangerous animal? There is no easy answer, only a challenge of pressing importance (Lench, 2004). The solution will undoubtedly involve the best efforts of thinkers and researchers from many disciplines.

For the immediate future, it is clear that we need more people who are willing to engage in helpful, altruistic, prosocial behavior. As we saw with bystander apathy earlier in this chapter there are forces that operate to prevent people from helping others. In the next section we will examine some of the other forces that operate to prevent people from helping others. Also discussed are a few glimmerings about how to encourage prosocial behavior.

Prejudice—Attitudes That Injure

Gateway Question: What causes prejudice?

Love and friendship bring people together. Prejudice, which is marked by suspicion, fear, or hatred, has the opposite effect. Prejudice is an all too common part of daily life. What are the origins of prejudice? How can prejudice and hurtful attitudes be reduced? Psychologists have provided valuable insights into these questions. (See "I'm Not Prejudiced, Right?")

Prejudice is a negative emotional attitude held toward members of a specific social group. Prejudices may be reflected in the

Desensitization A reduction in emotional sensitivity to a stimulus.

Anger control Personal strategies for reducing or curbing anger.

Prejudice A negative emotional attitude held against members of a particular group of people.

DISCOVERING PSYCHOLOGY

I'm Not Prejudiced, Right?

Are you prejudiced against women working outside the family home? Keep in mind your answer to this question as you read on.

Below you will find a list of 12 words. Your job is to categorize the words. Suppose, for example, that one of the words is "factory." If you feel that "factory" belongs in the category "Male or Career," then you would touch (or mark) the O to the left of the word. Otherwise, you would mark the O to the right of "factory."

Now, take 20 seconds to classify each of the words in the list. Place them into the correct categories as quickly and accurately as you can. Got the idea? Ready, set, go!

Male or Career		Female or Family
O	Daniel	O
O	Sally	O
O	House	O
O	Kitchen	O
O	Merchant	O
O	Company	O
O	Emily	O
O	Relatives	O
O	Employment	O
O	Baby	O
O	Steven	O
O	Executive	O

Now try it again with 12 new words. The only difference is that the categories have changed. Ready, set, go!

Male or Family		Female or Career
O	Home	O
O	Manager	O
O	Domestic	O
O	Andrew	O
O	In-laws	O
O	Jane	O
O	Workplace	O
O	Sarah	O
O	Office	O
O	Corporation	O
O	Siblings	O
O	John	O

Many people notice that it takes longer to do the second list and that they make more mistakes. Even people who claim they are not prejudiced against women working outside the home will nevertheless be slower and less accurate in classifying words into the categories "Male or Family" as opposed to "Female or Career." Why is there a difference? For many people, "Female" and "Family" seem to go together better than "Female" and "Career" do.

You just completed a pencil-and-paper version of an *implicit association test* (adapted from Nosek, Greenwald, & Banaji, 2005). If you Google the web, you will find that similar tests have been constructed for race, age, religion, ethnicity, disability, sexual orientation, weight, and many other stereotyped categories of people (Blair, 2001; Hofmann et al., 2005; Kite et al., 2005). Apparently, we can harbor implicit (hidden) prejudices even when we do not explicitly own up to them.

---

policies of police departments, schools, or government institutions (Dovidio, Glick, & Rudman, 2005). In such cases, prejudice is referred to as **racism, sexism, ageism,** or **heterosexism,** depending on the group affected. Because sexism, ageism, and heterosexism were discussed in earlier chapters, let's focus on racism.

Both racial prejudice and racism lead to **discrimination,** or unequal treatment of people who should have the same rights as others. Discrimination prevents people from doing things they should be able to do, such as buying a house, getting a job, voting, or attending a high-quality school. For example, in many cities, African-American drivers have been the target of "racial profiling" in which they are stopped by police without reason. Sometimes they are merely questioned, but many are cited for minor infractions, such as a cracked taillight or an illegal lane change. For many law-abiding citizens, being detained in this manner is a rude awakening (Plous, 2003). It's also one reason why many African Americans and other persons of color in America distrust police and the legal system (Dovidio et al., 2002).

Becoming Prejudiced

How do prejudices develop? One major theory suggests that prejudice is a form of **scapegoating** (blaming a person or a group for the actions of others or for conditions not of their making). Scape-

goating, you may recall, is a type of **displaced aggression** in which hostilities triggered by frustration are redirected at "safer" targets (Nelson, 2006). One interesting classic test of this hypothesis was conducted at a summer camp for young men. The men were given a difficult test they were sure to fail. Additionally, completing the test caused them to miss a trip to the movies, which was normally the high point of their weekly entertainment. Attitudes toward Mexicans and Japanese were measured before the test and after the men had failed the test and missed the movie. Subjects in this study, all European Americans, consistently rated members of the two ethnic groups lower after being frustrated (Miller & Bugelski, 1970). This effect has been easy to observe since the September 11, 2001, terrorist attacks in the United States, when people who looked "foreign" became targets for displaced anger and hostility.

At times, the development of prejudice (like other attitudes) can be traced to direct experiences with members of the rejected group. A child who is repeatedly bullied by members of a particular ethnic group might develop a lifelong dislike for all members of the group. Yet even subtle influences, such as parents' attitudes, the depiction of people in books and on TV, and exposure to children of other races, can have an impact. By the time they are 3 years of age, many children show signs of race bias (Katz, 2003). Sadly, once prejudices are established, they prevent us from accepting more positive experiences that could reverse the damage (Wilder, Simon, & Faith, 1996).

Distinguished psychologist Gordon Allport (1958) concluded that there are two important sources of prejudice. **Personal prejudice** occurs when members of another social group are perceived as a threat to one's own interests. For example, members of another group may be viewed as competitors for jobs. **Group prejudice** occurs when a person conforms to group norms. Let's say, for instance, that you have no personal reason for disliking out-group members. Nevertheless, your friends, acquaintances, or coworkers expect it of you.

The Prejudiced Personality

Other research suggests that prejudice can be a general personality characteristic. Theodore Adorno and his associates (1950) carefully probed what they called the *authoritarian* (ah-thor-ih-TARE-ee-un) *personality*. These researchers started out by studying anti-Semitism. In the process, they found that people who are prejudiced against one group tend to be prejudiced against *all* out-groups (Perreault & Bourhis, 1999).

What are the characteristics of the prejudice-prone personality? The **authoritarian personality** is marked by rigidity, inhibition, prejudice, and oversimplification (black-and-white thinking). Authoritarians also tend to highly value social conformity (Feldman, 2003) and hence to be very *ethnocentric*. **Ethnocentrism** refers to placing one's own group "at the center," usually by rejecting all other groups. Put more simply, authoritarians consider their own ethnic group superior to others. In fact, authoritarians think they are superior to everyone who is different, not just other ethnic groups (Altemeyer, 2004; Whitley, 1999).

In addition to rejecting out-groups, authoritarians are overwhelmingly concerned with power, authority, and obedience. To measure these qualities, the *F scale* was created (the *F* stands for "fascism"). This scale is made up of statements such as the ones that follow—to which authoritarians readily agree (Adorno et al., 1950):

Authoritarian Beliefs
- Obedience and respect for authority are the most important virtues children should learn.
- People can be divided into two distinct classes: the weak and the strong.
- If people would talk less and work more, everybody would be better off.
- What this country needs most, more than laws and political programs, is a few courageous, tireless, devoted leaders, in whom the people can put their faith.
- Nobody ever learns anything really important except through suffering.
- Every person should have complete faith in some supernatural power whose decisions are obeyed without question.
- Certain religious sects that refuse to salute the flag should be forced to conform to such patriotic action or else be abolished.

As you can see, authoritarians are rather close-minded (Butler, 2000). As children, most were severely punished. As a result, they learned to fear authority (and to covet it) at an early age. In general, people are more likely to express authoritarian beliefs when they feel threatened (Doty, Peterson, & Winter, 1991). An example would be calling for more severe punishment in schools when

the economy is bad and job insecurities are high. Authoritarians are not happy people.

It should be readily apparent from the list of authoritarian beliefs that the F scale is slanted toward politically conservative authoritarians. To be fair, psychologist Milton Rokeach (1918–1988) noted that rigid and authoritarian personalities can be found at both ends of the political scale. Rokeach, therefore, preferred to describe rigid and intolerant thinking as *dogmatism*. (**Dogmatism** is an unwarranted certainty in matters of belief or opinion.) Dogmatic persons find it difficult to change their beliefs, even when the evidence contradicts them (Davies, 1993).

Even if we discount the obvious bigotry of the authoritarian personality, racial prejudice runs deep in many nations. Let's probe deeper into the roots of such prejudiced behavior.

◖◗ Intergroup Conflict— The Roots of Prejudice

Gateway Question: What can be done about prejudice and intergroup conflict?

An unfortunate by-product of group membership is that it often limits contact with people in other groups. In addition, groups themselves may come into conflict. Both events tend to foster hatred and prejudice toward the out-group. The bloody clash of opposing forces in Israel, Ireland, Africa, and Hometown, U.S.A., are reminders that intergroup conflict is widespread. Daily, we read of jarring strife between political, religious, or ethnic groups.

Racism Racial prejudice that has become institutionalized (that is, it is reflected in government policy, schools, and so forth) and that is enforced by the existing social power structure.

Sexism Institutionalized prejudice against members of either sex, based solely on their gender.

Ageism An institutionalized tendency to discriminate on the basis of age; prejudice based on age.

Heterosexism The belief that heterosexuality is better or more natural than homosexuality.

Discrimination Treating members of various social groups differently in circumstances where their rights or treatment should be identical.

Scapegoating Blaming a person or a group for the actions of others or for conditions not of their making.

Displaced aggression Redirecting aggression to a target other than the actual source of one's frustration.

Personal prejudice Prejudicial attitudes held toward persons who are perceived as a direct threat to one's own interests.

Group prejudice Prejudice held out of conformity to group views.

Authoritarian personality A personality pattern characterized by rigidity, inhibition, prejudice, and an excessive concern with power, authority, and obedience.

Ethnocentrism Placing one's own group or race at the center—that is, tending to reject all other groups but one's own.

Dogmatism An unwarranted positiveness or certainty in matters of belief or opinion.

HUMAN DIVERSITY

Choking on Stereotypes

Bill, a retired aircraft mechanic, has agreed to talk to a group of high school students about the early days of commercial aviation. During his talk, Bill is concerned that any slip in his memory will confirm stereotypes about older people being forgetful. Because he is anxious and preoccupied about possible memory lapses, Bill actually does have problems with his memory (Chasteen et al., 2005).

As Bill's example suggests, negative stereotypes can have a self-fulfilling quality. This is especially true in situations in which a person's abilities are evaluated. For example, African Americans must often cope with negative stereotypes about their academic

abilities (Steele & Aronson, 1995). Could such stereotypes actually impair school performance?

Psychologist Claude Steele has amassed evidence that victims of stereotyping tend to feel *stereotype threat*. They can feel threatened when they think they are being judged in terms of a stereotype. The anxiety that this causes can then lower performance, seemingly confirming the stereotype. An experiment Steele did demonstrates this effect. In the study, African-American and European-American college students took a very difficult verbal test. Some students were told the test measured *academic ability*. Others

were told that the test was a laboratory *problem-solving task* unrelated to ability. In the ability condition, African-American students performed worse than European Americans. In the problem-solving condition they performed the same as European Americans (Steele, 1997; Steele & Aronson, 1995). A similar effect occurred with women, who scored lower on a math test after being reminded of the stereotype that "women aren't good at math" (Cadinu et al., 2005; Keller, 2002).

In light of such findings, Steele and others are currently working on ways to remove stereotype threat, so that all students can use their potentials more fully (Steele, 1997).

Shared beliefs concerning *superiority, injustice, vulnerability,* and *distrust* are common triggers for hostility between groups. Pick almost any group in conflict with others and you will find people thinking along these lines: "We are special people who are superior to other groups, but we have been unjustly exploited, wronged, or humiliated [superiority and injustice]. Other groups are a threat to us [vulnerability]. They are dishonest and have repeatedly betrayed us [distrust]. Naturally, we are hostile toward them. They don't deserve our respect or cooperation" (Eidelson & Eidelson, 2003).

In addition to hostile beliefs about other groups, conflicts are almost always amplified by stereotyped images of out-group members (Bar-Tal & Labin, 2001).

What exactly is a stereotype? **Social stereotypes** are oversimplified images of people in various groups. There is a good chance that you have stereotyped images of some of the following: African Americans, European Americans, Hispanics, Jews, women, Christians, old people, men, Asian Americans, blue-collar workers, rednecks, politicians, business executives, teenagers, and billionaires. In general, the top three categories on which most stereotypes are based are sex, age, and race (Fiske, 1993; Fiske et al., 2002). (● Figure 17.7).

Stereotypes tend to simplify people into "us" and "them" categories. Actually, aside from the fact that they always oversimplify, stereotypes often include a mixture of *positive* and *negative* qualities (Fiske et al., 2002). Even though stereotypes sometimes include positive traits, they are mainly used to maintain control over other people. When a person is stereotyped, the easiest thing for her or him to do is to abide by others' expectations—even if those expectations are demeaning. That's why no one likes to be stereotyped. Being forced into a small, distorted social "box" by stereotyping is limiting and insulting. Stereotypes rob people of their individuality (Maddox,

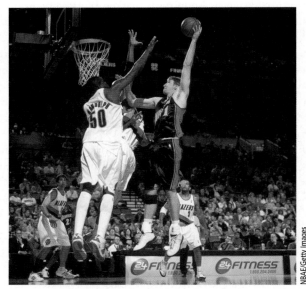

● **Figure 17.7** Racial stereotypes are common in sports. For example, one study confirmed that many people actually do believe that "white men can't jump." This stereotype implies that African-American basketball players are naturally superior in athletic ability. European-American players, in contrast, are falsely perceived as smarter and harder working than African Americans. Such stereotypes set up expectations that distort the perceptions of fans, coaches, and sportswriters. The resulting misperceptions, in turn, help perpetuate the stereotypes (Stone, Perry, & Darley, 1997).

2004). (See "Choking on Stereotypes.") Without stereotypes there would be far less hate, prejudice, exclusion, and conflict.

Today's racism is often disguised by **symbolic prejudice.** That is, many people realize that crude and obvious racism is socially unacceptable. However, this may not stop them from expressing prejudice in thinly veiled forms when they state their opinions

CRITICAL THINKING

Terrorists, Enemies, and Infidels

During times of war, normal people are called upon to kill other humans. How do they turn off their emotions and moral standards? Actually, they don't. Instead, they convince themselves that their actions are just (Osofsky, Bandura, & Zimbardo, 2005). For example, violence may be seen as necessary to eradicate evil; to serve God; or to protect honor, virtue, justice, or freedom.

Whether it's Israelis and Palestinians, Sinhalese and Tamil in Sri Lanka, or al-Qaeda and the United States, each side believes that attack or counterattack is morally justified. And, whether they are right or wrong, both sides use the same psychological mechanisms to justify violence (Wilmot & Hocker, 2007). In violent conflicts between groups, "the enemy" is always portrayed as evil, monstrous, or less than human. Dehumanizing others makes it seem that they *deserve* hatred and even death. Undoubtedly, this

provides a degree of emotional insulation that makes it easier for soldiers to harm other humans. However, it also makes terrorism, torture, murder, and genocide possible (Anderson & Bushman, 2002). Recent examples are the bloody executions of foreigners and indiscriminate suicide attacks by al-Qaeda and Iraqi insurgents in Iraq and the torture of prisoners under American control in facilities like Abu Ghraib prison (Hooks & Mosher, 2005).

A danger in demonizing "the enemy" is that it can lead to misperceptions of the motives and actions of other nations or groups (Silverstein, 1989). Many of the bloodiest conflicts in history have been fueled, in part, by treating "the enemy" as evil and subhuman. Those who actually do hold the moral high ground must be careful not to succumb to the same kind of blind hatred that leads to wanton violence and terrorism. It is also wise

to remember that ethnic jokes, racial stereotypes, degrading names, and out-group slurs are small-scale examples of the damage that "enemy" images can do.

The United Nations had declared that the current military conflict in the Darfur region of the Sudan is a genocide in which hundreds of thousands of mothers, fathers, daughters, and sons have been slaughtered.

---

about affirmative action, busing, immigration, crime, and so on. In effect, modern racists find ways to rationalize their prejudice so that it seems to be based on issues other than raw racism. For instance, an African-American candidate and an European-American candidate apply for a job. Both are only moderately qualified for the position. If the person making the hiring decision is European American, who gets the job? As you might guess, the European-American candidate is much more likely to be hired. In other words, the European-American candidate will be given "the benefit of the doubt" about his or her abilities, whereas the African-American candidate won't. People making such decisions often believe that they aren't being prejudiced, but they unconsciously discriminate against minorities (Dovidio et al., 2002).

Stereotypes held by the prejudiced tend to be unusually irrational. When given a list of negative statements about other groups, prejudiced individuals agree with most of them. It's particularly revealing that they often agree with conflicting statements. Thus, a prejudiced person may say that Jews are both "pushy" and "standoffish" or that African Americans are both "ignorant" and "sly." In one study, prejudiced persons even expressed negative attitudes toward two nonexistent groups, the "Piraneans" and the "Danirians." (See "Terrorists, Enemies, and Infidels" for further information.) Note, too, that when a prejudiced person meets a pleasant or likable member of a rejected group, the out-group member tends to be perceived as "an exception to the rule," not as evidence against the stereotype. Even when such "exceptional" experiences begin to stack up, a preju-

diced person may not change his or her stereotyped belief (Fiske, 1993; Wilder, Simon, & Faith, 1996). Because some elements of prejudice are unconscious, they are very difficult to change (Dovidio et al., 2002).

Ethnic pride is gradually replacing stereotypes and discrimination. For example, the African-American festival of Kwanzaa, a holiday celebrated in late December, emphasizes commitment to family, community, and African culture. However, despite affirmations of ethnic heritage, the problem of prejudice is far from solved.

Social stereotypes Oversimplified images of the traits of individuals who belong to a particular social group.

Symbolic prejudice Prejudice that is expressed in disguised fashion.

HUMAN DIVERSITY

Is America Purple?

As research shows, it is easy to create prejudice. Pick any simplistic way to divide a group of people into "us" and "them" and popularize it. That's what teacher Jane Elliott did when she divided her class into the brown-eyed kids and the blue-eyed kids. In no time at all, the groups were prejudiced against each other.

But that was just an experiment. It couldn't happen in the real world, right? According to psychologists Conor Seyle and Matthew Newman (2006), we are witnessing just such a real-world example in America today. In order to graphically convey the outcome of the presidential vote in the 2000 election, *USA Today* created a state-by-state map, color coded red and blue to denote states that had voted for the Republican candidate or the Democratic candidate.

Just a few years later, "red" and "blue" have become a national shorthand for dividing Americans into opposing camps. The "reds" are supposed to be Republican, conservative, middle-class, rural, religious, and live in the American heartland. The "blues" are supposed to be Democrat, liberal, upper class, urban, nonreligious, and live on the coasts. The end result is that the complex American social world is reduced to two oversimplified stereotypes, leading to an increase in between-group prejudice (Mundy, 2004).

This oversimplification ignores the fact that, in many states, the presidential votes are very close. Thus, a state that is "red" by 51 percent is nevertheless 49 percent "blue." Besides, many different combinations exist. Former President Bill Clinton is originally from Arkansas (a "red" state), identifies himself as a Southern Baptist, and worships in a Methodist church. Is he "blue"? How do you categorize someone from California (a "blue" state) who is an economic conservative, attends church occasionally, lives in San Francisco, supports gay marriage, and yet votes Republican?

● **Figure 17.8** Purple America map. Counties within states voting more than 70 percent Republican appear in red; areas voting more than 70 percent Democratic appear in blue. Shades of purple represent intermediate percentages of voters. (Reprinted by permission of the authors, Michael Gastner, Cosma Shalizi, and Mark Newman, University of Michigan.)

According to Seyle & Newman (2006), a better approach is to recognize that America is made up of a full spectrum of political, social, religious, and economic views and that most Americans are "purple." Thinking this way also highlights the fact that Americans of all political persuasions share more similarities than they do differences when compared with the citizens of other countries. This more tolerant, less polarizing view of America is reflected in the "purple America" map (● Figure 17.8) (Gastner, Shalizi, & Newman, 2005). Thinking purple just might result in a more productive national discussion about the important issues facing America today.

How do stereotypes and intergroup tensions develop? Two experiments, both in unlikely settings and both using children as subjects, offer some insight into these problems.

Experiments in Prejudice

What is it like to be discriminated against? In a unique experiment, elementary school teacher Jane Elliot sought to give her pupils direct experience with prejudice. On the first day of the experiment, Elliot announced that brown-eyed children were to sit in the back of the room and that they could not use the drinking fountain. Blue-eyed children were given extra recess time and got to leave first for lunch. At lunch, brown-eyed children were prevented from taking second helpings because they would "just waste it." Brown-eyed and blue-eyed children were kept from mingling, and the blue-eyed children were told they were "cleaner" and "smarter" (Peters, 1971).

Eye color might seem like a trivial basis for creating prejudices. However, people primarily use skin color to make decisions about the race of another person (Brown, Dane, & Durham, 1998). Surely this is just as superficial a way of judging people as eye color is, especially given recent biological evidence that it does not even make genetic sense to talk about "races" (Bonham, Warshauer-Baker, & Collins, 2005). (See this chapter's Psychology in Action section for further information about the concept of race.)

At first, Elliot made an effort to constantly criticize and belittle the brown-eyed children. To her surprise, the blue-eyed children rapidly joined in and were soon outdoing her in the viciousness of their attacks. The blue-eyed children began to feel superior, and the brown-eyed children felt just plain awful. Fights broke out. Test scores of the brown-eyed children fell.

How lasting were the effects of this experiment? The effects were short lived, because two days later the roles of the children were reversed. Before long, the same destructive effects occurred again, but this time in reverse. The implications of this experiment are unmistakable. In less than one day it was possible to get children to hate each other because of eye color and **status inequalities** (differences in power, prestige, or privileges). Certainly the effects of a lifetime of real racial or ethnic prejudice are infinitely more powerful and destructive. Racism is a major source of stress in the lives of many people of color. Over time, prejudice can have a negative impact on a person's physical and emotional health (Clark et al., 1999). (See "Is America Purple?")

Equal-Status Contact

What can be done to combat prejudice? Progress has been made through attempts to educate the general public about the lack of justification for prejudice. Changing the belief component of an attitude is one of the most direct means of changing the entire attitude. Thus, when people are made aware that members of various racial and ethnic groups share the same goals, ambitions, feelings, and frustrations as they do, intergroup relations may be improved.

However, this is not the whole answer. As we noted earlier, there is often a wide difference between attitudes and actual behavior. Until nonprejudiced behavior is engineered, changes can be quite superficial. Several lines of thought (including cognitive dissonance theory) suggest that more frequent *equal-status contact* between groups in conflict should reduce prejudice and stereotyping (Olson & Zanna, 1993 Wernet et al., 2003).

Equal-status contact refers to interacting on an equal footing, without obvious differences in power or status. Much evidence suggests that equal-status contact does, in fact, lessen prejudice. In one early study, European-American women who lived in integrated and segregated housing projects were compared for changes in attitude toward their African-American neighbors. Women in the integrated project showed a favorable shift in attitudes toward members of the other racial group. Those in the segregated project showed no change or actually became more prejudiced than before (Deutsch & Collins, 1951). In other studies, mixed-race groups have been formed at work, in the laboratory, and at schools. The conclusion from such research is that personal contact with a dis-liked group will induce friendly behavior, respect, and liking. However, these benefits occur only when personal contact is cooperative and on an equal footing (Grack & Richman, 1996).

To test the importance of equal-status contact directly, Gerald Clore and his associates set up a unique summer camp for children. The camp was directed by one European-American male, one European-American female, one African-American male, and one African-American female. Each campsite had three African-American and three European-American campers and one African-American and one European-American counselor. Thus, African-Americans and European-Americans were equally divided in number, power, privileges, and duties. Did the experience make a difference? Apparently it did: Testing showed that the children had significantly more positive attitudes toward opposite-race children after the camp than they did before (Clore, 1976).

Superordinate Goals

Let us now consider a revealing study done with 11-year-old boys. When the boys arrived at a summer camp, they were split into two groups and housed in separate cabins. At first the groups were kept apart to build up separate group identities and friendships. Soon each group had a flag and a name (the "Rattlers" and the "Eagles") and each had staked out its territory. At this point the two groups were placed in competition with each other. After a number of clashes, disliking between the groups bordered on hatred: The boys baited each other, started fights, and raided each other's cabins (Sherif et al., 1961).

Were they allowed to go home hating each other? As an experiment in reducing intergroup conflict, and to prevent the boys from remaining enemies, various strategies to reduce tensions were tried. Holding meetings between group leaders did nothing. When the groups were invited to eat together, the event turned into a free-for-all. Finally, emergencies that required *cooperation* among members of both groups were staged at the camp. For example, the water supply was damaged so that all the boys had to work together to repair it. Creating this and other *superordinate goals* helped restore peace between the two groups. (A **superordinate goal** exceeds or overrides other lesser goals.)

Cooperation and shared goals seem to help reduce conflict by encouraging people in opposing groups to see themselves as members of a single, larger group (Gaertner et al., 2000). Superordinate goals, in other words, have a "we're all in the same boat" effect on perceptions of group membership (Olson & Zanna, 1993). The power of superordinate goals can be seen in the unity that prevailed in the United States (and throughout much of the rest of

Many school districts in the United States have begun requiring students to wear uniforms. Appearance (including gang colors) is one of the major reasons why kids treat each other differently. Uniforms help minimize status inequalities and in-group/out-group distinctions. In Long Beach, California, a switch to uniforms was followed by a 91 percent drop in student assaults, thefts, vandalism, and weapons and drug violations (Ritter, 1998).

Mary Kate Denny/PhotoEdit

Status inequalities Differences in the power, prestige, or privileges of two or more persons or groups.

Equal-status contact Social interaction that occurs on an equal footing, without obvious differences in power or status.

Superordinate goal A goal that exceeds or overrides all others; a goal that renders other goals relatively less important.

the world) for months after the September 11 terrorist attacks. Superordinate goals are also an important factor in helping peacekeepers constructively engage with people from other nationalities (Boniecki & Britt, 2003).

Can such goals exist on a global scale? One example might be a desire to deal with the current global energy and food crisis. Another that comes to mind is the need to preserve the natural environment on a global scale. Still another is the continuing threat posed by terrorism and religious extremism. Politically, such goals may be far from universal. But their superordinate quality is clearly evident.

"Jigsaw" Classrooms

Contrary to the hopes of many, integrating public schools often has little positive effect on racial prejudice. In fact, prejudice may be made worse, and the self-esteem of minority students frequently decreases (Aronson, 1992).

If integrated schools provide equal-status contact, shouldn't prejudice be reduced? Theoretically, yes. But in practice, minority-group children often enter schools unprepared to compete on an equal footing. The competitive nature of schools almost guarantees that children will *not* learn to like and understand each other.

With the preceding in mind, social psychologist Elliot Aronson pioneered a way to apply superordinate goals to ordinary classrooms. According to Aronson, such goals are effective because they create **mutual interdependence.** That is, people must depend on one another to meet each person's goals. When individual needs are linked, cooperation is encouraged (Deutsch, 1993).

How has that idea been applied? Aronson has successfully created "jigsaw" classrooms that emphasize cooperation rather than competition. The term "jigsaw" refers to the pieces of a jigsaw puzzle. In a **jigsaw classroom,** each child is given a "piece" of the information needed to complete a project or prepare for a test.

In a typical session, children are divided into groups of five or six and given a topic to study for a later exam. Each child is given

his or her "piece" of information and asked to learn it. For example, one child might have information on Thomas Edison's invention of the light bulb; another, facts about his invention of the long-playing phonograph record; and a third, information about Edison's childhood. After the children have learned their parts, they teach them to others in the group. Even the most competitive children quickly realize that they cannot do well without the aid of everyone in the group. Each child makes a unique and essential contribution, so the children learn to listen to and respect each other.

Does the jigsaw method work? Compared with children in traditional classrooms, children in jigsaw groups are less prejudiced, they like their classmates more, they have more positive attitudes toward school, their grades improve, and their self-esteem increases (Aronson, 2008; Walker & Crogan, 1998). Such results are quite encouraging. As distinguished African-American psychologist Kenneth Clark said, "Racial prejudice . . . debases all human beings—those who are its victims, those who victimize, and in quite subtle ways, those who are merely accessories."

To summarize, prejudice will be reduced when:

- Members of different groups have equal status *within the situation* that brings them together.
- Members of all groups seek a common goal.
- Group members must cooperate to reach the goal.
- Group members spend enough time together for cross-group friendships to develop.

Sports teams are an excellent example of a situation in which all these conditions apply. The close contact and interdependent effort required in team sports often creates lifelong friendships and breaks down the walls of prejudice.

A Look Ahead

The Psychology in Action section of this chapter takes a look at multiculturalism and offers some further thoughts about how to promote tolerance. Don't miss this interesting conclusion to our discussion of social psychology.

Jonathan Nourok/PhotoEdit

In a "jigsaw" classroom, children help each other prepare for tests. As they teach each other what they know, the children learn to cooperate and to respect the unique strengths of each individual.

KNOWLEDGE BUILDER
Prejudice and Intergroup Conflict
RECITE

1. As a basis for prejudice, _____ is frequently related to frustration and displaced _____.
2. The authoritarian personality tends to be prejudiced against all outgroups, a quality referred to as _____.
3. Social stereotypes may be both positive and negative. T or F?
4. The stereotypes underlying racial and ethnic prejudice tend to evolve from the superordinate goals that often separate groups. T or F?
5. The term "symbolic prejudice" refers to racism or prejudice that is expressed in disguised or hidden form. T or F?

Continued

6. Jane Elliot's classroom experiment in prejudice showed that children could be made to dislike one another
   a. by setting up group competition
   b. by imposing status inequalities
   c. by role-playing
   d. by frustrating all the students
7. Research suggests that prejudice and intergroup conflict may be reduced by _____ interaction and _____ _____ goals.

REFLECT

Critical Thinking

8. In court trials, defense lawyers sometimes try to identify and eliminate prospective jurors who have authoritarian personality traits. Can you guess why?

Relate

Mentally scan over the events of the last week. How would they have changed if prejudices of all types ceased to exist?

Think of the most rigid or dogmatic person you know. Does he or she match the profile of the authoritarian personality?

Stereotypes exist for many social categories, even ordinary ones such as "college student" or "unmarried young adult." What stereotypes do you think you face in daily life?

The director of a youth recreation center is concerned about the amount of conflict she is seeing between boys and girls from different racial and ethnic groups. What advice can you give the director?

Answers: 1. scapegoating, aggression **2.** ethnocentrism **3.** T **4.** F **5.** F **6.** b **7.** equal-status, superordinate **8.** Because authoritarians tend to believe that punishment is effective, they are more likely to vote for conviction.

PSYCHOLOGY IN ACTION

Multiculturalism—Living with Diversity

Gateway Question: How can we promote multiculturalism and social harmony?

Today's society is more like a "tossed salad" than a cultural "melting pot." Rather than expecting everyone to be alike, psychologists believe that we must learn to respect and appreciate our differences. **Multiculturalism,** as this is called, gives equal status to different ethnic, racial, and cultural groups. It is a recognition and acceptance of human diversity (Moghaddam, 2007).

Breaking the Prejudice Habit

Most people publicly support policies of equality and fairness. Yet, many still have lingering biases and negative images of African Americans, Latinos, Asian Americans, and other ethnic minorities. How can we make sense of such conflicting attitudes? A decision to forsake prejudice does not immediately eliminate prejudiced thoughts and feelings. People who are not consciously prejudiced may continue to respond emotionally to members of other ethnic groups (Nosek, Greenwald, & Banaji, 2005). Quite likely this reflects lingering stereotypes and prejudices learned in childhood (Dion, 2003).

For many people, becoming less prejudiced begins by accepting the value of *openness to the other,* the ability to genuinely appreciate those who differ from us culturally (Fowers & Davidov, 2006). It is important to

remember that being open to someone else does not mean that you have to agree with that person or turn your back on your own culture. Openness, in turn, leads to the acceptance of the values of tolerance and equality. People who value tolerance resist intolerant thoughts or feelings, which motivates them to try to alter their own biased reactions (Dovidio & Gaertner, 1999; Zuwerink et al., 1996). But doing so is not easy. Typically, it requires repeated efforts to learn to think, feel, and act differently. Nevertheless, many people have succeeded in overcoming the "prejudice habit" and becoming more open to life experiences in general (Fowers & Davidov, 2006). If you would like to be more open and tolerant, the following points may be helpful to you.

Beware of Stereotyping

Stereotypes make the social world more manageable. But placing people in categories almost always causes them to appear more similar than they really are. As a result, we tend to see out-group members as very much alike, even when they are as varied as our friends and family. People who are not prejudiced work hard to actively inhibit stereotyped thoughts and to emphasize fairness and equality. A good way to tear down stereotypes is to get to know individuals from various ethnic and cultural groups (Giliovich, Keltner, & Nisbett, 2005).

Seek Individuating Information

When are we most tempted to apply stereotypes? Typically it is when we only have minimal information about a person. Stereotypes help us guess what a person is like and how she or he will act. Unfortunately, these inferences are usually wrong.

One of the best antidotes for stereotypes is **individuating information,** which helps us see a person as an individual, rather than as a member of a group (Cameron & Trope, 2004). Anything that keeps us from placing a person in a particular social category tends to negate stereotyped thinking. When you meet individuals from various backgrounds, focus on the *person,* not the *label* attached to her or him.

Mutual interdependence A condition in which two or more persons must depend on one another to meet each person's needs or goals.

Jigsaw classroom A method of reducing prejudice; each student receives only part of the information needed to complete a project or prepare for a test.

Multiculturalism Giving equal status, recognition, and acceptance to different ethnic and cultural groups.

Individuating information Information that helps define a person as an individual, rather than as a member of a group or social category.

A good example of the effects of individuating information comes from a Canadian study of English-speaking students in a French language program. Students who were "immersed" (spent most of their waking hours with French Canadians) became more positive toward them. Immersed students were more likely to say they had come to appreciate and like French Canadians, they were more willing to meet and interact with them, and they saw themselves as less different from French Canadians (Lambert, 1987). In fact, with more subtle kinds of symbolic prejudice, such contact may be the best way to reduce intergroup conflict (Dovidio & Gaertner, 1999).

Don't Fall Prey to Just-World Beliefs

Do you believe that the world is basically fair? Even if you don't, you may believe that the world is sufficiently just so that people generally get what they deserve. It may not be obvious, but such beliefs can directly increase prejudiced thinking (Hafer & Bègue, 2005).

As a result of discrimination, social conditions, and circumstances (such as recent immigration), minorities may occupy lower socioeconomic positions. **Just-world beliefs** (belief that people generally get what they deserve) can lead us to assume that minority group members wouldn't be in such positions if they weren't inferior in some way. This bit of faulty thinking amounts to blaming people who are *victims* of prejudice and discrimination for their plight. For example, assuming that a poor person is lazy may overlook the fact that discrimination in hiring has made it very difficult for him or her to find a job.

Be Aware of Self-Fulfilling Prophecies

You may recall from Chapter 1 that people tend to act in accordance with the behavior expected by others. If you hold strong stereotypes about members of various groups, a vicious cycle can occur. When you meet someone who is different from yourself, you may treat her or him in a way that is consistent with your stereotypes. If the other person is influenced by your behavior, she or he may act in ways that seem to match your stereotype. For example, a person who believes that members of another ethnic group are hostile and unfriendly will probably treat people in that group in ways that provoke hostile and unfriendly response. This creates a self-fulfilling prophecy and reinforces belief in the stereotype. (A **self-fulfilling prophecy** is an expectation that prompts people to act in ways that make the expectation come true.)

Remember, Different Does Not Mean Inferior

Some conflicts between groups cannot be avoided. What *can* be avoided is unnecessary **social competition** (rivalry among groups, each of which regards itself as superior to others). The concept of social competition refers to the fact that some individuals seek to enhance their self-esteem by identifying with a group. However, this works only if the group can be seen as superior to others. Because of social competition, groups tend to view themselves as better than their rivals (Baron, Byrne, & Branscombe, 2007). In one survey, every major ethnic group in the United States rated itself as better than any other group (Njeri, 1991).

A person who has high self-esteem does not need to treat others as inferior in order to feel good about himself or herself. Similarly, it is not necessary to degrade other groups in order to feel positive about one's own group identity (Fowers & Davidov, 2006). In fact, each ethnic group has strengths that members of other groups could benefit from emulating. For instance, African Americans, Asian Americans, and Latinos emphasize family networks that help buffer them from some of the stresses of daily life (Suinn, 1999).

Understand That Race Is a Social Construction

From the viewpoint of modern genetics, the concept of race has absolutely no meaning (Bonham, Warshauer-Baker, & Collins, 2005; Sternberg, Grigorenko, & Kidd, 2005). Members of various groups are so varied genetically and human groups have intermixed for so many centuries that it is impossible to tell, biologically, to what "race" any given individual belongs. Thus, race is an illusion based on superficial physical differences and learned ethnic identities. Certainly people *act as if* different races exist. But this is a matter of social labeling, not biological reality. To assume that any human group is biologically superior or inferior is simply wrong. In fact, the best available evidence suggests that all people are descended from the same ancient ancestors. The origins of our species lie in Africa, about 100,000 years ago. Among early human populations, darker skin was a protective adaptation to sun exposure near the equator (Jablonski & Chaplin, 2000). Biologically, we are all brothers and sisters under the skin (Graves, 2001; Smedley & Smedley, 2005).

Look for Commonalities

We live in a society that puts a premium on competition and individual effort. One problem with this is that competing with others fosters desires to demean, defeat, and vanquish them. When we cooperate with others we tend to share their joys and suffer when they are in distress (Aronson, 2008; Lanzetta & Englis, 1989). If we don't find ways to cooperate and live in greater harmony, everyone will suffer. That, if nothing else, is one thing that we all have in common. Everyone knows what it feels like to be different. Greater tolerance comes from remembering those times.

Set an Example for Others

People who act in a tolerant fashion can serve as models of tolerance for others. An example is the use of newsletters to promote understanding at an ethnically diverse high school in Houston, Texas. Students wrote stories for the newsletter about situations in which cooperation led to better understanding. For instance, a story about a Hispanic-Anglo friendship in a sports team had this headline: "Don't judge somebody until you know them. The color of the skin doesn't matter." Other stories emphasized the willingness of students to get acquainted with people from other ethnic groups and the new perceptions they had of their abilities. After just 5 months of modeling tolerance, hostility between campus ethnic groups was significantly reduced (McAlister et al., 2000).

Tolerance and Cultural Awareness

Living comfortably in a multicultural society means getting to know a little about other groups. Getting acquainted with a person whose cultural background is different from your own can be a wonderful learning experience. No one culture has all the answers or the best ways of doing things. Multicultural populations enrich a community's food, music, arts, and philosophy. Likewise, openness toward learning about different racial, cultural, and ethnic groups can be personally rewarding (Fowers & Davidov, 2006).

The importance of cultural awareness often lies in subtleties and details. For example, in large American cities, many small stores are owned by Korean immigrants. Some of these Korean-American merchants have been criticized for being cold and hostile to their customers. Refusing to place change directly in customers' hands, for instance, helped trigger an African-American boycott of Korean grocers in New York City. The core of the problem was a lack of cultural awareness on both sides.

In America, if you walk into a store, you expect the clerk to be courteous to you. One way of showing politeness is by smiling. But in the Confucian-steeped Korean culture, a smile is reserved for family members and close friends. If a Korean or Korean American has no reason to smile, he or she just

doesn't smile. There's a Korean saying: "If you smile a lot, you're silly." Expressions such as "thank you" and "excuse me" are also used sparingly and strangers rarely touch each other—not even to return change.

Here's another example of how ignorance of cultural practices can lead to needless friction and misunderstanding: An African-American woman who wanted to ease racial tensions took a freshly baked pie to her neighbors across the way, who were Orthodox Jews. At the front door the woman extended her hand, not knowing that Orthodox Jews don't shake women's hands, unless the woman is a close family member. Once she was inside, she picked up a kitchen knife to cut the pie, not knowing the couple kept a kosher household and used different knives for different foods. The woman's well-intentioned attempt at neighborliness ended in an argument! Knowing a little more about each other's cultures could have prevented both the conflicts just described.

If the Earth's population could be condensed to just 100 people, with all the current human ratios maintained, it would look like this:

- There would be 61 Asians, 14 Africans, 11 Europeans, and 14 from the Western Hemisphere, including North and South America.
- There would be 66 non-Christians and 33 Christians.
- More than half of the entire village's wealth would be in the hands of only ten people.
- Half the people in the village would suffer from malnutrition.
- Within the village would be enough weapons to kill everyone many times over.

When you consider the world from such a compressed perspective, the need for tolerance and understanding becomes readily apparent.

KNOWLEDGE BUILDER
Multiculturalism
RECITE
1. Multiculturalism refers to the belief that various subcultures and ethnic groups should be blended into a single emergent culture. T or F?
2. Many people who don't have prejudiced beliefs still have prejudiced thoughts and feelings in the presence of minority group individuals. T or F?
3. Individuating information tends to be a good antidote for stereotypes. T or F?
4. Just-world beliefs are the primary cause of social competition. T or F?

REFLECT
Critical Thinking
5. Why is it valuable to learn the terms by which members of various groups prefer to be addressed (for example, Mexican American, Latino [or Latina], Hispanic, or Chicano [Chicana])?

Relate
Which strategies for breaking the prejudice habit do you already use? How could you apply the remaining strategies to become more tolerant?

Answers: 1. F 2. T 3. T 4. F 5. Because labels might have negative meanings that are not apparent to persons outside the group. People who are culturally aware allow others to define their own identities, rather than imposing labels on them.

chapter in review
Gateways to Prosocial and Antisocial Behavior

Affiliation is tied to needs for approval, support, friendship, and information. Also, affiliation can reduce anxiety.
- Social comparison theory holds that we affiliate to evaluate our actions, feelings, and abilities. Social comparisons are also made for purposes of self-protection and self-enhancement.

Many social interactions can be understood as an exchange of attention, information, affection, or favors between two people.
- Interpersonal attraction is increased by physical proximity, frequent contact, physical attractiveness, competence, and similarity. A large degree of similarity on many dimensions is characteristic of mate selection.

- Self-disclosure occurs more when two people like one another. Self-disclosure follows a reciprocity norm: Low levels of self-disclosure are met with low levels in return, whereas moderate self-disclosure elicits more personal replies. However, overdisclosure tends to inhibit self-disclosure by others.

Just-world beliefs Belief that people generally get what they deserve.

Self-fulfilling prophecy An expectation that prompts people to act in ways that make the expectation come true.

Social competition Rivalry among groups, each of which regards itself as superior to others.

- According to social exchange theory, we tend to maintain relationships that are profitable; that is, those for which perceived rewards exceed perceived costs.

According to Sternberg's Triangular Theory of Love, liking involves a desire for intimacy with another person while love involves desiring intimacy as well as passion and/or commitment.

- Romantic love is based on feelings of both intimacy and passion. Companionate love involves feelings of both intimacy and commitment. Consummate love, involving intimacy, passion, and commitment, is the most complete form of love.
- Passionate love is also associated with greater mutual absorption between people.
- Adult love relationships tend to mirror patterns of emotional attachment observed in infancy and early childhood. Secure, avoidant, and ambivalent patterns can be defined on the basis of how a person approaches romantic and affectionate relationships with others.
- Evolutionary psychology attributes human mating patterns to the differing reproductive challenges faced by men and women during the course of evolution.

Four decision points that must be passed before a person gives help are noticing, defining an emergency, taking responsibility, and selecting a course of action. Helping is less likely at each point when other potential helpers are present.

- Understanding and removing barriers to prosocial behavior can encourage acts of helping and altruism.
- Helping is encouraged by general arousal, empathic arousal, being in a good mood, low effort or risk, and perceived similarity between the victim and the helper. For several reasons, giving help tends to encourage others to help too.

Aggression is a fact of life, but humans are not inevitably aggressive. The same factors that help explain aggression can form the basis for preventing it.

- Ethological explanations of aggression attribute it to inherited instincts. Biological explanations emphasize brain mechanisms and physical factors related to thresholds for aggression.
- According to the frustration-aggression hypothesis, frustration and aggression are closely linked. Frustration is only one of many aversive stimuli that can arouse a person and make aggression more likely. Aggression is especially likely to occur when aggression cues are present.
- Social learning theory has focused attention on the role of aggressive models in the development of aggressive behavior.

Prejudice is a negative attitude held toward members of various outgroups. One theory attributes prejudice to scapegoating. A second account says that prejudices may be held for personal reasons (personal prejudice) or simply through adherence to group norms (group prejudice).

- Prejudice, discrimination, intolerance, and stereotyping damage the lives of many people.
- Prejudiced individuals tend to have an authoritarian or dogmatic personality, characterized by rigidity, inhibition, intolerance, oversimplification, and ethnocentrism.
- Intergroup conflict gives rise to hostility and the formation of social stereotypes. Status inequalities tend to build prejudice. Equal-status contact tends to reduce it.

Prejudice is reduced by equal-status contact with other groups and by mutual interdependence, which promotes cooperation.

- Psychologists have emphasized the concept of superordinate goals as a key to reducing intergroup conflict, be it racial, religious, ethnic, or national. On a smaller scale, jigsaw classrooms (which encourage cooperation through mutual interdependence) have been shown to be an effective way of combating prejudice.

Multicultural harmony is attainable through conscious efforts to be more tolerant. Cultural awareness is a key element in promoting greater social harmony.

- Multiculturalism is a recognition and acceptance of human diversity.
- Greater tolerance can be encouraged by neutralizing stereotypes with individuating information; by looking for commonalities with others; and by avoiding the effects of just-world beliefs, self-fulfilling prophecies, and social competition.

Web Resources

For an up-to-date list of direct links to interesting sites, including those listed here, visit the student companion site for this book at www.cengage.com/psychology/coon

In Your Face Discusses research on facial attractiveness.

Center for Evolutionary Psychology A primer on evolutionary psychology, a reading list, and links.

Project Implicit Test yourself to see if you are unconsciously prejudiced.

Understanding Prejudice Explore different activities that illuminate the causes and consequences of prejudice.

Media Violence Explore the debate over media violence.

Multiculturalism Guidelines Read these guidelines from the American Psychological Association.

Diversity in College Read some relevant research about diversity in college.

Interactive Learning

Introduction to Psychology: Gateways to Mind and Behavior **Book Companion Website**
www.cengage.com/psychology/coon

Visit your book companion website, where you will find flash cards, practice quizzes, web links, and more to help you study.

CENGAGE**NOW**™ *Just what you need to know NOW!*

Spend time on what you need to master rather than on information you already have learned. Take a pre-test for this chapter, and CengageNOW will generate a personalized study plan based on your results. The study plan will identify the topics you need to review and direct you to online resources to help you master those topics. You can then take a post-test to help you determine the concepts you have mastered and what you will need to work on. Try it out! Go to www.cengage.com/login to sign in with an access code or to purchase access to this product.

CHAPTER 18

Applied Psychology

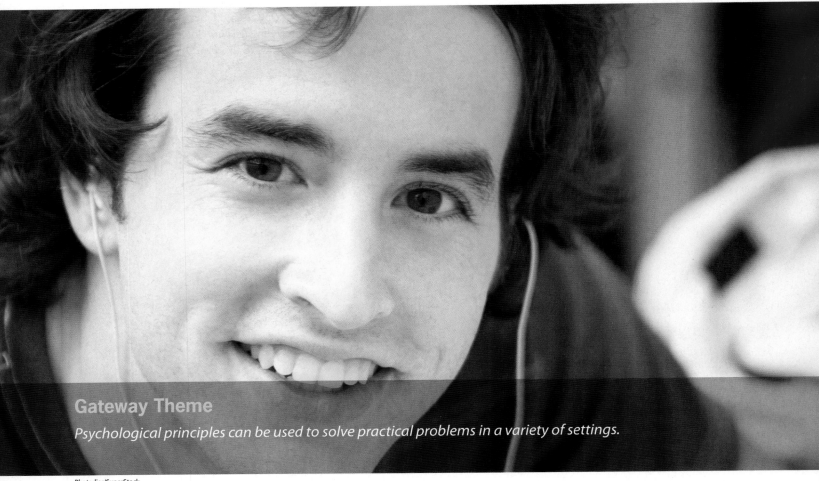

Gateway Theme

Psychological principles can be used to solve practical problems in a variety of settings.

Photodisc/SuperStock

Gateway Questions

- *How is psychology applied in business and industry?*
- *What have psychologists learned about the effects of our physical and social environments?*
- *How has psychology improved education?*
- *What does psychology reveal about juries and court verdicts?*
- *Can psychology enhance athletic performance?*
- *How are tools designed to better serve human needs?*

Insanely Great

By now we're all used to the arrival of yet another insanely great iPod model. But it's not so easy to ignore the impact the iPod has had in its short existence. Consumers have already bought more than 150 million of them, as well as more than 5 billion legal music downloads. The music business will never be the same.

New words like "podcast" and "vodcast" have been invented to describe the downloadable materials available from a growing number of organizations, including schools. Already, more than half of the nation's top 500 schools distribute educational materials digitally through iTunes U, Apple's higher education site. Many more are doing it on their own. For a change, it's not an exaggeration to call a product revolutionary.

Much of the iPod's success hinges on (rotates around?) a tiny device called a *click wheel*. This touch-sensitive ring lies at the heart of users' ability to quickly locate that one desired song among thousands. Whether it is the click wheel, the computer mouse, voice-activated computers, or computerized systems that disabled users can control, human factors psychologists depend on understanding human behavior to design better computer tools.

Applied psychology refers to the use of psychological principles and research methods to solve practical problems. Designing computer interfaces is only one way to apply psychology. The largest applied areas are clinical and counseling psychology, but there are many others, such as community psychology, educational psychology, military psychology, health psychology (discussed in Chapter 13), and space psychology. In this chapter we will focus on the application of psychology in five diverse fields: business, the environment, law, sports, and human factors.

⬤⬤ Industrial/Organizational Psychology—Psychology at Work

Gateway Question: How is psychology applied in business and industry?

Do you consider work a blessing? Or a curse? Whatever your attitude, the simple fact is that most adults work for a living. Whether you are employed now or plan to begin a career after college, it helps to know something about the psychology of work and organizations.

Industrial/organizational (I/O) psychologists study the behavior of people at work and in organizations (Aamodt, 2007). Very likely, their efforts will affect how you are selected for a job and tested, trained, or evaluated for promotion. Most I/O psychologists are employed by the government, industry, and businesses. Typically, they work in two major areas: (1) studying jobs to identify underlying skills, which can then guide efforts to select people and train them for those jobs (the *industrial* part); and (2) studying organizations to understand how to create structures and company cultures that will improve worker performance (the *organizational* part). To get a better idea of what I/O psychologists do, look at ● Table 18.1. As you can see, their interests are quite varied.

A key person in any organization is its leader. Family therapist and rabbi Edwin Friedman once remarked, "Leadership can be thought of as a capacity to define oneself to others in a way that clarifies and expands a vision of the future." How do great business leaders inspire their followers?

Table 18.1 ● Topics of Special Interest to Industrial/ Organizational Psychologists

Absenteeism	Minority workers
Decision making	Pay schedules
Design of organizations	Personnel selection
Employee stress	Personnel training
Employee turnover	Productivity
Interviewing	Promotion
Job enrichment	Task analysis
Job satisfaction	Task design
Labor relations	Work behavior
Leadership	Work environment
Machine design	Work motivation
Management styles	Worker evaluations

Theories of Leadership

During many lunch hours at a major computer game developer, most of the employees, including the top executives, eat together while playing computer games (and no, the "bosses" don't always win), talking, and joking. To say the least, these are unusual work-

Applied psychology The use of psychological principles and research methods to solve practical problems.

Industrial/organizational (I/O) psychology A field that focuses on the psychology of work and on behavior within organizations.

ing conditions. To understand the rationale behind them, let's consider two basic theories of leadership.

Theory X and Theory Y Leadership

One of the earliest attempts to improve worker efficiency was made in 1923 by Frederick Taylor, an engineer. To speed up production, Taylor standardized work routines and stressed careful planning, control, and orderliness. Today, versions of Taylor's approach are called *scientific management* (also known as **Theory X leadership,** for reasons explained shortly). **Scientific management** uses time-and-motion studies, task analysis, job specialization, assembly lines, pay schedules, and the like to increase productivity.

It sounds like scientific management treats people as if they were machines. Is that true? To some extent it is. In Taylor's day, many large companies were manufacturers with giant assembly lines. People had to be efficient cogs in the manufacturing machinery. Leaders who follow Theory X have a task orientation rather than a person orientation and tend to assume that workers must be goaded or guided into being productive. Many psychologists working in business, of course, are concerned with improving **work efficiency** (defined as maximum output at lowest cost). As a result, they alter conditions they believe will affect workers (such as time schedules, work quotas, bonuses, and so on). Some might even occasionally wish that people would act like well-oiled machines.

However, most recognize that psychological efficiency is just as important as work efficiency. **Psychological efficiency** refers to maintaining good morale, labor relations, employee satisfaction, and similar aspects of work behavior. Leadership styles that ignore or mishandle the human element can be devastatingly costly. Studies have consistently found that happy workers are productive workers (Cote, 1999; Wright & Cropanzano, 2000).

The term *Theory X* was coined by psychologist Douglas McGregor (1960) as a way to distinguish the leadership style asso-

ciated with scientific management from *Theory Y*, a newer approach, which emphasizes human relations at work.

How is this approach different? **Theory Y leaders** have a person orientation rather than a task orientation and tend to assume that workers enjoy autonomy and are willing to accept responsibility. They also assume that a worker needs and goals can be meshed with the company's goals, and that people are not naturally passive or lazy. In short, Theory Y assumes that people are industrious, creative, and rewarded by challenging work.

Over the last 50 years, manufacturing has declined in North America while *knowledge companies* have become much more common (Drucker, 1993). That is, employees are becoming **knowledge workers.** These are people who add value to a company by creating and manipulating information. Some examples are bankers, teachers, lawyers, computer engineers, writers, and scientists. Today in North America, 4 of every 5 persons in the workforce are knowledge workers. It appears that given the proper conditions of freedom and responsibility, many people *will* work hard to gain competence and use their talents. This is especially true for knowledge workers, who usually think of their work as a career rather than as a job.

Consider Armando, who is a software engineer. He has been working long hours trying to develop a new way to more quickly predict hurricane activity for a satellite weather system. The work efficiency of Armando's job cannot easily be measured or improved. Instead, his success depends on his own initiative, creativity, and commitment to his work. Armando quit his last job because the leaders of that company made him feel like he was "punching the clock," which is something Armando does not want to do. The woman who is the chief executive officer of his current company impresses Armando. In fact, he wonders whether women might not make better business leaders. (See "From Glass Ceiling to Labyrinth.")

A Honda plant at Marysville, Ohio, illustrates many features of Theory Y. As you may already know, the automobile industry has a long history of labor-management clashes and worker discontent. In fact, outright sabotage by assembly line workers is not uncommon. To avoid such problems, Honda initiated a series of simple, seemingly successful measures. They include the following practices.

- Regardless of their position, all employees wear identical white uniforms. This allows workers and supervisors to interact on a more equal footing and builds feelings of teamwork.
- To further minimize status differences, all employees hold the title *associate*.
- Private offices, separate dining halls, and reserved parking spaces for executives were abolished.
- Employees work alongside company executives, to whom they have easy access.
- Every employee has a say in, and responsibility for, quality control and safety.
- Departmental meetings are held daily. At this time, announcements are discussed, decisions are made, and thoughts are freely shared.

Charlie Chaplin captured the worker as machine perfectly in his 1936 film, *Modern Times.* Have you ever worked at a job that made you feel like this?

Chaplin/Unlimited Artists/The Kobal Collection

CRITICAL THINKING

From Glass Ceiling to Labyrinth

Aren't women more people-oriented than men? And doesn't that imply that women would make better Theory Y leaders? Good thinking. As person-oriented Theory Y leadership styles have become more popular, women are slowly gaining acceptance as leaders (Eagly, 2007). Nearly a quarter of all American organizations have female CEOs (Martin, 2007). Studies have even shown that companies with more women in leadership roles perform better financially (Carter, Simkins, & Simpson, 2003; Krishnan & Park, 2005).

And yet, according to psychologist Alice Eagly, women continue to face unique challenges. Increasingly, cracks are appearing in the *glass ceiling,* the invisible barrier that has prevented women from moving into leadership positions. But the glass ceiling is being replaced by a labyrinth created by a clash between leadership stereotypes and stereotypes of women (Eagly & Carli, 2007). On the one hand, most people expect good leaders to be *agentic*: independent, confi-

dent, ambitious, objective, dominant, and forceful. On the other hand, they expect women to be more *communal*: dependent, caring, nurturing, tender, sensitive, and sympathetic. According to traditional gender role stereotypes (see Chapter 11), it is men who are agentic, and therefore better leaders, despite evidence to the contrary (Eagly, 2007).

What does this mean for a woman who moves into a leadership role? If she practices communal, Theory Y leadership, she is seen as weak. She is "not tough enough" or does not "have the right stuff" to be a leader. Yet if she acts more assertively and confidently, she is scorned for "trying to be a man" (Martin, 2007). This conflict has been perfectly expressed by Carly Fiorina, a former CEO of Hewlett-Packard, who wrote, "In the chat rooms around Silicon Valley . . . I was routinely referred to as either a 'bimbo' or a 'bitch'—too soft or too hard, and presumptuous, besides" (Fiorina, 2006, p. 173).

As traditional gender stereotypes fade, and as Theory Y styles gain wider acceptance, perhaps women will add escaping the leadership labyrinth to their many other successes.

As the CEO of Hewlett-Packard, Carley Fiorina constantly faced the incongruity between leadership stereotypes and stereotypes of women (Fiorina, 2006).

Justin Sullivan/Getty Images

Leadership Strategies

Two techniques that make Theory Y leadership methods effective are *shared leadership* and *management by objectives.* In **shared leadership (participative management),** employees at all levels are

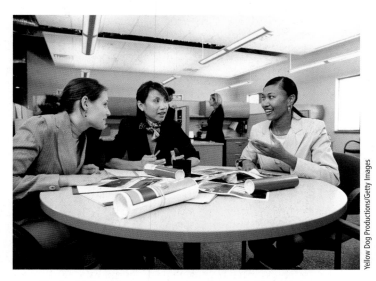

Shared leadership techniques encourage employees at all levels to become involved in decision making. Quite often this arrangement leads to greater job satisfaction.

Yellow Dog Productions/Getty Images

directly involved in decision making. By taking part in decisions that affect them, employees like those at the Honda factory come to see work as a cooperative effort—not as something imposed on them by an egotistical leader. The benefits include greater productivity, more involvement in work, greater job satisfaction, and less job-related stress (Kim, 2002; Pearce, Conger, & Locke, 2007).

What does "management by objectives" refer to? In **management by objectives,** workers are given specific goals to meet, so they can

Theory X leadership (scientific management) An approach to leadership that emphasizes work efficiency.

Work efficiency Maximum output (productivity) at lowest cost.

Psychological efficiency Maintenance of good morale, labor relations, employee satisfaction, and similar aspects of work behavior.

Theory Y leadership A leadership style that emphasizes human relations at work and that views people as industrious, responsible, and interested in challenging work.

Knowledge workers Workers who add value to their company by creating and manipulating information.

Shared leadership (participative management) A leadership approach that allows employees at all levels to participate in decision making.

Management by objectives A management technique in which employees are given specific goals to meet in their work.

tell if they are doing a good job. Typical objectives include reaching a certain sales total, making a certain number of items, or reducing waste by a specific percentage. In any case, workers are free to choose (within limits) how they will achieve their goals. As a result, they feel more independent and take personal responsibility for their work. Workers are especially productive when they receive feedback about their progress toward goals. Clearly, people like to know what the target is and whether they are succeeding (Neubert, 1998).

Many companies also give *groups* of workers even greater freedom and responsibility. This is typically done by creating self-managed teams. A **self-managed team** is a group of employees who work together toward shared goals. Self-managed teams can typically choose their own methods of achieving results, as long as they are effective. Self-managed teams tend to make good use of the strengths and talents of individual employees. They also promote new ideas and improve motivation. Most of all, they encourage cooperation and teamwork within organizations (Lewis, Goodman, & Fandt, 1995). Workers in self-managed teams are much more likely to feel that they are being treated fairly at work (Chansler, Swamidass, & Cammann, 2003) and to develop a positive team atmosphere (Zárraga & Bonache, 2005).

How can workers below the management level be involved more in their work? One answer is the use of **quality circles.** These are voluntary discussion groups that seek ways to solve business problems and improve efficiency (Aamodt, 2007). In contrast to self-managed teams, quality circles usually do not have the power to put their suggestions into practice directly. But good ideas speak for themselves and many are adopted by company leaders. Quality circles have many limitations. Nevertheless, studies verify that greater personal involvement can lead to better performance and job satisfaction (Beyer et al., 2003; Geehr, Burke, & Sulzer, 1995).

Job Satisfaction

It often makes perfect sense to apply Theory X methods to work. However, doing so without taking worker needs into account can be a case of winning the battle while losing the war. That is, immediate productivity may be enhanced while job satisfaction is lowered. And when job satisfaction is low, absenteeism skyrockets, morale falls, and there is a high rate of employee turnover, leading to higher training costs and inefficiency (Wright & Bonett, 2007).

Understandably, many of the methods used by enlightened Theory Y leaders ultimately improve **job satisfaction,** or the degree to which a person is pleased with his or her work. Job satisfaction is well worth cultivating because positive moods are associated with more cooperation, better performance, a greater willingness to help others, more creative problem solving, and less absenteeism (Brief & Weiss, 2002).

Under what conditions is job satisfaction highest? Basically, job satisfaction comes from a good fit between work and a person's interests, abilities, needs, and expectations (Landy & Conte, 2007). Think of a job you have held. It's likely that the more these

factors were present, the higher your job satisfaction was (adapted from Aamodt, 2007, p. 349):

1. My job meets my expectations.   Y or N?
2. My needs, values, and wants are met by my job.   Y or N?
3. The tasks I have to do are enjoyable.   Y or N?
4. I enjoy my supervisors and coworkers.   Y or N?
5. My coworkers are outwardly happy.   Y or N?
6. I am rewarded fairly for doing a good job.   Y or N?
7. I have a chance to grow and be challenged.   Y or N?

We should note that job satisfaction is not entirely a matter of work conditions. Anyone who has ever been employed has probably encountered at least one perpetually grumpy co-worker. In other words, workers don't leave their personalities at home. Happy people are more often happy at work, and they are more likely to focus on what's good about their job, rather than what's bad (Brief & Weiss, 2002). Understandably, the most productive employees are those who are happy at work (Aamodt, 2007; Elovainio et al., 2000). This connection can be seen clearly in the research reported in "Flexible Work."

Flexible Work

If you've ever worked "9 to 5" in an office, you know that traditional time schedules can be confining. They also doom many workers to a daily battle with rush-hour traffic (Lucas & Heady, 2002). To improve worker morale, I/O psychologists recommend the use of a variety of flexible work arrangements, of which the best known is **flextime,** or flexible working hours. The basic idea of flextime is that starting and quitting times are flexible, as long as employees are present during a core work period (Aamodt, 2007). For example, employees might be allowed to arrive between 7:30 AM and 10:30 AM and

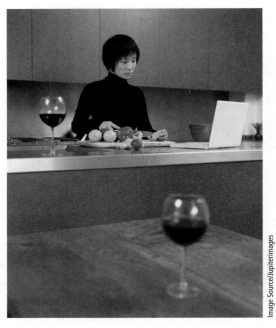

Connecting with work through the Internet makes it possible to telecommute, or work from home (Golden, Veiga, & Simsek, 2006).

Image Source/Jupiterimages

depart between 3:30 PM and 6:30 PM In a variation called a **compressed workweek,** employees might work fewer days but put in more hours per day.

A different approach to flexible work involves working at home. In knowledge companies, employees are often allowed to **telecommute,** by using a computer to remain connected to the office throughout the work day (Golden, Veiga, & Simsek, 2006).

Is flexible work really an improvement? Generally speaking, yes. For example, flextime typically has a positive effect on workers' productivity, job satisfaction, absenteeism, and comfort with their work schedules (Baltes et al., 1999). Similarly, telecommuting is especially effective when it allows valued employees to maintain their homes in other cities (Atkin & Lau, 2007). Psychologists theorize that flexible work lowers stress and increases feelings of independence, both of which increase productivity and job satisfaction.

Of course, not everyone wants a compressed workweek or to work from home. Ideally, flexible working arrangements should fit the needs of employees (Rothbard, Phillips, & Dumas, 2005). Regardless, most large organizations now use flexible work arrangements. Perhaps we can conclude that it is better, when possible, to bend working arrangements instead of people.

Job Enrichment

For years, the trend in business and industry was to make work more streamlined and efficient and to tie better pay to better work. There is now ample evidence that incentives such as bonuses, earned time off, and profit sharing can increase productivity. However, in recent years far too many jobs have become routine, repetitive, boring, and unfulfilling. To combat the discontent this can breed, many psychologists recommend a strategy called *job enrichment.*

Job enrichment involves making a job more personally rewarding, interesting, or intrinsically motivating. Large corporations such as IBM, Maytag, Western Electric, Chrysler, and Polaroid have used job enrichment with great success. It usually leads to lower production costs, increased job satisfaction, reduced boredom, and less absenteeism (Lewis, Goodman, & Fandt, 1995; Niehoff et al., 2001).

How is job enrichment done? Merely assigning a person more tasks is usually not enriching. Overloaded workers just feel stressed, and they tend to make more errors. Instead, job enrichment applies many of the principles we have discussed. Usually it involves removing some of the controls and restrictions on employees, giving them greater freedom, choice, and authority. In some cases, employees also switch to doing a complete cycle of work. That is, they complete an entire item or project, instead of doing an isolated part of a larger process. Whenever possible, workers are given direct feedback about their work or progress.

True job enrichment increases workers' *knowledge.* That is, workers are encouraged to continuously learn a broad range of skills and information related to their occupations (Campion &

McClelland, 1993; Sessa & London, 2006). In short, most people seem to enjoy being good at what they do.

bridges

Job enrichment can be thought of as a way of increasing intrinsic motivation. **See Chapter 10, page 339.**

Organizational Culture

Businesses and other organizations, whether they are large or small, develop distinct cultures. **Organizational culture** refers to a blend of customs, beliefs, values, attitudes, and rituals. These characteristics give each organization its unique "flavor." Organizational culture includes such things as how people are hired and trained, disciplined, and dismissed. It encompasses how employees dress, communicate, resolve conflicts, share power, identify with organizational goals and values, negotiate contracts, and celebrate special occasions.

People who fit well into a particular organization tend to contribute to its success in ways that are not specifically part of their job description. For example, they are helpful, conscientious, and courteous. They also display good sportsmanship by avoiding pettiness, gossiping, complaining, and making small problems into big ones. (See "Desk Rage and Healthy Organizations.") Like good citizens, the best workers keep themselves informed about organizational issues by attending meetings and taking part in discussions. Workers with these characteristics display what could be called **organizational citizenship.** Understandably, managers and employers highly value workers who are good organizational citizens (Muchinsky, 2006).

Self-managed team A work group that has a high degree of freedom with respect to how it achieves its goals.

Quality circle An employee discussion group that makes suggestions for improving quality and solving business problems.

Job satisfaction The degree to which a person is comfortable with or satisfied with his or her work.

Flextime A work schedule that allows flexible starting and quitting times.

Compressed workweek A work schedule that allows an employee to work fewer days per week by putting in more hours per day.

Telecommuting An approach to flexible work that involves working from home but using a computer to stay connected to the office throughout the workday.

Job enrichment Making a job more personally rewarding, interesting, or intrinsically motivating; typically involves increasing worker knowledge.

Organizational culture The social climate within an organization.

Organizational citizenship Making positive contributions to the success of an organization in ways that go beyond one's job description.

THE CLINICAL FILE

Desk Rage and Healthy Organizations

Like road rage on the highways, "desk rage," or workplace anger, is becoming a frequent occurrence and all too often erupts into workplace violence (Martinko, Douglas, & Harvey, 2006). It's not difficult to understand the common triggers for workplace anger: Intense anger is frequently triggered by job-related stresses such as feeling that one has been treated unfairly, perceived threats to one's self-esteem, and work-related conflicts with others (Glomb, 2002; Spector, 2005).

What can be done about anger and aggression at work? Most larger companies now offer mental health services to troubled employees and trauma counseling if violence erupts in the workplace. More importantly, healthy organizations actively promote the well-being of people. They do this through trust, by openly confronting problems; empowering employees; and encouraging participation, cooperation, and full use of human potential. Healthy organizations also support well-being in the following ways (Fuqua & Newman, 2002):

- Rather than always complaining and blaming, group members express sincere gratitude for the efforts of others.
- Everyone makes mistakes. The culture in caring organizations includes a capacity to forgive.
- Everyone needs encouragement at times. Encouragement can inspire workers and give them hope, confidence, and courage.
- Showing sensitivity to others can dramatically change the work environment.

Sensitivity can take the form of expressing interest in others and in how they are doing. It also includes respecting the privacy of others.
- Compassion for others is a good antidote for destructive competitiveness and petty game playing.
- People have very different needs, values, and experiences. Tolerance and respect for the dignity of others goes a long way toward maintaining individual well-being.

The economic pressures that organizations face can lead to hostile and competitive work environments. However, productivity and quality of life at work are closely intertwined. Effective organizations seek to optimize both (Fuqua & Newman, 2002).

Personnel Psychology

Companies can also enhance their chances of success by hiring the right employees in the first place. **Personnel psychology** is concerned with testing, selection, placement, and promotion of employees (Muchinsky, 2006). At present, 9 out of 10 people are or will be employed in business or industry. Thus, nearly everyone who holds a job is sooner or later placed under the "psychological microscope" of personnel selection. Clearly, there is value in knowing how selection for hiring and promotion is done.

Job Analysis

How do personnel psychologists make employee selections? Personnel selection begins with **job analysis,** a detailed description of the skills, knowledge, and activities required by a particular job (Dierdorff & Wilson, 2003; Landy & Conte, 2007). A job analysis may be done by interviewing expert workers or supervisors, giving them questionnaires, directly observing work, or identifying *critical incidents.* **Critical incidents** are situations with which competent employees must be able to cope. The ability to deal calmly with a mechanical emergency, for example, is a critical incident for airline pilots. Once job requirements are known, psychologists can state what skills, aptitudes, and interests are needed (● Figure 18.1). In addition, some psychologists are now doing a broader "work analysis." In this case, they try to identify general characteristics that a person must have to succeed in a variety of work roles, rather than in just a specific job (Hough & Oswald, 2000).

● **Figure 18.1** Analyzing complex skills has also been valuable to the U.S. Air Force. When million-dollar aircraft and the lives of pilots are at stake, it makes good sense to do as much training and research as possible on the ground. Air Force psychologists use flight simulators like the one pictured here to analyze the complex skills needed to fly jet fighters. Skills can then be taught without risk on the ground. The General Electric simulator shown here uses a computer to generate full-color images that respond realistically to a pilot's use of the controls.

Courtesy of the General Electric Company

Selection Procedures

After desirable skills and traits are identified, the next step is to learn who has them. Today, the methods most often used for evaluating job candidates include collecting *biodata,* conducting *interviews,* giving *standardized psychological tests,* and employing the *assessment center* approach. Let's see what each entails.

DISCOVERING PSYCHOLOGY

Surviving Your Job Interview

Each year, clothing and cosmetics manufacturers spend huge sums to convince us that their products make us more attractive. Actually, such claims are somewhat justified. You might recall from Chapter 12, for instance, that physically attractive people are often given more positive evaluations in interviews—even on traits that have no connection with appearance.

In general, however, indirect efforts to make a good impression, like dressing well, wearing cologne, and flattering the interviewer, are less effective in interviews than direct efforts such as emphasizing your positive traits and past successes (Kristof-Brown, Barrick, & Franke, 2002). However, beware of blatant self-

promotion. Excessively "blowing your own horn" tends to lower interviewers' perceptions of competence and suitability for a job (Howard & Ferris, 1996). According to the U. S. Department of Labor (2007), the advice that follows will help you survive your job interview.

Make sure you are prepared for your interview. Know about the company and job for which you are interviewing. Review your job qualifications and your résumé. Think about the kinds of questions you may be asked at the interview and outline broad answers. Consider practicing the interview with a family member or friend.

Be on time for your interview and bring your Social Security card, résumé, and

references. Also, make sure you are well groomed, dressed appropriately, and well mannered. Don't smoke or chew gum. Learn your interviewer's name and shake his or her hand firmly. Relax and answer all questions politely, promptly, and concisely. Cooperate enthusiastically, use positive body language, and remember to avoid slang.

Don't be afraid to ask questions about the potential job and the company you might be working for. Just be sure the answers aren't already easily available on the company website. And avoid questions about salary and benefits unless a job offer is coming.

Biodata

As simple as it may seem, one good way to predict job success is to collect **biodata** (detailed biographical information) from applicants (Schultz & Schultz, 2006). The idea behind biodata is that looking at past behavior is a good way to predict future behavior. By learning in detail about a person's life, it is often possible to say whether the person is suited for a particular type of work (Hough & Oswald, 2000).

Some of the most useful items of biodata include past athletic interests, academic achievements, scientific interests, extracurricular activities, religious activities, social popularity, conflict with brothers and sisters, attitudes toward school, and parents' socioeconomic status (Muchinsky, 2006). (It is worth pointing out that there are civil liberty and privacy concerns around the collection of sensitive biodata.) Such facts tell quite a lot about personality, interests, and abilities. In addition to past experiences, a person's recent life activities also help predict job success (Schmidt, Ones, & Hunter, 1992). For instance, you might think that college grades are unimportant, but college grade point average (GPA) predicts success in many types of work (Hough & Oswald, 2000).

Interviews

The traditional personal interview is still one of the most popular ways to select people for jobs or promotions. In a **personal interview,** job applicants are questioned about their qualifications. At the same time, interviewers gain an impression of the applicant's personality (Schultz & Schultz, 2006). (Or personalities—but that's another story!)

As discussed in Chapter 12, interviews are subject to the halo effect and similar problems. (Recall that the *halo effect* is the ten-

dency of interviewers to extend favorable or unfavorable impressions to unrelated aspects of an individual's personality.) In addition, interviewees actively engage in *impression management,* seeking to portray a positive image to interviewers (Ellis et al., 2002). (See "Surviving Your Job Interview.")

It is for reasons like these that psychologists continue to look for ways to improve the accuracy of interviews. For instance, recent studies suggest that interviews can be improved by giving them more structure (Hough & Oswald, 2000; Tsai, Chen, & Chiu, 2005). For example, each job candidate should be asked the same questions (Campion, Palmer, & Campion, 1998). However, even with their limitations, interviews are a valid and effective way of predicting how people will perform on the job (Landy, Shankster, & Kohler, 1994).

Psychological Testing

What kinds of tests do personnel psychologists use? General mental ability tests (intelligence tests) tell a great deal about a person's chances of succeeding in various jobs (Schmidt & Hunter, 1998).

Personnel psychology Branch of industrial/organizational psychology concerned with testing, selection, placement, and promotion of employees.

Job analysis A detailed description of the skills, knowledge, and activities required by a particular job.

Critical incidents Situations that arise in a job, with which a competent worker must be able to cope.

Biodata Detailed biographical information about a job applicant.

Personal interview Formal or informal questioning of job applicants to learn their qualifications and to gain an impression of their personalities.

So do general personality tests and honesty tests (described in Chapter 10) (Hough & Oswald, 2000). In addition, personnel psychologists often use **vocational interest tests.** These paper-and-pencil tests assess people's interests and match them to interests found among successful workers in various occupations (Aamodt, 2007). Tests such as the *Kuder Occupational Interest Survey* and the *Strong-Campbell Interest Inventory* probe interests with items like the following:

> I would prefer to
> a. visit a museum
> b. read a good book
> c. take a walk outdoors

Interest inventories typically measure six major themes identified by John Holland (• Table 18.2). If you take an interest test and your choices match those of people in a given occupation, it is assumed that you, too, would be comfortable doing the work they do (Holland, 1997).

Aptitude tests are another mainstay of personnel psychology. Such tests rate a person's potential to learn tasks or skills used in various occupations. Tests exist for clerical, verbal, mechanical, artistic, legal, and medical aptitudes, plus many others (• Figure 18.2). For example, tests of clerical aptitude emphasize the capacity to do

rapid, precise, and accurate office work. One section of a clerical aptitude test might therefore ask a person to mark all identical numbers and names in a long list of pairs like those shown here.

49837266	49832766
Global Widgets, Inc.	Global Wigets, Inc.
874583725	874583725
Sevanden Corp.	Sevanden Corp.
Cengage Publishing	Cengage Puhlishing

> **bridges**
>
> Aptitude tests are related to intelligence tests. **See Chapter 9, pages 307–308, to learn how they differ.**

Paper-and-pencil tests sometimes seem far removed from the day-to-day challenges of work. In recent years, psychologists have tried to make employment testing more interesting and relevant. For example, personnel psychologists are developing **computerized tests,** which rely on computers to present realistic work situations. As potential employees watch typical work scenes unfold, the action freezes on various problems. The applicant is then asked what she or he would do in that situation. In addition to screening job applicants, computerized presentations can be used to improve the job skills of current employees (Landy, Shankster, & Kohler, 1994; Muchinsky, 2006).

After college, chances are good that you will encounter an *assessment center.* Many large organizations use **assessment centers**

Table 18.2 • **Vocational Interest Themes**

Themes	Sample College Majors	Sample Occupations
Realistic	Agriculture	Mechanic
Investigative	Physics	Chemist
Artistic	Music	Writer
Social	Education	Counselor
Enterprising	Business	Sales
Conventional	Economics	Clerk

Adapted from Holland, 1997.

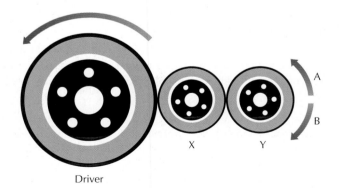

1. If the driver turns in the direction shown, which direction will wheel Y turn?   A   B

2. Which wheel will turn the slowest?   Driver   X   Y

• **Figure 18.2** Sample questions like those found on tests of mechanical aptitude. (The answers are A and the Driver.)

Bill Aron/PhotoEdit, Inc.

Aptitude tests are used to select job candidates and to advise people about what types of work they are likely to be good at.

to do in-depth evaluations of job candidates. This approach has become so popular that the list of businesses using it—Ford, IBM, Kodak, Exxon, Sears, and thousands of others—reads like a corporate *Who's Who.*

How do assessment centers differ from the selection methods already described? Assessment centers are primarily used to fill management and executive positions. First, applicants are tested and interviewed. Then they are observed and evaluated in simulated work situations. Specifically, **situational judgment tests** are used to present difficult but realistic work situations to applicants (Borman, Hanson, & Hedge, 1997; Lievens & Sackett, 2006). For example, in one exercise applicants are given an **in-basket test** that simulates the decision-making challenges executives face. The test consists of a basket full of memos, requests, and typical business problems. Each applicant is asked to quickly read all the materials and to take appropriate action. In another, more stressful test, applicants take part in a **leaderless group discussion.** This is a test of leadership that simulates group decision making and problem solving. While the group grapples with a realistic business problem, "clerks" bring in price changes, notices about delayed supplies, and so forth. By observing applicants, it is possible to evaluate leadership skills and to see how job candidates cope with stress.

> **bridges**
>
> Situational tests are also used to investigate personality differences. **See Chapter 12, pages 415–416.**

How well does this approach work? Assessment centers have had considerable success in predicting performance in a variety of jobs, careers, and advanced positions (Landy, Shankster, & Kohler, 1994).

Although we have only scratched the surface of industrial/organizational psychology, it is time to move on for a look at another applied area of great personal relevance. Before we begin, here's a chance to enhance your learning.

KNOWLEDGE BUILDER
Industrial/Organizational Psychology

RECITE

1. Theory X leadership, or scientific management, is concerned primarily with improving _____ _____.
2. Shared leadership management is often a feature of businesses with leaders who adhere to Theory Y. T or F?
3. For the majority of workers, job satisfaction is almost exclusively related to the amount of pay received. T or F?
4. Job enrichment is a direct expression of scientific management principles. T or F?
5. Identifying critical work incidents is sometimes included in a thorough _____ _____.
6. Detailed biographical information about a job applicant is referred to as _____.
7. The Strong-Campbell Inventory is a typical aptitude test. T or F?

8. A leaderless group discussion is most closely associated with which approach to employee selection?
   a. aptitude testing
   b. personal interviews
   c. job analysis
   d. assessment center

REFLECT

Critical Thinking

9. In what area of human behavior other than work would a careful task analysis be helpful?

Relate

If you were leading people in a business setting, which of the leadership concepts discussed in the text do you think you would be most likely to use?

Do you think women can make effective leaders? In business? In politics?

Think of a job you know well (something you have done yourself, or something a person you know does). Could job enrichment be applied to the work? What would you do to increase job satisfaction for people doing similar work?

Which of the various ways of evaluating job applicants do you regard as most valid? Which would you prefer to have applied to yourself?

Answers: 1. work (or task) efficiency **2.** T **3.** F **4.** F **5.** job analysis **6.** biodata **7.** F **8.** d **9.** One such area is sports psychology. As described later in this chapter, sports skills can be broken into subparts, so key elements can be identified and taught. Such methods are an extension of techniques first used for job analyses. To a large extent, attempts to identify the characteristics of effective teaching also rely on task analysis.

◐ Environmental Psychology— Life on Spaceship Earth

Gateway Question: What have psychologists learned about the effects of our physical and social environments?

Where do you think it is more likely that a fistfight would occur: in a church or a country-western bar? If the answer seems obvious, it is because specific environments have a significant impact on behavior. The reverse is also true: People have a significant impact

Vocational interest test A paper-and-pencil test that assesses a person's interests and matches them to interests found among successful workers in various occupations.

Aptitude test A test that rates a person's potential to learn skills required by various occupations.

Computerized test A test that uses a computer to present lifelike situations; test takers react to problems posed by the situations.

Assessment center A program set up within an organization to conduct in-depth evaluations of job candidates.

Situational judgment test Presenting realistic work situations to applicants in order to observe their skills and reactions.

In-basket test A testing procedure that simulates the individual decision-making challenges that executives face.

Leaderless group discussion A test of leadership that simulates group decision making and problem solving.

CRITICAL THINKING

Territoriality

In Chapter 16 we noted that powerful norms govern the use of the space immediately surrounding each person's body. As we move farther from the body, it becomes apparent that personal space also extends to adjacent areas that we claim as our "territory." **Territorial behavior** refers to actions that define a space as one's own or that protect it from intruders. For example, in the library, you might protect your space with a coat, handbag, book, or other personal belonging. "Saving a place" at a theater or a beach also demonstrates the tendency to identify a space as "ours." Even sports teams are territorial, usually showing a home team advantage by playing better on their own home territory than while playing in another team's territory (Neave & Wolfson, 2003).

Respect for the temporary ownership of space is also widespread. It is not unusual for a person to "take over" an entire table or study room by looking annoyed when others intrude. Your own personal territory may include your room, specific seats in many of your classes, or a particular table in the campus center or library that "belongs" to you and your friends.

Researchers have found that the more attached you are to an area, the more likely you are to adorn it with obvious **territorial markers** that signal your "ownership." Typical markers include decorations, plants, photographs, or posters. College dorms and business offices are prime places to observe this type of territorial marking. Interestingly, burglars are less likely to break into houses that have lots of obvious territorial markers, such as fences (even if small), parked cars, lawn furniture, exterior lights, and security signs (Brown & Bentley, 1993). "Gated communities" have sprung up in many cities because they mark out a "defensible space" that discourages intrusions (Low, 2001; Tijerino, 1998). (A highly territorial bulldog may help, too.)

Graffiti, one of the blights of urban life, is an obvious form of territorial marking.

---

on environments, both natural and constructed. Because of this second possibility, *environmental psychologists* are concerned with some of the most serious problems facing humanity.

Environmental psychology is the specialty concerned with the relationship between environments and human behavior (Bell et al., 2006). Environmental psychologists are interested in both **physical environments** (natural or constructed) and **social environments** (defined by groups of people, such as a dance, business meeting, or party). They also give special attention to **behavioral settings** (smaller areas within an environment whose use is well defined, such as an office, locker room, church, casino, or classroom). As you have no doubt noticed, various environments and behavioral settings tend to "demand" certain actions. Consider, for example, the difference between a library and a campus center lounge. In which would a conversation be more likely to occur?

Other major interests of environmental psychologists are personal space, territorial behavior (discussed in "Territoriality"), stressful environments, architectural design, environmental protection, and many related topics (● Table 18.3).

Various behavioral settings place strong demands on people to act in expected ways.

Table 18.3 ● **Topics of Special Interest to Environmental Psychologists**

Architectural design	Noise
Behavioral settings	Personal space
Cognitive maps	Personality and environment
Constructed environments	Pollution
Crowding	Privacy
Energy conservation	Proxemics
Environmental stressors	Resource management
Heat	Territoriality
Human ecology	Urban planning
Littering	Vandalism
Natural environment	

Environmental Influences

Much of our behavior is controlled, in part, by specific types of environments. For example, many shopping malls and department stores are designed like mazes. Their twisting pathways encourage shoppers to linger and wander while looking at merchandise. Likewise, in every city more assaults and burglaries take place near the few restaurants or bars where likely offenders tend to hang out (Buchanan, 2008). Even public bathrooms influence behavior. Because the seating is limited, few people hold meetings there!

Psychologists have found that a variety of environmental factors influence the amount of vandalism that occurs in public places. On the basis of psychological research, many architects now "harden" and "de-opportunize" public settings to discourage vandalism and graffiti. Some such efforts limit opportunities for vandalism (doorless toilet stalls, tiled walls). Others weaken the lure of likely targets. (Strangely enough, raised flowerbeds around signs helps protect them because people resist trampling the flowers to get to the sign.)

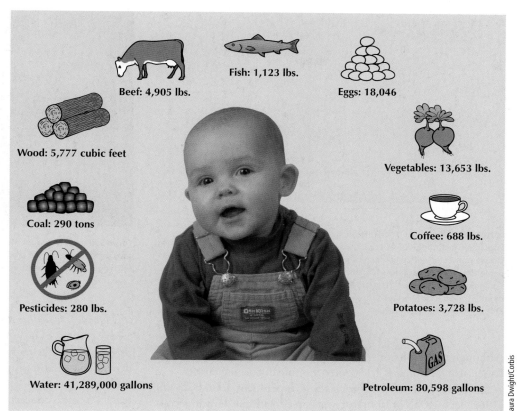

What will it cost the world to provide for a baby born in the year 2000? Over a lifetime, a person born in North America will consume, on average, the resources shown here ("Bringing Up Baby," 1999).

Given the personal impact that environments have, it is important to know how we are affected by stressful or unhealthy environments—a topic we will consider next.

Stressful Environments

Large cities are usually thought of as stressful places to live. Traffic congestion, pollution, crime, and impersonality are urban problems that immediately come to mind. To this list psychologists have added crowding, noise, and overstimulation as major sources of urban stress. Psychological research has begun to clarify the impact of each of these conditions on human functioning (Marsella, 1998).

Crowding

Overpopulation ranks as one of the most serious problems facing the world today. World population has exploded in the last 150 years (● Figure 18.3). The world's population is now more than 6 billion people and may exceed 10 billion by 2050 (UN, 2004).

Experts estimate that the maximum sustainable population of the Earth is between 5 billion and 20 billion persons. This means the Earth has already entered the lower range of its carrying capacity (Cohen, 1995). Further population increases at the present rate could be disastrous. How many more people can the forests, oceans, croplands, and atmosphere support? The most pessimistic

experts believe we have *already* exceeded the number of people the Earth can sustain indefinitely (Global Footprint Network, 2006; Oskamp, 2000).

Nowhere are the effects of overpopulation more evident than in the teeming cities of many underdeveloped nations. Closer to home, the jammed buses, subways, and living quarters of our own large cities are ample testimony to the stresses of crowding.

Is there any way to assess the effect crowding has on people? One approach is to study the effects of overcrowding among animals.

Territorial behavior Any behavior that tends to define a space as one's own or that protects it from intruders.

Territorial markers Objects and other signals whose placement indicates to others the "ownership" or control of a particular area.

Environmental psychology The formal study of how environments affect behavior.

Physical environments Natural settings, such as forests and beaches, as well as environments built by humans, such as buildings, ships, and cities.

Social environment An environment defined by a group of people and their activities or interrelationships (such as a parade, revival meeting, or sports event).

Behavioral setting A smaller area within an environment whose use is well defined, such as a bus depot, waiting room, or lounge.

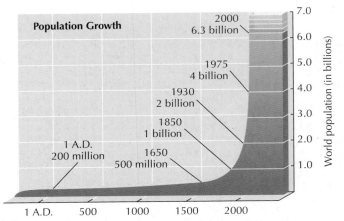

● **Figure 18.3** Population growth has exploded since 1850 (graph source: Population Institute, 2006). Overpopulation and rapid population growth are closely connected with environmental damage, international tensions, and rapid depletion of nonrenewable resources. Some demographers predict that if population growth is not limited voluntarily before it reaches 10 billion, it will be limited by widespread food shortages, disease, infant mortality, and early death (Erlich & Erlich, 1990). (Population Institute)

Times Square in New York, New Year's Eve, 2008. High densities do not automatically produce feelings of crowding. The nature of the situation and the relationships among crowd members are also important.

Although the results of animal experiments cannot be considered conclusive for humans, they point to some disturbing effects.

For example? In an interesting classic experiment, John Calhoun (1962) let a group of laboratory rats breed without limit in a confined space. Calhoun provided plenty of food, water, and nesting material for the rats. All that the rats lacked was space. At its peak, the colony numbered 80 rats. Yet it was housed in a cage designed to comfortably hold about 50. Overcrowding in the cage was heightened by the actions of the two most dominant males. These rascals staked out private territory at opposite ends of the cage, gathered harems of 8 to 10 females, and prospered. Their actions forced the remaining rats into a small, severely crowded middle area.

What effect did crowding have on the animals? A high rate of pathological behavior developed in both males and females. Females gave up nest building and caring for their young. Pregnancies decreased, and infant mortality ran extremely high. Many of the animals became indiscriminately aggressive and went on rampaging attacks against others. Abnormal sexual behavior was rampant, with some animals displaying hypersexuality and others total sexual passivity. Many of the animals died, apparently from stress-caused diseases. The link between these problems and overcrowding is unmistakable.

But does that apply to humans? Many of the same pathological behaviors can be observed in crowded inner-city ghettos. It is therefore tempting to assume that violence, social disorganization, and declining birthrates as seen in these areas are directly related to crowding. However, the connection has not been so clearly demonstrated with humans. People living in the inner city suffer disadvantages in nutrition, education, income, and health care. These, more than crowding, may deserve the blame. In fact, most laboratory studies using human subjects have failed to produce any serious ill effects by crowding people into small places. Most likely, this is because *crowding* is a psychological condition that is separate from **density** (the number of people in a given space).

How does crowding differ from density? **Crowding** refers to subjective feelings of being overstimulated by social inputs or a loss of privacy. Whether high density is experienced as crowding may depend on relationships among those involved. In an elevator, subway, or prison, high densities may be uncomfortable. In contrast, a musical concert, party, or reunion may be most pleasant at high density levels. Thus, physical crowding may interact with situations to intensify existing stresses or pleasures (Evans, Lercher, & Kofler, 2002). However, when crowding causes a *loss of control* over one's immediate social environment, stress is likely to result (Pandey, 1999).

Stress probably explains why death rates increase among prison inmates and mental hospital patients who live in crowded conditions. Even milder instances of crowding can have a negative impact. People who live in crowded conditions often become more aggressive or guarded and withdrawn from others (Regoeczi, 2003).

Overload

One unmistakable result of high densities and crowding is a state that psychologist Stanley Milgram called **attentional overload.** This is a stressful condition that occurs when sensory stimulation, information, and social contacts make excessive demands on attention. Large cities, in particular, tend to bombard residents with continuous input. The resulting sensory and cognitive overload can be quite stressful.

Milgram (1970) believed that city dwellers learn to prevent attentional overload by engaging only in brief, superficial social contacts, by ignoring nonessential events, and by fending off others with cold and unfriendly expressions. In short, many city dwellers find that a degree of callousness is essential for survival.

Kind or Callous?

Is there any evidence that such strategies are actually adopted? A fascinating study suggests they are. In several large American cities and smaller nearby towns, a young child stood on a busy street corner and asked passing strangers for help, saying, "I'm lost. Can you call my house?" About 72 percent of those approached in small towns offered to help. Only about 46 percent of those who were asked for help in the cities gave aid. In some cities (Boston and Philadelphia) only about one third were willing to help (Takooshian, Haber, & Lucido, 1977). An analysis of 65 studies confirmed that country people are more likely to help than city people (Steblay, 1987). The least helpful city tested was New York, where the crime rate is high and people are densely packed together (Levine, 2003). Thus, a blunting of sensitivity to the needs of others may be one of the more serious costs of urban stresses and crowding. As described next, noise also contributes to the sensory assault many people endure in urban environments.

The High Cost of Noise

How serious are the effects of daily exposure to noise? A classic study of children attending schools near Los Angeles International Airport suggests that constant noise can be quite damaging. Children from the noisy schools were compared with similar students attending schools farther from the airport (Cohen et al., 1981). The comparison students were from families of comparable social and economic makeup. Testing showed that children attending the noisy schools had higher blood pressure than those from the quieter schools. They were more likely to give up attempts to solve a difficult puzzle. And they were poorer at proofreading a printed paragraph—a task that requires close attention and concentration. Other studies of children living near other airports or in noisy neighborhoods have found similar signs of stress, poor reading skills, and other damaging effects (Evans, 2006; Haines et al., 2001).

The tendency of the noise-battered children to give up or become distracted is a serious handicap. It may even reveal a state of "learned helplessness" (described in Chapter 13, pages 442–443 for details) caused by daily, uncontrollable blasts of sound. Even if such damage proves to be temporary, it is clear that **noise pollution** (annoying and intrusive noise) is a major source of environmental stress (Staples, 1996).

Toxic Environments

Human activities drastically change the natural environment. We burn fossil fuels; destroy forests; use chemical products; and strip, clear, and farm the land. In doing so, we alter natural cycles, animal populations, and the very face of the Earth. The long-range impact of such activities is already becoming evident through global warming; the extinction of plants and animals; a hole in the ozone layer; and polluted land, air, water, and oceans (Oskamp, 2002; Winter & Koger, 2004).

On a smaller scale there is plenty of evidence that unchecked environmental damage will be costly to our children and descendants. For example, exposure to toxic hazards, such as radiation, pesticides, and industrial chemicals, leads to an elevated risk of physical and mental disease (Evans, 2006).

As the late Carl Sagan once said, "When you look closely, you find so many things going wrong with the environment, you are forced to reassess the hypothesis of intelligent life on Earth."

Sustainable Lifestyles

A worldwide ecological crisis is brewing and humans must change course to avoid vast human misery and permanent damage. Of course, corporations and governments do much environmental damage. Thus, many of the solutions will require changes in politics and policies. Ultimately, it will also require changes in individual behavior. Most of the environmental problems we face can be traced back to the human tendency to overuse natural resources (Global Footprint Network, 2006; Oskamp & Schultz, 2006; Winter & Koger, 2004).

Wasted Resources

The rapid worldwide consumption of natural resources is a devastating social problem. Resource consumption can be measured as an **ecological footprint,** the amount of land and water area required to replenish the resources that a human population consumes. According to the Global Footprint Network (2006), humans are already consuming more than the Earth can regener-

Density The number of people in a given space or, inversely, the amount of space available to each person.

Crowding A subjective feeling of being overstimulated by a loss of privacy or by the nearness of others (especially when social contact with them is unavoidable).

Attentional overload A stressful condition caused when sensory stimulation, information, and social contacts make excessive demands on attention.

Noise pollution Stressful and intrusive noise; usually artificially generated by machinery, but also including noises made by animals and humans.

Ecological footprint The amount of land and water area required to replenish the resources that a human population consumes.

Shown here are the Skeen family of Pearland, Texas, and the Yadev family of Ahraura, India. Each was photographed by the Material World Project, which documented typical families and their possessions around the world. Developed countries presently have much larger ecological footprints. However, population growth is fastest in developing countries and their hunger for material possessions is rapidly expanding. Achieving sustainable levels of population and consumption are two of the greatest challenges of this century. (From Menzel et al., 1994.)

ate. Industrialized nations, in particular, are consuming world resources at an alarming rate. North America, for instance, has an ecological footprint about 10 times higher than that of Asia or Africa. In the face of projected shortages and squandered resources, what can be done to encourage conservation on a personal level?

Conservation

Try as you might to reduce your use of resources (electricity, for instance), you may find it difficult to do. Environmental psychologists have long known that a lack of prompt *feedback* is a major barrier (Abrahamse et al., 2005). (See Chapter 7, page 232, for details.) For example, feedback about electricity use (the monthly electricity bill) arrives long after the temptation to turn up the heat or to leave lights on. Psychologists aware of this problem have shown that lower energy bills result from simply giving families daily feedback about their use of gas or electricity.

Conservation is especially elusive when feedback is entirely unavailable. For example, electricity use in some apartment complexes is "master-metered." In such apartments, families do not receive individual bills for their utilities. Consequently, they consume about 25 percent more energy than they would in an individually metered apartment (McClelland & Cook, 1980). Simply providing individual meters can result in improved conservation

and considerable cost reduction. Savings are magnified further with the addition of programs that give monetary rewards for energy conservation.

Effective feedback about resource use is finally becoming widely available as several organizations provide *ecological footprint calculators,* websites that allow individuals to calculate, and therefore track, their individual resource consumption (Global Footprint Network, 2006). With growing public concern over global warming, many people are now calculating their individual **carbon footprint,** the volume of greenhouse gases individual consumption adds to the atmosphere (The Nature Conservancy, 2008).

It is now easier than ever to conserve energy (by installing energy efficient lights, for example) and see an immediate reduction in your carbon footprint. It is also becoming more popular to offset some *carbon debt*—by planting trees, for example. Prompt and accurate information and feedback about energy use is making it possible to aspire to a *carbon-neutral lifestyle,* in which your energy consumption is reduced and the remainder offset so that your overall impact on global warming is zero.

Similar factors can greatly increase recycling, as described in "Reuse and Recycle."

Social Dilemmas

Why is it so difficult to get people to take better care of the environment? A pattern of behavior called a *social dilemma* contributes to many environmental problems. A **social dilemma** is any social situation that rewards actions that have undesired effects in the long run (Van Vugt, 2002). In a typical social dilemma, no one individual intentionally acts against the group interest, but if many people act alike, collective harm is done. For example, the rapid transit systems in many large cities are underused. At the same time, the roads are jammed. Why? Because too many people decide that it is convenient to own and drive a separate car (in order to run errands and so on). However, each person's behavior affects the welfare of others. Because everyone wants to drive for "convenience," driving becomes inconvenient: The mass of cars in most cities causes irritating traffic snarls and a lack of parking spaces. Each car owner has been drawn into a dilemma.

The Tragedy of the Commons

Social dilemmas are especially damaging when we are enticed into overuse of scarce resources that must be shared by many people. Again, each person acts in his or her self-interest. But collectively, everyone ends up suffering. Ecologist Garrett Hardin (1968) calls such situations the **tragedy of the commons.** An example we have already discussed is the lack of individual incentives to conserve gasoline, water, or electricity. Whenever personal comfort or convenience is involved, it is highly tempting to "let others worry about it." Yet in the long run everyone stands to lose.

Why does such misguided behavior so often prevail? Again, we see a social dilemma at work: If one person pollutes a river or trashes the roadside, it has little noticeable effect. But as many people do the same, problems that affect everyone quickly mount. Throwing away one plastic bag may seem inconsequential, but

DISCOVERING PSYCHOLOGY

Reuse and Recycle

While reducing consumption can lighten the environmental impact of our "throw-away" society, personally reusing products and materials that would normally be thrown away is also important. In addition, we can recycle materials such as paper, steel, glass, aluminum, and plastic that can be used to make new products.

What can be done to encourage people to recycle? Psychological research has shown that all of the following strategies promote

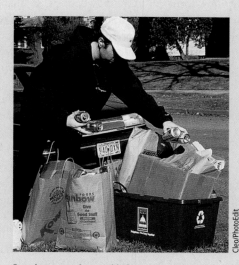

People are much more likely to recycle if proper attention is given to psychological factors that promote recycling behavior.

recycling (Oskamp, 1995; Schmuck & Vlek, 2003; Winter & Koger, 2004).

- **Educate.** Learning about environmental problems and pro-environment values at school has been one of the most effective ways to encourage pro-environmental behavior including recycling (Schmuck & Vlek, 2003; Zelezny, 1999).
- **Provide monetary rewards.** As mentioned before, monetary rewards encourage conservation. Requiring refundable deposits on glass bottles is a good example of using incentives to increase recycling.
- **Remove barriers.** Anything that makes recycling more convenient helps. A good example is cities that offer curbside pickup of household recyclables. Some cities even accept unsorted recycling materials, which greatly increases participation in recycling programs. On campus, simply putting marked containers in classrooms is a good way to encourage recycling (Ludwig, Gray, & Rowell, 1998; Winter & Koger, 2004).
- **Use persuasion.** Many recycling programs benefit from media campaigns to persuade people to participate.
- **Obtain public commitment.** People who feel they have committed themselves to recycling are more likely to follow through and actually recycle.

Sometimes, people are asked to sign "pledge cards" on which they promise to recycle. Another technique involves having people sign a list committing themselves to recycling. Such lists may or may not be published in a local newspaper. They are just as effective either way.

- **Encourage goal setting.** People who set their own goals for recycling tend to meet them. Goal setting has been used successfully with families, dorms, neighborhoods, offices, factories, and so forth.
- **Give feedback.** To reiterate, feedback proves to be very valuable. Recycling typically increases when families, work groups, dorms, and the like are simply told, on a weekly basis, how much they recycled (Schultz, 1999). Even impersonal feedback can be effective. In one study, signs were placed on recycling containers on a college campus. The signs showed how many aluminum cans had been deposited in the previous week. This simple procedure increased recycling by 65 percent (Larson, Houlihan, & Goernert, 1995).
- **Revise attitudes.** Even people who believe that recycling is worthwhile are likely to regard it as a boring task. Thus, people are most likely to continue recycling if they emphasize the sense of satisfaction they get from contributing to the environment (Werner & Makela, 1998).

---

across the world 500 billion plastic bags are used every year and it takes hundreds of years for the environment to recycle them. Plastic bags are major polluters of the world's oceans.

As another example, consider the farmer who applies pesticides to a crop to save it from insect damage. The farmer benefits immediately. However, if other farmers follow suit, the local water system may be permanently damaged. In most cases of environmental pollution there are immediate benefits for polluting and major, but delayed, long-term costs. What can we do to avoid such dilemmas?

Escaping Dilemmas

Persuasion and education have been used with some success to get individuals and businesses to voluntarily reduce destructive activities. Effective appeals may be based on self-interest (cost savings), the collective good (protecting one's own children and future gen-

erations), or simply a personal desire to take better care of the planet (Stern, 1992; Winter & Koger, 2004). It really helps if conservation is seen as a group effort. There is evidence that in most social dilemmas, people are more likely to restrain themselves when they believe others will, too (Messick et al., 1983). Otherwise they are likely to think, "Why should I be a sucker? I don't

Carbon footprint The volume of greenhouse gases individual consumption adds to the atmosphere.

Social dilemma A social situation that tends to provide immediate rewards for actions that will have undesired effects in the long run.

Tragedy of the commons A social dilemma in which individuals, each acting in his or her immediate self-interest, overuse a scarce group resource.

think anyone else is going to conserve" (fuel, electricity, water, paper, or whatever).

In some cases it is possible to dismantle social dilemmas by rearranging rewards and costs. For example, many companies are tempted to pollute because it saves them money and increases profits. To reverse the situation, a pollution tax could be levied so that it would cost more, not less, for a business to pollute. Likewise, incentives can be offered for responsible behavior. An example is the rebates offered for installing insulation or buying energy-efficient appliances (Dwyer et al., 1993; Schmuck & Vlek, 2003).

Some problems may be harder to solve. What, for instance, can be done about truck drivers who cause dangerous traffic jams because they will not pull over on narrow roads? How can littering be discouraged or prevented? How would you make carpooling or using public transportation the first choice for most people? Or how could people simply be encouraged to stagger their departure times to and from work? All these and more are social dilemmas that need solving. It is important that we not fall into the trap of ignoring them.

Environmental Problem Solving

How do psychologists find solutions to problems like overcrowding, pollution, and overuse of resources? Solutions can more easily be found by doing **environmental assessments** to see how environments influence the behavior and perceptions of the people using them.

For example, anyone who has ever lived in a college dorm knows that at times a dorm hall can be quite a "crazy house." In one well-known environmental assessment, Baum and Valins (1977) found that students housed in long, narrow, corridor-design dormitories often feel crowded and stressed. The crowded students tended to withdraw from others and even made more trips to the campus health center than students living in less-crowded buildings.

Through **architectural psychology,** the study of the effects buildings have on behavior, psychologists are often able to suggest design changes that solve or avoid problems (Zeisel, 2006). For example, Baum and Valins (1979) studied two basic dorm arrangements. One dorm had a long corridor with one central bathroom. As a result, residents were constantly forced into contact with one another. The other dorm had rooms clustered in threes. Each of these suites shared a small bathroom. Even though the amount of space available to each student was the same in both dorms, students in the long-corridor dorm reported feeling more crowded. They also made fewer friends in their dorm and showed greater signs of withdrawing from social contact.

What sort of solution does this suggest? A later study showed that small architectural changes can greatly reduce stress in high-density living conditions. Baum and Davis (1980) compared students living in a long-corridor dorm housing 40 students with those living in an altered long-corridor dorm. In the altered dorm, Baum and Davis divided the hallway in half with unlocked doors and made three center bedrooms into a lounge area (● Figure 18.4). At the end of the term, students living in the divided dorm reported less stress from crowding. They also formed more friendships and were more open to social contacts. In comparison, students in the long-corridor dorm felt more crowded, stressed, and unfriendly, and they kept their doors shut much more frequently—presumably because they "wanted to be alone."

Similar improvements have been made by altering the interior design of businesses, schools, apartment buildings, mental hospitals, and prisons. In general, the more spaces one must pass through to get from one part of a building to another, the less stressed and crowded people feel (Evans, Lepore, & Schroeder, 1996; Zeisel, 2006).

Conclusion

We have had room here only to hint at the creative and highly useful work being done in environmental psychology. Although many environmental problems remain, it is encouraging to see that behavioral solutions exist for at least some of them. Surely, creating and maintaining healthy environments is one of the major challenges facing coming generations (Gifford, 2002; Oskamp & Schultz, 2006).

We have discussed work and the environment at some length because both have major effects on our lives. To continue exploring the diversity of applied psychology, let's briefly sample four additional topics of interest: educational psychology, legal psychology, sports psychology, and human factors psychology.

(a)   (b)

◼ Bedroom   ◻ Bathroom   ◼ Lounge

● **Figure 18.4** An architectural solution for crowding. Psychologists divided a dorm hall like that shown in the left diagram *(a)* into two shorter halls separated by unlocked doors and a lounge area *(b)*. This simple change minimized unwanted social contacts and greatly reduced feelings of crowding among dorm residents. (Adapted from Baum & Davis, 1980.)

Environmental Psychology

RECITE

1. Although male rats in Calhoun's crowded animal colony became quite pathological, female rats continued to behave in a relatively normal fashion. T or F?
2. To clearly understand behavior, it is necessary to make a distinction between crowding and _____ (the number of people in a given space).
3. Milgram believed that many city dwellers prevent attentional overload by limiting themselves to superficial social contacts. T or F?
4. Performing an environmental _____ might be a good prelude to redesigning college classrooms to make them more comfortable and conducive to learning.
5. Using ecological footprint calculators to provide feedback is one effective approach for bringing about energy conservation. T or F?
6. So far, the most successful approach for bringing about energy conservation is to add monetary penalties to monthly bills for excessive consumption. T or F?

REFLECT

Critical Thinking

7. Many of the most damaging changes to the environment being caused by humans will not be felt until sometime in the future. How does this complicate the problem of preserving environmental quality?

Relate

What is the nature of the natural environment, constructed environment, social environment, and behavioral setting you are in right now?

What forms of territorial behavior are you aware of in your own actions?

Have you ever experienced a stressful level of crowding? Was density or control the key factor?

Have you ever calculated your carbon footprint? Why not try it? You might be surprised by what you find.

Answers: 1. F **2.** density **3.** T **4.** assessment **5.** T **6.** F **7.** A delay of consequences (rewards, benefits, costs, and punishers) tends to reduce their impact on immediate behavior.

Table 18.4 ● Topics of Special Interest to Educational Psychologists

Aptitude testing	Language learning
Classroom management	Learning theory
Classroom motivation	Moral development
Classroom organization	Student adjustment
Concept learning	Student attitudes
Curriculum development	Student needs
Disabled students	Teacher attitudes
Exceptional students	Teaching strategies
Gifted students	Teaching styles
Individualized instruction	Test writing
Intellectual development	Transfer of learning
Intelligence testing	

Educational psychologists are interested in enhancing learning and improving teaching.

Educational Psychology—An Instructive Topic

Gateway Question: How has psychology improved education?

You have just been asked to teach a class of fourth-graders for a day. What will you do? (Assume that bribery, showing them movies, and a field trip to an amusement park are out.) If you ever do try teaching, you might be surprised at how challenging it is. Effective teachers must understand learning, instruction, classroom dynamics, and testing.

What are the best ways to teach? Is there an optimal teaching style for different age groups, topics, or individuals? These and related questions lie at the heart of educational psychology (● Table 18.4). Specifically, **educational psychology** seeks to understand how people learn and how teachers instruct.

Elements of a Teaching Strategy

Whether it's "breaking in" a new co-worker, instructing a friend in a hobby, or helping a child learn to read, the fact is, we all teach at times. The next time you are asked to share your knowledge, how

will you do it? One good way to become more effective is to use a specific **teaching strategy,** or planned method of instruction. The example that follows was designed for classroom use, but it applies to many other situations as well (Thornburg, 1984):

> **bridges**
> Many effective teaching strategies apply the basic principles of operant conditioning. **See Chapter 7, pages 226–241.**

Environmental assessment Measurement and analysis of the effects an environment has on the behavior and perceptions of people within that environment.

Architectural psychology Study of the effects buildings have on behavior and the design of buildings using behavioral principles.

Educational psychology The field that seeks to understand how people learn and how teachers instruct.

Teaching strategy A plan for effective teaching.

HUMAN DIVERSITY

Peanut Butter for the Mind: Designing Education for Everyone

"Education is the key to unlock the golden door of freedom," said George Washington Carver. Born in 1860, a son of slaves, he invented that universally popular food, peanut butter. In today's ever more complicated world, Carver's words ring truer than ever. Yet educators face an increasingly diverse mix of students: "regular" students, adult learners, students with disabilities, students who speak English as a second language, and students at risk for dropping out (Bowe, 2000). In response, educators have begun to apply an approach called *Universal Design for Instruction* (Scott, McGuire, & Shaw, 2003; Udvari-Solner, Villa, & Thousand, 2002). The basic idea is to design lessons so richly that they will benefit most, if not all, students.

One principle of Universal Design for Instruction is to use a variety of instructional methods, such as a lecture, a podcast of the lecture, a group activity, an Internet discussion list, and perhaps student blogs. That way, for example, hearing impaired or visually impaired students can find at least one learning approach they can use. Likewise, adult learners who can't always get to class, because of work or family responsibilities, can get course information in other ways. Ultimately, everyone benefits because we all learn better if we can choose among different ways of gaining knowledge.

Another principle is to make learning materials simple and intuitive by removing unnecessary complexity. For instance, students can be given clear grading standards, accurate and complete course outlines, and handbooks to guide them through difficult topics. Again, such materials are not just better for special groups of students. They make learning easier for all of us.

Are these principles being applied to learning in colleges and universities? In short, yes they are (McGuire, & Scott, 2002). Universal instruction has broad appeal—like peanut butter—but fortunately it won't stick to the roof of your mind!

Step 1: Learner preparation. Begin by gaining the learner's attention, and focus interest on the topic at hand.

Step 2: Stimulus presentation. Present instructional stimuli (information, examples, and illustrations) deliberately and clearly.

Step 3: Learner response. Allow time for the learner to respond to the information presented (by repeating correct responses or asking questions, for example).

Step 4: Reinforcement. Give positive reinforcement (praise, encouragement) and feedback ("Yes, that's right," "No, this way," and so on) to strengthen correct responses.

Step 5: Evaluation. Test or assess the learner's progress so that both you and the learner can make adjustments when needed.

Step 6: Spaced review. Periodic review is an important step in teaching because it helps strengthen responses to key stimuli.

Effects of Teaching Styles

As a student, I've encountered many different teaching styles. Do different styles affect classroom learning? There is little doubt that teachers can greatly affect student interest, motivation, and creativity. But what styles have what effects? To answer this question, psychologists have compared a number of teaching styles. Two of the most basic are *direct instruction* and *discovery learning.*

In **direct instruction,** factual information is presented by lecture, demonstration, and rote practice. In **discovery learning,** teachers create conditions that encourage students to discover or construct knowledge for themselves (Dean& Kuhn, 2007). As it turns out, both approaches have certain advantages. Students of direct instruction do slightly better on achievement tests than

students in discovery classrooms (Klahr & Nigam, 2004). However, students of discovery learning do somewhat better on tests of abstract thinking, creativity, and problem solving. They also tend to be more independent, curious, and positive in their attitudes toward school (Peterson, 1979; Scruggs & Mastropieri, 2007). At present, it looks as if a balance of teaching styles goes hand in hand with a balanced education.

Although we have viewed only a small sample of educational research, its value for improving teaching and learning should be apparent. Before we leave the topic of education, "Peanut Butter for the Mind: Designing Education for Everyone" offers a peek at where education is going in the new millennium.

Psychology and Law—Judging Juries

Gateway Question: What does psychology reveal about juries and court verdicts?

One of the best places to see psychology in action is the local courthouse. Jury trials are often fascinating studies in human behavior. Does the defendant's appearance affect the jury's decision? Do the personality characteristics or attitudes of jurors influence how they vote? These and many more questions have been investigated by psychologists interested in law. Specifically, the **psychology of law** is the study of the behavioral dimensions of the legal system (● Table 18.5).

Jury Behavior

When a case goes to trial, jurors must listen to days or weeks of testimony and then decide guilt or innocence. How do they reach their decision? Psychologists use **mock juries** (simulated juries) to

Table 18.5 ● Topics of Special Interest in the Psychology of Law

Arbitration	Juror attitudes
Attitudes toward law	Jury decisions
Bail setting	Jury selection
Capital punishment	Mediation
Conflict resolution	Memory
Criminal personality	Parole board decisions
Diversion programs	Police selection
Effects of parole	Police stress
Expert testimony	Police training
Eyewitness testimony	Polygraph accuracy
Forensic hypnosis	Sentencing decisions
Insanity plea	White-collar crime

probe such questions. In some mock juries volunteers are simply given written evidence and arguments to read before making a decision. Others watch videotaped trials staged by actors. Either way, studying the behavior of mock juries helps us understand what determines how real jurors vote (Kerr & Bray, 2005).

Some of the findings of jury research are unsettling (Levett et al., 2005). Studies show that jurors are rarely able to put aside their biases, attitudes, and values while making a decision (Devine et al., 2001). For example, jurors are less likely to find attractive defendants guilty (on the basis of the same evidence) than unattractive defendants (Perlman & Cozby, 1983). There is an interesting twist, however. If good looks helped a person commit a crime, it can work against her or him in court (Tedeschi, Lindskold, & Rosenfeld, 1985). An example would be a handsome man accused of swindling money from an unmarried middle-aged woman.

A second major problem is that jurors are not very good at separating evidence from other information, such as their perceptions of the defendant, attorneys, witnesses, and what they think the judge wants. For example, if complex scientific evidence is presented, jurors tend to be swayed more by the expertise of the witness than by the evidence itself (Cooper, Bennett, & Sukel, 1996). Similarly, today's jurors place too much confidence in DNA evidence because crime-solving programs like *CSI:* and *Forensic Files* make it seem simple (Myers, 2007). Further, jurors who have been exposed to pretrial publicity tend to inappropriately incorporate that information into their jury deliberations, often without being aware it has happened (Ruva, McEvoy, & Bryant, 2007).

Often the jurors' final verdict is influenced by inadmissible evidence, such as mention of a defendant's prior conviction. When jurors are told to ignore information that slips out in court, they find it very hard to do so. A related problem occurs when jurors take into account the severity of the punishment a defendant faces (Sales & Hafemeister, 1985). Jurors are not supposed to let this affect their verdict, but many do.

A fourth area of difficulty arises because jurors usually cannot suspend judgment until all the evidence is in. Typically, they form an opinion early in the trial. It then becomes hard for them to fairly judge evidence that contradicts their opinion.

Problems like these are troubling in a legal system that prides itself on fairness. However, all is not lost. The more severe the crime and the more clear-cut the evidence, the less a jury's quirks affect the verdict (Tedeschi, Lindskold, & Rosenfeld, 1985). Although it is far from perfect, the jury system works reasonably well in most cases.

Jury Selection

Before a trial begins, opposing attorneys are allowed to disqualify potential jurors who may be biased. For example, a person who knows anyone connected with the trial can be excluded. Beyond this, attorneys try to use jury selection to remove people who may cause trouble for them. For instance, juries composed of women are more likely to vote for conviction in child sexual assault trials (Golding et al., 2007). In many cases, the composition of a jury has a major effect on the verdict of a trial (Devine et al., 2001).

Only a limited number of potential jurors can be excused. As a result, many attorneys ask psychologists for help in identifying people who will favor or harm their efforts. In **scientific jury selection,** social science principles are applied to the process of choosing a jury (Seltzer, 2006). Several techniques are typically used. As a first step, *demographic information* may be collected for each juror. Much can be guessed by knowing a juror's age, sex, race, occupation, education, political affiliation, religion, and socioeconomic status. Most of this information is available from public records.

To supplement demographic information, a *community survey* may be done to find out how local citizens feel about the case. The assumption is that jurors probably have attitudes similar to people with backgrounds like their own. Although talking with potential jurors outside the courtroom is not permitted, other information networks are available. For instance, a psychologist may interview relatives, acquaintances, neighbors, and co-workers of potential jurors.

Back in court, psychologists also often watch for *authoritarian personality* traits in potential jurors. Authoritarians tend to believe that punishment is effective, and they are more likely to vote for conviction (Devine et al., 2001). At the same time, the psycholo-

Direct instruction Presentation of factual information by lecture, demonstration, and rote practice.

Discovery learning Instruction based on encouraging students to discover or construct knowledge for themselves.

Psychology of law Study of the psychological and behavioral dimensions of the legal system.

Mock jury A group that realistically simulates a courtroom jury.

Scientific jury selection Using social science principles to choose members of a jury.

CRITICAL THINKING

Death-Qualified Juries

People in a **death-qualified jury** must favor the death penalty or at least be indifferent to it. That way, jurors are capable of voting for the death penalty if they think it is justified.

In order for the death penalty to have meaning, death-qualified juries may be a necessity. However, psychologists have discovered that the makeup of such juries tends to be biased. Specifically, death-qualified juries are likely to contain a disproportionate number of people who are male, white, high income, conservative, and authoritarian. Given the same facts, jurors who favor the death penalty are more likely to read criminal intent into a defendant's actions (Goodman-Delahunty, Greene, & Hsiao, 1998) and are much more likely than average to convict a defendant (Allen, Mabry, & McKelton, 1998; Butler, 2007).

Could death-qualified juries be too willing to convict? It is nearly impossible to say how often the bias inherent in death-qualified juries results in bad verdicts. However, the possibility that some innocent persons have been executed may be one of the inevitable costs of using death as the ultimate punishment.

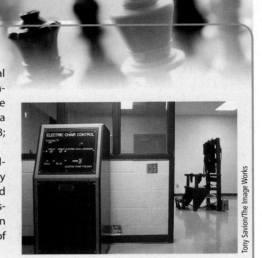

Tony Savino/The Image Works

gist typically observes potential jurors' *nonverbal behavior.* The idea is to try to learn from body language which side the person favors (Sales & Hafemeister, 1985).

> **bridges**
> Authoritarian personality traits are also related to ethnocentrism and racial prejudice. **See Chapter 17, pages 573–576.**

In the United States, murder trials require a special jury—one made up of people who are not opposed to the death penalty. "Death-Qualified Juries" examines the implications of this practice.

In the well-publicized case of O. J. Simpson, who was accused of brutally killing his wife and her friend, a majority of African Americans thought Simpson was innocent during the early stages of the trial. In contrast, the majority of European Americans thought he was guilty. The opinions of both groups changed little over the course of the yearlong trial. (Simpson was eventually acquitted, but he later lost a civil lawsuit brought by the victims' families.) The fact that emerging evidence and arguments had little effect on what people believed shows why jury makeup can sometimes decide the outcome of a trial (Brigham & Wasserman, 1999; ForsterLee et al., 2006).

Cases like Simpson's raise troubling ethical questions. Wealthy clients have the advantage of scientific jury selection—something most people cannot afford. Attorneys, of course, can't be blamed for trying to improve their odds of winning a case. And because both sides help select jurors, the net effect in most instances is probably a more balanced jury. At its worst, jury analysis leads to unjust verdicts. At its best, it helps to identify and remove only people who would be highly biased (Strier, 1999).

Jury research is perhaps the most direct link between psychology and law, but there are others. Psychologists evaluate people for sanity hearings, do counseling in prisons, profile criminals, advise

AFP/Getty Images

The behavior of juries and jurors has been extensively studied. The findings of such studies are applied by psychologists who act as advisers to attorneys during the jury selection process. Jury selection in the O. J. Simpson murder trial took 2 months, as defense and prosecution lawyers struggled for the advantage in jury makeup.

lawmakers on public policy, help select and train police cadets, and more (Brewer & Williams, 2005; Wrightsman & Fulero, 2005). In the future, it is quite likely that psychology will have a growing impact on law and the courts.

●● Sports Psychology—The Athletic Mind

Gateway Question: Can psychology enhance athletic performance?

What does psychology have to do with sports? **Sports psychology** is the study of the behavioral dimensions of sports performance (Cox, 2007). As almost all serious athletes soon learn, peak performance requires more than physical training. Mental and emotional "conditioning" are also important. Recognizing this fact, many teams, both professional and amateur, now include psychologists on their staffs. On any given day, a sports psychologist might teach an athlete how to relax, how to ignore distractions, or how to cope with emotions. The sports psychologist might also provide personal counseling for performance-lowering stresses and conflicts (LeUnes & Nation, 2002). Other psychologists are interested in studying factors that affect athletic achievement, such as skill learning, the personality profiles of champion athletes, the effects of spectators, and related topics (● Table 18.6). In short, sports psychologists seek to understand and improve sports performance and to enhance the benefits of participating in sports (Cox, 2007).

Sports often provide valuable information on human behavior in general. For example, one study of adolescents found a link between sports participation and physical self-esteem that was, in turn, linked with overall self-esteem (Bowker, 2006). In other work, psychologists have learned that such benefits are most likely to occur when competition, rejection, criticism, and the "one-winner mentality" are minimized. When working with children in sports, it is also important to emphasize fair play, intrinsic rewards, self-control of emotions, independence, and self-reliance.

Adults, of course, may also benefit from sports through reduced stress, better self-image, and improved general health (Williams, 2006). Researchers have reported, for instance, that running is associated with lower levels of tension, anxiety, fatigue, and depression than is found in the nonrunning population (Gondola & Tuckman, 1982).

Before the advent of sports psychology, it was debatable whether athletes improved because of "homespun" coaching methods or in spite of them. For example, in early studies of volleyball and gymnastics, it became clear that people teaching these sports had very little knowledge of crucial, underlying skills (Salmela, 1974, 1975).

How has psychology helped? An ability to do detailed studies of complex skills has been one of the major contributions. In a **task analysis,** sports skills are broken into subparts, so that key elements can be identified and taught. Such methods are an extension of techniques first used for job analyses, as described earlier. For example, it doesn't take much to be off target in the Olympic sport of marksmanship. The object is to hit a bull's-eye the size of a dime at the end of a 165-foot-long shooting range. Nevertheless,

Testing by psychologists has shown that umpires can call balls and strikes more accurately if they stand behind the outside corner of home plate. This position supplies better height and distance information because umpires are able to see pitches pass in front of the batter (Ford et al., 1999).

an average of 50 bull's-eyes out of 60 shots is not unusual in international competition (prone position).

What does it take—beyond keen eyes and steady hands—to achieve such accuracy? The answer is surprising. Sports psychologists have found that top marksmen consistently squeeze the trigger *between* heartbeats (● Figure 18.5). Apparently the tiny tremor

Table 18.6 ● Topics of Special Interest to Sports Psychologists

Achievement motivation	Hypnosis
Athletic personality	Mental practice
Athletic task analysis	Motor learning
Coaching styles	Peak performance
Competition	Positive visualization
Control of attention	Self-regulation
Coping strategies	Skill acquisition
Emotions and performance	Social facilitation
Exercise and mental health	Stress reduction
Goal setting	Team cooperation
Group (team) dynamics	Training procedures

● **Figure 18.5** The target on the left shows what happens when a marksman fires during the heart's contraction. Higher scores, as shown by the three shots on the right, are more likely when shots are made between heartbeats. (Adapted from Pelton, 1983.)

Death-qualified jury A jury composed of people who favor the death penalty or at least are indifferent to it.

Sports psychology Study of the psychological and behavioral dimensions of sports performance.

Task analysis Breaking complex skills into their subparts.

induced by a heartbeat is enough to send the shot astray (Pelton, 1983). Without careful psychological study, it is doubtful that this element of marksmanship would have been identified. Now that its importance is known, competitors have begun to use various techniques—from relaxation training to biofeedback—to steady and control their heartbeat. In the future, the best marksmen may be those who set their sights on mastering their hearts.

Motor Skills

Sports psychologists are very interested in how we learn motor skills. A **motor skill** is a series of actions molded into a smooth and efficient performance. Typing, walking, pole-vaulting, shooting baskets, playing golf, driving a car, writing, and skiing are all motor skills.

A basketball player may never make exactly the same shot twice in a game. This makes it almost impossible to practice every shot that might occur. How, then, do athletes become skillful? Typically, athletic performances involve learning *motor programs*. A **motor program** is a mental plan or model of what a skilled movement should be like. Motor programs allow an athlete—or a person simply walking across a room—to perform complex movements that fit changing conditions. If, for example, you have learned a "bike-riding" motor program, you can easily ride bicycles of different sizes and types on a large variety of surfaces.

Throughout life you will face the challenge of learning new motor skills. How can psychology make your learning more effective? Studies of sports skills suggest that you should keep the following points in mind for optimal skill learning:

1. Begin by observing and imitating a *skilled model*. Modeling provides a good mental picture of the skill. At this point, try simply to grasp a visual image of the skilled movement.
2. Learn *verbal rules* to back up motor learning. Such rules are usually most helpful in the early phases of skill learning. When first learning cross-country skiing, for example, it is helpful to say, "left arm, right foot, right arm, left foot." Later, as a skill becomes more automated, internal speech may actually get in the way.
3. Practice should be as *lifelike* as possible so that artificial cues and responses do not become a part of the skill. A competitive diver should practice on the board, not on a trampoline. If you want to learn to ski, try to practice on snow, not straw.
4. Get *feedback* from a mirror, videotape, coach, or observer. Whenever possible, get someone experienced in the skill to direct attention to *correct responses* when they occur.
5. When possible, it is better to practice *natural units* rather than breaking the task into artificial parts. When learning to type, it is better to start with real words rather than nonsense syllables.
6. Learn to *evaluate* and *analyze* your own performance. Remember, you are trying to learn a motor program, not just train your muscles. Motor skills are actually very mental.

The last point leads to one more suggestion. Research has shown that **mental practice,** or merely imagining a skilled performance, can aid learning (Short, Ross-Stewart, & Monsma, 2006). This technique seems to help by refining motor programs. Of course, mental practice is not superior to actual practice. Mental practice tends to be most valuable after you have mastered a task at a basic level (Tenenbaum, Bar-Eli, & Eyal, 1996). When you begin to get really good at a skill, give mental practice a try. You may be surprised at how effective it can be (Morris, Spittle, & Watt, 2005).

Positive Psychology: Peak Performance

One of the most interesting topics in sports psychology is the phenomenon of *peak performance.* During **peak performance,** physical, mental, and emotional states are harmonious and optimal. Many athletes report episodes during which they felt almost as if they were in a trance. The experience has also been called *flow* because the athlete becomes one with his or her performance and flows with it. At such times, athletes experience intense concentration, detachment, a lack of fatigue and pain, a subjective slowing of time, and feelings of unusual power and control (Csikszentmihalyi, Abuhamdeh, & Nakamura, 2005). It is at just such times that "personal bests" tend to occur.

A curious aspect of flow is that it cannot be forced to happen. In fact, if a person stops to think about it, the flow state goes away. Psychologists are now seeking to identify conditions that facilitate peak performance and the unusual mental state that usually accompanies it (Csikszentmihalyi, Abuhamdeh, & Nakamura, 2005).

Even though flow may be an elusive state, there is much that athletes can do mentally to improve performance (Porter, 2003). A starting point is to make sure that their *arousal level is appropriate for the task* at hand. For a sprinter at a track meet that may mean elevating arousal to a very high level. The sprinter could, for example, try to become angry by picturing a rival cheating. For a golfer or a gymnast, lowering arousal may be crucial, in order to avoid "choking" during a big event. One way of controlling arousal is to go through a *fixed routine* before each game or event. Athletes also learn to use *imagery and relaxation techniques* to adjust their degree of arousal (Gould & Udry, 1994).

> ## bridges
> Many of the mental strategies developed by sports psychologists are an extension of stress inoculation techniques. **See Chapter 13, page 456.**

Imaging techniques can be used to *focus attention* on the athlete's task and to *mentally rehearse* it beforehand. For example, golf great Jack Nicklaus "watches a movie" in his head before each shot. During events, athletes learn to *use cognitive-behavioral strategies to guide their efforts* in a supportive, positive way (Beauchamp et al., 1996). For instance, instead of berating herself for being behind in a match, a tennis player could use the time between points to savor a good shot or put an error out of mind. In general, athletes benefit from avoiding negative, self-critical thoughts that distract them and undermine their confidence (Cox, 2007). Finally, top athletes tend to use more *self-regulation strategies,* in which they evaluate their performance and make adjustments to keep it at optimum levels (Anshel, 1995; Kim, Singer, & Radlo, 1996).

At present, sports psychology is a very young field, and still much more an art than a science. Nevertheless, interest in the field is rapidly expanding (Petrie & Diehl, 1995).

A Look Ahead

Although we have sampled several major areas of applied psychology, they are by no means the only applied specialties. Others that immediately come to mind are community psychology, military psychology, and health psychology. The upcoming Psychology in Action section explores one of the most important applied fields, human factors psychology.

KNOWLEDGE BUILDER

Psychology Applied to Education, the Law, and Sports

RECITE

1. Evaluation of learning is typically the first step in a systematic teaching strategy. T or F?
2. Compared to direct instruction, discovery learning produces better scores on achievement tests. T or F?
3. Universal Design for Instruction aims to create educational materials that are useful to _____ students.
4. Despite their many limitations, one thing that jurors are good at is setting aside inadmissible evidence. T or F?

5. Which of the following is *not* commonly used by psychologists to aid jury selection?
   a. mock testimony
   b. information networks
   c. community surveys
   d. demographic data
6. Mental models, called _____ _____, appear to underlie well-learned motor skills.
7. Learning verbal rules to back up motor learning is usually most helpful in the early stages of acquiring a skill. T or F?
8. The flow experience is closely linked with instances of _____ performance.

REFLECT

Critical Thinking

9. When an athlete follows a set routine before an event, what source of stress has she or he eliminated?

Relate

You are going to tutor a young child in arithmetic. How could you use a teaching strategy to improve your effectiveness?

As a student, do you prefer direct instruction or discovery learning?

What advice would you give a person who is about to serve on a jury, if she or he wants to make an impartial judgment?

How could you apply the concepts of task analysis, mental practice, and peak performance to a sport you are interested in?

Answers: 1. F **2.** F **3.** all **4.** F **5.** a **6.** motor programs **7.** T **8.** peak **9.** As discussed in Chapter 15, stress is reduced when a person feels in control of a situation. Following a routine helps athletes maintain a sense of order and control so that they are not overaroused when the time comes to perform.

PSYCHOLOGY IN ACTION

Human Factors Psychology—Who's the Boss Here?

Gateway Question: How are tools designed to better serve human needs?

Should we serve machines or should they serve us? The demands that machines can make will be all too familiar if you have ever struggled with a new cell phone or failed to put together that "easy to assemble" home gym. Despite all they do for us, machines are of little value unless we humans can operate them effectively. An awkward pocket calculator might just as well be a paperweight. An automobile design that blocks large areas of the driver's vision could be deadly.

Designing for Human Use

The goal of **human factors psychology** (also known as **ergonomics**) is to design machines and work environments so they are *compatible* with our sensory and motor capacities (Gamache, 2004). For example, displays must be easy to perceive, controls must be easy to use, and the tendency to make errors must be minimized (● Figure 18.6). (A *display* is any dial, screen, light, or other device used to provide information about a machine's activity to a human user. A *control* is any knob, handle, button, lever, or other device used to alter the activity of a machine.)

Psychologist Donald Norman (1994) refers to successful human factors engineering as **natural design,** because it is based on perceptual signals that people understand naturally, without needing to learn them. An example is the row of vertical buttons in elevators that mimic the layout of the floors. This is simple, natural, and clear. One way to create more natural designs is to use *meta-*

Motor skill A series of actions molded into a smooth and efficient performance.

Motor program A mental plan or model that guides skilled movement.

Mental practice Imagining a skilled performance to aid learning.

Peak performance A performance during which physical, mental, and emotional states are harmonious and optimal.

Human factors psychology (ergonomics) A specialty concerned with making machines and work environments compatible with human perceptual and physical capacities.

Natural design Human factors engineering that makes use of naturally understood perceptual signals.

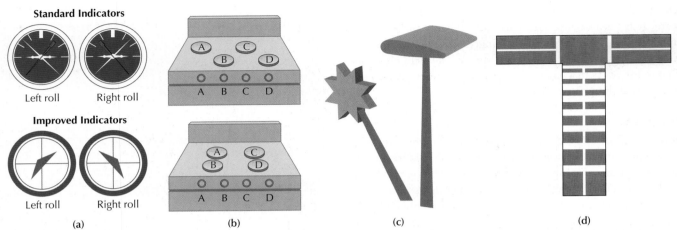

● **Figure 18.6** Human factors engineering. *(a)* Early roll indicators in airplanes were perceptually confusing and difficult to read (top). Improved displays are clear even to nonpilots. Which would you prefer if you were flying an airplane in heavy fog? *(b)* Even on a stove, the placement of controls is important. During simulated emergencies, people made no errors in reaching for the controls on the top stove. In contrast, they erred 38 percent of the time with the bottom arrangement (Chapanis & Lindenbaum, 1959). *(c)* Sometimes the shape of a control is used to indicate its function, to discourage errors. For example, the left control might be used to engage and disengage the gears of an industrial machine, whereas the right control might operate the landing flaps on an airplane. *(d)* This design depicts a street intersection viewed from above. Psychologists have found that painting white lines across the road makes drivers feel like they are traveling faster. This effect is even stronger if the lines get progressively closer together. Placing lines near dangerous intersections or sections of highway has dramatically lowered accident rates.

phors (one thing used to describe another) to create resemblances between different subjects. One famous example is the *desktop metaphor.* The design of all current personal computers presents a visual "desktop" with images of "files," "folders," and even a "trashcan." That way, you can use your knowledge of real desktops to immediately begin to use the virtual "desktop" on your computer. Earlier personal computer interfaces, which required you to type in coded instructions, were much harder to use. Similarly, digital cameras are designed to look a lot like film cameras. That way you can use your knowledge of how a mechanical camera works to start using a digital camera.

Effective design also provides *feedback* (information about the effect of making a response). The audible click designed into many computer keyboards is a good example. As Norman points out, the cause of many accidents is not just "human error." The real culprit is poor design. Human factors psychologists helped design many of the tools we rely on each day, such as "user-friendly" computers, home appliances, cameras, personal digital assistants (PDAs), airplane controls, and traffic signals.

Usability Testing

To design useful tools, human factors psychologists do **usability testing.** That is, they directly measure the ease with which people

can learn to use a machine (Norman & Panizzi, 2006). Health and safety are also important targets of usability testing. For example, construction workers who install steel rods in the floors of large buildings spend most of their work days awkwardly bent over. To avoid injuries and to minimize fatigue, machines have been designed that allow workers to do the job while standing upright. People using these machines are faster, and they spend less time in backbreaking positions (Vi, 2006).

One interesting form of usability testing is the *thinking aloud protocol.* In this case, people are asked to say everything they are thinking as they use a machine. By comparing their actual performance with what they were thinking, it is often possible to fine-tune the details of a design (Norman & Panizzi, 2006).

Human–Computer Interaction

Using human factors methods to design computers and software is referred to as **human–computer interaction (HCI).** Traditionally, machines were designed to make us stronger (such as the automobile, which moves us faster and farther than we could go on our own). In contrast, computers are meant to make us smarter (such as software that can balance a checkbook more quickly and accurately than you could on your own)

(Norman, 1994). In the world of HCI, controls are also called input devices and displays are called output devices. Humans communicate with computers through the *interface,* or set of input and output devices a computer provides.

The typical laptop computer today relies on a keyboard, touch pad, and perhaps voice recognition for input. Output is handled by a display screen and audio speakers. Many experts believe that current computer interfaces are too limited when compared with the richness of human communication. Accordingly, the search is on for ways to open up new channels of communication between humans and computers. As mentioned at the beginning of this chapter, the click wheel interface is a key to the success of the iPod. The Nintendo Wii game console is another example. The Wii wand allows players to interface with the game through hand and body movements. This is no small advance since it allows computer games to incorporate much more physical activity than is possible with traditional game controllers.

In addition to projecting a person's actions into a virtual world, computer interfaces can create a sense of being present in a remote location. *Telepresence,* as this is called, was illustrated in 2001 when a surgeon in New York used *telesurgery* to remove the diseased gallbladder of a patient an ocean away in France. In this instance, the surgeon con-

Human–computer interaction designers are actively seeking new ways to interface people with computers. The Nintendo Wii controller, which allows you to use body and hand movements for control, is one example.

trolled robotic hands to perform the surgery. Because a good surgeon relies on the sense of touch, it will be important to improve telepresence systems so they provide touch feedback to users (Lederman et al., 2004; Lederman & Klatsky, 2004).

Using Tools Effectively

Even the best designed tools, whether for the body or the mind, can be misused or underused. Do you feel like you are in control of the tools in your life or do you sometimes worry that they control you? Here are two tips for making sure you get the most out of the tools you use.

Understand Your Task

Using a tool like a digital camera, a cell phone, or a PDA can be challenging, especially if you are not sure what it can do. Begin by finding out more about what specific tasks your new tool is designed to help you accomplish. For example, if you are buying photo editing software for your digital camera, find out what tools it offers to adjust, improve, and transform photographs. In our hectic modern world, it is often tempting to **satisfice** or just get by, rather than doing things really well. Satisficing is not just a matter of being lazy. Getting by can be a survival skill, but it does not always take full advantage of the tools available to us. For example, if you know a little about photography and jump into using your new digital camera, you may be satisfied with just being able to take a basic photo. However, if you stop there, you will have used about 10 percent of what your camera is capable of doing.

Understand Your Tools

As tempting as it may be to just dive in and use your new tool, do take a peek at the instruction manual. Many modern tools, especially electronic devices, have valuable capacities hidden several layers down in menus. Without reading a manual, you might never find some of them, no matter how user friendly the device's interface may be.

Space Habitats

Let us conclude on a high note: Nowhere are the demands on human factors psychology greater than in space flight. Every machine, tool, and environment in a spacecraft must be carefully adapted for human use. Already, we have discovered that life on the International Space Station isn't easy, physically or mentally. For months at a time, residents are restricted to tiny living quarters with little privacy. These conditions, and other sources of stress, make it clear that the design of space habitats must take many human needs into account. For instance, researchers have learned that astronauts prefer rooms with clearly defined "up" and "down"—even in the weightlessness of space. This can be done by color-coding walls, floors, and ceilings, and by orienting furniture and controls so they all face the "ceiling" (Suedfeld & Steel, 2000).

Ideally there should be some flexibility in the use of living and work areas inside a space station. Behavior patterns change over time, and being able to control one's environment helps lower stress. At the same time, people need stability. Psychologists have found, for instance, that eating becomes an important high point in monotonous environments. Eating at least one meal together each day can help keep crew members working as a social unit.

Sleep cycles must be carefully controlled in space to avoid disrupting body rhythms (Suedfeld & Steel, 2000). In past space missions some astronauts found they couldn't sleep while other crew members continued to work and talk. Problems with sleep can be worsened by the constant noise on a space station. At first, such noise is annoying. After weeks or months, it can become a serious stressor. Researchers are experimenting with various earmuffs, eyeshades, and sleeping arrangements to alleviate such difficulties.

Assembly of the International Space Station by space shuttle crews began in 1998. The space station now provides a habitat in which men and women can live and work in space for extended periods. Solving the behavioral problems of living in space will be an important step toward human exploration of the solar system. (Art courtesy of NASA.)

Sensory Restriction

Sensory monotony can be a problem in space, even with the magnificent vistas of Earth below. (How many times would you have to see the North American continent before you lost interest?)

Researchers are developing stimulus environments that use music, movies, and other diversions to combat monotony and boredom. Again, they are trying to provide choice and control for space crews. Studies of confined living in the Arctic and elsewhere make it clear that one person's symphony is another's grating noise. Where music is concerned, individual earphones may be all that is required to avoid problems.

Most people in restricted environments find that they prefer solitary pastimes such as reading, listening to music, looking out windows, writing, and watching films or television. As much as anything, this preference may show the need for privacy. Reading or listening to music is a good way to psychologically withdraw from the group. Experiences with confining environments on Earth (such as Biosphere 2) suggest that including live animals and plants in space habitats could reduce stress and boredom (Suedfeld & Steel, 2000).

Usability testing The empirical investigation of the ease with which users can learn to use a machine.

Human–computer interaction (HCI) The application of human factors to the design of computers and computer software.

Satisficing Engaging in behavior that achieves a minimum result, rather than maximizing the outcome of that behavior.

Life on Spaceship Earth

It is curiously fitting that the dazzling technology of space travel has highlighted the inevitable importance of human behavior. Here on Earth, as in space, we cannot count on cleverly designed machines or technology alone to solve problems. The threat of nuclear war, social conflict, crime, prejudice, infectious disease, overpopulation, environmental damage, famine, homicide, economic disaster—these and most other major problems facing us are behavioral.

Will spaceship Earth endure? It's a psychological question.

KNOWLEDGE BUILDER
Human Factors Psychology

RECITE

1. Human factors psychologists are interested in finding ways to help people adapt to working with machines. T or F?
2. According to Donald Norman, successful human factors engineering makes use of perceptual signals that people understand naturally. T or F?

This fly is not real; it is painted onto this urinal from Amsterdam's Schiphol Airport. Why?

Maarten Udema Fotografie

3. Usability testing is used to empirically investigate machine designs. T or F?
4. To use tools effectively it is worth
   a. understanding your tool
   b. satisficing
   c. understanding your task
   d. overcoming writer's block
5. Researchers have learned that astronauts don't really care if living quarters have clearly defined "up" and "down" orientations. T or F?

REFLECT

Critical Thinking

6. Check out this photo of a men's urinal in Amsterdam's Schiphol Airport. Is that fly real? If not, why is it there?

Relate

Is there a machine whose design you admire? Can you express why the design works for you?

Have you thought about how you write? How does your approach differ from the one in this section? Are you using your word processor to your best advantage? What could you be improving?

Answers: 1. F **2.** T **3.** T **4.** a and c **5.** F **6.** Men tend to aim at the "fly" and hence are more accurate when they urinate. The result is much cleaner men's washrooms.

---

chapter in review   Gateways to Applied Psychology

Industrial/organizational psychologists enhance the quality of work by studying jobs to better match people to them and by studying organizational structures and culture to improve worker performance.

- Two basic leadership styles are Theory X (scientific management) and Theory Y (human relations approaches). Theory X is mostly concerned with work efficiency, whereas Theory Y emphasizes psychological efficiency.
- Theory Y methods include shared leadership (participative management), management by objectives, self-managed teams, and quality circles.
- Job satisfaction influences productivity, absenteeism, morale, employee turnover, and other factors that affect business efficiency.
- Job satisfaction comes from a good fit between work and a person's interests, abilities, needs, and expectations. Job enrichment tends to increase job satisfaction.

- To match people with jobs, personnel psychologists combine job analysis with selection procedures, such as gathering biodata, interviewing, giving standardized psychological tests, and using assessment centers.

Humans affect the environment and environments affect humans. Many problems can be solved by understanding both relationships.

- Environmental psychologists are interested in the effects of behavioral settings, physical or social environments, and human territoriality, among many other topics.
- Environmental problems such as crowding, pollution, and wasted resources are based on human behavior; they can only be solved by changing behavior patterns.
- Overpopulation is a major world problem, often reflected at an individual level in crowding.

- Animal experiments indicate that excessive crowding can be unhealthy. However, human research shows that psychological feelings of crowding do not always correspond to density.
- One major consequence of crowding is attentional overload.
- Providing feedback about resource use is an effective way to promote conservation. Research has shown that various psychological strategies can promote recycling.
- The origins of many environmental disasters lie in overpopulation and overconsumption (the tragedy of the commons).
- Environmental psychologists have offered solutions to many practical problems—from noise pollution to architectural design. Their work often begins with a careful environmental assessment.

Educational psychologists improve the quality of learning and teaching.

- Educational psychologists seek to understand how people learn and teachers instruct. They are particularly interested in teaching strategies, and teaching styles, such as direct instruction and discovery learning.

Psychological factors greatly affect the law and jury decisions.

- The psychology of law includes studies of courtroom behavior and other topics that pertain to the legal system. Psychologists also serve various consulting and counseling roles in legal, law enforcement, and criminal justice settings.
- Studies of mock juries show that jury decisions are often far from objective.
- Scientific jury selection is used in attempts to choose jurors who have particular characteristics. In some instances, this may result in juries that have a particular bias or that do not represent the community as a whole.
- A bias toward convicting defendants is characteristic of many death-qualified juries.

Sports psychologists enhance sports performance and the value of participating in sports.

- A careful task analysis of sports skills is one of the major tools for improving coaching and performance.
- A motor skill is a nonverbal response chain assembled into a smooth performance. Motor skills are guided by internal mental models called motor programs.
- Motor skills are refined through direct practice, but mental practice can also contribute to improvement.
- During moments of peak performance, or *flow*, physical, mental, and emotional states are optimal.
- Top performers in sports often use a variety of self-regulation strategies to focus their attention and maintain optimal levels of arousal.

Human factors psychologist (also known as ergonomists) design tools to be compatible with our sensory and motor capacities.

- Successful human factors engineering uses natural design, which makes use of perceptual signals that people understand naturally.

- Human factors psychologists rely on usability testing to empirically confirm that machines are easy to learn and use.
- Human–computer interaction (HCI) is the application of human factors to the design of computers and computer software.
- To use tools effectively it is useful to know something about the tool and the task you are using it to complete. Be aware of satisficing.
- Space habitats must be designed with special attention to the numerous human factors issues raised by space flight.

Web Resources

For an up-to-date list of direct links to interesting sites, including those listed here, visit the student companion site for this book at www.cengage.com/psychology/coon

Women in Management Read about how women are cracking the glass ceiling.

Job Interview Tips Further explore these tips from the U.S. Department of Labor.

Ecological Footprint Quiz Determine your ecological footprint with this quiz.

Carbon Calculator Determine your own carbon footprint.

The Innocence Project Read case studies of people wrongly convicted, often because of faulty eyewitness testimony.

Careers in Psychology and Law Find out about career opportunities in forensic psychology.

Sports Psychology Read sports training articles.

Bad Human Factors Designs Explore these examples of poor human factors design.

Interactive Learning

Introduction to Psychology: Gateways to Mind and Behavior Book Companion Website
www.cengage.com/psychology/coon

Visit your book companion website, where you will find flash cards, practice quizzes, web links, and more to help you study.

CENGAGENOW™ *Just what you need to know NOW!*

Spend time on what you need to master rather than on information you already have learned. Take a pre-test for this chapter, and CengageNOW will generate a personalized study plan based on your results. The study plan will identify the topics you need to review and direct you to online resources to help you master those topics. You can then take a post-test to help you determine the concepts you have mastered and what you will need to work on. Try it out! Go to www.cengage.com/login to sign in with an access code or to purchase access to this product.

Behavioral Statistics

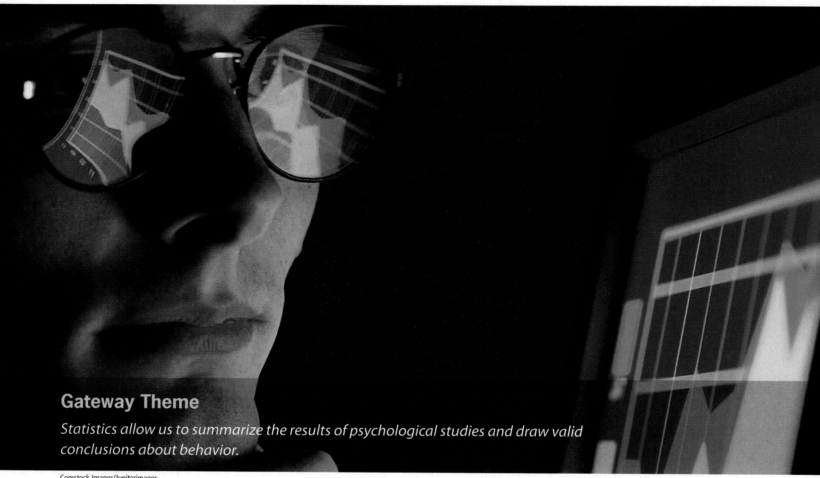

Gateway Theme

Statistics allow us to summarize the results of psychological studies and draw valid conclusions about behavior.

Comstock Images/Jupiterimages

Gateway Questions

- *What are descriptive statistics?*
- *How are correlations used in psychology?*
- *What are inferential statistics?*

preview — Statistics from "Heads" to "Tails"

Let's say a friend of yours invites you to try your hand at a "game of chance." He offers to flip a coin and pay you a dollar if the coin comes up heads. If the coin shows tails, you must pay him a dollar. He flips the coin: tails—you pay him a dollar. He flips it again: tails. Again: tails. And again: tails. And again: tails. For good luck, one more time: rats! tails!

At this point you are faced with a choice. Should you continue the game in an attempt to recoup your losses? Or should you assume that the coin is biased and quit before you really get "skinned"? Taking out your trusty pocket calculator (and, of course, the statistics book you carry with you at all times), you compute the odds of obtaining 6 tails in a row from an unbiased coin. The probability is 0.016 (less than 2 times out of 100).

If the coin really is honest, 6 consecutive tails is a rare event. Wisely, you decide that the coin is probably biased and refuse to play again. (Unless, of course, your "friend" is willing to take

"tails" for the next 6 tosses!) Perhaps a decision could have been made in this hypothetical example without using statistics. But notice how much clearer the situation becomes when it is expressed statistically.

The results of psychological studies are often expressed as numbers, which psychologists must summarize and interpret before they have any meaning. To do so, they use two major types of statistics. **Descriptive statistics** summarize or "boil down" numbers so they become more meaningful and easier to communicate to others. In comparison, **inferential statistics** are used for decision making, for generalizing from small samples, and for drawing conclusions. As was the case in the coin-flipping example, psychologists must often base decisions on limited data. Such decisions are much easier to make with the help of inferential statistics. Let's see how statistics are used in psychology.

Descriptive Statistics—Psychology by the Numbers

Gateway Question: What are descriptive statistics?

Let's say you have completed a study on human behavior. The results seem interesting, but can you really tell what your data reveal just by looking at a jumble of numbers? To get a clear picture of how people behaved, you will probably turn to descriptive statistics. By summarizing the results of your study, statistics will help you draw valid conclusions about what you observed.

Statistics bring greater clarity and precision to psychological thought and research (Gravetter & Wallnau, 2007). To see how, let's begin by considering three basic types of descriptive statistics: *graphical statistics,* measures of *central tendency,* and measures of *variability.* Let's start with **graphical statistics,** which present numbers pictorially, so they are easier to visualize.

Graphical Statistics

● Table A.1 shows simulated scores on a test of hypnotic susceptibility given to 100 college students. With such disorganized data, it is hard to form an overall "picture" of the differences in hypnotic susceptibility. But by using a *frequency distribution,* large amounts of information can be neatly organized and summarized. A **frequency distribution** is made by breaking down the entire range of

Descriptive statistics Mathematical tools used to describe and summarize numeric data.

Inferential statistics Mathematical tools used for decision making, for generalizing from small samples, and for drawing conclusions.

Graphical statistics Techniques for presenting numbers pictorially, often by plotting them on a graph.

Frequency distribution A table that divides an entire range of scores into a series of classes and then records the number of scores that fall into each class.

Table A.1 ● Raw Scores of Hypnotic Susceptibility

55	86	52	17	61	57	84	51	16	64
22	56	25	38	35	24	54	26	37	38
52	42	59	26	21	55	40	59	25	57
91	27	38	53	19	93	25	39	52	56
66	14	18	63	59	68	12	19	62	45
47	98	88	72	50	49	96	89	71	66
50	44	71	57	90	53	41	72	56	93
57	38	55	49	87	59	36	56	48	70
33	69	50	50	60	35	67	51	50	52
11	73	46	16	67	13	71	47	25	77

possible scores into classes of equal size. Next, the number of scores falling into each class is recorded. In ● Table A.2, the raw data from ● Table A.1 have been condensed into a frequency distribution. Notice how much clearer the pattern of scores for the entire group becomes.

Frequency distributions are often shown *graphically* to make them more "visual." A **histogram,** or graph of a frequency distribution, is made by labeling class intervals on the *abscissa* (X axis or horizontal line) and frequencies (the number of scores in each class) on the *ordinate* (Y axis or vertical line). Next, bars are drawn for each class interval; the height of each bar is determined by the number of scores in each class (● Figure A.1). An alternate way of graphing scores is the more familiar **frequency polygon** (● Figure A.2). Here, points are placed at the center of each class interval to indicate the number of scores. Then the dots are connected by straight lines.

Measures of Central Tendency

Notice in ● Table A.2 that more scores fall in the range 40–59 than elsewhere. How can we show this fact? A measure of **central tendency** is simply a number describing a "typical score" around which other scores fall. A familiar measure of central tendency is the mean, or "average." But as we shall see in a moment, other types

Table A.2 ● Frequency Distribution of Hypnotic Susceptibility Scores

Class Interval	Number of Persons in Class
0–19	10
20–39	20
40–59	40
60–79	20
80–99	10

● **Figure A.1** Frequency histogram of hypnotic susceptibility scores contained in ● Table A.2.

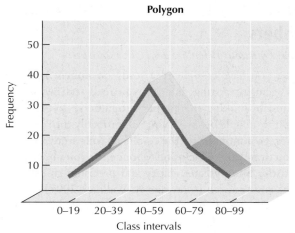

● **Figure A.2** Frequency polygon of hypnotic susceptibility scores contained in ● Table A.2.

of "averages" can be used. To illustrate each we need an example: ● Table A.3 shows the raw data for an imaginary experiment in which two groups of subjects were given a test of memory. Assume that one group was given a drug that might improve memory (let's call the drug Rememberine). The second group received a placebo. Is there a difference in memory scores between the two groups? It's difficult to tell without computing an average.

The Mean

As one type of "average," the **mean** is calculated by adding all the scores for each group and then dividing by the total number of scores. Notice in ● Table A.3 that the means reveal a difference between the two groups.

Table A.3 ● Raw Scores on a Memory Test for Subjects Taking Rememberine or a Placebo

Subject	Group 1 Rememberine	Group 2 Placebo
1	65	54
2	67	60
3	73	63
4	65	33
5	58	56
6	55	60
7	70	60
8	69	31
9	60	62
10	68	61
Sum	650	540
Mean	65	54
Median	66	60

$$\text{Mean} = \frac{\Sigma X}{N} \text{ or } \frac{\text{Sum of all scores, } X}{\text{number of scores}}$$

$$\text{Mean Group 1} = \frac{65 + 67 + 73 + 65 + 58 + 55 + 70 + 69 + 60 + 68}{10}$$
$$= \frac{650}{10} = 65$$

$$\text{Mean Group 2} = \frac{54 + 60 + 63 + 33 + 56 + 60 + 60 + 31 + 62 + 61}{10}$$
$$= \frac{540}{10} = 54$$

Median = the middle score or the mean of the two middle scores*

Median Group 1 = 55 58 60 65 ⎡65 67⎤ 68 69 70 73
$$= \frac{65 + 67}{2} = 66$$

Median Group 2 = 31 33 54 56 60 ⎡60 60⎤ 61 62 63
$$= \frac{60 + 60}{2} = 60$$

*⎡   ⎤ indicates middle score(s).

The mean is sensitive to extremely high or low scores in a distribution. For this reason it is not always the best measure of central tendency. (Imagine how distorted it would be to calculate average yearly incomes from a small sample of people that happened to include a multimillionaire, such as actor Johnny Depp.) In such cases the middle score in a group of scores—called the *median*—is used instead.

The Median

The **median** is found by arranging scores from the highest to the lowest and selecting the score that falls in the middle. In other words, half the values in a group of scores fall below the median and half fall above. Consider, for example, the following weights obtained from a small class of college students: 105, 111, 123, 126, 148, 151, 154, 162, 182. The median for the group is 148, the middle score. Of course, if there is an even number of scores, there will be no "middle score." This problem is handled by averaging the two scores that "share" the middle spot. This procedure yields a single number to serve as the median. (See bottom panel of ● Table A.3.)

The Mode

A final measure of central tendency is the *mode*. The **mode** is simply the most frequently occurring score in a group of scores. If you were to take the time to count the scores in ● Table A.3, you would find that the mode of Group 1 is 65, and the mode of Group 2 is 60. The mode is usually easy to obtain. However, the mode can be an unreliable measure, especially in a small group of scores. The mode's advantage is that it gives the score actually obtained by the greatest number of people.

Measures of Variability

Let's say a researcher discovers two drugs that lower anxiety in agitated patients. However, let's also assume that one drug consistently lowers anxiety by moderate amounts, whereas the second

Histogram A graph of a frequency distribution in which the number of scores falling in each class is represented by vertical bars.

Frequency polygon A graph of a frequency distribution in which the number of scores falling in each class is represented by points on a line.

Central tendency The tendency for a majority of scores to fall in the midrange of possible values.

Mean A measure of central tendency calculated by adding a group of scores and then dividing by the total number of scores.

Median A measure of central tendency found by arranging scores from the highest to the lowest and selecting the score that falls in the middle. That is, half the values in a group of scores fall above the median and half fall below.

Mode A measure of central tendency found by identifying the most frequently occurring score in a group of scores.

sometimes lowers it by large amounts, sometimes has no effect, or may even increase anxiety in some patients. Overall, there is no difference in the *average* (mean) amount of anxiety reduction. Even so, an important difference exists between the two drugs. As this example shows, it is not enough to simply know the average score in a distribution. Usually, we would also like to know if scores are grouped closely together or scattered widely.

Measures of **variability** provide a single number that tells how "spread out" scores are. When the scores are widely spread, this number gets larger. When they are close together it gets smaller. If you look again at the example in ● Table A.3, you will notice that the scores within each group vary widely. How can we show this fact?

The Range

The simplest way would be to use the **range,** which is the difference between the highest and lowest scores. In Group 1 of our experiment, the highest score is 73 and the lowest is 55; thus, the range is 18 ($73 - 55 = 18$). In Group 2, the highest score is 63 and the lowest is 31; this makes the range 32. Scores in Group 2 are more spread out (are more variable) than those in Group 1.

The Standard Deviation

A better measure of variability is the **standard deviation** (an index of how much a typical score differs from the mean of a group of scores). To obtain the standard deviation, we find the deviation (or difference) of each score from the mean and then square it (multiply it by itself). These squared deviations are then added and averaged (the total is divided by the number of deviations). Taking the square root of this average yields the standard deviation (● Table A.4). Notice again that the variability for Group 1 (5.4) is smaller than that for Group 2 (where the standard deviation is 11.3).

Standard Scores

A particular advantage of the standard deviation is that it can be used to "standardize" scores in a way that gives them greater meaning. For example, John and Heather both took psychology midterms, but in different classes. John earned a score of 118, and Heather scored 110. Who did better? It is impossible to tell without knowing what the average score was on each test, and whether John and Heather scored at the top, middle, or bottom of their classes. We would like to have one number that gives all this information. A number that does this is the *z-score.*

To convert an original score to a **z-score,** we subtract the mean from the score. The resulting number is then divided by the standard deviation for that group of scores. To illustrate, Heather had a score of 110 in a class with a mean of 100 and a standard deviation of 10. Therefore, her z-score is $+1.0$ (● Table A.5). John's score of 118 came from a class having a mean of 100 and a standard deviation of 18; thus his z-score is also $+1.0$. (See ● Table A.5.) Originally it looked as if John did better on his midterm than Heather did. But we now see that relatively speaking, their scores were equivalent. Compared with other students, each was an equal distance above average.

Table A.4 ● Computation of the Standard Deviation

Score Mean	Deviation (d)	Deviation Squared (d^2)
Group 1 Mean = 65		
$65 - 65 =$	0	0
$67 - 65 =$	2	4
$73 - 65 =$	8	64
$65 - 65 =$	0	0
$58 - 65 =$	-7	49
$55 - 65 =$	-10	100
$70 - 65 =$	5	25
$69 - 65 =$	4	16
$60 - 65 =$	-5	25
$68 - 65 =$	3	9
		292

$$SD = \sqrt{\frac{\text{sum of } d^2}{n}} = \sqrt{\frac{292}{10}} = \sqrt{29.2} = 5.4$$

Score Mean	Deviation (d)	Deviation Squared (d^2)
Group 2 Mean = 54		
$54 - 54 =$	0	0
$60 - 54 =$	6	36
$63 - 54 =$	9	81
$33 - 54 =$	-21	441
$56 - 54 =$	2	4
$60 - 54 =$	6	36
$60 - 54 =$	6	36
$31 - 54 =$	-23	529
$62 - 54 =$	8	64
$61 - 54 =$	7	49
		1276

$$SD = \sqrt{\frac{\text{sum of } d^2}{n}} = \sqrt{\frac{1276}{10}} = \sqrt{127.6} = 11.3$$

The Normal Curve

When chance events are recorded, we find that some outcomes have a high probability and occur very often, others have a lower probability and occur infrequently; still others have little probability and occur rarely. As a result, the distribution (or tally) of chance events typically resembles a *normal curve* (● Figure A.3). A **normal curve** is bell-shaped, with a large number of scores in the middle, tapering to very few extremely high and low scores.

Table A.5 ● Computation of a z-score

$$z = \frac{X - \bar{X}}{SD} = \text{or} \quad \frac{\text{score} - \text{mean}}{\text{standard deviation}}$$

$$\text{Susan: } z = \frac{110 - 100}{10} = \frac{+10}{10} = +1.0$$

$$\text{John: } z = \frac{118 - 100}{18} = \frac{+18}{18} = +1.0$$

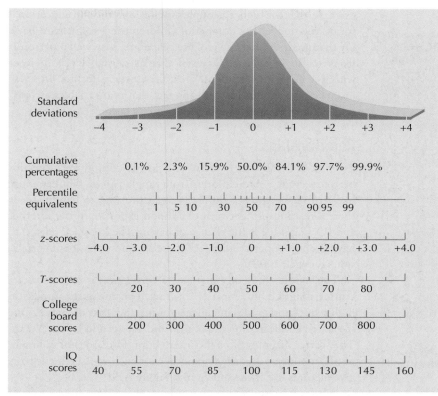

● Figure A.3 The normal curve. The normal curve is an idealized mathematical model. However, many measurements in psychology closely approximate a normal curve. The scales you see here show the relationship of standard deviations, z-scores, and other measures to the curve.

One valuable property concerns the relationship between the standard deviation and the normal curve. Specifically, the standard deviation measures off set proportions of the curve above and below the mean. For example, in ● Figure A.4, notice that roughly 68 percent of all cases (IQ scores, memory scores, heights, or whatever) fall between one standard deviation above and below the mean (± 1 SD); 95 percent of all cases fall between ± 2 SD; and 99 percent of the cases can be found between ± 3 SD from the mean.

● Table A.6 gives a more complete account of the relationship between z-scores and the percentage of cases found in a particular area of the normal curve. Notice, for example, that 93.3 percent of all cases fall below a z-score of +1.5. A z-score of 1.5 on a test (no matter what the original, or "raw," score was) would be a good performance, because roughly 93 percent of all scores fall below this mark. Relationships between the standard deviation (or z-scores) and the normal curve do not change. This makes it possible to compare various tests or groups of scores if they come from distributions that are approximately normal.

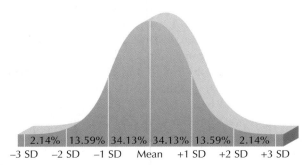

● Figure A.4 Relationship between the standard deviation and the normal curve.

Most psychological traits or events are determined by the action of a large number of factors. Therefore, like chance events, measures of psychological variables tend to roughly match a normal curve. For example, direct measurement has shown such characteristics as height, memory span, and intelligence to be distributed approximately along a normal curve. In other words, many people have average height, memory ability, and intelligence. However, as we move above or below average, fewer and fewer people are found.

It is very fortunate that so many psychological variables tend to form a normal curve, because much is known about the curve.

Variability The tendency for a group of scores to differ in value. Measures of variability indicate the degree to which a group of scores differ from one another.

Range The difference between the highest and lowest scores in a group of scores.

Standard deviation An index of how much a typical score differs from the mean of a group of scores.

z-score A number that tells how many standard deviations above or below the mean a score is.

Normal curve A bell-shaped distribution, with a large number of scores in the middle, tapering to very few extremely high and low scores.

Table A.6 ● Computation of a z-score

z-Score	Percentage of Area to the Left of This Value	Percentage of Area to the Right of This Value
23.0 SD	00.1	99.9
−2.5 SD	00.6	99.4
−2.0 SD	02.3	97.7
−1.5 SD	06.7	93.3
−1.0 SD	15.9	84.1
−0.5 SD	30.9	69.1
0.0 SD	50.0	50.0
+0.5 SD	69.1	30.9
+1.0 SD	84.1	15.9
+1.5 SD	93.3	06.7
+2.0 SD	97.7	02.3
+2.5 SD	99.4	00.6
+3.0 SD	99.9	00.1

6. A z-score of −1 tells us that a score fell one standard deviation below the mean in a group of scores. T or F?

7. In a normal curve, 99 percent of all scores can be found between +1 and −1 standard deviations from the mean. T or F?

REFLECT

Critical Thinking

8. You are asked to calculate the mean income of the following annual salaries: $2,000,000, $33,000, $27,000, $22,000, $21,000. Why might you refuse? What statistic might you propose to calculate instead?

Relate

Let's say you ask 100 people how long they sleep each night and record their answers. How could you show these scores graphically?

To find the average amount of sleep for your subjects, would you prefer to know the most frequent score (the mode), the middle score (the median), or the arithmetic average (the mean)?

How could you determine how much sleep times vary? That is, would you prefer to know the highest and lowest scores (the range), or the average amount of variation (the standard deviation)?

How would you feel about receiving your scores on classroom tests in the form of z-scores?

Do you think the distribution of scores in your study of sleep would form a normal curve? Why or why not?

Answers: 1. Descriptive, inferential 2. T 3. mode 4. T 5. F 6. T 7. F 8. The single large salary in this small group will distort the mean. In cases like this, the median is a better measure of central tendency.

Correlation—Rating Relationships

Gateway Question: How are correlations used in psychology?

As we noted in Chapter 1, many of the statements that psychologists make about behavior do not result from the use of experimental methods. Rather, they come from keen observations and measures of existing phenomena. A psychologist might note, for example, that the higher a couple's socioeconomic and educational status, the smaller the number of children they are likely to have. Or that grades in high school are related to how well a person is likely to do in college. Or even that as rainfall levels increase within a given metropolitan area, crime rates decline. In these instances, we are dealing with the fact that two variables are **correlating** (varying together in some orderly fashion).

Relationships

Psychologists are very interested in describing relationships between events: Are children from single-parent families more likely to misbehave at school? Is wealth related to happiness? Is there a relationship between childhood exposure to the Internet and IQ at age 20? Is the chance of having a heart attack related to having a hostile personality? All these are questions about correlation (Howell, 2008).

The simplest way of visualizing a correlation is to construct a **scatter diagram.** In a scatter diagram, two measures (grades in high school and grades in college, for instance) are obtained. One measure is indicated by the X axis and the second by the Y axis. The scatter diagram plots the intersection (crossing) of each pair of measurements as a single point. Many such measurement pairs give pictures like those shown in ● Figure A.5.

Figure A.5 also shows scatter diagrams of three basic kinds of relationships between variables (or measures). Graphs *A*, *B*, and *C* show *positive relationships* of varying strength. As you can see, in a **positive relationship,** increases in the X measure (or score) are matched by increases on the Y measure (or score). An example would be finding that higher IQ scores (X) are associated with higher college grades (Y). A **zero correlation** suggests that no relationship exists between two measures. (See graph *D*.) This might be the result of comparing subjects' hat sizes (X) to their college grades (Y). Graphs *E* and *F* both show a **negative relationship** (or correlation). Notice that as values of one measure increase, those of the second become smaller. An example might be the relationship between amount of alcohol consumed and scores on a test of coordination: Higher alcohol levels are correlated with lower coordination scores.

The Correlation Coefficient

The strength of a correlation can also be expressed as a **coefficient of correlation.** This coefficient is simply a number falling somewhere between +1.00 and −1.00. If the number is zero or close to zero, it indicates a weak or nonexistent relationship. If the correlation is +1.00, a **perfect positive relationship** exists; if the correlation is −1.00, a **perfect negative relationship** has been discovered. The most commonly used correlation coefficient is called the Pearson *r*. Calculation of the Pearson *r* is relatively simple, as shown in ● Table A.7. (The numbers shown are hypothetical.)

As stated in Chapter 1, correlations in psychology are rarely perfect. Most fall somewhere between zero and plus or minus 1. The closer the correlation coefficient is to +1.00 or −1.00, the stronger the relationship. An interesting example of some typical

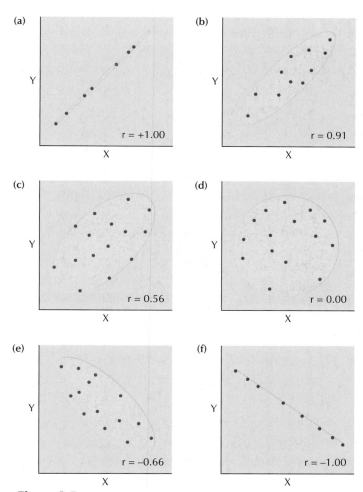

● **Figure A.5** Scatter diagrams showing various degrees of relationship for a positive, zero, and negative correlation.

For example, most colleges have formulas that use multiple correlations to decide which applicants have the best chances for success. Usually the formula includes such predictors as high school grade point average (GPA), teacher ratings, extracurricular activities, and scores on the *SAT Reasoning Test* (SAT) or some similar test. Although no single predictor is perfectly correlated with success in college, together the various predictors correlate highly and provide a useful technique for screening applicants.

There is an interesting "trick" you can do with correlations that you may find useful. It works like this: If you *square* the correlation coefficient (multiply *r* by itself), you will get a number telling the **percent of variance** (amount of variation in scores) accounted for by the correlation. For example, the correlation between IQ scores and college grade point average is .5. Multiplying .5 times .5 gives .25, or 25 percent. This means that 25 percent of the variation in college grades is accounted for by knowing IQ scores. In other words, with a correlation of .5, college grades are "squeezed" into an oval like the one shown in graph C, ● Figure A.5*c*. IQ scores take away some of the possible variation in corresponding grade point averages. If there were no correlation between IQ and grades, grades would be completely free to vary, as shown in graph D, ● Figure A.5*d*.

Along the same line, a correlation of +1.00 or −1.00 means that 100 percent of the variation in the Y measure is accounted for by knowing the X measure: If you know a person's X score, you can tell exactly what the Y score is. An example that comes close to this state of affairs is the high correlation (.86) between the IQs of identical twins. In any group of identical twins, 74 percent of the variation in the "Y" twins' IQs is accounted for by knowing the IQs of their siblings (the "Xs").

Squaring correlations to obtain the *percent variance* accounted for is a useful tool for interpreting the correlations encountered in the media and the psychological literature. For example, sweeping pronouncements about relationships are occasionally made on the

correlations is provided by a study that compared the IQs of adopted children with the IQs of their biological mothers. At age 4, the children's IQs correlated .28 with their biological mothers' IQs. By age 7 the correlation was .35. And by age 13 it had grown to .38. Over time, the IQs of adopted children become more similar to the IQs of their biological mothers.

Prediction

Correlations often provide highly useful information. For instance, it is valuable to know that there is a correlation between cigarette smoking and lung cancer rates. Another example is the fact that higher consumption of alcohol during pregnancy is correlated with lower birth weight and a higher rate of birth defects. There is a correlation between the number of recent life stresses experienced and the likelihood of emotional disturbance. Many more examples could be cited, but the point is, correlations help us to identify relationships that are worth knowing.

Correlations are particularly valuable for making *predictions*. If we know that two measures are correlated, and we know a person's score on one measure, we can predict his or her score on the other.

Correlation The existence of a consistent, systematic relationship between two events, measures, or variables.

Scatter diagram A graph that plots the intersection of paired measures; that is, the points at which paired X and Y measures cross.

Positive relationship A mathematical relationship in which increases in one measure are matched by increases in the other (or decreases correspond with decreases).

Zero correlation The absence of a (linear) mathematical relationship between two measures.

Negative relationship A mathematical relationship in which increases in one measure are matched by decreases in the other.

Coefficient of correlation A statistical index ranging from −1.00 to +1.00 that indicates the direction and degree of correlation.

Perfect positive relationship A mathematical relationship in which the correlation between two measures is +1.00.

Perfect negative relationship A mathematical relationship in which the correlation between two measures is −1.00.

Percent of variance A portion of the total amount of variation in a group of scores.

Table A.7 ● IQ and Grade Point Average for Computing Pearson r

Student No.	IQ (X)	Grade Point Average (Y)	X Score Squared (X²)	Y Score Squared (Y²)	X Times Y (XY)
1	110	1.0	12,100	1.00	110.0
2	112	1.6	12,544	2.56	179.2
3	118	1.2	13,924	1.44	141.6
4	119	2.1	14,161	4.41	249.9
5	122	2.6	14,884	6.76	317.2
6	125	1.8	15,625	3.24	225.0
7	127	2.6	16,124	6.76	330.2
8	130	2.0	16,900	4.00	260.0
9	132	3.2	17,424	10.24	422.4
10	134	2.6	17,956	6.76	348.4
11	136	3.0	18,496	9.00	408.0
12	138	3.6	19,044	12.96	496.8
Total	1503	27.3	189,187	69.13	3488.7

$$r = \frac{\sum XY - \frac{(\sum X)(\sum Y)}{N}}{\sqrt{\left[\sum X^2 - \frac{(\sum X)^2}{N}\right]\left[\sum Y^2 - \frac{(\sum Y)^2}{N}\right]}}$$

$$= \frac{3488.7 - \frac{1503(27.3)}{12}}{\sqrt{\left[189,187 - \frac{(1503)^2}{2}\right]\left[69.13\,2\frac{(27.3)^2}{12}\right]}}$$

$$= \frac{69.375}{81.088} = 0.856 = 0.86$$

basis of correlations in the .25 to .30 range even though the values mean that only 6 to 9 percent of the variance is accounted for by the observed correlation. Such correlations may document relationships worth noting, but they are rarely something to get excited about.

Correlation and Causation

It is very important to reiterate that finding a correlation between two measures does not automatically mean that one **causes** the other: Correlation does not demonstrate causation. When a correlation exists, the best we can say is that two variables are related. Of course, this does not mean that it is impossible for two correlated variables to have a cause-and-effect relationship. Rather, it means that we cannot *conclude,* solely on the basis of correlation, that a causal link exists. To gain greater confidence that a cause-and-effect relationship exists, an experiment must be performed. (See Chapter 1.)

Often, two correlated measures are related as a result of the influence of a third variable. For example, we might observe that the more hours students devote to studying, the better their grades. Although it is tempting to conclude that more studying produces (causes) better grades, it is possible (indeed, it is probable) that grades and the amount of study time are both related to the amount of motivation or interest a student has.

The difference between cause-and-effect data and data that reveal a relationship of unknown origin is one that should not be forgotten. Because we rarely run experiments in daily life, the information on which we act is largely correlational. This should make us more humble and more tentative in the confidence with which we make pronouncements about human behavior.

Inferential Statistics—Significant Numbers

Gateway Question: What are inferential statistics?

You would like to know if boys are more aggressive than girls. You observe a group of 5-year-old boys and girls on a playground. After collecting data for a week you find that the boys committed more aggressive acts than the girls. Could this difference just be a meaningless fluctuation in aggression? Or does it show conclusively that boys are more aggressive than girls? Inferential statistics were created to answer just such questions (Sprinthall, 2007).

Let's say that a researcher studies the effects of a new therapy on a small group of depressed individuals. Is she or he interested only in these particular individuals? Usually not, because except in rare instances, psychologists seek to discover general laws of behavior that apply widely to humans and animals. Undoubtedly the researcher would like to know if the therapy holds any promise for all depressed people. As stated earlier, *inferential statistics* are techniques that allow us to make inferences. That is, they allow us to generalize from the behavior of small groups of subjects to that of the larger groups they represent.

Samples and Populations

In any scientific study, we would like to observe the entire set, or **population,** of subjects, objects, or events of interest. However, this is usually impossible or impractical. Observing all terrorists, all cancer patients, or all mothers-in-law could be both impractical (because all are large populations) and impossible (because people change political views, may be unaware of having cancer, and change their status as relatives). In such cases, **samples** (smaller cross sections of a population) are selected, and observations of the sample are used to draw conclusions about the entire population.

For any sample to be meaningful, it must be **representative.** That is, the sample group must truly reflect the membership and characteristics of the larger population. In our earlier hypothetical study of a memory drug, it would be essential for the sample of 20 people to be representative of the general population. A very important aspect of representative samples is that their members are chosen at **random.** In other words, each member of the population must have an equal chance of being included in the sample.

Significant Differences

In our imaginary drug experiment, we found that the average memory score was higher for the group given the drug than it was for persons who didn't take the drug (the placebo group). Certainly this result is interesting, but could it have occurred by chance? If two groups were repeatedly tested (with neither receiving any drug), their average memory scores would sometimes differ. How much must two means differ before we can consider the difference "real" (not due to chance)?

Notice that the question is similar to one discussed earlier: How many tails in a row must we obtain when flipping a coin before we can conclude that the coin is biased? In the case of the coin, we noted that obtaining 6 tails in a row is a rare event. Thus, it became reasonable to assume that the coin was biased. Of course, it is possible to get 6 tails in a row when flipping an honest coin. But because this outcome is unlikely, we have good reason to suspect that something other than chance (a loaded coin, for instance) caused the results. Similar reasoning is used in tests of statistical significance.

Tests of **statistical significance** provide an estimate of how often experimental results could have occurred by chance alone. The results of a significance test are stated as a probability. This probability gives the odds that the observed difference was due to chance. In psychology, any experimental result that could have occurred by chance 5 times (or less) out of 100 (in other words, a probability of .05 or less) is considered *significant*. In our memory experiment, the probability is .025 ($p = .025$) that the group means would differ as much as they do by chance alone. This allows us to conclude with reasonable certainty that the drug actually did improve memory scores.

appendix in review
Gateways to Behavioral Statistics

Descriptive statistics such as graphical statistics, measures of central tendency, and measures of variability organize and summarize numbers.

- Summarizing numbers visually, by using various types of graphs such as histograms and frequency polygons, makes it easier to see trends and patterns in the results of psychological investigations.
- Measures of central tendency define the "typical score" in a group of scores.
- The mean is found by adding all the scores in a group and then dividing by the total number of scores.
- The median is found by arranging a group of scores from the highest to the lowest and selecting the middle score.
- The mode is the score that occurs most frequently in a group of scores.
- Measures of variability provide a number that shows how much scores vary.
- The range is the difference between the highest score and the lowest score in a group of scores.
- The standard deviation shows how much, on average, all the scores in a group differ from the mean.
- To change an original score into a standard score (or z-score), you must subtract the mean from the score and then divide the result by the standard deviation.
- Standard scores (z-scores) tell, in standard deviation units, how far above or below the mean a score is. This allows meaningful comparisons between scores from different groups.
- Scores that form a normal curve are easy to interpret because the properties of the normal curve are well known.

When there is a correlation, or consistent relationship, between scores on two measures, knowing a person's score on one measure allows us to predict his or her score on the second measure.

- Pairs of scores that vary together in an orderly fashion are said to be correlated.
- The relationship between two variables or measures can be positive or negative.
- Correlation coefficients tell how strongly two groups of scores are related.
- Correlation alone does not demonstrate cause-and-effect links between variables or measures.

Inferential statistics can be used to generalize results from samples to populations, to draw conclusions, and to tell if the results of a study could have occurred by chance.

- Most studies in psychology are based on samples. Findings from representative samples are assumed to also apply to entire populations.

- In psychology experiments, differences in the average performance of groups could occur purely by chance. Tests of statistical significance tell us if the observed differences between groups are common or rare. If a difference is large enough to be improbable, it suggests that the results did not occur by chance alone.

Web Resources

For an up-to-date list of direct links to interesting sites, including those listed here, visit the student companion site for this book at www.cengage.com/psychology/coon

Frequency Distribution of Tossing Coins and Dice Automatically calculate frequency distributions for tossing coins or dice and plot the results as a frequency polygon.

Descriptive Statistics Further explore descriptive statistics.

Concepts and Applications of Inferential Statistics Browse this full online statistics textbook.

Correlations Vary the correlations and view the corresponding scatter diagram.

Interactive Learning

Introduction to Psychology: Gateways to Mind and Behavior **Book Companion Website**
www.cengage.com/psychology/coon

Visit your book companion website, where you will find flash cards, practice quizzes, web links, and more to help you study.

CENGAGENOW™ *Just what you need to know NOW!*

Spend time on what you need to master rather than on information you already have learned. Take a pre-test for this chapter, and CengageNOW will generate a personalized study plan based on your results. The study plan will identify the topics you need to review and direct you to online resources to help you master those topics. You can then take a post-test to help you determine the concepts you have mastered and what you will need to work on. Try it out! Go to www.cengage.com/login to sign in with an access code or to purchase access to this product.

glossary

Ablation (ab-LAY-shun)   Surgical removal of tissue.

Absolute threshold   The minimum amount of physical energy necessary to produce a sensation.

Abstract   Research reports begin with a very brief summary of the study and its findings. The abstract allows you to get an overview without reading the entire article.

Accessibility (in memory)   Memories currently stored in memory, which can be retrieved when necessary, are both available and accessible.

Accommodation (perceptual)   Changes in the shape of the lens of the eye.

Accommodation (Piaget)   In Piaget's theory, the modification of existing mental patterns to fit new demands (that is, mental schemes are changed to accommodate new information or experiences).

Acculturative stress   Stress caused by the many changes and adaptations required when a person moves to a foreign culture.

Acetylcholine (ah-SEET-ul-KOH-leen)   The neurotransmitter released by neurons to activate muscles.

Acquaintance (date) rape   Forced intercourse that occurs in the context of a date or other voluntary encounter.

Acquisition   The period in conditioning during which a response is reinforced.

Action component   How one tends to act toward the object of an attitude.

Action potential   The nerve impulse.

Activation-synthesis hypothesis   An attempt to explain how random activity in lower brain centers results in the manufacture of relatively bizarre dreams by higher brain centers.

Active listener   A person who knows how to maintain attention, avoid distractions, and actively gather information from lectures.

Actor–observer bias   The tendency to attribute the behavior of others to internal causes while attributing one's own behavior to external causes (situations and circumstances).

Acute stress disorder   A psychological disturbance lasting up to 1 month following stresses that would produce anxiety in anyone who experienced them.

Adaptive behaviors   Actions that aid attempts to survive and adapt to changing conditions.

Adjustment disorder   An emotional disturbance caused by ongoing stressors within the range of common experience.

Adolescence   The culturally defined period between childhood and adulthood.

Adrenal glands   Endocrine glands that arouse the body, regulate salt balance, adjust the body to stress, and affect sexual functioning.

Adrenaline   A hormone produced by the adrenal glands that tends to arouse the body.

Affectional needs   Emotional needs for love and affection.

Ageism   An institutionalized tendency to discriminate on the basis of age; discrimination or prejudice based on a person's age.

Aggression cues   Stimuli or signals that are associated with aggression and that tend to elicit it.

Aggression   Any action carried out with the intention of causing harm; hurting another person or achieving one's goals at the expense of another person.

Aggressive pornography   Media depictions of sexual violence or of forced participation in sexual activity.

Agnosia   An inability to grasp the meaning of stimuli, such as words, objects, or pictures.

Agoraphobia (ah-go-rah-FOBE-ee-ah) **(without panic)**   The fear that something extremely embarrassing will happen if one leaves the house or enters unfamiliar situations.

Alarm reaction   First stage of the GAS, during which bodily resources are mobilized to cope with a stressor.

Alcohol myopia (my-OH-pea-ah)   Shortsighted thinking and perception that occurs during alcohol intoxication.

Algorithm   A learned set of rules that always leads to the correct solution of a problem.

All-or-nothing thinking   Classifying objects or events as absolutely right or wrong, good or bad, acceptable or unacceptable, and so forth.

Alpha waves   Large, slow brain waves associated with relaxation and falling asleep.

Altered state of consciousness (ASC)   A condition of awareness distinctly different in quality or pattern from waking consciousness.

Alzheimer's (ALLS-hi-merz) **disease**   An age-related disease characterized by memory loss, mental confusion, and, in its later stages, a nearly total loss of mental abilities.

Ambivalence   Mixed positive and negative feelings or simultaneous attraction and repulsion.

Ambivalent attachment   An emotional bond marked by conflicting feelings of affection, anger, and emotional turmoil.

Amygdala (ah-MIG-dah-luh)   A part of the limbic system (within the brain) associated with fear responses.

Anal stage   The psychosexual stage corresponding roughly to the period of toilet training (ages 1 to 3).

Anal-expulsive personality   A disorderly, destructive, cruel, or messy person.

Anal-retentive personality   A person who is obstinate, stingy, or compulsive, and who generally has difficulty "letting go."

Androgen (an-dro-JEN)   Any of a number of male sex hormones, especially testosterone.

Androgyny (an-DROJ-ih-nee)   The presence of both "masculine" and "feminine" traits in a single person (as masculinity and femininity are defined within one's culture).

Anger control   Personal strategies for reducing or curbing anger.

Anhedonia (an-he-DAWN-ee-ah)   An inability to feel pleasure.

Anima   An archetype representing the female principle.

Animal model   In research, an animal whose behavior is used to derive principles that may apply to human behavior.

Animus   An archetype representing the male principle.

Anorexia nervosa (AN-uh-REK-see-yah ner-VOH-sah)   Active self-starvation or a sustained loss of appetite that has psychological origins.

Antecedents   Events that precede a response.

Anthropomorphic error (AN-thro-po-MORE-fik)   The error of attributing human thoughts, feelings, or motives to animals, especially as a way of explaining their behavior.

Antidepressants   Mood-elevating drugs.

Antipsychotics   Drugs that, in addition to having tranquilizing effects, also tend to reduce hallucinations and delusional thinking. (Also called **major tranquilizers.**)

Antisocial behavior   Any behavior that has a negative impact on other people.

Antisocial personality   A person who lacks a conscience; is emotionally shallow, impulsive, and selfish; and tends to manipulate others.

Anxiety disorder   Disruptive feelings of fear, apprehension, or anxiety, or distortions in behavior that are anxiety related.

Anxiety reduction hypothesis   Explains the self-defeating nature of avoidance responses as a result of the reinforcing effects of relief from anxiety.

Anxiety   Apprehension, dread, or uneasiness similar to fear but based on an unclear threat.

Anxiolytics   Drugs (such as Valium) that produce relaxation or reduce anxiety.

Aphasia (ah-FAZE-yah)   A speech disturbance resulting from brain damage.

Apparent-distance hypothesis   An explanation of the moon illusion stating that the horizon seems more distant than the night sky.

Applied psychology   The use of psychological principles and research methods to solve practical problems.

Approach-approach conflict   Choosing between two positive, or desirable, alternatives.

Approach-avoidance conflict   Being attracted to and repelled by the same goal or activity.

Aptitude test   A test that rates a person's potential to learn skills required by various occupations.

Archetype   A universal idea, image, or pattern, found in the collective unconscious.

Architectural psychology   Study of the effects buildings have on behavior and the design of buildings using behavioral principles.

Arousal theory   Assumes that people prefer to maintain ideal, or comfortable, levels of arousal.

Artificial intelligence (AI)   Any artificial system (often a computer program) that is capable of human-like problem solving or intelligent responding.

Assertiveness training   Instruction in how to be self-assertive.

Assessment center   A program set up within an organization to conduct in-depth evaluations of job candidates.

Assimilation   In Piaget's theory, the application of existing mental patterns to new situations (that is, the new situation is assimilated to existing mental schemes).

Association area (association cortex)   All areas of the cerebral cortex that are not primarily sensory or motor in function.

Associative learning   The formation of simple associations between various stimuli and responses.

Astigmatism (ah-STIG-mah-tiz-em)   Defects in the cornea, lens, or eye that cause some areas of vision to be out of focus.

Attention   Voluntarily focusing on a specific sensory input.

Attention deficit/hyperactivity disorder (ADHD) A behavioral problem characterized by short attention span, restless movement, and impaired learning capacity.

Attentional overload A stressful condition caused when sensory stimulation, information, and social contacts make excessive demands on attention.

Attitude scale A collection of attitudinal statements with which respondents indicate agreement or disagreement.

Attitude A learned tendency to respond to people, objects, or institutions in a positive or negative way.

Attribution The mental process of assigning causes to events, including making inferences about the causes of one's own behavior, and that of others. In emotion, the process of attributing arousal to a particular source.

Authenticity In Carl Rogers's terms, the ability of a therapist to be genuine and honest about his or her own feelings.

Authoritarian parents Parents who enforce rigid rules and demand strict obedience to authority.

Authoritarian (ah-thor-ih-TARE-ee-un) **personality** A personality pattern characterized by rigidity, inhibition, prejudice, and an excessive concern with power, authority, and obedience.

Authoritative parents Parents who supply firm and consistent guidance combined with love and affection.

Autism Spectrum Disorders A range of disorders, from less to more severe, involving mutism, sensory spin-outs, sensory blocking, tantrums, unresponsiveness to others, and other difficulties.

Autokinetic effect The apparent movement of a stationary pinpoint of light displayed in a darkened room.

Autonomic nervous system (ANS) The system of nerves connecting the brain to and carrying information to and from the internal organs and glands.

Autonomy versus shame and doubt A conflict created when growing self-control (autonomy) is pitted against feelings of shame and doubt.

Availability (in memory) Memories currently stored in memory are available.

Aversion therapy Suppressing an undesirable response by associating it with aversive (painful or uncomfortable) stimuli.

Aversive stimulus A stimulus that is painful or uncomfortable.

Avoidance learning Learning to make a response in order to postpone or prevent discomfort.

Avoidance-avoidance conflict Choosing between two negative, undesirable alternatives.

Avoidant attachment An emotional bond marked by a tendency to resist commitment to others.

Axon (AK-sahn) Fiber that carries information away from the cell body of a neuron.

Axon terminals Bulb-shaped structures at the ends of axons that form synapses with the dendrites and somas of other neurons.

Bait shyness An unwillingness or hesitation on the part of animals to eat a particular food.

Barnum effect The tendency to consider a personal description accurate if it is stated in very general terms.

Base rate The basic rate at which an event occurs over time; the basic probability of an event.

Basic anxiety A primary form of anxiety that arises from living in a hostile world.

Basic needs The first four levels of needs in Maslow's hierarchy; lower needs tend to be more potent than higher needs.

Basic suggestion effect The tendency of hypnotized persons to carry out suggested actions as if they were involuntary.

Behavior modification The application of learning principles to change human behavior, especially maladaptive behavior.

Behavior therapy Any therapy designed to actively change behavior.

Behavioral assessment Recording the frequency of various behaviors.

Behavioral contract A formal agreement stating behaviors to be changed and consequences that apply.

Behavioral dieting Weight reduction based on changing exercise and eating habits, rather than temporary self-starvation.

Behavioral genetics The study of inherited behavioral traits and tendencies.

Behavioral medicine The study of behavioral factors in medicine, physical illness, and medical treatment.

Behavioral personality theory Any model of personality that emphasizes learning and observable behavior.

Behavioral risk factors Behaviors that increase the chances of disease, injury, or premature death.

Behavioral setting A smaller area within an environment whose use is well defined, such as a bus depot, waiting room, or lounge.

Behaviorism The school of psychology that emphasizes the study of overt, observable behavior.

Belief component What a person thinks or believes about the object of an attitude.

Beta waves Small, fast brain waves associated with being awake and alert.

Beta-endorphin (BAY-tah-en-DOR-fin) A natural, painkilling brain chemical similar to morphine.

Biased sample A subpart of a larger population that does not accurately reflect characteristics of the whole population.

Bilingualism An ability to speak two languages.

Binge drinking Consuming five or more drinks in a short time (four drinks for women).

Binocular depth cues Perceptual features that impart information about distance and three-dimensional space which require two eyes.

Biodata Detailed biographical information about a job applicant.

Biofeedback Information given to a person about his or her ongoing bodily activities; aids voluntary regulation of bodily states.

Biological biasing effect Hypothesized effect that prenatal exposure to sex hormones has on development of the body, nervous system, and later behavior patterns.

Biological motives Innate motives based on biological needs.

Biological perspective The attempt to explain behavior in terms of underlying biological principles.

Biological predisposition The presumed hereditary readiness of humans to learn certain skills, such as how to use language, or a readiness to behave in particular ways.

Biological rhythm Any repeating cycle of biological activity, such as sleep and waking cycles or changes in body temperature.

Bipolar disorders Emotional disorders involving both depression and mania or hypomania.

Bipolar I disorder A mood disorder in which a person has episodes of mania (excited, hyperactive, energetic, grandiose behavior) and also periods of deep depression.

Bipolar II disorder A mood disorder in which a person is mostly depressed (sad, despondent, guilt ridden) but has also had one or more episodes of mild mania (hypomania).

Bisexual A person romantically and erotically attracted to both men and women.

Blind spot An area of the retina lacking visual receptors.

Bottom-up processing Organizing perceptions by beginning with low-level features.

Brainstem The lowest portions of the brain, including the cerebellum, medulla, pons, and reticular formation.

Brainwashing Engineered or forced attitude change involving a captive audience.

Brief psychodynamic therapy A modern therapy based on psychoanalytic theory but designed to produce insights more quickly.

Brightness constancy The apparent (or relative) brightness of objects remains the same as long as they are illuminated by the same amount of light.

Broca's area (BRO-cahs) A language area related to grammar and pronunciation.

Broken record A self-assertion technique involving repeating a request until it is acknowledged.

Browser Software that facilitates access to text, images, sounds, video, and other information stored in formats used on the Internet.

Bulimia (bue-LIHM-ee-yah) **nervosa** Excessive eating (gorging) usually followed by self-induced vomiting and/or taking laxatives.

Burnout A job-related condition of mental, physical, and emotional exhaustion.

Bystander apathy Unwillingness of bystanders to offer help during emergencies or to become involved in others' problems.

Caffeinism Excessive consumption of caffeine, leading to dependence and a variety of physical and psychological complaints.

Cannon-Bard theory States that activity in the thalamus causes emotional feelings and bodily arousal to occur simultaneously.

Carbon footprint The volume of greenhouse gases individual consumption adds to the atmosphere

Cardinal trait A personality trait so basic that all of a person's activities relate to it.

Case study An in-depth focus on all aspects of a single person.

Castration Surgical removal of the testicles or ovaries.

Cataplexy (CAT-uh-plex-see) A sudden temporary paralysis of the muscles.

Catatonic schizophrenia Schizophrenia marked by stupor, rigidity, unresponsiveness, posturing, mutism, and, sometimes, agitated, purposeless behavior.

Causation The act of causing some effect.

Central nervous system (CNS) The brain and spinal cord.

Central tendency The tendency for a majority of scores to fall in the midrange of possible values.

Central traits The core traits that characterize an individual personality

Cerebellum (ser-ah-BEL-uhm) A brain structure that controls posture and coordination.

Cerebral cortex (seh-REE-brel or ser-EH-brel) The outer layer of the brain.

Cervix (SER-vix) The lower end of the uterus that projects into the vagina.

Character Personal characteristics that have been judged or evaluated; a person's desirable or undesirable qualities.

Chromosomes Thread-like "colored bodies" in the nucleus of each cell that are made up of DNA.

Chronological age   A person's age in years.

Circadian rhythms (SUR-kay-dee-AN)   Cyclical changes in bodily functions and arousal levels that vary on a schedule approximating a 24-hour day.

Clairvoyance   The purported ability to perceive events at a distance or through physical barriers.

Classical conditioning   A form of learning in which reflex responses are associated with new stimuli.

Client-centered (or person-centered) therapy   A nondirective therapy based on insights gained from conscious thoughts and feelings; emphasizes accepting one's true self.

Clinical case study   A detailed investigation of a single person, especially one suffering from some injury or disease.

Clinical method   Studying psychological problems and therapies in clinical settings.

Clinical psychologist   A psychologist who specializes in the treatment of psychological and behavioral disturbances or who does research on such disturbances.

Clitoris (KLIT-er-iss)   Small, sensitive organ made up of erectile tissue; located above the vaginal opening.

Coefficient of correlation   A statistical index ranging from −1.00 to +1.00 that indicates the direction and degree of correlation.

Coercion   Being forced to change your beliefs or your behavior against your will.

Coercive power   Social power based on the ability to punish others.

Cognition   The process of thinking or mentally processing information (images, concepts, words, rules, and symbols).

Cognitive behaviorism   An approach that combines behavioral principles with cognition (perception, thinking, anticipation) to explain behavior.

Cognitive dissonance   An uncomfortable clash between self-image, thoughts, beliefs, attitudes, or perceptions and one's behavior.

Cognitive interview   Use of various cues and strategies to improve the memory of eyewitnesses.

Cognitive learning   Higher-level learning involving thinking, knowing, understanding, and anticipation.

Cognitive map   Internal images or other mental representations of an area (maze, city, campus, and so forth) that underlie an ability to choose alternative paths to the same goal.

Cognitive therapy   A therapy directed at changing the maladaptive thoughts, beliefs, and feelings that underlie emotional and behavioral problems.

Collective unconscious   A mental storehouse for unconscious ideas and images shared by all humans.

Color blindness   A total inability to perceive colors.

Color weakness   An inability to distinguish some colors.

Commitment   The determination to stay in a long-term relationship with another person.

Common traits   Personality traits that are shared by most members of a particular culture.

Community health campaign   A community-wide education program that provides information about how to lessen risk factors and promote health.

Community mental health center   A facility offering a wide range of mental health services, such as prevention, counseling, consultation, and crisis intervention.

Companionate love   Form of love characterized by intimacy and commitment but not passion.

Comparison level   A personal standard used to evaluate rewards and costs in a social exchange.

Compensation   Counteracting a real or imagined weakness by emphasizing desirable traits or seeking to excel in the area of weakness or in other areas.

Compliance   Bending to the requests of a person who has little or no authority or other form of social power.

Compressed workweek   A work schedule that allows an employee to work fewer days per week by putting in more hours per day.

Computed tomographic scan (CT scan)   Computed tomography scan; a computer-enhanced X-ray image of the brain or body.

Computerized test   A test that uses a computer to present life-like situations; test takers react to problems posed by the situations.

Concentrative meditation   Mental exercise based on attending to a single object or thought.

Concept formation   The process of classifying information into meaningful categories.

Concept   A generalized idea representing a category of related objects or events.

Concrete operational stage   Period of intellectual development during which children become able to use the concepts of time, space, volume, and number, but in ways that remain simplified and concrete, rather than abstract.

Condensation   Combining several people, objects, or events into a single dream image.

Conditioned emotional response (CER)   An emotional response that has been linked to a previously nonemotional stimulus by classical conditioning.

Conditioned response (CR)   A learned response elicited by a conditioned stimulus.

Conditioned stimulus (CS)   A stimulus that evokes a response because it has been repeatedly paired with an unconditioned stimulus.

Conditions of worth   Internal standards used to judge the value of one's thoughts, actions, feelings, or experiences.

Conductive hearing loss   Poor transfer of sounds from the eardrum to the inner ear.

Cones   Visual receptors for colors and daylight visual acuity.

Conflict   A stressful condition that occurs when a person must choose between incompatible or contradictory alternatives.

Conformity   Bringing one's behavior into agreement or harmony with norms or with the behavior of others in a group.

Congenital problems   Problems or defects that originate during prenatal development in the womb.

Conjunctive concept   A class of objects that have two or more features in common. (For example, to qualify as an example of the concept an object must be both red *and* triangular.)

Connotative meaning   The subjective, personal, or emotional meaning of a word or concept.

Conscience   The part of the superego that causes guilt when its standards are not met.

Conscious   The region of the mind that includes all mental contents a person is aware of at any given moment.

Consciousness   Mental awareness of sensations, perceptions, memories, and feelings.

Consequences   Effects that follow a response.

Conservation   In Piaget's theory, mastery of the concept that the weight, mass, and volume of matter remains unchanged (is conserved) even when the shape or appearance of objects changes.

Consistency   With respect to child discipline, the maintenance of stable rules of conduct.

Consolidation   Process by which relatively permanent memories are formed in the brain.

Constructive processing   Reorganizing or updating memories on the basis of logic, reasoning, or the addition of new information.

Consummate love   Form of love characterized by intimacy, passion, *and* commitment.

Contact comfort   A pleasant and reassuring feeling human and animal infants get from touching or clinging to something soft and warm, usually their mother.

Context   Information surrounding a stimulus.

Continuous reinforcement   A schedule in which every correct response is followed by a reinforcer.

Control group   In a controlled experiment, the group of subjects exposed to all experimental conditions or variables *except* the independent variable.

Control questions   In a polygraph exam, questions that almost always provoke anxiety.

Control   Altering conditions that influence behavior; where pain is concerned, refers to an ability to regulate the pain stimulus.

Conventional moral reasoning   Moral thinking based on a desire to please others or to follow accepted rules and values.

Convergent thinking   Thinking directed toward discovery of a single established correct answer; conventional thinking.

Conversion disorder   A bodily symptom that mimics a physical disability but is actually caused by anxiety or emotional distress.

Conviction   Beliefs that are important to a person and that evoke strong emotion.

Coping statements   Reassuring, self-enhancing statements that are used to stop self-critical thinking.

Correlation   The existence of a consistent, systematic relationship between two events, measures, or variables.

Correlational method   Making measurements to discover relationships between events.

Correlational study   A nonexperimental study designed to measure the degree of relationship (if any) between two or more events, measures, or variables.

Corticalization (KORE-tih-kal-ih-ZAY-shun)   An increase in the relative size of the cerebral cortex.

Counseling psychologist   A psychologist who specializes in the treatment of milder emotional and behavioral disturbances.

Counselor   A mental health professional who specializes in helping people with problems not involving serious mental disorder; for example, marriage counselors, career counselors, or school counselors.

Counterirritation   Using mild pain to block more intense or long-lasting pain.

Covert reinforcement   Using positive imagery to reinforce desired behavior.

Covert sensitization   Use of aversive imagery to reduce the occurrence of an undesired response.

Cowper's glands   Two small glands that secrete a clear fluid into the urethra during sexual excitement.

Cranial nerves   Major nerves that leave the brain without passing through the spinal cord.

Creative self   The "artist" in each of us that creates a unique identity and style of life.

Crisis intervention   Skilled management of a psychological emergency.

Critical incidents   Situations that arise in a job, with which a competent worker must be able to cope.

Critical situations   Situations during childhood that are capable of leaving a lasting imprint on personality.

Critical thinking An ability to reflect on, evaluate, compare, analyze, critique, and synthesize information.

Crowding A subjective feeling of being overstimulated by a loss of privacy or by the nearness of others (especially when social contact with them is unavoidable).

Cue External stimuli that guide responses, especially by signaling the presence or absence of reinforcement.

Cult A group that professes great devotion to some person and follows that person almost without question; cult members are typically victimized by their leaders in various ways.

Cultural relativity The idea that behavior must be judged relative to the values of the culture in which it occurs.

Culturally skilled therapist A therapist who has the awareness, knowledge, and skills necessary to treat clients from diverse cultural backgrounds.

Culture An ongoing pattern of life, characterizing a society at a given point in history.

Culture-fair test A test (such as an intelligence test) designed to minimize the importance of skills and knowledge that may be more common in some cultures than in others.

Curve of forgetting A graph that shows the amount of memorized information remembered after varying lengths of time.

Cyclothymic (SIKE-lo-THY-mik) **disorder** Moderate manic and depressive behavior that persists for 2 years or more.

Dark adaptation Increased retinal sensitivity to light.

Death-qualified jury A jury composed of people who favor the death penalty or at least are indifferent to it.

Declarative memory That part of long-term memory containing specific factual information.

Deductive thought Thought that applies a general set of rules to specific situations; for example, using the laws of gravity to predict the behavior of a single falling object.

Deep lesioning (LEE-zhun-ing) Removal of tissue within the brain by use of an electrode.

Deep sleep Stage 4 slow-wave sleep; the deepest form of normal sleep.

Defense mechanism A habitual and often unconscious psychological process used to reduce anxiety.

Deinstitutionalization Reduced use of full-time commitment to mental institutions to treat mental disorders.

Delta waves Large, slow brainwaves that occur in deeper sleep (stages 3 and 4).

Delusion A false belief held against all contrary evidence.

Delusional disorder A psychosis marked by severe delusions of grandeur, jealousy, persecution, or similar preoccupations.

Dementia (duh-MEN-sha) A serious mental impairment in old age caused by physical deterioration of the brain.

Demonology In medieval Europe, the study of demons and the treatment of persons "possessed" by demons.

Dendrites (DEN-drytes) Neuron fibers that receive incoming messages.

Denial Protecting oneself from an unpleasant reality by refusing to perceive it.

Denotative meaning The exact, dictionary definition of a word or concept; its objective meaning.

Density The number of people in a given space or, inversely, the amount of space available to each person.

Dependent variable In an experiment, the condition (usually a behavior) that is affected by the independent variable.

Depressant (downer) A substance that decreases activity in the body and nervous system.

Depression A state of despondency marked by feelings of powerlessness and hopelessness.

Depressive disorders Emotional disorders primarily involving sadness, despondency, and depression.

Deprivation In development, the loss or withholding of normal stimulation, nutrition, comfort, love, and so forth; a condition of lacking.

Depth cues Perceptual features that impart information about distance and three-dimensional space.

Depth perception The ability to see three-dimensional space and to accurately judge distances.

Description In scientific research, the process of naming and classifying.

Descriptive statistics Mathematical tools used to describe and summarize numeric data.

Desensitization Reducing fear or anxiety by repeatedly exposing a person to emotional stimuli while the person is deeply relaxed.

Determinism The idea that all behavior has prior causes that would completely explain one's choices and actions if all such causes were known.

Detoxification In the treatment of alcoholism, the withdrawal of the patient from alcohol.

Developmental level An individual's current state of physical, emotional, and intellectual development.

Developmental psychology The study of progressive changes in behavior and abilities from conception to death.

Developmental task Any skill that must be mastered, or personal change that must take place, for optimal development.

Deviation IQ An IQ obtained statistically from a person's relative standing in his or her age group; that is, how far above or below average the person's score was relative to other scores.

Difference threshold A change in stimulus intensity that is detectable to an observer.

Diffusion of responsibility Spreading the responsibility to act among several people; reduces the likelihood that help will be given to a person in need.

Direct instruction Presentation of factual information by lecture, demonstration, and rote practice.

Direct observation Assessing behavior through direct surveillance.

Discovery learning Instruction based on encouraging students to discover or construct knowledge for themselves; learning based on insight and understanding.

Discrimination Treating members of various social groups differently in circumstances where their rights or treatment should be identical.

Discriminative stimuli Stimuli that precede rewarded and nonrewarded responses in operant conditioning.

Discussion The results of the study are discussed in relation to the original question. Implications of the study are explored and further studies may be proposed.

Disease-prone personality A personality type associated with poor health; marked by persistent negative emotions, including anxiety, depression, and hostility.

Dishabituation A reversal of habituation.

Disinhibition The removal of inhibition; results in acting out behavior that normally would be restrained.

Disjunctive concept A concept defined by the presence of at least one of several possible features; for example, to qualify an object must be either blue *or* circular.

Disorganized schizophrenia Schizophrenia marked by incoherence, grossly disorganized behavior, bizarre thinking, and flat or grossly inappropriate emotions.

Displaced aggression Redirecting aggression to a target other than the actual source of one's frustration.

Displacement Directing emotions or actions toward safe or unimportant dream images.

Dissociative amnesia Loss of memory (partial or complete) for important information related to personal identity.

Dissociative disorder Temporary amnesia, multiple personality, or depersonalization.

Dissociative fugue Sudden travel away from home, plus confusion about one's personal identity.

Dissociative identity disorder The presence of two or more distinct personalities (multiple personality).

Disuse Theory that memory traces weaken when memories are not periodically used or retrieved.

Divergent thinking Thinking that produces many ideas or alternatives; a major element in original or creative thought.

Divided attention Allotting mental space or effort to various tasks or parts of a task.

DNA Deoxyribonucleic acid, a molecular structure that contains coded genetic information.

Dogmatism An unwarranted positiveness or certainty in matters of belief or opinion.

Dominant gene A gene whose influence will be expressed each time the gene is present.

Dominant hemisphere A term usually applied to the side of a person's brain that produces language.

Door-in-the-face effect The tendency for a person who has refused a major request to subsequently be more likely to comply with a minor request.

Double approach-avoidance conflict Being simultaneously attracted to and repelled by each of two alternatives.

Double standard Applying different standards for judging the appropriateness of male and female sexual behavior.

Double-blind experiment An arrangement in which both participants and experimenters are unaware of whether participants are in the experimental group or the control group, including who might have been administered a drug or a placebo.

Downward comparison Comparing yourself with a person who ranks lower than you on some dimension.

Dream processes Mental filters that hide the true meanings of dreams.

Dream symbols Images in dreams that serve as visible signs of hidden ideas, desires, impulses, emotions, relationships, and so forth.

Drive The psychological expression of internal needs or valued goals. For example, hunger, thirst, or a drive for success.

Drug interaction A combined effect of two drugs that exceeds the addition of one drug's effects to the other.

Drug tolerance A reduction in the body's response to a drug.

Dynamic touch Touch experienced when the body is in motion; a combination of sensations from skin receptors, muscles, and joints.

Dysosmia (dis-OZE-me-ah) Loss or impairment of the sense of smell.

Dyspareunia (DIS-pah-ROO-nee-ah) Genital pain before, during, or after sexual intercourse.

Dysthymic (dis-THY-mik) **disorder** Moderate depression that persists for 2 years or more.

Echoic memory A brief continuation of sensory activity in the auditory system after a sound is heard.

Ecological footprint The amount of land and water area required to replenish the resources that a human population consumes.

Educational psychology The field that seeks to understand how people learn and how teachers instruct.

Ego ideal The part of the superego representing ideal behavior; a source of pride when its standards are met.

Ego The executive part of personality that directs rational behavior.

Egocentric thought Thought that is self-centered and fails to consider the viewpoints of others.

Eidetic (eye-DET-ik) **imagery** The ability to retain a "projected" mental image long enough to use it as a source of information.

Ejaculation The release of sperm and seminal fluid by the male at the time of orgasm.

Elaborative encoding Encoding that links new information with existing memories and knowledge.

Electra conflict A girl's sexual attraction to her father and feelings of rivalry with her mother.

Electrical stimulation of the brain (ESB) Direct electrical stimulation and activation of brain tissue.

Electroconvulsive shock (ECS) An electric current passed directly through the brain, producing a convulsion.

Electroconvulsive therapy (ECT) A treatment for severe depression, consisting of an electric shock passed directly through the brain, which induces a convulsion.

Electrode Any device (such as a wire, needle, or metal plate) used to electrically stimulate or destroy nerve tissue or to record its activity.

Electroencephalograph (eh-LEK-tro-en-SEF-uh-lo-graf) **(EEG)** A device designed to detect, amplify, and record electrical activity in the brain.

Emblems Gestures that have widely understood meanings within a particular culture.

Emotion A state characterized by physiological arousal, changes in facial expression, gestures, posture, and subjective feelings.

Emotional appraisal Evaluating the personal meaning of a stimulus or situation.

Emotional attachment An especially close emotional bond that infants form with their parents, caregivers, or others.

Emotional component One's feelings toward the object of an attitude.

Emotional expression Outward signs that an emotion is occurring.

Emotional feelings The private, subjective experience of having an emotion.

Emotional intelligence The ability to perceive, use, understand, and manage emotions.

Emotion-focused coping Managing or controlling one's emotional reaction to a stressful or threatening situation.

Empathic arousal Emotional arousal that occurs when you feel some of another person's pain, fear, or anguish.

Empathy A capacity for taking another's point of view; the ability to feel what another is feeling.

Empathy-helping relationship Observation that we are most likely to help someone else when we feel emotions such as empathy and compassion.

Encoding failure Failure to store sufficient information to form a useful memory.

Encoding Converting information into a form in which it will be retained in memory.

Encounter group A group experience that emphasizes intensely honest interchanges among participants regarding feelings and reactions to one another.

Endocrine system Glands whose secretions pass directly into the bloodstream or lymph system.

Endogenous (en-DODGE-eh-nus) **depression** Depression that appears to be produced from within (perhaps by chemical imbalances in the brain), rather than as a reaction to life events.

Enrichment In development, deliberately making an environment more stimulating, nutritional, comforting, loving, and so forth.

Environment ("nurture") The sum of all external conditions affecting development, including especially the effects of learning.

Environmental assessment Measurement and analysis of the effects an environment has on the behavior and perceptions of people within that environment.

Environmental psychology The formal study of how environments affect behavior.

Epididymis (ep-ih-DID-ih-mus) A coiled structure at the top of the testes in which sperm are stored.

Epinephrine (ep-eh-NEF-rin) An adrenal hormone that tends to arouse the body; epinephrine is associated with fear. (Also known as adrenaline.)

Episodic (ep-ih-SOD-ik) **drive** A drive that occurs in distinct episodes.

Episodic (ep-ih-SOD-ik) **memory** A subpart of declarative memory that records personal experiences that are linked with specific times and places.

Equal-status contact Social interaction that occurs on an equal footing, without obvious differences in power or status.

Erectile disorder An inability to maintain an erection for lovemaking.

Erogenous zones (eh-ROJ-eh-nus) Areas of the body that produce pleasure and/or provoke erotic desire.

Eros Freud's name for the "life instincts."

Escape Reducing discomfort by leaving frustrating situations or by psychologically withdrawing from them.

Escape learning Learning to make a response in order to end an aversive stimulus.

Estrogen Any of a number of female sex hormones.

Estrus Changes in the sexual drives of animals that create a desire for mating; particularly used to refer to females in heat.

Ethnocentrism Placing one's own group or race at the center—that is, tending to reject all other groups but one's own.

Ethologist A person who studies the natural behavior patterns of animals.

Evolutionary psychology Study of the evolutionary origins of human behavior patterns.

Excitement phase The first phase of sexual response, indicated by initial signs of sexual arousal.

Exhibitionism "Flashing," or displaying the genitals to unwilling viewers

Existential therapy An insight therapy that focuses on the elemental problems of existence, such as death, meaning, choice, and responsibility; emphasizes making courageous life choices.

Expectancy An anticipation concerning future events, relationships or about the effect a response will have, especially regarding reinforcement.

Experiment A formal trial undertaken to confirm or disconfirm a hypothesis about cause and effect.

Experimental group In a controlled experiment, the group of subjects exposed to the independent variable or experimental condition.

Experimental method Investigating causes of behavior through controlled experimentation.

Experimental subjects Humans (also referred to as **participants**) or animals whose behavior is investigated in an experiment.

Expert power Social power derived from possession of knowledge or expertise.

Explicit memory A memory that a person is aware of having; a memory that is consciously retrieved.

Expressive behaviors Behaviors that express or communicate emotion or personal feelings.

External cause A cause of behavior that is assumed to lie outside a person.

External urethral orifice (yoo-REE-thral OR-ih-fis) The opening at the tip of the penis through which urine and semen pass.

Extinction The weakening of a conditioned response through removal of reinforcement.

Extracellular thirst Thirst caused by a reduction in the volume of fluids found between body cells.

Extraneous variables Conditions or factors excluded from influencing the outcome of an experiment.

Extrasensory perception The purported ability to perceive events in ways

that cannot be explained by known capacities of the sensory organs.

Extrinsic motivation Motivation based on obvious external rewards, obligations, or similar factors.

Extroversion Ego attitude in which energy is mainly directed outward.

Extrovert A person whose attention is directed outward; a bold, outgoing person.

Eye movement desensitization and reprocessing (EMDR) A technique for reducing fear or anxiety; based on holding upsetting thoughts in mind while rapidly moving the eyes from side to side.

Facial agnosia Inability to perceive familiar faces.

Facial feedback hypothesis States that sensations from facial expressions help define what emotion a person feels.

Factor analysis A statistical technique used to correlate multiple measurements and identify general underlying factors.

Fallacy of positive instances The tendency to remember or notice information that fits one's expectations while forgetting discrepancies.

Fallopian tube (feh-LOPE-ee-en) One of two tubes that carry eggs from the ovaries to the uterus.

Family therapy Technique in which all family members participate, both individually and as a group, to change destructive relationships and communication patterns.

Fantasy Fulfilling unmet desires in imagined achievements or activities.

Feedback Information returned to a person about the effects a response has had; also known as knowledge of results.

Feeling of knowing A feeling that allows people to predict beforehand whether they will be able to remember something.

Female orgasmic disorder A persistent inability to reach orgasm during lovemaking.

Female sexual arousal disorder A lack of physical arousal to sexual stimulation.

Fetishism Sexual arousal associated with inanimate objects

Figure-ground organization Part of a stimulus appears to stand out as an object (figure) against a less prominent background (ground).

Five-factor model Proposes that there are five universal dimensions of personality.

Fixation A lasting conflict developed as a result of frustration or over-indulgence; the tendency to repeat wrong solutions or faulty responses, especially as a result of becoming blind to alternatives.

Fixed interval (FI) schedule A reinforcer is given only when a correct response is made after a set amount of time has passed since the last reinforced response. Responses made during the time interval are not reinforced.

Fixed ratio (FR) schedule   A set number of correct responses must be made to get a reinforcer. For example, a reinforcer is given for every four correct responses.

Flashbulb memories   Memories created at times of high emotion that seem especially vivid.

Flexibility   In tests of creativity, flexibility is indicated by the number of different types of solutions produced.

Flextime   A work schedule that allows flexible starting and quitting times.

Fluency   In tests of creativity, *fluency* refers to the total number of solutions produced.

Foot-in-the-door effect   The tendency for a person who has first complied with a small request to be more likely later to fulfill a larger request.

Forcible rape   Sexual intercourse carried out against the victim's will, under the threat of violence or bodily injury.

Formal operations stage   Period of intellectual development characterized by thinking that includes abstract, theoretical, and hypothetical ideas.

Fovea (FOE-vee-ah)   An area at the center of the retina containing only cones.

Framing   In thought, the terms in which a problem is stated or the way that it is structured.

Free association   In psychoanalysis, the technique of having a client say anything that comes to mind, regardless of how embarrassing or unimportant it may seem.

Free will   The idea that human beings are capable of freely making choices or decisions.

Frequency distribution   A table that divides an entire range of scores into a series of classes and then records the number of scores that fall into each class.

Frequency polygon   A graph of a frequency distribution in which the number of scores falling in each class is represented by points on a line.

Frequency theory   Holds that tones up to 4,000 hertz are converted to nerve impulses that match the frequency of each tone.

Frontal lobes   A brain area associated with movement, the sense of self, and higher mental functions.

Frotteurism   Sexually touching or rubbing against a nonconsenting person, usually in a public place such as a subway.

Frustration   A negative emotional state that occurs when one is prevented from reaching a goal.

Frustration-aggression hypothesis   States that frustration tends to lead to aggression.

Fully functioning person   A person living in harmony with her or his deepest feelings, impulses, and intuitions.

Functional fixedness   A rigidity in problem solving caused by an inability to see new uses for familiar objects.

Functional MRI (fMRI)   Functional magnetic resonance imaging that records brain activity.

Functional solution   A detailed, practical, and workable solution.

Functionalism   The school of psychology concerned with how behavior and mental abilities help people adapt to their environments.

Fundamental attribution error   The tendency to attribute the behavior of others to internal causes (personality, likes, and so forth).

Galvanic skin response (GSR)   A change in the electrical resistance (or inversely, the conductance) of the skin, due to sweating.

Gate control theory   Proposes that pain messages pass through neural "gates" in the spinal cord.

Gender bias (in research)   A tendency for females and female issues to be underrepresented in research, psychological or otherwise.

Gender identity   One's personal, private sense of maleness or femaleness as expressed in appearance, behavior, and attitudes.

Gender role socialization   The process of learning gender behaviors considered appropriate for one's sex in a given culture.

Gender role stereotypes   Oversimplified and widely held beliefs about the basic characteristics of men and women.

Gender role   The pattern of behaviors that are regarded as "male" or "female" by one's culture; sometimes also referred to as a sex role.

Gender   Psychological and social characteristics associated with being male or female; defined especially by one's gender identity and learned gender roles.

General adaptation syndrome (GAS)   A series of bodily reactions to prolonged stress; occurs in three stages: alarm, resistance, and exhaustion.

General solution   A solution that correctly states the requirements for success but not in enough detail for further action.

Generalized anxiety disorder   A chronic state of tension and worries about work, relationships, ability, or impending disaster.

Generativity versus stagnation   A conflict of middle adulthood in which self-interest is countered by an interest in guiding the next generation.

Genes   Specific areas on a strand of DNA that carry hereditary information.

Genetic disorders   Problems caused by defects in the genes or by inherited characteristics.

Genetic sex   Sex as indicated by the presence of *XX* (female) or *XY* (male) chromosomes.

Genital sex   Sex as indicated by the presence of male or female genitals.

Genital stage   Period of full psychosexual development, marked by the attainment of mature adult sexuality.

Gestalt psychology   A school of psychology emphasizing the study of thinking, learning, and perception in whole units, not by analysis into parts.

Gestalt therapy   An approach that focuses on immediate experience and awareness to help clients rebuild thinking, feeling, and acting into connected wholes; emphasizes the integration of fragmented experiences.

g-factor   A general ability factor or core of general intellectual ability that involves reasoning, problem-solving ability, knowledge, memory, and successful adaptation to one's surroundings.

Giftedness   The possession of a high IQ or special talents or aptitudes.

Glans penis (glanz PEA-nis)   The tip of the penis.

Goal   The target or objective of motivated behavior.

Gonadal sex   Sex as indicated by the presence of ovaries (female) or testes (male).

Gonads   The primary sex glands—the testes in males and ovaries in females.

Grammar   A set of rules for combining language units into meaningful speech or writing.

Graphical statistics   Techniques for presenting numbers pictorially, often by plotting them on a graph.

Group cohesiveness   The degree of attraction among group members or their commitment to remaining in the group.

Group intelligence test   Any intelligence test that can be administered to a group of people with minimal supervision.

Group prejudice   Prejudice held out of conformity to group views.

Group sanctions   Rewards and punishments (such as approval or disapproval) administered by groups to enforce conformity among members.

Group structure   The network of roles, communication pathways, and power in a group.

Group therapy   Psychotherapy conducted in a group setting to make therapeutic use of group dynamics.

Groupthink   A compulsion by members of decision-making groups to maintain agreement, even at the cost of critical thinking.

Growth hormone   A hormone, secreted by the pituitary gland, that promotes body growth.

Growth needs   In Maslow's hierarchy, the higher-level needs associated with self-actualization.

Guided imagery   Intentional visualization of images that are calming, relaxing, or beneficial in other ways.

Gustation   The sense of taste.

Habit   A deeply ingrained, learned pattern of behavior.

Habituation   A decrease in perceptual response to a repeated stimulus.

Hair cells   Receptor cells within the cochlea that transduce vibrations into nerve impulses.

Halfway house   A community-based facility for individuals making the transition from an institution (mental hospital, prison, and so forth) to independent living.

Hallucination   An imaginary sensation, such as seeing, hearing, or smelling something that does not exist in the external world.

Hallucinogen (hal-LU-sin-oh-jin)   A substance that alters or distorts sensory impressions.

Halo effect   The tendency to generalize a favorable or unfavorable first impression to unrelated details of personality.

Handedness   A preference for the right or left hand in most activities.

Hardy personality   A personality style associated with superior stress resistance.

Hassle (microstressor)   Any distressing, day-to-day annoyance.

Health psychology   Study of the ways in which behavioral principles can be used to prevent illness and promote health.

Heredity ("nature")   The transmission of physical and psychological characteristics from parents to offspring through genes.

Heterosexism   The belief that heterosexuality is better or more natural than homosexuality.

Heterosexual   A person romantically and erotically attracted to members of the opposite sex.

Heuristic (hew-RIS-tik)   Any strategy or technique that aids problem solving, especially by limiting the number of possible solutions to be tried.

Hidden observer   A detached part of the hypnotized person's awareness that silently observes events.

Hierarchy of human needs   Abraham Maslow's ordering of needs, based on their presumed strength or potency.

Hierarchy   A rank-ordered series of higher and lower amounts, levels, degrees, or steps.

Higher order conditioning   Classical conditioning in which a conditioned stimulus is used to reinforce further learning; that is, a CS is used as if it were a US.

Hippocampus (HIP-oh-CAMP-us)   A part of the limbic system in the brain associated with emotion, storing memories, and the transfer of information from short-term memory to long-term memory.

Histogram   A graph of a frequency distribution in which the number of scores falling in each class is represented by vertical bars.

Homeostasis (HOE-me-oh-STAY-sis)   A steady state of bodily equilibrium.

Homogamy (huh-MOG-ah-me)   Marriage of two people who are similar to one another.

Homosexual   A person romantically and erotically attracted to same-sex persons.

Hormonal sex   Sex as indicated by a preponderance of estrogens (female) or androgens (male) in the body.

Hormone   A glandular secretion that affects bodily functions or behavior.

Human factors psychology (ergonomics)   A specialty concerned with making machines and work environments compatible with human perceptual and physical capacities.

Human nature   Those traits, qualities, potentials, and behavior patterns most characteristic of the human species.

Human–computer interaction (HCI)   The application of human factors to the design of computers and computer software.

Humanism   An approach to psychology that focuses on human experience, problems, potentials, and ideals.

Hyperopia (HI-per-OPE-ee-ah)   Difficulty focusing on nearby objects (farsightedness).

Hypersomnia (hi-per-SOM-nee-ah)   Excessive daytime sleepiness. This can result from depression, insomnia, narcolepsy, sleep apnea, sleep drunkenness, periodic limb movements, drug abuse, and other problems.

Hypnosis   An altered state of consciousness characterized by narrowed attention and increased suggestibility.

Hypnotic susceptibility   One's capacity for becoming hypnotized.

Hypoactive sexual desire   A persistent, upsetting loss of sexual desire.

Hypochondriac (HI-po-KON-dree-ak)   A person who complains about illnesses that appear to be imaginary.

Hypochondriasis (HI-po-kon-DRY-uh-sis)   A preoccupation with fears of having a serious disease. Ordinary physical signs are interpreted as proof that the person has a disease, but no physical disorder can be found.

Hypothalamus (HI-po-THAL-ah-mus)   A small area at the base of the brain that regulates many aspects of motivation and emotion, especially hunger, thirst, and sexual behavior.

Hypothesis   The predicted outcome of an experiment or an educated guess about the relationship between variables.

Iconic (eye-KON-ick) **memory**   A mental image or visual representation.

Id   The primitive part of personality that remains unconscious, supplies energy, and demands pleasure.

Ideal self   An idealized image of oneself (the person one would like to be).

Identification   Taking on some of the characteristics of an admired person, usu-

ally as a way of compensating for perceived personal weaknesses or faults.

Identity versus role confusion   A conflict of adolescence, involving the need to establish a personal identity.

Illogical thought   Thought that is intuitive, haphazard, or irrational.

Illusion   A misleading or distorted perception.

Illustrators   Gestures people use to illustrate what they are saying.

Image   Most often, a mental representation that has picture-like qualities; an icon.

I-message   A message that states the effect someone else's behavior has on you.

Imitation   An attempt to match one's own behavior to another person's behavior.

Implicit memory   A memory that a person does not know exists; a memory that is retrieved unconsciously.

Inattentional blindness   Failure to perceive a stimulus that is in plain view, but not the focus of attention.

In-basket test   A testing procedure that simulates the individual decision-making challenges that executives face.

Incentive value   The value of a goal above and beyond its ability to fill a need.

Incongruence   State that exists when there is a discrepancy between one's experiences and self-image or between one's self-image and ideal self.

Independent variable   In an experiment, the condition being investigated as a possible cause of some change in behavior. The values that this variable takes are chosen by the experimenter.

Individual intelligence test   A test of intelligence designed to be given to a single individual by a trained specialist.

Individual traits   Personality traits that define a person's unique individual qualities.

Individuating information   Information that helps define a person as an individual, rather than as a member of a group or social category.

Inductive thought   Thinking in which a general rule or principle is gathered from a series of specific examples; for instance, inferring the laws of gravity by observing many falling objects.

Industrial/organizational psychology   A field that focuses on the psychology of work and on behavior within organizations.

Industry versus inferiority   A conflict in middle childhood centered around lack of support for industrious behavior, which can result in feelings of inferiority.

Inferential statistics   Mathematical tools used for decision making, for generalizing from small samples, and for drawing conclusions.

Information bits   Meaningful units of information, such as numbers, letters, words, or phrases.

Information chunks   Information bits grouped into larger units.

Informational view   Perspective that explains learning in terms of information imparted by events in the environment.

In-group   A group with which a person identifies.

Initiative versus guilt   A conflict between learning to take initiative and overcoming feelings of guilt about doing so.

Insanity   A legal term that refers to a mental inability to manage one's affairs or to be aware of the consequences of one's actions.

Insecure-ambivalent attachment   An anxious emotional bond marked by both a desire to be with a parent or caregiver and some resistance to being reunited.

Insecure-avoidant attachment   An anxious emotional bond marked by a tendency to avoid reunion with a parent or caregiver.

Insight   A sudden mental reorganization of a problem that makes the solution obvious.

Insomnia   Difficulty in getting to sleep or staying asleep; also, not feeling rested after sleeping.

Instrumental behaviors   Behaviors directed toward the achievement of some goal; behaviors that are instrumental in producing some effect.

Integrity versus despair   A conflict in old age between feelings of integrity and the despair of viewing previous life events with regret.

Intellectual disability (formerly **mental retardation**)   The presence of a developmental disability, a formal IQ score below 70, or a significant impairment of adaptive behavior.

Intellectualization   Separating emotion from a threatening or anxiety-provoking situation by talking or thinking about it in impersonal "intellectual" terms.

Intelligence quotient (IQ)   An index of intelligence defined as a person's mental age divided by his or her chronological age and multiplied by 100.

Intelligence   An overall capacity to think rationally, act purposefully, and deal effectively with the environment.

Interference   The tendency for new memories to impair retrieval of older memories, and the reverse.

Internal cause   A cause of behavior assumed to lie within a person—for instance, a need, preference, or personality trait.

Internet   An electronic network of interlinked computers.

Interpersonal attraction   Social attraction to another person.

Interpersonal psychotherapy (IPT)   A brief dynamic psychotherapy designed to help people by improving their relationships with other people.

Interpretation   Where pain is concerned, the meaning given to a stimulus.

Intersexual person   A person who has genitals suggestive of both sexes.

Interview (personality)   A face-to-face meeting held for the purpose of gaining information about an individual's personal history, personality traits, current psychological state, and so forth.

Intimacy versus isolation   The challenge of overcoming a sense of isolation by establishing intimacy with others.

Intimacy   Feelings of connectedness and affection for another person.

Intimate distance   The most private space immediately surrounding the body (up to about 18 inches from the skin).

Intracellular thirst   Thirst triggered when fluid is drawn out of cells due to an increased concentration of salts and minerals outside the cell.

Intrinsic motivation   Motivation that comes from within, rather than from external rewards; motivation based on personal enjoyment of a task or activity.

Introduction   The introduction describes the question to be investigated. It also provides background information by reviewing prior studies on the same or related topics.

Introspection   To look within; to examine one's own thoughts, feelings, or sensations.

Introversion   Ego attitude in which energy is mainly directed inward.

Introvert   A person whose attention is focused inward; a shy, reserved, self-centered person.

Intuition   Quick, impulsive thought that does not make use of formal logic or clear reasoning.

Intuitive thought   Thinking that makes little or no use of reasoning and logic.

Ion (EYE-on) **channels**   Tiny openings through the axon membrane.

Iris   Circular muscle that controls the amount of light entering the eye.

Isolation   Separating contradictory thoughts or feelings into "logic-tight" mental compartments so that they do not come into conflict.

James-Lange theory   States that emotional feelings follow bodily arousal and come from awareness of such arousal.

Jigsaw classroom   A method of reducing prejudice; each student receives only part of the information needed to complete a project or prepare for a test.

Job analysis   A detailed description of the skills, knowledge, and activities required by a particular job.

Job enrichment   Making a job more personally rewarding, interesting, or intrinsically motivating; typically involves increasing worker knowledge.

Job satisfaction   The degree to which a person is comfortable with or satisfied with his or her work.

Just noticeable difference (JND) Any noticeable difference in a stimulus.

Just-world beliefs Belief that people generally get what they deserve.

Keyword method As an aid to memory, using a familiar word or image to link two items.

Kinesics (kih-NEEZ-iks) Study of the meaning of body movements, posture, hand gestures, and facial expressions; commonly called body language.

Kinesthetic senses The senses of body movement and positioning.

Knowledge of results (KR) Informational feedback.

Knowledge workers Workers who add value to their company by creating and manipulating information.

Labia majora (LAY-bee-ah mah-JOR-ah) The larger outer lips of the vulva.

Labia minora (LAY-bee-ah mih-NOR-ah) Inner lips of the vulva, surrounding the vaginal opening.

Language Words or symbols, and rules for combining them, that are used for thinking and communication.

Large-group awareness training Any of a number of programs (many of them commercialized) that claim to increase self-awareness and facilitate constructive personal change.

Latency According to Freud, a period in childhood when psychosexual development is more or less interrupted.

Latent dream content The hidden or symbolic meaning of a dream, as revealed by dream interpretation and analysis.

Latent learning Learning that occurs without obvious reinforcement and that remains unexpressed until reinforcement is provided.

Lateralization Differences between the two sides of the body, especially differences in the abilities of the brain hemispheres.

Law of effect Responses that lead to desirable effects are repeated; those that produce undesirable results are not.

Leaderless group discussion A test of leadership that simulates group decision making and problem solving.

Learned helplessness A learned inability to overcome obstacles or to avoid punishment; learned passivity and inaction to aversive stimuli.

Learned motives Motives based on learned needs, drives, and goals.

Learning Any relatively permanent change in behavior that can be attributed to experience.

Legitimate power Social power based on a person's position as an agent of an accepted social order.

Libido (lih-BEE-doe) In Freudian theory, the force, primarily pleasure oriented, that energizes the personality.

Life skills training A program that teaches stress reduction, self-protection, decision making, self-control, and social skills.

Lifestyle disease A disease related to health-damaging personal habits.

Light sleep Stage 1 sleep, marked by small irregular brainwaves and some alpha waves.

Liking A relationship based on intimacy, but lacking passion and commitment.

Limbic system A system in the forebrain that is closely linked with emotional response.

Links Connections built into websites that let you "jump" from one site to the next.

Lobes of the cerebral cortex Areas on the cortex bordered by major fissures or defined by their functions.

Localization of function The research strategy of linking specific structures in the brain with specific psychological or behavioral functions.

Lock and key theory of olfaction Holds that odors are related to the shapes of chemical molecules.

Logical consequences Reasonable consequences that are defined by parents.

Logical thought Drawing conclusions on the basis of formal principles of reasoning.

Long-term memory (LTM) The memory system used for relatively permanent storage of meaningful information.

Lowball technique A strategy in which commitment is gained first to reasonable or desirable terms, which are then made less reasonable or desirable.

Lucid dream A dream in which the dreamer feels awake and capable of normal thought and action.

Magnetic resonance imaging (MRI) A three-dimensional image of the brain or body, based on its response to a magnetic field.

Maintenance rehearsal Silently repeating or mentally reviewing information to hold it in short-term memory.

Major depressive disorder A mood disorder in which the person has suffered one or more intense episodes of depression.

Major mood disorders Disorders marked by lasting extremes of mood or emotion and sometimes accompanied by psychotic symptoms.

Maladaptive behavior Behavior that makes it difficult to adapt to the environment and meet the demands of day-to-day life.

Male orgasmic disorder A persistent inability to reach orgasm during lovemaking.

Management by objectives A management technique in which employees are given specific goals to meet in their work.

Management techniques Combining praise, recognition, approval, rules, and reasoning to enforce child discipline.

Mandala A circular design representing balance, unity, and completion.

Manifest dream content The surface, "visible" content of a dream; dream images as they are remembered by the dreamer.

Massed practice Practice done in a long, uninterrupted study session.

Mastery training Reinforcement of responses that lead to mastery of a threat or control over one's environment.

Masturbation Self-stimulation that causes sexual pleasure or orgasm.

Maternal influences The aggregate of all psychological effects mothers have on their children.

Maturation The physical growth and development of the body and nervous system.

Mean A measure of central tendency calculated by adding a group of scores and then dividing by the total number of scores.

Mechanical solution A problem solution achieved by trial and error or by a fixed procedure based on learned rules.

Median A measure of central tendency found by arranging scores from the highest to the lowest and selecting the score that falls in the middle. That is, half the values in a group of scores fall above the median and half fall below.

Meditation A mental exercise for producing relaxation or heightened awareness.

Medulla (meh-DUL-ah) The structure that connects the brain with the spinal cord and controls vital life functions.

Melatonin (mel-ah-TONE-in) Hormone released by the pineal gland in response to daily cycles of light and dark.

Memory cue Any stimulus associated with a particular memory. Memory cues usually enhance retrieval.

Memory decay The fading or weakening of memories assumed to occur when memory traces become weaker.

Memory task Any task designed to test or assess memory.

Memory traces Physical changes in nerve cells or brain activity that take place when memories are stored.

Memory The mental system for receiving, encoding, storing, organizing, altering, and retrieving information.

Mental age The average mental ability people display at a given age.

Mental disorder A significant impairment in psychological functioning.

Mental hospitalization Placing a person in a protected, therapeutic environment staffed by mental health professionals.

Mental images Internal images or visual depictions used in memory and thinking.

Mental practice Imagining a skilled performance to aid learning.

Mere presence The tendency for people to change their behavior just because of the presence of other people.

Meta-analysis A statistical technique for combining the results of many studies on the same subject.

Meta-needs In Maslow's hierarchy, needs associated with impulses for self-actualization.

Method This section of a research report tells how and why observations were made. It also describes the specific procedures used to gather data. That way, other researchers can repeat the study to see if they get the same results.

Microsleep A brief shift in brain-wave patterns to those of sleep.

Mindfulness A state of open, nonjudgmental awareness of current experience.

Mindfulness meditation Mental exercise based on widening attention to become aware of everything experienced at any given moment.

Minnesota Multiphasic Personality Inventory-2 (MMPI-2) One of the best-known and most widely used objective personality questionnaires.

Mirror neuron A neuron that becomes active when a motor action is carried out *and* when another organism is observed carrying out the same action.

Mirror technique Observing another person re-enact one's own behavior, like a character in a play; designed to help persons see themselves more clearly.

MMPI-2 profile A graphic representation of an individual's scores on each of the primary scales of the MMPI-2.

Mnemonic (nee-MON-iks) Any kind of memory system or aid.

Mock jury A group that realistically simulates a courtroom jury.

Mode A measure of central tendency found by identifying the most frequently occurring score in a group of scores.

Model A person who serves as an example in observational learning.

Monocular depth cues Perceptual features that impart information about distance and three-dimensional space which require just one eye.

Mood disorder A major disturbance in mood or emotion, such as depression or mania.

Mood A low-intensity, long-lasting emotional state.

Moon illusion The apparent change in size that occurs as the moon moves from the horizon (large moon) to overhead (small moon).

Moral anxiety Apprehension felt when thoughts, impulses, or actions conflict with the superego's standards.

Moral development The development of values, beliefs, and thinking abilities that act as a guide regarding what is acceptable behavior.

Morphemes (MOR-feems) The smallest meaningful units in a language, such as syllables or words.

Motherese (or parentese) A pattern of speech used when talking to infants, marked by a higher-pitched voice; short, simple sentences; repetition, slower speech; and exaggerated voice inflections.

Motivation Internal processes that initiate, sustain, and direct activities.

Motor program A mental plan or model that guides skilled movement.

Motor skill A series of actions molded into a smooth and efficient performance.

Müller-Lyer (MEOO-ler-LIE-er) **illusion** Two equal-length lines tipped with inward or outward pointing Vs appear to be of different lengths.

Multiculturalism Giving equal status, recognition, and acceptance to different ethnic and cultural groups.

Multiple approach-avoidance conflict Being simultaneously attracted to and repelled by each of several alternatives.

Multiple intelligences Howard Gardner's theory that there are several specialized types of intellectual ability.

Munchausen syndrome by proxy An affected person fakes the medical problems of someone in his or her care in order to gain attention.

Munchausen syndrome An affected person fakes his or her own medical problems in order to gain attention.

Mutual absorption With regard to romantic love, the nearly exclusive attention lovers give to one another.

Mutual interdependence A condition in which two or more persons must depend on one another to meet each person's needs or goals.

Myelin (MY-eh-lin) A fatty layer coating some axons.

Myopia (my-OPE-ee-ah) Difficulty focusing on distant objects (nearsightedness).

Narcolepsy (NAR-koe-lep-see) Sudden, irresistible, daytime sleep attacks that may last anywhere from a few minutes to a half hour. Victims may fall asleep while standing, talking, or even driving.

Natural consequences The effects that naturally tend to follow a particular behavior.

Natural design Human factors engineering that makes use of naturally understood perceptual signals.

Natural selection Darwin's theory that evolution favors those plants and animals best suited to their living conditions.

Naturalistic observation Observing behavior as it unfolds in natural settings.

Need for achievement (nAch) The desire to excel or meet some internalized standard of excellence.

Need for power The desire to have social impact and control over others.

Need to affiliate The desire to associate with other people.

Need An internal deficiency that may energize behavior.

Negative after-potential A drop in electrical charge below the resting potential.

Negative correlation A statistical relationship in which increases in one measure are matched by decreases in the other.

Negative reinforcement Occurs when a response is followed by an end to discomfort or by the removal of an unpleasant event.

Negative relationship A mathematical relationship in which increases in one measure are matched by decreases in the other.

Negative self-statements Self-critical thoughts that increase anxiety and lower performance.

Negative transfer Mastery of one task conflicts with learning or performing another.

Neo-Freudian A psychologist who accepts the broad features of Freud's theory but has revised the theory to fit his or her own concepts.

Nerve A bundle of neuron fibers.

Network model A model of memory that views it as an organized system of linked information.

Neurilemma (NOOR-rih-LEM-ah) A layer of cells that encases many axons.

Neurocognitive dream theory Proposal that dreams reflect everyday waking thoughts and emotions.

Neurogenesis (noor-oh-JEN-uh-sis) The production of new brain cells.

Neurological soft signs Subtle behavioral signs of brain dysfunction, including clumsiness, an awkward gait, poor hand–eye coordination, and other perceptual and motor problems.

Neuron (NOOR-on) An individual nerve cell.

Neuropeptides (NOOR-oh-PEP-tides) Brain chemicals that regulate the activity of neurons, such as enkephalins and endorphins.

Neuroplasticity The capacity of our brains to change in response to experience.

Neurosis An outdated term once used to refer, as a group, to anxiety disorders, somatoform disorders, dissociative disorders, and some forms of depression.

Neurotic anxiety Apprehension felt when the ego struggles to control id impulses.

Neurotransmitter (NOOR-oh-TRANS-mit-ers) Any chemical released by a neuron that alters activity in other neurons.

Neutral stimulus (NS) A stimulus that does not evoke a response.

Night blindness Blindness under conditions of low illumination.

Night terror A state of panic during NREM sleep.

Nightmare disorder Vivid, recurrent nightmares that significantly disturb sleep.

Nightmare A bad dream that occurs during REM sleep.

Noise pollution Stressful and intrusive noise; usually artificially generated by machinery, but also including noises made by animals and humans.

Noise-induced hearing loss Damage caused by exposing the hair cells to excessively loud sounds.

Non-homeostatic drive A drive that is relatively independent of physical deprivation cycles or bodily need states.

Non-REM (NREM) sleep Non–rapid eye movement sleep characteristic of stages 2, 3, and 4.

Norepinephrine An adrenal hormone that tends to arouse the body; norepinephrine is associated with anger. (Also known as noradrenaline.)

Norm A widely accepted (but often unspoken) standard of conduct for appropriate behavior.

Normal curve A bell-shaped curve characterized by a large number of scores in a middle area, tapering to very few extremely high and low scores.

Obedience Conformity to the demands of an authority.

Object permanence Concept, gained in infancy, that objects continue to exist even when they are hidden from view.

Objective test A test that gives the same score when different people correct it.

Observational learning Learning achieved by watching and imitating the actions of another or noting the consequences of those actions.

Observational record A detailed summary of observed events or a videotape of observed behavior.

Observer bias The tendency of an observer to distort observations or perceptions to match his or her expectations.

Observer effect Changes in a person's behavior brought about by an awareness of being observed.

Obsessive-compulsive disorder An extreme preoccupation with certain thoughts and compulsive performance of certain behaviors.

Occipital lobes (awk-SIP-ih-tal) Portion of the cerebral cortex where vision registers in the brain.

Oedipus conflict A boy's sexual attraction to his mother, and feelings of rivalry with his father.

Olfaction The sense of smell.

Open-ended interview An interview in which persons are allowed to freely state their views.

Operant conditioning chamber (Skinner box) An apparatus designed to study operant conditioning in animals; a Skinner box.

Operant conditioning Learning based on the consequences of responding.

Operant extinction The weakening or disappearance of a nonreinforced operant response.

Operant reinforcer Any event that reliably increases the probability or frequency of responses it follows.

Operant stimulus discrimination The tendency to make an operant response when stimuli previously associated with reward are present and to withhold the response when stimuli associated with nonreward are present.

Operant stimulus generalization The tendency to respond to stimuli similar to those that preceded operant reinforcement.

Operational definition Defining a scientific concept by stating the specific actions or procedures used to measure it. For example, "hunger" might be defined as "the number of hours of food deprivation."

Opponent-process theory (of color vision) Theory of color vision based on three coding systems (red or green, yellow or blue, black or white).

Opponent-process theory (of emotions) States that strong emotions tend to be followed by an opposite emotional state; also the strength of both emotional states changes over time.

Oral stage The period when infants are preoccupied with the mouth as a source of pleasure and means of expression.

Oral-aggressive personality A person who uses the mouth to express hostility by shouting, cursing, biting, and so forth. Also, one who actively exploits others.

Oral-dependent personality A person who wants to passively receive attention, gifts, love, and so forth.

Organ of Corti (KOR-tee) Center part of the cochlea, containing hair cells, canals, and membranes.

Organic mental disorder A mental or emotional problem caused by brain diseases or injuries.

Organismic valuing A natural, undistorted, full-body reaction to an experience.

Organizational citizenship Making positive contributions to the success of an organization in ways that go beyond one's job description.

Organizational culture The social climate within an organization.

Orgasm A climax and release of sexual excitement.

Orientation response Bodily changes that prepare an organism to receive information from a particular stimulus.

Originality In tests of creativity, *originality* refers to how novel or unusual solutions are.

Out-group A group with which a person does not identify.

Ovary (OH-vah-ree) One of the two female reproductive glands; ovaries are the source of hormones and eggs.

Overgeneralization Blowing a single event out of proportion by extending it to a large number of unrelated situations.

Overlearning Learning or practice that continues after initial mastery of a skill.

Overly permissive parents Parents who give little guidance, allow too much freedom, or do not require the child to take responsibility.

Pain disorder Pain that has no identifiable physical cause and appears to be of psychological origin.

Panic disorder (with agoraphobia) A chronic state of anxiety and brief moments of sudden panic. The person fears that these panic attacks will occur in public places or unfamiliar situations.

Panic disorder (without agoraphobia) A chronic state of anxiety and also has brief moments of sudden, intense, unexpected panic.

Paranoid psychosis A delusional disorder centered especially on delusions of persecution.

Paranoid schizophrenia Schizophrenia marked by a preoccupation with delusions or by frequent auditory hallucinations related to a single theme, especially grandeur or persecution.

Paraphilias (PAIR-eh-FIL-ih-ahs) Compulsive or destructive deviations in sexual preferences or behavior.

Paraprofessional An individual who works in a near-professional capacity under the supervision of a more highly trained person.

Parapsychology The study of extranormal psychological events, such as extrasensory perception.

Parasympathetic branch A part of the autonomic system that quiets the body and conserves energy.

Parasympathetic rebound Excess activity in the parasympathetic nervous system following a period of intense emotion.

Parental styles Identifiable patterns of parental caretaking and interaction with children.

Parietal lobes (puh-RYE-ih-tal) Area of the brain where body sensations register.

Partial hospitalization An approach in which patients receive treatment at a hospital during the day, but return home at night.

Partial reinforcement effect Responses acquired with partial reinforcement are more resistant to extinction.

Partial reinforcement A pattern in which only a portion of all responses are reinforced.

Passion Deep emotional and/or sexual feelings for another person.

Passive compliance Passively bending to unreasonable demands or circumstances.

Paternal influences The aggregate of all psychological effects fathers have on their children.

Peak experiences Temporary moments of self-actualization.

Peak performance A performance during which physical, mental, and emotional states are harmonious and optimal.

Pedophilia Sex with children, or child molesting.

Peer counselor A nonprofessional person who has learned basic counseling skills.

Pelvic bone One of the bones at the front of the pelvis (the pelvis connects the spine with the legs).

Percent of variance A portion of the total amount of variation in a group of scores.

Perception The mental process of organizing sensations into meaningful patterns.

Perceptual construction A meaningful mental model of external events.

Perceptual expectancy (or set) A readiness to perceive in a particular manner, induced by strong expectations.

Perceptual features Important elements of a stimulus pattern, such as lines, shapes, edges, spots, and colors.

Perceptual habits Well-established patterns of perceptual organization and attention.

Perceptual hypothesis An initial guess regarding how to organize (perceive) a stimulus pattern.

Perceptual learning Changes in how we construct sensory information into percepts that can be attributed to prior experience.

Perfect negative relationship A mathematical relationship in which the correlation between two measures is −1.00.

Perfect positive relationship A mathematical relationship in which the correlation between two measures is +1.00.

Performance intelligence Intelligence measured by solving puzzles, assembling objects, completing pictures, and other nonverbal tasks.

Periodic limb movement syndrome Muscle twitches (primarily affecting the legs) that occur every 20 to 40 seconds and severely disturb sleep.

Peripheral nervous system (PNS) All parts of the nervous system outside the brain and spinal cord.

Peripheral vision Vision at the edges of the visual field.

Persona The "mask" or public self presented to others.

Personal distance The distance maintained when interacting with close friends (about 18 inches to 4 feet from the body).

Personal interview Formal or informal questioning of job applicants to learn their qualifications and to gain an impression of their personalities.

Personal prejudice Prejudicial attitudes held toward persons who are perceived as a direct threat to one's own interests.

Personal space An area surrounding the body that is regarded as private and subject to personal control.

Personal unconscious A mental storehouse for a single individual's unconscious thoughts.

Personality A person's unique and relatively stable behavior patterns.

Personality disorder A maladaptive personality pattern.

Personality questionnaire A paper-and-pencil test consisting of questions that reveal aspects of personality.

Personality theory A system of concepts, assumptions, ideas, and principles used to understand and explain personality.

Personality trait A stable, enduring quality that a person shows in most situations.

Personality type A style of personality defined by a group of related traits.

Personnel psychology Branch of industrial/organizational psychology concerned with testing, selection, placement, and promotion of employees.

Persuasion A deliberate attempt to change attitudes or beliefs with information and arguments.

PET scan Positron emission tomography; a computer-generated image of brain activity based on glucose consumption in the brain.

Phallic personality A person who is vain, exhibitionistic, sensitive, and narcissistic.

Phallic stage The psychosexual stage (roughly ages 3 to 6) when a child is preoccupied with the genitals.

Phantom limb The illusory sensation that a limb still exists after it is lost through accident or amputation.

Pharmacotherapy (FAR-meh-koe-THER-eh-pea) The use of drugs to treat psychopathology.

Pheromone An airborne chemical signal.

Phonemes (FOE-neems) The basic speech sounds of a language.

Phototherapy A treatment for seasonal affective disorder that involves exposure to bright, full-spectrum light.

Physical dependence (addiction) Physical addiction, as indicated by the presence of drug tolerance and withdrawal symptoms.

Physical environments Natural settings, such as forests and beaches, as well as environments built by humans, such as buildings, ships, and cities.

Physiological changes (in emotion) Alterations in heart rate, blood pressure, perspiration, and other involuntary responses.

Pictorial depth cues Features found in paintings, drawings, and photographs that impart information about space, depth, and distance.

Pineal gland Gland in the brain that helps regulate body rhythms and sleep cycles.

Pituitary gland The "master gland" whose hormones influence other endocrine glands.

Place theory Theory that higher and lower tones excite specific areas of the cochlea.

Placebo (plah-SEE-bo) An inactive substance given in the place of a drug in psychological research or by physicians who wish to treat a complaint by suggestion.

Placebo effect Changes in behavior due to participant's expectations that a drug (or other treatment) will have some effect.

Plateau phase The second phase of sexual response during which physical arousal is further heightened.

Pleasure principle A desire for immediate satisfaction of wishes, desires, or needs.

Polygenic characteristics (pol-ih-JEN-ik) Personal traits or physical properties that are influenced by many genes working in combination.

Polygraph A device for recording heart rate, blood pressure, respiration, and galvanic skin response; commonly called a "lie detector."

Pons An area on the brainstem that acts as a bridge between the medulla and other structures.

Population An entire group of animals or people belonging to a particular category (for example, all college students or all married women).

Positive correlation A statistical relationship in which increases in one measure are matched by increases in the other (or decreases correspond with decreases).

Positive psychology The study of human strengths, virtues, and effective functioning.

Positive reinforcement Occurs when a response is followed by a reward or other positive event.

Positive relationship A mathematical relationship in which increases in one measure are matched by increases in the other (or decreases correspond with decreases).

Positive self-regard Thinking of oneself as a good, lovable, worthwhile person.

Positive transfer Mastery of one task aids learning or performing another.

Possible self   A collection of thoughts, beliefs, feelings, and images concerning the person one could become.

Postconventional moral reasoning   Moral thinking based on carefully examined and self-chosen moral principles.

Postpartum depression   A mild to moderately severe depression that begins within 3 months following childbirth.

Posttraumatic stress disorder (PTSD)   A psychological disturbance lasting more than 1 month following stresses that would produce anxiety in anyone who experienced them.

Power assertion   The use of physical punishment or coercion to enforce child discipline.

Precognition   The purported ability to accurately predict future events.

Preconscious   An area of the mind containing information that can be voluntarily brought to awareness.

Preconventional moral reasoning   Moral thinking based on the consequences of one's choices or actions (punishment, reward, or an exchange of favors).

Prediction   An ability to accurately forecast behavior.

Prefrontal area (prefrontal cortex)   The very front of the frontal lobes; involved in sense of self, reasoning, and planning.

Prejudice   A negative emotional attitude held against members of a particular group of people.

Premack principle   Any high-frequency response can be used to reinforce a low-frequency response.

Premature ejaculation   Ejaculation that consistently occurs before the man and his partner want it to occur.

Preoperational stage   Period of intellectual development during which children begin to use language and think symbolically, yet remain intuitive and egocentric in their thought.

Presbyopia (prez-bee-OPE-ee-ah)   Farsightedness caused by aging.

Pressure   A stressful condition that occurs when a person must meet urgent external demands or expectations.

Primary appraisal   Deciding if a situation is relevant to oneself and if it is a threat.

Primary auditory area   Part of the temporal lobe where auditory information is first registered.

Primary emotions   According to Robert Plutchik's theory, the most basic emotions are fear, surprise, sadness, disgust, anger, anticipation, joy, and acceptance.

Primary motor area (primary motor cortex)   A brain area associated with control of movement.

Primary reinforcers   Nonlearned reinforcers; usually those that satisfy physiological needs.

Primary sexual characteristics   Sex as defined by the genitals and internal reproductive organs.

Primary somatosensory area (primary somatosensory cortex) (SO-mat-oh-SEN-so-ree)   A receiving area for body sensations.

Primary visual area   The part of occipital lobe that first receives input from the eyes.

Priming   Facilitating the retrieval of an implicit memory by using cues to activate hidden memories.

Private self-consciousness   Preoccupation with inner feelings, thoughts, and fantasies.

Proactive (pro-AK-tiv) **interference**   The tendency for old memories to interfere with the retrieval of newer memories.

Problem-focused coping   Directly managing or remedying a stressful or threatening situation.

Procedural memory   Long-term memories of conditioned responses and learned skills.

Programmed instruction   Any learning format that presents information in small amounts, gives immediate practice, and provides continuous feedback to learners.

Progressive relaxation   A method for producing deep relaxation of all parts of the body.

Projection   Attributing one's own feelings, shortcomings, or unacceptable impulses to others.

Projective tests   Psychological tests making use of ambiguous or unstructured stimuli.

Prosocial behavior   Any behavior that has a positive impact on other people.

Prostate (PROSS-tate)   A gland located at the base of the urinary bladder that supplies most of the fluid that makes up semen.

Prototype   An ideal model used as a prime example of a particular concept.

Proxemics (prok-SEE-miks)   Systematic study of the human use of space, particularly in social settings.

Pseudopsychology (SUE-doe-psychology)   Any false and unscientific system of beliefs and practices that is offered as an explanation of behavior.

Psi (sigh) **phenomena**   Events that seem to lie outside the realm of accepted scientific laws.

Psyche (sigh-KEY)   The mind, mental life, and personality as a whole.

Psychiatric social worker   A mental health professional trained to apply social science principles to help patients in clinics and hospitals.

Psychiatrist   A medical doctor with additional training in the diagnosis and treatment of mental and emotional disorders.

Psychoactive drug   A substance capable of altering attention, memory, judg-ment, time sense, self-control, mood, or perception.

Psychoanalysis   A Freudian therapy that emphasizes the use of free association, dream interpretation, resistances, and transference to uncover unconscious conflicts.

Psychoanalyst   A mental health professional (usually a medical doctor) trained to practice psychoanalysis.

Psychoanalytic theory   Freudian theory of personality that emphasizes unconscious forces and conflicts.

Psychodrama   A therapy in which clients act out personal conflicts and feelings in the presence of others who play supporting roles.

Psychodynamic theory   Any theory of behavior that emphasizes internal conflicts, motives, and unconscious forces.

Psychogenic   Having psychological origins, rather than physical causes.

Psychokinesis   The purported ability to mentally alter or influence objects or events.

Psychological dependence   Drug dependence that is based primarily on emotional or psychological needs.

Psychological efficiency   Maintenance of good morale, labor relations, employee satisfaction, and similar aspects of work behavior.

Psychological perspective   The traditional view that behavior is shaped by psychological processes occurring at the level of the individual.

Psychological situation   A situation as it is perceived and interpreted by an individual, not as it exists objectively.

Psychological trauma   A psychological injury or shock, such as that caused by violence, abuse, neglect, separation, and so forth.

Psychologist   A person highly trained in the methods, factual knowledge, and theories of psychology.

Psychology of law   Study of the psychological and behavioral dimensions of the legal system.

Psychology   The scientific study of behavior and mental processes.

Psychoneuroimmunology   Study of the links among behavior, stress, disease, and the immune system.

Psychopathology   The scientific study of mental, emotional, and behavioral disorders; also, abnormal or maladaptive behavior.

Psychophysics   Study of the relationship between physical stimuli and the sensations they evoke in a human observer.

Psychosexual stages   The oral, anal, phallic, and genital stages, during which various personality traits are formed.

Psychosis   A withdrawal from reality marked by hallucinations and delusions, disturbed thought and emotions, and personality disorganization.

Psychosocial dilemma   A conflict between personal impulses and the social world.

Psychosomatic (SIKE-oh-so-MAT-ik) **disorders**   Illnesses in which psychological factors contribute to bodily damage or to damaging changes in bodily functioning.

Psychosurgery   Any surgical alteration of the brain designed to bring about desirable behavioral or emotional changes.

Psychotherapy   Any psychological technique used to facilitate positive changes in a person's personality, behavior, or adjustment.

Psychotic disorder   A severe mental disorder characterized by a retreat from reality, by hallucinations and delusions, and by social withdrawal.

PsycINFO   A searchable, online database that provides brief summaries of the scientific and scholarly literature in psychology.

Puberty   The biologically defined period during which a person matures sexually and becomes capable of reproduction.

Public distance   Distance at which formal interactions, such as giving a speech, occur (about 12 feet or more from the body).

Public self-consciousness   Intense awareness of oneself as a social object.

Punisher   Any event that decreases the probability or frequency of responses it follows.

Punishment   Any event that follows a response and *decreases* its likelihood of occurring again.

Pupil   The opening at the front of the eye through which light passes.

Quality circle   An employee discussion group that makes suggestions for improving quality and solving business problems.

Racism   Racial prejudice that has become institutionalized (that is, it is reflected in government policy, schools, and so forth) and that is enforced by the existing social power structure.

Random assignment   The use of chance (for example, flipping a coin) to assign subjects to experimental and control groups.

Random search strategy   Trying possible solutions to a problem in a more or less random order.

Random selection   Choosing a sample so that each member of the population has an equal chance of being included in the sample.

Range   The difference between the highest and lowest scores in a group of scores.

Rape myths   False beliefs about rape that tend to blame the victim and increase the likelihood that some men will think that rape is justified.

Rapid eye movements (REMs)   Swift eye movements during sleep.

Rating scale   A list of personality traits or aspects of behavior on which a person is rated.

Rational-emotive behavior therapy (REBT)   An approach that states that irrational beliefs cause many emotional problems and that such beliefs must be changed or abandoned.

Rationalization   Justifying your behavior by giving reasonable and "rational," but false, reasons for it.

Reaction formation   Preventing dangerous impulses from being expressed in behavior by exaggerating opposite behavior.

Reaction range   The limits environment places on the effects of heredity.

Readiness   A condition that exists when maturation has advanced enough to allow the rapid acquisition of a particular skill.

Reality principle   Delaying action (or pleasure) until it is appropriate.

Reality testing   Obtaining additional information to check on the accuracy of perceptions.

Recall   To supply or reproduce memorized information with a minimum of external cues.

Receptor sites   Areas on the surface of neurons and other cells that are sensitive to neurotransmitters or hormones.

Recessive gene   A gene whose influence will be expressed only when it is paired with a second recessive gene.

Reciprocal inhibition   The presence of one emotional state can inhibit the occurrence of another, such as joy preventing fear or anxiety inhibiting pleasure.

Recoding   Reorganizing or modifying information to assist storage in memory.

Recognition memory   An ability to correctly identify previously learned information.

Rectum   The lowest section of the large intestine.

Redintegration (ruh-DIN-tuh-GRAY-shun)   Process by which memories are reconstructed or expanded by starting with one memory and then following chains of association to other, related memories.

Reference group   Any group that an individual identifies with and uses as a standard for social comparison.

Referent power   Social power gained when one is used as a point of reference by others.

Referred pain   Pain that is felt in one part of the body but comes from another.

Reflection   In client-centered therapy, the process of rephrasing or repeating thoughts and feelings expressed by clients so they can become aware of what they are saying.

Reflex arc   The simplest behavior, in which a stimulus provokes an automatic response.

Reflex   An innate, automatic response to a stimulus; for example, an eyeblink.

Refractory period   A short period after orgasm during which males are unable to again reach orgasm.

Refusal skills training   Program that teaches youths how to resist pressures to begin smoking. (Can also be applied to other drugs, and health risks.)

Regression   Retreating to an earlier level of development or to earlier, less demanding habits or situations.

Reinforcement   Any event that increases the probability that a particular response will occur.

Reinforcement value   The subjective value a person attaches to a particular activity or reinforcer.

Relational concept   A concept defined by the relationship between features of an object or between an object and its surroundings (for example, "greater than," "lopsided").

Relaxation response   The pattern of internal bodily changes that occurs at times of relaxation.

Relearning   Learning again something that was previously learned. Used to measure memory of prior learning.

Reliability   The ability of a test to yield nearly the same score each time it is given to the same person.

REM behavior disorder   A failure of normal muscle paralysis, leading to violent actions during REM sleep.

REM rebound   The occurrence of extra rapid eye movement sleep following REM sleep deprivation.

REM sleep   Sleep marked by rapid eye movements and a return to stage 1 EEG patterns.

Reminding system   Pain based on small nerve fibers; reminds the brain that the body has been injured.

Replicate   To reproduce or repeat.

Representative sample   A small, randomly selected part of a larger population that accurately reflects characteristics of the whole population.

Representativeness heuristic (hew-RIS-tik)   A tendency to select wrong answers because they seem to match preexisting mental categories.

Repression   The unconscious process by which memories, thoughts, or impulses are held out of awareness.

Research method   A systematic approach to answering scientific questions.

Research participant bias   Changes in the behavior of research participants caused by the unintended influence of their own expectations.

Researcher bias   Changes in subjects' behavior caused by the unintended influence of a researcher's actions.

Resistance   A blockage in the flow of free association; topics the client resists thinking or talking about.

Resolution   The fourth phase of sexual response, involving a return to lower levels of sexual tension and arousal.

Respondent reinforcement   Reinforcement that occurs when an unconditioned stimulus closely follows a conditioned stimulus.

Response chaining   The assembly of separate responses into a series of actions that lead to reinforcement.

Response cost   Removal of a positive reinforcer after a response is made.

Response   Any muscular action, glandular activity, or other identifiable aspect of behavior.

Resting potential   The electrical charge of a neuron at rest.

Restless legs syndrome   An irresistible urge to move the legs to relieve sensations of creeping, tingling, prickling, aching, or tension.

Restricted Environmental Stimulation Therapy (REST)   A form of sensory deprivation that results in a variety of psychological benefits.

Results   The outcome of the investigation is presented. Data may be graphed, summarized in tables, or statistically analyzed.

Reticular activating system (RAS) (reh-TICK-you-ler)   A part of the reticular formation that activates the cerebral cortex.

Reticular formation (RF) (reh-TICK-you-ler)   A network within the medulla and brainstem; associated with attention, alertness, and some reflexes.

Retina   The light-sensitive layer of cells at the back of the eye.

Retrieval   Recovering information from storage in memory.

Retroactive (RET-ro-AK-tiv) **interference**   The tendency for new memories to interfere with the retrieval of old memories.

Reward   Anything that produces pleasure or satisfaction; a positive reinforcer.

Reward power   Social power based on the capacity to reward a person for acting as desired.

Rods   Visual receptors for dim light that produce only black and white sensations.

Role conflict   Trying to occupy two or more roles that make conflicting demands on behavior.

Role reversal   Taking the role of another person to learn how one's own behavior appears from the other person's perspective.

Romantic love   Love that is associated with high levels of interpersonal attraction, heightened arousal, mutual absorption, and sexual desire.

Rorschach Technique   A projective test comprised of 10 standardized inkblots.

Rote learning   Learning that takes place mechanically, through repetition and memorization, or by learning rules.

Run of luck   A statistically unusual outcome (as in getting five heads in a row when flipping a coin) that could still occur by chance alone.

Saltatory conduction   The process by which nerve impulses conducted down the axons of neurons coated with myelin jump from gap to gap in the myelin layer.

Sample   A smaller subpart of a population.

Satisficing   Engaging in behavior that achieves a minimum result, rather than maximizing the outcome of that behavior.

Scaffolding   The process of adjusting instruction so that it is responsive to a beginner's behavior and supports the beginner's efforts to understand a problem or gain a mental skill.

Scapegoating   Blaming a person or a group for the actions of others or for conditions not of their making.

Scatter diagram   A graph that plots the intersection of paired measures; that is, the points at which paired X and Y measures cross.

Schachter's cognitive theory   States that emotions occur when physical arousal is labeled or interpreted on the basis of experience and situational cues.

Schedule of reinforcement   A rule or plan for determining which responses will be reinforced.

Schizophrenia   A psychosis characterized by delusions, hallucinations, apathy, and a "split" between thought and emotion.

Scientific jury selection   Using social science principles to choose members of a jury.

Scientific method   A form of critical thinking based on careful measurement and controlled observation.

Scientific observation   An empirical investigation structured to answer questions about the world in a systematic and intersubjective fashion (observations can be reliably confirmed by multiple observers).

Scrotum (SKROE-tehm)   The sac-like pouch that holds the testes.

Seasonal affective disorder (SAD)   Depression that occurs only during fall and winter; presumably related to decreased exposure to sunlight.

Secondary appraisal   Deciding how to cope with a threat or challenge.

Secondary elaboration   Making a dream more logical and complete while remembering it.

Secondary reinforcer   A learned reinforcer; often one that gains reinforcing properties by association with a primary reinforcer.

Secondary sexual characteristics   Sexual features other than the genitals and reproductive organs—breasts, body shape, facial hair, and so forth.

Secondary traits   Traits that are inconsistent or relatively superficial.

Secure attachment A stable and positive emotional bond.

Selective attention Giving priority to a particular incoming sensory message.

Selective perception Perceiving only certain stimuli among a larger array of possibilities.

Self A continuously evolving conception of one's personal identity.

Self archetype An unconscious image representing, unity, wholeness, completion, and balance.

Self-actualization The ongoing process of fully developing one's personal potential.

Self-assertion A direct, honest expression of feelings and desires.

Self-concept A person's perception of his or her own personality traits.

Self-disclosure The process of revealing private thoughts, feelings, and one's personal history to others.

Self-efficacy Belief in your capacity to produce a desired result.

Self-esteem Regarding oneself as a worthwhile person; a positive evaluation of oneself.

Self-fulfilling prophecy An expectation that prompts people to act in ways that make the expectation come true.

Self-handicapping Arranging to perform under conditions that usually impair performance, so as to have an excuse for a poor showing.

Self-help group A group of people who share a particular type of problem and provide mutual support to one another.

Self-image Total subjective perception of one's body and personality (another term for self-concept).

Self-managed team A work group that has a high degree of freedom with respect to how it achieves its goals.

Self-recording Self-management based on keeping records of response frequencies.

Self-regulated learning Deliberately reflective and active, self-guided study.

Self-reinforcement Praising or rewarding oneself for having made a particular response (such as completing a school assignment).

Self-testing Evaluating learning by posing questions to yourself.

Semantic memory A subpart of declarative memory that records impersonal knowledge about the world.

Semantics The study of meanings in words and language.

Seminal vesicles (SEM-in-uhl VES-ih-kuhlz) These two small organs (one on each side of the prostate) supply fluid that becomes part of semen.

Sensate focus A form of therapy that directs a couple's attention to natural sensations of sexual pleasure.

Sensation A sensory impression; also, the process of detecting physical energies with the sensory organs.

Sensitive period During development, a period of increased sensitivity to environmental influences. Also, a time during which certain events must take place for normal development to occur.

Sensitivity group A group experience consisting of exercises designed to increase self-awareness and sensitivity to others.

Sensorimotor stage Stage of intellectual development during which sensory input and motor responses become coordinated.

Sensorineural hearing loss Loss of hearing caused by damage to the inner ear hair cells or auditory nerve.

Sensory adaptation A decrease in sensory response to an unchanging stimulus.

Sensory analysis Separation of sensory information into important elements.

Sensory coding Codes used by the sense organs to transmit information to the brain.

Sensory conflict theory Explains motion sickness as the result of a mismatch between information from vision, the vestibular system, and kinesthesis.

Sensory deprivation (SD) Any major reduction in the amount or variety of sensory stimulation.

Sensory gating Alteration of sensory messages in the spinal cord.

Sensory memory The first stage of memory, which holds an exact record of incoming information for a few seconds or less.

Sensory neuron A nerve cell that carries information from the senses toward the CNS.

Separation anxiety Distress displayed by infants when they are separated from their parents or principal caregivers.

Serial position effect The tendency to make the most errors in remembering the middle items of an ordered list.

Set point The proportion of body fat that tends to be maintained by changes in hunger and eating.

Sex drive The strength of one's motivation to engage in sexual behavior.

Sex One's biological classification as female or male.

Sexism Institutionalized prejudice against members of either sex, based solely on their gender.

Sexual and gender identity disorders Any of a wide range of difficulties with sexual identity, deviant sexual behavior, or sexual adjustment.

Sexual aversion Persistent feelings of fear, anxiety, or disgust about engaging in sex.

Sexual masochism Desiring pain and/or humiliation as part of the sex act

Sexual orientation One's degree of emotional and erotic attraction to members of the same sex, opposite sex, or both sexes.

Sexual sadism Deriving sexual pleasure from inflicting pain and/or humiliation

Sexual script An unspoken mental plan that defines a "plot," dialogue, and actions expected to take place in a sexual encounter.

Sexually transmitted disease (STD) A disease that is typically passed from one person to the next by intimate physical contact; a venereal disease.

Shape constancy The perceived shape of an object is unaffected by changes in its retinal image.

Shaping Gradually molding responses to a final desired pattern.

Shared leadership (Participative management) A leadership approach that allows employees at all levels to participate in decision making.

Short-term memory (STM) The memory system used to hold small amounts of information for relatively brief time periods.

Shyness A tendency to avoid others plus uneasiness and strain when socializing.

Sidedness A combination of preference for hand, foot, eye, and ear.

Signal In early language development, any behavior, such as touching, vocalizing, gazing, or smiling, that allows nonverbal interaction and turn-taking between parent and child.

Simultaneous color contrast Changes in perceived hue that occur when a colored stimulus is displayed on backgrounds of various colors.

Single-blind experiment An arrangement in which participants remain unaware of whether they are in the experimental group or the control group.

Situational demands Unstated expectations that define desirable or appropriate behavior in various settings and social situations.

Situational determinants External conditions that strongly influence behavior.

Situational judgment test Presenting realistic work situations to applicants in order to observe their skills and reactions.

Situational test Simulating real-life conditions so that a person's reactions may be directly observed.

Size constancy The perceived size of an object remains constant, despite changes in its retinal image.

Size-distance invariance The strict relationship between the distance an object lies from the eyes and the size of its image.

Skin receptors Sensory organs for touch, pressure, pain, cold, and warmth.

Skin senses The senses of touch, pressure, pain, heat, and cold.

Sleep apnea (AP-nee-ah) During sleep, breathing stops for 20 seconds or more until the person wakes a little, gulps in air,

and settles back to sleep; this cycle may be repeated hundreds of times per night.

Sleep deprivation Being prevented from getting desired or needed amounts of sleep.

Sleep drunkenness A slow transition to clear consciousness after awakening; sometimes associated with irritable or aggressive behavior.

Sleep hormone A sleep-promoting substance found in the brain and spinal cord.

Sleep patterns The order and timing of daily sleep and waking periods.

Sleep spindles Distinctive bursts of brainwave activity that indicate a person is asleep.

Sleep stages Levels of sleep identified by brain-wave patterns and behavioral changes.

Sleep terror disorder The repeated occurrence of night terrors that significantly disturb sleep.

Sleep-deprivation psychosis A major disruption of mental and emotional functioning brought about by sleep loss.

Sleep-wake schedule disorder A mismatch between the sleep-wake schedule demanded by a person's bodily rhythm and that demanded by the environment.

Sleepwalking disorder Repeated incidents of leaving bed and walking about while asleep.

Social anxiety A feeling of apprehension in the presence of others.

Social comparison Making judgments about ourselves through comparison with others.

Social competition Rivalry among groups, each of which regards itself as superior to others.

Social development The development of self-awareness, attachment to parents or caregivers, and relationships with other children and adults.

Social dilemma A social situation that tends to provide immediate rewards for actions that will have undesired effects in the long run.

Social distance scale A rating of the degree to which a person would be willing to have contact with a member of another group.

Social distance Distance at which impersonal interaction takes place (about 4 to 12 feet from the body).

Social environment An environment defined by a group of people and their activities or interrelationships (such as a parade, revival meeting, or sports event).

Social exchange theory Theory stating that rewards must exceed costs for relationships to endure.

Social exchange Any exchange between two people of attention, information, affection, favors, or the like.

Social facilitation The tendency to perform better when in the presence of others.

Social influence   Changes in a person's behavior induced by the presence or actions of others.

Social learning theory   Combines learning principles with cognitive processes, socialization, and modeling to explain behavior.

Social loafing   The tendency of people to work less hard when part of a group than when they are solely responsible for their work.

Social motives   Learned motives acquired as part of growing up in a particular society or culture.

Social nonconformity   Failure to conform to societal norms or the usual minimum standards for social conduct.

Social norms   Rules that define acceptable and expected behavior for members of a group.

Social phobia   An intense, irrational fear of being observed, evaluated, embarrassed, or humiliated by others in social situations.

Social power   The capacity to control, alter, or influence the behavior of another person.

Social psychology   The scientific study of how individuals behave, think, and feel in social situations.

Social Readjustment Rating Scale (SRRS)   A scale that rates the impact of various life events on the likelihood of illness.

Social reinforcement   Praise, attention, approval, and/or affection from others.

Social reinforcer   Reinforcement based on receiving attention, approval, or affection from another person.

Social role   Expected behavior patterns associated with particular social positions (such as daughter, worker, student).

Social smile   Smiling elicited by social stimuli, such as seeing a parent's face.

Social stereotypes   Oversimplified images of the traits of individuals who belong to a particular social group.

Social support   Close, positive relationships with other people.

Sociocultural perspective   The focus on the importance of social and cultural contexts in influencing the behavior of individuals.

Soma (SOH-mah)   The main body of a neuron or other cell.

Somatic nervous system (SNS)   The system of nerves linking the spinal cord with the body and sense organs.

Somatic pain   Pain from the skin, muscles, joints, and tendons.

Somatic therapy   Any bodily therapy, such as drug therapy, electroconvulsive therapy, or psychosurgery.

Somatization (som-ah-tuh-ZAY-shun) **disorder**   Afflicted persons have numerous physical complaints. Typically, they have consulted many doctors, but no organic cause for their distress can be identified.

Somatoform (so-MAT-oh-form) **disorder**   Physical symptoms that mimic disease or injury for which there is no identifiable physical cause.

Somesthetic sense   Sensations produced by the skin, muscles, joints, viscera, and organs of balance.

Somnambulists (som-NAM-bue-lists)   People who sleepwalk; occurs during NREM sleep.

Source traits   Basic underlying traits, or dimensions, of personality; each source trait is reflected in a number of surface traits.

Spaced practice   A practice schedule that alternates study periods with brief rests.

Specific goal   A goal with a clearly defined and measurable outcome.

Specific phobia   An intense, irrational fear of specific objects, activities, or situations.

Spinal nerves   Major nerves that carry sensory and motor messages in and out of the spinal cord.

"Split-brain" operation   Cutting the corpus callosum.

Spontaneous recovery   The reappearance of a learned response after its apparent extinction.

Sports psychology   Study of the psychological and behavioral dimensions of sports performance.

SQ4R method   An active study-reading technique based on these steps: survey, question, read, recite, reflect, and review.

Squeeze technique   A method for inhibiting ejaculation by compressing the tip of the penis.

Stage ESP   The simulation of ESP for the purpose of entertainment.

Stage hypnosis   Use of hypnosis to entertain; often, merely a simulation of hypnosis for that purpose.

Stage of exhaustion   Third stage of the GAS, at which time the body's resources are exhausted and serious health consequences occur.

Stage of resistance   Second stage of the GAS, during which bodily adjustments to stress stabilize, but at a high physical cost.

Standard deviation   An index of how much a typical score differs from the mean of a group of scores.

State-dependent learning   Memory influenced by one's bodily state at the time of learning and at the time of retrieval. Improved memory occurs when the bodily states match.

Statistical abnormality   Abnormality defined on the basis of an extreme score on some dimension, such as IQ or anxiety.

Statistical significance   The degree to which an event (such as the results of an experiment) is unlikely to have occurred by chance alone.

Status inequalities   Differences in the power, prestige, or privileges of two or more persons or groups.

Status   An individual's position in a social structure, especially with respect to power, privilege, or importance.

Stereoscopic vision   Perception of space and depth caused chiefly by the fact that the eyes receive different images.

Sterilization   Medical procedures such as vasectomy or tubal ligation that make a man or a woman infertile.

Stimulant (upper)   A substance that increases activity in the body and nervous system.

Stimulus control   Stimuli present when an operant response is acquired tend to control when and where the response is made.

Stimulus discrimination   The learned ability to respond differently to similar stimuli.

Stimulus drives   Drives based on needs for exploration, manipulation, curiosity, and stimulation.

Stimulus generalization   The tendency to respond to stimuli similar to, but not identical to, a conditioned stimulus.

Stimulus motives   Innate needs for stimulation and information.

Stimulus   Any physical energy sensed by an organism.

Storage   Holding information in memory for later use.

Stress disorder   A significant emotional disturbance caused by stresses outside the range of normal human experience.

Stress inoculation   Use of positive coping statements to control fear and anxiety.

Stress management   The application of cognitive and behavioral strategies to reduce stress and improve coping skills.

Stress reaction   The physical response to stress, consisting mainly of bodily changes related to autonomic nervous system arousal.

Stress   The mental and physical condition that occurs when a person must adjust or adapt to the environment.

Stressor   A specific condition or event in the environment that challenges or threatens a person.

Stress-vulnerability model   Attributes mental disorders such as psychosis to a combination of environmental stress and inherited susceptibility.

Striving for superiority   According to Adler, this basic drive propels us toward perfection.

Stroboscopic movement (strobe-oh-SKOP-ik)   Illusion of movement in which an object is shown in a rapidly changing series of positions.

Structuralism   The school of thought concerned with analyzing sensations and personal experience into basic elements.

Style of life   The pattern of personality and behavior that defines the pathway each person takes through life.

Subcortex   All brain structures below the cerebral cortex.

Subjective experience   Reality as it is perceived and interpreted, not as it exists objectively.

Subjective well-being   General life satisfaction combined with frequent positive emotions and relatively few negative emotions.

Sublimation (sub-lih-MAY-shun)   Working off unmet desires, or unacceptable impulses, in activities that are constructive.

Subliminal perception   Perception of a stimulus below the threshold for conscious recognition.

Substance-related disorder   Abuse of or dependence on a mood- or behavior-altering drug.

Sudden infant death syndrome (SIDS)   The sudden, unexplained death of an apparently healthy infant.

Superego   A judge or censor for thoughts and actions.

Superordinate goal   A goal that exceeds or overrides all others; a goal that renders other goals relatively less important.

Superstitious behavior   A behavior repeated because it seems to produce reinforcement, even though it is actually unnecessary.

Suppression   A conscious effort to put something out of mind or to keep it from awareness.

Surface traits   The visible or observable traits of one's personality.

Surrogate mother   A substitute mother (often an inanimate dummy in animal research).

Survey method   The use of public polling techniques to answer psychological questions.

Symbolic prejudice   Prejudice that is expressed in disguised fashion.

Symbolization   The nonliteral expression of dream content.

Sympathetic branch   A part of the ANS that activates the body at times of stress.

Synapse (SIN-aps)   The microscopic space between two neurons, over which messages pass.

Syntax   Rules for ordering words when forming sentences.

Systematic desensitization   A reduction in fear, anxiety, or aversion brought about by planned exposure to aversive stimuli.

Task analysis   Breaking complex skills into their subparts.

Taste aversion   An active dislike for a particular food.

Taste bud   The receptor organ for taste.

Teaching strategy   A plan for effective teaching.

Telecommuting   An approach to flexible work that involves working from home but using a computer to stay connected to the office throughout the workday.

Telepathy   The purported ability to directly know another person's thoughts.

Temperament   The physical core of personality, including emotional and perceptual sensitivity, energy levels, typical mood, and so forth.

Temporal lobes   Areas on each side of the brain where hearing registers in the brain.

Tension-release method   A procedure for systematically achieving deep relaxation of the body.

Teratogen (teh-RAT-uh-jen)   Radiation, a drug, or other substance capable of altering fetal development in nonheritable ways that cause birth defects.

Term schedule   A written plan that lists the dates of all major assignments for each of your classes for an entire semester or quarter.

Territorial behavior   Any behavior that tends to define a space as one's own or that protects it from intruders.

Territorial markers   Objects and other signals whose placement indicates to others the "ownership" or control of a particular area.

Test anxiety   High levels of arousal and worry that seriously impair test performance.

Testis (TES-tis, singular; testes, plural)   One of the two male reproductive glands; the testes are a source of hormones and sperm.

Testosterone (tes-TOSS-teh-rone)   A male sex hormone, secreted mainly by the testes and responsible for the development of many male sexual characteristics.

Thalamus (THAL-uh-mus)   A brain structure that relays sensory information to the cerebral cortex.

Thanatologist (THAN-ah-TOL-oh-jist)   A specialist who studies emotional and behavioral reactions to death and dying.

Thanatos   The death instinct postulated by Freud.

Thematic Apperception Test (TAT)   A projective test consisting of 20 different scenes and life situations about which respondents make up stories.

Theory X leadership (scientific management)   An approach to leadership that emphasizes work efficiency.

Theory Y leadership   A leadership style that emphasizes human relations at work and that views people as industrious, responsible, and interested in challenging work.

Theory   A system of ideas designed to interrelate concepts and facts in a way that

summarizes existing data and predicts future observations.

Therapeutic alliance   A caring relationship that unites a therapist and a client in working to solve the client's problems.

Therapy placebo effect   Improvement caused not by the actual process of therapy but by a client's expectation that therapy will help.

Thought stopping   Use of aversive stimuli to interrupt or prevent upsetting thoughts.

Threshold   The point at which a nerve impulse is triggered.

Thyroid gland   Endocrine gland that helps regulate the rate of metabolism.

Tip-of-the-tongue (TOT) state   The feeling that a memory is available but not quite retrievable.

Token economy   A therapeutic program in which desirable behaviors are reinforced with tokens that can be exchanged for goods, services, activities, and privileges.

Token reinforcer   A tangible secondary reinforcer such as money, gold stars, poker chips, and the like.

Top-down processing   Applying higher-level knowledge to rapidly organize sensory information into a meaningful perception.

Tragedy of the commons   A social dilemma in which individuals, each acting in his or her immediate self-interest, overuse a scarce group resource.

Trait profile   A graph of the scores obtained on several personality traits.

Trait theorist   A psychologist interested in classifying, analyzing, and interrelating traits to understand personality.

Trait-situation interaction   The influence that external settings or circumstances have on the expression of personality traits.

Tranquilizer   A drug that lowers anxiety and reduces tension.

Transducers   Devices that convert one kind of energy into another.

Transference   The tendency of patients to transfer feelings to a therapist that correspond to those the patient had for important persons in his or her past.

Transformation rules   Rules by which a simple declarative sentence may be changed to other voices or forms (past tense, passive voice, and so forth).

Transformation   The ability to mentally change the shape or form of a mental image or idea.

Transition period   Time span during which a person leaves an existing life pattern behind and moves into a new pattern.

Transsexual   A person with a deep conflict between his or her biological sex and preferred psychological and social gender roles.

Transvestic fetishism   Achieving sexual arousal by wearing clothing of the opposite sex.

Traumatic stresses   Extreme events that cause psychological injury or intense emotional pain.

Trichromatic theory   Theory of color vision based on three cone types: red, green, and blue.

Trust versus mistrust   A conflict early in life about learning to trust others and the world.

Twin study   A comparison of the characteristics of twins who were raised together or separated at birth; used to identify the relative impact of heredity and environment.

Two-way bilingual education   A program in which English-speaking children and children with limited English proficiency are taught half the day in English and half in a second language.

Type A personality   A personality type with an elevated risk of heart disease; characterized by time urgency, anger, and hostility.

Type B personality   All personality types other than Type A; a low-cardiac-risk personality.

Unconditional positive regard   An unqualified, unshakable acceptance of another person.

Unconditioned response (UR)   An innate reflex response elicited by an unconditioned stimulus.

Unconditioned stimulus (US)   A stimulus innately capable of eliciting a response.

Unconscious   Contents of the mind that are beyond awareness, especially impulses and desires not directly known to a person.

Uncritical acceptance   The tendency to believe generally positive or flattering descriptions of oneself.

Understanding   In problem solving, a deeper comprehension of the nature of the problem. In psychology, understanding is achieved when the causes of a behavior can be stated.

Undifferentiated schizophrenia   Schizophrenia lacking the specific features of catatonic, disorganized, or paranoid types.

Upward comparison   Comparing yourself with a person who ranks higher than you on some dimension.

Urethra (yoo-REE-thra)   The tube through which urine drains as it leaves the body. In males, semen also passes through the urethra.

Urinary bladder   The sac that collects urine before it is eliminated from the body.

Usability testing   The empirical investigation of the ease with which users can learn to use a machine.

Uterus (YOO-ter-us)   The pear-shaped muscular organ in which the fetus develops during pregnancy; also known as the womb.

Vagina (vah-JINE-ah)   Tube-like structure connecting the external female genitalia with the uterus.

Vaginismus (VAJ-ih-NIS-mus)   Muscle spasms of the vagina.

Validity   The ability of a test to measure what it purports to measure.

Validity scales   Scales that tell whether test scores should be invalidated for lying, inconsistency, or "faking good."

Variability   The tendency for a group of scores to differ in value. Measures of variability indicate the degree to which a group of scores differ from one another.

Variable interval (VI) schedule   A reinforcer is given for the first correct response made after a varied amount of time has passed since the last reinforced response. Responses made during the time interval are not reinforced.

Variable ratio (VR) schedule   A varied number of correct responses must be made to get a reinforcer. For example, a reinforcer is given after three to seven correct responses; the actual number changes randomly.

Variable   Any condition that changes or can be made to change; a measure, event, or state that may vary.

Vas deferens (vaz DEH-fur-enz)   The duct that carries sperm from the testes to the urethra.

Verbal intelligence   Intelligence measured by answering questions involving vocabulary, general information, arithmetic, and other language- or symbol-oriented tasks.

Vestibular senses   The senses of balance, position in space, and acceleration.

Vicarious classical conditioning   Classical conditioning brought about by observing another person react to a particular stimulus.

Vicarious desensitization   A reduction in fear or anxiety that takes place vicariously ("secondhand") when a client watches models perform the feared behavior.

Virtual reality exposure   Use of computer-generated images to present fear stimuli. The virtual environment responds to a viewer's head movements and other inputs.

Visceral pain   Pain originating in the internal organs.

Visible spectrum   The narrow spread of the electromagnetic spectrum to which the eyes are sensitive.

Visual acuity   The sharpness of visual perception.

Visual agnosia (ag-KNOW-zyah)   Inability to identify seen objects.

Vocational interest test   A paper-and-pencil test that assesses a person's interests and matches them to interests found among successful workers in various occupations.

Voyeurism   "Peeping," or viewing the genitals of others without their permission.

Waking consciousness   A state of clear, organized alertness.

Warning system   Pain based on large nerve fibers; warns that bodily damage may be occurring.

Weapons effect   The observation that weapons serve as strong cues for aggressive behavior.

Weber's law   The just noticeable difference is a constant proportion of the original stimulus intensity.

Weekly time schedule   A written plan that allocates time for study, work, and leisure activities during a one-week period.

Wellness   A positive state of good health; more than the absence of disease.

Wernicke's area (VER-nick-ees)   A temporal lobe brain area related to language comprehension.

Wish fulfillment   Freudian belief that many dreams express unconscious desires.

Withdrawal of love   Withholding affection to enforce child discipline.

Withdrawal symptoms   Physical illness and discomfort following the withdrawal of a drug.

Work efficiency   Maximum output (productivity) at lowest cost.

Working memory   Another name for short-term memory, especially when it is used for thinking and problem solving.

World Wide Web (WWW)   A system of information "sites" accessible through the Internet.

X chromosome   The female chromosome contributed by the mother; produces a female when paired with another X chromosome, and a male when paired with a Y chromosome.

Y chromosome   The male chromosome contributed by the father; produces a male when paired with an X chromosome. Fathers may give either an X or a Y chromosome to their offspring.

Yerkes-Dodson law   A summary of the relationships among arousal, task complexity, and performance.

You-message   Threatening, accusing, bossing, lecturing, or criticizing another person.

Zener cards   A deck of 25 cards bearing various symbols and used in early parapsychological research.

Zero correlation   The absence of a (linear) mathematical relationship between two measures.

Zone of proximal development   Refers to the range of tasks a child cannot yet master alone, but that she or he can accomplish with the guidance of a more capable partner.

z-score   A number that tells how many standard deviations above or below the mean a score is.

references

AACAP. (2008). *Child sexual abuse.* Washington, DC: American Academy of Child and Adolescent Psychiatry. Retrieved May 14, 2008, from http://www.aacap.org/cs/root/facts_for_families/child_sexual_abuse.

AAIDD. (2004). *Montreal declaration on intellectual disabilities.* Washington, DC: American Association on Mental Retardation. Retrieved June 25, 2007, from http://www.aaidd.org/pdf/DeclarationMTL.pdf.

Aamodt, M. G. (2007). *Industrial/organizational psychology: An applied approach* (5th ed.). Belmont, CA: Cengage Learning/Wadsworth.

Abe, N., Suzuki, M., Mori, E., Itoh, M., et al. (2007). Deceiving others: Distinct neural responses of the prefrontal cortex and amygdala in simple fabrication and deception with social interactions. *Journal of Cognitive Neuroscience, 19,* 2, 287–295.

Abel, G. G., Wiegel, M., & Osborn, C. A. (2007). Pedophilia and other paraphilias. In L. VandeCreek, F. L. Peterson. Jr., et al. (Eds.), *Innovations in clinical practice: Focus on sexual health. Innovations in clinical practice.* Sarasota: Professional Resource Press.

Abraham, W. C. (2006). Memory maintenance: The changing nature of neural mechanisms. *Current Directions in Psychological Science, 15*(1), 5–8.

Abrahamse, W., Steg, L., Vlek, C., & Rothengatter, T. (2005). A review of intervention studies aimed at household energy conservation. *Journal of Environmental Psychology, 25*(3), 273–291.

Abrahamson, D. J., Barlow, D. H., & Abrahamson, L. S. (1989). Differential effects of performance demand and distraction on sexually functional and dysfunctional males. *Journal of Abnormal Psychology, 98*(3), 241–247.

Abrams, D. B., Brown, R., Niaura, R. S., Emmons, K., et al. (2003). *The tobacco dependence treatment handbook: A guide to best practices.* New York: Guilford.

Accordino, D. B., Accordino, M. P., & Slaney, R. B. (2000). An investigation of perfectionism, mental health, achievement, and achievement motivation in adolescents. *Psychology in the Schools, 37*(6), 535–545.

ACT Against Violence (2005a). *Facts related to media violence.* Washington, DC: Adults and Children Against Violence Together. Retrieved July 18, 2008, from http://www.actagainstviolence.com/materials/handouts/FamilyMV1.pdf.

ACT Against Violence (2005b). *Early violence prevention.* Washington, DC: Adults and Children Against Violence Together. Retrieved July 18, 2008, from http://www.actagainstviolence.com/violprevent/index.html.

Adams, J. (1988). *Conceptual blockbusting.* New York: Norton.

Adamson, K. (2004). *Kate's journey: Triumph over adversity.* Redondo Beach, CA: Nosmada Press.

Addis, K. M., & Kahana, M. J. (2004). Decomposing serial learning: What is missing from the learning curve? *Psychonomic Bulletin & Review, 11*(1), 118–174.

Adler, S. A., & Orprecio, J. (2006). The eyes have it: Visual pop-out in infants and adults. *Developmental Science, 9,* 189–206.

Adorno, T. W., Frenkel-Brunswik, E., Levinson, D. J., & Sanford, R. N. (1950). *The authoritarian personality.* New York: Harper.

Afifi, T. O., Brownridge, D. A., Cox, B. J., & Sareen, J. (2006). Physical punishment, childhood abuse and psychiatric disorders. *Child Abuse & Neglect, 30*(10), 1093–1103.

Ahima. R. S., & Osei, S. Y. (2004). Leptin signaling. *Physiology & Behavior, 81,* 223–241.

Ajzen, I. (2005). *Attitudes, personality and behaviour* (2nd ed.). New York: McGraw-Hill.

Åkerstedt, T. (2007). Altered sleep/wake patterns and mental performance. *Physiology & Behavior, 90*(2–3), 209–218.

Albarracín, D., Johnson, B. T., & Zanna, M. P. (Eds.) (2005). *The handbook of attitudes.* Mahwah, NJ: Erlbaum.

Alberti, R., & Emmons, M. (2001). *Your perfect right* (8th ed.). San Luis Obispo, CA: Impact.

Alberto, P. A., & Troutman, A. C. (2006). *Applied behavior analysis for teachers* (7th ed.). Englewood Cliffs, NJ: Prentice Hall.

Alcock, J. E. (2003). Give the null hypothesis a chance: Reasons to remain doubtful about the existence of psi. *Journal of Consciousness Studies, 10*(6–7), 29–50.

Alcock, J. E., Burns, J., & Freeman, A. (2003). *Psi wars: Getting to grips with the paranormal.* Exeter, UK: Imprint Academic Press.

Allen, D., Carlson, D., & Ham, C. (2007). Well-being: New paradigms of wellness-inspiring positive health outcomes and renewing hope. *American Journal of Health Promotion, 21*(3), 1–9.

Allen, K., Blascovich, J., & Mendes, W. B. (2002). Cardiovascular reactivity in the presence of pets, friends, and spouses: The truth about cats and dogs. *Psychosomatic Medicine, 64*(5), 727–739.

Allen, M., Mabry, E., & McKelton, D. (1998). Impact of juror attitudes about the death penalty on juror evaluations of guilt and punishment: A meta-analysis. *Law & Human Behavior, 22*(6), 715–731.

Allgower, A., Wardle, J., & Steptoe, A. (2001). Depressive symptoms, social support, and personal health behaviors in young men and women. *Health Psychology, 20*(3), 223–227.

Allik, J. (2000). Available and accessible information in memory and vision. In E. Tulving (Ed.), *Memory, consciousness, and the brain: The Tallinn Conference.* Hove, UK: Psychology Press.

Allport, G. W. (1958). *The nature of prejudice.* Garden City, NY: Anchor Books, Doubleday.

Allport, G. W. (1961). *Pattern and growth in personality.* New York: Holt, Rinehart, and Winston.

Alsaker, F. D. (1995). Is puberty a critical period for socialization? *Journal of Adolescence, 18*(4), 427–444.

Altemeyer, B. (2004). Highly dominating, highly authoritarian personalities. *Journal of Social Psychology, 144*(4), 421–447.

Altman, L. K. (2002). AIDS threatens to claim 65M more lives by '20. *Arizona Daily Star,* July 3, A7.

Altschuler, G. C. (2001). Battling the cheats. *The New York Times: Education,* Jan. 7, 15.

Alvarado, N. (1994). Empirical validity of the Thematic Apperception Test. *Journal of Personality Assessment, 63*(1), 59–79.

Alvino, J., & the Editors of *Gifted Children Monthly* (1996). *Parents' guide to raising a gifted child.* New York: Ballantine.

Alwin, D. F., Cohen, R. L., & Newcomb, T. M. (1991). *Political attitudes over the life span: The Bennington women after fifty years.* Madison, WI: University of Wisconsin Press.

Amabile, T., Hadley, C. N., & Kramer, S. J. (2002). Creativity under the gun. *Harvard Business Review, 80*(8), 52–61.

Amato, P. R., & Fowler, F. (2002). Parenting practices, child adjustment, and family diversity. *Journal of Marriage & Family, 64*(3), 703–716.

Ambady, N., & R. Rosenthal, R. (1993). Half a minute: Predicting teacher evaluations from thin slices of nonverbal behavior and physical attractiveness. *Journal of Personality & Social Psychology, 64,* 431–441.

American Lung Association (2006). *Smokeless tobacco fact sheet.* Retrieved June 6, 2007, from http://www.lungusa.org/site/pp.asp?c=dvLUK9O0E&b=1694879.

Ancis, J. R., Chen, Y., & Schultz, D. (2004). Diagnostic challenges and the so-called culture-bound syndromes. In J. R. Ancis (Ed.), *Culturally responsive interventions: Innovative approaches to working with diverse populations.* New York: Brunner-Routledge.

Anderson, C. A. (1989). Temperature and aggression. *Psychological Bulletin, 106,* 74–96.

Anderson, C. A. (2004). An update on the effects of violent video games. *Journal of Adolescence, 27,* 113–122.

Anderson, C. A., & Bushman, B. J. (2001). Effects of violent video games on aggressive behavior, aggressive cognition, aggressive affect, physiological arousal, and prosocial behavior: A meta-analytic review of the scientific literature. *Psychological Science, 12*(5), 353–359.

Anderson, C. A., & Bushman, B. J. (2002). Human aggression. *Annual Review of Psychology, 53,* 27-51.

Anderson, C. A., Anderson, K. B., & Deuser, W. E. (1996). Examining an affective aggression framework. *Personality & Social Psychology Bulletin, 22*(4), 366–376.

Anderson, C. A., Berkowitz, L. Donnerstein, E., Huesmann, L. R., et al. (2003). The influence of media violence on youth. *Psychological Science in the Public Interest, 4,* 1–30.

Anderson, C. A., Berkowitz, L. Donnerstein, E., Huesmann, L. R., et al. (2003). The influence of media violence on youth. *Psychological Science in the Public Interest, 4,* 1–30.

Anderson, C. A., Carnagey, N. L., & Eubanks, J. (2003). Exposure to violent media: The effects of songs with violent lyrics on aggressive thoughts and feelings. *Journal of Personality & Social Psychology, 84*(5), 960–971.

Anderson, J. R. (2005). *Cognitive psychology and its implications* (6th ed.). New York: Worth.

Anderson, M. C. (2001). Active forgetting: Evidence for functional inhibition as a source of memory failure. *Journal of Aggression, Maltreatment & Trauma, 4*(2), 185–210.

Anderson, M. C., & Bell, T. (2001). Forgetting our facts: The role of inhibitory processes in the loss of propositional knowledge. *Journal of Experimental Psychology: General, 130*(3), 544–570.

Anderson, M. C., & Green, C. (2001). Suppressing unwanted memories by executive control. *Nature, 410*(6826), 366–369.

Anderson, M. C., Ochsner, K. N., Kuhl, B., Cooper, J., et al. (2004). Neural systems underlying the suppression of unwanted memories. *Science, 303,* 232–235.

Andrasik, F. (2003). Behavioral treatment approaches to chronic headache. *Neurological Sciences, 24*(Suppl2), S80–S85.

André, C., Jaber-Filho, J. A., Carvalho, M., Jullien, C., et al. (2003). Predictors of recovery following involuntary hospitalization of violent substance abuse patients. *The American Journal on Addictions, 12*(1), 84–89.

Andresen, J. (2000). Meditation meets behavioural medicine: The story of experimental research on meditation. *Journal of Consciousness Studies, 7*(11–12), 17–73.

Andrews, J. D. (1989). Integrating visions of reality. *American Psychologist, 44*(5), 803–817.

Anekonda, T. S. (2006). Resveratrol: A boon for treating Alzheimer's disease? *Brain Research Reviews, 52*(2), 316–326.

Annett, M. (2002). *Handedness and brain asymmetry: The right shift theory.* Hove, UK: Psychology Press.

Annett, M., & Manning, M. (1990). Arithmetic and laterality. *Neuropsychologia, 28*(1), 61–69.

Anshel, M. H. (1995). An examination of self-regulatory cognitive-behavioural strategies of Australian elite and non-elite competitive male swimmers. *Australian Psychologist, 30*(2), 78–83.

Antle, M. C., & Mistlberger, R. E. (2005). Circadian rhythms. In I. Q. Whishaw & B. Kolb (Eds.), *The behavior of the laboratory rat: A handbook with tests.* London: Oxford.

Antony. M. M. (2004). *10 simple solutions to shyness: How to overcome shyness, social anxiety & fear of public speaking.* Oakland, CA: New Harbinger.

APA. (2000). *2000 APA directory survey.* Washington, DC: American Psychological Association. Retrieved May 18, 2007, from http://research.apa.org/2000membership4.pdf.

APA. (2002). Ethical principles of psychologists and code of conduct. *American Psychologist, 57,* 1060–1073. Retrieved May 18, 2007, from http://www.apa.org/ethics/homepage.html.

APA. (2003). Guidelines on multicultural education, training, research, practice, and organizational change for psychologists. *American Psychologist, 58*(5), 377–402.

APA. (2004). *Sexual orientation and homosexuality.* Washington, DC: American Psychological Association. Retrieved July 29, 2007, from http://www.apahelpcenter.org/articles/article.php?id=31.

APA. (2005). *2005 APA directory survey.* Washington, DC: American Psychological Association. Retrieved May 18, 2007, from http://research.apa.org/profile2005t3.pdf.

APA. (2007). *Report of the APA Task Force on the sexualization of girls.* Washington, DC: American Psychological Association/ Retrieved July 26, 2007, from http://www.apa.org/pi/wpo/sexualization.html.

Arbona, C. B., Osma, J., Garcia-Palacios, A., Quero, S., et al. (2004). Treatment of flying phobia using virtual reality: Data from a 1-year follow-up using a multiple baseline design. *Clinical Psychology & Psychotherapy, 11*(5), 311–323.

Ariely, D., & Loewenstein, G. (2006). The heat of the moment: The effect of sexual arousal on sexual decision making. *Journal of Behavioral Decision Making, 19*(2), 87–98.

Ariely, D., & Wertenbroch, K. (2002). Procrastination, deadlines, and performance: Self-control by precommitment. *Psychological Science, 13*(3), 219–224.

Armeli, S., Gunthert, K. C., & Cohen, L. H. (2001). Stressor appraisals, coping, and post-event outcomes: The dimensionality and antecedents of stress-related growth. *Journal of Social & Clinical Psychology, 20*(3), 366–395.

Arndt, J., Allen, J. J. B., & Greenberg, J. (2001). Traces of terror. *Motivation & Emotion, 25*(3), 253–277.

Arnett, J. J. (2000). Emerging adulthood. *American Psychologist, 55*(5), 469–480.

Arnett, J. J. (2001). Conceptions of the transition to adulthood. *Journal of Adult Development, 8*(2), 133–143.

Arnett, J. J. (2004). *Emerging adulthood: The winding road from late teens through the twenties.* New York: Oxford University Press.

Arnett, J. J., & Galambos, N. L. (Eds.). (2003). *New directions for child and adolescent development: Exploring cultural conceptions of the transition to adulthood.* San Francisco: Jossey-Bass.

Arnett, J. J., & Tanner, J. L. (Eds.). (2006). *Emerging adults in America: Coming of age in the 21st century.* Washington, DC: American Psychological Association.

Aronoff, J., Barclay, A. M., & Stevenson, L. A. (1988). The recognition of threatening facial stimuli. *Journal of Personality & Social Psychology, 54*(4), 647–655.

Aronow, E., Altman Weiss, K., & Reznikoff, M. (2001). *A practical guide to the Thematic Apperception Test: The TAT in clinical practice.* New York: Brunner-Routledge.

Aronson, E. (1969). Some antecedents of interpersonal attraction. In W. J. Arnold, & D. Levine (Eds.), *Nebraska Symposium on Motivation.* Lincoln: University of Nebraska Press.

Aronson, E. (1992). *The social animal.* San Francisco: W. H. Freeman.

Aronson, E. (2008). *The social animal* (10th ed.). New York: Worth.

Aronson, E., Wilson, T. D., & Akert, R. M. (2007). *Social psychology* (6th ed.). Englewood Cliffs, NJ: Prentice Hall.

Arthur, W., & Doverspike, D. (2001). Predicting motor vehicle crash involvement from a personality measure and a driving knowledge test. *Journal of Prevention & Intervention in the Community, 22*(1), 35–42.

Artz, S. (2005). To die for: Violent adolescent girls' search for male attention. In D. J. Pepler, K. C. Madsen, et al. (Eds.), *The development and treatment of girlhood aggression.* Mahwah, NJ: Erlbaum.

Ary, D. V., Duncan, T. E., Biglan, A., Metzler, C. W., et al. (1999). Development of adolescent problem behavior. *Journal of Abnormal Child Psychology, 27*(2), 141–150.

Asch, S. E. (1956). Studies of independence and conformity: A minority of one against a unanimous majority. *Psychological Monographs, 70*(416).

Ash, D. W., & Holding, D. H. (1990). Backward versus forward chaining in the acquisition of a keyboard skill. *Human Factors, 32*(2), 139–146.

Ashby, F. G., & Maddox, W. T. (2005). Human category learning. *Annual Review of Psychology, 56,* 149–278.

Ashton, M. C. (2007). *Individual differences and personality.* San Diego: Elsevier.

Asmundson, G. J. G., & Taylor, S. (2005). *It's not all in your head.* London: Psychology Press.

Assanand, S., Pinel, J. P. J., & Lehman, D. R. (1998). Personal theories of hunger and eating. *Journal of Applied Social Psychology, 28*(11), 998–1015.

Athenasiou, R., Shaver, P., & Tavris, C. (1970). Sex. *Psychology Today, 4*(2), 37–52.

Atkin, D. J., & Lau, T. Y. (2007). Information technology and organizational telework. In C. A. Lin, & D. J Atkin (Eds.), *Communication technology and social change: Theory and implications.* Mahwah, NJ: Erlbaum.

Atkinson, R. C. & Schiffrin, R. M. (1968). Human memory: A proposed system and its control processes. In K. W. Spence, & J. T. Spence (Eds.), *The psychology of learning and motivation* (Vol. 2). London: Academic Press.

Atwood, J. D. (2006). Mommy's little angel, daddy's little girl: Do you know what your pre-teens are doing? *American Journal of Family Therapy, 34*(5), 447–467.

Aucoin, K. J., Frick, P. J., & Bodin, S. D. (2006). Corporal punishment and child adjustment. *Journal of Applied Developmental Psychology, 27*(6), 527–541.

Ausubel, D. P. (1978). In defense of advance organizers: A reply to the critics. *Review of Educational Research, 48,* 251–257.

Avery, D. H., Eder, D. N., Bolte, M. A., Hellekson, C. J., et al. (2001). Dawn simulation and bright light in the treatment of SAD. *Biological Psychiatry, 50*(3), 205–216.

Awadallah, N., Vaughan, A., Franco, K., Munir, F., et al. (2005). Munchausen by proxy: A case, chart series, and literature review of older victims. *Child Abuse & Neglect, 29*(8), 931–941.

Ayers, L., Beaton, S., & Hunt, H. (1999). The significance of transpersonal experiences, emotional conflict, and cognitive abilities in creativity. *Empirical Studies of the Arts, 17*(1), 73–82.

Ayllon, T. (1963). Intensive treatment of psychotic behavior by stimulus satiation and food reinforcement. *Behavior Research & Therapy, 1,* 53–61.

Ayllon, T., & Azrin, N. H. (1965). The measurement and reinforcement of behavior of psychotics. *Journal of the Experimental Analysis of Behavior, 8,* 357–383.

Baard, P. P., Deci, E. L., & Ryan, R. M. (2004). Intrinsic need satisfaction: A motivational basis of performance and well-being in two work settings. *Journal of Applied Social Psychology, 34*(10), 2045–2068.

Bachman, J. G., & Johnson, L. D. (1979). The freshmen. *Psychology Today, 13,* 78–87.

Baddeley, A. D. (2003). Working memory: Looking back and looking forward. *Nature Reviews Neuroscience, 4*(10), 829–839.

Baer, J. M. (1993). *Creativity and divergent thinking.* Hillsdale, NJ: Erlbaum.

Bailey, C. H., & Kandel, E. R. (2004). Synaptic growth and the persistence of long-term memory: A molecular perspective. In M. S. Gazzaniga (Ed.), *The cognitive neurosciences* (3rd ed.). Cambridge, MA: MIT Press.

Bailey, L. M., & McKeever, W. F. (2004). A large-scale study of handedness and pregnancy/birth risk events: Implications for genetic theories of handedness. *Laterality: Asymmetries of Body, Brain & Cognition, 9*(2), 175–188.

Bailis, D. S. (2001). Benefits of self-handicapping in sport. *Canadian Journal of Behavioural Science, 33*(4), 213–223.

Baillargeon, R. (1991). Reasoning about the height and location of a hidden object in 4.5- and 6.5-month-old infants. *Cognition, 38*(1), 13–42.

Baillargeon, R. (2004). Infants' reasoning about hidden objects: Evidence for event-general and event-specific expectations. *Developmental Science. 7*(4), 391–424.

Baillargeon, R., De Vos, J., & Graber, M. (1989). Location memory in 8-month-old infants in a non-search AB task. *Cognitive Development, 4,* 345–367.

Bain, S. K., & Allin, J. D. (2005). Stanford-Binet Intelligence Scales, Fifth Edition. *Journal of Psychoeducational Assessment, 23*(1), 87–95.

Bajracharya, S. M., Sarvela, P. D., & Isberner, F. R. (1995). A retrospective study of first sexual intercourse experiences among undergraduates. *Journal of American College Health, 43*(4), 169–177.

Baker, T. B., Brandon, T. H., & Chassin, L. (2004). Motivational influences on cigarette smoking. *Annual Review of Psychology, 55,* 463–491.

Bakich, I. (1995). Hypnosis in the treatment of sexual desire disorders. *Australian Journal of Clinical & Experimental Hypnosis, 23*(1), 70–77.

Baldo, O., & Eardley, I. (2005). Diagnosis and investigation of men with erectile dysfunction. *Journal of Men's Health & Gender, 2*(1), 79–86.

Balk, D. E., Lampe, S., Sharpe, B., Schwinn, S., et al. (1998). TAT results in a longitudinal study of bereaved college students. *Death Studies, 22*(1), 3–21.

Balsam, K. F., & Mohr, J. J. (2007). Adaptation to sexual orientation stigma: A comparison of bisexual and lesbian/gay adults. *Journal of Counseling Psychology, 54*(3), 306–319.

Baltes, B. B., Briggs, T. E., Huff, J. W., Wright, J. A., et al. (1999). Flexible and compressed workweek schedules. *Journal of Applied Psychology, 84*(4), 496–513.

Bandura, A. (1971). *Social learning theory.* New York: General Learning Press.

Bandura, A. (2001). Social cognitive theory. *Annual Review of Psychology, 52,* 1–26.

Bandura, A., & Walters, R. (1959). *Adolescent aggression.* New York: Ronald.

Bandura, A., Blanchard, E. B., & Ritter, B. (1969). Relative efficacy of desensitization and modeling approaches for inducing behavioral, affective, and attitudinal changes. *Journal of Personality & Social Psychology, 13*(3), 173–199.

Bandura, A., Ross, D., & Ross, S. A. (1963). Vicarious reinforcement and imitative learning. *Journal of Abnormal and Social Psychology, 67,* 601–607.

Banich, M. T. (2004). *Cognitive neuroscience and neuropsychology* (2nd ed.). Boston: Houghton Mifflin.

Bank, B. J., & Hansford, S. L. (2000). Gender and friendship: Why are men's best same-sex friendships less intimate and supportive? *Personal Relationships, 7*(1), 63–78.

Banks, A., & Gartrell, N. K. (1995). Hormones and sexual orientation: A questionable link. *Journal of Homosexuality, 28*(3–4), 247–268.

Barabasz, A. (2000). EEG markers of alert hypnosis. *Sleep & Hypnosis, 2*(4), 164–169.

Barber, T. X. (2000). A deeper understanding of hypnosis: Its secrets, its nature, its essence. *American Journal of Clinical Hypnosis, 42*(3–4), 208–272.

Bard, C., Fleury, M., & Goulet, C. (1994). Relationship between perceptual strategies and response adequacy in sport situations. *International Journal of Sport Psychology, 25*(3), 266–281.

Bargh, J. A., McKenna, K. Y. A., & Fitzsimons, G. M. (2002). Can you see the real me? Activation and expression of the "true self" on the Internet. *Journal of Social Issues, 58*(1), 33–48.

Barkataki, I., Kumari, V., Das, M., Taylor, P., et al. (2006). Volumetric structural brain abnormalities in men with schizophrenia or antisocial personality disorder. *Behavioural Brain Research, 169*(2), 239–247.

Barlow, D. H. (2000). Unraveling the mysteries of anxiety and its disorders from the perspective of emotion theory. *American Psychologist, 55,* 1247–1263.

Barlow, D. H. (2002). *Anxiety and its disorders* (2nd ed.). New York: Guilford.

Barlow, D. H. (2004). Psychological treatments. *American Psychologist, 59*(9), 869–878.

Barnett, J., Behnke, S. H., Rosenthal, S., & Koocher, G. (2007). In case of ethical dilemma, break glass: Commentary on ethical decision making in practice. *Professional Psychology: Research & Practice, 38*(1), 7–12.

Barnier, A. J., McConkey, K. M., & Wright, J. (2004). Posthypnotic amnesia for autobiographical episodes: Influencing memory accessibility and quality. *International Journal of Clinical and Experimental Hypnosis, 52*(3), 260–279.

Baron, R. A., Byrne, D., & Branscombe, N. R. (2007). *Mastering social psychology.* Boston: Pearson/Allyn and Bacon.

Baron, R. S. (2005). So right it's wrong: Groupthink and the ubiquitous nature of polarized group decision making. In M. P. Zanna, (Ed.), *Advances in experimental social psychology* (Vol. 37). San Diego: Elsevier.

Baron, R. S. (2005). So right it's wrong: Groupthink and the ubiquitous nature of polarized group decision making. In M. P. Zanna, (Ed.), *Advances in experimental social psychology* (Vol. 37). San Diego: Elsevier.

Barrett, D. (1993). The "committee of sleep": A study of dream incubation for problem solving. *Dreaming, 3*(2), 115–122.

Barrett, D., Greenwood, J. G., & McCullagh, J. F. (2006). Kissing laterality and handedness. *Laterality: Asymmetries of Body, Brain & Cognition, 11*(6), 573–579.

Barrick, M. R., Moun, M. K., & Judge, T. A. (2001). Personality and performance at the beginning of the new millennium. *International Journal of Selection & Assessment, 9*(1–2), 9–30.

Barron, F. (1958). The psychology of imagination. *Scientific American, 199*(3), 150–170.

Barrowcliff, A. L., & Haddock, G. (2006). The relationship between command hallucinations and factors of compliance: A critical review of the literature. *Journal of Forensic Psychiatry & Psychology, 17*(2), 266–298.

Bar-Tal, D., & Labin, D. (2001). The effect of a major event on stereotyping: Terrorist attacks in Israel and Israeli adolescents' perceptions of Palestinians, Jordanians and Arabs. *European Journal of Social Psychology, 31*(3), 265–280.

Bartholow, B. D., & Anderson, C. A. (2002). Effects of violent video games on aggressive behavior. *Journal of Experimental Social Psychology, 38*(3), 283–290.

Bartholow, B. D., Bushman, B. J., & Sestir, M. A. (2006). Chronic violent video game exposure and desensitization to violence: Behavioral and event-related brain potential data. *Journal of Experimental Social Psychology, 42*(4), 532–539.

Bartholow, B. D., Sestir, M. A., & Davis, E. B. (2005). Correlates and consequences of exposure to video game violence: Hostile personality, empathy, and aggressive behavior. *Personality and Social Psychology Bulletin, 31*(11), 1573–1586.

Bartoshuk, L. M. (2000). Psychophysical advances aid the study of genetic variation in taste. *Appetite, 34*(1), 105.

Bartoshuk, L. M., Duffy, V. B., Green, B. G., Hoffman, H. J., et al. (2004). Valid across-group comparisons with labeled scales: The gLMS versus magnitude matching. *Physiology & Behavior, 82*(1), 109–114.

Bartram, B. (2006). An examination of perceptions of parental influence on attitudes to language learning. *Educational Research, 48*(2), 211–222.

Basson, R., Brotto, L. A., Laan, E., Redmond, G., et al. (2005). Assessment and management of women's sexual dysfunctions: Problematic desire and arousal. *Journal of Sexual Medicine, 2*(3), 291–300.

Bastian, B., & Haslam, N. (2006). Psychological essentialism and stereotype endorsement. *Journal of Experimental Social Psychology, 42*(2), 228–235.

Bath, H. (1996). Everyday discipline or control with care. *Journal of Child & Youth Care, 10*(2), 23–32.

Batson, C. D. (2006). "Not all self-interest after all": Economics of empathy-induced altruism. In D. De Cremer, M. Zeelenberg, et al. (Eds.), *Social psychology and economics.* Mahwah, NJ: Erlbaum.

Batson, C. D., & Powell, A. A. (2003). Altruism and prosocial behavior. In T. Millon, & M. J. Lerner (Eds.), *Handbook of psychology: Personality and social psychology* (Vol. 5). New York: Wiley.

Batterham, R. L., Cohen, M. A., Ellis, S. M., Le Roux, C. E., et al. (2003). Inhibition of food intake in obese subjects by peptide YY3–36. *New England Journal of Medicine, 349*(Sept. 4), 941–948.

Bauer, J. J., McAdams, D. P., & Pals, J. L. (2008). Narrative identity and eudaimonic well-being. *Journal of Happiness Studies, 9*(1), 81–104.

Baum, A., & Davis, G. E. (1980). Reducing the stress of high-density living: An architectural intervention. *Journal of Personality & Social Psychology, 38,* 471–481.

Baum, A., & Posluszny, D. M. (1999). Health psychology. *Annual Review of Psychology, 50,* 137–163.

Baum, A., & Valins, S. (1979). Architectural mediation of residential density and control: Crowding and the regulation of social contact. *Advances in Experimental & Social Psychology, 12,* 131–175.

Baum, A., & Valins, S. (Eds.). (1977). *Human response to crowding: Studies of the effects of residential group size.* Mahwah, NJ: Erlbaum.

Bauman, L. J., Karasz, A., & Hamilton, A. (2007). Understanding failure of condom use intention among adolescents: Completing an intensive preventive intervention. *Journal of Adolescent Research, 22*(3), 248–274.

Baumeister, R. F., & Bushman, B. (2008). *Social psychology and human nature.* Belmont, CA: Cengage Learning/Wadsworth.

Baumeister, R. F., Campbell, J. D., Krueger, J. I., & Vohs, K. D. (2003). Does high self-esteem cause better performance, interpersonal success, happiness, or healthier lifestyles? *Psychological Science in the Public Interest, 4*(1), 1–44.

Baumrind, D. (1991). The influence of parenting style on adolescent competence and substance use. *Journal of Early Adolescence, 11*(1), 56–95.

Baumrind, D. (2005). Patterns of parental authority and adolescent autonomy. In J. Smetana (Ed.), *New directions for child development: Changes in parental authority during adolescence.* San Francisco: Jossey-Bass.

Baumrind, D., Larzelere, R. E., & Cowan, P. A. (2002). Ordinary physical punishment: Is it harmful? *Psychological Bulletin, 128*(4), 580–589.

Bearman, P. S., Moody, J., & Stovel, K. (2004). Chains of affection: The structure of adolescent romantic and sexual networks. *American Journal of Sociology, 110*(1), 44–91.

Beauchamp, P. H., Halliwell, W. R., Fournier, J. F., & Koestner, R. (1996). Effects of cognitive-behavioral psychological skills training on the motivation, preparation, and putting performance of novice golfers. *Sport Psychologist, 10*(2), 157–170.

Beaulieu, C. M. J. (2004). Intercultural study of personal space: A case study. *Journal of Applied Social Psychology, 34*(4), 794–805.

Beck, A. T. (1991). Cognitive therapy. *American Psychologist, 46*(4), 368–375.

Beck, A. T. (2004). Cognitive patterns in dreams and daydreams. In R. I. Rosner,

& W. J. Lyddon (Eds.), *Cognitive therapy and dreams.* New York: Springer Publishing.

Beck, A. T., & Greenberg, R. L. (1974). *Coping with depression.* New York: Institute For Rational Living.

Beck, A. T., Brown, C., Berchick, R. J., Stewart, B. L., et al. (1990). Relationship between hopelessness and ultimate suicide. *American Journal of Psychiatry, 147*(2), 190–195.

Beck, B. L., Koons, S. R., & Milgrim, D. L. (2000). Correlates and consequences of behavioral procrastination. *Journal of Social Behavior & Personality, 15*(5), 3–13.

Beck, J. S. (2002). Beck therapy approach. In M. Hersen, & W. H. Sledge (Eds.), *Encyclopedia of psychotherapy.* San Diego: Academic Press.

Beck, R. C. (2004). *Motivation: Theories and principles* (5th ed.). Englewood Cliffs, NJ: Prentice Hall.

Becker, S. W., & Eagly, A. H. (2004). The heroism of women and men. *American Psychologist, 59*(3), 163–178.

Beebe, B., Gerstman, L., Carson, B., Dolins, M., et al. (1982). Rhythmic communication in the mother–infant dyad. In M. Davis (Ed.), *Interaction rhythms, periodicity in communicative behavior.* New York: Human Sciences Press.

Beeber, L. S., Chazan-Cohen, R., Squires, J., Harden, B. J., et al. (2007). The Early Promotion and Intervention Research Consortium (E-PIRC): Five approaches to improving infant/toddler mental health in Early Head Start. *Infant Mental Health Journal, 28*(2), 130–150.

Beeman, M. J., & Chiarello, C. (1998). Complementary right- and left-hemisphere language comprehension. *Current Directions in Psychological Science, 7*(1), 2–8.

Beersma, D. G. M., & Gordijn, M. C. M. (2007). Circadian control of the sleep-wake cycle. *Physiology & Behavior, 90*(2–3), 190–195.

Behrend, D. A., Beike, D. R., & Lampinen, J. M. (2004). *The self and memory.* Hove, UK: Psychology Press.

Beirne-Smith, M., Patton, J., & Shannon, K. (2006). *Mental retardation: An introduction to intellectual disability* (7th ed.). Englewood Cliffs, NJ: Prentice Hall.

Belenky, G., Wesensten, N. J., Thorne, D. R., Thomas, M. L., et al. (2003). Patterns of performance degradation and restoration during sleep restriction and subsequent recovery: A sleep dose-response study. *Journal of Sleep Research, 12*(1), 1–12.

Beljan, J. R., Rosenblatt, L. S., Hetherington, N. W., Layman, J., et al. (1972). *Human performance in the aviation environment.* NASA Contract no 2-6657, Pt. Ia, 253–259.

Bell, P. A., Greene, T., Fisher, J., & Baum, A. S. (1996). *Environmental psychology* (5th ed.). Mahwah, NJ: Erlbaum.

Bellezza, F. S., Six, L. S., & Phillips, D. S. (1992). A mnemonic for remembering long strings of digits. *Bulletin of the Psychonomic Society, 30*(4), 271–274.

Belsky, J. (1996). Parent, infant, and social-contextual antecedents of father-son attachment security. *Developmental Psychology, 32*(5), 905–913.

Bem, S. L. (1974). The measurement of psychological androgyny. *Journal of Consulting & Clinical Psychology, 42*(2), 155–162.

Bem, S. L. (1975). Androgyny vs. the tight little lives of fluffy women and chesty men. *Psychology Today*, Sept., 58–62.

Bem, S. L. (1981). Gender schema theory. A cognitive account of sex typing. *Psychological Review, 88,* 354–364.

Benbow, C. P. (1986). Physiological correlates of extreme intellectual precocity. *Neuropsychologia, 24*(5), 719–725.

Benjafield, J. G. (2004). *A history of psychology* (2nd ed.). Boston: Allyn & Bacon.

Benloucif, S., Bennett, E. L., & Rosenzweig, M. R. (1995). Norepinephrine and neural plasticity: The effects of xylamine on experience-induced changes in brain weight, memory, and behavior. *Neurobiology of Learning & Memory, 63*(1), 33–42.

Bensafi, M., Zelano, C., Johnson, B., Mainland, J., Khan, R., et al. (2004). Olfaction: From sniff to percept. In M. S. Gazzaniga (Ed.), *The cognitive neurosciences* (3rd ed.). Cambridge, MA: MIT Press.

Ben-Shakhar, G., & Dolev, K. (1996). Psychophysiological detection through the guilty knowledge technique: Effect of mental countermeasures. *Journal of Applied Psychology, 81*(3), 273–281.

Bensley, L., & Van Eenwyk, J. (2001). Video games and real-life aggression. *Journal of Adolescent Health, 29*(4), 244–257.

Benson, E. (2002). Pheromones, in context. *Monitor on Psychology*, Oct., 46–48.

Benson, H. (1977). Systematic hypertension and the relaxation response. *The New England Journal of Medicine, 296,* 1152–1156.

Benson, J., Greaves, W., O'Donnell, M., & Taglialatela, J. (2002). Evidence for symbolic language processing in a Bonobo (Pan paniscus). *Journal of Consciousness Studies, 9*(12), 33–56.

Bergeron, S., & Lord, M. J. (2003). The integration of pelvi-perineal reeducation and cognitive-behavioral therapy in the multidisciplinary treatment of the sexual pain disorders. *Sexual & Relationship Therapy, 18,* 135–141.

Bergin, A.E. (1991). Values and religious issues in psychotherapy and mental health. *American Psychologist, 46*(4), 394-403

Berman, S. L., Weems, C. F., & Stickle, T. R. (2006). Existential anxiety in adolescents: Prevalence, structure, association with psychological symptoms and identity development. *Journal of Youth & Adolescence, 35*(3), 303–310.

Bernat, J. A., Calhoun, K. S., & Stolp, S. (1998). Sexually aggressive men's responses to a date rape analogue. *Journal of Sex Research, 35*(4), 41–348.

Berne, E. (1964). *Games people play.* New York: Grove.

Bernstein H. J., Beale M. D., Burns C., & Kellner C. H. (1998). Patient attitudes about ECT after treatment. *Psychiatric Annals, 28*(9), 524–527.

Bernthal, M. J. (2003) The effects of professional wrestling viewership on children. *The Sport Journal, 6*(3). Retrieved June 6, 2007, from http://www.thesportjournal.org/2003Journal/Vol6-No3/wrestling.htm.

Berntsen, D., & Thomsen, D. K. (2005). Personal memories for remote historical events: Accuracy and clarity of flashbulb memories related to World War II. *Journal of Experimental Psychology: General, 134*(2), 242–257.

Berry, D. S., & Miller, K. M. (2001). When boy meets girl: Attractiveness and the five-factor model in opposite-sex interactions. *Journal of Research in Personality, 35*(1), 62–77.

Berry, J. W. (1990). The psychology of acculturation. In R. A. Dienstbier, & J. J. Berman (Eds.), *Nebraska Symposium on Motivation 1989: Cross-cultural perspectives, 37.* Lincoln: University of Nebraska Press.

Berry, J. W., Phinney, J. S, Sam, D. L., & Vedder, P. (2005). *Immigrant youth in cultural transition.* Mahwah, NJ: Erlbaum.

Berscheid, E. (2000). Attraction. In A. Kazdin (Ed.), *Encyclopedia of psychology.* Washington, DC: American Psychological Association.

Berscheid, E., & Regan, P. (2005). *The psychology of interpersonal relationships.* Englewood Cliffs, NJ: Prentice Hall.

Bersoff, D. M. (1999). Why good people sometimes do bad things: Motivated reasoning and unethical behavior. *Personality & Social Psychology Bulletin, 25*(1), 28–39.

Bertenthal, B. I., & Longo, M. R. (2007). Is there evidence of a mirror system from birth? *Developmental Science, 10*(5), 526–529.

Bertsch, G. J. (1976). Punishment of consummatory and instrumental behavior: A review. *Psychological Record, 26,* 13–31.

Besnard, D., & Cacitti, L. (2005). Interface changes causing accidents: An empirical study of negative transfer. *International Journal of Human-Computer Studies, 62*(1), 105–125.

Best, D. (2002). Cross-cultural gender roles. In J. Worell (Ed.), *Encyclopedia of women and gender.* New York: Oxford.

Betancur, C., Velez, A., Cabanieu, G., le Moal, M., et al. (1990). Association between left-handedness and allergy: A reappraisal. *Neuropsychologia, 28*(2), 223–227.

Beyer, M., Gerlach, F. M., Flies, U., Grol, R., et al. (2003). The development of quality circles/peer review groups as a tool for quality improvement in Europe: Results of a survey in 26 European countries. *Family Practice, 20,* 443–451.

Bhushan, B., & Khan, S. M. (2006). Laterality and accident proneness: A study of locomotive drivers. *Laterality: Asymmetries of Body, Brain & Cognition, 11*(5), 395–404.

Bialystok, E. (2001). *Bilingualism in development: Language, literacy, and cognition.* New York: Cambridge.

Binder, J. L. (2004). *Key competencies in brief dynamic psychotherapy: Clinical practice beyond the manual.* New York: Guilford.

Binik, Y. M. (2005). Should dyspareunia be retained as a sexual dysfunction in DSM-V? A painful classification decision. *Archives of Sexual Behavior, 34*(1), 11–21.

Birch, J., & McKeever, L. M. (1993). Survey of the accuracy of new pseudoisochromatic plates. *Ophthalmic & Physiological Optics, 13*(1), 35–40.

Birnbaum, M. H. (2004). Human research and data collection via the Internet. *Annual Review of Psychology, 55,* 803–832.

Bisson, J. I., Ehlers, A., Matthews, R., Pilling, S., et al. (2007). Psychological treatments for chronic post-traumatic stress disorder: Systematic review and meta-analysis. *British Journal of Psychiatry, 190*(2), 97–104.

Blackmore, S. (2001). What can the paranormal teach us about consciousness? *Skeptical Inquirer, 25,* 22–27.

Blackmore, S. (2004). *Consciousness: An introduction.* New York: Oxford University Press.

Blackwell, D. L., & Lichter, D. T. (2004). Homogamy among dating, cohabiting, and married couples. *Sociological Quarterly, 45*(4), 719–737.

Blair, I. V. (2001). Implicit stereotypes and prejudice. In G. B. Moscowitz (Ed.), *Cognitive social psychology.* Mahwah, NJ: Erlbaum.

Blair, K. S., Richell, R. A., Mitchell, D. G. V., Leonard, A., et al. (2006). They know the words, but not the music: Affective and semantic priming in individuals with psychopathy. *Biological Psychology, 73*(2), 114–123.

Blakemore, C., & Cooper, G. (1970). Development of the brain depends on the visual environment. *Nature, 228,* 477–478.

Blanchard, D. C., & Blanchard, R. J. (2003). What can animal aggression research tell us about human aggression? *Hormones & Behavior, 44*(3), 171–177.

Blanchard, E. B., Kuhn, E., Rowell, D. L., Hickling, E. J., et al. (2004). Studies of the vicarious traumatization of college students by the September llth attacks: Effects of proximity, exposure and connectedness. *Behaviour Research & Therapy, 42*(2), 191–205.

Blatner, A. (2006). Current trends in psychodrama. *International Journal of Psychotherapy, 10*(3), 43–53.

Bloch, M., Daly, R. C., Rubinow, D. R. (2003). Endocrine factors in the etiology of postpartum depression. *Comprehensive Psychiatry, 44*(3), 234–246.

Bloch, S. (2006). *Introduction to the psychotherapies* (4th ed.). New York: Oxford University Press.

Blood, A. J., & Zatorre, R. J. (2001). Intensely pleasurable responses to music correlate with activity in brain regions implicated in reward and emotion. *Proceedings National Academy of Sciences, 98*(20) 11818–11823.

Bloom, B. (1985). *Developing talent in young people.* New York: Ballantine.

Bloom, C. M., & Lamkin, D. M. (2006). The Olympian struggle to remember the cranial nerves: Mnemonics and student success. *Teaching of Psychology, 33*(2), 128–129.

Bloom, J. W. (1998). The ethical practice of WebCounseling. *British Journal of Guidance & Counselling, 26*(1), 53–59.

Blunt, A., & Pychyl, T. A. (2005). Project systems of procrastinators: A personal project-analytic and action control perspective. *Personality & Individual Differences, 38*(8), 1771–1780.

Bockting, W. O., & Coleman, E. (Eds.). (2003). *Masturbation as a means of achieving sexual health.* New York: Haworth Press.

Boergers, J., Spirito, A., & Donaldson, D. (1998). Reasons for adolescent suicide attempts. *Journal of the American Academy of Child & Adolescent Psychiatry, 37*(12), 1287–1293.

Bohannon, J. N., & Stanowicz, L. B. (1988). The issue of negative evidence: Adult responses to children's language errors. *Developmental Psychology, 24*(5), 684–689.

Boivin, D. B., Czeisler, C. A., & Waterhouse, J. W. (1997). Complex interaction of the sleep-wake cycle and circadian phase modulates mood in healthy subjects. *Archives of General Psychiatry, 54*(2), 145–152.

Boldero, J. M., Moretti, M. M., Bell, R. C., & Francis, J. J. (2005). Self-discrepancies and negative affect: A primer on when to look for specificity, and how to find it. *Australian Journal of Psychology, 57*(3), 139–147.

Bonanno, G. A., Papa, A., Lalande, K., Westphal, M., et al. (2004). The importance of being flexible. *Psychological Science, 15*(7), 482–487.

Bond, R., & Smith, P. B. (1996). Culture and conformity: A meta-analysis of studies using Asch's (1952, 1956) line judgment task. *Psychological Bulletin, 119*(1), 111–137.

Bond, T., & Wooten, V. (1996). The etiology and management of insomnia. *Virginia Medical Quarterly, 123*(4), 394–255.

Bongard, S., al'Absi, M., & Lovallo, W. R. (1998). Interactive effects of trait hostility and anger expression on cardiovascular reactivity in young men. *International Journal of Psychophysiology, 28*(2), 181–191.

Bonham, V., Warshauer-Baker, E., & Collins, F. S. (2005). Race and ethnicity in the genome era: The complexity of the constructs. *American Psychologist, 60*(1), 9–15.

Boniecki, K. A., & Britt, T. W. (2003). Prejudice and the peacekeeper. In T. W. Britt, & A. B Adler (Eds.), *The psychology of the peacekeeper: Lessons from the field.* Westport, CT: Praeger.

Bood, S., Sundequist, U., Kjellgren, A., Norlander, T., et al. (2006). Eliciting the relaxation response with the help of flotation-REST (Restricted Environmental Stimulation Technique) in patients with stress-related ailments. *International Journal of Stress Management, 13*(2), 154–175.

Booker, J. M., & Hellekson, C. J. (1992). Prevalence of seasonal affective disorder in Alaska. *American Journal of Psychiatry, 149*(9), 1176–1182.

Bootzin, R. R., & Epstein, D. R. (2000). Stimulus control. In K. L. Lichstein, & C. M. Morin. *Treatment of late life insomnia.* Thousand Oaks, CA: Sage.

Borlongan, C. V., Sanberg, P. R., Freeman, T. B. (1999). Neural transplantation for neurodegenerative disorders. *Lancet, 353*(Suppl 1), S29–30.

Borman, W. C., Hanson, M. A., & Hedge, J. W. (1997). Personnel psychology. *Annual Review of Psychology, 48,* 299–337.

Bornstein, M. H., & Tamis-LeMonda, C. S. (2001). Mother-infant interaction. In A. Fogel, & G. Bremmer (Eds.), *Blackwell handbook of infant development.* London: Blackwell.

Bornstein, R. F. (1996). Sex differences in dependent personality disorder prevalence rates. *Clinical Psychology: Science & Practice, 3*(1), 1–12.

Borod, J. C., Bloom, R. L., Brickman, A. M., Nakhutina, L., et al. (2002). Emotional processing deficits in individuals with unilateral brain damage. *Applied Neuropsychology, 9*(1), 23–36.

Botes, A. (2000). A comparison between the ethics of justice and the ethics of care. *Journal of Advanced Nursing, 32*(5), 1071–1075.

Bouchard, Jr., T. J. (1983). Twins—Nature's twice-told tale. *Yearbook of science and the future,* 66–81. Chicago: Encyclopedia Britannica.

Bouchard, Jr., T. J. (2004). Genetic influence on human psychological traits: A survey. *Current Directions in Psychological Science, 13*(4), 148–151.

Bouchard, Jr., T. J., Lykken, D. T., McGue, M., Segal, N. L., et al. (1990). Sources of human psychological differences: The Minnesota study of twins reared apart. *Science, 250,* 223–228.

Bourne, E. J. (2005). *The anxiety & phobia workbook* (4th ed.). Oakland, CA: New Harbinger.

Bovbjerg, D. H., Redd, W. H., Jacobsen, P. B., Manne, S. L., et al. (1992). An experimental analysis of classically conditioned nausea during cancer chemotherapy. *Psychosomatic Medicine, 54*(6), 623–637.

Bowe, F. (2000). *Universal Design in education: Teaching nontraditional students.* Westport, CT: Bergin & Garvey.

Bower, G. H. (1973). How to…uh…remember. *Psychology Today,* 63–70.

Bower, G. H. (1981). Mood and memory. *American Psychologist, 36,* 129–148.

Bower, G. H., & Springston, F. (1970). Pauses as recoding points in letter series. *Journal of Experimental Psychology, 83,* 421–430.

Bowker, A. (2006). The relationship between sports participation and self-esteem during early adolescence. *Canadian Journal of Behavioural Science, 38*(3), 214–229.

Boyle, S. H., Williams, R. B., Mark, D., Brummett, B. H., et al. (2004). Hostility as a predictor of survival in patients with coronary artery disease. *Psychosomatic Medicine, 66*(5), 629–632.

Brach, T. (2003). *Radical acceptance.* New York: Bantam Books

Bradley, R. H., & Corwyn, R. F. (2002). Socioeconomic status and child development. *Annual Review of Psychology, 53,* 377–399.

Bradley, R., Greene, J., Russ, E., Dutra, L., et al. (2005). A multidimensional meta-analysis of psychotherapy for PTSD. *American Journal of Psychiatry, 162*(2), 214–227.

Bradshaw, S. D. (2006). Shyness and difficult relationships: Formation is just the beginning. In D. C. Kirkpatrick, D. S. Duck, et al. (Eds.), *Relating difficulty: The processes of constructing and managing difficult interaction.* Mahwah, NJ: Erlbaum.

Brainerd, C. J. (2003). Jean Piaget, learning research, and American education. In B. J. Zimmerman, & D. H. Schunk (Eds.), *Educational psychology: A century of contributions.* Mahwah, NJ: Erlbaum.

Bramerson, A., Johansson, L., Ek, L., et al. (2004). Prevalence of olfactory dysfunction: The Skovde population-based study. *Laryngoscope, 114*(4), 733–737.

Brannon, L. (1996). *Gender.* Boston: Allyn & Bacon.

Brannon, L., & Feist, J. (2007). *Health psychology: An introduction to behavior and health* (6th ed.). Belmont, CA: Cengage Learning/Wadsworth.

Bransford, J. D., & McCarrell, N. S. (1977). A sketch of cognitive approach to comprehension: Some thoughts about understanding what it means to comprehend. In P. N. Johnson-Laird, & P. C. Wason (Eds.), *Thinking: Readings in cognitive science.* Cambridge, UK: Cambridge University Press.

Bratter, T. E. (2007). The myth of ADHD and the scandal of Ritalin: Helping John Dewey students succeed in medicine-free college preparatory and therapeutic high school. *International Journal of Reality Therapy, 27*(1), 4–13.

Braun, A. R., Balkin, T. J., & Herscovitch, P. (1998). Dissociated pattern of activity in visual cortices and their projections during human rapid eye movement sleep. *Science, 279*(5347), 91–95.

Braun, K. A., Ellis, R., & Loftus, E. F. (2002). Make my memory: How advertising can change memories of the past. *Psychology and Marketing, 19,* 1–23.

Braun, S. (2001). Seeking insight by prescription. *Cerebrum, 3*(2), 10–21.

Braun-LaTour, K. A., & LaTour, M. S. (2004). Assessing the long-term impact of a consistent advertising campaign on consumer memory. *Journal of Advertising, 33*(2), 49–61.

Breckler, S. J., Olson, J., & Wiggins, E. (2006). *Social psychology alive.* Belmont, CA: Cengage Learning/Wadsworth.

Breedlove, S. M., Cooke, B. M., & Jordan, C. L. (1999). The orthodox view of brain sexual differentiation. *Brain, Behavior & Evolution, 54*(1), 8–14.

Brehm, S. S., Kassin, S. M., & Fein, S. (2005). *Social psychology* (6th ed.). Boston: Houghton Mifflin.

Brennan, F. X., Beck, K. D., & Servatius, R. J. (2003). Lever press escape/avoidance conditioning in rats: Safety signal length and avoidance performance. *Integrative Physiological & Behavioral Science, 38*(1), 36–44.

Breslau, N., Johnson, E. O., Hiripi, E., & Kessler, R. (2001). Nicotine dependence in the United States. *Archives of General Psychiatry, 58*(9), 810–816.

Bressan, P., & Pizzighello, S. (2008). The attentional cost of inattentional blindness. *Cognition, 106*(1), 370–383.

Bressi, C., Albonetti, S., & Razzoli, E. (1998). "Communication deviance" and schizophrenia. *New Trends in Experimental & Clinical Psychiatry, 14*(1), 33–39.

Bretherton, R., & Orner, R. J. (2004). Positive psychology and psychotherapy: An existential approach. In P. A. Linley, & S. Joseph (Eds.), *Positive psychology in practice.* New York: Wiley.

Brewer, J. S. (1981). Duration of intromission and female orgasm rates. *Medical Aspects of Human Sexuality, 15*(4), 70–71.

Brewer, K. R., & Wann, D. L. (1998). Observational learning effectiveness as a function of model characteristics. *Social Behavior & Personality, 26*(1), 1–10.

Brewer, N., & Wells, G. L. (2006). The confidence-accuracy relationship in eyewitness identification: Effects of lineup instructions, foil similarity, and target-absent base rates. *Journal of Experimental Psychology: Applied, 12*(1), 11–30.

Brewer, N., & Williams, K. D. (Eds.). (2005). *Psychology and law: An empirical perspective.* New York: Guilford.

Bridges, K. M. B. (1932). Emotional development in early infancy. *Child Development, 3,* 324–334.

Bridges, L. J. (2003). Trust, attachment, and relatedness. In M. H. Bornstein, L. Davidson, et al. (Eds.), *Well-being: Positive development across the life course.* Mahwah, NJ: Erlbaum.

Brief, A. P., & Weiss, H. M. (2002). Organizational behavior. *Annual Review of Psychology, 53,* 279–307.

Brigham, J. C., & Wasserman, A. W. (1999). The impact of race, racial attitude, and gender on reactions to the criminal trial of O. J. Simpson. *Journal of Applied Social Psychology, 29*(7), 1333–1370.

Bringing up baby. (1999). *Sierra,* Jan–Feb, 17.

Brinton, R. D., & Wang, J. M. (2006). Therapeutic potential of neurogenesis for prevention and recovery from Alzheimer's disease: Allopregnanolone as a proof of concept neurogenic agent. *Current Alzheimer Research, 3*(3), 185–190.

Brisbois, T. D., Hutton, J. L., Baracos, V. E., et al. (2006). Taste and smell abnormalities as an independent cause of failure of food intake in patients with advanced cancer: An argument for the application of sensory science. *Journal of Palliative Care, 22*(2), 111–114.

Brock, T. C., & Green, M. C. (Eds.). (2005). *Persuasion: Psychological insights and perspectives* (2nd ed.). Thousand Oaks, CA: Sage.

Brodley, B. T. (2006). Non-directivity in client-centered therapy. *Person-Centered & Experiential Psychotherapies, 5*(1), 36–52.

Brooks-Gunn, J., & Warren, M. P. (1988). The psychological significance of secondary sexual characteristics in nine- to eleven-year-old girls. *Child Development, 59*(4), 1061–1069.

Brothen, T., & Wambach, C. (2001). Effective student use of computerized quizzes. *Teaching of Psychology, 28*(4), 292–294.

Brower, A. M. (2002). Are college students alcoholics? *Journal of American College Health, 50*(5), 253–255.

Brown, A. E., Jeffcott, Jr., H. A. (1970). *Absolutely mad inventions.* New York: Dover Publications.

Brown, A. S. (2004). *The déjà vu experience.* New York: Psychology Press.

Brown, A. S., Cohen, P., Harkavy-Friedman, J., Babulas, V., et al. (2001). Prenatal rubella, premorbid abnormalities, and adult schizophrenia. *Biological Psychiatry, 49*(6), 473–486.

Brown, B. B., & Bentley, D. L. (1993). Residential burglars judge risk. *Journal of Environmental Psychology, 13*(1), 51–61.

Brown, K. W., & Ryan, R. M. (2003). The benefits of being present. *Journal of Personality and Social Psychology, 84*(4), 822–848

Brown, L. M. (2005). *Girlfighting: Betrayal and rejection among girls.* New York: New York University Press.

Brown, P. (1990). The name game. *Journal of Mind and Behavior, 11,* 385–406.

Brown, R. L., Leonard, T., Saunders, L. A., & Papasouiotis, O. (1997). A two-item screening test for alcohol and other drug problems. *Journal of Family Practice, 44*(2), 151–160.

Brown, R., & Kulik, J. (1977). Flashbulb memories. *Cognition, 5,* 73–99.

Brown, R., & McNeill, D. (1966). The "tip of the tongue" phenomenon. *Journal of Verbal Learning and Verbal Behavior, 5,* 325–337.

Brown, S. A., Tapert, S. F., Granholm, E., & Delis, D. C. (2000). Neurocognitive functioning of adolescents: Effects of protracted alcohol use. *Alcoholism: Clinical & Experimental Research, 24*(2), 164–171.

Brown, S. G., Roy, E., Rohr, L., & Bryden, P. (2006). Using hand performance measures to predict handedness. *Laterality: Asymmetries of Body, Brain & Cognition, 11*(1), 1–14.

Brown, T. A., & Barlow, D. H. (2007). *Casebook in abnormal psychology* (3rd ed.). Belmont, CA: Cengage Learning/Wadsworth

Brown, T. D., Dane, F. C., & Durham, M. D. (1998). Perception of race and ethnicity. *Journal of Social Behavior & Personality, 13*(2), 295–306.

Browne, B. A. (1998). Gender stereotypes in advertising on children's television in the 1990s. *Journal of Advertising, 27*(1), 83–96.

Browne, N., & Keeley, S. (2007). *Asking the right questions: A guide to critical thinking* (8th ed.). Englewood Cliffs, NJ: Prentice Hall.

Brownell, K. D. (2003). *Food fight.* New York: McGraw-Hill.

Bruch, M. A. (2001). Shyness and social interaction. In R. Crozier, & L. Alden (Eds.), *International handbook of social anxiety.* Sussex, England: Wiley.

Bruer, J. T. (2001). A critical and sensitive period primer. In D. B. Bailey, Jr., J. T. Bruer, et al. (Eds.), *Critical thinking about critical periods.* Baltimore: Paul H. Brookes.

Bruner, J. (1973). *Going beyond the information given.* New York: Norton.

Bruner, J. (1983). *Child's talk.* New York: Norton.

Bryden, P. J., Bruyn, J., & Fletcher, P. (2005). Handedness and health: An examination of the association between different handedness classifications and health disorders. *Laterality: Asymme-*

tries of Body, Brain & Cognition, 10(5), 429–440.

Buchanan, M. (2008). Sin cities: The geometry of crime. *New Scientist, 2654* (April 30), 36–39.

Buchwald, A. (1965). Psyching out. *The Washington Post,* June 20.

Buckhout, R. (1974). Eyewitness testimony. *Scientific American, 231,* 23–31.

Buddie, A. M. (2004). Alternatives to twelvestep programs. *Journal of Forensic Psychology Practice, 4*(3), 61–70.

Budney, A. J., & Hughes, J. R. (2006). The cannabis withdrawal syndrome. *Current Opinion in Psychiatry, 19*(3), 233–238.

Buehner, M. J., & May, J. (2003). Rethinking temporal contiguity and the judgement of causality: Effects of prior knowledge, experience, and reinforcement procedure. *Quarterly Journal of Experimental Psychology: Human Experimental Psychology, 56A*(5), 865–890.

Buller, D. J. (2005). *Adapting minds: Evolutionary psychology and the persistent quest for human nature.* Cambridge, MA: MIT Press.

Bunde, J., & Suls, J. (2006). A quantitative analysis of the relationship between the cook-medley hostility scale and traditional coronary artery disease risk factors. *Health Psychology, 25*(4), 493–500.

Bunn, G. C. (2007). Spectacular science: The lie detector's ambivalent powers. *History of Psychology, 10*(2), 156–178.

Burchinal, M. R., Roberts, J. E., Riggins, R., Zeisel, S. A., et al. (2000). Relating quality of center-based child care to early cognitive and language development longitudinally. *Child Development, 71*(2), 339–357.

Burger, J. M. (2008). *Personality* (7th ed.). Belmont, CA: Cengage Learning/Wadsworth.

Burger, J. M., & Lynn, A. L. (2005). Superstitious behavior among American and Japanese professional baseball players. *Basic & Applied Social Psychology, 27*(1), 71–76.

Burgess, C. A., & Kirsch, I. (1999). Expectancy information as a moderator of the effects of hypnosis on memory. *Contemporary Hypnosis, 16*(1), 22–31.

Burgess, M. C. R., & Weaver, G. E. (2003). Interest and attention in facial recognition. *Perceptual & Motor Skills, 96*(2), 467–480.

Burke, D., Hickie, I., Breakspear, M., & Götz, J. (2007). Possibilities for the prevention and treatment of cognitive impairment and dementia. *British Journal of Psychiatry, 190,* 371–372.

Burlingame, G. M., & Davies, R. (2002). Self-help groups. In M. Hersen, & W. H. Sledge (Eds.), *Encyclopedia of psychotherapy.* San Diego: Academic Press.

Burlingame, G. M., Fuhriman, A., & Mosier, J. (2003). The differential effectiveness of group psychotherapy: A meta-analytic perspective. *Group Dynamics: Theory, Research, & Practice, 7*(1), 3–12.

Burnett, R. C., Medin, D. L., Ross, N. O., & Blok, S. V. (2005). Ideal is typical. *Canadian Journal of Experimental Psychology. Special Issue on 2003 Festschrift for Lee R. Brooks, 59*(1), 3–10.

Burns, D. D., & Persons, J. (1982). Hope and hopelessness: A cognitive approach. In L. E. Abt, & I. R. Stuart (Eds.), *The newer therapies: A sourcebook.* New York: Van Nostrand Reinhold.

Burns, T. (2004). *Community mental health teams: A guide to current practices.* New York: Oxford University Press.

Burt, S. A., McGue, M., Carter, L. A., & Iacono, W. G. (2007). The different origins of stability and change in antisocial personality disorder symptoms. *Psychological Medicine, 37*(1), 27–38.

Burton, C. M., & King, L. A. (2004). The health benefits of writing about intensely positive experiences. *Journal of Research in Personality, 38*(2), 150–163.

Burton, D. L. (2008). An exploratory evaluation of the contribution of personality and childhood sexual victimization to the development of sexually abusive behavior. *Sexual Abuse: Journal of Research & Treatment, 20*(1), 102–115.

Burtt, H. E. (1941). An experimental study of early childhood memory: Final report. *Journal of General Psychology, 58,* 435–439.

Bushman, B. J., & Anderson, C. A. (2001). Media violence and the American public. *American Psychologist, 56*(6/7), 477–489.

Bushnell, L. W., Sai, F., & Mullin, L. T. (1989). Neonatal recognition of the mother's face. *British Journal of Developmental Psychology, 7*(1), 3–15.

Bushnell, M. C., Villemure, C., & Duncan, G. H. (2004). Psychophysical and neurophysiological studies of pain modulation by attention. In D. D. Price, & M. C. Bushnell (Eds.), *Psychological methods of pain control: Basic science and clinical perspectives.* Seattle: IASP Press.

Buss, D. M. (1985). Human mate selection. *American Scientist, 73,* 47–51.

Buss, D. M. (2000). *The dangerous passion.* New York: Free Press.

Buss, D. M. (2004). *Evolutionary psychology: The new science of the mind* (2nd ed.). Boston: Allyn & Bacon.

Buss, D. M. (2007). The evolution of human mating. *Acta Psychologica Sinica, 39*(3), 502–512.

Butcher, J. N. (2005). *A beginner's guide to the MMPI-2* (2nd ed.). Washington, DC: American Psychological Association.

Butcher, J. N., Mineka, S., & Hooley, J. (2007). *Abnormal psychology and modern life* (13th ed.). Boston: Allyn & Bacon.

Butkovic, A., & Bratko, D. (2003). Generation and sex differences in sensation seeking: Results of the family study. *Perceptual and Motor Skills, 97*(3, Pt 1), 965–970.

Butler, B. (2007). The role of death qualification in capital trials involving juvenile defendants. *Journal of Applied Social Psychology, 37*(3), 549–560.

Butler, J. C. (2000). Personality and emotional correlates of right-wing authoritarianism. *Social Behavior & Personality, 28*(1), 1–14.

Butler, M. G. (2001). *Overcoming social anxiety and shyness: A self-help guide using cognitive behavioral techniques.* New York: New York University Press.

Butler, R. (1954). Curiosity in monkeys. *Scientific American, 190*(18), 70–75.

Byrne, S. M., & McLean, N. J. (2002). The cognitive-behavioral model of bulimia nervosa: A direct evaluation. *International Journal of Eating Disorders, 31,* 17–31.

Byrnes, J. P., Miller, D. C., & Schafer, W. D. (1999). Gender differences in risk taking: A meta-analysis. *Psychological Bulletin, 125*(3), 367–383.

Cadinu, M., Maass, A., Rosabianca, A., & Kiesner, J. (2005). Why do women underperform under stereotype threat? Evidence for the role of negative thinking. *Psychological Science, 16*(7), 572–578.

Caharel, S., Fiori, N., Bernard, C., et al. (2006). The effects of inversion and eye displacements of familiar and unknown faces on early and late-stage ERPs. *International Journal of Psychophysiology, 62*(1), 141–151.

Cahill, S. P., Carrigan, M. H., & Frueh, B. C. (1999). Does EMDR work? and if so, why? *Journal of Anxiety Disorders, 13*(1–2), 5–33.

Cahn, B. R., & Polich, J. (2006). Meditation states and traits: EEG, ERP, and neuroimaging studies. *Psychological Bulletin, 132*(2), 180–211.

Calhoun, J. B. (1962). A "behavioral sink." In E. L. Bliss (Ed.), *Roots of behavior.* New York: Harper & Row.

Callahan, C. M. (2006). Giftedness. In G. G. Bear, & K. M. Minke, (Eds.), *Children's needs III: Development, prevention, and intervention.* Washington, DC: National Association of School Psychologists.

Cameron, J. A., & Trope, Y. (2004). Stereotype-biased search and processing of information about group members. *Social Cognition, 22*(6), 650–672.

Cameron, J., & Pierce, W. D. (2002). *Rewards and intrinsic motivation: Resolving the controversy.* Westport, CO: Bergin & Garvey.

Campbell, L., Campbell, B., & Dickinson, D. (2003). *Teaching and learning through multiple intelligences* (3rd ed.). Boston: Allyn & Bacon.

Campion, M. A., & McClelland, C. L. (1993). Follow-up and extension of interdisciplinary costs and benefits of enlarged jobs. *Journal of Applied Psychology, 78*(3), 339–351.

Campion, M. A., Palmer, D. K., & Campion, J. E. (1998). Structuring employment interviews to improve reliability, validity and users' reactions. *Current Directions in Psychological Science, 7*(3), 77–82.

Canli, T., Desmond, J. E., Zhao, Z., Glover, G., et al. (1998). Hemispheric asymmetry for emotional stimuli detected with fMRI. *Neuroreport, 9*(14) 3233–3239.

Cannon, W. B. (1932). *The wisdom of the body.* New York: Norton.

Cannon, W. B. (1934). Hunger and thirst. In C. Murchinson (Ed.), *Handbook of general experimental psychology.* Worcester, MA: Clark University Press.

Cannon, W. B., & Washburn, A. L. (1912). An exploration of hunger.

American Journal of Physiology, 29, 441–454.

Caplan, P. J. (1995). *They say you're crazy.* Reading, MA: Addison-Wesley.

Capuzzi, D. (2003). *Approaches to group counseling.* Englewood Cliffs, NJ: Prentice Hall.

Cardoso, S. H. (2000). Our ancient laughing brain. *Cerebrum, 2*(4), 15–30.

Carducci, B. J., & Fields, T. H. (2007). *The shyness workbook for teens.* Champaign, IL: Research Press.

Carey, J. C., Stanley, D. A., & Biggers, J. (1988). Peak alert time and rapport between residence hall roommates. *Journal of College Student Development, 29*(3), 239–243.

Carlbring, P., Gunnarsdóttir, M., Hedensjö, L., Andersson, G., et al. (2007). Treatment of social phobia: Randomised trial of internet-delivered cognitive-behavioural therapy with telephone support. *British Journal of Psychiatry, 190*(2), 123–128.

Carlson, M., Marcus-Hewhall, A., & Miller, N. (1990). Effects of situational aggression cues: A quantitative review. *Journal of Personality & Social Psychology, 58*(4), 622–633.

Carlson, N. R. (2005). *Physiology of behavior* (8th ed.). Boston: Allyn & Bacon.

Carlson, N. R. (2007). *Physiology of behavior* (9th ed.). Boston: Allyn & Bacon.

Carnagey, N. L., & Anderson, C. A. (2004). Violent video game exposure and aggression: A literature review. *Minerva Psichiatrica, 45*(1), 1–18.

Carnagey, N. L., Anderson, C. A., & Bushman, B. J. (2007). The effect of video game violence on physiological desensitization to real-life violence. *Journal of Experimental Social Psychology, 43*(3), 489–496.

Carney, R. N., & Levin, J. R. (2001). Remembering the names of unfamiliar animals: Keywords as keys to their kingdom. *Applied Cognitive Psychology, 15*(2), 133–143.

Carney, R. N., & Levin, J. R. (2003). Promoting higher-order learning benefits by building lower-order mnemonic connections. *Applied Cognitive Psychology, 17*(5), 563–575.

Carroll, D. W. (2008). *Psychology of language* (5th ed.). Belmont, CA: Cengage Learning/Wadsworth.

Carroll, J. L. (2007). *Sexuality now: Embracing diversity* (2nd ed.). Belmont, CA: Cengage Learning/Wadsworth.

Carroll, J. M., & Russell, J. A. (1996). Do facial expressions signal specific emotions? Judging emotion from the face in context. *Journal of Personality & Social Psychology, 70*(2), 205–218.

Carroll, K. M., & Rounsaville, B. J. (2007). W(h)ither empirically supported therapies (ESTS)? Reply to commentaries. *Addiction, 102*(6), 867–869.

Carskadon, M. A., Acebo, C., & Jenni, O. C. (2004). Regulation of adolescent sleep: Implications for behavior. *Annals of the New York Academy of Science, 1021,* 276–291.

Carter, D. A., Simkins, B. J., & Simpson, W. G. (2003). Corporate governance, board diversity, and firm value. *Financial Review, 38,* 33–53.

Cartwright, D. (2002a). *Psychoanalysis, violence and rage-type murder: Murdering minds.* New York: Brunner-Routledge.

Cartwright, D. (2002b). The narcissistic exoskeleton: The defensive organization of the rage-type murderer. *Bulletin of the Menninger Clinic, 66*(1), 1–18.

Cartwright, R., & Lamberg, L. (1992). *Crisis dreaming.* New York: Harper-Collins.

Casey, P. (2001). Multiple personality disorder. *Primary Care Psychiatry, 7*(1), 7–11.

Caspi, A., Roberts, B. W., & Shiner, R. L. (2005). Personality development: Stability and change. *Annual Review of Psychology, 56,* 453–484.

Caspi, A., Sugden, K., Moffitt, T. E., Taylor, A., et al. (2003). Influence of life stress on depression: Moderation by a polymorphism in the 5-HTT gene. *Science, 301*(5631), 386–389.

Cassady, J. C. (2004). The influence of cognitive test anxiety across the learning-testing cycle. *Learning & Instruction, 14*(6), 569–592.

Castro, J., Gila, A., Gual, P., Lahortiga, F., et al. (2004). Perfectionism dimensions in children and adolescents with anorexia nervosa. *Journal of Adolescent Health, 35*(5), 392–398.

Castro, J. R., & Rice, K. G. (2003). Perfectionism and ethnicity: Implications for depressive symptoms and self-reported academic achievement. *Cultural Diversity and Ethnic Minority Psychology, 9*(1), 64–78.

Catalano, R., Novaco, R., & McConnell, W. (1997). A model of the net effect of job loss on violence. *Journal of Personality & Social Psychology, 72*(6), 1440–1447.

Cattell, R. B. (1965). *The scientific analysis of personality.* Baltimore: Penguin.

Cattell, R. B. (1973). Personality pinned down. *Psychology Today,* July, 40–46.

Cautela, J. R., & Kearney, A. J. (1986). *The covert conditioning handbook.* New York: Springer.

Cavaco, S., Anderson, S. W., Allen, J. S., Castro-Caldas, A., et al. (2004). The scope of preserved procedural memory in amnesia. *Brain: A Journal of Neurology, 127*(8), 1853–1867.

CDC. (2002a). *Overweight, obesity, and healthy weight among persons 20 years of age and over, according to sex, age, race, and Hispanic origin: United States, 1960–62, 1971–74, 1976–80, 1988–94, and 1999–2000.* Atlanta: Centers for Disease Control and Prevention. Retrieved July 8, 2007, from http://www.cdc.gov/nchs/data/hus/tables/2002/02hus070.pdf.

CDC (2002b). *Teenagers in the United States: sexual activity, contraceptive use, and childbearing, 2002.* Atlanta: Centers for Disease Control and National Center for Health Statistics, National Vital Statistics System. Retrieved July 30, 2007, from http://0-www.cdc.gov.mill1.sjlibrary.org:80/nchs/data/series/sr_23/sr23_024.pdf.

CDC. (2003). *Deaths, percent of total deaths, and death rates for 15 leading causes of death in 5-year age groups, by race and sex: United State, 2000.* Atlanta: Centers for Disease Control and

National Center for Health Statistics, National Vital Statistics System. Retrieved July 25, 2007, from http://www.cdc.gov/nchs/datawh/statab/unpubd/mortabs/lcwk1_10.htm.

CDC. (2005). Annual smoking–attributable mortality, years of potential life lost, and productivity losses: United States, 1997–2001. *Centers for Disease Control and Prevention Morbidity and Mortality Weekly Report, 54*(25), 625–628.

CDC. (2007). *Sexual violence: Fact sheet.* Atlanta: National Center for Injury Prevention and Control. Retrieved July 29, 2007, from http://www.cdc.gov/ncipc/factsheets/svfacts.htm.

Chabas, D., Taheri, S., Renier, C., & Mignot, E. (2003). The genetics of narcolepsy. *Annual Review of Genomics and Human Genetics, 4,* 459–483.

Chakos, M. H., Alvir, J. M. J., Woerner, M., & Koreen, A. (1996). Incidence and correlates of tardive dyskinesia in first episode of schizophrenia. *Archives of General Psychiatry, 53*(4), 313–319.

Chamberlin, J. (2004). Survey says: More Americans are seeking mental health treatment. *Monitor on Psychology,* July/Aug., 17.

Chamberlin, J., & Rogers, J. A. (1990). Planning a community-based mental health system. *American Psychologist, 45*(11), 1241–1244.

Chambers, R. A., Taylor, J. R., & Potenza, M. N. (2003). Developmental neurocircuitry of motivation in adolescence: A critical period of addiction vulnerability. *American Journal of Psychiatry, 160*(6), 1041–1052.

Chambless, D. L., & Ollendick, T. H. (2001). Empirically supported psychological interventions. *Annual Review of Psychology, 52,* 685–716.

Chamorro-Premuzic, T., & Furnham, A. (2003). Personality predicts academic performance. *Journal of Research in Personality, 37*(4), 319–338.

Chan, G. C.-K., Hinds, T. R., Impey, S., & Storm, D. R. (1998). Hippocampal neurotoxicity of Δ-sup-9-tetrahydrocannabinol. *Journal of Neuroscience, 18*(14), 5322–5332.

Chance, P. (2006). *Learning and behavior* (5th ed.). Belmont, CA: Wadsworth.

Chandrashekar, J., Hoon, M. A., Ryba, N. J. P., & Cammann, C. (2006). The receptors and cells for mammalian taste. *Nature, 444*(7117), 288–294.

Chansler, P. A., Swamidass, P. M., & Cammann, C. (2003). Self-managing work teams: An empirical study of group cohesiveness in "natural work groups" at a Harley-Davidson Motor Company plant. *Small Group Research, 34*(1), 101–120.

Chao, R., & Tseng, V. (2002). Parenting of Asians. In M. H. Bornstein (Ed.), *Handbook of parenting* (Vol. 4): *Social conditions and applied parenting* (2nd ed.). Mahwah, NJ: Erlbaum.

Chapanis, A., & Lindenbaum, L. E. (1959). A reaction time study of four control-display linkages. *Human Factors, 1,* 1–7.

Chapman, R. A. (Ed.). (2006). *The clinical use of hypnosis in cognitive behavior therapy: A practitioner's casebook.* New York: Springer Publishing.

Chartrand, T. L., & Bargh, J. A. (1999). The chameleon effect: The perception-behavior link and social interaction. *Journal of Personality & Social Psychology, 76*(6), 893–910.

Chassin, L., Presson, C. C., Sherman, S. J., & Kim, K. (2003). Historical changes in cigarette smoking and smoking-related beliefs after 2 decades in a Midwestern community. *Health Psychology, 22*(4), 347–353.

Chasteen, A. L., Bhattacharyya, S., Horhota, M., Tam, R., et al. (2005). How feelings of stereotype threat influence older adults' memory performance. *Experimental Aging Research, 31*(3), 235–260.

Chaves, J. F. (2000). Hypnosis. In A. Kazdin (Ed.), *Encyclopedia of psychology.* Washington, DC: American Psychological Association.

Check, J. V. P., & Malamuth, N. M. (1983). Sex role stereotyping and reactions to depictions of stranger versus acquaintance rape. *Journal of Personality & Social Psychology, 45,* 344–356.

Cheek, J., & Buss, A. H. (1979). *Scales of shyness, sociability and self-esteem and correlations among them.* Unpublished research, University of Texas. (Cited by Buss, 1980.)

Chen, Z., Lawson, R. B., Gordon, L. R., & McIntosh, B. (1996). Groupthink: Deciding with the leader and the devil. *Psychological Record, 46*(4), 581–590.

Chen, Z., Mo, L., & Honomichl, R. (2004). Having the memory of an elephant. *Journal of Experimental Psychology: General, 133*(3), 415–433.

Cheng, H., Cao, Y., & Olson, L. (1996). Spinal cord repair in adult paraplegic rats: Partial restoration of hind limb function. *Science, 273*(5274), 510.

Chess, S., & Thomas, A. (1986). *Know your child.* New York: Basic.

Chester, A., & Glass, C. A. (2006). Online counselling: A descriptive analysis of therapy services on the internet. *British Journal of Guidance & Counselling, 34*(2), 145–160.

Cheyne, J. A. (2005). Sleep paralysis episode frequency and number, types, and structure of associated hallucinations. *Journal of Sleep Research, 14*(3), 319–324.

Cheyne, J. A., Rueffer, S. D., & Newby-Clark, I. R. (1999). Hypnagogic and hypnopompic hallucinations during sleep paralysis: Neurological and cultural construction of the nightmare. *Consciousness & Cognition, 8,* 319–337.

Chisolm, T. H., Willott, J. F., & Lister, J. J. (2003). The aging auditory system: Anatomic and physiologic changes and implications for rehabilitation. *International Journal of Audiology, 42*(Suppl2), 2S3–2S10.

Chomsky, N. (1975). *Reflections on language.* New York: Pantheon.

Chomsky, N. (1986). *Knowledge of language.* New York: Praeger.

Christakis, N. A., & Fowler, J. H. (2007). The spread of obesity in a large social network over 32 years. *New England Journal of Medicine, 357*(4), 370–379.

Christakis, N. A., & Fowler, J. H. (2008). The collective dynamics of smoking in a large social network. *New England Journal of Medicine, 358*(21), 2249–58.

Christensen, A., & Jacobson, N. S. (1994). Who (or what) can do psychotherapy. *Psychological Science, 5*(1), 8–14.

Christian, K. M., & Thompson, R. F. (2005). Long-term storage of an associative memory trace in the cerebellum. *Behavioral Neuroscience, 119*(2), 526–537.

Christophersen, E. R., & Mortweet, S. L. (2003). *Parenting that works: Building skills that last a lifetime.* Washington, DC: American Psychological Association.

Chua, H. F., Boland, J. E., & Nisbett, R. E. (2005). Cultural variation in eye movements during scene perception. *Proceedings of the National Academy of Sciences of the United States of America, 102*(35), 12629–12633.

Chua, P., & Fujino, D. C. (1999). Negotiating new Asian-American masculinities: Attitudes and gender expectations. *Journal of Men's Studies, 7*(3), 391–413.

Cialdini, R. B. (2001). *Influence: Science and practice* (4th ed.). Boston: Allyn & Bacon.

Cialdini, R. B., Eisenberg, N., & Green, B. L., Rhoads, K., et al. (1998). Undermining the undermining effect of reward on sustained interest. *Journal of Applied Social Psychology, 28*(3), 249–263.

Cialdini, R. B., & Goldstein, N. J. (2004). Social influence: Compliance and conformity. *Annual Review of Psychology, 55,* 591–621.

Cialdini, R. B., Reno, R. R., & Kallgren, C. A. (1990). A focus theory of normative conduct: Recycling the concept of norms to reduce littering in public places. *Journal of Personality & Social Psychology, 58*(6), 1015–1026.

Ciarrochi, J., Dean, F. P., & Anderson, S. (2002). Emotional intelligence moderates the relationship between stress and mental health. *Personality & Individual Differences, 32*(2), 197–209.

Cinciripini, P. M., Wetter, D. W., & McClure, J. B. (1997). Scheduled reduced smoking. *Addictive Behaviors, 22*(6), 759–767.

Clark, D., Boutros, N., & Mendez, M. (2005). *The brain and behavior* (2nd ed.). Cambridge, MA: Cambridge University Press.

Clark, R., Anderson, N. B., Clark, V. R., & Williams, D. R. (1999). Racism as a stressor for African Americans. *American Psychologist, 54*(10), 805–816.

Clayton, N. S., Yu, K. S., & Dickinson, A. (2001). Scrub jays (Aphelocoma coerulescens) form integrated memories of the multiple features of caching episodes. *Journal of Experimental Psychology: Animal Behavior Processes, 27,* 17–29.

Clearfield, M. W., & Nelson, N. M. (2006). Sex differences in mothers' speech and play behavior with 6-, 9-, and 14-month-old infants. *Sex Roles, 54*(1–2), 127–137.

Clements, A. M., Rimrodt, S. L., Abel, J. R., Blankner, J. G., et al. (2006). Sex differences in cerebral laterality of language and visuospatial processing. *Brain & Language, 98*(2), 150–158.

Cline, V. B., Croft, R. G., & Courrier, S. (1972). Desensitization of children to television violence. *Journal of Personality & Social Psychology, 27,* 360–365.

Clore, G. L. (1976). Interpersonal attraction: An overview. In *Contemporary topics in social psychology.* Morristown, NJ: General Learning Press.

Cnattingius, S., Signorello, L. B., Ammerén, G., Clausson, B., et al. (2000). Caffeine intake and the risk of first-trimester spontaneous abortion. *New England Journal of Medicine, 343*(25), 1839–845.

Cochran, S. D. (2001). Emerging issues in research on lesbians' and gay men's mental health. *American Psychologist, 56*(11), 931–947.

Cohen, D. J., & Bennett, S. (1997). Why can't most people draw what they see? *Journal of Experimental Psychology: Human Perception and Performance, 23*(3), 609–621.

Cohen, J. E. (1995). *How many people can the earth support?* New York: Norton.

Cohen, N. L., Waltzman, S. B., & Fisher, S. G. (1993). A prospective, randomized study of cochlear implants. *New England Journal of Medicine, 328*(4), 233–237.

Cohen, S., Evans, G. W., Krantz, D. S., & Stokols, D. (1981). Cardiovascular and behavioral effects of community noise. *American Scientist, 69,* 528–535.

Colapinto, J. (2000). *As nature made him: The boy who was raised as a girl.* New York: HarperCollins.

Cole, J. (1995). *Pride and a daily marathon.* Cambridge, MA: MIT Press.

Coles, C. D., & Black, M. M. (2006). Introduction to the special issue. *Journal of Pediatric Psychology. Special Issue: Prenatal Substance Exposure: Impact on Children's Health, Development, School Performance, and Risk Behavior, 31*(1), 1–4.

Colin, A. K., Moore, K., & West, A. N. (1996). Creativity, oversensitivity, and rate of habituation. *EDRA: Environmental Design Research Association, 20*(4), 423–427.

Collins, A. M., & Quillian, M. R. (1969). Retrieval time from semantic memory. *Journal of Verbal Learning & Verbal Behavior, 8,* 240–247.

Collins, N. L., Cooper, M. L., Albino, A., & Allard, L. (2002). Psychosocial vulnerability from adolescence to adulthood: A prospective study of attachment style differences in relationship functioning and partner choice. *Journal of Personality, 70*(6), 965–1008.

Collins, W. A., & Gunnar, M. R. (1990). Social and personality development. *Annual Review of Psychology, 41,* 387–416.

Collop, N. A. (2005). Obstructive sleep apnea: Treatment overview and controversies. In P. R. Carney, J. D. Geyer, & R. B. Berry (Eds.), *Clinical sleep disorders.* Philadelphia: Lippincott Williams & Wilkins.

Comer, R. J. (2005). *Fundamentals of abnormal psychology* (4th ed.). New York: Worth.

Comperatore, C. A., Lieberman, H. R., Kirby, A. W., & Adams, B. (1996). *Melatonin* efficacy in aviation missions requiring rapid deployment and night

operations. *Aviation, Space, & Environmental Medicine, 67*(6), 520–524.

Compton, W. C. (2005). *An introduction to positive psychology.* Belmont, CA: Cengage Learning/Wadsworth.

Conway, A. R. A., Cowan, N., & Bunting, M. F. (2001). The cocktail party phenomenon revisited. *Psychonomic Bulletin & Review, 8*(2), 331–335.

Conway, M. A., Cohen, G., & Stanhope, N. (1992). Very long-term memory for knowledge acquired at school and university. *Applied Cognitive Psychology, 6*(6), 467–482.

Coolican, H., Cassidy, T., Dunn, O., Sharp, R., et al. (2007). *Applied psychology* (2nd ed.). London: Hodder Education.

Cooper, J., Bennett, E. A., & Sukel, H. L. (1996). Complex scientific testimony: How do jurors make decisions? *Law & Human Behavior, 20*(4), 379–394.

Cooper, J., Mirabile, R., & Scher, S. J. (2005). Actions and attitudes: The theory of cognitive dissonance. In T. C. Brock, & M. C. Green (Eds.), *Persuasion: Psychological insights and perspectives* (2nd ed) Thousand Oaks, CA: Sage.

Cooper, M. J. (2005). Cognitive theory in anorexia nervosa and bulimia nervosa: Progress, development and future directions. *Clinical Psychology Review, 25*(4), 511–531.

Cooper, P. J., & Murray, L. (2001). The treatment and prevention of postpartum depression and associated disturbances in child development. *Archives of Women's Mental Health, 3*(suppl 2), 5.

Cooper, R. P., Abraham, J., Berman, S., & Staska, M. (1997). The development of infants' preference for motherese. *Infant Behavior and Development, 20*(4), 477–488.

Corballis, M. C. (2002). *From hand to mouth: The origins of language.* Princeton, NJ: Princeton University Press.

Corbin, W. R., & Fromme, K. (2002). Alcohol use and serial monogamy as risks for sexually transmitted diseases in young adults. *Health Psychology, 21*(3), 229–236.

Coren, S. (1992). *The left-hander syndrome.* New York: Free Press.

Coren, S. (1996). *Sleep thieves.* New York: Free Press.

Coren, S., Ward, L. M., & Enns, J. T. (2004). *Sensation and perception* (6th ed.). New York: Wiley.

Corey, G. (2008). *Theory and practice of group counseling* (7th ed.). Belmont, CA: Cengage Learning/Wadsworth.

Corkin, S. (2002). What's new with the amnesic patient H.M.? *Nature Reviews Neuroscience, 3,* 153–160.

Cormier, J. F., & Thelen, M. H. (1998). Professional skepticism of multiple personality disorder. *Professional Psychology: Research and Practice, 29*(2), 163–167.

Cornsweet, T. N. (1970). *Visual perception.* New York: Academic.

Correa-Chávez, M., Rogoff, B., & Arauz, R. M. (2005). Cultural patterns in attending to two events at once. *Child Development, 76*(3), 664–678.

Corrigan, P. W., & Penn, D. L. (1999). Lessons from social psychology on dis-

crediting psychiatric stigma. *American Psychologist, 54*(9), 765–776.

Corrigan, P. W., & Watson, A. C. (2005). Findings from the National Comorbidity Survey on the frequency of violent behavior in individuals with psychiatric disorders. *Psychiatry Research, 136*(2–3), 153–162.

Corsini, R. J. (2001). *Handbook of innovative therapy* (2nd ed.). New York: Wiley.

Costa, Jr., P. T., & McCrae, R. R. (2006). Trait and factor theories. In J. C. Thomas, D. L. Segal, et al. (Eds.), *Comprehensive handbook of personality & psychopathology* (Vol. 1): *Personality and everyday functioning.* New York: Wiley.

Côté, J. E. (2006a). Emerging adulthood as an institutionalized moratorium: Risks and benefits to identity formation. In J. J. Arnett & J. L. Tanner (Eds.), *Emerging adults in America: Coming of age in the 21st century.* Washington, DC: American Psychological Association.

Côté, J. E. (2006b). Identity studies: How close are we to developing a social science of identity? An appraisal of the field. *Identity: An International Journal of Theory & Research, 6,* 3–26.

Côté, J. E., & Levine, C. (2002). *Identity formation, agency, and culture.* Mahwah, NJ: Erlbaum.

Cote, S. (1999). Affect and performance in organizational settings. *Current Directions in Psychological Science, 8*(2), 65–68.

Coursey, R. D., Ward-Alexander, L., & Katz, B. (1990). Cost-effectiveness of providing insurance benefits for posthospital psychiatric halfway house stays. *American Psychologist, 45*(10), 1118–1126.

Court, J. H., & Court, P. C. (2001). Repression: R. I. P. *Australian Journal of Clinical & Experimental Hypnosis, 29*(1), 8–16.

Cover, J. D. (1995). The effects of social contact on prejudice. *Journal of Social Psychology, 135*(3), 403–405.

Cowan, G., Heiple, B., Marquez, C., Khatchadourian, D., et al. (2005). Heterosexuals' attitudes toward hate crimes and hate speech against gays and lesbians: Old-fashioned and modern heterosexism. *Journal of Homosexuality, 49*(2), 67–82.

Cowan, N. (2005). *Working memory capacity.* Hove, UK: Psychology Press.

Cowden, C. R. (2005). Worry and its relationship to shyness. *North American Journal of Psychology, 7*(1), 59–69.

Cowles, J. T. (1937). Food tokens as incentives for learning by chimpanzees. *Comparative Psychology,* Monograph, 14(5, Whole No. 71).

Cox, J. J., Reimann, F., Nicholas, A. K., et al. (2006). An SCN9A channelopathy causes congenital inability to experience pain. *Nature, 444,* 894–898.

Cox, R. H. (2007). *Sport psychology: Concepts and applications* (6th ed.). New York: McGraw-Hill.

Craig, L. (2006). Does father care mean fathers share? A comparison of how mothers and fathers in intact families spend time with children. *Gender & Society, 20*(2), 259–281.

Craig, T. Y., & Kelly, J. R. (1999). Group cohesiveness and creative performance. *Group Dynamics, 3*(4), 243–256.

Craik, F. I. M. (1970). The fate of primary items in free recall. *Journal of Verbal Learning and Verbal Behavior, 9,* 143–148.

Craik, F. I. M., & Bialystok, E. (2005). Intelligence and executive control: Evidence from aging and bilingualism. *Cortex, 41*(2), 222–224.

Crano, W. D. (2000). Milestones in the psychological analysis of social influence. *Group Dynamics: Theory, Research, and Practice, 4*(1), 68–80.

Cravatt, B. F., Prospero-Garcia O., Siuzdak G., Gilula, N. B., et al. (1995). Chemical characterization of a family of brain lipids that induce sleep. *Science, 268*(5216), 1506–1509.

Crawley, S. B., & Sherrod, K. B. (1984). Parent-infant play during the first year of life. *Infant Behavior & Development, 7,* 65–75.

Crencavage, L. M., & Norcross, J. C. (1990). Where are the commonalities among the therapeutic common factors? *Professional Psychology: Research & Practice, 21*(5), 372–378.

Crisp, A., Gowers, S., Joughin, N., McClelland, L., et al. (2006). The enduring nature of anorexia nervosa. *European Eating Disorders Review, 14*(3), 147–152.

Crocker, J., & Park, L. E. (2004). The costly pursuit of self-esteem. *Psychological Bulletin, 130*(3), 392–414.

Cromdal, J. (1999). Childhood bilingualism and metalinguistic skills. *Applied Psycholinguistics, 20*(1), 1–20.

Crooks, R., & Baur, K. (2008). *Our sexuality* (10th ed.). Belmont, CA: Cengage Learning/Wadsworth.

Cropley, A. (2006). In praise of convergent thinking. *Creativity Research Journal, 18,* 391–404.

Crosby, R. A., & Yarber, W. L. (2001). Perceived versus actual knowledge about correct condom use among U.S. adolescents: Results from a national study. *Journal of Adolescent Health, 28*(5), 415–420.

Crown, C. L., Feldstein, S., Jasnow, M. D., Beebe, B., et al. (2002). The cross-modal coordination of interpersonal timing. *Journal of Psycholinguistic Research, 31*(1), 1–23.

Crowther, J. H., Sanftner, J., Bonifazi, D. Z., & Shepherd, K. L. (2001). The role of daily hassles in binge eating. *International Journal of Eating Disorders, 29,* 449–454.

Csikszentmihalyi, M. (1997). *Creativity.* New York: HarperCollins.

Csikszentmihalyi, M., Abuhamdeh, S., Nakamura, J. (2005). Flow. In A. J. Elliot, & C. S. Dweck, (Eds.), *Handbook of competence and motivation.* New York: Guilford.

Cull, M. (2002). Treatment of intersex needs open discussion. *British Medical Journal, 324*(7342), 919.

Cull, W. L., Shaughnessy, J. J., & Zechmeister, E. B. (1996). Expanding understanding of the expanding-pattern-of-retrieval mnemonic. *Journal of Experimental Psychology: Applied, 2*(4) 365–378.

Culver, R. & Ianna, P. (1988). *Astrology: True or false?* Buffalo, NY: Prometheus Books.

Cumming, B. G., & DeAngelis, G. C. (2001). The physiology of stereopsis. *Annual Review of Neuroscience, 24,* 203–238.

Cummings, M. R. (2006) *Human heredity: Principles and issues* (7th ed.). Belmont CA: Cengage Learning/ Wadsworth.

Cummins, D. D. (1995). *The other side of psychology.* New York: St. Martins.

Curci, A., & Luminet, O. (2006). Follow-up of a cross-national comparison on flashbulb and event memory for the September 11th attacks. *Memory, 14*(3), 329–344.

Czeisler, C. A., Duffy, J. F., Shanahan, T. L., Brown, E. N., et al. (1999). Stability, precision, and near-24-hour period of the human circadian pacemaker. *Science, 284*(5423), 2177–2181.

Czeisler, C. A., Richardson, G. S., Zimmerman, J. C., Moore-Ede, M. C., et al. (1981). Entrainment of human circadian rhythms by light-dark cycles: A reassessment. *Photochemistry, Photobiology, 34,* 239–247.

Dahlquist, L. M., McKenna, K. D., Jones, K. K., et al. (2007). Active and passive distraction using a head-mounted display helmet: Effects on cold pressor pain in children. *Health Psychology, 26*(6), 794–801.

Dane, S., & Erzurumluoglu, A. (2003). Sex and handedness differences in eye-hand visual reaction times in handball players. *International Journal of Neuroscience, 113*(7), 923–929.

Daniels, H. (2005). Vygotsky and educational psychology: Some preliminary remarks. *Educational & Child Psychology, 22*(1), 6–17.

Danziger, N., Prkachin, K. M., & Willer, J.-C. (2006). Is pain the price of empathy? The perception of others' pain in patients with congenital insensitivity to pain. *Brain: A Journal of Neurology, 129*(9), 2494–2507.

Darley, J. M. (2000). Bystander phenomenon. In A. E. Kazdin (Ed.), *Encyclopedia of psychology* (Vol. 1). Washington, DC: American Psychological Association.

Darley, J. M., & Latané, B. (1968). Bystander intervention in emergencies: Diffusion of responsibility. *Journal of Personality & Social Psychology, 8,* 377–383.

Darling, C. A., Davidson, J. K., & Passarello, L. C. (1992). The mystique of first intercourse among college youth: The role of partners, contraceptive practices, and psychological reactions. *Journal of Youth & Adolescence, 21*(1), 97–117.

Darou, W. S. (1992). Native Canadians and intelligence testing. *Canadian Journal of Counselling, 26*(2), 96–99.

Daruna, J. H. (2004). *Introduction to psychoneuroimmunology.* Amsterdam: Elsevier.

Darwin, C. (1872). *The expression of emotion in man and animals.* Chicago: University of Chicago Press.

Das, A. (2007). Masturbation in the United States. *Journal of Sex & Marital Therapy, 33,* 301–317.

Das, J. P. (2000). Mental retardation. In A. Kazdin (Ed.), *Encyclopedia of psychology.* Washington, DC: American Psychological Association.

Dauvilliers, Y., Cervena, K, Carlander, B., Espa, F., et al. (2004). Dissociation in circadian rhythms in a pseudohypersomnia form of fatal familial insomnia. *Neurology, 63*(12), 2416–2418.

Davidovitch, N., & Milgram, R. M. (2006). Creative thinking as a predictor of teacher effectiveness in higher education. *Creativity Research Journal, 18,* 385–390.

Davidson, P. R., & Parker, K. C. H. (2001). Eye movement desensitization and reprocessing (EMDR): A meta-analysis. *Journal of Consulting & Clinical Psychology, 69*(2), 305–316.

Davidson, R. J., Kabat-Zinn, J., Schumacher, J., Rosenkranz, M., et al. (2003). Alternations in brain and immune function produced by mindfulness meditation. *Psychosomatic Medicine, 65*(4), 564–570.

Davidson, T. L. (2000). Latent learning. In A. E. Kazdin (Ed.), *Encyclopedia of psychology* (Vol. 4). Washington, DC: American Psychological Association.

Davies, M. F. (1993). Dogmatism and the persistence of discredited beliefs. *Personality & Social Psychology Bulletin, 19*(6), 692–699.

Davies, M., & McCartney, S. (2003). Effects of gender and sexuality on judgements of victim blame and rape myth acceptance in a depicted male rape. *Journal of Community & Applied Social Psychology, 13*(5), 391–398.

Davis, D., & Follette, W. C. (2002). Rethinking the probative value of evidence. *Law & Human Behavior, 26*(2), 133–158.

Davis, K. C., Morris, J., George, W. H., Martell, J., et al. (2006). Men's likelihood of sexual aggression: The influence of alcohol, sexual arousal, and violent pornography. *Aggressive Behavior, 32*(6), 581–589.

Davis, M. J., & Bibace, R. (1999). Dating couples and their relationships: Intimacy and contraceptive use. *Adolescence, 34*(133), 1–7.

Davis, M. R., McMahon, M., & Greenwood, K. M. (2005). The efficacy of mnemonic components of the cognitive interview: Towards a shortened variant for time-critical investigations. *Applied Cognitive Psychology, 19*(1), 75–93.

Davison, G. C., & Neale, J. M. (2006). *Abnormal psychology* (10th ed.). San Francisco: Jossey-Bass.

Day, S., & Schneider, P. L. (2002). Psychotherapy using distance technology. *Journal of Counseling Psychology, 49*(4), 499–503.

de C. Hamilton, A. F. (2008). Emulation and mimicry for social interaction: A theoretical approach to imitation in autism. *The Quarterly Journal of Experimental Psychology, 61*(1), 101–111.

de Jong, P. J., & Muris, P. (2002). Spider phobia. *Journal of Anxiety Disorders, 16*(1), 51–65.

de las Fuentes, C., & Vasquez, M. J. T. (1999). Immigrant adolescent girls of color. In N. G. Johnson, M. C. Roberts, et al. (Eds.), *Beyond appearance.* Washington, DC: American Psychological Association.

de Leon, C. F. M. (2005). Social engagement and successful aging. *European Journal of Ageing, 2*(1), 64–66.

de Rios, M. D., & Grob, C. S. (2005). Editors' introduction: Ayahuasca use in cross-cultural perspective. *Journal of Psychoactive Drugs, 37*(2), 119–121.

Dean, D., Jr., & Kuhn, D. (2007). Direct instruction vs. discovery: The long view. *Science Education, 91*(3), 384–397.

Deardorff, J., Hayward, C., Wilson, K. A., Bryson, L., et al. (2007). Puberty and gender interact to predict social anxiety symptoms in early adolescence. *Journal of Adolescent Health, 41*(1), 102–104.

DeArmond, S., Tye, M., Chen, P. Y., Krauss, A., et al. (2006). Age and gender stereotypes: New challenges in a changing workplace and workforce. *Journal of Applied Social Psychology, 36*(9), 2184–2214.

Deckers, L. (2005). *Motivation: Biological, psychological, and environmental* (2nd ed.). Boston: Allyn & Bacon.

Deckro, G. R., Ballinger, K. M., Hoyt, M., Wilcher, M., et al. (2002). The evaluation of a mind/body intervention to reduce psychological distress and perceived stress in college students. *Journal of American College Health, 50*(6), 281–287.

Deco, G., Rolls, E. T., & Horwitz, B. (2004). "What" and "where" in visual working memory: A computational neurodynamical perspective for integrating fMRI and single-neuron data. *Journal of Cognitive Neuroscience, 16*(4), 683–701.

Deeb, S. S. (2004). Molecular genetics of color-vision deficiencies. *Visual Neuroscience, 21*(3), 191–196.

DeGaetano, G. (2005). The impact of media violence on developing minds and hearts. In S. Olfman (Ed.), *Childhood lost: How American culture is failing our kids.* Westport, CT: Praeger Publishers.

deGroot, G. (1994). Psychologists explain Barney's power. *APA Monitor,* June, 4.

Dein, S., & Littlewood, R. (2005). Apocalyptic suicide: From a pathological to an eschatological interpretation. *International Journal of Social Psychiatry, 51*(3), 198–210.

Deinzer, R., Kleineidam, C., Stiller-Winkler, R., Idel, H., et al. (2000). Prolonged reduction of salivary immunoglobulin A (sIgA) after a major academic exam. *International Journal of Psychophysiology, 37,* 219–232.

Delgado, B. M., & Ford, L. (1998). Parental perceptions of child development among low-income Mexican American families. *Journal of Child & Family Studies, 7*(4), 469–481.

Delpero, W. T., O'Neill, H., Casson, E., & Hovis, J. (2005). Aviation-relevent epidemiology of color vision deficiency. *Aviation, Space, & Environmental Medicine, 76*(2), 127–133.

Demos, J. N. (2005). *Getting started with neurofeedback.* New York: Norton.

Denmark, F. L., Rabinowitz, V. C., & Sechzer, J. A. (2005). *Engendering psychology: Women and gender revisited* (2nd ed.). Boston: Allyn & Bacon.

Denollet, J., & Van Heck, G. L. (2001). Psychological risk factors in heart disease. *Journal of Psychosomatic Research, 51*(3), 465–468.

Deregowski, J. B. (1972, Nov.). Pictorial perception and culture. *Scientific American,* 82–88.

Derlega, V. J., Winstead, B. A., & Jones, W. H. (2005). *Personality: Contemporary theory and research* (3rd ed.). Belmont, CA: Wadsworth.

Deutsch, M. (1993). Educating for a peaceful world. *American Psychologist, 48*(5), 510–517.

Deutsch, M., & Collins, M.E. (1951). *Interracial housing.* Minneapolis: University of Minnesota.

Devine, D. J., Clayton, L. D., Dunford, B. B., Seying, R., et al. (2001). Jury decision making: 45 years of empirical research on deliberating groups. *Psychology, Public Policy, & Law, 7*(3), 622–727.

Devlin, B., Daniels, M., & Roeder, K. (1997). The heritability of IQ. *Nature, 388*(6641), 468–471.

Devoto, A., Lucidi, F., Violani, C., & Bertini, M. (1999). Effects of different sleep reductions on daytime sleepiness. *Sleep, 22*(3), 336–343.

Di Forti, M., Lappin, J. M., & Murray, R. M. (2007). Risk factors for schizophrenia: All roads lead to dopamine. *European Neuropsychopharmacology, 17*(Suppl 2), S101–S107.

Di Marzo, V., Goparaju, S. K., Wang, L., Liu, J., et al. (2001). Leptin-regulated endocannabinoids are involved in maintaining food intake. *Nature, 410*(6830), 822–825.

Diamond, L. M. (1998). Development of sexual orientation among adolescent and young adult women. *Developmental Psychology, 34*(5), 1085–1095.

Diano, S., Farr, S. A., Benoit, S. C., McNay, E. C., et al. (2006). Ghrelin controls hippocampal spine synapse density and memory performance. *Nature Neuroscience, 9,* 381–388.

Dickens, W. T., & Flynn, J. R. (2001). Heritability estimates versus large environmental effects: The IQ paradox resolved. *Psychological Review, 108,* 346–369.

Dickerson, F. B., Tenhula, W. N., & Green-Paden, L. D. (2005). The token economy for schizophrenia: Review of the literature and recommendations for future research. *Schizophrenia Research, 75*(2–3), 405–416.

Dickinson, D. K., & Tabors, P. O. (Eds.). (2001). *Beginning literacy with language.* Baltimore: Paul H. Brookes.

Dick-Niederhauser, A. & Silverman, W. K. (2006). Separation anxiety disorder. In J. E. Fisher, & W. T. O'Donohue (Eds.), *Practitioner's guide to evidence-based psychotherapy.* New York: Springer.

Diener, E., Suh, E. M., Lucas, R. E., & Smith, H. L. (1999). Subjective well-being: Three decades of progress. *Psychological Bulletin, 125*(2), 276–302.

Dierdorff, E. C., & Wilson, M. A. (2003). A meta-analysis of job analysis reliability. *Journal of Applied Psychology, 88*(4), 635–646.

Dieterich, S. E., Assel, M. A., Swank, P., Smith, K. E., et al. (2006). The impact of early maternal verbal scaffolding and child language abilities on later decoding and reading comprehension skills. *Journal of School Psychology, 43*(6), 481–494.

Dignon, A. M. (1996). Acceptability of a computer-administered psychiatric interview. *Computers in Human Behavior, 12*(2), 177–191.

Dinan, T. G. (2001). Stress, depression and cardiovascular disease. *Stress & Health: Journal of the International Society for the Investigation of Stress, 17*(2), 65–66.

Dingus, T. A., Klauer, S. G., Neale, V. L., Petersen, A., et al. (2006). The 100-Car Naturalistic Driving Study, Phase II—Results of the 100-car field experiment. *National Highway Traffic Safety Administration Report No.* DOT HS 810 593. Retrieved May 18, 2007, from http://www-nrd.nhtsa.dot.gov/departments/nrd-13/driver-distraction/PDF/100CarMain.pdf.

Dinkmeyer, D., Sr., McKay, G. D., & Dinkmeyer, D., Jr. (1997). *The parent's handbook.* Circle Pines, MN: American Guidance Service.

Dion, K. L. (2003). Prejudice, racism, and discrimination. In T. Millon, & M. J. Lerner (Eds.), *Personality and social psychology. The comprehensive handbook of psychology* (Vol. 5). New York: Wiley.

Dirkzwager, A. J. E., Bramsen, I., & Van Der Ploeg, H. M. (2001). The longitudinal course of posttraumatic stress disorder symptoms among aging military veterans. *Journal of Nervous & Mental Disease, 189*(12), 846–853.

Distin, K. (2006). *Gifted children: A guide for parents and professionals.* London: Jessica Kingsley Publishers.

Dixon, M. J., Smilek, D., & Merikle, P. M. (2004). Not all synaesthetes are created equal: Projector versus associator synaesthetes. *Cognitive, Affective, & Behavioral Neuroscience, 4*(3), 335–343.

Dixon, S. V., Graber, J, A., & Brooks-Gunn, J. (2008). The roles of respect for parental authority and parenting practices in parent-child conflict among African American, Latino, and European American families. *Journal of Family Psychology, 22*(1), 1–10.

Dobson, K. S., Backs-Dermott, G. J., & Dozois, D. J. A. (2000). Cognitive and cognitive-behavioral therapies. In C. R. Snyder, & R. E. Ingram (Eds.), *Handbook of psychological change: Psychotherapy processes and practices for the 21st century.* New York: Wiley.

Dodds, P. S., Muhamad, R., & Watts, D. J. (2003). An experimental study of search in global social networks. *Science, 301*(5634), 827–829.

Doidge, N. (1997). Empirical evidence for the efficacy of psychoanalytic psychotherapies and psychoanalysis. *Psychoanalytic Inquiry,* Suppl., 102–150.

Dollard, J., & Miller, N. E. (1950). *Personality and psychotherapy: An analysis in terms of learning, thinking and culture.* New York: McGraw-Hill.

Domhoff, G. W. (2001). A new neurocognitive theory of dreams. *Dreaming, 11,* 13–33.

Domhoff, G. W. (2003). *The scientific study of dreams: neural networks, cognitive development, and content analysis.*

Washington, DC: American Psychological Association.

Domhoff, G. W. (2005). Refocusing the neurocognitive approach to dreams: A critique of the Hobson versus Solms debate. *Dreaming, 15*(1), 3–20.

Domingo, R. A., & Goldstein-Alpern, N. (1999). "What dis?" and other toddler-initiated, expressive language-learning strategies. *Infant-Toddler Intervention, 9*(1), 39–60.

Domjan, M. (2006). *The principles of learning and behavior* (5th ed.). Belmont, CA: Cengage Learning/Wadsworth.

Donate-Bartfield, E., & Passman, R. H. (2004). Relations between children's attachments to their mothers and to security blankets. *Journal of Family Psychology, 18*(3), 453–458.

Donnerstein, E. (2001). Media violence. In J. Worell (Ed.), *Encyclopedia of gender and women.* San Diego: Academic Press.

Donnerstein, E. I., & Linz, D. G. (1986). The question of pornography. *Psychology Today,* Dec., 56–59.

Dooling, D. J., & Lachman, R. (1971). Effects of comprehension on retention of prose. *Journal of Experimental Psychology, 88,* 216–222.

Doran, S. M., Van Dongen, H. P., & Dinges, D. F. (2001). Sustained attention performance during sleep deprivation. *Archives of Italian Biology, 139,* 253–267.

Dorman, M. F., & Wilson, B. S. (2004). The design and function of cochlear implants. *American Scientist, 92*(Sept–Oct), 436–445.

Dosher, B. A., & Ma, J. (1998). Output loss or rehearsal loop? *Journal of Experimental Psychology: Learning, Memory, & Cognition, 24*(2), 316–335.

Doty, R. M., Peterson, B. E., & Winter, D. G. (1991). *Journal of Personality & Social Psychology, 61*(4), 629–640.

Dougall, A. L., & Baum, A. (2003). Stress, coping, and immune function. In M. Gallagher, & R. J. Nelson (Eds.), *Handbook of psychology: Biological psychology* (Vol. 3). New York: John Wiley.

Dougherty, D. D., Baer, L., Cosgrove, G. R., Cassem, E. H., et al. (2002). Prospective long-term follow-up of 44 patients who received cingulotomy for treatment-refractory obsessive-compulsive disorder. *American Journal of Psychiatry, 159*(2), 269–275.

Douvan, E. (1997). Erik Erikson: Critical times, critical theory. *Child Psychiatry & Human Development, 28*(1), 15–21.

Dovidio, J. F., Allen, J. L., & Schroeder, D. A. (1990). Specificity of empathy-induced helping: Evidence for altruistic motivation. *Journal of Personality & Social Psychology, 59*(2), 249–260.

Dovidio, J. F., & Gaertner, S. L. (1999). Reducing prejudice: Combating intergroup biases. *Current Directions in Psychological Science, 8*(4), 101–105.

Dovidio, J. F., Gaertner, S. L., Kawakami, K., & Hodson, G. (2002). Why can't we just get along? *Cultural Diversity and Ethnic Minority Psychology, 8*(2), 88–102.

Dovidio, J. F., Glick, P., & Rudman, L. A. (Eds.). (2005). *On the nature of prejudice: Fifty years after Allport.* Malden, MA: Blackwell.

Dovidio, J. F., & Penner, L. A. (2001). Helping and altruism. In M. Hewstone, & M. Brewer (Eds.), *Handbook of social psychology.* London: Blackwell.

Dovidio, J. F., Piliavin, J. A., Schroeder, D. A., & Penner, L. A. (2006). *The social psychology of prosocial behavior.* Mahwah, NJ: Erlbaum.

Dowling, K. W. (2005). The effect of lunar phases on domestic violence incident rates. *Forensic Examiner, 14*(4), 13–18.

Dozois, D. J. A., & Dobson, K. S. (2002). Depression. In M. M. Antony, & D. H. Barlow (Eds.), *Handbook of assessment and treatment planning for psychological disorders.* New York: Guilford.

Dozois, D. J. A., & Dobson, K. S. (Eds.). (2004). *The prevention of anxiety and depression: Theory, research, and practice.* Washington, DC: American Psychological Association.

Draguns, J. G., Gielen, U. P., & Fish, J. M. (2004). Approaches to culture, healing, and psychotherapy. In U. P. Gielen, J. M. Fish, et al. (Eds.), *Handbook of culture, therapy, and healing.* Mahwah, NJ: Erlbaum.

Drigotas, S. M., Rusbult, C. E., Wieselquist, J., & Whitton, S. W. (1999). Close partner as sculptor of the ideal self: Behavioral affirmation and the Michelangelo phenomenon. *Journal of Personality & Social Psychology, 77*(2), 293–323.

Driver, J. L., & Gottman, J. M. (2004). Daily marital interactions and positive affect during marital conflict among newlywed couples. *Family Process, 43*(3), 301–314.

Drolet, G., Dumont, E. C., Gosselin, I., Kinkead, R., et al. (2001). Role of endogenous opioid system in the regulation of the stress response. *Progress in Neuro-Psychopharmacology & Biological Psychiatry, 25*(4), 729–741.

Drucker, P. (1993). *Post-capitalist society.* New York: HarperCollins.

Druckman, D., & Bjork, R. A. (1994). *Learning, remembering, believing: Enhancing human performance.* Washington, DC: National Academy Press.

Drummond, M., Douglas, J., & Olver, J. (2007). Anosmia after traumatic brain injury: A clinical update. *Brain Impairment, 8*(1), 31–40.

DSM-IV (1994). *Global Assessment of Functioning Scale.* DSM-IV: Diagnostic and statistical manual of mental disorders (4th ed.). Washington, DC: American Psychiatric Association.

DSM-IV-TR: Diagnostic and statistical manual of mental disorders (5th ed.). (2000). Washington, DC: American Psychiatric Association.

Duclos, S. E., & Laird, J. D. (2001). The deliberate control of emotional experience through control of expressions. *Cognition and Emotion, 15,* 27–56.

Duffy, J. F., & Wright, Jr., K. P. (2005). Entrainment of the human circadian system by light. *Journal of Biological Rhythms, 20*(4), 326–338.

Duffy, J. F., Rimmer, D. W., & Czeisler, C. A. (2001). Association of intrinsic cir-

cadian period with morningness-eveningness, usual wake time, and circadian phase. *Behavioral Neuroscience, 115*(4), 895–899.

Dulewicz, V., & Higgs, M. (2000). Emotional intelligence. *Journal of Managerial Psychology, 15*(4), 341–372.

Duncan, J. (2005). Frontal lobe function and general intelligence: Why it matters. *Cortex, 41*(2), 215–217.

Duncker, K. (1945). On problem solving. *Psychological Monographs, 58*(270).

Durand, V. M., & Barlow, D. H. (2006). *Essentials of abnormal psychology* (4th ed.). Belmont, CA: Cengage Learning/Wadsworth.

Durham, M. D., & Dane, F. C. (1999). Juror knowledge of eyewitness behavior. *Journal of Social Behavior & Personality, 14*(2), 299–308.

Durham, M. G. (2008). *The Lolita Effect.* New York: Overlook Press.

Durrant, J. E., & Janson, S. (2005). Legal reform, corporal punishment and child abuse: The case of Sweden. *International Review of Victimology, 12,* 139–158.

Dutta, T., & Mandal, M. K. (2005). The relationship of handedness and accidents: A meta-analytical review of findings. *Psychological Studies, 50*(4), 309–316.

Dutton, D. G., & Aron, A. P. (1974). Some evidence for heightened sexual attraction under conditions of high anxiety. *Journal of Personality & Social Psychology, 30,* 510–517.

Dwyer, W. O., Leeming, F. C., Cobern, M. K., Porter, B. E. et al. (1993). Critical review of behavioral interventions to preserve the environment. *Environment and Behavior, 25*(3), 275–321.

Dyer, K. A. (2001). Dealing with death and dying in medical education and practice. *Journey of Hearts.* www.journeyofhearts.org.

Dywan, J., & Bowers, K. S. (1983). The use of hypnosis to enhance recall. *Science, 222,* 184–185.

Dzokoto, V. A., & Adams, G. (2005). Understanding genital-shrinking epidemics in West Africa: Koro, juju, or mass psychogenic illness? *Culture, Medicine and Psychiatry, 29*(1), 53–78.

Eagly, A. H. (2000). Gender roles. In A. Kazdin (Ed.), *Encyclopedia of psychology.* Washington, DC: American Psychological Association.

Eagly, A. H. (2001). Social role theory of sex differences and similarities. In J. Worell (Ed.), *Encyclopedia of women and gender.* San Diego: Academic Press.

Eagly, A. H. (2007). Female leadership advantage and disadvantage: Resolving the contradictions. *Psychology of Women Quarterly, 31*(1), 1–12.

Eagly, A. H., & Carli, L. L. (2007). *Through the labyrinth: The truth about how women become leaders.* Watertown, MA: HBS Press Book.

Ebbinghaus, H. (1885). *Memory: A contribution to experimental psychology.* Translated by H. A. Ruger, & C. E. Bussenius, 1913. New York: New York Teacher's College, Columbia University.

Ebster, C., & Kirk-Smith, M. (2005). The effect of the human pheromone androstenol on product evaluation. *Psychology & Marketing, 22*(9), 739–749.

Eckardt, M. H. (2005). Karen Horney: A portrait. The 120th anniversary, Karen Horney, September 16, 1885. *American Journal of Psychoanalysis, 65*(2), 95–101.

Eckerman, D. A. (1999). Scheduling reinforcement about once a day. *Behavioural Processes, 45*(1–3), 101–114.

Eddy, K. T., Dutra, L., Bradley, R., & Westen, D. (2004). A multidimensional meta-analysis of psychotherapy and pharmacotherapy for obsessive-compulsive disorder. *Clinical Psychology Review, 24*(8), 1011–1030.

Eichenbaum, H., & Fortin, N. J. (2005). Bridging the gap between brain and behavior: Cognitive and neural mechanisms of episodic memory. *Journal of the Experimental Analysis of Behavior, 84*(3), 619–629.

Eidelson, R. J., & Eidelson, J. I. (2003). Dangerous ideas. *American Psychologist, 58*(3), 182–192.

Eifert, G. H., & Lejuez, C. W. (2000). Aversion therapy. In A. E. Kazdin (Ed.), *Encyclopedia of psychology*. Washington, DC: American Psychological Association.

Eimas, P. D., Quinn, P. C., & Cowan, P. (1994). Development of exclusivity in perceptually based categories of young infants. *Journal of Experimental Child Psychology, 58*(3), 418–431.

Eisenberg, N., Valiente, C., Fabes, R. A., Smith, C. L., et al. (2003). The relations of effortful control and ego control to children's resiliency and social functioning. *Developmental Psychology, 39*(4), 761–776.

Eisler, I., Simic, M., Russell, G. F. M., & Dare, C. (2007). A randomised controlled treatment trial of two forms of family therapy in adolescent anorexia nervosa: A five-year follow-up. *Journal of Child Psychology & Psychiatry, 48*(6), 552–560.

Eisler, J. A., Justice, Jr., J. B., & Neill, D. B. (2004). Individual differences in reward sensitivity: Implications for psychostimulant abuse vulnerability. *North American Journal of Psychology, 6*(3), 527–544.

Ekman, P. (1993). Facial expression and emotion. *American Psychologist, 48*(4), 384–392.

Ekman, P. (2001). *Telling lies: Clues to deceit in the marketplace, politics, and marriage*. New York: Norton.

Ekman, P., Levenson, R. W., & Friesen, W. V. (1983). Autonomic nervous system activity distinguishes among emotions. *Science, 221*, 1208–1210.

Ekman, P., & O'Sullivan, M. (1991). Who can catch a liar? *American Psychologist, 46*(9), 913–920.

Elder, P. (2006). *Critical thinking: Learn the tools the best thinkers use*. Englewood Cliffs, NJ: Prentice-Hall.

Eliot, L. (1999). *What's going on in there?* New York: Bantam

Elli, K. A., & Nathan, P. J. (2001). The pharmacology of human working memory. *International Journal of Neuropsychopharmacology, 4*(3), 299–313.

Ellickson, P. L., Martino, S. C., & Collins, R. L. (2004). Marijuana use from adolescence to young adulthood. *Health Psychology, 23*(3), 299–307.

Elliott, M., Browne, K., & Kilcoyne, J. (1995). Child sexual abuse prevention: What offenders tell us. *Child Abuse & Neglect, 19*(5), 579–594.

Elliott, M., & Williams, D. (2003). The client experience of counselling and psychotherapy. *Counselling Psychology Review, 18*(1), 34–38.

Ellis, A. (1979). The practice of rational-emotive therapy. In A. Ellis, & J. Whiteley (Eds.), *Theoretical and empirical foundations of rational-emotive therapy*. Monterey, CA: Brooks/Cole.

Ellis, A. (1995). Changing rational-emotive therapy (RET) to rational emotive behavior therapy (REBT). *Journal of Rational-Emotive & Cognitive Behavior Therapy, 13*(2), 85–89.

Ellis, A. (2004). Why rational emotive behavior therapy is the most comprehensive and effective form of behavior therapy. *Journal of Rational-Emotive & Cognitive Behavior Therapy, 22*(2), 85–92.

Ellis, P. J., West, B. J., Ryan, A. M., & Deshon, R. P. (2002). The use of impression management tactics in structured interviews: A function of question type. *Journal of Applied Psychology, 87*, 1200–1208.

Elovainio, M., Kivimaeki, M., Steen, N., & Kalliomaeki-Levanto, T. (2000). Organizational and individual factors affecting mental health and job satisfaction. *Journal of Occupational Health Psychology, 5*(2) 269–277.

Emmorey, K., Grabowski, T., Mc-Cullough, S., Damasio, H., et al. (2003). Neural systems underlying lexical retrieval for sign language. *Neuropsychologia, 41*(1), 85–95.

Emurian, H. H. (2005). Web-based programmed instruction: Evidence of rule-governed learning. *Computers in Human Behavior, 21*(6), 893–915.

Engber, D. (2006). The mystery of Sonar Boy. *Slate*, December 1. Retrieved February 28, 2008, from http://www.slate.com/id/2154696/.

Engle, D. E., & Arkowitz, H. (2006). *Ambivalence in psychotherapy: Facilitating readiness to change*. New York: Guilford.

Enns, J. T., & Coren, S. (1995). The box alignment illusion. *Perception & Psychophysics, 57*(8), 1163–1174.

Enns, M. W., Cox, B. J., & Clara, I. P. (2005). Perfectionism and neuroticism: A longitudinal study of specific vulnerability and diathesis-stress models. *Cognitive Therapy and Research, 29*(4), 463–478.

Erickson, C. D., & Al-Timimi, N. R. (2001). Providing mental health services to Arab Americans. *Cultural Diversity and Ethnic Minority Psychology, 7*(4), 308–327.

Ericsson, K. A. (2000). How experts attain and maintain superior performance. *Journal of Aging & Physical Activity, 8*(4), 366–372.

Ericsson, K. A., & Charness, N. (1994). Expert performance. *American Psychologist, 49*(8), 725–747.

Ericsson, K. A., & Chase, W. G. (1982). Exceptional memory. *American Scientist, 70*, 607–615.

Ericsson, K. A., Delaney, P. F., Weaver, G., & Mahadevan, R. (2004). Uncovering the structure of a memorist's superior "basic" memory capacity. *Cognitive Psychology, 49*(3), 191–237.

Erikson, E. H. (1963). *Childhood and society*. New York: Norton.

Erlacher, D., & Schredl, M. (2004). Dreams reflecting waking sport activities: A comparison of sport and psychology students. *International Journal of Sport Psychology, 35*(4), 301–308.

Erlich, P. R., & Erlich, A. H. (1990). The population explosion. *The Amicus Journal*, Winter, 18–29.

Ernst, E. (1994). Is acupuncture effective for pain control? *Journal of Pain & Symptom Management, 9*(2), 72–74.

Eron, L. D. (1987). The development of aggressive behavior from the perspective of a developing behaviorism. *American Psychologist, 42*, 435–442.

Eschholz, S., Chiricos, T., & Gertz, M. (2003). Television and fear of crime: Program types, audience traits, and the mediating effect of perceived neighborhood racial composition. *Social Problems, 50*(3), 395–415.

Espie, C. A. (2002). Insomnia. *Annual Review of Psychology, 53*, 215–243.

Esterling, B. A., L'Abate, L., Murray, E. J., & Pennebaker, J. W. (1999). Empirical foundations for writing in prevention and psychotherapy: Mental and physical health outcomes. *Clinical Psychology Review, 19*(1), 79–96.

Ethier, K. A., Kershaw, T., Niccolai, L., Lewis, J. B., et al. (2003). Adolescent women underestimate their susceptibility to sexually transmitted infections. *Sexually Transmitted Infections, 79*, 408–411.

Evans, G. W. (2006). Child development and the physical environment. *Annual Review of Psychology, 57*, 423–451.

Evans, G. W., Lercher, P., & Kofler, W. W. (2002). Crowding and children's mental health: the role of house type. *Journal of Environmental Psychology, 22*, 221–231.

Evans, G.W., Lepore, S. J., & Schroeder, A. (1996). The role of interior design elements in human responses to crowding. *Journal of Personality & Social Psychology, 70*(1), 41–46.

Evans, G. W., & Wener, R. E. (2007). Crowding and personal space invasion on the train: Please don't make me sit in the middle. *Journal of Environmental Psychology, 27*(1), 90–94.

Evardone, M., Alexander, G. M., & Morey, L. C. (2007). Hormones and borderline personality features. *Personality & Individual Differences, 44*(1), 278–287.

Everly, G. S. (2002). Thoughts on peer (paraprofessional) support in the provision of mental health services. *International Journal of Emergency Mental Health, 4*(2), 89–92.

Ewen, R. B. (2003). *An introduction to theories of personality* (6th ed.). Mahwah, NJ: Erlbaum.

Ewing, G. (2001). Altruistic, egoistic, and normative effects on curbside recycling. *Environment & Behavior, 33*(6), 733–764.

Eysenck, H. J. (Ed.). (1981). *A model for personality*. New York: Springer-Verlag.

Eysenck, H. J. (1994). The outcome problem in psychotherapy: What have we learned? *Behaviour Research & Therapy, 32*(5), 477–495.

Fabrega, Jr., H. (2004). Culture and the origins of psychopathology. In U. P. Gielen, J. M., Fish, et al. (Eds.), *Handbook of culture, therapy, and healing*. Mahwah, NJ: Erlbaum.

Fagan, J. F., & Holland, C. R. (2007). Racial equality in intelligence: Predictions from a theory of intelligence as processing. *Intelligence, 35*(4), 319–334.

Fahim, C., Stip, E., Mancini-Marie, A., Mensour, B., et al. (2005). Brain activity during emotionally negative pictures in schizophrenia with and without flat affect: An fMRI study. *Psychiatry Research: Neuroimaging, 140*(1), 1–15.

Fahle, M., & Poggio, T. (Eds.). (2002). *Perceptual learning*. Cambridge, MA: MIT Press.

Fain, G. L. (2003). *Sensory transduction*. Sunderland, MA: Sinauer.

Faith, M. S., Wong, F. Y., & Carpenter, K. M. (1995). Group sensitivity training: Update, meta-analysis, and recommendations. *Journal of Counseling Psychology, 42*(3), 390–399.

Falkowski, C. (2000). *Dangerous drugs*. Center City, MN: Hazelden Information Education.

Farah, M. J. (2004). *Visual agnosia* (2nd ed.). Cambridge, MA: MIT Press.

Farah, M. J. (2006). Prosopagnosia. In M. J. Farah, & T. E. Feinberg (Eds.), *Patient-based approaches to cognitive neuroscience* (2nd ed.). Cambridge, MA: MIT Press.

Farb, N. A. S., Segal, Z. V., Mayberg, H., et al. (2007). Attending to the present: Mindfulness meditation reveals distinct neural modes of self-reference. *Social Cognitive & Affective Neuroscience, 2*(4), 313–322.

Farrimond, T. (1990). Effect of alcohol on visual constancy values and possible relation to driving performance. *Perceptual & Motor Skills, 70*(1), 291–295.

Farroni, T., Massaccesi, S., Pividori, D., & Johnson, M. H. (2004). Gaze following in newborns. *Infancy, 5*(1), 39–60.

FBI. (2005). *Crime in the United States, 2005*. Washington, DC: Federal Bureau of Investigation. Retrieved July 18, 2008, from http://www.fbi.gov/ucr/05cius/.

Feingold, A. (1990). Gender differences in effects of physical attractiveness on romantic attraction. *Journal of Personality & Social Psychology, 59*(5), 981–993.

Feingold, A. (1992). Gender differences in mate selection preferences. *Psychological Bulletin, 111*, 304–341.

Feldhusen, J. F., & Goh, B. E. (1995). Assessing and accessing creativity: An integrative review of theory, research, and development. *Creativity Research Journal, 8*(3), 231–247.

Feldman, D. H. (2004). Piaget's stages: The unfinished symphony of cognitive development. *New Ideas in Psychology, 22*(3), 175–231.

Feldman, S. (2003). Enforcing social conformity: A theory of authoritarianism. *Political Psychology, 24*(1), 41–47.

Fellous, J.-M., & Ledoux, J. E. (2005). Toward basic principles for emotional processing: What the fearful brain tells the robot. In J.-M. Fellous, & M. A. Arbib (Eds.), *Who needs emotions? The brain meets the robot*. New York: Oxford University Press.

Fenn, K. M., Nusbaum, H. C., & Margoliash, D. (2003). Consolidation during sleep of perceptual learning of spoken language. *Nature, 425*(6958), 614–616.

Fenton, G. W. (1998). Neurosurgery for mental disorder. *Irish Journal of Psychological Medicine, 15*(2), 45–48.

Fernald, A. (1989). Intonation and communicative intent in mothers' speech to infants: Is the melody the message? *Child Development, 60*(6), 1497–1510.

Fernald, A., Perfors, A., & Marchman, V. A. (2006). Picking up speed in understanding: Speech processing efficiency and vocabulary growth across the 2nd year. *Developmental Psychology, 42*(1), 98–116.

Féron, F., Perry, C., Cochrane, J., Licina, P., et al. (2005). Autologous olfactory ensheathing cell transplantation in human spinal cord injury. *Brain: A Journal of Neurology, 128*(12), 2951–2960.

Ferrari, J. R., & Scher, S. J. (2000). Toward an understanding of academic and nonacademic tasks procrastinated by students: The use of daily logs. *Psychology in the Schools, 37*(4), 359–366.

Festinger, L. (1957). *A theory of cognitive dissonance*. Stanford, CA: Stanford University Press.

Festinger, L., & Carlsmith, J. M. (1959). Cognitive consequences of forced compliance. *Journal of Abnormal & Social Psychology, 58*, 203–210.

Ficca, G., & Salzarulob, P. (2004). What in sleep is for memory. *Sleep Medicine, 5*, 225–230.

Field, C. E., Nash, H. M., Handwerk, M. L., & Friman, P. C. (2004). A modification of the token economy for nonresponsive youth in family-style residential care. *Behavior Modification, 28*(3), 438–457.

Fields, R. D. (2007). The shark's electric sense. *Scientific American, 297*(8), 74–81.

Fields, R. M., & Margolin, J. (2001). *Coping with trauma*. Washington, DC: American Psychological Association.

Figueredo, A. J., Sefcek, J. A., & Jones, D. N. (2006). The ideal romantic partner personality. *Personality & Individual Differences, 41*(3), 431–441.

Fink, M. (2000). Electroshock revisited. *American Scientist, 88*(March–April), 162–167.

Fink, M., & Taylor, M. A. (2003). *Catatonia: A clinician's guide to diagnosis and treatment*. London: Cambridge University Press.

Fiore, D., Dimaggio, G., Nicoló, G., Semerari, A., et al. (2008). Metacognitive interpersonal therapy in a case of obsessive-compulsive and avoidant personality disorders. *Journal of Clinical Psychology, 64*(2), 168–180.

Fiorina, C. (2006). *Tough choices: A memoir*. New York: Penguin.

Fireman, G., Kose, G., & Solomon, M. J. (2003). Self-observation and learning: The effect of watching oneself on problem solving performance. *Cognitive Development, 18*(3), 339–354.

Firestone, P., Kingston, D. A., Wexler, A., & Bradford, J. M. (2006). Long-term follow-up of exhibitionists: Psychological, phallometric, and offense characteristics. *Journal of the American Academy of Psychiatry & the Law, 34*(3), 349–359.

First, M. B., & Pincus, H. A. (2002). The DSM-IV text revision: Rationale and potential impact on clinical practice. *Psychiatric Services, 53*, 288–292.

Fischer, A. H., Manstead, A. S. R., Rodriquez Mosquera, P. M., & van Vianen, A. E. M. (2004). Gender and culture differences in emotion. *Emotion, 4*(1), 87–94.

Fisher, B. S., Cullen, F. T., & Daigle, L. E. (2005). The discovery of acquaintance rape: The salience of methodological innovation and rigor. *Journal of Interpersonal Violence, 20*(4), 493–500.

Fisher, R. P., & Geiselman, R. E. (1987). Enhancing eyewitness memory with the cognitive interview. In M. M. Grunegerg, P. E. Morris, et al. (Eds.), *Practical aspects of memory: Current research and issues*. Chinchester, UK: Wiley.

Fisher, S. (1973). *The female orgasm*. New York: Basic.

Fiske, S. T. (1993). Social cognition and social perception. *Annual Review of Psychology, 44*, 155–194.

Fiske, S. T., Cuddy, A. J. C., Glick, P., & Xu, J. (2002). A model of (often mixed) stereotype content. *Journal of Personality & Social Psychology, 82*(6), 878–902.

Flanagan, M. B., May, J. G., & Dobie, T. G. (2004). The role of vection, eye movements and postural instability in the etiology of motion sickness. *Journal of Vestibular Research: Equilibrium & Orientation, 14*(4), 335–346.

Flannery, D. J., Rowe, D. C., & Gulley, B. L. (1993). Impact of pubertal status, timing, and age on adolescent sexual experience and delinquency. *Journal of Adolescent Research, 8*(1), 21–40.

Flavell, J. H. (1992). Cognitive development: Past, present, and future. *Developmental Psychology, 28*(6), 998–1005.

Fleming, J. (1974). Field report: The state of the apes. *Psychology Today*, Jan., 46.

Flowe, H. D., & Ebbese, E. B. (2007). The effect of lineup member similarity on recognition accuracy in simultaneous and sequential lineups. *Law & Human Behavior, 31*(1), 33–52.

Flynn, J. R. (2007). *What is intelligence? Beyond the Flynn Effect*. New York: Cambridge.

Flynn, K. J., & Fitzgibbon, M. (1998). Body images and obesity risk among black females: A review of the literature. *Annals of Behavioral Medicine, 20*(1), 13–24.

Fobair, P. (1997). Cancer support groups and group therapies. *Journal of Psychosocial Oncology, 15*(3–4), 123–147.

Fochtmann, L. J. (1995). Intractable sneezing as a conversion symptom. *Psychosomatics, 36*(2), 103–112.

Fogel, S. M., Nader, R., Cote, K. A., & Smith, C. T. (2007). Sleep spindles and learning potential. *Behavioral Neuroscience, 121*(1), 1–10.

Folkman, S., & Moskowitz, J. T. (2004). Coping. *Annual Review of Psychology, 55*, 745–774.

Follett, K., & Hess, T. M. (2002). Aging, cognitive complexity, and the fundamental attribution error. *Journals of Gerontology: Series B: Psychological Sciences and Social Sciences, 57B*(4), 312–323.

Fontaine, K. R., Redden, D. T., Wang, C., Westfall, A. O., et al. (2003). Years of life lost due to obesity. *Journal of the American Medical Association, 289*, 187–193.

Fontenelle, D. H. (1989). *How to live with your children*. Tucson, AZ: Fisher Books.

Foo, P., Warren, W. H., Duchon, A., & Tarr, M. J. (2005). Do humans integrate routes into a cognitive map? Map- versus landmark-based navigation of novel shortcuts. *Journal of Experimental Psychology: Learning, Memory, & Cognition, 31*(2), 195–215.

Foot, M., & Koszycki, D. (2004). Gender differences in anxiety-related traits in patients with panic disorder. *Depression & Anxiety, 20*(3), 123–130.

Forbes, G. B., & Adams-Curtis, L. E. (2001). Experiences with sexual coercion in college males and females. *Journal of Interpersonal Violence, 16*(9), 865–889.

Forbes, G. B., Adams-Curtis, L. E., & White, K. B. (2004). First- and second-generation measures of sexism, rape myths and related beliefs, and hostility toward women: Their interrelationships and association with college students' experiences with dating aggression and sexual coercion. *Violence Against Women, 10*(3), 236–261.

Ford, D. Y., & Moore, J. L. (2006). Being gifted and adolescent: Issues and needs of students of color. In F. A. Dixon, & S. M. Moon (Eds.), *The handbook of secondary gifted education*. Waco, TX: Prufrock Press.

Ford, G. G., Gallagher, S. H., Lacy, B. A., Bridwell, A. M., et al. (1999). Repositioning the home plate umpire to provide enhanced perceptual cues and more accurate ball-strike judgments. *Journal of Sport Behavior, 22*(1), 28–44.

Forney, W. S., Forney, J. C., & Crutsinger, C. (2005). Developmental stages of age and moral reasoning as predictors of juvenile delinquents' behavioral intention to steal clothing. *Family & Consumer Sciences Research Journal, 34*(2), 110–126.

ForsterLee, R., ForsterLee, L., Horowitz, I. A., & King, E. (2006). The effects of defendant race, victim race, and juror gender on evidence processing in a murder trial. *Behavioral Sciences & the Law, 24*(2), 179–198.

Forsyth, D. R. (2006). *Group dynamics* (4th ed.). Belmont, CA: Cengage Learning/Wadsworth.

Forsyth, J. P., & Savsevitz, J. (2002). Behavior therapy: Historical perspective and overview. In M. Hersen, & W. H. Sledge (Eds.), *Encyclopedia of psychotherapy*. San Diego: Academic Press.

Fosse, R., Stickgold, R., & Hobson, J. A. (2001). The mind in REM sleep: Reports of emotional experience. *Sleep: Journal of Sleep & Sleep Disorders Research, 24*(8), 947–955.

Foster, C. A., Witcher, B. S., Campbell, W. K., & Green, J. D. (1998). Arousal and attraction. *Journal of Personality & Social Psychology, 74*(1), 86–101.

Foster, G., & Ysseldyke, J. (1976). Expectancy and halo effects as a result of artificially induced teacher bias. *Contemporary Educational Psychology, 1*, 37–45.

Fowers, B. J., & Davidov, B. J. (2006). The virtue of multiculturalism: Personal transformation, character, and openness to the other. *American Psychologist, 61*(6), 581–594.

Foxhall, K. (2000). Suddenly, a big impact on criminal justice. *APA Monitor*, Jan., 36–37.

Fraley, R. C. (2002). Attachment stability from infancy to adulthood: Meta-analysis and dynamic modeling of developmental mechanisms. *Personality and Social Psychology Review, 6*(2), 123–151.

Fraley, R. C., & Shaver, P. R. (2000). Adult romantic attachment: Theoretical developments, emerging controversies, and unanswered questions. *Review of General Psychology. Special Issue: Adult Attachment, 4*(2), 132–154.

Frank, J. D., & Frank, J. (2004). Therapeutic components shared by all psychotherapies. In A. Freeman, M. J. Mahoney, et al. (Eds.), *Cognition and psychotherapy* (2nd ed.). New York: Springer.

Frank, M. G. (2002). Smiles, lies, and emotion. In M. H. Abel (Ed.), *An empirical reflection on the smile. Mellen studies in psychology* (Vol. 4). Lewiston, NY: Edwin Mellen Press.

Frank, M. G., & Ekman, P. (2004). Appearing truthful generalizes across different deception situations. *Journal of Personality and Social Psychology, 86*(3), 486–495.

Franken, R. E. (2007). *Human motivation* (6th ed.). Belmont, CA: Cengage Learning/Wadsworth.

Frankl, V. (1955). *The doctor and the soul*. New York: Knopf.

Franzoi, S. L., & Klaiber, J. R. (2007). Body use and reference group impact: With whom do we compare our bodies? *Sex Roles, 56*(3–4), 205–214.

Fraser, C. (2002). Fact and fiction: A clarification of phantom limb phenomena. *British Journal of Occupational Therapy, 65*(6), 256–260.

Fredrickson, B. L. (2003). The value of positive emotions. *American Scientist, 91*, 330–335.

Fredrickson, B. L., & Branigan, C. (2005). Positive emotions broaden the scope of attention and thought-action repertoires. *Cognition & Emotion, 19*(3), 313–332.

Fredrickson, B. L., Roberts, T., Noll, S. M., Quinn, D. M., et al. (1998). That swimsuit becomes you. *Journal of Personality & Social Psychology, 75*(1), 269–284.

Freeman, D., & Garety, P. A. (2004). *Paranoia: The psychology of persecutory delusions*. New York: Routledge.

Freize, I. H. (1987). The female victim. In VandenBos, G. R., & Bryant, B. K. (Eds.), *Cataclysms, crises, and catastrophes: Psychology in action*. Washington, DC: American Psychological Association.

French, C. C., Fowler, M., McCarthy, K., & Peers, D. (1991). A test of the Barnum effect. *Skeptical Inquirer, 15*(4), 66–72.

French, S. E., Kim, T. E., & Pillado, O. (2006). Ethnic identity, social group membership, and youth violence. In N. G. Guerra, & E. P. Smith (Eds.), *Preventing youth violence in a multicultural society*. Washington, DC: American Psychological Association.

Freud, S. (1900). *The interpretation of dreams*. London: Hogarth.

Freud, S. (1949). *An outline of psychoanalysis*. New York: Norton.

Frey, M. C., & Detterman, D. K. (2004). Scholastic assessment or g? The relationship between the scholastic assessment test and general cognitive ability. *Psychological Science, 15*(6), 373–378.

Fried, P. A., & Smith, A. M. (2001) A literature review of the consequences of prenatal marihuana exposure. *Neurotoxicology and Teratology, 23*(1), 1–11.

Friedman, H. S. (2002). *Health psychology* (2nd ed.). Englewood Cliffs, NJ: Prentice-Hall.

Friedman, L. (2006). What is psychoanalysis? *Psychoanalytic Quarterly, 75*(3), 689–713.

Friedman, L. J. (2004). Erik Erikson on generativity: A biographer's perspective. In E. de St. Aubin, D. P. McAdams, et al. (Eds.), *The generative society: Caring for future generations*. Washington, DC: American Psychological Association.

Friedman, M., & Rosenman, R. H. (1983). *Type A behavior and your heart*. New York: Knopf.

Friedman, R. C., Bucci, W., Christian, C., Drucker, P., et al. (1998). Private psychotherapy patients of psychiatrist psychoanalysts. *American Journal of Psychiatry, 155,* 1772–1774.

Fritz, C. O., Morris, P. E., Acton, M., Voelkel, A. R., et al. (2007). Comparing and combining retrieval practice and the keyword mnemonic for foreign vocabulary learning. *Applied Cognitive Psychology, 21*(4), 499–526.

Froehlich, T.E., Lanphear, B. P., Epstein, J. N., Barbaresi, W. J., et al. (2007). Prevalence and treatment of ADHD in a national sample of U.S. Children. *Archives of Pediatrics & Adolescent Medicine, 161*(9), 857–864.

Froufe, M., & Schwartz, C. (2001). Subliminal messages for increasing selfesteem: Placebo effect. *Spanish Journal of Psychology, 4*(1), 19–25.

Fryar, C. D., Hirsch, R., Porter, K. S., Kottiri, B., et al. (2007). Drug use and sexual behaviors reported by adults: United States, 1999–2002. *Advance data from vital and health statistics; no. 384*. Hyattsville, MD: National Center for Health Statistics. Retrieved May 17, 2008, from http://www.cdc.gov/nchs/data/ad/ad384.pdf.

Frydman, M. (1999). Television, aggressiveness and violence. *International Journal of Adolescent Medicine & Health, 11*(3–4), 335–344.

Fu, J. H., Morris, M. W., Lee, S., Chao, M., et al. (2007). Epistemic motives and cultural conformity: Need for closure, culture, and context as determinants of conflict judgments. *Journal of Personality & Social Psychology, 92*(2), 191–207.

Fukuda, K., & Ishihara, K. (2001). Age-related changes of sleeping pattern during adolescence. *Psychiatry & Clinical Neurosciences, 55*(3), 231–232.

Funder, D. C. (2006). *The personality puzzle* (4th ed.). New York: Norton.

Funk, J. B. (2005). Children's exposure to violent video games and desensitization to violence. *Child and Adolescent Psychiatric Clinics of North America, 14*(3), 387–404.

Fuqua, D. R., & Newman, J. L. (2002). Creating caring organizations. *Consulting Psychology Journal: Practice & Research, 54*(2), 131–140.

Furnham, A., Chamorro-Premuzic, T., & Callahan, I. (2003). Does graphology predict personality and intelligence? *Individual Differences Research, 1*(2), 78–94.

FVPF. (2007). Domestic violence is a serious, widespread social problem in America: The facts. Family Violence Prevention Fund. Retrieved July 29, 2007, from http://www.endabuse.org/resources/facts/.

Gable, S. L., Reis, H. T., Impett, E. A., & Asher, E. R. (2004). What do you do when things go right? *Journal of Personality & Social Psychology, 87*(2), 228–245.

Gabrieli, J. D. E. (1998). Cognitive neuroscience of human memory. *Annual Review of Psychology, 49,* 87–115.

Gadzella, B. M. (1995). Differences in processing information among psychology course grade groups. *Psychological Reports, 77,* 1312–1314.

Gaertner, S. L., Dovidio, J. F., Banker, B. S., Houlette, M., et al. (2000). Reducing intergroup conflict: From superordinate goals to decategorization, recategorization, and mutual differentiation. *Group Dynamics, 4*(1), 98–114.

Galambos, N. L., Barker, E. T., & Tilton-Weaver, L. C. (2003). Who gets caught at maturity gap? A study of pseudomature, immature and mature adolescents. *International Journal of Behavioral Development, 27*(3), 253–263.

Galanter, M., Hayden, F., Castañeda, R, & Franco, H. (2005). Group therapy, self-help groups, and network therapy. In R. J. Frances, S. I. Miller, et al. (Eds.), *Clinical textbook of addictive disorders* (3rd ed.). New York: Guilford.

Galati, D., Scherer, K. R., & Ricci-Bitti, P. E. (1997). Voluntary facial expression of emotion: Comparing congenitally blind with normally sighted encoders. *Journal of Personality & Social Psychology, 73*(6), 1363–1379.

Galea, S., Ahern, J., Resnick, H., Kilpatrick, D., et al. (2002). Psychological sequelae of the September 11 terrorist attacks in New York City. *New England Journal of Medicine, 346*(13), 982–987.

Galea, S., & Resnick, H. (2005). Posttraumatic stress disorder in the general population after mass terrorist incidents: Considerations about the nature of exposure. *CNS Spectrums, 10*(2), 107–115.

Gamache, G. (2004). *Essentials in human factors*. San Mateo, CA: Usernomics.

Ganis, G., Thompson, W. L., & Kosslyn, S. M. (2004). Brain areas underlying visual mental imagery and visual perception: An fMRI study. *Cognitive Brain Research, 20*(2), 226–241.

Ganster, D. C., Fox, M. L., & Dwyer, D. J. (2001). Explaining employees' health care costs: A prospective examination of stressful job demands, personal control, and physiological reac-

tivity. *Journal of Applied Psychology, 86,* 954–964.

Garbarino, S., Beelke, M., Costa, G., Violani, C., et al. (2002). Brain function and effects of shift work: Implications for clinical neuropharmacology. *Neuropsychobiology, 45,* 50–56.

Garbarino, S., Mascialino, B., Penco, M. A., Squarcia, S., et al. (2004). Professional shift-work drivers who adopt prophylactic naps can reduce the risk of car accidents during night work. *Sleep: Journal of Sleep & Sleep Disorders Research, 27*(7), 1295–1302.

García-Junco-Clemente, P., Linares-Clemente, P., & Fernández-Chacón, R. (2005). Active zones for presynaptic plasticity in the brain. *Molecular Psychiatry, 10*(2), 185–200.

Gardner, H. (2003). *Multiple intelligences after twenty years*. Invited Address, American Educational Research Association, April, 2003. Retrieved December 6, 2005, from http://www.pz.harvard.edu/PIs/HG_MI_after_20_years.pdf.

Gardner, H. (2004). *Frames of mind* (Tenth-anniversary edition). New York: Basic.

Gardner, R. A., & Gardner, B. T. (1989). *Teaching sign language to chimpanzees*. Albany, NY: State University of New York Press.

Garland, A. F., & Zigler, E. (1993). Adolescent suicide prevention. *American Psychologist, 48*(2), 169–182.

Garlow, S. J., Purselle, D. C., & Heninger, M. (2007). Cocaine and alcohol use preceding suicide in African American and White adolescents. *Journal of Psychiatric Research, 41*(6), 530–536.

Garnets, L. D. (2002). Sexual orientation in perspective. *Cultural Diversity & Ethnic Minority Psychology, 8*(2), 115–129.

Garnets, L. D., & Kimmel, D. (1991). Lesbian and gay male dimensions in the psychological study of human diversity. *Psychological perspectives on human diversity in America*. Washington, DC: American Psychological Association.

Gass, R. H., & Seiter, J. S. (2007). Persuasion: Social influence and compliance gaining (3rd ed.). Boston: Allyn & Bacon.

Gastner, M. T., Shalizi, C. R., & Newman, M. E. J. (2005). Maps and cartograms of the 2004 US presidential election results. *Advances in Complex Systems, 8*(1), 117–123.

Gates, A. I. (1958). Recitation as a factor in memorizing. In J. Deese (Ed.), *The psychology of learning*. New York: McGraw-Hill.

Gathcel, R. J., & Oordt, M. S. (2003). Insomnia. In R. J. Gatchel, & M. S. Oordt (Eds.), *Clinical health psychology and primary care: Practical advice and clinical guidance for successful collaboration*. Washington, DC: American Psychological Association.

Gatz, M. (2007). Genetics, dementia, and the elderly. *Current Directions in Psychological Science, 16*(3), 123–127.

Gauquelin, M. (1970). *Astrology and science*. London: Peter Davies.

Gayle, H. (2000). An overview of the global HIV/AIDS epidemic, with a focus on the United States. *AIDS, 14*(Suppl 2), S8–S17.

Gazzaniga, M. S. (1970). *The bisected brain*. New York: Plenum.

Geary, N. (2004). Endocrine controls of eating: CCK, leptin, and ghrelin. *Physiology & Behavior, 81*(5), 719–733.

Gedo, J. E. (2002). The enduring scientific contributions of Sigmund Freud. *Perspectives in Biology & Medicine, 45,* 200–211.

Geehr, J. L., Burke, M. J., & Sulzer, J. L. (1995). Quality circles: The effects of varying degrees of voluntary participation on employee attitudes and program efficacy. *Educational & Psychological Measurement, 55*(1), 124–134.

Gegenfurtner, K. R., & Kiper, D. C. (2003). Color vision. *Annual Review of Neuroscience, 26,* 181–206.

Geiselman, R. E., Fisher, R. P., MacKinnon, D. P., & Holland, H. L. (1986). Eyewitness memory enhancement with the cognitive interview. *American Journal of Psychology, 99,* 385–401.

Geliebter, A., & Aversa, A. (2003). Emotional eating in overweight, normal weight, and underweight individuals. *Eating Behaviors, 3*(4), 341–347.

Genesee, F., Paradis., J., & Crago, M. (2004). *Dual language development and disorders: A handbook on bilingualism and second language learning*. Baltimore: Paul H. Brookes.

George, A. (2006). Living online: The end of privacy? *New Scientist, 2659*(Sept 18), 50–51.

Georgiades, A., Serwood, A., Gullette, E. C., Babyak, M. A., et al. (2000). Effects of exercise and weight loss on mental stress-induced cardiovascular responses in individuals with high blood pressure. *Hypertension, 36,* 171–176.

Gerardi, M., Rothbaum, B. O., Ressler, K., Heekin, M., et al. (2008). Virtual reality exposure therapy using a virtual Iraq: Case report. *Journal of Traumatic Stress, 21*(2), 209–213.

Germain, A., Krakow, B., Faucher, B., Zadra, A., et al. (2004). Increased mastery elements associated with imagery rehearsal treatment for nightmares in sexual assault survivors with PTSD. *Dreaming, 14*(4), 195–206.

German, T. P., & Barrett, H. C. (2005). Functional fixedness in a technologically sparse culture. *Psychological Science, 16*(1), 1–5.

German, T. P., & Defeyter, M. A. (2000). Immunity to functional fixedness in young children. *Psychonomic Bulletin & Review, 7*(4), 707–712.

Gersh, R. D. (1982). Learning when not to shoot. *Santa Barbara News Press,* June 20.

Gershoff, E. T. (2002). Corporal punishment by parents and associated child behaviors and experiences: A meta-analytic and theoretical review. *Psychological Bulletin, 128*(4), 539–579.

Gerstein, E. R. (2002). Manatees, bioacoustics, and boats. *American Scientist, 90*(March–April), 154–163.

Gerwood, J. B. (1998). The legacy of Viktor Frankl. *Psychological Reports, 82*(2), 673–674.

Geschwind, N. (1979). Specializations of the human brain. *Scientific American, 241,* 180–199.

Gewirtz, J. C., & Davis, M. (1998). Application of Pavlovian higher-order conditioning to the analysis of the neural substrates of fear conditioning. *Neuropharmacology, 37*(4–5), 453–459.

Giarratano, J. C., & Riley, G. (2005). *Expert systems, principles and programming* (4th ed.). Belmont, CA: Cengage Learning/Wadsworth.

Gibbons, F. X., Lane, D. J., Gerrard, M., Reis-Bergan, M., et al. (2002). Comparison-level preferences after performance: Is downward comparison theory still useful? *Journal of Personality & Social Psychology, 83*(4), 865–880.

Gibson, B., & Werner, C. M. (1994). The airport as a behavior setting: The role of legibility in communicating the setting program. *Journal of Personality and Social Psychology, 66,* 1049–1060.

Gibson, E. J., & Walk, R. D. (1960). The "visual cliff." *Scientific American, 202*(4), 67–71.

Gibson, K. R. (2002). Evolution of human intelligence: The roles of brain size and mental construction. *Brain, Behavior & Evolution, 59*(1–2), 10–20.

Gifford, R. (2002). *Environmental psychology: Principles and practice* (3rd ed.). Colville, WA: Optimal Books.

Gilbert, A. N., & Wysocki, C. J. (1987). The smell survey results. *National Geographic,* Oct., 514–524.

Gilbert, P. (2001). *Overcoming depression.* New York: Oxford University Press.

Gilovich, T., Keltner, D., & Nisbett, R. (2005). *Social psychology.* New York: Norton.

Gillespie, C. F., & Nemeroff, C. B. (2007). Corticotropin-releasing factor and the psychobiology of early-life stress. *Current Directions in Psychological Science, 16*(2), 85–89.

Gilligan, C. (1982). *In a different voice.* Cambridge, MA: Harvard University Press.

Gilligan, C., & Attanucci, J. (1988). Two moral orientations: Gender differences and similarities. *Merrill-Palmer Quarterly, 34*(3), 223–237.

Gilman, S. E., Cochran, S. D., Mays, V. M., Hughes, M., et al. (2001). Risk of psychiatric disorders among individuals reporting same-sex sexual partners in the National Comorbidity Survey. *American Journal of Public Health, 91*(6), 933–939.

Ginet, M., & Py, J. (2001). A technique for enhancing memory in eyewitness testimonies for use by police officers and judicial officials: The cognitive interview. *Travail Humain, 64*(2), 173–191.

Ginott, H. G. (1965). *Between parent and child: New solutions to old problems.* New York: Macmillan.

Ginsberg, D. L. (2006). Fatal agranulocytosis four years after clozapine discontinuation. *Primary Psychiatry, 13*(2), 32–33.

Giuseppe, R. (2005). Virtual reality in psychotherapy: Review. *CyberPsychology & Behavior. Special Use of Virtual Environments in Training and Rehabilitation: International Perspectives, 8*(3), 220–230.

Gladstone, G. L., & Parker, G. B. (2002). When you're smiling, does the whole world smile for you? *Australasian Psychiatry, 10*(2), 144–146.

Gladwell, M. (2005). Blink: *The power of thinking without thinking.* New York: Little, Brown.

Gleason, J. B. (2005). *The development of language* (6th ed.). Boston: Allyn & Bacon.

Glisky, M. L., Williams, J. M., & Kihlstrom, J. F. (1996). Internal and external mental imagery perspectives and performance on two tasks. *Journal of Sport Behavior, 19*(1), 3–18.

Global Footprint Network (2006). *Ecological footprint: Overview.* Retrieved July 11, 2008, from http://www.footprintnetwork.org/gfn_sub.php?content=footprint_overview.

Glomb, T. M. (2002). Workplace anger and aggression. *Journal of Occupational Health Psychology, 7*(1), 20–36.

Glover, R. J. (2001). Discriminators of moral orientation: Gender role or personality? *Journal of Adult Development, 8*(1), 1–7.

Gobet, F. (2005). Chunking models of expertise: Implications for education. *Applied Cognitive Psychology, 19*(2), 183–204.

Gobet, F., & Simon, H. A. (1996). Recall of random and distorted chess positions: Implications for the theory of expertise. *Memory & Cognition, 24*(4), 493–503.

Godnig, E. C. (2003). Tunnel vision: It's causes & treatment strategies. *Journal of Behavioral Optometry, 14*(4), 95–99.

Goel, V., & Dolan, R. J. (2004). Differential involvement of left prefrontal cortex in inductive and deductive reasoning. *Cognition, 93*(3), 109–121.

Gogate, L. J., Bahrick, L. E., & Watson, J. D. (2000). A study of multimodal motherese: The role of temporal synchrony between verbal labels and gestures. *Child Development, 71*(4), 878–894.

Goldberg, C. (2001). Of prophets, true believers, and terrorists. *The Dana Forum on Brain Science, 3*(3), 21–24.

Goldberg, R. (2006). *Drugs across the spectrum* (5th ed.). Belmont, CA: Cengage Learning/Wadsworth.

Golden, J. (2005). *Message in a bottle: The making of fetal alcohol syndrome.* Cambridge, MA: Harvard University Press.

Golden, T. D., Veiga, J. F., & Simsek, Z. (2006). Telecommuting's differential impact on work-family conflict: Is there no place like home? *Journal of Applied Psychology, 91*(6), 1340–1350.

Goldenberg, H., & Goldenberg, I. (2004). *Family therapy: An overview* (6th ed.). Pacific Grove, CA: Brooks/Cole.

Goldfried, M. R. (2001). Integrating gay, lesbian, and bisexual issues into mainstream psychology. *American Psychologist,* Nov., 977–987.

Golding, J. M., Bradshaw, G. S., Dunlap, E. E., & Hodell, E. C. (2007). The impact of mock jury gender composition on deliberations and conviction rates in a child sexual assault trial. *Child Maltreatment, 12*(2), 182–190.

Goldman, H. H. (1998). Deinstitutionalization and community care. *Harvard Review of Psychiatry, 6*(4), 219–222.

Goldstein, E. B. (2007). *Sensation and perception* (7th ed.). Belmont, CA: Cengage Learning/Wadsworth.

Goldstein, E. B. (2008). *Cognitive psychology: Connecting mind, research and everyday experience* (2nd ed.). Belmont, CA: Cengage Learning/Wadsworth.

Goldston, D. B., Molock, S. D., Whitbeck, L. B., Murakami, J. L., et al. (2008). Cultural considerations in adolescent suicide prevention and psychosocial treatment. *American Psychologist, 63*(1), 14–31.

Goleman, D. (1995). *Emotional intelligence.* New York: Bantam.

Gomez, R., & McLaren, S. (2007). The inter-relations of mother and father attachment, self-esteem and aggression during late adolescence. *Aggressive Behavior, 33*(2), 160–169.

Gondola, J. C., & Tuckman, B. W. (1982). Psychological mood state in "average" marathon runners. *Perceptual and Motor Skills, 55,* 1295–1300.

Goodale, M. A., Milner, A. D., Jakobson, L. S., & Carey, D. P. (1991). A neurological dissociation between perceiving objects and grasping them. *Nature, 349,* 154–156.

Goode, E. (1996). Gender and courtship entitlement: Responses to personal ads. *Sex Roles, 34*(3–4), 141–169.

Goodman-Delahunty, J. Greene, E., & Hsiao, W. (1998). Construing motive in videotaped killings: The role of jurors' attitudes toward the death penalty. *Law & Human Behavior, 22*(3), 257–271.

Goodwin, R. D., Fergusson, D. M., & Horwood, L. J. (2005). Childhood abuse and familial violence and the risk of panic attacks and panic disorder in young adulthood. *Psychological Medicine, 35*(6), 881–890.

Goodwin, S. A., & Fiske, S. T. (2001). Power and gender. In R. K. Unger (Ed.), *Handbook of the psychology of women and gender.* New York: Wiley.

Gopnik, A., Meltzoff, A. N., & Kuhl, P. K. (2000). *The scientist in the crib: What early learning tells us about the mind.* New York: HarperCollins.

Gordon, A. K., & Kaplar, M. E. (2002). A new technique for demonstrating the actor-observer bias. *Teaching of Psychology, 29*(4), 301–303.

Gordon, T. (2000). *Parent effectiveness training: The proven program for raising responsible children.* New York: Three Rivers Press.

Gorman, J. M. (1996). *The essential guide to mental health.* New York: St. Martin's Griffin.

Gottlieb, G. (1998). Normally occurring environmental and behavioral influences on gene activity: From central dogma to probabilistic epigenesis. *Psychological Review, 105*(4), 792–802.

Gottman, J. M. (1994). *Why marriages succeed or fail.* New York: Simon & Schuster.

Gottman, J. M., & Krokoff, L. J. (1989). Marital interaction and satisfaction: A longitudinal view. *Journal of Consulting & Clinical Psychology, 57*(1), 47–52.

Gould, D., & Udry, E. (1994). Psychological skills for enhancing performance: Arousal regulation strategies. *Medicine & Science in Sports & Exercise, 26*(4), 478–485.

Gould, E., & Gross, C. G. (2002). Neurogenesis in adult mammals: Some progress and problems. *Journal of Neuroscience, 22*(3), 619–623.

Gould, R. (1975). Growth toward self-tolerance. *Psychology Today,* Feb., 74–78.

Grabe, M. (2006). *Integrating technology for meaningful learning.* Boston: Houghton Mifflin.

Grabill, K., Merlo, L., Duke, D., Harford, K.-L., et al. (2008). Assessment of obsessive-compulsive disorder: A review. *Journal of Anxiety Disorders, 22*(1), 1–17.

Grack, C., & Richman, C. L. (1996). Reducing general and specific heterosexism through cooperative contact. *Journal of Psychology & Human Sexuality, 8*(4), 59–68.

Grande, T., Rudolf, G., Oberbracht, C., & Pauli-Magnus, C. (2003). Progressive changes in patients' lives after psychotherapy. *Psychotherapy Research, 13*(1), 43–58.

Grandner, M. A., & Kripke, D. F. (2004). Self-reported sleep complaints with long and short sleep: A nationally representative sample. *Psychosomatic Medicine, 66,* 239–241.

Granrud, C. E. (2004). Visual metacognition and the development of size constancy. In D. T. Levin (Ed.), *Thinking and seeing: Visual metacognition in adults and children.* Cambridge, MA: MIT Press.

Granrud, C. E. (2006). Size constancy in infants: 4-month-olds' responses to physical versus retinal image size. *Journal of Experimental Psychology: Human Perception & Performance, 32*(6), 1398–1404.

Grant, B. F., & Dawson, D. A. (1997). Age at onset of alcohol use and its association with DSM-IV alcohol abuse and dependence. *Journal of Substance Abuse, 9,* 103.

Grant, B. F., Hasin, D. S., Stinson, F. S., Dawson, D. A., et al. (2006). The epidemiology of DSM-IV panic disorder and agoraphobia in the United States: Results from the National Epidemiologic Survey on Alcohol and Related Conditions. *Journal of Clinical Psychiatry, 67*(3), 363–374.

Grant, I., Gonzalez, R., Carey, C., & Natarajan, L. (2001). Long-term neurocognitive fconsequences of marijuana. In *National Institute on Drug Abuse Workshop on Clinical Consequences of Marijuana,* August 13, 2001, Rockville, MD.

Graves, J. L. (2001). *The emperor's new clothes.* Piscataway, NJ: Rutgers University Press.

Gravetter, F. J., & Wallnau, L. B. (2007). *Statistics for the behavioral sciences* (7th ed.). Belmont, CA: Cengage Learning/Wadsworth.

Gray, J. M., & Wilson, M. A. (2007). A detailed analysis of the reliability and validity of the sensation seeking scale in a UK sample. *Personality & Individual Differences, 42*(4), 641–651.

Graziottin, A. (1998). The biological basis of female sexuality. *International Clinical Psychopharmacology, 13*(Suppl 6), S15–S22.

Greenberg, D. L. (2004). President Bush's false "flashbulb" memory of 9/11/01. *Applied Cognitive Psychology, 18*(3), 363–370.

Greene, D., & Lepper, M. R. (1974). How to turn play into work. *Psychology Today,* Sept., 49.

Greenfield, P. M. (1997). You can't take it with you: Why abilities assessments don't cross cultures. *American Psychologist, 52,* 1115–1124.

Greenglass, E. R., Burke, R. J., & Konarski, R. (1998). Components of burnout, resources, and gender-related differences. *Journal of Applied Social Psychology, 28*(12), 1088–1106.

Greenglass, E. R., Burke, R. J., & Moore, K. A. (2003). Reactions to increased workload: Effects on professional efficacy of nurses. *Applied Psychology: An International Review, 52*(4), 580–597.

Greenwald, R. (2006). Eye movement desensitization and reprocessing with traumatized youth. In N. B. Webb (Ed.), *Working with traumatized youth in child welfare: Social work practice with children and families.* New York: Guilford.

Greenwood, J. G., Greenwood, J. J. D., McCullagh, J. F., Beggs, J., et al. (2006). A survey of sidedness in Northern Irish schoolchildren: The interaction of sex, age, and task. *Laterality: Asymmetries of Body, Brain & Cognition, 12*(1), 1–18.

Gregory, R. L. (1990). *Eye and brain: The psychology of seeing.* Princeton, NJ: Princeton University Press.

Gregory, R. L. (2000). Visual illusions. In A. Kazdin (Ed.), *Encyclopedia of psychology.* Washington, DC: American Psychological Association.

Gregory, R. L. (2003). Seeing after blindness. *Nature Neuroscience, 6*(9), 909–910.

Grenier, G., & Byers, E. S. (1995). Rapid ejaculation: A review of conceptual, etiological, and treatment issues. *Archives of Sexual Behavior, 24*(4), 447–472.

Griffin, D. R. (1992). *Animal minds.* Chicago: University of Chicago Press.

Griffin, W. A. (2002). Family therapy. In M. Hersen, & W. H. Sledge (Eds.), *Encyclopedia of psychotherapy.* San Diego: Academic Press.

Grigorenko, E. L. (2005). The inherent complexities of gene-environment interactions. *Journals of Gerontology: Series B: Psychological Sciences & Social Sciences. Special Research on Environmental Effects in Genetic Studies of Aging, 60B*(1,SpecIssue), 53–64.

Grigorenko, E. L., & Sternberg, R. J. (2003). The nature-nurture issue. In A. Slater, & G. Bremner (Eds.), *An introduction to developmental psychology.* Malden, MA: Blackwell.

Gross, J. J. (2001). Emotion regulation in adulthood: Timing is everything. *Current Directions in Psychological Science, 10*(6), 214–219.

Grubin, D., & Madsen, L. (2005). Lie detection and the polygraph: A historical review. *Journal of Forensic Psychiatry & Psychology, 16*(2), 357–369.

Grunbaum, J. A., Kann, L., Kinchen, S., & Ross, J., et al. (2004). Youth risk behavior surveillance: United States, 2003. *Centers for Disease Control and Prevention Morbidity and Mortality Weekly Report Surveillance Summary, 53*(SS02), 1–96.

Gruner, C. R., & Tighe, M. R. (1995). Semantic differential measurements of connotations of verbal terms and their doublespeak facsimiles in sentence contexts. *Psychological Reports, 77*(3, Pt 1) 778.

Grzegorek, J. L., Slaney, R. B., Franze, S., & Rice, K. G. (2004). Self-criticism, dependency, self-esteem, and grade point average satisfaction among clusters of perfectionists and nonperfectionists. *Journal of Counseling Psychology, 51*(2), 192–200.

Guastello, D. D., & Guastello, S. J. (2003). Androgyny, gender role behavior, and emotional intelligence among college students and their parents. *Sex Roles, 49*(11–12), 663–673.

Guéguen, N. (2002). Status, apparel and touch: Their joint effects on compliance to a request. *North American Journal of Psychology, 4*(2), 279–286.

Guéguen, N., & Pascual, A. (2003). Status and people's tolerance towards an ill-mannered person: A field study. *Journal of Mundane Behavior, 4*(1). Retrieved August 4, 2007, from http://www.mundanebehavior.org/issues/v4n1/gueguen-pascual.htm.

Guéguen, N., Pascual, A., & Dagot, L. (2002). Low-ball and compliance to a request: An application in a field setting. *Psychological Reports, 91*(1), 81–84.

Gullette, D. L., & Lyons, M. A. (2005). Sexual sensation seeking, compulsivity, and HIV risk behaviors in college students. *Journal of Community Health Nursing, 22*(1), 47–60.

Gump, B. B., & Kulik, J. A. (1997). Stress, affiliation, and emotional contagion. *Journal of Personality & Social Psychology, 72*(2), 305–319.

Gur, R. E., Cowell, P., Turetsky, B. I., Gallacher, F., et al. (1998). A follow-up magnetic resonance imaging study of schizophrenia. *Archives of General Psychiatry, 55*(2), 145–152.

Gurung, R. (2006). *Health psychology: A cultural approach.* Belmont, CA: Cengage Learning/Wadsworth.

Gustavson, C. R., & Garcia, J. (1974). Pulling a gag on the wily coyote. *Psychology Today,* May, 68–72.

Gustavsson, J. P., Weinryb, R. M., Göransson, S., Pedersen, N. L., et al. (1997). Stability and predictive ability of personality traits across 9 years. *Personality & Individual Differences, 22*(6), 783–791.

Guthrie, R. V. (2004). *Even the rat was white: A historical view of psychology* (2nd ed.). Boston: Allyn & Bacon.

Haas, B. W., Omura, K., Constable, R. T., & Canli, T. (2007). Is automatic emotion regulation associated with agreeableness? A perspective using a social neuroscience approach. *Psychological Science, 18*(2), 130–132.

Haber, R. N. (1969). Eidetic images; with biographical sketches. *Scientific American, 220*(12), 36–44.

Haber, R. N. (1970, May). How we remember what we see. *Scientific American,* 104–112.

Haber, R. N., & Haber, L. (2000). Eidetic imagery. In A. E. Kazdin, (Ed.), *Encyclopedia of psychology* (Vol. 3). Washington, DC: American Psychological Association.

Haddad, S. (2003). Islam and attitudes toward U.S. policy in the Middle East: Evidence from survey research in Lebanon. *Studies in Conflict & Terrorism, 26*(2), 135–154.

Hadwin, A. F., Kirby, J. R., & Woodhouse, R. A. (1999). Individual differences in notetaking, summarization and learning from lectures. *Alberta Journal of Educational Research, 45*(1), 1–17.

Haenschel, C., Vernon, D. J., Dwivedi, P., Gruzelier, J. H., et al. (2005). Event-related brain potential correlates of human auditory sensory memory-trace formation. *Journal of Neuroscience, 25*(45), 10494–10501.

Hafer, C. L., & Bègue, L. (2005). Experimental research on just-world theory: Problems, developments, and future challenges. *Psychological Bulletin, 131*(1), 128–167.

Haier, R. J., Jung, R. E., Yeo, R. A., Head, K, & Alkire, M. T. (2004). Structural brain variation and general intelligence. *NeuroImage, 23,* 425–433.

Haier, R. J., Siegel, B. V., Nuechterlein, K. H., Hazlett, E., et al. (1988). Cortical glucose metabolic rate correlates of abstract reasoning and attention studied with positron emission tomography. *Intelligence, 12,* 199–217.

Haier, R. J., White, N. S., & Alkire, M. T. (2003). Individual differences in general intelligence correlate with brain function during nonreasoning tasks. *Intelligence, 31*(5), 429–441.

Haines, M. M., Stansfeld, S. A., Job, R. F. S., Berglund, B., et al. (2001). Chronic aircraft noise exposure, stress responses, mental health and cognitive performance in school children. *Psychological Medicine, 31*(2), 265–277.

Halbert, J., Crotty, M., & Cameron, I. D. (2002). Evidence for the optimal management of acute and chronic phantom pain. *Clinical Journal of Pain, 18*(2), 84–92.

Hall, C. (1966). *The meaning of dreams.* New York: McGraw-Hill.

Hall, C. (1974). What people dream about. In R. L. Woods, & H. B. Greenhouse (Eds.), *The new world of dreams: An anthology.* New York: Macmillan.

Hall, E. T. (1966). *The hidden dimension.* Garden City, NY: Doubleday.

Hall, J. (2006). *What is clinical psychology?* (4th ed.). New York: Oxford University Press.

Hall, J. A. (1996). Touch, status, and gender at professional meetings. *Journal of Nonverbal Behavior, 20*(1), 23–44.

Hall, J. A., Coats, E. J., & LeBeau, L. S. (2005). Nonverbal behavior and the vertical dimension of social relations: A meta-analysis. *Psychological Bulletin, 131*(6), 898–924.

Hall, N. C., Perry, R. P., Goetz, T., et al. (2007). Attributional retraining and elaborative learning: Improving academic development through writing-based interventions. *Learning & Individual Differences, 17*(3), 280–290.

Hallahan, D. P., & Kauffman, J. M. (2006). *Exceptional learners* (10th ed.). Boston: Allyn & Bacon.

Halpern, D. F. (2001). Sex difference research: Cognitive abilities. In J. Worell (Ed.), *Encyclopedia of women and gender.* New York: Oxford University Press.

Halpern, D. F. (2003). *Thought and knowledge: An introduction to critical thinking* (4th ed.). Mahwah, NJ: Erlbaum.

Hamilton, V. L., & Sanders, J. (1995). Crimes of obedience and conformity in the workplace. *Journal of Social Issues, 51*(3), 67–88.

Hammer, J. C., Fisher, J. D., Fitzgerald, P., & Fisher, W. A. (1996). When two heads aren't better than one: AIDS risk behavior in college-age couples. *Journal of Applied Social Psychology, 26*(5), 375–397.

Hammer, L. B., Grigsby, T. D., & Woods, S. (1998). The conflicting demands of work, family, and school among students at an urban university. *Journal of Psychology, 132*(2), 220–226.

Hancock, P. A., & Ganey, H. C. N. (2003). From the inverted-U to the extended-U: The evolution of a law of psychology. *Journal of Human Performance in Extreme Environments, 7*(1), 5–14.

Handsfield, H. H. (2001). Resurgent sexually transmitted diseases among men who have sex with men. *Medscape Infectious Disease, July.* Retrieved October 2, 2008, from https://profreg.medscape.com/px/getlogin.do?urlCache=aHR0cDovL3d3dy5tZWRzY2FwZS5jb20vdmlld2FydGljbGUvNDA4MzAx.

Hanley, S. J., & Abell, S. C. (2002). Maslow and relatedness: Creating an interpersonal model of self-actualization. *Journal of Humanistic Psychology, 42*(4), 37–56.

Hannigan, S. L., & Reinitz, M. T. (2001). A demonstration and comparison of two types of inference-based memory errors. *Journal of Experimental Psychology: Learning, Memory, and Cognition, 27*(4), 931–940.

Hansell, J. H. (2007). *Abnormal psychology: The enduring issues* (2nd ed.). New York: Wiley.

Hansen, C. J., Stevens, L. C., & Coast, J. R. (2001). Exercise duration and mood state. *Health Psychology, 20*(4), 267–275.

Hansen, N. B., Lambert, M. J., & Forman, E. M. (2002). The psychotherapy dose-response effect and its implications for treatment delivery services. *Clinical Psychology: Science & Practice, 9*(3), 329–343.

Hanton, S., Mellalieu, S. D., & Hall, R. (2004). Self-confidence and anxiety interpretation: A qualitative investigation. *Psychology of Sport & Exercise, 5*(4), 477–495.

Hardaway, C. A., & Gregory, K. B. (2005). Fatigue and sleep debt in an operational navy squadron. *International Journal of Aviation Psychology, 15*(2), 157–171.

Hardin, G. (1968). The tragedy of the commons. *Science, 162,* 1243–1248.

Harding, D. J., Fox, C., & Mehta, J. D. (2002). Studying rare events through qualitative case studies. *Sociological Methods & Research, 31*(2), 174–217.

Harding, R. W., Morgan, F. H., Indermaur, D., Ferrante, A. M., et al. (1998). Road rage and the epidemiology of violence. *Studies on Crime & Crime Prevention, 7*(2), 221–238.

Hare, R. D. (2006). Psychopathy: A clinical and forensic overview. *Psychiatric Clinics of North America, 29*(3), 709–724.

Harker, L., & Keltner, D. (2001). Expressions of positive emotion in women's college yearbook pictures and their relationship to personality and life outcomes across adulthood. *Journal of Personality & Social Psychology, 80*(1), 112–124.

Harlow, H. F., & Harlow, M. K. (1962). Social deprivation in monkeys. *Scientific American, 207,* 136–146.

Harlow, J. M. (1868). Recovery from the passage of an iron bar through the head. *Publications of the Massachusetts Medical Society, 2,* 327–347.

Harm, D. L. (2002). Motion sickness neurophysiology, physiological correlates, and treatment. In K. M. Stanney (Ed.), *Handbook of virtual environments: Design, implementation, and applications.* Hillsdale, NJ: Erlbaum.

Harrigan, J. A. (2005). Proxemics, kinesics, and gaze. In J. A. Harrigan, R. Rosenthal, et al. (Eds.), *The new handbook of methods in nonverbal behavior research.* New York: Oxford University Press.

Harris, C. (2004). The evolution of jealousy. *American Scientist, 92,* 62–71.

Harris, J. A., Rushton, J. P., Hampson, E., & Jackson, D. N. (1996). Salivary testosterone and self-report aggressive and pro-social personality characteristics in men and women. *Aggressive Behavior, 22*(5), 321–331.

Harris, J. C. (2003). Pinel delivering the insane. *Archives of General Psychiatry, 60*(6), 552.

Harris, J. R., & Liebert, R. M. (1991). *The child.* Englewood Cliffs, NJ: Prentice Hall.

Harrison, P. J., & Weinberger, D. R. (2005). Schizophrenia genes, gene expression, and neuropathology: On the matter of their convergence. *Molecular Psychiatry, 10*(1), 40–68.

Hart, B., & Risley, T. R. (1999). *The social world of children learning to talk.* Baltimore: Paul H. Brookes.

Hart, D., & Carlo, G. (2005). Moral development in adolescence. *Journal of Research on Adolescence. 15*(3), 223–233.

Hartgens, F., & Kuipers, H. (2004). Effects of androgenic-anabolic steroids in athletes. *Sports Medicine, 34*(8), 513–554.

Hartlep, K. L., & Forsyth, G. A. (2000). The effect of self-reference on learning and retention. *Teaching of Psychology, 27*(4), 269–271.

Hartmann, P., Reuter, M., & Nyborg, H. (2006). The relationship between date of birth and individual differences in personality and general intelligence: A large scale study. *Personality & Individual Differences, 40*(7), 1349–1362.

Harvey, C. A., Curson, D. A., Pantelis, C., & Taylor, J. (1996). Four behavioural syndromes of schizophrenia. *British Journal of Psychiatry, 168*(5), 562–570.

Harway, M. (Ed.). (2004). *Handbook of couples therapy.* San Francisco: Jossey-Bass.

Hashibe, M., Straif, K., Tashkin, D. P., Morgenstern, H., et al. (2005). Epidemiologic review of marijuana use and cancer risk. *Alcohol, 35*(3), 265–275.

Hashimoto, I., Suzuki, A., Kimura, T., Iguchi Y., et al. (2004). Is there training-dependent reorganization of digit representations in area 3b of string players? *Clinical Neurophysiology, 115*(2), 435–447.

Hauck, F. R., Moore, C. M., Herman, S. M., Donovan, M., et al. (2002). The contribution of prone sleeping position to the racial disparity in sudden infant death syndrome. *Pediatrics, 110,* 772–780.

Hauri, P., & Linde, S. (1990). *No more sleepless nights.* New York: Wiley.

Hawks, J., Wang, E. T., Cochran, G. M., et al. (2007). Recent acceleration of human adaptive evolution. *Proceedings of the National Academy of Sciences, 104*(52), 20753–20758.

Hayes, C. (1951). *The ape in our house.* New York: Harper & Row.

Hayne, H., & Rovee-Collier, C. (1995). The organization of reactivated memory in infancy. *Child Development, 66*(3), 893–906.

Hays, W. S. T. (2003). Human pheromones: Have they been demonstrated? *Behavioral Ecology & Sociobiology, 54*(2), 89–97.

Hearold, S. L. (1987). Meta-analysis of the effects of television on social behavior. In G. Comstock (Ed.), *Public communication and behavior* (Vol. 1). New York: Academic.

Heath, R. G. (1963). Electrical self-stimulation of the brain in man. *American Journal of Psychiatry, 120,* 571–577.

Hebl, M. R., King, E. G., & Lin, J. (2004). The swimsuit becomes us all: Ethnicity, gender, and vulnerability to selfobjectification. *Personality & Social Psychology Bulletin, 30,* 1322–1331.

Hecht, J. (2007). *The happiness myth: Why what we think is right is wrong.* New York: HarperCollins.

Heiby, E. M. (1983). Assessment of frequency of self-reinforcement. *Journal of Personality & Social Psychology, 44,* 1304–1307.

Heiman, J. R. (2002). Sexual dysfunction: Overview of prevalence, etiological factors, and treatments. *Journal of Sex Research. Special Promoting Sexual Health And Responsible Sexual Behavior, 39*(1), 73–78.

Heimann, M., & Meltzoff, A. N. (1996). Deferred imitation in 9-and 14-month-old infants. *British Journal of Developmental Psychology, 14*(Mar.), 55–64.

Heinrichs, R. W. (2001). *In search of madness: Schizophrenia and neuroscience.* New York: Oxford University Press.

Heisel, M. J., Flett, G. L., & Hewitt, P. L. (2003). Social hopelessness and college student suicide ideation. *Archives of Suicide Research, 7*(3), 221–235.

Held, R. (1971). Plasticity in sensory-motor systems. In *Contemporary psychology.* San Francisco: Freeman.

Helgeson, V. S. (2005). *The psychology of gender* (2nd ed.). Englewood Cliffs, NJ: Prentice Hall.

Hellerstein, D. J., Rosenthal, R. N., Pinsker, H., Samstag, L. W., et al. (1998). A randomized prospective study comparing supportive and dynamic therapies. *Journal of Psychotherapy Practice & Research, 7*(4), 261–271.

Hellige, J. B. (1993). *Hemispheric asymmetry.* Cambridge, MA: Harvard University Press.

Helson, R., & Srivastava, S. (2002). Creative and wise people. *Personality & Social Psychology Bulletin, 28*(10), 1430–1440.

Helton, W. S. (2007). Skill in expert dogs. *Journal of Experimental Psychology: Applied, 13*(3), 171–178.

Helwig, A. A. (1998). Gender-role stereotyping: Testing theory with a longitudinal sample. *Sex Roles, 38*(5–6), 403–423.

Henderson, N. D. (1982). Human behavior genetics. *Annual Review of Psychology, 33,* 403–440.

Henman, L. D. (2001). Humor as a coping mechanism. *Humor: International Journal of Humor Research, 14*(1), 83–94.

Henningsen, D. D., Henningsen, M. L. M., Eden, J., & Cruz, M. G. (2006). Examining the symptoms of groupthink and retrospective sensemaking. *Small Group Research, 37*(1), 36–64.

Hepper, P. G., Wells, D. L., & Lynch, C. (2005). Prenatal thumb sucking is related to postnatal handedness. *Neuropsychologia, 43*(3), 313–315.

Hepper, P. G., McCartney, G. R., & Shannon, E. A. (1998). Lateralised behaviour in first trimester human foetuses. *Neuropsychologia, 36*(6), 531–534.

Hergenhahn, B. R. (2005). *An introduction to the history of psychology* (5th ed.). Belmont, CA: Cengage Learning/Wadsworth.

Hergenhahn, B. R., & Olson, M. (2005). *Introduction to the theories of learning* (7th ed.). Englewood Cliffs, NJ: Prentice Hall.

Hergenhahn, B. R., & Olson, M. (2007). *An introduction to theories of personality* (7th ed.). Englewood Cliffs, NJ: Prentice Hall.

Heriot, S. A., & Pritchard, M. (2004). "Reciprocal Inhibition as the Main Basis of Psychotherapeutic Effects" by Joseph Wolpe (1954). *Clinical Child Psychology & Psychiatry, 9*(2), 297–307.

Hermann, B., Seidenberg, M., Sears, L., Hansen, R., et al. (2004). Cerebellar atrophy in temporal lobe epilepsy affects procedural memory. *Neurology, 63*(11), 2129–2131.

Hernstein, R., & Murray, C. (1994). *The bell curve.* New York: Free Press.

Herrmann, D. J., Yoder, C. Y., Gruneberg, M., & Payne, D. G. (2006). *Applied cognitive psychology: A textbook.* Mahwah, NJ: Erlbaum.

Herxheimer, A., & Waterhouse, J. (2003). The prevention and treatment of jet lag. *British Medical Journal, 326*(7384), 296–297.

Herz, R. S. (2001). Ah sweet skunk! *Cerebrum, 3*(4), 31–47.

Hettich, P. I. (2005). *Connect college to career: Student guide to work and life transition.* Belmont, CA: Cengage Learning/Wadsworth.

Higbee, K. L. (1997). Novices, apprentices, and mnemonists: Acquiring expertise with the phonetic mnemonic. *Applied Cognitive Psychology, 11*(2), 147–161.

Higbee, K. L., Clawson, C., DeLano, L., & Campbell, S. (1990). Using the link mnemonic to remember errands. *Psychological Record, 40*(3), 429–436.

Higgins, S. T., Heil, S. H., & Lussier, J. P. (2004). Clinical implications of reinforcement as a determinant of substance use disorders. *Annual Review of Psychology, 55,* 431–461.

Higham, P. A., & Gerrard, C. (2005). Not all errors are created equal: Metacognition and changing answers on multiple-choice tests. *Canadian Journal of Experimental Psychology, 59*(1), 28–34.

Hilgard, E. R. (1968). *The experience of hypnosis.* New York: Harcourt Brace Jovanovich.

Hilgard, E. R. (1977). *Divided consciousness.* New York: Wiley.

Hilgard, E. R. (1994). Neodissociation theory. In S. J. Lynn, & J. W. Rhue (Eds.), *Dissociation: Clinical, theoretical and research perspectives.* New York: Guilford.

Hilsenroth, M. J. (2000). Rorschach test. In A. Kazdin (Ed.), *Encyclopedia of psychology.* Washington, DC: American Psychological Association.

Hinkel, E. (Ed.). (2005). *Handbook of research in second language teaching and learning.* Mahwah, NJ: Erlbaum.

Hinterberger, T., Kübler, A., Kaiser, J., Neumann, N., et al. (2003). A brain–computer interface (BCI) for the locked-in: Comparison of different EEG classifications for the thought translation device. *Clinical Neurophysiology, 114*(3), 416–425.

Hintzman, D. L. (2005). Memory strength and recency judgments. *Psychonomic Bulletin & Review, 12*(5), 858–864.

Hirshbein, L., & Sarvananda, S. (2008). History, power, and electricity: American popular magazine accounts of electroconvulsive therapy, 1940–2005. *Journal of the History of the Behavioral Sciences, 44*(1), 1–18.

Hirstein, W. (2005). *Brain fiction: Self-deception and the riddle of confabulation.* Cambridge, MA: MIT Press.

Hiscock, M., Perachio, N., & Inch, R. (2001). Is there a sex difference in human laterality? *Journal of Clinical & Experimental Neuropsychology, 23*(2), 137–148.

Hobson, J. A. (2000). Dreams: Physiology. In A. Kazdin (Ed.), *Encyclopedia of psychology.* Washington, DC: American Psychological Association.

Hobson, J. A. (2001). *Consciousness.* New York: Freeman.

Hobson, J. A. (2005). Sleep is of the brain, by the brain and for the brain. *Nature, 437*(7063), 1254–1256.

Hobson, J. A., Pace-Schott, E. F., & Stickgold, R. (2000). Dream science 2000. *Behavioral & Brain Sciences, 23*(6), 1019–1035; 1083–1121.

Hochstenbach, J., Mulder, T., van Limbeek, J., Donders, R., et al. (1998). Cognitive decline following stroke: A comprehensive study of cognitive decline following stroke. *Journal of Clinical & Experimental Neuropsychology, 20*(4), 503–517.

Hodapp, R. M. (1994). Mental retardation. *Encyclopedia of human behavior* (Vol. 3). San Diego: Academic Press.

Hodgson, R., & Miller, P. (1982). *Self-watching.* New York: Facts on File.

Hofer, B. K., & Yu, S. L. (2003). Teaching self-regulated learning through a "Learning to Learn" course. *Teaching of Psychology, 30*(1), 30–33.

Hoff, E. (2006). How social contexts support and shape language development. *Developmental Review, 26*(1), 55–88.

Hoff, E., & Tian, C. (2005). Socioeconomic status and cultural influences on language. *Journal of Communication Disorders, 38*(4), 271–278.

Hoffart, A. (2005). Interpersonal therapy for social phobia: Theoretical model and review of the evidence. In M. E. Abelian (Ed.), *Focus on psychotherapy research.* Hauppauge, NY: Nova Science Publishers.

Hoffer, A., & Youngren, V. R. (2004). Is free association still at the core of psychoanalysis? *International Journal of Psychoanalysis, 85*(6), 1489–1492.

Hoffman, D. D. (1999). *Visual intelligence.* New York: Norton.

Hoffman, H. G., Garcia-Palacios, A., Carlin, A., Furness, T. A., et al. (2003). Interfaces that heal: Coupling real and virtual objects to treat spider phobia. *International Journal of Human–Computer Interaction, 16*(2), 283–300.

Hoffman, H. G., Patterson, D. R., Carrougher, & Sharar, S. (2001). The effectiveness of virtual reality pain control with multiple treatments. *Clinical Journal of Pain, 17*(3), 229–235.

Hofmann, W., Gawronski, B., Gschwendner, T., Le, H., et al. (2005). A meta-analysis on the correlation between the implicit association test and explicit self-report measures. *Personality & Social Psychology Bulletin, 31*(10), 1369–1385.

Hogan, E. H., Hornick, B. A., & Bouchoux, A. (2002). Focus on communications: Communicating the message: Clarifying the controversies about caffeine. *Nutrition Today, 37,* 28–35.

Hogben, D., & Lawson, M. J. (1992). Superiority of the keyword method for backward recall in vocabulary acquisition. *Psychological Reports, 71*(3, Pt 1), 880–882.

Hoge, C. W., Castro, C. A., Messer, S. C., McGurk, D., et al. (2004). Combat duty in Iraq and Afghanistan, mental health problems, and barriers to care. *New England Journal of Medicine, 351*(1), 13–22.

Hohwy, J., & Rosenberg, R. (2005). Unusual experiences, reality testing and delusions of alien control. *Mind & Language, 20*(2), 141–162.

Holden, C. (1980). Twins reunited. *Science 80,* Nov., 55–59.

Holland, J. L. (1997). *Making vocational choices.* Odessa, FL: Psychological Assessment Resources.

Hollon, S. D., Stewart, M. O., & Strunk, D. (2006). Enduring effects for cogni-

tive behavior therapy in the treatment of depression and anxiety. *Annual Review of Psychology, 57,* 285–315.

Holman, E. A., Silver, R. C., Poulin, M., Andersen, J., et al. (2008). Terrorism, acute stress, and cardiovascular health: A 3-year national study following the September 11th attacks. *Archives of General Psychiatry, 65*(1), 73–80.

Holmes, J., & Adams, J. W. (2006). Working memory and children's mathematical skills: Implications for mathematical development and mathematics curricula. *Educational Psychology, 26*(3), 339–366.

Holmes, M. (2002). Rethinking the meaning and management of intersexuality. *Sexualities, 5*(2), 159–180.

Holmes, P. S., & Collins, D. J. (2001). The PETTLEP approach to motor imagery: A functional equivalence model for sport psychologists. *Journal of Applied Sport Psychology, 13*(1), 60–83.

Holmes, T. H., & Rahe, R. H. (1967). The social readjustment rating scale. *Journal of Psychosomatic Research, 11*(2), 213–218.

Holstein, M. (1997). Reflections on death and dying. *Academic Medicine, 72*(10), 848–855.

Holtzen, D. W. (2000). Handedness and professional tennis. *International Journal of Neuroscience, 105*(1–4), 101–111.

Holzinger, B., LaBerge, S., & Levitan, L. (2006). Psychophysiological correlates of lucid dreaming. *Dreaming, 16*(2), 88–95.

Hooks, G., & Mosher, C. (2005). Outrages against personal dignity: Rationalizing abuse and torture in the war on terror. *Social Forces, 83*(4), 1627–1646.

Horgan, J. (2005). The forgotten era of brain chips. *Scientific American, 293*(4), 66–73.

Horn, R. R., Williams, A. M., Scott, M. A., & Hodges, N. J. (2005). Visual search and coordination changes in response to video and point-light demonstrations without KR. *Journal of Motor Behavior, 37*(4), 265–274.

Horne, R. S. C., Andrew, S., Mitchell, K., Sly, D. J., et al. (2001). Apnoea of prematurity and arousal from sleep. *Early Human Development, 61*(2), 119–133.

Hortman, G. (2003). What do facial expressions convey? *Emotion, 3*(2), 150–166.

Horvath, L. S., Milich, R., Lynam, D., Leukefeld, C., et al. (2004) Sensation seeking and substance use: A cross-lagged panel design. *Individual Differences Research, 2*(3), 175–183.

Hosch, H. M., & Cooper, D. S. (1982). Victimization as a determinant of eyewitness accuracy. *Journal of Applied Psychology, 67,* 649–652.

Hough, L. M., & Oswald, F. L. (2000). Personnel selection. *Annual Review of Psychology, 51,* 631–664.

Hove, P., Riley, M. A., & Shockley, K. (2006). Perceiving affordances of hockey sticks by dynamic touch. *Ecological Psychology, 18*(3), 163–189.

Howard, A., Pion, G. M., Gottfredson, G. D., Flattau, P. E., et al. (1986). The changing face of American psychology. *American Psychologist, 41,* 1311–1327.

Howard, I. P., & Rogers, B. J. (2001a). *Seeing in depth* (Vol. I): *Basic mechanisms.* Toronto: Porteous.

Howard, I. P., & Rogers, B. J. (2001b). *Seeing in depth* (Vol. II): *Depth perception.* Toronto: Porteous.

Howard, J. L., & Ferris, G. R. (1996). The employment interview context. *Journal of Applied Social Psychology, 26*(2), 112–136.

Howell, D. C. (2008). *Fundamental statistics for the behavioral sciences* (6th ed.). Belmont, CA: Cengage Learning/Wadsworth.

Howes, C. (1997). Children's experiences in center-based child care as a function of teacher background and adult:child ratio. *Merrill-Palmer Quarterly, 43*(3), 404–425.

Howitt, D., Craven, G., Iveson, C., Kremer, J., et al. (1977). The misdirected letter. *British Journal of Social and Clinical Psychology, 16,* 285–286.

Hsia, Y., & Graham, C. H. (1997). Color blindness. In A. Byrne, D. R. Hilbert, et al., (Eds.), *Readings on color* (Vol. 2): *The science of color.* Cambridge, MA: MIT Press.

Hsiung, P. (1990). Expansion of field of view via wide angle imaging. Unpublished document.

Hu, S., Pattatucci, A. M., Patterson, C., Li. L., et al. (1995). Linkage between sexual orientation and chromosome Xq28 in males but not in females. *Nature Genetics 11*(3), 248–256.

Hubble, M.A., Duncan, B. L., & Miller, S. D. (Eds.). (1999). *The heart and soul of change: What works in therapy.* Washington, DC: American Psychological Association.

Hubel, D.H., & Wiesel, W. N. (2005). *Brain & visual perception: The story of a 25-year collaboration.* New York: Oxford University Press.

Hubel, D. H. (1979). The visual cortex of normal and deprived monkeys. *American Scientist, 67,* 532–543.

Hubel, D. H., & Wiesel, T. N. (1979). Brain mechanisms of vision. *Scientific American, 241,* 150–162.

Hübner, R., & Volberg, G. (2005). The integration of object levels and their content: A theory of global/local processing and related hemispheric differences. *Journal of Experimental Psychology: Human Perception & Performance, 31*(3), 520–541.

Huesmann, L. R., Moise-Titus, J., Podolski, C., & Eron, L. D. (2003). Longitudinal relations between children's exposure to TV violence and their aggressive and violent behavior in young adulthood: 1977-1992. *Developmental Psychology, 39*(2), 201–221.

Hughes, J. N., & Hasbrouck, J. E. (1996). Television violence: Implications for violence prevention. *School Psychology Review, 25*(2), 134–151.

Hughes, J. R., Oliveto, A. H., Liguori, A., Carpenter, J., et al. (1998). Endorsement of DSM-IV dependence criteria among caffeine users. *Drug & Alcohol Dependence, 52*(2), 99–107.

Huguet, P., Dumas, F., Monteil, J. M., & Genestoux, N. (2001). Social comparison choices in the classroom: Further evidence for students' upward comparison tendency and its beneficial impact

on performance. *European Journal of Social Psychology, 31*(5), 557–578.

Huijbregts, S. C., Séguin, J. R., Zelazo, P. D., Parent, S., et al. (2006). Interrelations between maternal smoking during pregnancy, birth weight and sociodemographic factors in the prediction of early cognitive abilities. *Infant & Child Development, 15*(6), 593–607.

Human Rights Watch. (2003). *Ill-equipped: U.S. prisons and offenders with mental illness.* New York: Human Rights Watch.

Hunt, R. R., & Ellis, H. C. (2004). *Fundamentals of cognitive psychology* (7th ed.). New York: McGraw-Hill.

Hunter, E. (1998). Adolescent attraction to cults. *Adolescence, 33*(131), 709–714.

Hunter, J. P., Katz, J., & Davis, K. D. (2003). The effect of tactile and visual sensory inputs on phantom limb awareness. *Brain, 126*(3), 579–589.

Hutchinson, S. R. (2004). Survey research. In K. deMarrais, & S. D. Lapan (Eds.), Foundations for research: *Methods of inquiry in education and the social sciences. Inquiry and pedagogy across diverse contexts.* Mahwah, NJ: Erlbaum.

Hutchinson, S., Lee, L. H. L., Gaab, N., Schlaug, G. (2003). Cerebellar volume of musicians. *Cerebral Cortex, 13*(9), 943–949.

Hutchison, K. E., McGeary, J., Smolen, A., Bryan, A., et al. (2002). The DRD4 VNTR polymorphism moderates craving after alcohol consumption. *Health Psychology, 21*(2), 139–146.

Hyde, J. S. (2004). *Half the human experience: The psychology of women* (6th ed.). Boston: Houghton Mifflin.

Hyde, J. S., & DeLamater, J. D. (2006). *Understanding human sexuality* (9th Ed.). New York: McGraw-Hill.

Hyman, R. (1996a). Evaluation of the military's twenty-year program on psychic spying. *Skeptical Inquirer, 20*(2), 21–23.

Hyman, R. (1996b). The evidence for psychic functioning: Claims vs. reality. *Skeptical Inquirer, 20*(2), 24–26.

Hyman, R. (2007). Talking with the dead, communicating with the future and other myths created by cold reading. In S. Della Sala (Ed.), *Tall tales about the mind & brain: Separating fact from fiction.* New York: Oxford University Press.

Hysenbegasi, A., Hass, S. L., & Rowland, C. R. (2005). The impact of depression on the academic productivity of university students. *Journal of Mental Health Policy & Economics, 8*(3), 145–151.

Ida, Y., & Mandal, M. K. (2003). Cultural differences in side bias: Evidence from Japan and India. *Laterality: Asymmetries of Body, Brain & Cognition, 8*(2), 121–133.

Impett, E. A. Strachman, A., Finkel, E. J., & Gable, S. L. (2008). Maintaining sexual desire in intimate relationships: The importance of approach goals. *Journal of Personality & Social Psychology, 94*(5), 808–823.

Ingham, A. G, Levinger, G, Graves, J., & Peckham, V. (1974). The Ringelmann effect: Studies of group size and group performance. *Journal of Personality & Social Psychology, 10,* 371–384.

Ingram, V. (2003). Alzheimer's disease. *American Scientist, 91,* 312–321.

Iosif, A., & Ballon, B. (2005). Bad moon rising: The persistent belief in lunar connections to madness. *Canadian Medical Association Journal, 173*(12), 1498–1500.

Ivanco, T. L., & Racine, R. J. (2000). Long-term potentiation in the pathways between the hippocampus and neocortex in the chronically implanted, freely moving, rat. *Hippocampus, 10,* 143–152.

Iversen, L. (2006). *Speed, Ecstasy, Ritalin: The science of amphetamines.* New York: Oxford University Press.

Izard, C. E. (1977). *Human emotions.* New York: Plenum.

Izard, C. E. (1990). Facial expressions and the regulation of emotions. *Journal of Personality & Social Psychology, 58*(3), 487–498.

Izard, C. E., Fantauzzo, C. A., Castle, J. M., Haynes, O. M., et al. (1995). The ontogeny and significance of infants' facial expressions in the first 9 months of life. *Developmental Psychology, 31*(6), 997–1013.

Jablonski, N.G., & Chaplin, G. (2000). The evolution of human skin coloration. *Journal of Human Evolution, 39*(1), 57–106.

Jackson, G. R., Owsley, C., & McGwin, G. Jr. (1999). Aging and dark adaptation. *Vision Research, 39*(23), 3975–3982.

Jackson, S. L. (2008). *Research methods: A modular approach.* Belmont, CA: Cengage Learning/Wadsworth.

Jackson, T., Fritch, A., Nagasaka, T., & Gunderson, J. (2002). Towards explaining the association between shyness and loneliness. *Social Behavior & Personality, 30*(3), 263–270.

Jackson, T., Towson, S., & Narduzzi, K. (1997). Predictors of shyness. *Social Behavior & Personality, 25*(2), 149–154.

Jacob, A., Prasad, S., Boggild, M., & Chandratre, S. (2004). Charles Bonnet syndrome: Elderly people and visual hallucinations. *British Medical Journal, 328*(7455), 1552–1554.

Jacob, S., Hayreh, D. J. S., & McClintock, M. K. (2001). Context-dependent effects of steroid chemosignals on human physiology and mood. *Physiology & Behavior, 74*(1–2), 15–27.

Jacobs, M. (2003). *Sigmund Freud.* Thousand Oaks, CA: Sage.

Jacobs, M. K., Christensen, A., Snibbe, J. R., Dolezal-Wood, S., et al. (2001). A comparison of computer-mediated versus traditional individual psychotherapy. *Professional Psychology: Research & Practice, 32*(1), 92–96.

Jacobs, S. R., & Dodd, D. K. (2003). Student burnout as a function of personality, social support, and workload. *Journal of College Student Development, 44*(3), 291–303.

Jacobsen, P. B., Bovbjerg, D. H., Schwartz, M. D., Andrykowski, M. A., et al. (1993). Formation of food aversions in cancer patients receiving repeated infusions of chemotherapy. *Behavior Research & Therapy, 31*(8), 739–748.

Jaeggi, S. M., Buschkuehl, M., Jonides, J., & Perrig, W. J. (2008). Improving fluid intelligence with training on working memory. *Proceedings of the National Academy of Sciences,* April 28, 10.1073/pnas.0801268105.

Jaffe, J., Beatrice, B., Feldstein, S., Crown, C. L., et al. (2001). Rhythms of dialogue in infancy. *Monographs of the Society for Research in Child Development, 66*(2), vi–131.

James, T. W., Culham, J., Humphrey, G. K., Milner, A. D., et al. (2003). Ventral occipital lesions impair object recognition but not object-directed grasping: An fMRI study. *Brain, 126*(11), 2463–2475.

Jamison, K. R. (2001). Suicide in the young: An essay. *Cerebrum, 3*(3), 39–42.

Janis, I. L. (1989). *Crucial decisions.* New York: Free Press.

Janowsky, J. S. (2006). Thinking with your gonads: Testosterone and cognition. *Trends in Cognitive Sciences, 10*(2), 77–82.

Janssen, S. A., & Arntz, A. (2001). Real-life stress and opioid-mediated analgesia in novice parachute jumpers. *Journal of Psychophysiology, 15*(2), 106–113.

Janus, S. S., & Janus, C. L. (1993). *The Janus report.* New York: Wiley.

Jarvin, L., & Sternberg, R. J. (2003). Alfred Binet's contributions to educational psychology. In B. J. Zimmerman, & D. H. Schunk (Eds.), *Educational psychology: A century of contributions.* Mahwah, NJ: Erlbaum.

Jawahar, I. M., Stone, T. H., & Kisamore, J. L. (2007). Role conflict and burnout: The direct and moderating effects of political skill and perceived organizational support on burnout dimensions. *International Journal of Stress Management, 14*(2), 142–159.

Jay, T. B. (2003). *Psychology of language.* Upper Saddle River, NJ: Prentice Hall.

Jeffery, R. W., & Wing R. R. (2001). The effects of an enhanced exercise program on long-term weight loss. *Obesity Research, 9*(3), O193.

Jenkins, J. G., & Dallenbach, K. M. (1924). Oblivescence during sleep and waking. *American Journal of Psychology, 35,* 605–612.

Jennings, L., & Skovholt, T. M. (1999). The cognitive, emotional, and relational characteristics of master therapists. *Journal of Counseling Psychology, 46*(1), 3–11.

Jerabek, I., & Standing, L. (1992). Imagined test situations produce contextual memory enhancement. *Perceptual & Motor Skills, 75*(2), 400.

Joffe, R. T. (2006). Is the thyroid still important in major depression? *Journal of Psychiatry & Neuroscience, 31*(6), 367–368.

Johnson, B. T. (1991). Insights about attitudes: Meta-analytic perspectives. *Personality & Social Psychology Bulletin, 17*(3), 289–299.

Johnson, K. E., & Mervis, C. B. (1997). Effects of varying levels of expertise on the basic level of categorization. *Journal of Experimental Psychology: General, 126*(3), 248–277.

Johnson, K. J., & Fredrickson, B. L. (2005). "We all look the same to me": Positive emotions eliminate the own-race bias in face recognition. *Psychological Science, 16*(11), 875–881.

Johnson, S. (2005). *Everything bad is good for you: How today's popular culture is actually making us smarter.* New York: Riverhead.

Johnson, T. J. (2002). College students' self-reported reasons for why drinking games end. *Addictive Behaviors, 27*(1), 145–153.

Johnson, W., Jung, R. E., Colom, R., & Haier, R. J. (2008).Cognitive abilities independent of IQ correlate with regional brain structure. *Intelligence, 36*(1), 18–28.

Jones, E. E., & Nisbett, R. E. (1971). The actor and observer: Divergent perceptions of the causes of behavior. In E. E. Jones, D. E. Kanouse, et al. (Eds.), *Attribution: Perceiving the causes of behavior.* Morristown, NJ: General Learning Press.

Jones, G. V., & Martin, M. (2001). Confirming the X-linked handedness gene as recessive, not additive. *Psychological Review, 108*(4), 811–813.

Jones, L., & Petruzzi, D. C. (1995). Test anxiety: A review of theory and current treatment. *Journal of College Student Psychotherapy, 10*(1), 3–15.

Jones, M. E., Russell, R. L., & Bryant, F. B. (1998). The structure of rape attitudes for men and woman. *Journal of Research in Personality, 32*(3), 331–350.

Jones, M. K., & Menzies, R. G. (1998). Danger ideation reduction therapy (DIRT) for obsessive-compulsive washers. *Behaviour Research & Therapy, 36*(10), 959–970.

Jones, R. N. (2003). Racial bias in the assessment of cognitive functioning of older adults. *Aging & Mental Health, 7*(2), 83–102.

Jones, R., Yates, W. R., & Zhou, M. (2002). Readmission rates for adjustment disorders: Comparison with other mood disorders. *Journal of Affective Disorders, 71*(1–3), 199–203.

Jones, S. S., & Hong, H.-W. (2001). Onset of voluntary communication: Smiling looks to mother. *Infancy, 2*(3), 353–370.

Jonides, J., Lewis, R. L., Nee, D. E., et al. (2008). The mind and brain of short-term memory. *Annual Review of Psychology, 59,* 193–224.

Jorm, A. F., Korten, A. E., Rodgers, B., Jacomb, P. A., et al. (2002). Sexual orientation and mental health. *British Journal of Psychiatry, 180*(5), 423–427.

Jourard, S. M. (1963). *Personal adjustment.* New York: Macmillan.

Jourard, S. M. (1974). *Healthy personality.* New York: Macmillan.

Jouvet, M. (1999). *The paradox of sleep.* Boston, MA: MIT Press.

Jowett, G. S. (2006). Brainwashing: The Korean POW controversy and the origins of a myth. In G. S. Jowett, & V. O'Donnell (Eds.), *Readings in propaganda and persuasion: New and classic essays.* Thousand Oaks, CA, Sage.

Joyce, P., & Sills, C. (2001). *Skills in Gestalt counseling & psychotherapy.* Newbury Park: Sage.

Julesz, B. (1971). *Foundations of cyclopean perception.* Chicago: University of Chicago Press.

Juliano, L. M., & Griffiths, R. R. (2004). A critical review of caffeine withdrawal: Empirical validation of symptoms and signs, incidence, severity, and associated features. *Psychopharmacology, 176*(1), 1–29.

Julien, R. M. (2005). *A primer of drug action: A comprehensive guide to the actions, uses, and side effects* (10th ed.). New York: Worth.

Jung, C. G. (1961). *Memories, dreams, reflections.* New York: Pantheon.

Jussim, L., & Harber, K. D. (2005). Teacher expectations and self-fulfilling prophecies: Knowns and unknowns, resolved and unresolved controversies. *Personality & Social Psychology Review, 9*(2), 131–155.

Kadosh, R. C, & Henik, A. (2007). Can synaesthesia research inform cognitive science? *Trends in Cognitive Sciences, 11*(4), 177–184.

Kagan, J. (1971). *Change and continuity in infancy.* New York: Wiley.

Kagan, J. (2004). New insights into temperament. *Cerebrum, 6*(1), 51–66.

Kagan, J. (2005). Personality and temperament: Historical perspectives. In M. Rosenbluth, S. H. Kennedy, et al. (Eds.), *Depression and personality: Conceptual and clinical challenges.* Washington, DC: American Psychiatric Publishing.

Kahneman, D. (2003). A perspective on judgment and choice. *American Psychologist, 58*(9), 697–720.

Kahneman, D., & Tversky, A. (1972). Subjective probability: A judgment of representativeness. *Cognitive Psychology, 3,* 430–454.

Kahneman, D., & Tversky, A. (1973). On the psychology of prediction. *Psychological Review, 80,* 237–251.

Kahneman, D., Krueger, A. B., Schkade, D., Schwarz, N. et al. (2004). A survey method for characterizing daily life experience: The day reconstruction method. *Science, 306*(5702), 1776–1780.

Kahneman, D., Slovic, P., & Tversky, A. (1982). *Judgment under uncertainty: Heuristics and biases.* Cambridge, MA: Cambridge University Press.

Kalat, J. W. (2007). *Biological psychology* (8th ed.). Belmont, CA: Cengage Learning/Wadsworth.

Kalat, J. W., & Shiota, M. N. (2007). *Emotion.* Belmont, CA: Cengage Learning/Wadsworth.

Kallio, S., & Revonsuo, A. (2003). Hypnotic phenomena and altered states of consciousness: A multilevel framework of description and explanation. *Contemporary Hypnosis, 20*(3), 111–164.

Kamimori, G. H., Johnson, D., Thorne, D., & Belenky, G. (2005). Multiple caffeine doses maintain vigilance during early morning operations. *Aviation, Space, & Environmental Medicine, 76*(11), 1046–1050.

Kamin, L. J. (1981). *The intelligence controversy.* New York: Wiley.

Kandel, E. R., Schwartz, J. H., & Jessell, T. M. (2003). *Principles of neuroscience* (5th ed.). New York: McGraw-Hill.

Kaplan, H. S. (1974). *The new sex therapy.* New York: Brunner/Mazel.

Kaplan, P. S. (1998). *The human odyssey.* Pacific Grove, CA: Brooks/Cole.

Kapleau, P. (1966). *The three pillars of Zen.* New York: Harper & Row.

Kapur, S., & Lecrubier, Y. (Eds.). (2003). *Dopamine in the pathophysiology and treatment of schizophrenia: New findings.* Washington, DC: Taylor & Francis.

Karim, A. A., Hinterberger, T., Richter, J, Mellinger, J., et al. (2006). Neural internet: Web surfing with brain potentials for the completely paralyzed. *Neurorehabilitation & Neural Repair, 20*(4), 508–515.

Karon, B. P., & Widener, A. J. (1997). Repressed memories and World War II: Lest we forget! *Professional Psychology: Research & Practice, 28*(4), 338–340.

Karremans, J. C., Stroebe, W., & Claus, J. (2006). Beyond Vicary's fantasies: The impact of subliminal priming and brand choice. *Journal of Experimental Social Psychology, 42*(6), 792–798.

Kasser, T., & Ryan, R. M. (1993). A dark side of the American dream: Correlates of financial success as a central life aspiration. *Journal of Personality & Social Psychology, 65*(2), 410–422.

Kasser, T., & Ryan, R. M. (1996). Further examining the American dream: Differential correlates of intrinsic and extrinsic goals. *Personality & Social Psychology Bulletin, 22*(3), 280–287.

Kassin, S. M. (2005). On the psychology of confessions: Does innocence put innocents at risk? *American Psychologist, 60*(3), 215–228.

Kassin, S. M., Fein, S., & Markus, H. R. (2008). *Social psychology* (7th ed.). Boston: Houghton Mifflin.

Kassin, S. M., Tubb, V. A., Hosch, H. M., & Memon, A. (2001). On the "general acceptance" of eyewitness testimony research. *American Psychologist, 56*(5), 405–416.

Kataria, S. (2004). A clinical guide to pediatric sleep: Diagnosis and management of sleep problems. *Journal of Developmental & Behavioral Pediatrics, 25*(2), 132–133.

Katz, P. A. (2003). Racists or tolerant multiculturalists? *American Psychologist, 58*(11), 897–909.

Kaufman, A. S. (2000). Intelligence tests and school psychology: Predicting the future by studying the past. *Psychology in the Schools, 37*(1), 7–16.

Kaufman, L., & Kaufman, J. H. (2000). Explaining the moon illusion. *Proceedings of the National Academy of Sciences, 97*(1), 500–505.

Kaufmann, J. (2007). Transfiguration: A narrative analysis of male-to-female transsexual. *International Journal of Qualitative Studies in Education, 20*(1), 1–13.

Kawai, K., Sugimoto, K., Nakashima, K., Miura, H., et al. (2000). Leptin as a modulator of sweet taste sensitivities in mice. *Proceedings: National Academy of Sciences, 97*(20), 11044–11049.

Kawasaki, H., Adolphs, R., Oya, H., Kovach, C. et al. (2005). Analysis of single-unit responses to emotional scenes in human ventromedial prefron-

tal cortex. *Journal of Cognitive Neuroscience, 17*(10), 1509–1518.

Kearney, C. A., Sims, K. E., Pursell, C. R., & Tillotson, C. A. (2003). Separation anxiety disorder in young children: A longitudinal and family analysis. *Journal of Clinical Child & Adolescent Psychology, 32*(4), 593–598.

Kebbell, M. R., & Wagstaff, G. F. (1998). Hypnotic interviewing: The best way to interview eyewitnesses? *Behavioral Sciences & the Law, 16*(1), 115–129.

Keefe, F. J., Abernethy, A. P., & Campbell, L. C. (2005). Psychological approaches to understanding and treating disease-related pain. *Annual Review of Psychology, 56*, 601–630.

Keel, P. K., & Klump, K. L. (2003). Are eating disorders culture-bound syndromes? Implications for conceptualizing their etiology. *Psychological Bulletin, 129*(5), 747–769.

Keller, J. (2002). Blatant stereotype threat and women's math performance. *Sex Roles, 47*(3–4), 193–198.

Keller, M. C., & Young, R. K. (1996). Mate assortment in dating and married couples. *Personality & Individual Differences, 21*(2), 217–221.

Kellermann, A. L., Rivara, F. P., Rushforth, N. B., Banton, J. G., et al. (1993). Gun ownership as a risk factor for homicide in the home. *New England Journal of Medicine, 329*(15), 1084–1091.

Kelley, H. H. (1967). Attribution in social psychology. *Nebraska Symposium on Motivation, 15*, 192–238.

Kellogg, W. N. (1962). Sonar system of the blind. *Science, 137*, 399–404.

Kelly, I. W. (1999). "Debunking the debunkers": A response to an astrologer's debunking of skeptics. *Skeptical Inquirer*, Nov.–Dec., 37–43.

Kelly, M. P., Strassberg, D. S., & Turner, C. M. (2006). Behavioral assessment of couples' communication in female orgasmic disorder. *Journal of Sex & Marital Therapy, 32*(2), 81–95.

Kempermann, G. (2005). *Adult neurogenesis: Stem cells and neuronal development in the adult brain.* New York: Oxford University Press.

Kendler, K. S., Thornton, L. M., & Prescott, C. A. (2001). Gender differences in the rates of exposure to stressful life events and sensitivity to their depressogenic effects. *American Journal of Psychiatry, 158*(4), 587–593.

Kennaway, D. J., & Wright, H. (2002). Melatonin and circadian rhythms. *Current Topics in Medicinal Chemistry, 2,* 199–209.

Kenneth, M., Carpenter, K. M., & Hasin, D. S. (1998). Reasons for drinking alcohol. *Psychology of Addictive Behaviors, 12*(3), 168–184.

Kenny, P. J., & Markou, A. (2006). Nicotine self-administration acutely activates brain reward systems and induces a long-lasting increase in reward sensitivity. *Neuropsychopharmacology, 31*(6), 1203–1211.

Kensinger, E. A. (2007). Negative emotion enhances memory accuracy: Behavioral and neuroimaging evidence. *Current Directions in Psychological Science, 16*(4), 213–218.

Kerr, N. L., & Bray, R. M. (2005). Simulation, realism, and the study of the jury.

In N. Brewer, & K. D. Williams (Eds.), *Psychology and law: An empirical perspective.* New York: Guilford.

Kety, S. S. (1979). Disorders of the human brain. *Scientific American, 241*(Sept.), 202–214.

Key, W. B. (1973). *Subliminal seduction: Ad media's manipulation of a not so innocent America.* Englewood Cliffs, NJ: Prentice Hall.

Keyes, C. L. M., & Haidt, J. (2003). Introduction: Human flourishing. In C. L. M. Keyes, & J. Haidt (Eds.), *Flourishing.* Washington, DC: American Psychological Association.

Keysers, C., Xiao, D.–K., Földiák, P., & Perrett, D. I. (2005). Out of sight but not out of mind: The neurophysiology of iconic memory in the superior temporal sulcus. *Cognitive Neuropsychology, 22*(3–4), 316–332.

Kida, T. E. (2006). *Don't believe everything you think.* Buffalo, NY: Prometheus.

Kiecolt-Glaser, J. K., McGuire, L. Robles, T. F., & Glaser, R. (2002). Emotions, morbidity, and mortality. *Annual Review of Psychology, 53,* 83–107.

Kim, J., Singer, R. N., & Radlo, S. J. (1996). Degree of cognitive demands in psychomotor tasks and the effects of the five-step strategy on achievement. *Human Performance, 9*(2), 155–169.

Kim, S. (2000). Bogglers. *Discover,* Dec., 98.

Kim, S. (2002). Participative management and job satisfaction: Lessons for management leadership. *Public Administration Review, 62*(2), 231–241.

Kimble, C. E., & Hirt, E. R. (2005). Self-focus, gender, and habitual self-handicapping: Do they make a difference in behavioral self-handicapping? *Social Behavior & Personality, 33*(1), 43–56.

Kim-Cohen, J., Moffitt, T. E., Caspi, A., & Taylor, A. (2004). Genetic and environmental processes in young children's resilience and vulnerability to socioeconomic deprivation. *Child Development, 75*(3), 651–668.

King, B. E. (2005). *Human sexuality today* (5th ed.). Englewood Cliffs, NJ: Prentice Hall.

King, H. E. (1961). Psychological effects of excitation in the limbic system. In D. E. Sheer (Ed.), *Electrical stimulation of the brain.* Austin: University of Texas Press.

King, N. J., Muris, P., & Ollendick, T. H. (2005). Childhood fears and phobias: Assessment and treatment. *Child & Adolescent Mental Health, 10*(2), 50–56.

Kingsley, C. H., & Lambert, K. G. (2006). The maternal brain. *Scientific American, 294*(1), 72–79.

Kinnunen, L. H., Moltz, H., Metz, J., & Cooper, M. (2004). Differential brain activation in exclusively homosexual and heterosexual men produced by the selective serotonin reuptake inhibitor, fluoxetine. *Brain Research, 1024*(1–2), 251–254.

Kinsey, A., Pomeroy, W., & Martin, C. (1948). *Sexual behavior in the human male.* Philadelphia: Saunders.

Kinsey, A., Pomeroy, W., & Martin, C. (1953). *Sexual behavior in the human female.* Philadelphia: Saunders.

Kipper, D. A. (1992). The effect of two kinds of role playing on self-evaluation of improved assertiveness. *Journal of Clinical Psychology, 48*(2), 246–250.

Kirsch, I., & Lynn, S. J. (1995). The altered state of hypnosis. *American Psychologist, 50*(10), 846–858.

Kirsch, I., & Sapirstein, G. (1998). Listening to Prozac but hearing placebo: A meta–analysis of antidepressant medication. *Prevention & Treatment, 1*, art. 0002a. Retrieved May 18, 2007, from http://journals.apa.org/prevention/volume1/pre0010002a.html.

Kirsch, I., (2005). The flexible observer and neodissociation theory. *Contemporary Hypnosis, 22*(3), 121–122.

Kirsh, S. J. (2005). *Children, adolescents, and media violence: A critical look at the research.* Newbury Park, CA: Sage.

Kirveskari, E., Salmelin, R., & Hari, R. (2006). Neuromagnetic responses to vowels vs. tones reveal hemispheric lateralization. *Clinical Neurophysiology, 117*(3), 643–648.

Kiser, L. J., Heston, J. D., & Paavola, M. (2006). Day treatment centers/Partial hospitalization settings. In T. A. Petti, & C. Salguero (Eds.), *Community child & adolescent psychiatry: A manual of clinical practice and consultation.* Washington, DC: American Psychiatric Publishing.

Kisilevsky, B. S., Hains, S. M. J., Jacquet, A.-Y., Granier-Deferre, C., et al. (2004). Maturation of fetal responses to music. *Developmental Science, 7*(5), 550–559.

Kitayama, S., Markus, H. R., & Kurokawa, M. (2000). Culture, emotion, and wellbeing: Good feelings in Japan and the United States. *Cognition and emotion, 14,* 93–124.

Kite, M. E., Russo, N. F., Brehm, S. S., Fouad, N. A., et al. (2001). Women psychologists in academe. *American Psychologist, 56*(12), 1080–1098.

Kite, M. E., Stockdale, G. D., Whitley, B. E., Jr., & Johnson, B. T. (2005). Attitudes toward younger and older adults: An updated meta-analytic review. *Journal of Social Issues, 61*(2), 241–266.

Klahr, D., & Nigam, M. (2004). The equivalence of learning paths in early science instruction: Effects of direct instruction and discovery learning. *Psychological Science, 15,* 661–667.

Klein, B., Richards, J. C., & Austin, D. W. (2006). Efficacy of internet therapy for panic disorder. *Journal of Behavior Therapy & Experimental Psychiatry, 37*(3), 213–238.

Klein, D. W., & Kihlstrom, J. F. (1986). Elaboration, organization, and the self-reference effect in memory. *Journal of Experimental Psychology: General, 115,* 26–38.

Klein, K., & Boals, A. (2001a). The relationship of life event stress and working memory capacity. *Applied Cognitive Psychology, 15*(5), 565–579.

Klein, K., & Boals, A. (2001b). Expressive writing can increase working memory capacity. *Journal of Experimental Psychology: General, 130*(3), 520–533.

Klein, R. M. (2004). On the control of visual orienting. In M. I. Posner (Ed.), *Cognitive neuroscience of attention.* New York: Guilford.

Kleinke, C. L., Peterson, T. R., & Rutledge, T. R. (1998). Effects of self-generated facial expressions on mood. *Journal of Personality and Social Psychology, 74*(1), 272–279.

Kleinplatz, P. J. (1996). The erotic encounter. *Journal of Humanistic Psychology, 36*(3), 105–123.

Klohnen, E. C., & Luo, S. (2003). Interpersonal attraction and personality: What is attractive—self similarity, ideal similarity, complementarity or attachment security? *Journal of Personality & Social Psychology, 85*(4), 709–722.

Knaus, W. J., & Ellis, A. (2002). *The procrastination workbook: Your personalized program for breaking free from the patters that hold you back.* Oakland, CA: New Harbinger Press.

Knickmeyer, R. C., & Baron-Cohen, S. (2006). Fetal testosterone and sex differences. *Early Human Development, 82*(12), 755–760.

Knight, J. (2005). The truth about lying. *Nature, 428,* 692–694.

Knoops, K. T. B., de Groot, L. C., Kromhout, D., Perrin, A., et al. (2004). Mediterranean diet, lifestyle factors, and 10-year mortality in elderly European men and women. *Journal of the American Medical Association, 292*(12), 1433–1439.

Koch, C. (2004). *The quest for consciousness: A neurobiological approach.* Englewood, CO: Roberts and Co.

Koch, W. H., & Pratarelli, M. E. (2004). Effects of intro/extraversion and sex on social internet use. *North American Journal of Psychology, 6*(3), 371–382.

Kohlberg, L. (1969). The cognitive-developmental approach to socialization. In A. Goslin (Ed.), *Handbook of socialization theory and research.* Chicago: Rand McNally.

Kohlberg, L. (1981). *Essays on moral development* (Vol. I): *The philosophy of moral development.* San Francisco: Harper.

Kohler, I. (1962). Experiments with goggles. *Scientific American,* Offprint No. 465, 62–72.

Kohn, C. S., & Antonuccio, D. O. (2002). Treatment of kleptomania using cognitive and behavioral strategies. *Clinical Case Studies, 1*(1), 25–38.

Köke, A., Schouten J. S., Lamerichs-Geelen. M. J. H., Lipsch J. S. M., et al. (2004). Pain reducing effect of three types of transcutaneous electrical nerve stimulation in patients with chronic pain: A randomized crossover trial. *Pain, 108*(1–2), 36–42.

Kolb, B. (1990). Recovery from occipital stroke: A self-report and an inquiry into visual processes. *Canadian Journal of Psychology, 44*(2), 130–147.

Kolb, B., & Whishaw, I.Q. (2006). *Introduction to brain and behavior* (2nd ed.). New York: Freeman-Worth.

Kolb, B., Gibb, R., & Gorny, G. (2003). Experience-dependent changes in dendritic arbor and spine density in neocortex vary with age and sex. *Neurobiology of Learning & Memory, 79*(1), 1–10.

Kopta, M. S. Lueger, R. J., Saunders, S. M., & Howard, K. I. (1999). Individual psychotherapy outcome and process research. *Annual Review of Psychology, 50,* 441–469.

Kornhaber, M. L., & Gardner, H. (2006). Multiple intelligences: Developments in implementation and theory. In M. A. Constas, & R. J. Sternberg (Eds.), *Translating theory and research into educational practice: Developments in content domains, large-scale reform, and intellectual capacity.* Mahwah, NJ: Erlbaum.

Korol, C., Craig, K. D., & Firestone, P. (2003). Dissociative and somatoform disorders. In P. Firestone, & W. L. Marshall (Eds.), *Abnormal psychology: Perspectives* (2nd ed.). Toronto: Prentice Hall.

Koss, M. P. (2000). Blame, shame, and community: Justice responses to violence against women. *American Psychologist,* Nov., 1332–1343.

Kosslyn, S. M. (1983). *Ghosts in the mind's machine.* New York: Norton.

Kosslyn, S. M. (1985). Stalking the mental image. *Psychology Today,* May, 23–28.

Kosslyn, S. M. (2005). Mental images and the brain. *Cognitive Neuropsychology, 22*(3–4), 333–347.

Kosslyn, S. M., Ball, T. M., & Reiser, B. J. (1978). Visual images preserve metric spatial information: Evidence from studies of image scanning. *Journal of Experimental Psychology: Human Perception and Performance, 4,* 47–60.

Kosslyn, S. M., Thompson, W. L., Costantini-Ferrando, M. F., Alpert, N. M., et al. (2000). Hypnotic visual illusion alters color processing in the brain. *American Journal of Psychiatry, 157*(8), 1279–1284.

Kosson, D. S., Suchy, Y., Mayer, A. R., & Libby, J. (2002). Facial affect recognition in criminal psychopaths. *Emotion, 2*(4), 398–411.

Kotkin, M., Daviet, C., & Gurin, J. (1996). The Consumer Reports mental health survey. *American Psychologist, 51*(10), 1080–1082.

Kottler, J. A. (2004). *Introduction to therapeutic counseling.* Belmont, CA: Cengage Learning/Wadsworth.

Kowert, P. A. (2002). *Groupthink or deadlock: When do leaders learn from their advisors? SUNY series on the presidency.* Albany, NY: State University of New York Press.

Kozart, M. F. (2002). Understanding efficacy in psychotherapy. *American Journal of Orthopsychiatry, 72*(2), 217–231.

Krakow, B., & Zadra, A. (2006). Clinical management of chronic nightmares: Imagery rehearsal therapy. *Behavioral Sleep Medicine, 4*(1), 45–70.

Krall, E. A., Garvey, A. J., & Garcia, R. I. (2002). Smoking relapse after 2 years of abstinence: Findings from the VA Normative Aging Study. *Nicotine & Tobacco Research, 4*(1), 95–100.

Krantz, D. S., & McCeney, M. K. (2002). Effects of psychological and social factors on organic disease. *Annual Review of Psychology, 53,* 341–369.

Krishnan, H. A., & Park, D. (2005). A few good women—on top management teams. *Journal of Business Research, 58,* 1712–1720.

Kristof-Brown, A. L., Barrick, M. R., & Franke, M. (2002). Applicant impression management: Dispositional influences and consequences for recruiter perceptions of fit and similarity. *Journal of Management, 28,* 27–46.

Krosnick, J. A., Betz, A. L., Jussim, L. J., & Lynn, A. R. (1992). Subliminal conditioning of attitudes. *Personality & Social Psychology Bulletin, 18*(2), 152–162.

Ksir, C. J., Hart, C. L., & Ray, O. S. (2006). *Drugs, society, and human behavior* (11th ed.). New York: McGraw-Hill.

Kübler-Ross, E. (1975). *Death: The final stage of growth.* Englewood Cliffs, NJ: Prentice-Hall.

Kuczka, K. K., & Treasure, D. C. (2005). Self-handicapping in competitive sport: Influence of the motivational climate, self-efficacy, and perceived importance. *Psychology of Sport and Exercise, 6*(5), 539–550.

Kuehner, C. (2003). Gender differences in unipolar depression: an update of epidemiological findings and possible explanations. *Acta Psychiatrica Scandinavica, 108*(3), 163–174.

Kuhl, P. K. (2004). Early language acquisition: Cracking the speech code. *Nature Reviews Neuroscience, 5*(11), 831–841.

Kuhn, C. M., & Wilson, W. A. (2001). Our dangerous love affair with Ecstasy. *Cerebrum, 3*(2), 22–33.

Kulik, J., Mahler, H. I. M., & Moore, P. J. (2003). Social comparison affiliation under threat: Effects on recovery from major surgery. In P. Salovey, & A. J. Rothman (Eds.), *Social psychology of health: Key readings in social psychology.* New York: Psychology Press.

Kumaran, D., & Maguire, E. A. (2005). The human hippocampus: Cognitive maps or relational memory? *Journal of Neuroscience, 25*(31), 7254–7259.

Kunkel, M. A. (1993). A teaching demonstration involving perceived lunar size. *Teaching of Psychology, 20*(3), 178–180.

Laan, E., Everaerd, W., van Bellen, G., & Hanewald, G. J. F. P. (1994). Women's sexual and emotional responses to male- and female-produced erotica. *Archives of Sexual Behavior, 23*(2), 153–169.

LaBar, K. S. (2007). Beyond fear: Emotional memory mechanisms in the human brain. *Current Directions in Psychological Science, 16*(4), 173–177.

LaBar, K. S., & LeDoux, J. E. (2002). Emotional learning circuits in animals and man. In R. J. Davidson, K. R. Scherer, et al. (Eds.), *Handbook of affective sciences.* New York: Oxford University Press.

LaBerge, S. (2000). Lucid dreaming: Evidence and methodology. In F. E. Pace-Schott, M. Solms, et al. (Eds.), *Sleep and dreaming: Scientific advances and reconsiderations.* Cambridge, UK: Cambridge University Press.

Labov, W. (1973). The boundaries of words and their meanings. In C. J. N. Bailey, & R. W. Shuy (Eds.). *New ways of analyzing variation in English.* Washington, DC: Georgetown University Press.

LaBrie, R. A., & Shaffer, H. J. (2007). Gambling with adolescent health. *Journal of Adolescent Health, 40*(5), 387–389.

Lacayo, A. (1995). Neurologic and psychiatric complications of cocaine abuse. *Neuropsychiatry, Neuropsychology, & Behavioral Neurology, 8*(1), 53–60.

Lachman, M. E. (2004). Development in midlife. *Annual Review of Psychology, 55,* 305–331.

Lackner, J. R., & DiZio, P. (2005). Vestibular, proprioceptive, and haptic contributions to spatial orientation. *Annual Review of Psychology, 56,* 115–147.

Lakin, J. L., Jefferis, V. E., Cheng, C. M., & Chartrand, T. L. (2003). The chameleon effect as social glue: Evidence for the evolutionary significance of nonconscious mimicry. *Journal of Nonverbal Behavior, 27*(3), 145–162.

Lamb, M. R., & Yund, E. W. (1996). Spatial frequency and attention. *Perception & Psychophysics, 58*(3), 363–373.

Lambert, M. J., & Cattani-Thompson, K. (1996). Current findings regarding the effectiveness of counseling. *Journal of Counseling & Development, 74*(6), 601–608.

Lambert, M. J., & Ogles, B. M. (2002). The efficacy and effectiveness of psychotherapy. In M. J. Lambert (Ed.), *Handbook of psychotherapy and behavior change* (5th ed.). New York: Wiley.

Lambert, W. E. (1987). The effects of bilingual and bicultural experiences on children's attitudes and social perspectives. In P. Homel, M. Palij, & D. Aaronson (Eds.), *Childhood bilingualism.* Hillsdale, NJ: Erlbaum.

Lance, C. E., LaPointe, J. A., & Stewart, A. M. (1994). A test of the context dependency of three causal models of halo rater error. *Journal of Applied Psychology, 79*(3), 332–340.

Landau, J. D., & Bavaria A. J. (2003). Does deliberate source monitoring reduce students's misconceptions about psychology? *Teaching of Psychology, 30,* 311–314.

Landy, F. J., & Conte, J. M. (2007). *Work in the 21st century: An introduction to industrial and organizational psychology* (2nd ed.). Malden, MA: Blackwell.

Landy, F. J., Shankster, L. J., & Kohler, S. S. (1994). Personnel selection and placement. *Annual Review of Psychology, 45,* 261–296.

Langer, E. J. (2000). Mindful learning. *Current Directions in Psychological Science, 9*(6), 220–223.

Langer, E. J., & Abelson, R. P. (1974). A patient by any other name: Clinician group difference in labeling bias. *Journal of Consulting and Clinical Psychology, 42*(1), 4–9.

Langleben, D. D. (2008). Detection of deception with fMRI: Are we there yet? *Legal & Criminological Psychology, 13*(1), 1–9.

Langleben, D. D., Dattilio, F. M., & Gutheil, T. G. (2006). True lies: Delusions and lie-detection technology. *Journal of Psychiatry & Law, 34*(3), 351–370.

Langleben, D. D., Loughead, J. W., Bilker, W. B., Ruparel, K., et al. (2005). Telling truth from lie in individual subjects with fast event-related fMRI. *Human Brain Mapping, 26*(4), 262–272.

Langleben, D. D., Schroeder, L, Maldjian, J. A., Gur, R. C., et al. (2002). Brain activity during simulated deception: An event-related functional magnetic resonance study. *NeuroImage 15*, 727–732.

Langone, M. D. (2002). Cults, conversion, science, and harm. *Cultic Studies Review, 1*(2), 178–186.

Lanzetta, J. T., & Englis, B. G. (1989). Expectations of cooperation and competition and their effects on observers' vicarious emotional responses. *Journal of Personality & Social Psychology, 56*(4), 543–554.

Larsen, R. J., & Buss, D. M. (2005). *Personality psychology* (2nd ed.). New York: McGraw-Hill.

Larsen, R. J., & Kasimatis, M. (1990). Individual differences in entrainment of mood to the weekly calendar. *Journal of Personality & Social Psychology, 58*(1), 164–171.

Larsen, R.J., & Prizmic, Z. (2004) Affect regulation. In R. Baumeister, & K. D. Voohs (Eds.), *Handbook of self-regulation: Research, theory, and applications*. New York: Guilford.

Larson, M. E., Houlihan, D., & Goernert, P. N. (1995). Effects of informational feedback on aluminum can recycling. *Behavioral Interventions, 10*(2), 111–117.

Larsson, B., Carlsson, J., Fichtel, Å., & Melin, L. (2005). Relaxation treatment of adolescent headache sufferers: Results from a school-based replication series. *Headache: The Journal of Head & Face Pain, 45*(6), 692–704.

Larsson, J.-O., Larsson, H., & Lichtenstein, P. (2004). Genetic and environmental contributions to stability and change of ADHD symptoms between 8 and 13 years of age: A longitudinal twin study. *Journal of the American Academy of Child & Adolescent Psychiatry, 43*(10), 1267–1275.

Latané, B., Nida, S. A., & Wilson, D. W. (1981). The effects of group size on helping behavior. In J. P. Rushton, & R. M. Sorrentino (Eds.), *Altruism and helping behavior: Social, personality and developmental perspectives*. Mahwah, NJ: Erlbaum.

LaTour, M. S., & Henthorne, T. L. (2003). Nudity and sexual appeals: Understanding the arousal process and advertising response. In T. Reichert & J. Lambioase (Eds.), *Sex in advertising: Perspectives on the erotic appeal*. Mahwah, NJ: Erlbaum.

Lattal, K. A., Reilly, M. P., & Kohn, J. P. (1998). Response persistence under ratio and interval reinforcement schedules. *Journal of the Experimental Analysis of Behavior, 70*(2), 165–183.

Latty-Mann, H., & Davis, K. E. (1996). Attachment theory and partner choice. *Journal of Social & Personal Relationships, 13*(1), 5–23.

Laub, J. H., & Sampson, R. J. (2003). *Shared beginnings, divergent lives: Delinquent boys to age 70*. Cambridge, MA: Harvard University Press.

Laumann, E., Michael, R., Michaels, S., & Gagnon, J. (1994). *The social organization of sexuality*. Chicago: University of Chicago Press.

Laurent, G., Stopfer, M., Friedrich, R. W., Rabinovich, M. I., et al. (2001). Odor encoding as an active, dynamical process. *Annual Review of Neuroscience, 24*, 263–297.

Laureys, S, & Boly. M. (2007). What is it like to be vegetative or minimally conscious? *Current Opinion in Neurology, 20*, 609–613.

Lavie, P. (2001). Sleep-wake as a biological rhythm. *Annual Review of Psychology, 52*, 277–303.

Lawson, H. M., & Leck, K. (2006). Dynamics of Internet dating. *Social Science Computer Review, 24*(2), 189–208.

Lay, C., & Verkuyten, M. (1999). Ethnic identity and its relation to personal self-esteem. *Journal of Social Psychology, 139*(3), 288–299.

Lazar, S. W. (2005). Mindfulness research. In C. K. Germer, R. D. Siegel, et al. (Eds.), *Mindfulness and psychotherapy*. New York: Guilford.

Lazar, S. W., Bush, G., Gollub, R. L., Fricchione, G. L., et al. (2000). Functional brain mapping of the relaxation response and meditation. *Neuroreport, 11*(7), 1581–1585.

Lazarus, R. S. (1991a). Progress on a cognitive-motivational-relational theory of emotion. *American Psychologist, 46*(8), 819–834.

Lazarus, R. S. (1991b). Cognition and motivation in emotion. *American Psychologist, 46*(4), 352–367.

Lazev, A. B., Herzog, T. A., & Brandon, T. H. (1999). Classical conditioning of environmental cues to cigarette smoking. *Experimental and Clinical Psychopharmacology, 7*(1), 56–63.

Leal, M. C., Shin, Y. J., Laborde, M.-L., Calmels, M.-N., et al. (2003). Music perception in adult cochlear implant recipients. *Acta Oto-Laryngologica, 123*(7), 826–835.

Leavens, D. A., & Hopkins, W. D. (1998). Intentional communication by chimpanzees. *Developmental Psychology, 34*(5), 813–822.

LeBlanc, G., & Bearison, D. J. (2004). Teaching and learning as a bi-directional activity: Investigating dyadic interactions between child teachers and child learners. *Cognitive Development, 19*(4), 499–515.

Lederman, S. J., & Klatzky, R. L. (2004). Haptic identification of common objects: Effects of constraining the manual exploration process. *Perception & Psychophysics, 66*(4), 618–628.

Lederman, S. J., Howe, R. D., Klatzky, R. L., & Hamilton, C. (2004). Force variability during surface contact with bare finger or rigid probe. *Twelfth International Symposium on Haptic Interfaces for Virtual Environment and Teleoperator Systems*, 154–160.

LeDoux, J. (1999). The power of emotions. In R. Conlan (Ed.), *States of mind*. New York: Wiley.

LeDoux, J. E. (2000). Emotion circuits in the brain. *Annual Review of Neuroscience, 23*, 155–184.

LeDoux, J. E., & Gorman, J. M. (2001). A call to action: Overcoming anxiety through active coping. *American Journal of Psychiatry, 158*(12), 1953–1955.

Lee, J. M., Ku, J. H., Jang, D. P., Kim, D., et al. (2002). Virtual reality system for treatment of the fear of public speaking using image-based rendering and moving pictures. *CyberPsychology & Behavior, 5*(3), 191–195.

Lee, M., Zimbardo, P. G., & Bertholf, M. (1977). Shy murderers. *Psychology Today*, Nov.

Leenaars, A. A., Lester, D., & Wenckstern, S. (2005). Coping with suicide: The art and the research. In R. I. Yufit, & D. Lester (Eds.), *Assessment, treatment, and prevention of suicidal behavior*. New York: Wiley.

Leeper, R. W. (1935). A study of a neglected portion of the field of learning: The development of sensory organization. *Pedagogical Seminary and Journal of Genetic Psychology, 46*, 41–75.

Lefcourt, H. M. (2003). Humor as a moderator of life stress in adults. In C. E. Schaefer (Ed.), *Play therapy with adults*. New York: Wiley.

Lefkowitz, E. S., & Zeldow, P. B. (2006). Masculinity and femininity predict optimal mental health: A belated test of the androgyny hypothesis. *Journal of Personality Assessment, 87*(1), 95–101.

Lefrançois, G. R. (2006). *Theories of human learning: What the old woman said* (5th ed.). Belmont, CA: Cengage Learning/Wadsworth.

Lehman, D. R., Chiu, C., & Schaller, M. (2004). Psychology and culture. *Annual Review of Psychology, 55*, 689–714.

Leichtman, M. (2004). Projective tests: The nature of the task. In M. J. Hilsenroth, & D. L. Segal (Eds.), *Comprehensive handbook of psychological assessment* (Vol. 2): *Personality assessment*. New York: Wiley.

Leiter, M. P., & Maslach, C. (2005). *Banishing burnout: Six strategies for improving your relationship with work*. San Francisco: Jossey-Bass.

Lejuez, C. W., Eifert, G. H., Zvolensky, M. J., & Richards, J. B. (2000). Preference between onset predictable and unpredictable administrations of 20% carbon-dioxide-enriched air: Implications for better understanding the etiology and treatment of panic disorder. *Journal of Experimental Psychology: Applied, 6*(4), 349–358.

Lench, H. C. (2004). Anger management: Diagnostic differences and treatment implications. *Journal of Social & Clinical Psychology, 23*(4), 512–531.

Lenton, A. P., & Bryan, A. (2005). An affair to remember: The role of sexual scripts in perceptions of sexual intent. *Personal Relationships, 12*(4), 483–498.

Lenzenweger, M. F., & Gottesman, I. I. (1994). Schizophrenia. In V. S. Ramachandran (Ed.), *Encyclopedia of human behavior*. San Diego: Academic.

Leor, J., Poole, W. K., & Kloner, R. A. (1996). Sudden cardiac death triggered by earthquake. *New England Journal of Medicine, 334*(7), 413.

Lepage, J.-F., & Théret, H. (2007). The mirror neuron system: Grasping others' actions from birth? *Developmental Science, 10*(5), 513–523.

Lepore, F. E. (2002). When seeing is not believing. *Cerebrum, 4*(2), 23–38.

Leslie, K., & Ogilvie, R. (1996). Vestibular dreams: The effect of rocking on dream mentation. *Dreaming: Journal of the Association for the Study of Dreams, 6*(1), 1–16.

Lessow-Hurley, J. (2005). *Foundations of dual language instruction* (4th ed.). Boston: Allyn & Bacon.

Lester, D. (2006). Sexual orientation and suicidal behavior. *Psychological Reports, 99*(3), 923–924.

Lester, D., & Yang, B. (2005). Regional and time-series studies of suicide in nations of the world. *Archives of Suicide Research, 9*(2), 123–133.

Lettvin, J. Y. (1961). Two remarks on the visual system of the frog. In W. Rosenblith (Ed.), *Sensory communication*. Cambridge, MA: MIT Press.

LeUnes, J., & Nation, J. R. (2002). *Sport psychology* (3rd ed.). Belmont, CA: Cengage Learning/Wadsworth.

Levant, R. F. (1996). The new psychology of men. *Professional Psychology: Research & Practice, 27*(3), 259–265.

Levant, R. F. (2001). Men and masculinity. In J. Worell (Ed.), *Encyclopedia of women and gender*. San Diego: Academic Press.

Levant, R. F. (2003). Treating male alexithymia. In L. B. Silverstein, & T. J. Goodrich (Eds.), *Feminist family therapy: Empowerment in social context*. Washington, DC: American Psychological Association.

Levant, R. F., Good, G. E., Cook, S. W., O'Neil, J. M., et al. (2006). The Normative Male Alexithymia Scale: Measurement of a gender-linked syndrome. *Psychology of Men & Masculinity, 7*(4), 212–224.

LeVay, S. (1993). *The sexual brain*. Cambridge, MA: MIT Press.

LeVay, S., & Valente, S. M. (2005). *Human sexuality* (2nd ed.). Sunderland, MA: Sinauer Associates.

Levenston, G. K., Patrick, C. J., Bradley, M. M., & Lange, P. J. (2000). The psychopathic observer. *Journal of Abnormal Psychology, 109*, 373–385.

Leventhal, E. A., Leventhal, H., Shacham, S., & Easterling, D. V. (1989). Active coping reduces reports of pain from childbirth. *Journal of Consulting & Clinical Psychology, 57*(3), 365–371.

Levesque, M. J., Steciuk, M., & Ledley, C. (2002). Self-disclosure patterns among well-acquainted individuals. *Social Behavior & Personality, 30*(6), 579–592.

Levett, L. M., Danielsen, E. M., Kovera, M. B., & Cutler, B. L. (2005). The psychology of jury and juror decision making. In N. Brewer, & K. D. Williams, (Eds.), *Psychology and law: An empirical perspective*. New York: Guilford.

Levi, A. M. (1998). Are defendants guilty if they were chosen in a lineup? *Law & Human Behavior, 22*(4), 389–407.

Levin, B. E. (2006). Metabolic sensing neurons and the control of energy homeostasis. *Physiology & Behavior, 89*(4), 486–489.

Levin, R., & Fireman, G. (2002). Nightmare prevalence, nightmare distress, and selfreported psychological disturbance. *Sleep: Journal of Sleep & Sleep Disorders Research, 25*(2), 205–212.

Levine, M., & Harrison, K. (2004). Media's role in the perpetuation and prevention of negative body image and disordered eating. In J. K. Thompson (Ed.), *Handbook of eating disorders and obesity*. New York: Wiley.

Levine, R. V. (2003). The kindness of strangers. *American Scientist, 91*(May–June), 226–233.

Levinson, D. J. (1986). A conception of adult development. *American Psychologist, 41*(1), 3–13.

Levinson, D. J., & Levinson, J. D. (1996). *The seasons of a woman's life.* New York: Knopf.

Levis, D. J. (1989). The case for a return to a two-factor theory of avoidance: The failure of non-fear interpretations. In S. B Klein, & R. R. Mower (Eds.), *Contemporary learning theories.* Hillsdale, NJ: Erlbaum.

Levitsky, D. A., Nussbaum, M., Halbmaier, C.A., Mrdjenovic, G. (2003). The Freshman 15: a model for the study of techniques to curb the "epidemic" of obesity. *Society for the Study of Ingestive Behavior: Annual Meeting,* July, 15–19, University of Groningen, Haren, The Netherlands.

Levy, D. A. (2003). *Tools of critical thinking: Metathoughts for psychology.* Long Grove, IL: Waveland Press.

Levy, J., & Reid, M. (1976). Cerebral organization. *Science,* 337–339.

Lewandowski, G. W., Jr., Aron, A., & Gee, J. (2007). Personality goes a long way: The malleability of opposite-sex physical attractiveness. *Personal Relationships, 14*(4), 571–585.

Lewchanin, S., & Zubrod, L. A. (2001). Choices in life: A clinical tool for facilitating midlife review. *Journal of Adult Development, 8*(3), 193–196.

Lewis, M. (1995). Self-conscious emotions. *American Scientist, 83*(Jan–Feb), 68–78.

Lewis, P. S., Goodman, S. H., & Fandt, P. M. (1995). *Management.* St. Paul, MN: West.

Lewy, A. J., Bauer V. K., Cutler, N. L., Sack, R. L., et al. (1998). Morning vs evening light treatment of patients with winter depression. *Archives of General Psychiatry, 55*(10), 890–896.

Leyendecker, B., Harwood, R. L., Comparini, L., & Yalçinkaya, A. (2005). Socioeconomic status, ethnicity, and parenting. In T. Luster, & L. Okagaki (Eds.), *Parenting: An ecological perspective* (2nd ed.). Mahwah, NJ: Erlbaum.

Lichtman, A. H., & Martin, B. R. (2006). Understanding the pharmacology and physiology of cannabis dependence In R. Roffman, & R. S. Stephens (Eds.), *Cannabis dependence. Its nature, consequences and treatment.* New York: Cambridge University Press.

Liddell, S. K. (2003). *Grammar, gesture and meaning in American Sign Language.* Cambridge, UK: Cambridge University Press.

Lidz, C. W., Banks, S., Simon, L., Schubert, C., et al. (2007). Violence and mental illness: A new analytic approach. *Law & Human Behavior, 31*(1), 23–31.

Lieberman, D. A. (2004). *Learning and memory: An integrative approach.* Belmont, CA: Wadsworth.

Lievens, F., & Sackett, P. R. (2006). Video-based versus written situational judgment tests: A comparison in terms of predictive validity. *Journal of Applied Psychology, 91*(5), 1181–1188.

Lilienfeld, S. O. (1999). Projective measures of personality and psychopathol-ogy. *Skeptical Inquirer,* (Sept./Oct.), 32–39.

Lilienfeld, S. O. (2005). Pseudoscience, nonscience, and nonsense in clinical psychology: Dangers and remedies. In K. A. Fowler, J. M. Lohr et al. (Eds.), *Destructive trends in mental health: The well–intentioned path to harm.* New York: Routledge.

Lilienfeld, S. O., Fowler, K. A., Lohr, J. M., & Lynn, S. (2005). Pseudoscience, non-science & nonsense in clinical psychology: Dangers and remedies. In R. H. Wright, & N. A. Cummings (Eds.), *Destructive trends in mental health: The well-intentioned path to harm.* New York: Routledge.

Lindemann, B. (2001). Receptors and transduction in taste. *Nature, 413,* 219–25.

Linden, W. (2005). *Stress management: From basic science to better practice.* Thousand Oaks, CA: Sage.

Linderoth, B., & Foreman, R. D. (2006). Mechanisms of spinal cord stimulation in painful syndromes: Role of animal models. *Pain Medicine, 7*(Suppl 1), S14–S26.

Lindsay, E. W., Mize, J., & Pettit, G. S. (1997). Differential pay patterns of mothers and fathers of sons and daughters. *Sex Roles, 37*(9–10), 643–661.

Lipsey, M. W., & Wilson, D. B. (1993). The efficacy of psychological, educational, and behavioral treatment: Confirmation from meta-analysis. *American Psychologist, 48,* 1181–1209.

Liu, X., Matochik, J. A., Cadet, J., & London, E. D. (1998). Smaller volume of prefrontal lobe in polysubstance abusers. *Neuropsychopharmacology, 18*(4), 243–252.

Liu, Y., Gao, J., Liu, H., & Fox, P. T. (2000). The temporal response of the brain after eating revealed by functional MRI. *Nature, 405,* 1058–1062.

Locke, B. D., & Mahalik, J. R. (2005). Examining masculinity norms, problem drinking, and athletic involvement as predictors of sexual aggression in college men. *Journal of Counseling Psychology, 52*(3), 279–283.

Loeber, R., & Hay, D. (1997). Key issues in the development of aggression and violence from childhood to early adulthood. *Annual Review of Psychology, 48,* 371–410.

Loehlin, J. C., McCrae, R. R., Costa, P. T., & John, O. (1998). Heritabilities of common and measure-specific components of the Big Five personality factors. *Journal of Research in Personality, 32*(4), 431–453.

Loftus, E. & Loftus, G. (1980). On the permanence of stored information in the human brain. *American Psychologist, 35,* 409–420.

Loftus, E. F. (2003a). Make-believe memories. *American Psychologist, 58*(11), 867–873.

Loftus, E. F. (2003b). Memory in Canadian courts of law. *Canadian Psychology, 44*(3), 207–212.

Loftus, E. F., & Bernstein, D. M. (2005). Rich false memories: The royal road to success. In A. F. Healy, (Ed.), *Experimental cognitive psychology and its applications.* Washington, DC: American Psychological Association.

Loftus, E. F., & Ketcham, K. (1994). *The myth of repressed memory: False memories and allegations of abuse.* New York: St. Martin's Press.

Loftus, E., & Palmer, J. C. (1974). Reconstruction of automobile destruction: An example of interaction between language and memory. *Journal of Verbal Learning and Verbal Behavior, 13,* 585–589.

Loftus, G. R., & Mackworth, N. H. (1978). Cognitive determinants of fixation location during picture viewing. *Journal of Experimental Psychology: Human Perception and Performance, 4,* 565–572.

LoLordo, V. M. (2001). Learned helplessness and depression. In M. E. Carroll, & J. B. Overmier (Eds.), *Animal research and human health: Advancing human welfare through behavioral science.* Washington, DC: American Psychological Association.

Long, E. C., & Andrews, D. W. (1990). Perspective taking as a predictor of marital adjustment. *Journal of Personality & Social Psychology, 59*(1), 126–131.

Long, V. O. (1989). Relation of masculinity to self-esteem and self-acceptance in male professionals, college students, and clients. *Journal of Counseling Psychology, 36*(1), 84–87.

López, S. R., & Guarnaccia, P. J. J. (2000). Cultural psychopathology. *Annual Review of Psychology, 51,* 571–598.

Lorenz, K. (1966). *On aggression.* Translated by M. Kerr-Wilson. New York: Harcourt Brace Jovanovich.

Lorenz, K. (1974). *The eight deadly sins of civilized man.* Translated by M. Kerr-Wilson. New York: Harcourt Brace Jovanovich.

Lovaas, O., & Simmons, J. (1969). Manipulation of self-destruction in three retarded children. *Journal of Applied Behavior Analysis, 2,* 143–157.

Low, K. G., & Feissner, J. M. (1998). Seasonal affective disorder in college students: Prevalence and latitude. *Journal of American College Health, 47*(3), 135–137.

Low, S. M. (2001). The edge and the center: Gated communities and the discourse of urban fear. *American Anthropologist, 103*(1), 45–58.

Lucas, F., & Sclafani, A. (1990). Hyperphagia in rats produced by a mixture of fat and sugar. *Physiology & Behavior, 47*(1), 51–55.

Lucas, J. L., & Heady, R. B. (2002). Flextime commuters and their driver stress, feelings of time urgency, and commute satisfaction. *Journal of Business & Psychology, 16*(4), 565–572.

Luchins, D. J., Cooper, A. E., Hanrahan, P., & Rasinski, K. (2004). Psychiatrists' attitudes toward involuntary hospitalization. *Psychiatric Services, 55*(9), 1058–1060.

Ludwig, T. D., Gray, T. W., & Rowell, A. (1998). Increasing recycling in academic buildings. *Journal of Applied Behavior Analysis, 31*(4), 683–686.

Lumley, M. A. (2004). Alexithymia, emotional disclosure, and health: A program of research. *Journal of Personality. Special Emotions, Personality, and Health, 72*(6), 1271–1300.

Lundh, L., Berg, B., Johansson, H., Nilsson, L., et al. (2002). Social anxiety is associated with a negatively distorted perception of one's own voice. *Cognitive Behaviour Therapy, 31*(1), 25–30.

Luppa, M., Heinrich, S., Angermeyer, M. C., König, H.-H., et al. (2007). Cost-of-illness studies of depression A systematic review. *Journal of Affective Disorders, 98*(1–2), 29–43.

Luria, A. R. (1968). *The mind of a mnemonist.* New York: Basic.

Lustig, C., May, C. P., Hasher, L. (2001). Working memory span and the role of proactive interference. *Journal of Experimental Psychology: General, 130*(2), 199–207.

Luyben, P. D., Hipworth, K., & Pappas, T. (2003). Effects of CAI on the academic performance and attitudes of college students. *Teaching of Psychology, 30*(2), 154–158.

Lykken, D. T. (1998). *A tremor in the blood: Uses and abuses of the lie detector.* New York: Plenum.

Lykken, D. T. (2001). Lie detection. In W. E. Craighead, & C. B. Nemeroff (Eds.), *The Corsini encyclopedia of psychology and behavioral science* (3rd ed.). New York: Wiley.

Lynch, K. B., Geller, S. R., & Schmidt, M. G. (2004). Multi-year evaluation of the effectiveness of a resilience-based prevention program for young children. *Journal of Primary Prevention, 24*(3), 335–353.

Lynch, T. R., Robins, C. J., Morse, J. Q., & MorKrause, E. D. (2001). A mediational model relating affect intensity, emotion inhibition, and psychological distress. *Behavior Therapy, 32*(3), 519–536.

Lynn, J. (2001). Serving patients who may die soon and their families. *Journal of the American Medical Association, 285*(7), 925–932.

Lynn, S. J., & Kirsch, I. (2006). Introduction: Definitions and early history. In S. J. Lynn, & I. Kirsch (Eds.), *Essentials of clinical hypnosis: An evidence-based approach.* Washington, DC: American Psychological Association.

Lyons, A. C., & Chamberlain, K. (2006). *Health psychology.* Cambridge, MA: Cambridge University Press.

Lyubomirsky, S., & Tucker, K. L. (1998). Implications of individual differences in subjective happiness for perceiving, interpreting, and thinking about life events. *Motivation & Emotion, 22*(2), 155–186.

Maas, J. (1999). *Power Sleep.* New York: HarperCollins.

Maccoby, E. E. (1990). Gender and relationships: A developmental account. *American Psychologist, 45*(4), 513–520.

Mack, A. (2002). Is the visual world a grand illusion? *Journal of Consciousness Studies, 9*(5–6), 102–110.

Mack, A., & Rock, I. (1998). *Inattentional blindness.* Cambridge, MA: MIT Press.

Mackintosh, N. J. (2003). Pavlov and associationism. *Spanish Journal of Psychology, 6*(2), 177–184.

Macklin, C. B., & McDaniel, M. A. (2005). The bizarreness effect: Dissociation between item and source memory. *Memory, 13*(7), 662–689.

MacLeod, C. M. (2005). The Stroop task in cognitive research. In A. Wenzel, & D. C. Rubin (Eds.), *Cognitive methods and their application to clinical research.* Washington, DC: American Psychological Association.

Maddi, S. R. (2006). Hardiness: The courage to grow from stresses. *Journal of Positive Psychology, 1*(3), 160–168.

Maddock, J. E., Laforge, R. G., Rossi, J. S., & O'Hare, T. (2001). The College Alcohol Problems Scale. *Addictive Behaviors, 26,* 385–398.

Maddox, K. B. (2004). Perspectives on racial phenotypicality bias. *Personality & Social Psychology Review, 8*(4), 383–401.

Maguire, E. A., Frackowiak, R. S. J., & Frith, C. D. (1997). Recalling routes around London: Activation of the hippocampus in taxi drivers. *The Journal of Neuroscience, 17*(8), 7103.

Maguire, E. A., Valentine, E. R., Wilding, J. M., et al. (2003). Routes to remembering: The brains behind superior memory. *Nature Neuroscience, 6*(1), 90–95.

Mah, K., & Binik, Y. M. (2001). The nature of human orgasm: A critical review of major trends. *Clinical Psychology Review, 21*(6), 823–856.

Mahay, J., & Laumann, E. O. (2004). Meeting and mating over the life course. In E. O. Laumann, & R. Michael (Eds.), *The sexual organization of the city.* Chicago: University of Chicago Press.

Maheu, M. M., Pulier, M. L., Wilhelm, F. H., McMenamin, J. P., et al. (2004). *The mental health professional and the new technologies: A handbook for practice today.* Mahwah, NJ: Erlbaum.

Maier, N. R. F. (1949). *Frustration.* New York: McGraw-Hill.

Maier, S. F. (2001). Exposure to the stressor environment prevents the temporal dissipation of behavioral depression/learned helplessness. *Biological Psychiatry, 49*(9), 763–773.

Mailis-Gagnon, A., & Israelson, D. (2005). *Beyond pain: Making the mind-body connection.* Ann Arbor, MI: University of Michigan Press.

Major, B., Schmidlin, A. M., & Williams, L. (1990). Gender patterns in social touch: The impact of setting and age. *Journal of Personality & Social Psychology, 58*(4), 634–643.

Malamuth, N. M., & Donnerstein, E. (1982). The effects of aggressive-pornographic of mass media stimuli. In L. Berkowitz (Ed.), *Advances in experimental social psychology* (Vol. 15). New York: Academic Press.

Malamuth, N. M., Addison, T., & Koss, M. (2000). Pornography and sexual aggression: Are there reliable effects and can we understand them? *Annual Review of Sex Research, 11,* 26–91.

Malaspina, D., Reichenberg, A., Weiser, M., Fennig, S., et al. (2005). Paternal age and intelligence: Implications for age-related genomic changes in male germ cells. *Psychiatric Genetics, 15*(2), 117–125.

Maloney, A. (1999). Preference ratings of images representing archetypal themes. *Journal of Analytical Psychology, 44*(1) 101–116.

Mamen, M. (2004). *Pampered child syndrome: How to recognize it, how to manage it and how to avoid it.* Carp, ON: Creative Bound.

Manalo, E. (2002). Uses of mnemonics in educational settings: A brief review of selected research. *Psychologia: An International Journal of Psychology in the Orient, 45*(2), 69–79.

Manber, R., Kraemer, H. C., Arnow, B. A., Trivedi, M. H., et al. (2008). Faster remission of chronic depression with combined psychotherapy and medication than with each therapy alone. *Journal of Consulting & Clinical Psychology, 76*(3), 459–467.

Mandler, J. M., & McDonough, L. (1998). On developing a knowledge base in infancy. *Developmental Psychology, 34*(6), 1274–1288.

Mangan, M. A. (2004). A phenomenology of problematic sexual behavior occurring in sleep. *Archives of Sexual Behavior, 33*(3), 287–293.

Mangels, J. A., Picton, T. W., & Craik, F. I. M. (2001). Attention and successful episodic encoding: An event-related potential study. *Brain Research, 11,* 77–95.

Manning, R., Levine, M, & Collins, A. (2007). The Kitty Genovese murder and the social psychology of helping: The parable of the 38 witnesses. *American Psychologist, 62,* 555–562.

Manschreck, T. C. (1996). Delusional disorder: The recognition and management of paranoia. *Journal of Clinical Psychiatry, 57*(3, Suppl), 32–38.

Mansouri, A., & Adityanjee. (1995). Delusion of pregnancy in males: A case report and literature review. *Psychopathology, 28*(6), 307–311.

Mantyla, T. (1986). Optimizing cue effectiveness: Recall of 600 incidentally learned words. *Journal of Experimental Psychology: Learning, Memory, and Cognition, 12*(1), 66–71.

Marcus, E. (2002). Psychoanalytic psychotherapy and psychoanalysis: An overview. In M. Hersen & W. H. Sledge (Eds.), *Encyclopedia of psychotherapy.* San Diego: Academic Press.

Margolin, G., & Gordis, E. B. (2000). The effects of family and community violence on children. *Annual Review of Psychology, 51,* 445–479.

Marion, S. L., Shayka, J. J., & Marcus, S. C. (1996). A short computer interview for obtaining psychiatric diagnoses. *Psychiatric Services, 47*(3), 293–297.

Marks, D. F. (2000). *The psychology of the psychic.* Buffalo, NY: Prometheus.

Markus, H. R., Uchida, Y., Omoregie, H., Townsend, S. S. M., et al. (2006). Going for the gold: Models of agency in Japanese and American contexts. *Psychological Science, 17*(2), 103–112.

Markus, H., & Nurius, P. (1986). Possible selves. *American Psychologist, 41,* 954–969.

Marmarosh, C., Holtz, A., & Schottenbauer, M. (2005). Group cohesiveness, group-derived collective self-esteem, group-derived hope, and the well-being of group therapy members. *Group Dynamics: Theory, Research, & Practice, 9*(1), 32–44.

Marsella, A. J. (1998). Urbanization, mental health, and social deviancy. *American Psychologist, 53*(6), 624–634.

Marshall, R. D., Bryant, R. A., Amsel, L., Suh, E. J., et al. (2007). The psychology of ongoing threat: Relative risk appraisal, the September 11 attacks, and terrorism-related fears. *American Psychologist, 62*(4), 304–316.

Marsiglia, F. F., Kulis, S., Hecht, M. L., & Sills, S. (2004). Ethnicity and ethnic identity as predictors of drug norms and drug use among preadolescents in the US southwest. *Substance Use & Misuse, 39*(7), 1061–1094.

Martens, R., & Trachet, T. (1998). *Making sense of astrology.* Amherst, MA: Prometheus.

Martin, A. J., & Marsh, H. W. (2003). Fear of failure: Friend or foe? *Australian Psychologist, 38*(1), 31–38.

Martin, C. L., & Fabes, R. A. (2001). The stability and consequences of young children's same-sex peer interactions. *Developmental Psychology, 37*(3), 431–446.

Martin, E. K., Taft, C. T., & Resick, P. A. (2007). A review of marital rape. *Aggression & Violent Behavior, 12*(3), 329–347.

Martin, G., & Pear, J. (2007). *Behavior modification: What it is and how to do it* (8th ed.). Upper Saddle River, NJ: Prentice-Hall.

Martin, L. R., Friedman, H. S., & Schwartz, J. E. (2007). Personality and mortality risk across the life span: The importance of conscientiousness as a biopsychosocial attribute. *Health Psychology, 26*(4), 428–436.

Martin, S. (2007). The labyrinth of leadership. *Monitor on Psychology,* July/Aug., 90–91.

Martin, W. L. B., & Freitas, M. B. (2002). Mean mortality among Brazilian left- and right-handers: Modification or selective elimination. *Laterality, 7*(1), 31–44.

Martinez-Gonzalez, M. A., Gual, P., Lahortiga, F., Alonso, Y., et al. (2003). Parental factors, mass media influences, and the onset of eating disorders in a prospective population-based cohort. *Pediatrics, 111,* 315–320.

Martinko, M. J., Douglas, S. C., & Harvey, P. (2006). Understanding and managing workplace aggression. *Organizational Dynamics, 35*(2), 117–130

Marx, B. P., Gross, A. M., & Adams, H. E. (1999). The effect of alcohol on the responses of sexually coercive and noncoercive men on an experimental rape analogue. *Sexual Abuse: Journal of Research & Treatment, 11*(2), 131–145.

Mashour, G. A., Walker, E. E., & Martuza, R. L. (2005). Psychosurgery: Past, present, and future. *Brain Research Reviews, 48*(3), 409–419.

Masi, G., Mucci, M., & Millepiedi, S. (2001). Separation anxiety disorder in children and adolescents. *CNS Drugs, 15*(2), 93–104.

Maslach, C., Schaufeli, W. B., & Leiter, M. P. (2001). Job burnout. *Annual Review of Psychology, 52,* 397–422.

Maslow, A. H. (1954). *Motivation and personality.* New York: Harper.

Maslow, A. H. (1967). Self-actualization and beyond. In J. F. T. Bugental (Ed.), *Challenges of humanistic psychology.* New York: McGraw-Hill.

Maslow, A. H. (1968). *Toward a psychology of being.* New York: Van Nostrand.

Maslow, A. H. (1969). *The psychology of science.* Chicago: Henry Regnery.

Maslow, A. H. (1970). *Motivation and personality.* New York: Harper & Row.

Maslow, A. H. (1971). *The farther reaches of human nature.* New York: Viking.

Masse, L. C. & Tremblay, R. E. (1997). Behavior of boys in kindergarten and the onset of substance use during adolescence. *Archives of General Psychiatry, 54*(1), 62.

Masten, A. S. (2001). Ordinary magic: Resilience processes in development. *American Psychologist, 56*(3), 227–238.

Masters, W. H., & Johnson, V. E. (1966). *Human sexual response.* Boston: Little, Brown.

Masters, W. H., & Johnson, V. E. (1970). *The pleasure bond: A new look at sexuality and commitment.* Boston: Little, Brown.

Matheny, K. B., Brack, G. L., McCarthy, C. J., Penick, J. M. (1996). The effectiveness of cognitively-based approaches in treating stress-related symptoms. *Psychotherapy, 33*(2), 305–320.

Matossian, M. K. (1982). Ergot and the Salem witchcraft affair. *American Scientist, 70,* 355–357.

Matson, J. L., Sevin, J. A., Fridley D., & Love, S. R. (1990). Increasing spontaneous language in three autistic children. *Journal of Applied Behavior Analysis, 23*(2), 223–227.

Matthews, G., Deary, I. J., & Whiteman, M. C. (2003). *Personality traits* (2nd ed.). New York: Cambridge University Press.

Matthews, P. H., & Matthews, M. S. (2004). Heritage language instruction and giftedness in language minority students: Pathways toward success. *Journal of Secondary Gifted Education, 15*(2), 50–55.

Mayberg, H., Lozano, A., Voon, V., McNeely, H., et al. (2005). Deep brain stimulation for treatment-resistant depression. *Neuron, 45*(5), 651–660.

Mayer, E. L. (2002). Freud and Jung: the boundaried mind and the radically connected mind. *Journal of Analytical Psychology, 47,* 91–99.

Mayer, J. D., Salovey, P., Caruso, D. R., & Sitarenios, G. (2001). Emotional intelligence as standard intelligence. *Emotion, 1*(3), 232–242.

Mayer, R. E. (1995). *Thinking, problem solving, and cognition.* New York: Freeman.

Mayer, R. E. (2004). Should there be a three-strikes rule against pure discovery learning? *American Psychologist, 59*(1), 14–19.

Mazur, J. E. (2006). *Learning and behavior* (6th ed.). Englewood Cliffs, NJ: Prentice Hall.

McAdams, D. P., & Pals, J. L. (2006). A new Big Five: Fundamental principles for an integrative science of personality. *American Psychologist, 61*(3), 204–217.

McAlister, A. L., Ama, E., Barroso, C., Peters, R. J., et al. (2000). Promoting tolerance and moral engagement through peer modeling. *Cultural Diversity & Ethnic Minority Psychology, 6*(4), 363–373.

McBride, W. J., Murphy, J. M., & Ikemoto, S. (1999). Localization of brain reinforcement mechanisms. *Behavioural Brain Research, 101*(2), 129–152.

McCabe, C., & Rolls, E. T. (2007). Umami: A delicious flavor formed by convergence of taste and olfactory pathways in the human brain. *European Journal of Neuroscience, 25*(6), 1855–1864.

McCabe, M. P. (1992). A program for the treatment of inhibited sexual desire in males. *Psychotherapy, 29*(2), 288–296.

McCabe, M. P., & Ricciardelli, L. A. (2004). Weight and shape concerns of boys and men. In Thompson, J. K. (Ed.), *Handbook of eating disorders and obesity.* New York: Wiley.

McCall, W. V., Prudic, J., Olfson, M., & Sackeim, H. (2006). Health-related quality of life following ECT in a large community sample. *Journal of Affective Disorders, 90*(2–3), 269–274.

McCarthy, B. W. (1995). Bridges to sexual desire. *Journal of Sex Education & Therapy, 21*(2), 132–141.

McCarthy, B. W., & Fucito, L. M. (2005). Integrating medication, realistic expectations, and therapeutic interventions in the treatment of male sexual dysfunction. *Journal of Sex & Marital Therapy, 31*(4), 319–328.

McCaul, K. D., & Malott, J. M. (1984). Distraction and coping with pain. *Psychological Bulletin, 95,* 516–533.

McClelland, D. C. (1961). *The achieving society.* New York: Van Nostrand.

McClelland, D. C. (1965). Achievement and entrepreneurship. *Journal of Personality & Social Psychology, 1,* 389–393.

McClelland, D. C. (1975). *Power: The inner experience.* New York: Irvington.

McClelland, D. C. (1994). The knowledge-testing-educational complex strikes back. *American Psychologist, 49*(1), 66–69.

McClelland, D. C., & Cheriff, A. D. (1997). The immunoenhancing effects of humor on secretory IgA and resistance to respiratory infections. *Psychology & Health, 12*(3), 329–344.

McClelland, D. C., & Pilon, D. A. (1983). Sources of adult motives in patterns of parent behavior in early childhood. *Journal of Personality & Social Psychology, 44,* 564–574.

McClelland, J. L., & Rogers, T. T. (2003). The parallel distributed processing approach to semantic cognition. *Nature Reviews Neuroscience, 4*(4), 310–322.

McClelland, L., & Cook, S. W. (1980). Promoting energy conservation in master-metered apartments through group financial incentives. *Journal of Applied & Social Psychology, 10,* 20–31.

McCluskey, U. (2002). The dynamics of attachment and systems-centered group psychotherapy. *Group Dynamics, 6*(2), 131–142.

McCoy, N. L., & Pitino, L. (2002). Pheromonal influences on sociosexual behavior in young women. *Physiology & Behavior, 75*(3), 367–375.

McCrae, R. R., & Costa, P. T. (2001). A five-factor theory of personality. In L. A. Pervin, & O. P. John (Eds.), *Handbook of personality.* New York: Guilford.

McCrae, R. R., & Terracciano, A. (2005). Universal features of personality traits from the observer's perspective: Data from 50 cultures. *Journal of Personality & Social Psychology, 88*(3), 547–561.

McDaniel, M. A., Maier, S. F., & Einstein, G. O. (2002). "Brain-specific" nutri-

ents: A memory cure? *Psychological Science in the Public Interest, 3*(1), 12–38.

McDermott, R., Johnson, D., Cowden, J., & Rosen, S. (2007). Testosterone and aggression in a simulated crisis game. *Annals of the American Academy of Political and Social Science, 614*(1), 15–33.

McDonald, J. K., Yanchar, S. C., & Osguthorpe, R. (2005). Learning from programmed instruction: Examining implications for modern instructional technology. *Educational Technology Research & Development, 53*(2), 84–98.

McGregor, D. (1960). *The human side of enterprise.* New York: McGraw-Hill.

McGregor, I., McAdams, D. P., & Little, B. R. (2006). Personal projects, life stories, and happiness: On being true to traits. *Journal of Research in Personality, 40*(5), 551–572.

McGuffin, P., Rijsdijk, F., Andrew, M., Sham, P., et al. (2003). The heritability of bipolar affective disorder and the genetic relationship to unipolar depression. *Archives of General Psychiatry, 60*(5), 497–502.

McGuire, J., & Scott, S. (2002). Universal Design for Instruction: A promising new paradigm for higher education. *Perspectives, 28,* 27–29.

McIntosh, W. D., Harlow, T. F., & Martin, L. L. (1995). Linkers and nonlinkers: Goal beliefs as a moderator of the effects of everyday hassles on rumination, depression, and physical complaints. *Journal of Applied Social Psychology, 25*(14), 1231–1244.

McKay, A. (2005). Sexuality and substance use: The impact of tobacco, alcohol, and selected recreational drugs on sexual function. *Canadian Journal of Human Sexuality, 14*(1–2), 47–56.

McKeever, L. (2006). Online plagiarism detection services: Saviour or scourge? *Assessment & Evaluation in Higher Education, 31*(2), 155–165.

McKeever, W. F. (2000). A new family handedness sample with findings consistent with X-linked transmission. *British Journal of Psychology, 91*(1), 21–39.

McKeever, W. F., Cerone, L. J., Suter, P. J., & Wu, S. M. (2000). Family size, miscarriage-proneness, and handedness. *Laterality, 5*(2), 111–120.

McKenna, M. W., & Ossoff, E. P. (1998). Age differences in children's comprehension of a popular television program. *Child Study Journal, 28*(1), 52–68.

McKenzie, K., Serfaty, M., & Crawford, M. (2003). Suicide in ethnic minority groups. *British Journal of Psychiatry, 183*(2), 100–101.

McKim, W. A. (2007). *Drugs and behavior* (6th ed.). Englewood Cliffs, NJ: Prentice Hall.

McKone, E., Brewer, J. L., MacPherson, S., et al. (2007). Familiar other-race faces show normal holistic processing and are robust to perceptual stress. *Perception, 36*(2), 244–248.

McLewin, L. A., & Muller, R. T. (2006). Childhood trauma, imaginary companions, and the development of pathological dissociation. *Aggression & Violent Behavior, 11*(5), 531–545.

McLoyd, V. C., & Smith, J. (2002). Physical discipline and behavior problems in

African American, European American, and Hispanic children: Emotional support as a moderator. *Journal of Marriage & Family, 64*(1), 40–53.

McMahon, S., & Koltzenburg, M. (2005). *Wall & Melzack's textbook of pain* (5th ed.). London: Churchill Livingstone.

McNally, R. J., & Clancy, S. A. (2005). Sleep paralysis, sexual abuse, and space alien abduction. *Transcultural Psychiatry, 42*(1), 113–122.

McNally, R. J., Clancy, S. A., & Barrett, H. M. (2004). Forgetting trauma? In D. Reisberg, & P. Hertel (Eds.), *Memory & emotion.* New York: Oxford University Press.

McNamara, D. S., & Scott, J. L. (2001). Working memory capacity and strategy use. *Memory & Cognition, 29*(1), 10–17.

McRobbie, H., & Hajek, P. (2007). Effects of rapid smoking on post-cessation urges to smoke. *Addiction, 102*(3), 483–489.

Mead, M. (1935). *Sex and temperament in three primitive societies.* New York: Morrow.

Medhus, E. (2001). *Child rearing challenges.* Retrieved May 25, 2007, from http://www.drmedhus.com/childchallenges.htm.

Mehl, M. R., Vazire, S., Ramírez-Esparza, N., Slatcher, R. B., et al. (2007). Are women really more talkative than men? *Science, 317*(5834), 82.

Mehrabian, A. (2000). Beyond IQ. *Genetic Social, and General Psychology Monographs, 126,* 133–239.

Mehrabian, A., & Blum, J. S. (2003). Physical appearance, attractiveness, and the mediating role of emotions. In N. J. Pallone (Ed.), *Love, romance, sexual interaction: Research perspectives from Current Psychology.* New Brunswick, NJ: Transaction Publishers.

Meichenbaum, D., Henshaw, D., & Himel, N. (1982). Coping with stress as a problem-solving process. In H. W. Krohne, & L. Laux (Eds.), *Achievement, stress, and anxiety.* New York: Hemisphere.

Meier, P. S., Donmall, M. C., McElduff, P., Barrowclough, C., et al. (2006). The role of the early therapeutic alliance in predicting drug treatment dropout. *Drug & Alcohol Dependence, 83*(1), 57–64.

Meltzoff, A. N. (2005). Imitation and other minds: The "Like Me" Hypothesis. In S. Hurley, & N. Chater (Eds.), *Perspectives on imitation: From neuroscience to social science* (Vol. 2): *Imitation, human development, and culture.* Cambridge, MA: MIT Press.

Meltzoff, A. N., & Prinz, W. (2002). *The imitative mind: Development, evolution, and brain bases.* Cambridge, MA: Cambridge University Press.

Melzack, R. (1999). From the gate to the neuromatrix. *Pain. Special A tribute to Patrick D. Wall,* Suppl 6, S121–S126.

Melzack, R., & Katz, J. (2004). The gate control theory: Reaching for the brain. In T. Hadjistavropoulos, & K. D. Craig (Eds.), *Pain: Psychological perspectives.* Mahwah, NJ: Erlbaum.

Melzack, R., & Katz, J. (2006). Pain in the 21st century: The neuromatrix and beyond. In G. Young, A. W. Kane, et al.

(Eds.), *Psychological knowledge in court: PTSD, pain, and TBI.* New York: Springer.

Melzack, R., & Wall, P. D. (1996). *The challenge of pain.* Harmondworth, UK: Penguin.

Mendolia, M. (2002). An index of self-regulation of emotion and the study of repression in social contexts that threaten or do not threaten self-concept. *Emotion, 2*(3), 215–232.

Meneses, G. D., & Beerlipalacio, A. (2005). Recycling behavior: A multidimensional approach. *Environment & Behavior, 37*(6), 837–860.

Menzel, P., Eisert, S., Mann, C. C., & Kennedy, P. (1994). *Material world: A global family portrait.* San Francisco: Sierra Club Books

Mercer, J. (2006). *Understanding attachment: Parenting, child care, and emotional development.* Westport, CT: Praeger.

Merhi, O., Faugloire, E., Flanagan, M, et al. (2007). Motion sickness, console video games, and head-mounted displays. *Human Factors, 49*(5), 920–934.

Merritt, J. M., Stickgold, R., Pace-Schott, E., Williams, J., et al. (1994). Emotion profiles in the dreams of men and women. *Consciousness & Cognition, 3*(1), 46–60.

Mesquita, B., & Markus, H. R. (2004). Culture and emotion: Models of agency as sources of cultural variation in emotion. In A. S. R. Manstead, S. R. Antony, et al. (Eds.), *Feelings and emotions: The Amsterdam symposium.* New York: Cambridge University Press.

Messer, S. B., & Kaplan, A. H. (2004). Outcomes and factors related to efficacy of brief psychodynamic therapy. In D. P. Charman (Ed.), *Core processes in brief psychodynamic psychotherapy: Advancing effective practice.* Mahwah, NJ: Erlbaum.

Messick, D. M., Wilke, H., Brewer, M., Kramer, R. M., et al. (1983). Individual adaptations and structural change as solutions to social dilemmas. *Journal of Personality & Social Psychology, 44,* 294–309.

Meunier, M., Monfardini, E., & Boussaoud, D. (2007). Learning by observation in rhesus monkeys. *Neurobiology of Learning and Memory, 88*(2), 243–248.

Meyer, G. J., Finn, S. E., Eyde, L. D., Kay, G. G., et al. (2001). Psychological testing and psychological assessment. *American Psychologist, 56*(2) 128–165.

Meyer-Bisch, C. (1996). Epidemiological evaluation of hearing damage related to strongly amplified music (Personal cassette players, discotheques, rock concerts). *Audiology, 35*(3), 121–142.

Meyers, L. (2006). Behind the scenes of the "Dr. Phil" show. *Monitor on Psychology, 37*(9), 63.

Michael, D., & Chen, S. (2006). *Serious games: Games that educate, train, and inform.* Boston: Cengage Learning/Course Technology.

Michaels, J. W., Blommel, J. M., Brocato, R. M., Linkous, R. A., et al. (1982). Social facilitation and inhibition in a natural setting. *Replications in Social Psychology, 2,* 21–24.

Michalak, E. E., & Lam, R. W. (2002). Seasonal affective disorder: The latitude hypothesis revisited. *Canadian Journal of Psychiatry, 47*(8), 787–788.

Michalko, M. (1998). *Cracking creativity.* Berkeley, CA: Ten Speed Press.

Michel, C., Caldara, R., & Rossion, B. (2006). Same-race faces are perceived more holistically than other-race faces. *Visual Cognition, 14*(1), 55–73.

Michelangelo, I., Stefania, B., Donatella, P., Maria, C. Z., et al. (2006). Electrocortical effects of MDMA are potentiated by acoustic stimulation in rats. *BMC Neuroscience,* doi :10.1186/1471-2202-7-13. Retrieved May 25, 2007, from http://www. biomedcentral.com/content/ pdf/1471-2202-7-13.pdf.

Mickelson, K. D., Kessler, R. C., & Shaver, P. R. (1997). Adult attachment in a nationally representative sample. *Journal of Personality & Social Psychology, 73*(5), 1092–1106.

Middaugh, S. J., & Pawlick, K. (2002). Biofeedback and behavioral treatment of persistent pain in the older adult: A review and a study. *Applied Psychophysiology & Biofeedback, 27*(3), 185–202.

Mielke, H. W. (1999). Lead in the inner cities. *American Scientist, 87*(Jan.–Feb.), 62–73.

Mignot, E. (2001). A hundred years of narcolepsy research. *Archives of Italian Biology, 139,* 207–220.

Mikulincer, M., & Nachshon, O. (1991). Attachment styles and patterns of self-disclosure. *Journal of Personality & Social Psychology, 61*(2), 321–331.

Milgram, S. (1963). Behavioral study of obedience. *Journal of Abnormal and Social Psychology, 67,* 371–378.

Milgram, S. (1965). Some conditions of obedience and disobedience to authority. *Human Relations, 18,* 57–76.

Milgram, S. (1967). The small-world problem. *Psychology Today,* May, 61–67.

Milgram, S. (1970). The experience of living in the cities: A psychological analysis. *Science, 167,* 1461–1468.

Milgram, S., Bickman, L., & Berkowitz, L. (1969). Note on the drawing power of crowds of different size. *Journal of Personality & Social Psychology, 13,* 79–82.

Miller, D. T. (2006). *An invitation to social psychology.* Belmont, CA: Cengage Learning/Wadsworth.

Miller, E. K., & Cohen, J. D. (2001). An integrative theory of prefrontal cortex function. *Annual Review of Neuroscience, 24,* 167–202.

Miller, G. A. (1956). The magical number seven, plus or minus two: Some limits on our capacity for processing information. *Psychological Review, 63,* 81–87.

Miller, G. A. (1999). On knowing a word. *Annual Review of Psychology, 50,* 1–19.

Miller, G. E., Cohen, S., & Ritchey, A. K. (2002). Chronic psychological stress and the regulation of pro-inflammatory cytokines. *Health Psychology, 21*(6), 531–541.

Miller, M., Hemenway, D., & Azraela, D. (2007). State-level homicide victimization rates in the US in relation to survey measures of household firearm ownership, 2001–2003. *Social Science & Medicine, 64*(3), 656–664.

Miller, N. E. (1944). Experimental studies of conflict. In J. McV. Hunt (Ed.), *Per-*

sonality and the behavior disorders (Vol. 1). New York: Ronald Press.

Miller, N. E., & Bugelski. R. (1970). The influence of frustration imposed by the in-group on attitudes expressed toward out-groups. In R. I. Evans, & R. M. Rozelle (Eds.), *Social psychology in life.* Boston: Allyn & Bacon.

Miller, N., Pedersen, W. C., Earleywine, M., & Pollock, V. E. (2003). A theoretical model of triggered displaced aggression. *Personality & Social Psychology Review, 7*(1), 75–97.

Miller, R., Perlman, D., & Brehm, S. S. (2007). *Intimate relationships* (4th ed.). New York: McGraw-Hill.

Miller, S. J., & Binder, J. L. (2002). The effects of manual-based training on treatment fidelity and outcome. *Psychotherapy: Theory, Research, Practice, Training, 39*(2), 184–198.

Miller, W. R., & Munoz, R. F. (2005). *Controlling your drinking: Tools to make moderation work for you.* New York: Guilford.

Millet, K., & Dewitte, S. (2007). Digit ratio (2D:4D) moderates the impact of an aggressive music video on aggression. *Personality & Individual Differences, 43*(2), 289–294.

Millman, R. B., & Ross, E. J. (2003). Steroid and nutritional supplement use in professional athletes. *American Journal on Addictions, 12*(Suppl 2), S48–S54.

Millon, T. (1981). *Disorders of personality: DSM-III: Axis II.* New York: Wiley.

Milne, R., & Bull, R. (2002). Back to basics: A componential analysis of the original cognitive interview mnemonics with three age groups. *Applied Cognitive Psychology, 16*(7), 743–753.

Milner, B. (1965). Memory disturbance after bilateral hippocampal lesions. In P. Milner, & S. Glickman (Eds.), *Cognitive processes and the brain.* Princeton, NJ: Van Nostrand.

Miltenberger, R. G. (2008). *Behavior modification: Principles and procedures* (4th ed.). Belmont, CA: Cengage Learning/Wadsworth.

Miltner, W. H. R., Krieschel, S., Hecht, H., Trippe, R., et al. (2004). Eye movements and behavioral responses to threatening and nonthreatening stimuli during visual search in phobic and nonphobic subjects. *Emotion, 4*(4), 323–339.

Milton, J., & Wiseman, R. (1997). *Guidelines for extrasensory perception research.* Hertfordshire, UK: University of Hertfordshire Press.

Milton, J., & Wiseman, R. (1999). A meta-analysis of mass-media tests of extrasensory perception. *British Journal of Psychology, 90*(2), 235–240.

Minda, J. P., & Smith, J. D. (2001). Prototypes in category learning. *Journal of Experimental Psychology: Learning, Memory, & Cognition, 27*(3), 775–799.

Minton, H. L. (2000). Psychology and gender at the turn of the century. *American Psychologist, 55*(6), 613–615.

Miotto, K., Darakjian, J., Basch, J., Murray, S., et al. (2001). Gamma-hydroxybutyric acid: Patterns of use, effects and withdrawal. *American Journal on Addictions, 10*(3), 232–241.

Miranda, R., & Kihlstrom, J. F. (2005). Mood congruence in childhood and re-

cent autobiographical memory. *Cognition & Emotion, 19*(7), 981–998.

Mirsky, A. F., & Duncan, C. C. (2005). Pathophysiology of mental illness: A view from the fourth ventricle. *International Journal of Psychophysiology, 58*(2–3), 162–178.

Mirsky, A. F., Bieliauskas, L. M., Van Kammen, D. P., Jonsson, E., et al. (2000). A 39-year followup of the Genain quadruplets. *Schizophrenia Bulletin, 3,* 5–18.

Mischel, W. (2004). Toward an integrative science of the person. *Annual Review of Psychology, 55,* 1–22.

Mischel, W., & Shoda, Y. (1998). Reconciling processing dynamics and personality dispositions. *Annual Review of Psychology, 49,* 229–258.

Mischel, W., Shoda, Y., & Smith, R. E. (2004). *Introduction to personality: Toward an integration* (7th ed.). Hoboken, NJ: Wiley.

Mistlberger, R. E. (2005). Circadian regulation of sleep in mammals: Role of the suprachiasmatic nucleus. *Brain Research Reviews, 49*(3), 429–454.

Mitchell, D. (1987). Firewalking cults: Nothing but hot air. *Laser,* Feb., 7–8.

Mitchell, L. A., MacDonald, R. A.R., Knussen, C., et al. (2007). A survey investigation of the effects of music listening on chronic pain. *Psychology of Music, 35*(1), 37–57.

Miyake, A. (2001). Individual differences in working memory. *Journal of Experimental Psychology: General, 130*(2), 163–168.

Moerman, D. E. (2002). The meaning response and the ethics of avoiding placebos. *Evaluation & the Health Professions. Special Recent Advances in Placebo Research, 25*(4), 399–409.

Mogg, K., Bradley, B. P., Hyare, H., & Lee, S. (1998). Selective attention to food-related stimuli in hunger. *Behaviour Research & Therapy, 36*(2), 227–237.

Moghaddam, B. (2002). Stress activation of glutamate neurotransmission in the prefrontal cortex. *Biological Psychiatry, 51*(10), 775–787.

Moghaddam, F. M. (2007). *Multiculturalism and intergroup relations: Psychological implications for democracy in global context.* Washington, DC: American Psychological Association.

Mohr, D. C., Hart, S. L., Julian, L., Catledge, C., et al. (2005). Telephone-administered psychotherapy for depression. *Archives of General Psychiatry, 62*(9), 1007–1014.

Mokdad, A. H., Marks, J. S., Stroup, D. F., & Gerberding, J. L. (2004). Actual causes of death in the United States, 2000. *Journal of the American Medical Association, 291*(March 10), 1238–1245.

Monahan, J., Steadman, H. J., Silver, E., Appelbaum, P. S., et al. (2001). *Rethinking risk assessment: The MacArthur Study of Mental Disorder and Violence.* New York, Oxford University Press, 2001.

Montgomery, P., & Dennis, J. (2004). A systematic review of non-pharmacological therapies for sleep problems in later life. *Sleep Medicine Reviews, 8*(1), 47–62.

Moor, J. (Ed.). (2003). *The Turing test: The elusive standard of artificial intelligence.* London: Kluwer Academic Publishers.

Moore, S. A., & Zoellner, L. A. (2007). Overgeneral autobiographical memory and traumatic events: An evaluative review. *Psychological Bulletin, 133*(3), 419–437.

Moore, T. O. (2001). Testosterone and male behavior: Empirical research with hamsters does not support the use of castration to deter human sexual aggression. *North American Journal of Psychology, 3*(3), 503–520.

Moore-Ede, M. C., Sulzman, F. M., & Fuller, C. A. (1982). *The clocks that time us.* Cambridge, MA: Harvard University Press.

Moran, J. M., Macrae, C. N., Heatherton, T. F., Wyland, C. L. et al. (2006). Neuroanatomical evidence for distinct cognitive and affective components of self. *Journal of Cognitive Neuroscience, 18*(9), 1586–1594.

Moras, K. (2002). Research on psychotherapy. In M. Hersen, & W. H. Sledge (Eds.), *Encyclopedia of psychotherapy.* San Diego: Academic Press.

Moreno, J. L. (1953). *Who shall survive?* New York: Beacon.

Morgan, J. P. (Ed.). (2005). *Psychology of aggression.* Hauppauge, NY: Nova Science Publishers.

Morgan, M. J., Hole, G. J., & Glennerster, A. (1990). Biases and sensitivities in geometrical illusions. Special Issue: Optics, physiology and vision. *Vision Research, 30*(11), 1793–1810.

Morgenstern, J., Labouvie, E., McCrady, B. S., Kahler, C. W., et al. (1997). Affiliation with Alcoholics Anonymous after treatment. *Journal of Consulting & Clinical Psychology, 65*(5), 768–777.

Moriarty, T. (1975). A nation of willing victims. *Psychology Today,* April, 43–50.

Morisse, D., Batra, L., Hess, L., & Silverman, R. (1996). A demonstration of a token economy for the real world. *Applied & Preventive Psychology, 5*(1), 41–46.

Moritz, A. P., & Zamchech, N. (1946). Sudden and unexpected deaths of young soldiers. *American Medical Association Archives of Pathology, 42,* 459–494.

Morr Serewicz, C. M., & Gale, E. (2008). First-date scripts: Gender roles, context, and relationship. *Sex Roles, 58*(3–4), 149–164.

Morris, T., Spittle, M., & Watt, T. (2005). *Imagery in sport.* Champaign, IL: Human Kinetics.

Morrison, R. G., & Wallace, B. (2001). Imagery vividness, creativity and the visual arts. *Journal of Mental Imagery, 25*(3–4), 135–152.

Morsella, E., & Krauss, R. M. (2004). The role of gestures in spatial working memory and speech. *American Journal of Psychology, 117*(3), 411–424.

Mosher, W. D., Chandra, C., & Jones, J. (2005). *Sexual behavior and selected health measures: Men and women 15–44 years of age, United States, 2002.* Atlanta: Centers for Disease Control. Retrieved August 25, 2006, from http://www.cdc.gov/nchs/data/ad/ ad362.pdf.

Most, S. B., Scholl, B. J., Clifford, E. R., & Simons, D. J. (2005). What you see is what you set: Sustained inattentional blindness and the capture of awareness. *Psychological Review, 112*(1), 217–242.

Motivala, S. J., & Irwin, M. R. (2007). Sleep and immunity: Cytokine pathways linking sleep and health outcomes. *Current Directions in Psychological Science, 16*(1), 21–25.

Mshelia, A. Y., & Lapidus, L. B. (1990). Depth picture perception in relation to cognitive style and training in non-Western children. *Journal of Cross-Cultural Psychology, 21*(4), 414–433.

Muchinsky, P. M. (2006). *Psychology applied to work* (8th ed.). Belmont, CA: Cengage Learning/Wadsworth.

Mundy, A. (2004). Divided we stand. *American Demographics, 26*(5), 26–31.

Munsey, C. (2006). RxP legislation made historic progress in Hawaii. *APA Monitor,* June, 42.

Murray, B. (2001). A daunting unbelievable experience. *Monitor on Psychology,* Nov., 18.

Murray, C. B., & Warden, M. R. (1992). Implications of self-handicapping strategies for academic achievement. *Journal of Social Psychology, 132*(1), 23–37.

Murray, J. B. (2002). Phencyclidine (PCP): A dangerous drug, but useful in schizophrenia research. *Journal of Psychology, 136*(3), 319–327.

Murray, S. L., & Holmes, J. G. (1993). Seeing virtues in faults. *Journal of Personality & Social Psychology, 65*(4), 707–722.

Murray, S. L., Holmes, J. G., & Griffin, D. W. (1996). The self-fulfilling nature of positive illusions in romantic relationships. *Journal of Personality & Social Psychology, 71*(6), 1155–1180.

Murray, S., Holmes, J. G., & Griffin, D. W. (2003). Reflections on the self-fulfilling effects of positive illusions. *Psychological Inquiry, 14*(3–4), 2003, 289–295.

Murrell, A. R., Christoff, K. A., & Henning, K. R. (2007). Characteristics of domestic violence offenders: Associations with childhood exposure to violence. *Journal of Family Violence, 22*(7), 523–532.

Mussen, P. H., Conger, J. J., Kagan, J., & Geiwitz, J. (1979). *Psychological development: A life span approach.* New York: Harper & Row.

Musso, M., Weiller, C., Kiebel, S., Muller, S. P., et al. (1999). Training-induced brain plasticity in aphasia. *Brain, 122,* 1781–1790.

Mustanski, B. S., Chivers, M. L., & Bailey, J. M. (2002). A critical review of recent biological research on human sexual orientation. *Annual Review of Sex Research, 13,* 89–140.

Myers, H. F., Lesser, I., Rodriguez, N., Mira, C. B. et al. (2002). Ethnic differences in clinical presentation of depression in adult women. *Cultural Diversity & Ethnic Minority Psychology, 8*(2), 138–156.

Myers, L. (2007). The problem with DNA. *Monitor on Psychology,* June, 52–53.

NAFE (2004). Salary survey. *National Association for Female Executives Magazine, 27*(4), 20–21.

Nagel, T. (1974). What is it like to be a bat? *The Philosophical Review, 83,* 435–450.

Nairne, J. S. (2002). Remembering over the short-term. *Annual Review of Psychology, 53,* 53–81.

Naitoh, P., Kelly, T. L., & Englund, C. E. (1989). *Health effects of sleep deprivation.* U.S. Naval Health Research Center Report, No. 89–46.

Nakamichi, M. (2004). Tool-use and tool-making by captive, group-living orang-utans (Pongo pygmaeus abelii) at an artificial termite mound. *Behavioural Processes, 65*(1), 87–93.

Nakamura, J., & Csikszentmihalyi, M. (2003). The motivational sources of creativity as viewed from the paradigm of positive psychology. In L. G. Aspinwall, & U. M. Staudinger (Eds.), *A psychology of human strengths: Fundamental questions and future directions for a positive psychology.* Washington, DC: American Psychological Association.

National Academy of Sciences. (2002). *The polygraph and lie detection.* Washington, DC.: The National Academies Press.

Nau, S. D., & Lichstein, K. L. (2005). Insomnia: Causes and treatments. In P. R. Carney, J. D. Geyer, et al. (Eds.), *Clinical sleep disorders.* Philadelphia: Lippincott Williams & Wilkins.

Naveh-Benjamin, M., Guez, J., & Sorek, S. (2007). The effects of divided attention on encoding processes in memory: Mapping the locus of interference. *Canadian Journal of Experimental Psychology, 61*(1), 1–12.

NCCDPHP (National Center for Chronic Disease Prevention and Health Promotion). (2004). *Health effects of cigarette smoking.* Retrieved July 19, 2006, from http://www.cdc.gov/Tobacco/factsheets/HealthEffectsofCigaretteSmoking_Factsheet.htm.

Neath, I., & Surprenant, A. (2003). *Human memory* (2nd ed.). Belmont, CA: Cengage Learning/Wadsworth.

Neave, N., & Wolfson, S. (2003). Testosterone, territoriality, and the "home advantage." *Physiology & Behavior, 78*(2), 269–275.

Needles, D. J., & Abramson, L. Y. (1990). Positive life events, attributional style, and hopefulness: Testing a model of recovery from depression. *Journal of Abnormal Psychology, 99*(2), 156–165.

Nehlig, A. (Ed.). (2004). *Coffee, tea, chocolate, and the brain.* Boca Raton, FL: CRC Press.

Neisser, U., Boodoo, G., Bouchard, T. J., Boykin, A. W. et al. (1996). Intelligence: Knowns and unknowns. *American Psychologist, 51*(2), 77–101.

Nelson, C. A. (1999). How important are the first 3 years of life? *Applied Developmental Science, 3*(4), 235–238.

Nelson, G., & and Prilleltensky, I. (Eds.). (2005). *Community psychology: In pursuit of liberation and well-being.* New York: Palgrave MacMillan.

Nelson, T. D. (2005). Ageism: Prejudice against our feared future self. *Journal of Social Issues, 61*(2), 207–221.

Nelson, T. D. (2006). *The psychology of prejudice* (2nd ed.). Needham Heights, MA: Allyn and Bacon.

Nemeroff, C. B., Bremner, J. D., Foa, E. B., Mayberg, H. S., et al. (2006). Posttrau-matic stress disorder: A state-of-the-science review. *Journal of Psychiatric Research, 40*(1), 1–21.

Neter, E., & Ben-Shakhar, G. (1989). The predictive validity of graphological inferences: A meta-analytic approach. *Personality & Individual Differences, 10*(7), 737–745.

Nettle, D. (2006). The evolution of personality variation in humans and other animals. *American Psychologist, 61*(6), 622–631.

Nettle, D. (2008). The personality factor: What makes you unique? *New Scientist, 2642* (Feb. 9), 36–39.

Neubert, M. J. (1998). The value of feedback and goal setting over goal setting alone and potential moderators of this effect: A meta-analysis. *Human Performance, 11*(4), 321–335.

Neufeld, R. W. (1970). The effect of experimentally altered cognitive appraisal on pain tolerance. *Psychonomic Science, 20*(2), 106–107.

Neufeld, R. W. J., Carter, J. R., Nicholson, I. R., & Vollick, D. N. (2003). Schizophrenia. In P. Firestone, & W. L. Marshall (Eds.), *Abnormal psychology: Perspectives* (2nd ed.). Toronto: Prentice Hall.

Neumeister, A. (2004). Neurotransmitter depletion and seasonal affective disorder: Relevance for the biologic effects of light therapy. *Primary Psychiatry. Special Neurotransmitter Depletion, 11*(6), 44–48.

Nevid, J. S., & Greene, B. (2005). *Abnormal psychology in a changing world, media and research update* (5th ed.). Upper Saddle River, NJ: Prentice Hall.

Newman, A. W., & Thompson, J. W. (2001). The rise and fall of forensic hypnosis in criminal investigation. *Journal of the American Academy of Psychiatry & the Law, 29*(1), 75–84.

Ng, S. H. (2002). Will families support their elders? Answers from across cultures. In T. Nelson (Ed.), *Ageism: Stereotyping and prejudice against older persons.* Cambridge, MA: MIT Press.

Niaura, R., Todaro, J. F., Stroud, L., Spiro, A., et al. (2002). Hostility, the metabolic syndrome, and incident coronary heart disease. *Health Psychology, 21*(6), 588–593., from http://www.nichd.nih.gov/health/topics/sudden_infant_death_syndrome.cfm.

NICHD Early Child Care Reseach Network. (1999). Child outcomes when child care center classes meet recommended standards for quality. *American Journal of Public Health, 89,* 1072–1077.

NICHD (2006). *Research on sudden infant death syndrome (SIDS).* Bethesda, MD: National Institute of Child Health and Human Development. Retrieved March 24, 2008, from http://www.nichd.nih.gov/health/topics/sudden_infant_death_syndrome.cfm.

Nickell, J. (2001). John Edward: Hustling the bereaved. *Skeptical Inquirer,* Nov.–Dec., 19–22.

Nickerson, R. S., & Adams, M. J. (1979). Long-term memory for a common object. *Cognitive Psychology, 11,* 287–307.

NIDA. (2006). *Tobacco addiction.* National Institute on Drug Abuse, NIH Publication Number 06-4342. Retrieved July 24, 2006, from http://www.nida.nih.gov/PDF/RRTobacco.pdf.

Niedzwienska, A. (2004). Metamemory knowledge and the accuracy of flash-bulb memories. *Memory, 12*(5), 603–613.

Niehaus, D. J. H., Stein, D. J., Koen, L., Lochner, C., et al. (2005). A case of "If-ufunyane": A Xhosa culture-bound syndrome. *Journal of Psychiatric Practice, 11*(6), 411–413.

Niehoff, B. P., Moorman, R. H., Blakely, G., & Fuller, J. (2001). The influence of empowerment and job enrichment on employee loyalty in a downsizing environment. *Group & Organization Management, 26*(1), 93–113.

Nielsen, D. M., & Metha, A. (1994). Parental behavior and adolescent self-esteem in clinical and nonclinical samples. *Adolescence, 29*(115), 525–542.

Nielsen, M., & Dissanayake, C. (2004). Pretend play, mirror self-recognition and imitation: A longitudinal investigation through the second year. *Infant Behavior & Development, 27*(3), 342–365.

NIMH. (2003). *In harm's way: Suicide in America.* Bethesda, MD: National Institute of Mental Health. Retrieved July 25, 2007, from http://www.nimh.nih.gov/publicat/harmsway.cfm.

NIMH. (2005). *Getting help: Locate services.* Bethesda, MD: National Institute of Mental Health. Retrieved August 20, 2007, from http://www.nimh.nih.gov/tools/contactus.cfm.

NIMH. (2006a). *Facts about Anxiety Disorders.* Bethesda, MD: National Institute of Mental Health. Retrieved July 25, 2007 from http://www.nimh.nih.gov/publicat/anxiety.cfm.

NIMH. (2006b). *The numbers count: Mental disorders in America.* Bethesda, MD: National Institute of Mental Health. Retrieved July 25, 2007, from http://www.nimh.nih.gov/publicat/numbers.cfm.

NIMH. (2008). *Attention deficit hyperactivity disorder.* Bethesda, MD: National Institute of Mental Health. Retrieved July 10, 2008, from http://www.nimh.nih.gov/health/publications/adhd/complete-publication.shtml.

NINDS. (2007). *Brain basics: Understanding sleep.* Bethesda, MD: National Institute of Neurological Disorders and Stroke. Retrieved March 23, 2008, from http://www.ninds.nih.gov/disorders/brain_basics/understanding_sleep.htm

Nisbett, R. E. (2005). Heredity, environment, and race differences in IQ: A commentary on Rushton and Jensen (2005). *Psychology, Public Policy, and Law, 11*(2), 302–310.

Nisbett, R. E., & Miyamoto, Y. (2005). The influence of culture: holistic versus analytic perception. *Trends in Cognitive Sciences, 9*(10), 467–473.

Njeri, I. (1991). Beyond the melting pot. *Los Angeles Times,* Jan. 13, E-1, E-8.

Noble, K. D., Subotnik, R. F., & Arnold, K. D. (1996). A new model for adult female talent development. In K. D. Arnold, K. D. Noble, et al. (Eds.), *Remarkable women.* Cresskill, NJ: Hampton Press.

Noice, H., & Noice, T. (1999). Long-term retention of theatrical roles. *Memory, 7*(3), 357–382.

Noland, J. S., Singer, L. T., Short, E. J., Minnes, S., et al. (2005). Prenatal drug exposure and selective attention in preschoolers. *Neurotoxicology & Teratology, 27*(3), 429–438.

Nolen-Hoeksema, S. (2007). *Abnormal psychology* (4th ed.). New York: McGraw-Hill.

Norcross, J. C. (2005). A primer on psychotherapy integration. In J. C. Norcross, & M. R. Goldfried (Eds.), *Handbook of psychotherapy integration* (2nd ed.). London: Oxford.

Norcross, J. C., Hedges, M., & Prochaska, J. O. (2002). The face of 2010: A Delphi poll on the future of psychotherapy. *Professional Psychology: Research & Practice, 33*(3), 316–322.

Norem, J. K. (2002). *The positive power of negative thinking: Using defensive pessimism to harness anxiety and perform at your peak.* New York: Basic Books.

Norenzayan, A., & Nisbett, R.E. (2000). Culture and causal cognition. *Current Directions in Psychological Science, 9,* 132–135.

Nori, G. (1998). Glucagon and the control of meal size. In: Smith, G. P. (Ed.), *Satiation: From gut to brain.* New York: Oxford University Press.

Norlander, T., Bergman, H., & Archer, T. (1998). Effects of flotation rest on creative problem solving and originality. *Journal of Environmental Psychology, 18*(4), 399–408.

Norlander, T., Bergman, H., & Archer, T. (1999). Primary process in competitive archery performance: Effects of flotation REST. *Journal of Applied Sport Psychology, 11*(2), 194–209.

Norman, D. A. (1994) *Things that make us smart.* Menlo Park, CA: Addison-Wesley.

Norman, K. L., & Panizzi, E. (2006). Levels of automation and user participation in usability testing. *Interacting with Computers, 18*(2), 246–264.

Norris, R. M., & Weinman, J. A. (1996). Psychological change following a long sail training voyage. *Personality & Individual Differences, 21*(2), 189–194.

North, C. S. (1987). *Welcome silence.* New York: Simon & Schuster.

North, C. S., King, R. V., Fowler, R. L., Polatin, P., et al. (2008). Psychiatric disorders among transported Hurricane evacuees: Acute-phase findings in a large receiving shelter site. *Psychiatric Annals, 38*(2), 104–113.

Northcutt, R. G. (2004). Taste buds: Development and evolution. *Brain, Behavior & Evolution, 64*(3), 198–206.

Norton, P. (2003). *Teaching with technology: Designing opportunities to learn.* Belmont, CA: Cengage Learning/Wadsworth.

Nosek, B. A., Greenwald, A. G., & Banaji, M. R. (2005). Understanding and using the implicit association test: II. Method variables and construct validity. *Personality and Social Psychology Bulletin, 31*(2), 166–180.

Nurnberger, J. I., & Zimmerman, J. (1970). Applied analysis of human behaviors: An alternative to conventional motivational inferences and unconscious determination in therapeutic programming. *Behavior Therapy, 1,* 59–69.

Nuttin, B., Cosyns, P., Demeulemeester, H., Gybels, J., et al. (1999). Electrical stimulation in anterior limbs of internal capsules in patients with obsessive-compulsive disorder. *The Lancet, 354*(9189), 1526.

O'Conner, T. G., Marvin, R. S., Rutter, M., Olrick, J. T., et al. (2003). Child-parent attachment following early institutional deprivation. *Development & Psychopathology, 15*(1), 19–38.

O'Connor, M. G., Sieggreen, M. A., Bachna, K., et al. (2000). Long-term retention of transient news events. *Journal of the International Neuropsychological Society, 6*(1), 44–51.

O'Craven, K. M., & Kanwisher, N. (2000). Mental imagery of faces and places activates corresponding stimulus-specific brain regions. *Journal of Cognitive Neuroscience, 12*(6), 1013–1023.

O'Keeffe, C., & Wiseman, R. (2005). Testing alleged mediumship: Methods and results. *British Journal of Psychology, 96*(2), 165–179.

O'Neill, B. (2003). *Don't believe everything you read online.* BBC News. Retrieved May 18, 2007, from http://newswww.bbc.net.uk/1/hi/magazine/3151595.stm.

O'Neill, P. (2005). The ethics of problem definition. *Canadian Psychology, 46,* 13–20.

O'Roark, A. M. (2001). Personality assessment, projective methods and a triptych perspective. *Journal of Projective Psychology & Mental Health, 8*(2), 116–126.

Oakley R. (2004). How the mind hurts and heals the body. *American Psychologist, 59*(1), 29–40.

Oakley, D. A., Whitman, L. G., & Halligan, P. W. (2002). Hypnotic imagery as a treatment for phantom limb pain. *Clinical Rehabilitation, 16*(4), 368–377.

Oberauer, K., & Göthe, K. (2006). Dual-task effects in working memory: Interference between two processing tasks, between two memory demands, and between storage and processing. *European Journal of Cognitive Psychology, 18*(4), 493–519.

Ochoa, J. G., & Pulido, M. (2005). Parasomnias. In P. R. Carney, J. D. Geyer, et al. (Eds.), *Clinical sleep disorders.* Philadelphia: Lippincott Williams & Wilkins.

Ofosu, H. B., Lafreniere, K. D., & Senn, C. Y. (1998). Body image perception among women of African descent: A normative context? *Feminism & Psychology, 8*(3), 303–323.

Ogden C. L., Carroll M. D., McDowell M. A., & Flegal K. M. (2007). *Obesity among adults in the United States—No change since 2003–2004.* Hyattsville, MD: National Center for Health Statistics. Retrieved May 3, 2008, from http://www.cdc.gov/nchs/data/databriefs/db01.pdf.

Ogloff, J. R. P. (2006). Psychopathy/antisocial personality disorder conundrum. *Australian & New Zealand Journal of Psychiatry, 40*(6), 519–528.

Ohayon, M. M., Guilleminault, C., & Priest, R. G. (1999). Night terrors, sleepwalking, and confusional arousals in the general population. *Journal of Clinical Psychiatry, 60*(4), 268–276.

Okiishi, J., Lambert, M. J., Nielsen, S. L., & Ogles, B. M. (2003). Waiting for superskink: An empirical analysis of therapist effects. *Clinical Psychology & Psychotherapy, 10*(6), 361–373.

Olds, M. E., & Fobes, J. L. (1981). The central basis of motivation: Intracranial self-stimulation studies. *Annual Review of Psychology, 32,* 523–574.

O'Leary, E. (2006). Person-centred gestalt therapy. In E. O'Leary, & M. Murphy (Eds.), *New approaches to integration in psychotherapy.* New York: Routledge.

Olio, K. A. (2004). The truth about "false memory syndrome." In P. J. Caplan, & L. Cosgrove (Eds.), *Bias in psychiatric diagnosis. A project of the association for women in psychology.* Northvale, NJ: Jason Aronson.

Olson, J. M., & Zanna, M. P. (1993). Attitudes and attitude change. *Annual Review of Psychology, 44,* 117–154.

Olson-Buchanan, J. B., & Drasgow, F. (2006). Multimedia situational judgment tests: The medium creates the message. In J. A. Weekley & R. E. Ployhart (Eds.), *Situational judgment tests: Theory, measurement, and application.* Mahwah, NJ: Erlbaum.

Olsson, A., Nearing, K, & Phelps, E. A. (2007). Learning fears by observing others: The neural systems of social fear transmission. *Social Cognitive & Affective Neuroscience, 2*(1), 3–11.

Olsson, M. J., Lundström, J. N., Diamantopoulou, S., et al. (2006). A putative female pheromone affects mood in men differently depending on social context. *European Review of Applied Psychology, 56*(4), 279–284.

Olszewski, P. K., Li, D., Grace, M. K., Billington, C. J., et al. (2003). Neural basis of orexigenic effects of ghrelin acting within lateral hypothalamus. *Peptides, 24*(4), 597–602.

Onweugbuzie, A. J. (2000). Academic procrastinators and perfectionistic tendencies among graduate students. *Journal of Social Behavior & Personality, 15*(5), 103–109.

Ooki, S. (2005). Genetic and environmental influences on the handedness and footedness in Japanese twin children. *Twin Research & Human Genetics, 8*(6), 649–656.

Oppliger, P. A. (2007). Effects of gender stereotyping on socialization. In R. W. Preiss, B. M. Gayle, et al. (Eds.), *Mass media effects research: Advances through meta-analysis.* Mahwah, NJ: Erlbaum.

Ord, T. J., Martins E. P., Thakur S., Mane K. K., et al. (2005). Trends in animal behaviour research (1968–2002): Ethoinformatics and the mining of library databases. *Animal Behaviour, 69*(6), 1399–1413.

Orleans, C. T. (2000). Promoting the maintenance of health behavior change. *Health Psychology, 19*(Suppl. 1), 76–83.

Orleans, C. T., Gruman, J., & Hollendonner, J. K. (1999). Rating our progress in population health promotion: Report card on six behaviors. *American Journal of Health Promotion, 14*(2), 75–82.

Ormay, T. (2006). Cybertherapy: Psychotherapy on the Internet. *International Journal of Psychotherapy, 10*(2), 51–60.

Ornstein, R., & Ehrlich, P. (1989). *New world new mind.* New York: Simon & Schuster.

Ornstein, S., & Isabella, L. (1990). Age vs. stage models of career attitudes of women: A partial replication and extension. *Journal of Vocational Behavior, 36,* 1–19.

Oskamp, S. (1995). Resource conservation and recycling: Behavior and policy. *Journal of Social Issues, 51*(4), 157–177.

Oskamp, S. (2000). A sustainable future for humanity? *American Psychologist, 55*(5), 496–508.

Oskamp, S. (2002). Summarizing sustainability issues and research approaches. In P. Schmuck, & W. P. Schultz (Eds.), *Psychology of sustainable development.* Dordrecht, Netherlands: Kluwer.

Oskamp, S., & Schultz, P. W. (2005). *Attitudes and opinions* (3rd ed.). Mahwah, NJ: Erlbaum.

Oskamp, S., & Schultz, P. W. (2006). Using psychological science to achieve ecological sustainability. In S. I. Donaldson, D. E. Berger, et al. (Eds.), *Applied psychology: New frontiers and rewarding careers.* Mahwah, NJ: Erlbaum.

Osofsky, M. J., Bandura, A., & Zimbardo, P. G. (2005). The role of moral disengagement in the execution process. *Law and Human Behavior, 29*(4), 371–393.

Oster, H. (2005). The repertoire of infant facial expressions: a ontogenetic perspective. In J. Nadel, & D. Muir (Eds.), *Emotional development: Recent research advances.* New York: Oxford University Press.

Overmier, J. B., & LoLordo, V. M. (1998). Learned helplessness. In O'Donohue, W. T. (Ed.), *Learning and behavior therapy.* Boston: Allyn & Bacon.

Oyserman, D., Bybee, D., Terry, K., & Hart-Johnson, T. (2004). Possible selves as roadmaps. *Journal of Research in Personality, 38*(2), 130–149.

Page, K. (1999, May 16). The graduate. *Washington Post Magazine, 152,* 18–20.

Page, M. P. A., Madge, A., Cumming, N., et al. (2007). Speech errors and the phonological similarity effect in short-term memory: Evidence suggesting a common locus. *Journal of Memory & Language, 56*(1), 49–64.

Pagnin, D., de Queiroz, V., Pini, S., & Cassano, G. B. (2004). Efficacy of ECT in depression: A meta-analytic review. *Journal of ECT, 20*(1), 13–20.

Palm, K., & Gibson, P. (1998). Recovered memories of childhood sexual abuse: Clinicians' practices and beliefs. *Professional Psychology: Research & Practice, 29*(3), 257–261.

Palmer, S. E., & Beck, D. M. (2007). The repetition discrimination task: An objective method for studying perceptual grouping. *Perception & Psychophysics, 69*(1), 68–78.

Pals, J. L. (2006). Narrative identity processing of difficult life experiences: Pathways of personality development and positive self-transformation in adulthood. *Journal of Personality, 74*(4), 1079–1110.

Pandey, S. (1999). Role of perceived control in coping with crowding. *Psychological Studies, 44*(3), 86–91.

Panksepp, J., & Pasqualini, M. S. (2005). The search for the fundamental brain/mind sources of affective experience. In J. Nadel, & D. Muir (Eds.), *Emotional development: Recent research advances.* New York: Oxford University Press.

Papa, F. J., Aldrich, D., & Schumacker, R. E. (1999). The effects of immediate online feedback upon diagnostic performance. *Academic Medicine, 74*(Suppl. 10), S16–S18.

Papanicolaou, A. C. (Ed.) (2006). *The amnesias: A clinical textbook of memory disorders.* New York: Oxford University Press.

Paquette, V., Lévesque, J., Mensour, B., Leroux, J.-M., et al. (2003). "Change the mind and you change the brain": Effects of cognitive-behavioral therapy on the neural correlates of spider phobia. *NeuroImage, 18,* 401–409.

Paquette, V., Lévesque, J., Mensour, B., Leroux, J.-M., et al. (2003). "Change the mind and you change the brain": Effects of cognitive-behavioral therapy on the neural correlates of spider phobia. *NeuroImage, 18,* 401–409.

Paradis, C. M., Solomon, L. Z., Florer, F., et al. (2004). Flashbulb memories of personal events of 9/11 and the day after for a sample of New York City residents. *Psychological Reports, 95*(1), 304–310.

Park, N., Peterson, C., & Seligman, M.E.P. (2004). Strengths of character and well-being. *Journal of Social & Clinical Psychology, 23*(5), 603–619.

Parke, R. D. (2004). Development in the family. *Annual Review of Psychology, 55,* 365–399.

Parker, A., Ngu, H., & Cassaday, H. J. (2001). Odour and Proustian memory. *Applied Cognitive Psychology, 15*(2), 159–171.

Parker, J. D. A. (2005). The relevance of emotional intelligence for clinical psychology. In R. Schulze, & R. D. Roberts (Eds.), *Emotional intelligence: An international handbook.* (pp. 271–287). Ashland, OH: Hogrefe & Huber.

Pascual, A., & Guéguen, N. (2005). Foot-in-the-door and door-in-the-face: A comparative meta-analytic study. *Psychological Reports, 96*(1), 122–128.

Passman, R. H. (1987). Attachments to inanimate objects: Are children who have security blankets insecure? *Journal of Consulting and Clinical Psychology, 55*(6), 825–830.

Pasupathi, M., & Staudinger, U. M. (2001). Do advanced moral reasoners also show wisdom? *International Journal of Behavioral Development, 25*(5), 401–415.

Patterson, C. J. (2002). Lesbian and gay parenthood. In M. Bornstein (Ed.), *Handbook of Parenting, 3, 4, 5.* Mahwah, NJ: Erlbaum.

Paulhus, D. L. (1998). Interpersonal and intrapsychic adaptiveness of trait self-enhancement. *Journal of Personality and Social Psychology, 74*(5), 1197–1208.

Paulsson, T., & Parker, A. (2006). The effects of a two-week reflection-intention training program on lucid dream recall. *Dreaming, 16*(1), 22–35.

Pavlidis, I., Eberhardt, N. L., & Levine, J. A. (2002). Seeing through the face of deception. *Nature, 415*(6867), 35.

Pavlov, I. P. (1927). *Conditioned reflexes.* Translated by G. V. Anrep. New York: Dover.

Pearce, C. L., Conger, J. A., & Locke, E. A. (2007). Shared leadership theory. *Leadership Quarterly, 18*(3), 281–288.

Pelton, T. (1983). The shootists. *Science 83, 4*(4), 84–86.

Penfield, W. (1957). Brain's record of past a continuous movie film. *Science News Letter,* April 27, 265.

Penfield, W. (1958). *The excitable cortex in conscious man.* Springfield, IL: Charles C. Thomas.

Pennebaker, J. W. (2004). *Writing to heal: A guided journal for recovering from trauma and emotional upheaval.* Oakland, CA: New Harbinger Press.

Pennebaker, J. W., & Chung, C. K. (2007). Expressive writing, emotional upheavals, and health. In H. S. Friedman, & R. C. Silver (Eds.), *Foundations of health psychology.* New York: Oxford University Press.

Penner, L. A., Dovidio, J. F., Piliavin, J. A., & Schroeder, D. A. (2005). Prosocial behavior: Multilevel perspectives. *Annual Review of Psychology, 56,* 365–392.

Peplau, L. A. (2003). Human sexuality: How do men and women differ? *Current Directions in Psychological Science, 12*(2), 37–40.

Perin, C. T. (1943). A quantitative investigation of the delay of reinforcement gradient. *Journal of Experimental Psychology, 32,* 37–51.

Perlman, D., & Cozby, P. C. (1983). *Social psychology.* New York: Holt, Rinehart & Winston.

Perls, F. (1969). *Gestalt therapy verbatim.* Lafayette, CA: Real People.

Perreault, S., & Bourhis, R. Y. (1999). Ethnocentrism, social identification, and discrimination. *Personality & Social Psychology Bulletin, 25*(1), 92–103.

Perry, R. P. (2003). Perceived (academic) control and causal thinking in achievement settings. *Canadian Psychology, 44*(4), 312–331.

Perry, R. P., Hladkyj, S., Pekrun, R. H., & Pelletier, S. T. (2001). Academic control and action control in the achievement of college students: A longitudinal field study. *Journal of Educational Psychology, 93*(4), 776–789.

Pervin, L. A., Cervone, D., & John, O. P. (2005). *Personality: Theory and research* (9th ed.). New York: Wiley.

Pesant, N., & Zadra, A. (2006). Dream content and psychological well-being: A longitudinal study of the continuity hypothesis. *Journal of Clinical Psychology, 62*(1), 111–121.

Pescatello, L. S. (2001). Exercising for health. *Western Journal of Medicine, 174*(2), 114–118.

Peters, E., Västfjäll, D., Gärling, T., & Slovic, P. (2006). Affect and decision making: A "hot" topic. *Journal of Behavioral Decision Making, 19*(2), 79–85.

Peters, L., Clark, D., & Carroll, F. (1998). Are computerized interviews equivalent to human interviewers? *Psychological Medicine, 28*(4), 893–901.

Peters, W. A. (1971). *A class divided.* Garden City, NY: Doubleday.

Peterson, C., & Chang, E. C. (2003). Optimism and flourishing. In C. L. M. Keyes, & J. Haidt (Eds.), *Flourishing.*

Washington, DC: American Psychological Association.

Peterson, C., & Seligman, M. E. P. (2004). *Character strengths and virtues.* Washington, DC: American Psychological Association.

Peterson, C., & Vaidya, R. S. (2001). Explanatory style, expectations, and depressive symptoms. *Personality & Individual Differences, 31*(7), 1217–1223.

Peterson, D. R. (2001). Choosing the PsyD. In S. Walfish, & A. K. Hess (Eds.), *Succeeding in graduate school: The career guide for psychology students.* Mahwah, NJ: Erlbaum.

Peterson, L. R., & Peterson, M. J. (1959). Short-term retention of individual verbal items. *Journal of Experimental Psychology, 58,* 193–198.

Peterson, P. L. (1979). Direct instruction: Effective for what and for whom? *Educational Leadership, 37,* 46–48.

Peterson, S. E. (1992). The cognitive functions of underlining as a study technique. *Reading Research & Instruction, 31*(2), 49–56.

Petrie, T. A., & Diehl, N. S. (1995). Sport psychology in the profession of psychology. *Professional Psychology: Research & Practice, 26*(3), 288–291.

Pett, M. A., & Johnson, M. J. M. (2005). Development and psychometric evaluation of the Revised University Student Hassles Scale. *Educational & Psychological Measurement, 65*(6), 984–1010.

Peverly, S. T., Brobst, K. E., Graham, M., & Shaw, R. (2003). College adults are not good at self-regulation. *Journal of Educational Psychology, 95*(2), 335–346.

Phillips, D. P., Liu, G. C., Kwok, K., Jarvinen, J., et al. (2001). The Hound of the Baskervilles effect: Natural experiment on the influence of psychological stress on timing of death. *British Medical Journal, 323*(7327), 1443–1446

Piaget, J. (1951, original French, 1945). *The psychology of intelligence.* New York: Norton.

Piaget, J. (1952). *The origins of intelligence in children.* New York: International University Press.

Pickel, K. L., French, T. A., & Betts, J. M. (2003). A cross-modal weapon focus effect: The influence of a weapon's presence on memory for auditory information. *Memory, 11*(3), 277–292.

Piek, J. P. (2006). *Infant motor development.* Champaign, IL: Human Kinetics Publishers.

Pierce, W. D., & Cheney, C. D. (2004). *Behavior analysis and learning* (3rd ed.). Mahwah, NJ: Erlbaum.

Pierrehumbert, B., Ramstein, T., Karmaniola, A., Miljkovitch, R., et al. (2002). Quality of child care in the preschool years. *International Journal of Behavioral Development, 26*(5), 385–396.

Piliavin, I. M., Rodin, J., & Piliavin, J. A. (1969). Good samaritanism: An underground phenomenon? *Journal of Personality & Social Psychology, 13,* 289–299.

Piliavin, J. A. (2003). Doing well by doing good: Benefits to the benefactor. In C. L. M. Keyes, & J. Haidt (Eds.), *Flourishing,* Washington, DC: American Psychological Association.

Pillow, D. R., Zautra, A. J., & Sandler, I. (1996). Major life events and minor

stressors: Identifying mediational links in the stress process. *Journal of Personality & Social Psychology, 70*(2), 381–394.

Pinel, J. P. J., Assanand, S., & Lehman, D. R. (2000). Hunger, eating, and ill health. *American Psychologist, 55*(10), 1105–1116.

Pines, A. M., Ben-Ari, A., Utasi, A., & Larson, D. (2002). A cross-cultural investigation of social support and burnout. *European Psychologist, 7*(4), 256–264.

Pinker, S., & Jackendoff, R. (2005). The faculty of language: What's special about it? *Cognition, 95*(2), 201–236.

Pizam, A., Jeong, G.-H., Reichel, A., Van Boemmel, H., et al. (2004). The relationship between risk-taking, sensation-seeking, and the tourist behavior of young adults: A cross-cultural study. *Journal of Travel Research, 42,* 251–260.

Plassmann, H., O'Doherty, J., Shiv, B., et al. (2008). Marketing actions can modulate neural representations of experienced pleasantness. *Proceedings of the National Academy of Sciences, 105*(3), 1050–1054.

Plazzi, G., Vetrugno, R., Provini, F., Montagna, P. (2005). Sleepwalking and other ambulatory behaviours during sleep. *Neurological Sciences, 26*(Suppl. 3), s193–s198.

Pliner, P., & Mann, N. (2004). Influence of social norms and palatability on amount consumed and food choice. *Appetite, 42*(2), 227–237.

Plous, S. (2003). *Understanding prejudice and discrimination.* New York: McGraw-Hill.

Plutchik, R. (2003). *Emotions and life.* Washington, DC: American Psychological Assocation.

Poland, J., & Caplan, P. J. (2004). The deep structure of bias in psychiatric diagnosis. In P. J. Caplan, & L. Cosgrove (Eds.), *Bias in psychiatric diagnosis. A project of the association for women in psychology.* Lanham, MD: Jason Aronson.

Polemikos, N., & Papaeliou, C. (2000). Sidedness preference as an index of organization of laterality. *Perceptual & Motor Skills, 91*(3, Pt 2), 1083–1090.

Polivy, J., & Herman, C. P. (2002). Causes of eating disorders. *Annual Review of Psychology, 53,* 187–213.

Pollner, M. (1998). The effects of interviewer gender in mental health interviews. *Journal of Nervous & Mental Disease, 186*(6), 369–373.

Pollock, V. E., Briere, J., Schneider, L., Knop, J., et al. (1990). Childhood antecedents of antisocial behavior. *American Journal of Psychiatry, 147*(10), 1290–1293.

Pomaki, G., Supeli, A., & Verhoeven, C. (2007). Role conflict and health behaviors: Moderating effects on psychological distress and somatic complaints. *Psychology & Health, 22*(3), 317–335.

Pope, H. G., Gruber, A. J., & Yurgelun-Todd, D. (1995). The residual neuropsychological effects of cannabis. *Drug & Alcohol Dependence, 38*(1), 25–34.

Popma, A., Vermeiren, R., Geluk, C., Rinne, T., et al. (2007). Cortisol moderates the relationship between testosterone and aggression in delinquent male adolescents. *Biological Psychiatry, 61*(3), 405–411.

Porter, K., (2003). *The mental athlete: Inner training for peak performance in all sports.* Champaign, IL: Human Kinetics.

Porter, S., Campbell, M. A., Birt, A. R., et al. (2003). "He said, she said": A psychological perspective on historical memory evidence in the courtroom. *Canadian Psychology, 44*(3), 190–206.

Posada, G., Jacobs, A., Richmond, M. K., Carbonell, O. A., et al. (2002). Maternal caregiving and infant security in two cultures. *Developmental Psychology, 38*(1), 67–78.

Powell, A. L., & Thelen, M. H. (1996). Emotions and cognitions associated with bingeing and weight control behavior in bulimia. *Journal of Psychosomatic Research, 40*(3), 317–328.

Powell, R. A., Symbaluk, D. G., & Macdonald, S. E. (2005). *Introduction to learning and behavior.* Belmont, CA: Wadsworth.

Pratkanis, A. R. (1992). The Cargo-cult science of subliminal persuasion. *Skeptical Inquirer, 16*(Spring), 260–272.

Pratkanis, A. R., & Aronson, E. (2001). *Age of propaganda: The everyday use and abuse of persuasion.* New York: Henry Holt.

Preckel, F., Holling, H., & Wiese, M. (2006). Relationship of intelligence and creativity in gifted and non-gifted students: An investigation of threshold theory. *Personality & Individual Differences, 40*(1), 159–170.

Premack, A. J., & Premack, D. (1972). Teaching language to an ape. *Scientific American,* Oct., 92–99.

Premack, D., & Premack, A. J. (1983). *The mind of an ape.* New York: Norton.

Prentice, D. A., & Miller, D. T. (1993). Pluralistic ignorance of alcohol use on campus. *Journal of Personality and Social Psychology, 64*(2), 243–256.

Pressley, M. (1987). Are key-word method effects limited to slow presentation rates? An empirically based reply to Hall and Fuson (1986). *Journal of Educational Psychology, 79*(3), 333–335.

Price, M. (2007). Star-crossed lovers quit West Bank. BBC News, Feb 28. Retrieved July 16, 2008, from http://news.bbc.co.uk/2/hi/middle_east/6405799.stm.

Prigerson, H. G., Maciejewski, P.K., & Rosenheck, R. A. (2002). Population attributable fractions of psychiatric disorders and behavioral outcomes associated with combat exposure among US men. *American Journal of Public Health, 92,* 59–63.

Priluck, R., & Till, B. D. (2004). The role of contingency awareness, involvement, and need for cognition in attitude formation. *Journal of the Academy of Marketing Science, 32*(3), 329–344.

Prinstein, M. J., Meade, C. S. & Cohen, G. L. (2003). Adolescent oral sex, peer popularity, and perceptions of best friends' sexual behavior. *Journal of Pediatric Psychology, 28, 4,* 243–249.

Pritchard, R. M. (1961). A collimator stabilizing system. *Quarterly Journal of Experimental Psychology, 13,* 181–183.

Prochaska, J. O., & Norcross, J. C. (2007). *Systems of psychotherapy: A transtheoretical analysis* (6th ed.). Belmont, CA: Cengage Learning/Wadsworth.

Provencher, M. D., Dugas, M. J., & Ladouceur, R. (2004). Efficacy of problem-solving training and cognitive exposure in the treatment of generalized anxiety disorder: A case replication series. *Cognitive & Behavioral Practice, 11*(4), 404–414.

Puca, R. M., & Schmalt, H. (1999). Task enjoyment: A mediator between achievement motives and performance. *Motivation & Emotion, 23*(1), 15–29.

Pychyl, T. A., Lee, J. M., Thibodeau, R., & Blunt, A. (2000). Five days of emotion: An experience sampling study of undergraduate student procrastination. *Journal of Social Behavior & Personality, 15*(5), 239–254.

Quednow, B. B., Jessen, F., Kühn, K.-W., Maier, W., et al. (2006). Memory deficits in abstinent MDMA (Ecstasy) users: Neuropsychological evidence of frontal dysfunction. *Journal of Psychopharmacology, 20*(3), 373–384.

Quigley, B. M., & Leonard, K. E. (2000). Alcohol, drugs, and violence. In V. B. Van Hasselt, & M. Hersen (Eds.), *Aggression and violence: An introductory text.* Boston: Allyn & Bacon.

Quinn, P. C., Bhatt, R. S., & Hayden, A. (2008). Young infants readily use proximity to organize visual pattern information. *Acta Psychologica, 127*(2), 289–298.

Raag, T., & Rackliff, C. L. (1998). Preschoolers' awareness of social expectations of gender: Relationships to toy choices. *Sex Roles, 38*(9–10), 685–700.

Rabius, V., McAlister, A. L., Geiger, A., Huang, P., et al. (2004). Telephone counseling increases cessation rates among young adult smokers. *Health Psychology, 23*(5), 539–541.

Rachman, S. (2004). *Anxiety* (2nd. ed.). New York: Routledge.

Rahman, Q., & Wilson, G. D. (2003). Born gay? The psychobiology of human sexual orientation. *Personality & Individual Differences, 34*(8), 1337–1382.

Rainville, P. (2004). Pain & emotions. In D. D. Price, & M. C. Bushnell (Eds.), *Psychological methods of pain control: Basic science and clinical perspectives.* Seattle: IASP Press.

Ramachandran, V. S. & Oberman, L. (2006). Broken mirrors: A theory of autism. *Scientific American,* October, 63–69.

Ramachandran, V. S. (1995). 2-D or not 2-D—that is the question. In R. Gregory, J. Harris, P. et al. (Eds.), *The artful eye.* Oxford, UK: Oxford University Press.

Ramsay, M. C., Reynolds, C. R., & Kamphaus, R. W. (2002). *Essentials of behavioral assessment.* New York: Wiley.

Randi, J. (1997). *An encyclopedia of claims, frauds, and hoaxes of the occult and supernatural.* New York: St. Martin's Press.

Rathus, R., Nevid, J., & Fichner-Rathus, L. (2005). *Human sexuality in a world of diversity* (6th ed.). Boston: Allyn & Bacon.

Rau, H., Bührer, M., & Weitkunat, R. (2003). Biofeedback of R-wave-to-pulse interval normalizes blood pressure. *Applied Psychophysiology and Biofeedback, 28*(1), 37–46.

Rau, P. R. (2005). *Drowsy driver detection and warning system for commercial vehicle drivers: Field operational test design, data analyses, and progress.* National Highway Traffic Safety Administration Paper Number 05-0192. Retrieved July 24, 2006, from http://www-nrd.nhtsa.dot.gov/pdf/nrd-01/esv/esv19/05-0192-W.pdf.

Rau, W., & Durand, A. (2000). The academic ethic and college grades: Does hard work help students to "make the grade"? *Sociology of Education, 73*(1), 19–38.

Raun, K., von Voss, P., & Knudsen, L. B. (2007). Liraglutide, a once-daily human glucagon-like peptide-1 analog, minimizes food intake in severely obese minipigs. *Obesity, 15*(7), 1710–1716.

Raven, B. H. (1974). *The analysis of power and power preference.* In J. T. Tebeschi (Ed.), *Prospectus on social power.* Chicago: Aldine.

Read, J. (1995). Female sexual dysfunction. *International Review of Psychiatry, 7*(2), 175–182.

Reed, J. D., & Bruce, D. (1982). Longitudinal tracking of difficult memory retrievals. *Cognitive Psychology, 14,* 280–300.

Reed, S. K. (2007). *Cognition: Theory and applications* (7th ed.). Belmont, CA: Cengage Learning/Wadsworth.

Reevy, G. M., & Maslach, C. (2001). Use of social support: Gender and personality differences. *Sex Roles, 44*(7–8), 437–459.

Regan, P. C., Levin, L., Sprecher, S., Christopher, F. S., et al. (2000). Partner preferences: What characteristics do men and women desire in their short-term sexual and long-term romantic partners? *Journal of Psychology & Human Sexuality, 12*(3), 1–21.

Regev, L. G., Zeiss, A., & Zeiss, R. (2006). Orgasmic disorders. In J. E. Fisher, & W. T. O'Donohue (Eds.), *Practitioner's guide to evidence-based psychotherapy.* New York: Springer Science.

Regoeczi, W. C. (2003). When context matters: A multilevel analysis of household and neighbourhood crowding on aggression and withdrawal. *Journal of Environmental Psychology, 23*(4), 457–470.

Reid, M. R., Mackinnon, L. T., & Drummond, P. D. (2001). The effects of stress management on symptoms of upper respiratory tract infection, secretory immunoglobulin A, and mood in young adults. *Journal of Psychosomatic Research, 51*(6), 721–728.

Reid, P. T. (2002). Multicultural psychology. *Cultural Diversity & Ethnic Minority Psychology, 8*(2), 103–114.

Reiff, S. Katkin, E. S., & Friedman, R. (1999). Classical conditioning of the human blood pressure response. *International Journal of Psychophysiology, 34*(2), 135–145.

Reifman, A. S., Larrick, R. P., & Fein, S. (1991). Temper and temperature on the diamond: The heat-aggression relationship in major league baseball. *Personality & Social Psychology Bulletin, 17*(5), 580–585.

Reisner, A. D. (2006). A case of Munchausen syndrome by proxy with subsequent stalking behavior. *International Journal of Offender Therapy & Comparative Criminology, 50*(3), 245–254.

Reiss, M., Tymnik, G., Koegler, P., Koegler, W., et al. (1999). Laterality of hand, foot, eye, and ear in twins. *Laterality, 4*(3), 287–297.

Reiss, S., & Havercamp, S. M. (2005). Motivation in developmental context: A new method for studying self-actualization. *Journal of Humanistic Psychology, 45*(1), 41–53.

Reissing, E. D., Binik, Y. M., Khalifé, S., Cohen, D., et al. (2003). Etiological correlates of vaginismus: Sexual and physical abuse, sexual knowledge sexual self-schema and relationship adjustment. *Journal of Sex & Marital Therapy, 29*(1), 47–59.

Reissing, E. D., Binik, Y. M., Khalifé, S., Cohen, D., et al. (2004). Vaginal spasm, pain, and behavior: An empirical investigation of the diagnosis of vaginismus. *Archives of Sexual Behavior, 33*(1), 5–17.

Reiterman, T. (1993). Parallel roads led to Jonestown, Waco. *The Los Angeles Times,* April 23, A24.

Reitman, D., Murphy, M. A., Hupp, S. D. A., & O'Callaghan, P. M. (2004). Behavior change and perceptions of change: Evaluating the effectiveness of a token economy. *Child & Family Behavior Therapy, 26*(2), 17–36.

Remland, M. S., Jones, T. S., & Brinkman, H. (1991). Proxemic and haptic behavior in three European countries. *Journal of Nonverbal Behavior, 15*(4), 215–232.

Renner, M. J., & Mackin, R. S. (1998). A life stress instrument for classroom use. *Teaching of Psychology, 25*(1), 46–48.

Rentfrow, P. J. & Gosling, S. D. (2003). The do re mi's of everyday life: The structure and personality correlates of music preferences. *Journal of Personality & Social Psychology, 84*(6), 1236–1256.

Rentfrow, P. J., & Gosling, S. D. (2007). The content and validity of music-genre stereotypes among college students. *Psychology of Music, 35*(2), 306–326.

Reppucci, N. D., Woolard, J. L., & Fried, C. S. (1999). Social, community, and preventive interventions. *Annual Review of Psychology, 50,* 387–418.

Rescorla, R. A. (1987). A Pavlovian analysis of goal-directed behavior. *American Psychologist, 42,* 119–126.

Rescorla, R. A. (2004). Spontaneous recovery. *Learning & Memory, 11*(5), 501–509.

Restak, R. M. (2001). *The secret life of the brain.* New York: Dana Press.

Rhine, J. B. (1953). *New world of the mind.* New York: Sloane.

Rhodewalt, F. (1994). Conceptions of ability, achievement goals, and individual differences in self-handicapping behavior. *Journal of Personality, 62*(1), 67–85.

Rice, M. E. (1997). Violent offender research and implications for the criminal justice system. *American Psychologist, 52*(4), 414–423.

Richards, J. M., & Gross, J. J. (2000). Emotion regulation and memory: The cognitive costs of keeping one's cool. *Jour-*

nal of Personality & Social Psychology, 79(3), 410–424.

Richardson, D. R., Green, L. R. (1999). Social sanction and threat explanations on gender effects in direct and indirect aggression. *Aggressive Behavior, 25,* 425–434.

Richmond, L. J. (2004). When spirituality goes awry: Students in cults. *Professional School Counseling, 7*(5), 367–375.

Ricketts, M. S., & Galloway, R. E. (1984). Effects of three different one-hour single-session treatments for test anxiety. *Psychological Reports, 54,* 113–119.

Ridenour, T. A., Maldonado-Molina M., Compton, W. M., Spitznagel, E. L., et al. (2005). Factors associated with the transition from abuse to dependence among substance abusers: Implications for a measure of addictive liability. *Drug & Alcohol Dependence, 80*(1), 1–14.

Ridings, C. M., & Gefen, D. (2004). Virtual community attraction: Why people hang out online. *Journal of Computer-Mediated Communication, 10*(1).

Riefer, D. M., Keveri, M. K., & Kramer, D. L. (1995). Name that tune: Eliciting the tip-of-the-tongue experience using auditory stimuli. *Psychological Reports, 77*(3) (Pt 2), 1379–1390.

Riley, W., Jerome, A., Behar, A., & Zack, S. (2002). Feasibility of computerized scheduled gradual reduction for adolescent smoking cessation. *Substance Use & Misuse, 37*(2), 255–263.

Rind, B., Tromovitch, P., & Bauserman, R. (1998). A meta-analytic examination of assumed properties of child sexual abuse using college samples. *Psychological Bulletin, 124*(1), 22–53.

Riquelme, H. (2002). Can people creative in imagery interpret ambiguous figures faster than people less creative in imagery? *Journal of Creative Behavior, 36*(2), 105–116.

Ritter, J. (1998). Uniforms changing the culture of the nation's classrooms. *USA Today,* Oct. 15, 1A, 2A.

Riva, G., & Wiederhold, B. K. (2006). Emerging trends in cybertherapy: Introduction to the special issue. *Psychology Journal, 4*(2), 121–128.

Rizzolatti, G., & Craighero, L. (2004). The mirror-neuron system. *Annual Review of Neuroscience, 27,* 169–192.

Rizzolatti, G., Fogassi, L., & Gallese V. (2006). Mirrors in the mind. *Scientific American,* Nov., 54–61.

Roberti, J. W. (2004). A review of behavioral and biological correlates of sensation. seeking. *Journal of Research in Personality, 38,* 256–279.

Roberts, B. W., & Mroczek, D. (2008). Personality trait change in adulthood. *Current Directions in Psychological Science, 17*(1), 31–35.

Roberts, B. W., Kuncel, N. R., Shiner, R., & Caspi, A., et al. (2007). The power of personality: The comparative validity of personality traits, socioeconomic status, and cognitive ability for predicting important life outcomes. *Perspectives on Psychological Science, 2*(4), 313–345.

Roberts, D. F., Foehr, U. G., & Rideout, V. (2005). *Generation M: Media in the lives of 8–18 year-olds.* Kaiser Family Foundation. Retrieved June 6, 2007, from http://www.kff.org/entmedia/7251.cfm.

Roberts, R. E., Phinney, J. S., Masse, L. C., Chen, Y. R., et al. (1999). The structure of ethnic identity of young adolescents from diverse ethnocultural groups. *Journal of Early Adolescence, 19*(3), 301–322.

Roberts, W. A. & Roberts, S. (2002). Two tests of the stuck-in-time hypothesis. *Journal of General Psychology, 129*(4), 415–429.

Roberts, W. A. (2002). Are animals stuck in time? *Psychological Bulletin, 128*(3), 473–489.

Robertson, I. S. (2001). *Problem solving.* Hove, UK: Psychology Press.

Robertson, L. C., & Sagiv, N, (2005). *Synesthesia: Perspectives from cognitive neuroscience.* New York: Oxford.

Robins, R. W., Gosling, S. D., & Craik, K. H. (1998). Psychological science at the crossroads. *American Scientist, 86*(July–Aug.), 310–313.

Robinson, A., & Clinkenbeard, P. R. (1998). Giftedness. *Annual Review of Psychology, 49,* 117–139.

Robinson, B., Frye, E. M., & Bradley, L. J. (1997). Cult affiliation and disaffiliation. *Counseling & Values, 41*(2), 166–173.

Robinson, D. N. (2008). *Consciousness and mental life.* New York: Columbia University Press.

Robinson, T. E., & Berridge, K. C. (2003). Addiction. *Annual Review of Psychology, 54,* 25–53.

Robinson, T. N., Wilde, M. L., Navracruz, L. C., Haydel, K. F., et al. (2001). Effects of reducing children's television and video game use on aggressive behavior. *Archives of Pediatrics and Adolescent Medicine, 155*(1), 17–23.

Robinson-Riegler, B., & McDaniel, M. (1994). Further constraints on the bizarreness effect: Elaboration at encoding. *Memory & Cognition, 22*(6), 702–712.

Rock, A. (2004). *The mind at night: The new science of how and why we dream.* New York: Basic Books.

Rodd, Z. A., Bell, R. L., McQueen, V. K., Davids, M. R., et al. (2005). Chronic ethanol drinking by alcohol-preferring rats increases the sensitivity of the posterior ventral tegmental area to the reinforcing effects of ethanol. *Alcoholism: Clinical & Experimental Research, 29*(3), 358–366.

Roeckelein, J. E. (2004). *Imagery in psychology: A reference guide.* Westport, CT: Praeger.

Roediger, H. L., & McDermott, K. B. (1995). Creating false memories: Remembering words not presented on lists. *Journal of Experimental Psychology: Learning, Memory, and Cognition, 21*(4), 803–814.

Roediger, III., H. L., & Amir, N., (2005). Implicit memory tasks: Retention without conscious recollection. In A. Wenzel, & D. C. Rubin (Eds.), *Cognitive methods and their application to clinical research.* Washington, DC: American Psychological Association.

Rogers, C. R. (1959). A theory of therapy, personality, and interpersonal relationships, as developed in the client-centered framework. In S. Koch (Ed.), *Psychology: A study of a science* (Vol. 3). New York: McGraw-Hill.

Rogers, C. R. (1961). *On becoming a person: A therapist's view of psychotherapy.* Boston: Houghton Mifflin.

Rogers, S., & Silver, S. M. (2002). Is EMDR an exposure therapy? A review of trauma protocols. *Journal of Clinical Psychology, 58*(1), 43–59.

Rohsenow, D. J., & Smith R. E. (1982). Irrational beliefs as predictors of negative affective states. *Motivation and Emotion, 6,* 299–301

Roid, G. (2003). *Technical manual: Stanford-Binet Intelligence Scales* (5th ed.). Itasca, IL: Riverside.

Roney, J. R. (2003). Effects of visual exposure to the opposite sex: Cognitive aspects of mate attraction in human males. *Personality & Social Psychology Bulletin, 29,* 393–404.

Roos, P. E., & Cohen, L. H. (1987). Sex roles and social support as moderators of life stress adjustment. *Journal of Personality & Social Psychology, 52,* 576–585.

Rosch, E. (1977). Classification of real-world objects: Origins and representations in cognition. In P. N. Johnson-Laird, & P. C. Wason (Eds.), *Thinking: Reading in cognitive science.* Cambridge, UK: Cambridge University Press.

Rosen, G., Hugdahl, K., Ersland, L., Lundervold, A., et al. (2001). Different brain areas activated during imagery of painful and non-painful "finger movements" in a subject with an amputated arm. *Neurocase, 7*(3), 255–260.

Rosenberg, L. B. (1994). The effect of interocular distance upon depth perception when using stereoscopic displays to perform work within virtual and telepresent environments. *USAF AMRL Technical Report (Wright-Patterson),* July, AL/CF-TR-1994-0052.

Rosenberg, S. S., & Lynch, J. E. (2002). Fritz Perls revisited: A micro-assessment of a live clinical session. *Gestalt Review, 6*(3), 184–202.

Rosenblum, L. D., Gordon, M. S., & Jarquin, L. (2000). Echolocating distance by moving and stationary listeners. *Ecological Psychology, 12*(3), 181–206.

Rosenfeld, P., Giacalone, R. A., & Tedeschi, J. T. (1983). Cognitive dissonance vs. impression management. *Journal of Social Psychology, 120,* 203–211.

Rosenhan, D. L. (1973). On being sane in insane places. *Science, 179,* 250–258.

Rosenkranz, M.A., Jackson, D. C., Dalton, K. M., Dolski, I., et al. (2003). Affective style and in vivo immune response: Neurobehavioral mechanisms. *Proceedings of the National Academy of Sciences, 100,* 11148–11152.

Rosenman, R. H., Brand, R. J., Jenkins, C. D., Friedman, M., et al. (1975). Coronary heart disease in the Western Collaborative Group Study: Final follow-up experience of 8½ years. *Journal of the American Medical Association, 233,* 872–877.

Rosenthal, D., & Quinn, O. W. (1977). Quadruplet hallucinations: Phenotypic variations of a schizophrenic genotype. *Archives of General Psychiatry, 34*(7), 817–827.

Rosenthal, R. (1973). The Pygmalion effect lives. *Psychology Today,* Sept., 56–63.

Rosenthal, R. (1994). Science and ethics in conducting, analyzing, and reporting psychological research. *Psychological Science, 5,* 127–134.

Rosenthal, R., & DiMatteo, M. R. (2001). Meta-analysis: Recent developments in quantitative methods for literature reviews. *Annual Review of Psychology, 52,* 59–62.

Rosenthal, S. L., Von Ranson, K. M., Cotton, S., Biro, F. M., et al. (2001). Sexual initiation: Predictors and developmental trends. *Sexually Transmitted Diseases, 28*(9), 527–532.

Rosenthal, T. L. (1993). To soothe the savage breast. *Behavior Research & Therapy, 31*(5), 439–462.

Rosenthal, T. L., & Rosenthal, R. (1980). *The vicious cycle of stress reaction.* Memphis: Stress Management Clinic, Department of Psychiatry, University of Tennessee College of Medicine.

Rosenzweig, M. R., Breedlove, S. M., & Watson, N. V. (2004). Biological psychology: *An introduction to behavioral and cognitive neuroscience* (4th ed.). Sunderland, MA: Sinauer Associates.

Rosnow, R. L. (2006). *Writing papers in psychology: A student guide to research papers, essays, proposals, posters, and handouts* (7th Ed.). Belmont, CA: Cengage Learning/Wadsworth.

Ross, H. E., & Plug. C. (2002). *The mystery of the moon illusion.* Oxford, UK: Oxford University Press.

Ross, M., Heine, S. J., Wilson, A. E., & Sugimori, S. (2005). Cross-cultural discrepancies in self-appraisals. *Personality and Social Psychology Bulletin, 31*(9), 1175–1188.

Ross, P. E. (2006). The expert mind. *Scientific American, 294*(7), 64–71.

Roth, W. T., Breivik, G., Jorgensen, P. E., & Hofmann, S. (1996). Activation in novice and expert parachutists while jumping. *Psychophysiology, 33*(1), 63–72.

Rothbard, N. P., Phillips, K. W., & Dumas, T. L. (2005). Managing multiple roles: Work-family policies and individuals' desires for segmentation. *Organization Science, 16*(3), 243–258.

Rothbart, M. K. (2007). Temperament, development, and personality. *Current Directions in Psychological Science, 16*(4), 207–212.

Rothschild, B., & Rand, M. (2006). *Help for the helper: The psychophysiology of compassion fatigue and vicarious trauma.* New York: Norton.

Rotter, J. B. & Hochreich, D. J. (1975). *Personality.* Glenview, IL: Scott, Foresman.

Rowe, B. (2007). *College awareness guide: What students need to know to succeed in college.* Englewood Cliffs, NJ: Prentice Hall.

Rowland, D. L. (2007). Sexual health and problems: Erectile dysfunction, premature ejaculation, and male orgasmic disorder. In J. E. Grant, & M. N. Potenza (Eds.), *Textbook of men's mental health.* Washington, DC: American Psychiatric Publishing.

Rozin, P., Kabnick, K., Pete, E., Fischler, C., et al. (2003). The ecology of eating:

Smaller portion sizes in France than in the United States help explain the French paradox. *Psychological Science, 14*(5), 450–454.

Rubenstein, C. (1983). The modern art of courtly love. *Psychology Today, 17*(7), 43–49.

Rubenstein, C. (2002). What turns you on? *My Generation,* July–Aug., 55–58.

Rubenstein, J., & Tavris, C. (1987). Special survey results: 2600 women reveal the secrets of intimacy. *Redbook, 159,* 147–149.

Rubin, D. C. (1985). The subtle deceiver: Recalling our past. *Psychology Today,* Sept., 38–46.

Rudd, M. D., Joiner, Jr., T. E., & Rajab, M. H. (2001). *Treating suicidal behavior.* New York: Guilford.

Rueckl, J. G., & Galantucci, B. (2005). The locus and time course of long-term morphological priming. *Language & Cognitive Processes, 20*(1), 115–138.

Rummens, J., Beiser, M., & Noh, S. (Eds.). (2003). *Immigration, ethnicity and health.* Toronto: University of Toronto Press.

Runco, M. A. (2003). *Critical creative processes.* Cresskill, NJ: Hampton Press.

Runco, M. A. (2004). Creativity. *Annual Review of Psychology, 55,* 657–687.

Ruscio, J., Whitney, D. M., & Amabile, T. M. (1998). Looking inside the fishbowl of creativity. *Creativity Research Journal, 11*(3), 243–263.

Rushton, J. P., & Jensen, A. R. (2005). Thirty years of research on race differences in cognitive ability. *Psychology, Public Policy, & Law, 11,* 235–294.

Russell, S., & Norvig, P. (2003). *Artificial intelligence: A modern approach* (2nd. ed.). Englewood Cliffs, NJ: Prentice Hall.

Russell, T. G., Rowe, W., & Smouse, A. D. (1991). Subliminal self-help tapes and academic achievement: An evaluation. *Journal of Counseling & Development, 69*(Mar.–Apr.), 359–362.

Russo, M. B., Brooks, F. R., Fontenot, J., Dopler, D. M., et al. (1998). Conversion disorder presenting as multiple sclerosis. *Military Medicine, 163*(10), 709–710.

Rutledge, T., & Linden, W. (1998). To eat or not to eat: Affective and physiological mechanisms in the stress–eating relationship. *Journal of Behavioral Medicine, 21*(3), 221–240.

Rutz, C., Bluff, L.A., Weir, A.A.S., & Kacelnik, A. (2007). Video cameras on wild birds. *Science, 318,* 765.

Ruva, C., McEvoy, C., & Bryant, J. B. (2007). Effects of pre-trial publicity and jury deliberation on juror bias and source memory errors. *Applied Cognitive Psychology, 21*(1), 45–67.

Ryan, M. P. (2001). Conceptual models of lecture learning. *Reading Psychology, 22*(4), 289–312.

Ryan, R. M., & Deci, E. L. (2000). Self-determination theory and the facilitation of intrinsic motivation, social development, and well-being. *American Psychologist, 55*(1), 68–78.

Ryckman, R. M. (2008). *Theories of personality* (9th ed.). Belmont, CA: Cengage Learning/Wadsworth.

Ryff, C. D. (1995). Psychological well-being in adult life. *Current Directions in Psychological Science, 4*(4), 99–104.

Ryff, C. D., & Keyes, C. L. (1995). The structure of psychological well-being revisited. *Journal of Personality & Social Psychology, 69*(4), 719–727.

Ryff, C. D., & Singer, B. (2000). Interpersonal flourishing. *Personality & Social Psychology Review, 4,* 30–44.

Ryff, C. D., Singer, B. H., & Palmersheim, K. A. (2004). Social inequalities in health and well-being: The role of relational and religious protective factors. In O. G. Brim, C. D. Ryff, et al. (Eds.), *How healthy are we? A national study of wellbeing at midlife.* Chicago, IL: University of Chicago Press.

Saadeh, W., Rizzo, C. P., & Roberts, D. G. (2002). Spanking. *Clinical Pediatrics, 41*(2), 87–88.

Sackeim, H. A., Haskett, R. F., Mulsant, B. H., Thase, M. E., et al. (2001). Continuation pharmacotherapy in the prevention of relapse following electroconvulsive therapy. *Journal of the American Medical Association, 285,* 1299–1307.

Sahelian, R. (1998). *5-HTP.* Wakefield, RI: Moyer Bell.

Saksida, L. M., & Wilkie, D. M. (1994). Time-of-day discrimination by pigeons. *Animal Learning & Behavior, 22,* 143–154.

Sales, B. D., & Hafemeister, T. L. (1985). Law and psychology. In E. M. Altmeir, & M. E. Meyer (Eds.), *Applied specialties in psychology.* New York: Random House.

Salmela, J. H. (1974). An information processing approach to volleyball. *C.V.A. Technical Journal, 1,* 49–62.

Salmela, J. H. (1975). Psycho-motor task demands of artistic gymnastics. In J. H. Salmela (Ed.), *The advanced study of gymnastics: A textbook.* Springfield, IL: Charles C Thomas.

Salmon, P. (2001). Effects of physical exercise on anxiety, depression, and sensitivity to stress: A unifying theory. *Clinical Psychology Review, 21*(1), 33–61.

Salovey, P., & Mayer, J. (1997). *Emotional development and emotional intelligence.* New York: Basic.

Salthouse, T. A. (2004). What and when of cognitive aging. *Current Directions in Psychological Science, 13*(4), 140–144.

SAMHAS (Substance Abuse and Mental Health Services Administration). (2005). *Overview of findings from the 2004 National Survey on Drug Use and Health.* Rockville, MD: Office of Applied Studies, NSDUH Series H-27, DHHS Publication No. SMA 05-4061. Retrieved June 6, 2007, from http://www.oas.samhsa.gov/nsduh/2k4nsduh/2k4overview/2k4overview.pdf.

Sankofa, B. M., Hurley, E. A., Allen, B. A., & Boykin, A. W. (2005). Cultural expression and black students' attitudes toward high achievers. *Journal of Psychology: Interdisciplinary & Applied, 139*(3), 247–259.

Santrock, J. W. (2007). *Child development* (11th ed.). New York: McGraw-Hill.

Santrock, J. W., & Halonen, J. S. (2007). *Connections to college success.* Belmont, CA: Cengage Learning/Wadsworth.

Sarason, I. G., & Sarason, B. R. (2005). *Abnormal psychology* (11th ed.). Mahwah, NJ: Prentice Hall.

Sateia, M. J., & Nowell, P. D. (2004). Insomnia. *Lancet, 364*(9449), 1959–1973.

Saunders, T., Driskell, J. E., Johnston, J. H., Salas, E. (1996). The effect of stress inoculation training on anxiety and performance. *Journal of Occupational Health Psychology, 1*(2), 170–186.

Savage-Rumbaugh, S., & Lewin, R. (1996). *Kanzi.* New York: Wiley.

Savage-Rumbaugh, S., Murphy, J., Sevcik, R. A., Brakke, K. E., et al. (1993). Language comprehension in ape and child. *Monographs of the Society for Research in Child Development, 58*(3–4), v–221.

Savage-Rumbaugh, S., Sevcik, R. A., Brakke, K. E., Rumbaugh, D. M., et al. (1990). Symbols: Their communicative use, comprehension, and combination by bonobos (Pan paniscus). *Advances in Infancy Research, 6,* 221–278.

Savage-Rumbaugh, S., Shanker, S., & Taylor, T. (1998). *Apes, language, and mind.* New York: Oxford.

Sawyer, R. G., & Smith, N. G. (1996). A survey of situational factors at first intercourse among college students. *American Journal of Health Behavior, 20*(4), 208–217.

Saxton, M., Houston-Price, C., & Dawson, N. (2005). The prompt hypothesis: Clarification requests as corrective input for grammatical errors. *Applied Psycholinguistics, 26*(3), 393–414.

Saxvig, I. W., Lundervold, A. J., Gronli, J., et al. (2008). The effect of a REM sleep deprivation procedure on different aspects of memory function in humans. *Psychophysiology, 45*(2), 309–317.

Saywitz, K. J., Mannarino, A. P., Berliner, L., & Cohen, J. A. (2000). Treatment for sexually abused children and adolescents. *American Psychologist, 55*(9), 1040–1049.

Schachter, S. (1959). *Psychology of affiliation.* Stanford, CA: Stanford University Press.

Schachter, S., & Wheeler, L. (1962). Epinephrine, chlorpromazine and amusement. *Journal of Abnormal and Social Psychology, 65,* 121–128.

Schacter, D. L. (1996). *Searching for memory: The brain, the mind, and the past.* New York: Basic Books.

Schacter, D. L. (2000). Memory: Memory systems. In A. Kazdin (Ed.), *Encyclopedia of psychology.* Washington, DC: American Psychological Association.

Schacter, D. L. (2001). *The seven sins of memory.* Boston: Houghton Mifflin.

Schacter, D. L., Norman, K. A., & Koutstaal, W. (1998). The cognitive neuroscience of constructive memory. *Annual Review of Psychology, 49,* 289–318.

Schafer, M., & Crichlow, S. (1996). Antecedents of groupthink: A quantitative study. *Journal of Conflict Resolution, 40*(3), 415–435.

Schaie, K. W. (1994). The course of adult intellectual development. *American Psychologist, 49*(4), 304–313.

Schaie, K. W. (2005). *Developmental influences on adult intelligence: The Seattle longitudinal study.* New York: Oxford University Press.

Scheck, B., Neufeld, P., & Dwyer, J. (2000). *Actual innocence.* New York: Doubleday.

Scheinkman, M. (2008). The multi-level approach: A road map for couples therapy. *Family Process, 47*(2), 197–213.

Schenck, C. H., & Mahowald, M. W. (2005). Rapid eye movement and non-REM sleep parasomnias. *Primary Psychiatry, 12*(8), 67–74.

Schick, T., & Vaughn, L. (1995). *How to think about weird things: Critical thinking for a new age.* Mountain View, CA: Mayfield.

Schick, T., & Vaughn, L. (2001). *How to think about weird things: Critical thinking for a new age.* New York: McGraw-Hill.

Schick, T., & Vaughn, L. (2004). *How to think about weird things: Critical thinking for a new age* (4th ed.). New York: McGraw-Hill.

Schilling, M. A. (2005). A "Small-World" network model of cognitive insight. *Creativity Research Journal, 17*(2–3), 131–154.

Schiraldi, G. R., & Brown, S. L. (2001). Primary prevention for mental health: Results of an exploratory cognitive-behavioral college course. *Journal of Primary Prevention, 22*(1), 55–67.

Schlaepfer, T. E., Cohen, M. X., Frick, C., Kosel, M., et al. (2008). Deep brain stimulation to reward circuitry alleviates anhedonia in refractory major depression. *Neuropsychopharmacology, 33*(2), 368–377.

Schleicher, S. S., & Gilbert, L. A. (2005). Heterosexual dating discourses among college students: Is there still a double standard? *Journal of College Student Psychotherapy, 19*(3), 7–23.

Schlosberg, H. (1954). Three dimensions of emotion. *Psychological Review, 61,* 81–88.

Schmidt, F. L., & Hunter, J. E. (1998). The validity and utility of selection methods in personnel psychology. *Psychological Bulletin, 124*(2), 262–274.

Schmidt, F. L., Ones, D. S., & Hunter, J. E. (1992). Personnel selection. *Annual Review of Psychology, 43,* 627–670.

Schmitt, D. P., & Allik, J. (2005). Simultaneous administration of the Rosenberg Self-Esteem Scale in 53 nations: Exploring the universal and culture-specific features of global self-esteem. *Journal of Personality and Social Psychology, 89*(4), 623–642.

Schmolck, H., Buffalo, E. A., & Squire, L. R. (2000). Memory distortions develop over time. *Psychological Science, 11*(1), 39–45.

Schmuck, P., & Vlek, C. (2003). Psychologists can do much to support sustainable development. *European Psychologist, 8*(2), 66–76.

Schneider, K. J. (2002). Humanistic psychotherapy. In M. Hersen, & W. H. Sledge (Eds.), *Encyclopedia of psychotherapy.* San Diego: Academic Press.

Schneider, K. J., Bugental, J. F. T., & Pierson, J. F. (2001). Introduction. *The handbook of humanistic psychology.* Thousand Oaks, CA: Sage.

Schneiderman, N., Antoni, M. H., Saab, P. G., & Ironson, G. (2001). Health psychology: Psychological and biobehavioral aspects of chronic disease management. *Annual Review of Psychology, 52,* 555–580.

Schooler, C. (1998) Environmental complexity and the Flynn effect. In U. Neisser (Ed.), *The rising curve: Long-term gains in IQ and related measures.* Washington, DC: American Psychological Association.

Schopp, L. H., Demiris, G., & Glueckauf, R. L. (2006). Rural backwaters or front-runners? Rural telehealth in the vanguard of psychology practice. *Professional Psychology: Research & Practice, 37*(2), 165–173.

Schreiber, E. H., & Schreiber, D. E. (1999). Use of hypnosis with witnesses of vehicular homicide. *Contemporary Hypnosis, 16*(1), 40–44.

Schreiber, F. R. (1973). *Sybil.* Chicago: Regency.

Schroeder, J. E. (1995). Self-concept, social anxiety, and interpersonal perception skills. *Personality & Individual Differences, 19*(6), 955–958.

Schroeder, S. (2008). Stranded in the periphery The increasing marginalization of smokers *New England Journal of Medicine, 35*(821), 2284.

Schuel, H., Chang, M. C., Burkman, L. J., Picone, R. P., et al. (1999). Cannabinoid receptors in sperm. In G. Nahas, K. M. Sutin, et al. (Eds.), *Marihuana and medicine.* Totowa, NJ: Humana Press.

Schuetze, P., & Eiden, R. D. (2006). The association between maternal cocaine use during pregnancy and physiological regulation in 4- to 8-week-old infants: An examination of possible mediators and moderators. *Journal of Pediatric Psychology, 31*(1), 15–26.

Schuiling, G. A. (2004). Death in Venice: The homosexuality enigma. *Journal of Psychosomatic Obstetrics & Gynecology, 25*(1), 67–76.

Schultheiss, O. C., Wirth, M. M., & Stanton, S. J. (2004). Effects of affiliation and power motivation arousal on salivary progesterone and testosterone. *Hormones and Behavior, 46*(5), 592–599.

Schultz, D. P., & Schultz, S. E. (2005). *Theories of personality* (8th ed.). Belmont, CA: Cengage Learning/ Wadsworth.

Schultz, D. P., & Schultz, S. E. (2006). *Psychology and work today* (9th ed.). Englewood Cliffs, NJ: Prentice Hall

Schultz, D. P., & Schultz, S. E. (2008). *A history of modern psychology* (9th ed.). Belmont, CA: Cengage Learning/ Wadsworth.

Schultz, H. T. (2004). Good and bad movie therapy with good and bad outcomes. *The Amplifier: Official Newsletter of APA Division 46, Media Psychology,* Fall/ Winter. Retrieved May 18, 2007, from http://www.apa.org/divisions/ div46/Amp%20Winter%2005/ for%20Website/ampwinter05. html#therapy.

Schultz, P. W. (1999). Changing behavior with normative feedback interventions. *Basic & Applied Social Psychology, 21*(1), 25–36.

Schum T. R., Kolb, T. M., McAuliffe T. L., Simms, M., et al. (2002). Sequential ac-

quisition of toilet-training skills: A descriptive study of gender and age differences in normal children. *Pediatrics, 3,* e48. Retrieved May 25, 2007, from http://pediatrics.aappublications.org/ cgi/content/abstract/109/3/e48.

Schum, T. R., McAuliffe, T. L., Simms, M. D., Walter, J. A., et al. (2001). Factors associated with toilet training in the 1990s. *Ambulatory Pediatrics, 1*(2), 79–86.

Schuster, M. A., Stein, B. D., Jaycox, L. H., Collins, R. L., et al. (2001). A national survey of stress reactions after the September 11, 2001, terrorist attacks. *New England Journal of Medicine, 345*(20), 1507–1512.

Schwartz, B. L. (2002). *Tip-of-the-tongue states: Phenomenology, mechanism, and lexical retrieval.* Mahwah, NJ: Erlbaum.

Schwartz, M. S., & Andrasik, F. (Eds.). (2003) *Biofeedback: A practitioner's guide* (3rd ed.). New York: Guilford.

Schwartz, S. J. (2008). Self and identity in early adolescence: Some reflections and an introduction to the special issue. *Journal of Early Adolescence, 28*(1), 5–15.

Schwinghammer, S. A., Stapel, D. A., & Blanton, H. (2006). Different selves have different effects: Self-activation and defensive social comparison. *Personality & Social Psychology Bulletin, 32*(1), 27–39.

Sclafani, A., & Springer, D. (1976). Dietary obesity in adult rats: Similarities to hypothalamic and human obesity syndromes. *Psychology and Behavior, 17,* 461–471.

Scoboria, A., Mazzoni, G., Kirsch, I., et al. (2002). Immediate and persisting effects of misleading questions and hypnosis on memory reports. *Journal of Experimental Psychology: Applied, 8*(1), 26–32.

Scott, J. P., & Ginsburg, B. E. (1994). The Seville statement on violence revisited. *American Psychologist, 49*(10), 849–850.

Scott, L., & O'Hara, M. W. (1993). Self-discrepancies in clinically anxious and depressed university students. *Journal of Abnormal Psychology, 102*(2), 282–287.

Scott, S. S., McGuire, J. M., & Shaw, S. F. (2003). Universal design for instruction: A new paradigm for adult instruction in postsecondary education. *Remedial and Special Education. Special Issue: Adults with Learning Disabilities, 24*(6), 369–379.

Scruggs, T. E. & Mastropieri, M. A. (2007). Science learning in special education: The case for constructed versus instructed learning. *Exceptionality, 15*(2), 57–74.

Scully, J. A., Tosi, H., & Banning, K. (2000). Life event checklists: Revisiting the Social Readjustment Rating Scale after 30 years. *Educational & Psychological Measurement, 60*(6), 864–876.

Scurfield, R. M. (2002). Commentary about the terrorist acts of September 11, 2001: Posttraumatic reactions and related social and policy issues. *Trauma Violence & Abuse, 3*(1), 3–14.

Searcy, W. A., & Nowicki, S. (2005). *The evolution of animal communication: Re-*

liability and deception in signaling systems. Princeton, NJ: Princeton University Press.

Seckel, A. (2000). *The art of optical illusions.* London: Carlton Books.

Segerdahl, P., Fields, W., & Savage-Rumbaugh, S. (2005). *Kanzi's primal language: The cultural initiation of primates into language.* New York: Palgrave MacMillan.

Segerstrom, S., & Miller, G. E. (2004). Psychological stress and the human immune system: A meta-analytic study of 30 years of inquiry. *Psychological Bulletin, 130*(4), 601–630.

Segraves, R. T., & Segraves, K. B. (1995). Human sexuality and aging. *Journal of Sex Education & Therapy, 21*(2), 88–102.

Segraves, R., & Woodard, T. (2006). Female hypoactive sexual desire disorder: History and current status. *Journal of Sexual Medicine, 3*(3), 408–418.

Segraves, T., & Althof, S. (2002). Psychotherapy and pharmacotherapy for sexual dysfunctions. In P. E. Nathan, & J. M. Gorman, (Eds.), *A guide to treatments that work* (2nd ed.). London: Oxford.

Seidler, G. H., & Wagner, F. E. (2006). Comparing the efficacy of EMDR and trauma-focused cognitive-behavioral therapy in the treatment of PTSD: A meta-analytic study. *Psychological Medicine, 36*(11), 1515–1522.

Seidman, B. F. (2001). Medicine wars. *Skeptical Inquirer,* Jan.–Feb., 28–35.

Seitz, A., & Watanabe, T. (2005). A unified model for perceptual learning. *Trends in Cognitive Sciences, 9*(7), 329–334.

Sekuler, R., & Blake, R. (2006). *Perception* (5th ed.). New York: McGraw-Hill.

Seligman, M. E. P. (1972). For helplessness: Can we immunize the weak? In *Readings in psychology today* (2nd ed.). Del Mar, CA: CRM.

Seligman, M. E. P. (1989). *Helplessness.* New York: Freeman.

Seligman, M. E. P. (1994). *What you can change and what you can't.* New York: Knopf.

Seligman, M. E. P. (1995). The effectiveness of psychotherapy. *American Psychologist, 50*(12), 965–974.

Seligman, M. E. P. (1998). Why therapy works. *APA Monitor, 29*(12), 2.

Seligman, M. E. P. (2002). *Authentic happiness.* New York: Free Press.

Seligman, M. E. P. (2003). Positive psychology: Fundamental assumptions. *Source Psychologist, 16*(3), 126–127.

Seligman, M. E. P., & Csikszentmihalyi, M. (2000). Positive psychology: An introduction. *American Psychologist, 55,* 5–14.

Seltzer, R. (2006). Scientific jury selection: Does it work? *Journal of Applied Social Psychology, 36*(10), 2417–2435.

Selye, H. (1976). *The stress of life.* New York: Knopf.

Senécal, C., Julien, E., & Guay, F. (2003). Role conflict and academic procrastination: A self-determination perspective. *European Journal of Social Psychology, 33*(1), 135–145.

Service, R. F. (1994). Will a new type of drug make memory-making easier? *Science, 266,* 218–219.

Sessa, V. I., & London, M. (2006). *Continuous learning in organizations: Individual, group, and organizational perspectives.* Mahwah, NJ: Erlbaum.

Seto, M. C. (2008). *Pedophilia and sexual offending against children: Theory, assessment, and intervention.* Washington, DC: American Psychological Association.

Seto, M. C., Cantor, J. M., & Blanchard, R. (2006). Child pornography offenses are a valid diagnostic indicator of pedophilia. *Journal of Abnormal Psychology, 115*(3), 610–615.

Seybolt, D. C., & Wagner, M. K. (1997). Self-reinforcement, gender-role, and sex of participant in prediction of life satisfaction. *Psychological Reports, 81*(2) 519–522.

Seyle, D. C., & Newman, M. L. (2006). A house divided? The psychology of red and blue America. *American Psychologist, 61*(6), 571–580.

Shaffer, D. R. (2002). *Developmental psychology.* Belmont, CA: Wadsworth.

Shaffer, J. B., & Galinsky, M. D. (1989). *Models of group therapy.* Englewood Cliffs, NJ: Prentice Hall.

Shafir, E. (1993). Choosing versus rejecting: Why some options are both better and worse than others. *Memory and Cognition, 21,* 546–556.

Shafton, A. (1995). *Dream reader.* Albany, NY: SUNY Press.

Shakesby, A. C., Anwyl, R., & Rowan, M. J. (2002). Overcoming the effects of stress on synaptic plasticity in the intact hippocampus: Rapid actions of serotonergic and antidepressant agents. *Journal of Neuroscience, 22,* 3638–3644.

Shapiro, C. M., Trajanovic, N. N., & Fedoroff, J. P. (2003). Sexsomnia: A new parasomnia? *Canadian Journal of Psychiatry, 48*(5), 311–317.

Shapiro, D. A., Barkham, M., Stiles, W. B., Hardy, G. E., et al. (2003). Time is of the essence: A selective review of the fall and rise of brief therapy research. *Psychology & Psychotherapy: Theory, Research & Practice, 76*(3), 211–235.

Shapiro, F. (2001). *Eye movement desensitization and reprocessing: Basic principles, protocols and procedures* (2nd ed.). New York: Guilford.

Shapiro, F., & Forrest, M. S. (2004). *EMDR: The breakthrough therapy for overcoming anxiety, stress, and trauma.* New York: Basic Books.

Shapiro, J. M. (2006). A "memory-jamming" theory of advertising. *Social Science Research Network.* Retrieved June 20, 2007, from http://ssrn.com/ abstract=903474.

Shapiro, S. L., & Walsh, R. (2006). The meeting of meditative disciplines and Western psychology: A mutually enriching dialogue. *American Psychologist, 61*(3), 227–239.

Sharf, R. S. (2008). *Theories of psychotherapy & counseling: Concepts and cases* (4th ed.). Belmont, CA: Cengage Learning/Wadsworth.

Sharkey, K. M., & Eastman, C. I. (2002). Melatonin phase shifts human circadian rhythms in a placebo-controlled simulated night-work study. *American Journal of Physiology: Regulatory, Integrative, and Comparative Physiology, 282,* R454–R463.

Sharot, T., Martorella, E. A., Delgado, M. R., et al. (2007). How personal experience modulates the neural circuitry of memories of September 11. *PNAS Proceedings of the National Academy of Sciences of the United States of America, 104*(1), 389–394.

Shaw, J. S. (1996). Increases in eyewitness confidence resulting from postevent questioning. *Journal of Experimental Psychology: Applied, 2*(2), 126–146.

Shaywitz, B. A, Shaywitz, S. E., Pugh, K. R., Constable, R. T., et al. (1995). Sex differences in the functional organization of the brain for language. *Nature, 373*, 607–609.

Shaywitz, S. E., & Gore, J. C. (1995). Sex differences in functional organization of the brain for language. *Nature, 373*(6515), 607.

Sheehy, M., & Cournos, F. (1992). What is mental illness? In F. I. Kass, J. M. Oldham, et al. (Eds.), *The Columbia University College of Physicians and Surgeons complete home guide to mental health.* New York: Sharpe Communications/Henry Holt.

Sheldon, K. M., Ryan, R. M., Rawsthorne, L. J., & Ilardi, B. (1997). Trait self and true self: Cross-role variation in the Big-Five personality traits and its relations with psychological authenticity and subjective well-being. *Journal of Personality & Social Psychology, 73*(6), 1380–1393.

Shen, J., Botly, L. C. P., Chung, S. A., Gibbs, A. L., et al. (2006). Fatigue and shift work. *Journal of Sleep Research, 15*(1), 1–5.

Shepard, R. N. (1975). Form, formation, and transformation of internal representations. In R. L. Solso (Ed.), *Information processing and cognition: The Loyola Symposium.* Hillsdale, NJ: Erlbaum.

Shepherd, G. M. (2006). Smell images and the flavour system in the human brain. *Nature, 444*(7117), 316–321.

Sherif, M., Harvey, O. J., White, B. J., Hood, W. R., et al. (1961). *Intergroup conflict and cooperation: The Robbers Cave experiment.* University of Oklahoma, Institute of Group Relations.

Shiffman, S., Scharf, D. M., Shadel, W. G., Gwaltney, C. J., et al. (2006). Analyzing milestones in smoking cessation: Illustration in a nicotine patch trial in adult smokers. *Journal of Consulting & Clinical Psychology, 74*(2), 276–285.

Shires, A., & Miller, D. (1998). A preliminary study comparing psychological factors associated with erectile dysfunction in heterosexual and homosexual men. *Sexual & Marital Therapy, 13*(1), 37–49.

Shneerson, J. M. (2005). *Sleep medicine: A guide to sleep and its disorders* (2nd ed.). London: Blackwell.

Shneidman, E. S. (1987a). At the point of no return. *Psychology Today,* March, 54–58.

Shneidman, E. S. (1987b). Psychological approaches to suicide. In VandenBos, G. R., & Bryant, B. K. (Eds.), *Cataclysms, crises and catastrophes: Psychology in action.* Washington, DC: American Psychological Association.

Shore, H. (2003). Personal communication.

Short, S. E., Ross-Stewart, L., & Monsma, E. V. (2006). Onwards with the evolution of imagery research in sport psychology. *Athletic Insight: Online Journal of Sport Psychology, 8*(3), 1–15.

Shrum, L. J. (2004). *The psychology of entertainment media: Blurring the lines between entertainment and persuasion.* Mahwah, NJ: Erlbaum.

Shulman, B. H. (2004). Cognitive therapy and the individual psychology of Alfred Adler. In A. Freeman, M. J. Mahoney, et al. (Eds.), *Cognition and psychotherapy* (2nd ed.). New York: Springer.

Shurkin, J. N. (1992). *Terman's kids.* Boston: Little, Brown.

Sieber, J. E., & Saks, M. J. (1989). A census of subject pool characteristics and policies. *American Psychologist, 44*(7), 1053–1061.

Siegel, R. K. (2005). *Intoxication: The universal drive for mind-altering substances.* Rochester, VT: Park Street Press.

Siegler, R. S. (2004). *Children's thinking* (4th ed.). Mahwah, NJ: Erlbaum.

Siegler, R. S., DeLoache, J. S., & Eisenberg, N. (2006). *How children develop* (2nd ed.). New York: Worth.

Siever, L. J., & Koenigsberg, H. W. (2000). The frustrating no-man's-land of borderline personality disorder. *Cerebrum, 2*(4), 85–99.

Sigelman, C. K., & Rider, E. A. (2006). *Life-span human development* (5th ed.). Belmont, CA: Cengage Learning/Wadsworth.

Silver, S. M., Rogers, S., Knipe, J., & Colelli, G. (2005). EMDR therapy following the 9/11 terrorist attacks: A community-based intervention project in New York City. *International Journal of Stress Management, 12*(1), 29–42.

Silverstein, B. (1989). Enemy images. *American Psychologist, 44*(6), 903–913.

Simeon, D., Guralnik, O., Knutelska, M., & Schmeidler, J. (2002). Personality factors associated with dissociation: Temperament, defenses, and cognitive schemata. *American Journal of Psychiatry, 159*, 489–491.

Simister, J., & Cooper, C. (2005). Thermal stress in the U.S.A.: Effects on violence and on employee behaviour. *Stress &Health, 21, 3–15.*

Simner, M. L., & Goffin, R. D. (2003). A position statement by the international graphonomics society on the use of graphology in personnel selection testing. *International Journal of Testing, 3*(4), 353–364.

Simon, G. E, Ludman, E. J., Tutty, S., Operskalski, B., et al. (2004). Telephone psychotherapy and telephone care management for primary care patients starting antidepressant treatment. *Journal of the American Medical Association, 292,* 935–942.

Simons, D. J., & Chabris, C. F. (1999). Gorillas in our midst: Sustained inattentional blindness for dynamic events. *Perception, 28,* 1059–1074.

Simons, D. J., & Levin, D. T. (1998). Failure to detect changes to people during a real-world interaction. *Psychonomic Bulletin & Review, 5*(4), 644–649.

Simons, J. S., Dodson, C. S., Bell, D., & Schacter, D. L. (2004). Specific- and partial-source memory: Effects of aging. *Psychology & Aging, 19*(4), 689–694.

Simonton, D. K., & Baumeister, R. F. (2005). Positive psychology at the summit. *Review of General Psychology, 9*(2), 99–102.

Simpson, D. D., Joe, G. W., Fletcher, B. W., Hubbard, R. L, et al. (1999). A national evaluation of treatment outcomes for cocaine dependence. *Archives of General Psychiatry, 57*(6), 507–514.

Simpson, K. J. (2002). Anorexia nervosa and culture. *Journal of Psychiatric & Mental Health Nursing, 9,* 65–71.

Singer, J. D. (2005). Explaining foreign policy: U.S. decision-making and the Persian Gulf War. *Political Psychology, 26*(5), 831–834.

Singer, M. T. (2003). *Cults in our midst: The continuing fight against their hidden menace* (rev. ed.). San Francisco: Jossey-Bass.

Singer, M. T., & Addis, M. E. (1992). Cults, coercion, and contumely. *Cultic Studies Journal, 9*(2), 163–189.

Singleton, J. L., & Newport, E. L. (2004). When learners surpass their models: The acquisition of American Sign Language from inconsistent input. *Cognitive Psychology, 49*(4), 370–407.

Sinha, R., Garcia, M., Paliwal, P., Kreek, M. J., et al. (2006). Stress-induced cocaine craving and hypothalamic-pituitary-adrenal responses are predictive of cocaine relapse outcomes. *Archives of General Psychiatry, 63*(3), 324–331.

Sipos, A., Rasmussen, F., Harrison, G., Tynelius, P., et al. (2004), Paternal age and schizophrenia: A population based cohort study. *British Medical Journal, 329*(7474), 1070.

Sirkin, M. I. (1990). Cult involvement: A systems approach to assessment and treatment. *Psychotherapy, 27*(1), 116–123.

Skeels, H. M. (1966). Adult status of children with contrasting early life experiences. *Monograph of the Society for Research in Child Development, 31*(3), 105.

Skillsoft (2006). *IT pros more like to suffer from stress, says new survey.* Retrieved July 17, 2007 from http://www.skillsoft.com/EMEA/news/19-May-06.asp

Skinner, B. F. (1938). *The behavior of organisms.* Englewood Cliffs, NJ: Prentice-Hall.

Skipton, L. H. (1997). The many faces of character. *Consulting Psychology Journal: Practice & Research, 49*(4), 235–245

Slaby, A. E., Garfinkel, B. D., & Garfinkel, L. F. (1994). *No one say my pain.* New York: Norton.

Slater, A., Mattock, A., & Brown, E. (1990). Size constancy at birth: Newborn infants' responses to retinal and real size. *Journal of Experimental Child Psychology, 49*(2), 314–322.

Slater, A., Mattock, A., Brown, E., & Bremner, J. G. (1991). Form perception at birth: Cohen and Younger (1984) revisited. *Journal of Experimental Child Psychology, 51*(3), 395–406.

Slijper, F. M. E., Drop, S. L. S., Molenaar, J. C.; de Muinck, K., et al. (2000). "Long-term psychological evaluation of intersex children": Reply. *Archives of Sexual Behavior, 29*(1), 119–121.

Slot, L. A. B., & Colpaert, F. C. (1999). Recall rendered dependent on an opiate state. *Behavioral Neuroscience, 113*(2), 337–344.

Smedley, A., & Smedley, B. D. (2005). Race as biology is fiction, racism as a social problem is real. *American Psychologist, 60*(1), 16–26.

Smith, A. P. (2005). Caffeine at work. *Human Psychopharmacology: Clinical & Experimental, 20*(6), 441–445.

Smith, A. P., Clark, R., & Gallagher, J. (1999). Breakfast cereal and caffeinated coffee: Effects on working memory, attention, mood and cardiovascular function. *Physiology & Behavior, 67*(1), 9–17.

Smith, C., Carey, S., & Wiser, M. (1985). On differentiation: A case study of the development of the concepts of size, weight, and density. *Cognition, 21*(3), 177–237.

Smith, E., & Delargy, M (2005). Locked-in syndrome. *British Medical Journal, 330,* 406–409.

Smith, J. L., & Cahusac, P. M. B. (2001). Right-sided asymmetry in sensitivity to tickle. *Laterality, 6*(3), 233–238.

Smith, K. H., & Rogers, M. (1994). Effectiveness of subliminal messages in television commercials: Two experiments. *Journal of Applied Psychology, 79*(6), 866–874.

Smith, L. F. (2002). The effects of confidence and perception of test-taking skills on performance. *North American Journal of Psychology, 4*(1), 37–50.

Smith, M. L., Cottrell, G. W., Gosselin, F., & Schyns, P. G. (2005). Transmitting and decoding facial expressions. *Psychological Science, 16*(3), 184–189.

Smith, S. M, McIntosh, W. D., & Bazzini, D. G. (1999). Are the beautiful good in Hollywood? *Basic & Applied Social Psychology, 21*(1), 69–80.

Smith, T. W. (1990). *Adult sexual behavior in 1989: Number of partners, frequency, and risk.* Paper presented to the American Association for the Advancement of Science, February, 1990, New Orleans.

Smith, T. W., Glazer, K., Ruiz, J. M., & Gallo, L. C. (2004). Hostility, anger, aggressiveness, and coronary heart disease: An interpersonal perspective on personality, emotion, and health. *Journal of Personality, 72*(6), 1217–1270.

Smith, T. W., Ruiz, J. M., & Uchino, B. N. (2004). Mental activation of supportive ties, hostility, and cardiovascular reactivity to laboratory stress in young men and women. *Health Psychology, 23*(5), 476–485.

Smyth, M. M., & Waller, A. (1998). Movement imagery in rock climbing. *Applied Cognitive Psychology, 12*(2), 145–157.

Snow, C. P. (1961). Either-or. *Progressive,* Feb., 24.

Snyder, A., Bahramali, H., Hawker, T., et al. (2006). Savant-like numerosity skills revealed in normal people by magnetic pulses. *Perception, 35*(6), 837–845.

Sobel, E., Shine, D., DiPietro, D., & Rabinowitz, M. (1996). Condom use among HIV/infected patients in South Bronx, New York. *AIDS, 10*(2), 235–236.

Sobolewski, J. M., & Amato, P. R. (2005). Economic hardship in the family of origin and children's psychological well-being in adulthood. *Journal of Marriage and Family, 67*(1), 141–156.

Soderstrom, M. (2007). Beyond babytalk: Re-evaluating the nature and content of speech input to preverbal infants. *Developmental Review, 27*(4), 501–532.

Solomon, J. L., Marshall, P., & Gardner, H. (2005). Crossing boundaries to generative wisdom: An analysis of professional work. In R. J. Sternberg, & J. Jordan (Eds.), *A handbook of wisdom: Psychological perspectives*. New York: Cambridge University Press.

Solomon, R. C., & Wynne, L. C. (1953). Traumatic avoidance learning: Acquisition in normal dogs. *Psychological Monographs, 67*(4, Whole No. 354).

Solomon, R. L. (1980). The opponent-process theory of acquired motivation. *American Psychologist*, Aug., 691–721.

Solowij, N., Stephens, R. S., Roffman, R. A., & the Marijuana Treatment Project Research Group. (2002). Cognitive functioning of long-term heavy cannabis users seeking treatment. *Journal of the American Medical Association, 287*, 1123–1131.

Solso, R. L., MacLin, M. K., & MacLin, O. H. (2008). *Cognitive psychology* (8th ed). Boston: Allyn and Bacon.

Somberg, D. R., Stone, G., & Claiborn, C. D. (1993). Informed consent: Therapist's beliefs and practices. *Professional Psychology: Research & Practice, 24*(2), 153–159.

Sommers-Flanagan, J., & Sommers-Flanagan, R. (2002). *Clinical interviewing* (3rd ed.). New York: Wiley.

Soussignan, R. (2002). Duchenne smile, emotional experience, and autonomic reactivity. *Emotion, 2*(1), 52–74.

Soyez, V., & Broekaert, E. (2003). How do substance abusers and their significant others experience the re-entry phase of therapeutic community treatment: a qualitative study. *International Journal of Social Welfare, 12*(3), 211–220.

Spalding, K. L., Arner, E., Westermark, P. O., Buchholz, B. A., et al. (2008). Dynamics of fat cell turnover in humans. *Nature, May 4*, doi:10.1038/ nature06902.

Spano, R. (2005). Potential sources of observer bias in police observational data. *Social Science Research, 34*(3), 591–617.

Spector, P. E. (2005). *Industrial and organizational psychology: Research and practice* (4th ed.). New York: Wiley.

Spence, S., & David, A. (Eds.). (2004). *Voices in the brain: The cognitive neuropsychiatry of auditory verbal hallucinations*. London: Psychology Press.

Sperry, R. W. (1968). Hemisphere deconnection and unity in conscious awareness. *American Psychologist, 23,* 723–733.

Spiegler, M. D., & Guevremont, D. C. (2003). *Contemporary behavior therapy*. Belmont, CA: Wadsworth

Spinella, M. (2005). Compulsive behavior in tobacco users. *Addictive Behaviors, 30*(1), 183–186.

Spiro Wagner, P., & Spiro, C. S. (2005). *Divided minds: Twin sisters and their journey through schizophrenia*. New York, St. Martin's Press, 2005

Sporer, S. L. (2001). Recognizing faces of other ethnic groups. *Psychology, Public Policy, and Law, 7*(1), 36–97

Sprecher, S. (1998). Insiders' perspectives on reasons for attraction to a close other. *Social Psychology Quarterly, 61*(4), 287–300.

Sprecher, S., & Hatfield, E. (1996). Premarital sexual standards among U.S. college students. *Archives of Sexual Behavior, 25*(3), 261–288.

Springer, S. P., & Deutsch, G. (1998). *Left brain, right brain*. New York: Freeman.

Sprinthall, R. C. (2007). *Basic statistical analysis* (8th ed.). Boston: Allyn & Bacon.

Squire, L. R. (2004). Memory systems of the brain: A brief history and current perspective. *Neurobiology of Learning & Memory, 82,* 171–177.

Squire, L. R., & Kandel, E. R. (2000). *Memory: From mind to molecule*. New York: Worth.

Sroufe, L. A., Egeland, B., Carlson, E., & Collins, W. A. (2005). Placing early attachment experiences in developmental context: The Minnesota Longitudinal Study. In K. E. Grossmann, K. Grossmann, et al. (Eds.), *Attachment from infancy to adulthood: The major longitudinal studies*. New York: Guilford.

Staats, P., Hekmat, H., & Staats, A. (1998). Suggestion/Placebo effects on pain: Negative as well as positive. *Journal of Pain & Symptom Management, 15*(4), 235–243.

Staemmler, F.-M. (2004). Dialogue and interpretation in Gestalt therapy: Making sense together. *International Gestalt Journal, 27*(2), 33–57.

Stanovich, K. E. (2007). *How to think straight about psychology* (8th ed.). Boston: Allyn & Bacon.

Stapel, D. A., & Marx, D. M. (2007). Distinctiveness is key: How different types of self-other similarity moderate social comparison effects. *Personality & Social Psychology Bulletin, 33*(3), 439–448.

Staples, S. L. (1996). Human response to environmental noise. *American Psychologist, 51*(2), 143–150.

Steblay, N. M. (1987). Helping behavior in rural and urban environments: A meta-analysis. *Psychological Bulletin, 102*(3), 346–356.

Steele, C. M. (1997). A threat in the air. *American Psychologist, 52*(6), 613–629.

Steele, C. M., & Aronson, J. (1995). Stereotype threat and the intellectual test performance of African Americans. *Journal of Personality & Social Psychology, 69*(5), 797–811.

Steiger, A. (2007). Neurochemical regulation of sleep. *Journal of Psychiatric Research, 41*, 537–552.

Stein, L. M., & Memon, A. (2006). Testing the efficacy of the cognitive interview in a developing country. *Applied Cognitive Psychology, 20*(5), 597–605.

Stein, M. B., & Stein, Dan J. (2008). Social anxiety disorder. *Lancet, 371*(9618), 1115–1125.

Stein, M. D., & Friedmann, P. D. (2005). Disturbed sleep and its relationship to alcohol use. *Substance Abuse, 26*(1), 1–13.

Stein, M. T., & Ferber, R. (2001). Recent onset of sleepwalking in early adolescence. *Journal of Development, Behavior, and Pediatrics, 22,* S33–S35.

Steinberg, L (2001). Adolescent development. *Annual Review of Psychology, 52,* 83–110.

Stemler, S. E., & Sternberg, R. J. (2006). Using situational judgment tests to measure practical intelligence. In J. A. Weekley, & R. E. Ployhart (Eds.), *Situational judgment tests: Theory, measurement, and application*. Mahwah, NJ: Erlbaum.

Stephens, K., Kiger, L., Karnes, F. A., & Whorton, J. E. (1999). Use of nonverbal measures of intelligence in identification of culturally diverse gifted students in rural areas. *Perceptual & Motor Skills, 88*(3, Pt 1), 793–796.

Stern, P. C. (1992). Psychological dimensions of global environmental change. In M. R. Rosenzweig, & L. W. Porter (Eds.), *Annual Review of Psychology, 43,* 269–302.

Stern, S. L., Dhanda, R., & Hazuda, H. P. (2001). Hopelessness predicts mortality in older Mexican and European Americans. *Psychosomatic Medicine, 63*(3), 344–351.

Sternberg, E. M. (2000). *The balance within: The science of connecting health with emotions*. New York: Freeman.

Sternberg, R. J. (1988). *The triangle of love*. New York: Basic.

Sternberg, R. J. (2004). Culture and intelligence. *American Psychologist, 59*(5), 325–338.

Sternberg, R. J. (2007). Race and intelligence: Not a case of black and white. *New Scientist, 2627*(Oct. 27), 16.

Sternberg, R. J., & Davidson, J. D. (1982). The mind of the puzzler. *Psychology Today*, June, 37–44.

Sternberg, R. J., & Grigorenko, E. L. (2005). Cultural explorations of the nature of intelligence. In A. F. Healy, (Ed.), *Experimental cognitive psychology and its applications*. Washington, DC: American Psychological Association.

Sternberg, R. J., & Grigorenko, E. L. (2006). Cultural intelligence and successful intelligence. *Group & Organization Management, 31*(1), 27–39.

Sternberg, R. J., & Lubart, T. I. (1995). *Defying the crowd*. New York: The Free Press.

Sternberg, R. J., Grigorenko, E. L., & Kidd, K. K. (2005). Intelligence, race, and genetics. *American Psychologist, 60*(1), 46–59.

Sternberg, W. F., Bailin, D., Grant, M., & Gracely, R. H. (1998). Competition alters the perception of noxious stimuli in male and female athletes. *Pain, 76*(1–2), 231–238.

Steuer, F. B., & Hustedt, J. T. (2002). *TV or No TV? A primer on the psychology of television*. Lanham, MD: University Press of America.

Stewart, A. J., & Ostrove, J. M. (1998). Women's personality in middle age. *American Psychologist, 53*(11), 1185–1194.

Stewart, A. J., & Vandewater, E. A. (1999). "If I had it to do over again . . .": Midlife review, midcourse corrections, and women's well-being in midlife. *Journal of Personality & Social Psychology, 76*(2), 270–283.

Stewart-Williams, S. (2004). The placebo puzzle: Putting together the pieces. *Health Psychology, 23*(2), 198–206.

Stickgold, R., & Walker, M. (2004). To sleep, perchance to gain creative insight? *Trends in Cognitive Sciences, 8*(5), 191–192.

Stinson, F. S., Dawson, D. A., Chou, S. P., Smith, S., et al. (2007). The epidemiology of DSM-IV specific phobia in the USA: Result from the National Epidemiologic Survey on Alcohol and Related Conditions. *Psychological Medicine, 37*(7), 1047–1059.

Stipek, D. (2001). *Motivation to learn* (4th ed.). Boston: Allyn & Bacon.

Stöber, J. (2004). Dimensions of test anxiety: Relations to ways of coping with pre-exam anxiety and uncertainty. *Anxiety, Stress & Coping: An International Journal, 17*(3), 213–226.

Stockhorst, U., Klosterhalfen, S., & Steingrueber, H. (1998). Conditioned nausea and further side-effects in cancer chemotherapy. *Journal of Psychophysiology, 12*(Suppl. 1), 14–33.

Stokes, D. M. (2001). The shrinking file-drawer. *Skeptical Inquirer*, May–June, 22–25.

Stokoe, W. C. (2001). *Language in hand: Why sign came before speech*. Washington, DC: Gallaudet University Press.

Stolerman, I. P., & Jarvis, M. J. (1995) The scientific case that nicotine is addictive. *Psychopharmacology, 117*(1), 2–10.

Stone, J., Perry, Z. W., & Darley, J. M. (1997). "White men can't jump." *Basic and Applied Social Psychology, 19*(3), 291–306.

Stoppard, J. M., & McMullen, L. M. (Eds.). (2003). *Situating sadness: Women and depression in social context*. New York: New York University Press.

Strack. F., Martin, L. L., & Stepper, S. (1988). Inhibiting and facilitating conditions of facial expressions: A nonobtrusive test of the facial feedback hypothesis. *Journal of Personality & Social Psychology, 54*, 768–777.

Straneva, P. A., Maixner, W., Light, K. C., Pedersen, C. A., et al. (2002). Menstrual cycle, beta-endorphins, and pain sensitivity in premenstrual dysphoric disorder. *Health Psychology, 21*(4), 358–367.

Strange, J. R. (1965). *Abnormal psychology*. New York: McGraw-Hill.

Straub, R. (2006). *Health psychology* (2nd ed.) New York: Worth.

Strayer, D. L., Drews, F. A., & Crouch, D. J. (2006). A comparison of the cell phone driver and the drunk driver. *Human Factors, 48*(2), 381–391.

Strickler, E. M., & Verbalis, J. G. (1988). Hormones and behavior: The biology of thirst and sodium appetite. *American Scientist*, May–June, 261–267.

Strier, F. (1999). Whither trial consulting? Issues and projections. *Law & Human Behavior, 23*(1), 93–115.

Strong, B., & DeVault, C. (1994). *Understanding our sexuality*. St. Paul, MN: West.

Strongman, K. T. (2003). *The psychology of emotion: From everyday life to theory* (5th Ed.). New York: Wiley.

Strote, J., Lee, J. E., & Wechsler, H. (2002). Increasing MDMA use among college students: Results of a national survey.

Journal of Adolescent Health, 30(1), 64–72.

Strubbe, M. J. (2005). What did Triplett really find? A contemporary analysis of the first experiment in social psychology. *American Journal of Psychology, 118,* 271–286.

Sturges, J. W., & Sturges, L. V. (1998). In vivo *systematic desensitization* in a single-session treatment of an 11-year old girl's elevator phobia. *Child & Family Behavior Therapy, 20*(4), 55–62.

Stuss, D. T., & Alexander, M. P. (2000). The anatomical basis of affective behavior, emotion and self-awareness: A specific role of the right frontal lobe. In G. Hatano, N. Okada, & H. Tanabe (Eds.), *Affective minds. The 13th Toyota conference.* Amsterdam: Elsevier.

Stuss, D. T., & Knight, R. T. (2002). *Principles of frontal lobe function.* New York: Oxford University Press.

Stuss, D. T., & Levine, B. (2002). Adult clinical neuropsychology. *Annual Review of Psychology, 53,* 401–433.

Sue, D., Sue, D. W., & Sue, S. (1996). *Understanding abnormal behavior.* Boston: Houghton Mifflin.

Suedfeld, P. & Steel, G. D. (2000). The environmental psychology of capsule habitats. *Annual Review of Psychology, 51,* 227–253.

Suedfeld, P., & Borrie, R. A. (1999). Health and therapeutic applications of chamber and flotation restricted environmental stimulation therapy (REST). *Psychology & Health, 14*(3), 545–566.

Sugihara, Y., & Warner, J. A. (1999). Endorsements by Mexican-Americans of the Bem Sex-Role Inventory: Cross-ethnic comparison. *Psychological Reports, 85*(1), 201–211.

Sugimoto, K., & Ninomiya, Y. (2005). Introductory remarks on umami research: Candidate receptors and signal transduction mechanisms on umami. *Chemical Senses, 30*(Suppl. 1), p i21–i22, 2005.

Suinn, R. M. (1975). *Fundamentals of behavior pathology* (2nd ed.). New York: Wiley.

Suinn, R. M. (1999). Scaling the summit: Valuing ethnicity. *APA Monitor,* March, 2.

Suinn, R. M. (2001). The terrible twos—Anger and anxiety. *American Psychologist, 56*(1), 27–36.

Sumathipala, A., Siribaddana, S. H., & Bhugra, D. (2004). Culture-bound syndromes: The story of dhat syndrome. *British Journal of Psychiatry, 184*(3), 200–209.

Sumerlin, J. R., & Bundrick, C. M. (1996). Brief Index of Self-Actualization: A measure of Maslow's model. *Journal of Social Behavior & Personality, 11*(2), 253–271.

Sumi, K., & Kanda, K. (2002). Relationship between neurotic perfectionism, depression, anxiety, and psychosomatic symptoms. *Personality & Individual Differences, 32*(5), 817–826.

Sunnafrank, M., Ramirez, A., & Metts, S. (2004). At first sight: Persistent relational effects of get-acquainted conversations. *Journal of Social & Personal Relationships, 21*(3), 361–379.

Sutherland, R. J., Lehmann, H., Spanswick, S. C., et al. (2006). Growth points in research on memory and hippocampus. *Canadian Journal of Experimental Psychology, 60*(2), 166–174.

Suzuki, L., & Aronson, J. (2005). The cultural malleability of intelligence and its impact on the racial/ethnic hierarchy. *Psychology, Public Policy, & Law, 11,* 320–327.

Svartdal, F. (2003). Extinction after partial reinforcement: Predicted vs. judged persistence. *Scandinavian Journal of Psychology, 44*(1), 55–64.

Swaak, J., de Jong, T., & van Joolingen, W. R. (2004). The effects of discovery learning and expository instruction on the acquisition of definitional and intuitive knowledge. *Journal of Computer Assisted Learning, 20*(4), 225–234.

Swann, W. B., Jr., Chang-Schneider, C., & Larsen McClarty, K. (2007). Do people's self-views matter? Self-concept and self-esteem in everyday life. *American Psychologist, 62*(2), 84–94.

Synhorst, L. L., Buckley, J. A., Reid, R., Epstein, M. H. et al. (2005). Cross informant agreement of the Behavioral and Emotional Rating Scale—2nd Edition (BERS-2) parent and youth rating scales. *Child & Family Behavior Therapy, 27*(3), 1–11.

Szabo, A. (2003). The acute effects of humor and exercise on mood and anxiety. *Journal of Leisure Research, 35*(2), 152–162.

Takooshian, H., Haber, S., & Lucido, D. J. (1977). Who wouldn't help a lost child? You, maybe. *Psychology Today,* Feb., 67.

Talbot, N. L., & Gamble, S. A. (2008). IPT for women with trauma histories in community mental health care. *Journal of Contemporary Psychotherapy, 38*(1), 35–44.

Talbott, J. A. (2004). Deinstitutionalization: Avoiding the disasters of the past. *Psychiatric Services, 55*(10), 1112–1115.

Talley, P. F., Strupp, H. H., & Morey, L. C. (1990). Matchmaking in psychotherapy: Patient–therapist dimensions and their impact on outcome. *Journal of Consulting & Clinical Psychology, 58*(2), 182–188.

Tal-Or, N., & Papirman, Y. (2007). The fundamental attribution error in attributing fictional figures' characteristics to the actors. *Media Psychology, 9*(2), 331–345.

Tamis-LeMonda, C. S., Bornstein, M. H., & Baumwell, L. (2001). Maternal responsiveness and children's achievement of language milestones. *Child Development, 72,* 748–767.

Tamis-LeMonda, C. S., Shannon, J. D., Cabrera, N. J., & Lamb, M. E. (2004). Fathers and mothers at play with their 2- and 3-year-olds: Contributions to language and cognitive development. *Child Development, 75*(6), 1806–1820.

Tanner, J. M. (1973). Growing up. *Scientific American,* Sept., 34–43.

Taraban, R., Rynearson, K., & Kerr, M. (2000). College students' academic performance and self-reports of comprehension strategy use. *Reading Psychology, 21*(4), 283–308.

Tardif, T. Z., & Sternberg, R. J. (1988). What do we know about creativity? In R. J. Sternberg (Ed.), *The nature of creativity.* Cambridge University Press.

Taris, T. W., Bakker, A. B., Schaufeli, W. B., Stoffelsen, J., et al. (2005). Job control and burnout across occupations. *Psychological Reports, 97*(3), 955–961.

Taub, E. (2004). Harnessing brain plasticity through behavioral techniques to produce new treatments in neurorehabilitation. *American Psychologist, 59*(8), 692–704.

Tausig, M., Michello, J., & Subedi, S. (2004). *A sociology of mental illness* (2nd ed.). Englewood Cliffs, NJ: Prentice Hall.

Tavris, C., & Aronson, E. (2007). *Mistakes were made (but not by me): Why we justify foolish beliefs, bad decisions, and hurtful acts.* New York: Harcourt.

Taylor, G. J., & Taylor-Allan, H. L. (2007). Applying emotional intelligence in understanding and treating physical and psychological disorders: What we have learned from alexithymia. In R. Bar-On, M. J. G. Reuven, et al. (Eds.), *Educating people to be emotionally intelligent.* Westport, CT: Praeger.

Taylor, K. (2004). *Brainwashing: The science of thought control.* New York: Oxford University Press.

Taylor, S. E. (2002). Classical conditioning. In M. Hersen, & W. H. Sledge (Eds.), *Encyclopedia of psychotherapy.* San Diego: Academic Press.

Taylor, S. E. (2006). *Health psychology* (6th ed.). New York: McGraw-Hill.

Taylor, S. E., Kemeny, M. E., Reed, G. M., Bower, J. E., et al. (2000). Psychological resources, positive illusions, and health. *American Psychologist, 55*(1), 99–109.

Taylor, S. E., Lerner, J. S., Sherman, D. K., Sage, R. M., et al. (2003). Are self-enhancing cognitions associated with healthy or unhealthy biological profiles? *Journal of Personality & Social Psychology, 85*(4), 605–615.

Taylor-Seehafer, M., & Rew, L. (2000). Risky sexual behavior among adolescent women. *Journal of Social Pediatric Nursing, 5*(1), 15–25.

Tedeschi, J. T., Lindskold, S., & Rosenfeld, P. (1985). *Introduction to social psychology.* St. Paul: West Publishing.

Tenenbaum, G., Bar-Eli, M., & Eyal, N. (1996). Imagery orientation and vividness: Their effect on a motor skill performance. *Journal of Sport Behavior, 19*(1), 32–49.

Tennesen, M. (2007). Gone today, hear tomorrow. *New Scientist, 2594*(March 10), 42–45.

Terman, L. M., & Merrill, M. A. (1937, revised, 1960). *Stanford-Binet Intelligence Scale.* Boston: Houghton Mifflin.

Terman, L. M., & Oden, M. (1959). *The gifted group in mid-life* (Vol. 5): *Genetic studies of genius.* Stanford, CA: Stanford University Press.

Terry, C. (2006). History of treatment of people with mental illness. In J. R. Matthews, C. E. Walker, et al. (Eds.), *Your practicum in psychology: A guide for maximizing knowledge and competence.* Washington, DC: American Psychological Association.

Terry, D. J., & Hogg, M. A. (1996). Group norms and the attitude-behavior relationship. *Personality & Social Psychology Bulletin, 22*(8), 776–793.

Thase, M. E. (2006). Major depressive disorder. In F. Andrasik (Ed.), *Comprehensive handbook of personality and psychopathology* (Vol. 2): *Adult psychopathology.* New York: Wiley.

The Nature Conservancy (2008). *Carbon calculator.* Retrieved July 11, 2008, from http://www.nature.org/initiatives/climatechange/calculator/.

Thelen, E. (2000). Infancy: Perception and motor development. In A. Kazdin (Ed.), *Encyclopedia of psychology.* Washington, DC: American Psychological Association.

They'd kill for $1 million. (1991). *The Los Angeles Times,* July 1, A8.

Thiessen, E. D., Hill, E. A., & Saffran, J. R. (2005). Infant-directed speech facilitates word segmentation. *Infancy, 7*(1), 53–71.

Thomas, E. M. (2004). *Aggressive behaviour outcomes for young children: Change in parenting environment predicts change in behaviour.* Ottawa, ON: Statistics Canada. Retrieved June 6, 2007, from http://www.statcan.ca/cgi-bin/downpub/listpub.cgi?catno=89-599-MIE2004001.

Thompson, A., Boekhoorn, K., Van Dam, A. M., & Lucassen, P. J. (2008). Changes in adult neurogenesis in neurodegenerative diseases: Cause or consequence? *Genes, Brain & Behavior, 7*(Suppl. 1), 28–42.

Thompson, C. P., Cowan, T. M., & Frieman, J. (1993). *Memory search by a memorist.* Hillsdale, NJ: Lawrence Erlbaum.

Thompson, R. A., & Nelson, C. A. (2001). Developmental science and the media. *American Psychologist, 56*(1), 5–15.

Thompson, R. F. (2005). In search of memory traces. *Annual Review of Psychology, 56,* 1–23.

Thornburg, H. D. (1984). *Introduction to educational psychology.* St. Paul, MN: West.

Thorpy, M. J. (2006). Cataplexy associated with narcolepsy: Epidemiology, pathophysiology and management. *CNS Drugs, 20*(1), 43–50.

Thorson, J. A., & Powell, F. C. (1990). Meanings of death and intrinsic religiosity. *Journal of Clinical Psychology, 46*(4), 379–391.

Thyen, U., Richter-Appelt, H., Wiesemann, C., Holterhus, P. M., et al. (2005). Deciding on gender in children with intersex conditions: Considerations and controversies. *Treatments in Endocrinology, 4*(1), 1–8.

Tidwell, M. O., Reis, H. T., & Shaver, P. R. (1996). Attachment, attractiveness, and social interaction. *Journal of Personality & Social Psychology, 71*(4), 729–745.

Tierney, S. (2008). Creating communities in cyberspace: Pro-anorexia web sites and social capital. *Journal of Psychiatric & Mental Health Nursing, 15*(4), 340–343.

Tijerino, R. (1998). Civil spaces: A critical perspective of defensible space. *Journal of Architectural & Planning Research, 15*(4), 321–337.

Till, B. D., & Priluck, R. L. (2000). Stimulus generalization in classical conditioning: An initial investigation and extension. *Psychology & Marketing, 17*(1), 55–72.

Timmerman, C. K., & Kruepke, K. A. (2006). Computer-assisted instruction, media richness, and college student performance. *Communication Education, 55*(1), 73–104.

Timmerman, I. G. H., Emmelkamp, P. M. G., & Sanderman, R. (1998). The effects of a stress-management training program in individuals at risk in the community at large. *Behaviour Research & Therapy, 36*(9), 863–875.

Tipples, J., Atkinson, A. P., & Young, A. W. (2002). The eyebrow frown: A salient social signal. *Emotion, 2*(3), 288–296.

Tobler, N. S., Roona, M. R., Ocshorn, P., Marshall, D. G., et al. (2000). School-based adolescent drug prevention programs: 1998 meta-analysis. *Journal of Primary Prevention, 20,* 275–337.

Tolman, E. C., & Honzik, C. H. (1930). Introduction and removal of reward and maze performance in rats. *University of California Publications in Psychology, 4,* 257–275.

Tolman, E. C., Ritchie, B. F., & Kalish, D. (1946). Studies in spatial learning: II. Place learning versus response learning. *Journal of Experimental Psychology, 36,* 221–229.

Tomasello, M. (2003). *Constructing a language: A usage-based theory of language acquisition.* Cambridge, MA: Harvard University Press.

Toneatto, T. (2002). Cognitive therapy for problem gambling. *Cognitive & Behavioral Practice, 9*(3), 191–199.

Toneatto, T., Sobell, L. C., Sobell, M. B., & Rubel, E. (1999). Natural recovery from cocaine dependence. *Psychology of Addictive Behaviors, 13*(4), 259–268.

Tononi, G., & Cirelli, C. (2003). Sleep and synaptic homeostasis: A hypothesis. *Brain Research Bulletin, 62*(2), 143–150.

Toro, C. T., & Deakin, J. F. W. (2007). Adult neurogenesis and schizophrenia: A window on abnormal early brain development? *Schizophrenia Research, 90*(1–3), 1–14.

Torrey, E. F. (1996). *Out of the shadows.* New York: John Wiley & Sons.

Tourangeau, R. (2004). Survey research and societal change. *Annual Review of Psychology, 55,* 775–801.

Toyota, H., & Kikuchi, Y. (2005). Encoding richness of self-generated elaboration and spacing effects on incidental memory. *Perceptual & Motor Skills, 101*(2), 621–627.

Trainor, L. J., & Desjardins, R. N. (2002). Pitch characteristics of infant-directed speech affect infants' ability to discriminate vowels. *Psychonomic Bulletin & Review, 9*(2), 335–340.

Travis, F., Arenander, A., & DuBois, D. (2004). Psychological and physiological characteristics of a proposed objectreferral/self-referral continuum of self awareness. *Consciousness & Cognition, 13,* 401–420.

Treffert, D. A., & Christensen, C. D. (2005). Inside the mind of a savant. *Scientific American, 293*(6), 108–113.

Trehub, S. E., Unyk, A. M., & Trainor, L. J. (1993a). Adults identify infant-directed music across cultures. *Infant Behavior & Development, 16*(2), 193–211.

Trehub, S. E., Unyk, A. M., & Trainor, L. J. (1993b). Maternal singing in cross-cultural perspective. *Infant Behavior & Development, 16*(3), 285–295.

Trepel, C., & Racine, R. J. (1999). Blockade and disruption of neocortical long-term potentiation following electroconvulsive shock in the adult, freely moving rat. *Cerebral Cortex, 9*(3), 300–305.

Triandis, H. C., & Suh, E. M. (2002). Cultural influences on personality. *Annual Review of Psychology, 53,* 133–160.

Trocmé, N., MacLaurin, B., Fallon, B., et al. (2001). *Canadian Incidence Study of Reported Child Abuse and Neglect.* Ottawa, ON: National Clearinghouse on Family Violence. Retrieved April 5, 2008, from http://www.phac-aspc.gc.ca/publicat/cissr-ecirc/.

Troll, L. E., & Skaff, M. M. (1997). Perceived continuity of self in very old age. *Psychology & Aging, 12*(1), 162–169.

Truax, S. R. (1983). Active search, mediation, and the manipulation of cue dimensions: Emotion attribution in the false feedback paradigm. *Motivation and Emotion, 7,* 41–60.

Trull, T. (2005). *Clinical psychology* (7th ed.). Belmont, CA: Cengage Learning/Wadsworth.

Tsai, C., Hoerr, S. L., & Song, W. O. (1998). Dieting behavior of Asian college women attending a US university. *Journal of American College Health, 46*(4), 163–168.

Tsai, G., & Coyle, J. T. (2002). Glutamatergic mechanisms in schizophrenia. *Annual Review of Pharmacology & Toxicology, 42,* 165–179.

Tsai, W-C., Chen, C.-C., & Chiu, S-F. (2005). Exploring boundaries of the effects of applicant impression management tactics in job interviews. *Journal of Management, 31*(1), 108–125.

Tse, L. (1999). Finding a place to be: Ethnic identity exploration of Asian Americans. *Adolescence, 34*(133), 121–138.

Tugade, M. M., Fredrickson, B. L., & Barrett, L. F. (2004). Psychological resilience and positive emotional granularity: Examining the benefits of positive emotions on coping and health. *Journal of Personality, 72*(6), 1161–1190.

Tulving, E. (1989). Remembering and knowing the past. *American Scientist, 77*(4), 361–367.

Tulving, E. (2002). Episodic memory. *Annual Review of Psychology, 53,* 1–25.

Turiel, E. (2006).Thought, emotions, and social interactional processes in moral development. In M. Killen, & J. G. Smetana, (Eds.), *Handbook of moral development.* Mahwah, NJ: Erlbaum.

Turk, D. C., & Melzack. R. (2001). *Handbook of pain assessment.* New York: Guilford.

Turkheimer, E., Haley, A., Waldron, M., D'Onofrio, B. M., et al. (2003). Socioeconomic status modifies heritability of IQ in young children. *Psychological Science, 14,* 623–628.

Turner, S. J. M. (1997). The use of the reflective team in a psychodrama therapy group. *International Journal of Action Methods, 50*(1) 17–26.

Turvey, M. T. (1996). Dynamic touch. *American Psychologist, 51*(11), 1134–1152.

Tversky, A., & Kahneman, D. (1981). The framing of decisions and the psychology of choice. *Science, 211,* 453–458.

Tversky, A., & Kahneman, D. (1982). Judgments of and by representativeness. In D. Kahneman, P. Slovic, et al. (Eds.), *Judgment under uncertainty: Heuristics and biases.* Cambridge, UK: Cambridge University Press.

Twenge, J. M., & Campbell, W. K. (2001). Age and birth cohort differences in self-esteem. *Personality & Social Psychology Review, 5*(4), 321–344.

Tye-Murray, N., Spencer, L., & Woodworth, G. G. (1995). Acquisition of speech by children who have prolonged cochlear implant experience. *Journal of Speech & Hearing Research, 38*(2), 327–337.

Tyler, J. M., & Feldman, R. S. (2006). Deflecting threat to one's image: Dissembling personal information as a self-presentation strategy. *Basic and Applied Social Psychology, 27*(4), 371–378.

Tzeng, M. (1992). The effects of socioeconomic heterogamy and changes on marital dissolution for first marriages. *Journal of Marriage & Family, 54,* 609–619.

U.S. Department of Energy Human Office of Science. (2005). *About the Human Genome Project.* Washington, DC: U.S. Department of Energy. Retrieved May 25, 2007, from http://www.ornl.gov/sci/techresources/Human_Genome/project/about.shtml.

U.S. Department of Labor. (2007). *Occupational Outlook Handbook job interview tips.* Washington, DC: U.S. Department of Labor. Retrieved July 11, 2008, from http://www.bls.gov/oco/oco20045.htm.

Udvari-Solner, A., Villa, R. A., & Thousand, J. S. (2002). Access to the general education curriculum for all: The universal design process. In J. S. Thousand, R. A. Villa, et al. (Eds.), *Creativity and collaborative learning: The practical guide to empowering students, teachers, and families* (2nd ed.). Baltimore: Paul H. Brookes.

UN. (2004). *World population in 2300.* New York: United Nations. Retrieved July 12, 2008, from http://www.un.org/esa/population/publications/longrange2/2004worldpop2300reportfinalc.pdf.

UNAIDS. (2006). *UNAIDS/WHOAIDS epidemic update: December 2006.* New York: United Nations. Retrieved July 27, 2007, from http://www.unaids.org/en/HIV_data/epi2006/default.asp.

Underwood, B. J. (1957). Interference and forgetting. *Psychological Review, 64,* 49–60.

UNESCO. (1990). The Seville statement on violence. *American Psychologist, 45*(10), 1167–1168.

United States Bureau of Census. (2007). *Minority population tops 100 million.* New York: U. S. Census Bureau News, CB07-70. Retrieved January 19, 2008, from http://www.census.gov/Press-Release/www/releases/archives/population/010048.html.

Unsworth, G., & Ward, T. (2001). Video games and aggressive behaviour. *Australian Psychologist, 36*(3), 184–192.

Urbina, S. (2004). *Essentials of psychological testing.* New York: Wiley.

Urdan, T., & Midgley, C. (2001). Academic self-handicapping. *Educational Psychology Review, 13*(2), 115–138.

USDHHS (U.S. Department of Health and Human Services). (2004). *The health consequences of smoking: A report of the Surgeon General, Executive summary.* Washington, DC: Department of Health and Human Services. Retrieved June 6, 2007, from http://www.cdc.gov/tobacco/data_statistics/sgr/sgr_2004/00_pdfs/executivesummary.pdf.

Uwe P. Gielen, U. P., Fish, J. M., & Draguns, J. G. (Eds.) (2006). *Handbook of culture, therapy, and healing.* Mahwah, NJ: Erlbaum.

Uziel, L. (2007). Individual differences in the social facilitation effect: A review and meta-analysis. *Journal of Research in Personality, 41*(3), 579–601.

Vaillant, G. E. (2002). *Aging well.* Boston: Little, Brown.

Vaillant, G. E. (2005). Alcoholics Anonymous: Cult or cure? *Australian & New Zealand Journal of Psychiatry, 39*(6), 431–436.

Vaillant, G. E., & Mukamal, K. (2001). Successful aging. *American Journal of Psychiatry, 158*(6), 839–847.

Valins, S. (1966). Cognitive effects of false heart-rate feedback. *Journal of Personality & Social Psychology, 4,* 400–408.

Valins, S. (1967). Emotionality and information concerning internal reactions. *Journal of Personality & Social Psychology, 6,* 458–463.

Vallerand, A. H., Saunders, M. M., & Anthony, M. (2007). Perceptions of control over pain by patients with cancer and their caregivers. *Pain Management Nursing, 8*(2), 55–63.

Van den Bergh, B., & Dewitte, S. (2006). Digit ratio (2D:4D) moderates the impact of sexual cues on men's decisions in ultimatum games. *Proceedings of the Royal Society of London B, 273,* 2091–2095.

Van der Hart, O., Lierens, R., & Goodwin, J. (1996). Jeanne Fery: A sixteenth-century case of dissociative identity disorder. *Journal of Psychohistory, 24*(1), 18–35.

Van Deurzen, E., & Kenward, R. (2005). *Dictionary of existential psychotherapy and counselling.* Thousand Oaks, CA: Sage.

Van Dierendonck, D., & Te Nijenhuis, J. (2005). Flotation restricted environmental stimulation therapy (REST) as a stress-management tool: A meta-analysis. *Psychology & Health, 20*(3), 405–412.

Van Elst, L. T., Valerius, G., Büchert, M., Thiel, T., et al. (2005). Increased prefrontal and hippocampal glutamate concentration in schizophrenia: Evidence from a magnetic resonance spectroscopy study. *Biological Psychiatry, 58*(9), 724–730.

Van Goozen, S. H. M., Cohen-Kettenis, P. T., Gooren, L. J. G., & Frijda, N. H. (1995). Gender differences in behaviour: Activating effects of cross-sex hormones. *Psychoneuroendocrinology, 20*(4) 343–363.

Van Lawick-Goodall, J. (1971). *In the shadow of man.* New York: Houghton Mifflin.

Van Rooij, J. J. F. (1994). Introversion–extraversion: Astrology versus psychology. *Personality & Individual Differences, 16*(6), 985–988.

Van Vugt, M. (2002). Central, individual, or collective control? Social dilemma strategies for natural resource management. *American Behavioral Scientist, 45*(5), 783–800.

Vandell, D. L. (2004). Early child care: The known and the unknown. *Merrill-Palmer Quarterly. Special The maturing of the human developmental sciences: Appraising past, present, and prospective agendas, 50*(3), 387–414.

Vasa, R. A., Carlino, A. R., & Pine, D. S. (2006). Pharmacotherapy of depressed children and adolescents: Current issues and potential directions. *Biological Psychiatry, 59*(11), 1021–1028.

Vecera, S. P., Vogel, E. K., & Woodman, G. F. (2002). Lower region: A new cue for figure-ground assignment. *Journal of Experimental Psychology: General, 131*(2), 194–205.

Velakoulis, D., & Pantelis, C. (1996). What have we learned from functional imaging studies in schizophrenia? *Australian & New Zealand Journal of Psychiatry, 30*(2), 195–209.

Venezia, M., Messinger, D. S., Thorp, D., & Mundy, P. (2004). The development of anticipatory smiling. *Infancy, 6*(3), 397–406.

Vi, P. (2006). A field study investigating the effects of a rebar-tying machine on trunk flexion, tool usability and productivity. *Ergonomics, 49*(14), 1437–1455.

Videon, T. M. (2005). Parent-child relations and children's psychological well-being: Do dads matter? *Journal of Family Issues, 26*(1), 55–78.

Viegener, B. J., Perri, M. G., Nezu, A. M., Renjilian, D. A., et al. (1990). Effects of an intermittent, low-fat, low-calorie diet in the behavioral treatment of obesity. *Behavior Therapy, 21*(4), 499–509.

Viveros, M. P., Llorente, R., Moreno, E., & Marco, E. M. (2005). Behavioural and neuroendocrine effects of cannabinoids in critical developmental periods. *Behavioural Pharmacology, 16*(5–6), 353–362.

Vogel, E. K., Woodman, G. F., & Luck, S. J. (2006). The time course of consolidation in visual working memory. *Journal of Experimental Psychology: Human Perception and Performance, 32*(6), 1436–1451.

Vogler, R. E., & Bartz, W. R. (1982). *The better way to drink.* New York: Simon and Schuster.

Vogler, R. E., & Bartz, W. R. (1992). *Teenagers and alcohol.* Philadelphia: Charles Press.

Vogler, R. E., Weissbach, T. A., Compton, J. V., & Martin, G. T. (1977). Integrated behavior change techniques for problem drinkers in the community.

Journal of Consulting and Clinical Psychology, 45, 267–279.

Volkow, N. D., Gillespie, H., Mullani, N., & Tancredi, L. (1996). Brain glucose metabolism in chronic marijuana users at baseline and during marijuana intoxication. *Psychiatry Research: Neuroimaging, 67*(1), 29–38.

Volpicelli, J. R., Ulm, R. R., Altenor, A., & Seligman, M. E. P. (1983). Learned mastery in the rat. *Learning and Motivation, 14,* 204–222.

Vygotsky, L. S. (1962). *Thought and language.* Cambridge, MA: MIT Press.

Vygotsky, L. S. (1978). *Mind in society.* Cambridge, MA: Harvard University Press.

Wager, T. D., Rilling, J. K., Smith, E. E., Sokolik, A., et al. (2004). Placebo-induced changes in fMRI in the anticipation and experience of pain. *Science, 303*(Feb. 20), 1162–1166.

Wagstaff, G., Brunas-Wagstaff, J., Cole, J., & Wheatcroft, J. (2004). New directions in forensic hypnosis: Facilitating memory with a focused meditation technique. *Contemporary Hypnosis, 21*(1), 14–27.

Waid, W. M., & Orne, M. T. (1982). The physiological detection of deception. *American Scientist, 70*(July/Aug.), 402–409.

Wainright, J. L., Russell, S. T., & Patterson, C. J. (2004). Psychosocial adjustment, school outcomes, and romantic relationships of adolescents with same-sex parents. *Child Development, 75*(6), 1886–1898.

Wakefield, J. C. (1992). The concept of mental disorder. *American Psychologist, 47*(3), 373–388.

Wald, J., & Taylor, S. (2000). Efficacy of virtual reality exposure therapy to treat driving phobia. *Journal of Behavior Therapy & Experimental Psychiatry, 31*(3–4), 249–257.

Waldvogel, J. A. (1990). The bird's eye view. *American Scientist, 78*(4), 342–353.

Walker, E., Kestler, L. Bollini, A., & Hochman, K. M. (2004). Schizophrenia: Etiology and course. *Annual Review of Psychology, 55,* 401–430.

Walker, I., & Crogan, M. (1998). Academic performance, prejudice, and the jigsaw classroom. *Journal of Community & Applied Social Psychology, 8*(6), 381–393

Walker, M. P., & Stickgold, R. (2006). Sleep, memory, and plasticity. *Annual Review of Psychology, 57,* 139–166.

Wallach, M. A., & Kogan, N. (1965). *Modes of thinking in young children.* New York: Holt.

Walster, E. (1971). Passionate love. In B. I. Murstein (Ed.), *Theories of attraction and love.* New York: Springer.

Walton, C. E., Bower, M. L., & Bower, T. G. (1992). Recognition of familiar faces by newborns. *Infant Behavior & Development, 15*(2), 265–269.

Wampold, B. E., Minami T., Tierney, S. C., Baskin, T. W., et al. (2005). The placebo is powerful: Estimating placebo effects in medicine and psychotherapy from randomized clinical trials. *Journal of Clinical Psychology, 61*(7), 835–854.

Wampold, B. E., Mondin, G. W., Moody, M., Stich, E., et al. (1997). A meta-analysis of outcome studies comparing

bona fide psychotherapies. *Psychological Bulletin, 122*(3), 203–215.

Wandersman, A., & Florin, P. (2003). Community interventions and effective prevention. *American Psychologist, 58*(6/7), 441–448.

Wang, Q., & Conway, M. A. (2004). The stories we keep: Autobiographical memory in American and Chinese middle-aged adults. *Journal of Personality, 72*(5), 911–938.

Wang, S. S., & Brownell, K. D. (2005). Public policy and obesity: The need to marry science with advocacy. *Psychiatric Clinics of North America, 28*(1), 235–252.

Ward, C., & Rana-Deuba, A. (1999). Acculturation and adaptation revisited. *Journal of Cross-Cultural Psychology, 30*(4), 422–442.

Ward, J. (2006). *The student's guide to cognitive neuroscience.* Hove, UK: Psychology Press.

Ward, L. M. (2004). Wading through the stereotypes: Positive and negative associations between media use and black adolescents' conceptions of self. *Developmental Psychology, 40,* 284–294.

Wargo, E. (2007). Understanding the have-knots: The role of stress in just about everything. *APS Observer, 20*(11), 18–23.

Wark, G. R., & Krebs, D. L. (1996). Gender and dilemma differences in real-life moral judgment. *Developmental Psychology, 32*(2), 220–230.

Warren, D. J., & Normann, R. A. (2005). Functional reorganization of primary visual cortex induced by electrical stimulation in the cat. *Vision Research, 45,* 551–565.

Waterfield, R. (2002). *Hidden depths: The story of hypnosis.* London: Macmillan.

Watson, D. L., & Tharp, R. G. (2007). *Self-directed behavior* (9th ed.). Belmont, CA: Cengage Learning/Wadsworth.

Watson, J. B. (1913/1994). Psychology as the behaviorist views it. *Psychological Review, 101*(2), 248–253.

Way, I., vanDeusen, K. M., Martin, G., Applegate, B., et al. (2004). Vicarious trauma: A comparison of clinicians who treat survivors of sexual abuse and sexual offenders. *Journal of Interpersonal Violence, 19*(1), 49–71.

Wechsler, H., & Wuethrich, B. (2002). *Dying to drink.* Emmaus, PA: Rodale Books.

Wechsler, H., Lee, J. E., Kuo, M., Seibring, M., et al. (2002). Trends in college binge drinking during a period of increased prevention efforts. *Journal of American College Health, 50*(5), 203–217.

Wedding, D., & Corsini, R. J. (2005). *Case studies in psychotherapy* (4th ed.). Belmont, CA: Cengage Learning/Wadsworth.

Weekley, J. A., & Jones, C. (1997). Video-based situational testing. *Personnel Psychology, 50*(1), 25–49.

Weems, C. F. (1998). The evaluation of heart rate biofeedback using a multielement design. *Journal of Behavior Therapy & Experimental Psychiatry, 29*(2), 157–162.

Wehr, T. A., Duncan, W. C., Sher, L., Aeschbach, D., et al. (2001). A circa-

dian signal of change of season in patients with seasonal affective disorder. *Archives of General Psychiatry, 58*(12), 1108–1114.

Weidenhammer, W., Linde, K., Streng, A., et al. (2007). Acupuncture for chronic low back pain in routine care: A multi-center observational study. *Clinical Journal of Pain, 23*(2), 128–135.

Weinberg, R. A. (1989). Intelligence and IQ. *American Psychologist, 44*(2), 98–104.

Weinstein, R. S., Gregory, A., & Strambler, M. J. (2004). Intractable self-fulfilling prophesies. *American Psychologist, 59*(6), 511–520.

Weintraub, M. I. (1983). *Hysterical conversion reactions.* New York: SP Medical & Scientific Books.

Weishaar, M. E. (2006). A cognitive-behavioral approach to suicide risk reduction in crisis intervention. In A. R. Roberts, & K. R. Yeager, (Eds.), *Foundations of evidence-based social work practice.* New York: Oxford University Press.

Weisskirch, R. S. (2005). Ethnicity and perceptions relationship to ethnic identity development. *International Journal of Intercultural Relations, 29*(3), 355–366.

Weissman, A. M., Jogerst, G. J., & Dawson, J. D. (2003). Community characteristics associated with child abuse in Iowa. *Child Abuse & Neglect, 27*(10), 1145–1159.

Weiten, W. (1998). Pressure, major life events, and psychological symptoms. *Journal of Social Behavior & Personality, 13*(1), 51–68.

Weitzenhoffer, A. M., & Hilgard, E. R. (1959) *Stanford Hypnotic Susceptibility Scale: Forms A and B.* Palo Alto, CA: Consulting Psychologists Press.

Weitzman, E. R. (2004). Poor mental health, depression, and associations with alcohol consumption, harm, and abuse in a national sample of young adults in college. *Journal of Nervous & Mental Disease, 192*(4), 269–277.

Wellings, K., Collumbien, M., Slaymaker, E., Singh, S., et al. (2006). Sexual behaviour in context: A global perspective. *Lancet, 368*(9548), 1706–1738.

Wells, B. E., & Twenge, J. M. (2005). Changes in young people's sexual behavior and attitudes, 1943–1999: A cross-temporal meta-analysis. *Review of General Psychology, 9*(3), 249–261.

Wells, G. L. (2001). Police lineups: Data, theory, and policy. *Psychology, Public Policy, & Law, 7*(4), 791–801.

Wells, G. L., & Olsen, E. A. (2003). Eyewitness testimony. *Annual Review of Psychology, 54,* 277–295.

Wells, G. L., Memon, A., & Penrod, S. D. (2006). Eyewitness evidence: Improving its probative value. *Psychological Science in the Public Interest, 7*(2), 45–75.

Weltzin, T. E., Weisensel, N., Franczyk, D., Burnett, K., et al. (2005). Eating disorders in men: Update. *Journal of Men's Health & Gender, 2*(2), 186–193.

Werner, C. M., & Makela, E. (1998). Motivations and behaviors that support recycling. *Journal of Environmental Psychology, 18*(4), 373–386.

Wernet, S. P., Follman, C., Magueja, C., & Moore-Chambers, R. (2003). Building bridges and improving racial harmony: An evaluation of the Bridges Across Racial Polarization Program. In J. J. Stretch, E. M. Burkemper, et al. (Eds.), *Practicing social justice*. New York: Haworth Press.

Wertheimer, M. (1959). *Productive thinking*. New York: Harper & Row.

Wesensten, N. J., Belenky, G., Kautz, M. A., Thorne, D. R., et al. (2002). Maintaining alertness and performance during sleep deprivation: Modafinil versus caffeine. *Psychopharmacology, 159*(3), 238–247.

Wessel, I., & Wright, D. B. (Eds.). (2004). *Emotional memory failures*. Hove, UK: Psychology Press.

West, L. J. (1993). A psychiatric overview of cult-related phenomena. *Journal of the American Academy of Psychoanalysis, 21*(1), 1–19.

West, R., & Sohal, T. (2006). "Catastrophic" pathways to smoking cessation: Findings from national survey. *British Medical Journal, 332*(7539), 458–460.

West, T. G. (1991). *In the mind's eye*. Buffalo, NY: Prometheus.

Westen, D., & Bradley, R. (2005). Empirically supported complexity: Rethinking evidence-based practice in psychotherapy. *Current Directions in Psychological Science, 14*(5), 266–271.

Wester, A. E., Böcker, K. B. E., Volkerts, E. R., Verstera, C. (2008). Event-related potentials and secondary task performance during simulated driving. *Accident Analysis & Prevention, 40*(1), 1–7.

Westrin, Å., & Lam, R. W. (2007a). Seasonal affective disorder: A clinical update. *Annals of Clinical Psychiatry, 19*(4), 239–246.

Westrin, Å., & Lam, R. W. (2007b). Long-term and preventative treatment for seasonal affective disorder. *CNS Drugs, 21*(11), 901–909.

Wethington, E. (2000). Expecting stress: Americans and the "midlife crisis." *Motivation & Emotion, 24*(2), 85–103.

Wethington, E. (2003). Turning points as opportunities for psychological growth. In C. L. M. Keyes & J. Haidt (Eds.), *Flourishing*. Washington, DC: American Psychological Association.

Wethington, E., Kessler, R. C., & Pixley, J. E. (2004). Turning points in adulthood. In O. G. Brim, C. D. Ryff, et al. (Eds.), *How healthy are we? A national study of well-being at midlife*. Chicago: University of Chicago Press.

Wexler, M. N. (1995). Expanding the groupthink explanation to the study of contemporary cults. *Cultic Studies Journal, 12*(1), 49–71.

Whipple, B. (2000). Beyond the G spot. *Scandinavian Journal of Sexology, 3*(2), 35–42.

Whitaker, B. G. (2007). Internet-based attitude assessment: Does gender affect measurement equivalence? *Computers in Human Behavior, 23*(3), 1183–1194.

White, G. L., & Taytroe, L. (2003). Personal problem-solving using dream incubation: Dreaming, relaxation, or waking cognition? *Dreaming, 13*(4), 193–209.

White, J. (2006). *Intelligence, destiny and education: The ideological roots of intelligence testing*. New York: Brunner-Routledge.

Whitehouse, A. J. O., Maybery, M. T., & Durkin, K. (2006). The development of the picture-superiority effect. *British Journal of Developmental Psychology, 24*(4), 767–773.

Whitley, B. E. (1999). Right-wing authoritarianism, social dominance orientation, and prejudice. *Journal of Personality & Social Psychology, 77*(1), 126–134.

Whitton, E. (2003). *Humanistic approach to psychotherapy*. New York: Wiley.

Whyte, G. (2000). Groupthink. In A. E. Kazdin (Ed.), *Encyclopedia of psychology* (Vol. 4). Washington, DC: American Psychological Association.

Widiger, T. A. (2005). Classification and diagnosis: Historical development and contemporary issues. In J. E. Maddux, & B. A. Winstead (Eds.), *Psychopathology: Foundations for a contemporary understanding*. Mahwah, NJ: Erlbaum.

Widner, Jr., R. L., Otani, H., & Winkelman, S. E. (2005). Tip-of-the-tongue experiences are not merely strong feeling-of-knowing experiences. *Journal of General Psychology, 132*(4), 392–407.

Wiederhold, B. K., & Wiederhold, M. D. (2005). Acrophobia. In B. K. Wiederhold, & M. D. Wiederhold, *Virtual reality therapy for anxiety disorders: Advances in evaluation and treatment*. Washington, DC: American Psychological Association.

Wiederman, M. W. (1999). Volunteer bias in sexuality research using college student participants. *Journal of Sex Research, 36*(1), 59–66.

Wiederman, M. W. (2001). Gender differences in sexuality: Perceptions, myths, and realities. *Family Journal—Counseling & Therapy for Couples & Families, 9*(4), 468–471.

Wigfield, A., & Eccles, J. (Eds.). (2002). *Development of achievement motivation*. San Diego: Academic Press.

Wilber, M. K., & Potenza, M. N. (2006). Adolescent gambling: Research and clinical implications. *Psychiatry, 3*(10), 40–46.

Wilder, D. A., Simon, A. F., & Faith, M. (1996). Enhancing the impact of counterstereotypic information. *Journal of Personality & Social Psychology, 71*(2), 276–287.

Wilding, J., & Valentine, E. (1994). Memory champions. *British Journal of Psychology, 85*(2), 231–244.

Wilkinson, D., & Abraham, C. (2004). Constructing an integrated model of the antecedents of adolescent smoking. *British Journal of Health Psychology, 9*(3), 315–333.

Wilkinson, M. (2006). The dreaming mindbrain: A Jungian perspective. *Journal of Analytical Psychology, 51*(1), 43–59.

Williams, G., Cai, X. J., Elliott, J. C., Harrold, J. A. (2004). Anabolic neuropeptides. *Physiology & Behavior. Special Reviews on Ingestive Science, 81*(2), 211–222.

Williams, J. M. (2006). *Applied sport psychology: Personal growth to peak performance* (5th ed.). New York: McGraw-Hill.

Williams, L. M., Senior, C. David, A. S., Loughland, C. M., et al. (2001). In search of the "Duchenne Smile": Evidence from eye movements. *Journal of Psychophysiology, 15*(2), 122–127.

Williams, N. (2002). The imposition of gender: Psychoanalytic encounters with genital atypicality. *Psychoanalytic Psychology, 19*(3), 455–474.

Williams, R. (1989). *The trusting heart: Great news about Type A behavior*. New York: Random House.

Williams, R., & Vinson, D. C. (2001). Validation of a single screening question for problem drinking. *The Journal of Family Practice, 50*(4), 307–312.

Williams, R. B., Barefoot, J. C., & Schneiderman, N. (2003). Psychosocial risk factors for cardiovascular disease: More than one culprit at work. *JAMA: Journal of the American Medical Association, 290*(16), 2190–2192.

Williams, R. L., & Eggert, A. (2002). Notetaking predictors of test performance. *Teaching of Psychology, 29*(3)

Williams, R. L., & Long, J. D. (1991). *Toward a self-managed life style*. Boston: Houghton Mifflin.

Williams, R. L., Agnew, H. W., & Webb, W. B. (1964). Sleep patterns in young adults: An EEG study. *Electroencephalography & Clinical Neurophysiology, 17*, 376–381.

Williamson, D. A., Ravussin, E., Wong, M.-L., Wagner, A. et al. (2005). Microanalysis of eating behavior of three leptin deficient adults treated with leptin therapy. *Appetite, 45*, 75–80.

Willoughby, T., Wood, E., Desmarais, S., et al. (1997). Mechanisms that facilitate the effectiveness of elaboration strategies. *Journal of Educational Psychology, 89*(4), 682–685.

Wilmot, W. W., & Hocker, J. L. (2007). *Interpersonal conflict* (7th ed.). Boston: McGraw-Hill.

Wilson, F. L. (1995). The effects of age, gender, and ethnic/cultural background on moral reasoning. *Journal of Social Behavior & Personality, 10*(1), 67–78.

Wilson, S. L. (2003). Post-institutionalization: The effects of early deprivation on development of Romanian adoptees. *Child & Adolescent Social Work Journal, 20*(6), 473–483.

Wilson, T. D. (2002). *Strangers to ourselves: Discovering the adaptive unconscious*. Cambridge, MA: Harvard University Press.

Winger, G., Woods, J. H., Galuska, C. M., & Wade-Galuska, T. (2005). Behavioral perspectives on the neuroscience of drug addiction. *Journal of the Experimental Analysis of Behavior, 84*(3), 667–681.

Wingood, G.M., DiClemente, R.J., Bernhardt, J.M., Harrington, K., et al. (2003). A prospective study of exposure to rap music videos and African American female adolescents' health. *American Journal of Public Health, 93*, 437–439.

Winner, E. (2003). Creativity and talent. In M. H. Bornstein, L. Davidson, et al. (Eds.), *Well-being: Positive development across the life course*. Mahwah, NJ: Erlbaum.

Winstead, B. A., & Sanchez, J. (2005). Gender and psychopathology. In J. E. Maddux & B. A. Winstead (Eds.), *Psychopathology: Foundations for a contemporary understanding*. Mahwah, NJ: Erlbaum.

Winter, D. D. N., & Koger, S. M. (2004). *The psychology of environmental problems* (2nd ed.). Mahwah, NJ: Erlbaum.

Wise, R. A., & Safer, M. A. (2004). What US judges know and believe about eyewitness testimony. *Applied Cognitive Psychology, 18*(4), 427–443.

Wiseman, R., & Watt, C. (2006). Belief in psychic ability and the misattribution hypothesis: A qualitative review. *British Journal of Psychology, 97*(3), 323–338.

Witelson, S. F., Beresh, H., & Kigar, D. L. (2006). Intelligence and brain size in 100 postmortem brains: Sex, lateralization and age factors. *Brain: A Journal of Neurology, 129*(2), 386–398.

Witherington, D. C., Campos, J. J., Anderson, D. I., Lejeune, L., et al. (2005). Avoidance of heights on the visual cliff in newly walking infants. *Infancy, 7*(3), 285–298.

Withers, N. W., Pulvirenti, L., Koob, G. F., & Gillin, J. C. (1995). Cocaine abuse and dependence. *Journal of Clinical Psychopharmacology, 15*(1), 63–78.

Witt, S. D. (1997). Parental influences on children's socialization to gender roles. *Adolescence, 32*(126), 253–259.

Wixted, J. T. (2004). The psychology and neuroscience of forgetting. *Annual Review of Psychology, 55*, 235–269.

Wixted, J. T. (2005). A theory about why we forget what we once knew. *Current Directions in Psychological Science, 14*(1), 6–9.

Wolfe, J. B. (1936). Effectiveness of token rewards for chimpanzees. *Comparative Psychology Monographs, 12*(5), Whole No. 60.

Wolpe, J. (1974). *The practice of behavior therapy* (2nd ed.). New York: Pergamon.

Wolpin, M., Marston, A., Randolph, C., & Clothier, J. (1992). Individual difference correlates of reported lucid dreaming frequency and control. *Journal of Mental Imagery, 16*(3–4), 231–236.

Wong, A. M., Hodges, H., & Horsburgh, K. (2005). Neural stem cell grafts reduce the extent of neuronal damage in a mouse model of global ischaemia. *Brain Research, 1063*(2), 140–150.

Wood, E., & Willoughby, T. (1995). Cognitive strategies for test-taking. In E. Wood, V. Woloshyn, et al. (Eds.), *Cognitive strategy instruction for middle and high schools*. Cambridge, MA: Brookline Books.

Wood, J. M., Nezworski, M. T., Lilienfeld, S. O., & Garb, H. N. (2003). The Rorschach Inkblot test, fortune tellers, and cold reading. *Skeptical Inquirer, 27*(4), 29–33.

Woodhill, B. M., & Samuels, C. A. (2004). Desirable and undesirable androgyny: A prescription for the twenty-first century. *Journal of Gender Studies, 13*(1), 15–28.

Woods, S. C., Schwartz, M. W, Baskin, D. G., & Seeley, R J. (2000). Food intake and the regulation of body weight. *Annual Review of Psychology, 51*, 255–277.

Worthen, J. B., & Marshall, P. H. (1996). Intralist and extralist sources of distinctiveness and the bizarreness effect. *American Journal of Psychology, 109*(2), 239–263.

Wraga, M., Shephard, J. M., Church, J. A., Inati, S., et al. (2005). Imagined rotations of self versus objects: An fMRI study. *Neuropsychologia, 43*(9), 1351–1361.

Wright, J. P., Dietrich, K. N., Ris, M. D., Hornung, R. W., et al. (2008). Association of prenatal and childhood blood lead concentrations with criminal arrests in early adulthood. *PNAS Proceedings of the National Academy of Sciences of the United States of America, 5*(5), e101 doi:10.1371/journal.pmed.0050101. Retrieved October 2, 2008, from http://medicine.plosjournals.org/perlserv/?request=getdocument&doi=10.1371%2Fjournal.pmed.0050101.

Wright, T. A., & Bonett, D. G. (2007). Job satisfaction and psychological wellbeing as nonadditive predictors of workplace turnover. *Journal of Management, 33*(2), 141–160.

Wright, T. A., & Cropanzano, R. (2000). Psychological well-being and job satisfaction as predictors of job performance. *Journal of Occupational Health Psychology, 5*(1), 84–94.

Wrightsman, L. S., & Fulero, S. M. (2005). *Forensic psychology* (2nd ed.). Belmont, CA: Cengage Learning/Wadsworth.

Wu, C. W.H., & Kaas, J. H. (2002). The effects of long-standing limb loss on anatomical reorganization of the somatosensory afferents in the brainstem and spinal cord. *Somatosensory & Motor Research, 19*(2), 153–163.

Wulf, G., McConnel, N., Gärtner, M., & Schwarz, A. (2002). Enhancing the learning of sport skills through externalfocus feedback. *Journal of Motor Behavior, 34*(2), 171–182.

Wyatt, J. W., Posey, A., Welker, W., & Seamonds, C. (1984). Natural levels of similarities between identical twins and between unrelated people. *The Skeptical Inquirer, 9,* 62–66.

Wynne, C. D. L. (2004). The perils of anthropomorphism. *Nature, 428*(6983), 606.

X Day, S., & Schneider, P. L. (2002). Psychotherapy using distance technology. *Journal of Counseling Psychology, 49*(4), 499–503.

Yahnke, B. H., Sheikh, A. A., & Beckman, H. T. (2003). Imagery and the treatment of phobic disorders. In A. A. Sheikh (Ed.), *Healing images: The role of imagination in health.* Amityville, NY: Baywood Publishing.

Yarmey, A. D. (2003). Eyewitness identification: Guidelines and recommendations for identification procedures in the United States and in Canada. *Canadian Psychology, 44*(3), 181–189.

Yedidia, M. J., & MacGregor, B. (2001). Confronting the prospect of dying. *Journal of Pain & Symptom Management, 22*(4), 807–819.

Yeh, C. J. (2003). Age, acculturation, cultural adjustment, and mental health symptoms of Chinese, Korean, and Japanese immigrant youths. *Cultural Diversity & Ethnic Minority Psychology, 9*(1), 34–48.

Yip, P. S. F., & Thorburn, J. (2004). Marital status and the risk of suicide: Experience from England and Wales, 1982–1996. *Psychological Reports, 94*(2), 401–407.

Yokota, F., & Thompson, K. M. (2000). Violence in G-rated animated films. *Journal of the American Medical Association, 283*(20), 2716.

Yonas, A., Elieff, C. A., & Arterberry, M. E. (2002). Emergence of sensitivity to pictorial depth cues: Charting development in individual infants. *Infant Behavior & Development, 25*(4), 495–514.

Yoshida, M. (1993). Three-dimensional electrophysiological atlas created by computer mapping of clinical responses elicited on stimulation of human subcortical structures. *Stereotactic & Functional Neurosurgery, 60*(1–3), 127–134.

Yost, W. A. (2007) *Fundamentals of hearing: An introduction* (5th ed.). San Diego: Elsevier.

Young, R. (2005). Neurobiology of savant syndrome. In C. Stough (Ed.), *Neurobiology of exceptionality.* New York: Kluwer Academic Publishers.

Young, S. M., & Pinsky, D. (2006). Narcissism and celebrity. *Journal of Research in Personality, 40*(5), 463–471.

Yuille, J. C., & Daylen, J. (1998). The impact of traumatic events on eyewitness memory. In C. Thompson, D. Herrmann, et al. (Eds.), *Eyewitness memory: Theoretical and applied perspectives.* Mahwah, NJ: Erlbaum.

Zarcadoolas, C., Pleasant, A., & Greer, D. S. (2006). *Advancing health literacy: A framework for understanding and action.* San Francisco: Jossey-Bass.

Zarraga, C., & Bonache, J. (2005). The impact of team atmosphere on knowledge outcomes in self-managed teams. *Organization Studies, 26*(5), 661–681.

Zeisel, J. (2006). *Inquiry by design: Environment/behavior/neuroscience in architecture, interiors, landscape, and planning.* New York: Norton.

Zeki, S. (1991). Cerebral akinetopsia (visual motion blindness): A review. *Brain, 114,* 811–824.

Zelezny, L. C. (1999). Educational interventions that improve environmental behaviors: A meta-analysis. *Journal of Environmental Education, 31*(1), 5–14.

Zellner, D. A., Harner, D. E., & Adler, R. L. (1989). Effects of eating abnormalities and gender on perceptions of desirable body shape. *Journal of Abnormal Psychology, 98*(1), 93–96.

Zemishlany, Z., Aizenberg, D., & Weizman, A. (2001). Subjective effects of MDMA ("Ecstasy") on human sexual function. *European Psychiatry, 16*(2), 127–130.

Zentall, T. R. (2002). A cognitive behaviorist approach to the study of animal behavior. *Journal of General Psychology. Special Issue: Animal Behavior, 129*(4), 328–363.

Zentall, T. R. (2005). Animals may not be stuck in time. *Learning and Motivation, 36*(2), 208–225.

Zhang R. L., Zhang Z. G., & Chopp, M. (2005). Neurogenesis in the adult ischemic brain: Generation, migration, survival, and restorative therapy. *Neuroscientist, 11*(5), 408–416.

Zhang, A. Y., & Snowden, L. R. (1999). Ethnic characteristics of mental disorders in five U.S. communities. *Cultural Diversity and Ethnic Minority Psychology, 5*(2), 134–146.

Zimbardo, P. (2007). *The Lucifer Effect: Understanding how good people turn evil.* New York: Random House.

Zimbardo, P. G., Haney, C., & Banks, W. C. (1973). A Pirandellian prison. *The New York Times Magazine,* April 8.

Zimbardo, P. G., Pilkonis, P. A., & Norwood, R. M. (1978). The social disease called shyness. In *Annual editions, personality and adjustment 78/79.* Guilford CT: Dushkin.

Zohar, D. (1998). An additive model of test anxiety: Role of exam-specific expectations. *Journal of Educational Psychology, 90,* 330–340.

Zola, S. M., & Squire, L. R. (2001). Relationship between magnitude of damage to the hippocampus and impaired recognition in monkeys. *Hippocampus, 11,* 92–98.

Zucker, A. (1995). Rights and the dying. In H. Wass, & R. A. Neimeyer (Eds.), *Dying: Facing the facts.* Washington, DC: Taylor & Francis.

Zuckerman, M. (1990). The psychophysiology of sensation seeking. *Journal of Personality, 58*(1), 313–345.

Zuckerman, M. (1996). Item revisions in the Sensation Seeking Scale Form V (SSS-V). *EDRA: Environmental Design Research Association, 20*(4), 515.

Zuckerman, M. (2000). Sensation seeking. In A. Kazdin (Ed.), *Encyclopedia of psychology.* Washington, DC: American Psychological Association.

Zuckerman, M. (2002). Genetics of sensation seeking. In J. Benjamin, R. P. Ebstein, et al. (Eds.), *Molecular genetics and the human personality.* Washington, DC: American Psychiatric Publishing.

Zuckerman, M., & Tsai, F-R. (2005). Costs of self-handicapping. *Journal of Personality, 73*(2), 411–442.

Zuckerman, M., Kieffer, S. C., & Knee, C. R. (1998). Consequences of selfhandicapping. *Journal of Personality & Social Psychology, 74*(6), 1619–1628.

Zuwerink, J. R., Devine, P. G., Monteith, M. J., & Cook, D. A. (1996). Prejudice toward Blacks: With and without compunction? *Basic & Applied Social Psychology, 18*(2), 131–150.

name index

subject index

Ablation, 57–58
Abnormality, statistical, 460, 461
Absolute threshold, 119–120
Abuse, drug, 199–210
  alcohol, 207–210
  amphetamine, 201–202
  barbiturates, 206
  caffeine, 204–205
  cocaine, 203–204
  gamma-hydroxybutyrate, 206–207
  hallucinogens, 210–211
  MDMA, 204
  nicotine, 205
  patterns of, 200
  tranquilizers, 207
Acceptance
  of death, 111
  uncritical, 18
Accessibility in memory, 266, 267
Accommodation, 97, 124, 125, 162
Acculturative stress, 448, 449
Acetylcholine, 51
Achievement, need for, 336–337
Acquaintance rape, 377
Acquired strategies, 294
Acquisition, 222, 223
Acromegaly, 71
Action component, 536
Action potential, 49
Action therapy, 496
Activation-synthesis hypothesis of
  dreaming, 192–193
Active listening, 516
Actor-observer bias, 535
Acupuncture, 143
Acute stress disorder, 483
Adaptability, androgyny and, 367–
  368
Adaptation
  dark, 131
  desensitization and, 505
  sensory, 142, 143
Adaptive behaviors, 341
Addiction, 200, 201
Adjustment disorder, 480–481
Adler, Alfred, 402
Adolescence, 102–104
Adorno, Theodore, 573
Adrenal glands, 70, 71, 72, 73
Adrenaline, 341
Adulthood
  late, 108
  later, 108–110
  middle, 108
  young, 102–104
Aerial perspective, 163
Affectional needs, 91
Affiliation, 557–558
African-American, intelligence testing of,
  315–316
African-American family, 93
After-potential, negative, 49
Afterimages, 128
Age
  chronological, 305
  mental, 305
  sex drive and, 370
  sleep and, 184–185
  suicide and, 491
Age regression, hypnosis and, 196
Ageism, 110, 111, 572, 573

Aggression, 436–437, 566–571
  biological factors in, 567
  displaced, 572, 573
  frustration causing, 567–568
  instincts and, 567
  prevention of, 570–571
  social learning and, 568
  television and, 244–245, 568–570
Aggression cues, 568, 569
Aggressive behavior, 552
Aggressive pornography, 569
Aging, 110
Agnosia, visual, 66, 67
Agoraphobia, 481–482
Agreeableness, 396
Alarm reaction, 431
Alcohol
  abuse of, 207–210
  aversion therapy for, 504
  effects of, 202–203
  sex drive and, 370
Alcohol myopia, 207
Alcoholics Anonymous, 209
Algorithm, 293
All-or-nothing thinking, 510
Alpha waves, 186, 187
Altered states of consciousness
  drugs causing, 199–210. *See also*
    Drug-altered consciousness
  hypnosis and, 194–197
  meditation and, 197–198
  sensory deprivation causing, 198–199
  sleep and, 182–194. *See also* Sleep
Alternate responses, 248
Alzheimer's disease, 469
Ambady, Nalini, 301
Ambivalence, 439
Ambivalent attachment, 562, 563
Ambivalent attachment style, 91
American Psychological Association
  specialties in psychology and, 32
  website of, 9–10
American Sign Language, 290–291
Amnesia
  dissociative, 484, 485
  hypnosis and, 196
Amok, 466
Amphetamines, 201–202
Amplitude of sound waves, 133
Ampulla, 140
Amygdala, 69, 342, 343
Anal-expulsive personality, 401
Anal-retentive personality, 401
Anal stage, 401
Androgens, 72, 332, 333, 358, 359
Androgyny, 367–368
Anesthesia, glove, 485
Angel dust, 210
Anger, as reaction to dying, 111
Anger control, 570
Anhedonia, 204, 205
Anima, 403–404
Animal language, 291
Animal model, 14, 15
Animus, 403–404
Anorexia nervosa, 329–330
Anorgasmic woman, 384
Antecedents, 219–220
  in behavioral self-management, 248
Anterograde amnesia, 270
Anthropomorphic error, 38, 39

Anticipation, sexual, 381
Antidepressant, 518, 519
Antipsychotic, 518, 519
Antismoking program, 429
Antisocial behavior
  aggression as, 566–571
  multiculturalism and, 579–581
  prejudice as, 571–578
Antisocial personality disorders, 487–
  489
Anxiety, 440, 441
  basic, 402
  moral, 400
  neurotic, 400
  pain and, 145
  separation, 90, 91
  social, 421
  test, 335
Anxiety disorder, 464, 465, 480–487
  adjustment, 480–481
  agoraphobia, 481–482
  behavioral approaches to, 486–487
  cognitive approaches to, 487
  dissociative, 484
  generalized, 481
  humanistic-existential approaches to,
    486
  obsessive-compulsive, 482–483
  panic disorder, 481–482
  phobia as, 482
  psychodynamic approach to, 486
  social phobia as, 482
  somatoform, 484–485
  stress, 483
Anxiety reduction hypothesis, 487
Anxiolytic, 518, 519
APA. *See* American Psychological
  Association
Apathy, bystander, 564, 565
Aphasia, 63–64
  fluent, 65
  receptive, 65
Aphrodisiac, 370
Aplysia, 272
Apnea, sleep, 189
Applied psychology, 585–611
  educational, 601–602
  environmental, 593–601
  human factors, 607–610
  industrial, 585–593
  law and, 602–604
  sports, 604–607
Applied research, 32
Appraisal, emotional, 350, 351
Approach-approach conflict, 438, 439
Aptitude test, 592, 593
Arab-American family, 93
Arc, reflex, 54
Archetypes, 403
Architectural psychology, 600, 601
Area
  association, 63
  Broca's, 63–64
Arousal
  empathic, 565
  levels of, 334–335
  sexual, 369
Arousal disorders, 382, 383–384
Arousal theory, 333–334
Artificial intelligence, 311–312
Asch experiment, 543–544

Asian-American family, 93
Assertiveness training, 551–553
Assessment
  behavioral, 415
  environmental, 600, 601
Assessment center, 592, 593
Assigned sex, 358, 359, 360
Assignment, random, 33
Assimilation, 97, 448, 449
Association areas, 63
Associative learning, 219–220
Astigmatism, 124, 125
Astrology, 18
Attachment, 89
  love and, 562
  quality of, 90
Attention
  divided, 151
  pain and, 146
  perception and, 151–154
  selective, 151, 470
Attention deficit hyperactivity disorder,
  152, 153
Attention seeking, negative, 229
Attentional overload, 596, 597
Attitude, 535–536
  behavior and, 536–537
  change in, 537–538
  prejudice and, 571–578
Attitude scale, 537
Attraction, interpersonal, 558–563
Attractiveness, 559
Attribution, 349, 532–533
Attribution error, fundamental, 535
Auditory area, primary, 65
Auditory ossicles, 133
Authentic smile, 347
Authenticity, 500, 501
Authoritarian parents, 91
Authoritative parents, 92, 93
Autokinetic effect, 532, 533
Automatic processing, 294
Autonomic nervous system, 53–54, 343
Autonomy *vs.* shame and doubt, 107
Autosuggestion, 194
Availability in memory, 266, 267
Aversion
  sexual, 383
  taste, 327
Aversion therapy, 504, 505
Aversive stimulus, 229, 568, 569
Avoidance-avoidance conflict, 438–439
Avoidance learning, 239, 486–487
Avoidant attachment, 562, 563
Awareness
  levels of, 400
  perceptual, 177–178
Awareness training, large-group, 513
Axon terminals, 48, 49
Axons, 48, 49

Babbling, 94
Bait shyness, 327
Barbiturates, 202–203, 206
Bargaining
  compliance and, 546
  as reaction to dying, 111
Barnum effect, 19
Barriers to problem solving, 297
Base rate, 302, 303
Basic anxiety, 402